FACTITIOUS DISORDERS

Factitious Disorder
Factitious Disorder NOS

DISSOCIATIVE DISORDERS

Dissociative Amnesia
Dissociative Fugue
Dissociative Identity Disorder
Depersonalization Disorder
Dissociative Disorder NOS

SEXUAL DYSFUNCTIONS

Sexual Desire Disorders
    Hypoactive Sexual Desire Disorder
    Sexual Aversion Disorder
Sexual Arousal Disorders
    Female Sexual Arousal Disorder
    Male Erectile Disorder
Orgasmic Disorders
    Female Orgasmic Disorder
    Male Orgasmic Disorder
    Premature Ejaculation
Sexual Pain Disorders
    Dyspareunia (Not Due to a General Medical Condition)
    Vaginismus (Not Due to a General Medical Condition)
Sexual Dysfunction Due to a General Medical Condition [Specify Further]
Substance-Induced Sexual Dysfunction
Sexual Dysfunction NOS

PARAPHILIAS

Exhibitionism
Fetishism
Frotteurism
Pedophilia
Sexual Masochism
Sexual Sadism
Transvestic Fetishism
Voyeurism
Paraphilia NOS

GENDER IDENTITY DISORDERS

Gender Identity Disorder
Gender Identity Disorder NOS
Sexual Disorder NOS

EATING DISORDERS

Anorexia Nervosa
Bulimia Nervosa
Eating Disorder NOS

SLEEP DISORDERS

Primary Sleep Disorders
    Dyssomnias
        Primary Insomnia
        Primary Hypersomnia
        Narcolepsy
        Breathing-Related Sleep Disorder
        Circadian Rhythm Sleep Disorder
        Dyssomnia NOS
    Parasomnias
        Nightmare Disorder
        Sleep Terror Disorder
        Sleepwalking Disorder
        Parasomnia NOS
Sleep Disorders Related to Another Mental Disorder
    Insomnia Related to [Indicate Axis I or Axis II disorder]
    Hypersomnia Related to [Indicate Axis I or Axis II disorder]
Other Sleep Disorders
    Sleep Disorder Due to a General Medical Condition
    Substance-Induced Sleep Disorder

IMPULSE-CONTROL DISORDERS NOT ELSEWHERE CLASSIFIED

Intermittent Explosive Disorder
Kleptomania
Pyromania
Pathological Gambling
Trichotillomania
Impulse-Control Disorder NOS

ADJUSTMENT DISORDERS

Adjustment Disorder with Depressed Mood
Adjustment Disorder with Anxiety
Adjustment Disorder with Mixed Anxiety and Depressed Mood
Adjustment Disorder with Disturbance of Conduct
Adjustment Disorder with Mixed Disturbance of Emotions and Conduct

OTHER CONDITIONS THAT MAY BE A FOCUS OF CLINICAL ATTENTION

PSYCHOLOGICAL FACTORS AFFECTING MEDICAL CONDITION

MEDICALLY INDUCED MOVEMENT DISORDERS

OTHER MEDICALLY INDUCED DISORDERS

RELATIONAL PROBLEMS

Relational Problem Related to a Mental Disorder or General Medical Condition
Parent-Child Relational Problem
Partner Relational Problem
Sibling Relational Problem

PROBLEMS RELATED TO ABUSE OR NEGLECT

Physical Abuse of Child
Sexual Abuse of Child
Neglect of Child
Physical Abuse of Adult
Sexual Abuse of Adult

ADDITIONAL CONDITIONS THAT MAY BE A FOCUS OF CLINICAL ATTENTION

Noncompliance with Treatment
Malingering
Adult Antisocial Behavior
Child or Adolescent Antisocial Behavior
Borderline Intellectual Functioning
Age-Related Cognitive Decline
Bereavement
Academic Problem
Occupational Problem
Identity Problem
Religious or Spiritual Problem
Acculturation Problem
Phase of Life Problem

AXIS II

MENTAL RETARDATION

Mild Mental Retardation
Moderate Mental Retardation
Severe Mental Retardation
Profound Mental Retardation

PERSONALITY DISORDERS

Paranoid Personality Disorder
Schizoid Personality Disorder
Schizotypal Personality Disorder
Antisocial Personality Disorder
Borderline Personality Disorder
Histrionic Personality Disorder
Narcissistic Personality Disorder
Avoidant Personality Disorder
Dependent Personality Disorder
Obsessive-Compulsive Personality Disorder
Personality Disorder NOS

Abnormal Psychology

Michael L. Raulin
State University of New York at Buffalo

In collaboration with
Scott O. Lilienfeld and
Edward S. Katkin

Boston   New York   San Francisco
Mexico City   Montreal   Toronto   London   Madrid   Munich   Paris
Hong Kong   Singapore   Tokyo   Cape Town   Sydney

Series Editor:	Kelly M. May
Senior Development Editor:	Lisa McLellan
Marketing Manager:	Wendy Gordon
Production Administrator:	Susan Brown
Editorial/Production Services:	Kathleen Deselle
Text Designer:	The Davis Group, Inc.
Photo Researcher:	Martha Shethar
Formatting/Page Layout:	Shelley Smigelski
Composition Buyer:	Linda Cox
Manufacturing Buyer:	Megan Cochran

For related titles and support materials, visit our online catalog at www.ablongman.com.

Between the time Website information is gathered and then published, it is not unusual for some sites to have closed. Also, the transcription of URLs can result in unintended typographical errors. The publisher would appreciate notification where these errors occur so that they may be corrected in subsequent editions.

Library of Congress Cataloging-in-Publication Data

Raulin, Michael L.
   Abnormal psychology / Michael L. Raulin.
      p. cm.
   Includes bibliographical references and index.
   ISBN 0-205-37580-4
   1. Psychology, Pathological.   I. Title.

RC439 .R24 2002
616.89—dc21

                 2002027654

Printed in the United States of America
0 9 8 7 6 5 4 3 2 1   VHP   07 06 05 04 03 02

To Loren and Jean Chapman

Whose graduate school mentorship taught me the importance of precision in research

To Paul Meehl

Whose stimulating and provocative writings taught me that it is better for scientists to be clear, but wrong, than to be vague and, therefore, unable to know when they are wrong

To Sher

My wife and best friend, whose partnership and love has made my life infinitely more rewarding

Brief Contents

Contents

PART I *Understanding Psychopathology*

CHAPTER 1
Understanding Abnormal Behavior 2

CHAPTER 2
Diagnosis and Assessment 24

PART II *The Disorders*

CHAPTER 5
Schizophrenia and Other Psychotic Disorders   102

CHAPTER 6
The Study of Schizophrenia   134

CHAPTER 7
Mood Disorders 166

CHAPTER 13
Disorders First Apparent in Childhood   394

PART III *Closing Issues*

CHAPTER 16

Contemporary Issues and Future Directions 512

Feature List

FOCUS

MODERN Myths

ADVANCES

- Seeing Into the Mind (Chapter 2, p. 44)
- The Human Genome Project (Chapter 4, p. 73)
- Brain Images of Discordant Twins (Chapter 5, p. 120)
- A PDP Model of Schizophrenic Deficits (Chapter 6, p. 162)
- Transcranial Magnetic Stimulation (Chapter 7, p. 190)
- A Window on the Brains of People with OCD (Chapter 8, p. 229)
- Psychoneuroimmunology (Chapter 9, p. 259)
- Studying Eating Disorders Prospectively (Chapter 10, p. 300)
- Rape from an Evolutionary Perspective (Chapter 11, p. 356)
- Psychometric Determination of Personality Disorders (Chapter 12, p. 372)
- Evaluating Specific Genes (Chapter 13, p. 427)
- Sexual Predators (Chapter 16, p. 516)

CLIENT Snapshots
(found on accompanying CD)

- Welcoming Message from Mike Raulin
- Chapter 1: Discussion of Abnormality
- Chapter 2: Discussion of Diagnosis and Assessment
- Chapter 3: Discussion of Historical Perspectives
- Chapter 4: Discussion of Current Perspectives
- Chapter 5: Interview with Rodney (schizophrenia)
- Chapter 7: Three Client Interviews
      Helen (major depression)
      Nathan (cyclothymia)
      William (double depression)
- Chapter 8: Five Client Interviews
      John (obsessive-compulsive disorder)
      Margo (obsessive-compulsive disorder)
      Larry (panic disorder)
      Donald (panic disorder)
      Carl (social phobia)
- Chapter 9: Interview with Elizabeth (chronic fatigue syndrome)
- Chapter 10: Two Client Interviews
      Kim (anorexia nervosa)
      Roberta (insomnia)
- Chapter 11: Discussion of Sexual Disorders
      Interview with an Anonymous Pedophile
- Chapter 12: Discussion of Personality Disorders
      Interview with Janna (borderline personality disorder)
- Chapter 13: Interview with Adrian (mental retardation)
- Chapter 14: Interview with Kathy (substance abuse)
- Chapter 15: Discussion of Cognitive and Dissociative Disorders
      Judy (dementia)
      Connie (head injury)
- Chapter 16: Interview with Adrian's Guardian on Fighting for Her Treatment

COVERAGE OF CROSS-CULTURAL ISSUES

COVERAGE OF GENDER ISSUES

COVERAGE OF THE EVOLUTIONARY PERSPECTIVE

Preface to the Instructor

Few areas of human activity generate as much interest, curiosity, and mystery as psychopathology. My goal in writing this book was to capture each of these elements in a balanced presentation of this rapidly evolving field. I draw from a combination of classic and cutting-edge research to illustrate the dynamics of the field. This research is frequently presented from the point of view of the researcher, emphasizing for students the inherent excitement of satisfying one's curiosity by unraveling the mysteries and mechanisms behind abnormal behavior. I address the students' questions about psychopathology with a sensitive portrayal of psychiatric disorders and with an emphasis on the progress made in understanding and treating these disorders. I include dozens of case examples, many drawn from my own clinical experience, to illustrate real people living meaningful lives despite their disorders.

THEMES

The primary theme of this text is that a scientific approach provides the strongest tool for studying psychopathology and for developing effective treatments. I want my students to appreciate the excitement of scientific discovery. The text employs the traditional theoretical perspectives to explain psychopathology, such as physiological, cognitive-behavioral, and sociocultural, but it also adds an evolutionary perspective in a way that is rarely presented in psychopathology textbooks. This evolutionary perspective often provides unique insights into various forms of psychopathology. Finally, several things were done to make the material consistently accessible to students, including using an engaging writing style, frequent case studies integrated into the chapters, and several pedagogical features to enhance learning.

EXCITEMENT OF RESEARCH

Scientific research has consistently produced the most significant breakthroughs in understanding psychopathology.

This theme shaped the textbook in several ways. First, I cover topics with the strongest scientific background, rather than that which has the widest play in popular markets. Second, actual research is presented throughout the text (and in the *Examining the Evidence* feature) to give students a feel for the research process and to help them appreciate the excitement of scientific discovery. Third, scientific critiques are employed to help students realize that there are still many questions that remain unanswered and that some of the existing theories are suspect and may change when better research is available. Fourth, cutting-edge research is presented frequently, even when its value is still unclear. Scientific controversies are not avoided, but rather highlighted, as are the mechanisms by which those controversies will be resolved. Finally, the presentation of research concepts is unique in that it is discussed within the context of a specific disorder (Chapter 6: The Study of Schizophrenia), rather than in the abstract, as is typically done in other texts.

THEORETICAL PERSPECTIVES

Each form of psychopathology is explored from several theoretical perspectives, but unlike some other texts, no effort is made to cover every disorder from every perspective. In fact, except in rare instances, disorders are covered *only* from those perspectives that have made the greatest contribution to understanding and treatment. The only exceptions are a few cases in which a perspective has great historical interest. I emphasize this approach by covering the perspectives in two chapters—one dedicated to historically important perspectives and another to the currently dominant perspectives.

I have chosen to include a perspective normally left out of abnormal psychology texts—the cognitive neuroscience perspective. This perspective has been a central part of research in schizophrenia for half a century but has recently been incorporated into research in other disorders. Borrowing heavily from cognitive psychology, the cognitive neuroscience perspective investigates the perceptual and cognitive underpinnings of disorders and seeks to relate these variables to their physiological mechanisms. For example, it has long been known that anxious people seem to be remarkably capable of finding things to be anxious about. What perceptual, memory, or thought processes might be contributing to this phenomenon, and what brain mechanisms are implicated? The traditional cognitive perspective acknowledged such factors but never attempted to explain the mechanisms behind them.

Whenever the understanding of a phenomenon is sufficient to permit integration of theoretical perspectives, that integration is included in the text. For example, if specific brain mechanisms are identified that generate psychological experiences central to a phenomenon, those overlapping elements are highlighted in the text. That is the case, for example, with panic disorder, in which the brain mechanisms behind the psychological and physiological experience of panic are known and the specific impact of psychological experiences on brain functioning is beginning to be understood. This text does *not* favor biological reductionism but rather strives for an integration of theoretical perspectives as different ways of viewing the same phenomena.

EVOLUTIONARY IMPACT

This is the first book in the field to examine and integrate the evolutionary perspective. Some people have used evolutionary theory as a plausible, but generally untestable, explanation for phenomena. This text, however, studiously avoids using the evolutionary perspective in this way. Evolution is *not* used as the explanation for psychopathology. The evolutionary significance of emotional experiences, such as anxiety and depression, is first introduced in Chapter 1 and revisited repeatedly in the text, and the idea that the forces of natural selection change as the environment changes is emphasized throughout the book. The benefit of the evolutionary perspective is that it provides a coherent integrating theme that ties biological, psychological, and environmental variables together to explain the functioning of organisms. Anxiety disorders provide an excellent example of this integration. The obvious survival value of anxiety-driven avoidance of dangerous situations makes the psychological phenomena associated with anxiety disorders understandable. The biological mechanisms that evaluate the potential danger and produce the emotional and behavioral responses evolved because they increased the likelihood of survival.

ACCESSIBLE PRESENTATION

Making psychopathology accessible for students was my top priority in this text. I try to engage students with plenty of examples, especially case studies. The case studies do not simply illustrate symptoms but rather present real

people dealing with specific psychopathologies, and several of these people are interviewed on the CD-ROM that accompanies this text. Many of the cases were drawn from my own practice or cases that I had supervised.

ORGANIZATION OF THE TEXT

The DSM is the de facto standard in the field of psychopathology and, as such, provides the organizational structure for the disorders chapters. The diagnostic criteria for each disorder is described concisely, leaving out the detail and differential diagnostic issues included in the DSM manual. Students are not expected to use this text as a basis for making clinical diagnoses, as these skills are typically taught at a graduate level. Instead, it is more important for students to understand the diagnostic process and the dynamic and changing nature of any diagnostic system.

Using the DSM as an organizational tool does not imply a blind acceptance of the diagnostic system. In fact, in several cases, such as several personality disorders, the categorical nature of the diagnostic system is challenged with data that support a more dimensional view. For example, an obsessive-compulsive personality disorder is more likely an extreme version of meticulousness rather than a separate category different from the norm. Nevertheless, the DSM does provide a traditional organization.

The text is divided conceptually into three parts: an introduction, the disorders, and a closing section.

▶ **Part I: Introduction (Chapters 1–4).** This section provides an overview to psychopathology, a brief discussion of the diagnostic system and assessment procedures, and a description of several theoretical perspectives on abnormal psychology.

▶ **Part II: Disorders (Chapters 5–15).** The disorders are covered with a chapter organization largely based on the DSM. Although Chapter 6 is in this section, it is really part of the introductory chapters in that it covers research methodology.

▶ **Part III: Closing Issues (Chapter 16).** This section covers legal, ethical, and practical issues in abnormal psychology and looks into the future, outlining the current trends in the field and how those trends are shaping the direction of research and theory.

FEATURES OF THE TEXT

Several features are included in this text to enhance the presentation of the material.

Examining the Evidence. These integrated features explore the research evidence on a particular topic and the rationale behind the interpretation of the data. They are intended to give students an appreciation for the evidential basis for some of the information reported in the text.

Evolutionary Impact Commentaries. Every chapter includes several discussions of the evolutionary significance of the topics discussed in the chapter. Some commentaries focus on survival value of behaviors, even behaviors that might be maladaptive in other respects. Others focus on the way in which an evolutionary perspective refocuses questions from "What is wrong?" to "How could such problems develop?" Finally, some focus on the impact of a changing environment on natural selection and how some psychopathologies might have been functional earlier in human evolutionary history.

Case Studies. Every chapter begins with one or more thought-provoking case studies, which illustrate many of the key topics of the chapter. These case studies, which are revisited throughout the chapter, illustrate the human cost of psychopathology.

Focus. These boxes highlight hot topics within abnormal psychology, by focusing on research that does a particularly good job of conceptually integrating (1) different theoretical perspectives on a disorder, (2) different research areas, or (3) common elements in several disorders. They are also used to highlight interesting examples of research questions or the research process. For example, the *Focus* box in Chapter 7 discusses the possible link between creativity and mania and the potential mechanism that might account for the link.

Advances. These boxes highlight exciting new research approaches that hold promise for answering difficult questions. For example, the *Advances* box in Chapter 8 discusses how PET scans and functional MRIs have demonstrated specific functional brain abnormalities suspected of contributing to OCD and that these abnormalities disappear after successful treatment.

Modern Myths. Unfortunately, students are often exposed to misinformation about psychopathology that is promulgated through television and the media. *Modern Myth* boxes highlight popular, but erroneous, beliefs, such as "Only Depressed Individuals Commit Suicide" (Chapter 8), and show how inadequate data or a misinterpretation of data can lead to inaccurate conceptualizations.

Check Yourself (with Ponder this . . . questions). Each major section concludes with a brief set of questions designed to encourage students to evaluate their understanding of the material that they just read. In addition, to facilitate active learning, each *Check Yourself* section includes one thought-provoking *Ponder this* question. Some of these questions ask students to speculate about the impact of a certain pathology on functioning. Others encourage students to integrate ideas from different sources into a more coherent view of a disorder.

Glossary. A running glossary is included in the text. In addition, a complete glossary of terms is included at the end of the text.

SUPPLEMENTS PACKAGE

The text includes several supplemental items to enhance the experience of both instructors and students. Listed below are the key elements in this package.

FOR THE INSTRUCTOR

Instructor's Manual. Written by David Wasieleski of Valdosta State University, this is a wonderful tool for classroom preparation and management. Each chapter includes

an At-A-Glance grid (with detailed pedagogical information linking to other available supplements), a detailed chapter outline, teaching objectives, key terms, and lecture material—including demonstrations and activities, discussion questions pertaining to the CD-ROM, and web links. In addition, an appendix includes a comprehensive list of handouts.

Test Bank. Written by Suzanne deBeaumont and Michael Raulin, this extensive test bank includes challenging questions that target key concepts. Each chapter contains more than 100 multiple-choice questions—each with an answer justification. Page references and type designation are available for each question. I co-authored the test bank, because I wanted to assure the highest quality and accuracy for the items.

Computerized Test Bank. The test-item file is also available to instructors in electronic form. The TestGen-EQ program (available in both Windows and Mac versions) allows instructors to add, delete, and modify items, and to construct classroom tests.

PowerPoint Lectures. This CD-ROM is an exciting interactive classroom presentation tool. Each chapter includes key points covered in the textbook, images from the textbook (including Flash animation), a link to the companion web site for corresponding activities, and the electronic Instructor's Manual.

The Digital Media Archive for Abnormal Psychology. This classroom presentation software CD-ROM contains electronic images from the text and other sources. It also contains video and lecture outlines.

Transparencies for Abnormal Psychology. Approximately 110 full-color acetates are available to enhance classroom lecture and discussion.

CourseCompass. Powered by Blackboard, this course management system uses a powerful suite of tools so instructors can create an online presence for any course.

Allyn & Bacon APPI Video Series. Adopters of the Raulin text are eligible to receive select videos produced by APPI. *DSM-IV: New Diagnostic Issues Videotape Series* is a series of clinical programs containing enactments of actual patient interviews and a discussion of the DSM-IV diagnostic criteria currently in use. *Treatments of Psychiatric Disorders Videotape* contains four clinicians presenting recent information on treatments for psychiatric disorders.

FOR THE STUDENT

Grade Aid Study Guide. Written by Marjorie Hardy at Eckerd College, this is a comprehensive and interactive study guide. Each chapter includes: "Before You Read," with a brief chapter summary and chapter learning objectives; "As You Read," a collection of demonstrations, activities, and exercises; "After You Read," containing three short practice quizzes and one comprehensive practice test; and "When You Have Finished," with short answer and essay questions to reiterate concepts.

Companion Web Site. This is a unique resource for connecting the textbook to the Internet. Each chapter includes learning objectives, a chapter summary, flashcards (with glossary terms from the text), updated and annotated web links for additional sources of information, learning activities, online practice tests (including multiple choice, fill-in-the-blank, true/false, and essay questions), and research updates.

Client Snapshots CD-ROM. This multimedia tool allows students to experience firsthand the human side of psychopathology. The CD-ROM includes video clips of Dr. Raulin interviewing his own clients, many of whom are featured as case studies in the text. Raulin also provides a brief background statement about each of the clients interviewed, in order to give students more of a context to understand the video clips and to get a better sense of the person behind the disorder. Each clip is followed by thought questions for students to consider. The CD-ROM also contains chapter objectives, learning activities, and links directly to the companion web site.

iSearch: Abnormal Psychology. Designed to help students select and evaluate research from the web to find the best and most credible information available. This booklet includes a practical and to-the-point discussion of search engines, detailed information on evaluating online sources, citation guidelines for web resources, web activities for abnormal psychology, web links for abnormal psychology, and a guide to ContentSelect.

Allyn & Bacon ContentSelect for Psychology. Allyn & Bacon and EBSCO Publishing, leaders in the development of electronic journal databases, have exclusively collaborated to develop the Psychology ContentSelect Research Database, an online collection of leading scholarly and peer-reviewed journals in the discipline. Students can have unlimited access to a customized, searchable collection of discipline-specific articles from top-tier academic publications.

ACKNOWLEDGMENTS

No project of this size could ever be done well by a single person. Two outstanding development editors helped shape this project from beginning to end. I cannot thank enough my development editor at Allyn & Bacon, Lisa McLellan, who seamlessly managed this project through every phase. Prior to Lisa, Dawn Groundwater worked with me on the first two chapters. Both were enormously helpful in setting the highest of standards and helping me to achieve more than I realized was possible. During the course of this project, I worked with three editors: Rebecca Pascal, Carolyn Merrill, and Eric Stano. Each provided critical advice at various stages and helped coordinate the entire process. I also had two partners on this project—Scott Lilienfeld from Emory University and Ed Katkin from the State University of New York at Stony Brook. They are two of the finest scholars I know, and I am proud to say that each is a close friend. They reviewed everything that was written, from initial drafts through the final versions, and provided invaluable suggestions on content, style, and tone. Their involvement allowed me to create a text with a single voice, while still maintaining the broader perspective characteristic of a text with multiple authors. The production staff at Allyn & Bacon were incredible, handling the hundreds of details with such skill and efficiency that they almost seemed to happen magically. The major contributors included Susan Brown (Production Supervisor), Kathleen Deselle (Production Editor), Erin Liedel (Supplements Editor), Lisa Black (Permissions Editor), Connie Day (Copyeditor), and Martha Shethar (Photo Researcher). Finally, I want to thank my wife, Sher, for her support, love, and patience during several years of writing and revisions.

Several scholars reviewed every chapter, providing valuable suggestions and feedback. These people are the unsung heroes of textbook projects in that they quietly find the mistakes, point out omissions, and gently remind me when I am not connecting to the intended audience—their students. Listed below are those who reviewed one or more chapters. Most reviewed several chapters, and some reviewed multiple drafts of chapters. I want to single out Tom Kwapil, whose reviews were more thorough, insightful, and helpful than any I have ever seen in my years of textbook writing.

Jean F. Ayers, Towson University

C. Peter Bankhart, Wabash College

Dorothy M. Bianco, Rhode Island College

Paul H. Blaney, Emory & Henry College

JoAnne Brewster, James Mason University

Eric Cooley, Western Ontario University

Laurie Corey, Westchester Community College

Joanne Davila, State University of New York at Stony Brook

Joan Duer, University of West Florida

Mitchell Earleywine, University of Southern California

Kenneth L. Farr, University of Texas at Arlington

Perilou Goddard, Northern Kentucky University

Steen Halling, Seattle University

Marjorie Hardy, Eckerd College

William P. Hetrick, Indiana University

Michael Hirt, Kent State University

April Hollenhorst, Indian Hills Community College

Stephen Kahoe, El Paso Community College

Thomas R. Kwapil, University of North Carolina, Greensboro

Charles LaJeunesse, College Misercordia

Marvin W. Lee, Shenandoah University

Jane Ellen Maddy, University of Minnesota, Duluth

James A. Marley, Loyola University, Chicago

Patricia Owen, St. Mary's University

Ralph G. Pifer, Sauk Valley Community College

Michelle Pilati, Rio Hondo College

Neva Sanders, Canisius College

Janet Smith, Pittsburgh State University

Ari Solomon, Williams College

John Suler, Rider University

Mary Ann Swiatek, Lafayette College

Michael Wierzbicki, Marquette University

Michael Zvolensky, University of Vermont

FEEDBACK

A work of this magnitude benefits tremendously from faculty feedback. I am interested in your ideas, suggestions, and complaints, and I will make every effort to incorporate your ideas into future editions. I have established an e-mail discussion list for instructors to share ideas about teaching this course and using the text and supplementary materials more effectively. If you would like to be included in this discussion list, contact me at the e-mail address listed below. If you have questions or problems, feel free to contact me; I will do everything that I can to help.

Mike Raulin
MichaelRaulin@aol.com

To the Student

Welcome to the exciting field of abnormal psychology. There are few areas that have as much inherent interest and are so critical to the well being of millions of people. This textbook introduces you to the nature of psychopathology, what is known about its causes, and how it is best treated. It is likely that you know someone who suffers from one or more of the disorders discussed in this text; perhaps you suffer from a psychological disorder. It is my sincere hope that the information included in these pages will provide insights that will increase your ability to understand and manage stresses in your own life and in the lives of those you love.

LEARNING TOOLS

In each chapter you will find a set of features designed to enhance learning. These include:

New terms highlighted in the text and defined when first introduced

An outline of the chapter content at the beginning of each chapter

Definitions of new terms included at the bottom of each page

A brief summary at the end of the chapter

It may seem silly to tell a college student like yourself how to use a textbook. After all, you have been using them for some time. But have you ever spent most of an evening reading a textbook, only to realize at some point that you do not remember a thing you read? Most students have, because reading is so easy and automatic for them that they can do it without thinking. Unfortunately, one may be able to read without thinking, but one cannot learn without thinking. This book was carefully constructed to not just provide you with information but rather to provide it in a manner that is likely to enhance your learning. If you understand how to use these features, you can reduce the amount of study time while actually increasing the amount you learn. I will briefly describe these learning tools, describe some of the key features of the textbook, and finally outline a set of study tactics to increase your efficiency.

Check Yourself questions at the end of each section to test your knowledge of key points

A *Ponder this* question at the end of each section to encourage you to think beyond the material covered

A list of key terms at the end of the chapter and a glossary with definitions at the end of the text

A list of suggested readings at the end of each chapter for those who wish to learn more about a topic

TEXTBOOK FEATURES

The material in this text is carefully organized to enhance both your enjoyment and your learning. The text features that implement these goals include:

Case studies to bring the disorders to life and to help you understand what it is like to suffer from a disorder

Focus boxes to highlight hot topics in abnormal psychology or to integrate two or more areas of study

Modern Myths boxes to dispel commonly held, but erroneous, ideas about psychopathology

Advances boxes to describe cutting-edge research or technology that is changing our understanding of a disorder

In addition to the features included in the chapters, the following supplementary materials are available with this text:

▶ A **companion web site**, which includes learning objectives, a chapter summary, flashcards (with glossary terms from the text), updated and annotated web links for additional sources of information, learning activities, online practice tests, and research updates.

▶ **Client Snapshots,** a CD-ROM that includes interviews of clients with specific disorders, discussions of other disorders, and critical thinking questions on each video segment.

▶ The **Grade Aid Student Study Guide** can be purchased separately. It provides a hands-on, structured approach to enhance reading and later preparation for examinations.

Evolutionary Impact commentaries to provide information about how the disorders might have evolved, why they may be problematic now but were not so in the past, or how symptomatic behavior may be beneficial in the right situation

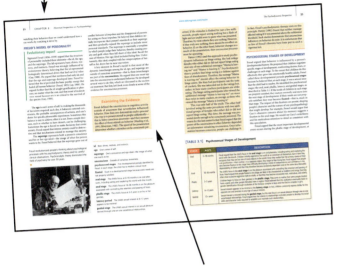

Examining the Evidence features to illustrate specific research on a given topic

STUDY STRATEGIES

What is the best way to learn new material? The discipline of psychology has been studying this question for more than a century. The information in this section is not just opinion, but rather is backed up by this extensive body of research on learning. Listed below are some study strategies, the rationale behind them, and how the learning features of the textbook are designed to encourage their use.

▶ **Get the big picture and learn the details within the context of the big picture**. Every chapter begins with an outline. Take a minute to review it so that you can visualize the organization and coverage of the chapter. Each chapter begins with one or more case studies that illustrate the material covered in the chapter. These cases not only make the material more vivid but also provide a subtle organizational tool for material covered in the text.

▶ **Review the material for optimal learning**. Reading material is an inefficient learning strategy. The real learning comes from reviewing the material. The *Check Yourself* questions at the end of each section provide this review. The two to three minutes they will take you to complete will dramatically improve retention of the material and will prevent those long study sessions in which you learn absolutely nothing. The summary at the end of each chapter provides an

additional opportunity for review. The running list of new terms and their definitions makes it easy to review these items. The frequent case studies in the text help you to review or preview concepts discussed in the text.

▶ **Relate new material to things you already know**. This book is filled with examples, many of them vividly portrayed in graphs and pictures with captions. Every picture and graph was selected or developed with a specific learning objective in mind. Looking at the pictures and reading the captions not only helps review the material but also helps relate the material to experiences in your own life. A concept that you might forget in an hour will stay with you for years if it can be remembered in the context of your own life experiences. The *Ponder this* questions at the end of each section often encourage you to find your own links between the new material covered in the section and your previous experiences.

▶ **Avoid cramming**. Spending twelve hours studying the day before the exam is horribly inefficient, not to mention stressful. You would learn a lot more by studying one hour each day for the six days prior to the exam than cramming for twelve straight hours the day before. Spreading out the learning improves efficiency. Studying in different ways will further increase learning efficiency. Do not just reread a chapter in preparation for an exam. Use the chapter outlines and summaries, the *Check Yourself* questions, and the list of key terms and their running definitions in the text to stimulate your thinking and enhance your recall of these concepts. Even looking at the pictures helps if you are actively thinking during the process. The more different ways you review the material, the more likely you will recall it when necessary, such as during the exam.

▶ **Don't study all the time**. Study for short periods, perhaps no more than twenty minutes at a time. When you study, concentrate on understanding the material, not memorizing it. Then take a few minutes to clear your head before you return to studying. You need not have the book in front of you to study. Reviewing the concepts you just read or learned about in lecture while you walk to your car or your apartment or dorm room will dramatically enhance learning, without cutting into your social life. Optimizing learning involves creating the right balance of work, recreation, socialization, and sleep. Pulling all-nighters is a virtual waste of time. Spend half the time studying a half hour a day and you will learn much more and will be rested enough to actually recall it for the exam. Study for shorter periods, but study intensely. Talk with friends during breaks or get some exercise. Get enough sleep. You will learn in Chapter 10 that college students are, on average, seriously sleep-deprived. Sleep-deprived individuals do not think clearly or learn efficiently. Most students would be better off spending less time studying and more time sleeping, provided that they have a disciplined and consistent study plan.

FEEDBACK

Good textbooks are written for students, with features designed to enhance a student's learning experience. Through most of the writing, and all of the rewriting, I tried to feel my students standing behind me and reacting to every sentence. Does it make sense? Is it interesting? What is its relevance? As hard as I try to do this, however, there is no substitute for the real thing. Therefore, I want to extend an open invitation to contact me about your experiences with the text and your ideas for improvement. The web site for the text has an evaluation section as a place to provide such feedback. You can use either the formal or informal evaluation form to e-mail me comments. I will save and sort every comment, using your ideas in the next edition.

Good luck with your course. I hope that this text will enhance your learning experience and, perhaps, also turn you on to a truly exciting and important field of study.

Mike Raulin

About the Author

Michael Raulin is a clinical associate professor at the State University of New York at Buffalo, where he has been a faculty member since 1978. He received his BS and Ph.D. from the University of Wisconsin at Madison. At Buffalo, he was the director of the Psychological Services Center—the research and training clinic for the Ph.D. program in clinical psychology—and also headed the Ph.D. clinical psychology program for several years. He founded and directed the department's Anxiety Disorders Clinic and has maintained a small private practice since 1984.

Dr. Raulin's research has always focused on psychopathology, with most of his work on risk factors in schizophrenia. He has published 30 articles or chapters and is co-author of a successful research methods textbook with Anthony Graziano (now in its fourth edition). He served on the editorial board of the *Journal of Consulting and Clinical Psychology* and the *Journal of Abnormal Psychology* and reviewed papers for nearly 20 different journals and grant applications for the National Institute of Health (NIH) and the Social Sciences and Humanities Research Council of Canada. He has been active in psychological affairs locally, regionally, and nationally. He was president of the Psychological Association of Western New York, chaired the program committees for the Society for Research in Psychopathology and the Eastern Psychological Association, and was president of the National Association of Directors of Psychology Training Clinics and secretary of the Society for Research in Psychopathology. He has an excellent reputation for his teaching, with evaluations that consistently place him among the top instructors at the university. He has won awards for teaching and public service and is listed in *Who's Who Among Rising Young Americans*, *Who's Who Among Health Service Professionals*, *Who's Who in Science and Engineering*, and *Who's Who in Medicine and Health Care*. When time and weather permit, he can be found on the golf course.

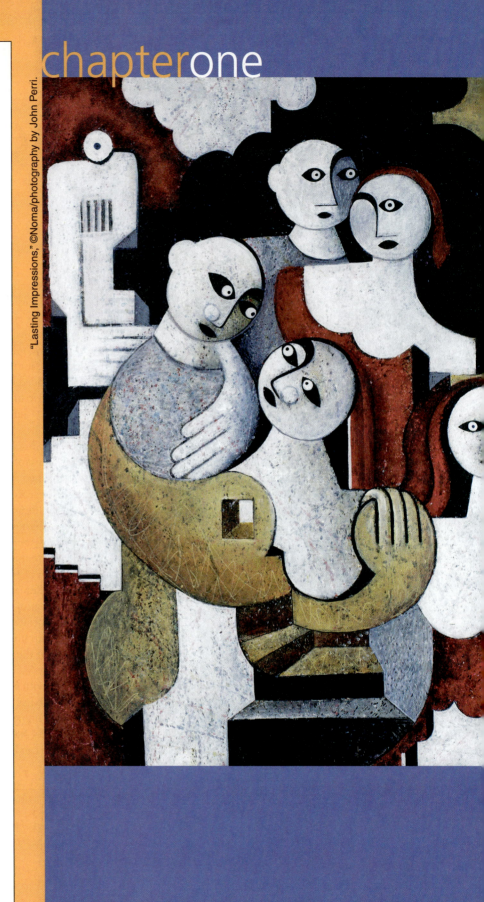

chapterone

"Lasting Impressions," ©Noma/photography by John Perri.

Understanding Abnormal Behavior

A Life So Promising

KEVIN Kevin was a bright, sensitive teenager and a gifted artist. Yet at the age of 21, with a promising life in front of him, he slowly slipped into a psychiatric disorder. Voices that only he could hear told him what to do. His thoughts became so scrambled that he spoke in gibberish. His facial expressions were often grossly distorted, his emotions unpredictable, and his mood increasingly somber. His sensitivity to the feelings of others—once his trademark—was completely lost. The artwork that had won him several awards became grotesque and bizarre, and eventually he just stopped painting. He ceased bathing and sometimes wore the same clothes for weeks. He at times would rant and rave about wild conspiracies and at other times would sit motionless, apparently oblivious to the world around him. Yet Kevin had no idea anything was wrong. His parents begged him to see a doctor, but he refused. When he finally did see a doctor several months later, he looked twice his age and spent most of his days staring into space or carrying on conversations with people who were not there.

How does a person like Kevin go from being sensitive, caring, and immensely talented to being self-absorbed, bizarre, and unable to function? The reasons are complex and will be the focus of this text. One can sometimes see clues in the history of people like Kevin. For example, Kevin was adopted, and the only thing Kevin's adoptive parents were told about his biological parents was that his biological mother was "very high strung," a phrase that is sometimes a nice way of saying that there was severe psychopathology. Kevin's early development was normal, although he was quiet and shy, but by the third grade, Kevin was so uncomfortable in school that he was virtually mute. A child psychologist helped him discover his artistic and musical talent. Joining the school band in the fifth grade boosted Kevin's self-confidence. He played the trumpet beautifully and with a dramatic flair that gained him considerable respect from his peers.

A shy, socially awkward student in junior high school, Kevin became a favorite target of school bullies, who took his lunch money, tripped him in the hall, threw his books out the window, ripped up his homework, and threatened to push him down the stairs. Kevin would feign illness to avoid going to school and facing these roughnecks. A case of pneumonia his freshman year of high school kept Kevin out of school for three months. When he was healthy enough to return, he simply refused, and no amount of effort could get him back in class.

Kevin's grades remained high on home study, but his parents were increasingly concerned about his behavior. He became extremely meticulous about his grooming, spending four to five hours a day on it. His daydreaming took on a reality of its own. Kevin would imagine himself as a rock star, with admiring groupies begging for his attention—not a bad fantasy, except at times Kevin would talk as though it were true.

By the time Kevin entered his senior year in high school he was a virtual prisoner in his own home. His anxiety was so intense that he rarely ventured outside at all, and when he did, it was only into his backyard. With intense therapy, he was able to leave his house, and he even went to his senior prom. However, he never returned to classes, and he remained uncomfortable around most of his peers.

How would you describe Kevin? You might be inclined to describe him as an unusual child who became even more unusual as he matured. Kevin's symptoms capture our attention; they jump out at us and make us uncomfortable. Therefore, many people want to dismiss individuals like Kevin as very different from themselves. They want to label someone like Kevin as crazy, as though that single term could capture all of the critical elements of his being. But Kevin was much more than someone with a serious psychological problem. He clearly had a number of strengths. He was bright and artistically skilled. Even while completely housebound, he maintained two close friendships. Yet the stress of attending school was more than he could handle. For all practical purposes, Kevin's world during his high school years was reduced to the confines of a three-bedroom home. Like most high school seniors, he took his grooming seriously; unlike most high school seniors, he performed grooming rituals for several hours each day. Even before the onset of his more severe symptoms, Kevin's behavior was unusual. But when did his behavior cross the line from being unusual to being abnormal? When did his shyness and sensitivity become something more troublesome? Finally, were there signs in his early behavior that would have warned of the serious psychological problems that awaited him just a few years later?

Kevin's symptoms are referred to as psychopathology. **Psychopathology** covers a range of disturbed behavior, including severe depression and anxiety, substance abuse, consistent emotional or behavioral overreactions to life stresses, and disruption in thought processes, emotional functioning, and behavior. Sometimes psychopathology is subtle—barely noticeable except to the person experiencing it. In this category are mild depression, specific fears, and avoidance of certain situations. Psychopathology is inherently interesting to people, although it can be frightening. One reason for this interest may be a voyeuristic curiosity about an unusual phenomenon. What are these people like? How did they get that way? How does it feel to have such symptoms? Those are legitimate questions, and they may well serve as part of your motivation for reading this book. But there may be other motivations. Perhaps you know someone who has suffered from a psychological disorder. Perhaps you yourself have struggled with one or more of these conditions and know firsthand the impact such disorders can have. If you are like most people, you do not qualify for any of the more than 250 diagnostic conditions that are listed in the official diagnostic manual. But there may be times when you question your own mental health. Sometimes you get anxious and avoid situations that make you anxious. You probably get depressed at times and find it hard to stay productive. Your thinking may not always be as clear and focused as you would like. You may daydream about being successful, wealthy, attractive, or all of the above. You may experience anger so intense that you

psychopathology A range of disturbed behavior, including severe depression and anxiety, substance abuse, consistent emotional or behavioral overreactions to life stresses, and disruption in thought processes, emotional functioning, and behavior.

At times, psychopathology can be so dramatic that it blinds people to the fact that a person is suffering. Psychopathology is something that a person must deal with; it is not something that defines the person.

cannot think of anything else. You may occasionally engage in such superstitious rituals as knocking on wood. So how different are you from Kevin?

People are enormously resilient. Through stresses and strains of all sorts, they manage to function well—at least most of the time. When that functioning breaks down, however, a variety of behaviors may result. Some of this behavior makes sense. For example, withdrawing from situations that make one anxious, although potentially problematic, is certainly understandable. Other abnormal behavior is harder to understand because it is clearly outside the realm of everyday experience. For example, a client with a condition called obsessive-compulsive disorder believed that his parents would die if he did not turn around twice and say "never" to himself three times whenever he heard the word *hell*. Such unusual behavior is common in some psychopathology.

This text will be asking the question "When is behavior abnormal?" As you will see shortly, it is a difficult question to answer. This chapter discusses the problem of defining abnormal behavior. Later chapters address other questions, such as "How is psychopathology classified?" and "How do these behaviors develop?" Never forget, however, that each person with a psychological disorder is unique. Each is struggling with life and, for the moment at least, losing the battle. To drive this point home, case studies of real people dealing with their disorders are presented throughout the text.

Some types of psychopathology are better understood than others. Areas that are still puzzling to scientists despite years of research will not be glossed over in this text, and the controversies that exist among those who study abnormal behavior will not be ignored. This is a dynamic field, where research constantly enhances our understanding and often challenges previous conceptualizations. You should not expect simple explanations for psychopathology. However, you can expect interesting ideas, provocative questions, and intriguing examples.

This chapter begins with a discussion of *adaptability,* which is the ability to change one's behavior to meet the demands of new situations. The ability to adapt to an ever-changing environment is a critical component of normal functioning, and psychopathology can seriously impair adaptation. The focus then shifts to failures at adaptation, as the various ways of defining abnormality are described. A brief history of how psychopathology has been viewed and treated provides a basis for understanding the current conceptualizations of psychopathology. The final section of this chapter describes the various mental health professionals who deal daily with psychopathology.

RESPONDING TO ENVIRONMENTAL CHALLENGES

Human beings are remarkable creatures, capable of doing so many things. They are the result of hundreds of millions of years of evolution—evolution that continues to this day. **Evolution** refers to the gradual changes in a species that occur across generations and are shaped by the environmental demands placed on that species. The mechanism by which these changes occur is covered in the nearby Focus box. The complexity and functionality of human beings are almost miraculous. Yet in spite of their wondrous nature, human beings are challenged every day, and their survival and success will depend on how well they respond to that challenge. One cannot understand psychopathology without first understanding the constant pressures that people face daily and the ways in which they handle those pressures. Our species's adaptation to environmental demands is a critical element in evolutionary theory, which is one of the themes of this textbook.

ADAPTING TO THE ENVIRONMENT

Human beings are animals—similar in many ways to other animals. On some dimensions, such as abstract reasoning, humans are more advanced than other animals. Humans have created an incredibly complex culture and technology based largely on their ability to think and to communicate abstract ideas and information via language. Like all animals, humans take advantage of particular environmental niches—places and situations that are well suited to their

survival. Unlike other animals, however, humans are able to take advantage of a vast range of environmental settings. No other mammal covers so much of the planet or is so successful in adapting to a variety of conditions. People are even adaptable enough to leave this planet and survive in the hostile environment of outer space (Diamond, 1992).

Evolutionary Impact

All animals, including human beings, respond and adapt to the environment. Adapting to the environment involves adjusting behavior to increase the likelihood of positive consequences or to decrease the likelihood of negative consequences. Animals might adapt by learning to avoid places that their predators frequent or to seek out places that their prey frequent. Humans might adapt by building shelters for protection or cultivating crops for food. If an organism adapts effectively, it survives; if it does not, it will probably die prematurely. Of course, life is rarely that black and white. Some people do a marvelous job of adapting to their surroundings, but despite their efforts they die young. For example, they may work hard to get good jobs and provide security for their families only to be hit and killed by a careless driver. Other people adapt rather poorly but get lucky and survive anyway. For example, those careless drivers might never be seriously hurt, in spite of causing repeated accidents. Nevertheless, on average, people who adapt well tend to survive longer than those who adapt less effectively, and therefore, they are more likely to raise offspring and thus pass on their genes.

This last point is worth emphasizing. Each individual organism is involved in its own personal struggle to survive and reproduce. Evolution is not driven by these individual events, however, but rather by the *collective* experience of all the organisms of a given species in a given region. If those that survive and reproduce have a specific genetically influenced characteristic, such as coloring, the genes affecting that characteristic will be more common in the next generation—that is, more of the members of the species will carry these genes than carried them in the previous generation. As Darwin was able to deduce from his observations of birds and other species, once a subset of a population becomes geographically isolated from the rest of the population, it will follow its own evolutionary course. In that way, a single species might diverge in its characteristics in different locations to the point where two different species

evolution   The gradual changes in a species that occur across generations and are shaped by the environmental demands placed on that species.

FOCUS Evolutionary perspective and psychology

Evolutionary theory, independently articulated by Charles Darwin and Alfred Russel Wallace nearly 150 years ago, emphasizes how an organism's characteristics influence its survival and reproduction. This process, which is called **natural selection,** affects the distribution of genes in the next generation. Genes that increase the likelihood of an organism's surviving and reproducing will be more heavily represented in the next generation than genes that do not confer such an advantage. For example, if certain genes enhance the ability to learn to avoid danger, the organisms with those genes will have a better chance of surviving long enough to pass the genes on. Organisms without those genes will tend to die early, before they have offspring. The result is that in the next generation, the genes that contribute to this critical learning will be more common. Even a small selective advantage—say a 1 or 2% better

chance of survival—is more than enough to increase rapidly the frequency of genes that impart that advantage (Mitton, 1997; Ridley, 1996).

Natural selection frequently is misunderstood by the general public. It is based on the simple principle that some organisms die prematurely, thus limiting their reproductive success. Sometimes the premature death is random and has nothing to do with the organism. Nonetheless, the organism's genes are less well represented in the population in the succeeding generation, because it produced few if any offspring. However, subtle differences in the organism's behavior or functioning may have contributed to the premature death. For example, organisms that blend in with their surroundings are less likely to be detected by predators. To the extent that genes influence such beneficial features, the frequency of those genes in the next generation tends to increase. In contrast, genes that decrease the organism's chance for survival tend to

decrease because the organism may not live long enough to pass them on. Subtle differences may affect survival in small but significant ways. What is surprising to most students is how the slightest selective advantage can lead to a substantial change in gene frequency over just a few dozen generations.

Evolutionary theory has shaped much of modern psychology by emphasizing the twin themes of (1) the function of behavior and (2) the similarity between human behavior and that of other animals. Understanding how behaviors might evolve requires a thorough study of how the behaviors serve the organism. Effective behavior is at least as critical to survival as the shape of an organism's mouth or the sensitivity of its hearing. Many animals, including human beings, share the drives that propel behavior, such as hunger and fear. The principles of learning and adaptation also appear to be similar across species. By studying the func-

are formed. Humans show some divergence in that those who evolved in the hot sun of Africa have darker skin than those who evolved in the northern regions of Europe. This occurred because dark skin protects people from the intense African sun. However, humans never diverged into separate species, and such surface characteristics as skin color, although valuable adaptations to the environment, are trivial traits that differentiate one human being from another only superficially.

Like all advanced animals, people are inherently hedonic creatures—that is, they seek pleasure and avoid pain. These hedonic tendencies are the primary motivator of adaptive responses. People learn complex behaviors through a process of interacting with the environment, observing the impact of their behavior on the environment and the consequences to themselves, and then modifying their behavior to improve the outcome. Behavior that produces positive outcomes is said to be **adaptive;** behavior that produces negative outcomes is said to be **maladaptive.** For example, failing to find sufficient food will lead to starvation, which is clearly mal-

adaptive. On the other hand, identifying locations that provide adequate food sources and moving on to other locations when the food supply in one location is no longer adequate is clearly adaptive. However, these deceptively simple definitions become complicated in the complex reality of life. Because most behaviors have multiple consequences, judging how adaptive they are can be difficult. For example, finding a location with abundant food supplies would appear to be adaptive, but if that location harbors an equally abundant supply of predators, the long-term consequences of foraging for food there may far outweigh the short-term advantage. Nevertheless, many behaviors are either clearly adaptive or maladaptive.

The example of adapting to the environment by finding new food sources suggests that the organism is simply responding to the environment passively. That need not be the case, and for human beings, it is rarely the case. Organisms can adapt by changing the environment or by changing the way they interact with it. For example, squirrels improve their chance of living tionality, purpose, and flexibility of behavior, psychologists can explore how behavioral mechanisms might have developed and thus provide insights into the limitations of the mechanisms.

There is certainly controversy among nonscientists regarding evolutionary theory (Berra, 1990; Firenze, 1997). For example, there are some who believe that this theory must be wrong because it contradicts the account of creation in the Bible. However, there is little controversy among scientists, who are convinced, by abundant evidence, that organisms evolve (Ridley, 1996). Scientists accept the basic tenets of evolutionary theory because evolutionary theory organizes thousands of specific pieces of information into a coherent explanation of those diverse observations. Many of the religious objections to evolutionary theory have recently been softened or dropped in the face of the overwhelming evidence for the general concept of evolution. For exam-

ple, the Catholic church, which once opposed the concept, now acknowledges that living creatures constantly evolve and that human beings evolved from other organisms. Even if you are uncomfortable accepting the concept of evolution, you will still find the organizational advantages of the theory helpful in minimizing the effort needed to remember the hundreds of diverse facts presented in this text.

There is a potential problem with evolutionary theory, however. It is very easy to use an overly simplistic notion of the theory to create an endless supply of post hoc—after the fact—explanations for almost any phenomenon. For example, it is not hard to make up a reasonable evolutionary scenario that might explain the existence of a given phenomenon, such as depression. Scientists know that such post hoc explanations are virtually useless *unless* they also generate strong predictions that can be subjected to experiment and disproved if they are not valid. Evolutionary theory

can do just that when it is used properly. Therefore, in addition to being an organizational tool, it can provide guidance for useful research. Of course, it can also provide the pseudoscientific explanations that have made it popular among those who want support for their pet beliefs. For example, it was once widely invoked to support the belief that certain nationalities were superior to other nationalities—a theory called *social Darwinism*. In effect, evolutionary theory was used as a justification for racism. In this case, not only was evolutionary theory misapplied, but the data presented in support of the theory were seriously flawed and deliberately distorted. This textbook will not pervert evolutionary theory in any such manner. To do so would be to take a valid and serviceable scientific theory and dress it up like a clown.

through the winter by finding and storing food during late summer and fall. Humans manipulate every aspect of the environment to provide safe and relatively comfortable living situations in climates that are generally hostile, such as the Arctic Circle. They decrease their risk of starvation by systematically cultivating crops and animals and storing food for a later time. These active adaptations are particularly effective because they can be applied to a wider variety of environmental conditions than the more passive adaptations geared to taking advantage of a given environment.

People who consistently are unable to adapt and function effectively in a variety of conditions are classified as **abnormal.** Of course, there are limits to adaptability in everyone. It is a challenge to adapt to a new boss or a new job; it is a greater challenge to adapt to losing one's job. It is a challenge to adapt to new surroundings, with new demands and new requirements; it is a greater challenge if those new surroundings are a prisoner-of-war camp where torture is routine. It is challenge to adapt to the ever-

increasing demands of the outside world as you grow from a toddler, to a preschooler, to an adolescent; it is a greater challenge to adapt to those situations while being abused or neglected by those who should be caring for you. Whether a failure to adapt is classified as abnormal depends on the severity of the situation and on whether most people could adapt to the situation. Some situations may be so severe that few people could adapt to them, in which case, failing to adapt would not be considered abnormal.

The concepts of abnormal and maladaptive may seem simple, but they can become complex and confusing. What

natural selection   How an organism's characteristics influence its survival and reproduction. This process affects the distribution of genes in the next generation.

adaptive   Behavior that produces positive outcomes.

maladaptive   Behavior that produces negative outcomes.

abnormal   A term applied to people who consistently are unable to adapt and function effectively in a variety of conditions.

is adaptive in one setting may not be adaptive in others. Adaptive behavior is not static. Whales born and raised in an aquarium may be perfectly adapted to the setting in which they reside. But release those whales into their natural environment, and their life expectancy may be sharply limited because they have never learned how to catch their food.

Even subtle changes can make an enormous difference in whether a behavior is adaptive. Think about the changes students face moving from high school to college. Although they were already well suited and prepared for college, much of their previously effective behavior no longer works. A one-hour cram session is no longer enough to ensure a good grade on an exam. Furthermore, behaviors that may previously have been ineffective now work well. For example, they are no longer considered strange for spending an entire afternoon in the library. As adaptable creatures, most of them make the transition to college, and within a matter of weeks, they feel like seasoned college students.

Adapting successfully to the world around you does not mean that you will not make mistakes along the way. No one possesses the wisdom and insight to predict correctly the most adaptive response under all circumstances. If people's first attempts at dealing with a new situation are ineffective, that does not mean that they are maladapted; it simply means that they have not *yet* adapted. The environment is dynamic, always changing, and people have to be dynamic as well. Therefore, one should never make a judgment about how well adapted someone is by looking at just a few behaviors. When we look at the broader picture, we discover that the adaptability of individuals has to be defined by specifying the range of situations in which they can function.

FACTORS THAT AFFECT ADAPTATION

Many factors contribute to how effectively people adapt to a given environment. Four key factors are the individual's (1) genetic makeup, (2) physical condition, (3) learning and reasoning, and (4) socialization.

Genetic Makeup. Each person, unless he or she has an identical twin, is endowed at conception with a unique genetic heritage, which influences appearance, development, and behavioral tendencies. For example, a genetic heritage that results in strong spatial skills, the ability to control anxiety in dangerous situations, and the intellectual capacity to learn complex material and recall it quickly under demanding circumstances may prepare someone to be a fighter pilot. Other combinations of attributes may prepare other people for other roles.

Genetic makeup affects many aspects of a person, including physical characteristics, temperament, and the behavioral tendencies called personality traits (Plomin et al., 1990). For example, people whose genes make them prone to be overweight may fatigue easily just from meet-

ing the demands of everyday life, whereas other people may simply have high energy levels regardless of the situation. Genes can also affect intellectual capacity and the ability to reason (Gregory, 1992). They may affect tendencies to respond to stresses with anxiety, to give up easily, or to focus on one thing to the exclusion of others. Scientists are only now beginning to appreciate all the ways in which genes affect human functioning.

Genetically influenced characteristics often affect adaptability, although the effect may depend on other factors. For example, some people seem predisposed to be sensitive to others and may often worry excessively about how others respond to them. Is such behavior adaptive or maladaptive? It depends on the situation and on your perspective about what is important. Such a trait is likely to lead to the development of effective interpersonal skills, permitting the person to tune in easily to the feelings of others. There are many occupations, such as clinical psychology, in which such a trait would be adaptive. However, such a trait could also predispose the individual to being easily hurt by little things that people say and do. This could lead in turn to social withdrawal, which can be maladaptive. Virtually every personality trait is a double-edged sword—adaptive in some situations and maladaptive in others. If people are fortunate enough to have sufficient talent and opportunities, they are often able to select for themselves environments that fit their personality and abilities.

The role of genes in shaping human behavior has always been controversial. At one time, most psychologists and psychiatrists flatly denied the proposition that genetic factors influence the risk for psychiatric disorders (Gottesman, 1991). Today, most professionals readily accept the role of genetic factors in such disorders.

Physical Condition. Adaption is a function of both stable and fluctuating aspects of the organism. For example, such stable factors as size, strength, and appearance can increase or decrease adaptation. Fluctuating factors, such as fatigue and physical health, also affect adaptation.

The biological makeup of the organism, including temperament, can have enormous influence on adaptability. For example, a large and strong animal is generally better able to adapt to the demands of the environment than a small and weak animal of the same species. However, this principle is not absolute. A large animal may be able to compete more successfully for scarce resources, but in times of famine, a large animal has a much higher caloric demand and therefore may not be able to find enough food to survive. A large animal may be able to fight off attacks more readily or capture prey more effectively, but a smaller animal may be harder to detect and may be able to hide more effectively when hiding places are scarce. A bold animal may be able to venture out more readily to find food, but such boldness may increase its risk from predators. Even such factors as coloring can be significant. Dull coloring may increase survivability by providing camouflage. Bright colors may not enhance survivability directly, but they could be genetically favored because they enhance mating success.

Such transient features as fatigue or health also affect adaptation. Someone who is fatigued will not function as effectively as someone who is well rested. Physical health and adequate food and sleep increase physical energy. It is difficult to function when a virus has turned your digestive system into a war zone. Hormonal influences may either increase or decrease the level of energy available. During times of stress, people adapt by producing hormones, such as adrenaline, that temporarily increase the available energy. After a prolonged period without sleep, biological influences decrease one's energy reserves, forcing one to sleep (Walsh & Lindblom, 1997). Over the course of a normal day, energy reserves fluctuate. At 4 a.m. most people have relatively low energy reserves, whereas at 10 a.m. or 6 p.m. people's energy reserves tend to be higher (Campbell, 1997). Energy levels are also influenced by external events. If the Publisher's Clearinghouse representative surprises you with a ten-million-dollar check, chances are you will be full of energy no matter how little sleep you got the night before. Such psychological responses to environmental events are mediated by specific physiological mechanisms, which will be discussed in Chapter 4.

Adequate energy is critical if people are to adapt to changing environments. What may be less obvious is that having too much energy can be as problematic as having too little. Have you ever been wound up too tight to be

No one is capable of always being effective in handling day-to-day stresses. Momentary lapses in effectiveness are expected, and such lapses are not considered a sign of psychopathology.

able to focus on a problem? Have you ever been too anxious to think clearly? Both of these situations represent high-energy states—states that may inhibit one's ability to respond.

Learning and Reasoning. One of the richest and most useful of adaptive resources is a person's ability to keep a personal record of his or her history. A key to adaptability is that people learn from past experiences and remember what they have learned. What they learn is complex and can be adapted to a variety of situations. People do not simply learn that behavior A will lead to consequence B in situation C. People naturally group behaviors, consequences, and situations into categories (Gazzaniga et al., 1998). If a set of possible behaviors has been effective in a certain set of situations, then one has a basis for selecting a potentially successful response when faced with a new, but similar, situation. The more experience people have in a situation, the more likely they are to have an effective response for any environmental demand.

One usually thinks of learning as an asset, and in most cases it clearly is. The more information people have, the more likely they will have the resources to adapt to new situations. Sometimes, however, learning gets in the way of an adaptive response (Meichenbaum & Turk, 1987). People may be reluctant to give up a previously effective response to try something new, even if their current response is not working. For example, people who have learned to avoid being held responsible for mistakes by acting naïve and childlike may be reluctant to change this approach, even though it is preventing their advancement at work. It matters little that changing one's approach would be advantageous. The avoidance behavior is too comfortable for the individual to risk another approach.

Experiences and the learning that comes from them clearly affect later responses. However, human beings also have the ability to think beyond experience, to speculate and to reason, and, consequently, to create new and effective solutions based on abstract principles (Matlin, 1998). People would never tolerate an engineer who built a bridge with a "let's see if this will be strong enough" attitude. They expect engineers to know exactly how strong a given design will be and whether it will be strong enough to meet the demands of the situation. Knowing in advance how strong the bridge will be is possible because abstract principles exist that enable the engineer to make these computations.

People's ability to reason permits them to solve daily problems that might well threaten their existence if they went unsolved. For example, they can develop new food resources or increase their ability to store food against a potential famine. In today's modern world, getting and keeping a good job depends on one's ability to learn new things associated with that job. If people fail, they lose their ability to provide for themselves, and they are at the mercy of others.

One's ability to reason is affected by many variables, including motivation, emotional state, and psychological health. People make most of their everyday decisions without conducting a thorough analysis because they have little motivation to do so (Myers, 1999). However, if they are contemplating a major decision, such as which career to pursue, they may be motivated to gather relevant data and weigh all options. People's thinking can become very disorganized when they are emotionally upset or frightened. For example, it is common for people who have just had someone close to them die to "go around in circles" trying to figure out what they should do next (Staudacher, 1991). Finally, specific psychological disorders can reduce the reasoning capacity of individuals, dramatically undermining their ability to adapt to the world (Gottesman, 1991).

Socialization. Not every organism is dependent on social interactions to enhance adaptability, but human beings clearly are. Human beings are social by nature, and their success as a species is largely due to their cooperative nature. Neither modern civilizations nor even primitive hunter-gatherer societies would be possible without such cooperation. There are many who believe that the primary pressure shaping the evolution of the human brain is the value of social cooperation, which requires extensive communication (Deacon, 2000). Modern brain-imaging studies show that face-to-face communication activates more areas of the brain than any other activity (Grabowski & Damasio, 2000).

Social cooperation contributes to adaptability in several ways besides enhancing activities, such as hunting, that were once critical to survival. Human beings readily supply social support to one another, building up the spirits of disheartened individuals and encouraging those people who are discouraged, fearful, or unmotivated. Think of times when a teammate essentially gave you a pat on the back, saying, "You can do it" or "We are all counting on you." Such supportive gestures and the physical help people receive from one another enhance adaptability in many different situations. As you will see throughout the text, social support often decreases the risk of psychopathology or mitigates its impact on people. Furthermore, some forms of psychopathology interfere with socialization, thereby exacerbating some of the symptoms experienced.

Check Yourself 1.1

Responding to Environmental Challenges

1. What process fuels evolution?
2. What factors contribute to adaptation?

Ponder this . . . *Adaptation requires constant struggle—a struggle that each person engages in daily. Think about times when you felt you were adapting well and other times when you felt you were not adapting well. Identify the factors that might have accounted for the difference in those situations. Judging on the basis of your analysis, what might you do to increase your effectiveness in the future?*

DEFINING ABNORMALITY

Defining abnormal behavior is a challenge. As Supreme Court Justice Potter Stewart said in a landmark ruling on obscenity, "I know it when I see it." Most people believe that they know obscenity when they see it, but definitions vary considerably from person to person. To a degree, the same is true of the concept of abnormality.

At first glance, the task of defining abnormal behavior appears trivial. But to be scientifically useful, the definition of abnormality has to be specific. Several definitions of abnormal behavior have been suggested. They include (1) statistically unusual behavior, (2) socially unacceptable behavior, (3) dysfunctional behavior, and (4) personally distressing behavior. Some of these definitions (dysfunctional and personally distressing) are based on the individual's perspective, whereas others (statistically unusual and socially unacceptable) look at the behavior from the perspective of society. Each definition has advantages and disadvantages. No single definition underlies all the different forms of psychopathology. Collectively, however, these definitions help delineate what is meant by *abnormal*. These definitions are briefly summarized in Table 1.1.

[TABLE 1.1] Defining Abnormality

Several criteria that are used to define abnormality are briefly described here.

Statistically unusual behavior: Behavior that occurs infrequently.

Socially unacceptable behavior: Behavior that is considered unacceptable within a given culture. Note that behaviors that are unacceptable in one culture may be perfectly acceptable in another.

Dysfunctional behavior: Behavior that is ineffective in meeting a person's goals. The related concept of harmful dysfunction employs two criteria. The first is harm, which is a societal judgment that the behavior is undesirable. The second is that a system is failing to perform the function that natural selection shaped it to handle.

Personally distressing behavior: Behavior or feelings that are uncomfortable or upsetting to the person experiencing them.

STATISTICALLY UNUSUAL BEHAVIOR

Implicit in most conceptualizations of abnormality is that it is rare or unusual. Therefore, it makes sense to employ a statistical definition as a way of objectifying abnormality. For example, one could define as abnormal anything unusual enough that no more than 2% of the population behaves that way. Kevin's inability to attend high school, his spending several hours each day on grooming, and his eventual psychological deterioration are all statistically unusual events.

On the surface, this seems a clean, objective way of defining abnormality. However, there are complications. First, human behavior is complex, and classifying it with enough precision to employ such a statistical analysis is not easy. Second, some disorders, such as depression and substance abuse, are unfortunately not rare. Finally, statistical improbability alone is often insufficient to define abnormality. By the statistical improbability definition, Albert Einstein, Tiger Woods, and Mother Teresa would have to be classified as abnormal. Their accomplishments are extremely unusual. However, most people would call them exceptional, remarkable, or impressive instead of abnormal. A statistical definition alone does not capture psychopathology well, because most people have a sense that one end of the statistical distribution is more pathological than the other. For example, low IQs are usually considered more pathological than high IQs. Accordingly, we must combine statistical considerations with other criteria to arrive at an accepted definition of abnormality. Yet despite these problems, statistical criteria are critical to many concepts of abnormality. For example, extreme sadness is considered normal for a period after the death of a loved one, because it is a common grief reaction. Persistently exhibiting that same reaction in everyday situations, in which few people respond that way, is labeled depression and is considered abnormal.

SOCIALLY UNACCEPTABLE BEHAVIOR

The definition of abnormal behavior should always be tied to one's cultural background. People learn what is normal or acceptable by observing society's response to behaviors or by learning explicit rules and regulations. People who frequently violate social norms find themselves at odds with the rest of society.

What is considered normal or socially acceptable varies from one culture to the next. For example, in some ethnic groups, such as among Russians, openly showing one's emotions is considered inappropriate (Wierzbicka, 1998); in other ethnic groups, such as among Italians, *not* showing one's emotions is considered inappropriate. In most cultures, engaging in sexual relationships with one's children is both illegal and strongly condemned. However, in some

Whether a given behavior is considered normal depends on the context of that behavior, and cultural norms often define the context. The revealing outfit is perfectly acceptable in many cultures, but other cultures insist on more modest dress at all times for women.

Polynesian cultures, the norm is for the parents to initiate their children into sex, much as parents might teach their children to drive a car (Danielsson, 1956). Is one culture right and the other culture wrong? It is tempting to be egocentric and view other cultures as weird and pathological, but that is an unreasonable stance, given what is known about cultural diversity. A better approach is always to judge the appropriateness of behavior by taking into account the specific norms of the individual's culture.

The fact that a behavior is acceptable in one culture does not mean it is normal in any culture. The existence of cultural differences in what is judged abnormal does not mean that these distinctions are arbitrary. Cultures are complex, and individual behaviors cannot be interpreted out of a cultural context. For example, arguing that sexual activity with children is normal because there are cultures that accept it ignores the fact that there are dramatic differences in the respective cultures—differences that affect the impact of behaviors. In Western cultures, the way in which adults and children interact and the way in which sexual behavior is viewed make the impact of adult/child sexual behavior on children negative, sometimes devastatingly so.

Another problem with defining abnormal behavior culturally is that it depends on one's perspective. You might be unwilling to consider cheating an elderly couple out of their life savings as effective, but a swindler may consider such a con very effective indeed. Such vastly different perspectives, even within a culture, lead to disagreements about the abnormality of specific behavior. Most people think of criminal behavior as abnormal; career criminals rarely do.

Another important point to recognize is that cultural norms change over time. Homosexuality is a good example.

Homosexuality was once widely condemned in the United States, and there are still people with strong negative views on homosexuality. The question of whether homosexuality was abnormal, and therefore should be a diagnostic category, was once hotly debated in psychiatry and psychology (Schmidt, 1995). Homosexuality is now more widely accepted, and it is no longer considered a psychiatric disorder. Many companies now extend benefits to same sex partners much as they have to heterosexual partners in the past (Collison, 1993). Also, some states now grant adoption rights to same sex couples, and other states are moving toward legalizing homosexual marriage. Clearly attitudes have changed.

Even behaviors that appear unambiguous may be difficult to classify. For example, suppose someone is hearing things that are not there, which is referred to as an auditory hallucination. Most people would judge that person abnormal because his or her behavior suggests a loss of contact with reality. At one point, Kevin heard voices, and the voices were very real to him. However, many of the prophets who have shaped religions claimed to have heard the voice of God. Whether they are labeled as prophets or crazy will depend on how credible one finds their claim that God spoke to them (Szasz, 1961).

DYSFUNCTIONAL BEHAVIOR

This definition of abnormal behavior focuses on whether a person's behavior meets minimal required standards or helps to advance the person's goals. The case of Kevin provides several examples of behavior that fits this definition. Kevin was unable to attend school. In fact, for three years he was unable to leave the house. Therefore, he was unable to live up to societal expectations. Furthermore, his avoidance behavior prevented him from learning critical social skills, a deficit that handicapped him later. By his early 20s, Kevin was almost totally unable to function and could not even take care of himself. People who are unable to perform sexually, unable to function effectively in a social situation, or unable to think clearly might meet criteria for one or more diagnostic categories. Of course, any definition of abnormality in terms of dysfunctional behavior cannot be too broad or it will include everyone. Everyone has done things that were dysfunctional. Every time people go on a job interview and fail to get the job, every time they fail to convince someone of their point of view, every time they mess up a task by forgetting an important step, and every time they lose a tennis match their actions are dysfunctional in that they are ineffective. But these things happen to everyone. Therefore, the definition of abnormality has to take into account the degree of dysfunction and the importance of the behavior involved.

Evolutionary Impact

Recently, the concept of harmful dysfunction was advanced as a way to objectify the process of deciding what is normal and what is abnormal (Wakefield, 1992). In this model, harm is viewed as a societal judgment of the undesirability of a condition. Dysfunction is defined as a failure of a system to perform the natural function for which it was designed by natural selection. For example, if someone's brain is compromised by a disorder, such as Alzheimer's disease, clearly the brain is not functioning the way it was designed to function, and society would judge such a dysfunction harmful. Hence it would qualify as abnormal. The harmful-dysfunction criterion provides a unique perspective on abnormality. More than any other perspective, it focuses on the evolutionary significance of behavior. One must determine the functional purpose of the behavior in order to decide whether it is dysfunctional.

On the surface, this approach appears to be more objective than relying primarily on social judgment of abnormality, but like all the other approaches, it fails to define all the various types of psychopathologies. For example, posttraumatic stress disorder—a response to life-threatening trauma that is covered in Chapter 8—may represent adaptive functioning that was shaped through natural selection (Lilienfeld & Marino, 1995). However, the world has changed substantially since the time when this response was adaptive, and consequently, it no longer is adaptive. Nevertheless, the harmful-dysfunction approach has led to considerable discussion of the criteria for defining abnormality, and in that respect it has had a positive influence on the field of psychopathology.

An evolutionary perspective provides a variation on this theme of effectiveness. From an evolutionary perspective, effectiveness is judged on the basis of survival and reproduction, and the factors that affect these variables may change over time. From this perspective, anxiety is normal if it promotes survival by enhancing the organism's vigilance, but it is abnormal if it prevents the organism from doing things that are critical to survival, such as searching for food. This is often a delicate balance, which can change quickly in nature as predators wander into and out of an area. Today, people do not have to worry about being literally eaten for lunch. Nevertheless, survival and reproduction still involve competing in environments that can be hostile and demanding. Knowing when to argue and when to avoid conflict may affect whether one keeps a job or maintains social status. The nearby Focus box outlines some of the issues that arise in applying an evolutionary theme to psychopathology.

FOCUS

Evolutionary perspective and psychopathology

Evolutionary perspectives have been applied to the field of psychopathology in a number of ways. This perspective is unique in that it integrates other perspectives by focusing researchers on critical factors, including (1) genetic influences, (2) biological mechanisms, (3) adaptive functioning and the purpose of behavior, (4) flexibility of behavior, and (5) the role of the environment in determining whether behavior is adaptive. All of these factors will be addressed in this text.

Evidence is growing that genes influence many types of psychopathology. Not too long ago, scientists might have considered such genetic factors as inherently pathological traits that have yet to be eliminated by the process of natural selection. However, researchers are now questioning whether some pathological conditions may have been either less pathological or actually advantageous in another era. Could a condition such as depression, which on the surface appears to have little survival value, have been advantageous at one time? Martin Seligman thinks it might have, and he has argued that the behavior associated with depression may sometimes be an effective way of conserving energy that might otherwise be wasted (Seligman, 1975). Similar arguments have been made for disorders such as panic disorder and posttraumatic stress disorder, which will be discussed in later chapters.

It is only a small step from theorizing about the evolutionary advantages of behavior to theorizing about the current advantages of such behavior. People tend to classify behavior as either advantageous or pathological, but the world is not that simple. The effectiveness of behavior often depends on many variables. The tendency of depressed individuals to give up easily when confronted with difficult tasks would indeed conserve energy if the tasks were virtually impossible, but the effectiveness of this strategy rests on the accuracy of the individual's evaluation of the situation. People once thought that depressed individuals tend to see the world *more pessimistically* than is warranted. However, research shows that depressed people may see the world *more accurately* than nondepressed people (Alloy and Abramson, 1979, 1988). This surprising finding has triggered considerable research and controversy. The situation is clearly more complex than was once thought, as you will see in the discussion of depression in Chapter 7. Perhaps it was not an accident that this classic study was performed by two psychologists who studied with Dr. Seligman, because it is one of the things one might investigate if one were viewing the issue from an evolutionary perspective. This is just one of many examples of how thinking about psychopathology from an evolutionary perspective opens up entirely new avenues for research—productive avenues that lead to useful new ways of understanding and treating psychopathology.

PERSONALLY DISTRESSING BEHAVIOR

There is yet another way of defining abnormality. People can define feelings that are uncomfortable or distressing as abnormal, even if the feelings have little impact on their functioning. People who feel stressed out, see no point in life, and are just "going through the motions" may see themselves as suffering from a psychological problem, even though they may still be handling their responsibilities adequately.

Like the Supreme Court justice who could not define obscenity but knew it when he saw it, we are often faced with the same problem in defining abnormal behavior. In building a complex diagnostic system, researchers have relied on a number of definitions. In some cases, statistical rarity or consensus of opinion is what defines abnormality. In others, abnormality is defined in terms of dysfunctional behavior. In yet other cases, the person's discomfort defines abnormality. But most often, behaviors are classified as abnormal on the basis of a combination of these elements. Examples of all of these situations will be included in the discussions of disorders covered in this textbook.

Check Yourself 1.2

Defining Abnormality

1. What are the four primary methods of defining abnormality?

2. Describe the harmful-dysfunction approach to defining abnormality.

Ponder this . . . *Everyone occasionally behaves in ways that might be regarded as abnormal. Select a situation in which you felt that your behavior might qualify as abnormal, such as overreacting in an argument with a family member. Now select a behavior that you believe is clearly normal, such as expressing displeasure at a roommate's inconsiderate action. Finally, select a grossly abnormal behavior that you have personally witnessed in someone else. How do these behaviors stack up against the criteria for abnormality? Do the criteria appear to be too narrow or too broad to encompass what you think of as abnormal?*

HISTORY OF ABNORMAL BEHAVIOR

Mental health professionals deal with psychopathology today in much the same way in which doctors deal with physical disorders. There are hospital wards and entire

MODERN Myths

Misconceptions OF Psychopathology

Even though researchers have learned a great deal about psychopathology, there is much more to learn. Modern perspectives emphasize such factors as genetics, biological influences, learning histories, and cultural influences, but many misconceptions still cloud the general population's view of psychopathology. People like to think of themselves as sophisticated and enlightened, but their behavior and emotional responses often tell a different story.

Why are people so uncomfortable with psychopathology? If people really believe that psychopathology is caused by such factors as learning history and biological influences, why do they get so uncomfortable when they are around someone with serious psychopathology? The reason may be that their gut is telling them something else—something that is untrue. Mental disorders are not contagious; being near someone with a mental disorder will not put you at risk for developing the disorder. Mental disorders are not a sign of evil; people with the disorders are not possessed, and they did not do anything evil to warrant their disorder. Mental disorders are not a sign of character weakness.

Why is it so difficult to talk with someone who has severe psychopathology? It is interesting to watch people interact with individuals who suffer from serious psychopathology. Their conversations are often more tentative, more cautious, and more impersonal. They rarely seem to connect to the person; instead, their conversation seems to "talk around" the psychopathology without explicitly mentioning it. Individuals with mental disorders are still people, and they have feelings, views on life, and aspirations. You can talk to them. They are often willing to talk about their illness. They usually know that something is wrong, although some severely disturbed individuals do not realize there is a problem.

Why do people tend to blame people for their mental disorder? It is common for people to assume that the person with a mental disorder is somehow responsible for the disorder. This misconception is especially prevalent among family members of the affected person, perhaps because having a family member with a psychological problem embarrasses them. With few exceptions, people are not responsible for their psychiatric disorders. They did not bring the dis-

orders on themselves and are rarely capable of just making the disorders go away.

Why is it so frightening to imagine experiencing psychopathology? Psychopathology is more common than many believe; in fact, some disorders affect up to 10% of the population. Anyone could be affected by one or more psychopathological conditions sometime during his or her life. Nevertheless, people tend to deny that possibility. Being so depressed that one seriously considers suicide, so anxious that one is unable to perform routine tasks, or so confused and disoriented that one's sentences make no sense to other people is a terrifying thought. No wonder people avoid considering the possibility. Yet these are real and treatable disorders, and they do occur to ordinary people. In many ways, they are similar to other disabling disorders, such as gout or diabetes, which can strike people without warning, forcing major changes in their lives. Like physical disorders, they can be managed; sometimes they can even be cured. People can, and do, learn to live with the disorder and to live a normal life.

hospitals devoted to treating psychiatric problems. Medications and psychotherapy are the major treatment options. Psychiatric problems are attributed to physical and psychological causes. Abnormal behavior is considered a natural, understandable phenomenon. It has not always been this way, however. To appreciate the modern view of abnormal behavior, one has only to consider how such behavior has been viewed historically. Even in today's science-based society, abnormal behavior often makes people uncomfortable, as discussed in the nearby Modern Myths box. If people still feel uncomfortable with abnormal behavior, given all that is now known about it, one can only imagine what feelings they may have had in more primitive societies. Knowledge is a defense against many fears. Today a solar eclipse is a predictable, awe-inspiring event. However, without today's understanding of the phenomenon, a solar eclipse was often interpreted as the beginning of the end of the earth or a sign of anger from the gods. This section will briefly review how abnormal behavior has been seen historically, what its causes were thought to be, and how people with mental illness were regarded and treated. It was not always a pretty picture. Ignorance and fear can lead to cruel and inhumane responses.

PREHISTORIC CONCEPTUALIZATIONS

Archaeological evidence suggests that ancient humans believed that gods, demons, or evil forces caused a variety of otherwise unexplained phenomena, including psychopathology. Because people believed that abnormality was due to possession by evil spirits, treatments focused on driving the evil spirits out. Some treatments were barbaric. Archaeologists have found skulls with holes in them that do not appear to be the result of an accident or a battle wound. They believe that such holes were drilled in the skull deliberately, perhaps as a way of treating individuals thought to be possessed. This procedure, called **trephination,** may be one of the earliest known treatments for abnormal behavior. Imagine what it would have been like to be emotionally disturbed 10,000 years ago when such beliefs and treatments were prevalent. As your own sanity slipped away, both you and the people around you would suspect demonic possession. Would you be shunned or harassed? Would you willingly submit to trephination? Or would you be held down while the doctors of the time drilled a hole in your head to release the evil spirits? Would people be compassionate, or would they blame you for your disorder? Could you ever be accepted back into society,

....

trephination   The deliberate drilling of holes in the skull, perhaps as a way of treating individuals thought to be possessed. This procedure may be one of the earliest known treatments for abnormal behavior.

This skull, found in Peru, shows signs of trephining. The hole has begun to close, which suggests that the person survived this procedure long enough to permit healing.

even after treatment? Scientists do not know the answers to any of these questions; they can only speculate. They do know that many of the skulls discovered with such holes show signs of healing, which suggests that at least some people survived the procedure. What was a person's life like after such treatment?

EARLY SCIENTIFIC CONCEPTUALIZATIONS

Some of the earliest recorded speculations about the causes of abnormal behavior are attributed to Greek philosophers. Early Greeks apparently believed that psychopathology was a punishment inflicted by the gods. However, in the fourth century B.C., Hippocrates challenged that notion by suggesting that both physical and psychiatric disorders resulted from natural causes. He believed that health depended on the proper balance of four body substances—yellow bile, black bile, blood, and phlegm—and that disrupting this balance produced symptoms. He argued that giving the person the right combination of natural elements would restore the balance and dispel the symptoms. For example, he suggested treating depression with relaxation, proper diet, healthful activities, and abstinence from alcohol and sexual activity (Lewis, 1941).

Hippocrates' conceptualization was a huge step forward in that it focused for the first time on natural causes of psychopathology. Hippocrates is often regarded as the father of modern medicine. His contributions to the understanding of psychopathology were remarkable. He correctly identified the critical role of the brain in determining behavior (Lewis, 1941). From today's perspective, this observation seems trivial, but other scholars, including

The ancient pharaohs of Egypt often had organs removed as part of their burial process. The heart was carefully embalmed and laid with the body. The brain, in contrast, was typically removed and apparently discarded. Perhaps this culture considered the brain to be of little importance to the pharaoh in his long trip into eternity.

Aristotle, argued that behavior was controlled by such organs as the heart, the lungs, or even the bowels. Hippocrates also described many psychiatric conditions still seen today, including depression, mania, and epilepsy (Gottesman, 1991). In spite of his insights, his treatments were ineffective, which is not surprising given how little was known about physiology and psychopathology at the time. Furthermore, his ideas appeared to have little impact on the thinking of the general public about psychopathology. Because the public believed that mental illness was a punishment from the gods, it is safe to assume that there was considerable stigma associated with it during that era.

Much of the wisdom attributed to the early Greeks had minimal impact in Western Europe, but some of those traditions were maintained and expanded in Middle Eastern cultures (Polvan, 1969). These Arab cultures were the first to establish hospitals specifically for the treatment of individuals with mental illness (Gottesman, 1991).

THE MIDDLE AGES AND EARLY RENAISSANCE

During the Middle Ages and even into the early Renaissance (approximately the sixth through fourteenth centuries), there continued to be a widespread belief in demons and possession, and mental illness was typically attributed to demonic possession (Hunter and Macalpine, 1963; Rose, 1991). "Talking crazy," carrying on conversations with people who were not there, or showing wild fluctuations in mood might well be considered evidence of possession. People believed that demons could be driven out. Exorcisms were routine, and in extreme cases, possessed people were

burned at the stake to drive out demons. Simply being accused of being possessed was hazardous. The commonly used test for possession at the time was dunking, where the individual was dropped into a pond or river and weighted down. Drowning was proof of innocence. Surviving this ordeal, on the other hand, was positive proof that the person was possessed—and therefore led to the treatments previously described.

These treatments and others were described in a book by Father Henry Kramer and Father James Sprenger entitled the *Malleus Maleficarum* (*The Witches' Hammer*), published in 1484. This book detailed the theoretical and theological underpinnings of demonic possession and argued that abnormal behavior was evidence of demonic possession. It was essentially a manual for diagnosis and treatment of a range of conditions and, in some sense, was

In sixteenth-century Europe, a person who behaved abnormally might have been labeled a witch or a warlock—that is, possessed by the devil—and then burned at the stake to force the devil out.

a precursor to modern diagnostic manuals. It should be noted that the best available evidence suggests that most people who were accused of being possessed probably did not suffer from psychiatric disorders (Schoeneman, 1984), although clearly at least some people with mental illness were singled out for such barbaric treatment (Zilboorg & Henry, 1941).

As you consider such cruel treatment, remember that people believed the person's immortal soul was at stake. Being possessed by demons was construed as a spiritual crisis demanding drastic action. Then, as now, diagnosis and treatment were based on the prevailing theory of what was wrong.

REEMERGENCE OF SCIENCE AND THE RISE OF ASYLUMS

The belief in demons and possession, so prevalent in the Middle Ages and early Renaissance, began to give way to more benign beliefs as the Renaissance progressed (the sixteenth through eighteenth centuries). By the middle of the Renaissance there were significant changes in attitudes toward the mentally ill. Recognizing mental illness as a physical, and not a spiritual, problem eliminated some of the barbaric treatments, but it did little to provide effective alternatives. Seriously disturbed people still could not function in society. **Asylums**—institutions for housing seriously disturbed people—were established but were given little financial support. The facilities were often crude, little more than warehouses, and people considered dangerous were often chained or placed in straitjackets (Pinel, 1801/1962). There was neither the knowledge nor the financial resources to provide treatment.

The first asylums were created around 800 B.C. in the Arab world (Gottesman, 1991). The first asylums in Europe were established in Spain in the fifteenth century, and such facilities gradually spread across Europe over the next century (Hunter & Macalpine, 1963). A particularly notorious asylum—St. Mary's of Bethlehem Hospital—was established in London in the middle of the sixteenth century. The Bethlehem Hospital quickly became overcrowded. Because of the overcrowding, people were typically chained, and their cries could be heard for some distance (Allderidge, 1985). Bethlehem was referred to in slang as Bet'lem, which eventually became *bedlam*, a word that now is used to denote general mayhem. This asylum, as well as others across Europe, became tourist attractions. Tickets were actually sold to members of the public who wanted to observe the bizarre behavior of the people who lived in the asylums, and the money was used to support their operation.

As the Renaissance continued and rational and scientific approaches became more dominant, several significant advances were made in the understanding of abnormal

This drawing illustrates activity at the St. Mary's of Bethlehem Hospital in the heart of London (about 1550). This hospital was well known to the citizens of London because of the constant wailing from the people confined there.

behavior. For example, Paul Broca (1824–1880) identified an area of the brain, now known as *Broca's area*, that is critical to the processing of language. His discovery was based on careful observation of individuals with brain injuries. Broca's discovery was the first of dozens of discoveries about the organization and functioning of the human brain (Golden et al., 2000). Emil Kraepelin (1856–1926) identified a subset of disturbed individuals who appeared to suffer from a single disorder—a disorder he labeled dementia praecox, which is now called schizophrenia. *Dementia praecox* literally means "early loss of the mind." Kraepelin recognized that abnormal behavior was not a single disorder, and his efforts to identify individual disorders form the basis for the modern diagnostic system.

Not all of the early speculations about the natural causes for abnormal behavior have stood the test of time. Franz Anton Mesmer (1734-1815) proposed a theory of **animal magnetism.** He believed that each person or animal emitted a magnetic field and was affected by the magnetic fields of others. He developed treatments based on these ideas that were essentially **placebos**—that is, treatments that were effective solely because of the power of suggestion. Another idea conceived during this period, and long

asylums   Institutions for housing seriously disturbed people.

animal magnetism   A theory that each person or animal emits a magnetic field and is affected by the magnetic fields of others.

placebos   Treatments that are effective solely because of the power of suggestion.

since relegated to historical interest only, is the concept of **phrenology.** Phrenology drew on two areas of scientific inquiry: the role of the brain in controlling behavior and the recognition of stable personality characteristics. Phrenology was based on the concept that personality traits, like other functions, were localized in the brain. It was assumed that the strength of any personality trait was proportional to the size of the part of the brain that controlled that trait. This led to a method of assessing personality by measuring the location of bumps on the head. These bumps were thought to reflect an enlargement of the brain below that region of the skull and hence to indicate a strong dose of whatever personality trait was assumed to be localized in that region. Few people take phrenology seriously anymore, but it was taken very seriously at one time (Hunt, 1993).

REFORM MOVEMENTS

The overcrowding and inhumane conditions of the early asylums may have been a step forward from the burnings at the stake of the Middle Ages and early Renaissance, but they were still a long way from respecting the dignity of people with psychiatric problems. These conditions cried out for reform, and by the eighteenth and nineteenth centuries, reform movements were starting to make a difference.

One of the first reformers, Philippe Pinel (1748–1826), led the reform movement in France (Selling, 1943). He was a respected physician in charge of a major asylum, who argued for sympathetic and humane care for the mentally disturbed, a proposition that many viewed as outrageous. He unchained the people under his care and allowed them free access to the grounds. He insisted that people in asylums be treated with dignity and that they no longer be tortured to keep them in line. This approach, which became known as **moral treatment,** gradually spread across Europe and the United States.

The early asylums were meant to isolate disturbed individuals from society more than to provide them with treatment. In America, disturbed people were routinely isolated from the population by jailing them, but reform movements changed that. The jailing of disturbed individuals gradually gave way to their placement in treatment facilities. An American physician, Benjamin Rush (1745–1813), is credited with developing some of the first treatments for mental illness (Hunter & Macalpine, 1963). By modern standards, his treatments were ineffective and uncomfortable. For example, he would draw considerable amounts of blood from disturbed and excited individuals, a

This may look more like a medieval torture device, but it is one of many contraptions developed by Dr. Benjamin Rush. His devices and procedures were intended to be state-of-the-art treatment for people with serious mental disorders.

practice called *blood letting,* or would spin them for several minutes in a chair (Hunter & Macalpine, 1963). These procedures calmed his patients, who probably just emerged too weak or dizzy to be disruptive. But whatever the validity of Rush's treatments, his efforts reinforced the idea that psychiatric disorders should be treated in a hospital setting.

Reform of psychiatric care in America was also stimulated by the efforts of Dorothea Dix (1802–1887) and Clifford Beers (1876–1943). Dorothea Dix was a schoolteacher who was acutely concerned about the way in which prisoners, the poor, and mentally disturbed individuals were being treated. She lobbied across the country for new laws to protect these people. Her efforts led to the development of a number of modern treatment facilities for people with mental illness. Clifford Beers learned about mental illness from the inside. He spent considerable time in the hospital as a psychiatric patient. In an influential book entitled *A Mind That Found Itself,* Beers described his experiences in vivid detail (Beers, 1908/1970). He talked about being chained and beaten and gave numerous examples of humiliating treatment. The shocking accounts by Dix and

....

phrenology   Obsolete field that attempted to relate people's personality traits to the bumps on their heads.

moral treatment   Treating people in asylums with respect.

Dorothea Dix spent 40 years leading a series of reform movements in the United States. Her efforts greatly improved the lot of people with mental illness, resulting in their being moved out of prisons and into treatment facilities.

Beers of conditions in mental hospitals and asylums stimulated reform that continues even today.

The reform movements changed attitudes about how seriously disturbed individuals should be treated. The focus on moral treatment restored some of the human dignity that was lost in the chains of the early asylums. People with mental illness were treated as human beings, but unfortunately, there were few effective treatments available. In time, the limitations of moral treatment became painfully obvious, the asylums and hospitals became increasingly overcrowded, and the quality of care deteriorated. This set the stage for the next significant advance—one that was grounded in both the good intentions of the reform movements and the power of scientific investigation. The scientific focus led to the development of specific diagnoses and, in time, to vastly improved treatments.

MODERN CONCEPTUALIZATIONS

The reform movements set the stage for the rapid development seen in the late nineteenth and twentieth centuries. Improving the environment in psychiatric institutions was only the first step. What was needed were new ideas about what caused psychiatric disorders and how they could be treated. The development of psychiatric diagnosis in the late nineteenth century was a major step. No longer was the hospitalized person simply considered mad or a lunatic; instead, recognizing specific types of madness allowed for the later development of specific treatments. This was the first time that a real effort was made to differentiate people on the basis of their pattern of symptoms.

The advent of psychoactive drugs in the early 1950s was the most significant change in psychiatric treatment during the twentieth century (Gottesman, 1991). The drug chlorpromazine (brand name: Thorazine), although it was not a cure, significantly reduced the symptoms of schizophrenia in many individuals. The advent of effective medications meant that many people who had previously been incapable of living outside the hospital were now able to return to the community. Prior to this breakthrough, it was common for people with schizophrenia to spend their entire lives in the hospital. Psychiatric hospitals, once overflowing, now had fewer patients. With fewer patients, it was possible to offer more active treatment. Efforts at psychological rehabilitation were expanded, and support systems were developed to help the people who recovered sufficiently to leave the hospital.

Around 1970 there was a push to limit psychiatric hospitalization. This was a revolutionary idea. Until then, people with psychiatric disorders were routinely hospitalized, even when the hospitalization was of little benefit. This effort to limit hospitalization, which is known as **deinstitutionalization,** was based on the idea that institutional living tends to decrease a person's adaptive skills. Deinstitutionalization was supposed to replace hospital treatment with effective community care, and many programs that provided such community care proved effective (Honkonen et al., 1999). However, some programs were so totally mismanaged that people were, in effect, dumped onto the street without treatment or support (Westermeyer, 1987). Furthermore, the funding for quality treatment programs in the community often did not materialize, leaving even well-intentioned mental health professionals without the resources to care for these previously hospitalized individuals. Many of these people quickly deteriorated and had to be rehospitalized; others joined the ranks of the homeless (Leeper, 1988). It was no coincidence that the problem of homelessness increased dramatically once deinstitutionalization became common. The mistakes of the deinstitutionalization efforts have led to further reforms. The norm now is to treat individuals in the

deinstitutionalization   An effort to limit hospitalization, based on the idea that institutional living tends to decrease a person's adaptive skills.

The crowded, inhumane conditions of the early asylums have largely been replaced by modern hospital settings like this one, where people are treated with a combination of medications, psychological interventions, and emotional support before they return to the community.

least restrictive environment possible, but there is a growing sense that society has an obligation to provide treatment.

The field of psychopathology has come a long way in understanding seriously disturbed individuals and their problems. People with severe emotional disturbance now can expect humane and usually effective treatment in modern hospitals, clinics, and community rehabilitation residences. But there is one area in which progress has been slow. There is still considerable stigma attached to mental problems, and people are still distressed by the behavior of seriously disturbed individuals. It does not seem to matter that psychiatric problems are understandable and treatable. People still seem to have trouble accepting abnormality.

Check Yourself 1.3

History of Abnormal Behavior

1. What culture was the first to attribute diseases, including mental disorders, to natural causes?
2. What was believed to be the cause of mental disorders during the Middle Ages?
3. What were the strengths and the weaknesses of asylums?
4. How did the reform movements affect the people with mental illness?

Ponder this . . . *Imagine what it would have been like to have a severe mental disorder during the various periods of history described in this section. Imagine how people would have looked at you, how you would have been treated, and the impact that your illness would have had on your life.*

MENTAL HEALTH PRACTITIONERS

Many different professionals work with individuals suffering from psychopathology. These professionals differ in their training and in the roles they play in the mental health arena, as summarized in Table 1.2. This section describes these professions.

Psychiatrists are physicians who have completed medical school and a specialized residency program in psychiatry. As physicians, they can prescribe medications and administer other medical procedures, such as electroshock therapy. When people with emotional problems have deteriorated to the point of requiring hospitalization, psychiatrists are usually the professionals who arrange and manage the hospital treatment. They often handle some of the most severe cases of psychopathology—cases that are likely to

psychiatrists Physicians who have completed medical school and a specialized residency program in psychiatry.

[TABLE 1.2] Mental Health Professionals

PROFESSIONAL	EDUCATION	ROLE
Psychiatrist	M.D. degree plus three or more years of a residency in psychiatry	Prescribes medications; supervises hospital stays; psychotherapy
Clinical psychologist	Either a Master's degree or a Ph.D., plus a one-year internship, although in most states only a person with a Ph.D. can practice independently	Provides psychotherapy, which may follow one or more theoretical orientations, such as psychodynamic or behavioral
Counseling psychologist	Either a Master's degree or a Ph.D., plus a one-year internship, although in most states only a person with a Ph.D. can practice independently	Most often helps people make career choices or other changes in their lives, but sometimes provides psychotherapy as well
Psychoanalyst	Either a Ph.D. or an M.D., plus specialized training in psychoanalysis	Conducts psychoanalytic psychotherapy
Psychiatric social worker	Either a Bachelor's or a Master's degree in social work, plus several years of supervised experience working in the psychiatric field	Manages the case for people in treatment, such as referring the person for financial, educational, or job placement; psychotherapy
Psychiatric nurse	Either a Bachelor's or a Master's degree in nursing, plus several years of supervised experience working in the psychiatric field	Works with hospitalized psychiatric patients to improve functioning and manages various aspects of treatment
Nurse practitioner	Typically a Bachelor's degree in nursing, plus a Master's degree to prepare to be a nurse practitioner	Works in the office of a supervising psychiatrist, assessing clients and prescribing medication as needed
Pastoral counselor	Typically a Bachelor's degree in divinity, plus specialized training in counseling	Provides a variety of supportive counseling primarily to people in the counselor's congregation who are going through difficult times

require medication and occasional hospitalization. Psychiatrists may do psychotherapy, although many psychiatrists today devote the majority of their professional time to medication and hospital management.

Clinical psychologists have advanced training in psychology, usually having earned a Ph.D., Psy.D., or Master's degree. They apply the principles of psychology to understanding and treating emotional disturbance. They are trained in the assessment and psychological treatment of individuals with mental illness. They are typically trained to perform one or more forms of **psychotherapy**—nonmedical therapies that help clients understand their problems and develop the skills to manage them. Because research is routinely included in programs for clinical psychologists, they often are involved in the development and evaluation of treatment programs. **Counseling psychologists** sometimes play the same role, but their training is geared more to helping people with little psychopathology make beneficial changes in their lives.

The terms **psychoanalyst** and **analyst** refer to someone who has received advanced training in the delivery of psychodynamic psychotherapy. The base training for analysts is usually either psychiatry or psychology, but conceivably any mental health professional could be trained to be a psychoanalyst. Note that these terms only apply to those therapists who provide psychodynamic therapy, not to therapists who provide other kinds of psychological treatment.

Psychiatric social workers usually have either a college degree or a Master's degree in social work (M.S.W.) and considerable field experience in working with psychopathology. The traditional role of social workers has been to provide the link between the person in treatment and the resources of the community. This may include connecting people with outpatient mental health services, informing them of available benefits, and coordinating services with their families. Increasingly, psychiatric social workers are being trained to do psychotherapy and other

clinical psychologists   People with advanced training in psychology who apply the principles of psychology to understanding and treating emotional disturbance.

psychotherapy   Nonmedical approach that helps clients understand their problems and develop the skills to manage them.

counseling psychologists   Psychologists trained to help people who have little psychopathology to make beneficial changes in their lives.

psychoanalyst or **analyst**   Someone who is trained in the delivery of psychodynamic psychotherapy.

psychiatric social workers   People who usually have either a college degree or a Master's degree in social work, along with considerable field experience in working with psychopathology.

services that have traditionally been handled by clinical psychologists.

Psychiatric nurses have completed nursing training and have specialized in working with psychopathological populations. They tend to work in institutional settings with more severely disturbed individuals, although the roles available to psychiatric nurses have expanded recently.

Nurse practitioners are nurses with advanced training in medicine. They often work with doctors to provide a range of routine medical services that in the past have been provided exclusively by doctors. Increasingly, they are working with psychiatrists to provide the same type of service to those suffering from psychopathology. Nurse practitioners often have **prescription privileges**,

....

psychiatric nurses Nurses who have completed nursing training and have specialized in working with psychopathological populations.

nurse practitioners Nurses with advanced training in medicine.

prescription privileges The legal authority to prescribe medications, which has been extended in many states to nurse practitioners.

pastoral counselors Religious personnel (priests, ministers, rabbis) who are trained to address the emotional needs of the people in their ministry.

which means that, like doctors, they can write prescriptions, although the limits on such privileges vary from state to state.

Pastoral counselors are religious personnel (priests, ministers, rabbis) who are trained to counsel to the emotional needs of the people in their ministry. Depending on their training and interest, these counselors may handle things ranging from marital problems and grief reactions to the most severe forms of psychopathology. They often work with families who are dealing with severe psychopathology in one of their members.

Check Yourself 1.4

Mental Health Practitioners

1. What is the difference between a psychologist and a psychiatrist?
2. What is the difference between a psychiatric nurse and a nurse practitioner?

Ponder this . . . *With so many different mental health professionals, how might an individual who is having emotional difficulties find the right person to provide the necessary treatment?*

 SUMMARY

RESPONDING TO ENVIRONMENTAL CHALLENGES

- Psychopathology can interfere with a person's ability to adapt.
- The effectiveness of people's adaptation depends on their genetic makeup, physical condition, learning history and ability to reason, and level of social support. Because everyone behaves maladaptively at times, maladaptive behavior must be consistent or significantly disruptive before it is classified as psychopathological.

DEFINING ABNORMALITY

- Defining abnormality is more difficult than it first appears. Abnormality has been defined in terms of many criteria, such as statistical considerations, cultural norms, level of dysfunction, and personal distress. Many behaviors could be defined as either normal or abnormal, depending on the situation in which they occur.

HISTORY OF ABNORMAL BEHAVIOR

- Perspectives on abnormal behavior have changed considerably over time. The earliest conceptualizations emphasized demonic possession. Some early enlightened cultures, such as the ancient Greeks, offered more naturalistic explanations for abnormality. However, demonic explanations continued to dominate into the early Renaissance. In the last 200 years, a combination of scientific thought and reform movements has changed dramatically the way in which psychopathology is understood and treated.

MENTAL HEALTH PRACTITIONERS

- A variety of mental health professionals treat psychopathology, including psychiatrists, clinical and counseling psychologists, psychiatric social workers, psychiatric nurses, nurse practitioners, and pastoral counselors. These professionals differ in the nature of their training and in the roles they play.

KEY TERMS

abnormal   (7)
adaptive   (6)
animal magnetism   (17)
asylums   (17)
clinical psychologists   (21)
counseling psychologists   (21)
deinstitutionalization   (19)
evolution   (5)
maladaptive   (6)
natural selection   (6)
nurse practitioners   (22)
moral treatment   (18)

pastoral counselors   (22)
phrenology   (18)
placebos   (17)
prescription privileges   (22)
psychiatric social workers   (21)
psychiatric nurses   (22)
psychiatrists   (20)
psychoanalyst or analyst   (21)
psychopathology   (4)
psychotherapy   (21)
trephination   (15)

SUGGESTED READINGS

Gottesman, I. I. (1991). *Schizophrenia genesis: The origins of madness.* New York: W. H. Freeman. This is a fascinating review of the history of our understanding of schizophrenia. It has won several awards and has been translated into more than a dozen different languages.

Micale, M. S., & Porter, R. (Eds.). (1994). *Discovering the history of psychiatry.* New York: Oxford University Press. This book covers dozens of topics in the history of psychiatry, with particular emphasis on the last 200 years of development.

Nesse, R. M., & Williams, G. C. (1994). *Why we get sick: The new science of Darwinian medicine.* New York: Vintage Books. This best-seller reconceptualizes many topics in medicine and psychology in terms of an evolutionary perspective. Its thoughtful analysis challenges some of the current diagnostic and treatment practices and suggests a number of fruitful lines for additional research.

"Two Face," Noma & Jim Bliss/©SIS.

chaptertwo

Diagnosis and Assessment

A Victim Once Removed

HARRIET

Harriet was not hurt in the World Trade Center and Pentagon attacks, and she did not know anyone who was killed. In fact, she lived hundreds of miles away. She was in treatment for depression when the September 11 tragedies happened. For the first week, her sleep was restless, and some nights she could not sleep at all. She was able to get to work and take care of her children, but she worried constantly and found herself staring at any plane she spotted. The first report of anthrax troubled her but added little to her trauma. Then one Saturday evening, after watching a news channel special on anthrax and other biological agents, she started crying uncontrollably. Initially, it just looked like she was frightened, especially for her three children. But over the next couple of days, she completely lost control. She would scream, "They're coming!" and would accuse strangers of being terrorists. When her husband came home and found her huddled in the basement with the kids, holding his loaded hunting rifle, he decided it was time to seek hospitalization. Three days in the hospital, a heavy dose of medication, and supportive counseling were sufficient to calm Harriet down and enable her to return to her responsibilities at home.

Hating the Limelight

CAL

Cal had never enjoyed public speaking. Even in school he would avoid classes that required oral presentations. When forced to speak, he would literally shake, his mind would go blank, and his voice would crack. The experience would leave him embarrassed for months afterward. But now he was being asked to chair a banquet with nearly 200 people. The thought terrified him. He considered quitting his job to avoid the banquet, but decided that he could not do that. Instead, he sought out a therapist to help him handle the stress of public speaking.

Not Quite Right

NORMA

At the insistence of her children, Norma sought the advice of her doctor. For the last couple of years, she had been having increasing difficulty remembering things. Always independent and dependable, she had lived alone since her husband died 12 years earlier. Retired for the last 4 years, she continued to be active, volunteering at the local hospital and playing cards regularly with friends. But recently she had forgotten some of her outings, had failed to pay her bills, and had once left the house with an entire meal cooking in the oven. The burned roast set off the smoke detector, which was part of a home security alarm, so the fire department came before anything worse happened. Her doctor could find nothing physically wrong but referred Nora to a neurologist for additional testing.

Harriet, Cal, and Norma are all experiencing difficulties. Harriet's difficulty is clearly emotional—an intense response to a powerful stressor. Cal's difficulty is more situational. He functions fine as long as he does not have to speak in front of people. Norma's problem is more ambiguous. Her recent lapses of memory are uncharacteristic. She has always been well organized and has never been forgetful in the past. She may be distracted by life's everyday hassles, or there may be something else going on. Her doctor was not sure, so she referred Norma to a specialist for further evaluation. All of these individuals, and the people who love them, want to know what is wrong and what can be done about it.

This chapter addresses the first steps in providing help to people who may be experiencing psychological problems. The chapter begins with a discussion of the process of diagnosis and the current psychiatric diagnostic system. It then turns to the process of assessment, which is critical to diagnosis. Various methods of psychological, behavioral, and biological assessment are described.

THE DIAGNOSTIC SYSTEM

Strictly speaking, diagnosing a person is applying a label, but the diagnostic label should never be arbitrary. It should be based on the observation of a specific pattern of behaviors or symptoms, and it should describe the person's symptoms accurately. Often included in the diagnosis is an implicit assumption that similar sets of symptoms reflect the same cause, or **etiology.** For some current diagnoses, such an assumption is supported by research; for other diagnoses, there is little or no evidence to suggest a common etiology.

There are a number of reasons to make a diagnosis. Diagnostic labels facilitate communication among professionals responsible for the care of individuals. Instead of it being necessary to describe all of the detailed observations of the person, one or two diagnostic labels may capture the essential features of the pathology she or he shows. Diagnostic labels emphasize the commonalties among different people with the same disorder. This allows well-trained professionals to predict which treatments are likely to be effective. The relationship between diagnosis and response to treatment is critical. If a diagnosis leads to the selection of a treatment procedure that alleviates the problem, then the diagnostic system is working. Although facilitating the selection of effective treatments is the point of making a diagnosis, current diagnoses do not always predict what treatments will be optimal. There have, however, been tremendous advances in treatments over the last two decades.

A good diagnostic system does more than classify individuals and guide treatment. It also helps in the conceptualization of disorders, organizing them into categories and permitting exploration of their possible causes. In this way, the diagnostic system is like other organizational systems in

science. The periodic table of elements, for example, organizes the various elements in a way that enables chemists to see quickly how elements are related and to predict how elements will react with one another. The periodic table is much more than just a series of labels for elements, just as the diagnostic system used for mental disorders is much more than just a series of diagnostic labels. Of course, human beings are much more complicated and variable than elements, so the diagnostic system is more complex than the periodic table. Furthermore, the diagnostic system does not capture the uniqueness of individuals nearly so effectively as the periodic table captures the uniqueness of elements. Psychopathology researchers are constantly questioning and refining the organization of the diagnostic system, exploring whether revised definitions for disorders provide better explanations for the pathology (Raulin & Lilienfeld, 1999). This research process may lead to subdividing one diagnostic category into two or more diagnostic categories, or it may lead to combining two diagnostic categories into a single category.

Nothing advanced the field of psychopathology more than the recognition that there were different subtypes of psychopathology. Until that breakthrough, treatments had to be generic, suitable for every type of pathology. However, there are no treatments that help all people regardless of their diagnosis. The modern diagnostic system is a work in progress in that diagnostic criteria and diagnostic categories are constantly being modified on the basis of new research. This section will introduce the current diagnostic system and how it is used today.

THE DSM

The diagnostic system used in the United States is called DSM-IV-TR (American Psychiatric Association, 2000), which stands for the ***Diagnostic and Statistical Manual of Mental Disorders*** (4th edition, text revision). This manual is a compendium of diagnostic conditions and the criteria required for each diagnosis. Unlike earlier diagnostic manuals, the current DSM strives to be atheoretical—that is, the disorders and the criteria for diagnosis are not based on any one theoretical orientation. Earlier versions of the DSM were based on particular theories of what caused psychopathology, and therefore the diagnoses were less relevant for professionals who had a different theoretical orientation. Chapters 3 and 4 will describe the primary theoretical orientations that have been applied to the field of psychopathology.

The DSM is published by the American Psychiatric Association and is used by psychiatrists, psychologists, social workers, psychiatric nurses, and a variety of other mental health professionals. Insurance companies insist that professionals diagnose each patient or client using either the current DSM or the international diagnostic

----

etiology The cause or causes of a disease or abnormality.

Diagnostic and Statistical Manual of Mental Disorders **(DSM)** A compendium of diagnostic conditions and the criteria for each diagnosis.

manual, the ***International Classification of Diseases*** or **ICD.** The DSM and ICD manuals are similar in coverage and diagnostic criteria for psychiatric disorders.

The DSM does much more than list diagnoses and the criteria for making those diagnoses. It provides guidance on how to differentiate among diagnostic conditions that may superficially appear similar. This process is referred to as **differential diagnosis.** In addition, the DSM lists other disorders that are likely to accompany a specific disorder; this information can guide the clinician in making a more systematic assessment of the case. Diagnostic conditions that occur together in the same individual are referred to as **comorbid conditions.** Finally, the DSM lists information about each disorder. This information may include the base rate, incidence and prevalence rates, typical age of onset, causal or contributing factors (if known), and expected course. The **base rate** is the frequency of the disorder in the population. **Incidence** is the percentage of new cases that develop during a specified period (Regier & Burke, 1985). **Prevalence** is the percentage of the population afflicted with the disorder over a specified period. **Lifetime prevalence** is the percentage of the population that will experience the disorder sometime during their lifetime. Finally, the **age of onset** is the age at which the disorder first develops, and the **course** of the disorder is the change in symptomatology over time.

The process of diagnosis developed out of a medical framework. In this framework, the doctor identifies the symptoms, tries to match that pattern of symptoms to known diseases, and then uses whatever technologies are available to treat or prevent that disease. Implicit in this model is that diagnoses are *categories,* which differ in kind, rather than degree, from other conditions. Take the disease called AIDS (acquired immune deficiency syndrome). The diagnosis of AIDS is based on the presence of a particular class of viruses called human immunodeficiency virus (HIV) as well as on a progression of symptoms, in individuals with this virus, to a specific severity. People are not diagnosed with AIDS, even if they have some of the symptoms of AIDS, unless they are HIV+—that is, unless they carry the HIV virus. HIV+ status is categorical—people either meet the criterion or they don't.

Sometimes disorders are clearly categorical, and a classification system predicated on establishing categories functions well. But nature is not always organized that way. Take, for example, depression. There are clearly degrees of depression. Some people are so depressed that they are literally unable to get out of bed or take care of themselves. Others suffer from milder, but still disruptive, depression. Milder depressions may come and go, depending on the stresses faced by the individual. Disorders such as depression may more properly be thought of as lying on a continuum, although, as is true of many issues in psychopathology, the data are not entirely conclusive yet (Haslam & Beck, 1994).

These distinctions between dimensional and categorical diagnoses are illustrated in Figure 2.1. A pure categorical distinction is shown in Figure 2.1a, in which only two scores are represented: no depression and serious depression. The evidence suggests that depression does not fit the pure categorical model. In Figure 2.1b, the depression scores are distributed across a wide range, with most of the scores clustered in the middle. This is a classic dimensional model, in which the diagnosis of depression is made for the small group of people who have unusually high depression scores. Finally, Figure 2.1c shows a bimodal distribution, in which there are two clusters of depression scores representing two categories—depressed and nondepressed people—with variability within those clusters. Most categories in nature show this kind of distribution. Note that if the mean scores for the two clusters are too close together, the clusters will blend together, making it hard to discern the categorical nature of the data without using sophisticated mathematical procedures (Waller & Meehl, 1998).

Many of the disorders covered in this textbook are probably dimensional, or distributed along a continuum, rather than categories. One implication of this fact is that mild levels of the symptoms on which a diagnosis is based are often found in perfectly normal people. Almost everyone experiences anxiety, depression, or confusion at various times and under specific circumstances. Harriet and Cal, whom we met at the beginning of this chapter, were anxious, and Norma was confused. It is the intensity of these symptoms and the range of situations in which they occur that determine whether the symptoms are abnormal. What do you think? Was Harriet's response to terrorism excessive? When did it pass from understandable to

---

International Classification of Diseases **(ICD)**   A manual similar to the DSM in coverage and diagnostic criteria.

differential diagnosis   The process of determining the correct diagnosis when the superficial symptom pattern suggests several possible diagnoses.

comorbid conditions   Diagnostic conditions that occur together in the same individual.

base rate   The frequency of a disorder in the population.

incidence   The percentage of new cases of a disorder that develop during a specified period.

prevalence   The percentage of the population afflicted with a disorder over a specified period.

lifetime prevalence   The percentage of the population that will experience a disorder sometime in their lifetime.

age of onset   The age at which a disorder first develops.

course   The change in symptomatology of a disorder over time.

abnormal? What about Cal's fear of public speaking and Norma's forgetfulness?

This brief introduction to diagnosis will cover the structure of the diagnostic system and how diagnoses are

[FIGURE 2.1]

Categorical versus Dimensional Conditions

These graphs illustrate three types of diagnostic situations. The top panel illustrates pure categories; there are only two levels, and all people are at one of those levels. The middle panel illustrates a dimensional model, with considerable variability across the population. In this case, the diagnosis of depression might be arbitrarily set at a score of 16 or higher (approximately the top 5% of the population on the depression measure). The bottom panel illustrates a categorical situation, in which there is variability within each category. For example, most nondepressed people show little depression, but some show depression almost as high as the depressed group.

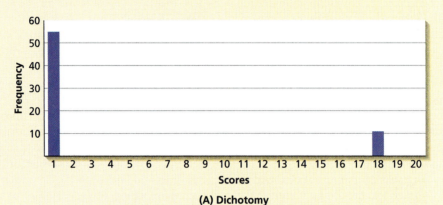

(A) Dichotomy

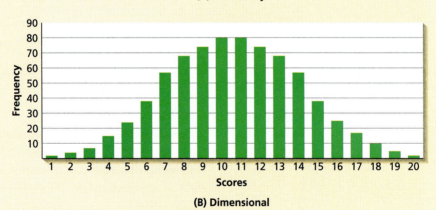

(B) Dimensional

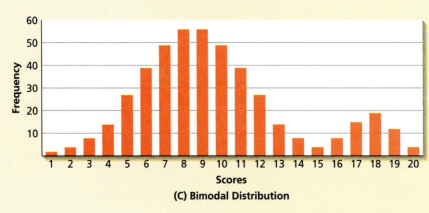

(C) Bimodal Distribution

used and evaluated. The coverage of specific disorders in later chapters will be organized around the current DSM manual.

MULTIAXIAL DIAGNOSIS

The current diagnostic manual utilizes a **multiaxial diagnosis**—that is, it breaks the process of diagnosis into five distinct dimensions, referred to as **axes,** as shown in Table 2.1. This approach provides a systematic way of coding multiple features of an individual in a succinct, effective manner. Each axis codes different information. The person's psychiatric diagnoses are recorded on Axis I. Axis II lists stable personal characteristics that affect functioning, such as personality disorders or mental retardation. *Personality disorders* represent rigid personality styles that may interfere with functioning and may even contribute to the development or exacerbation of an Axis I disorder. Axes III through V list features that are important in understanding the total person. Axis III lists medical conditions, which can often affect a person's functioning or limit treatment options. For example, cancer and its treatment may have enormous effects on both the physical and the psychological well-being of the person. Axis IV lists psychosocial and environmental problems, such as job or family stresses, which often increase stress and may even be part of the reason for the current psychiatric problem. The information on Axis IV would be critical in understanding the behavior of someone like Harriet. Finally, Axis V gives an overall rating of the person's clinical functioning. This rating is made on a scale called the **Global Assessment of Functioning** or **GAF.** GAF ratings range from 1 to 100, where higher ratings represent higher levels of functioning (see Table 2.1). A thorough diagnostic workup requires classification on all five of these axes, not just a single label of a psychiatric disorder.

The DSM divides the more than 250 individual disorders into 17 broad categories. Most of the disorders in these broad categories are coded on Axis I. These categories are primarily for organizational purposes and are based on similarity of symptoms. Table 2.1 also lists these categories and the chapters in which the disorders will be covered.

USING A DIAGNOSIS

The point of a diagnosis is to describe the dysfunction that the person is experiencing in a manner that will aid mental health professionals in selecting the most appropriate treatment. It is helpful if the diagnosis is also related to the underlying cause, or etiology, of the disorder, although this is not strictly necessary. A diagnosis unrelated to etiology can still be the basis for treatment decisions, although treatments tend to be more powerful, effective, and focused when the underlying causes are understood.

Creating a useful diagnostic system is more than arbitrarily dividing individuals into categories. The categories must be developed on the basis of evidence that they represent meaningful subgroups of individuals. Diagnoses are based on symptoms and signs. **Symptoms** are maladaptive, ineffective, or even bizarre experiences that are typically unobservable but can be reported by the individual. **Signs** are observable features, such as a sad face, excited behavior, and psychological test performance. Groups of symptoms and signs may cluster in individuals, so that a person who shows one or two of them is likely to show others in the cluster. Such a cluster of symptoms and signs is known as a **syndrome.** The identification of a reliable syndrome is often the basis for a preliminary diagnostic category. It is considered "preliminary" because more than just a clustering of symptoms is required to have confidence that a useful diagnostic entity has been identified.

RELIABILITY AND VALIDITY

To be useful, diagnoses must be clearly defined so that well-trained professionals can agree that a given individual qualifies for a given diagnosis. **Reliability** is the degree of consistency in the diagnostic process or any other assessment situation. The form of reliability most critical in diagnosis is interrater reliability. A diagnostic category has **interrater reliability** when professionals consistently agree on a person's diagnosis. For example, if two professionals can agree on which people have schizophrenia and which people have other disorders, then that category has good interrater reliability. In contrast, if five different professionals interview the same person and come up with five different diagnoses, the diagnostic system they are using is unreliable. Imagine how chaotic it would be if the diagnostic system did not have interrater reliability. No two professionals could agree on what was wrong with a person, much less on what course of treatment to follow.

---

multiaxial diagnosis   A diagnostic procedure that breaks diagnoses into several distinct dimensions.

axes   The distinct dimensions of a multiaxial diagnosis.

global assessment of functioning (GAF)   A scale, utilized in the DSM, whereon the individual's overall clinical functioning is rated on a scale of 1 to 100.

symptoms   Internal experiences that are maladaptive, ineffective, or bizarre.

syndrome   A cluster of symptoms. A person who shows one or two of these symptoms is likely to show the other symptoms in the cluster.

signs   External characteristics that often accompany a disorder.

reliability   The degree of consistency in the diagnostic process or any other assessment situation.

interrater reliability   The degree to which professionals agree on a person's diagnosis.

[TABLE 2.1] DSM-IV Multiaxial Diagnosis

One of the major advances in diagnoses, first introduced with the DSM-III, was the multiaxial diagnosis. For the first time, it was possible to provide a reasonably comprehensive picture of the person in a standardized diagnostic format. Listed here are the five axes of the DSM-IV, with a brief explanation of each.

AXIS	DESCRIPTION
I	This axis codes all psychiatric diagnoses except for personality disorders and mental retardation. It is possible to list more than one Axis I diagnosis. In fact, it is common for people to qualify for more than one psychiatric diagnosis. ◆ Disorders usually first diagnosed in infancy, childhood, or adolescence (*excluding mental retardation, which is coded on Axis II*) (Chapter 13) ◆ Delirium, dementia, and amnestic and other cognitive disorders (Chapter 15) ◆ Mental disorders due to a general medical condition not elsewhere classified ◆ Substance-related disorders (Chapter 14) ◆ Schizophrenia and other psychotic disorders (Chapters 5 & 6) ◆ Mood disorders (Chapter 7) ◆ Anxiety disorders (Chapter 8) ◆ Somatoform disorders (Chapter 9) ◆ Factitious disorders ◆ Dissociative disorders (Chapter 15) ◆ Sexual and gender identity disorders (Chapter 11) ◆ Eating disorders (Chapter 10) ◆ Sleep disorders (Chapter 10) ◆ Impulse-control disorders not elsewhere classified ◆ Adjustment disorders ◆ Other conditions that may be a focus of clinical attention
II	This axis codes personality disorders and mental retardation. These are stable features of the person that are likely to affect the clinical situation. ◆ Mental retardation (*listed among disorders usually first diagnosed in infancy, childhood, or adolescence*) (Chapter 13) ◆ Personality disorders (Chapter 12)
III	This axis codes any relevant medical conditions (conditions that may have an impact on the Axis I disorders or affect the person's ability to cope). When in doubt, it is best to list all current medical conditions here.

Researchers could not study a disorder because a sample of people with the disorder would be impossible to identify. In other words, without interrater reliability, nothing else is possible.

Two other types of reliability, test-retest reliability and internal consistency reliability, assess different types of consistency. These types of reliability are more often applied to psychological testing than to diagnosis. **Test-retest reliability** reflects how consistent a measure is over time, and **internal consistency reliability** reflects the degree to which the items that make up a test all measure the same thing. Whether these types of reliability are relevant depends on what is being measured. For example, some characteristics, such as intelligence, are thought to be stable. Hence a measure of intelligence should provide consistent scores at different points in time; that is, it should have high test-retest reliability.

Note that reliability is not dichotomous—a test is not simply either reliable or unreliable. Rather, reliability is measured on a continuum. For example, some diagnoses can be made with nearly perfect agreement, so those diagnoses have very high interrater reliability. Other diagnoses are more difficult to agree on, so their interrater reliability is correspondingly lower.

....

test-retest reliability   How consistent a measure is over time.

internal consistency reliability   The degree to which the items that make up a test all measure the same thing.

[TABLE 2.1] *Continued*

AXIS	DESCRIPTION
IV	This axis lists psychosocial and environmental problems and stressors. These stressors may or may not have precipitated the Axis I disorder, but invariably they contribute to current emotional problems and will have an impact on treatment planning.
V	This axis lists the rating for the person on the Global Assessment of Functioning Scale (GAF). {For rating the GAF scale, consider psychological, social, and occupational functioning on a hypothetical continuum of mental health–illness. Do not include impairment in functioning due to physical (or environmental) limitations).

Code	Description[1]
91–100	Superior functioning in a wide range of activities, life's problems never seem to get out of hand, is sought out by others because of his or her many positive qualities. No symptoms.
81–90	Absent or minimal symptoms (e.g., mild anxiety before an exam), good functioning in all areas, interested and involved in a wide range of activities, socially effective, generally satisfied with life, no more than everyday problems or concerns (e.g., an occasional argument with family members).
71–80	If symptoms are present, they are transient and expectable reactions to psychosocial stressors (e.g., difficulty concentrating after family argument); no more than slight impairment in social, occupational, or school functioning (e.g., temporarily falling behind in schoolwork).
61–70	Some mild symptoms (e.g., depressed mood and mild insomnia) OR some difficulty in social, occupational, or school functioning (e.g., occasional truancy, or theft within the household), but generally functioning pretty well, has some meaningful interpersonal relationships.
51–60	Moderate symptoms (e.g., flat affect and circumstantial speech, occasional panic attacks) OR moderate difficulty in social, occupational, or school functioning (e.g., few friends, conflicts with peers or co-workers).
41–50	Serious symptoms (e.g., suicidal ideation, severe obsessional rituals, frequent shoplifting) OR any serious impairment in social, occupational, or school functioning (e.g., no friends, unable to keep a job).
31–40	Some impairment in reality testing or communication (e.g., speech is at times illogical, obscure, or irrelevant) OR major impairment in several areas, such as work or school, family relations, judgment, thinking, or mood (e.g., depressed man avoids friends, neglects family, and is unable to work; child frequently beats up younger children, is defiant at home, and is failing at school).
21–30	Behavior is considerably influenced by delusions or hallucinations OR serious impairment in communication or judgment (e.g., sometimes incoherent, acts grossly inappropriately, suicidal preoccupation) OR inability to function in almost all areas (e.g., stays in bed all day; no job, home, or friends).
11–20	Some danger of hurting self or others (e.g., suicide attempts without clear expectation of death; frequently violent; manic excitement) OR occasionally fails to maintain minimal personal hygiene (e.g., smears feces) OR gross impairment in communication (e.g., largely incoherent or mute).
1–10	Persistent danger of severely hurting self or others (e.g., recurrent violence) OR persistent inability to maintain minimal personal hygiene OR serious suicidal act with clear expectation of death.

[1] *Unfamiliar terms in the GAF will be defined as the various psychiatric conditions are described later in the text.*

A diagnosis or a psychological test must be reliable to be useful. However, a reliable diagnosis or test by itself is not enough. For example, if a magician saws an assistant in half before a large audience, most audience members will report seeing the same phenomenon: A person is cut in two, and seconds later an intact, whole person reappears. The reports are reliable, but they describe an illusion and not what actually happened. Magicians deflect audience attention from what is actually happening, and thus they induce the audience to reliably misreport events. So it is with diagnosis. Sometimes a set of symptoms may appear to be something they are not, and a group of professionals may reliably arrive at a diagnosis that is not correct. For example, during the Salem witch-hunts, most observers reported that the devil possessed particular members of their community. The diagnosis was reliable but not valid.

Validity means that what is being measured is real and is related to critical variables. In addition to being reliable, a diagnosis or a psychological test must be valid. In the assessment of some psychological variables, validity is easy to establish. For instance, IQ tests were initially developed to predict performance in school. Therefore, to be valid an IQ test should correlate with performance in school—that is, these two variables should be related to one another. The

validity   The property a test exhibits when the thing being measured is real and is related to critical variables.

higher the correlation, the more valid the test is said to be. Similarly, the validity of a diagnosis of pathology must be correlated with some expected behaviors. Unfortunately, it is difficult to specify the expected behaviors in psychopathology with the same precision with which one can specify performance in school. After all, school performance can be reduced to an average grade. Complex pathological behavior cannot so easily be reduced to a number. However, there is one prediction that is always important in a diagnostic system: The diagnosis should predict treatment response so that it can help professionals select an effective treatment.

There are several types of validity. **Concurrent validity** reflects the relationship of a measure or diagnosis to some variable that is currently present. For example, an IQ test has concurrent validity if it predicts current school performance. In contrast, **predictive validity** refers to the relationship of a measure or diagnosis to some future event. The IQ test would have predictive validity if it predicted school performance years later. Because IQ is presumed to be stable, one would expect it to have both concurrent and predictive validity. However, other psychological variables, such as anxiety and depression, may come and go. Consequently, these variables may have concurrent validity but, because of their unstable nature, little predictive validity. Both concurrent and predictive validities are **criterion-related validities** in that they are concerned with the strength of the relationship between the measure or diagnosis and some criterion measure, such as school performance.

Two other validities are content and face validity, which are often confused with one another. **Content validity** reflects how well a test or measure covers the relevant content of interest. It is most easily demonstrated in a classroom examination. If an instructor gives an examination on Chapters 5–10, but most of the questions come from Chapter 8, then the content of the examination does not cover the material to be examined very well. If the instructor includes ten questions from each of the assigned chapters instead, then the content is being covered more reasonably and the test is said to have content validity. **Face validity** reflects to what degree a test is measuring what it appears to measure. The content-valid classroom examination just mentioned would also have face validity, because students are likely to say that it measures knowledge from those chapters. However, as you will see later in this chapter, there are situations in which is it desirable to avoid face validity. Content validity and face validity are usually judgment calls—that is, the professional looks at the items in the measure and judges whether they cover the content domain or measure what they appear to measure.

Validity, like reliability, is not an all-or-nothing phenomenon. In addition to specifying the strength of the relationship, one should specify what variables are related to the diagnosis or test score. For example, demonstrating that individuals with mental retardation show not only poor performance on IQ measures but also social insensitivity could validate this diagnostic category. However, researchers might also find that the mental retardation diagnosis is not related to happiness. In this case, the mental retardation diagnosis is a valid predictor of IQ test performance and social insensitivity but is not a valid predictor of happiness.

Finally, a diagnosis can be reliable without being valid, as illustrated in the magician example. However, a diagnosis can never be valid without also being reliable.

ADVANTAGES OF THE CURRENT DSM

There were five previous editions of the DSM: DSM-I (APA, 1952), DSM-II (APA, 1968), DSM-III (APA, 1980), DSM-III-R (APA, 1987), and DSM-IV (APA, 1994). Both the third edition and the fourth were revised, but the revisions were not sufficient to call them new editions. The first two editions of the DSM were slim volumes, which listed a few dozen disorders. The criteria for diagnosis in these early editions were vague and often required the clinician to make inferences about underlying causes of the symptoms. Not surprisingly, the interrater reliability of these early diagnostic manuals was low (Spitzer & Fleiss, 1974).

DSM-III ushered in a new era. The number of diagnoses increased dramatically in DSM-III, and the diagnostic process also changed. The movement toward symptom-based diagnoses with DSM-III dramatically improved interrater reliability, because the bases for the diagnosis—the symptoms and signs—were observable (APA, 1980; Spitzer et al., 1975; Spitzer & Williams, 1988). This was a step forward from a diagnostic system that required so many inferences about what was going on inside the person that interrater reliability was often embarrassingly low

concurrent validity The relationship of a measure or diagnosis to some variable that is currently present.

predictive validity The relationship of a measure or diagnosis to some future event.

criterion-related validities Validities concerned with the strength of the relationship between the measure or diagnosis and some criterion measure, such as school performance.

content validity How well a test or measure covers the relevant content.

face validity The degree to which a test is measuring what it appears to measure.

(Spitzer & Fleiss, 1974). Nevertheless, further improvement was possible, and to a degree it has been achieved in later editions (Kirk & Kutchins, 1994). Improved reliability made possible better evaluations of the validity of the diagnostic system. An explosion of research has occurred since the publication of DSM-III. DSM-III-R, DSM-IV, and DSM-IV-TR continue to use symptom-based diagnoses, and all have benefited from ongoing research, refining the diagnostic categories. These refinements are not merely academic exercises; they often have led to improved treatment.

LIMITATIONS OF DIAGNOSES

People are so accustomed to the concept of diagnosis that they frequently do not recognize the problems associated with creating and using a diagnostic system. Of course, the diagnosis should be shown to be reliable and valid before it is accepted as standard practice. However, there are other issues that should be addressed as part of the process of studying psychopathology and developing and refining a diagnostic system.

The effectiveness of a diagnostic system rests on the precision with which each diagnosis is defined. A problem, however, is that the nature of symptoms associated with disorders may vary from culture to culture or may vary as a function of the person's age, sex, or history. For example, symptoms of depression vary among cultures and are different in adults and children (APA, 2000; Marsella, 1987). However, these differences appear to be surface variations and not evidence for different kinds of depression in these different groups. The field is not yet at a stage where the psychological equivalent of a blood test can yield a definitive diagnosis. As a consequence, the diagnostic system must be flexible enough to take into account secondary factors that may affect symptom patterns, while still maintaining sufficient specificity to produce high interrater reliability.

The diagnostic system has led to significant improvements in treatment of people with mental disorders, but these improvements have not been achieved without costs. One of the most significant costs is the negative effect of labeling people with a diagnosis. There is nothing inherently wrong with such diagnostic labeling, but unfortunately, there is still considerable stigma associated with a psychiatric diagnosis (Crisp, 2001), and the stigma can have real consequences. People may be denied opportunities for employment, may be shunned by peers, or may find themselves unable to get insurance coverage because of a previous diagnosis. This stigma is often reinforced by the portrayal of mental illness in the media, which is discussed in the nearby Modern Myths box. In some cases, these prejudices become so powerful that steps must be taken to protect people who are in treatment. Sometimes that has involved changing the labels. For example, the terms *idiot, imbecile,* and *moron* were once official diagnostic labels for levels of mental retardation. Over time they became insults, so new diagnostic labels were created (mild, moderate, severe, and profound mental retardation). Mental health professionals must be acutely aware of the negative effects of such labels. They should take steps to protect their clients by using diagnostic labels only in those contexts in which the label will be unlikely to have adverse consequences, such as in communicating to other mental health professionals.

Another problem is that a psychiatric diagnostic system has the potential to become a tool for repression. In the former Soviet Union, psychiatric hospitalization was routinely used as a way of controlling dissidents (Yegorov, 1992). Hospitalizing and drugging such people was every bit as effective as imprisoning them, while allowing the government to maintain at least a pretense of caring about the well-being of its victims. Even in the United States, early laws allowed families to have problematic members locked up "for their own good." Chapter 16 will cover changes in laws designed to protect people against such abuses. Any system can be abused; it takes vigilance and effort to minimize the possibility of abuse and correct abuses when they are detected.

Check Yourself 2.1

The Diagnostic System

1. What is the name of the current diagnostic system used for mental disorders in the United States?
2. What are the five axes that make up the DSM?
3. What are the different types of reliability, and which one is most relevant to diagnosis?
4. What are the advantages of the current diagnostic system?

Ponder this . . .   *The difficult part of validating a concept, such as a diagnostic category, is to decide what relationships should exist and what relationships should not exist. Take a concept that you probably have at least some familiarity with, such as the common cold. How would you go about validating a diagnosis of a cold? In other words, what relationships do you expect between that diagnosis and the behavior and experiences of people with that diagnosis? This process is covered in considerable detail in Chapter 6, but see if you can reason out the steps now.*

MODERN Myths

Psychopathology AND Dangerousness

Well before you signed up for this course or began reading this textbook, you had a sense of what it meant to be abnormal from television, movies, and other media. Your notion of abnormality may have been fuzzy, but you did know something about the consequences of behaving abnormally. You knew, for example, that if your behavior was too outrageous, "men in white coats would come to take you away to a padded cell." That, of course, is not literally what happens today, although 60 years ago it might have happened.

One area in which the media has done a disservice to people with mental disorders is in depicting such people as dangerous. The media do not do this deliberately or systematically, but when they cover on the evening news only people with mental illness who are violent, it gives viewers the impression that mental illness and dangerousness "go together." The portrayal of people with mental illness in movies and on TV has this same bias. Consider Hannibal Lecter

from *The Silence of the Lambs* or Kahn from *Star Trek II: The Wrath of Kahn*. The result of this distortion is often devastating to people who suffer from a mental disorder. Watch people react to seriously disturbed individuals. Watch their eyes, and you can often see the fear. Granted that the person's behavior may be unpredictable, but unpredictability alone is unlikely to arouse such fear.

Of course, some people with mental disorders are clearly dangerous. Consider David Berkowitz (the Son of Sam killer), John Hinkley (who attempted to kill President Reagan), and Jeffrey Dalmer (who killed and cannibalized two dozen victims). They made the front page, and our memories of them remain vivid even though they have been locked up for some time (or, in the case of Dalmer, are now dead). Unfortunately, when mentally disturbed individuals do become violent, their violence has a bizarre quality that makes it more newsworthy and more frightening. There are millions of people with psychopathology every bit as severe as that experienced by these notorious individuals,

yet none of them has committed heinous crimes. Nevertheless, people still tend to view disturbed individuals as far more dangerous than they truly are (Monahan, 1992; Teplin, 1985).

Although the occasional disturbed individual who becomes violent gets all the media coverage, it is far more common for people with mental illness to be the victims of violence (Marley & Buila, 2001). In many ways, they are easy targets. They often fail to discern the self-serving motives of others, they may be less able to understand the consequences of their actions, and they often have more difficulty convincing friends, family, and the authorities that they have been victimized.

Imagine how difficult it is to return to your home following a serious psychiatric disturbance, having to deal with your symptoms and with the embarrassment of having displayed them. Now imagine how much more difficult it is when your neighbors and co-workers virtually shun you because they think you may be dangerous. These distortions are not innocuous; they affect real people every day.

PSYCHOLOGICAL ASSESSMENT

Psychological assessment involves measuring such psychological variables as diagnosis, skills or personality traits. This section focuses on five broad classes of such measures: structured interviews, intelligence tests, neuropsychological tests, objective psychological tests, and projective tests.

STRUCTURED INTERVIEWS

In the field of psychopathology, **structured interviews** are the workhorses of diagnosis. They are formalized inter-

views, which incorporate precisely worded questions with rules for how the interviewer should select the questions to be asked. They are used extensively in research to enhance the reliability and validity of diagnoses. Structured interviews are contrasted with unstructured and semi-structured interviews. **Unstructured interviews** allow the interviewer to ask any question and to follow up on any answer. Many therapy sessions are essentially unstructured interviews, in which the course of the session is determined by the nature of the information exchanged. **Semi-structured interviews** have a specific agenda, but no strict format dictates what will be asked, how the questions will be asked, and in what order. Most diagnostic interviews in clinical practice are of this type. The clinician has a clear idea of what general areas need to be covered but starts by following the lead of the client. Most such interviews start with a request like "What prompted you to call for an appointment?" If the client reports depression, the therapist will explore that area but will later explore other topics, such as substance abuse, family history of psychopathology, and level of social support. The order of topics is selected to make the interview flow, but the topics to be covered are determined by what needs to be covered in a thorough diagnostic interview.

A structured interview offers three major advantages for diagnosis. (1) Such interviews obtain precise information from individuals in a consistent manner. This means that the interview will have generally good interrater reliability. (2) The interview questions are carefully worded to avoid ambiguity and minimize defensiveness. That improves the accuracy of the information and thus increases validity. (3) The systematic nature of the interview ensures that all relevant information is obtained.

In a simple structured interview, the professional asks all of the questions in the interview. More commonly, the professional asks subsets of questions, in which the subset depends on the information offered in response to earlier questions. Structured interviews typically include several semi-independent sections. Each section begins with one or more screening questions. For example, the screening questions for schizophrenia might include

> Now I am going to ask you about some unusual experiences that people sometimes have.... Did it ever seem that people were talking about you or taking special notice of you? . . . What about receiving special messages from the TV, radio, or newspaper, or from the way things were arranged around you? . . . What about anyone going out of their way to give you a hard time or hurting you? . . .

If the person answers no to all such screening questions, the professional skips to the next section because it is unlikely that the person qualifies for the diagnosis of schizophrenia. If, on the other hand, the person answers yes to any of these questions, then further questioning is warranted.

With any assessment device, there is always the possibility of error. Two types of errors are possible, false negatives and false positives (see Table 2.2). **False positives,** also known as false alarms, occur when one predicts a specific situation, such as a diagnosis, and the prediction is wrong. **False negatives,** also known as misses, occur when one predicts that a situation, such as a diagnosis, does not exist, and the prediction is wrong. This concept can be applied to any prediction. For example, a psychologist

The clinical interview is one of the most flexible and powerful assessment devices in psychopathology. Researchers rely primarily on structured clinical interviews, whereas clinicians tend to use semi-structured and unstructured interviews.

may predict that a person will attempt suicide. This example illustrates how the costs of each error may be different. A false positive in the suicide example means that the prediction of suicide is wrong. The cost is that the psychologist worried needlessly and perhaps took unnecessary precautions. A false negative means that a person whom the psychologist thought was not suicidal commits suicide. The cost here is the person's death and the fact that the psychologist will probably never stop wondering whether he or she overlooked a warning sign. Which error would you be more willing to tolerate?

The relationship between false positives and false negatives is complex, but in general, as one error increases in frequency, the frequency of the other error decreases. How common each error is depends on the criterion for the decision. For example, using strict criteria for the diagnosis

structured interviews Formal interviews that incorporate precisely worded questions with rules for how the interviewer should select the questions to be asked.

unstructured interviews Interviews in which the interviewer can ask any question and follow up on any answer.

semi-structured interviews Interviews that have a specific agenda but no strict format for what will be asked, how it will be asked, or in what order the questions will be asked.

false positives Occur when one predicts a specific situation, such as a diagnosis, and the prediction is wrong. Also known as false alarms.

false negatives Occur when one predicts that a situation, such as a diagnosis, does not exist, and the prediction is wrong. Also known as misses.

[TABLE 2.2] **Decisions and Errors**

		TRUE STATE OF AFFAIRS	
		Person has schizophrenia.	Person does not have schizophrenia.
DECISION	Person has schizophrenia.	Hit	False positive
	Person does not have schizophrenia.	False *negative*	Valid *negative*

Every assessment decision can be either right or wrong. In this example, the assessment task is to diagnose people who may or may not have schizophrenia. The two types of errors that one could make are false negatives (sometimes called misses) and false positives (sometimes called false alarms), as shown in the table.

of schizophrenia minimizes false positives but produces many false negatives. In other words, virtually everyone who qualifies for the diagnosis under these strict criteria will indeed have schizophrenia, but a fair number of people who fail to meet the criteria will be misdiagnosed as *not* having schizophrenia. In contrast, using broad criteria for diagnosis reduces false negatives but does so at the expense of many false positives. Normally, the criteria is set on the basis of the cost of the errors. For example, in structured interviews, the screening questions are worded to produce few false negatives, and false positives are common. The only cost of false positives is that additional questions will be asked. In contrast, false negatives mean that an important diagnosis may be overlooked. In the suicide example, the obvious choice is to err on the side of caution: Assume suicide potential if there are any signs, and take appropriate measures to reduce the risk.

Structured interviews have been developed for virtually every type of diagnostic assessment. There are general diagnostic interviews, such as the *Structured Clinical Interview for DSM-IV* (SCID-P; First et al., 1995). There are diagnostic interviews that focus specifically on personality disorders (Pfohl et al., 1997; Trull et al., 1998), anxiety disorders (Brown et al., 1994), dissociative disorders (Ross et al., 1989), and psychotic disorders (Orvaschel & Puig-Antich, 1986; Spitzer & Endicott, 1977), to name but a few. There are even simplified structured interviews designed

for physicians to use in screening for mental disorders that may require referral to a mental health professional (Spitzer et al., 1994).

INTELLIGENCE TESTS

Intelligence is the ability to think and solve problems. One often associates it with school performance, but of course, intelligence contributes to success in many endeavors. **Intelligence tests,** often referred to as **IQ tests,** were developed to measure the abilities believed to be at the core of intelligence. IQ is short for *intelligence quotient,* a term based on how the IQ score was first computed. Intelligence tests are most frequently used by schools for the selection and placement of students.

Intelligence tests originated in France, where they were introduced by Alfred Binet as a standardized way of identifying children with intellectual deficits severe enough to warrant special schooling. The technique was adapted and standardized for an American population at Stanford University by Terman (1919), who created the *Stanford-Binet Intelligence Test,* which is still in use in a revised form today. A number of other intelligence measures have been developed over the years, including the *Wechsler Adult Intelligence Scale* (WAIS) and the *Wechsler Intelligence Scale for Children* (WISC), both now in their third edition. Universities use group-administered intelligence tests, such as the *Scholastic Assessment Test* (SAT) and the *Graduate Record Exam* (GRE) to help them select among applicants to college and graduate school, respectively. Intelligence measures are a critical part of the diagnostic procedure for mental retardation (covered in Chapter 13) and are part of a neuropsychological test battery for the diagnosis of brain impairment (covered later in this section).

Intelligence tests represent samples of behavior—primarily academic behavior. For example, most intelligence tests measure verbal and mathematical ability, problem

intelligence The ability to think and solve problems.

intelligence test or IQ test A measure of the abilities believed to be at the core of intelligence. IQ is short for *intelligence quotient.*

neuropsychological tests Tests that measure detailed functioning in people in order to *infer* something about the functioning of their brains.

solving skill, and memory. All of these skills are thought to be a part of the concept of intelligence, and the fact that scores on each of these measures tend to be highly correlated is consistent with the idea that all the measures assess a single concept (Matarazzo, 1972). It is not surprising that the vast majority of so-called intelligence tests measure academic ability, because such tests are used most often in academic settings for selection and placement. However, one might question, as many people have (Ceci & Roazzi, 1994; Sternberg, 1994, 2001), whether academic skills are the only elements of intelligence. Is a person with "street smarts" intelligent or something else? Is a person with unusual skill in reading the motives of others intelligent or just socially perceptive? These questions about the nature of intelligence have occasioned considerable debate (Sternberg, 2001; Sternberg & Wagner, 1994).

NEUROPSYCHOLOGICAL TESTS

Neuropsychological tests are designed to measure detailed functioning in people in order to *infer* something about the functioning of their brains. They are used most fre-

quently to evaluate people with possible brain injury or dysfunction. Norma—one of the cases that opened the chapter—was given neuropsychological tests to assess her forgetfulness. Neuropsychological tests also have been used in research to document subtle aspects of behavior that may indicate a neurological deficit underlying a disorder. For example, such use is common in research on schizophrenia (Green, 1998).

Neuropsychological testing involves giving clients a battery of tests, each of which requires specific skills (Golden, 1978, 1990; Lezak, 1995). Most perceptual, motor, and cognitive behavior is composed of numerous individual elements. By carefully examining the client's pattern of performance on the test battery, neuropsychologists are able to identify specific elements that are disordered and hence can infer what brain structures are likely to be dysfunctional. This is an indirect measure of brain pathology in that it measures the results of the pathology—the deficits in functioning. Because this is one of the most sophisticated uses of psychological testing, it is impossible to cover the principles in detail here. A typical neuropsychological test is shown in Figure 2.2.

[FIGURE 2.2]
The Tactual Performance Test

The Tactual Performance Test is one of several standard neuropsychological tests. The task is to place the blocks into the correct holes on the form-board while blindfolded. It measures the ability to discern shapes by feel and to remember the location of holes on the form-board.

OBJECTIVE PSYCHOLOGICAL TESTS

There are literally hundreds of **objective psychological tests** available to measure almost every conceivable psychological concept. In objective psychological tests, the person selects, from a limited number of choices, the answer that seems most appropriate. For example, the test may include items in which the person responds with either "true" or "false" to each of a series of statements. The scoring of the test is entirely objective in that rules for scoring are completely spelled out; no subjective judgment is required or allowed. Many objective tests can be purchased through companies that specialize in the distribution of psychological tests, and others are available to researchers and clinicians free of charge (Fischer & Corcoran, 1994a, 1994b). Basic validational data are always available for standardized tests, and some of the best-known psychological tests have thousands of published validational studies to support their use.

The MMPI. The most widely used psychological test is the **Minnesota Multiphasic Personality Inventory** or **MMPI.** The MMPI is one of several **personality inventories,** which are psychological tests designed to assess a number of personality or diagnostic variables simultaneously. Such inventories can provide a reasonably comprehensive psychological picture of a person. Personality inventories are routinely computer-scored these days. Currently in its second edition (MMPI-2), the MMPI consists of 567 true/false items. It originally included 10 clinical diagnostic scales and 3 validity scales, but it is currently scored on nearly 100 scales representing a variety of psychopathological and personality characteristics. The original clinical scales are described in Table 2.3. They were developed via an **empirical approach to test development,** in which groups of people with the pathology that was assessed by each scale were compared with groups of people without that pathology

....

objective psychological tests   Tests in which the person selects, from a limited number of choices, the answer that seems most appropriate.

Minnesota Multiphasic Personality Inventory (MMPI)
The most widely used psychological test.

personality inventories   Psychological tests designed to assess a number of personality or diagnostic variables simultaneously.

empirical approach to test development   A test development technique that selects items based on their ability to differentiate people with and without a specified personality trait or diagnosis.

projective tests   Tests in which people are asked to respond to vague stimuli.

Rorschach Inkblot Test   A test in which people are asked what a series of inkblots resemble.

Thematic Apperception Test (TAT)   A test in which people are asked to tell stories based on pictures they are shown.

on their responses to items. This information determined whether an item was included in the scale. For example, if people with depression respond differently than people without depression to an item such as "I have a lot of energy," then that item would be included in the depression scale. Depressed people are more likely to say "false" to this item, so the item is keyed false for depression—that is, a "false" response increases the score on the depression scale. This procedure identifies items that *empirically* discriminate one diagnostic group from another. Some items are obvious, such as the depression item just mentioned, so they are said to be face valid. Other items are less obvious. For example, an item such as "Many people cut corners instead of doing what is right" is likely to discriminate people with paranoia from other people, paranoid individuals being more likely to respond "true." Subtle items have a potential advantage because defensive individuals may not recognize that such items assess psychopathology.

The profile for the MMPI-2 is typically graphed as shown in Figure 2.3. Scores at or above the 93rd percentile are considered in the pathological range. Interpreting MMPI profiles involves looking at the pattern of elevated scores—specifically, the highest two or three scores on the clinical scales. This pattern of elevated scores is called the *codetype.* In Figure 2.3, the codetype is 8-6 (highest elevations on scales 8 and 6). This codetype is commonly found in people who qualify for a diagnosis of paranoid schizophrenia. The original names of the clinical scales of the MMPI were replaced with numbers when research indicated that patterns of scores were more effective than single scales in diagnosing individuals. Published manuals exist to help clinicians interpret the most commonly found codetypes for the MMPI-2 (Butcher, 1990; Graham, 1990; Greene, 1991).

Other Self-Report Measures.   The MMPI-2 is only one of hundreds of self-report measures. Some are personality inventories, such as the *Millon Clinical Multiaxial Inventory* (MCMI-III), the *16 Personality Factors* (16PF), and the *Personality Research Form* (PRF). Most are single-purpose measures.

An advantage of self-report measures is that they are easy to administer and score. In most cases, the person responds in a specific format, such as true/false or a rating scale, to a series of items. The scoring involves simply counting responses. A disadvantage of self-report measures is that the people taking them may deliberately underreport or overreport pathology. Many measures include validity scales as a way of detecting such responding. The projective techniques covered in the next section were designed in part to overcome this problem.

PROJECTIVE TESTS

With **projective tests,** people are asked to respond to vague stimuli. For example, in the **Rorschach Inkblot Test,** people

[TABLE 2.3]   The Scales of the MMPI-2

Listed below are the original ten clinical scales and the three most widely used validity scales of the MMPI, complete with sample items. The names of the clinical scales have more recently been replaced by numbers (shown in parentheses).

CLINICAL SCALES	VALIDITY SCALES
Hypochondriasis (1): A tendency to report vague and nonspecific complaints about body functioning. [*The top of my head sometimes feels tender.* (true)]	**L Scale**: A tendency to deliberately avoid answering questions in a frank and truthful manner. The items tap admirable, but highly implausible, behaviors or feelings. [*At times I feel like swearing.* (false)]
Depression (2): A tendency to report depressive symptomatology, including hopelessness and dissatisfaction with one's life. [*I usually feel that life is worthwhile.* (false)]	**F Scale**: A tendency to answer in a deviant manner. The items tap unusual or pathological behavior that was reported by less than 10% of the original standardization sample. [*When I am with people, I am bothered by hearing very strange things.* (true)]
Hysteria (3): A tendency to experience general physical complaints, coupled with a tendency to present oneself as well socialized and adjusted. [*I often wonder what hidden reasons another person may have for doing something nice for me.* (false)]	**K Scale**: A tendency to minimize or deny psychopathology. Scores on this scale are used to correct scores on five of the ten clinical scales. [*I have very few quarrels with members of my family.* (true)]
Psychopathic deviance (4): A tendency to complain about authority figures and to present oneself as socially alienated and bored. [*My way of doing things is apt to be misunderstood by others.* (true)]	
Masculinity/femininity (5): A tendency to endorse stereotypically cross-sex interests and behavior. High scores indicate more stereotypically feminine interests. This scale is graphed in opposite directions for males and females (high scores are deviant for males, and low scores are deviant for females). [*I think I would like the work of a librarian.* (true)]	
Paranoia (6): A tendency to show excessive interpersonal sensitivity, suspiciousness, or self-righteousness. [*I have no enemies who really wish to harm me.* (false)]	
Psychasthenia (7): A tendency toward obsessive-compulsive behavior, excessive guilt, abnormal anxiety and fears, and excessive self-criticism. [*I feel anxiety about something or someone almost all the time.* (true)]	
Schizophrenia (8): A tendency to report a variety of unusual thoughts, perceptions, and experiences, social and family alienation, difficulties in concentration and impulse control, sexual difficulties, and poor sense of self-worth and self-identity. [*I often feel as if things are not real.* (true)]	
Hypomania (9): A tendency to report elated but unstable mood, rapid flow of thoughts, and constant and rapid activity. [*When I get bored I like to stir up some excitement.* (true)]	
Social introversion (0): A tendency to report social anxiety and a preference for social withdrawal. [*Whenever possible I avoid being in a crowd.* (true)]	

SOURCE: *From* The MMPI-2/MMPI: An Interpretive Manual *by R. L. Greene. Copyright © 1991. Reprinted by permission of Allyn and Bacon.*

are asked what a series of inkblots resemble (Exner, 1985, 1993; Rorschach, 1942). In the **Thematic Apperception Test (TAT),** people are asked to tell stories based on pictures they are shown. It is assumed that people taking such tests will have to "project" their experiences and personality onto the stimuli. For example, telling a story about feeling controlled by one's mother in response to the picture shown on page 41 may reveal something about the storyteller's own experiences and feelings.

Projective tests have a long and contentious history in clinical psychology, and in some ways they have become the symbol of psychological testing. Unfortunately, they have also been used in clinical situations in which their validity is either untested or has been shown to be clearly lacking (Chapman & Chapman, 1967, 1969; Wood et al., 2001). For example, early manuals for scoring the Rorschach (Rorschach, 1942) routinely suggested that certain observations were indicative of certain personality characteristics, even though there were no scientific data to support such claims. Recent manuals (Exner, 1993) rely more on scientific data, but there are few psychologically significant variables that are predicted well by the Rorschach. An example

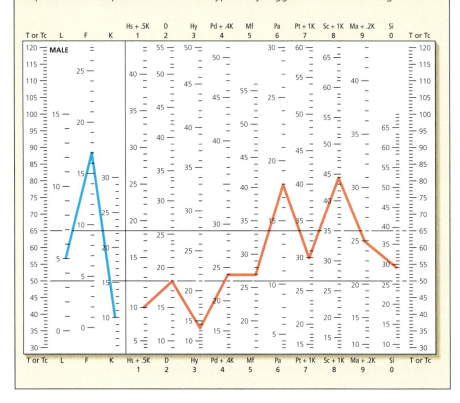

[FIGURE 2.3]

An Example of an MMPI-2 Profile

This MMPI-2 profile shows the validity and primary clinical scales. In this case, the person shows an 8-6 codetype, with the highest scores on scale 8 (schizophrenia) and scale 6 (paranoia). This pattern is typical of a person who would qualify for a diagnosis of paranoid schizophrenia. Other codetypes may suggest other clinical diagnoses.

of a prediction that *is* scientifically supported is that people with schizophrenia consistently respond to the Rorschach in ways that are easily distinguished from the responses of people without this disorder (Rapaport et al., 1946). These responses include obvious perceptual and cognitive distortions, such as reporting perceptions that don't look anything like the inkblot, telling detailed and bizarre personal stories about the inkblot, employing unusual and strange wording in describing the inkblots, and even fusing objects into implausible hybrids (for example, "the face of a bug-ox," a combination of a bug and an ox). These well-validated signs of schizophrenia have often been combined into a single schizophrenia index (Watkins & Stauffacher, 1952). However, one hardly needs to spend two hours administering and scoring a psychological test to diagnose schizophrenia reliably. Thus, although supported by data, this application makes little sense. A more useful role for the Rorschach is identifying individuals who may be at risk for schizophrenia but are not currently psychotic (Chapman et al., 1978b; Gunderson & Singer, 1975). In fact, these pathological signs may actually be more dramatic in

individuals at risk for schizophrenia than in people with schizophrenia (Rorschach, 1942), although the reason for this startling finding is unclear. Here again, however, other tests that detect risk for schizophrenia (Chapman et al., 1994) are much easier to administer. Whether the Rorschach adds useful information to what these instruments provide has yet to be established. Techniques such as the Rorschach may also be useful for detecting narrow concepts, such as interpersonal dependency (Bornstein, 1999). Nevertheless, there is little evidence to support its widespread use for general psychological assessment.

The TAT has also been used extensively in research. For example, content scoring is used to measure motivational variables on the basis of the themes of the stories, such as the need for achievement (McClelland, 1985). The TAT has also been used to provide a standardized method of generating speech samples. For example, several investigators have used the TAT to generate speech samples for scoring communication deviance in people with psychiatric disorders and their families (Singer & Wynne, 1963; Tompson et al., 1990). Clinically, the TAT tends to be used

In the Thematic Apperception Test, or TAT, people are asked to tell stories about pictures that are deliberately vague like this one. It is assumed that people project their experiences or personality onto the pictures, so their comments give the clinician or researcher insights into their thoughts, emotions, and experiences.

for generating hypotheses about what might be bothering the person. The clinician looks for consistent themes in the stories and then uses that information to guide later interviewing and therapy. Used in this way, the TAT is a relatively low-cost assessment, but is not relied on to provide strong predictions or a specific diagnosis.

Check Yourself 2.2

Psychological Assessment

1. How do structured, semi-structured, and unstructured interviews differ?
2. What was the reason for the initial development of intelligence tests?
3. What is the most commonly used objective psychological test?

Ponder this . . . What is the difference between being "school smart" (doing well in school) and being

"street smart" (doing well in the real world)? What skills contribute to both? Do you think a school smart person would be more or less likely than a randomly selected person to be street smart as well?

BEHAVIORAL ASSESSMENT

The thing that most people want to know about other people is how those other people will behave. You may spend considerable time and energy trying to understand what people are thinking and feeling, but if you pause for a moment and contemplate, you will realize that the reason why you want to know what is going on inside of them is so that you can predict their next moves. If one is interested in predicting behavior, why not directly observe the behavior and use it as a basis for prediction? That is the premise behind **behavioral assessment,** which is the observation of people's behavior in specified situations. This section discusses two behavioral assessment techniques: behavioral observation and role-playing.

BEHAVIORAL OBSERVATION

Behavioral observation involves watching and recording key aspects of a person's behavior. This can be done in almost any setting, including the person's natural environment. Many psychological laboratories utilize one-way mirrors to permit easy observation. For example, a playroom may be equipped with such facilities so that observers can monitor the social interactions of children during play. One advantage of observing behind a one-way mirror is that the observer is not obvious. (In general, people tend to behave differently when they know they are being observed.) Behavior can be recorded on videotape as a permanent record or coded as it occurs. The more complex the behavior of interest, the more difficult it is to code in real time, and thus the more important it is to have a permanent record. *Coding* the behavior involves classifying it into categories or scores. For example, if someone interacts with a member of his or her family, the nature of that interaction could be coded on many dimensions. This approach has been used to measure the level of hostility in a family to assess its impact on symptomatology in schizophrenia (Vaughn & Leff, 1976b; Mottaghipour et al., 2001) and several other psychological and physical disorders (Blair et al., 1995; Chambless et al., 2001; Liakopoulou et al., 2001).

behavioral assessment   Observing the behavior of people in specified situations.

behavioral observation   Watching and recording key aspects of a person's behavior.

It is common to include one-way observation windows in psychological laboratories to facilitate the unobtrusive observation of behavior. The observer can see the participants clearly, but the participants see a mirror.

ROLE-PLAYING

Some behaviors occur infrequently in natural situations, but one still wants to observe the person in such situations. The best way to do this is to place people in situations and observe their behavior or, alternatively, ask them to imagine that they are in situations and to behave accordingly. This latter strategy is referred to as **role-playing.** Role-playing is used most often to evaluate a person's skills. For example, if a person complains about feeling uncomfortable around other people, the psychologist might role-play a social interaction with the person to see how well she or he recognizes and responds to the demands of the situation. The advantage of a role-play situation is that it can provide valuable information about the person without risking embarrassment. Role-playing often requires little more than the imagination and encouragement of the psychologist. Role-playing can also draw on technology. The flight simulators that are routinely used to train airline crews are multi-million-dollar re-creations of flight, which enable pilots to role-play hundreds of potentially dangerous situations. This example illustrates another aspect of role-playing: It not only evaluates a person's skill but can also be used to enhance skills. For example, virtual reality programs have recently been used to treat fear of heights or of flying by giving people the sense that they are up high without their ever leaving the therapist's office (Muehlberger et al., 2001; Regenbrecht et al., 1998). Role-playing was used to teach Cal how to control his anxiety about public speaking. Role-

role-playing Behavioral assessment strategy that involves observing how people behave in imagined situations.

structural brain abnormalities Visible changes in the size and shape of brain areas.

playing has also been used to assess and encourage social skills in students (Taylor, 2001), in people with schizophrenia (Goldsmith & McFall, 1975; Wixted et al., 1988), and in people at risk for schizophrenia (Haberman et al., 1979).

Check Yourself 2.3

Behavioral Assessment

1. Why might a researcher want to hide, from the participants in a study, the fact that behavioral assessment is being done?
2. What behavioral assessment approach is most appropriate when a situation is unlikely to arise very often in the natural environment?

Ponder this . . . *Say you were asked to coach your son's or daughter's soccer team. How might you use the methods of behavioral assessment to evaluate the skills of the players and later improve those skills?*

BIOLOGICAL ASSESSMENT

This section describes some of the techniques used to evaluate biological processes that may underlie psychopathology. Studying biological factors is inherently difficult, and until recently the procedures available have been primitive. However, tremendous advances in technology have opened new avenues for research into psychopathology. This section covers current biological assessment strategies for investigating both structural and functional abnormalities. Several techniques of historical interest are also covered because they illustrate the logic of biological assessment.

STRUCTURAL BRAIN ABNORMALITIES

Structural brain abnormalities are visible changes in the size and shape of brain areas. They can result from injury, deterioration, or abnormal development of certain regions of the brain. Norma's doctor suspected that such brain abnormalities were causing her memory problems and so referred her to a neurologist for evaluation. In general, structural brain abnormalities tend to lead to severe and irreversible pathology. Until the mid-twentieth century, such abnormalities were detectable only at autopsy. In the last 50 years, increasingly sophisticated and accurate imaging techniques have been developed.

Autopsy. A detailed autopsy, wherein the pathologist dissects the brain piece by piece, was the first procedure devised for studying brain abnormalities. The quality of the data from autopsies is excellent, but timeliness is problematic. Autopsies are performed only after a person dies. With diseases that lead to a quick death, the autopsy usually provides valuable information about the disease process. However, it is common for people to develop a disorder early in life but to live out a normal life expectancy. An autopsy conducted on people who die at age 75 tells little about the condition of their brains at age 25, when the symptoms may have first appeared. Given these limitations, it is not surprising that autopsies have contributed little to the understanding of psychopathology, although there have been exceptions. For example, many people with schizophrenia tend to show damage to the neurological reward mechanisms of the brain (Wise & Stein, 1973) and a decrease in the number of nicotinic receptors in the hippocampus (Freedman et al., 1995).

Imaging Techniques. The X-ray machine revolutionized medicine by making it possible to photograph internal structures without surgery. X-rays are great for imaging bones, but they are less effective for imaging tissue because various tissues differ so little in density. X-rays of the brain clearly show the skull but reveal little in the way of detail of the brain, with one exception. The ventricles of the brain are fluid-filled cavities of much lower density than the surrounding brain tissue. Hence they do show up on X-rays. Filling the ventricles with air instead of the fluid that normally fills them can enhance X-ray images. This is the logic behind *pneumoencephalograms.* However, pneumoencephalograms provided crude images, and obtaining them was both painful and potentially dangerous.

The early imaging techniques have been completely replaced by CAT scans and MRIs, which are discussed in the nearby Advances box. These techniques use sophisticated mathematics to reconstruct a three-dimensional image of the brain from hundreds of individual pictures. The difference between the two techniques lies in how the images are formed. **Computerized axial tomography (CAT scan)** uses X-ray pictures, whereas **magnetic resonance imaging (MRI)** sets up a magnetic field and forms images based on the varying magnetic properties of different brain tissues. Because data from the multiple images are converted into a three-dimensional matrix, it is relatively easy to show any section of the brain as though a slice were taken through that section. Examining such brain slices is the traditional

way in which physiologists have studied details of specific regions of the brain, but previously the technique could be applied only at autopsy. With the CAT scan and MRI, multiple sections can be inspected with minimal risk to the person and without doing damage to the brain.

FUNCTIONAL BRAIN ABNORMALITIES

Although there is evidence for structural brain abnormalities in some psychiatric disorders, of more interest is the functioning of the brain. A brain may be intact but still not function as it should. Measuring the functioning of the brain has been a dream of science for decades, and the techniques for doing so have been gradually improving. This section covers two approaches to measuring brain activity: psychophysiology and imaging techniques.

Psychophysiological Techniques. **Psychophysiological techniques** measure the activity of body organs, including the brain, as the person is engaged in behavior (Lykken, 1982). Dozens of individual measures have been developed to study relevant organ systems. In general, these procedures rely on measuring electrical or mechanical activity and recording that activity for later analysis.

The modern psychophysiological laboratory can measure a dozen or more physiological variables while the person is comfortably performing a task or responding to stimuli.

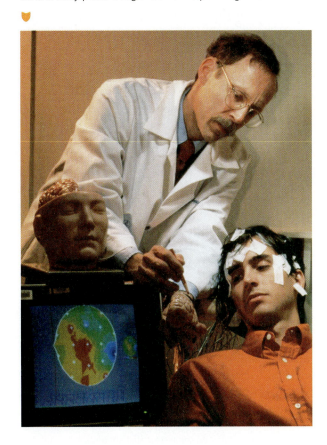

---

computerized axial tomography (CAT scan)   X-ray pictures used to view a person's body.

magnetic resonance imaging (MRI)   The use of a magnetic field to form images based on the varying magnetic properties of different body tissues.

psychophysiological techniques   Measurements of the activity of body organs, including the brain, as the person is engaged in behavior.

ADVANCES Seeing Into the Mind

Throughout this text, Advances boxes will cover cutting-edge technology, research, and theory that offer new insights into psychopathology. Nowhere is that more evident than in the tremendous advances over the last 20 years in brain-imaging technology.

Much of early psychology involved studying the relationships between external variables and behavior. There is no doubt that such research has led to a sophisticated understanding of how behavior is influenced both by external contingencies and by one's perception of the world. It is clearly the brain that mediates these behaviors, but until recently, technological procedures for studying how the brain mediates behavior were limited. Researchers could observe people with specific brain damage and see how that brain damage affected their functioning. From those observations, they could infer what each part of the brain did. However, it was often hard to know exactly what parts of the brain were damaged in someone with a head injury, tumor, or stroke. Today, CAT scans (computerized axial

tomography) and MRIs (magnetic resonance imaging) produce detailed pictures of the brain, that clearly show most structural abnormalities (see Figure 2.4). Researchers can then correlate those structural brain abnormalities with behavior. This technology has advanced our understanding of brain functioning and its relationship to specific forms of psychopathology.

Even more exciting is the ability to measure brain activity. Such procedures as the CAT scan can locate brain damage, but they cannot show dysfunction in the brain that is not associated with some structural abnormality. Such **functional brain abnormalities** *can* be assessed with newer technology such as the PET scan (positron emission tomography) and the fMRI (functional magnetic resonance imaging). These techniques make it possible to measure the activity level of specific brain regions and correlate it with behavior. Furthermore, in the field of psychopathology, these techniques can compare the patterns of brain activity in people with and people without a specified disorder, thus providing insight into what might underlie the

observed psychopathology. An older technology called EEG (electroencephalogram) provides another way to observe brain activity by measuring the electrical activity generated by the brain at the surface of the skull. Taken together, these techniques enable investigators to look at the relationship between brain and behavior in ways only dreamed about a couple of decades ago. They have confirmed suspicions about the brain mechanisms involved in several forms of psychopathology and, even more important, have yielded new insights into some forms of psychopathology that would have been difficult to obtain any other way. We will see numerous examples of this in later discussions of specific disorders.

Physiological arousal, which may indicate psychological stress, can be measured by changes in heart rate, muscle tension, or sweating of the palms. Heart rate can be measured with the *electrocardiogram* (EKG), which measures heart activity by monitoring the large electrical impulses associated with the muscular contractions of the heart. Muscle tension can be measured with the *electromyogram* (EMG), which monitors the electrical activity of muscles when they contract. Sweating on the palms can be monitored by observing changes in *skin conductance*. A small electric current is passed between two electrodes on the palm, and the amount of current passing between the electrodes changes as the conductance rises because of

sweating. All of these techniques are safe, noninvasive, and relatively easy to obtain without affecting the behavior of the person being monitored. In fact, some of this equipment is so portable and non-intrusive that participants can wear it throughout the day (Trimble, 1996).

Measuring brain activity is more complicated than measuring physiological arousal in the peripheral organs of the body. The brain is a complex organ, in which hundreds of thousands of things go on simultaneously. Because nerve cells transmit information through electrical impulses, brain activity creates electrical fields, which can be monitored by electrodes placed on the surface of the skin—a measurement known as the *electroencephalogram* (EEG). You have probably seen the traces from an EEG on TV. They are the half-dozen or more squiggly lines that are written on a constantly moving sheet of paper. Today those lines are typically recorded electronically for later analysis.

functional brain abnormalities Dysfunction in the brain that is not associated with some structural abnormality.

[FIGURE 2.4]
Brain Imaging

Modern technology provides a window on the brain and its functioning that has never before been available. CAT scans and MRIs produce three-dimensional images of the brain, which can be viewed in slices as shown (left) to provide the doctor or researcher with precise information about the condition of each region of the brain. PET scans and fMRIs produce three-dimensional images that represent activity levels, with colors illustrating the level of biological activity in each region of the brain, as shown (right).

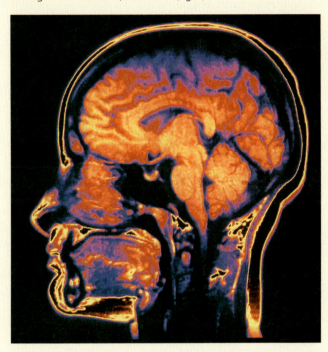

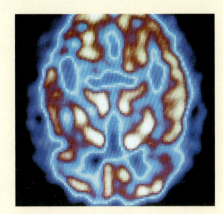

One way of simplifying the EEG is to look at the dominant frequencies. The frequencies of the EEG are classified into broad ranges. Delta waves are 1–3 cycles per second, or hertz (Hz); theta waves are 4–7 Hz; alpha waves are 8–12 Hz; and beta waves are 13 Hz and above. Mathematical procedures can analyze the complex waveforms of the EEG to see just how much of the total electrical signal falls in each of those frequency ranges.

Another way to simplify the voluminous amount of data in the EEG is to measure what are called *event-related potentials* (ERP). The ERP is a waveform that represents the specific activity of the brain that is elicited by a specific event. To obtain a measure of the ERP, the researcher has to present a specific stimulus repeatedly and monitor the activity of the brain each time. Averaging the complex electrical signal of the brain across repeated presentations of the event will produce a waveform that would otherwise be buried in the complex brain activity. The ERP is believed to provide a relatively pure measure of the brain's response to a stimulus. The first 100 milliseconds or so of the ERP is thought to represent sensory processing, whereas the later components of the ERP are thought to measure cognitive interpretation of the signal.

Imaging Techniques. Just as the CAT scan and MRI revolutionized the measurement of brain structure, the PET scan and fMRI revolutionized the measurement of brain functioning. **Positron emission tomography (PET**

....

positron emission tomography (PET scan)   A way to measure the relative activity of various parts of the brain by measuring the absorption of a harmless radioactive isotope into the cells of the brain.

scan) measures the relative activity of various parts of the brain by measuring the absorption of a harmless radioactive isotope into the brain cells. The more active a brain area is, the more of the isotope is absorbed. **Functional magnetic resonance imaging (fMRI)** measures the activity level of various parts of the brain by measuring changes in the magnetic properties of brain tissue. The fMRI does not require as long an exposure as the PET scan to record brain activity reliably. Consequently, fMRI has become the preferred method of measuring brain activity. Dozens of researchers have used functional brain imaging to study the brain activity of people with a variety of psychiatric disorders.

. . . .

functional magnetic resonance imaging (fMRI) A way to measure changes in the activity level of various parts of the brain by measuring the magnetic properties of brain tissue.

Check Yourself 2.4

Biological Assessment

1. What is the distinction between structural and functional brain abnormalities?
2. What is the difference between an MRI and an fMRI?
3. What kinds of variables can be measured using psychophysiological techniques?

Ponder this . . . *How much of an advantage is it to be able to image brain functioning, as opposed to imaging brain structure alone?*

SUMMARY

THE DIAGNOSTIC SYSTEM

- The diagnostic system for psychological disorders used in the United States is outlined in the fourth edition of the *Diagnostic and Statistical Manual of Mental Disorders* (DSM-IV). The international version is the *International Classification of Diseases* (ICD).

- The DSM encourages diagnoses on five axes, which code different aspects of a person's functioning: (1) psychiatric disorders, (2) personality disorders, (3) relevant medical disorders, (4) current psychosocial and environmental problems, and (5) an overall rating of level of functioning.

- When using any diagnostic system, one should be concerned with both interrater reliability (whether independent clinicians can agree on the appropriate diagnosis) and validity (whether the diagnosis is predictive of critical issues such as response to treatment). The current diagnostic system relies strictly on observable symptoms, which improves interrater reliability. There are several types of reliability and validity.

- Because of the stigma associated with psychopathology, diagnostic labeling can have a negative impact on people being diagnosed.

PSYCHOLOGICAL ASSESSMENT

- There are a number of routinely used psychological measurement procedures. The structured interview is one of the most flexible assessment strategies and is a mainstay of the field of psychopathology. Intelligence tests measure the skills that are critical in academic situations. Neuropsychological tests assess behaviors that give indications of brain functioning. Objective psychological tests ask people to respond to standardized stimuli with a limited number of responses. Projective tests ask people to respond to deliberately vague stimuli, a situation that causes them to project their experiences and personality onto the stimulus.

BEHAVIORAL ASSESSMENT

- Behavioral assessment involves directly observing the behavior of people in relevant situations. The strategies used most often are behavioral observation and role-playing.

BIOLOGICAL ASSESSMENT

- Structural brain abnormalities can be studied with procedures that range from autopsies to the CAT scans and MRIs of today. The modern scanning procedures provide accurate pictures of brain structures with minimal risk to the person.

- Psychophysiological techniques can monitor aspects of physiological arousal, such as heart rate, muscle tension, and palmar sweating; they can also monitor brain activity. Specialized scanning techniques, such as the PET scan and the fMRI, can also monitor brain activity.

KEY TERMS

age of onset   (27)
axes   (29)
base rate   (27)
behavioral assessment   (41)
behavioral observation   (41)
comorbid conditions   (27)
computerized axial tomography or CAT scan   (43)
concurrent validity   (32)
content validity   (32)
criterion-related validity   (32)
course   (27)
Diagnostic and Statistical Manual of Mental Disorders
   or DSM-IV   (26)
differential diagnosis   (27)
empirical approach to test development   (38)
etiology   (26)
face validity   (32)
false negatives   (35)
false positives   (35)
functional brain abnormalities   (44)
functional magnetic resonance imaging or fMRI   (46)
Global Assessment of Functioning or GAF   (29)
incidence   (27)
intelligence   (36)
intelligence tests or IQ tests   (36)
internal consistency reliability   (30)
International Classification of Diseases or ICD   (27)

interrater reliability   (29)
lifetime prevalence   (27)
magnetic resonance imaging or MRI   (43)
Minnesota Multiphasic Personality Inventory
   or MMPI   (38)
multiaxial diagnosis   (29)
neuropsychological tests   (36)
objective psychological tests   (38)
personality inventories   (38)
positron emission tomography or PET scan   (45)
predictive validity   (32)
prevalence   (27)
projective tests   (38)
psychophysiological techniques   (43)
reliability   (29)
role-playing   (42)
Rorschach Inkblot Test   (38)
semi-structured interviews   (35)
signs   (29)
structural brain abnormalities   (42)
structured interviews   (35)
symptoms   (29)
syndrome   (29)
test-retest reliability   (30)
Thematic Apperception Test or TAT   (39)
unstructured interviews   (35)
validity   (31)

 ## SUGGESTED READINGS

Millon, T., Blaney, P. H., & Davis, R. D. (Eds.). (1999). *Oxford Textbook of Psychopathology*. New York: Oxford University Press. This book, which offers chapters written by leading scholars in the field, provides state-of-the-art reviews of many topics in psychopathology. It was intended as a text for advanced undergraduates or students entering graduate school and as an up-to-date review for practitioners. Reading it is a great way for students to go beyond the basics in a particular topic.

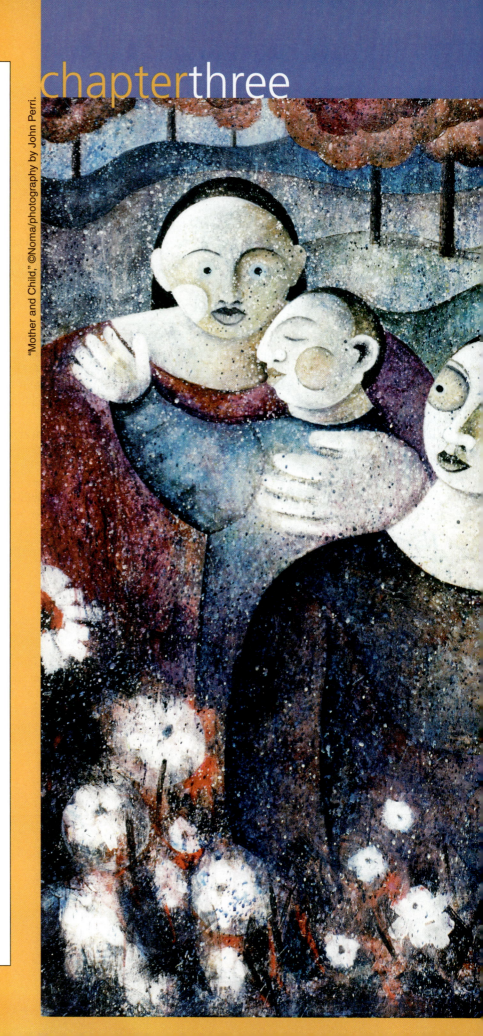

"Mother and Child," ©Noma/photography by John Perri.

chapterthree

Historical Perspectives on Psychopathology

DAN

Losing the Battle with Depression

No one will ever know exactly what Dan was feeling as he sat in a deserted park with a shotgun resting on his lap. Was he afraid of what would come next or relieved that the suffering would soon be over? Was he sure of his intentions or still debating what to do? He had left his suicide note in his apartment, where he knew police and family would find it. The only identification on him was a handwritten note listing his name, address, and next of kin, which he neatly covered in plastic and pinned to his jacket. Just minutes after 2:00 a.m. on that cold April morning, he rested the gun butt on the ground, leaned over, placed his mouth around the barrel, and pulled the trigger, ending his life in a split second. At 43, single, and feeling like a failure, he may have thought he had little choice. The fact that he was bright, capable, successful, and well liked was obviously inconsequential to him.

GARY

Obsessed with His Memory

Gary was 61 when he decided to retire. He was the most successful negotiator in his company, who often worked on several multi-million-dollar deals simultaneously. Retirement was an abrupt change for Gary, who suddenly went from 60- to 70-hour workweeks to staying at home and playing a little golf. Within a month of retirement, he knew he had made a mistake, and within three months he had slipped into a deep depression. He responded well to medication for the depression, but as his depression improved, he began to obsess about his memory. Within months, he started taking notes about everything, sometimes filling 50 sheets of paper in a single day. He stopped throwing out newspapers in case he forgot something in them. He felt compelled to read everything in the newspaper including the classifieds, every day. If he forgot the name of someone he met years earlier, he would be frantic until he could track it down. By the time he sought professional help, his basement was filled with newspapers and over 50 boxes of notes.

MONICA

Never Thin Enough

Monica was a wonderful daughter and a great student. She was popular with the boys in her class, but in her mind she was fat, so she dieted. When she started her diet at age 15, she weighed 118 pounds. A year later, down to 86 pounds, she continued to diet. Her parents were worried about her and encouraged her to eat more. She usually picked at her food, sometimes skipping meals altogether. If she did eat a normal meal, she would subsequently force herself to vomit. When her parents could not convince her to stop her excessive dieting, they insisted that she see a therapist. Monica liked the therapist, but little progress was made on her eating. She was hospitalized for the first time just before her seventeenth birthday because she was down to 78 pounds. An aggressive eating and intravenous nutrition program stabilized her weight, but within a month of her release, she started losing weight again. By now, even Monica knew that something was wrong, yet she still could not bring herself to eat more, and her weight continued to drop. She was hospitalized three more times over the next ten months. Her family and friends felt helpless, unable to alter what seemed a dangerous course.

What could possibly bring a successful individual like Dan to such despair that he took his own life? Why would someone as talented and effective as Gary obsess about his memory to the point where he was spending ten hours a day reading every word in the newspaper and taking pages of notes? Why would a vivacious young woman believe she was so fat that she dieted to the point of endangering her own life? These cases are both heart-wrenching and puzzling. So much was going on in the lives of these people that it is hard to know what elements are critical to understanding their behavior. Psychologists organize such complexity by looking at these cases from different perspectives. Each perspective gives a different view and highlights a different set of variables. The terms *model, theoretical orientation,* and *paradigm* are often used interchangeably with the term *perspective.*

A perspective is like a map, which gives selected information about an area. The nature of the information depends on the purpose of the map. For example, a road map includes roads and major landmarks but is unlikely to list tall objects. An aviation map locates airports and major landmarks and also gives elevations of the land and the position and height of objects that could affect aviation.

Any map simplifies an area by presenting information selectively, as shown in Figure 3.1. By simplifying, the map provides, in an easy-to-read format, information that is useful for a specified task.

Like a map, perspectives on psychopathology simplify the complexity of an individual by focusing on selected features that may give the professional insights into what is wrong. Perspectives are simply different ways of looking at psychopathology. They do not change the nature of the psychopathology any more than a map changes an area that it represents. However, perspectives often affect treatment decisions.

Chapters 3 and 4 discuss the perspectives that have had the most impact on the field of psychopathology. This chapter covers historically significant perspectives, and Chapter 4 covers the currently dominant ones. Some of the perspectives we describe in this chapter (psychodynamic and humanistic) continue to influence treatment, although there is little controlled research on their effectiveness

[FIGURE 3.1]
Perspectives as Maps

These two maps emphasize different features. The street map gives street names and is drawn to precise scale, whereas the tourist map gives approximate locations of attractions and is drawn with less precision. Perspectives are like maps. Because perspectives focus on different aspects, they may seem to represent different systems, but they are really just different ways of looking at the same thing.

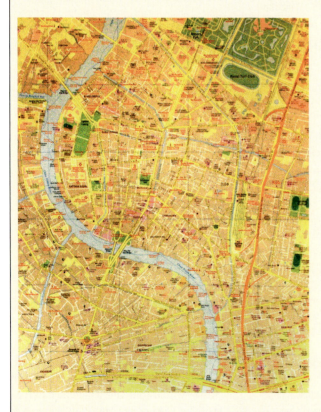

FOCUS   Science and psychopathology

In our review of the perspectives discussed in this chapter, and in our coverage of disorders in later chapters, the focus will be scientific. **Science** combines two processes: rationalism and empiricism. **Rationalism** uses a system of logical inference to generate new knowledge, whereas **empiricism** relies on observation. When the two are combined, logic is used to develop theories and derive predictions from them, and empiricism is used to test those predictions. A **theory** is a statement about how one thinks something works. In science, theories organize ideas and provide a basis for predicting what will happen in new situations. Having a logical theory is not enough; the the-

ory must make accurate predictions, and, even more important, those predictions must be falsifiable (able to be proved wrong if they *are* wrong). A theory that can explain any result is scientifically useless because it can never predict what will happen. Scientists want their theories to be challenged. If theories are seriously challenged and still survive, one can have confidence in them. Scientists also have a preference, all other things being equal, for theories that are parsimonious. One theory is more **parsimonious** than another if it provides a simpler explanation for a phenomenon or if it explains more phenomena.

Scientific values dominate this text because the most successful per-

spectives have all had a strong scientific basis. In fact, the stronger the scientific basis for a perspective, the greater the contribution it has made. That is not an accident. In a hundred other fields, work with a strong scientific basis leads to useful discoveries more readily that work that lacks such a basis. This is not to say that science should be the only criterion for judging a perspective. But it should be a major criterion, because the social and personal costs of psychopathology are so high that it is unacceptable to use anything other than the very best methods for studying it and finding effective treatments.

(Chambless & Ollendick, 2001). Other perspectives (behaviorism) have evolved significantly. But the historical perspectives covered in this chapter have little current impact on research on the causes of specific psychological disorders. The coverage of each perspective includes a brief overview of its central tenets, definitions of key concepts, treatment approaches, and an evaluation of its scientific strengths and weaknesses. The rationale for emphasizing the scientific approach is discussed in the nearby Focus box.

THE PSYCHODYNAMIC PERSPECTIVE

Imagine sitting by yourself having lunch at a restaurant. You have finished your meal and have another 20 minutes before you have to return to work. As you wait for your check, you notice a server bringing two incredible hot fudge sundaes to the next table. Rich and creamy, they look like works of art. You love hot fudge sundaes, but you are on a diet. Still, those sundaes look wonderful, and you have been so good about your diet. Surely, one little sundae would be all right. You had both a light breakfast and a light lunch, and maybe if you have a light dinner, the sundae will fit right into your diet! Decisions, decisions, decisions. Suddenly, your server interrupts your train of thought by asking whether she can get you anything else. You look up, give her a faint smile, and say, "No, just the check please."

The facts of this scenario are straightforward: You finish your lunch; the server asks whether you would like anything else; you say no and ask for the check. However, anyone who has been there knows that these facts do not begin to tell the whole story. **Psychodynamic theory** is based on the idea that behavior may be the end product of a long, often contentious internal discussion about how one should behave. According to Freud, most of this contentious discussion is outside of awareness, although in our example, we made the critical thoughts and feelings explicit for the sake of illustration. Furthermore, most dynamic interchanges involve matters more important to one's identity than whether to have dessert. Psychodynamic theorists argue that we can no more understand people by

science   The combined use of rationalism, to develop theories and derive predictions, and empiricism, to test the predictions.

rationalism   The use of a system of logical inference to generate new knowledge.

empiricism   Using observation to generate new knowledge.

theory   A statement about how one thinks something works.

parsimonious theory   A theory that either offers a simple explanation for a phenomenon or explains several phenomena.

psychodynamic theory   The idea that behavior may be the end product of a long, often contentious and often unconscious discussion about how one should behave.

watching their behavior than we could understand how a car works by watching it drive by.

FREUD'S MODEL OF PERSONALITY

Evolutionary Impact

Sigmund Freud (1856–1939) argued that the structure of personality included three elements—the id, the ego, and the superego. The **id** represents basic drives, motives, and instincts. Freud was strongly influenced by evolutionary theory, believing that the id represented biologically determined drives that had survival value (Gay, 1988). He argued that newborns had only ids and that the ego and superego developed later. Freud believed that the id provided the basic psychic energy that fueled all human behavior (Freud, 1933; Gay, 1988). He argued further that the id sought gratification or pleasure, no matter what the cost, and that most id instincts were sexual because sex is so critical to the survival of the species (Gay, 1988).

The **ego** is one's sense of self. In making the thousands of decisions required each day, it balances external constraints, the probable consequences of actions, and one's desire for specific pleasurable experiences. Sometimes this balance is easy to achieve; often it is not. Even a simple decision, such as whether to have dessert, can be challenging. Sometimes the ego is forced to make decisions that create anxiety. Freud argued that intense anxiety could be destructive and that mechanisms existed to manage this anxiety.

The **superego** represents both a person's conscience and his or her *ego ideal*—the image of what the person wants to be. Freud believed that the superego grew out of

conflict between id impulses and the disapproval of parents for acting on those impulses. He believed that children initially incorporate their parent's standards as their superego and then gradually expand the superego to include more personal standards. The superego is essentially a template by which people judge their behavior, thereby creating anxiety and guilt when they fall short of this ideal. Recall the case of Monica. Her ego ideal included being thin. Unfortunately, this ideal, coupled with her misperception of herself as fat, drove her to near starvation.

A key element in Freud's model is that most of the dynamic interchanges among the id, ego, and superego are outside of conscious awareness—that is, these interchanges are part of the **unconscious.** He argued that one must tap into the unconscious to understand behavior. He developed several ways to do this, which are discussed in the section on treatment. But first, let's look more closely at some of the evidence for unconscious processes.

Examining the Evidence

Freud defined the unconscious as cognitive activity outside of awareness that nevertheless influenced behavior. How does one demonstrate such a process? One way is to present stimuli to people subliminally—that is, below conscious awareness—and then measure the effect of those stimuli on behavior (Masling et al., 1991; Silverman, 1983). The speed of the presentation determines whether a stimulus can be consciously per-

---

Freud revolutionized people's thinking about psychological processes with his psychodynamic theory and his careful clinical observations. Psychoanalytic theory dominated the field of psychiatry for over 50 years.

id Basic drives, motives, and instincts.

ego One's sense of self.

superego One's conscience and ego ideal—the image of what one wants to be.

unconscious Outside of conscious awareness.

psychosexual stages Five developmental periods identified by Freud. In each stage, the child has to resolve a sexual issue.

fixated Stuck in a developmental stage because one's needs are not properly satisfied.

oral stage The child's focus at 0–18 months is on oral pleasures, including eating and exploring the world with the mouth.

anal stage The child's focus at 18–36 months is on the pleasure associated with controlling the retention and passing of feces.

phallic stage The child's focus at 3–5 years is on his or her genitals.

latency period The child's sexual interest at 6–12 years appears to be minimal.

genital stage The child's sexual interest is on sexual pleasure derived through one-on-one social/sexual relationships.

ceived. If the stimulus is flashed for just a few milliseconds, people report seeing nothing but a flash of light and are unable even to guess what was presented. Therefore, by most criteria they saw nothing. However, if they truly saw nothing, there should be no effect on behavior. If, on the other hand, behavior changes as a result of the presentation, then *unconscious processes* must be operating.

Patton (1992) used this approach to study psychodynamic influences on binge eating. She had college females who either did or did not report binge eating view one of two subliminal messages: "Mama is leaving me" and "Mama is loaning it." Psychodynamic theory predicts that binge eating is a defense against fears of abandonment. Therefore, the message "Mama is leaving me" should affect the eating behavior in binge eaters. She then had participants rate the taste of crackers. She was interested not in the ratings but, rather, in how many crackers participants ate while rating. The binge-eating participants who viewed the subliminal message "Mama is leaving me" ate more than twice as many crackers, on average, as those who viewed the message "Mama is loaning it."

This was only half of the study. The other half involved using the same procedures with two additional groups of females who either did or did not report binge eating. This time, the message was presented slowly enough to be consciously perceived. The reason for this last control is that Freud argued that the power of the unconscious to affect behavior depended on information remaining unconscious. Once information becomes conscious, people can challenge it.

In fact, Freud's psychodynamic therapy rests on this principle. Patton (1992) found that neither message affected eating if it was presented above the subliminal threshold. Such studies demonstrate that unconscious influences on behavior do exist. It is unfortunate that so few of Freud's theories have been put to such a rigorous test.

PSYCHOSEXUAL STAGES OF DEVELOPMENT

Freud argued that behavior is influenced by a person's developmental history. He proposed that children negotiate specific stages of development, confronting desires, fears, or challenges at each stage. To the extent that children do this effectively, they grow into emotionally healthy adults. Freud called these developmental periods **psychosexual stages** because he believed that, at each stage, it was a sexual issue that the child had to resolve. He identified five psychosexual stages: the oral, anal, phallic, latency, and genital stages, as described in Table 3.1. If the needs of children in each stage are properly satisfied, they mature normally and move into the next stage of development. If their needs are not properly satisfied, they may become **fixated**—that is, stuck in that stage. The impact of this fixation can persist, shaping people's character and the nature of any psychopathology that might develop. For example, Freud would argue that Gary's obsessive concern about his memory suggests a fixation in the anal stage. He would see Gary's orderliness and his meticulous attention to detail as consistent with this speculation.

Freud argued that the most important developmental event occurs during the phallic stage of development, at

[TABLE 3.1]   Psychosexual Stages of Development

STAGE	AGES	DESCRIPTION
Oral	0–18 months	Freud argued that the child's focus in the **oral stage** is on oral pleasures, including eating and exploring the world with the mouth. Children initially experience the world as an extension of themselves, but in time they recognize that they are but one of many objects in the world. Once they realize that the primary source of their oral gratification—their mother—is a separate object, they begin to fear losing her. Freud argued that people who become fixation in this stage have difficulty developing a sense of independence and confidence in the dependability of others and that they therefore become excessively dependent and at the same time distrustful.
Anal	18–36 months	The child's focus in the **anal stage** is on the pleasure associated with controlling the retention and passing of feces. Freud argued that people fixated in this stage are likely to be characterized as stubborn and stingy, that they often show a passive-aggressive style as adults, or that they may become excessively neat, meticulous, and orderly.
Phallic	3–5 years	Children begin to focus on their genitals in the **phallic stage.** They come to realize that some people (males) have a penis and other people (females) have a vagina. Freud believed that this realization eventually leads to gender identification through resolution of the Oedipus complex in boys and the Electra complex in girls.
Latency	6–12 years	Sexual interest appears to be minimal in the **latency stage.** In fact, children commonly express dislike for the opposite sex and aversion to any sign of sexual interest.
Genital	12+ years	Sexual interest is renewed during the **genital stage,** but the new focus is on sexual pleasure through one-on-one social/sexual relationships. Freud argued that the interest in relationships motivates people to develop the social skills and character traits required to establish and maintain such relationships.

Freud argued that the first sexual experience of infants is the oral gratification they receive at the mother's breast. The mother's breast not only banishes their hunger pangs but also provides comfort, security, and warmth.

about age four. This is when children first feel sexual longings for another person, and the object of their longings is the opposite-sex parent. Acting on such desires risks severe reprisals from the same-sex parent, so the child tries to bury those feelings. This process is referred to as the **Oedipus complex** in boys and as the **Electra complex** in girls. This is a pivotal point in the child's development. Freud argued that the child typically resolved this complex by identifying with the same-sex parent but that failure to resolve this complex could lead to a variety of sexual, emotional, and relationship problems in adulthood.

Children who successfully negotiate the early stages of psychosexual development are free, in the genital stage, to learn how to build relationships with the opposite sex, a complex process that most young people are ill prepared to handle. This fact makes the teenage years awkward, terrifying, and unbelievably exciting—sometimes all at the same time. Nevertheless, the sexual drive is a powerful motivator

. . . .

Oedipus complex   A boy's first sexual longings for another, in the person of his mother.

Electra complex   A girl's first sexual longings for another, in the person of her father.

defense mechanisms   Strategies for reducing anxiety caused by thoughts, desires, or impulses.

ego psychology   Erikson's theory that psychological development involves the maturation of the ego to handle social demands.

psychosocial stages of development   Social developmental stages proposed by Erikson.

object relations theory   A recent psychodynamic development that focuses on social relationships as critical to psychological development and functioning.

for young men and women to build social and dating skills, to experiment with relationships, and to learn to commit themselves to another person as part of a relationship. Freud would argue that Monica was in the genital stage when her eating disorder began. She was attractive and popular with the boys, but perhaps she did not feel she could handle such attention. Some specialists in eating disorders believe that Monica's disorder is a means that adolescent girls unconsciously use to make themselves less sexual (Wiederman, 1996). The weight loss minimizes such secondary sexual characteristics as breasts, and severe weight loss prevents ovulation.

DEFENSE MECHANISMS

Perhaps Freud's most enduring legacy was his identification of **defense mechanisms,** which are strategies for reducing anxiety aroused by thoughts, desires, or impulses. Freud viewed defense mechanisms as psychological reflexes that are triggered whenever anxiety becomes excessive. They permit the ego to regulate anxiety when id impulses clash with superego restrictions. Which defenses are activated depends on the person's psychological maturity and developmental history, as well as on the intensity of anxiety. Table 3.2 defines the most common defense mechanisms.

Defense mechanisms protect the ego from what might otherwise be overwhelming anxiety. Some defenses do this without compromising other functioning; others are considered primitive because they involve behavior that appears immature or irrational. Therapists from many theoretical persuasions recognize defense mechanisms, although some view defense mechanisms as conscious efforts at coping rather than unconscious reflexes. Consequently, they may differ on whether the goal of therapy is to strengthen defenses or weaken them (Wachtel, 1977).

NEO-ANALYTIC PERSPECTIVES

Freud's psychodynamic theory has stimulated considerable discussion and debate. Some theorists were impressed with Freud's ideas but disagreed with certain tenets of his theory. For example, Erik Erikson (1902–1994) is credited with playing an important role in the development of **ego psychology.** He believed that psychological development involved the maturation of the ego to handle social demands. He de-emphasized the sexual focus of Freud's psychodynamic theory in favor of this social focus. He outlined several **psychosocial stages of development,** which he thought reflected development more accurately. Like Freud, Erikson believed that failure to negotiate developmental stages could have life-long consequences.

A more recent psychodynamic development is **object relations theory,** which focuses on social relationships as critical to psychological development and functioning. The "objects" in this theory are other people, who exist in the external world but are also represented in the internal world of one's psyche. The way in which these external

[TABLE 3.2]   Defense Mechanisms

One of the most widely accepted contributions of Freud is his delineation of defense mechanisms. Several defense mechanisms are described here, along with an example of each.

Regression is a retreat to an earlier stage of development. This primitive defense is hypothesized to be the process behind severe psychopathology. *(Regression is often seen in young children who are lost in a strange city; they will often sit down and cry for their mother like a baby.)*

Denial involves behaving as though things were different than they really are. In extreme forms, denial borders on the delusional. *(A husband whose wife is about to leave him because of severe problems in their marriage steadfastly refuses to believe that she would ever go or that anything significant is wrong.)*

Repression represents a motivated forgetting in that thoughts that would create anxiety are prevented from reaching awareness. Freud argued that, unlike forgetting, the repressed thought is still there and that considerable emotional energy is required to maintain the repression. *(A woman's desire to cheat on her husband with the husband of her best friend is so upsetting to her that she completely represses the thought.)*

Projection involves attributing one's own unacceptable feelings to another person—that is, projecting those feelings onto that person. In some cases, projection is used as an excuse for one's feelings. For example, if you do not like someone, you may see her or him as not liking you, which gives you an excuse for your feelings. *(The woman just described who wanted to have an affair with her best friend's husband might believe that her best friend had a desire to have an affair with her husband.)*

Rationalization involves reinterpreting an unacceptable desire by creating an acceptable reason for that desire. *(You are planning a party and working on your invitation list. You feel obliged to invite certain friends but are embarrassed by them and do not want your other friends to see you associate with them. You rationalize that "they really aren't the party type" and would only feel obliged to come to the party if you invited them. Therefore, you leave them off the guest list.)*

Displacement involves taking unacceptable feelings toward one person and projecting them onto another person. Unfortunately, the displaced feelings often end up being refocused onto loved ones. *(A totally unreasonable boss makes you so angry that you want to scream. Instead of making a scene with the boss, which could jeopardize your job, you go home and snap at your spouse or kids.)*

Reaction formation involves behaving in a manner that is opposite to the underlying, often repressed feeling that one has. *(Parents who feel that their children have prevented them from having the life they really wanted may respond by being excessively loving and overprotective of the children.)*

Sublimation is considered one of the most mature and effective defenses. It involves channeling unacceptable impulses into socially appropriate activities, thus using the energy in more productive ways. *(A person may channel angry impulses into a single-minded drive to become the best at something.)*

objects are represented affects one's social relationships. Object relations theorists believe that the ability to form meaningful and fulfilling attachments is often influenced

by the effectiveness of the first attachment with one's primary caregiver.

Heinz Kohut (1913–1981) formulated **self-psychology,** which focuses on the individual's developing awareness of her or his identity (Kohut, 1977). He believed that self-awareness develops out of the interaction with such primary caregivers as parents. Initially, young children experience parents as part of themselves—what Kohut called selfobjects. If parents provide a nurturing and supportive environment, children eventually recognize themselves as distinct from selfobjects. However, children find it threatening to think of themselves as separate individuals because they feel so vulnerable. Therefore, they initially idealize caregivers, viewing them as perfect, strong, and completely willing to protect them. Of course, no parent is that perfect, and in time children begin to realize and accept this. A key axiom of self-psychology is that relationships are critical to the emotional health of people. These relationships provide support, empathy, and a sense of belonging. The manner in which people establish and maintain relationships is influenced by how successfully they developed a valid and secure sense of themselves during their formative years.

Recall the case of Dan and his battle with depression. Dan illustrates many of the concepts of self-psychology. He clearly needed the support of social relationships but found it difficult to form such relationships. He had several medical problems when he was young, which separated him for months at a time from his friends. Perhaps these problems prevented him from developing the ability to form lasting relationships. For most of his adult life, he relied primarily on the emotional support of his parents. Perhaps their

· ·

regression   A retreat to an earlier stage of development.

denial   Behaving as though things were different than they really are and refusing to acknowledge that reality, even to oneself.

repression   A motivated forgetting in that thoughts that would create anxiety are prevented from reaching awareness.

projection   Attributing one's own unacceptable feelings to another person.

rationalization   Reinterpreting an unacceptable desire by creating an acceptable reason for that desire.

displacement   Taking unacceptable feelings toward one person and projecting them onto another person.

reaction formation   Behaving in a manner that is opposite to the underlying, often repressed, feeling that one has.

sublimation   Channeling unacceptable impulses into socially appropriate activities.

self-psychology   A perspective developed by Heinz Kohut that focuses on the individual's developing awareness of her or his identity.

death just two years before his own left him feeling alone and vulnerable.

TREATMENT

Psychodynamic therapies fall into the general category of insight-oriented therapies. The goal of these therapies is to help clients develop insight into the reasons behind their behavior, with the implicit assumption that such insight will inspire behavioral change. Freud believed that the key to developing insight is to help clients make unconscious processes conscious, and he developed several procedures to accomplish this goal. One was *dream analysis,* in which the content of dreams is analyzed to identify themes that reflect unconscious desires and impulses (Freud, 1900). In another technique, *free association,* clients are encouraged to say whatever comes to mind. Freud argued that free association relaxed the usual psychic defenses, thus allowing clients to discover unconscious material. Freud also argued that unconscious material can "slip out," during conversation, in what are known as *Freudian slips* (see Figure 3.2). If, for example, someone inadvertently referred to the police force as the "police farce," Freud would argue that the person might be revealing his or her real—perhaps unconscious—feelings about the police. Finally, the rela-

tionship that a client develops with the therapist often mirrors critical relationships in the person's life. By looking carefully at the client/therapist relationship, which is called the **transference relationship,** clients can develop insights into other important relationships.

Early forms of psychodynamic therapy, referred to as **psychoanalysis,** were intense and expensive. Clients came to therapy daily and free-associated. The therapist reflected on what the client said and guided the client in a process of self-discovery. Such intensive therapies, although they are still practiced occasionally, have largely been replaced by short-term dynamic approaches. These approaches use the concepts and techniques of psychoanalysis but narrow the focus to one or two specific issues (Binder et al., 1995; Davanloo, 1996; Luborsky et al., 1996). Narrowing the focus and telling the client that therapy will last for a fixed number of sessions encourages clients to address key issues quickly. This problem-focused psychodynamic approach shows promise for treating such common psychological problems as relationship issues, although it has rarely been tested with severe psychopathology.

EVALUATION

Psychodynamic theory was the dominant perspective in psychiatry for the first 60 years of the twentieth century. Its influence is still strong in some treatment circles, and the effect it has had on literature and culture is undeniable. For example, twentieth-century novels routinely explore the motives and internal dynamics of characters, whereas such exploration was rare before the influential writings of Freud. However, its current impact on the field of psychopathology is minimal, largely because many psychodynamic concepts lack a scientific foundation. Furthermore, even when scientific evidence has been available, it has had little impact on clinical practice (Schachter & Luborsky, 1998).

A major problem with psychodynamic theory is that it requires that the therapist draw inferences about what unseen dynamic processes underlie a person's actions. The complexity of psychodynamic theory makes it possible to draw several inferences from a single set of behaviors. Hence it is difficult to obtain interrater reliability among professionals. DSM-II (APA, 1968), which relied heavily on psychodynamic theory, had low interrater reliability (Spitzer & Fleiss, 1974). The more symptom-based diagnoses outlined in later editions of the DSM have good reliability and have stimulated fruitful research.

Another problem is that psychodynamic concepts are not always scientifically testable. For a theory to be tested scientifically, the theory must make predictions that are *falsifiable*—that is, predictions that could be shown to be

---

[FIGURE 3.2]
Freudian Slips Are Everywhere

Freud argued that there is no such thing as an innocent verbal mistake. Those slips of the tongue often reveal more about people's feelings than they might like to admit. How does the man really feel about the bride he wants to "cuss" instead of "kiss"?

SOURCE: *By permission of Sidney Harris,* http://www.ScienceCartoonsPlus.com.

---

transference relationship   The client/therapist relationship.

psychoanalysis   Early forms of psychodynamic therapy.

false. Psychodynamic theory is often so flexible that it can explain any result. For example, negative feelings about a person could result in either negative behavior toward that person or positive behavior due to reaction formation. A similar problem exists with the theory of fixation, because Freud argued that either too much or too little gratification could result in fixation. In fairness, Freud was not interested in doing controlled research; he treated clients and developed theories to guide treatment. His theories were interesting, and some of them may well be valid. Unfortunately, although some researchers have done so (Masling & Bornstein, 1993), few psychodynamic theorists have taken up the challenge of testing those theories, refining them on the basis of new data, and extending them into new areas. When systematic research has been done, the findings have often been inconsistent with psychodynamic theory (Fisher & Goldberg, 1996; Holmes, 1974, 1978).

Psychodynamic therapy tends to use the same treatment techniques regardless of the diagnosis, which is distinctly different from the current trend toward using specific treatments for specific disorders (Chambless & Ollendick, 2001). One reason is that psychodynamic treatment focuses on underlying problems rather than on specific symptoms. In fact, for many years psychodynamic therapists argued that treating surface symptoms would just result in other symptoms appearing—a process known as *symptom substitution*. However, data show that symptom substitution rarely occurs (Erwin, 1978). Although there is nothing to prevent the scientific evaluation of psychodynamic treatment for specific disorders, few scientifically rigorous tests have been done.

Check Yourself 3.1

The Psychodynamic Perspective

1. What are the two principles that underlie the psychodynamic perspective?
2. What are the three elements of Freud's structure of the personality?
3. What are the five stages of psychosexual development?
4. What is the difference between a primitive and a healthy defense?
5. What distinguishes Freud's psychodynamic perspective from the neo-analytic perspectives of Erikson and Kohut?

Ponder this ...   *Imagine a difficult decision, such as whether to buy an expensive object that you really want but can't really afford. Identify the many feelings, the external factors and their impact on your feelings, and the process of arriving at your decision. Label each of these component*

feelings using Freud's personality elements: id, ego, and superego. What outcome is likely for you in this scenario?

THE BEHAVIORAL PERSPECTIVE

Behaviorism, which developed early in the twentieth century, argued that psychology could be scientific only if it restricted research to observable events (Watson, 1913). Concepts now taken for granted—memory, emotion, and thoughts—were excluded from study because they could not be directly observed. This position, which is formally known as *methodological behaviorism,* now seems extreme; although memory, for example, cannot be observed, evidence of its existence is obvious. Behaviorism was a response to two perspectives common at the time. The dominant position in mainstream psychology at the time was *structuralism,* which studied psychological processes by asking participants to describe how they performed various psychological tasks. Modern research shows that many psychological processes are outside of people's awareness, so even the most careful and motivated individuals could not possibly describe them. A less extreme form of behaviorism, called *radical behaviorism,* included the self-report of thoughts and feelings but conceptualized these self-reports as overt behaviors. That is, radical behaviorism included these self-reports but did not assume that they represented real internal events. Behaviorism also challenged the psychodynamic perspective, which relied more heavily on inference than on observable data. In contrast to these perspectives, behaviorism relied exclusively on observable events and avoided speculation about unseen processes.

Evolutionary Impact

Behaviorism often focused on **learning**—that is, changing behavior to fit the needs of the situation better. Adaptation through learning takes place quickly and requires neither the multiple generations nor the demise of millions of ill-prepared individuals that is characteristic of natural selection. Therefore, it is not surprising that the ability to learn has been favored by natural selection. Most of the early research on learning was conducted with animals. The pioneering work of scientists such as John Watson (1878–1958), Ivan Pavlov (1849–1936), B. F. Skinner (1904–1990), and Neal Miller (b. 1909) demonstrated the phenomenal adaptability of animals.

behaviorism   The conviction that psychology can be scientific only if it restricts research to observable events. Behaviorism was focused mostly on learning principles.

learning   Changing one's behavior to fit the needs of the situation better.

CLASSICAL CONDITIONING

Pavlov is credited with identifying the process of **classical conditioning,** in which a response elicited *unconditionally* by one stimulus will in time be elicited by a second stimulus *on the condition that* the two stimuli consistently occur together. For example, if you are distressed by loud noises and your neighbor's young son likes to blow his stadium horn, in time just the sight of your neighbor's son will cause distress.

Pavlov was a Russian physiologist who studied salivation in dogs (see Figure 3.3). Dogs were excellent subjects because they salivate immediately whenever meat is presented. Such outstanding experimental control made it easy to study salivation, but as often happens in science, things did not work out quite as planned. Pavlov noticed that over time, his dogs began to salivate well before the meat was presented. It was as though the dog were anticipating the food when the researcher walked into the room, salivating in response to that anticipation, and in the process disrupting the experiment. A less gifted scientist might have been annoyed at this turn of events and might have focused on developing procedures to eliminate this aberration. But as Skinner argued, a scientist who runs onto something interesting should "drop everything else and study it" (Skinner, 1956), which is exactly what Pavlov did.

Pavlov took control of the variables he believed were affecting his dogs and, in doing so, was able to identify the key components of this new phenomenon. He already knew that presenting meat produced the innate response of salivation. He discovered that presenting the meat at the same time that a bell was rung resulted eventually in the animal salivating in response to the sound of the bell alone. Pavlov called the stimulus that produced the response without any need for conditioning the **unconditioned stimulus (US)**—meat in this case. The response to this stimulus—salivation in this example—was called the **unconditioned response (UR).** The neutral stimulus that later came to elicit the response (the bell) was called the **conditioned stimulus (CS),** and the response produced by this stimulus (salivation) was called the **conditioned response (CR).** Pavlov's research suggested that the conditioned and unconditioned responses were virtually identical except for the stimulus that elicited them.

The paradigm for classical conditioning is diagrammed below. Before conditioning, the unconditioned stimulus produces the unconditioned response, but the conditioned stimulus produces no response. After repeated pairings of

[FIGURE 3.3]
Pavlov's Research on Salivation in Dogs

This is the setup for Pavlov's studies of classical conditioning of salivation in dogs. The dogs were placed in a comfortable harness to prevent them from moving extensively during the study. Food (the unconditioned stimulus, or US) was presented, and salivation was measured using a small, flexible tube surgically implanted in the dog's cheek. This arrangement caused the dog no pain and made possible the experimental study of behavior that would be difficult or impossible to investigate outside the laboratory.

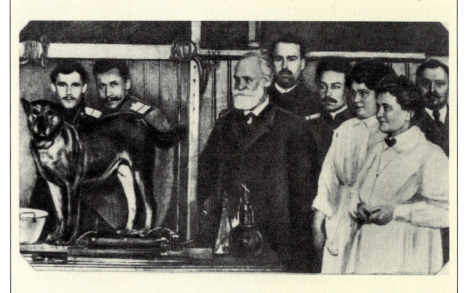

the CS and US, the ability of the conditioned stimulus to produce a response is evaluated.

Before Conditioning

CS (e.g., a bell)   →   No response

US (e.g., meat)   →   UR (e.g., salivation)

After Conditioning

CS (e.g., a bell)   →   CR (e.g., salivation)

Evolutionary Impact

Pavlov discovered several principles of conditioning. For example, the stronger the UR (all other things being equal), the faster the conditioning. This explains, for example, why people can develop an instant fear of driving after being involved in a terrifying accident. Pavlov also discovered that the conditioned response can be "unlearned"—that is, the CS comes to no longer produce the CR. This process, which is called **extinction,** occurs when the CS and the US are no longer paired. If someone develops a fear of driving after a terrifying accident, that fear gradually extinguishes after he or she has driven many times without experiencing another accident. However, people tend to learn fears quickly and to unlearn them slowly, a pattern that has enormous survival value.

Classical conditioning may account for many learned emotional responses. Some fears appear to be instinctual, such as fear of heights, but others may develop because of their association with already feared stimuli; examples include fear of climbing ladders and fear of flying, which are both associated with heights. Emotional responses to people are probably shaped by one's history of interactions with them. For example, when certain people are consistently associated with positive feelings, in time their mere presence creates positive feelings. Classical conditioning probably played a significant role in the development and maintenance of Dan's low self-esteem and depression. He reported dozens of things that made him feel inadequate. These feelings may have been the first step in a cascade of emotional responses that led to his severe bouts of depression.

Pavlov discovered that behavior conditioned to one stimulus can generalize to other stimuli. **Generalization** occurs when stimuli that have never been conditioned produce the same response as the CS because they are physically or functionally similar to the original CS. For example, someone who has learned to fear riding in cars as the result of a severe traffic accident may also fear riding in buses. **Discrimination** is essentially the opposite of generalization. People discriminate between two stimuli when they respond differently to them. A person who fears riding in cars, but not riding on trains, is discriminating between

these vehicles. Some of the principles of classical conditioning are illustrated in the following case study.

DR. RAULIN

Target of a stalker

A few years ago, a former client of mine, 20 years older than I, became convinced that I loved her and began to stalk me. She would stand outside my office window, wait for me by my car, come into my office and refuse to leave, send gifts and love letters, and make endless phone calls to my office. Initially I tried to be patient, but her behavior was annoying and distressing, and after months of this behavior, just the sight of her elicited significant distress. Nothing I could do would stop my negative emotional response to her, and unfortunately, nothing my attorney or I could do seemed to stop her positive emotional response to me. I was surprised, although I probably should not have been, that my emotional response generalized to other white-haired older women, including a close friend and even my mother. With my attorney's help, I was able to end the stalking. Over two months, my attorney gradually increased the legal pressure on her until she stopped, although it took several arrests. By this time, even the places where she frequently waited for me were generating the same negative feelings that she generated. With her no longer stalking me, my emotional responses gradually extinguished, but the extinction took months. However, about twice a year for several years she would resume her stalking behavior. Fortunately for me, another kind of conditioning—operant conditioning (discussed next)—was affecting her behavior. Her experience with the legal system was apparently aversive enough that a single letter from my attorney threatening legal action was now sufficient to deter her.

---

classical conditioning   Credited to Pavlov, a process in which a response elicited *unconditionally* by one stimulus will in time be elicited by a second stimulus *on the condition that* the two stimuli consistently occur together.

unconditioned stimulus (US)   A stimulus that produces a response without any need for conditioning.

unconditioned response (UR)   The response to an unconditioned stimulus.

conditioned stimulus (CS)   A neutral stimulus that later comes to elicit a response.

conditioned response (CR)   The response produced by a conditioned stimulus.

extinction   The process of "unlearning" a conditioned response so that the CS no longer produces the CR.

generalization   Occurs when stimuli that have never been conditioned produce the same response as the CS because they are physically or functionally similar to the original CS.

discrimination   Essentially the opposite of generalization; occurs when people respond differently to two stimuli.

INSTRUMENTAL CONDITIONING

In **instrumental conditioning,** which is sometimes called **operant conditioning,** behavior is modified by its consequences. The principles of instrumental conditioning rest on the law of effect, first articulated by Edward L. Thorndike (1874–1949), which states that behaviors followed by positive consequences tend to be repeated and that behaviors followed by negative consequences tend not to be repeated. Skinner (1972) extended the work of Thorndike, identifying many of the principles of instrumental conditioning. He defined a *positive reinforcer* as any stimulus that, when presented immediately after a behavior, increased the probability of that behavior occurring in the future. Note that the definition of a positive reinforcer does not depend on the characteristics of the stimulus but, instead, depends solely on the effect it has on behavior. For example, say you "punish" your daughter for not eating her dinner by making her go to her room, but her behavior of not eating dinner increases instead of decreases. Then, by definition, sending her to her room is a positive reinforcer.

Using positive reinforcers is only one way to influence behavior. Table 3.3 shows how the systematic application or removal of a stimulus following a behavior can either increase or decrease the behavior, depending on the nature of the stimulus. For example, you can increase the likelihood of a behavior by either applying a positive reinforcer following the behavior, which is called **positive reinforcement,** or by removing an already present aversive stimulus, which is called **negative reinforcement.** Negative reinforcement is often confused with **punishment,** which involves the application of an aversive stimulus after a behavior. Punishment decreases behavior, but removing a positive reinforcer can also decrease behavior, which is called **response cost.** Some examples may clarify these distinctions. Saying "good job" is positive reinforcement. Criticizing someone's work is punishment. Taking an aspirin when one has a headache is negatively reinforced, because the aversive stimulus (the headache) is removed by the behavior of taking the aspirin. Finally, getting a speeding ticket is a response cost for driving too fast in that you have to surrender a positive reinforcer (your money).

Skinner found that the animals in his studies not only could learn to increase specific behaviors to obtain desired rewards but also could discriminate situations in which reinforcement was possible from situations in which it was not possible. Stimuli that signal the availability of reinforcement are called **discriminative stimuli.** If one friend, but not another, praises you for being funny, than the presence of the first friend is a discriminative stimulus for "joking around"; in other words, you are more inclined to joke with the first friend because that behavior is more likely to be rewarded.

Extinction occurs in operant conditioning when behavior is no longer reinforced. The pace of extinction depends on the history of reinforcement. If reinforcement has been **continuous**—that is, given for every response—extinction is rapid; if reinforcement has been **intermittent**—that is, given for some responses but not for every one—extinction is slower. This principle is easy to remember if you compare human behavior at a vending machine and a slot machine. The vending machine gives continuous reinforcement. Every time you insert money, you expect to receive the item requested. A slot machine operates on an

The Skinner box is a semi-automated apparatus for measuring learning in animals. Pictured here is a box designed to train rats to press bars. Skinner demonstrated that complex learning is often composed of a series of simple behaviors. Therefore, studying simple laboratory behaviors often provides insights into more complex behaviors.

[TABLE 3.3]   Reinforcement and Punishment

One can either increase or decrease a behavior by presenting or removing a stimulus as shown in this table.

	Positive Reinforcer	**Aversive Stimulus**
Apply the Stimulus	Positive reinforcement (increases behavior)	Punishment (decreases behavior)
Remove the Stimulus	Response cost (decreases behavior)	Negative reinforcement (increases behavior)

intermittent-reinforcement schedule. You win only occasionally when you insert money. If both machines malfunctioned so that neither gives reinforcement, you would probably stop putting your money in the vending machine quickly, but you would be likely to put considerably more money in the slot machine before you gave up on it.

Maladaptive behavior, like all behavior, is subject to reinforcement. A hyperactive child whose misbehavior gets him out of classes that he dislikes will be more likely to engage in such behavior in the future when he wants to avoid class. It does not matter that other factors are contributing to his hyperactivity. If behavior results in reinforcement, it will tend to be repeated. Many maladaptive behaviors are extremely resistant to extinction because they are reinforced on an intermittent-reinforcement schedule. Parents who ignore most temper tantrums in their child, but give in when they are too tired to argue, will find that their child continues to throw temper tantrums. In fact, children are likely to detect the discriminative stimuli in the situation, recognizing that a temper tantrum is most effective when their parents are fatigued. There is virtually no behavior that does not produce, at least intermittently, consequences. Therefore, operant conditioning principles are likely to apply to the maintenance of virtually every form of psychopathology, even if conditioning had little or nothing to do with its original cause.

Skinner boxes exist outside of the laboratory. The device shown here reinforces behavior on an intermittent-reinforcement schedule. Slot machine behavior is therefore resistant to extinction—that is, people continue to play the slots even during prolonged losing periods. In contrast, vending machines give continuous reinforcement. When a vending machine stops functioning, people stop putting money into it almost immediately.

instrumental conditioning   Sometimes called operant conditioning; based on the principle that behavior is modified by its consequences.

operant conditioning   Sometimes called instrumental conditioning; based on the principle that behavior is modified by its consequences.

positive reinforcement   A positive reinforcer applied following a behavior to increase the likelihood of the desired behavior occurring again.

negative reinforcement   The removal of an aversive stimulus to increase the likelihood of a desired behavior occurring again.

punishment   The application of an aversive stimulus after a behavior to decrease the likelihood of the behavior occurring again.

response cost   The removal of a positive reinforcer; imposed to decrease behavior.

discriminative stimuli   Stimuli that signal the availability of reinforcement.

continuous reinforcement   Reinforcement given for every response.

intermittent reinforcement   Reinforcement given for some, but not all responses.

Operant conditioning probably affected Dan, Gary, and Monica. When Dan's depression was strong, being around people was painful and aversive. His response was to withdraw, but his withdrawal reduced his access to the normal reinforcers that shape day-to-day behavior, thus reducing his productivity and enhancing his sense of failure. Gary's compulsion to save every newspaper and magazine was probably driven by the reduction in anxiety that he experienced because he knew he could potentially look up anything. Monica's dieting may initially have been reinforced by compliments about her appearance. Her case is interesting because it shows the limits of the behavioral perspective. At some point as she lost weight, Monica stopped being complimented on her figure and started to receive expressions of disapproval or concern. Nevertheless, her strict dieting continued.

TREATMENT

The behavioral perspective has led to several effective treatments. This section introduces the logic of these treatments. Specific treatments will be discussed in later chapters, in the context of the disorders they address.

Conditioning and Counterconditioning.
Conditioning and counterconditioning are used to change the emotional response to objects or situations. For example, **systematic desensitization** is a treatment that reduces the anxiety that specific objects or situations elicit by using gradual exposure to the feared stimulus while the person maintains a relaxed state. The logic of this procedure is that it is impossible to be both relaxed and anxious at the same time. Therefore, pairing the relaxation with whatever normally makes one anxious blocks the anxiety and builds new, nonanxious associations to the stimulus. Both imaginal and actual exposure to the feared stimulus have proved effective (Bandura, 1969; Chambless & Ollendick, 2001).

Aversive conditioning is a counterconditioning strategy designed to increase negative affect to specific situations. This procedure has been used, for example, to treat alcohol abuse. Specifically, alcohol consumption is paired with the aversive stimulus of stomach distress and vomiting. This aversive stimulus can be achieved with drugs that react to alcohol consumption by inducing immediate and intense nausea.

Contingency Management.
The basic operant conditioning treatment strategy involves (1) identifying maladaptive behavior, (2) identifying the contingencies that maintain it, (3) extinguishing the maladaptive behavior, and (4) replacing the maladaptive behavior by reinforcing more adaptive behaviors. This strategy is particularly applicable when one has considerable control over contingencies. Hence it is frequently used to treat childhood problems, both in school and at home, where teachers and parents control most of the child's rewards. It has also been used successfully in psychiatric hospitals to treat seriously disturbed individuals (Paul & Lentz, 1977).

Many people manage their own contingencies. By setting up desired rewards that are contingent on completing a task, people can move themselves toward better functioning. For example, people who want to lose weight might plan to reward themselves by buying new clothes once they have lost 15 pounds. Most often, these strategies are used as a bridge to get to a point where natural rewards take over (Hartmann & Atkinson, 1973). For example, it is assumed that the "15-pounds-lighter" look will elicit compliments or yield more positive social interactions.

EVALUATION

The tremendous success of behaviorism in uncovering principles of learning prompted theorists to extend these principles to many areas, including psychopathology. However, like many promising new theories, the behavioral approach was oversold. For example, behaviorists argued that the symptoms of schizophrenia, which have strong genetic and biological contributions, were learned responses (Ullmann & Krasner, 1975). People were presumably reinforced for such disturbed behavior because they were able to avoid everyday demands of life. Such effects might well be there, but it is not justified to conclude that those effects are the primary cause of a disorder, especially when there is clear evidence for genetic influences (Meehl, 1962).

The biggest problem with the behavioral perspective is that it refused to study the thought processes that are so critical in understanding human behavior. Thought processes were excluded on philosophical grounds because they were not observable. Yet many concepts in science, such as gravity, cannot be directly observed. Nevertheless, scientists are able to work with the concept of gravity because its effects can be observed. Thought processes are so clearly involved in behavior that it seems ridiculous to exclude them. The cognitive-behavioral perspective, which is covered in Chapter 4, maintains the strong scientific grounding of the traditional behavioral perspective but does not exclude such unseen processes as memory and thought. Furthermore, it comfortably acknowledges the role of biological factors, while recognizing that even pathological behavior is subject to reinforcement. This modified behavioral perspective continues to be a major contributor to the understanding of psychopathology, whereas other, once-dominant perspectives play a minor role. This is largely

systematic desensitization A treatment that reduces anxiety to specific objects or situations via the person's gradual exposure to the feared stimulus in a relaxed state.

aversive conditioning A counterconditioning strategy designed to increase negative affect to specific situations.

because the scientific culture of the behavioral perspective allowed it to weed out flawed theories and replace them with better ones.

Check Yourself 3.2

The Behavioral Perspective

1. How was behaviorism different from the psychodynamic and structuralist perspectives?
2. What is the difference between classical conditioning and instrumental conditioning?
3. What is the difference between negative reinforcement and punishment?
4. Name some of the treatments that were developed from a behavioral perspective.

Ponder this . . .   *Many intensely emotional situations lead to classically conditioned responses. The terrorist attack on September 11, 2001, and the events that followed were exactly such kinds of incidents. What was your response to these events? What stimuli elicited an emotional response in you (planes, tall buildings, mail)?*

THE HUMANISTIC AND EXISTENTIAL PERSPECTIVES

The humanistic and existential perspectives provided alternatives to the dominant behavioral and psychodynamic perspectives.

HUMANISTIC PERSPECTIVE

The **humanistic perspective** grew out of dissatisfaction with perspectives that viewed humans as little more than complex animals, responding in much the same way as any other animal. It was argued that humans are more capable than other animals and that this additional capability translates into the individual's unique awareness of the world and appreciation for the role that she or he plays in it. The defining characteristic of the humanistic perspective is the belief that human beings are basically good and, if allowed to develop normally, will mature into emotionally healthy adults.

Rogers's View of People.   Carl Rogers (1902–1987) is often considered the father of the humanistic perspective. He noted that clients often responded well to a strongly supportive therapy that he called **client-centered therapy** (Rogers & Sanford, 1989). People in client-centered therapy are given **unconditional positive regard**—a nonjudgmen-

Carl Rogers is often considered the father of humanistic psychology. He believed that each person was capable of positive change and growth if provided a nurturing environment. His client-centered therapy sought to provide that nurturing environment by giving clients unconditional positive regard—a positive affirmation of their worth as human beings.

tal acceptance of their worth as human beings (Rogers, 1951, 1961, 1967). The positive impact of this treatment approach led Rogers to speculate that human beings had a natural tendency to find a satisfying and productive role in society. This perspective contrasted with the most influential perspective of the time, the psychoanalytic perspective. Freud had argued that human behavior was driven by id impulses and that proper social behavior involved taming those id impulses. Rogers argued that rather than taming human impulses, one should allow them to develop naturally. He called this process of fulfilling one's human potential **self-actualization.**

humanistic perspective   The view that humans are more capable than other animals and are uniquely aware of the world and of their role in it.

client-centered therapy   A strongly supportive therapy designed to nourish the natural development of the client.

unconditional positive regard   A nonjudgmental acceptance of the client's worth as a human being.

self-actualization   The process of fulfilling one's human potential.

Maslow's Hierarchy of Needs. **Maslow's hierarchy of needs** represented a rethinking of human potential and linked some of the humanistic ideals with other perspectives, such as the sociocultural perspective. Maslow's insight was that self-actualization was a complex process that could never be achieved unless more basic needs were met first (Maslow, 1968). For example, worrying about improving one's self-esteem is not likely to occur in people who are starving or are in fear for their life. He arranged those needs in a hierarchy, arguing that until lower-level needs are met, higher-level needs cannot even be addressed. This hierarchy is illustrated in Figure 3.4.

EXISTENTIAL PERSPECTIVE

The **existential perspective** shares with the humanistic perspective a belief in the uniqueness of human beings relative to other animals (Yalom, 1980). However, the existential and humanistic perspectives differ on a number of critical variables. The existential perspective on psychopathology grew out of the European existential philosophical movement. Its major premise is that each person is responsible for finding meaning in life. Some people are willing to accept that responsibility and are rewarded with a more ful-

filling existence; others are not. Each decision made, each path selected, and each thing that happens shape people's lives. Some of these elements can be controlled, although many cannot. Healthy people accept that life may not be completely controllable but accept individual responsibility, making choices within the constraints imposed by their situation. From the existential perspective, when people give up responsibility, letting others choose for them, they lose the chance to develop their full potential. In the words of existential philosophy, they become *inauthentic*. They are no longer the real people that they should be, and pathology is the result.

TREATMENT

Rogers and others argued that the processes that led to normal development are universal, provided that the right environment is available to nurture the person (Rogers, 1961). The focus was on providing this nurturing environment in therapy to overcome the impact of a less supportive environment earlier in the person's development. The therapist focused on the client's responses in therapy as the most precise index of how well the client was functioning (Perls, 1969). A client who can interact with a therapist in a

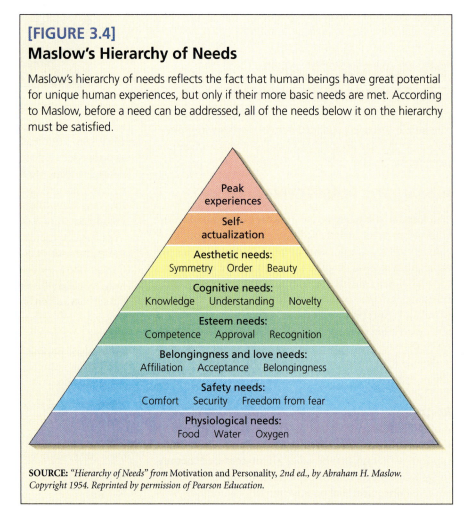

[FIGURE 3.4]
Maslow's Hierarchy of Needs

Maslow's hierarchy of needs reflects the fact that human beings have great potential for unique human experiences, but only if their more basic needs are met. According to Maslow, before a need can be addressed, all of the needs below it on the hierarchy must be satisfied.

Peak experiences

Self-actualization

Aesthetic needs:
Symmetry   Order   Beauty

Cognitive needs:
Knowledge   Understanding   Novelty

Esteem needs:
Competence   Approval   Recognition

Belongingness and love needs:
Affiliation   Acceptance   Belongingness

Safety needs:
Comfort   Security   Freedom from fear

Physiological needs:
Food   Water   Oxygen

SOURCE: *"Hierarchy of Needs"* from Motivation and Personality, *2nd ed., by Abraham H. Maslow. Copyright 1954. Reprinted by permission of Pearson Education.*

No other issue in existential philosophy is more powerful than death. All people eventually die. One's fears about death may drive one's behavior throughout life, and the inevitability of death often raises profound questions about the meaning of life.

warm, sincere manner, with little defensiveness, is functioning at a high level. The hallmark of client-centered therapy was that therapists never told their clients what they should do; rather, therapists provided the environment that allowed their clients to find their own solutions.

Existential therapy tries to help clients accept responsibility for their lives and make their own choices to achieve their full potential (Yalom, 1980). It acknowledges that life is not always controllable, but challenges clients to exercise control whenever possible. Like the client-centered approach of Rogers, existential therapy is supportive and seeks to foster personal growth in clients. Its techniques vary little from one pathology to another, and in general, existential therapy tends to be used with general disaffection with life, rather than with more severe psychopathology.

EVALUATION

The humanistic and existential perspectives have influenced psychological treatment, but they have had little effect on the field of psychopathology. This is partly because many humanists and existentialists have been opposed to scientific research, although Rogers himself spent over two decades doing research on client-centered psy-

chotherapy (Rogers & Sanford, 1989). Both humanists and existentialists argue that research oversimplifies the complexity of human beings. They are correct, of course, but rarely does one need to know everything about a person to make effective interventions. Another reason for their limited impact is that neither the humanistic nor the existential perspective has accepted the detailed classification system that has helped define psychopathology since the publication of DSM-III. For one thing, much of humanistic and existential writing was done prior to the advent of DSM-III, which was really the first diagnostic system to achieve wide acceptance. But more fundamentally, both perspectives are less interested in the diagnostic process inherent in the DSM than in striving to understand the uniqueness of each individual.

Even so, the humanist and existential perspectives influence therapists of many persuasions. Many therapists readily accept the notion that each person is unique and that everyone needs to find meaning in life. And many therapists who are guided by these values are likely to use techniques that have proved effective for treating the kinds of disorders covered in this text.

Maslow's hierarchy of needs   A model reflecting awareness that self-actualization can be achieved only if more basic needs are met first.

existential perspective   A belief that each person is responsible for finding meaning in life.

Check Yourself 3.3

The Humanistic and Existential Perspectives

1. What were the contributions of Rogers to the humanistic perspective?

2. Describe the concept of a hierarchy of needs as defined by Maslow.

3. What is the basic premise of the existential perspective?

Ponder this . . .   *From the brief description provided in this section, what advice do you think Rogers would give parents about raising their children?*

CHANGING PERSPECTIVES

At one time or another, each of the perspectives covered in this chapter has had a significant impact on the field of psychopathology. The behavioral perspective remains influential, although the strict behavioral perspective has been replaced with a perspective that includes cognitive elements. All of these perspectives continue to influence psychological treatment, although, as you will see throughout the text, treatments based on the modern perspectives are generally more effective and promising than the traditional treatment approaches derived from the perspectives covered in this chapter (Chambless & Ollendick, 2001).

The diverse perspectives discussed in this chapter share one characteristic: They viewed all psychopathology, regardless of its nature, as the result of a single underlying process, whether it be fixation in one of the psychosexual stages of development (the psychodynamic perspective), an inappropriate learning history (the behavioral perspective), failure to self-actualize (the humanistic perspective), or failure to accept personal responsibility (the existential perspective). The available data simply do not support such a contention. This "one cause for everything" philosophy that dominated the early perspectives has been largely replaced by a view that features two concepts. The first is that each disorder may very well have its own cause(s). The second is that most disorders are likely to have multiple causes. Accepting that different disorders may have different causes has dramatically increased the emphasis on making precise diagnoses, which can isolate unique disorders with specific causes.

The tremendous changes in the diagnostic system from DSM-II to DSM-III reflect this new attitude. And the impressive growth in the understanding of specific psychopathologies that has occurred since the publication of DSM-III confirms the wisdom of this conceptual shift. Accepting that most disorders have multiple causes has had an even more significant impact. This model is often referred to as the **diathesis-stress model** of psychopathology. It argues that specific features—the diathesis—predispose people to specific psychopathology but that psychopathology develops only if triggered by sufficient life stresses. For example, research shows that genes influence

risk for schizophrenia and so represent a diathesis. However, genes are not sufficient to cause schizophrenia. For example, in identical twins with identical genes, sometimes one develops schizophrenia whereas the other does not. Clearly, nongenetic factors also play a role.

If you read the research and theoretical papers that are based on the perspectives covered in this chapter, you will be struck by the fact that other perspectives are almost never mentioned. In fact, the tendency is for each perspective to have its own unique terminology for psychological phenomena, which makes it difficult to integrate perspectives. There were efforts to overcome this parochial bias. For example, Wachtel (1977) published a landmark book noting the overlap between the dominant models of the time—the psychodynamic and behavioral perspectives. Although highly regarded, the book had little impact on these disciplines. Psychodynamic theorists were no more likely to interpret their findings in terms of learning, and behaviorists were no more likely to acknowledge any evidence of unconscious influences to emerge from their studies. In contrast, scientists who study psychopathology today actively strive to integrate perspectives. They might, for example, acknowledge that genetic factors may affect the level of arousal for some people, which would influence their psychological experience of events, which would alter the reinforcing quality of the events and hence their responses, thus changing their expectations of what might happen in the future. This approach makes complete sense if you remember that the different perspectives represent different maps of the person, not different processes within the person. The nearby Modern Myths box deals with one implication of failing to recognize this fact.

There is room within the diathesis-stress approach for some of the historically significant perspectives to contribute additional insights into psychopathology. The "one cause for everything" concept is clearly dead, but that does not mean that perspectives that once espoused that concept have nothing to contribute to the more sophisticated diathesis-stress models that are dominant today. There is a strong tendency today to borrow from other perspectives and thereby to create a more sophisticated understanding of psychopathology. This process is facilitated by the fact that the modern perspectives share the terminology for common aspects of a disorder, which makes communication between perspectives easier and less confusing.

· ·

diathesis-stress model   The theory that specific features—the diathesis—predispose people to specific psychopathology but that psychopathology develops only if triggered by sufficient life stresses.

MODERN Myths

If It's Biological, Psychological Treatments Won't Work

We introduced our discussion of perspectives on abnormal behavior by noting that these perspectives represent different maps of complex behavior. They simplify the behavior by focusing on some specific details while glossing over others. As such, they make the situation manageable, even if a bit oversimplified.

A problem inherent in using perspectives is that people tend to forget that each perspective represents a simplified picture of a complex human being. Instead, people tend to see the perspectives as different parts of the human being, much like the liver and kidney are different body parts. If one falls into this trap, logical fallacies may follow. For example, if a person has a disease of the kidney, you treat the kidney, not the liver. And that makes sense, *unless* there is evidence that the liver may be contributing to the kidney disease. Similarly, people infer that if

a disorder is biological—that is, if it involves biological processes that are disordered—then one has to use biological treatments. As reasonable as this seems, it is not correct—either logically or empirically.

People are integrated units, capable of behaving and functioning in a variety of situations. Processes that people think of as psychological or biological are simply abstractions—ideas that people created to organize the complexity of the person. There are no such things in reality. Psychological processes are also biological in that psychological experiences involve biological processes. Biological processes are also psychological in that one's biology is affected by one's psychological experiences.

Therefore, it should not be surprising that any effective treatment affects both biological and psychological functioning. Most people can accept that biological treatments affect psychological functioning. Take

a tranquilizer (a biological treatment) and you feel more relaxed (a psychological effect). However, the reverse is also true. If you relax yourself, your biology changes as a result of your efforts. In fact, you will see later in this text that when psychological treatments are effective, they appear to have the same biological effects on the person as effective biological treatments. This finding shocks many students; sometimes it even shocks mental health professionals. It shouldn't. A person is a single entity, in whom biological and psychological functioning are fully integrated. These are not different processes but simply different maps of the same complex process, life. The real breakthroughs of the last 20 years in psychopathology have increasingly rested on the realization that biology and psychology are just different ways of viewing the complexity of the person.

Check Yourself 3.4

Changing Perspectives

1. What did all the perspectives discussed in this chapter have in common?
2. Describe the diathesis-stress model of psychopathology.

Ponder this . . . *What are the advantages of using multiple perspectives and integrating these perspectives whenever possible in studying something as complex as psychopathology?*

 ## SUMMARY

THE PSYCHODYNAMIC PERSPECTIVE

- The psychodynamic perspective suggests that behavior is the result of a complex and dynamic interplay among

different aspects of a person's personality. Freud called these aspects the id, ego, and superego. Although some of this interplay is conscious, most is unconscious. Freud argued that most id impulses were sexual and that human development was characterized by a focus on various sexual experiences at different stages, which he called psychosexual stages of development.

- People use psychological defense mechanisms to deal with excessive anxiety.

- Erikson challenged the psychosexual stages of development, proposing instead that the term *psychosocial development* more accurately described the maturational process. Object relations theory also focused on social development, studying how relationships from childhood through adulthood shape personality and behavior. Finally, self-psychology focused on how people develop a sense of identity and how that sense shapes their behavior.

THE BEHAVIORAL PERSPECTIVE

- The behavioral perspective rejected the study of such unseen concepts as memory and the unconscious.

- Classical conditioning involves learning to respond to a stimulus with the same response previously given to another stimulus. Instrumental conditioning involves changing behavior on the basis of its consequences.

THE HUMANIST AND EXISTENTIAL PERSPECTIVES

- The humanist believes that people are inherently social creatures, with a natural tendency to develop into contributing and caring members of society. The existential perspective focuses on how people must accept responsibility for their own life choices if they are to develop to their full potential. The humanist and existential perspectives have contributed little to the understanding of specific forms of psychopathology.

CHANGING PERSPECTIVES

- The perspectives discussed in this chapter argued that all psychopathology was the result of a common underlying process. There was little effort to integrate perspectives or to differentiate among disorders that might differ in etiology. In contrast, most modern psychopathologists use several perspectives, always trying to integrate the perspectives.

● KEY TERMS

anal stage   (53)
aversive conditioning   (62)
behaviorism   (57)
classical conditioning   (59)
client-centered therapy   (63)
conditioned response, or CR   (59)
conditioned stimulus, or CS   (59)
continuous reinforcement   (61)
defense mechanisms   (54)
denial   (55)
diathesis-stress model   (66)
discrimination   (59)
discriminative stimuli   (61)
displacement   (55)
ego   (52)
ego psychology   (54)
Electra complex   (54)
empiricism   (51)
existential perspective   (65)
extinction   (59)
fixated   (53)
generalization   (59)
genital stage   (53)
humanistic perspective   (63)
id   (52)
instrumental conditioning   (61)

intermittent reinforcement   (61)
latency period   (53)
learning   (57)
Maslow's hierarchy of needs   (65)
negative reinforcement   (61)
object relations theory   (54)
Oedipus complex   (54)
operant conditioning   (61)
oral stage   (53)
parsimonious theory   (51)
phallic stage   (53)
positive reinforcement   (61)
projection   (55)
psychodynamic theory   (51)
psychoanalysis   (56)
psychosexual stages   (53)
psychosocial stages of development   (54)
punishment   (61)
rationalism   (51)
rationalization   (55)
reaction formation   (55)
regression   (55)
repression   (55)
response cost   (61)
science   (51)
self-actualization   (63)

SUGGESTED READINGS

Masling, J. M., & Bornstein, R. F. (Eds.) (1993). *Psycho-analytic perspectives on psychopathology.* Washington, DC: American Psychological Association. This edited volume contains several reviews of psychoanalytic concepts and the research supporting them.

Rogers, C. R. (1961). *On becoming a person.* Boston: Houghton Mifflin. This widely read book outlines the basic principles behind client-centered therapy.

Skinner, B. F. (1956). A case history in scientific method. *American Psychologist, 11,* 221–233. Reprinted in B. F. Skinner, *Cumulative record: A selection of papers* (3rd ed.). New York: Appleton-Century-Crofts, published in 1972. This article provides a wonderfully funny and informative look inside the research of a true genius.

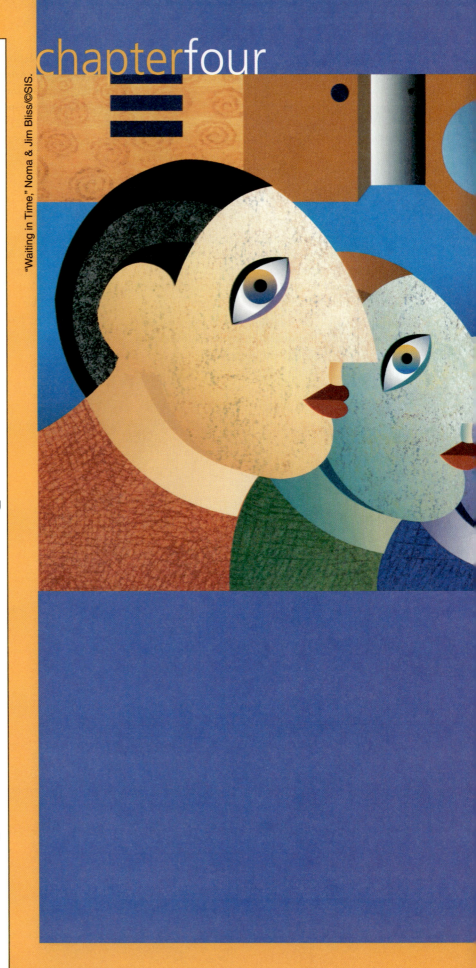

chapterfour

"Waiting in Time," Noma & Jim Bliss/©SIS.

Current Perspectives on Psychopathology

Let's revisit the cases of Dan, Gary, and Monica from Chapter 3.

The Seeds of Depression

DAN

Dan's life had always been a struggle. He had had half a dozen major operations on his hips and knees before he graduated from high school. Yet he managed to become an All-Conference football player, an accomplished debater, and a top student. He was well liked but had few friends, and his relationship with his family was often strained. He barely spoke with his father in high school and often fought with his two older brothers. Over the years, he would get close to a family member and then abruptly break it off in anger. He shared his father's sensitivity and intensity but lacked his father's ability to bond with other people. Always shy, he dated little and rarely went out with friends. His father also experienced depression, but was able to handle it better because of the strong support of his wife. Dan did not have such support, and the more depressed he got, the more he withdrew from friends and family.

Not Ready for Retirement

GARY

Gary loved his work and enjoyed the prestige of being the best at what he did. He was a loving father and husband, but he did not feel that he really excelled at those roles, and Gary needed to excel. He felt empty and useless when he retired, and it took only a few months for him to sink into a deep depression. He was not ready for retirement, so he approached his employer about working part-time—a request that his employer supported enthusiastically. With aggressive treatment and his return to work, he quickly stabilized and then began the task of preparing for the fulfilling retirement that he had always imagined.

Always the Perfect Girl

MONICA

Monica was caring and thoughtful; she always tried to be what others expected of her. She was one of the most popular kids in her class. Somewhat shy by nature, she pushed herself to be outgoing. Her parents could not have been more proud. The oldest daughter, she was always the responsible one. Therefore, when Monica started to diet, no one thought much of it. She did not need to diet, but she did lots of things that she did not need to do. Staying on her strict diet was entirely in character for her. The only thing that was not in character was that she did not stop dieting when friends and family voiced concern. Never before had she failed to respond to the wishes of others.

Chapter 3 reviewed historically significant perspectives on psychopathology. This chapter reviews the perspectives that are contributing significantly to today's psychopathology research. These include the physiological, cognitive-behavioral, cognitive neuroscience, sociocultural, and evolutionary perspectives. As in Chapter 3, we will use the case studies of Dan, Gary, and Monica, as well as other cases we will introduce later, to illustrate key concepts.

THE PHYSIOLOGICAL PERSPECTIVE

Evolutionary Impact

The **physiological perspective** focuses on how physiological mechanisms affect behavior, including abnormal behavior. In some ways, the physiological perspective is one of the oldest. Hippocrates speculated almost 2500 years ago about physiological causes for psychiatric disorders, and Kraepelin argued over 100 years ago that dementia praecox was a physiological disorder, yet the psychoanalytic perspective dominated psychiatry during the early part of the twentieth century. The rebirth of the physiological perspective occurred in the middle of the twentieth century, spurred by (1) research showing that genes contributed to some psychiatric disorders, (2) discovery of the first effective medications for psychiatric disorders, and (3) the development of brain-imaging techniques. In the last 50 years, tremendous advances in technology have fueled advances in the scientific understanding of physiological functioning and its contributions to psychopathology.

Our discussion of the physiological perspective begins with an introduction to genetics, which is followed by brief discussions of the central nervous system, the autonomic nervous system, the endocrine system, and physiological treatments. Although students are often intimidated by the study of physiology, understanding abnormal behavior requires at least a rudimentary understanding of these systems.

GENETIC INFLUENCES

At one time, every person was a single cell—a fertilized egg. That cell contained the genetic information that served as the blueprint for a person. This section presents some of the basic principles of genetics, especially as they relate to psychopathology.

Most animals, including humans, reproduce sexually—that is, they combine genetic material from two parents to form an offspring. Combining genes from two parents produces an unfathomable number of possible

....

physiological perspective   Looks at how physiological mechanisms affect behavior, including abnormal behavior.

Mendelian inheritance   The mechanism of single-gene transmission, identified by Gregor Mendel.

dominant gene   A gene for which only a single dose is needed to obtain the trait that the gene specifies.

recessive gene   A gene for which a double dose is needed to obtain the trait that the gene specifies.

polygenic   Caused, or contributed to, by several genes.

combinations, which is why, with the exception of identical twins, each person is genetically unique. Genes affect almost every aspect of physical and psychological development, from the things that make people similar (internal organs, sensory systems, general shape of the body) to the elements that make each person unique (appearance, skills, temperament). People readily accept that genes affect appearance, but genes also affect risk for dozens of diseases, such as heart disease, diabetes, and cancer. Genes also contribute to many psychiatric disorders.

The simplest genetic trait is one that is influenced by a single gene. The Austrian monk Gregor Mendel (1822–1884) identified the mechanism of single-gene transmission—a process known as **Mendelian inheritance**—through a brilliant series of studies on garden peas. Mendel's work provided the basis for much of the current understanding of gene action. He correctly inferred from his data that there must be a pair of genes for each of the traits that he studied. With some traits, which are called **dominant,** only a single dose of the gene was needed to obtain the trait; with other traits, called **recessive,** a double dose was necessary. Mendel knew nothing about DNA, which wasn't discovered until nearly a century later, or about the chromosomes that carried the DNA or the mechanism by which each parent contributed a single set of chromosomes to form an offspring. He knew nothing about the complex process by which genes influence characteristics through the control of protein synthesis. Yet his observations created the framework that stimulated many of these later advances.

Single genes are responsible for two psychiatric disorders. The disorder phenylketonuria, better known as PKU, results from the action of a single recessive gene that causes an enzyme deficiency that, if not recognized and dealt with early, will result in severe retardation. PKU is a perfect example of a diathesis-stress model. The PKU gene affects metabolism (the diathesis), but the metabolic dysfunction leads to a problem only if certain foods are consumed (the stress). The details of this process are discussed in Chapter 13. A single dominant gene causes another disorder, Huntington's disease, which involves intellectual and motor deterioration and early death. The details of Huntington's disease are discussed in Chapter 15.

Most psychiatric disorders are thought to be **polygenic**—that is, several genes contribute to an increased risk for the disorder. Scientists almost never know what genes are involved, although cutting-edge technology, such as the Human Genome Project, may soon provide this information. The Human Genome Project is discussed in the nearby Advances box. Polygenic influences are probably cumulative, each influence weakening the person's adaptive ability and thus increasing the risk of his or her developing one or more specific disorders. It is important to realize that it is not the disorder that is inherited, but rather a predisposition to develop the disorder.

ADVANCES   The Human Genome Project

One of the most exciting advances in twentieth-century science was the human genome project, which mapped the location of every human gene. This project, launched in 1990, was finished well ahead of schedule—and under the $3 billion proposed budget. An unthinkable task just a couple of decades ago, the human genome project has the potential to revolutionize genetic research. Being able to pinpoint the location of genes enables researchers to bridge the huge gap between knowing that genes influence a condition and understanding the biological mechanisms by which that influence is exerted. Thanks to this and other

recent advances, scientists may soon be able to develop wholesale gene therapies to correct hundreds of currently untreatable genetic disorders. Even in the early stages of its application, the human genome project is generating exciting new possibilities. Already, the project has made it possible to screen for dozens of genetic illnesses, an ability that has raised a number of ethical issues (Beardsley, 1996; Cook-Deegan, 1996). Nevertheless, the potential for understanding the genetics of psychiatric disorders is enormous (Grodin & Laurie, 2000).

In the field of psychopathology, many disorders are known to be influenced by genes, but the genes involved and their locations are

unknown. That may change in the near future. Most psychopathologies appear to have polygenic influences—that is, several genes contribute to the risk for the disorder. Each gene that is discovered will provide clues about what other genes are involved and about what biological mechanisms predispose the person to a given psychopathology. Putting the pieces together is the equivalent of assembling the largest jigsaw puzzle ever, but the early results with other genetically influenced disorders are promising. In the next couple of decades, our understanding of genetic contributions to psychopathology may well expand dramatically.

Some polygenic traits are difficult to identify as genetic because they do not run in families as single-gene and polygenic traits do. These **emergenic traits** (Lykken et al., 1992) are the result of specific *combinations* of characteristics, and they do not appear unless *all* of the elements are present. To help illustrate this concept, consider what makes a person's face attractive. Many people have faces that are considered

attractive, and each is different. So what makes them attractive? It isn't having a particular eye color or a specific mouth or nose or cheekbone. Rather, it is having a combination of characteristics that is harmonious and pleasing. To get this combination, you have to have just the right combination of genes. Change one feature and the balance may be lost.

Although emergenic traits do not generally run in families, there are ways of detecting them. Identical twins share not only traits due to single genes and to typical polygenic combinations but also emergenic traits. This may explain some of the striking similarities observed in identical twins that were separated as newborns (Bouchard et al., 1990). Systematic and controlled study of these twins at the University of Minnesota has shown that many personality characteristics have a strong genetic influence (Bouchard et al., 1990; Lykken et al, 1992; Segal, 1999).

There is moderate to strong evidence that genes contribute to the risk for dozens of psychiatric disorders, including each of the disorders suffered by Dan, Gary, and Monica. For most disorders, however, scientists currently know little about what is inherited or how it contributes to risk. Furthermore, the genetic contributions to psychopathology are likely to differ from one person to the next.

Identical twins not only look alike but are alike in every respect that is influenced by genes. Twins are a "natural laboratory" for studying genetic influences, and twin studies have contributed significantly to the understanding of psychopathology.

emergenic traits Traits that result from specific *combinations* of characteristics, *all* of which must be present.

THE BUILDING BLOCKS OF THE NERVOUS SYSTEM

All behavior is mediated by the nervous system. Understanding the nervous system requires a basic understanding of individual nerve cells, how they connect, and how they communicate with one another. The nervous system is composed of billions of specialized cells called **neurons.** Figure 4.1 illustrates a typical neuron. Neurons receive information and transmit it to other locations. They receive input at branchlike structures on the cell body, called *dendrites,* and transmit information down a tail-like structure, called the *axon,* to branchlike structures at the end of the axon, called *axon terminals.* Neurons do not physically connect with other neurons. Instead there is a small gap, called the **synapse,** between the axon terminal of one neuron and the dendrite of the next, as shown in Figure 4.2. The firing of a cell releases chemicals, called **neurotransmitters,** from the axon terminals. After they are released, one of three things can happen to the neurotransmitters: (1) They can migrate across the small area of the synapse and stimulate specific chemical receptors in the dendrite of the next cell; (2) they can be reabsorbed, in a process called reuptake,

by the cell that released them; or (3) they can break down before either of these events occurs. Many different neurotransmitters are present in the brain, although specific neurotransmitters may dominate specific regions of the brain.

Neurotransmitters appear to play significant roles in either the etiology or the maintenance of several forms of psychopathology, and most of the medications used to treat psychopathology affect specific neurotransmitters. For example, fluoxetine (brand name: Prozac) inhibits the reuptake of serotonin by the neuron that released it, and it is generally effective in treating depression. Dan took Prozac to help his depression, although it provided only limited relief of symptoms for him. Prozac and other drugs in the same class are also used to treat the disorders suffered by Gary and Monica.

THE CENTRAL NERVOUS SYSTEM

Although textbooks typically make a distinction between the central nervous system and the autonomic nervous system, this distinction can be misleading. It implies that these are separate units that function independently, when they are actually different aspects of a single, integrated nervous

---

[FIGURE 4.1]
Neurons

Neurons are the building blocks of the nervous system. A typical neuron contains hundreds of branchlike structures call dendrites, which accept information, a tail-like structure called the axon, and more branchlike structures at the end of the axon called axon terminals. Information passes from the dendrite down the axon to the axon terminals.

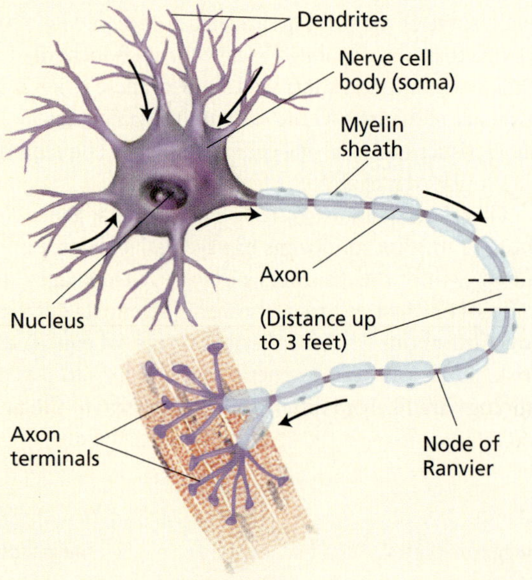

[FIGURE 4.2]
The Synapse

The synapse is the point where neurons communicate with one another. Neurons do not physically touch. Instead, information is passed from one neuron to another through the release of chemicals called neurotransmitters. Disruption in the operation of neurotransmitters has been implicated in several forms of psychopathology.

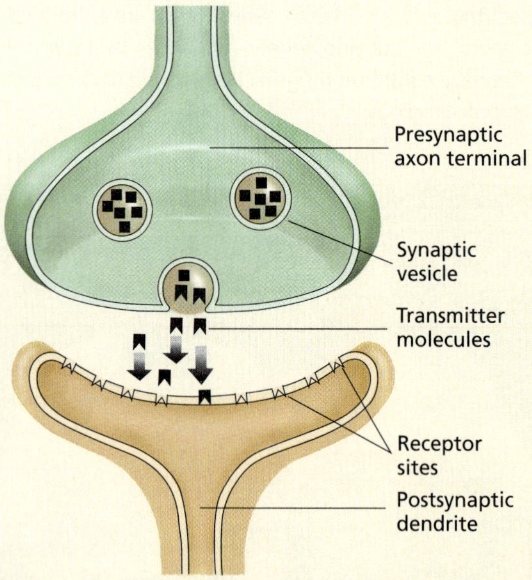

[FIGURE 4.3]

The Human Brain

This drawing illustrates the major elements of the human brain. Many areas of the brain are specialized to perform certain types of tasks. Understanding how brain abnormalities could contribute to psychopathology requires that scientists first understand how the normal brain functions.

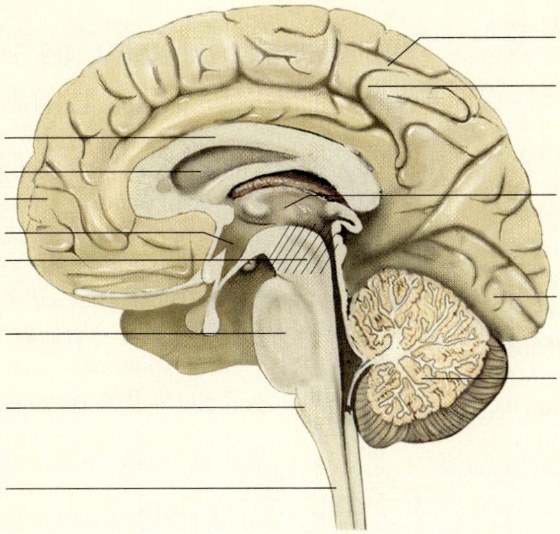

Labels: Parietal lobe, Cerebral cortex, Corpus callosum, Lateral ventricle, Frontal lobe, Hypothalamus, Midbrain, Thalamus, Pons, Occipital lobe, Medulla, Cerebellum, Spinal cord

system. Even so, we will discuss these systems separately because this approach helps students to understand the immense complexity of the nervous system.

The **central nervous system** consists of the brain and the spinal cord. It evaluates incoming information, selects suitable responses, and implements those responses. The brain is a highly specialized organ, in which particular regions handle particular functions. Figure 4.3 shows the overall structure of the human brain. The **cerebral cortex** processes perceptions, memories, and thoughts and also implements behavior. Below the cerebral cortex are **midbrain structures,** and below those is the **brain stem.** Midbrain structures perform a variety of functions, including regulating hunger and thirst, generating emotions, and serving as a relay center for signals from other parts of the brain. The brain stem controls some of the most critical life functions—functions so vital that damage to the brain stem usually results in immediate death. Just below the cerebral cortex in the back of the brain is the **cerebellum.** The cerebellum controls fine motor coordination, although there is evidence that disorders of the cerebellum may be associated with a severe psychiatric disorder in children called autism (Ciaranello & Ciaranello, 1995; Courchesne, 1997).

A critically important part of the brain is a set of subcortical (below the cortex) structures known as the limbic system. The **limbic system** includes such structures as the cingulate gyrus, amygdala, hypothalamus, thalamus, and basal ganglia. The primary functions of the limbic system are emotion processing, learning, and memory, and dysfunctions in the limbic system have been implicated in at

neuron   A specialized cell that makes up the nervous system.

synapse   The small gap between the axon terminal of one neuron and the dendrite of the next.

neurotransmitters   Chemicals released from the axon terminals by the firing of a neuron.

central nervous system   The brain and the spinal cord.

cerebral cortex   The part of the brain that processes perceptions, memories, and thoughts and also implements behavior.

midbrain structures   The parts of the brain that regulate such body functions as hunger and thirst, generate emotions, and serve as a relay center for signals from other parts of the brain.

brain stem   The part of the brain that controls some of the most critical life functions. Damage to the brain stem usually results in immediate death.

cerebellum   The part of the brain that controls fine motor coordination.

limbic system   The subcortical structures of the brain that control emotional processing, learning, and memory.

least a dozen psychological disorders. The role of the individual structures and their functions in specific psychopathologies will be discussed in later chapters.

Evolutionary Impact

The single most important factor differentiating humans from other species is the size of the cerebral cortex, which is a relatively recent evolutionary development. Understanding its role in determining human behavior requires an understanding of both how the cerebral cortex functions and how it interacts with other brain regions. The cerebral cortex is divided into right and left hemispheres. The right cerebral hemisphere controls the left side of the body and generally receives sensory input from the left side of the body, whereas the left cerebral hemisphere controls the right side of the body and generally receives sensory input from the right side of the body. This differentiation of the functions of the left and right cerebral hemispheres is called **lateralization.** Advanced cortical functions are also lateralized. For example, the functional use of language is coordinated by the left cerebral cortex in the vast majority of people, although a few people (mostly left-handers) may have this lateralization reversed. Lateralization appears to be relevant in emotion and in certain forms of psychopathology (Davidson, 1995). For example, depressed individuals show less brain activity on the left side of the brain than do nondepressed individuals (Henriques & Davidson, 1990).

Much of the cerebral cortex seems to be specialized for perception. For example, the *occipital lobe* processes visual information, the *parietal lobe* processes somatosensory (touch) information, and the *temporal lobe* processes auditory information (see Figure 4.3). The *frontal lobe* is critical in sequencing behavior in order to produce the complex and purposeful behavior of everyday life. People with damage to the frontal lobe, for example, often find it difficult to accomplish tasks that require many steps. It is as though

they forget what they were doing and therefore are unable to remember what step comes next. Such advanced cortical functions as memory and problem solving appear to be distributed throughout the cerebral cortex. The cerebral cortex is so central to everyday functioning that it would be hard to imagine its not playing a significant role in psychopathology. As we will see later, the cerebral cortex has been implicated, both directly and indirectly, in several types of psychopathology.

THE AUTONOMIC NERVOUS SYSTEM

One of the remarkable things about living organisms is their ability to adapt quickly to changes in their environment. A major contributor to this adaptive functioning is the **autonomic nervous system,** which links the central nervous system and the peripheral organs of the body. Its name reflects the fact that this system is largely automatic. In fact, at one time scientists believed that voluntary control of this system was impossible. However, research suggests that it is possible to exert limited, indirect control over this system (Lang & Twentyman, 1974; Schwartz & Olson, 1995).

Evolutionary Impact

The role of the autonomic nervous system is to prime the functioning of peripheral organs to facilitate appropriate action. The autonomic nervous system is divided conceptually into two units: the sympathetic and parasympathetic branches. The **sympathetic nervous system** tends to arouse such organs as the heart. Its name reflects the fact that the units of the sympathetic nervous system are "ganged" and therefore often act together. In other words, they act "in sympathy." In contrast, the **parasympathetic nervous system** tends to calm organs. The specific actions of the parasympathetic nervous system are not "ganged" in the same way as those of the sympathetic nervous system; the actions are more localized, serving the needs of a specific organ and situation. The sympathetic nervous system prepares the body for action in situations in which potential danger is perceived, and it is central in the **fight-or-flight response**— a complex survival reflex that mobilizes the body for defensive action in life-or-death situations. Sympathetic activation increases heart rate and the intensity of the heartbeat, thus moving more blood to muscles that may require the additional energy for rapid escape or battle. It also stimulates the release of hormones that are circulated through the bloodstream and provide long-term stimulation of critical body functions. At the same time, the sympathetic nervous system inhibits digestive functioning and stimulates the release of glucose by the liver. In effect, the body is devoting all of its resources to dealing with the current crisis and is not devoting resources to long-term maintenance. Such mobilization can be

---

lateralization   Differentiation of the functions of the left and right cerebral hemispheres.

autonomic nervous system   Composed of the sympathetic and parasympathetic branches, this system links the central nervous system and the peripheral organs of the body.

sympathetic nervous system   The nerves that tend to arouse such organs as the heart.

parasympathetic nervous system   The nerves that tend to calm organs.

fight-or-flight response   A complex survival reflex that mobilizes the body for defensive action in life-or-death situations.

the difference between living and dying. In contrast, the parasympathetic nervous system slows the heart and stimulates body functions that promote long-term health, such as digestion of food and removal of wastes. These functions are critical to survival, but in times of danger or stress they can be postponed to allot maximal resources to dealing with the danger.

Proper functioning of the autonomic nervous system is crucial to survival. Clearly people need to mobilize resources during times of potential danger, and they need to care for their bodies when there is no immediate danger. The functioning of the autonomic nervous system can be disrupted by such psychological problems as anxiety disorders (discussed in Chapter 8), and other psychological problems, such as psychophysiological disorders (discussed in Chapter 9), may stem primarily from disruptions in this critical system. Individual differences in the sensitivity of this system, in reaction time, and in the intensity of responses may shape emotional responding. For example, people who are easily aroused may be perceived as anxious and emotional.

THE ENDOCRINE SYSTEM

The autonomic nervous system prepares organisms to respond to changing surroundings, but it often relies on the endocrine system to carry its message. The **endocrine system** includes a variety of glands, each of which secretes one or more chemicals, called **hormones,** into the bloodstream. A single hormone, circulating through the body, can affect several organs, regulating and coordinating their actions. In most cases, these hormones maintain a delicate balance for the organism. For example, the pancreas regulates blood sugar by controlling the release of insulin. The endocrine system can also release hormones that facilitate emergency reactions, maintaining the aroused state initiated by the organism's sympathetic nervous system.

Evolutionary Impact

The endocrine system has two critical characteristics. First, compared to the central and autonomic nervous systems, it is slow to respond. Whereas the response time of the central nervous system is measured in fractions of a second, the response time of the endocrine system is measured in seconds because the hormones must circulate throughout the body. This delay is of no consequence for regulating such body functions as blood

sugar level, but it can have enormous consequences in an emergency situation. Natural selection probably favored initiating an emergency response with a relatively fast system (the autonomic nervous system). A second characteristic of the endocrine system is that it is slow to shut down. Once the hormones are released, they continue to exert their effects until they either break down or are filtered from the system—a process that can take hours.

Two common situations will illustrate these characteristics. Imagine that you narrowly avoid a life-threatening car accident. The very real danger is sensed and the autonomic nervous system is activated, although the activation probably does not occur until a second or two after the danger has passed. Remember that humans evolved in a world where one does not travel at such speeds and danger does not disappear so quickly. The autonomic nervous system stimulates the adrenal gland to release stress hormones. All of this occurs in the few seconds it takes to avoid the potential accident, but the endocrine effects are still several seconds from being felt, illustrating the slow startup of the system. With the danger gone, you take a deep breath, but a few seconds later you feel your body react to the hormones and experience a second wave of emotion. If this experience happens on your way home late at night, the arousal and hormones associated with it may prevent you from sleeping for several hours, illustrating the slow shutdown of the system.

When the individual encounters a life-threatening situation, the autonomic nervous system facilitates an all-out survival response. Part of this response includes stimulating the endocrine system to release hormones that maintain a longer-term emergency response. This may result in intense emotions long after the danger has passed.

---

endocrine system   A variety of glands, each of which secretes one or more chemicals into the bloodstream.

hormones   The chemicals secreted by the glands of the endocrine system.

TREATMENT

Several effective biological treatments have been developed for specific psychiatric disorders. These include psychoactive medications, psychosurgery, and electroconvulsive therapy.

Medication. The most common biological treatment for any kind of psychological disorder is medication. Powerful medications have been developed to treat mood disorders, anxiety disorders, schizophrenia, and attention-deficit/hyperactivity disorder, to name but a few. Medications can reduce symptoms, although there are usually some individuals who do not respond. In general, the effects of medication tend to persist only as long as the person takes them. It is often useful to combine medication and psychological treatments so that the medication provides quick relief of symptoms and the psychological treatment provides strategies for symptom control without the need for long-term medication.

Medications have had an enormous impact on the fields of psychiatry and psychology. In fact, the advent of effective medications shifted the dominant perspective in psychiatry from psychodynamic to physiological. People who had previously been unable to function on their own were often able to function adequately with the right medication. This has been particularly true for disorders such as schizophrenia and depression. Even so, medications are no panacea. Many have significant side effects, and some have significant risks. Some are overused, perhaps because people want an easy answer to their everyday problems. Pharmacology is now a multi-billion-dollar industry that mounts numerous TV and print ad campaigns for its products. It is unclear whether such promotions will improve or degrade treatment.

Until recently, developing effective medications was essentially a trial-and-error activity. As the understanding of neurochemistry has increased, scientists have been able to develop drugs with chemical characteristics that make them promising for treatment of specific conditions. As you will see throughout the text, knowing which drugs work often provides clues about the biological mechanisms behind a disorder and in turn can lead to the development of even more effective medications.

....

psychosurgery The removal or modification of portions of the brain that are thought to be involved in creating a psychiatric disorder.

prefrontal lobotomy A crude operation practiced in the 1940s that involved destroying portions of the frontal lobe.

electroconvulsive therapy (ECT) Producing a seizure in a person by passing an electric current through the brain. Also called *electroshock therapy*.

Psychosurgery. **Psychosurgery** involves the removal or modification of portions of the brain thought to be involved in creating a psychiatric disorder. The most infamous of psychosurgery techniques was the **prefrontal lobotomy** (Moniz, 1937/1994), a crude operation practiced in the 1940s that involved destroying portions of the frontal lobe (Swayze, 1995). Although some individuals improved, many got worse and some became virtually incapacitated (Jasper, 1995). The risks clearly outweighed the potential gains, and the frontal lobotomies were stopped. As barbaric as they seem today, lobotomies were once considered a medical breakthrough and won Dr. Moniz the Nobel Prize in medicine (Tierney, 2000).

The psychosurgeries of today are infinitely more sophisticated than lobotomies. They are based on a much better understanding of how the brain functions and of what brain mechanisms might be involved in a particular disorder. Some can be done without even using a scalpel; the surgeon instead trains microwaves on a single focal point to destroy the target without damaging adjacent tissue (Spangler et al., 1996). Nevertheless, psychosurgery continues to be the method of last resort, to be used only in those severe cases that have responded to nothing else.

Electroconvulsive Therapy. **Electroconvulsive therapy (ECT),** also known as **electroshock therapy,** involves producing a seizure in a person by passing an electric current through the brain. It is used most often to treat severely depressed individuals who have not responded to antidepressant medication. Although not without its critics (Breggin, 1991), ECT is an effective alternative to other treatments, and there is little evidence of long-term

Although it was once widely used, ECT has been largely replaced by medications. However, some people with depression fail to respond to antidepressant medications but do respond to ECT. Note that the electrode placement has both electrodes on the righthand side of the head. This placement minimizes side effects, such as memory loss, while still providing relief from symptoms.

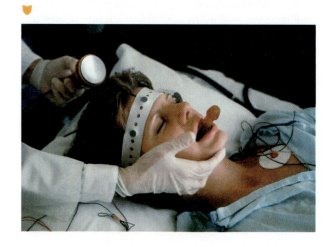

side effects, although some memory losses are reported (Sackeim, 1989). Modern ECT is now safer because muscle relaxants decrease the intensity of physical movements during the seizure, and electrode placement minimizes memory loss (Prudic et al., 2001; Sackeim, 1989). Unfortunately, however, research has shown that many psychiatrists are not using the most effective and safe ECT procedures (Prudic et al., 2001).

You might wonder how anyone could dream up ECT as a treatment. The logic of ECT was based on the idea that seizure disorders appeared to protect individuals from developing schizophrenia (Kiloh, 1982). Hence, it was reasoned that inducing a seizure disorder in people with schizophrenia might reduce their symptoms or even cure them. ECT was the safest procedure for inducing seizures. As it turned out, the original idea that seizures protected individuals from schizophrenia was false, but ECT nonetheless showed promise (Kalinowski, 1982), especially for the treatment of severe depression (Sackeim, 1989). Yet it remains controversial, despite the evidence for its efficacy and general safety (Fink, 2001).

Even today, the exact mechanism of ECT is unknown. Many mechanisms have been proposed over the years, but most have not been borne out by research findings (O'Connor, 1993). There is some evidence for changes in the concentration of TRH (thyroid-releasing hormone) following ECT, especially in the limbic and frontal regions of the brain (Sattin, 1999), but it would be premature to say that this accounts for ECT's treatment efficacy.

EVALUATION

The physiological perspective has made enormous contributions to the understanding of specific forms of psychopathology and the mechanisms behind them. The 1990s were declared the decade of the brain, and advances in understanding brain functioning were impressive. New technologies, such as PET scans and fMRIs, now permit scientists to watch the brain in action in ways that were unimaginable just a generation ago. Many areas of functioning are still not well understood, and new data are always challenging existing theories. This situation should be viewed as a sign of a healthy, vibrant science. The greatest advances in understanding have occurred when scientists have integrated findings from multiple perspectives, including the physiological perspective, and it is safe to assume that such advances will continue.

The greatest danger in using the physiological perspective is the problem of **biological reductionism,** which is the belief that one can understand the complexity of human behavior by understanding the biological mechanisms that underlie it. This belief was at one time widely held, but such simplistic notions are less common today as cognitive scientists and neuroscientists strive to understand the delicate interaction between physiological and psychological experiences. Although trying to reduce human behavior, including abnormal behavior, to physiological processes is a scientific dead end, not trying to integrate physiological and psychological findings is a serious mistake as well. We will witness more of this effort as the technology improves and as the scientific understanding of behavior advances.

Check Yourself 4.1

The Physiological Perspective

1. Define Mendelian, polygenic, and emergenic inheritance.
2. How is information transmitted across the synapse?
3. What parts of the brain are involved in perceptual processes?
4. What is the difference between the sympathetic and parasympathetic nervous systems?
5. What is the most common biological treatment for psychological disorders?

Ponder this . . .   *The autonomic nervous system is tremendously valuable in that it allows the organism to mobilize maximal resources to deal with stress. One might ask, however, why the organism should not be mobilized for action all the time, constantly capable of putting out 100%. Wouldn't such an organism be more effective and therefore have an evolutionary advantage? What, on the other hand, are the costs to the organism of maintaining an essentially constant state of sympathetic arousal?*

THE COGNITIVE-BEHAVIORAL PERSPECTIVE

The **cognitive-behavioral perspective** is both an outgrowth of the behavioral perspective and a reaction to it. It is essentially a behavioral perspective, acknowledging that people's thoughts have a powerful impact on their behavior (Leahey, 1980). For example, people who inadvertently hurt someone's feelings may receive no overt aversive consequences but may well punish themselves for "being a jerk." Hence their future behavior changes because feeling like a jerk is aversive. The cognitive-behavioral perspective

biological reductionism   The belief that one can thoroughly understand human behavior just by understanding the biological mechanisms that underlie it.

cognitive-behavioral perspective   A behavioral perspective that incorporates the realization that people's thoughts have a powerful impact on their behavior.

is richer in its description of reinforcement than the early behaviorist perspectives, which often limited descriptions to observable behavior. However, the concerns of behaviorists remain; scientists must be cautious in their interpretations because thoughts are unobservable. Consequently, there is potential for building theories on uncertain ground unless great care is taken to tie those theories to observable data.

This section begins by outlining early cognitive models of abnormal behavior and then revisiting classical and instrumental conditioning from a cognitive perspective. Next, a type of learning—modeling—not even considered within the behaviorist perspective is discussed. Finally, the cognitive-behavioral treatment approach is outlined.

EARLY COGNITIVE PERSPECTIVE ON PSYCHOPATHOLOGY

The premise behind the cognitive perspective is that the way people respond to their environment is largely a function of how they perceive and interpret it. To appreciate this premise, consider a common situation. Have you ever made an innocent comment to someone who responded by getting upset? Puzzled, you ask what is wrong. When you are told, it is clear that the person misinterpreted your comment or read something into it that was never intended. People do not respond to the objective world; they respond to their interpretation of it. One's interpretation of the world starts with the information gathered, is next sorted according to preexisting conceptualizations, and then is interpreted on the basis of one's assumptions. These steps leave considerable room for error or distortion, which could easily cause problems.

Aaron Beck focused on specific thought distortions in his cognitive theory of depression, arguing that during a typical day, people experience hundreds of **automatic thoughts** that are triggered by the day's events (Beck, 1976, 1993a). Some are commentaries on one's actions, such as "I can't believe I said that." Others are memories, such as "I lost confidence again, just like last week." Still others are conclusions based on observations about the current situation, such as "She thinks I am too outspoken." More examples are included in Table 4.1.

Beck's concept of automatic thoughts is similar to the psychodynamic concept of the unconscious. This similarity to psychodynamic theory is not surprising, given that Dr. Beck was originally trained as a psychoanalyst. Any thought or action can become automatic if it is repeated enough, and once it becomes automatic, the person has little or no awareness of it. Beck's automatic thoughts are typically unconscious, but unlike the psychodynamic uncon-

[TABLE 4.1] **Automatic Thoughts and Irrational Assumptions**

Beck's Automatic Thoughts
◆ I am worthless.
◆ Everyone hates me.
◆ I never do anything right.

Beck's Errors in Logic
◆ **Arbitrary inference:** Drawing unwarranted conclusions on the basis of little or no evidence.
◆ **Selective abstraction:** Drawing conclusions on the basis of a single piece of data while ignoring contradictory data.
◆ **Overgeneralization:** Drawing a general conclusion on the basis of a single, sometimes insignificant, event.
◆ **Magnification or minimization:** Overestimating the importance of negative events and/or underestimating the importance of positive events.
◆ **Personalization:** Taking the blame for something that is clearly not one's fault.

Ellis's Irrational Assumptions
◆ I must always do well or very well.
◆ I must be approved and accepted by people I find important.
◆ I can't stand it when life is unfair.
◆ I am a bad, unlovable person if I get rejected.

SOURCE: Based on A. T. Beck, Cognitive Therapy and the Emotional Disorders. *(New York: International Universities Press, 1976); and A. Ellis and W. Dryden, The Practice of Rational-Emotive Therapy (RET). (New York: Springer, 1987.)*

scious, automatic thoughts can be made conscious with a little effort. If these automatic thoughts are predominantly negative and self-deprecating, then they might well lead to depression. Furthermore, people who develop depression often have habitual logical distortions in their thinking (Beck, 1976, 1993a); these are summarized in Table 4.1. In recent years, Beck's ideas have been extended to forms of psychopathology other than depression, such as anxiety disorders (Butler & Mathews, 1983; Clark, 1986) and schizophrenia (Beck, 1999).

Dan's depression seemed to be fueled by cognitive distortions. He felt like a failure in spite of extensive evidence to the contrary. With hundreds of successes for every failure in his life, it took considerable distortion to conclude that he was a failure, with no hope of future success. Nevertheless, when Dan was depressed, that is exactly how he felt. His beliefs may have been inaccurate, but they nevertheless had a powerful impact on Dan, eventually robbing him of all hope.

Beck's cognitive perspective has broad appeal because it fits one's experiences well. When people are down, they get discouraged easily and often feel terrible about themselves. They also tend to remember every mistake they have ever made and find it hard to remember any of their

---

automatic thoughts Beck's term for thoughts that are triggered by the day's events.

accomplishments (Beck et al., 1983). Furthermore, evidence from laboratory studies suggest that manipulating these thought processes or assumptions can lead to depression or anxiety (Rimm & Litvak, 1969).

Albert Ellis (1962, 1991) proposed a different cognitive distortion theory, arguing that people often hold **irrational assumptions** about the world and themselves. These assumptions are rarely recognized as irrational because people are often unaware of them. For example, some people feel intense distress whenever someone dislikes them. Ellis would argue that this distress is the result of holding an irrational assumption such as "I must be loved and respected by everyone who knows me." Such assumptions set a person up for failure because no one can live up to them. Several other irrational assumptions are listed in Table 4.1.

Gary probably harbored the irrational assumption "I must remember everyone's name and every detail or people will think less of me," and thus he suffered considerable anxiety whenever he could not remember a name or event. On one occasion, he spent six hours frantically making over 100 phone calls to track down the name of a neighborhood store owner from his childhood who had been dead for over 50 years.

It is hard to argue with Ellis's contention that people hold irrational assumptions that predispose them to experience psychological distress. You probably have found yourself thinking things similar to the statements found in Table 4.1. One might question whether the irrational nature of these self-statements or their content is the critical element. Could people have other irrational assumptions that actually shield them from psychological distress? For example, some people have a strong tendency to attribute their every failure to factors beyond their control, even when a more reasonable interpretation is that the failure results from their own inadequacies (Arkin et al., 1980; Bradley, 1978; Silvia & Duval, 2001). These individuals tend to blame others for their own failings. Ever meet someone like that?

A COGNITIVE INTERPRETATION OF CLASSICAL CONDITIONING

Classical conditioning is more complex than that first envisioned by Pavlov, who was influenced heavily by research on physiological reflexes in which conditioning was conceptualized as a transfer of control from one stimulus to another. Modern research suggests that classical conditioning involves more complicated learning of relationships among events. Let's look as some of that research.

irrational assumptions Ellis's term for distorted assumptions that people often hold about the world and themselves without being aware of it.

Examining the Evidence

Rescorla (1988) conducted a series of clever studies of classical conditioning, which revealed some surprisingly complicated nuances. The key elements of his argument are illustrated in Figure 4.4 on page 82. The horizontal lines in this figure represent time lines—that is, movement from left to right represents the passage of time. The top line, labeled Condition 1, shows the traditional classical conditioning pairings. A light, the conditioned stimulus, or CS, is turned on periodically for 5 seconds. Like any CS before conditioning, the light produces no response. The unconditioned stimulus, or US, is a burst of loud noise, which produces the unconditioned response of cringing. The CS and US are paired; the light goes on, followed immediately by a burst of noise. Under such circumstances, conditioning is rapid. In very little time, the onset of the light will produce a cringing response. Participants in this study would probably explain that they were anticipating the loud noise and that is why they cringed. Is there a way of testing whether their subjective impressions are accurate? If participants are truly anticipating the noise whenever the light goes on, one should be able to change that anticipation by manipulating the variables appropriately. For example, the second time line, labeled Condition 2, represents a different set of conditioning trials. Note that the light comes on in exactly the same pattern as before and that the bursts of noise when the light is on are identical. However, additional noise bursts have been added randomly in Condition 2 so that the light is no longer a signal that a loud noise is imminent. Furthermore, the light being off is no longer a "safe signal"—a signal that no noise will occur. In this condition, the light provides no information about the probability of the aversive noise because the noise occurs randomly, sometimes when the light is on and sometimes when it is off. If it is just the pairing of the CS and US that produces conditioning, as Pavlov hypothesized, then conditioning should occur in this second condition, just as it did in the first. However, that is not what happens. No conditioning occurs in the second condition. Clearly, the participant is doing something more complicated during conditioning—something that involves higher cognitive functions.

Other observations also suggest that thought processes affect classical conditioning. One of the most powerful is the effect of instructions. Instructions are verbal statements about what to expect. If conditioning does not involve thought processes, one would expect such instructions to have minimal effect. However, informing participants that

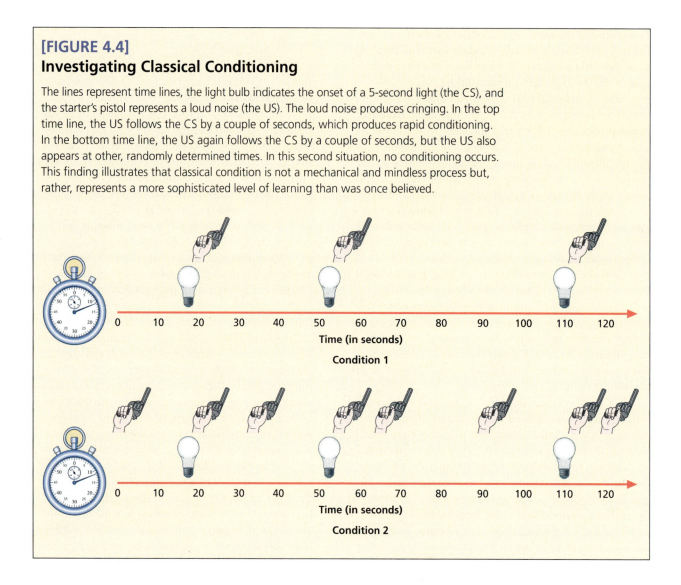

[FIGURE 4.4]

Investigating Classical Conditioning

The lines represent time lines, the light bulb indicates the onset of a 5-second light (the CS), and the starter's pistol represents a loud noise (the US). The loud noise produces cringing. In the top time line, the US follows the CS by a couple of seconds, which produces rapid conditioning. In the bottom time line, the US again follows the CS by a couple of seconds, but the US also appears at other, randomly determined times. In this second situation, no conditioning occurs. This finding illustrates that classical condition is not a mechanical and mindless process but, rather, represents a more sophisticated level of learning than was once believed.

the aversive stimulus (the US) will no longer appear dramatically speeds extinction (Grings, 1973). In Chapter 3, I related a case of a former client who stalked me. When this former client was in jail or in the hospital, my classically conditioned response to such events as going to my car quickly extinguished. I felt safe because I knew she could not be waiting for me. In contrast, when she was no longer stalking me but was at home, my response extinguished slowly. Clearly, knowledge about the situation affected my classically conditioned responses.

A COGNITIVE INTERPRETATION OF OPERANT CONDITIONING

In operant conditioning, one needs to know only what people experienced, not what they were thinking. This system works, especially when dealing with such nonverbal subjects as young children or animals. Nevertheless, a wealth of information is lost when one does not study the thoughts of the people involved. One also loses the chance to increase the effectiveness of reinforcement by making the contin-

gencies explicit. For example, if a father wanted to increase the study behavior of his ten-year-old daughter, he might allow her to watch TV only after she had completed her homework. Telling his daughter that this was the new contingency for watching TV would speed the process. Making her guess about what she had to do before she could watch TV would be pointless. She might spend days or weeks trying to figure out what was expected of her, when a ten-word sentence could end the confusion.

MODELING

Evolutionary Impact ⎯⎯⎯⎯⎯

People are quite capable of learning from the experience of others. If you observe several people being stopped for speeding, you are likely to watch your speed more carefully, even though you have not personally experienced the aversive consequences of getting a speeding ticket. Such learning from observing the consequences experienced by others is referred to as **modeling** or

observational learning. If you think about it, observational learning has a tremendous evolutionary advantage in that people do not have to jump over a cliff themselves to learn about the negative consequences of such action. Observational learning is not unique to humans. For example, Mineka and Cook (1993) found that rhesus monkeys learned to fear snakes by observing the fear in other monkeys or by even viewing a videotape of fearful monkeys (Cook & Mineka, 1990).

Bandura showed that many behaviors including aggression, can be learned through modeling (Bandura, 1969, 1973, 1976; Bandura et al., 1963). One's attitudes, fears, and behaviors are all influenced by observation of one's parents and other family members. Observational learning can even cross species. For example, it is common for people who are fearful of thunderstorms to have pets who show the same fear.

TREATMENT

The cognitive-behavioral treatment approaches in use today borrow heavily from early behaviorism and from the cognitive approaches of Ellis and Beck. This section outlines traditional cognitive therapies and the more modern cognitive-behavioral approaches that combine several elements into a treatment protocol.

Early Cognitive-Behavioral Therapies. The assumption behind all cognitive therapies is that thoughts affect feelings and actions. When those effects are maladaptive, a specific therapeutic effort is made to identify and challenge the thoughts, replacing them with more functional ones. In **Beck's cognitive-behavioral therapy (CBT),** the therapist explores daily events with the client, looking for instances in which automatic thoughts may be counterproductive. Automatic thoughts are typically out of the person's awareness, but by exploring the links between events and the person's reactions to them, the therapist gradually uncovers these problematic thoughts. For example, a person who typically responds with hopelessness whenever he makes a mistake may be magnifying this single failure into more general statements such as "I can't do anything right." Awareness of these statement enables the person to challenge them.

Ellis's idea that irrational assumptions contribute to many negative feelings led to the development of **rational emotive behavior therapy (REBT).** The goal of REBT is to help clients identify and then change their irrational assumptions. Identifying these assumptions requires considerable practice, and so, like many CBT therapists, REBT therapists often give homework assignments to encouraged clients to identify and challenge their irrational assumptions.

Bandura showed that children readily learn to be aggressive from watching aggressive material on television.

Modern Cognitive-Behavioral Approaches. Modern cognitive-behavioral treatment uses many of the behavioral techniques introduced in Chapter 3, such as conditioning, counterconditioning, and contingency management, as well as the cognitive techniques of Ellis and Beck. For example, David Clark (1986) uses cognitive strategies to help clients with uncontrolled panic to avoid making catastrophic misinterpretations of their panic, such as "I am going to die" or "I will lose all control." By challenging these cognitive misinterpretations while facing the fearful situations, clients are able to decrease their fear of panic. In addition, modeling is often used to correct such

....

modeling   Learning from observing the consequences experienced by others. Also called *observational learning*.

Beck's cognitive-behavioral therapy (CBT)   Therapy in which the therapist explores daily events with the client, looking for instances in which automatic thoughts may be counterproductive.

rational emotive behavior therapy (REBT)   Therapy in which the therapist tries to help clients identify and then change their irrational assumptions.

behavioral problems as deficits in social skills (Bandura, 1969, 1976).

Education is a major component of many cognitive-behavioral treatments. Most people come into treatment with preconceived ideas about what is wrong with them, what is responsible for the problem, and what should be done about the problem. Often they have unrealistic fears about the problem—fears that increase their anxiety, thus exacerbating symptoms. Education about the problem often reduces these fears and convinces people that they can reassume control of their lives.

The current cognitive-behavioral approaches tend to be specialized for the treatment of specific disorders. These treatment packages, known as **treatment protocols,** combine specific elements to handle the range of symptoms exhibited by people with a particular disorder. Cognitive-behavioral treatment protocols have been developed for numerous disorders, including depression (Clark & Beck, 1999), panic disorder (Barlow & Craske, 2000; Clark, 1986), and generalized anxiety disorder (Craske et al., 1992). These treatment protocols typically require only a few weeks to a few months to complete. This approach is now being extended to disorders once thought to be resistant to cognitive-behavioral treatment, such as schizophrenia (Beck, 1999) and obsessive-compulsive disorder (Clark & Purdon, 1993).

EVALUATION

The cognitive-behavioral perspective expands on the strength of behaviorism by adding the element of human thought and interpretation. The strong scientific tradition on which the behavioral perspective was built has continued to be a part of the cognitive-behavioral perspective. Consequently, the hypotheses developed within this perspective are routinely submitted to scientific challenge and replaced when they fail to stand up to the challenge. The cognitive-behavioral perspective has produced several effective treatments for psychological disorders. Nevertheless, it lost a major opportunity by not drawing more heavily on the sophisticated understandings of how humans perceive and think that were developed in other areas of psychology. Knowing how memory functions to solve problems and how people develop cognitive biases that speed up normal processing of material, but at the expense of occasionally producing inaccurate perceptions or interpretations, would have yielded even more insights into

treatment protocols   Treatment packages that combine specific elements to handle the range of symptoms shown by people with a particular disorder.

cognitive neuroscience perspective   Looks at how people with a given disorder differ from other people in the way they perceive and think about the world and at how those differences may contribute to the onset or maintenance of a disorder.

psychopathology. The cognitive neuroscience perspective covered in the next section addresses many of these issues.

Check Yourself 4.2

The Cognitive-Behavioral Perspective

1. What do Beck's automatic thoughts and Ellis's irrational assumptions have in common?
2. What is the evidence that classical conditioning is not just the result of the pairing of CS and US as originally proposed by Pavlov?
3. What is the evolutionary advantage of modeling?
4. What characterizes modern cognitive-behavioral treatments?

Ponder this . . .   *The best way to understand cognitive distortion is to recognize that everyone has them, including you. Think about incidents in which you were distressed and ask, "What must I be telling myself to get me so upset?" Once you determine what you are telling yourself, think about what you should do about it. The treatment section will give you more ideas on this second step.*

THE COGNITIVE NEUROSCIENCE PERSPECTIVE

The **cognitive neuroscience perspective** focuses on how people with a given disorder differ from other people in the way they perceive and think about the world and on how those differences may contribute to the onset or maintenance of a disorder. A constant source of confusion for students is the distinction between the cognitive-behavioral perspective just discussed and the cognitive neuroscience perspective. The cognitive-behavioral perspective relied on the idea that thoughts and environmental contingencies influence emotions and behaviors. For example, if you think you are failing at something, you may become demoralized and give up. In contrast, the cognitive neuroscience perspective is more interested in the details of such cognitive processes as memory, perception, and thought, as well as in the brain mechanisms that contribute to these processes. In other words, the cognitive-behavioral approach looks at the big picture—how the person conceptualizes the world and reacts to it. The cognitive neuroscience approach looks at how the details come together to form the big picture—how memory and perception influence the thoughts that influence behavior.

In this section, you will learn about cognitive psychology and how the methods of cognitive psychology have been modified for the study of psychopathology. Several aspects of cognitive functioning are discussed, including memory, perceptual biases, and controlled versus automatic processing.

COGNITIVE PSYCHOLOGY

Evolutionary Impact

Cognitive psychologists study human perceptual and thought processes with the goal of understanding these processes and their limitations. Note that cognitive psychologists are *not* the people who practice CBT. This overlap in terminology can be confusing. Understanding cognitive processes and their limitations is critical as humans continue to move into environments that are vastly different from the environment of human evolutionary history. For example, there is nothing in human evolutionary history that prepared people to fly planes, so several limitations of human perception had to be addressed to make flying safe. For example, humans tell up from down by orienting to gravity, which pulls them toward the earth. However, when a plane banks to turn, the combined force of gravity and the force exerted by the plane to bank gives people the impression that down is tilted by the amount of the bank. That is, people feel like they are still sitting upright, even though they are tilted with respect to the earth. You may have noticed that you do not feel turns in a plane the way you do in a car. This is a dangerous problem when there is no visual reference, as is the case when a plane is flying through clouds. Fortunately, instruments provide accurate information when the senses are undependable.

Technology forces people to deal every day with hundreds of things that evolution never prepared humans for. Every time you look at the jumble of information on a computer screen, drive a car, or operate your remote control, you are using technology that had to be designed with the perceptual and cognitive limitations of the human brain in mind. However, technological changes are not the only thing that strains mental resources. The complex societies of today demand so much from people, who must evaluate and interact each day with dozens or even hundreds of individuals from a variety of cultural backgrounds. Just a thousand generations ago—a split second in evolutionary terms—humans typically dealt with only a few dozen members of their nomadic tribe and had occasional encounters with other tribes. In addition, the complexity of the decisions is much greater and the price of incorrect decisions much higher in a world were conflicts could kill millions of people. The nature of risks and the way those risks are managed have changed as well. When the risk is becoming some predator's lunch, avoiding the predator was a simple solution. When the risk is losing one's job, what does one do? These dramatic changes strain the individual's ability to adapt. Understanding cognitive limitations helps scientists to predict what situations are likely to lead to breakdown and what approaches might minimize the impact when people are stressed beyond their ability to cope.

Cognitive psychologists have uncovered numerous aspects of human thought and perception that have contributed to improving human functioning in a variety of contexts, from airplane safety to computer operation. These psychologists are interested in finding processes shared by virtually everyone. In other words, they want to know how human beings are similar to one another in their perception and thought processes. In contrast, scientists who study psychopathology are interested in the things that make some people different from other people—more specifically, in what things contribute to psychopathology. Why do anxious people see so many scary things? Are there differences in the way depressed people perceive and think about the world? Why do people with schizophrenia hear imaginary voices? These are questions about **individual differences**—that is, the natural differences between human beings.

MEMORY

Evolutionary Impact

Memory is the ability to encode information for later use. Most people think of memory as a single thing, but it is more complicated than that. For example, psychologists distinguish declarative from procedural memory. **Declarative memories** are the memories of events, whereas **procedural memories** are memories of how to do things. Amnesia, or loss of memory, is more likely to disrupt declarative memory than procedural memory (Glisky et al., 1986; Kapur, 1997; Schacter & Tulving, 1982). Nature may have developed a way to encode procedural memories more securely because of their importance to survival. Psychologists also distinguish implicit from explicit memories (Schacter, 1992). **Explicit memories** are memories that people can recount because they are aware of them, whereas **implicit memories** are memories that people are unaware of. Most

cognitive psychologists Psychologists who study human perceptual and thought processes with the goal of understanding these processes and their limitations.

individual differences The natural differences between human beings.

memory The ability to encode information for later use.

declarative memories The memories of events.

procedural memories Memories of how to do things.

explicit memories Memories that people can recount because they are aware of them.

implicit memories Memories that people are unaware of.

students wonder how you can call it a memory if the person does not "remember" it? If one can show that the person is changed by the event, then there must be a memory for the event, even if the person has no recollection of it. Jacoby (Jacoby, 1983; Jacoby et al., 1992) and others (Toth et al., 1994; Kihlstrom, 1999) have clearly demonstrated such implicit memories. This research confirms the existence of cognitive mechanisms that could create the unconscious influences hypothesized in both psychodynamic and cognitive-behavioral perspectives.

Memory is so much a part of everyday life that it is inconceivable that it is not related to psychopathology. The more psychologists learn about memory, the more valuable the concept of memory becomes for understanding a variety of symptoms. As we will see, memory biases are common in depression and anxiety disorders. Memory effectiveness is compromised in other disorders, such as schizophrenia and Alzheimer's disease. This section will introduce several key concepts associated with memory that are relevant to one or more psychopathologies.

Limitations of Memory. Some memories are so vivid that they never seem to fade. Many people can tell you where they were when they first heard about President Kennedy's assassination, or the space shuttle Challenger explosion, or the attack on the World Trade Center. These critical historical events create memories so vivid and clear that they have often been referred to as **flashbulb memories**—as though they were imprinted on one's mind for eternity. But how "eternal" are these memories?

Examining the Evidence

Neisser and Harsch (1992) wanted to evaluate the accuracy of flashbulb memories, so they asked 44 college students the day after the Challenger explosion to write down how they heard about the explosion and what they did when they found out. Thirty months later, they again asked these students to do the same thing. None of the participants gave exactly the same account on the two occasions, and over a third gave dramatically different accounts. Even more striking, most participants were certain that their memories at 30 months were accurate, and there was essentially no relationship between their confidence in the memory's accuracy and its actual accuracy. Some participants were amazed when they were presented with

their own, hand-written accounts written the day after the tragedy. This study and many others illustrate that memories, even the most vivid memories, are much more fragile and far less accurate than most people believe (Loftus & Ketcham, 1991, 1994).

Evolutionary Impact

Although memory is not so reliable as one would like, it does serve people's needs reasonably well. Like every other functional capacity, memory was shaped by natural selection. Absolute accuracy is less important from a natural selection perspective than whether the memories guide more functional behavior—that is, behavior that increases the likelihood of survival. Memory clearly plays a huge role in how people function, and this is a testament to its inherent value. Whether it is reliable

Events such as the attack on the World Trade Center have a powerful impact on people. It feels as though the experience is indelibly fixed in memory, but research shows that even these powerful memories are subject to distortion over time.

flashbulb memories Vivid memories of a critical event that are so clear they seem to be etched in one's mind forever.

enough to make people good witnesses is another matter (Loftus & Ketcham, 1991). Of more importance to the field of psychopathology is whether memory is reliable enough to serve human beings in today's complex and rapidly changing world.

Memory as Sequences. Understanding memory processes is critical to understanding how memory affects psychopathology. Memory evolved to guide behavior. Most behaviors are really behavioral sequences; they represent a series of behaviors that the individual must perform in a particular order to achieve a goal. Therefore, it should not be surprising that many things are learned as sequences. For example, people can easily name the months of the year in chronological order, but most find it difficult to name them in alphabetical order. Learning a sequence has a number of functional advantages. If you always do a series of tasks in a particular order and you are interrupted, you only need to remember one thing (the last item completed) to know everything that you have done already and everything that still needs to be done.

This sequencing of memories can be either exaggerated or disrupted in various forms of psychopathology. Ritualistic behavior—behavior that is constantly repeated in exactly the same way—is found in several forms of psychopathology, from severe disorders of childhood to anxiety disorders. Gary performed such rituals when his obsessions were particularly severe. If interrupted, he would have to repeat the ritual from the beginning. People with schizophrenia often show severe disruption in the ability to sequence ideas, and this sometimes makes their communication nonsensical.

Cued Memories. Most memories are connected to other memories, and those other memories serve as cues for recall. Naming the months of the year in order is easy, because January is the cue for February and February is the cue for March. April is not a good cue for August (the next month in alphabetical order) unless the months were learned in alphabetical order. Memory cues are associations that either are specifically learned or have some conceptual relationship to the new memory. Classically conditioned fears can be conceptualized as cued memories, which helps to explain such phenomena as generalization. The associations on which generalization is based are part of a person's existing memories.

Memory cues have relevance to psychopathology in several ways. First, many psychopathological responses are cued by specific situations, which are usually determined by past learning history. For example, someone afraid of speaking in public may vividly remember a past speaking occasion that went badly. Emotional states can serve as memory cues. For example, people who worry constantly

often remember thousands of "close calls" that other people would have long ago forgotten. Their worry reminds them of other things they worried about in the past.

Evolutionary Impact

Memory Biases. **Memory biases** reflect the tendency to recall certain memories more readily than others. For example, people tend to remember more quickly things that are associated with danger—a bias that has obvious survival value. Not only do memory biases exist, but they vary depending on the situation. This effect is called **priming**, which refers to an enhancement in the likelihood of memory recall as a function of context. Memories that are most likely to be useful in a given context are the memories that are most easily recalled. Unfortunately, psychopathology provides its own context, which may prime memories that lead to maladaptive behavior. For example, depressed individuals, such as Dan, often suffer from selective memory. When depressed, they are more likely to remember past failures than past successes, which can reinforce their feeling of worthlessness. When depressed, Dan could remember only his failures, although his successes outnumbered them by at least 50 to 1.

Memory and Stress. Every student knows about the effect of stress on memory. How many times have you walked out of an exam and suddenly remembered an answer that had eluded you just moments before? Stress reduces one's ability to recall information. Many forms of psychopathology are triggered or exacerbated by stress. Gary's rituals increased dramatically during stressful periods. Stress clearly affects memory, but until recently, there was virtually no research on this critical phenomenon in people with psychological disorders. This aspect of memory has had the greatest impact on treatment, which is often a stressful time for clients. Many treatment packages now use overlearning of critical elements to increase the likelihood that they will actually be remembered when the person is feeling overwhelmed by symptoms.

PERCEPTUAL BIASES

To be able to perceive anything, people must focus their attention. **Attention,** focusing on one thing while ignoring other things, is constantly shifted from one target to

....

memory biases   The tendency to recall certain memories more readily than others.

priming   An enhancement in the likelihood of memory recall as a function of context.

attention   The process by which people focus on one thing while ignoring other things.

another as people evaluate and respond to their surroundings. However, there are too many potential targets for people to evaluate. Hence people automatically select targets most likely to be relevant. For example, when you walk into a room, your attention is most likely to be drawn to animate objects, such as people or pets, and less likely to be drawn to inanimate objects. Certain inanimate objects, such as obstructions that need to be avoided, capture your attention more readily than others. It is not likely that you will notice wall outlets unless your purpose is to find an outlet. These are examples of **perceptual biases**—the tendency to perceive some objects more readily than others. Some perceptual biases represent obvious distortion, such as noticing every speck of dirt in a nearly spotless room. Some people with the same disorder as Gary show this distortion.

Perceptual biases focus attention on items most likely to be relevant. To the extent that those decisions on relevance are accurate, these biases increase perceptual efficiency. Some biases are learned. For example, upon entering a crime scene, a seasoned detective focuses on critical evidence that most people would not notice. Other biases are affected by the situation. For example, fearful people often notice potential danger. Perceptual biases are common in psychopathology. Monica displayed an extreme perceptual bias in which she saw herself as fat, even as she was wasting away. Dan felt that everyone was judging him negatively when he spoke in public. The key question is "Are these perceptual biases a cause or an effect (or both) of psychopathology?"

CONTROLLED VERSUS AUTOMATIC PROCESSING

Cognitive psychologists make the distinction between controlled and automatic processing (Matlin, 1998; Reisberg, 1997). Automatic processing occurs without the need for attention, whereas controlled processing requires attention. Any behavior can become automatic. Because attention is required for controlled-processing tasks, people can normally do only one such task at a time. Controlled processing is required when one is first learning a task, but with sufficient practice, the task can become automatic. When you first learned to drive, it required considerable concentration, but with practice, driving became automatic. Tasks can become so automatic that it is frightening how little attention is needed. Have you ever driven home, only to realize that you do not remember a thing about the drive?

The advantage of automatic processing is that it requires less cognitive resources, and therefore the person is free to use cognitive resources for other tasks. The disadvantage is that because the task is performed without thinking, the person typically has less control over it. Most behaviors, when learned well enough, become automatic. This is also true for pathological behaviors. Beck's automatic thoughts are a good example. Once these thoughts are learned, they often occur without awareness. Changing automatic thoughts and behaviors requires considerable effort. Gary found that his compulsive reading of every article in the newspaper was largely automatic. Helping him cease this behavior required making him aware of what he was doing.

LINKING COGNITIVE PROCESSES TO BRAIN MECHANISMS

The real strength of the cognitive neuroscience perspective is that it is likely to be the link between the physiological perspective and the other perspectives. Knowing what basic cognitive functions underlie advanced human behavior and thought and knowing what brain mechanisms are responsible for these basic cognitive functions will help scientists to fill in details of the causal chain. Again, one should avoid biological reductionism—the belief that every behavior can be understood in terms of its biological underpinnings. Causation does not go in one direction only, from biology to thoughts and behavior. Thoughts and behavior affect biology, which in turn affects later thoughts and behavior. Until scientists understand how all these mechanisms work together, they will not be able to develop the kind of specific theories that are likely to lead to truly effective treatments. This would be like studying the operation of a factory by observing only the materials that are brought into the factory and the finished products that are shipped out. One could never hope to improve the operation of the factory without knowing what was going on inside. In the same way, scientists must understand what is going on inside the person at many different levels in order to understand and treat psychopathology. The cognitive neuroscience perspective, one of the newest perspectives to be applied to the field, will eventually provide some critical insights.

Since its inception, the goal of cognitive neuroscience has been to understand the relationship between thoughts and behavior on the one hand and brain mechanisms on the other. Early models did assume that the relationship flowed just one way—brain mechanisms creating thoughts and behavior (Marshall & Magoun, 1998), although more recent models recognize the bidirectional nature of this relationship (Gazzaniga et al., 1998). This is partly because early research focused on simple behaviors, such as motor activity, whereas current cutting-edge research focuses on such complex activities as memory, emotion, and language (Purves et al., 2001). The incredible advances of neuroscience in understanding brain/behavior relationships, especially over the past 15 years, could not possibly be covered in the space available here. However, you will see several examples throughout the text of how this research

perceptual biases The tendency to perceive some objects more readily than others.

formed the basis for sophisticated reinterpretations of psychological disorders.

TREATMENT

Most of the research from the cognitive neuroscience perspective has focused on determining what cognitive processes are disturbed, in what ways are they disturbed, and how this disturbance contributes to the symptoms shown by the individual. To date, there has been little direct effort to apply the principles of cognitive neuroscience to the treatment of psychopathology, although some specific cognitive-behavioral protocols are beginning to use information derived from the cognitive neuroscience perspective in the development of specific elements of their treatment. For example, the rehearsal repetition of many cognitive-behavioral approaches is designed to make the new behavior automatic and dominant so that the behavior will be cued without thinking, even during stressful periods.

EVALUATION

The cognitive neuroscience perspective has been a lost stepchild in the field of psychopathology. Researchers studying schizophrenia have used this perspective for the last 50 years, probably because cognitive processes are so obviously disturbed in schizophrenia. However, only recently has the focus on basic perceptual and cognitive processes in other disorders become commonplace. It is likely that the cognitive neuroscience perspective will become increasingly important in the study of psychopathology, providing a link between thoughts and behavior and basic brain processes. The complex thoughts and behavior of psychopathology are composed of hundreds of basic perceptual and cognitive functions, which are mediated by physiological processes. Furthermore, behavior and thoughts affect the operation of the physiological processes and thus the basic cognitive processes. If scientists hope ever to understand the development and maintenance of psychopathology from the behavioral level down to the level of the cell, the cognitive neuroscience perspective will be a critical link.

Check Yourself 4.3

The Cognitive Neuroscience Perspective

1. What do cognitive psychologists do?
2. What is the difference between declarative and procedural memory? Which is more durable if a person suffers brain damage?
3. What are flashbulb memories and how trustworthy are they?
4. What is the distinction between controlled and automatic processing?

Ponder this . . .   From an evolutionary perspective, memory need not be a completely accurate record of specific events to have survival value. How might memory serve an organism despite being less than perfectly accurate?

THE SOCIOCULTURAL PERSPECTIVE

Many social factors influence people's behavior, including family, culture, and religious and national values. These factors create the foundation for people's lives and affect every aspect of functioning, both normal and pathological. The **sociocultural perspective** focuses on how institutions and cultural norms influence the likelihood of psychological disorders and shape the pattern of symptoms when those disorders develop. Sociocultural influences interact with biological and psychological factors in shaping psychopathology.

This section begins with a discussion of culture and cultural diversity and then considers several societal influences, including social class, social and gender roles, social stresses, cultural factors, and the family. The sociocultural perspective has influenced family therapy and spawned community psychology.

CULTURAL DIVERSITY

Former U.S. senator J. William Fulbright argued that the greatest arrogance was to assume that one's own cultural perspective had universal validity. In a world that is constantly growing smaller, culture still separates people, sometimes more effectively than oceans once did. **Culture** consists of the common expectations, experiences, and perspectives of a group of people living together. The experiences of men and women, although they live and work together, can also differ so much as to represent different cultures.

The diversity of cultural experience provides opportunities for naturalistic studies of psychopathology. Studying the rates and nature of psychopathology across cultures enables scientists to identify factors that may increase or decrease risk. These studies have demonstrated that every culture has both advantages and disadvantages relative to other cultures. Aspects of each culture may protect its members from some forms of psychopathology while increasing the risk for other forms of psychopathology.

sociocultural perspective   Looks at how institutions and cultural norms influence the likelihood of psychological disorders and shape the pattern of symptoms when those disorders develop.

culture   The common expectations, experiences, and perspectives of a group of people living together.

Cultural diversity is more than just looking different. People from different cultures are raised with different values, have had different experiences, and have learned different expectations. All of these factors could affect the likelihood of the individual developing a psychopathology or could influence the nature of the psychopathology that develops.

SOCIAL INFLUENCES

Social scientists have studied many social influences on behavior, including social class, gender roles, social stresses, and cultural factors.

Social Class. **Social class** is defined by a combination of education level and occupation (Hollingshead, 1957). For example, doctors are in the highest social class because they have extensive education and a prestigious career. Although social class is moderately correlated with income, income is not the defining characteristic.

The risk for some forms of psychopathology varies as a function of social class (APA, 2000). Schizophrenia, for example, is much more common in the lowest social class than in the middle and upper classes (Hollingshead & Redlich, 1958). Why does this pattern exist? Is there something about growing up in the lower class that increases the risk for schizophrenia? Could the combination of poverty, poor education, random violence, and crowding that often plagues lower-class neighborhoods be responsible? Alternatively, perhaps social class is the result of psychopathology (Goldberg & Morrison, 1963). For example, poor functioning due to psychopathology may limit the achievements that define social class. Answering these questions is critical if one is to understand schizophrenia.

Evolutionary Impact

Social and Gender Roles. Everyone plays dozens of social roles. A person might be a student or a teacher; a son, a daughter, or a parent; a worker, a golfer, a lover, or a teammate. People behave differently in each of these roles because each is associated with different expectations for behavior. Roles provide guidelines on how people should behave and on what behavior people can expect from others. Gender defines a social role that no one can escape. Depending on the culture and era in which one grew up, expectations are different for men and women. For example, in the United States today, there is considerable pressure on women to be thin. This is a recent trend but certainly a powerful one. Men do not experience the same pressure. This social pressure may have contributed to Monica's eating disorder. The role expectations of men and women, perhaps shaped by their different evolutionary roles in the family, affect the way they address many aspects of life. It is hard to imagine that such pronounced differences in role expectations would not affect people and their risk for various forms of psychopathology. For example, alcoholism is five times more common in American men than women (APA, 2000). Could social roles account for this difference? Heavy drinking is more readily accepted in American men than women, although there is evidence that biological factors may also play a role (Dawson & Grant, 1998; Rosenfield, 1999).

Social Stresses. Stress seems to have a cumulative effect in increasing the risk for a variety of psychological problems (Leighton, 1998). Some events are obviously stressful, such as the death of a loved one or the loss of a job. Surprisingly, even such positive events as getting married or getting a promotion can be stressful because they require adaptation (Holmes and Rahe, 1967/1989). Some people seem to face stress more often than others. Such factors as poverty, unemployment, high crime rates, and racial bigotry can dramatically increase the stress in a person's life (Banyard & Graham-Bermann, 1998; Paschall & Hubbard, 1998), and all of these factors have been associated with an increase in psychological disorders (Luthar, 1999). There was a point in recent history when it was common to blame such sociological problems for just about everything from crime to psychopathology. Today, few sci-

social class A grouping of people on the basis of education level and occupation.

community psychology A field that focuses on understanding how social factors affect individual behavior, with an eye toward positive intervention.

primary prevention Preventive strategies applied to the entire population.

secondary prevention Preventive strategies applied to groups that are known to be at risk, such as crisis interventions with rape victims.

entists argue that social stresses are the primary cause of psychopathology. Rather, they believe that these stresses decrease coping and thus increase the risk for many problems, including psychopathology.

The cumulative effects of the daily hassles of life may be the greatest source of stress (Kanner et al., 1981). Everyone experiences daily hassles, but they affect some people more than others. Many factors account for this, including constitutional factors. Some people just respond more strongly to things than others, and these differences may be genetically influenced. However, social support can be a significant buffer against stress (DeLongis et al., 1988). Unfortunately, many forms of psychopathology, such as depression and schizophrenia, are associated with social withdrawal and isolation. That certainly was true for Dan, who completely isolated himself whenever he was depressed.

Cultural Factors. The differences among cultures in experiences, attitudes, and family dynamics can be enormous. Given such variability, it is not surprising that one often sees cultural differences in the rates of specific forms of psychopathology. Alcoholism, for example, is more common in cultures that accept heavy drinking, such as Irish and some Native American cultures, than in cultures that discourage heavy drinking, such as Jewish and Chinese American cultures (APA, 2000). The nature of a culture can also affect the symptom pattern for a disorder. For example, the way in which depression is manifested is different in Western cultures than in some Eastern cultures (APA, 2000). In Western cultures, sadness and guilt are prominent, whereas a sense of weakness or tiredness is prominent in many Eastern cultures. Furthermore, some cultures discourage, whereas others encourage, the display of such emotions as depression, a difference that complicates the process of diagnosis (APA, 2000). Severe disorders, such as schizophrenia, show consistent risk and similar symptom patterns across cultures (Gottesman, 1991).

FAMILY INFLUENCES

Families have considerable influence on the individual's development and therefore may affect the development of psychopathology. Family theorists have generally had more of an impact on the field of psychotherapy than on psychopathology (Minuchin et al., 1996; Nichols & Minuchin, 1999), although evidence of family influences on some forms of psychopathology does exist.

Families are dynamic organizations, in which each member is implicitly assigned social roles (Minuchin et al., 1996). For example, one member might be the peacemaker, who always tries to resolve family disagreements. Another might be the "bad sheep"—the one who is constantly in trouble. Another might be the "good boy or girl"—the one who never misbehaves and is always dependable. These roles are rarely played out as consistently as they may appear. More likely than not, people's expectations about how each person will behave distort their perceptions of the actual behavior. Nevertheless, once these roles are established, they influence behavior and—just as important—influence how others react to the behavior.

TREATMENT

The sociocultural perspective has spawned two areas of intervention: community psychology and family therapy. **Community psychology** is an outgrowth of both sociology and clinical psychology (Levine & Perkins, 1997). Its focus is on understanding how social factors affect individual behavior, with an eye toward positive intervention. Although traditional treatment is possible within a community psychology framework, the greatest emphasis is on prevention. Preventive strategies that are applied to the entire population are referred to as **primary prevention.** For example, Seligman (1992) has suggested that specific interventions with children, applied as a routine part of the school curriculum, might stem the rising tide of teenage depression. **Secondary prevention** consists of strategies that are applied to groups known to be at risk. Crisis interventions with rape and assault victims represent secondary prevention. Assault victims are at high risk for a condition

One of the most important sociocultural influences is the family. The family unit is where most people learn about the expectations of their culture.

called posttraumatic stress disorder (PTSD), but early intervention can reduce this risk.

Family therapy is a variation on traditional individual therapy, with some dramatically different assumptions. Family therapists believe that the dynamics of a family has powerful influences on individual members and that treating a psychological problem of one member without taking into account the impact of the family makes it unlikely that any change will occur. Furthermore, problems encountered by one family member affect other family members. For example, problems in the relationship between parents affect children, and problems with one child affect the other children and the parents (Dadds et al., 1987; Jouriles et al., 1988; Sanders et al., 1997; Walker et al., 1996). However, some family therapists believe that the links between pathology and families run deeper still. They argue that the family constrains behavior because of the interconnected dynamics of the situation (Nichols & Minuchin, 1999). They might question, for example, what the impact of a wife overcoming her fears of driving might have on the marital relationship. Would her newfound mobility create jealousy in her husband? To the extent that these questions have relevance, family therapy endeavors to resolve them.

EVALUATION

Studying the impact of the sociocultural environment is inherently difficult because of its complexity and because of ethical constraints. For example, one cannot ethically assign couples to divorce or stay married to determine whether divorce increases risk for depression. Without that level of control, it is impossible to know whether divorce increased the risk for depression, whether early manifestations of depression increased the risk for divorce, or whether some other factor, such as drinking or excessive anger, contributed to both the divorce and the depression. Despite these constraints, however, sociocultural research has contributed to the understanding of many forms of psychopathology.

....

family therapy   A variation on traditional individual therapy, based on the belief that the dynamics of a family have powerful influences on individual members and that treating a psychological problem of one member without taking into account the impact of the family makes it difficult for any change to occur.

evolutionary perspective   Looks at how psychopathology evolves across generations, whether it was once adaptive, and what contributions the environment makes.

evolution   The theory that the nature of living things changes over generations in response to specific environmental pressures.

natural selection   The process whereby genetic traits that foster survival and reproduction increase in frequency across generations because the organisms that exhibit those traits survive longer and reproduce more successfully.

Sociocultural research provides clues about factors that may contribute to psychopathology. These clues can focus more specific research from other perspectives. For example, if alcoholism runs in families and is more common in men and in certain socioeconomic groups, research can begin to narrow down the possibilities. Genetic research can determine whether genes or family influences account for the tendency of the alcoholism to run in families. Evaluating cultural differences may uncover possible factors, such as attitudes toward drinking. However, because studying sociocultural influences is so difficult, scientists must be cautious in their interpretations of sociocultural data.

Check Yourself 4.4

The Sociocultural Perspective

1. How is social class defined? What is the relationship between social class and schizophrenia?
2. How do cultural factors affect psychopathology?
3. What is the difference between primary prevention and secondary prevention?

Ponder this . . .   *More than a dozen forms of psychopathology show a significant difference between the proportions of males and females affected. Give some thought to how the role expectations of men and women differ and to how those differences might affect the rates of psychopathology. What symptoms might you expect to be more common in males and what symptoms more common in females?*

THE EVOLUTIONARY PERSPECTIVE

Evolutionary Impact

All living creatures are born with specific characteristics dictated by their genetic code. Humans share about 99.8% of their genes with all other human beings (Gould, 1995) and 98.4% of their genes with chimpanzees (Diamond, 1992). In other words, humans differ from chimps in fewer than 2% of their genes. One's basic shape and features, organs and the way they function, and perceptual and neurological systems are virtually identical from person to person and are remarkably similar to those of other species. These features evolved over millions of years.

Rather than focus on the immediate cause of abnormality, the **evolutionary perspective** asks how psychopathology evolves across generations, whether it was once adaptive, and what contributions the environment makes. In this section, you will learn the basics of evolutionary theory and how this theory can provide unique insights into psychopathology. As you will see, the evolutionary perspective integrates other perspectives and yet is completely dependent on those other perspectives to explain specific disorders in specific individuals.

THE CONCEPT OF EVOLUTION

The theory of evolution has had an enormous influence on both biology and psychology. **Evolution** is based on the principle that the nature of living things changes over generations in response to specific environmental pressures. Charles Darwin (1809–1882) is credited with formulating the theory of evolution (Darwin, 1859), although he was not the first to propose it. Alfred Russel Wallace, another eminent naturalist, proposed a similar theory at about the same time as Darwin, and the ancient Greeks proposed crude evolutionary concepts centuries earlier. However, Darwin's concepts provided the best conceptual framework for organizing and explaining a vast array of observations.

Darwin's concept of evolution is based on a process called **natural selection.** He observed that there is variability in the characteristics of organisms, both within and across species. In the day-to-day struggle to survive, organisms draw on strengths and struggle to overcome weaknesses. Significant weaknesses lead to an early death, thus preventing reproduction. Those genetic traits that foster survival and reproduction increase in frequency across generations, because the organisms endowed with those traits survive longer and reproduce. Note that survival and reproduction, not happiness, drive natural selection. This point will be critical in later discussions of specific psychopathologies. From the perspective of natural selection, a miserably unhappy person who survives and has children is more genetically "fit" than a happy, productive person who never reproduces.

An evolutionary perspective on psychopathology focuses on the question of why apparently maladaptive behavior exists at all. How would such behavior develop and why hasn't natural selection eliminated it long ago? Wouldn't people like Dan or Gary or Monica be less likely to survive and reproduce—not just in today's world but also in the much harsher world of several thousand years ago? If genes contributed to such symptoms, shouldn't natural selection reduce their frequency? Could currently maladaptive behaviors have been adaptive—or at least less maladaptive—in another era? These questions go beyond the immediate causes of abnormal behavior, forcing scientists to view abnormal behavior within the context of the everyday struggle to survive.

Criticisms of Evolution. Although evolution is a well-established scientific theory, it does have its critics. The 1925 Scopes Monkey Trial, in which Clarence Darrow defended the right of John T. Scopes to teach evolution in the state of Tennessee, is perhaps the most celebrated of the challenges to evolution. The state of Tennessee had made it illegal to teach evolution in public schools, and Scopes, a high school biology teacher, defied the law. Although Scopes lost the case because he clearly broke the law, he succeeded in spurring a national debate that continues today. Challenges to the presentation of evolutionary concepts in grade school and high school textbooks still occur frequently (Firenze, 1997). Nevertheless, the theory of evolution has established itself in science by providing coherent and parsimonious explanations of thousands of phenomena (Ridley, 1996). Fields as divergent as biology geology, psychology, and genetics all build theories around the concept of evolution. The concept of evolution organizes this vast array of data in a way that no other theory has done (Keeling, 1997). Of course, scientists routinely disagree about the specifics of evolution. Such healthy debates are common in science, and they do not mean that scientists reject evolution (Berra, 1990). It may be that much of the controversy surrounding the theory of evolution arises from a misunderstanding of the concept, as illustrated in the nearby Modern Myths box.

Factors That Affect Survival. Survival is the driving force behind evolution. If an organism fails to

Few people have had more impact on science than Charles Darwin. His theory of evolution has shaped the thinking of scientists in dozens of disciplines and has helped scientists to integrate findings from diverse scientific fields.

MODERN Myths

Humans Descended FROM Apes

No theory has been more misunderstood by the public than the theory of evolution. This may be because, like all complex scientific theories, the theory of evolution does not translate well into everyday language, and yet the public wants to know about this theory, because it represents a view of human beings that seems at odds with other philosophical perspectives.

Humans did not descend from apes, as many people believe. Rather, the best evidence suggests that apes and humans descended from a common ancestor (Diamond, 1992; Zimmer, 2001). Evolution is character-

ized by these splits, in which a species diverges into separate lines, often after groups become geographically isolated. This geographic isolation allows the normal changes over time to accumulate until the groups evolve into different species. Perhaps because the term *evolution* implies evolving from one species into another, many people mistakenly believe that humans must have evolved from species that still exist. Not so. The species from which both modern apes and humans evolved is long gone, but its genetic legacy lives on.

Darwin was able to see many examples of the process of divergence in his living record of animals and

plants. This monumental achievement occurred almost a century before the discovery of DNA. On the basis of the similarities he observed among species, he was able to make reasonable guesses about the evolutionary path for each species. Today, scientists make more precise judgments about evolutionary history by comparing the overlap in DNA between species (Diamond, 1992; Atherly et al., 1999). The extensive fossil record, advances in DNA technology, and careful analysis of every clue gleaned from living organisms and fossilized remains have provided the information on which scientists have pieced evolutionary history together.

---

survive and reproduce, natural selection has limited its influence on succeeding generations. Genes shape many things that contribute to survival, such as appearance, which may provide camouflage. However, the most important element in survival is behavior. Listed below are a few examples.

▶ An animal with keen senses may be more successful than others at finding food.

▶ Some animals rely on social cooperation. Ants and bees, for example, have evolved elaborate social structures in which each member has a specific role.

▶ Some animals, such as dogs, survive by developing mutually beneficial relationships with other species. In exchange for affection, protection, and specialized work, such as herding sheep or tracking game, these animals have linked their fortune to a powerful and uniquely adapted group—human beings.

▶ Parenting contributes to the survival of the parents' genes because having offspring is of little value unless those offspring survive to reproduce. Parenting is especially critical in humans because human infants are completely helpless at birth.

▶ Adaptable organisms have an enormous advantage over organisms that do not adapt. Learning what

is dangerous and how to minimize the danger dramatically increases the likelihood of survival.

ANIMAL AND HUMAN BEHAVIOR

Natural selection constantly tests the make-up of species. Successful species may branch out into variations of the species and may in time become so distinct that new species evolve. Not surprisingly, a new species brings with it most of the characteristics of the old. This process can be complex and exceedingly difficult to recreate after the fact. Fossil records provide clues to some of the pathways of evolution. Figure 4.5 gives a graphical illustration of the best guess for the recent evolutionary ancestry of human beings. It is worth noting that if one could construct the evolutionary history of all species, it would be several million times the size of Figure 4.5.

Surviving in a complex, constantly changing, and often hostile environment requires just the right collection of characteristics. Some characteristics prove to be so valuable that they quickly come to dominate a species and then remain critical as the species diverges into other species. These characteristics form the basis on which not one but many species build their survival. For example, tens of thousands of species use a circulatory system very similar to that found in humans. Such a circulatory system is so effective at distributing nutrients

[FIGURE 4.5]

The Evolution of Human Beings

This chart illustrates scientists' best guess for the recent evolutionary development of human beings. Of course, such charts are constantly revised as new data provide a more detailed picture of evolutionary development.

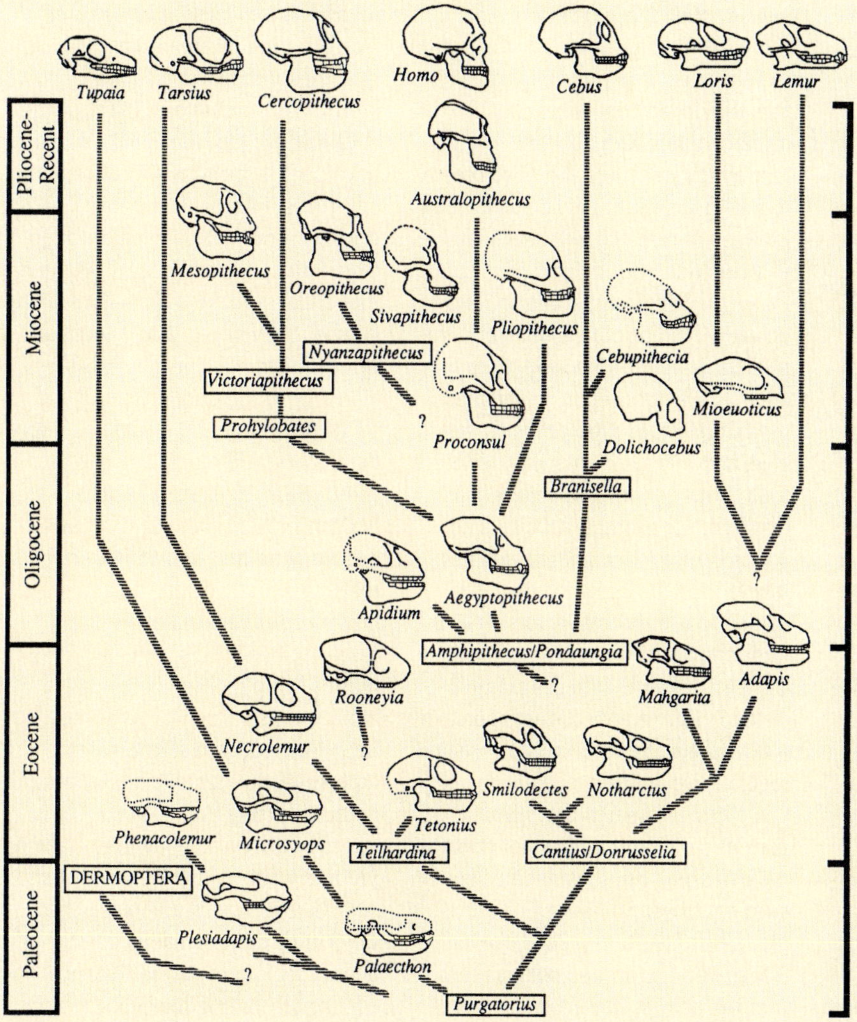

SOURCE: *Fig. 2.28, p. 97 from* The Human Career *by R. G. Klein. Copyright © 1999. Reprinted by permission of The University of Chicago Press.*

and oxygen throughout the body that this adaptation has survived millions of years of evolutionary pressure (Ridley, 1996).

The fact that humans are similar in many ways to other species means that scientists can learn about human functioning by studying other species. The human brain is considerably larger than the brains of most other species, yet many of the structures of the brain and their functioning are identical in humans, dogs, cats, and rats, and this enables scientists to learn about human functioning by carefully studying animals. As we saw earlier, humans have the ability to adapt to momentary demands of the situation, and they can also learn from their experiences. Animal models have helped scientists to understand these processes. This text will draw frequently on information from animal studies. The careful study of humans, combined with information gleaned from animal research, has produced significant insights into several forms of psychopathology. Research with animals, like research with humans, must be guided by ethical principles. The nearby Focus box discusses some of these ethical issues.

FOCUS The ethics of animal research

Today, there is a heightened concern for ethical principles in the conduct of any research project, but that was not always the case. Prior to World War II, there were no real ethical guidelines for research and no appointed bodies whose job it was to oversee the ethics of ongoing research projects. The combination of the ethical atrocities committed in the name of "research" by Nazi scientists and the growing realization that a few researchers in the United States and elsewhere were conducting research using ethically questionable procedures led to the development of formal ethical principles for human research and to the formation of Institutional Review Boards—bodies that review research projects to ascertain that each upholds the letter and the spirit of these ethical principles. These ethical principles have been gradually expanded and clarified over the past 50 years and are a critical element in all human research. The American Psychological Association (APA) took the lead in this effort and continues to have one of the most comprehensive and sensitive sets of ethical principles (APA, 1998).

Although the early ethical focus was on human research, there has also been considerable discussion and debate about the ethical principles that should apply to animal research.

Every major professional organization that relies on animal research has published and/or endorsed a comprehensive set of ethical guidelines. Again, the APA has taken a lead in this area; its formation of professional committees to address concerns about animal research dates back to 1925. The current ethical principles and government regulations seek to provide all animals involved in research with adequate and humane housing and care, to minimize discomfort and pain, and to do everything possible to minimize the number of animals involved. Currently, animals are not used in research and teaching if other alternatives are available, and this has dramatically reduced the number of animals involved in research. For example, 30 years ago it was common for undergraduates taking their first research methods course to use laboratory rats. That is rare today. When research questions can be answered with cell cultures instead of a live animal, that approach is now used. But some animal research requires live animals.

Animal research may always be controversial, and it does not hurt to have periodic vigorous debates about such controversial issues. For example, Ulrich (1991), a former animal researcher, has argued persuasively that the animal research practices of the 1970s and 1980s were insensitive to the animals and, like many aspects

of the society, tended to be wasteful and thoughtless. He and others like him have argued for a more thoughtful and sensitive use of animals in research, and those arguments have been heeded. But as Neal Miller (1985) has pointed out, many of the advances derived from animal research have been enormous and would not otherwise have been possible. There is virtually no medical breakthrough that did not depend heavily on information learned from animal research (Carroll & Overmier, 2001). Animal research has also contributed substantially to the understanding and treatment of several psychiatric disorders, as we will see later in the text (Dess, 2001; Zinbarg & Mineka, 2001). Furthermore, not only have people benefited, but so have animals. Veterinary care is substantially better today because of animal research. In addition, the management of wildlife has been much improved as a result of what has been learned from animal research. Of course, the benefits do not automatically justify the research. The ethics of all research involves making judgments about benefits and costs. Animal researchers, like researchers who study human beings, must always seek to minimize the negative consequences and maximize the positive consequences of their work.

THE EVOLUTION OF INTELLIGENCE

Although most human brain structures are remarkably similar to those of other species, the cerebral cortex is greatly enlarged in humans. It is interesting to speculate on how this rapid evolution of the cerebral cortex occurred. Some scientists believe that the development of crude language in early humans put a huge premium on cerebral development (Diamond, 1992; Wills, 1993). An enlarged, more capable brain could enhance communication—and thus enhance survival—in such

social creatures as humans. The human cortex is massive, containing roughly 30 billion neurons and 300 trillion neuronal connections. In contrast, the rat cortex is approximately 1/500 this size, and the cortex of the chimpanzee is approximately 1/4 as large.

The cerebral cortex is enormously important in people's day-to-day functioning. Most perceptual processing is done in the cortex. The identification of meaning in the environment and the communication of that meaning to others would not be possible without the cerebral cortex. Humans have created extensive technology by observing and reasoning about nature and, most important, by communicating that knowledge to others. Were it not for communication, every generation would literally have to reinvent the wheel. In fact, every generation would have to reinvent every technology. Creating stone tools is far from simple, and it is not likely that people who had to develop those crafts from scratch in each generation would ever get beyond stone tools.

Thought processes are critical to human survival and central to many forms of psychopathology. Some disorders disrupt thought processes. Other disorders may be exacerbated or even caused by thought processes. As critical as the intellect is to humans, it is a fragile asset that can be disrupted in many ways. There is no form of psychopathology in which intellectual processes are irrelevant. Even if thought processes are not affected by the pathology, they may have contributed to it or they may be relevant in treating it. At the very least, people observe and react to their own behavior, sometimes making things better and sometimes making things worse.

HAVE HUMAN BEINGS OUTPACED EVOLUTION?

Natural selection weeds out characteristics that are not well suited to the environment. Species become extinct or change across generations in the face of such pressure. Natural selection typically operates over thousands or millions of years. Environments may change over such long periods, but the change is often gradual, and organisms typically have time to evolve. There are exceptions. Evidence suggests that the dinosaurs, along with half the other species on earth, were driven to extinction 65 million years ago by a cataclysmic collision of an asteroid with the earth (Kerr, 1996). This collision created a huge dust cloud that encircled the earth, cutting off the sunlight critical to plant growth and thus breaking the food chain. As a result, the process of natural selection was given a good swift kick. Many scientists believe that evolution is characterized by such swift kicks—a process known as **punctuated equilibrium** (Gould & Eldredge, 1993).

Human beings may be creating changes in the environment every bit as dramatic as the changes that eliminated half the earth's species 65 million years ago (Nesse & Williams, 1994). Humans have developed tools, a social structure, and a language sufficiently powerful to communicate ideas across time and space. They have constructed vast societies that collectively are able to achieve much more than small groups could ever ac-

complish. They have also created technologies that have changed people's lives and the nature of this planet. Bodies and minds that evolved through millions of years have been forced to take on a world that changes more in a single lifetime than one might normally expect in a millennium. There is now a mismatch between the human species that evolved over millions of years and the environment that humans have created over the last few hundred years. Think about how work has changed. Early humans were hunters and gatherers. Even 300 years ago, most of human effort focused on the production of food and shelter. In the United States, 3% of the population now produce more than enough food to feed the entire country (Famighetti, 1997). Today people work in offices and factories, which forces them to change their social interactions and imposes new adaptation demands. Computers and telecommunications,

In the blink of an eye in evolutionary terms, human beings have gone from a hunter-gatherer environment to the complex technological environment of today. People are facing today's world with bodies that have probably evolved little since our species wandered grassy plains in search of food. Perhaps some of what is called psychopathology today was actually adaptive in the world in which humans evolved but is no longer adaptive in today's vastly more complex world.

punctuated equilibrium The theory that evolution occurs rapidly at times when massive environmental changes affect natural selection.

mass transit, and incredible advances in the health care system have an enormous impact on everyday lives. Without medicine, optometry, and dentistry, human life expectancies would be much shorter. An increase in the average life expectancy changes social systems. You are in the middle of these rapid changes, struggling to adapt with a body and mind only slightly different from that possessed by ancestors who used stone tools to carve out a living. Therefore, it is surprising that psychopathologies are not more common. The ability of humans to adapt to such a rapidly changing culture is remarkable, though not unlimited. This **mismatch theory**—the mismatch between what humans have evolved to handle and what they are required to handle today—may be critical in understanding psychopathology.

EVOLUTION AS AN INTEGRATIVE PERSPECTIVE

Evolution is a unique perspective on psychopathology in two ways. The first is that, unlike other perspectives, evolution forces one to think beyond individuals and try to understand how pathology evolved. Stepping back to question how things developed across generations leads to insights that may inspire research into the mechanisms behind a particular pathology. The second is that evolution integrates other perspectives. Because evolutionary theory does little to explain why a particular individual is behaving abnormally now, scientists must turn to other perspectives for answers to that question. For example, are there genetic influences that contribute to pathology? If so, what are the biological mechanisms that translate those genetic influences into behavior? How does the behavior affect others, and how do the consequences of the behavior affect future behavior? How do people interpret what is happening to them, and what effects are those thoughts having? How does the social environment affect the behavior? These questions must be addressed to explain the pathology of a specific individual, and they all come from the other theoretical perspectives. These questions address the **proximal causes** of the pathology—those factors that are immediately responsible for an event. For example, if a person slips and falls off a ladder, the proximal causes may include gravity, a slippery substance on the steps of the ladder, and perhaps the distracting effect of hornets buzzing around the person's head. **Distal causes** are more remote factors that set up the conditions leading to the event. For example, distal causes might focus on why there were so many hornets that season, how the ladder step became slippery, and whether using a different type of ladder could have prevented that problem. Most perspectives are concerned with proximal causes for psychopathology. The evolutionary perspective ties them all together by focusing on common distal causes—why and how these factors evolved to produce the pathology.

TREATMENT

Although the evolutionary perspective is enormously helpful in understanding psychopathology, it has so far contributed little to treatment. However, animal research, which follows logically from an evolutionary perspective, has contributed to both the physiological and behavior perspectives, which have made significant contributions to treatment.

EVALUATION

The strength of the evolutionary perspective is that it provides a set of integrating principles. Other perspectives deal with how psychopathology develops in an individual and what might be done to help that individual regain normal functioning. In contrast, the evolutionary perspective focuses on how the processes and structures that contribute to psychopathology evolved and why behavior that may once have been adaptive may have become maladaptive. Although the evolutionary perspective is unique in its ability to integrate ideas from other perspectives, caution must be exercised. Most of the course of human evolution is unknown, and probably much of it will remain unknown because no permanent evidence was left behind. Nevertheless, the evolutionary perspective can stimulate broader conceptualizations about psychopathology, and thus it may contribute to creative ideas that can then be tested within other perspectives.

Check Yourself 4.5

The Evolutionary Perspective

1. What process drives evolution?
2. How can behavior affect natural selection?
3. What does it mean that humans may have outpaced their evolution?
4. What is the difference between distal and proximal causes?

---

mismatch theory   The theory that there is a mismatch between what humans have evolved to handle and what they are required to handle today.

proximal causes   Those factors that are immediately responsible for an event.

distal causes   Remote factors that set up the conditions leading to an event.

Ponder this . . .   *Think about Dan's severe depression and the behavior associated with it. Could depression have survival value? What do you predict would happen to the rate of depression over time if it had no survival value?*

USING THESE PERSPECTIVES

The advantage of having multiple perspectives is that each perspective provides a simplified map of the complexity of human behavior. Scientists have no choice but to rely on such simplifications, because behavior is far too complex to try to make sense of it as a whole. Each of the simplified views that the various perspectives represent focuses on only a portion of behavior. Nevertheless, if scientists choose a perspective wisely and apply it to a given psychopathology, they are often rewarded with a surprisingly useful understanding of that pathology. More important, this understanding often translates into effective treatment, which is the ultimate goal. Because no perspective incorporates every aspect of a person, it is desirable to apply more than one perspective to develop multiple insights.

The perspectives discussed in Chapter 3 and 4 have been applied to most forms of psychopathology. Therefore, one could look at every form of psychopathology from each of the perspectives. That will *not* be the approach of this text, however. Not every perspective has led to fruitful research and provided an understanding that could form the basis for effective treatment or prevention. Therefore, only those perspectives that have made major contributions to understanding a disorder will be featured in the chapters on the various disorders. Sometimes this is a judgment call. More often, the research data make it clear what perspectives have been most productive. This does not mean that the other perspectives have not been applied or that they might not lead to the next breakthrough; it means only that so far, their contributions have been more modest.

 ## SUMMARY

THE PHYSIOLOGICAL PERSPECTIVE

- The physiological perspective focuses on the biological mechanisms behind behavior and on the factors that influenced those mechanisms, such as genetics.
- The central nervous system gathers information, selects appropriate responses, and implements those responses. The autonomic nervous system provides a link between the central nervous system and the peripheral organs. When people are faced with a threatening situation, the sympathetic branch of the autonomic nervous system is activated, preparing and coordinating a number of organs for defensive action. The parasympathetic branch of the autonomic nervous system activates individual organs to perform body maintenance tasks.
- The endocrine system uses hormones that are secreted by glands to regulate and coordinate the activities of groups of organs.

THE COGNITIVE-BEHAVIORAL PERSPECTIVE

- The cognitive-behavioral perspective expands on the behavioral perspective by including a person's thoughts in the analysis of behavior.
- Beck and Ellis presented cognitive models that emphasized the role of automatic thoughts and irrational assumptions, respectively, in determining feelings and behavior.
- Factoring in the role of thoughts increases one's understanding of classical and operant conditioning.
- Modeling requires no direct experience with contingencies but, rather, relies on observing what happens to others.

THE COGNITIVE NEUROSCIENCE PERSPECTIVE

- The cognitive neuroscience perspective focuses on such cognitive processes as perception and memory and the brain mechanisms behind these processes.
- Memory is a critical element of all cognitive activity, but memory limitations and biases may underlie many forms of psychopathology.
- Perceptual biases enhance the efficiency with which people scan and process the environment, but they may also contribute to psychopathology.
- Many cognitive functions are overlearned so that they become automatic. Automatic processes require little conscious thought and therefore can be performed with little effort. However, a pathological automatic process can be difficult to reverse.

THE SOCIOCULTURAL PERSPECTIVE

- The sociocultural perspective argues that the social environment shapes behavior.

- Social scientists have studied a number of sociocultural factors, including social class, social and gender roles, social stresses, and family dynamics.
- The sociocultural perspective has spawned two interventions: community psychology and family therapy.

THE EVOLUTIONARY PERSPECTIVE

- The concept of evolution is based on the principle of natural selection.
- Evolution is the logical link that explains why animal research has been such a valuable contributor to the scientific understanding of human behavior.
- Intellectual functioning in humans is an impressive evolutionary achievement, but it is fragile and is often affected by psychopathology.

- Human beings have so dramatically reshaped the world that they may have outpaced their own evolutionary development.
- The evolutionary perspective integrates ideas from other perspectives. It focuses on distal causes for psychopathology, such as how it evolved and what purpose it might have once served. Other perspectives address proximal causes for psychopathology.

USING THESE PERSPECTIVES

- This text will emphasize only those perspectives that have contributed significantly to the understanding of a given psychopathology.

 KEY TERMS

attention   (87)
automatic thoughts   (80)
autonomic nervous system   (76)
Beck's cognitive-behavioral therapy or CBT   (83)
biological reductionism   (79)
brain stem   (75)
central nervous system   (75)
cerebellum   (75)
cerebral cortex   (75)
cognitive-behavioral perspective   (79)
cognitive neuroscience perspective   (84)
cognitive psychologists   (85)
community psychology   (90)
culture   (89)
declarative memories   (85)
distal causes   (98)
dominant gene   (72)
electroconvulsive therapy (ECT), or
   electroshock therapy   (78)
emergenic traits   (73)
endocrine system   (77)
evolution   (92)
evolutionary perspective   (92)
explicit memories   (85)
family therapy   (92)
fight-or-flight response   (76)
flashbulb memories   (86)
hormones   (77)
implicit memories   (85)
individual differences   (85)
irrational assumptions   (81)

lateralization   (76)
limbic system   (75)
memory   (85)
memory biases   (87)
Mendelian inheritance   (72)
midbrain structures   (75)
mismatch theory   (98)
modeling, or observational learning   (83)
natural selection   (92)
neuron   (75)
neurotransmitters   (75)
parasympathetic nervous system   (76)
perceptual biases   (88)
physiological perspective   (72)
polygenic   (72)
prefrontal lobotomy   (78)
primary prevention   (90)
priming   (87)
procedural memories   (85)
proximal causes   (98)
psychosurgery   (78)
punctuated equilibrium   (97)
rational emotive behavior therapy, or REBT   (83)
recessive gene   (72)
secondary prevention   (90)
social class   (90)
sociocultural perspective   (89)
sympathetic nervous system   (76)
synapse   (75)
treatment protocols   (84)

SUGGESTED READINGS

Nesse, R. M., & Williams, G. (1994). *Why we get sick: The new science of Darwinian medicine.* New York: New York Times Books. This fascinating and thoughtful review of medical and psychological pathologies from an evolutionary perspective raises questions about the wisdom of some current treatment approaches.

chapterfive

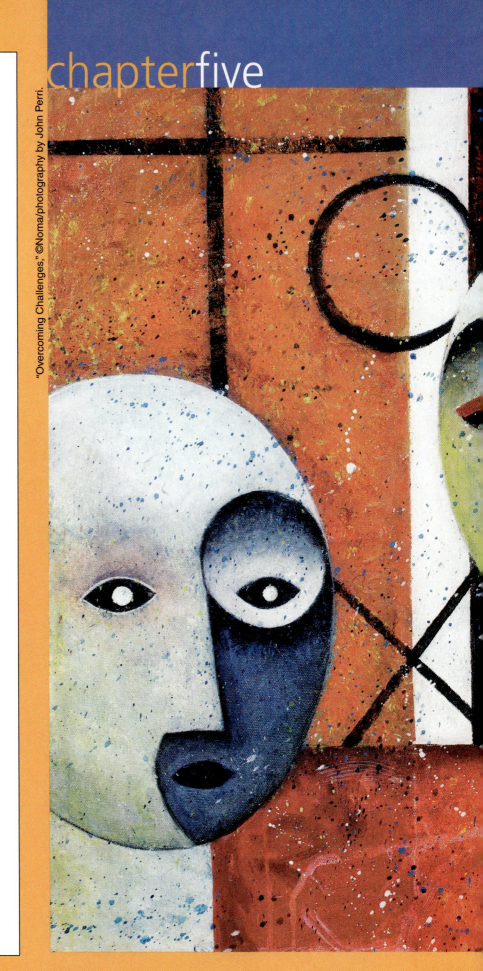

"Overcoming Challenges," ©Noma/photography by John Perri.

Schizophrenia and Other Psychotic Disorders

Could Not Get Control

JAMES James, a 28-year-old, single man, has lived most of the last 9 years in mental hospitals or residential care facilities. He was first diagnosed with schizophrenia at age 18, although emotional problems were apparent long before then. His teachers consistently described him as "spacey," and his classmates largely avoided him. He never dated, has no friends, and has had strained relationships with family members since high school. James's grades slipped badly during his junior year, and his class contributions became increasingly bizarre. By the end of his junior year, he was telling everyone about the great powers given to him by God and how he would use them for the betterment of humanity. He was arrested at age 17 for harassing restaurant patrons, telling them they were evil and that God would punish them. The judge gave him probation on the condition that he seek psychiatric treatment. Instead, he disappeared, living on the street and sleeping in alleys or dumpsters. On rare occasions when he visited home, his parents would beg him to go for treatment, but he always refused.

Two years later, James was spotted standing on a park bench in his underwear talking gibberish to a group of onlookers. After a court-ordered psychiatric evaluation, James spent the next 26 months in a psychiatric hospital. During that time, he improved with medication and a supportive environment, and he has required only brief hospitalizations since that time. He is currently living in a residential facility for people with severe psychiatric disorders. He spends most of his day at a day treatment facility and most evenings in his room by himself. He still has bizarre and unusual ideas and often talks to imaginary figures. Most often he sits quietly, apparently unaware of much of what is going on around him. He tried living with his parents twice, but each time he was back in the hospital in a few weeks with severe psy-

chotic symptoms. The quiet pace of the residential facility and the day treatment program seems to serve him well.

On the Edge

SUZANNE Everyone who knew Suzanne knew that she was fragile. She had good, supportive friends and a stable job, although she was underemployed as a clerk, given her three years of college. She had experienced two serious breakdowns previously, but was able to return to work in less than two weeks each time. One of these episodes required a four-day psychiatric hospitalization. Now 35, she had just gone through the breakup of a two-year relationship, which had pushed her over the edge. She was hearing voices that told her that her boyfriend had really been a plant from the CIA. She talked at length with friends who visited her in the hospital, but her conversation made very little sense. She was very paranoid and angry one moment, strangely jovial the next, and tearful the next. Her voice was animated, but her face showed no response. The episode lasted nearly three weeks this time, and it was nearly six weeks before Suzanne was strong enough to return to work.

Schizophrenia is one of the most dramatic and frightening of all psychiatric disorders. It is characterized by disruption of normal perceptual and thought processes, personality, and **affect,** the external expression of emotion. Schizophrenia is classified as a psychotic disorder.

affect The external expression of emotion.

Psychotic disorders involve such severe symptomatology that the person has essentially lost touch with reality. In general, the earlier a person develops schizophrenia, the worse the prognosis or likelihood of recovery. James is a good example of early-onset schizophrenia. He is stable now and out of the hospital, but he is unable to hold a job, plan for the future, or even carry on a meaningful conversation. Suzanne is an example of a milder case of schizophrenia. Although there were subtle indications of pathology prior to Suzanne's most recent episode, she had functioned adequately before, and she recovered reasonably from even this most recent episode. Nevertheless, her brush with schizophrenia significantly affected her life. Schizophrenia is often a devastating disorder, which dramatically affects the lives of those afflicted as well as the lives of their loved ones.

Approximately 1% of the population will develop schizophrenia during their lifetime (APA, 2000; Narrow et al., 2002). It occurs equally often in men and women and is found in all cultures. Although small variations occur (Katz et al., 1988; Maslowski, 1988), the symptoms of schizophrenia are generally consistent across cultures (Taleb et al., 1996). However, schizophrenia is dramatically overrepresented in the lower social classes (Hollingshead & Redlich, 1958). Most people who develop schizophrenia develop it early in their adult life. Curiously, women tend to develop the disorder about 5 years later, on average, than men, and women tend to have a slightly less severe course and a better prognosis (APA, 2000; Hambrecht et al., 1992; Saugstad, 1989). One can obtain a visual idea of when a disorder develops by constructing an age-of-risk curve, as illustrated in Figure 5.1. The age-of-risk curve shows the age at which people first develop the disorder. It is sometimes graphed as a cumulative proportion curve, which shows at a glance how many of the people who will eventually develop the

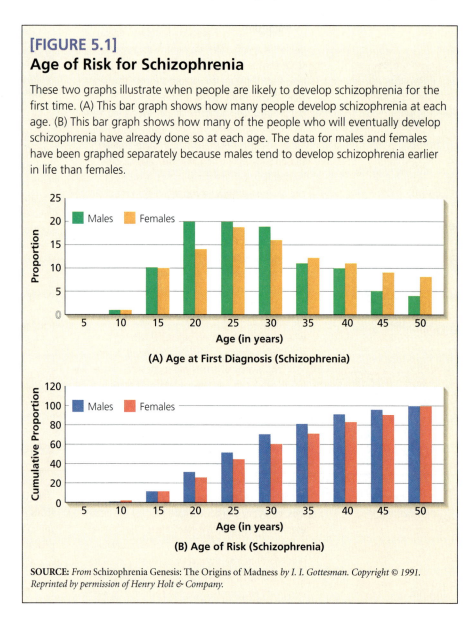

[FIGURE 5.1]
Age of Risk for Schizophrenia

These two graphs illustrate when people are likely to develop schizophrenia for the first time. (A) This bar graph shows how many people develop schizophrenia at each age. (B) This bar graph shows how many of the people who will eventually develop schizophrenia have already done so at each age. The data for males and females have been graphed separately because males tend to develop schizophrenia earlier in life than females.

(A) Age at First Diagnosis (Schizophrenia)

(B) Age of Risk (Schizophrenia)

SOURCE: *From* Schizophrenia Genesis: The Origins of Madness *by I. I. Gottesman. Copyright © 1991. Reprinted by permission of Henry Holt & Company.*

FOCUS | What is schizophrenia?

Emil Kraepelin was the first to identify a subgroup of individuals whose symptoms closely resemble the modern diagnosis of schizophrenia. To refer to this group, he used the term *dementia praecox* which literally means "early-onset intellectual deterioration." He considered this progressive deterioration to be a defining characteristic and speculated that the disorder had a biological cause. Eugen Bleuler, who coined the term *schizophrenia* to refer to this group, noted that some people with the symptoms of dementia praecox did not show the predicted deteriorating course, nor did they always develop symptoms early in life. He argued that early onset and continual deterioration were not inevitable in schizophrenia. Some, like James, show the deteriorating course described by Kraepelin,

whereas others, like Suzanne, show nearly complete recovery.

Virtually no term in the field of psychopathology has been misused in modern speech as often as *schizophrenia*. People talk about their attitude toward something as being "schizophrenic," when what they really mean is that they are ambivalent. (For example, someone might strongly oppose government intervention in people's lives but also believe that seatbelt laws should be enforced because they save lives.) Another misuse of the term *schizophrenic* is to confuse it with the term *split personality.* The concept of split personality, which is known as dissociative identity disorder in the DSM, will be discussed in Chapter 15. Bleuler coined the term *schizophrenia,* which literally means "splitting of the mind," as a way of emphasizing not a split in personality but,

rather, a disconnect between thoughts and feelings.

Interestingly, there is a rationale for using the term *schizophrenic* to refer to ambivalence, although it has nothing to do with the current colloquial use of the term. Eugen Bleuler (1911/1950) coined both terms in the same classic paper on the topic. His use of the term *ambivalence* emphasized the dramatic contradictions in feelings expressed by people with schizophrenia, apparently with little awareness or concern for these contradictions. The schizophrenic ambivalence described by Bleuler was much stronger than the occasional ambivalence that most people experience. For people with this pathological level of ambivalence, their feelings about a topic were so strong and so dramatically opposite to each other that it was almost as though they were talking about two entirely different things.

The Oscar-winning movie *A Beautiful Mind* provided an accurate portrayal of many of the symptoms of schizophrenia. More importantly, it showed that it is possible to make a life for oneself despite a constant struggle with this disorder.

disorder have done so at each age. For example, about half of all males who will develop schizophrenia have already developed the disorder by about age 25, and about 90% have developed it by age 40.

The nearby Focus box gives a little of the history of the disorder and discusses the meaning of the term *schizophrenia.* This chapter provides an overview of schizophrenia, including descriptions of symptoms, subtypes, possible causes, and current treatment. Also covered in this chapter are two other psychotic disorders: delusional disorder and schizoaffective disorder. Chapter 6 also covers schizophrenia, but with an entirely different purpose. Chapter 6 uses schizophrenia as an example to illustrate research strategies in the field of psychopathology.

psychotic disorders   Disorders so severe that the person has essentially lost touch with reality. Schizophrenia is classified as a psychotic disorder.

SYMPTOMS OF SCHIZOPHRENIA

People with schizophrenia may show a variety of symptoms, although many of these symptoms are not unique to schizophrenia. A person diagnosed with schizophrenia rarely shows all of the symptoms discussed here. Symptoms may vary in intensity from person to person, and milder forms of these symptoms can be found in individuals who are not psychotic.

Psychiatrists make a distinction between positive and negative symptoms of schizophrenia (Andreasen & Olsen, 1982). **Positive symptoms** are clearly deviant behaviors, such as delusions, hallucinations, and thought disorder. **Negative symptoms** are deficit symptoms—that is, they represent a *lack* of normal functioning. Typical negative symptoms are flat affect and loss of capacity for pleasure. As we will see, the distinction between positive and negative symptoms not only helps to organize symptoms but may also have significance in identifying meaningful subgroups of schizophrenia. Our presentation of schizophrenic symptoms will be organized in terms of this positive/negative dichotomy.

POSITIVE SYMPTOMS

This section will describe several positive symptoms of schizophrenia, including thought disorder, delusions, hallucinations, and attentional deficits.

Thought Disorder. **Thought disorder** represents a disruption of normal cognitive functioning and is the most dramatic and obvious symptom of schizophrenia. It involves a collection of symptoms that all seem to represent difficulty in thinking clearly or in expressing thoughts.

- -

positive symptoms   Clearly deviant behaviors, such as delusions, hallucinations, and thought disorder.

negative symptoms   Deficit symptoms—that is, symptoms that represent a lack of normal functioning.

thought disorder   A disruption of normal cognitive functioning; the most dramatic and obvious symptom of schizophrenia.

loosening of associations   Jumping from one topic to another, sometimes in mid-sentence; the most common form of thought disorder in schizophrenia.

word salad   Associations so loose that the words seem random.

neologisms   Made-up words.

clang associations   Ideas strung together on the basis of the sound of the words.

delusions   Beliefs that are not objectively true, that would not be accepted as true within the person's culture, and that the person holds firmly in spite of contradictory evidence.

These symptoms may include loosening of associations, word salad, neologisms, and clang association.

The most common form of thought disorder in schizophrenia is **loosening of associations.** People who show loose associations jump from one topic to another, sometimes in mid-sentence, to the point where it is difficult or impossible to follow their conversation. James showed a loosening of associations so serious that he often made no sense. Comprehending such speech is extremely difficult and frustrating. One is often left with the impression that it would all make sense if only one could listen just a little harder, but that is rarely the case. The point of talking to someone is to communicate something, and many people with schizophrenia are unable to achieve this primary goal. The following example illustrates how dramatic the loosening of associations in schizophrenia can be.

> "I wanted to go, you know. It is no good. . . . She was a beauty. . . . Nobody knew me then, even though I was very old. Ah, why did they have to do that? I would have helped. My grandfather told me about the big one—it was good, in a bad sort of way. She must have been there. I have been hounded and hated since that day of infamy. You don't understand—it hurts!"

Sometimes associations become so loose that the words seem random, a phenomenon called **word salad:**

> "I am the fresh prince elect for god almighty and never again until life do us part."

Although loosening of associations is the most common form of thought disturbance, other disturbances of thought are also found in schizophrenia. Some people with schizophrenia make up words, which are known as **neologisms.** For example, one individual referred to people she thought were plotting against her as "clandestites," a term that is apparently based on the word *clandestine* but has no meaning except to this individual. Others string ideas together on the basis of the sound of the words, creating **clang associations.** The following is a classic example of a clang association. Note that this example also includes several neologisms.

> "She loved to sing, ding, fling, ming, and ping, but never zing bing."

Thought disorder may vary over time. Sometimes, people with schizophrenia may show considerable thought disturbance. At other times, they may be lucid and clear. Sometimes, they are aware that their thoughts are disorganized. At other times, they seem to be totally unaware that anything is wrong.

Delusions. **Delusions** are beliefs that are not objectively true, that would not be accepted as true within the person's culture, and that the person holds firmly in spite of contradictory evidence. People may believe, for example, that other people are plotting against them. Such a belief would be called a **paranoid delusion.** For example, one person with schizophrenia believed that organized crime members had implanted electrodes in his brain so that they could control his behavior. He believed that they implanted these electrodes because they wanted to take over the nightclub he managed. This is an especially interesting example because it illustrates how one must be cautious about what is labeled a delusion. In this case, there were no implanted electrodes, but organized crime had indeed taken over his club, along with half a dozen other downtown clubs in the city. Another common type of delusion is the **delusion of grandeur,** in which people believe they are special or have special powers. James had such delusions, believing that God and chosen him to rid the world of evil.

Believing in magical powers may or may not be delusional, depending on the general beliefs of the person's culture. Belief in Voodoo, which is widely accepted in some cultures, is not delusional in someone from such a culture. People who show severe loosening of associations may also show delusional thinking. The delusions in such individuals are often disorganized, have a bizarre quality, and typically change over time. James's religious delusions fell into this category. They changed constantly and often made no sense. For example, he told his doctor that he knew God had chosen him when he realized that the road signs turned into crosses whenever he passed by. Other people with schizophrenia show a **fixed delusional system,** in which the delusions remain constant over time. These people seem to interpret everything that happens to them in the context of their delusional system. Interestingly, such individuals often show less thought disorder and can appear normal when you talk with them about matters unrelated to their delusional system. However, once you start talking about their delusions, they will quickly impress you as seriously disturbed.

All symptoms should be evaluated within the individual's cultural context. Believing in Voodoo, for example, may be delusional in some cultures but perfectly acceptable in others.

Hallucinations. People with schizophrenia often show **hallucinations,** which are perceptual experiences that feel real even though there is nothing there to perceive. For example, they may see things that are not there (*visual hallucinations*), hear things that are not there (*auditory hallucinations*), or feel things that are not there (*tactile hallucinations*). The most common hallucinations in schizophrenia are auditory, usually voices that speak to the person, although in some cultures—Kenyan, for example—visual hallucinations are common (Ndetei & Singh, 1983). James often heard voices, and at times he believed that one of the voices was that of God. Suzanne also heard voices during her brief schizophrenic episode. The voices seemed real to both James and Suzanne, and they responded to these voices in the same way they would have responded to anyone talking to them. Like most people who hallucinate, neither thought it unusual that they could not see the person talking or that others could not hear the voices.

Thinking is essential internal speech, which is apparent when people think out loud, talking to themselves. However, most people know that their thoughts are not a disembodied voice talking to them. There is evidence that hallucinatory voices may represent subvocal speech—that is, speech that is not audible. Let's look at the research on this question.

Examining the Evidence

Subvocal speech is common. What evidence is there that it could be the basis of auditory hallucinations? For one thing, small movements in the voice apparatus typically, though not always, occur when people with schizophrenia report auditory hallucinations (Bick & Kinsbourne, 1987; Green & Kinsbourne, 1990; Junginger & Rauscher, 1987). In addition, the brain areas that are normally active when a person is producing speech are active during auditory hallucinations (McGuire et al., 1993, 1996). Furthermore, occupying the voice system by having the person hum a single note will often block hallucinations (Gallagher et al., 1994; Green & Kinsbourne, 1990), although this technique does not always work (Levitt & Waldo, 1991).

paranoid delusion   A false belief that other people are plotting against one.

delusion of grandeur   A belief that one is special or has special powers.

fixed delusional system   Delusions that remain constant over time.

hallucinations   Perceptual experiences that feel real although there is nothing there to perceive.

People with schizophrenia are often surprised that they can block the voices so easily.

Although such data suggest that subvocalization may be part of the mechanism of auditory hallucinations, it is clear that other elements are also necessary. Most people subvocalize when they read, but they do not experience those subvocalizations as hallucinatory voices. To experience subvocalizations as voices, there has to be a source attribution error—that is, the person must experience the subvocalization as coming from some other place than the self. How much evidence is there that such misattributions are found in schizophrenia? To date, there is only limited evidence. People with schizophrenia are more likely to misattribute the source of words they hear than people without the disorder, and those individuals with schizophrenia who were actively hallucinating were more likely than nonhallucinating people with schizophrenia to make such errors (Brebion et al., 2000). However, additional studies of this source misattribution will be required before one can have confidence that it partially explains hallucinations.

Evolutionary Impact

The existence of hallucinations suggests that there is a basic breakdown in the perceptual processing system. Human perceptual systems are remarkable in their efficiency. They have evolved to process information rapidly and to use that information to formulate appropriate action. Remembering the source of the information is as critical as remembering the information. For example, if you daydreamed about winning the lottery, you certainly want to remember that this thought was only a daydream, not a real event. Otherwise, you might be tempted to spend money you do not have. People generate and process images and thoughts all the time to help them solve everyday problems or think hypothetically about problems that might appear in the future. In most cases, people easily distinguish their thoughts from real events, although there is mounting evidence that everyone tends to blur these distinctions over time (Loftus & Ketcham, 1991, 1994). People with schizophrenia, however, appear to be unable to distinguish real from imagined events. Scientists do not know the mechanism behind this problem, but it is clear that some of the symptoms of schizophrenia, such as hallucinations, can be understood as stemming from this problem (Brebion et al., 2000; Keefe et al., 1999a).

Attentional Deficits. People with schizophrenia often complain of difficulty focusing their attention, especially during the early stages of the disorder (Chapman & Chapman, 1973). Some describe feeling bombarded by

stimuli from every direction. Although such attentional problems are typically considered a positive symptom of schizophrenia, some argue that they are better regarded as a negative symptom—specifically, the inability to focus attention.

Most people do not appreciate how critical attention is to functioning. To read this paragraph, you must ignore all of the interesting things that may be going on around you because those distractions would interfere with your reading. Some distractions are internal. For example, if you are upset about an argument you just had with a friend, it may be difficult to concentrate. Likewise, pain from a sprained ankle affects concentration. One way to appreciate what it might be like to suffer from schizophrenia is to set up a situation in which you are bombarded by two channels of information. Sit between two radios, each tuned to a different talk show. You will instantly feel overwhelmed and will find it almost impossible to pay attention to either show. With tremendous effort, you might be able to focus on one show, but often the two shows will get intermixed. Now imagine what it would be like to have 20 channels of information bombarding you simultaneously—not just people talking, but movements by people or objects, sounds from cars, kids playing, the hum from the ventilation system, the smell of the room, and all the feelings in your body. Shutting out these distractions is difficult or impossible for many people with schizophrenia (Freedman, 1974; Freedman & Chapman, 1973; McGhie & Chapman, 1961). One person described his attentional problems in this way:

> Dispersal is the word that I keep thinking of . . . dispersal meaning from the center out in all directions . . . there is a circle and arrows all heading outward and meeting many different objects. So your attention is just whew—360 degrees. (Freedman & Chapman, 1973, p. 50)

anhedonia   The inability to experience pleasure.

avolition   Apathy or an energy deficit.

alogia   A negative thought disorder in which there is either a poverty of speech or a poverty of content to the speech.

asociality   A lack of interest in social relations.

flat or blunted affect   A lack of emotional display.

catatonia   A psychomotor disturbance of movement and posture.

catatonic stupor   A condition of being mute and apparently unaware of what is going on.

waxy flexibility   A property of catatonic stupor, exhibited when a person's limbs can be moved by someone and he or she will maintain the new position.

inappropriate affect   Unusual and sometimes bizarre emotional responses.

NEGATIVE SYMPTOMS

Negative symptoms of schizophrenia represent behavioral deficits. For example, **anhedonia** is the inability to experience pleasure. People with this deficit often show little interest in activities because they do not experience the rewards normally associated with those activities. **Avolition** represents apathy or an energy deficit. People with this symptom often do not care about critical behaviors such as self-grooming. Consequently, they are often unkempt and may spend day after day doing nothing. **Alogia** represents a negative thought disorder in that there is either a poverty of speech or a poverty of content to the speech. People with alogia rarely talk, and when they do, their speech is often disappointingly sparse. For example, when one person with schizophrenia was asked to express her feelings about the tragic death of her sister, her answer was "It's bad." **Asociality** is a lack of interest in social relations. People with asociality often have no friends and apparently have no desire to make friends. Finally, **flat or blunted affect** is a lack of emotional display. People with flat affect appear to have no emotion, although recent evidence suggests that they may feel emotions but not be able to express them (Dworkin et al., 1996). Some people with schizophrenia show flat affect from the very beginning of their illness; others show a more volatile affect initially and then show blunted affect as the disorder progresses (APA, 2000).

James showed several negative symptoms. He had very little energy (avolition), and there was nothing that he enjoyed doing (anhedonia). Early in his illness he showed the positive symptoms of thought disorder, hallucinations, and delusions, but within a few years these more dramatic symptoms were gradually replaced by alogia and an almost frighteningly flat affect, which together made him appear like a zombie at times. He was asocial well before other symptoms were apparent. Even as a child, he had little desire to be around other people. In contrast, Suzanne showed almost no negative symptomatology. Prior to her severe psychotic episode, she appeared normal, although perhaps a bit shy and withdrawn. During the episode, her symptoms were almost exclusively positive symptoms. Some people with schizophrenia show predominantly negative symptoms, whereas others, like Suzanne, show predominantly positive symptoms (Andreasen & Olsen, 1982; Andreasen et al., 1990). Some, like James, show positive symptoms at one point in their illness but exhibit a more negative symptom pattern later in the illness (APA, 2000). As we will see later in this chapter and in Chapter 6, the positive/negative symptom distinction is important in several ways. It predicts both prognosis and response to medications (Davis et al., 1989). It may even reflect different subtypes of schizophrenia (Andreasen et al., 1982).

OTHER SYMPTOMS

Not all symptoms of schizophrenia fit neatly into the categories of positive and negative symptoms. This section will briefly review some that do not fit, including catatonia, inappropriate affect, lack of insight, and psychological dysfunction.

Catatonia. **Catatonia** is a psychomotor disturbance of movement and posture. More specifically, people with catatonia often remain "frozen" in an unusual posture for prolonged periods. During such periods, the person is often mute and appears to be unaware of what is going on—a condition referred to as a **catatonic stupor.** During a stupor, people may show **waxy flexibility,** which means that their limbs can be moved by another person and they will maintain the new position.

Inappropriate Affect. Flat affect is not the only affective disturbance found in schizophrenia. Some people with this disorder show what is called **inappropriate affect,** which involves unusual and sometimes even bizarre

This is the kind of unusual posture often found in catatonia. These positions can be held for hours. Many people with catatonia also show waxy flexibility—that is, their positions can be changed by another person and they will maintain that new position.

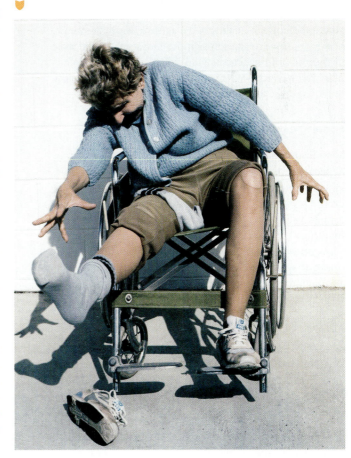

emotional responses. They may giggle while discussing something tragic or break into tears for no reason at all. Their emotions may be volatile and apparently unconnected to their thoughts or statements. This behavior is one of the reasons why Bleuler coined the term *schizophrenia*, which reflects the lack of connection between thoughts and feelings that he observed in many of the people he treated.

Lack of Insight. People with psychotic disorders are often unaware that their experiences are unusual or abnormal, which is known as **lack of insight.** Both James and Suzanne showed this classic lack of insight, although Suzanne showed more insight than James. James believed that his thoughts made sense and that God was talking to him personally. No one could convince him otherwise. Suzanne knew there was something wrong, although during her schizophrenic episode she did not know exactly what. Lack of insight is not technically a symptom of schizophrenia. Rather, it can be characteristic of many disorders. However, lack of insight is almost always present in severe disorders such as schizophrenia.

Psychological Dysfunction. Like lack of insight, psychological dysfunction is not technically a symptom of schizophrenia. Rather, it is the result of the symptoms. For example, it is hard to get and hold a job if one is carrying on conversations with imaginary voices, making little sense when conversing, and not carrying out such basic self-care tasks as bathing. To qualify for a diagnosis of schizophrenia, however, people must show significant dysfunction because of their symptoms. People who hear voices and are paranoid, but nevertheless function adequately, do not qualify for a diagnosis of schizophrenia.

CLINICAL COURSE

Most disorders show a predictable **clinical course**—that is, a specific pattern of changes in symptomatology over time. For example, a cold virus might start with some sniffles, progress to a sore throat and coughing, and then settle into a chest cold before gradually improving. With schizophrenia, there is no single course, although certain patterns show up with some regularity. Some people show a rapid onset of symptoms and reasonably complete recovery, although this is not a common pattern for schizophrenia. Others show episodes of severe symptomatology with

....

lack of insight Lack of awareness that one's experiences are unusual or abnormal.

clinical course A specific pattern of changes in symptomatology over time.

prodromal phase The period before significant symptoms of a psychiatric disorder are apparent.

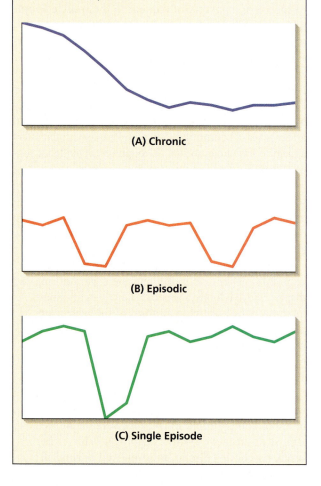

[FIGURE 5.2]
Typical Courses for Schizophrenia

The course of a disorder such as schizophrenia tends to follow one of three patterns. (A) Those with a chronic course show gradual onset and very poor prognosis. (B) Those with an episodic course have occasional episodes with nearly normal functioning between them. (C) The single-episode course, which is rare, involves a brief period of psychosis and nearly complete recovery with no other episodes.

(A) Chronic

(B) Episodic

(C) Single Episode

milder symptomatology present between these episodes. Suzanne's illness followed this course. Still others show a chronic course, in which the symptoms remain relatively stable for years. This was clearly the case for James. These typical courses are illustrated in Figure 5.2. Generally speaking, the earlier and more gradual the onset of symptoms, the worse the prognosis.

Researchers refer to three stages of a psychiatric disorder: the prodromal phase, the active phase, and the residual phase. The **prodromal phase** is the period before significant symptoms are apparent. During his prodromal phase, James displayed an odd quality and was socially ineffective. Suzanne appeared fragile and shy during her prodromal phase, but she had friends and functioned reasonably well. As we will see in Chapter 6, there is considerable research interest in the prodromal phase of schizophrenia because of its potential to illuminate the nature of the genetic influences for schizophrenia and how they interact with environmental stressors to increase risk for schizophrenia. The **active phase** is when the symptoms are most pronounced. The **residual phase** is when the primary symptoms of the disorder have subsided, but other symptoms may still be present. In schizophrenia, the residual phase is often characterized by significant negative symptomatology, with mild positive symptomatology. The majority of people with schizophrenia continue to show some symptoms during the residual phase (Cancro & Lehmann, 2000).

AN EVOLUTIONARY MYSTERY

Evolutionary Impact

The dramatic symptoms of schizophrenia raise an important evolutionary question. They significantly affect people's functioning, thus decreasing the likelihood of survival and reproduction. The current reproductive rate for people with schizophrenia in developed countries is about half the rate among the population at large (Ødegaard, 1972). Such a dramatic difference in reproductive rates between people with and people without schizophrenia should lead to a dramatic reduction in the genes that contribute to risk for the disorder. Of course, such a difference may not always have been present. In today's technological societies, children must complete substantial education in order to get good jobs, and therefore they are likely to marry and have their families later. In less technological societies, people are likely to start having children shortly after puberty, which is before the typical onset of schizophrenia. Nevertheless, there should still be negative selective pressure, because schizophrenic symptoms would be likely to reduce reproductive rates for young adults.

Genes with a negative impact on people may still be maintained in a population if they also have a positive impact; this phenomenon is known as a **balanced polymorphism.** The classic example of a balanced polymorphism is the recessive gene for sickle-cell anemia. People with two of these genes have deformed red blood cells that are inefficient in carrying oxygen, resulting in physical weakness and early death. This creates an obvious negative selective pressure for this gene. However, people who carry only a single copy of the gene are more resistant than other people to malaria. In regions of the world where malaria is common, such resistance is valuable, so there is a positive selective pressure for the sickle-cell gene. In the United States, the sickle-cell gene is more common in blacks because their ancestors came from regions in which malaria was widespread. However, malaria is rare in the United States, and therefore, the sickle-cell gene is dropping in frequency in the black

population because there is no longer a positive selective pressure.

Could there also be a basis for a balanced polymorphism in schizophrenia, which might explain why the obvious negative selective pressures on the genes for this disorder have not led to a dramatic reduction in this disorder over a few generations? One possibility is that carriers of the schizophrenic gene(s), such as first-degree relatives of people with schizophrenia, may have a higher reproductive rate than those who do not carry the genes. Such an elevated reproductive rate would balance the reduced reproductive rate in people with schizophrenia. However, there is no evidence for such an enhanced reproductive rate in gene carriers (Haverkamp et al., 1982).

Another possibility is that carrying the genes for schizophrenia reduces one's risk of contracting potentially life-threatening diseases. People with schizophrenia tend to smoke more heavily than people without the disorder, and yet some studies have found they have lower rates of lung cancer (Hoffer & Foster, 2000). What is more interesting from the balanced-polymorphism perspective is that Lichtermann et al. (2001) found that first-degree relatives of people with schizophrenia had reduced lung cancer rates. Could this be the source of the balanced polymorphism? Perhaps, but it seems unlikely. Lung cancer rarely develops in young adults, so most people who die of lung cancer are already past their reproductive years. Consequently, protection from lung cancer is unlikely to increase reproductive success. There is, however, some evidence for a decrease in the risk for rheumatoid arthritis, which can develop earlier in life and thus could affect survival (Tsuang et al., 1983). Furthermore, people with schizophrenia have higher concentrations of natural killer cells than people without the disorder (Yovel et al., 2000). This might well have provided sufficient selective advantage during periods of high disease rates to account for a balanced polymorphism.

Still another possibility is that some subtle factor associated with the genes for schizophrenia conferred at one time a selective advantage. One candidate is handedness. An unusually large number of people with schizophrenia and of people who show signs that suggest they might be at risk for schizophrenia exhibit mixed handedness—that is, they are able to use both hands for many tasks (Chapman & Chapman, 1987; Reilly et al.,

---

active phase   The period when symptoms are most pronounced.

residual phase   The period when the primary symptoms of the disorder have subsided but other symptoms may still be present.

balanced polymorphism   A phenomenon in which genes with a negative impact on people are maintained in a population because they also have a positive impact.

2001; Sommer et al., 2001). How could such a trait increase survival? Perhaps—and this is speculative—people with mixed handedness could function better when an arm was injured, thus increasing their chance of survival while healing occurred. It seems unlikely that this alone could account for a balanced polymorphism for schizophrenia, but remember, the reproductive rates that are observed today in people with schizophrenia may have been less affected in an earlier era when life expectancies were shorter and people had children earlier in life.

So the mystery remains. The current situation suggests that there is a strong negative selective pressure against the genes that increase risk for schizophrenia. It is not clear whether a balancing positive selective pressure existed in the past. But unless something changes, the genes responsible for this devastating disorder should gradually decrease in each new generation.

Check Yourself 5.1

Symptoms of Schizophrenia

1. How common is schizophrenia?
2. Distinguish between positive and negative symptoms of schizophrenia.
3. What is a delusion?
4. What kind of hallucination is most common in schizophrenia?
5. List the negative symptoms of schizophrenia.
6. Give the three phases of the schizophrenic course.

Ponder this . . . *Could any of the symptoms of schizophrenia have a positive impact on survival or reproduction?*

SUBTYPES OF SCHIZOPHRENIA

The tremendous diversity in the symptoms shown by people with schizophrenia is reflected in the subtypes of schizophrenia in the current DSM. The DSM subtypes are based largely on descriptions first provided by Kraepelin over 100 years ago. Although these subtypes help to organize the various symptom patterns found in schizophrenia, you should not think of them as separate disorders. It is common, for example, for people to show different symptom patterns at different points in their illness, thus qualifying for different subtype diagnoses. Furthermore, unlike other subtyping strategies, such as the distinction between positive and negative symptoms, the DSM subtypes described here do not predict such variables as course and

response to treatment. This section will describe the characteristics of the subtypes known as disorganized, catatonic, paranoid, undifferentiated, and residual schizophrenia.

DISORGANIZED SCHIZOPHRENIA

Disorganized schizophrenia, which was formerly called hebephrenic schizophrenia, is characterized by disorganized speech or behavior and by flat or inappropriate affect. The affect often includes silliness and laughter, which typically has little to do with the situation. There may be hallucinations and delusions. If delusions are present, they are typically bizarre and fragmented. People with this subtype of schizophrenia may also show facial grimacing and peculiar mannerisms. They often exhibit dramatic symptomatology, although these intense symptoms may fade with time (APA, 2000). Allen illustrates a case of an individual with a disorganized subtype of schizophrenia.

In a World of His Own

Allen was first diagnosed with disorganized schizophrenia when he was 23. He has been hospitalized continuously for the last three years, except for one brief three-week period. On a crowded psychiatric ward, Allen remains isolated. He rarely talks to anyone. When he talks, he makes no sense. He jumps from one topic to the next, making reference to things and people that could not possibly be real. For example, he told people that the planet Pluto came to earth to deliver Jesus Christ. At times, his speech is totally incomprehensible. Occasionally, there is urgency in his voice, but more often it sounds as though he is laughing at people. He will sit for several minutes talking to voices that no one else can hear. During these conversations, he will contort his face as though in pain. He walks with a bizarre sway, with his shoulders and lower arms typically raised and his elbows swinging well away from his body. He would stand out in a crowd, even without saying a word, because of the way he moves and the expressions on his face.

CATATONIC SCHIZOPHRENIA

The primary characteristic of **catatonic schizophrenia** is catatonia—the disturbance in movement and posture described earlier. The nature of the catatonia varies both from person to person and from time to time within a given person. Catatonic individuals often are "frozen" in an unusual posture for prolonged periods and show the waxy flexibility characteristic of catatonia. At other times, they may engage in excessive movement or move in a slow, deliberate manner, looking almost as though they were afraid they would break if they moved too quickly. Finally, these individuals may show *echolalia*, which is repeating whatever another person says, or *echopraxia*, which is repeating whatever another person does. These classic symptoms of catatonia are rarely seen today. Modern antipsychotic medica-

Disorganized schizophrenia is characterized by a variety of psychotic symptoms, including the kind of facial grimace shown here.

tions, sometimes coupled with sedatives, usually limit catatonic symptomatology (Cancro & Lehmann, 2000; Marder, 2000).

PARANOID SCHIZOPHRENIA

Paranoid schizophrenia is characterized by fixed delusions of being persecuted. The fixed delusions in people with paranoid schizophrenia remain stable over time, whereas the delusions in disorganized schizophrenia vary from day to day and are often bizarre or nonsensical. There may be other thought disturbance, but often there is less thought disorder than in other subtypes of schizophrenia. In fact, the person with paranoid schizophrenia may be able to describe the most implausible delusions in a wonderfully articulated and detailed fashion. Consequently, people with paranoid schizophrenia tend to be able to function better and often have a better prognosis (APA, 2000; Cancro & Lehmann, 2000; Ritzler, 1981). Hallucinations, if they occur, are usually related to the delusional material. The following is a brief history of a person suffering from paranoid schizophrenia.

soon she could no longer sit quietly and allow it to continue. She challenged students in the hall and professors in the classroom. After several faculty and student complaints to the dean, the medical school forced Barbara onto disability leave, encouraging her to seek treatment. Barbara initially refused to see a psychiatrist but finally went at the encouragement of her parents. Two weeks of hospitalization, a combination of medications, and the supportive therapy of a psychologist were sufficient to reduce the paranoia to the point where Barbara could typically challenge her feelings and evaluate the evidence for her beliefs. Nevertheless, when she attempted to return to medical school a year later, the delusions came back despite the medication and her weekly counseling sessions.

In Barbara's case, the onset of paranoid schizophrenia was rapid, and she responded well to medication and supportive therapy. She seemed to have recovered, although the symptoms returned a few months after she returned to medical school. She elected to take some time off from school in the hope that she could prepare herself to withstand the pressure of medical school. Although it is unclear how well Barbara will deal with her illness, people with paranoid schizophrenia generally have a good prognosis. It was people like Barbara that convinced Bleuler that schizophrenia did not always have a consistent deteriorating course.

UNDIFFERENTIATED SCHIZOPHRENIA

People who meet the criteria for schizophrenia but do not clearly fit into the paranoid, catatonic, or disorganized subtype are given the diagnosis of **undifferentiated schizophrenia.** The case of James that opened this chapter is an example. James showed signs of several subtypes—disorganized, paranoid, catatonic—but never to the point of meeting the criteria for a specific subtype. This pattern is common in people like James who show an early onset of the disorder. Some qualify for a diagnosis of undifferentiated schizophrenia from the very beginning of their disorder; others appear more undifferentiated as their disorder

The Pressure May Have Been Too Much

BARBARA

Barbara was described by many of her teachers as a brilliant, but strange, student. Her 4.0 undergraduate GPA actually understated her performance. But four weeks into medical school, she became completely convinced that teachers and students were conspiring to block her thinking and make her fail. These "realizations" came over her during a frustrating weekend of studying in which she found herself unable to concentrate. For a while, she kept quiet about this conspiracy, but

disorganized schizophrenia   Schizophrenia characterized by disorganized speech or behavior and by flat or inappropriate affect.

catatonic schizophrenia   Schizophrenia characterized by catatonia—the psychomotor disturbance of movement and posture.

paranoid schizophrenia   Schizophrenia characterized by fixed delusions of being persecuted.

undifferentiated schizophrenia   A diagnosis used for people who meet the criteria for schizophrenia but do not clearly fit into the paranoid, catatonic, or disorganized subtype.

becomes more chronic. The typical person with undifferentiated schizophrenia shows considerable negative symptomatology and occasional bizarre thinking.

RESIDUAL SCHIZOPHRENIA

Residual schizophrenia consists of the symptom patterns found during periods of relative remission in individuals with schizophrenia. These symptoms are typically milder forms of the symptoms described above. For example, a person may show some unusual thought patterns, but not the gross thought disorder characteristic of a full-blown schizophrenic episode. This milder form of thought disorder is referred to as **cognitive slippage.** In contrast to the blatant bizarreness of thought disorder, cognitive slippage involves subtle thought disturbances, which can make a person's speech or behavior appear odd. For example, it may include unusual or peculiar wording or conclusions that do not follow from the other information presented. Negative symptoms are often present in the residual phase of the disorder (APA, 2000). Although some individuals show complete recovery with no residual symptoms, most show residual symptoms during their periods of remission, although they may be functioning well in many respects (APA, 2000). Suzanne showed several residual symptoms between her brief episodes, although they were subtle and could be easily overlooked. Her thinking was a little odd, and she was anhedonic and socially withdrawn.

Check Yourself 5.2

Subtypes of Schizophrenia

1. Which subtype of schizophrenia is characterized by the most dramatic symptoms, such as thought disorder, hallucinations, delusions, and inappropriate affect?

2. Which subtype of schizophrenia tends to have the least thought disorder?

3. What are the characteristics of residual schizophrenia?

Ponder this . . . *The DSM subtypes of schizophrenia are purely descriptive. Ideally, what should a diagnostic subtyping system offer besides description?*

CAUSES OF SCHIZOPHRENIA

A disorder as dramatic and puzzling as schizophrenia is guaranteed to spawn theories designed to explain its unusual symptoms. Most theories focus either on the hypoth-

esized causes of schizophrenia or on factors that predispose individuals to schizophrenia. As we review the more prominent causal theories of schizophrenia, you might want to note two things. The first is that these theories are not mutually exclusive—that is, evidence for one theory's validity does not rule out the validity of other theories. Arguing that genetic factors increase risk for schizophrenia does not preclude the possibility that family interaction variables also contribute. Underlying psychodynamic processes do not preclude the possibility that differential learning histories also contribute. It is again useful to think in terms of the map analogy from Chapter 3. The second thing to note is that each theoretical perspective focuses on specific aspects of a person's behavior, rather than on the totality of that behavior. Of course, there is overlap in the theoretical maps, because all theories of schizophrenia are interested in explaining psychotic symptomatology. This section will review the genetic, physiological, environmental, psychodynamic, behavioral, and diathesis-stress perspectives on schizophrenia.

GENETIC VULNERABILITY

It has long been recognized that schizophrenia runs in families. Table 5.1 presents data on the risk for schizophrenia in relatives of people with schizophrenia. The risk of developing schizophrenia falls off sharply as the degree of genetic relationship declines. The identical twin of a person who has schizophrenia has a 48% chance of developing schizophrenia. In contrast, siblings of a person with schizophrenia, with whom they share half their genes, have only a 9% risk.

There is little argument that schizophrenia runs in families, but there have often been heated arguments about how to interpret this observation (Meehl, 1962). A disorder such as schizophrenia could run in families because of genes, environment, or both. People share both genes and environment with their close relatives. Separating those influences is impossible in a traditional family because the two are hopelessly confounded. Variables are **confounded** when they vary together. Consequently, when a relationship is discovered between the confounded variables and another variable, it is impossible to know which of the confounded variables is responsible. Say you have a cold, and one friend tells you to take Remedy A and a second tells you to take Remedy B. If you do both, the variables are confounded. If your cold goes away, you do not know

---

residual schizophrenia The symptom patterns found in individuals with schizophrenia during periods of relative remission.

cognitive slippage A milder form of thought disorder.

confounded variables Variables that vary together.

[TABLE 5.1] Schizophrenia in Families

DEGREE OF RELATIONSHIP	PROPORTION OF GENES SHARED ON AVERAGE	RISK FOR SCHIZOPHRENIA
Identical twins	100%	48%
First-degree relatives	50	
Parents		6
Siblings		9
Fraternal twins		17
Children		13
Second-degree relatives	25	
Half-siblings		6
Grandchildren		5
Uncles/aunts		2
Nieces/nephews		4
Third-degree relatives	12.5	
First cousins		2
No relationship	0	
General population		1
Spouses of patients		2

SOURCE: *From* Schizophrenia Genesis: The Origins of Madness *by I. I. Gottesman. Reprinted by permission of Henry Holt & Company.*

tion studies. **Twin studies** compare the risk of schizophrenia in both the identical and the fraternal twins of people with schizophrenia. If the person with schizophrenia has a twin who also has schizophrenia, the twin pair is said to be **concordant** for schizophrenia. If the person's twin does not have schizophrenia, the pair is said to be **discordant** for schizophrenia. Of course, not every person has a twin, so the sample is limited to people who have schizophrenia and also have a twin. Identical twins share 100% of their genes, whereas fraternal twins share 50% of their genes on average. Both sets of twins grow up together and, therefore, presumably share the same environment growing up. To make that assumption more likely to be true, the fraternal sample is usually restricted to same-sex twins, because parents often treat sons and daughters differently. The difference in the concordance rates for schizophrenia between the identical and the fraternal twins is an indication of the impact of genes on the disorder. Table 5.1 includes a summary of the key twin data. Studies have found that on average, identical twins are about three times more likely than fraternal twins to be concordant for schizophrenia. These results suggest that genes plays a significant role in schizophrenia.

One might hypothesize that identical twins, because they look and act the same, are treated more

whether Remedy A or Remedy B was responsible. If, on the other hand, you take Remedy A for the cold and do not take Remedy B and the cold goes away, and for the next cold you take Remedy B but do not take Remedy A and the cold does *not* go away, you might conclude that Remedy A may be the more effective treatment. Actually, as we shall see in the next chapter, it would be premature to draw this conclusion from such limited observations, but at least you would have eliminated the confounding of those variables by allowing only one to vary at a time.

It requires special research designs to measure the relative contributions of genetics and environment to a disorder and to reduce the natural confounding. The designs most commonly used are twin studies and adop-

twin studies   Comparisons of the risk of a specified disorder in both the identical and the fraternal twins of people with the disorder.

concordant   Twin pairs who both have a specified disorder.

discordant   Twin pairs only one of whom has a specified disorder.

The Genain quadruplets are among the most thoroughly studied people in psychiatric history. All four of them developed schizophrenia, although the age of onset and the symptom pattern varied among the four.

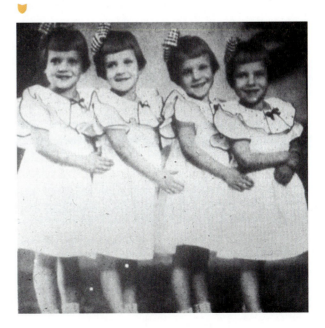

similarly than fraternal twins and that this may explain the higher concordance rates of schizophrenia in identical twins. This explanation seems unlikely, and it has also been discredited via adoption studies. **Adoption studies** take a different approach to separating the effects of genes and environment. Adopted individuals receive their genetic heritage from one family and their environmental heritage from another. Comparing the rates of schizophrenia in the biological and adopted relatives of people with schizophrenia who were adopted at birth provides an indication of the relative importance of these two factors in determining risk for schizophrenia. Kety and his colleagues (1968) used this approach and found that the risk for schizophrenia was substantially elevated in the biological, but not in the adoptive, families of people with schizophrenia, a result that again suggests that genes play a major role in this disorder. Furthermore, they found that not only schizophrenia was overrepresented in the biological relatives, but also a host of similar disorders, such as schizoaffective disorder and schizotypal and paranoid personality disorders. This group of disorders is referred to as **schizophrenic spectrum disorders** because they all appear to share a common genetic basis. Schizoaffective disorder is covered later in this chapter, and the personality disorders are covered in Chapter 12.

Other variations on the adoption study approach have supported the idea that genes contribute substantially to

risk for schizophrenia. For example, the rate of schizophrenia in children whose biological parents had schizophrenia, but whose adopted parents did not, is elevated nearly tenfold above a comparison group of adoptees whose biological and adoptive parents did not have schizophrenia (Rosenthal et al., 1968). Both the Kety et al. (1968) and the Rosenthal et al. (1968) studies, as well as dozens of other genetic studies, were conducted in Denmark because the quality of the national records enabled researchers to identify, find, and diagnose relatives with an efficiency that would have been impossible in other settings.

Data from both twin and adoption studies suggest that genes play a role in the development of schizophrenia. However, the twin study data also suggest that genes are only part of the picture. Half of the identical twins of people with schizophrenia never developed the disorder. If schizophrenia were caused solely by genetic factors, all of the identical twins of the people with schizophrenia should have developed schizophrenia. Therefore, other environmental factors *must* play a role.

Many people believe that if genes play a role in a disorder, there is nothing that can be done to prevent the disorder. Nothing could be further from the truth, as illustrated in the nearby Modern Myths box. The twin study research described above provides convincing evidence that both genes and environment currently play a role. Even if the data showed that environment was not cur-

MODERN Myths

Genetic Causes AND Environmental Contributions

A popular misconception is that conditions to which genes make a strong contribution cannot be affected by the environment. Nothing could be further from the truth. The evidence for a strong genetic contribution to schizophrenia is clear, but the same studies that demonstrate this genetic contribution also demonstrate that environment must also play a role. For example, twin studies have revealed that identical twins are three to five times more likely than fraternal twins to be concordant for schizophrenia. This is strong evidence

for genetic factors contributing to schizophrenia, yet the fact that 50% of identical twins are discordant for schizophrenia provides strong evidence for environmental contributions. If genes were the sole contributor to schizophrenia, then every identical twin of a person with schizophrenia should develop the disorder.

As you will learn throughout this text, many conditions with strong genetic components also have strong environmental components. In some cases, a properly adjusted environment can all but overcome a genetic problem that is normally devastating

to the individual. For example, a condition called PKU (discussed in Chapter 4) invariably leads to severe mental retardation in individuals with the PKU gene *unless* they are placed on a special diet for the first 10–20 years of their lives. This special diet prevents the retardation by blocking the biological mechanism underlying the disorder. As scientists learn more about how genetic factors contribute to a disorder, they become better able to identify systematic environmental manipulations that may prevent or reverse a genetic predisposition toward psychopathology.

rently having an impact, it would still be possible that systematic manipulation of the environment could reduce the toxic effects of the genes—and therefore reduce the likelihood of the disorder.

PHYSIOLOGICAL FACTORS

The physiological perspective on schizophrenia is really a collection of theories, some of them independent and others interrelated. Most people who study schizophrenia believe that it is a developmental brain disorder (Andreasen et al., 1999). Specifically, this hypothesis suggests that there is something fundamentally wrong with the functioning of the brain in schizophrenia and that this dysfunction interacts with external experiences to shape the symptoms of the disorder. The question is "What is dysfunctional and why is it dysfunctional?" This section will outline the three main biological theories that have been advanced to explain the brain dysfunction in schizophrenia: the role of dopamine, cerebral atrophy, and the neurodevelopmental hypothesis. (Chapter 6 will also cover several areas of biologically based research as examples of modern theorizing and research methodology in the field of psychopathology.) These theories are promising, but it is useful to approach them with a healthy amount of skepticism. Physiological functioning is enormously complicated, and at this point scientists have only discovered physiological correlates of schizophrenia. It is much too early to tell whether these correlates are causes or effects of the disorder.

Dopamine Hypothesis. The **dopamine hypothesis** argues that there is, in the brains of people with schizophrenia, either an excess of the neurotransmitter dopamine or, more likely, oversensitivity to dopamine. This does not mean that dopamine causes schizophrenia but, rather, that a dysregulation of dopamine is associated with schizophrenia. As we saw in Chapter 4, neurotransmitters are chemicals that the axon terminals of a neuron release as a way of stimulating the dendrite of another neuron. Dopamine is a major neurotransmitter used in the brain; it affects the functioning of several distinct brain regions and is critical to normal functioning. Although much of the evidence for the dopamine hypothesis is indirect, several lines of evidence point to the role of dopamine in schizophrenia.

One of the principal pieces of evidence suggesting the importance of dopamine in schizophrenia is the effect of phenothiazine medication on the symptoms of this disorder. These medications, which will be discussed later in the chapter, can have a profound impact on people with schizophrenia, often reducing their symptoms to the point where they can be discharged from the hospital. The fact that phenothiazines lower the dopamine level in the brain suggests that dopamine level and/or activity is excessive in

schizophrenia. This hypothesized excess of dopamine is also consistent with the theory that a chronic state of excess dopamine in schizophrenia damages the brain's reward mechanism, leading to the negative symptom anhedonia (Stein & Wise, 1971; Wise & Stein, 1973). Autopsy data from people with schizophrenia confirm the hypothesized deterioration in this neurological reward mechanism, although there is no evidence about what caused this deterioration (Wise & Stein, 1973).

Another source of indirect evidence for the dopamine hypothesis is the effect of high doses of amphetamines, which (1) produce symptoms remarkably similar to paranoid schizophrenia in people who do not have schizophrenia and (2) exacerbate psychotic symptoms in people with the disorder (Angrist et al., 1974). Amphetamines are known to increase levels of dopamine and norepinephrine (another neurotransmitter). The paranoid symptoms are apparently the result of an increase in the dopamine levels, because phenothiazine medication, which reduces dopamine levels, dramatically reduces these symptoms.

It may not be an excess of dopamine, but rather an overactivation or increased sensitivity of dopamine receptors, that is associated with schizophrenia. Imagine a synapse that relies on dopamine as one of its principal neurotransmitters (see Figure 5.3 on page 118). You can increase the probability that a cell will stimulate the adjacent cell by either releasing more dopamine into the synapse (the excess dopamine hypothesis shown in panel 2) or to have the cell release a specific amount of dopamine, but the adjacent cell has an unusually large number of dopamine receptors (the oversensitivity hypothesis shown in panel 3). Increasing either the amount of dopamine or the number of receptors increases the probability of a dopamine molecule finding a suitable receptor and stimulating the neuron. Both postmortem studies (Lee & Seeman, 1980) and PET scan studies (Wong et al., 1986) suggest that there may be an increase in the number of dopamine receptors in people with schizophrenia.

The five-year difference between men and women in average age of onset for schizophrenia has often puzzled researchers. Recent evidence suggests that this difference

----

adoption studies Comparisons of the rates of a specified disorder in the biological and adopted relatives of people with the disorder who were adopted at birth.

schizophrenic spectrum disorders A group of disorders: schizoaffective, schizotypal personality, and paranoid personality disorders.

dopamine hypothesis The argument that in the brains of people with schizophrenia, there is either an excess of the neurotransmitter dopamine or, more likely, oversensitivity to dopamine.

[FIGURE 5.3]
Dopamine and Schizophrenia

(A) A normal synapse, with a typical release of dopamine and the typical number of dopamine receptors in the dendrite of the next cell. (B) The excess dopamine hypothesis: Excess dopamine activity results when too much dopamine is released. (C) The oversensitivity hypothesis: Excess dopamine activity results when there is an excessive number of dopamine receptors. In either case, the likelihood of a dopamine molecule finding a dopamine receptor in the next cell is increased.

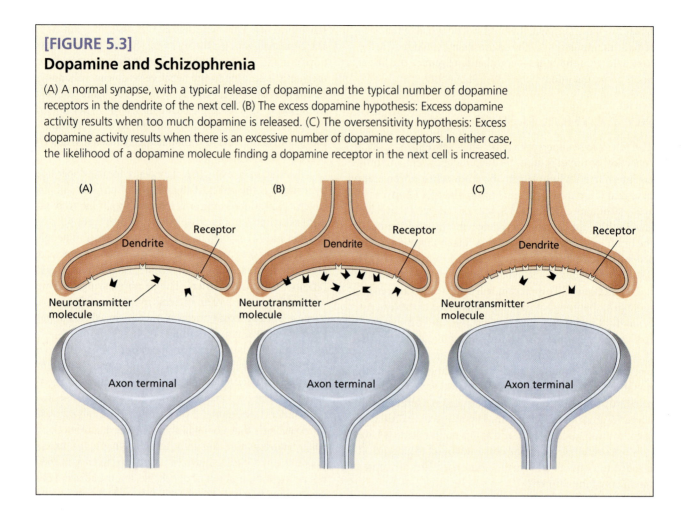

may be due to the effects of estrogen (Häfner et al., 1998). Estrogen reduces the sensitivity of dopamine receptors, thus, at least until menopause, protecting women to a degree from the increased dopamine sensitivity that is a part of schizophrenia. Once estrogen levels drop during menopause, the incidence of schizophrenia in women quickly catches up to the incidence in men, as is apparent in the age-of-risk curves in Figure 5.1.

Research is gradually helping scientists to zero in on the specific regions of the brain that are most involved in schizophrenia. For example, the excessive dopamine sensitivity in schizophrenia appears to be centered in the mesolimbic pathway (Csernansky & Bardgett, 1998). As shown in Figure 5.4, the mesolimbic pathway includes three critical brain areas: the ventral tegmental area, the hypothalamus, and the hippocampus. The neurons in some of these structures, such as the hippocampus, appear to be smaller than normal (Benes et al., 1991), although the significance of this finding is not yet clear. In addition, many of the connections from the mesolimbic pathway to the frontal cortex rely heavily on dopamine for transmission. Andreasen and colleagues (1995) argue that disruption in these brain regions is likely to be associated with positive symptoms, such as thought disorder and hallucinations, but not with negative symptoms. Weinberger (Egan & Weinberger, 1997; Weinberger & Gallhofer, 1997) argues that a dopamine insensitivity in the frontal lobes of the brain may be responsible for some of the negative symptoms of schizophrenia. Both of these theories are plausible and consistent with available data, but they should be regarded as speculative until additional confirming evidence is available. As technology for studying the brain improves, scientists will no doubt achieve a more detailed understanding of these complex processes.

Although dopamine has been implicated in schizophrenia, it may not be involved in all cases of schizophrenia. For example, Kornetsky (1976) found that amphetamines worsened the symptoms of schizophrenia for some, but not all, individuals. It has long been recognized that people with predominantly positive symptoms respond well to phenothiazine medications, whereas people with predominantly negative symptoms do not (Davis et al., 1989). It is possible that the disorder of schizophrenia is *heterogeneous*—that it is actually more than one disorder. It may be that some people show a dopamine dysfunction and others produce symptoms through an entirely different mecha-

[FIGURE 5.4]
Brain Mechanisms in Schizophrenia

Evidence suggests that excessive dopamine sensitivity in the mesolimbic pathway and in the pathways from those regions to the frontal lobes may characterize schizophrenia. The primary structures involved are shown here.

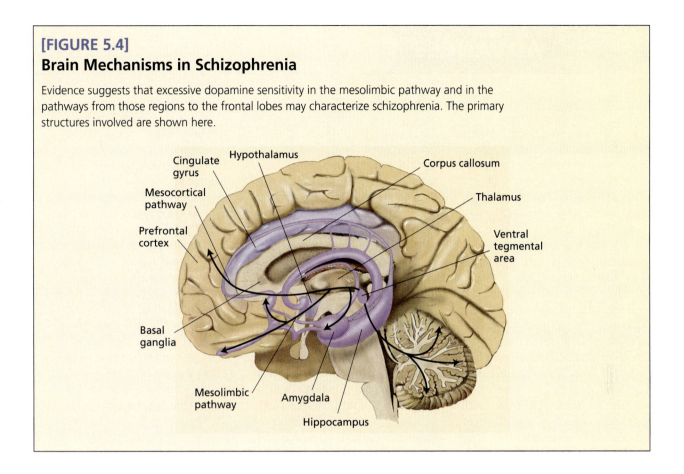

nism. This issue of possible heterogeneity and how to address it will be discussed in Chapter 6.

Cerebral Atrophy. Brain images from people with schizophrenia suggest that there is specific **cerebral atrophy**—that is, loss of brain tissue—associated with the disorder. Slow cerebral atrophy is a normal part of aging because brain cells die naturally across one's lifetime. However, in schizophrenia the atrophy is excessive and appears to be concentrated in certain regions. CAT scans and MRIs have shown that some people with schizophrenia, especially those with chronic and predominantly negative symptoms, show enlarged lateral ventricles and reduced volume in the limbic system (Gur & Pearlson, 1993). Three other brain regions have also received attention from schizophrenia researchers: the frontal lobes, the temporal lobes, and the basal ganglia (Egan & Weinberger, 1997; Finlay, 2001; Meador-Woodruff et al., 2001). Most of these brain regions are shown in Figure 5.4. In addition, imaging studies have suggested abnormalities in the thalamus, hippocampus, and corpus collosum of people with schizophrenia (Downhill et al., 2001; Finlay, 2001; Velakoulis et al., 2001). Some of this research will be discussed in Chapter 6 as examples of biological studies. The frontal lobe research is particularly promising (DeMyer et al., 1988; Weinberger et al., 1992), although the results have

been inconsistent. The degree of atrophy is generally predictive of long-term outcome, although not every study has found this effect (Staal et al., 1999).

One reason for the inconsistency in these studies is that people vary considerably in the relative sizes of various brain structures. This problem can be addressed in two ways. One is to use people as their own controls and take images of their brains before and after the start of the illness. (Of course, to do this, you have to be able to predict who will develop schizophrenia.) A second procedure uses the next best control, the person's identical twin. This strategy studies identical twins in whom one has developed schizophrenia and the other has not. The nearby Advances box illustrates this approach and the dramatic results obtained from one such study. Before this study, it had been believed that cerebral atrophy occurred only in people who had a chronic form of schizophrenia with predominantly negative symptom patterns. Now, the evidence suggests that excessive brain atrophy may be present in most individuals with schizophrenia and that it may be present early in the disorder.

cerebral atrophy   Loss of brain tissue.

ADVANCES Brain images of discordant twins

Sometimes the key to finding something elusive is to look in the right place. This seems so obvious, but it can be more difficult than you might imagine. Sometimes finding the right place to look is equivalent to hitting a grand-slam home run to win the deciding game of the World Series.

A case in point is the study of the brains of identical twins by Suddath and his colleagues (1990). They studied twin pairs in which one twin had developed schizophrenia and the other had not. Scientists had known for years that people with chronic forms of schizophrenia showed brain atrophy, which is seen most clearly in an enlargement of the lateral ventricles (Berman & Weinberger, 1989). Ventricles are natural spaces in the brain, and an enlargement of the ventricles indicates a loss of nearby brain tissue. Although this finding was important, it did not establish that the brain atrophy was a contributing factor to schizophrenia. Such atrophy had been found only in people with chronic schizophrenia, and it could have been due to something other than the disorder. For example, people with chronic schizophrenia are often prescribed large doses of antipsychotic medications over many years. It is possible that such powerful medications could have serious effects on the brain. Scientists know that heavy use

of antipsychotic medications over a long period of time can lead to permanent brain damage (Marder, 2000). The problem is that one would expect that the atrophy in less chronic individuals would be smaller because they (1) tend to have less severe symptoms and (2) are likely to be early in the disease process so that any atrophy would just be beginning. Detecting minimal brain atrophy is difficult because there is considerable natural variability among people in the size of various brain structures.

What was needed was a standard to judge whether the size of the ventricles in a recently diagnosed person with schizophrenia was an indication of atrophy or just a natural characteristic of the person. If one had a CAT scan from several years earlier for the patient, it could provide such a standard, but CAT scans are rare and are therefore unlikely to be available for comparison. Another strategy is to use a standard that already exists, and this is what Suddath et al. did. They used the identical twin of a person who had schizophrenia. Identical twins not only look alike but are also alike in virtually every other manner. By finding identical twins in whom only one of the twins has developed schizophrenia and taking brain scans of both twins, Suddath and his colleagues had the perfect control. They found clear evidence of brain atrophy

in the person who had developed schizophrenia in 14 of the 15 discordant twin pairs in their study. The amount of brain atrophy was so small that it would not have been detected without the brain scan of an identical twin for comparison. This study provided strong evidence that part of the neurodevelopmental course of schizophrenia involves atrophy of specific regions of the brain and that this atrophy occurs early in the disorder and continues in people with chronic forms of the disorder. Furthermore, because the people in this study were not chronic and therefore had not had long-term exposure to antipsychotic medications, medication was an unlikely cause of the atrophy in this study.

This approach has since been used to study the size of specific brain structures via MRI technology (Baare et al., 2001). Furthermore, obstetric complications were found to have been more common in those discordant twins who developed schizophrenia than in their co-twins, and the complications were specifically predictive of greater cerebral atrophy, especially in the hippocampus (McNeil et al., 2000). This clever use of discordant twins should continue, in the coming years, to provide more insights into the neurological mechanisms underlying schizophrenia.

Neurodevelopmental Hypothesis. The prenatal period of development is especially critical for the health of the individual. The development of the fetus is rapid, and any disruption of that development is likely to have serious consequences. The majority of brain development occurs during the second trimester of the pregnancy (the fourth month through the sixth month). During this period, billions of neurons form, migrate to their appropriate location in the brain, and begin to make the trillions of interconnections with other neurons. This process initially overwires the brain—that is, there are more neurons,

and more connections between neurons, than necessary. During early development, the useful neurons and connections are maintained while those that are unused are gradually pruned. Every stage of this neurological development and refinement is subject to disruption, and any disruption results in neurological dysfunction that could last a lifetime. Furthermore, disruptions could result in neurological deficits that do not become obvious until years later. Several lines of evidence suggest that disruptions of normal development during this period can have significant consequences for the child and may increase the risk for schizophrenia, a position known as the **neurodevelopmental hypothesis.**

The neurodevelopment of the child may be adversely affected during pregnancy in many ways. Viral infections, such as the flu, can affect both the mother's health and the health of the developing fetus. For example, the children of women who experience a serious case of the flu during the second trimester of their pregnancy have an elevated risk of schizophrenia (Mednick et al., 1988). Birth complications are found more frequently in people who developed schizophrenia than in those who did not, perhaps because birth complications increase the risk of brain damage by disrupting the blood supply, and therefore the availability of oxygen, to the fetus's brain (McNeil, 1987). The fact that different environmental insults to the brain can increase risk for schizophrenia suggests that generalized brain damage during this critical period must decrease neurological functioning in such a way as to increase the risk for psychopathology years later.

The neurodevelopmental hypothesis raises an interesting question. Why does this presumed neurological problem not show up until well into adulthood? Wouldn't one expect to see obvious signs of neurological problems from birth on? There is no simple answer to this question. Serious neurological problems in the developing fetus *are* evident at birth or shortly thereafter (Towbin, 1978). Furthermore, some serious neurological problems are *never* observed because the fetus is no longer viable and therefore is miscarried. In general, there is no evidence of serious neurological dysfunction in individuals who later develop schizophrenia (Green, 1998). However, there *is* evidence of subtle neurodevelopmental problems. Elaine Walker and her colleagues have discovered such evidence in young children by carefully examining childhood photographs and home movies of children who later developed schizophrenia (Walker et al., 1993, 1994). Evidence on handedness in those individuals who later develop schizophrenia is also consistent with the hypothesis that a neurodevelopmental problem underlies risk for this disorder. People who develop schizophrenia are more likely to show mixed handedness, such as writing with one hand but throwing with another (Green, 1998; Satz & Green, 1999). These studies and the logic behind them will be discussed in greater detail in Chapter 6. What is critical to remember here is that the neurodevelopmental dysfunctions hypothesized to underlie schizophrenia are likely to be subtle and not readily apparent, but there is a growing body of evidence suggesting that such dysfunctions exist.

ENVIRONMENTAL CONTRIBUTIONS

There are several potential environmental influences for a disorder such as schizophrenia. For example, one might hypothesize that a history of emotional abuse or a series of other life stresses might predispose someone to develop schizophrenia. To test such a hypothesis, scientists would see whether such events occur more often in the histories of people who develop schizophrenia than in those of people who do not. However, one has to be especially careful when interpreting such environmental information, because people are rarely just passive recipients of environmental events. For example, you probably know at least one or two people who experience a lot of hostility from other people, in part because they provoke it. Some people live through more than their share of broken relationships because they demand too much from the relationships, eventually driving others away. Some people experience success because they work hard and work smart; some experience love because they openly bestow their own. Of course, the direction of causation for these phenomena could be reversed: People may work hard and smart because they have been rewarded with success in the past. Most likely, these interrelationships are circular. People whose hard work brings success work harder in the future and are rewarded still more, and so on. People also choose their environments by choosing their jobs, neighborhoods, friends, and recreational activities. These choices may not always be within the individual's control, but people often have some control over them. However, young children have less control over their lives; parents and caregivers shape their early environment. Therefore, it is not surprising that most of the theories of environmental influences in schizophrenia focus on those early years.

Family Dynamics. Families shape the way people think and feel, and people's emotional security often depends on the quality and predictability of their early family relationships (Lieberman et al., 1999). Most parents do at least an adequate job of raising their children, but some don't, creating a negative environment for their children instead. Garmezy (1974) speculated that researchers might be wise to try to understand how someone could thrive in spite of a bad environment rather than focusing on how bad environments take their toll. Still, in trying to understand a disorder such as schizophrenia, investigators want to focus on variables that are presumed to be destructive enough to literally drive a person insane.

Early conceptualizations of family dynamics and their relationship to schizophrenia focused on the parents, especially the mother. Unfortunately, these early theories had little empirical support. They will be discussed in Chapter 6 as examples of theories that were invalidated by research. Other theories of family influences on schizophrenia have shown more promise. Here we will discuss two such theories, expressed emotion and affective style.

Clinicians who work with schizophrenia have long recognized that some of their clients relapse quickly when

neurodevelopmental hypothesis The theory that disruptions of normal development may increase the risk for schizophrenia.

released to their families—that is, their symptoms return and they often require rehospitalization. An exploration of this phenomenon led to the discovery of a pattern of family interaction known as **expressed emotion,** or **EE** (Leff & Vaughn, 1976; Vaughn & Leff, 1976a. Expressed emotion sounds like a positive thing. However, in coining this term, Vaughn and Leff were referring to the family's expression of a narrow range of emotion: hostile and critical comments directed at the person, coupled with overinvolvement in the person's life. Several studies have shown that people with schizophrenia who are released to families that show high EE relapse more quickly than those released to other settings, including those who are released to low-EE families (King & Dixon, 1999; Parker & Hadzi-Pavlovic, 1990). Relapse is predicted most strongly by the extent of hostile comments from fathers and the level of emotional overinvolvement of mothers (King & Dixon, 1999). More recent studies have tried to modify EE in the hope of reducing its toxic effect on people with schizophrenia, but they have had limited success (Goldstein, 1999; Nugter et al., 1997). EE is not something that can be easily reduced, and it tends to intensify during stressful periods.

The impact of EE seems to depend on at least three variables: (1) the level of EE in the family, (2) how much contact people with schizophrenia have with their family, and (3) whether the person with schizophrenia continues to take the prescribed antipsychotic medication. Those with a lot of contact who stop taking their medication usually relapse quickly. Those who have minimal contact and who continue to take their medication seem to avoid the toxic effects of the high-EE environment. Each time James, whose case is one of those that opened this chapter, returned home after being released from the hospital, he quickly deteriorated. His parents loved him, but they put such pressure on him to "pull himself together" that he quickly did just the opposite. Although it was once thought to be a specific stressor for schizophrenia, EE is better conceptualized as a general environmental stressor that increases risk for relapse in many disorders (Butzlaff & Hooley, 1998; O'Farrell et al., 1998; Simoneau et al., 1998).

A concept closely related to expressed emotion is **affective style** (Doanne et al., 1985). Affective style is based on the tendency of one or more relatives to make critical or guilt-inducing statements to individuals with schizophrenia or to make repeated statements about what those individuals are thinking. Examples might include "Why can't you be more dependable?" or "Don't lie to me; I know you are as upset as I am." Given its similarity to expressed emotion, it is not surprising that affective style is also a predictor of relapse (Miklowitz, 1994). However, considerably less research has been conducted on affective style than on expressed emotion.

Communication Deviance. Communication deviance is the degree to which a relative's communication

lacks clarity (Singer & Wynne, 1963; Wynne & Singer, 1963). It is scored from speech samples gathered in a standardized manner, such as having people tell stories about what is happening in a picture. For example, the person may be asked to tell a story in response to the picture shown in Figure 5.5. The following story is an example of abrupt shifts in perspective, which is one form of communication deviance.

> That boy with the violin has got the hands for it. I played very well when I was four, practicing, practicing every day. He'll give it up eventually. (Singer & Wynne, 1965, p. 194)

One could view communication deviance as a mild form of thought disorder, much like the cognitive slippage concept mentioned earlier. However, communication deviance and thought disorder appear to be independent concepts (Miklowitz, 1994). People with considerable thought

[FIGURE 5.5]
Assessing Communication Deviance

Singer and Wynne (1963) assessed communication deviance by asking people to tell stories in response to pictures like this one. They then scored the stories for instances of ineffective or unusual communication.

disorder can show little communication deviance, and people with little or no thought disorder can show significant communication deviance. Furthermore, it appears that communication deviance is more common in people who are at elevated genetic risk for schizophrenia but have never developed the disorder (Docherty et al., 1999). It is also more common in parents of people who develop schizophrenia than in parents of people who do not (Wynne et al., 1977). Biological parents who raised children who developed schizophrenia had more schizophrenic psychopathology than adoptive parents who raised children who developed schizophrenia, which is what one would predict from a genetic perspective (Wynne et al., 1976). However, the same study found no difference between adoptive and biological parents who raised children who eventually developed schizophrenia on the level of communication deviance, which suggests that this subtle variable characterized the upbringing of people who later developed schizophrenia. Thus communication deviance may be the kind of stressor that can increase the risk for schizophrenia, whatever the genetic risk.

Communication deviance is one of those fascinating concepts that has been very difficult to study because it is so difficult to measure. The fact that many investigators have been unable to achieve reasonable levels of reliability in their measures of communication deviance (Wender et al., 1977) has limited this construct's potential validity. Various scoring procedures have been tried, and some appear to be easier to use than others (Docherty, 1995). As difficult as this concept has been to measure, it still appears to have considerable value. It is pervasive enough to have a significant impact on a developing child, creating a degree of confusion in social interactions that increases anxiety and encourages divergent thinking about what is "really" being communicated. But unless the difficulty in measuring it is resolved, communication deviance may be just another great idea that never really delivers on its promise.

Communication deviance and expressed emotion, when they occur together in a family, may interact to create especially high risk for schizophrenia in the children. Goldstein (1992) found that the combination of communication deviance and expressed emotion predicted risk for schizophrenia, although individually these variables were not predictive. Furthermore, Docherty (1995) found that expressed emotion and communication deviance were correlated in relatives of people with schizophrenia, which suggests that a common variable may account for both factors. However, an alternative explanation may be that the stress of having to deal with communication deviance in one or more family members depletes people's adaptive resources, making it difficult for them to be patient and supportive of a family member with schizophrenia. Whatever the relationship, it is clear that the environmental variables associated with schizophrenia are not mutually exclusive but, rather, combine with one another in ways that are only now beginning to be explored.

Sociocultural Variables. One widely recognized finding in schizophrenia is that this disorder is not equally represented across social classes. In fact, the majority of people with schizophrenia come from the lower classes, and few come from the higher social classes (Faris & Dunham, 1939; Hollingshead & Redlich, 1958). The lower social classes include people who have a high school education or less and whose occupations require few skills and little training. The higher social classes include professionals and upper-management people, who typically have college degrees and often have postcollege education and advanced degrees. The disparity in the rates of schizophrenia across social classes is so dramatic that this finding demands an explanation. Could the stress of living in the lower social classes, with more poverty, more crime, less education, and less control over one's life, eventually result in schizophrenia? This is the hypothesis that was favored when this relationship was first discovered. However, there are other possibilities. Let's look at them and the data supporting them.

Examining the Evidence

What might account for the fact that schizophrenia is overrepresented in the lower social classes? Perhaps physical factors associated with poverty, such as malnutrition, limited medical care, and poor prenatal care increase the risk for neurodevelopmental damage. Could there be protective influences available to people in the upper classes, such as better education, that account for their low rates of schizophrenia? Could it be that, instead of social class influencing risk for schizophrenia, schizophrenia influences one's social class? Over a third of all people in the United States change social class during their lifetimes. People with schizophrenia often experience considerable difficulty in occupational and social functioning. Because the disorder tends to occur early in life, it may disrupt education and early career attainment. The **downward drift hypothesis** suggests not that being in the lower

---

expressed emotion (EE)   A family member's expression of hostile and critical comments directed at the person with psychopathology, coupled with an overinvolvement in the person's life.

affective style   The tendency of one or more relatives to make critical or guilt-inducing statements to individuals with schizophrenia or to make repeated statements about what those individuals are thinking.

communication deviance   The degree to which a relative's communication lacks clarity.

downward drift hypothesis   The idea that schizophrenia makes it hard for people to achieve educationally and occupationally and that they therefore drift into lower social classes.

social class that causes schizophrenia but that schizophrenia makes it hard for people to achieve educationally and occupationally and that they therefore drift into lower social classes. The data on whether people who develop schizophrenia drift into lower social classes has been mixed. Some researchers have found evidence for downward drift (Lystad, 1957; Turner & Wagonfeld, 1967), and others have failed to find such evidence (Dunham, 1965; Hollingshead & Redlich, 1958). However, one finding provides rather strong support for the downward drift hypothesis. Goldberg and Morrison (1963) found that the fathers and brothers of people with schizophrenia were distributed across the social classes, whereas the people with schizophrenia tended to be in lower social classes. These data are presented in Figure 5.6. People who developed schizophrenia were no more likely than other people to have been raised in lower social classes, and their siblings were no more likely than randomly selected individuals to end up in lower social classes. However, those who developed schizophrenia were more likely to be in lower social classes because their educational and occupational performance was not adequate to maintain their status in society. In other words, schizophrenia seems to contribute more to a person's social class than the other way around. You may have wondered about the obvious sexist nature of these data (looking only at fathers and brothers of people with schizophrenia). At the time of the study, two-career families were rare, and the social class of the family was typically determined by the occupation and education of the father.

That schizophrenia is as common in women as in men (APA, 2000) and that it is found throughout the world with roughly the same frequency (Gottesman, 1991) also suggest that sociocultural variables are not major contributing factors. The vast differences in sociocultural experiences among the many world cultures are at least as great as the differences between the lower and upper classes in the United States and England, where the studies on social class were performed. Furthermore, the variability in sociocultural experiences between men and women among the world's cultures is dramatic, and yet the male/female ratio is near 1.00 in just about every country studied. One cannot completely dismiss sociocultural factors on the basis of this evidence, but it seems unlikely that they contribute significantly to the risk of schizophrenia.

PSYCHODYNAMIC FACTORS

One would think that a disorder as dramatic as schizophrenia would have captured Freud's attention, but most of his psychodynamic theory focused on *neuroses,* the milder

[FIGURE 5.6]
Schizophrenia and Social Class

Schizophrenia is twice as common in the lower social classes than one would expect to occur by chance and is rare in the upper social classes relative to the typical distribution of social class (shown here as the "norms"). However, the fathers and brothers of people with schizophrenia are not overrepresented in the lower social classes. These data support the downward drift hypothesis, which suggests that people who develop schizophrenia have difficulty competing in school and in jobs, which is the basis for determining social class. Consequently, they are unable to avoid drifting into lower social classes.

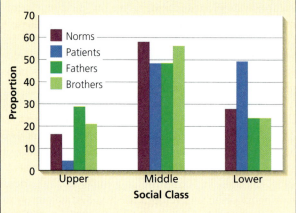

SOURCE: *After E. M. Goldberg and S. L. Morrison, "Schizophrenia and Social Class." British Journal of Psychiatry, 109 (1963): 785–802.*

anxiety-driven disorders. Freud speculated that schizophrenia represented regression to the stage that he called **primary narcissism,** which is the level of functioning of a newborn (Fenichel, 1945). According to Freud, the ego has not yet developed in infants, so they lack the necessary skills to deal with reality. With no ego to balance one's thoughts against reality, a person's thoughts *become* reality. Delusions and hallucinations are understandable within this context. Thoughts are disordered because there is little reason to make thoughts conform to the standards of accepted communication.

Freud's regression model for schizophrenia is intuitively appealing, but it does not address several key issues. For example, it does not explain why regression occurs. Contemporary psychoanalytic theorists have suggested that id impulses may be involved (Fenichel, 1945), especially aggressive impulses. People with schizophrenia often report being terrified of aggressive impulses (Silverman et al., 1976). However, it is not clear whether id impulses lead to psychotic symptoms or the emotional and cognitive deterioration of psychosis leads to id impulses.

primary narcissism The level of functioning of a newborn.

The work of Harry Stack Sullivan (1892–1949) and Frieda Fromm-Reichmann (1889–1957) contributed much to the understanding of schizophrenia (McGlashan & Hoffman, 2000). Both were gifted therapists who worked in a psychoanalytic framework with people who had schizophrenia. Sullivan believed that people with schizophrenia suffered from a fragile ego that simply could not deal with the stress of day-to-day life. He felt that interpersonal challenges overwhelmed these individuals, forcing them to regress as a way of avoiding adult responsibilities. Fromm-Reichmann saw people with schizophrenia as overwhelmed by early traumas. She argued that the social withdrawal typical of schizophrenia protected them from further trauma and that the bizarre symptoms of schizophrenia facilitated this withdrawal.

Although psychodynamic theory provides an interesting perspective from which to view schizophrenia, it lacks the detailed theoretical underpinnings and supporting data required for a true understanding of the disorder (McGlashan & Hoffman, 2000). The concept of regression is more descriptive than explanatory. Furthermore, much of the psychodynamic speculation about the nature of thought in infants and its alleged similarity to schizophrenic thought is difficult to confirm.

BEHAVIORAL FACTORS

The behavioral perspective hypothesizes that the symptoms of schizophrenia are the result of a complex learning history—that is, psychotic symptoms are reinforced in some manner (Ullmann & Krasner, 1975). For example, people who are uncomfortable in social situations may be reinforced for behaving strangely because doing so causes others to shy away from them. Every person experiences reinforcement contingencies, and those experiences shape behavior. But there are large individual differences in the responses to specific contingencies. Some people, for example, are anxious when they behave inappropriately, whereas others respond with little anxiety. Not surprisingly, people who naturally respond with anxiety are more likely to avoid anxiety-producing situations. Individuals who eventually develop schizophrenia show rapid shaping of avoidance behavior because they experience a rapid drop in anxiety once avoidance is initiated (Mednick & Schulsinger, 1968). Could this be the mechanism that shapes the social avoidance so common in schizophrenia? Mednick and Schulsinger (1968) speculated that this process could also reinforce "zoning out" to avoid thinking about anxiety-producing situations, which might eventually lead to loose thinking—retreating quickly from topics that produce anxiety to the shelter of other topics. This speculative hypothesis illustrates how physiological variables can interact with environmental events to create situations that foster psychopathology.

Although behavior principles clearly affect people with schizophrenia and may account for how and when some symptoms are manifested, it is too much of a leap to assume that a specific pattern of reinforcement by itself could lead to the dramatic symptoms of schizophrenia (Ullmann & Krasner, 1975). Scientists no longer accept this rather extreme position. Nevertheless, there is general recognition that learning principles may contribute to the maintenance of schizophrenia and that behavioral treatments can contribute to psychosocial rehabilitation (Paul & Lentz, 1977).

DIATHESIS-STRESS MODELS

None of the theories presented here completely accounts for the development of schizophrenia, and consequently, few researchers subscribe to a single theory. The evidence that both biological and environmental factors contribute to risk for schizophrenia is too strong to ignore. This position, which is termed the *diathesis-stress model*, hypothesizes that predisposing factors (the diathesis) interact with environmental experiences (the stress) to produce schizophrenic symptoms in a subset of individuals. Note that the nature of the diathesis and that of the stress have not been specified. The reason is simple; no one is sure what they are. There may be a range of genetic diatheses that predispose to schizophrenia (Gottesman et al., 1987) or a single primary genetic diathesis (Meehl, 1962, 1990). There almost certainly is a range of environmental stresses that might trigger deterioration in vulnerable individuals, such as viral infections during gestation (Mednick et al., 1988), pregnancy and birth complications (McNeil, 1987), communication patterns in families (Goldstein et al., 1992), level of expressed emotion (Vaughn & Leff, 1976a), and even season of birth (Torrey et al., 1997). Studying the interaction of two or more variables is inherently more difficult than studying the effects of individual variables. However, in the case of schizophrenia, studying the interaction of variables is likely to pay big dividends. Actually, the evidence is mounting that diathesis-stress models may be appropriate for virtually every psychiatric disorder (Millon et al., 1999).

Check Yourself 5.3

Causes of Schizophrenia

1. What is the best single source of evidence that both genes and environment contribute to risk for schizophrenia?
2. Which neurotransmitter has been strongly implicated in schizophrenia?
3. What family variables are associated with schizophrenic relapse?
4. What is the relationship between thought disorder and communication deviance?

5. What is the relationship between schizophrenia and social class?

Ponder this . . . *There is no question that expressed emotion increases the risk of relapse in schizophrenia. However, the way expressed emotion affects relapse is likely to be complex. Drawing from your own experience with people who are critical and hostile, explain what effect such behavior has on people? How might it increase risk of relapse in a person with schizophrenia?*

TREATING SCHIZOPHRENIA

Until the advent of antipsychotic medications in the early 1950s, treatment for schizophrenia involved hospitalization, psychosurgery, electroconvulsive therapy, and crude attempts to calm and control hospitalized individuals. These treatments were largely ineffective. The hospitals during that era were huge—the size of small towns. They were typically overflowing, with staffs much too small to provide any meaningful psychosocial treatment. Institutional treatment was the norm, and it was common for people with schizophrenia to be hospitalized for most of their adult lives. The development of effective medications ushered in a new treatment era. This section reviews current treatments, including medication, cognitive and behavioral treatments, and family therapies for schizophrenia.

MEDICATIONS

Drugs used to treat schizophrenia are called **antipsychotic medications.** Introduced in 1952, the first antipsychotic medication was chlorpromazine (brand name: Thorazine), which proved effective in reducing psychotic symptoms (Davis et al., 1989; Marder, 2000). Over time, other drugs in the same class—referred to as phenothiazines—were developed for treating schizophrenia, including such high-potency phenothiazines as haloperidol (Haldol). The phenothiazines were the main treatments for schizophrenia for years. A new class of medications, referred to as **atypical antipsychotics,** shows great promise for the treatment of schizophrenia (Kane et al., 1988; Taylor & Duncan-McConnell, 2000; Wirshing et al., 1999). Although there are risks associated with these drugs (Safferman et al., 1991), they generally are more effective and have fewer side effects than the earlier antipsychotic medications. Furthermore,

antipsychotic medications Drugs used to treat schizophrenia and other psychotic disorders.

atypical antipsychotics A new class of medications that show great promise for the treatment of schizophrenia.

tardive dyskinesia Abnormal, involuntary movements such as smacking of lips, sucking, and sideways jaw movements.

[TABLE 5.2] Antipsychotic Medications

Nearly a dozen medications have been used to treat the psychotic symptoms of schizophrenia. Listed below are their generic names and brand names.

GENERIC NAME	BRAND NAME
chlorpromazine	Thorazine
fluphenazine hydrochloride	Prolixin
haloperidol	Haldol
thiothixene	Navane
clozapine	Clozaril
olanzapine	Zyprexa
risperidone	Risperdal
ziprasidone hydrochloride	Geodon
quetiapine fumarate	Seroquel

the atypical antipsychotics not only reduce psychotic symptoms but also improve cognitive functioning (Keefe et al., 1999b; Kern et al., 1999; Meltzer & McGurk, 1999). Table 5.2 lists the various drugs used to treat schizophrenia.

Antipsychotic medications have had a tremendous impact on treatment. Before their widespread use, psychiatric hospitals were overflowing. In the early 1950s, there were over half a million people with schizophrenia in psychiatric hospitals in the United States. Within 15 years, that number was cut in half, and it continues to drop (Davis et al., 1989). The medications helped people control their symptoms sufficiently to allow discharge. The drop in the hospital census freed staff members to focus on helping clients prepare for living outside the hospital.

As critical a breakthrough as antipsychotic medications were, they are not a panacea. Most have serious side effects, some of them unbearable (Marder, 2000). The side effects include blurred vision, dry mouth, constipation, urinary retention, tremors, rigidity, a shuffling style of walking, and extreme motor restlessness. Some side effects are permanent, such as **tardive dyskinesia,** which involves such abnormal involuntary movements as smacking of lips, sucking, and sideways jaw movements. One of the newer medications—clozapine—has potentially life-threatening side effects. In a small percentage of individuals who take clozapine, the white blood cell count drops to dangerously low levels (Grace et al., 1996; Oyewumi & Al-Semaan, 2000; Safferman et al., 1991). If this drop is not recognized early and the medication is not immediately stopped, the person could die. For this reason, people on this drug have regular blood tests.

Although antipsychotic medications have been a tremendous asset in treatment, they are not a cure. They reduce schizophrenic symptoms but rarely eliminate them. They do little to improve the negative symptoms of schizophrenia, although the atypical antipsychotics do show promise in treating negative symptoms (Grace et al., 1996; Kane et al., 2001), especially when combined with other medications (Drapalsky et al., 2001; Jockers-Scheruebl et al., 2001). Given the side effects and the potential risks, better treatments are still needed.

PSYCHOLOGICAL INTERVENTIONS

Traditional psychotherapy is generally ineffective with schizophrenia (May, 1968; Bustillo et al., 2000). Before the advent of medications, psychotherapy was rarely used because there were so many people in the hospitals and so few people capable of administering psychotherapy. Behavioral approaches were more promising because professional staff were not required for the day-to-day implementation of the program (Paul & Lenz, 1977). More recently, cognitive therapy has shown promise for treating some of the symptoms of schizophrenia (Beck, 1999).

Behavioral Approach. The behavioral approach rests on the simple assumption that behavior is always controlled, at least to a degree, by its consequences. For example, most people are careful to avoid saying outrageous things because the people around them are likely to show disapproval. However, this assumption had often been questioned for schizophrenia because inappropriate behavior is common in this disorder in spite of its negative consequences. In the 1970s, Gordon Paul and his colleagues challenged that wisdom by setting up an experimental treatment unit in a state hospital (Paul & Lentz, 1977). They used behavioral principles to reduce the manifestation of symptoms and improve social functioning. As with most behavioral programs, punishment was rarely used. Behaviors that were rewarded tended to increase in frequency and gradually pushed less appropriate behaviors to the side. For example, the person might be reinforced for proper grooming, for making eye contact, or for doing such routine tasks as making her or his bed. This approach was formalized into a **token economy,** in which clients received tokens for performing desired behaviors, and the tokens could be redeemed for such goods as a candy bar or such activities as a walk around the grounds. The rules for earning the tokens were individually tailored to each person.

Progress with token economies in people with schizophrenia is slow, and there are definite limitations on how much progress can be made. For example, people with schizophrenia can be taught not to discuss their delusions, but the delusions are still there. Nevertheless, behaving more appropriately, even if it only masks symptoms, opens up opportunities that would not otherwise be available. Modern rehabilitative programs have thoroughly integrated behavioral principles into their operation. Training in appropriate behavior, social skills, and stress management improves the adaptive functioning of people with schizophrenia (Bellack & Mueser, 1993; Fenton

& McGlashan, 2000). Social skills training is especially critical, because many people with chronic schizophrenia have been socially withdrawn for years and therefore are unable to handle the most basic social situations (Liberman et al., 1989). Coupled with the therapeutic effects of medication, behavioral training often enables clients to live outside of the hospital—something that would be next to impossible without this treatment.

Cognitive Approach. The cognitive approach to the treatment of schizophrenia teaches clients to recognize and challenge irrational or inappropriate ideas. Of course, some people with schizophrenia are so seriously disturbed that they are unable even to consider such a strategy, but many have periods of relatively mild symptoms during which cognitive therapy is effective. For example, clients may be taught to label voices that others do not seem to hear as their own thoughts being experienced as voices. The person can then deal with these voices in the same way that other people deal with their thoughts. These approaches are effective in reducing schizophrenic symptoms (Shergill et al., 1998), and more important, these treatment gains persist (Klingberg et al., 1999). This therapy is typically slow and time-consuming. Consequently, it is fortunate that group therapy works, enabling a single therapist to treat several clients simultaneously (Wykes et al., 1999).

Cognitive treatment of schizophrenia is relatively new, and the extent to which this approach can help is not yet established. Nevertheless, early research suggests that psychological interventions long considered ineffective can be helpful. It also demonstrates that despite their dramatic symptoms, people with schizophrenia are capable of responding to psychological interventions.

FAMILY THERAPY

Family therapy is often a critical component in the overall treatment of schizophrenia, and in some cultures, such as some African cultures, it is the core of treatment (Peltzer & Machleidt, 1992). Although early theories of schizophrenia often blamed families for the disorder, modern theories recognize that other factors are the primary cause of the disorder. Furthermore, providing a supportive environment for a person with schizophrenia can be the difference between normal functioning and relapse (Vaughn & Leff, 1976a). Having a family member with schizophrenia is stressful. Parents and spouses often feel helpless in the face of psychotic symptoms, and this helpless frustration may contribute to a less tolerant attitude toward the affected person.

Family therapy is especially important in those families characterized by high levels of expressed emotion. When

· ·

token economy System in which clients who perform desired behaviors are given tokens as rewards that can be redeemed for goods or activities.

Family therapy for schizophrenia seeks to help family members deal more effectively with the person who has schizophrenia and avoid the hostility and overinvolvement typical of expressed emotion.

exposed to a high-EE environment, people with schizophrenia are likely to relapse. Family therapy educated family members about the biological nature of schizophrenia and provided them with constructive ways of dealing with the affected person, such as providing empathic encouragement instead of harsh criticism (Falloon et al., 1982, 1985). Early studies found such family interventions to be more effective than individual therapy in reducing relapse. It should be noted that one effect of family intervention is that it makes the person with schizophrenia more likely to take his or her medication. Because medication is a critical part of treatment and those who go off their medication often relapse, the effectiveness of family therapy may have been due to medication compliance. However, subsequent research that controlled for medication compliance found that family therapy did reduce both expressed emotion and relapse (Goldstein, 1999).

It is easy to look at the EE data and blame the family for the hostile environment that leads to relapse, but doing so shows little insight into the challenge of dealing with a family member who has schizophrenia. The case of Margaret illustrates how a person with schizophrenia can easily drive a caring family member to distraction.

Also Affected

MARGARET Margaret did not have schizophrenia, but she was certainly affected by it. Her husband Bob developed schizophrenia in his late twenties after five years of marriage and two children. Over a period of just a few weeks, Bob went from being a wonderful husband and father to someone who was unable to work, unable to think clearly, and unable even to take care of himself. Margaret noticed that Bob was feeling more anxious at work and less trusting of fellow employees, but she thought nothing of it at the time. Soon, however, Bob started recounting horrifying stories about how fellow employees wanted him dead. He would abruptly leave work for no apparent reason and got into increasingly frequent arguments at work. He would often stay up most of the night and would be talking about crazy things when Margaret and the kids got up. His behavior eventually got him fired, although his union intervened and had the dismissal changed to a forced disability leave.

Over a two-year period, Bob was hospitalized three times, but most of his time was spent at home. His behavior ranged from near normal to totally bizarre, and it was almost impossible to predict how he would behave on a given day. Margaret tried to be patient with Bob, but her patience was tested like never before. She was now the primary breadwinner. She not only had to take total responsibility for the kids but also had to protect them constantly from their father's unpredictable behavior. She would get frustrated when Bob stopped taking his medication or canceled appointments with his doctor. Bob said he was fine and did not need the medications, but Margaret could see otherwise. She could not reason with him; at times, she could not even carry on a conversation with him. When his behavior became too outrageous, she would lose control and yell at him.

Family therapy is usually combined with other approaches to provide optimal treatment. The family often can provide the monitoring of medication compliance, a supportive environment, and the encouragement to follow through with treatment recommendations. The family often needs support as well. Margaret benefited from occasional sessions with the social worker who was handling her husband's case. Those sessions gave her a chance to talk about the unique stress of living with someone who has schizophrenia and to learn ways of taking care of herself and her children while managing her husband's disorder.

HOSPITALIZATION AND BEYOND

Hospitalization is often a necessary part of treatment for people with schizophrenia. Although every effort is made today to minimize the use of hospitalization, there are times when people with schizophrenia are simply unable to function because of their symptoms. Hospitalization itself is not a treatment. It may be necessary to protect or stabilize the person. More often, it is the best way to provide the person with a supportive rehabilitative environment.

Protecting the Individual and Others. On rare occasions, people with schizophrenia present a danger to themselves or others. In such cases, the law provides for mandatory hospitalization, called *commitment*, until the risk has passed. Commitment procedures will be discussed in Chapter 16. For now, you should recognize that most people with schizophrenia do not represent an immediate threat and therefore are not committed by the court for treatment. When they *are* committed, it is based on evidence of imminent danger, not on some vague possibility of danger. The process of commitment is a formal procedure, with an attorney assigned to represent the person's

Hospitals are no longer used to "warehouse" individuals with such severe psychiatric disorders as schizophrenia. Instead, they provide an environment to stabilize and rehabilitate people in preparation for release back into the community.

rights, and the period of commitment is generally no more than a few months. The commitment is extended only if another hearing suggests that danger still exists.

Stabilizing the Individual. For the most part, the purpose of hospitalization is to stabilize individuals who are experiencing severe psychotic symptoms. Usually, a period of a few days to a few weeks is necessary to achieve this goal. If the person has the skills needed to function in the community and has a place to return to, hospitalization is likely to be brief. This approach to treatment is sometimes referred to unflatteringly as a revolving-door policy. If people are consistently returning to the hospital either because they never developed the skills to maintain themselves in the community or because they have not been adequately stabilized in the first place, this criticism is justified. However, if the person was released in a stable, though still psychotic, condition to an adequate placement, the use of occasional hospitalizations for reoccurrence of the symptoms is reasonable.

Rehabilitating the Individual. Some people with schizophrenia require considerable rehabilitation before they can be released with a reasonable chance of maintaining themselves in the community. This psychosocial rehabilitation focuses on teaching the person ways of managing stress, handling social situations, and avoiding behaviors that create problems. Some programs work with family members in an effort to establish a supportive environment for the person upon his or her release (Goldstein, 1999). Others emphasize acquisition of skills as part of a coordinated treatment program designed to complement medications (Grace et al., 1996; Mortimer, 2001). These programs usually take months or years, and they are not effective with every person. However, in combination with community support after release, these programs offer people with

schizophrenia the best opportunity to live reasonably independently outside the hospital.

Check Yourself 5.4

Treating Schizophrenia

1. What is the most common treatment for schizophrenia?
2. What two psychological interventions show promise for treating schizophrenia?
3. What is the purpose of hospitalization in the treatment of schizophrenia?

Ponder this . . .   *List some of the issues that might be addressed in family therapy for schizophrenia. What would be the best way to address each of these issues?*

OTHER PSYCHOTIC DISORDERS

Schizophrenia is only one of several psychotic disorders. The remaining psychotic disorders are summarized in Table 5.3 on page 130. This section will cover two of the more common psychotic disorders, delusional disorder and schizoaffective disorder.

DELUSIONAL DISORDERS

People suffering from **delusional disorders** show dramatic and stable delusions, but not the other symptoms typically found in schizophrenia. Unlike schizophrenia, which tends to develop early in adulthood, delusional disorders can develop at any time, even in old age (Manschreck, 2000). Delusional disorders are relatively rare, affecting less than one person in a thousand (APA, 2000). The several subtypes of delusional disorder are summarized in Table 5.4 on page 130.

The defining characteristic of delusional disorders is the presence of persistent, nonbizarre delusions that are not the result of some other physiological or psychological disorder. A nonbizarre delusion is one that could conceivably be true, even if it is unlikely or clearly not true. There may be mild hallucinations, but if these are present, they usually have little impact on the person's behavior. Thought disorder is minimal in these individuals. In fact, they often look and act normal except when they are preoccupied with their delusions. The delusions are often maintained in the face of enormous contradictory evidence and sometimes at great personal cost.

delusional disorders   Characterized by dramatic and stable delusions but few other psychotic symptoms.

[TABLE 5.3] Other Psychotic Disorders

Schizophreniform disorder: This disorder has the same criteria for diagnosis as schizophrenia except that the symptoms do not have to last a minimum of 6 months, nor do the psychotic symptoms have to cause social or occupational impairment.

Schizoaffective disorder: This disorder represents a blend of schizophrenic symptoms and mood disorder symptoms (either bipolar disorder or major depression).

Delusional disorder: This disorder is characterized by one or more nonbizarre delusions in an individual who has never met criteria for the diagnosis of schizophrenia.

Brief psychotic disorder: This disorder is characterized by one or more positive symptoms of schizophrenia that last between 1 and 30 days.

Shared psychotic disorder: This disorder involves a person accepting, in whole or in part, a delusional belief that was originally held by someone with whom the person has a close personal relationship.

Psychotic disorder due to a general medical condition: This is a psychotic disorder judged to be the direct physiological result of a medical condition.

Substance-induced psychotic disorder: This is a psychotic disorder judged to be the direct physiological result of one or more substances, such as medications, toxins, or street drugs.

Psychotic disorder not otherwise specified: This is a psychotic disorder that does not fit into any of the other psychotic diagnoses.

The behavior driven by a person's delusional thinking can be quite disruptive to both the person's life and to the lives of others. For example, people with erotomania believe that someone, typically someone of a higher status, is in love with them. Consequently, they may phone, write letters, send gifts, and even stalk their "lover." The talk-show host David Letterman was stalked for years by a woman

[TABLE 5.4] Subtypes of Delusional Disorders

Erotomanic type	Delusion that someone, typically of higher status, is in love with the person
Grandiose type	Delusion that one has special powers or knowledge or a special relationship to God or to powerful and important people
Jealous type	Delusion that one's sexual partner is unfaithful
Persecutory type	Delusion that one, or a close friend or family member, is being persecuted by powerful people
Somatic type	Delusion that one has a terrible physical defect or disease
Mixed type	Delusions representing more than one of the above categories
Unspecified type	Nature of delusional material not specified

A woman suffering from erotomania stalked David Letterman for years. She was convinced that he loved her, even though he had her arrested repeatedly for harassment and for breaking into his home.

suffering from erotomania—a woman who eventually committed suicide. She periodically broke into his apartment, apparently with the expectation that he would be delighted to see her. Of course, he was not, and in each case she was arrested, taken away, and subjected to both psychiatric and legal consequences for her behavior. Still, her delusion remained strong, apparently to the day she died. Another tragic case involved actress Rebecca Schaeffer, who was murdered by a man who was frustrated by what he experienced as her coy behavior when he "knew" that she really loved him. The following case of Judy is typical.

Love Was Not Enough[1]

JUDY

Judy's case looked routine when she sought therapy at the age of 57 for marital problems. She responded well to supportive therapy, sought advice from family members, and initiated a divorce from an emotionally abusive husband. However, her life remained stressful. In a six-month period, her son moved in with her following his divorce, she was fired from her job, and her son committed suicide, which left her depressed and increasingly delusional. For example, she thought people were sending her messages by having trucks drive by or planes fly over. She continued to receive supportive therapy, which helped her to regain control. She decided to sell her house and apply

---

[1]The case of Judy was discussed in Chapter 3 from the therapist's perspective. She was the person who stalked me off and on for several years.

for Social Security disability benefits. Therapy was terminated, and the case might have ended there—but it didn't.

Six months after therapy ended, Judy started writing letters to her former therapist expressing her gratitude. The weekly letters soon became daily rituals, and the letters became openly erotic. She started calling him, initially leaving messages on the answering machine once or twice a day, which quickly escalated to as many as 20 calls per day. She would deliver daily gifts, even once driving 40 miles in a blizzard to deliver a gift. Soon she was staking out his office, following him whenever he left. At one point, she came into a therapy session for another client and refused to leave until he made love to her. She was puzzled that he chose to call the police instead of acquiescing to her demand. She ignored threats of arrest, letters from his attorney, pleading from her family, and warnings from police officers, who were called on several occasions. Finally, charges were filed and she was arrested and committed to a psychiatric facility because she was found to be suicidal.

This case is interesting in several respects. Judy's belief that the therapist loved her persisted even when there was considerable evidence to the contrary. He told her that he did not love her on dozens of occasions, a message that was reinforced repeatedly by attorneys, the police, her family members, and eventually the judge who ordered her committed for psychiatric observation. Judy had never been hospitalized before, although at various points in her life she was clearly delusional. Her brother reported that her first husband was exceptionally supportive, possibly helping Judy to avoid more serious deterioration. At times during her life, she functioned well, but she also had periods of severe social dysfunction and delusional thinking. She had lost five jobs, each during one of these delusional periods. Several relatives had been diagnosed with schizophrenia or had exhibited significant delusional thinking. Curiously, Judy was remarkably objective in recognizing delusional thinking in her relatives, even though she could not recognize it in herself. Her thinking always had a delusional flavor, but Judy usually did not act on those delusions. This clinical course illustrates the role of psychosocial stressors in exacerbating her disorder.

Causes. Delusional disorders can be puzzling. Their principal symptom (delusions) is common in schizophrenia, yet there is no genetic link between schizophrenia and delusional disorders (Kendler et al., 1981; Kendler & Hays, 1981), although there is a genetic link between delusional disorders and both avoidant and paranoid personality disorders (APA, 2000; Kendler et al., 1985). These disorders will be covered in Chapter 12. We also know that relatives of people with delusional disorders tend to show suspiciousness, secretiveness, and jealousy (Winokur, 1985).

Delusional disorders are rare, usually occur later in life, and have an unpredictable course. Some people show a nearly complete recovery in a few months, whereas others show a very chronic course. The delusions are extremely resistant to logical arguments (Manschreck, 2000).

Treatment. Delusional disorders have proved difficult to treat. The evidence for the effectiveness of the antipsychotic medications that are used to treat schizophrenia is mixed at best (Manschreck, 2000), though there is some evidence that the new atypical antipsychotic agents may have promise (Songer & Roman, 1996). The popular wisdom, based on clinical case studies, is that the delusions are resistant to traditional psychotherapy, although no controlled treatment studies have been published to date. These people often get into legal trouble because they act on their delusional beliefs, which provides informal data on the impact of such aversive consequences as getting arrested and spending time in jail. It is clear that the delusions and the inappropriate behavior driven by the delusions will continue in some people for years, despite repeated and severe aversive consequences.

SCHIZOAFFECTIVE DISORDER

A diagnostic category marked by considerable controversy is **schizoaffective disorder.** This disorder involves a combination of schizophrenic symptoms and symptoms of either bipolar disorder or major depression, which are mood disorders that we will consider in Chapter 7. The controversy revolves around whether this disorder is better conceptualized as a separate disorder, distinct from either schizophrenia or mood disorders, or is a comorbid condition—two disorders in the same person (Procci, 1989). Although the data do not resolve this question, they tend to support the notion that schizoaffective disorder is the combination of two disorders. For example, the biological relatives of people with schizoaffective disorder tend to show increased risk for both schizophrenia and mood disorders (APA, 2000). The relatives of people with schizophrenia show increased risk for schizophrenia, but little increased risk for mood disorders, and a similar pattern is reported for people with mood disorders. This combination of results suggests that people with schizoaffective disorder carry genetic risk factors for both schizophrenia and mood disorders.

It is unclear how common schizoaffective disorder is, in part because there is little consensus on when to use this diagnostic category. It appears to be less common than schizophrenia, although it is not rare (APA, 2000). Onset is usually reported in early adulthood, much like schizophrenia, but late-adult onset is possible and much more common than in schizophrenia. The treatment of schizoaffective disorder typically involves a combination of medications, depending on the particular symptomatology present at the time (Lauriello et al., 2000). In general, the prognosis for schizoaffective disorder is better than for schizophrenia but not so good as for mood disorders (APA, 2000).

schizoaffective disorder   A controversial disorder involving a combination of schizophrenic symptoms and symptoms of either bipolar disorder or major depression.

Check Yourself 5.5

Other Psychotic Disorders

1. What is the primary difference between delusional disorders and schizophrenia?
2. What is the best treatment for delusional disorders?
3. Define the term *schizoaffective disorder*.

Ponder this . . . *The prognosis for schizoaffective disorder is generally better than that for schizophrenia. In general, when someone has two disorders instead of one, we would expect the overall prognosis to be worse. What could be going on to produce this curious finding?*

● SUMMARY

- Schizophrenia affects about 1% of the population, occurs equally often in men and women, and is found throughout the world. Onset is usually in early adulthood, and men develop the disorder on average five years earlier than women. It is overrepresented in the lower social classes and is rare in the upper classes.

SYMPTOMS OF SCHIZOPHRENIA

- The symptoms of schizophrenia include disturbances of thought, perception, attention, and emotion, as well as a variety of deficit, or negative, symptoms.
- Thought disorder is a positive symptom of schizophrenia. It includes loosening of associations, word salad, neologisms, and clang associations.
- Delusions are another positive symptom of schizophrenia. They involve believing things that are not true and that would be unreasonable within the culture.
- Hallucinations, another positive symptom of schizophrenia, involve perceptual experiences with no perceptual stimulus.
- People with schizophrenia often report severe problems focusing their attention on a single object or task, especially during the early phases of their disorder.
- Negative, or deficit, symptoms in schizophrenia include flat affect, anhedonia, avolition, alogia, and asociality.
- In addition to the positive and negative symptoms of schizophrenia, there are symptoms that do not neatly fit either of these categories, including catatonia, inappropriate affect, lack of insight, and psychological dysfunction.

SUBTYPES OF SCHIZOPHRENIA

- The DSM identifies five subtypes of schizophrenia, which are based largely on the original descriptions of Kraepelin.
- Disorganized schizophrenia is characterized by severe disruptions of thought and affect and by bizarre and fragmented hallucinations and delusions.
- Catatonic schizophrenia is characterized by disturbances in movement and posture.

- Paranoid schizophrenia is characterized by fixed paranoid delusions, with relatively little disturbance in thought and affect.
- Undifferentiated schizophrenia is the term applied to people with schizophrenia who do not meet the criteria for any specific subtype.
- Residual schizophrenia represents the mild symptoms typically found in people with schizophrenia during periods of relative remission.

CAUSES OF SCHIZOPHRENIA

- There is strong evidence for a genetic component that predisposes individuals to schizophrenia and to schizophrenic spectrum disorders.
- Several biological factors have been implicated in schizophrenia, including dopamine dysregulation, cerebral atrophy, and neurodevelopmental dysfunctions.
- Environmental factors that may contribute to schizophrenia include expressed emotion and communication deviance. The disproportionately high incidence of schizophrenia in the lower social class appears to be the result of downward drift in social class among people with this disorder.
- Psychodynamic theorists hypothesized that people with schizophrenia regressed to the earliest levels of infant development, but there is little support for this hypothesis.
- Behaviorists once argued that the symptoms of schizophrenia were learned, although the data to support this position are weak.
- The diathesis-stress model proposes that biological factors (the diathesis) increase risk and that environmental factors (the stress) trigger pathology in those at risk.

TREATING SCHIZOPHRENIA

- The primary treatment for schizophrenia is medication. Although generally effective, these drugs are not cures and have significant side effects.
- Traditional psychotherapy is ineffective in treating schizophrenia, although recent work with behavioral

and cognitive interventions is promising. Family therapy has been employed to help family members cope with the disorder. Hospitalization is used primarily to stabilize and protect people with severe psychiatric disorders.

OTHER PSYCHOTIC DISORDERS

- Delusional disorders are characterized by specific delusional thinking with few other psychotic symptoms. The recognized subgroups of delusional disorders are erotomanic type, grandiose type, jealous type, persecutory type, and somatic type.

- The evidence for a relationship between schizophrenia and delusional disorders is weak. Few treatments for delusional disorders show promise, although some of the newest antipsychotic medications may be helpful.

- Some people exhibit what is called schizoaffective disorder, wherein they show both symptoms of schizophrenia and symptoms of mood disorders. It is unclear whether this condition is a separate disorder. The prognosis for such individuals tends to be better than that for the typical person with schizophrenia.

 KEY TERMS

active phase   (111)
adoption studies   (116)
affect   (103)
affective style   (122)
alogia   (109)
anhedonia   (109)
antipsychotic medications   (126)
asociality   (109)
atypical antipsychotics   (126)
avolition   (109)
balanced polymorphism   (111)
catatonia   (109)
catatonic schizophrenia   (112)
catatonic stupor   (109)
cerebral atrophy   (119)
clang associations   (106)
clinical course   (110)
cognitive slippage   (114)
communication deviance   (122)
concordant   (115)
confounded variables   (114)
delusions   (106)
delusional disorders   (129)
delusion of grandeur   (107)
discordant   (115)
disorganized schizophrenia   (112)
dopamine hypothesis   (117)
downward drift hypothesis   (123)

expressed emotion, or EE   (122)
fixed delusional system   (107)
flat or blunted affect   (109)
hallucinations   (107)
inappropriate affect   (109)
lack of insight   (110)
loosening of associations   (106)
negative symptoms   (106)
neologisms   (106)
neurodevelopmental hypothesis   (121)
paranoid delusion   (107)
paranoid schizophrenia   (113)
positive symptoms   (106)
primary narcissism   (124)
prodromal phase   (110)
psychotic disorders   (104)
residual phase   (111)
residual schizophrenia   (114)
schizoaffective disorder   (131)
schizophrenic spectrum disorders   (116)
tardive dyskinesia   (126)
thought disorder   (106)
token economy   (127)
twin studies   (115)
undifferentiated schizophrenia   (113)
waxy flexibility   (109)
word salad   (106)

 SUGGESTED READINGS

Gottesman, I. I. (1991). *Schizophrenia genesis: The origins of madness.* New York: Freeman. This fascinating review of the history of our understanding of schizophrenia has won several awards and has been translated into more than a dozen languages.

Green, M. F. (1998). *Schizophrenia from a neurocognitive perspective: Probing the impenetrable darkness.* Boston: Allyn & Bacon. This technical, although quite readable, book describes some of the exciting work being done to bridge the gap between the neurological studies and the cognitive studies of schizophrenia. Dr. Green has a wonderful, engaging style in presenting the material.

"Roving Eye", Noma & Jim Bliss/©SIS.

chaptersix

6

The Study of Schizophrenia

Chapter 5 introduced schizophrenia—a devastating disorder that has been extensively studied over the last century. In fact, researchers studying schizophrenia developed most of the research paradigms in use today to study psychopathology. A **paradigm** is a research strategy that includes specific assumptions, research methods, and supporting data. This chapter introduces the logic and details of those research paradigms, using research on schizophrenia as illustrations.

There are many ways to study psychopathology, and the approach selected will depend on several factors. One factor is how much is already known. In the early stages of research on a disorder, basic questions are asked, and the research designs are selected accordingly. Later, as understanding of a disorder increases, more precise questions are asked and more specialized research designs are used. The long history of research on schizophrenia illustrates many research paradigms, includes a variety of theoretical perspectives, and offers examples of both successful and unsuccessful lines of research.

This chapter covers research methodology from basic conceptualization and measurement to methods for studying specific aspects of psychopathology, including cognitive processes and genetic, environmental, and physiological influences. Rather than just outlining the research approaches, this chapter emphasizes the logic of each approach and often describes how the research strategy was born.

SCHIZOPHRENIA AS A CONSTRUCT

To understand psychopathology research, one has to understand science. Scientists work with observations, constructs, hypotheses, and theories. **Constructs** are ideas about things that cannot be directly observed. Gravity is a construct. You cannot see it, but you can observe its effects. Furthermore, the construct of gravity explains many phenomena, from falling bodies to orbiting planets. Schizophrenia is also a construct. It is the idea that certain people exhibit a particular disorder characterized by a common symptom pattern, underlying etiology, course, and response to treatment. A **hypothesis** is a tentative statement about the relationship between things. Scientists test hypotheses by making observations to determine whether these observations are consistent with the predictions generated by the hypotheses. **Theories** are the detailed plans on which sciences are organized. Theories connect constructs with one another and with scientific observations. For example, the construct of schizophrenia suggests that it is a disorder characterized by psychotic symptoms. But scientists want to know more about schizophrenia, such as what causes it. They use theories to tie the construct of schizophrenia to other

---

paradigm   A research strategy that includes specific assumptions, research methods, and supporting data.

constructs   Ideas about things that cannot be directly observed.

hypothesis   A tentative statement about the relationship between things.

theories   The detailed plans that connect constructs with one another and with scientific observations.

constructs that might represent the cause(s), such as brain functioning or genes or parenting.

Studying a construct is known as **construct validation.** The construct validation of schizophrenia involves testing the predicted relationships between the diagnosis and such variables as brain functioning, course, and response to treatment. For example, research on brain functioning suggests that some of the symptoms of schizophrenia may result from a dysfunction in the mesolimbic pathways. If people with schizophrenia are shown to have this predicted dysfunction in the mesolimbic pathway, that provides one piece of construct validation. Construct validation is never completed. There are always more predictions to test.

How do researchers establish the construct validity of a disorder such as schizophrenia? The process of construct validation involves deriving predictions about the construct and testing whether those predictions are accurate. In an influential article, Robins and Guze (1970) outlined a comprehensive approach to establishing the construct validity of psychiatric diagnoses, arguing that a valid diagnosis must do five things:

1. Describe the clinical syndrome clearly enough so that professionals consistently agree on diagnoses of individuals (interrater reliability).
2. Predict the performance on laboratory measures for people with the diagnosis.
3. Predict such variables as premorbid history, course, and outcome for people with the diagnosis.
4. Predict family history of psychiatric syndromes for people with the diagnosis.
5. Differentiate the diagnosis from other, superficially similar diagnoses.

Although Robins and Guze did not mention it, a valid diagnosis should also

6. Predict response to treatment (Raulin & Lilienfeld, 1999).

Data on each of these six broad areas will offer evidence that the diagnostic category has construct validity if it predicts things of importance (Waldman et al., 1995). Applying the Robins and Guze approach to the construct of schizophrenia provides research guidance about what relationships are important. For example, existing research shows that

1. Trained clinicians can diagnose schizophrenia reliably.
2. People with schizophrenia perform differently than other people on many laboratory tasks and psychological tests.

3. Schizophrenia is generally, though not invariably, associated with a chronic course and a poor outcome.
4. Schizophrenia is associated with a family history of schizophrenia and of schizotypal and paranoid personality disorders.
5. The pattern reflected in the above findings is generally unique to schizophrenia and is not found in such superficially similar conditions as psychotic mood disorders.
6. People with schizophrenia generally respond positively to dopamine antagonist medications, such as Thorazine or Haldol.

Thus the evidence to date would suggest that schizophrenia is a valid construct.

The foregoing list of findings that support the construct validation of schizophrenia can be deceiving. One might conclude that every study of schizophrenia has been supportive of its construct validity, which is not the case. It is rare that the initial formulation of a construct, such as a psychiatric diagnosis, is so accurate that all of the elements of its construct validation fall into place. More commonly some studies are supportive, whereas others are not. In such cases, researchers modify the criteria defining the disorder to determine whether the modifications increase its construct validity. How that process works is the subject of the next section.

Check Yourself 6.1

Schizophrenia as a Construct

1. What are constructs?
2. Describe the key elements of construct validation.

Ponder this . . . *To appreciate the process of construct validation, consider the construct of love. What is it? How would you measure it? What would you predict its effects might be? Is love one construct or several? For example, is a parent's love for his or her children the same as the love parents have for one another?*

DEFINING AND REFINING THE SYNDROME

People who contemplate the world are struck by both its natural variability and its underlying order. Some aspects of the underlying order are easy to discover. For example, a quick glance around will reveal that there are two types of human beings—males and females. However, nature rarely gives up its secrets so easily. Scientists seek to identify order

construct validation Studying a construct.

in nature. The process of finding order typically requires an initial definition of a construct that hypothetically taps into that order, followed by a series of refinements of that definition on the basis of research data. This section includes a brief review of the history of this process for the construct of schizophrenia, from the early speculations of Kraepelin and Bleuler to the modern diagnostic refinements.

You learned in Chapter 5 about the early work of Kraepelin and Bleuler in defining the construct of schizophrenia. The wisdom of their initial definitions is illustrated by the fact that the current DSM diagnosis of schizophrenia is not dramatically different from what was first proposed, although there have been numerous refinements over the years. Classification systems often develop in this way. A dramatic, almost revolutionary rearrangement of thinking about the topic occurs and then is typically followed by a long period of refinement (Kuhn, 1962). In the case of schizophrenia, Kraepelin and Bleuler provided the revolutionary elements. Kraepelin started the revolution by identifying a relatively narrow syndrome characterized by severe dysfunction and a deteriorating course. He argued that this syndrome represented a distinct disorder, dementia praecox. The disorder was the proposed construct. Bleuler proposed a major refinement to this construct—so major that he suggested a new name, schizophrenia. He noted that many people who showed the same symptom pattern as people with dementia praecox did not show the deteriorating course. Bleuler's concept of schizophrenia was broader than Kraepelin's concept of dementia praecox and quickly became the norm in psychiatry.

Bleuler's broader concept of schizophrenia may have been too broad. Gradually, the diagnostic criteria for schizophrenia were tightened in Europe, because many people who met Bleuler's broader criteria showed differences in symptom pattern, course, or response to treatment. Nevertheless, Bleuler's broader conceptualization of schizophrenia remained dominant in the United States (Cooper et al., 1972). The advent of lithium treatment for manic depression changed things. Manic depression, which is now known as bipolar disorder, will be covered in Chapter 7. It is characterized by excessive energy and many of the psychotic symptoms found in schizophrenia, including hallucinations and delusions. Before the advent of lithium treatment, European psychiatrists took great pains to distinguish manic depression from schizophrenia, but American psychiatrists saw little point in this distinction and used the schizophrenia diagnosis for both groups. However, American psychiatrists later began to distinguish between manic depression and schizophrenia, because one group (people with manic depression) responded well to lithium and the other group (people with schizophrenia) did not (Gottesman, 1991).

This is an excellent example of how problems in the construct validation of a diagnosis lead to refinement of the construct. Because people who had previously been diagnosed with schizophrenia according to Bleuler's criteria showed an inconsistent response to treatment, scientists hypothesized that the criteria were too broad, thus including people who did not belong. Research results supported this hypothesis, and the diagnostic criteria for schizophrenia were revised—in this case, narrowed to exclude people with manic depression. Further refinement is occurring right now with the positive/negative symptom distinction introduced in Chapter 5, but the question is far from resolved (Ho & Andreasen, 2001; Moeller, 1995). Traditional antipsychotic medications are more effective in people with positive than in those with negative symptoms (Meltzer, 1999), whereas the new atypical antipsychotic medications appear to address both positive and negative symptoms (Kane et al., 2001). Furthermore, other data, such as the results of genetic studies, suggest that negative and positive forms of schizophrenia may represent somewhat different forms of schizophrenia, even though there may be some overlap in genetic risk (Baron et al., 1992; Cannon et al., 1991). So why is this distinction not included in the current DSM? So far, the data on this distinction are only promising. More construct validation research is needed before scientists are convinced that this is a valid diagnostic distinction. Nevertheless, these efforts may lead to further refinement of the syndrome of schizophrenia, which is one reason why they continue to receive attention.

Differentiating people with manic depression and schizophrenia was only one of several steps in the refinement of the diagnosis of schizophrenia. Decades earlier, a small group of individuals was identified who exhibited schizopheniclike symptoms and a distinctive course, which included a general weakening of the body, eventual paralysis, and death. Research ultimately showed that this group was suffering from an infection—an advanced case of the sexually transmitted disease syphilis. This condition, known as **general paresis,** is caused by the gradual destruction of brain tissue from the infection. People who show psychotic symptoms are now routinely screened for general paresis as part of a normal diagnostic work-up. As the understanding of the functioning of the human body improved, doctors began to recognize that certain toxic states could mimic the symptoms of schizophrenia. High doses of amphetamines, for example, produce paranoid symptoms that are often indistinguishable from paranoid schizophrenia. Deficiencies of certain vitamins, such as niacin, can also produce psychotic symptoms. Today, professionals can easily distinguish these conditions from schizophrenia.

This process of refining the concept of schizophrenia is ongoing. Continued research will probably identify, within schizophrenia, other distinctive subgroups that have unique etiologies and responses to treatment. Such refining of a broad category into several specific categories is common

....

general paresis Gradual destruction of brain tissue from the sexually transmitted disease syphilis.

in medicine. At one time, virtually all lung diseases were referred to as "consumption"—a broad category that included emphysema, lung cancer, tuberculosis, and pneumonia. Differential diagnosis has led to a better understanding of the causes of lung disorders and of the many ways in which a relatively simple organ, such as the lung, can be disrupted.

Check Yourself 6.2

Defining and Refining the Syndrome

1. What treatment innovation led to a narrowing of the construct of schizophrenia among American psychiatrists?
2. What conditions can cause psychotic symptoms that are similar to the symptoms found in schizophrenia?

Ponder this . . . *Suppose that a new treatment for schizophrenia is found to be very effective, but only for a portion of those with the disorder. A reasonable hypothesis might be that those who do respond actually represent a diagnostic category distinct from schizophrenia. How would scientists proceed to validate this proposed new diagnosis?*

TEST DEVELOPMENT AND VALIDATION

To study a phenomenon, researchers must be able to measure the variables associated with it. A **variable** is any characteristic that can take on different values. For example, diagnosis is a variable because different people can have different diagnoses. Age of onset is a variable because different people develop a disorder at different ages. Stress is a variable because people differ on their average level of stress, and a given person experiences different levels of stress at different times. The measurement of the variables significant in psychology poses unique challenges compared with measurement in other sciences. This section will outline the process of operationalizing a variable and developing and validating a psychological test to measure it.

OPERATIONALIZING A VARIABLE

To measure a variable, one must **operationalize** it, which involves specifying the procedures that one will follow to

measure it. For example, to operationalize the variable of weight, one might specify the scale to be used and the conditions under which it will be used. To operationalize a diagnosis, one would specify what symptoms must be present for the person to qualify for the diagnosis.

In the field of psychopathology, many variables are measured through *self-reports*—that is, people reporting about themselves. Self-reports may be derived from interviews, in which specific questions are asked, or psychological tests, in which people read statements and decide whether the statements accurately describe them. These two formats account for the vast majority of psychological measurement, and examples of each are described in this chapter. Some variables are measured by observing behavior. This approach is recommended, because in general, the best predictor of future behavior is past behavior in a similar situation. Finally, some operational definitions involve having the person respond to a prescribed set of stimuli. The best known of these techniques are the projective tests introduced in Chapter 2. Operationalizing a variable is only the first step in measurement. By far the more critical step is evaluating whether one's operational definition produces an accurate measure of the variable.

DEVELOPING AND EVALUATING PSYCHOLOGICAL INSTRUMENTS

Researchers often need to develop their own measures because no measures for the variables of interest exist. This section will describe the development of a scale to measure intense ambivalence—a trait hypothesized to be a critical symptom in schizophrenia by both Bleuler (1911/1950) and Paul Meehl (1962). Meehl is one of the most influential psychologists in the field of psychopathology. His theory of schizophrenia will be discussed later in this chapter. Table 6.1 presents several items from the Intense Ambivalence Scale (Raulin, 1984).

Recall from Chapter 2 that *reliability* refers to the consistency of a measure, whereas *validity* refers to how strongly the measure is related to other variables. These two concepts form the core of the construct validation of any measure. As we will see, the process of validating a new psychological test involves two steps. The first is identifying what characteristics the scale should have. The second is evaluating the extent to which the scale has those characteristics. Let's review the validational evidence for the Intense Ambivalence Scale.

---

variable Any characteristic that can take on different values.

operationalize To specify the procedures that one will follow to measure a variable.

Examining the Evidence

What characteristics should the Intense Ambivalence Scale have? Let's start with reliability. There are three types of reliability: interrater, test-retest, and internal consistency reliability. Should the Intense Ambivalence

[TABLE 6.1]   The Intense Ambivalence Scale

Many psychological scales ask people whether specific statements accurately describe their feelings. Several items from a scale designed to measure intense ambivalence are shown below. People are to answer true or false, depending on how accurately each item describes them. In parentheses at the end of the item is the response one would expect from an ambivalent person.

- I feel I can trust my friends. (false)
- Love and hate tend to go together. (true)
- Love never seems to last very long. (true)
- I don't mind too much the faults of people I admire. (false)
- I always seem to be the most unsure of myself at the same time that I am most confident of myself. (true)
- I often feel as though I cannot trust people whom I have grown to depend on. (true)
- I find that the surest way to start resenting someone is to just start liking them too much. (true)
- I usually know exactly how I feel about people I have grown close to. (false)

Scale have each of these reliabilities? The answer is "It depends." All psychological measures should have interrater reliability; the scores should be the same no matter who does the measuring. Test-retest reliability should exist only if the characteristic being measured is theoretically stable. Both Bleuler and Meehl argued that intense ambivalence is a stable characteristic of schizophrenia, and therefore the scale should have high test-retest reliability if it is an accurate measure of this construct. Finally, internal consistency reliability should exist only if the characteristic being measured is traitlike—that is, consistent across situations. Again, intense ambivalence is hypothesized to be a consistent trait, so high internal consistency is expected.

How does the Intense Ambivalence Scale stack up in terms of reliability? The Intense Ambivalence Scale is an objective test, in which scoring involves simply counting the number of items answered in the ambivalent direction. Therefore, interrater reliability is perfect. Data from college students and people with schizophrenia showed high test-retest reliability over periods as long as one year (Mahler et al., 1989; Raulin, 1984). Finally, internal consistency reliability was also found to be very high for both college students and people with schizophrenia (Raulin, 1984). In other words, the Intense Ambivalence Scale is clearly reliable in every sense that was theoretically required. The next step is determining the scale's validity.

To evaluate the validity of the Intense Ambivalence Scale, one must first identify the variables that should be related to scores on the scale. Two predictions from the construct of intense ambivalence are (1) that people who score high on the scale should behave ambivalently and (2) that people with schizophrenia should score higher on this scale than people without schizophrenia.

Do high scorers on this scale behave ambivalently? College students who scored high on the scale were found to contradict themselves about their feelings in a brief interview more than twice as often as students who scored in the normal range (Raulin, 1984). To avoid potential bias, the interviews and the scoring of the interviews were done **blind**—that is, without the researcher knowing the scores on the Intense Ambivalence Scale. A researcher who expected ambivalent individuals to contradict themselves more might be inclined to interpret ambiguous responses as contradictions or might ask questions in such a way as to elicit such contradictions. This effect is referred to as **experimenter bias,** and keeping the researcher blind effectively controls it.

Does intense ambivalence characterize people with schizophrenia? To address this question, a group of people with schizophrenia were compared to three other groups: (1) a nonpatient group that had approximately the same age, education, and social class as the schizophrenic sample, (2) a group of hospitalized depressed individuals, again of roughly the same age, sex, and social class, and (3) a sample of individuals seeking outpatient psychotherapy. It is common to have multiple comparison groups, because each comparison group controls for different confounding variables. A **confounding variable** is any variable, other than the variable of interest, on which the groups differ. If the groups being compared differ on more than one variable and a performance difference is discovered, the researcher will not know which of the variables was responsible for the performance difference. For example, the variable of interest in this study is the diagnosis of schizophrenia. If people with schizophrenia reported greater levels of ambivalence than a nonpatient comparison group, that difference might be

....

blind   Said of researchers who, in order to avoid potential bias, do not know the test scores of the people they interview.

experimenter bias   Occurs when a researcher expects a certain outcome and is inclined to interpret ambiguous responses as consistent with that expectation or ask questions in such a way as to elicit the expected result.

confounding variable   Any variable, other than the variable of interest, on which research groups differ.

due to schizophrenia, to hospitalization, to social class, to the stigma associated with having a mental disorder, or to some combination of these variables, because the two groups would probably differ on all these variables. The other two comparison groups in this study were included to "control for" some of these confounding variables. The people seeking outpatient psychotherapy were experiencing psychological distress and the stigma associated with a psychiatric diagnosis. The hospitalized depressed individuals controlled for these confounding variables, as well as for the variable of hospitalization. The people with schizophrenia did score higher than the nonpatient sample on the Intense Ambivalence Scale, but the depressed individuals scored higher than those with schizophrenia. These data clearly challenged the construct validity of the scale, suggesting that either the underlying theory was wrong or the scale was not measuring the construct of ambivalence as intended.

When faced with contradictory construct validation evidence, the researcher should modify either the construct or the measure. In fact, this is the type of finding that leads to refinements in constructs. In the case of the Intense Ambivalence Scale, item analyses revealed that a subset of items was strongly related to depression and another subset was strongly related to schizophrenia. Any item that referred to feelings changing from positive to negative was related to depression (*I can think of someone right now that I thought I could trust, but now I know I can't.*) In contrast, the items that discriminated individuals with schizophrenia from depressed individuals were matter-of-fact in their tone (*Love and hate tend to go together.*) Both types of items assessed ambivalence, but the emotional tone of some of the items meant that they also assessed depression, which is not what was intended. The scale was therefore modified so that it measured more effectively the intense ambivalence associated with schizophrenia (Raulin & Brenner, 1993).

Check Yourself 6.3

Test Development and Validation

1. How is a psychological measure validated?
2. When are test-retest reliability and internal consistency reliability relevant?

Ponder this . . . *When the validational data for the Intense Ambivalence Scale showed that depressed people scored higher than people with schizophrenia, the scale was modified because the construct of ambivalence as a unique symptom of schizophrenia was assumed to be valid. However, another approach would have been to reconsider the construct of intense ambivalence and accept the scale as it is. How might you modify the theoretical construct of ambivalence to take these data into account?*

DIATHESIS-STRESS MODELS

The diathesis-stress model, introduced in Chapter 3, is the most widely accepted model of psychopathology. Therefore, it is important to clarify the diathesis-stress model of schizophrenia before discussing the research on this disorder.

An analogy may help. If a bridge is built, but a key section of the bridge has defective steel, then the defective steel represents a diathesis, or risk factor, for structural failure. If the bridge is never really stressed during its lifetime, it may survive in spite of the weakness. However, if truck traffic on the bridge increases, thus adding a significant stress, the bridge may collapse because of the interaction of the structural weakness and the added heavy traffic. This analogy illustrates a simple diathesis-stress model. Now let's suppose both that the bridge has a section with defective steel and that one of the supports was constructed on land that is slowly sinking, thus gradually decreasing the bridge's support. This example illustrates multiple diatheses. Finally, suppose that the only risk factor for the bridge is a section with defective steel but that an earthquake moves one of the support towers enough to stress the entire structure. That movement, coupled with the heavy increase in traffic, sets the bridge up for eventual collapse. In this last example, there is a single diathesis and multiple stresses. At one time or another, diathesis-stress models for schizophrenia analogous to each of these examples have been proposed.

A bridge with a weakness may survive for decades if it is not subjected to sufficiently severe stress. In this analogy, the bridge weakness is the diathesis, and the heavy truck traffic is the stressor. Most theorists believe that conceptually similar diathesis-stress models may explain most forms of psychopathology.

This section starts by describing the most widely acknowledged diathesis-stress model for schizophrenia—the schizotaxia, schizotypy, schizophrenia model of Paul Meehl (1962). Then newer diathesis-stress models are described. The section ends with a discussion of how diathesis-stress models have shaped conceptualizations of schizophrenia and the resulting research.

SCHIZOTAXIA, SCHIZOTYPY, SCHIZOPHRENIA

Meehl (1962) suggested that there was a genetic risk factor that resulted in an integrative neural deficit that he called **schizotaxia.** He speculated that this defect involved a disruption in the functioning of individual neurons and that this subtle deficit interacted with environmental experiences to create more dramatic behavioral characteristics. Meehl's original formulation emphasized a single gene in schizophrenia, although he acknowledged that other genes might contribute (Meehl, 1962). In later formulations, he argued more strongly for additional genetic influences (Meehl, 1990). This schizotaxia was hypothesized to be a necessary, but not a sufficient, condition for schizophrenia. That is, it increased risk for schizophrenia but did not guarantee that schizophrenia would develop. Meehl further argued that anyone with this schizotaxia would develop a specific personality organization called **schizotypy,** characterized by such traits as cognitive slippage, magical thinking, anhedonia, and disturbance in one's body image (Meehl, 1962, 1964). In contrast to Meehl's model, Gottesman argues that the genetic diathesis is polygenic (Gottesman et al., 1987). In a polygenic model, it is hard to pinpoint a single diathesis, because there are many potential combinations of genes that can predispose a person to psychosis.

When Meehl delivered his landmark paper, environmental hypotheses dominated psychopathology, and many professionals either dismissed the genetic data or were unaware of it. What Meehl did was provide a framework for integrating genetic and environmental variables into a coherent model. Genes created an internal environment that fostered the development of a vulnerable personality style—schizotypy—but Meehl argued that only about 10% of people with this vulnerable personality ever went on to develop schizophrenia.

Meehl's diathesis-stress model focused researchers' attention on the question of what was inherited and, once inherited, how it affected the individual. The first step in studying these questions is to identify the individuals who have schizotaxia, because they could provide clues about how schizotaxia predisposes the individual to schizophrenia. There are several ways to identify such carriers. One is to study carefully the premorbid personalities of people who develop schizophrenia. Factors that differentiate these people from people who do not develop the disorder—factors referred to as *schizotypic signs*—may well be indica-

tors of the underlying schizotaxia. A second approach is to study people with schizophrenia during remissions. It is likely that the characteristics that are part of the schizotypal personality will remain even after the symptoms have disappeared. A third approach is to study family members, who are more likely to show schizotypic signs than randomly selected people. In particular, identical twins of people with schizophrenia who do not develop schizophrenia are ideal, because they must be carriers of the schizotaxia.

Scientists often state a hypothesis, derive predictions, and then test their accuracy. The more predictions that are confirmed, the more confidence one should have in the hypothesis. Let's look at the data on one such prediction.

Examining the Evidence

One prediction derived from Meehl's hypothesis is that individuals who do not have schizophrenia but have an identical twin with schizophrenia must still have the schizotaxia. Therefore, they should be as likely as their psychotic twins to pass it on to their children. On the face of it, this prediction is counterintuitive. It says that the risk for schizophrenia in the offspring of a person with schizophrenia will be the same as the risk from someone without the disorder, provided that the person without the disorder has an identical twin who has schizophrenia. An environmental hypothesis would never generate this prediction; only a genetic model like the one proposed by Meehl would. The data support this strong prediction; the rates of schizophrenia in the offspring of discordant identical twins are virtually identical (Fischer, 1971; Gottesman & Bertelsen, 1989). In contrast, the rates of schizophrenia in the offspring of discordant fraternal twins suggest that the twin without the disorder has no increased risk for schizophrenia. These data are illustrated in Figure 6.1 on page 142. This finding is not enough to prove Meehl's model, because other genetic models generate the same prediction, but it certainly increases one's confidence in the hypothesis that genes play a significant role in schizophrenia.

OTHER DIATHESIS-STRESS MODELS

In psychopathology, both multiple diatheses and multiple stresses are likely. Some of these factors may operate

schizotaxia   An integrative neural deficit linked to a genetic risk factor for schizophrenia.

schizotypy   A specific personality organization characterized by such traits as cognitive slippage, magical thinking, anhedonia, and disturbance in body image.

[FIGURE 6.1]
Risk for Schizophrenia in Offspring

Gottesman and Bertelsen (1989) found that the rates of schizophrenia in the offspring of discordant identical twins were virtually the same, which suggests that the unaffected co-twin must have carried the genetic risk factor for schizophrenia. By contrast, the offspring of the discordant fraternal twin of an individual with schizophrenia has no increased risk of schizophrenia.

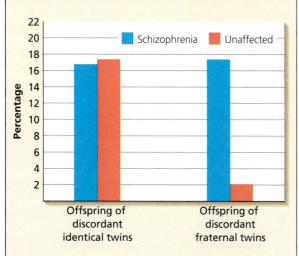

SOURCE: *Adapted from "Risk for Schizophrenia Offspring" in "Confirming Unexpressed Genotypes for Schizophrenia" by Gottesman and Bertelsen, Archives of General Psychiatry, 46, 1998. Copyright © 1998 by the American Medical Association. Reprinted by permission of the publisher.*

independently, each adding a bit more risk and making the person more vulnerable to psychopathology. This is the model proposed by Mednick et al. (1998). Their *two-hit model* proposes that multiple factors, such as a genetic diathesis and birth or pregnancy complications, combine to increase risk for schizophrenia. It is also likely that some factors will interact, such that the combination of the two factors is much worse than the sum of the negative effects of the factors when they occur independently. Meehl's (1990) current model of schizophrenia proposes that the specific risk factor for schizophrenia interacts with other genetic factors, environmental factors, or both. For example, Meehl argues that the trait of anhedonia (the inability to experience pleasure) interacts with the schizotaxia by reducing the inclination to engage in the pleasant activity of socializing. The resulting increase in social isolation reduces social support and decreases potential corrective feedback when the person's thoughts and ideas stray from normal. However, anhedonia is not presumed to be a risk factor by itself.

These more complex diathesis-stress models are becoming increasingly common. Although more difficult to test than the simple diathesis-stress models of the past, they are showing promise, and they probably represent a more

faithful representation of the reality of psychopathology. As research on diathesis-stress models continues, ever more sophisticated questions will be addressed. For example, does the diathesis combine with the stress in an additive fashion, or do the two interact? If it is an additive combination, the risk is the sum of the two effects. In this model, it is theoretically possible to have a diathesis strong enough to produce schizophrenia without a significant stressor or a stressor severe enough to produce schizophrenia without a genetic diathesis. In contrast, Meehl's model represents an interaction. With an interaction, the effect of the stress is different when the diathesis exists, and only people with the diathesis will respond strongly enough to develop schizophrenia. How risk factors interact is every bit as important as what the risk factors are. These questions will take time to answer, but the most sophisticated researchers are already considering them in formulating theories.

The available evidence suggests that there are multiple risk factors, some specific and others general. How these multiple factors combine to create a given disorder in a specific person is far from understood. Nevertheless, significant progress in understanding these factors is being made. Serious researchers and theorists have largely abandoned simple cause-effect models. **Developmental models of psychopathology,** which focus on how psychopathology develops over time, enable researchers to study where in the process each factor might be affecting the person (Leckman, 1999). It is naïve to say that schizophrenia is caused by a gene or by faulty parenting or by any other single factor. Psychopathologists have long since discarded such models in favor of the multifactorial models described in this section. Furthermore, there is increasing emphasis on studying people over time as a way of documenting the developmental course of a disorder.

It is highly unlikely that a single factor is responsible for any form of psychopathology. Even if scientists found, for example, that a specific region of the brain was always dysfunctional in people with schizophrenia, it would not mean that there is just one cause of the disorder. Such evidence might suggest a single proximal cause—that is, an immediate cause of the symptoms. However, there might be multiple distal causes—that is, different ways in which people could develop the proximal cause of the symptoms. The concept of *cause* in psychopathology is complex, sometimes frighteningly so. Nevertheless, with sufficient clarity about one's theories and with enough data, even the most complex of hypotheses can be tested.

To clarify some important distinctions, a given factor may be necessary, but not sufficient, to cause a disorder. Meehl's (1962, 1990) schizotaxia is in this category. Alternatively, a factor may be sufficient, but not necessary. For

developmental models of psychopathology Cause-effect models that focus on how psychopathology develops over time.

example, specific environmental trauma to the developing fetus, especially during the critical second trimester when the brain is developing, may be enough to lead to the neurodevelopmental problems that eventually result in schizophrenia (Green, 1998). However, if there are other ways in which schizophrenia can develop, this environmental trauma is clearly not necessary. Logically speaking, a factor could be both necessary and sufficient, but no one has proposed a model of schizophrenia with such a factor. In fact, the data from several sources would argue against such hypotheses. For example, the twin study data suggest that both genes and environment play critical roles. Finally, a factor can be neither necessary nor sufficient, in which case it is just one of many factors that increase risk for the disorder. Many of the **general risk factors** in psychopathology—such as reduced social support, psychological stress, and expressed emotion—fall into this category. These factors may add to the risk, but they are neither necessary nor sufficient, and they are not specific to a given disorder.

What kind of stress might contribute to schizophrenia and other psychological disorders? Could the stresses associated with being homeless contribute? What about family stresses, occupational stresses, and interpersonal stresses? These questions remain largely unanswered at this time.

Check Yourself 6.4

Diathesis-Stress Models

1. What is the hypothesized nature of Meehl's schizotaxia?
2. What evidence is there that the discordant identical twins of people with schizophrenia carry the genetic risk factor for schizophrenia?
3. What is the nature of current diathesis-stress models of schizophrenia?

Ponder this . . .   *In order to study the hypothesized construct of schizotaxia, one has to identify the characteristics of people who have this condition. What group of individuals would be ideal for studying the nature of schizotaxia? (Hint: It should be a group in which you know the people have the schizotaxia, even though they do not develop schizophrenia.)*

OVERVIEW OF RESEARCH DESIGNS

Several research strategies are used to study psychopathology. Five of them are introduced in this section: case studies, experimental studies, correlational studies, prospective and retrospective studies, and high-risk studies.

CASE STUDIES

Case studies involve the careful evaluation of a single person. Although they are a rich source of hypotheses, case studies are ill suited to uncovering general principles because each individual is unique (Raulin & Lilienfeld, 1999). For example, if a history of childhood abuse is found in someone with schizophrenia, it is unreasonable to conclude that the abuse caused the schizophrenia. The abuse experienced by this person may have had nothing to do with the later development of schizophrenia, and a case study cannot rule out that possibility. Furthermore, childhood abuse may be commonly experienced by people who do not develop schizophrenia. If one wanted to test the hypothesis that there is a link between childhood abuse and schizophrenia, one would have to compare groups of people with and without schizophrenia. Even this strategy does not establish causation, but it will determine whether abuse is more common in those who develop schizophrenia. This

general risk factors   Factors such as reduced social support, psychological stress, and expressed emotion that may add to the risk of schizophrenia. Nevertheless, they are neither necessary nor sufficient to cause the disease, nor are they specific to a given disorder.

case studies   Careful evaluations of individuals.

strategy will be discussed shortly. In spite of their limitations, case studies can provide useful hypotheses for further study, as illustrated with Angelo.

The Runt of the Litter

Angelo could never compete with his identical twin brother, Bobby, who always seemed to do a bit better at everything from school to playground activities. They looked the same and generally behaved the same, but there was always a subtle difference; if Angelo averaged a C+, Bobby would average a B. So no one took much note when Bobby became the more outgoing and popular one in high school and Angelo became increasingly shy. The subtle differences in grades became larger. Bobby decided to go to college, but Angelo thought it made more sense to get a job. Angelo's shyness increased after high school until he became socially isolated, spending nearly all nonworking hours in his room at home. His first schizophrenic episode occurred at age 24, after he lost his job when the company went bankrupt.

The case of Angelo is much more likely to be useful in generating hypotheses than most cases, because Angelo had an identical twin who did not develop schizophrenia. Are there clues in this case that might help explain the discordance in these twins? Clearly, Angelo was less successful than his twin brother throughout life, although the differences were small until late in high school. Could this have discouraged him and decreased his ability to cope emotionally? Perhaps, but both Angelo and Bobby were above average. It seems unlikely that being above average, even if your brother always did a bit better than you, could be a powerful enough factor to lead to schizophrenia. But there was another factor that may have contributed, and it goes back to before birth. There was nearly a 1.5-pound difference in the twins' birth weights. By age 2, this weight difference had been eliminated, but during the early stages of development, Angelo was always smaller and lagged 2–4 weeks behind in physical development. It is not uncom-

mon for one member of a twin pair to receive additional nourishment in the womb, often at the expense of the other twin (Plomin et al., 1990). Could this factor have been either a general risk factor or a risk factor that is specific to schizophrenia? This is a good question and an excellent research hypothesis. Answering it will take more than just a case study.

EXPERIMENTAL RESEARCH

The most powerful research strategy available to scientists is the experiment. In **experimental research,** participants are randomly assigned to one of two or more groups, each group is subjected to a particular treatment, and the groups are compared. For example, people with schizophrenia might be randomly assigned to two groups, each group given a different drug treatment, and the groups compared on treatment response. This strategy is effective because the process of randomly assigning participants to groups makes it likely that the groups are comparable at the beginning of the study (Graziano & Raulin, 2000). Therefore, any difference noted at the end of the study is probably due to the manipulation performed by the researcher. The variable that defines the groups is called the **independent variable.** The independent variable in this example is the type of drug treatment. The variable that is measured to determine whether the independent variable had an effect is called the **dependent variable.** The dependent variable in this example is the measure of treatment response.

If experiments are the best research strategy, why use anything but experiments? The reason is that in fields like psychopathology, experimental research is often impossible or unethical. There is no way to randomly assign people to be schizophrenic, and even if there were, it would not be ethical. The nearby Focus box addresses some of the most relevant ethical issues in psychopathology research.

CORRELATIONAL RESEARCH

Correlational research seeks to measure the relationship between variables. For example, a researcher studying negative symptomatology in schizophrenia might use a measure of the severity of negative symptoms and correlate it with the age of onset of the disorder. The correlation coefficient is the index of the strength of the relationship. It ranges from −1.00 to +1.00. The sign indicates the direction of the relationship, and the size indicates the strength of the relationship. For example, the correlation between severity of negative symptomatology and age of onset might be −0.58, which means that the later the age of onset, the less negative symptomatology the individual experiences, on average. Correlations can also be visualized in a scatter plot, as shown in Figure 6.2 on page 146. Scatter plots are created by taking the two scores for each individual and plotting the points on a two-dimensional graph. The stronger the correlation, the more these points cluster along a line.

experimental research   Studies in which participants are randomly assigned to one of two or more groups, each group is subjected to a particular treatment, and the groups are compared.

independent variable   The variable that defines the groups being studied.

dependent variable   The variables that are measured to see whether the independent variable had an effect.

informed consent   The right of each person to decide whether to participate after being fully informed about the nature of a research study.

correlational research   Research that measures the relationship between variables.

FOCUS · Ethical issues in psychopathology research

All researchers must be aware of ethical requirements when planning and conducting research. However, working in the field of psychopathology entails some special ethical issues. The following list is not exhaustive but merely highlights issues that are frequently encountered.

INFORMED CONSENT

The most critical safeguard in research is the concept of **informed consent,** which refers to the right of each person to decide whether to participate after having been fully informed about the nature of the study. With some forms of psychopathology, such as schizophrenia, it is not clear that the person has the ability to make a reasoned judgment about participation. In such cases, the person's consent alone is insufficient; consent from a legal guardian may also be required.

RISK TO PARTICIPANTS

No study is risk-free, but some studies involve more risk than others. For example, a surgical procedure has more risk than a clinical interview. However, not all risk is obvious. For example, a clinical interview usually involves little risk, but with some people, discussing the topics of the interview could be stressful and disruptive.

Researchers have a responsibility to minimize risk. Minimizing risk does not mean eliminating it; the only way

to eliminate risk is never to conduct research. Risk is always weighed against potential benefits. Valuable research that has clear risks is acceptable if participants are fully informed of the risks and, in possession of that information, decide to participate. Even with informed consent from participants, it is the obligation of researchers to anticipate problems and be prepared to handle them. For example, if a participant experiences distress during a study, the researcher must be qualified and prepared to handle the person's distress. Merely stopping the procedure and dismissing a distressed individual is ethically unacceptable. Some procedures, such as drug treatment studies, may entail medical risks. The researcher has the obligation to monitor potential risks and take immediate action if a problem develops.

Some research creates potential risks if specific procedures are not followed. For example, research on the effects of alcohol may involve having people consume alcohol. The researcher should not enlist people who are under age, problem drinkers, individuals who have health problems that would be exacerbated by drinking, or people who have little experience with drinking and therefore may respond strongly to consuming alcohol. In addition, the researcher must protect the welfare of the participants. Researchers in this area often insist that participants agree to stay in the laboratory for a fixed period after

the study is over to permit their blood alcohol to decrease to safe levels. If participants decide to leave early, the researcher has an obligation to offer a ride or offer to drive them to their destination in their car.

PROTECTING THE PARTICIPANT'S CONFIDENTIALITY

In research on psychopathology, potentially sensitive information is often gathered from participants. Researchers should protect the confidentiality of that information by storing it in locked cabinets and, as an additional safeguard, removing identifying information.

TAKING POSITIVE ACTION

Sometimes researchers uncover serious problems during a study. For example, the participant may report suicidal thoughts, or testing may reveal medical problems. Some of these risks are predictable, and researchers are required to have a standard response. For example, suicidal ideation is relatively common in depression. Therefore, the researcher should have an adequate plan for reducing the risk of suicide in people under study. Other problems are less predictable. Nevertheless, it is assumed that the researcher is qualified to identify and deal with problems or to make available experts who can deal with problems that may arise.

Researchers use correlations frequently in research on psychopathology to measure the strength of the relationship between variables.

One problem with correlational studies is that we must be cautious when we interpret them. If variables A and B are correlated, there are three potential interpretations. The first is that A causes B; the second is that B causes A; the third is that some other variable causes both A and B.

Let's consider the hypothetical correlation between age of onset and level of negative symptoms. Could earlier onset lead to stronger negative symptomatology? Could the negative symptomatology lead to an earlier age of onset? It is most likely that a third factor—possibly the nature of the illness itself—influences both variables. Some forms of schizophrenia may be characterized by both early onset and stronger negative symptoms. The point is that it is

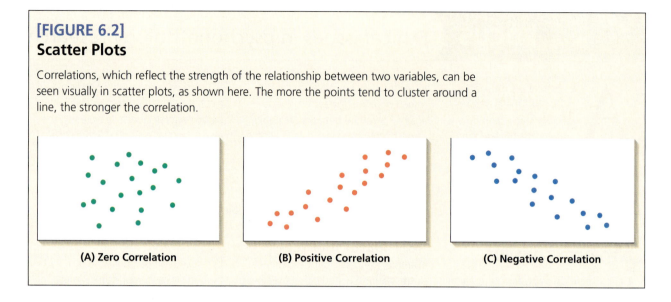

[FIGURE 6.2]
Scatter Plots

Correlations, which reflect the strength of the relationship between two variables, can be seen visually in scatter plots, as shown here. The more the points tend to cluster around a line, the stronger the correlation.

(A) Zero Correlation   **(B) Positive Correlation**   **(C) Negative Correlation**

impossible to tell from a simple correlation which of these interpretations is accurate.

Perhaps the most commonly used correlational research strategy in the field of psychopathology is to compare groups of individuals with and without a given disorder. For example, one might compare people with schizophrenia and people with bipolar disorder on the number of relatives who are diagnosed with schizophrenia. Although it may not be obvious, this strategy is a correlational approach because one is looking at the relationship between two variables—in this case, the relationship between diagnosis and the psychiatric status of relatives. This approach of comparing already-existing groups is referred to as **differential research.** This strategy was used in the validation of the Intense Ambivalence Scale discussed earlier in the chapter. Researchers hope that differences between people with and without a disorder will yield clues about what factors might be responsible for the disorder. For example, if people with schizophrenia were found to be more prone to making specific types of memory errors, one might hypothesize that this problem contributes to their risk for schizophrenia.

The problem with differential research is that these already-existing groups are likely to differ on many things—the concept called confounding that was introduced earlier. Because the groups differ in several ways, any observed differences between the groups could be due to any of those

differences. There is no easy way to eliminate confounding entirely in psychopathology research. Therefore, scientists select the best comparison groups available and are cautious about their conclusions. That is why several comparison groups were used in the validation of the Intense Ambivalence Scale. Each group controlled for different sources of confounding.

Other problems must also be considered when comparing groups to investigate psychopathology. For example, it is generally accepted that people with schizophrenia tend to do poorly on almost every task; the phenomenon is referred to as a **generalized deficit.** This does not occur in all psychiatric disorders, but it clearly occurs in schizophrenia. Because people with schizophrenia do worse on just about everything, it is not terribly interesting to find that they do worse on a new task that has never been studied in schizophrenia. Therefore, an approach called **differential deficit research** is used, in which people with schizophrenia are tested to see whether they do particularly poorly on one task compared with another. For example, a once popular theory of schizophrenia was that people with the disorder were so distressed when dealing with emotional material that their thought disorder increased and their performance decreased. More than a dozen studies of this phenomenon were published in the 1950s and 1960s (Chapman & Chapman, 1973a). For example, Woods (1961) asked people with and people without schizophrenia to sort emotional objects, such as a smiling face, and neutral objects, such as a book, into categories. Half of the items were emotional and the other half neutral. Woods found that people with schizophrenia did worse than those without the disorder on both emotional and neutral items but that they did particularly poorly on the emotional items.

This differential deficit design has been used hundreds of times to test dozens of hypotheses about schizophrenic deficits. Unfortunately, as Chapman and Chapman (1973b) showed in a classic paper, it is a design that can easily mis-

differential research   Research that compares already-existing groups.

generalized deficit   The tendency of people with schizophrenia to do poorly on almost every task.

differential deficit research   Studies in which people with schizophrenia are tested to see whether they do particularly poorly on one task compared with another.

lead investigators if proper precautions are not taken. None of the earlier researchers recognized the problem, so two decades of research on differential deficit was called into question. The Chapmans outlined procedures that would prevent the problem, but the procedures were cumbersome and created problems of their own (Knight & Silverstein, 2001). Their approach involved matching the two measures both on reliability and on the variability of scores, which is still regarded as the best solution (Strauss, 2001). This issue illustrates an important point: Conducting research in psychopathology requires a sophisticated understanding of both psychopathology and research methods. Anything less is a recipe for failure.

PROSPECTIVE AND RETROSPECTIVE STUDIES

Comparing diagnostic groups is an example of cross-sectional research. In **cross-sectional studies,** groups are compared at one point in time. Such comparisons may give clues to how the group differences might have developed, but they are not particularly good at helping to uncover the details of the developmental course for a disorder. To do that, one must study people over time to observe changes in their clinical status; in other words, one must conduct a **longitudinal study.**

Following people longitudinally to see whether they develop psychopathology, and to see what variables predict the development of psychopathology, is a powerful research strategy. The longitudinal approach to following people over time to see who develops psychopathology is called a **prospective study.** In contrast, a **retrospective study** involves examining the histories of people who develop a disorder to see what factors distinguish them from those who do not. You might think that these approaches are comparable because they both have the same objective, but they're not. Retrospective studies tend to be biased because the outcome can shape people's memories of past events. For example, people might be more likely to remember unusual behavior in someone who later developed schizophrenia than in someone who did not. These retrospective biases are well known, and they make most studies that rely on memory of past events suspect (Loftus & Loftus, 1980; Loftus, 2001). However, retrospective studies can be valuable in identifying factors that may be worth a closer look. In this way, they can provide the evidence to justify the greater time and expense of a prospective study.

Retrospective studies can minimize memory biases by using existing records that were made earlier, such as school report cards, medical records, and high school yearbooks (Barthell & Holmes, 1968). For example, Elaine Walker and her colleagues studied subtle neurodevelopmental problems in people who later developed schizophrenia by evaluating childhood home movies (Walker et al., 1993, 1994). As a control group, they used home movies of siblings who did not develop schizophrenia. All movies were evaluated blindly to avoid experimenter bias. As we saw in Chapter 5, Walker found clear evidence that children who go on to develop schizophrenia have subtle neurological deficits that are detectable in early childhood.

Prospective studies eliminate many of the biases inherent in retrospective studies, but they have the disadvantage of being expensive and time-consuming. It can cost millions of dollars to evaluate and follow hundreds of people, and only a small percentage of those people will develop psychopathology. For example, the base rate of schizophrenia in the general population is approximately 1%. About half of those who eventually develop schizophrenia do so by the age of 28. Therefore, if 1000 randomly selected people are followed from age 15 through age 28, approximately 5 of them will develop schizophrenia. Following 1000 people for 13 years is a lot of work for such a small yield of information. Furthermore, it is difficult to maintain contact with research participants over the several years that a longitudinal study may take. These numbers should quickly convince you that there has to be a better way, and there is. The better way is the high-risk study.

HIGH-RISK STUDIES

High-risk studies are prospective studies in which the people being followed are known to be at a higher than average risk for the disorder. For example, scientists know that schizophrenia runs in families. The offspring of parents who have schizophrenia are roughly ten times more likely than randomly selected individuals to develop schizophrenia. For low-base-rate disorders, such as schizophrenia, high-risk approaches are often the only financially feasible way of conducting a prospective study. This section will discuss two high-risk methodologies, the genetic and behavioral high-risk paradigms.

Genetic High-Risk Paradigms. The **genetic high-risk paradigm** selects participants on the basis of their

---

cross-sectional studies   Studies in which groups are compared at one point in time.

longitudinal studies   Studies in which people are followed over time to observe changes in their clinical status.

prospective study   The longitudinal approach to following people over time to see if psychopathology develops.

retrospective study   A study that looks into the history of people who develop a disorder to see what factors distinguish those who develop problems from those who do not.

high-risk studies   Prospective studies in which the people being followed are known to be at a higher than average risk for the disorder.

genetic high-risk paradigm   A study in which participants are selected on the basis of their genetic relationship to someone with a specified psychopathology.

MODERN Myths

Not Finding What You Expect IS a Failure

Most of the time, scientists are able to predict what they will find in their research. They can do that because research studies are rarely conducted in a vacuum. Rather, each study builds on dozens or even hundreds of earlier studies, and the theories that generated the research hypotheses have often been tested repeatedly. Past research and well-validated theories help scientists to make accurate predictions about what they will find. So what happens when a prediction is wrong? Do scientists throw out their theories or ignore the contradictory results? In extreme circumstances, scientists may well discard a theory when critical predictions derived from it are wrong. More often, scientists will rethink the theory, modify it as necessary, and then challenge the theory again with additional research. What good scientists *never* do is ignore contradictory results.

Mednick and Schulsinger (1968) measured psychophysiological functioning in their genetic high-risk study to identify early precursors of later psychiatric deterioration. They selected a measure of physiological arousal and presented each participant with a series of stimuli that normally increases arousal. They had predicted that the high-risk group would respond more strongly to the stimuli and would

recover more slowly, which would result in generally higher levels of chronic arousal. This arousal was hypothesized to be one of the factors that increased risk for eventual psychiatric deterioration. The theory made sense and was consistent with what was known at the time. The only problem was that the data disconfirmed it. The response to the arousing stimuli was not stronger in high-risk individuals, although they did not adapt to the stimulus the way low-risk individuals did in that they continued to react to each stimulus well after most people would have learned to ignore it. This increased their chronic arousal, but for a different reason than had been hypothesized. The most striking finding, however, was that high-risk individuals not only did not recover from arousal more slowly but actually recovered more quickly. This seems inconsistent with the observation that people who develop schizophrenia are generally more anxious and aroused before their symptoms appear. Nevertheless, the data must be taken seriously.

All important research findings should be replicated—that is, repeated to determine whether the findings are consistent—but once that replication shows that the findings are consistent, it is up to the researcher to make sense of them. These results may have

been surprising, but they are interpretable. The pattern of autonomic arousal has implications for learning. Stronger autonomic arousal to stimuli will result in quicker learning of responses. For example, if a situation creates more intense fear in one person than in another, the person who experiences the greater fear is likely to learn to avoid situations more quickly. Similarly, a rapid decrease in fear would strongly reinforce responses that trigger the decrease. For example, a person who recovers more quickly than another person from fear will experience greater reinforcement from withdrawal or avoidance behavior. Mednick and Schulsinger speculated that forcing oneself to think about something other than the immediate stimulus is a psychological form of withdrawal. The rapid drop in arousal in the high-risk participants would make such psychological withdrawal more reinforcing and therefore more likely to occur. Such rapid shifting of topics could be the precursor to the loose associations so common in schizophrenia. Mednick and Schulsinger's data forced researchers to reconceptualize and expand their developmental theories of schizophrenia. Whether this reconceptualization proves more promising than what preceded it will be determined by the results of the research it stimulates.

---

genetic relationship to someone with schizophrenia (Mednick & McNeil, 1968). The first genetic high-risk study compared the offspring of mothers who had schizophrenia to the offspring of mothers who did not have schizophrenia—the high-risk and low-risk groups, respectively (Mednick & Schulsinger, 1968). The high-risk and low-risk participants were matched on such potential confounding variables as age, education, social class, and where they were raised (urban or rural, family or institutional setting). All participants were evaluated at the beginning of

the study on variables that were thought to be predictive of eventual psychopathology and were then followed to determine who developed schizophrenia. Following the participants to determine who develops schizophrenia enables researchers to use information gathered before the onset of the disorder to identify factors that may increase risk.

Following participants for years is expensive. Consequently, it is critical to provide, at the outset, evidence that the information gleaned from a longitudinal study is likely to be useful. This can be done in several ways. The first is that the high- and low-risk groups provide a natural comparison because roughly 10% of the high-risk participants, but less than 1% of the low-risk participants, can be expected eventually to develop schizophrenia. Therefore, any factor that contributes to schizophrenia will be more frequent in the high-risk group. Mednick and Schulsinger (1968) compared their high- and low-risk participants on psychophysiological measures of emotional reactivity. What they found proved both interesting and surprising, as illustrated in the nearby Modern Myth box.

High-risk studies are ongoing projects, which often produce an incredible wealth of information as the study unfolds. For example, Mednick and Schulsinger's original sample has been followed continuously for years. Cannon et al. (1993a) found that the variables that predicted the development of schizophrenia were different for those individuals who developed primarily positive symptoms than for those who developed primarily negative symptoms. Those with positive symptoms were more likely to have had an unstable home life, whereas those with negative symptoms were more likely to have had pregnancy or birth complications and to have exhibited a flattened emotional response to stress at the beginning of the study. In a later study, brain scans showed cerebral atrophy in the high-risk participants who developed any schizophrenia spectrum disorder, but not in the low-risk participants or in the high-risk participants who did not develop a schizophrenia spectrum disorder (Cannon et al., 1994). Both the strength of genetic factors and a history of birth complications were associated with the degree of brain atrophy (Cannon et al., 1993b). This sample is still being followed, and it is likely that more insights will emerge from this work. Other major genetic high-risk studies are being conducted in New York and Israel, and like the Mednick study, they are providing extensive information about the developmental course of schizophrenia.

Behavioral High-Risk Paradigms. The genetic high-risk study was a breakthrough for investigating the developmental course of schizophrenia. However, there is a cost for the much greater efficiency of this paradigm. The cost is that the sample is inherently biased. In the Mednick and Schulsinger (1968) sample, all of the participants in the high-risk group had a mother who had schizophrenia, but only 5% of all individuals who develop schizophrenia have a mother with the disorder (Rosenthal, 1970). This biased-sample problem prompted Loren and Jean Chapman to propose a **behavioral high-risk paradigm** for schizophrenia (Chapman et al., 1978a), which identifies

participants not by their genetic relationship to someone with schizophrenia but, rather, on the basis of personality traits thought to be indicators of risk (Meehl, 1962, 1964). The Chapmans developed measures of some of the schizotypic signs proposed by Meehl (1962), such as physical anhedonia (Chapman et al., 1976), perceptual aberration (Chapman et al., 1978b), magical ideation (Eckblad & Chapman, 1983), and intense ambivalence (Raulin, 1984). Physical anhedonia is the inability to experience physical pleasure ("I have always enjoyed having my back massaged" keyed false). Perceptual aberration refers to unusual perceptual experiences, especially of one's body ("I have sometimes felt that some part of my body no longer belonged to me" keyed true). Magical ideation refers to magical beliefs ("I think I could learn to read others' minds if I wanted to" keyed true). These are characteristics that had informally been observed in people who developed schizophrenia and in people thought to be at risk for schizophrenia (Meehl, 1964). Some of the scales, such as the Perceptual Aberration Scale and the Magical Ideation Scale, are highly correlated, which suggests that they are assessing a common underlying characteristic. In contrast, the Physical Anhedonia Scale is uncorrelated with most of the other scales, which suggests that it assesses a different underlying characteristic. Let's look at the details of some of the studies that have been conducted using these scales.

---

behavioral high-risk paradigm   A study in which participants are selected not on the basis of their genetic relationship to someone with a specified psychopathology but on the basis of personality traits thought to be indicators of risk.

Examining the Evidence

The initial validation of the Chapman Scales focused on showing that individuals who scored high on the scales displayed characteristics similar to those found in schizophrenia. For example, high scorers on these scales reported psychoticlike experiences (Chapman et al., 1978a), poor social functioning (Beckfield, 1985), and cognitive processing deficits similar to those shown by people with schizophrenia (Simons, 1981). Psychoticlike experiences are milder forms of psychotic symptoms (Chapman & Chapman, 1980). For example, experiencing an auditory hallucination is hearing a voice that is different from one's own voice, that does not appear to be under one's control, and that seems to come from outside of one. However, some people hear their own thoughts as voices. Others experience these voices as different from their own, although they know that the voices are their own thoughts. Still others occasionally experience the voices as if they were different from their own thoughts, although they know they must be their own thoughts because the voices come from inside of their head. You can see how these experiences range from something that is clearly normal to something that is clearly psychotic, with many gradations in between.

In a 15-year period, over 50 studies conducted with these high-risk participants were published, and in the majority, the results were consistent with the hypothesis that these scales identified a group that might well be at risk for schizophrenia—an outcome that justified the time and expense for a follow-up study. The first 10-year follow-up confirmed that these scales did predict risk for schizophrenia, although they more accurately predicted risk for psychosis in general (Chapman et al., 1994). Specifically, in addition to finding a higher incidence of schizophrenia in the high-risk group, the Chapmans found an increased risk of psychotic mood disorders and other nonschizophrenic psychoses. Furthermore, high scorers on these scales who reported psychoticlike experiences in their late teens were ten times more likely to develop psychosis than either the low scorers or the high scorers who did not report psychoticlike experiences.

The focus now in the behavioral high-risk paradigm is on developing procedures that have more specificity for identifying people at risk for schizophrenia spectrum disorders. Recent work with other measures, such as the Social Anhedonia Scale, suggests that it may be possible to identify a group at specific risk for schizophrenia, although more research is clearly needed on this question (Kwapil, 1998). We noted earlier that efforts to refine the Intense Ambivalence Scale did increase the specificity of that scale (Kwapil et al., 2002). Extensive research with these measures of schizotypic signs continues in more than a dozen laboratories around the world.

Theoretically, any measurable characteristic could be used to identify a behavioral high-risk group. For example, the evidence reviewed earlier suggests that the experience of subtle psychoticlike experiences, such as hearing one's thoughts as voices, is a promising indication of risk (Chapman & Chapman, 1980; Chapman et al., 1994). People with schizophrenia are more likely to show mixed handedness—that is, they may write with their right hand but throw with their left (Green, 1998; Satz & Green, 1999). Could mixed handedness be used to define a behavioral high-risk group? This question raises an important issue. When evaluating any measure designed to classify individuals, one should examine both its sensitivity and its speci-

ficity. **Sensitivity** refers to the probability that a person with a characteristic, such as a specific diagnosis, will be correctly identified as having that characteristic. If a measure to screen for brain damage has a sensitivity of 90%, then 90% of the brain damaged individuals are correctly identified by the measure. In contrast, **specificity** refers to the probability that someone without a characteristic will be correctly identified as not having that characteristic. One needs both sensitivity and specificity in a measure that one intends to use to select a behavioral high-risk group. Without high sensitivity, one will miss many of the people one wants to identify; without high specificity, most of the people identified as high-risk will not be at risk. Mixed handedness has moderate sensitivity but rather low specificity—that is, most people with mix handedness are not at risk for schizophrenia. Modern behavioral high-risk studies often identify their high-risk samples by using multiple measures, from the schizotypal signs measured by the Chapman scales, to symptoms assessed in interviews, to biological measures known to be associated with schizophrenia.

Sometimes researchers modify measurement procedures to enhance the sensitivity and specificity of a measure. For example, the Perceptual Aberration Scale asks about perceptual distortions. The intent is to identify people who naturally experience these distortions. However, many street drugs produce perceptual distortions. This creates a problem, because drug users may endorse items describing their perceptual experiences while on drugs, when the intent was to assess perceptual experiences in a nondrug state. To avoid this problem, the Chapmans worded their instructions to indicate that one should report an experience *only* if it was experienced while *not* on drugs.

One final point is that rare conditions are much harder to detect accurately than more common conditions (Meehl & Rosen, 1955). Therefore, any measure designed to select a group at high risk for a rare disorder is likely to yield many false positives. This is not necessarily a problem if the goal of identifying a high-risk sample is to make a prospective study more efficient. One can still expect a higher yield of eventual psychopathology in a high-risk sample. However, it *is* a problem if one starts to think of all of the people in the sample as being at risk, which is not likely to be true.

High-risk research is continuing. These approaches are expensive and time-consuming, but they provide information about the development of psychopathology that cannot be obtained in any other way. The prospective high-risk study has several advantages. The first is that it enables researchers to study people at risk before they develop the devastating consequences of the disorder. When one studies an individual who already has the disorder, it is unclear whether what one finds is a cause or a consequence of the disorder. However, when characteristics precede the development of the disorder, one can rule out the possibility that they are consequences of it. A second advantage is that the prospective high-risk study facilitates the identification of

---

sensitivity   The probability that a person with a characteristic, such as a specific diagnosis, will be correctly identified as having that characteristic.

specificity   The probability that someone without a characteristic will be correctly identified as not having that characteristic.

markers for the disorder, thus helping to clarify the nature of the genetic diathesis. A third advantage is that it enables researchers to examine factors that may either increase or decrease the risk for the disorder. For example, if it emerges that those people who develop schizophrenia are more likely to be socially isolated as teenagers, this suggests that social isolation may increase the risk for schizophrenia. Finally, following individuals through a risk period to see who develops the disorder may provide information that can contribute to efforts at prevention. And looking at the experiences of those who do not develop the disorder may indicate variables that provide some protection from psychiatric deterioration.

Check Yourself 6.5

Research Designs

1. What is the value of a case study?
2. What is the most powerful research strategy available to researchers?
3. What problem must be considered in comparing groups that differ on diagnosis?
4. What is the difference between prospective and retrospective studies?
5. What is the difference between genetic and behavioral high-risk studies?

Ponder this . . . *As sophistication in the understanding of a disorder develops, researchers often move to developmental models to understand the disorder. What is the best way to study the developmental processes associated with any disorder?*

STUDYING COGNITIVE PROCESSING

The hallmark symptoms of schizophrenia are thought disorder and perceptual disturbance; that is, people with schizophrenia have difficulty thinking clearly and perceiving accurately. These complex symptoms are almost certainly the result of disruption in basic cognitive and perceptual processing, so it makes sense to investigate these areas to find clues about the underlying causes. Researchers are looking for something that is likely to be subtle, because if it were not subtle, they would have discovered it years ago. It is probably pervasive as well, because a subtle deficit that a person rarely experiences is unlikely to create the massive deterioration seen in schizophrenia. As we will see, the cognitive and perceptual disturbances that show the greatest promise fit this bill exactly—they are subtle and pervasive.

Cognitive processes are particularly relevant in schizophrenia because of the nature of schizophrenic symptomatology. However, cognitive processes are also important in other disorders, as we will see in later chapters. Basic processes, such as memory and attention, can dramatically affect a person's emotional and behavioral responses. For example, are anxious people more likely than others to remember certain events or more likely to notice certain things in the environment? Do those memories or perceptual biases affect their responses? Anxious people tend to be more vigilant, but is this increased vigilance the result of the increased anxiety or is the increased anxiety the result of the increased vigilance? Do anxious people just see more things to be anxious about? The strategy of studying cognitive and perceptual processes of people who have a disorder or are at risk for it has been employed with several disorders to untangle such questions.

The measures discussed in this section tap aspects of perceptual or cognitive processing that are presumed to have specific neurological mechanisms. Cognitive psychologists developed many of these tasks and have extensive normative information on them. Increasingly, there is an integration of cognitive and biological research as the field of cognitive neuroscience bridges the gap between these perspectives. Four neurocognitive measures have received considerable attention in schizophrenia: the continuous performance test, the span of apprehension test, backward masking, and measures of eye movement abnormalities. These examples illustrate both the logic and the techniques of research on cognitive processes in psychopathology.

CONTINUOUS PERFORMANCE TEST

Because people with schizophrenia report severe difficulties maintaining attention (Freedman, 1974; Freedman & Chapman, 1973; McGhie & Chapman, 1961), it makes sense to study attention in schizophrenia to identify how and when these processes are disrupted. The **Continuous Performance Test (CPT)** is a measure of attentional vigilance. The person views a series of stimuli on a screen and responds whenever a target stimulus appears. The target could be a single stimulus (such as the letter X) or a sequence of stimuli (such as the same letter appearing twice in a row, which is called identical pairs). People with schizophrenia consistently perform more poorly on this measure than people without the disorder (Nuechterlein, 1991). This performance difference is most pronounced when the task is made more difficult by either (1) using the sequence task described above (identical-pairs condition) or (2) making the stimuli fuzzy and therefore hard to identify (degraded-stimulus condition). These deficits are also found in people whose schizophrenia is in remission (Asarnow & MacCrimmon, 1978), in first-degree relatives of people with schizophrenia (Grove et al., 1991), in people thought to be at risk for schizophrenia (Cornblatt et al.,

....

Continuous Performance Test (CPT) A measure of attentional vigilance.

Many forms of psychological and cognitive testing are now done on computers. This person is taking the Continuous Performance Test. She must click the mouse whenever she sees the same letter appearing twice in a row.

1992), and in people with schizotypal traits (Lenzenweger et al., 1991). These findings suggest that the CPT might be a marker of schizophrenia risk, rather than just an indication of a schizophrenic deficit. A **marker** is a characteristic that is independent of the symptoms of the disorder, exists before the symptoms develop, and continues after the symptoms subside. It is assumed that a marker indicates something about the diathesis for the disorder. Identifying and validating markers is quite an enterprise, but their value in enhancing the scientific understanding of the disorder makes the effort worthwhile. Garver (1987) proposed several criteria that should be used in identifying a biological marker for schizophrenia; these are listed in Table 6.2.

SPAN OF APPREHENSION

People with schizophrenia often report feeling overwhelmed by stimuli and being unable to process them effectively (Freedman & Chapman, 1973; McGhie & Chapman, 1961). Therefore, it makes sense to study the processing of stimuli to see when it breaks down and what factors predict a breakdown. The span-of-apprehension test proved to be an effective measure of this phenomenon.

....

marker A characteristic that is independent of the symptoms of the disorder, exists before the symptoms develop, and continues after the symptoms subside.

span-of-apprehension test A test calling for a person to decide which target letter was included in an array of letters that is flashed briefly.

[TABLE 6.2] Criteria for a Biological Marker for Schizophrenia

Promising biological markers for schizophrenia should have the following characteristics:

1. The marker should be more common in people with schizophrenia than in people without the disorder.
2. The marker should be a stable trait.
3. The marker should occur more frequently in biological family members of people with schizophrenia than in the general population, and it should be associated with the presence of schizophrenia spectrum disorders in those family members.
4. The marker should occur more frequently in the offspring of people with schizophrenia, and it should be present before the onset of schizophrenia spectrum disorders in the offspring.
5. The presence of the marker should be predictive of later onset of schizophrenia spectrum disorders.
6. The marker should be easy to measure reliably.

SOURCE: *Adapted from "Criteria for a Biological Marker for Schizophrenia" in "Methodological Issues Facing the Interpretation of High-Risk Studies: Biological Heterogeneity" by Garver,* Schizophrenia Bulletin, *vol. 13, 1987.*

In the **span-of-apprehension test,** the task is to decide whether a T or an F (the target letter) was included in an array of letters that is flashed briefly. Only one target letter appears on each trial, and the array appears so briefly that there is insufficient time to scan it. Consequently, this task measures the ability to store and scan a visual image of the array. When the task is easy, such as when there is only a single letter in the array, people with schizophrenia do about as well as other people. However, as the size of the array increases, people with schizophrenia do worse than those without the disorder, whether they are psychotic or in remission (Green, 1998). The data are less clear when high-risk samples are studied; some researchers have found differences (Asarnow et al., 1977) and others have not (Harvey et al., 1985).

In an interesting study, Asarnow et al. (1983) used the span of apprehension to classify research participants obtained through a temporary-employment agency. Essentially, this was an attempt to determine whether the span-of-apprehension test could be useful in selecting a high-risk sample. This was a rather speculative hypothesis, given that there were so little data on the span-of-apprehension test in schizophrenia at the time. Nonetheless, it was a worthwhile endeavor because a measure of cognitive processing is likely be closer to the underlying genetic diathesis for schizophrenia than the self-report measures of schizotypic signs used by the Chapmans in their behavioral high-risk studies. The closer you can get to the diathesis, the less likely your measure is to be contaminated by other variables, such as life experiences or the tendency to overreport or underreport problems. None of the individuals in this study reported a history of psychopathology. Nevertheless, poor performers on the span-of-apprehension test showed elevations on the schizophrenia scale of the MMPI and the Magical Ideation Scale but did not show elevations on the other clinical scales of the MMPI. These findings suggest that the span-of-apprehension measure taps something specific to schizophrenia or schizophrenialike symptoms.

In an interesting variation on the span-of-apprehension task, Place and Gilmore (1980) asked people with and without schizophrenia to count the number of lines in a briefly presented display, as shown in Figure 6.3. In the homogeneous condition, the horizontal and vertical lines are grouped, which makes it easier for most people to count them. In the two heterogeneous conditions, the horizontal and vertical lines are not grouped. People who did not have schizophrenia counted the lines correctly 50% of the time

in the homogeneous condition and about 20% of the time in the heterogeneous conditions. In contrast, people with schizophrenia counted the lines correctly about 40% of the time in all three conditions. This is striking because people with schizophrenia almost never do better than people without the disorder, and here they outperformed those without the disorder in two of the three conditions.

Place and Gilmore argued that most people automatically group similar objects, which works well in the homogeneous condition. The grouping process fails in the heterogeneous conditions, and the person is forced to discard the grouping strategy in favor of a simple count of the lines. This takes extra time and decreases accuracy. In contrast, people with schizophrenia do not benefit from the grouping in the homogeneous condition; hence they do worse than people without the disorder. However, people with schizophrenia, who do not naturally group objects, are faster in the heterogeneous conditions because they do not waste time trying to organize the lines. This provides evidence that people with schizophrenia have a subtle but pervasive difference in what is called **preattentive processing,** the way they organize visual information in the first few milliseconds. This is an exciting finding, which has generated considerable research and theorizing among researchers (Knight & Silverstein, 2001).

BACKWARD MASKING

Backward masking is another way to study early stages of perceptual processing. In the span-of-apprehension test, a complex stimulus is presented briefly, and the person's ability to process it indicates her or his ability to hold an image and process its details. In contrast, in a **backward-masking task,** a simple target is presented for just a few milliseconds and is followed a few milliseconds later by a *mask,* which is another stimulus that appears in the same place. The task is to identify the target, but the mask prevents the person from maintaining the target image in memory long enough to process it fully. By manipulating the length of the delay between target and mask, researchers can learn how the stimulus is processed during those first few milliseconds. Masking always makes identification of a target more difficult, but the effect is stronger for people with schizophrenia (Knight, 1992), and this processing deficit remains during remission (Green, 1998). Furthermore, studies with relatives of people with schizophrenia suggested that masking deficits may be a marker for the disorder (Green et al., 1997).

[FIGURE 6.3]
Stimuli for Perceptual Organization Tasks

These stimuli are part of a clever study of early perceptual processing in schizophrenia conducted by Place and Gilmore (1980). The task is to count the number of lines. When similar lines are grouped together (the homogeneous condition), most people count the lines faster. People with schizophrenia do not seem to use the grouping information, so they count the lines equally quickly in all of these conditions.

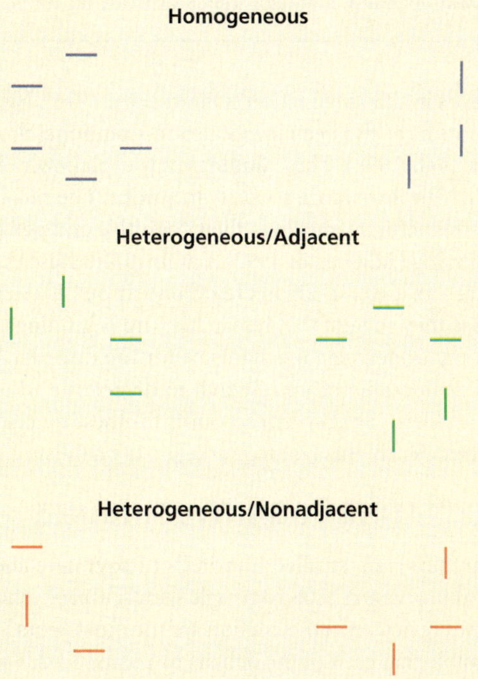

Homogeneous

Heterogeneous/Adjacent

Heterogeneous/Nonadjacent

SOURCE: *Figure, "Stimuli for Perceptual Organization Tasks" in "Perceptual Organization in Schizophrenia" by Place and Gilmore,* Journal of Abnormal Psychology, 89 *1980. Copyright © 1980 by the American Psychological Association. Reprinted with permission.*

preattentive processing   The way one organizes visual information in the first few milliseconds.

backward-masking task   A visual test in which a simple target is presented for just a few milliseconds and is followed a few milliseconds later by a mask, which is another stimulus that appears in the same place.

Findings like these provide clues about what might underlie the dramatic symptoms of schizophrenia. For example, it may be that deficits in early perceptual processing are central in schizophrenia, decreasing the efficiency of perceptual processing and thus straining the entire cognitive system. Of course, this is merely speculative, but it illustrates how a breakdown in basic cognitive functions could lead to multiple problems.

EYE MOVEMENT ABNORMALITIES

Eye movement abnormalities in people with schizophrenia were noted as early as the turn of the century (Diefendorf & Dodge, 1908). Since the 1970s (Holzman, 1975), the nature of this eye movement dysfunction has been studied extensively in people with schizophrenia, their relatives, and those thought to be at risk for schizophrenia (Lee et al., 2001; Levy et al., 2000). The type of eye movement abnormality studied most extensively is the **smooth-pursuit eye movement,** or **SPEM,** which involves visually following a target as it moves. People with schizophrenia have difficulty following moving objects, often falling behind or rushing ahead of the object and then making quick corrective eye movements, called *saccades,* as illustrated in the tracings of Figure 6.4.

Eye tracking dysfunction has been found in people with schizophrenia both during and after psychotic episodes (Levy et al., 2000). Furthermore, eye tracking dysfunction tends to run in the families of people with schizophrenia, is found in people with schizophrenic spectrum disorders (Siever et al., 1990), and is present in some, but not all, individuals who show personality traits thought to indicate risk for schizophrenia (Simons & Katkin, 1985). In general, nonpsychotic individuals who show eye tracking dysfunction show more symptomatology, such as flat or inappropriate affect, emotional constriction, oddness, and social isolation, than people with no eye tracking dysfunction (Kendler et al., 1991).

Drugs are a potential confounding variable in the study of eye tracking performance. Watch the eye movements of someone who is intoxicated to see a dramatic example of a smooth pursuit eye movement dysfunction. This is such a reliable indicator of intoxication that police officers routinely include it in their evaluation of suspected drunk drivers. The research participants in the eye movement studies were not intoxicated, but many were under the influence of powerful antipsychotic drugs. Fortunately, antipsychotic drugs seem not to affect eye tracking, although other commonly used drugs, such as nicotine, may have an effect (Levy et al., 2000). The fact that smoking decreases eye tracking dysfunction implicates nicotinic

smooth-pursuit eye movement (SPEM) Visually following a target as it moves.

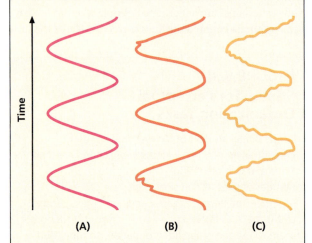

[FIGURE 6.4]
Smooth-Pursuit Eye Movement Dysfunction

These tracings represent the eye movements of people with schizophrenia and comparison subjects. A steady movement upward indicates the passage of time. (A) The smooth movement of a pendulum. (B) The typical eye tracking performance of a person with no history of schizophrenia. (C) The jerky eye tracking performance that is typical of people with schizophrenia and is also frequently found in their first-degree relatives.

(A)   (B)   (C)

SOURCE: *"Smooth-Pursuit Eye Movement Dysfunction" from "Eye Tracking Dysfunction and Schizophrenia: A Critical Perspective" by D. L. Levy, P. S. Matthysse, and N. R. Mendell,* Schizophrenia Bulletin, *vol. 19, 1993.*

receptors in this dysfunction (Olincy et al., 1996). Nicotinic receptors have also been implicated in attentional processes (Adler et al., 1998). These findings may explain why people with schizophrenia are so likely to smoke. The nicotine in cigarettes actually improves their cognitive and perceptual functioning (Adler et al., 1993). Findings like these that link research in diverse areas create enormous excitement, because they suggest that researchers are beginning to zero in on the underlying mechanisms for the disorder. It will take considerably more research to determine whether a single underlying problem accounts for these diverse findings, but clearly this research area looks promising.

INTEGRATING COGNITIVE FINDINGS

Researchers have studied hundreds of cognitive and perceptual processing tasks in people with schizophrenia, and the ones reviewed in this section are the most promising. It is possible that each of the deficits discussed in this section is independent of the others, although the data suggest otherwise. It is more likely that each represents a specific manifestation of a more basic underlying problem that has yet to be discovered. The task now is to identify mechanisms that could account for all of these deficits and that are consistent with other things known about schizophrenia, such as the biochemical findings. One promising area was introduced in this section—the role of nicotinic receptors of people with schizophrenia. The ultimate goal of any construct validation process is to understand the specific underlying mechanisms so clearly that one can accurately explain the details already observed and can accurately predict specific new observations. A recent effort at this integration will be presented later in this chapter.

Check Yourself 6.6

Studying Cognitive Processes

1. What characteristics would you expect the underlying causes of schizophrenia to have?
2. What is a marker for a psychiatric disorder?
3. What stages of perceptual processing are most likely to be disrupted in schizophrenia?
4. What is the nature of the eye movement dysfunction in schizophrenia, and how is it affected by nicotine?

Ponder this . . .   *Several cognitive processing and perceptual processing measures appear to be markers of schizophrenic risk. How could these markers be used to enhance prospective studies of schizophrenia?*

STUDYING GENETIC INFLUENCES

From the time of Kraepelin, professionals have recognized that schizophrenia runs in families. However, these observations were often informal, the data usually being gathered by questioning the person with schizophrenia or a family member (Hersen & Turner, 1985). Although these earlier observations were valuable, they fell short of providing information that would help unravel the causes of schizophrenia for two reasons. The first is that the observations were informal and therefore subject to a variety of observational biases. The second is that schizophrenia could run in families because of genes, environment, or both. Family members share both genes and environment, so these factors are confounded. However, the hypothesis that genes contribute to schizophrenia can be evaluated with the right research designs. Chapter 5 presented the evidence for a genetic influence in schizophrenia. This chapter will focus on the details of the research paradigms used to evaluate genetic contributions to psychological disorders. This section discusses three genetic research approaches: family studies, twin studies, and adoption studies. The

section ends with a brief discussion of the advances in genetic technology.

FAMILY STUDIES

The earliest genetic studies were designed to verify the casual observation that schizophrenia runs in families (Kallman, 1938). These investigations, which are called **family studies,** cannot rule out an environmental hypothesis, but they can rule out a genetic hypothesis because schizophrenia must run in families if genes contribute. Family studies start with people who have schizophrenia, called **probands.** The researcher then identifies and evaluates the proband's relatives. The least effective way of evaluating relatives is to rely on the report of others, such as a knowledgeable family member. A better way is to interview each relative. This procedure allows more precise diagnosis, but it is costly, especially if the family is spread over a wide geographic area. An alternative is to search existing records for information that would indicate the psychiatric status of each relative. Such a search is possible only in countries such as Denmark, where a national health care register is kept. This health care register lists every hospital admission and diagnosis. The cost of using the health care register is only a fraction of the cost of tracking down and interviewing relatives, and it enables researchers to evaluate people who have died. A comparison group and their relatives are also evaluated.

Breaking down the family study data by listing risk as a function of degree of genetic relatedness helps organize the findings. Table 5.1 on page 115 provided such a breakdown. That table showed a progression of risk as a function of degree of genetic overlap with the proband. Identical twins of probands have a roughly 50% chance of being diagnosed with schizophrenia, whereas first-degree relatives have a risk between 6% and 17%, and second-degree relatives have a risk between 2% and 6%. These data do not unambiguously establish that genes play a role, because the degree of genetic relatedness is usually confounded with the degree of overlap in the environment, but they do suggest that genes may play a role.

TWIN STUDIES

Twin studies were introduced in Chapter 5. They control for the impact of environment by holding the environment relatively constant. This approach starts with a proband who has schizophrenia and has a same-sex twin. Each twin

....

family studies   Genetic studies designed to verify that a specific psychopathology runs in families.

probands   People who have a specified disorder and are selected for a genetic study.

pair is classified as either **identical** (**MZ,** or **monozygotic**) or **fraternal** (**DZ,** or **dizygotic**), who share 100% and 50% of their genes, respectively. The samples are restricted to same-sex twins for two reasons. The first is that because girls and boys are often treated differently, the assumption of a similar environment is suspect for opposite-sex twins. The second is that genes on either the X or the Y chromosome may contribute to risk, and the study would not be controlled for this if opposite-sex twins were included. Typically, DNA, blood factors, or fingerprints are used to categorize twins as MZ or DZ; DNA analysis provides the most accurate determination. The co-twins are then diagnosed. If the co-twin has schizophrenia, the twins are concordant; otherwise, they are discordant. The statistical techniques can get rather sophisticated. For example, concordant twins are twice as likely as discordant twins to be sampled in a twin study because both concordant twins have schizophrenia, and therefore both could be identified as a proband. Genetic researchers often consider this potential bias in their calculations.

As we noted earlier, the average concordance rates for MZ and DZ twins in these studies are 48% and 17%, respectively (Gottesman, 1991). These figures provide more convincing evidence for a genetic risk factor than family studies, because there is little evidence that the environmental influences on most psychological traits are more similar in MZ than in DZ twins. However, these data also provide convincing evidence of environmental effects, because the MZ concordance rate is well short of 100%.

ADOPTION STUDIES

Adoption studies are the ultimate way of avoiding the confounding of genes and environment. In an adoption study, the proband is a person with schizophrenia who was adopted at or near birth. These probands have two sets of relatives—biological relatives who share genes, but not environment, and adoptive relatives who share environment, but not genes. To prevent confounding, probands who were adopted by a family member are excluded. A comparison group, consisting of individuals who were adopted at birth but who never developed schizophrenia, is also included.

As you learned in Chapter 5, Kety et al. (1968, 1971) identified 33 probands and 33 comparison subjects matched on such factors as age at adoption, social class of biological and adoptive parents, and birth complications. They utilized the birth and adoption registries of Denmark to identify probands and the psychiatric registry to identify which relatives had been diagnosed with schizophrenia.

The only people with an elevated risk for schizophrenia were biological relatives of the probands, which suggests that genes play a significant role in the development of schizophrenia. In another adoption study paradigm, the proband is a mother who has schizophrenia and who gave up her children for adoption. As we saw in Chapter 5, data obtained via this adoption paradigm also provided strong evidence for a genetic contribution to schizophrenia (Rosenthal et al., 1968).

STUDYING THE GENE

Scientists are increasingly able to study genetically influenced disorders such as schizophrenia at the level of the gene, and technological breakthroughs will probably continue to enhance this ability. The approach that is used most frequently is linkage analysis (Ott, 1991). In simple terms, linkage analysis involves identifying target traits that depend on specific genes with known locations on specific chromosomes and evaluating the co-transmission of these target traits with schizophrenia—that is, the frequency with which both the target trait and schizophrenia are passed on together to offspring. Traits that tend to be transmitted along with schizophrenia are more likely to be on a chromosome close to the gene responsible for schizophrenia. Linkage analysis has been used successfully in the study of simple Mendelian traits, but its usefulness with a disorder as complex as schizophrenia has been questioned (Kendler & Diehl, 1993). To date, linkage studies have provided no evidence that there is a single gene responsible for schizophrenia (Kendler & Diehl, 1993). There may be many reasons for this. One possibility is that the genetic diathesis for schizophrenia is due to several genes, rather than a single gene (Gottesman et al., 1987). Furthermore, most of the genes that are likely to affect the central nervous system have yet to be discovered (Kendler & Diehl, 1993). However, the Human Genome Project, which seeks to map all of

The human genetic material is organized on 23 pairs of chromosomes. Each chromosome contains millions of individual genes, which are in specific locations on the chromosome.

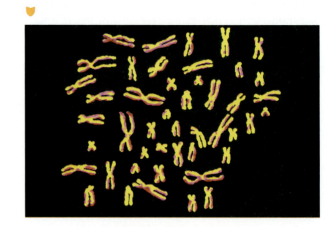

monozygotic (MZ, or identical) twins A pair of twins who share 100% of their genes.

dizygotic (DZ, or fraternal) twins A pair of twins who share 50% of their genes.

the genes on the 23 pairs of human chromosomes, may well provide the necessary foundation for the next generation of linkage studies. You may see within your lifetime a solid explanation of the genetic influences on schizophrenia, from the level of the gene to the symptoms of the disorder.

ANOTHER EVOLUTIONARY MYSTERY

Evolutionary Impact _____

In Chapter 5 you encountered an evolutionary mystery: Why is schizophrenia not decreasing in frequency? It appears that the rate of schizophrenia has remained relatively stable for at least the last 100 years, despite strong negative selective pressure (Gottesman, 1991). There is another evolutionary mystery: Where did schizophrenia come from in the first place? Ancient writings vividly describe depression, mania, epilepsy, and senile dementia but make no mention of a disorder that resembles schizophrenia (Gottesman, 1991). In fact, there is little evidence for the existence of schizophrenia before about 200 or 300 years ago. What could have caused the rapid rise in the frequency of schizophrenia 200 years ago?

There is no generally accepted answer to this question, but questions are the seeds of knowledge in science, and they should not be ignored. One speculative proposal is that there may be a viral infection that could trigger psychotic deterioration in those individuals who may be genetically predisposed to schizophrenia (Torrey, 1988). That suggestion may seem unreasonable because most known viruses tend to be fast-acting. You encounter someone who has a cold, pick up the virus, and in a few days get sick; then a couple of weeks later you are better. That course is typical for many common viruses, but slower-acting viruses exist, and more are being discovered all the time. An example is HIV (human immunodeficiency virus), which often takes years to announce its presence with the symptoms of AIDS. Scientists know that viruses can affect central nervous system development. For example, mothers exposed to the flu virus during the second trimester of pregnancy, when the fetal brain is undergoing rapid development, are more likely to have children who develop schizophrenia than mothers who do not get the flu during pregnancy (Cannon et al., 1991). It is only one further step to hypothesize a specific virus that leads to the neurodevelopmental problems that predispose people to schizophrenia. There is as yet no direct evidence for such a virus, but even if there were, the mystery of why schizophrenia is not decreasing in frequency would remain. Virus or no virus, the evidence is clear that genes play a role in schizophrenia and that the reproductive rates of people with schizophrenia are dramatically lower than the norm. Therefore, the genes should be disappearing and the rates of schizophrenia should be going down. Hence there are two evolutionary mysteries surrounding schizophrenia.

Check Yourself 6.7

Studying Genetic Influences

1. Which approach to studying genetic influences is *least* effective in controlling the confounding of genes and environment?

2. How is the proband selected in twin studies?

3. What are the two evolutionary mysteries surrounding schizophrenia?

Ponder this . . .   *To appreciate the task that researchers face, speculate on a possible developmental course for schizophrenia—from genes, to basic and subtle cognitive or emotional dysfunctions, to schizotypal traits, to interaction with the environment to create the symptoms of schizophrenia. Relax and be creative. Then, once you have articulated your model, look at all of the steps you would have to validate, and consider how much research evidence it would take to validate each of them.*

STUDYING BIOLOGICAL INFLUENCES

One of the most sophisticated areas of psychopathology research is the study of the biological underpinnings of abnormal behavior. What brain mechanisms are responsible for specific behavior or symptoms? Is there a biological abnormality that underlies the disorder? If there is, what is it and how does it interact with other factors to produce the symptoms observed? Understanding the biological contributions to a disorder often improves treatment, whether that treatment is biological or psychological.

There is a common misconception that biology and psychology are somehow separate realms. Nothing could be further from the truth. Biology and psychology are just different perspectives. Few would doubt that the effort you are expending now to learn the material in this chapter is somehow changing the operation of specific neurons in such a way that those neurons are storing what is learned. You are doing something psychological (learning), but your brain is doing something biological (probably modifying the strength of neuronal connections). Are two things going on then? No, only one—you are learning. Looking at the phenomenon from either a biological or a psychological perspective is simply choosing to look at it from a single point of view.

Ultimately, all behavior is biologically mediated, but that does not mean psychology is irrelevant. Psychology looks at the bigger picture; biology at the underlying details. An architect looks at the bigger picture when designing a building, whereas an engineer focuses on the details that make a building strong and functional. Can an architect afford to ignore engineering principles in order to design a building with flowing, graceful lines? If the architect does, and the building gets constructed that way, it is likely to collapse. Research that is well grounded in a thorough understanding of the underlying biology and the limitations that biology imposes will be more sophisticated and more likely to be fruitful.

This section reviews the research approaches that are used most commonly in biological research into psychopathology. It begins with the logic of comparing diagnostic groups on biological structure and functioning and then turns to drug studies and how they provide insights into underlying biochemical mechanisms. The section ends by discussing the integration of biological and psychological data.

COMPARING DIAGNOSTIC GROUPS

Although the advanced technology involved in biological research is impressive, the research designs are typically straightforward. Most biological studies use the differential research design, in which two or more groups are compared on specific variables. For example, people with and without schizophrenia have been compared on both functional (Gruzelier, 1999) and structural brain asymmetries (Petty, 1999). Several studies have shown that the brains of people with schizophrenia show a reduced left-side volume (Petty, 1999). The functional abnormalities are less consistent, and understanding them requires a refinement in the diagnosis. Specifically, the pattern of functional asymmetries in schizophrenia depends on whether the person shows primarily positive symptoms or primarily negative symptoms. In those with positive symptoms, there tends to be excessive left-brain activity, whereas those with negative symptoms show decreased left-brain activity (Gruzelier, 1999). The differentiation of functional brain asymmetries represents a refinement of the basic differential research design by looking for subgroups with different symptom patterns that show different relationships to the variables under study. In disorders in which there is substantial symptom variability among those affected, looking for such subgroups is a valuable technique. These analyses have often provided the first clues about potential new diagnostic entities (Raulin & Lilienfeld, 1999).

Some of the most interesting studies of schizophrenia have used people as their own controls. For example, individuals might be tested during a psychotic period and then again during a period of symptom remission. This design makes sense with only certain biological variables; for example, it is unlikely that cerebral atrophy will disappear during periods of remission. This approach has been used to identify many of the schizotypic signs that identify those

at risk for schizophrenia (Meehl, 1964). It has also been useful for the study of anxiety disorders (Barlow, 2002) and depression (Klein & Wender, 1993).

A variation on this design of using people as their own controls is the use of identical twins as controls. For example, the Advances box for Chapter 5 (see page 120) described a study of cerebral atrophy in MZ twins discordant for schizophrenia (Suddath et al., 1990). Employing a person's MZ twin provided a much more sensitive test of whether brain atrophy was characteristic of schizophrenia, because identical twins are normally physically identical in many ways, including the details of their brain anatomy. The fact that the twin with schizophrenia showed consistently more brain atrophy than the nonschizophrenic twin added strong evidence that atrophy contributes to the development of schizophrenia. Furthermore, because the inclusion of an identical twin as a control increased sensitivity, the study was able to show that such atrophy occurs in people not previously thought to have atrophy, such as people with a less chronic form of schizophrenia characterized by predominantly positive symptoms.

DRUG RESPONSE STUDIES

There is no question that the advent of medications for schizophrenia has had a tremendous positive impact on people with the disorder. Before these medications were available, many people with schizophrenia spent their entire lives in psychiatric hospitals. Now few people require constant hospitalization, and some are able to lead normal lives. However, the medications do more than just treat the disorder; they also give researchers insight into what biological factors could be contributing to the disorder.

Drugs exert their effect on brain functioning by affecting neurotransmitters at the synapse of the nerve cells. Drugs that enhance the activity of a neurotransmitter are called **agonists;** drugs that inhibit or block the activity of a neurotransmitter are called **antagonists.** The medications that are effective in treating schizophrenia are generally dopamine antagonists, which suggests that either an increased level of dopamine or an increase in the sensitivity of nerve cells to dopamine is involved in schizophrenia. The fact that amphetamines, which are dopamine agonists, tend to exacerbate the symptoms of schizophrenia and can even create psychotic symptoms in individuals who do not have schizophrenia adds more weight to the argument that dopamine plays a significant role in schizophrenia (Angrist et al., 1974). Until recently, the effectiveness of every drug used to reduce the symptoms of schizophrenia was roughly proportional to its strength as a dopamine antagonist. Some of the newer drugs used to treat schizophrenia, however, such as the atypical antipsychotics, affect both dopamine and serotonin, and this suggests that serotonin may also be involved in schizophrenia.

For several reasons, one must be careful in interpreting drug studies. The first is that drugs rarely affect just one

agonists Drugs that enhance the activity of a neurotransmitter.

antagonists Drugs that inhibit or block the activity of a neurotransmitter.

neurotransmitter. The second is that a positive treatment response does not mean necessarily that the treatment is addressing the cause. (For example, aspirin will often relieve a headache, but headaches are not caused by a shortage of aspirin.) The third is that one cannot be sure that a drug that is taken systemically—that is, ingested and allowed to distribute itself through the body—is having the intended result in the brain. In fact, evidence from animal studies suggests that drugs taken systemically often produce different effects than drugs that are delivered directly to a specific region of the brain (Givens & Olton, 1990). Delivering drugs through tiny tubes surgically implanted in the brain is not a workable solution in human research. Therefore, in the near term, scientists will have to rely on the body to distribute medications. It is worth noting that scanning technologies may soon allow scientists to monitor the distribution of medications, even if the scientists cannot fully control their distribution (Tauscher & Kapur, 2001).

INTEGRATING BIOLOGY AND BEHAVIOR

The most sophisticated biological research in the field of schizophrenia is heavily dependent on the available knowledge about the role of each brain mechanism on behavior. Certain brain regions are assumed to be more likely to be involved in schizophrenia because they control behavior that is known to be disordered in schizophrenia. The early biological and psychological studies of disorders such as schizophrenia were carried on rather independently, but that is no longer the case. Now scientists seek to understand how both the biological and the psychological manifestations of a disorder represent a single underlying problem (Green, 1998). Sophisticated fields such as neuropsychology provide the theoretical base for this understanding, as research provides new insights into the operation of the human brain (Gazzaniga et al., 1998). It is no accident that the advances in the scientific understanding of schizophrenia are accelerating, for they are building on a foundation of cognitive neuroscience that is of relatively recent origin. It isn't the impressive technology that drives this rapid advance. It is the basic knowledge that the technology has helped bring to light. This is an exciting time for cognitive neuroscience—and a hopeful time for those people suffering from psychological disorders.

Check Yourself 6.8

Studying Biological Influences

1. What is the relationship between schizophrenia and brain activity?
2. What is the difference between the effect of an agonist and that of an antagonist on a neurotransmitter?
3. Why is it dangerous to draw conclusions about the cause of a disorder from treatment data?

Ponder this . . . *What are the advantages of looking at a disorder from multiple perspectives simultaneously?*

STUDYING ENVIRONMENTAL INFLUENCES

In Chapter 5, we discussed three environmental factors that have shown a link to schizophrenia: communication deviance, affective style, and expressed emotion. The researchers who studied these environmental variables did not try to promise too much. They argued that these environmental variables contributed to, or exacerbated, symptoms, not that they caused schizophrenia. Furthermore, in the case of expressed emotion at least, the negative impact was not confined to schizophrenia but was also noted in depression (Butzlaff & Hooley, 1998), bipolar disorder (Simoneau et al., 1998), alcoholism (O'Farrell et al., 1998), and eating disorders (Butzlaff & Hooley, 1998). These lines of research were models of good science: They were carefully and systematically carried out, and they were not invoked to make broader claims than the data could support. However, not all studies of environmental variables lived up to these high standards. This section will review two environmental hypotheses—the schizophrenogenic mother hypothesis and the double-bind hypothesis—that were once widely accepted in the field. Neither is given much credence anymore. Nevertheless, these hypotheses illustrate three critical issues: (1) how hypotheses are formed; (2) the ease with which serious people can be misled by casual observations or faulty logic; and (3) how the scientific method eventually provides corrective feedback.

SCHIZOPHRENOGENIC MOTHER HYPOTHESIS

Frieda Fromm-Reichmann (1948), an unusually gifted therapist who treated many young people with schizophrenia, proposed the **schizophrenogenic mother hypothesis.** She noted that the parents of people with schizophrenia often showed significant psychopathology themselves. Furthermore, it was not uncommon for a person with schizophrenia who seemed to be making progress in therapy to return from a family visit grossly psychotic. Fromm-Reichmann speculated that the behavior of the parents, especially the mother, was psychologically toxic for the child. More specifically, she suggested that the mother's pathology was the cause of the schizophrenic pathology of her child—hence the term *schizophrenogenic mother.*

schizophrenogenic mother hypothesis   The discredited speculation that schizophrenia can be attributed to psychologically toxic effects of the individual's parents, especially the mother.

There are several problems with this hypothesis. First, it is based on casual observations and second-hand reports. Both of these data sources are unreliable and often biased. Therefore, the data on which the hypothesis was originally based are suspect. That is not necessarily a serious problem, because a hypothesis can be derived from any source. However, once formulated, hypotheses should be scientifically evaluated. The people who proposed the schizophrenogenic mother hypothesis never scientifically evaluated it. Another problem is that the observations of Fromm-Reichmann could be interpreted in different ways. For example, shared genes could account for these observations. It is also possible that the disturbed behavior of the people with schizophrenia took its toll on the family. The stress of dealing with an occasionally irrational child may have led to distorted and inappropriate behavior on the part of the parents. If the hypothesis that mildly abnormal behavior in parents can drive the child to become psychotic is considered plausible, it is certainly plausible that truly psychotic behavior in children can lead to mildly abnormal behavior in their parents.

These alternative hypotheses illustrate one of the most critical weaknesses in a simple observational procedure such as the case study method of Fromm-Reichmann. A correlation between two variables does not imply causality. The relationship between the child's psychosis (A) and the mother's behavior (B) may be due to B causing A, as Fromm-Reichmann speculated. However, it could just as easily be due to A causing B or to some third factor, such as genetic influences, causing both A and B. There is nothing wrong with speculating from a simple observation. However, a causal inference has to be backed up by more than simple observation to be taken seriously.

Scientifically evaluating environmental hypotheses such as the schizophrenogenic mother hypothesis is difficult. An experimental study would require the researcher to randomly assign children to be raised by schizophrenogenic or nonschizophrenogenic mothers—an approach that is clearly unethical. Therefore, researchers must rely on indirect evidence. Such indirect evidence can rarely establish the truth of a hypothesis, but it may well refute the hypothesis. The fact that most of the siblings of people with schizophrenia were raised by the same mother and yet never develop schizophrenia themselves raises doubt. The fact that most mothers of people who develop schizophrenia do not show schizophrenogenic traits raises even more doubt (Goldstein & Rodnick, 1975). Finally, both positive and negative evidence should be sought in the testing of scientific hypotheses. The schizophrenogenic mother hypothesis predicts not only that parents of children who later develop schizophrenia should have certain characteristics (positive evidence) but also that parents whose children do not develop schizophrenia should *not* have those characteristics (negative evidence). To illustrate this point, consider this extreme example, which might be called the "breathing parents hypothesis." It was observed that the parents of

people who develop schizophrenia all breathe, and therefore it was hypothesized that the breathing of the parents caused the schizophrenia in their children. Does this observation support the hypothesis? Not really, and the logical error is probably obvious. *All* parents breathe, which would be easy to confirm by looking at the negative evidence (parents of people who do not develop schizophrenia). For parental breathing to be a contributing factor in schizophrenia, it has to appear more often in parents of people who develop schizophrenia than in parents of people who do not develop the disorder. The alleged schizophrenogenic traits occur no more frequently in mothers whose children develop schizophrenia than in mothers whose children do not (Goldstein & Rodnick, 1975; Wynne et al., 1979).

Perhaps there are a few individuals whose psychosis can legitimately be attributed to the psychologically toxic effects of the environment their parents provided, but that does not seem to be generally true. Quite properly, scientists have laid the schizophrenogenic mother hypothesis to rest. Unfortunately, some hypotheses are not simply scientific tools but have real impact on the world around them. Family members of psychotic individuals are generally aware that many professionals—professionals who took this hypothesis seriously in spite of its scientific shortcomings—have blamed them for their children's problems. This awareness may have poisoned the relationship between the doctors and some families, thus further complicating treatment.

DOUBLE-BIND HYPOTHESIS

Bateson et al. (1956), in their **double-bind hypothesis,** speculated that conflicting communication by parents could have damaging psychological consequences on their children. The classic example of this conflicting communication is the parent who asks the child for a hug and kiss (a direct verbal message) but then tenses up and gives nonverbal cues about being uncomfortable with the child's show of affection (a contradictory nonverbal message). Children who read the nonverbal message correctly and back off from their display of affection may have the parent respond with "What's the matter? Don't you love me?" However, continuing to hug the parent evokes the clear nonverbal response "You are making me uncomfortable." The child is in a no-win situation.

Double-bind situations clearly exist. Everyone has received mixed messages from friends, family, and co-workers. Adults may be able to label the source of their discomfort, perhaps with the help and advice of a sympathetic or insightful friend. They can even challenge the mixed message if the power differential between them and

double-bind hypothesis The discredited speculation that conflicting communications by a parent psychologically damages children.

This child is enjoying a hug from his grandfather, and he can feel his grandfather's love. However, some children are caught in a double bind in their families. Their parents or grandparents ask for a hug but are clearly uncomfortable with the hug. When the child correctly reads the body language indicating discomfort and withdraws, the adult gives another mixed message by saying something like "Don't you love me?" Double-bind situations certainly occur, and they are uncomfortable, but there is no evidence that they can cause schizophrenia.

the people sending the contradictory messages is not too great. However, a child is unlikely to have the psychological maturity to handle such situations. Because even adults find such situations stressful and disruptive, the hypothesis that a defenseless child would be even more distressed has intuitive appeal. But does this hypothesis have scientific backing? The simple answer is no; there is no evidence to support the double-bind hypothesis. Double-bind situations occur about as often in the families of people with schizophrenia as in other families (Mishler & Waxler, 1968). Furthermore, even if positive findings had been reported, one could easily interpret the increased double-bind messages in the families that include a person who develops schizophrenia as a possible manifestation of a genetic diathesis for schizophrenia.

Check Yourself 6.9

Studying Environmental Influences

1. What environmental hypotheses have supporting data?
2. What evidence refutes the schizophrenogenic mother hypothesis?

Ponder this . . .   *Most siblings of people with schizophrenia do not develop schizophrenia, yet they share the same family environment. Does this preclude the possibility that family environment contributes to schizophrenia?*

PUTTING IT ALL TOGETHER

It is easy to be overwhelmed by the dozens of lines of research on schizophrenia. How do they all fit together? What research is most likely to lead to the next breakthrough? These two questions are actually closely connected. When researchers are able to think about a disorder from multiple perspectives and piece together divergent findings, they are far more likely to identify the truly promising areas of research. That can be a challenging task for an individual researcher, which is one reason why it is increasingly common for researchers from multiple perspectives to collaborate, both formally and informally. Such collaboration may be formal, as when two or more people with different skills carry out a project that they could not do individually. Funding agencies now encourage such collaboration because it results in more sophisticated and better integrated research. In addition, informal groups of investigators are now common. These may be universities with several people conducting schizophrenia research or regional groups of researchers that meet regularly. With the Internet and modern telecommunications, such collaboration can now occur among people who live halfway around the world from one another. You can see this collaboration in action when you conduct a literature search on any topic in psychopathology. Note how many of the articles have two or more authors and how many of those have authors who are at different institutions.

   Another kind of cross-fertilization, although it is less common, can change the direction of thought on a topic. This cross-fertilization occurs when a new idea or perspective integrates two or more ideas into an elegant reinterpretation of a long-familiar phenomenon. The work of Jonathan Cohen and his associates, which is featured in the nearby Advances box, is an excellent example. This study integrated information about the physiology of the brain, the neurochemistry of schizophrenia, and the perceptual and cognitive deficits in schizophrenia into a single conceptualization. Such elegant and parsimonious integrations are rare in science, but when they occur they are something special.

ADVANCES A PDP model of schizophrenic deficits

The goal in science is to integrate information from different sources to provide a coherent explanation for a phenomenon. This is a bit like piecing a massive puzzle together. In the field of schizophrenia, the following facts have been known for years: (1) Dopamine is involved in schizophrenia. (2) Dopamine modulates activity level in the brain. (3) People with schizophrenia have problems performing well on many cognitive and perceptual tasks. Cohen and Servan-Schreiber (1992) pulled all of these puzzle pieces together with a brilliant series of studies employing parallel distributed processing (PDP) models of cognitive performance.

PDP models are computer simulations of how a heavily interconnected system like the brain might work. What is special about these models is that they "learn" by being given examples of correct behavior. For example, a PDP model for forming the plural of nouns might be given the following input/output pairs: boy/boys, girl/girls, man/men, woman/women, light/lights, mouse/mice, window/windows, and so on. PDP models produce what appears to be rule-based behavior without ever being taught rules, and they seem to learn in much the same way as humans, even to the point of producing similar errors during learning. For example, the PDP model for forming plurals is likely to give *deers* as the plural of *deer* or *mices* as the plural of *mouse*—both errors that children commonly make as they learn the language.

Cohen and Servan-Schreiber (1992) used PDP models in a series of studies of schizophrenic psychopathology. Because dopamine has been implicated in schizophrenia and because this neurotransmitter is known to modulate activity level throughout the brain, they included in each of their simulations a "gain" parameter that increased or decreased the activity level of the PDP model, much as dopamine modulates activity level in the brain. They constructed three PDP models to simulate three different cognitive tasks: (1) the Stroop Test, (2) the Continuous Performance Test (CPT), and (3) a lexical ambiguity task. The Continuous Performance Test is a measure of vigilance that was discussed earlier in this chapter.

The Stroop Test is illustrated in Figure 6.5. The task is to name colors. In Condition 1, the colors are on rectangular blocks, and naming them is easy for most people. In contrast, Condition 2 is difficult because color words are printed in different colors, and people have to inhibit their tendency to read the words in order to perform the task of naming the color of the print. Give it a try and you will see that this is a challenge. People with schizophrenia show the same disruption as other people, but more severe. Finally, the lexical ambiguity task involves selecting the appropriate meaning of a word by using the context. For example, the word *pen* could mean either a writing implement or a barnyard enclosure. The sentences "You can't keep chickens without a pen" and "You can't write a check without a pen" make clear what meaning is appropriate. Nevertheless, people with schizophrenia select the most popular meaning—in this case, a writing instrument—more often than other people, even when the context would suggest a different meaning.

We won't go into the technical details, but Cohen and Servan-

---

 ## SUMMARY

SCHIZOPHRENIA AS A CONSTRUCT

- A diagnosis is a construct. Constructs cannot be seen, but they can be evaluated by testing the predictions that follow from them, a process known as construct validation.

- Robins and Guze (1970) outlined a procedure for evaluating a diagnostic construct by (1) establishing interrater reliability, (2) predicting laboratory measures, (3) predicting history and course, (4) predicting a positive family history, and (5) being able to differentiate the diagnosis from superficially similar diagnoses. An additional element is the ability to predict treatment response.

DEFINING AND REFINING THE SYNDROME

- The first step in the construct validation of a hypothesized disorder is to define the syndrome with sufficient precision to allow it to be studied. The process of construct validation will show whether the syndrome is likely to be valid and will guide refinements to the diagnostic criteria.

[FIGURE 6.5]
Stroop Test

Schreiber developed a model to simulate Stroop performance and "trained" it to perform the way most people were known to perform. They then adjusted the gain parameter until they produced the pattern of results shown by people with schizophrenia. Manipulating a single parameter that was designed to simulate the effect of dopamine was sufficient to take a model that reproduced the pattern of results found in most people and make that model reproduce the pattern of results found in people with schizophrenia. This in itself was impressive. Then they built and trained models to reproduce the performance of most people on the CPT and the lexical ambiguity task. Adjusting the gain function in these models to the same value that reproduced the schizophrenic pattern on the Stroop also reproduced the schizophrenic pattern of performance on these tasks. The finding that manipulating a single parameter can recreate the performance of people with schizophrenia on three different tasks is truly amazing. Previously, no single model could explain these results. Furthermore, this explanation was consistent with what is known about the neurochemistry of schizophrenia. Thus it provided for the first time a coherent, integrated picture of cognitive functioning in schizophrenia. As rare as a diamond, this kind of integration of findings into a single, parsimonious explanation for a phenomenon is the ultimate goal of science.

The research on PDP modeling of schizophrenic symptoms continues at an accelerated pace. Cohen and his associates continue their groundbreaking investigations (Braver et al., 1999; Cohen & Servan-Schreiber, 1993; Servan-Schreiber & Cohen, 1998), and others are adding to this exciting work (Amos, 2000; Hoffman et al., 1999; Mahurin, 1998). It remains to be seen whether these studies will lead to the next breakthrough in our understanding of schizophrenia.

TEST DEVELOPMENT AND VALIDATION

- A psychological test is an operationalization of a construct. Any new measure should be evaluated for its reliability and construct validity and then refined as necessary.

DIATHESIS-STRESS MODELS

- Meehl proposed an early model of a genetic diathesis for schizophrenia, although more recent models argue for multiple diatheses and multiple stressors. Prospective studies of the developmental course of disorders can lead to gradual refinements in diathesis-stress models.

OVERVIEW OF RESEARCH DESIGNS

- There are five general approaches to studying psychiatric disorders. Case studies are excellent at generating hypotheses but poor at testing them. Experimental research is the strongest approach, but ethical and practical problems limit its use in the field of psychopathology. Correlational research quantifies the relationship between variables. Differential research involves comparing diagnostic groups. Prospective and retrospective studies attempt to identify factors that reliably precede the development of a disorder and thus may provide clues about the developmental course. Finally, high-risk research is a more efficient way of conducting a prospective study, because a larger proportion of the sample is expected to develop the disorder.

STUDYING COGNITIVE PROCESSING

- Perceptual processing and cognitive processing are obviously disrupted in schizophrenia, although the exact nature of the disruption is not yet clear. Several areas of cognitive and perceptual processing have been studied, including vigilance, early perceptual processing, and eye movement dysfunction. That each of these aspects of functioning is disordered in schizophrenia and in unaffected relatives of people with schizophrenia suggests a genetic contribution.

STUDYING GENETIC INFLUENCES

- Three approaches have been used to verify genetic influences. Family studies determine the risk for a disorder in families of probands with the disorder. Twin studies control environment by comparing the concordance rates of MZ and DZ twins. Adoption studies separate environment and genetics by studying only those people with schizophrenia who were adopted at birth. By comparing the rates of schizophrenia in biological and adoptive families, one can get an indication of the relative strength of genetic and environmental factors.

- The technology is available to study individual genes through a procedure called linkage analysis. To date, no single gene has been implicated in schizophrenia, but advances in the understanding of the human genome may well increase the power of this approach in the near future.

- A major mystery in schizophrenia is why there is little evidence for the existence of schizophrenia before about 200 years ago.

STUDYING BIOLOGICAL INFLUENCES

- The most common research strategy in biological research is to compare diagnostic groups on biological variables.

- The neurochemistry of the brain can be evaluated by monitoring the specific effects of drugs that either enhance or block the action of specific neurotransmitters.

STUDYING ENVIRONMENTAL INFLUENCES

- Ethical constraints complicate the study of environmental factors in psychopathology. Nevertheless, it is possible to study such factors by carefully deriving predictions from theory and then testing them. The schizophrenogenic mother and double-bind hypotheses relied too heavily on casual observations and failed to consider critical data that would have discredited them.

PUTTING IT ALL TOGETHER

- The trend in psychopathology research is to integrate information and ideas from multiple perspectives, often by fostering active collaboration of researchers from different perspectives.

 KEY TERMS

agonists   (158)
antagonists   (158)
backward-masking task   (153)
behavioral high-risk paradigm   (149)
blind   (139)
case studies   (143)
confounding variable   (139)
constructs   (135)
construct validation   (136)
Continuous Performance Test, or CPT   (151)
correlational research   (144)
cross-sectional studies   (147)
dependent variable   (144)
developmental models of psychopathology   (142)
differential deficit research   (146)
differential research   (146)
dizygotic (DZ, or fraternal) twins   (156)

double-bind hypothesis   (160)
experimental research   (144)
experimenter bias   (139)
family studies   (155)
general paresis   (137)
general risk factors   (143)
generalized deficit   (146)
genetic high-risk paradigm   (147)
high-risk studies   (147)
hypothesis   (135)
independent variable   (144)
informed consent   (145)
longitudinal studies   (147)
marker   (152)
monozygotic (MZ, or identical) twins   (156)
operationalize   (138)
paradigm   (135)

SUGGESTED READINGS

Gottesman, I. I. (1991). *Schizophrenia genesis: The origins of madness.* New York: Freeman. This fascinating review of the history of our understanding of schizophrenia has won several awards and has been translated into more than a dozen languages.

Green, M. F. (1998). *Schizophrenia from a neurocognitive perspective: Probing the impenetrable darkness.* Boston: Allyn & Bacon. This technical, although quite readable, book describes some of the exciting work being done to bridge the gap between neurological and cognitive studies of schizophrenia. Dr. Green has a wonderful, engaging style in presenting the material.

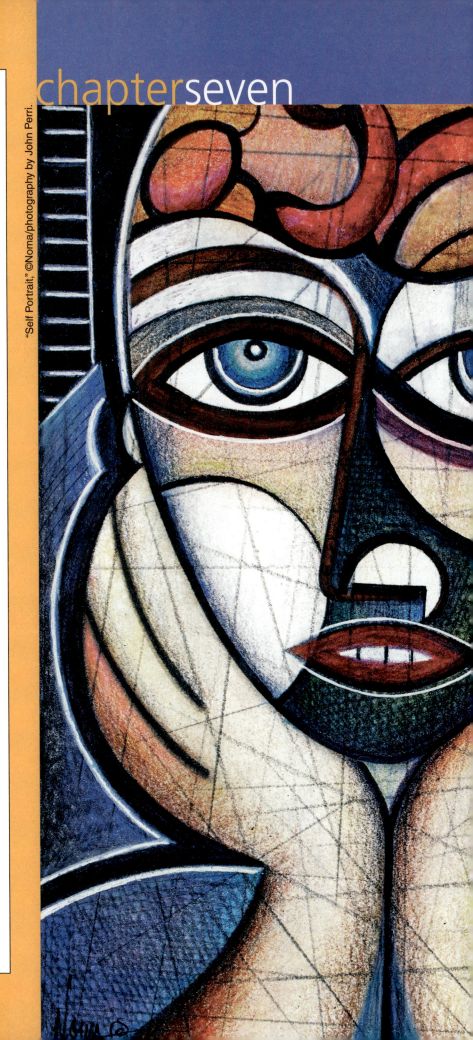

"Self Portrait," ©Noma/photography by John Perri.

chapterseven

Mood Disorders

A Life Lost for the Moment

ANNE

Anne never thought that she would be the one who needed help. For the first 26 years of her life, she was the one on whom everyone else depended for support. Yet for the last six months, her depression had gradually gotten worse until she could no longer take care of herself. She had stopped going to work a month ago, and she rarely even left her apartment. She stopped answering the phone and eventually unplugged it from the wall. She would sleep up to 16 hours a day and sometimes would just lie in bed for several hours, unable to muster the energy to get up. She barely ate and had lost over 25 pounds in the last six months. She had been depressed before; in fact, she had had several bouts of depression starting in early high school, but nothing like what she experienced now. She could not pinpoint when it started. It was like sinking slowly into a quicksand of despair. She felt that there was no reason to live and would lie in bed thinking that she would kill herself if only she had enough energy to do it.

A Wildfire Out of Control

LARRY

So far today, Larry has gotten into three screaming matches, threatened four different people with law suits, and come up with four "can't miss" business ideas—and it's not even 8:00 A.M. One can only imagine what he might do if he were not on a locked psychiatric ward. Larry did not sleep last night. He often skips sleeping when he is "cooking"—his term for the manic energy that periodically overtakes him. He is too wound up to sleep and too impatient to deal with the slow people around him. He has energy to burn and enough ideas to fill an encyclopedia. He talks so quickly that you can barely understand him and switches topics so frequently that his train of thought is impossible to follow. Ask him for clarification, and he is likely to scream at you, calling you an idiot. He says he feels great, and he looks like he is bubbling over with excitement, although in a flash he can turn frighteningly hostile. He tells the doctors that he does not need medication, but he takes it without complaining, saying it can't hurt. He checked himself into the hospital after his wife threatened to leave him and take the kids. Despite being the most productive sales rep in his company—outselling the next three sales reps put together—Larry was fired from his job for his outrageous behavior just a week before being hospitalized. It is not the first job he has lost, nor is it likely to be the last. Larry is supremely confident that he will get an even better job once he is out of the hospital, although a few weeks from now, when he comes down from his high, he will be terrified of having to put his life back together yet another time.

We all feel "down" occasionally, sometimes even depressed, but most people never get as depressed as Anne. She is so depressed that she can no longer take care of her most basic needs. Everyone has good days, when it is easy to feel confident and take on challenges, but most people never experience the out-of-control high that Larry experiences. These cases represent extreme examples of mood fluctuations. **Mood** is one's general emotional feeling that may vary gradually over time. For example, a person may feel sad or elated. The term **affect** refers to the more momentary behavioral manifestations of

mood   A general emotional feeling that may vary gradually over time.

affect   The more momentary behavioral manifestations of mood.

mood. For example, people who are depressed may still smile or laugh in certain situations. Their mood is depressed, but their affect is responsive to the situation. With severe depression, however, affect is no longer responsive to environmental circumstances. Mood fluctuations are normal, and they are usually responsive to the general pattern of life experiences. For example, if you win a big account at work, ace the most difficult course in your major, or go on the best date of your life, you have a right to feel good, and you probably will. On the other hand, if you find your work constantly coming up short, are turned down for graduate school, or have a fight with your best friend, you have a right to feel down, and you probably will. These momentary affective changes can influence a person's overall mood if the pattern is consistently positive or negative.

Shifts in mood are normal, but in some people the mood shifts are more dramatic, occur more frequently, or last longer. In such cases, the person is said to suffer from a **mood disorder. Depression** is a mood characterized by sadness and a loss of energy and enjoyment in life. In contrast, **mania** is a mood characterized by excessive energy, extreme confidence, euphoria, and irritability. The DSM distinguishes between unipolar depression and bipolar disorder. **Unipolar depression** is characterized by a pattern of serious depressive periods with no history of manic periods. In contrast, **bipolar disorder** is characterized by a pattern of mood fluctuations in which the mood is sometimes depressed and sometimes manic. One might expect there to be a third condition—unipolar mania—but this diagnosis does not exist. Individuals who have shown only manic episodes are given the diagnosis of bipolar disorder because they are assumed to be at risk for depression as well, and the research suggests that this assumption is justified (APA, 2000).

Although virtually everyone has experienced uncomfortable mood swings, most people do not experience the intense mood swings that occur in mood disorders. However, many famous figures have suffered from such mood disorders, and their struggles with these inner demons were

Abraham Lincoln was subject to severe periods of depression throughout his public life. Nevertheless, he is considered by many to be one of America's greatest presidents and was a capable leader during a very difficult time in history. Many capable people periodically experience depression and yet manage to lead fulfilling and rewarding lives.

apparently not enough to prevent them from achieving greatness. Two American presidents—Abraham Lincoln and Calvin Coolidge—suffered from recurrent depressions. A vice-presidential candidate—Thomas Eagleton—was forced off the ticket in 1972 when it was learned that he suffered recurrent severe depressions. Deep depressions were also a part of the lives of Mike Wallace and Joan Rivers. Bipolar disorder has plagued a number of artists and other creative people, including Vincent Van Gogh, Ernest Hemingway, Virginia Woolf, Eugene O'Neill, and Patty Duke (Andreasen, 1980).

This chapter will cover the two major classes of mood disorders—depression and bipolar disorders—including descriptions, theories about their causes, and current treatments. The chapter closes with a discussion of suicide.

CONCEPTUALIZING MOODS AND MOOD DISORDERS

Evolutionary Impact

What does it mean to be in a good mood or a bad mood? Moods clearly have an impact on people. Life is easy when you feel confident and positive; life is overwhelming when you feel down and hopeless. It is easy to see the beneficial effects of being in a good mood; it is hard to see any value in being depressed. So why do moods exist? More specifically, why has nature not selected only good moods, which seem to promote effective, productive behavior? If one looks casually at something like depression, one might well expect that natural selection would have eliminated it long ago.

mood disorder A disorder characterized by mood shifts that are more dramatic, more frequent, or last longer than what is considered normal.

depression A mood that is characterized by sadness and a loss of energy and enjoyment in life.

mania A mood characterized by excessive energy, extreme confidence, euphoria, and irritability.

unipolar depression A disorder characterized by a pattern of serious depressive periods with no history of manic or hypomanic periods.

bipolar disorder A pattern of mood fluctuations in which the mood is sometimes depressed and sometimes manic.

However, depression is vividly described in writings dating back thousands of years (Gottesman, 1991), and there is no indication that it will disappear anytime soon. In fact, it seems to be on the increase, especially among the young (Seligman, 1990; Surgeon General, 1999).

Thus mood disorders appear to be counterproductive and yet have not been eliminated by natural selection. *Why?* If mood disorders did not have a genetic component, that might explain the finding; but genes clearly do play a role in mood disorder. Therefore, it is likely that some benefit is associated with mood disorders, or at least that they exert no negative selective pressure (Nesse, 1990). We will return to this issue later in the chapter and address it from other perspectives.

One should expect many factors to influence something as critical to functioning as mood. Negative events, such as the loss of a job or the breakup of an important relationship, are capable of triggering a significant shift in a person's mood. The question here is *how*. What happens to trigger the changes in feelings? Some people rarely get depressed when faced with negative life events. The question here is *why*. Are there biological differences that account for some people getting depressed and others not? Can experiences increase or decrease people's risk for mood disorders? All these critical questions will be addressed in this chapter. For now, you should note that (1) mood swings are often, but not always, a response to environmental events; (2) there are large individual differences in susceptibility to these mood swings; and (3) a system so central to human functioning is likely to be affected by many factors.

In trying to understand the evolutionary significance of something like depression, one should look at the effect of depressive behavior on a depressed person as well as at the effect of the person's depressive posture and facial expressions on others.

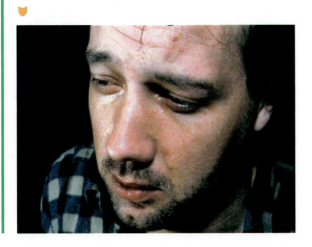

Check Yourself 7.1

Conceptualizing Moods and Mood Disorders

1. How long have mood disorders been around?
2. What factors trigger mood swings?

Ponder this . . .   *On the surface, depression appears to have little survival value, yet the fact that it does not seem to be disappearing suggests otherwise. Speculate about potential benefits of depression that may contribute to survival or reproduction.*

DEPRESSIVE DISORDERS

Everyone feels down and depressed occasionally. It may be unpleasant, but it is not necessarily pathological. However, more severe or long-lasting depression may qualify as a depressive disorder. Even severe depression that occurs as a result of a significant loss, such as the death of a close friend or relative, is not considered pathological unless it continues longer than is typical. For the first few weeks after such a loss, the grief can be every bit as intense as in clinical depression. For most people, however, the intense grief is replaced by a less intense sense of loss and an ability to resume normal activities. People do not qualify for a diagnosis of depression unless their intense grief lasts longer than two months (APA, 2000).

Two types of depressive conditions are recognized in the DSM. **Major depression** is an intense form of depression that occurs in episodes. It is called major depression to differentiate it from the normal depression that everyone experiences occasionally. **Dysthymic disorder** refers to a chronic form of depression—almost a depressive personality. In fact, there is considerable debate about whether dysthymia should be classified as a mood disorder or as a personality disorder (Ryder & Bagby, 1999). Occasionally, major depressive episodes occur in individuals who also suffer from the more chronic dysthymia, and this condition is known as **double depression** (Klein et al., 1988). This section will describe major depression and dysthymia as well as three additional variations on depression: seasonal affective disorder, postpartum depression, and childhood depression.

major depression   An intense form of depression that occurs in episodes.

dysthymic disorder   A chronic, lower-level depression.

double depression   A condition characterized by occasional major depressive episodes in individuals who also suffer from the more chronic dysthymia.

MAJOR DEPRESSION

Major depression occurs in episodes, which must last at least two weeks to qualify for the diagnosis (APA, 2000). The episodes last around six months on average, and it is rare for them to last longer than a year or two, even without treatment. A major depressive episode is characterized by a constellation of symptoms that are summarized in Table 7.1. Not every depressed individual shows every symptom, but most seriously depressed individuals show most of these symptoms.

Major depression usually develops over a period of days to weeks, often preceded by a prolonged period of increased anxiety or mild depressive symptoms. It seriously affects a person's ability to meet the demands of life, although many people with severe depression continue to function, albeit with little joy or enthusiasm for life. Major depression tends to recur, especially in those people who experience their first depression at a young age (Kessing et al., 2000), have other psychological problems (van Weel-Baumgarten et al., 2000), or have had several previous episodes (Hart et al., 2001). The majority of people with major depression never seek treatment (Alvidrez & Azocar, 1999; Surgeon General, 1999), especially among minority groups (Fellin, 1989; Munoz et al., 2000). One reason why so few people seek treatment for depression is that many people see it as untreatable, viewing it more as a character flaw. The characteristic distress, lack of motivation, and low self-esteem are viewed as things that should be overcome by sheer force of will. Such attitudes are more pronounced in some minority groups, which may partially explain the

dramatic undertreatment in these groups. Most people recover from major depressive episodes with few if any residual symptoms (APA, 2000).

The incidence of major depressive disorders is twice as great in women as in men (APA, 2000). Approximately 10 to 25% of women and 5 to 12% of men will develop major depression during their lifetimes (APA, 2000). This finding is so strong and so stable that the theories of depression have to address it. At any given point, approximately 5 to 9% of adults qualify for a diagnosis of major depression (Haarasilta et al., 2001). The average age of onset for depression has been decreasing dramatically in the United States, and depression in young people is now ten times more common than it was two generations earlier (Kessler et al., 2001; Seligman, 1990). This dramatic increase in childhood depression has not occurred in other cultures, which suggests that something about modern American culture may be **depressogenic**—that is, tending to create depression. Also interesting is the fact that the 2:1 female-to-male ratio is not found among children; boys are as likely as girls to develop severe depression (APA, 2000). The rates of depression tend to be highest during middle adulthood (25–44) and to drop off after age 65 for both men and women (APA, 2000; Bebbington et al., 1998).

Although depression appears to occur in every culture, there is considerable variation in how it is experienced (Kleinman & Good, 1985). For example, Latin cultures often complain of "nerves" and headaches, whereas Asian cultures complain of weakness, fatigue, and "imbalance," and Western cultures complain of sadness and hopelessness. Most researchers believe that these differences represent different cultural perspectives on what are the central symptoms of depression. Furthermore, depressive symptoms vary as a function of age. Young children may experience physical symptoms, irritability, and social withdrawal, whereas adolescents and adults are likely to experience slowed motor activity, excessive sleepiness, sadness, and guilt (APA, 2000).

DYSTHYMIC DISORDER

Dysthymic disorder is a chronic, lower-level depression that is present most of the day for at least two years (APA, 2000). The symptoms of dysthymia are similar to those of major depression; they include poor or excessive appetite, difficulty sleeping or excessive sleeping, fatigue or low energy, low self-esteem, difficulty in making decisions, and a feeling of hopelessness. The symptoms tend to be less severe in dysthymia than in major depression, but they are still uncomfortable and debilitating.

[TABLE 7.1] Symptoms of Major Depression

1. Depressed mood that lasts most of the day
2. Dramatic loss of interest and pleasure in most activities
3. Significant weight loss not associated with dieting, or significant increase or decrease in appetite
4. Difficulty in sleeping or excessive sleeping
5. Physical agitation so intense that one cannot sit still or a significant slowing of motor activity
6. Significant fatigue or loss of energy
7. Feelings of worthlessness or excessive guilt
8. Reduced ability to concentrate or to be decisive about normal matters
9. Recurrent thoughts of death or suicide

To qualify for the diagnosis of major depression, the individual must exhibit at least five of these symptoms for at least two weeks, and the symptoms must be apparent nearly every day.

depressogenic Tending to create depression.

Dysthymia can develop at any age and tends to be chronic once it develops. Most people with dysthymia report experiencing it the majority of their adult lives. There are some interesting differences between people who develop dysthymia early in adulthood and those who develop it later. Those with earlier onset are more likely to have a history of major depression, social phobia, panic disorder, and conversion disorder. In contrast, those with later onset are more likely to have had generalized anxiety disorder, substance abuse, and somatization disorder (Barzega et al., 2001). All of these disorders will be covered in later chapters. Just as in major depression, boys are as likely to develop dysthymia as girls, but by adulthood, females outnumber males by 2 or 3 to 1 (APA, 2000). The lifetime prevalence is approximately 6%, with approximately 3% of the population suffering from dysthymia at any given time (Angst, 1997). Few people with dysthymia seek treatment unless they develop a major depressive episode—the so-called double depression.

SEASONAL AFFECTIVE DISORDER

Some people experience depression that is tied to the season of the year—a condition known as **seasonal affective disorder,** or **SAD.** The typical course of SAD is for depression to develop sometime in late fall or early winter and continue until spring (Rosenthal, 1998; Rosenthal & Blehar, 1989). Except for its seasonal pattern, the depression in SAD appears to be like any other depression. The prevalence of SAD is approximately 3%, and another 8% show milder forms of the disorder but do not meet the full diagnostic criteria (Mersch et al., 1999).

What causes SAD? Because early winter in the United States is associated with the holidays, and the holidays have often been associated with depression, one cannot completely rule out psychological causes. However, the fact that the rates of SAD vary depending on latitude suggests that SAD is related to the length of the day, the average temperature, or both (Rosenthal & Blehar, 1989). The higher the latitude—that is, the farther north one goes in the Northern Hemisphere—the shorter the days during the winter, and generally the colder the winter weather. Curiously, however, seasonal affective disorder is rare in Iceland, a country in which you would expect high rates because it is so far north (Magnusson & Stefansson, 1993). In fact, the Icelandic population does not show the normal seasonal variation in mood found in virtually every other country in which it has been studied (Magnusson et al., 2000). One might speculate that there is something about Iceland that accounts for the low rate of SAD. However, the

fact that emigrants from Iceland to Canada also show low rates of SAD suggests that genetic factors are responsible (Magnusson & Axelsson, 1993).

Evolutionary Impact

The low rate of SAD in Iceland is a perfect example of evolution at work. The population of Iceland was geographically, and therefore genetically, isolated until the development of modern transportation. Hence the Icelandic population followed its own evolutionary course. In contrast, most other human populations were nomadic, spreading out over vast landmasses. To the extent that genes play a role in SAD, the people of Iceland would have been subjected to much stronger negative selective pressure on those genes, because the country is so far north and has such short days during the winter. Consequently, the genes that contribute to SAD would have been virtually eliminated. If Iceland were in the Caribbean, where winter days are long and not much different from summer days, there would have been little negative selective pressure to eliminate the genes responsible for SAD. Thus the combination of geographic isolation and strong negative selective pressure apparently changed one aspect of the genetic makeup of the people of Iceland.

SAD appears to be related to changes in hormones that are associated with changes in the season. For example, the level of melatonin increases during the winter months and decreases during the summer months. Melatonin, which is derived from the serotonin molecule (Terman & Schlager, 1990), suppresses a person's energy level, which may explain why many people experience greater energy levels during the summer and have less energy during the winter. It is hypothesized that this effect is stronger for people with SAD, and the data are partially supportive of that hypothesis. Specifically, males with SAD show more melatonin secretion during winter than summer, but females do not. This suggests that there may be different mechanisms underlying this disorder in males and females.

Most of the research on SAD has been conducted with Western populations. However, two studies have been conducted with Eastern populations—Chinese medical students (Han et al., 2000) and Japanese civil servants (Ozaki et al., 1995). In sharp contrast to the seasonal patterns found in most Western populations, the Chinese and Japanese show a strong seasonal variation with more depression during the summer months. To date, there is insufficient research to answer the obvious question of whether this pattern represents a completely different phenomenon from the SAD studied extensively in the West or essentially the same phenomenon with a different set of triggers.

seasonal affective disorder (SAD) Depression that develops consistently in late fall and continues until spring.

Most people with depression experience recurrent depressions, but few people experience depression with the same regularity as individuals with SAD. Thus SAD provides a natural laboratory for studying the developmental course of a disorder. Let's look at some of the data from such longitudinal studies.

Examining the Evidence

If you wanted to study the developmental course of a disorder, you could not find a better disorder to study than SAD, because it occurs in a select group of people on a regular schedule at predictable times. Researchers can take advantage of this regularity to study the phenomenon. By measuring critical variables that are theoretically related to risk for SAD over the course of the year, they can narrow their focus as they search for the mechanisms behind this condition. For example, Austen and Wilson (2001) found that as winter approached, heart rate and respiration slowed, blood pressure decreased, and there were changes in vagal tone in those at risk for SAD. These changes are similar to what is observed in animals that hibernate, which suggests that SAD may be a remnant of evolutionary history, when hibernation was a common way of dealing with winter.

Michael Young and his colleagues were able to demonstrate, in a pair of clever studies, the critical role of the length of the day in determining risk for SAD (Young et al., 1997). Specifically, they knew that SAD was related to the length of the day (sunrise to sunset), because it occurs during the time of year when the day is shortest and because it is more common in those parts of the earth where daylight during the winter is shortest. Other factors, of course, such as temperature, are confounded with the amount of sunlight, because the farther from the equator, the shorter the day *and* the colder the winter weather. However, weather varies from year to year and the length of the day does not. By inspecting data across several years, Young and his colleagues were able to show that the length of the day was a much better predictor of SAD onset than was temperature. Furthermore, even though the winter days are shorter the farther one goes from the equator, the days tend to shorten during winter everywhere except on the equator. Consequently, it is possible to look at the rate of SAD as a function of length of day at many different latitudes, each with different average temperatures, to determine whether the length of day is consistently predictive of risk. Again, the data suggested that the key variable is length of day (Young et al., 1997), although more recent data suggest that the impact of the absolute length of day is small (Haggarty

et al., 2001). This most recent finding suggests that SAD may be triggered less by the length of the day and more by the fact that the daylight hours are dwindling as winter approaches.

Until just a few years ago, SAD was acknowledged only in the conventional wisdom that some people seemed to get depressed during the winter. Careful scientific study has uncovered the primary variable (length of daylight) that triggers the depression, several tantalizing clues about what might be the mechanism for this disorder, and an effective treatment (light therapy). This disorder was tailor-made for research. Its regular pattern makes it ideal for prospective studies. The variables that are likely to be involved, such as social and biological variables, are easily measured. Research on SAD may eventually provide new insights into mood regulation and mood disorders.

POSTPARTUM DEPRESSION

Postpartum depression occurs in mothers during the first few weeks after delivery, which is referred to as the postpartum period.

It is important to note that postpartum depression must be distinguished from postpartum blues, which is a short phase of mild depression and mood swings occurring in the postpartum period. Postpartum blues are common, affecting 50 to 80% of women, and they probably represent a normal reaction to the immense stress and emotional volatility of pregnancy and delivery (Whiffen, 1992). The massive hormonal changes associated with pregnancy and delivery are the presumed trigger for postpartum blues (Parry & Newton, 2001). Mild to moderate depressive symptoms are also associated with several times of hormonal change in many, but not all, women, including the premenstrual phase of the menstrual cycle, the onset of puberty, menopause, and the start of the use of oral contraceptives.

Although postpartum depression has long been a part of the clinical vocabulary, it does not represent a separate diagnostic category; the best evidence suggests that it is simply a major depression that happens to occur shortly after giving birth (Whiffen, 1992; Whiffen & Gotlib, 1993). Furthermore, contrary to popular belief, depression is no more common during the postpartum period than in other periods of life (O'Hara et al., 1990). Given these facts, why would generations of clinicians and researchers single out postpartum depression as something different from other depressive disorders? Probably because a depression that is

postpartum depression A major depressive episode that occurs in a woman shortly after she gives birth.

experienced during what is normally a joyous time stands out dramatically, which makes it appear more common than it really is.

CHILDHOOD DEPRESSION

Depression is not a disorder confined to adults. It occurs with alarming frequency in children. In fact, depression appears to be occurring more frequently in children and at an earlier age than ever before (Seligman, 1990). Two questions are relevant to childhood depression. The first is whether childhood depression is different from adult depression, and the second is why the rate of childhood depression is increasing so rapidly. The first question is addressed here, and the second in the next section.

How similar are childhood and adult depressions? It is clear that depression is experienced in different ways in adults and children, as noted previously in this chapter. That difference in experience probably results from differences in cognitive and emotional development between adults and children. Are there more significant differences? Adults show a 2:1 female-to-male ratio in the rates of depression, which is remarkably stable across cultures (Jenkins et al., 1991). In sharp contrast, the rates of depression in young girls and boys are equal, not diverging until early adolescence (APA, 2000; Nolen-Hoeksema, 1990). Whether this divergence represents a hormonal effect that begins at puberty or a cultural difference between men and women has been the topic of vigorous debate (Elliot, 2001). Scientists do know that childhood depression is strongly predictive of adult depression, and this suggests that there is continuity between childhood and adult depression (Hammen & Rudolph, 1996). Perhaps biological factors play a larger role in childhood depression, but as children mature, social factors begin to play a greater

In the last 40 years, there has been a dramatic rise in the rates of depression among U.S. adolescents. Seligman argues that changes in educational philosophy may be one contributing factor.

role in determining risk for depression as they interact with these biological factors.

Check Yourself 7.2

Depressive Disorders

1. Define major depression, dysthymia, and seasonal affective disorder. How do they differ?
2. What are the symptoms of depression?
3. What is double depression?
4. What factors seem to account for seasonal affective disorder?
5. What is postpartum depression?
6. How is childhood depression different from depression in adults?

Ponder this . . . *Women outnumber men roughly 2 to 1 among those who experience depression, but this sex difference does not appear until adolescence. Speculate on possible explanations. How does the fact that this male-to-female ratio is roughly constant across cultures square with your speculations?*

EXPLAINING DEPRESSION

More than a dozen modern theories have been proposed to explain depression. This section will cover many of them under two general categories: biological and psychological. Of course, researchers recognize that both biological and psychological factors contribute to depression.

BIOLOGICAL THEORIES

Biological theories focus on the neural, biochemical, and physiological mechanisms underlying the risk for, the development of, and the maintenance of depression. In this section you will learn about neurobiological, neurophysiological, neuroendocrine, circadian, genetic, and evolutionary influences.

Neurobiological Influences. Three neurotransmitters have been implicated in depression: serotonin, norepinephrine, and, to a lesser extent, dopamine. Serotonin and norepinephrine have been the focus of research for almost 50 years, ever since drugs known to affect their levels and sensitivities proved effective in reducing depression. The data in support of the role of these neurotransmitters are indirect. For example, metabolites are the biological products that result from the breakdown of the neurotransmitters. They can often be measured in cerebrospinal fluid, blood, or urine. The levels of the metabolites of serotonin and norepinephrine are lower in depressed people than in nondepressed people (McNeal & Cimbolic, 1986; Muscettola et al., 1984). Metabolite levels do not always bear a strong relationship to the level of the neurotransmitters in the brain, however. Curiously, there is some evidence that there may be a sex difference in the role of serotonin in depression: Serotonin metabolites may differentiate depressed from nondepressed males, but not females (Neuger et al., 1999). Drugs that increase serotonin synthesis tend to decrease depression (Mendels et al., 1975), and drugs that decrease serotonin synthesis reduce the effectiveness of antidepressants (Shopsin et al., 1976), results that support the serotonin hypothesis. Furthermore, drugs that increase the availability of serotonin and/or norepinephrine in the synapse by inhibiting the normal reuptake of this neurotransmitter decrease depression (Beauclair et al., 2000; Kelsey & Nemeroff, 2000). *Reuptake* is a process by which the cell that originally released the neurotransmitter reabsorbs the excess that remains in the synapse. Even dietary changes that affect the production of serotonin have been shown to affect the level of depression (Delgado et al., 1990). Finally, recent PET scan evidence suggests that serotonin receptors in several areas of the brain are abnormal in depressed people (Drevets et al., 1999). As you will see when we discuss treatment, the most effective antidepressant medications tend to affect serotonin, norepinephrine, or both. The importance of these neurotransmitters in depression is generally undisputed, although their role appears to be complex and is far from fully understood.

Although serotonin and norepinephrine have received the greatest attention in the literature on depression, there is evidence that dopamine may also be involved. Recall from Chapter 5 that the general effect of dopamine is to modulate brain activity level. Could the passivity that is characteristic of many depressed people be due to low levels of dopamine? The answer is a cautious yes. In general, dopamine seems to be involved in some types of depression, such as seasonal affective disorder (Depue et al., 1989), and in some symptoms of depression, but it clearly does not account for all depression or all depressive symptoms (Diehl & Gershon, 1992). For example, the passive behavior of animals after they are placed in a situation in which they have no control is apparently mediated by a reduction in dopamine; dopamine antagonists, which block dopamine activity, increase this passive behavior, and dopamine agonists decrease it (Swerdlow & Koob, 1987). Furthermore, in selected individuals, dopamine agonists reduce depression or selected depressive symptoms. For example, people with bipolar depression tend to respond well to dopamine agonists, whereas most people with unipolar depression do not (Murphy et al., 1971). There is evidence that the depressive symptoms associated with withdrawal from alcohol may

be mediated by dopamine levels (Miller et al., 1986). Some individuals with depression show marked motor retardation—that is, they are barely able to move. Treatment with dopamine agonists dramatically reduces the motor retardation, although, interestingly, it has little effect on the depressed mood (van Praag & Korf, 1975). This suggests that the various symptoms of depression may be mediated by different biological mechanisms.

This situation, in which some symptoms of a disorder are affected, but not others, is called **response desynchrony.** Such response desynchrony is not uncommon in psychopathology, and it often provides critical clues about the underlying mechanisms of a disorder. In the case of depression, it suggests that multiple neurotransmitters are involved, each contributing different elements to the disorder. Such desynchrony is often a basis for subtyping disorders in such a way that treatment can be more effectively tailored to the needs of the individual.

Neurophysiological Influences. There is much interest in evaluating neurological functioning in an effort to understand the biological basis of depression. This relatively new research area borrows heavily from psychophysiology, functional brain imaging, and measures of cognitive and perceptual functioning. The research suggests that people with depression show a distinctive pattern of lateralized brain functioning, with greater alpha wave activity in the left frontal lobes than nondepressed individuals exhibit (Allen et al., 1993; Henriques & Davidson, 1990, 1991), although not every study finds this effect (Reid et al., 1998). Alpha wave activity is measured with an EEG. The presence of strong alpha waves generally indicates reduced cognitive activity and is normally associated with relaxation. The distinctive lateralized brain activation found in depression is coupled with distinctive patterns of performance on perceptual and cognitive tasks. This section presents some of this research.

A pattern of performance that indicates that one side of the brain is better than the other at a particular task is known as a **functional brain asymmetry.** The intensity of these asymmetries in depression is related to several factors. Functional brain asymmetries can be measured with tasks such as dichotic listening, which involves paying attention to the sounds (words or tones) in one ear while simultaneously ignoring sounds in the other ear. Depressed individuals consistently show a right-ear advantage on dichotic listening tests—that is, they do better when the target sounds are played in the right ear (Bruder et al., 1999).

....

response desynchrony A situation in which some symptoms of a disorder are affected by medication but others are not.

functional brain asymmetry A pattern of performance that indicates that one side of the brain is better than the other at a particular task.

Because perceptual processing crosses over in the brain, sounds heard in the right ear are processed by the left cerebral hemisphere. Therefore, a right-ear advantage means that the right hemisphere is performing more poorly than the left hemisphere. Interestingly, depressed individuals with a comorbid anxiety disorder show a left-ear advantage, which suggests a different pattern of brain activation (Bruder et al., 1999). This difference between anxious and nonanxious depressed individuals in lateralized activation patterns is confirmed by EEG studies of brain activity (Bruder et al., 1997a; Kentgen et al., 2000), and the nature of these brain asymmetries predicts who will benefit from such common treatments as cognitive therapy (Bruder et al., 1997b) and antidepressant medications (Bruder et al., 1996; Stewart et al., 1999). For example, those who respond best to cognitive therapy show more than twice the right-ear advantage of those who do not respond. Those individuals with a more dominant left hemisphere (greater right-ear advantage) may benefit more from cognitive treatment because they are more strongly controlled by verbal mediation—a process that depends primarily on left-hemisphere functioning.

Laterality effects show up in another way. The psychological impact of a stroke, which is the result of a vascular hemorrhage in the brain, depends on the location of the stroke. You would not be surprised to discover that people who have a stroke in the left cerebral hemisphere usually get depressed; you would expect anyone who suffers a stroke to be depressed about it. However, for people who suffer a stroke in the corresponding area of the right side of the brain, the likelihood of depression is much lower (Schramke et al., 1998). The loss of language capability associated with a left-hemisphere stroke, but not a right-hemisphere stroke, may account for this; language is so critical to human functioning that its loss may be more traumatic than other functional losses. However, it is also possible that the depression experienced with a left-hemisphere stroke is more than just a reaction to the medical problem. It may also represent a physiological response to the damage to the left side of the brain.

Neurophysiological data suggest some intriguing laterality effects in depression: Depressed people normally show decreased left-hemisphere activity, primarily in the frontal lobes (Marshall & Fox, 2000). However, there is considerable variability in these effects among individuals, which predicts such factors as comorbid anxiety disorders and response to treatment. This area of research promises to help researchers differentiate meaningful subgroups of depression.

There have been recent efforts to integrate the neuropsychological and cognitive research on depression (Gotlib & Neubauer, 2000). Dichotic listening tasks, for example, provide information not only on laterality differences but on attentional processes as well. Attentional processes can also be tapped by other tasks, such as the Stroop Color-Word test, in which the person is asked to name the color that a series of words are printed in. Depressed individuals are slower at naming depressive-content words, such as *sad* or *failure,* than nondepressed individuals (Gotlib & Cane, 1987). Other research suggests that depressed individuals are slower on a variety of emotional material, which implies that the attentional disruption is not specific to depressive content (Hill & Knowles, 1991). This latter finding, coupled with the observation that these attentional disruptions occur during depressive episodes but are not present during remission (Gotlib & Cane, 1987), raises the possibility that this cognitive process is affected by the depression rather than being a cause of the depression. Although these kinds of studies have not yet yielded a definitive understanding of how basic cognitive processes contribute to the formation and maintenance of depression, they are showing promising results and may add considerably to our understanding of depression in the near future (Gotlib & Neubauer, 2000).

Neuroendocrine Influences. Hormones regulate dozens of body functions, and there is increasing evidence that they can also affect mood. The fact that hormonal diseases, such as Cushing's syndrome and hypothyroidism, can lead to depression illustrates the impact of hormonal regulation on mood.

The hypothalamic-pituitary-adrenocortical axis (HPA axis) is part of the biological stress response mechanism and may play a central role in depression as well. This system is activated by stress and releases a variety of hormones to activate the body in preparation for dealing with the stress. One of these stress hormones is cortisol, which is consistently elevated in depressed individuals (Thase, 2000). In fact, this elevation of cortisol was once thought to be a biological marker for depression and led to the development of the dexamethasone suppression test (DST). Dexamethasone is a chemical that normally suppresses the secretion of cortisol, although some people with depression do not show this suppression effect (Nelson & Davis, 1997). The idea that a single biological test could diagnose depression proved to be simplistic, but the evidence that cortisol is involved in at least some forms of depression is irrefutable.

The role of cortisol and other stress hormones in depression is consistent with behavior observations of depression. It has long been recognized that anxiety and depression commonly occur together. It is extremely difficult to find people with depression who do not also show anxiety, and when one studies the developmental course of depression, anxiety often precedes depression. These findings and others led David Barlow (2002) to propose that anxiety and depression share a common underlying diathesis and may represent different stages in a disordered process. Anxiety represents a response that, if put into words, might read, "There is something out there that could be dangerous. I need to be prepared for it, but I am not sure I can handle it." In contrast, depression represents the following thought process: "There is something out there that could be dangerous. I need to be prepared for it, but I doubt that I can handle it." Essentially, depression represents a more hopeless cognitive response to the same threat stimulation. This model illustrates how the same biological diathesis could lead to different symptom patterns. It also explains why the treatment response of medications is nonspecific, whereas the treatment response of psychological interventions is more specific. As you will see, the same medications that effectively treat depression are often effective in treating anxiety disorders, but the psychological treatments are more closely tailored to the specific symptoms. This reinforces a key theme of this text: Psychological disorders are neither biological nor psychological but, rather, represent complex interactions of systems.

Circadian Rhythms and Sleep Disturbance.

A common physiological symptom of depression is sleep disturbance. Some people with depression sleep 15 or more hours a day, but most find it difficult to sleep. They may fall asleep readily but tend to awaken frequently. Furthermore, they often awaken 2 or 3 hours before their normal waking time and then find it impossible to go back to sleep. This **early morning awakening** is part of a general shift in circadian rhythms in depression (Akiskal, 2000). The term **circadian rhythms** refers to the normal pattern of biological changes that occur predictably throughout the day. Hormones regulate these rhythms, affecting such things as body temperature and energy level. In addition to the disruption of circadian rhythms, depressed individuals often show a marked shortening of their REM latency—that is, the time from first falling asleep to the first period of REM (rapid eye movement) sleep. REM sleep occurs several times each night and is the period in which dreams occur. In depressed individuals, the periods of REM sleep tend not only to come sooner but also to last longer and to be more intense—that is, the eye movements are stronger and faster. This earlier onset of REM sleep, or *reduced REM latency,* comes at the expense of the deeper stages of sleep, which may explain why depressed individuals often complain of being tired and sleepy (Akiskal, 2000; Kupfer, 1995). Deep sleep restores energy, and without it, people awaken weary and unrefreshed. The difference between the patterns of sleep in depressed and nondepressed individuals is illustrated in Figure 7.1.

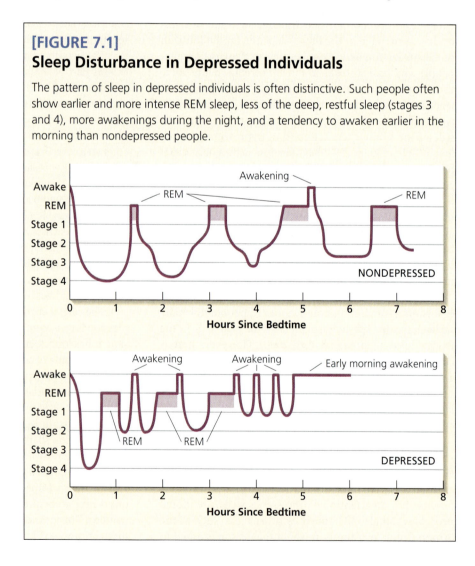

[FIGURE 7.1]
Sleep Disturbance in Depressed Individuals

The pattern of sleep in depressed individuals is often distinctive. Such people often show earlier and more intense REM sleep, less of the deep, restful sleep (stages 3 and 4), more awakenings during the night, and a tendency to awaken earlier in the morning than nondepressed people.

The sleep disturbance often found in depression has been studied at length. At one level, it appears to be a marker of the depressive episode in that the early morning awakening pattern tends to develop a few days or weeks before the onset of the depression and that it often remains for a while after the depression lifts (Buysse & Kupfer, 1993). However, other research shows that individuals who are prone to depression may show more chronic abnormal sleep patterns and that these abnormalities predict a poorer response to psychological treatment (Thase et al., 1996). Furthermore, sleep abnormalities, such as reduced REM latency, may provide valuable clues to the causes of depression. For example, Monroe et al. (1992) found that the reduced REM latency was more pronounced in individuals who did not experience a significant stressor before the onset of the depression than in depressed individuals whose depression appeared to be triggered by such a stressor. It may be that the reduced REM latency is a marker for a biological process capable of bringing on depression by itself. With such a process active, a stressor may be unnecessary as a trigger for depression, but in the absence of such an active biological process, an external stressor is necessary to trigger the depressive reaction. It is too early to tell whether this speculation is accurate, but it does raise several interesting questions worthy of further research.

Genetic Influences. The evidence that genetic factors figure in major depression is clear. For example, twin studies show concordance rates for major depression that are more than twice as high in monozygotic as in dizygotic twins (Bertelsen et al., 1977). However, these data only begin to tell the story. More recent studies have investigated factors that predict which depressed individuals show the strongest evidence of a genetic contribution. Those who show an earlier age of onset, a greater number of episodes, a greater duration of the longest episode, a higher level of impairment, and more frequent thoughts of death or suicide show the strongest evidence of genetic influences (Kendler et al., 1999). This relationship between severity and genetic risk suggests that major depression is probably polygenic—that is, it results from the combined influence of several genes. The more depressive genes people have, the worse their symptoms and the more the genetic risk is likely to be shared by relatives. Furthermore, adoption studies have generally confirmed that genes play a role in major depression (Mendlewicz & Rainer, 1977; Wender et al.,

1986), although curiously, one adoption study failed to find evidence for genetic factors (Von Knorring et al., 1983).

Evolutionary Impact

Evolutionary Influences. The central evolutionary question about depression is why it would exist at all. This is different from the question of why depression has not been eliminated by natural selection. Depression would be eliminated by natural selection only if the reproductive rates were lower in depressed individuals than in nondepressed individuals. Because depression tends to be episodic, there is plenty of opportunity for reproduction between episodes. Also, until the last 40 years or so (Seligman, 1990), depression was a disorder that began well into adulthood, after the typical period of maximum fertility, and hence had little effect on reproduction. Of course, one might reasonably ask whether depression would affect the quality of the parenting provided by affected individuals and would thus have an impact on the survivability of their offspring. One could also question whether severe depression would have increased mortality in an earlier era. Perhaps the passivity associated with such depression would decrease the normal vigilance that protects the person from danger.

The question considered here is "How would a process like depression evolve?" On the surface, depression appears to be entirely nonproductive. How could passivity, excessive sleeping, loss of interest in such pleasurable activities as sex, and loss of appetite contribute to survival and reproductive success? The answer, of course, is that in the short run they do not. In the long run, however, these behaviors may well be functional. There are situations in which struggling is a waste of energy because there is nothing to be achieved. (You will learn more about such situations in the section on learned helplessness.) The passivity exhibited in depression may be a mechanism by which the organism disengages from fruitless activities (Nesse, 1999). Such disengagement is the first step in redirecting efforts to more promising activity.

This concept of disengagement from fruitless activity is illustrated in an animal model of depression used to test the potential of new drugs to treat depression (Detke & Lucki, 1996). In this model, rats are placed in a water-filled cylinder from which escape is impossible. The rat's initial response is to swim vigorously, looking for a way to escape, but after a time, the rat stops swimming and quietly floats, with just its nose above the water. This shift to passive floating is considered an analogue of depression, and drugs that are effective in reducing depression in humans delay the onset of the passive-floating response in rats. This model works well in predicting which drugs are likely to reduce depression in humans, but it also illustrates the potential functional

. . . .

early morning awakening   A depressive symptom that manifests itself when an individual awakens two to three hours before the normal wake-up time and finds it impossible to go back to sleep.

circadian rhythms   The normal pattern of biological changes that occur predictably throughout the day.

value of depression. If an animal found itself in a similar situation in real life, what would be the optimal response? Certainly a period of effort trying to escape makes sense, but if no avenue of escape exists, conserving energy by floating and waiting for something to change may well be optimal. Perhaps a current will bring a branch within reach or move the animal closer to land. Surviving long enough to exploit such opportunity if it occurs is the only chance the animal has.

The foregoing scenario illustrates that depression may be functional at times. People often think that anything unpleasant is dysfunctional, but that view is short-sighted. Physical pain is uncomfortable, but it is rarely dysfunctional. Pain tells the organism that something is wrong and prompts activity to reduce the pain, which often facilitates healing. Consider the fact that some people are born with insensitivity to pain. These people have chewed off their lips, walked for days on broken legs, and suffered severe damage to internal organs, all without realizing that anything is wrong. They would

Although pain is unpleasant, it does motivate individuals to behave in ways that foster healing. Some people believe that depression serves the same function in the psychological realm.

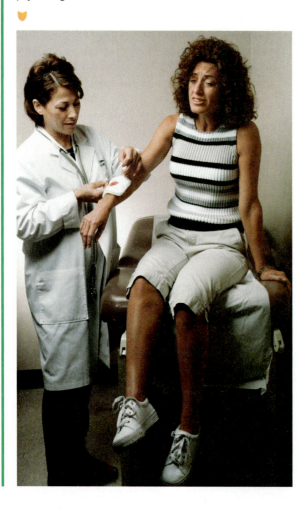

not have engaged in such self-destructive behavior if they had been able to feel pain as a signal of the damage they were doing.

Is such psychological pain as depression any less critical to motivating appropriate behavior? Some psychological theories, such as psychodynamic theory, note the similarity between depression and the grief we experience when someone dear to us dies. Grief is considered normal and generally is not treated with antidepressant medications. Should it be? The evolutionary perspective would say no. Grief is a necessary step in reorienting one's life when a critical person dies. It may be painful, but it eventually provides the disengagement necessary to rebuilding one's life around new people. This raises a controversial question. Could the treatment of depression interfere with a natural process and thus, in the long run, undermine the adaptability of the person? Anyone who has suffered from severe depression or knows someone who has would find the idea of denying treatment unreasonable. However, data show that the majority of people with depression never seek treatment, and yet most recover.

Postpartum depression raises several interesting questions about the evolutionary significance of depression. Remember from our earlier discussion that postpartum depression appears to be a major depression that just happens to occur during the postpartum period. This means that postpartum depression provides an excellent window into depression, and evolutionary theory makes some strong predictions about when such depression "should" occur. If depression is a disengagement mechanism, when would postpartum depression be most likely? From an evolutionary perspective, parenting a healthy baby in a supportive environment represents a worthwhile use of one's energy, because it means that one's genes will be passed on to a child who has a good chance of survival and reproductive success. However, if the child is sickly or the environment is so harsh that survival of the offspring is questionable, then investing one's resources in parenting may have little value for perpetuating one's genes. Of course, the idea of making a calculated decision to abandon a child because he or she is sick or the environment is too harsh is unthinkable. But not every evolutionary outcome reflects thought—or morality. Organisms that consciously or unconsciously managed their resources in this way would increase the likelihood that they would pass on their genes, and therefore a mechanism to accomplish that goal would be favored by natural selection. The passivity and lack of motivation associated with depression influence many behaviors, including the quality of mothering. Therefore, depression would provide a mechanism for reducing the mother's expenditure of energy on a child whose viability was in doubt.

Does the evidence support an evolutionary argument for postpartum depression? Is such depression more likely when there is insufficient support or when the child has potential health complications? The answer is a resounding yes. Hagen (1999) reviewed the published research on this issue and found that over a dozen published studies found relationships between deficits in social support, especially marital problems, and the probability of postpartum depression. Several studies reported a relationship between complications of pregnancy and birth (which usually translate into physical problems for the infant) and the probability of postpartum depression, although at least two studies found a higher incidence of postpartum depression in women who experienced less complicated deliveries (O'Hara et al., 1982; Paykel et al., 1980). Of course, in modern societies, the behaviors associated with postpartum depression—being less responsive and less sensitive to infant cues and less motivated to meet parental responsibilities—are often less threatening to the infant because others will step in and temporarily help out. However, these data might lead one to speculate about the impact of approximately half of all children being born to single mothers.

The evolutionary perspective addresses another critical issue that other perspectives fail to address. For the vast majority of people with depression, the depression is self-limiting—that is, it eventually goes away by itself. Most biological and psychological theories address how depression starts or how it is maintained, but not how people recover from it. The evolutionary perspective also provides no answer to the question of *how*, but it does address the question of *why*. To have any survival value, depression would have to lift after it had facilitated a necessary disengagement. Otherwise, the organism would die. The question of *how* must be approached from one of the other perspectives because answering it will involve identifying the proximate cause of remission. The evolutionary perspective merely highlights the importance of this question.

PSYCHOLOGICAL THEORIES

Several psychological theories have been proposed to explain the development and maintenance of depression. Although early theories, such as the psychodynamic and cognitive theories, sought a single explanation for all depression, more recent theories recognize that different people may become depressed for different reasons. This section will cover the psychodynamic, cognitive, behavioral, learned helplessness, hopelessness, and sociocultural models of depression.

Psychodynamic Model. Freud's (1917/1950) psychodynamic model of depression rests on the similarity between depression and grief. According to Freud, the loss of a loved one leads to regression to the oral stage while the mourner tries to incorporate the lost person

The similarity between grief and depression prompted Freud to suggest that depression was the result of a psychological loss. When it became clear that many people with depression appeared to suffer no obvious loss, Freud speculated about a symbolic loss.

psychologically. However, because most depressed people have not experienced a recent death of a loved one, Freud hypothesized that a symbolic loss could also lead to depression. These symbolic losses may include the end of a relationship or the loss of a job or may be only a potential loss that the person expects to experience. The symbolic-loss concept in the psychodynamic formulation is similar to concepts that are central to other psychological models, as we will see shortly.

Given the importance of developmental history in the psychodynamic model, it is not surprising that psychodynamic theorists emphasized early experiences as a psychological diathesis for depression. Specifically, both Freud (1917/1950) and Melanie Klein (1934) argued that the early loss of a mother or the failure of parents to satisfy the infant's early need for love could predispose individuals to depression. Melanie Klein (1934) also emphasized the importance of early mothering in depression. John Bowlby's (1969, 1973, 1980) work on the importance of early attachments stimulated the thinking of psychologists of many theoretical persuasions. Bowlby, who was originally trained as a psychoanalyst, was heavily influenced by the object relations perspective of psychodynamic theory. He noted that two personality types appear to be predisposed to depression. The first he called the *anxiously attached individual,* who is excessively dependent on people and therefore fears abandonment. Bowlby hypothesized that this personality developed as a result of parental neglect, although he acknowledged that the child's perception of neglect might be sufficient. The second he called the *compulsively self-reliant individual,* who shows little interest in social relationships. Bowlby believed that being rejected by parents could foster this personality style. These hypotheses are more specific and more readily tested than Freud's symbolic-loss hypothesis because they specify the presumed mechanism that shapes the cognitive diathesis for depression.

Cognitive Model. The cognitive model of depression was introduced in Chapter 4. Beck (1967, 1976) proposed that the critical element in the development of depression is the way in which depressed individuals tend to think about themselves and the world around them. Although others have offered cognitive models of depression (Ellis, 1962, 1991), Beck's model has been the most thoroughly elaborated and tested. Beck and his colleagues proposed a detailed model that hypothesized the existence of maladaptive attitudes, a cognitive triad of negative perceptions, specific errors in thinking, and automatic thoughts that increase the risk for depression.

Beck argued that the seeds of depression are maladaptive attitudes, or **schemas,** which are formed in childhood and continue to influence the person well into adulthood (Beck et al., 1990; Clark & Beck, 1999; Young et al., 1993). Schemas are cognitive structures that organize the world. They shape the way people experience life and hence the

way they feel about themselves and the world. Beck argued that if children form a set of negative schemas, those schemas will distort their perceptions and increase the likelihood of their experiencing depression. Note that this focus on developmental processes is similar to psychodynamic formulations.

Beck (1967) argued that the negative schemas developed during childhood could interact with the typical setbacks that most people experience in adulthood to form the cognitive triad. The **cognitive triad** consists of the distortion of (1) one's experiences, (2) oneself, and (3) one's future in ways that increase the likelihood of feeling depressed. For example, depressed individuals may experience normal challenges as excessive and unbearable, and therefore as more than they can handle. In addition, they often view themselves as deficient, especially in their ability to handle the stresses that others appear to handle easily. Finally, they may see the future as hopeless because the stresses and strains will never end and there is nothing they can do to change this. The cognitive triad is clearly represented in the case of Becky.

One Stress too Many

BECKY

Becky was never an optimistic person, but following her traffic accident at age 22, her pessimism simply overwhelmed her. Even though the accident had left her with chronic pain, physical weakness, and memory problems, by most standards she functioned well. Within two years of the accident, she met someone and married. They had two wonderful children and a reasonably stable relationship. However, Becky felt that life was a never-ending series of impossible challenges. When her husband could not attend their son's hockey banquet, she feared her son would be ruined for life. She believed that her husband did not love her and never would love her because of her injuries, although he had met and married her after the accident and knew all about her injuries. She felt that her children could not love her because her back problems prevented her from picking them up. She felt the future was hopeless, and this attitude colored every aspect of her life. Even during her happiest periods, a depressive cloud seemed to drain the joy out of her life.

Beck argued that the cognitive triad resulted from a series of errors in thinking, which systematically reinforced those negative beliefs (see Table 4.1 on page 80). These

schemas Cognitive structures, or attitudes, that form in childhood and thereafter serve to organize the individual's world.

cognitive triad The distortion of one's experiences, oneself, and one's future in ways that increase the likelihood of feeling depressed.

errors involve (1) arbitrary inference, (2) selective abstraction, (3) overgeneralization, (4) magnification or minimization, and (5) personalization. Becky's case illustrates how each of these errors can contribute to maintaining the cognitive triad. Becky constantly questioned the love of her husband and children, but she could almost never point to anything substantial to warrant such doubt (arbitrary inference). If her husband wanted to go out with the guys, she would assume that he was looking for another woman. When they argued, she became even more convinced that he was ready to dump her for another woman (selective abstraction). If her son threw a temper tantrum, she would conclude that she was a terrible mother and that her son would turn out to be an uncaring and selfish person (overgeneralization). If she made a single mistake at work, she would berate herself for being worthless and incompetent, ignoring the fact that she was a valuable employee who had been given several merit raises over the years (magnification and minimization). When her 7-year-old son lost a hockey game and broke down and cried on the ice, she was convinced that she had let him down by not cheering enough during the game (personalization). These errors so pervaded every aspect of Becky's thoughts that her chronic depression was nearly inevitable.

Behavioral Model. The behavioral model of depression emphasizes how the behaviors of depressed individuals enhance or maintain depressive feelings (Lewinsohn et al., 1970). Specifically, depressed people often withdraw from normally pleasurable social situations and activities because their depression robs them of the energy to cope with normal hassles and because nothing brings them pleasure. However, this withdrawal minimizes the chance that they will have pleasurable experiences thus depriving them of the very things that might help alleviate the depression. In other words, the depression is deepened by the lack of positive reinforcement. In some cases, social withdrawal may have been prompted by difficulties that the individual has had in social situations because of limited social skills (Lewinsohn et al., 1980; Teri & Lewinsohn, 1986). In such cases, social skills training may be helpful. Although they were formulated independently of the cognitive perspective, most of the concepts of the behavioral perspective have been incorporated into cognitive treatment.

Learned Helplessness Model. Feeling out of control and unable to change things for the better can lead to depression. This feeling of being helpless to control things

is the focal point of the learned helplessness model of Seligman (1975). The **learned helplessness model** suggests that depression results from being in aversive situations in which one has no control over the outcome. Placing people in such situations in the laboratory for only a few minutes is enough to increase their dysphoria and get them to give up on tasks that are well within their abilities (Peterson et al., 1993).

Evolutionary Impact

Seligman became interested in learned helplessness when he was studying escape behavior in dogs. These studies subjected dogs to mildly aversive stimuli, such as a shock from the floor of the cage. The dogs could easily escape from the shock by jumping to the other side of the cage. When a warning signal was added, such as a light that came on just before the shock, the dogs quickly learned to avoid the shock by jumping to the other side of the cage as soon as the warning signal appeared. Once the dogs had learned to avoid the shock, they experienced little distress, jumping nonchalantly to the other side of the cage whenever the warning signal appeared. The dogs recognized the aversive consequences and struggled to find a way to reduce or avoid those consequences, but their distress dropped dramatically once they learned to jump to the other side of the cage to avoid the shocks. This is an adaptive evolutionary mechanism. However, Seligman discovered that this mechanism could be defeated easily. If, on the day before testing, the dogs experienced shocks from which they could not escape, they did not learn to escape the next day when presented with the escapable shock. That is, the dogs learned to be helpless. Seligman was impressed by the fact that the dogs' behavior in this situation was similar to what is observed in human depression, so he began to study human responses to these kinds of situations.

From an evolutionary perspective, the phenomenon of learned helplessness looks counterproductive. An animal experiences some inescapable aversive consequences one day and then gives up trying to escape further aversive consequences—clearly not the best strategy for survival. Your first inclination, then, might be to dismiss learned helplessness as an aberration that occurs only in the laboratory. However, Seligman conducted this classic study because the phenomenon *does* occur in nature, and therefore understanding it is critical. Both humans and animals face inescapable aversive consequences frequently. What if you are caught in an open area when a hailstorm hits? There is no place to hide from the pounding of the hailstones. Is it thereafter in your best interest never to try to escape another hailstorm, even when protection is well within your reach, simply because of this one experience? The key to understanding this phenomenon is to recognize that

---

learned helplessness model   Seligman's proposal that depression results from being in aversive situations in which one has no control over the outcome.

learned helplessness has both advantages and disadvantages. What could be an advantage of this strategy?

Helplessness may be a reasonable strategy when there is nothing that the organism can do to escape. Making frantic and futile efforts at escape wastes valuable energy. Accepting the current negative consequences and conserving energy for situations in which the organism has a better chance of influencing its environment may well be an adaptive strategy. But how does an organism know that it is in an inescapable situation? It is tempting to suggest some sort of analytical process, but the cognitive capacity to perform such analyses is limited in many animals that clearly show learned helplessness, such as rats. It is more likely that nature equipped organisms with a simpler strategy—one that, if it could be verbalized, would go something like "If there was nothing I could do just a few hours ago and little has changed, there is probably little I can do now." That might explain the results of Seligman's (1975) first study, in which inescapable shocks the day before resulted in the dogs failing even to try to flee from escapable shocks the next day. Inescapable shocks delivered a month earlier have little effect.

Animals that have learned that they are helpless show the passivity typical of depression and give the appearance of being depressed, but is this phenomenon really depression? And would the same learned helplessness situations lead to depression in human beings? Psychologists know that conditions that foster helplessness, such as obsessive-compulsive disorder (covered in Chapter 8), often result in moderate depression, which often disappears once the symptoms has been successfully treated (Riggs & Foa, 1993; Steketee, 1993). However, without experimental control of the situation, it is impossible to say whether the helplessness was induced by the obsessive-compulsive symptoms or by some other factor, such as some shared biochemical process. The way to test this hypothesis is to manipulate helplessness experimentally and see what impact it has on people. Let's examine these findings more closely.

Examining the Evidence

Miller and Seligman (1975) created a learned helplessness situation by exposing college students to random aversive noise. They found that the noise increased depressive mood, but *only* if participants could do nothing to turn the noise off. Furthermore, the participants who could not control the noise not only showed more depressed mood but also performed poorly on an anagram task. The anagram task had nothing to do with the noise in the first part of the study, yet the helplessness induced by the inescapable noise carried over into the other realms, thus reducing performance. Later research showed that the critical element is whether individuals *believe* they have control (Benassi et al., 1988). If you give people the impression that they have control, even though they do not, they do not develop learned helplessness. Because there are many situations in life in which people have little control, this illusion-of-control phenomenon could have significant clinical utility. It might also explain the prevalence of magical rituals, which tend to be more common in situations over which people have little control, such as when one has to depend on the weather for one's safety (Malinowski, 1954; Zusne & Jones, 1989). For obvious ethical reasons, the manipulations in these studies are mild, and the dysphoria produced is both mild and short-lived.

Seligman and his colleagues later revised the learned helplessness model to take into account perceptions and, even more important, an individual's interpretation of his or her perceptions. They argued that the impact of a learned helplessness situation will depend on the type of attribution a person makes. An **attribution** is one's explanation for one's own behavior or that of others. For example, if you are anxious upon meeting someone, you might *attribute* your anxiety either to your being shy or to the other person's behavior making you uncomfortable. Seligman and his colleagues (Abramson et al., 1978) focused on three attributional dimensions: internal/external, global/specific, and stable/unstable. To illustrate these dimensions, assume that you have just failed a test. Blaming yourself for failing is an internal attribution; blaming the instructor for administering an unfair exam is an external attribution. Believing that the factors responsible for your failure occur in many other situations is a global attribution, whereas believing that those factors are unique to this particular situation is a specific attribution. Finally, expecting that the failure will occur again is a stable attribution, whereas expecting that the factors will not recur is an unstable attribution. Seligman and his colleagues argued that internal, global, and stable attributions are most likely to lead to depression. Table 7.2 illustrates attributions that one could make after a bad job interview, organized along these three dimensions. Can you see how the internal/global/stable attribution would leave the person feeling the most helpless and depressed?

Of course, people differ on the types of attributions they are likely to make, which is probably why some people react to a failure with depressive affect whereas others do not (Metalsky et al., 1987). Social psychologists have known for years that males tend to make external attributions and females internal attributions for failure (Beyer, 1998). Perhaps this difference between males and females contributes to the higher rate of depression in females.

[TABLE 7.2] Types of Attributions

Illustrated below are attributions for a bad job interview and failure to get the job. Each cell represents a different combination of internal/external, stable/unstable, and global/specific attributions.

	INTERNAL	EXTERNAL
Stable Global	I am so incompetent that I will never get hired.	The job interview is such an unfair way to assess the competence of prospective employees.
Stable Specific	I never interview well when I do not have enough time to prepare.	That interviewer likes to ask impossible questions so that she can reject candidates.
Unstable Global	I never do well at interviews.	They probably rejected me because they had another candidate in mind all along.
Unstable Specific	I was caught off guard by the focus of this interview and therefore made a bad impression.	I think the interviewer must have gotten up on the wrong side of the bed today, because he was simply nasty in the interview.

Evolutionary Impact

The learned helplessness model of depression is unique in several respects. First, it describes a phenomenon that occurs in both animals and humans and hence provides an evolutionary context. Yet the revised learned helplessness model also acknowledges that the advanced cognitive capabilities of humans modulate this basic response. The impact of aversive events depends on the way the person interprets the events, and there is substantial evidence that the manner in which people are likely to interpret events is a relatively stable part of their personality. These observations were part of the justification for another model of depression—the hopelessness model—that was proposed by two of Seligman's former students.

Hopelessness Model. Lyn Abramson, Lauren Alloy, and Gerald Metalsky proposed a refinement of the helplessness model called the **hopelessness model** of depression (Abramson et al., 1989, 1995). This model hypothesizes a subtype of depression—hopelessness depression—that results when people expect undesirable outcomes to occur and this expectation is confirmed by a series of negative events. For example, if (1) people expect others to reject them and (2) key relationships in their lives end, those

people are at risk for hopelessness depression because their pessimistic expectations have been confirmed. The cognitive diathesis in this model is the pessimistic expectations, and the key stressors are negative life events that are consistent with those expectations. Other elements, such as low self-esteem, can also increase the risk for hopelessness depression. This model is sometimes confused with the learned helplessness model, but there are several important distinctions. First, the hopelessness model emphasizes the diathesis—the person's expectations of negative outcomes—rather than focusing on the stressor. In that respect, it emphasizes the importance of individual differences and provides a rationale for a behavioral high-risk study. The hopelessness model predicts not only when depression is likely to occur but also what might happen when people who expect positive outcomes experience positive outcomes. Finally, the hopelessness model emphasizes that this is just one of several ways in which one might develop depression, thereby acknowledging the heterogeneity of depression.

One of the strengths of the hopelessness model is that it makes an explicit prediction about who is most at risk for depression and what factors are likely to trigger depression. These are strong predictions that can be tested with a longitudinal design. The approach is to identify at-risk and comparison groups on the basis of their attributional styles and then to follow the groups over time. The measure used for such identification is the *Attributional Styles Questionnaire* (*ASQ;* Peterson et al., 1982), which asks people to make attributions for six positive and six negative events. The attributions are rated on the internal/external, global/specific, and stable/unstable dimensions. High- and low-risk groups are selected on the basis of the scores on the ASQ and followed over time. Table 7.3 presents an item from the ASQ. Alloy and her colleagues (Alloy et al., 1999a,

attribution   A person's explanation for his or her behavior or the behavior of others.

hopelessness model   The hypothesis that hopelessness depression results when people expect undesirable outcomes to occur and this expectation is confirmed by a series of negative events.

[TABLE 7.3] The Attributional Styles Questionnaire

The Attributional Styles Questionnaire contains 12 hypothetical events—6 positive and 6 negative—to which the person attributes what he or she thinks is the most likely cause. The person then rates the cause along the three dimensions of internal/external, stable/unstable, and global/specific. Listed below are the general instructions for the ASQ, followed by a sample situation and the related ratings.

INSTRUCTIONS

Please try to vividly imagine yourself in the situations that follow. If such a situation happened to you, what would you feel would have caused it? While events may have many causes, we want you to pick only one—the major cause if this event happened to you. Please write this cause in the blank provided after each event. Next we want you to answer some questions about the cause. To summarize, we want you to:

1. Read each situation and vividly imagine it happening to you.
2. Decide what you feel would be the major cause of the situation if it happened to you.
3. Write one cause in the blank provided.
4. Answer three questions about the cause.
5. Go on to the next situation.

SAMPLE SITUATION

Event: You go out on a date and it goes badly.

1. Write down the one major cause for this event.

2. Is the cause of the date going badly due to something about you or something about other people or circumstances?

Due to other people								Due to me
	1	2	3	4	5	6	7	
			(Circle one number)					

3. In the future while dating, will this cause again be present?

Never again present								Always be present
	1	2	3	4	5	6	7	
			(Circle one number)					

4. Is the cause something that just influences dating or does it also influence other areas of your life?

Just this situation								All situations
	1	2	3	4	5	6	7	
			(Circle one number)					

SOURCE: *"The Attributional Styles Questionnaire"* from *"The Attributional Style Questionnaire"* by D. Peterson et al., Cognitive Therapy and Research, 6, 1982. Copyright © 1982. Reprinted by permission of Kluwer Academic/ Plenum Publishers.

1999b) found that naturally occurring negative life events were sufficient to trigger depression in the high-risk group but not in the low-risk group, an outcome that supported the hopelessness model.

Sociocultural Model. One of the strongest findings in the research literature is that stressful life events increase risk for psychopathology, and that seems to be especially true for depression (Kessler, 1997). Furthermore, social support seems to be a critical buffer that reduces the impact of stress on people (Gotlib & Hammen, 1992; Taylor & Aspinwall, 1996). Although the symptoms of depression and their impact on behavior can be significant stressors by themselves (Hammen, 1991), much of everyday stress comes from environmental sources. The level of stress that people face is often a function of the sociocultural demands on them and the sociocultural support systems available. There is an extensive literature on stress and depression but a surprisingly limited literature on sociocultural determinants of stress. Admittedly, this is a difficult research question, requiring researchers to study natural settings without the usual controls available in the laboratory. Nevertheless, understanding how sociocultural factors increase or decrease the impact of stress could suggest useful interventions. For example, understanding how crowding, increased time pressure, and frustrating loss of control from such things as traffic jams exacerbate stress could lead to cultural solutions instead of such individual solutions as stress management.

A major sociocultural issue that arises in studies of depression is the sex difference in the rate of depression. Depression is twice as common in women as in men (APA, 2000), and it is still not clear whether this is a biological phenomenon, a sociocultural phenomenon, or a combination of the two. If there are sociocultural components to this sex difference, it is important to identify the likely culprits. Several hypotheses have been offered, although evidence to support specific hypotheses is generally lacking. Several intriguing findings have been reported, however. For example, the rates of depression in children are equal in

One of the most important moderating factors in depression and in many other forms of psychopathology is social support. The support of family and friends helps people weather the hassles and traumas of life.

boys and girls but diverge sharply in adolescence (Nolen-Hoeksema, 1987; Nolen-Hoeksema & Girgus, 1994). It is during these years that young people begin to feel the pressure to conform to gender role expectations, although admittedly there are many other things—both biological and psychological—happening at this time in people's lives. Furthermore, it may be that the adolescent increase in depression in women is due to a greater increase in depressogenic factors in women or to an increase in depressogenic factors that are unique to women (Nolen-Hoeksema & Girgus, 1994). For example, factors that promote a feeling of helplessness, which increase risk for depression in both men and women, may increase more in women during adolescence. Alternatively, factors unique to women, such as the pressure to hide one's capabilities to avoid conflict in opposite-sex relationships, may be responsible. Currently, these are both viable hypotheses that await further research.

Seligman (1990) has offered an interesting sociocultural hypothesis to explain the dramatic increase in the rate of depression among young people in the United States (Surgeon General, 1999). He suggested that the educational philosophy in the public schools may be inadvertently setting students up for depression. Specifically, the modern educational philosophy emphasizes the importance of self-esteem as a motivator for learning. The idea is that people with higher self-esteem will be more successful in school and beyond, so the curriculum is structured to promote self-esteem by guaranteeing success. How do you guarantee success? You set things up so that failure is impossible by adjusting school standards. For example, inadequate school performance could result in students being assigned to a different learning track rather than failing the course. Seligman sees two problems with this model. The first is the assumption that self-esteem promotes success. He believes instead that success promotes self-esteem and argues that the children are too smart to be fooled by curriculum tricks intended to improve self-esteem. The second is that failure is part of life and that being able to bounce back from failure is critical to success. Eliminating failure from the curriculum deprives students of the chance to learn that they can bounce back. Whether Seligman is right or whether other factors are responsible for the dramatic increase in depression among the young, his ideas have prompted people to consider how social systems can contribute to psychological health.

Diathesis-Stress Models. The hopelessness model is an excellent example of a diathesis-stress model of depression. It hypothesizes that a specific cognitive diathesis will lead to depression under a specific set of circumstances. Most diathesis-stress models of psychopathology have not been so specific. This specificity, however, appears to be critical in understanding the development of depression (Blaney, 2000). Could there be many different personality types that are prone to depression, each requiring just

the right kind of stressor to trigger the depression? Let's look at the evidence.

Examining the Evidence

In an elegant study, Zuroff and Mongrain (1987) identified two groups of hypothetically at-risk individuals via a psychological questionnaire. One group was excessively dependent, and the other excessively self-critical. They then subjected these individuals to one of two negative mood induction states in the laboratory—a rejection scenario (your boyfriend or girlfriend breaking off the relationship) and a failure scenario (being rejected by a college). They found that the excessively self-critical group showed increased anxiety and depression in response to the failure scenario, whereas the excessively dependent groups showed increased anxiety and depression in response to the rejection scenario. Furthermore, the nature of the depressive feelings varied in the groups: The dependent group felt helpless and abandoned when imagining being rejected, and the self-critical group felt guilty and worthless when imagining failure. These different depressive states are a central theme in psychodynamic theories of depression (Blatt, 1974; Blatt et al., 1982). This study is an outstanding example of how integrating multiple perspectives can provide unique insights into a disorder. What is increasingly clear is that the study of depression will be more fruitful if researchers take into account the complex interaction of personality variables and stressors. What might be depressing to you may have little effect on the person next to you, whereas he or she might get depressed over events that have little effect on you.

The various psychological theories of depression emphasize both the predisposing factors and the life stresses that can increase risk for depression. Although each takes a different approach, as we have seen, they also share several concepts. The research has gradually illuminated this area, suggesting that different people may become depressed for different reasons. Probably no one theory of depression accounts for all cases, and research is likely to lead to additional reformulations and integrations of current theories.

Check Yourself 7.3

Theories of Depression

1. What neurotransmitters have been implicated in depression?

2. What is the evidence for genetic factors in depression?
3. What are the cognitive errors that Beck argued were central to depression?
4. Which model of depression relies heavily on animal research?
5. What types of attributions for failures are most likely to enhance risk for depression?
6. In what ways do the learned helplessness model and the hopelessness model differ?

Ponder this . . . *Suppose for the moment that you accept the contention of Seligman that the school system may be inadvertently contributing to the risk for depression in children. Based on what you learned in this section, how might you modify the school system to inoculate students from the adverse events of life that may otherwise trigger depression?*

TREATING DEPRESSION

Several effective treatments—both biological and psychological—exist for depression. This section outlines them and describes the evidence for their effectiveness.

BIOLOGICAL TREATMENTS

Biological treatments for depression seek to change the physiological functioning of the depressed individual in a manner that decreases the depressive symptoms. The most widely used biological treatments are medication, electroconvulsive therapy, and phototherapy.

Medication. Three major classes of medication reduce depression: the tricyclic antidepressants, the monoamine oxidase (MAO) inhibitors, and the selective serotonin reuptake inhibitors (SSRIs). The mechanisms of these medications differ slightly, but each appears to have an impact on the neurotransmitter serotonin, and two of them also affect the neurotransmitter norepinephrine.

The tricyclic antidepressants were at one time the primary treatment for depression, although they have been largely replaced by the SSRIs. The tricyclic antidepressants were so named because the chemical structures of these drugs all feature three rings, as shown in Figure 7.2. More than a dozen tricyclic antidepressants were marketed, but the two most widely used were imipramine (Tofranil) and amitriptyline (Elavil), both of which block the reuptake of norepinephrine and serotonin. These medications enter the system quickly, usually reaching their peak levels in 2 to 6 hours (Davis & Glassman, 1989). However, the treatment effect is delayed for 3 to 4 weeks (Physician's Desk Reference, or PDR, 2002; Rush, 2000) and for up to 12 weeks in the elderly (Reynolds et al., 1992, 1996). This delay provides clues to the treatment mechanism for these drugs. Specifically, blocking the reuptake of neurotransmitters results in increased amounts of those neurotransmitters in the synapse. The receptors for these neurotransmitters respond by reducing their sensitivity to compensate for the excess of norepinephrine or serotonin—a process called **down regulation.** This down regulation takes time; hence the delayed treatment effect. Unfortunately, however, the side effects of these medications are often experienced immediately. They may include dry mouth, blurred vision, constipation, drowsiness, and/or excessive weight gain. Many of these side effects decrease as the body grows accus-

[FIGURE 7.2]
Tricyclic Antidepressants

The chemical structures of all tricyclics have the characteristic three rings that give this group of medications its name.

Imipramine

Desipramine

Amitriptyline

Nortriptyline

Protriptyline

Doxepin

Trimipramine

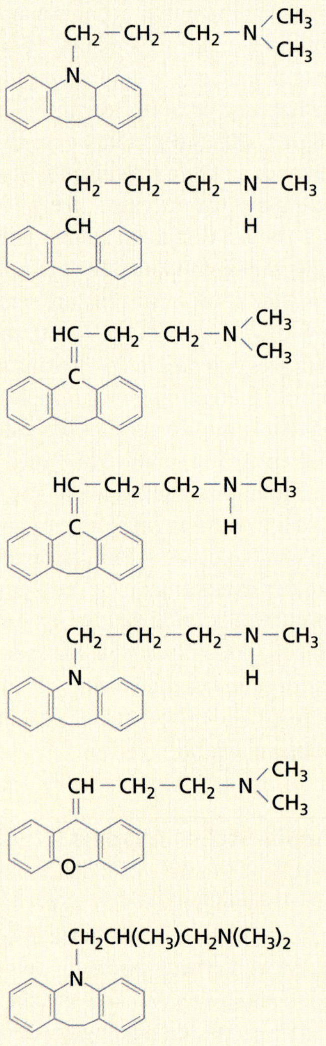

tomed to the new medications, but in some cases they are severe enough to force discontinuation of the drug (Davis & Glassman, 1989; Rush, 2000). Approximately half of all people with depression respond positively to tricyclic antidepressants (Depression Guideline Panel, 1993).

A second class of drugs used to treat depression consists of the MAO inhibitors. These drugs also increase the available norepinephrine and serotonin, but in a very different way than the tricyclics. The MAO inhibitors block the enzyme monoamine oxidase, which normally breaks down norepinephrine and serotonin (Davis & Glassman, 1989). Although they are effective for treating depression, MAO inhibitors are rarely the treatment of choice because they can interact with such common drugs as cold medications and with such foods and beverages as cheese, red wine, and beer. The interaction produces dramatic spikes in blood pressure that can be fatal. Nevertheless, MAO inhibitors do reduce depression significantly in about one-half to two-thirds of the people who take them (Rush, 2000). MAO inhibitors are often the preferred treatment for the depressive episodes in bipolar disorder, because they are less likely than SSRIs to trigger manic episodes (Post, 2000).

The third class of antidepressant drugs is made up of the selective serotonin reuptake inhibitors, or SSRIs. Unlike the tricyclics and MAO inhibitors, which block the reuptake of both serotonin and norepinephrine, the SSRIs, as their name implies, tend to block only the reuptake of serotonin. These relatively new drugs show considerable promise in the treatment of depression and some anxiety disorders. Some SSRIs are also effective in treating dysthymia (Ravindran et al., 1999). The best known of the SSRIs is fluoxetine, which is marketed as Prozac, a name that has become virtually synonymous with psychiatric medication. Whole books have been written about Prozac (Kramer, 1993), and it has been the subject of numerous talk shows and newspaper articles. Unfortunately, as so often happens when issues are widely covered in the popular press, the information on Prozac has often been biased or distorted; see the nearby Modern Myths box. There are now several SSRIs on the market (Celexa, Effexor, Luvox, Paxil, Prozac, Serzone, and Zoloft), and new ones are being released every year.

Curiously, sleep deprivation produces a short-term reduction in symptoms in over half of the people with major depression (Wu & Bunney, 1990). Depressed individuals who deliberately avoid sleeping often experience less depression the next day, although the depression returns after one or two nights of sleep (Post, 2000). Of course, this is not a practical treatment for depression because people cannot go very long without sleeping. However, there is now evidence that using sleep deprivation early in the pharmacological treatment of the elderly, who normally show a delayed response to drugs, significantly accelerates their treatment response (Smith et al., 1999). The exact mechanism for this effect is unknown, but PET studies suggest that both the drugs and the sleep deprivation tend to normalize functioning in the anterior cingulate cortex (Smith et al., 1999).

Electroconvulsive Therapy. Electroconvulsive therapy (ECT), also known as electroshock therapy, is a controversial treatment that involves triggering a seizure by passing a current between two electrodes placed on the person's head (Lilienfeld, 1995). Today, the intensity of the body movements associated with the seizure is controlled with muscle relaxants, thus preventing the muscle strains and occasional broken bones that resulted when ECT was first used. People who receive ECT are given a short-acting anesthetic and a muscle relaxant just before treatment. It is now customary to place both electrodes on the same side of the head. This *unilateral placement* (see Figure 7.3 on page 189) produces levels of symptom relief comparable to those achieved with *bilateral placement* (one electrode on each side of the head). Right-side placement minimizes temporary memory loss and so is preferred (Sackeim, 1989).

ECT is used today to treat severe depression, especially if psychotic symptoms are present (Rush, 2000). Depressed

This cartoon reflects one of the widespread misconceptions about medications for depression. They are not "happy pills." Instead they normalize a person's mood, making normal activity possible.

"I'LL HAVE TO GET DR. KENDRICK TO REDUCE HIS DOSAGE OF PROZAC."

SOURCE: *By permission of Sidney Harris,* http://www.ScienceCartoonsPlus.com.

down regulation   A reduction in neurotransmitter sensitivity, in response to medication, to compensate for an excess of the neurotransmitter.

MODERN Myths

Prozac: Marvel OR Menace?

When Prozac first became available, it was often touted as a wonder drug. It even made the covers of major news magazines. Although it did not give dramatically better results than existing treatments, Prozac often caused significantly fewer side effects and therefore could be tolerated by more people (PDR, 2002). However, shortly after Prozac became a widely used drug, it came under attack as dangerous. These attacks were leveled largely by members of the Church of Scientology, an organization that has often been at odds with psychiatry. These attacks, the alleged basis for them, and the effects of the attacks on the company that manufactures Prozac were the subject of a series of articles in the *Wall Street Journal* (Burton, 1991a, 1991b).

The campaign against Prozac was not based on careful scientific study. Instead, like many pseudoscientific claims, it was based on selected case studies (Graziano & Raulin, 2000). For example, it was claimed that Prozac produces suicidal and even homicidal ideation, the evidence for this claim being three or four people who had committed suicide while on Prozac. However, Prozac is used to treat depression, and depressed individuals are at markedly elevated risk for suicide. Therefore, this finding by itself is scientifically unimpressive. Furthermore, the arguments were not made in a scientific arena, where systematic study would have been invited. Instead, they were made on the talk-show circuit and in newspaper and magazine articles written by people who did not take the time to research the topic thoroughly. The spokespeople for this perspective were very convincing and seemed to have data backing up their position. To give this position even more credence, several attorneys have argued that Prozac drove their clients to commit murder (e.g., MacQuarrie, 2001). That argument rarely persuades juries, although the attorneys probably thought it was worth a try. After all, Dan White, a San Francisco supervisor who killed the mayor and a fellow supervisor in 1979, was acquitted because his lawyer convinced a jury he was driven to commit murder by the Twinkies he ate. A defense attorney does not have to have an argument grounded in solid research, only an argument that can raise reasonable doubt.

In part because of the powerful claims made in the press about the negative effects of Prozac, there has never been a drug more thoroughly studied for potential side effects. It is true that some people experience agitation from Prozac, and most of them simply decide to discontinue the drug and try something else (PDR, 2002). It is also true that some people on Prozac commit suicide, but the rate of suicide is no higher for those on Prozac than for those on other antidepressant medications or for those taking no medication at all (Leon et al., 1999). To claim that Prozac can drive people to commit suicide without having such comparative data is simple-minded at best, and deliberately misleading at worst.

Prozac is not a completely safe drug; no drug is. However, Prozac and other drugs in the same class have demonstrated their ability to relieve considerable suffering. Misinformation about available treatments can prey on the vulnerability of people who have to make difficult decisions about their health. How many people whom medication might have helped have had to endure depression because they were led to believe the medication was dangerous?

---

people with psychotic symptoms respond better to ECT than to medication (Weiner, 1989). In fact, research suggests that ECT tends to be generally more effective than antidepressant medications (Sackeim, 1989). Nevertheless, many doctors prefer medication because it is less drastic and is perceived as less dangerous. However, if medications are not effective, ECT can often provide symptom relief (Avery & Lubrano, 1979; Rush, 2000). ECT also produces an immediate drop in suicide risk, although it has no impact on the long-term risk of suicide (Prudic & Sackeim, 1999). The generally more rapid treatment response for ECT was one of the reasons why Senator Thomas Eagleton, the vice-presidential candidate dropped from the 1972 Democratic ticket when his history of depression was revealed, chose ECT over other treatments. He did not want his depression to interfere with his professional responsibilities, and his impressive accomplishments are a testament to how effectively he dealt with his occasional depressions. Recent evidence suggests that ECT may be the preferred treatment for the elderly (Tew et al., 1999). It is often faster and more effective than medications, and older people do not tolerate medications as well as younger people. Typically, a person receives between five and ten ECT treatments, with about two to three days between treatments

[FIGURE 7.3]

Electrode Placement for ECT

The preferred way to arrange the electrodes for ECT today is to place both electrodes on the same side of the head. This is called unilateral placement. The electrodes are normally placed on the nondominant side of the brain—the right side of the head for people who are right-handed and for the majority of people who are left-handed. Such placement avoids possible disruption to the language centers of the brain.

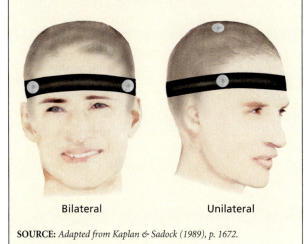

Bilateral   Unilateral

SOURCE: *Adapted from Kaplan & Sadock (1989), p. 1672.*

(Weiner, 1989). The exact number depends on the response. Generally, stopping treatments before the person has shown significant reduction in depression will lead to an early relapse (Weiner, 1989). Although ECT is generally safe if the person has been evaluated for medical complications, approximately 1 person in 5000 dies from the procedure, which is approximately the same rate expected from the anesthesia alone (Weiner, 1989).

Scientists still do not know how ECT works, although some of the earlier theories have been refuted. For example, it was once believed that ECT served as a punishment and that undergoing it enabled people experiencing significant guilt to feel they had paid for their failures. However, the facts that (1) ECT works about as well when the person is under anesthesia and therefore is unaware of the procedures, and (2) ECT works much better than a "sham" ECT suggest that the punishment theory is false. Sham ECTs provide every aspect of ECT treatment except for the electric shock. Most people cannot tell that they never received the shock, because they were unconscious when the shock would have been given. Modern theories of ECT's action

phototherapy   A treatment for SAD wherein the person spends approximately half an hour a day in front of a special light.

focus more on changes in brain chemistry and brain functioning. For example, the seizure associated with ECT is known to disrupt the blood-brain barrier temporarily, which normally separates brain tissue from the substances carried by the bloodstream. Although several theories have been advanced, there is still no conclusive understanding of how ECT works (Weiner, 1989).

A new procedure called transcranial magnetic stimulation is showing promise for the treatment of depression. The nearby Advances box describes some of the early research on this procedure.

Phototherapy. For those individuals suffering from SAD, phototherapy is often beneficial (Blehar & Rosenthal, 1989; Rush, 2000). In **phototherapy,** the person spends approximately half an hour a day in front of a special full-spectrum light—that is, a light that contains all visible wavelengths, much like the sun. The light also needs to be very bright (10,000 lux) to be effective. (The lux is a unit of brightness.) The best time to sit in front of the light is shortly before one would normally awaken (Eastman et al., 1998). This provides the optimal treatment effect and the most rapid treatment response. The exact mechanism of phototherapy is still unknown, but it is clear that phototherapy is generally ineffective for depressions that are not seasonal in nature. Phototherapy seems to reset the biological clock of the person with SAD and, in the process, reduces the depressive symptoms. That probably explains why the timing of the phototherapy is important, rather than just its duration. Consistent with this hypothesis is the fact that sitting in front of a bright light an hour before dawn in not so effective as sitting in front of a light that

In phototherapy a bright white light is used to treat seasonal affective disorder. It appears that the use of this light early in the morning tricks the body, making it seem that the time from sunup to sundown is longer than it really is and thus suggesting that winter is over.

ADVANCES Transcranial magnetic stimulation

Could the next advance in the treatment of depression be a brain stimulation process that is much less invasive than ECT? **Transcranial magnetic stimulation (TMS)** might be such a treatment, although it is much too early to say so with confidence (McNamara et al., 2001). TMS involves generating a magnetic field with an electric coil that is placed against the skull just in front of the left ear. Like ECT, the procedure is repeated every few days until either symptom relief is noted or it is clear that the treatment is having no effect. Controlled studies suggest that TMS may be effective for some people (Sackeim & Lisanby, 2001), although it is not so effective as current treatments (Wassermann & Lisanby, 2001) and is ineffective in the elderly (Manes et al., 2001). Like ECT, TMS is effective in treating those people who do not respond to antidepressant medications (Garcia-Toro et al., 2001). Hence it offers depressed individuals one more treatment option.

The rationale for TMS, which frankly at this point is rather primitive, is that the magnetic field affects the electrical activity of the brain, thus leading to desirable changes. In essence, it is a reverse EEG. You may remember from Chapter 2 that the EEG measures the electrical activity of the brain as a way to monitor brain activity. Here a magnetic field much more powerful than that produced by the brain itself is used to alter brain activity. The placement of the magnetic coil over the left prefrontal cortex is based on research showing dysfunction in this region of the brain in people with depression. There is no question that a strong magnetic field will alter the electrical activity of the brain, just as there is no question that the electric current used in ECT alters the electrical activity of the brain. The magnetic field's alteration of brain activity could perhaps be made more specific than an electrical alteration, thus minimizing undesirable side effects. Features such as the location of stimulation, the strength of the magnetic field, the pulse frequency of the field, and interactions with other variables have yet to be adequately investigated. Scientists have established that exposure to this magnetic field produces a small reduction in two hormones—cortisol and thyroid-stimulating hormone (Evers et al., 2001). This may or may not be the mechanism by which TMS affects mood. Nevertheless, it is important that research on TMS continue to focus on such variables, which may provide clues to the mechanism of action. Almost without exception, once the mechanism of action for a treatment is understood, the treatment can be fine-tuned to increase its effectiveness.

Transcranial magnetic stimulation is an interesting new approach that shows promise for the treatment of depression. Its current efficacy does not warrant its routine use, but further research may well improve its effectiveness. Until more research is completed, one should maintain a healthy dose of skepticism. Nevertheless, such innovations are one more reason why people who suffer from depression have reason for optimism.

gradually increases in intensity to simulate dawn (Avery et al., 2001). Interestingly, if a person is going to respond well to light therapy, there is a noticeable improvement after the first hour of the therapy (Sher et al., 2001). Although phototherapy is generally safe and effective, it does entail risks, especially to vision (Meesters & Letsch, 1998).

PSYCHOLOGICAL TREATMENTS

The psychological treatments for depression seek to change the person or the environment in a manner that decreases current symptoms and minimizes the chance of depression in the future. In that respect, psychological approaches

. . . .

transcranial magnetic stimulation (TMS) A brain stimulation process that utilizes a magnetic field to treat depression.

differ from biological approaches, which do not have as an explicit goal the minimization of future depressive episodes. This section reviews three widely used psychological approaches for the treatment of depression: the cognitive, behavioral, and psychodynamic approaches.

Cognitive Treatment. Beck and his colleagues (Beck, 1976, 1993b; Piasecki & Hollon, 1987) have developed a cognitive treatment approach that has become the dominant psychological treatment for depression. The goal of this therapy is to challenge and then change the maladaptive automatic thoughts that contribute to depression. For example, if a depressed individual overgeneralizes from a single failure, the therapist begins by pointing this out and then asks the client to analyze the statement more closely, questioning whether the evidence supports the conclusion that he or she is a total failure. Remember that these are overlearned thoughts—thoughts that have reached the point of being automatic. Therefore, changing them is difficult.

Although the rationale underlying cognitive therapy is straightforward, it demands patience and skill on the part of the therapist. The treatment is broken into several steps, as illustrated in Table 7.4. The goal is to convince depressed clients that their moods can be brought under control and show them how to identify the variables that control their moods and how to manipulate those variables to improve mood and prevent further depression. This relatively short-term therapy often requires no more than 20 sessions (Piasecki & Hollon, 1987).

Beck's cognitive therapy is effective in reducing depression (Hollon & Beck, 1994; Piasecki & Hollon, 1987), and it may even be more effective than medications (Rush et al., 1977). Furthermore, it prevents or reduces the intensity of later depressions (Blackburn et al., 1986; Hollon et al., 1992). Learning to challenge maladaptive automatic thoughts changes the explanatory style of the individual, thus reducing the likelihood of depressive cognitions in the future.

Seligman has also used cognitive approaches to decrease the risk for depression in young people. Concerned by what he called an "epidemic of depression in the young," he argued for interventions to reduce the risk of depression. Gillham et al. (1995) found that a brief cognitive intervention with 11- and 12-year-olds was sufficient to reduce the risk of depression substantially two years later. Although these data suggest that these children had cognitive styles that were potentially depressogenic, other naturalistic data cast doubt on whether depressogenic cognitive styles are the primary cause of depression in children (Nolen-Hoeksema et al., 1992). Nevertheless, these cognitive styles probably contribute to depression, and early cognitive intervention clearly shows promise as a preventive strategy.

Behavioral Treatment. The rationale behind behavioral treatment is that depression reduces a person's access to pleasurable activities, thus increasing negative mood or at least preventing a reversal of the negative mood. Two factors contribute to this process. The first is that depressed people often feel they do not have the energy to engage in activities. The second is that depressed people often withdraw from social contact. It is true that social contact can be stressful, and depressed people may feel unable to handle that stress. However, social contacts also provide the majority of positive experiences in a person's life. Increasing social contacts and engagement in pleasurable activities is effective in reducing depression, although the effect is not instantaneous (Lewinsohn et al., 1970; Teri & Lewinsohn, 1986). Clients often report that initially they are just going through the motions and get little or no pleasure from this activity. Therapists need to encourage depressed clients to continue the pleasurable activity, explaining that the benefits often take a few days or weeks to accrue. For some depressed individuals, the social withdrawal is motivated partly by a lack of social skills, in which case social skills training can be helpful (Teri & Lewinsohn, 1986). One of the most critical social relationships for most people is the relationship with their spouse or partner. Strains in a marriage or long-term relationship often take their toll in the form of depressed mood in one or both

[TABLE 7.4] The Steps of Cognitive Therapy for Depression

The effective use of cognitive therapy for the treatment of depression rests on the systematic work of the therapist. Listed below is an outline of the steps normally taken by cognitive therapists in the treatment of depression. This outline is an excellent model of how all psychotherapies should be structured.

1. **Providing a Rationale**. Here the therapist provides the rationale behind Beck's cognitive therapy. A cogent rationale will convince depressed individuals that the outcomes of therapy are worth the hard work involved.

2. **Training in Self-Monitoring**. Clients learn to record their mood and the events they experience systematically, as they occur, to avoid the problems associated with retrospective memory.

3. **Behavioral Activation Strategies**. Beck's cognitive therapy also includes behavioral components, such as encouraging clients to engage in pleasurable activities. The therapist will often problem-solve with the client to find ways to increase the effectiveness of the client's behavior.

4. **Training in Identifying Cognitions**. This is the core of Beck's approach. Clients are taught to identify automatic thoughts, which are often out of conscious awareness, by analyzing their emotional responses to situations. The self-monitoring records are critical at this point in providing the data for this analysis.

5. **Evaluating Beliefs**. Once the automatic thoughts have been identified, the client is taught to challenge them by evaluating their rationality and the evidence on which they are based. Furthermore, the client is taught to test the validity of those thoughts by making predictions based on them and evaluating whether these predictions are accurate.

6. **Exploring Underlying Assumptions**. Underlying assumptions are broad themes that often tie together many specific automatic thoughts. For example, a person may believe that any failure to achieve a goal, no matter how inconsequential the goal or how ambivalent the person is about the goal, is proof that he or she is worthless.

7. **Relapse Prevention**. Because depressed individuals are prone to later depressive episodes, the therapist prepares the person to recognize and respond to depressive cognitions and moods when they occur in the future, thus making future depression less likely.

SOURCE: *"The Steps of Cognitive Therapy for Depression" from "Cognitive Therapy For Depression: Unexplicated Schemata and Scripts" by J. Pianecki and S. D. Hollon in* Psychotherapists in Clinical Practice: Cognitive and Behavioral Perspectives, *ed. by Neil S. Jacobson. Copyright © 1987. Reprinted by permission of The Guilford Press.*

partners. Reducing the conflicts in a distressed relationship often has a significant impact on the mood of the parties involved (Jacobson et al., 1989), and it also tends to prevent recurrence of the depression (Jacobson et al., 1993).

You may have noticed that Beck's cognitive therapy includes behavioral elements and that cognitive elements are a part of behavior therapy for depression. Therapists often combined these approaches (Brunell, 1985).

Psychodynamic Treatment. Psychodynamic treatment for depression has been around longer than any other psychotherapy. Its goal is to enhance the insight of depressed individuals into the presumed underlying loss that led to the depression. For example, the depressed person may have been threatened by the increasing success of her or his spouse or partner, perhaps fearing that the partner will no longer need or want the relationship. Although the traditional psychoanalytic psychotherapy appears to be only modestly effective in the treatment of depression (Craighead et al., 1992), a variant of psychoanalytic treatment called **interpersonal therapy,** or **IPT,** shows considerable promise (Klerman et al., 1984; Weissman, 1995). IPT is a short-term neoanalytic approach that concentrates on helping clients appreciate how their interpersonal interactions may be preventing them from achieving satisfying social relationships. It focuses on how to improve social relationships as a means of increasing life satisfaction—and hence decreasing depression. The therapist may address such issues as how to resolve interpersonal disputes, how to deal emotionally with the loss of a relationship, and how to develop new relationships. If the depressed person is having difficulty with social relationships because of inadequate social skills, the therapist will address those deficits directly in therapy. IPT rests on the premise that social networks provide both satisfaction and social support, which offers a buffer against stress (Monroe & Johnson, 1992). The exact mechanism by which social support functions is unknown, but several researchers are studying this process (Veiel & Baumann, 1992). Note that the cognitive-behavioral approach and the dynamic approach of IPT—once close to polar opposites—now share many treatment elements.

The effectiveness of IPT for the treatment of depression was established in a major multisite study funded by the National Institute of Mental Health (Frank et al., 1990; Klerman, 1990). This study compared IPT, cognitive-behavioral treatment, and treatment with tricyclic anti-

depressants. All of the treatments were found to be equally effective. Although there were indications that medication was more effective than psychological treatments for severely depressed individuals, some have argued that this effect may be due more to the skill level of the therapists in this study than to any superiority of medications per se (Hollon, 1996; Hollon & Beck, 1994). The results of this major study were not all positive, however. The relapse rates in the first 18 months after treatment ranged from 70 to 80% (Shea et al., 1992). Although the technology for the treatment of depression has evolved significantly, there is still a need to find ways to reduce the risk of relapse.

Check Yourself 7.4

Treatment of Depression

1. What is the most widely used biological treatment for depression?
2. What neurotransmitters are affected by each of the various classes of antidepressant drugs?
3. What is the mechanism behind the antidepressant effect of ECT?
4. What type of depression responds to phototherapy?
5. What is the primary goal of cognitive therapy for depression?
6. What is the focus of interpersonal therapy (IPT)?

Ponder this . . .   *Most people with depression never seek treatment. Why do you think that is, and what might be done about it?*

BIPOLAR DISORDERS

Although depression is the most common mood disorder, some individuals experience an elevated and euphoric mood referred to as mania. Mania is characterized by excessive energy, decreased need for sleep, inappropriate confidence, rapid activity and speech, and impulsive, sometimes dangerous, behavior. Manic individuals may jump from one idea to another so quickly in a conversation that they are impossible to follow. They may engage in such impulsive behavior as spending sprees, risky investments, and sexual indiscretions. They often have a grandiose sense of themselves and show contempt for those they regard as inferior. The term **hypomania** refers to a less extreme level of mania, which may leave the person on the edge of control. This section describes bipolar disorder and cyclothymic disorder, which involves manic or hypomanic behavior.

Bipolar disorder is characterized by extreme mood shifts, from very high (mania) to very low (depression).

---

interpersonal therapy (IPT)   A short-term neoanalytic approach that focuses on helping clients appreciate how their interpersonal interactions may be preventing them from achieving satisfying social relationships.

hypomania   A less extreme level of mania, which may leave the person on the edge of control.

Patty Duke, who appeared in both television and the movies, has openly discussed her experiences with bipolar disorder. Her candid discussion of this powerful disorder has done a lot to inform the public and to give the disorder "a human face."

These periods of depression and/or mania may last anywhere from a few days to months. It is an emotional roller coaster for both the people with this disorder and their families and friends. The DSM distinguishes between bipolar I and bipolar II disorders. The diagnosis of **bipolar I disorder** is made when the person has had at least one clear manic episode. There is often a history of major depressive episodes in people with bipolar I disorder, but such episodes are not required for the diagnosis. The diagnosis of **bipolar II disorder** is made when there is a history of major depressive episodes and at least one hypomanic episode, but no full manic episode. Because the treatment strategies depend on the current symptom pattern, the diagnosis indicates the nature of the current episode (manic, hypomanic, depressed, or mixed).

Approximately 1% of the population will be diagnosed with bipolar I disorder, and 0.5% with bipolar II disorder, sometime during their lives (APA, 2000). Bipolar disorder occurs equally in men and women and is found in all races

bipolar I disorder   Diagnosis assigned when the individual has had at least one clear manic episode.

bipolar II disorder   Diagnosis assigned when there is a history of major depressive episodes and at least one hypomanic episode, but no full manic episode.

and cultures (APA, 2000). First-degree relatives of individuals with bipolar I disorder have elevated rates of bipolar I, bipolar II, and major depressive disorders (Wender et al., 1986). The first-degree relatives of individuals who have bipolar II disorder also show such elevated rates, although the rates are not as high as with bipolar I (APA, 2000). Both twin and adoption studies confirm that there is a strong genetic component to bipolar I disorder (Bertelsen et al., 1977; Mendelwicz, 1985; Mendelwicz & Rainer, 1977; Wender et al., 1986). Genes play a much stronger role in bipolar disorder than in major depression. Like many disorders, the earlier the age of onset of bipolar disorder, the more severe the symptoms and the more chronic the course (Carlson et al., 2000).

The course of bipolar disorder will vary, but certain patterns occur frequently. For example, although it is theoretically possible to have a single manic episode in bipolar disorder, most people tend to have multiple episodes of both depression and mania, separated by periods of relatively normal functioning (APA, 2000). The majority of individuals experience a manic episode either just before or just after a major depressive episode, and the pattern tends to be consistent within an individual. This pattern is illustrated in the case of Roseanne.

Struggling to Stay Above Water

Roseanne had seen the pattern before, but it never failed to frighten her. She was feeling good now—very good, in fact. She was able to work hard and was more outgoing than usual. However, she knew what was coming. During her last manic episode, two years earlier at the age of 58, she had spent over $75,000 of the money that she and her husband had saved for retirement. She was arrested three times for causing a disturbance before she was finally committed for "psychiatric observation." Her behavior was so outrageous at work—yelling at patients, throwing things around the office, and making lewd comments and passes at several men—that she was fired from her job as a medical secretary. Her behavior toward her husband and children was so ruthlessly insulting that her husband filed for divorce and her children disowned her. She still cries when she remembers that she was not even told of her daughter's wedding and is barred from seeing her grandchildren. She could not sleep for days on end during the last episode and so would wander the streets or frequent bars. In the bars she would vacillate from being a wild party animal to being verbally vicious. She lost count of the number of bars she was thrown out of during that episode. "Would this episode be as bad?" she wondered, "or could it be worse?"

Roseanne had experienced three previous manic episodes, each followed by two months of overpowering depression. This pattern is common in bipolar disorder. She had been hospitalized three times, once involuntarily after assaulting her husband and son. When she was younger, she dreaded the depression. Now she dreads the mania because she knows how damaging it can be to her life.

Cyclothymic disorder is a chronic disorder characterized by frequent mood swings, which include hypomanic and depressive periods. The mood swings are less dramatic and severe than in bipolar disorder but are nevertheless quite disruptive. Cyclothymia typically develops during adolescence and remains stable throughout adulthood. There is some evidence that people with cyclothymic disorder are at risk for bipolar disorder (Depue et al., 1981), although not all individuals with bipolar disorder show this more chronic mood fluctuation pattern. Cyclothymia is as common in males as in females, although females are more likely to seek treatment (APA, 2000). Approximately 0.4% of the general population will qualify for this diagnosis sometime during their lifetime (APA, 2000; Faravelli et al., 1990). First-degree family members of cyclothymic individuals show elevated rates of major depression and bipolar disorder, as well as elevated rates of substance abuse (APA, 2000; Brieger & Marneros, 1997). The impact of cyclothymia is illustrated in the case of Myron.

A Wild Ride

Your opinion of Myron would depend on when you met him. At times he was a sensitive, caring, and creative college student. Every few weeks, however, he would become so irritable that no one could stand being around him. During those periods, he would pick fights with his roommates, throw things around the apartment, and say outrageous and hurtful things to students and professors in his classes. He was typically hypersexual during those periods, frequenting as many as three prostitutes in a single evening and spending as much as $1000 in one day at a local strip club. He had learned to prevent his excessive spending by refusing to take the credit card his parents offered. Myron's depressive periods occurred every two to three weeks and usually lasted a few days. During those depressions, he would cry several hours at a time. He hides from people when depressed and is unable to work. He has never been fired from a job, but he has quit several when the hypomania or depression was bad, and now he is afraid even to get a job. If the timing for the semester is just right, his episodes do not severely affect his grades, but that is rarely the case. In the last six semesters, he has withdrawn twice and received GPAs of 4.0, 0.67, 3.85, and 2.25.

The case of Myron illustrates a critical aspect of cyclothymia. The mood swings of cyclothymia, which are typ-

· ·

cyclothymic disorder   A chronic disorder characterized by frequent mood swings.

ically milder than bipolar mood swings, can still have a major impact on the individual's life. Myron has contemplated suicide on many occasions, although he has never attempted it. It is not hard to understand why his situation leads him to feel hopeless at times.

Check Yourself 7.5

Bipolar Disorders

1. What is the difference between bipolar disorder and cyclothymia?
2. What is the difference between bipolar I disorder and bipolar II disorder?
3. What is the gender ratio for bipolar disorder and cyclothymic disorder?
4. What, if any, evidence exists for genetic factors in bipolar disorder?

Ponder this . . .   *Looking at the criteria for bipolar I and bipolar II disorders, as well as the data on these disorders, what do you think was the logic behind making a distinction between them?*

EXPLAINING BIPOLAR DISORDERS

There is no shortage of hypotheses about what causes bipolar disorder. Dozens have been proposed, although most either have not stood up well to research or have little research to support them. This section will outline some of the more widely accepted hypotheses.

BIOLOGICAL THEORIES

Most psychiatrists and psychologists believe that biological factors play a major role in bipolar disorder. This section addresses the evidence for genetic influences, biochemical abnormalities, body dysregulation, and brain dysfunction.

Genetic Contributions.   There is little doubt that genes make a strong contribution to bipolar disorder. The risk for bipolar disorder in first-degree relatives of people with bipolar disorder is approximately 10%—10 times higher than in the general population (Katz & McGuffin, 1993). Concordance rates for bipolar disorder are 3 times higher in monozygotic than in dizygotic twins (Bertelsen et al., 1977; Mendlewicz, 1985). Furthermore, adoption studies show an increased risk for mood disorders in biological, but not adoptive, families of people with bipolar disorder (Mendlewicz & Rainer, 1977; Wender et al., 1986). There is also an elevated risk for cyclothymia in relatives of individuals with bipolar disorder (Klein et al., 1985), which suggests that these disorders share a common genetic base and that people with cyclothymia are at risk for bipolar disorder (Depue et al., 1981).

Although much effort has recently been spent in an effort to locate a specific gene to account for the increased risk for bipolar disorder, there has been little success to date. The research suggests that more than one gene is involved, which makes the task of identifying specific "bipolar genes" prohibitively difficult with current genetic technology (Mathews & Freimer, 2000; McInnis, 1997; Mitchell et al., 1993). There is evidence that a dominant gene on the X chromosome may be involved, although the data have been inconsistent (Risch et al., 1986). Other studies have suggested that genes on chromosomes 18 and 21 may be linked to bipolar disorder (Berrettini & Pekkarinen, 1996). These findings should be treated as tentative, given that they have not generally been replicated. However, the work using linkage analysis continues and will probably yield insights into this disorder in the relatively near future (Mathews & Freimer, 2000).

Evolutionary Impact

One might look at the incredible disruption in the lives of people with bipolar disorder and wonder why natural selection did not long ago eliminate the gene(s) responsible. Remember, however, that natural selection selects genes not for health or happiness, but for reproductive success (Nesse & Williams, 1994). The reason why bipolar disorder still exists may be as simple as the fact that manic individuals tend to be hypersexual, engaging in more sexual contacts with more people in a short period of time. Such sexual behavior, although problematic from many perspectives, might well enhance the likelihood of passing on one's genes. Of course, this potential reproductive advantage might be offset by higher mortality rates due to either the impulsive behavior characteristic of mania or the passive behavior characteristic of depression.

Biochemical Abnormalities. The clear evidence for *deficiencies* of the neurotransmitters norepinephrine and serotonin in depressed individuals has led many researchers to suspect that there may be excesses of these neurotransmitters in individuals with bipolar disorder. Norepinephrine does appear to be elevated during manic states (Post et al., 1978), and the fact that lithium, which is an effective treatment for bipolar disorder, reduces norepinephrine activity provides further evidence for its involvement. However, there is no evidence that serotonin is elevated in mania; serotonin level is actually low in individuals who experience mania (Price, 1990).

It is unlikely that a single neurotransmitter is at the heart of something so critical as mood regulation. Three neurotransmitters appear to play significant and complex roles in shaping moods—serotonin, norepinephrine, and dopamine (Whybrow, 1997). You may remember from our earlier discussion of neurotransmitters in depression that dopamine has been linked to some of the passivity found in depression. The role of dopamine in mania has been less clear because of the unpredictable treatment response to dopamine antagonists in individuals with mania. However, recent research suggests that the atypical antipsychotic medication clozapine reduces mania in normally treatment-resistant individuals with bipolar disorder (Calabrese, 1996). Because clozapine is known to affect both serotonin and dopamine, this result raises the possibility that dopamine plays a secondary role in mania, at least for some individuals.

Evolutionary Impact

Unraveling the biological processes involved in any form of psychopathology requires evidence from many sources. Understanding normal processes and how they can be disrupted is a good start. The problem is that researchers are not sure what processes are involved in bipolar disorder. Animal models of a disorder can be helpful in uncovering critical variables. The series of studies that Seligman and his colleagues conducted with animals delineated many critical elements of the learned helplessness model, which provided valuable direction in research on depression (Seligman, 1975). An animal model of bipolar disorder that triggers mood cycling in rats via high doses of cocaine or amphetamines is currently under development (Antelman et al., 1998). The fact that mood swings can be triggered with drugs means little by itself, because many drugs can create symptoms that mimic specific disorders. Recall, for example, that high doses of amphetamines will trigger the paranoid symptomatology sometimes found in schizophrenia. What makes this animal model so promising is the fact that lithium blocks the action of these drugs in creating the mood cycles; that is, lithium appears to be an effective treatment for these rats, just as it is for humans suffering from bipolar disorder. If further evidence suggests that other effective treatments for bipolar disorder prevent these drug-induced mood cycles, then it will be reasonable to posit that similar processes are operating in both rats and bipolar individuals. It is unlikely that the biochemical mechanisms underlying bipolar disorder suddenly evolved for the first time in humans. It is more likely that these mechanisms are shared with other species, so animal models have the potential to provide useful insights.

Body Dysregulation. One of the most obvious facts about mania is that the person's body is not functioning as

Vincent van Gogh suffered from both the depths of depression and the heights of mania. During some of his hypomanic periods, he created masterful works of art at a feverish pace.

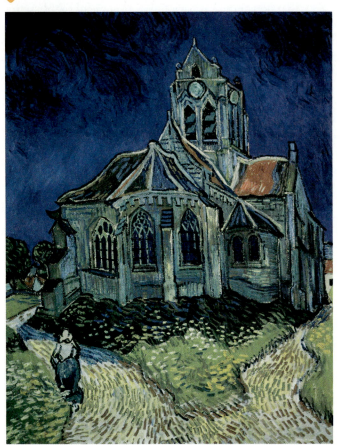

it should. The normal needs for sleep, food, and rest are distorted (APA, 2000). What accounts for this clear dysregulation of energy level? Could it be hormonal? Could it represent a problem in nervous system activity? Most important, why is the disruption episodic? The simple answer to these questions is that scientists still do not know, although many possible factors have been considered. Given the centrality of these symptoms in mania, it is remarkable that so little is known about the underlying mechanisms (Thase, 2000).

The body dysregulation that characterizes mania brings with it enormous energy. The question that one might raise is whether such energy may be beneficial. Imagine how much you could accomplish if you had unlimited energy and could go without sleeping for days. As noted in the nearby Focus box, at least some individuals with bipolar disorder can be enormously productive during a hypomanic, or even a manic, period. It is critical to realize, however, that this is not the norm for people with bipolar disorder. Most manic individuals find themselves afflicted with uncontrollable energy that cannot be focused in any constructive way.

Brain Dysfunction. Could brain abnormalities contribute to bipolar disorder? There is considerably less research on this question for bipolar disorder than for schizophrenia, although that is changing rapidly. For example, recent PET studies found a dysfunction in the prefrontal cortex in bipolar individuals (Blumberg et al., 1999). This finding is consistent with data showing that damage to the right prefrontal cortex often results in mania (Starkstein et al., 1990).

It is possible that, just as in schizophrenia, some of the brain dysfunction found in bipolar disorder may result from complications of pregnancy and birth, people with bipolar disorder are more likely than their siblings to have experienced such complications in their gestation and birth (Kinney et al., 1998). Whether this represents a biological stressor that increases the likelihood of the genetic diathesis leading to a disorder or whether it represents an alternative way in which bipolar disorder develops is currently unknown.

PSYCHOLOGICAL THEORIES

It is generally accepted that psychological factors are not the primary cause of bipolar disorder, but this does not mean that psychological factors do not contribute to the disorder or to its periodic episodes. This section discusses two factors that have been implicated: stressful life events and premorbid cognitive schemas.

Stressful Life Events. Studying the impact of stressful life events in bipolar individuals presents several challenges. The behavior of manic individuals often creates stressful situations, so it is important to exclude such events if one wants to investigate the potential triggering effects of stress (Johnson & Roberts, 1995). Furthermore, the mild mood swings associated with cyclothymia also increase the frequency of stressful events (Goplerud & Depue, 1985; Lovejoy & Steuerwald, 1997). Although stress does not appear to trigger manic episodes in general, it can trigger manic episodes in those people who are predisposed to bipolar disorder. Severe stress appears to be sufficient to trigger a manic episode for roughly half of the individuals with bipolar disorder, but stress seems to have little impact for the remaining individuals with the disorder (Hammen et al., 1992). Early research suggested that stress played a greater role for the first few episodes of mania, whereas later episodes were less likely to be precipitated by stress (Goodwin & Jamison, 1990; Ramana & Bebbington, 1995). However, more recent and better controlled research suggests that stress contributes as much to later episodes of mania as to the initial episodes (Hlastala et al., 2000). The stress that seems to have the greatest impact in triggering manic episodes is stress that either disrupts social interactions or is due to a disruption in social interactions (Malkoff-Schwartz et al., 1998, 2000). This finding is consistent with recent evidence

FOCUS Mania and creativity

You have perhaps heard about the supposed link between insanity and creativity. The idea is that the disordered, or "loose," thinking that is part of insanity enables artists and other creative individuals to develop new insights and to use those insights to produce wonderfully creative art, music, or literature. More than one casual visitor to a modern art display has probably contemplated the link between insanity and creativity. The evidence, however, suggests that the link is not between insanity and creativity, but rather between mania and creativity.

In a classic book on this topic, Kay Jamison (1992, 1996) reviews extensive examples of creative individuals who also suffered from mood disorders, especially bipolar disorder. Such legendary figures as Michelangelo, van Gogh, Tchaikovsky, and the poets Shelley and Whitman all suffered from periods of depression and mania. The life histories of these people often include periods of enormous productivity and other periods of little or no productivity. Their most creative works were usually generated during these productive periods, although that might be expected simply because most of their work was produced during those periods. When information about their psychiatric status is available, the creative times often emerge as hypomanic periods and the nonproductive times as depressed periods.

You might have expected that relationship from your own experience with mood fluctuations that are probably less severe. You may not feel productive or creative when you are mildly depressed and may be much more confident and creative when you are feeling especially good about yourself. The critical question is "What is it about manic and hypomanic periods that increases creativity?" To date, there is no good answer to that question. It may be the extra energy, which enables people to push themselves to new heights. It may be the loose thinking, which allows people to think things that they might otherwise never consider. It may be the sheer productivity, which results in a few creative ideas among hundreds of mundane ideas. Whatever it is, it is clear that creativity and moods are not always connected. There are many creative and productive individuals who do not appear to suffer from mood disorders, and there are lots of sufferers from mood disorders who are far from being creative.

There is a popular misconception associated with creativity and psychiatric disorders. Some people think of the supposed increase in creativity as the reason why psychiatric disorders have not been weeded out by natural selection. Remember that it is not creativity, but rather procreative activity, that determines whether genes are passed on to the next generation. Creativity might slightly enhance reproductive success because creative individuals might be more desirable mates. However, the evidence for this effect is weak at best. It makes more sense to argue that creativity has little to do with the selective pressure on genes associated with bipolar disorder.

---

suggesting that social support may help individuals with bipolar disorder to recover from episodes more quickly and that they are less prone to depressive affect when surrounded by adequate social support (Johnson et al., 1999). It is also consistent with the evidence that the stress of living in a home with high levels of expressed emotion—the hostile overinvolvement of family members in the person's life—is strongly predictive of relapse in people with bipolar disorder (Simoneau et al., 1998). Stress does not always precipitate a manic episode, but when it does, the severity of the manic symptoms is related to the severity of the stress (Hammen et al., 1992). Clearly, this is a complicated picture, and further research will be necessary to delineate the mechanisms by which stress precipitates manic episodes.

Premorbid Cognitive Schemas. Both the revised helplessness and the hopelessness models of depression hypothesize that a cognitive diathesis—a tendency to make internal, stable, and global attributions for negative life events—sets a person up for depression. What about people who have a predisposition to make internal, stable, and global attributions for positive life events? Could they be at risk for mania or hypomania? The logic of the argument is the same: A cognitive diathesis, coupled with the right set of events (in this case, a series of positive events), results in a hypomanic disorder. Recent data suggest that such premorbid cognitive schemas do increase risk for hypomania, although it is not clear whether they increase risk for mania (Reilly-Harrington et al., 1999).

Check Yourself 7.6

Theories of Mania

1. What is known about the genetic contributions to mania?

2. What brain dysfunctions have been found in bipolar disorder?

3. What is the role of stress in triggering manic episodes?

Ponder this . . . *The evidence for a strong genetic component for mania raises evolutionary issues. Think about the symptoms of mania. Are they likely to be more or less disruptive in today's environment than they were in the evolutionary past?*

TREATING BIPOLAR DISORDERS

Until recently, the only treatment for bipolar disorder was medication. Although medication is still the primary treatment approach, other treatments are now available.

MEDICATIONS

For the last 50 years, the primary treatment for bipolar disorder was a lithium salt (lithium carbonate). Lithium normally exists at low levels in the body, but at higher levels it appears to have a mood-stabilizing effect (Post, 2000). Although it was originally identified as a medication for mania, lithium is more accurately described as a mood-stabilizing drug because it reduces both the manic and the depressive episodes of bipolar disorder (Jefferson & Greist, 1989; Post, 2000). Most people with bipolar disorder are maintained on lithium even after the manic or depressive episode has passed, because staying on lithium dramatically reduces the risk of further episodes and suicide (Nemeroff & Schatzberg, 1998; Post, 2000; Viguera et al., 2000). Although lithium is effective in treating bipolar disorder, it is also a toxic substance at doses only slightly higher than the treatment dose (PDR, 2002; Post, 2000). Therefore, careful monitoring of blood levels is imperative, especially if the person is going through a mood shift (Jefferson & Greist, 1989). Lithium can also produce side effects, including tremor, weight gain, migraine headaches, rash, and impaired thyroid functioning (Post, 2000). However, these side effects are mild in most individuals. Lithium is often combined with an antidepressant medication when the person is in a depressive episode (Young et al., 2000).

The mechanism by which lithium normalizes mood in bipolar individuals is unclear, because lithium has multiple effects on systems that might be involved in mood regulation, right down to affecting the transcription of proteins from specific genes (Ikonomov & Manji, 1999). Consequently, it is difficult to determine which of these many effects are relevant.

Recently, a second class of drugs has proved effective in reducing the symptoms of bipolar disorder. Certain anticonvulsants, which are normally used to treat seizure disorders, have been applied successfully to treat bipolar symptoms (Nemeroff & Schatzberg, 1998). Both carbamazepine (Tegretol) and valproic acid (Depakote) are now used to treat mania (Lennkh & Simhandl, 2000; Mitchell, 1999b). These drugs are sometimes effective for people who do not respond well to lithium or cannot tolerate its side effects.

PSYCHOLOGICAL INTERVENTIONS

Traditional psychotherapy has not proved useful for either the treatment or the prevention of manic episodes. In fact, it is difficult even to have a conversation with a manic individual, let alone conduct psychotherapy. Until recently, the popular wisdom was that all psychological interventions were generally ineffective with bipolar disorder, although recent research is challenging that position.

The psychological intervention that has proved most beneficial for preventing relapse in bipolar disorder is family therapy aimed at reducing the level of expressed emotion in the family (George et al., 2000; Miklowitz, 1996). Family therapy does not replace medication, but in conjunction with appropriate medications, it can reduce the frequency of relapse.

Many people with bipolar disorder have benefited from the application of proven psychological treatment techniques for depression, such as Beck's cognitive therapy. These approaches can attenuate the depressive symptoms, although they tend to help little with the manic symptoms. In addition, people with bipolar disorder often spend considerable time in therapy between manic episodes to repair the damage that these episodes have done to their lives. It is common for manic individuals to behave in outrageous ways, which can ruin friendships, strain relationships of all sorts, and threaten job security. Furthermore, the impulsive behavior associated with manic and hypomanic periods can create huge financial obligations as a consequence of excessive spending, which may further strain family relationships. These real problems created by the manic behavior remain long after the manic episode has passed. The severity of these psychological "hangovers" following a manic period is illustrated in the case of George.

Paying the Price

GEORGE

George sits in his therapist's office in tears, recounting the problems he faces. He has seen this therapist four times over the last seven years, each time after a manic episode. He usually experiences hypomanic periods, in which he is enormously productive as a sales manager, followed by manic periods, in which his performance deteriorates dramatically and his behavior becomes outrageous. During his most recent manic episode, he screamed obscenities at two of his best customers; slept with two women from the office and two of the buyers he dealt with frequently; and, because he was sure it would lead to huge profits on the *next* deal, committed his company to a contract that will result in nearly $250,000 in losses. At home, his candor about sexual activities damaged his relationship with his wife and two teenage children. His wife obtained a legal separation and custody of the children, and he now lives alone in an apartment. If he were not one of the most productive and creative people in the company, he would have been fired long ago. He has been fired twice in the past and left another company because he could not handle the jokes about him that circulated behind his back after one particularly dramatic episode. This time he thinks that his wife has left him for good. With the help of his therapist, George will begin the hard work of repairing the mess he has made, just as he has done half a dozen times in the past.

Cases like that of George drive home the tremendous personal cost of bipolar disorder. The primary treatment is still medication, but supportive therapy is often necessary as the individual struggles to put his or her life back together after an episode. Bipolar disorder is an episodic condition, and the more one can stretch out the time between episodes, the fewer episodes one has to endure. This goal is best achieved by bolstering the person's social support network and reducing expressed emotion in the family.

Check Yourself 7.7

Treatment of Mania

1. What is the primary treatment approach for mania?
2. What role does traditional psychotherapy play in the treatment of bipolar disorder?
3. What is the focus of family therapy for bipolar disorder?

Ponder this . . .   *Imagine for a moment that you suffer from bipolar disorder. How would you deal emotionally with the periodic episodes and the fallout from those episodes?*

SUICIDE

Suicide—the deliberate taking of one's own life—is one of the most terrifying aspects of psychopathology. It is

suicide   The deliberate taking of one's own life.

The leader of the rock group Nirvana, Kurt Cobain, committed suicide at the height of his career. The reasons may never be known, but as is often true for people who commit suicide, drugs and alcohol appear to have been involved.

hard for most of us to imagine being driven to such despair and hopelessness that suicide seems the only solution. Although most people think of suicide as associated with depression, suicide is common in people with other psychiatric disorders, including schizophrenia (Roy, 1982, 1992), alcoholism (Cornelius et al., 1995), and borderline personality disorder (Linehan & Shearin, 1988). This section begins with an overview of suicide, followed by a discussion of the primary ways in which suicide has been studied. There is a brief discussion of physician-assisted suicide, one of the most controversial issues in this area. The section ends with a discussion of procedures designed to reduce the risk of suicide.

REALITY OF SUICIDE

In part because it is often hushed up, suicide is far more common than most people realize. There is considerable stigma associated with suicide, so families and friends often downplay the details of how a person who committed suicide died. It is estimated that at least 30,000 people a year commit suicide in the United States alone and nearly 1000 people a day worldwide (Roy, 2000); the actual figures are probably higher. It is likely that many single-car crashes, unexplained falls, and accidental overdoses actually have been suicides. Adolescent suicides, in particular, tend to be undercounted because of family efforts, often supported by doctors and coroners, to hide the cause of death (Holinger et al., 1994).

Most people who attempt suicide do not succeed (Shneidman, 1985), and in many of those cases, they may not really have wanted to die. Instead, their suicide attempts may have been a way to dramatize the severity of their distress—something that social service workers call a cry for help. However, many people who attempt suicide will make multiple attempts, and up to 65% have made prior attempts (Dorpat & Ripley, 1967; Farberow, 1994). The number of past suicide attempts is the single best predictor of who will commit suicide (Isometsä & Löennqvist, 1998; Maris, 1981). In the United States, women are about three times as likely to attempt suicide as men, although men are four to five times more likely than women to die from suicide (Stillion, 1985). The reason for this disparity is that men tend to choose more lethal means, such as guns or jumping from tall buildings, in which there is no way to reverse the action once it is taken. In contrast, an overdose of medication is less lethal than a gunshot, and medical treatment can often save the person's life; it takes a truly determined person to not seek treatment after ingesting pills. However, this gender difference in lethality of suicide attempts varies across cultures. For example, in Poland and Finland, suicide attempts by women are more likely to be lethal than attempts by men (Canetto, 1997).

Given the frightening nature of suicide, it is perhaps not surprising that many misconceptions have emerged. Some of the more prominent misconceptions are discussed in Table 7.5. The systematic study of suicide has debunked these myths and, in some cases, has provided the understanding necessary to implement effective prevention strategies. The approaches to the study of suicide are covered in the next section.

STUDYING SUICIDE

Understanding something as complex as suicide requires a variety of research techniques. The two most commonly used techniques involve epidemiological studies of suicide to identify general risk factors and "psychological autopsies" of people who have committed suicide to identify the individual factors that may have contributed in specific cases. Less common, but also important, is the study of genetic risk factors. All of these methods are covered in this section.

Epidemiological Studies. Being able to predict **suicidal ideation**—the feeling of wanting to commit suicide—is critical if one wants to prevent suicide. To understand the risk factors for suicide, researchers must first identify groups that are at high risk and then identify the

suicidal ideation The feeling of wanting to commit suicide.

[TABLE 7.5] Misconceptions about Suicide

1. Those who talk about suicide are unlikely to commit suicide.

Most people who commit suicide have given some indication of their suicidal feelings. They may have threatened suicide, suggested it as their best option, or actually attempted suicide (Isometsä & Löennqvist, 1998). Most people do not contemplate suicide casually. They have typically thought about it for some time and given some indication of their thoughts to at least a few people.

2. People who commit suicide are irrational.

Some people who commit suicide are irrational, but many are not. The clarity and poignancy of many suicide notes testify to the degree of thought that often goes into this fateful decision (Shneidman, 1979).

3. People who commit suicide are all very depressed.

Most people who commit suicide are depressed, but depression is not the only condition associated with suicide (Beck et al., 1985). Anything that makes a person feel hopeless can be associated with suicide. People with depression (Blair-West et al., 1999), schizophrenia (Roy, 1982, 1992), panic disorder (Friedman et al., 1992), alcoholism (Cornelius et al., 1995), and borderline personality disorder (Linehan & Shearin, 1988) are disproportionately represented among those who commit suicide.

4. Asking people whether they are feeling suicidal increases their risk of suicide.

This myth often makes new mental health workers anxious because they do not want to be the person who gave their client the idea of committing suicide. There is no evidence that asking a client about suicidal feelings increases suicidal risk. In fact, the evidence seems to favor the opposite, perhaps because the professional who assesses suicidal feelings is more likely to take appropriate treatment and management actions to reduce the risk of suicide (Shneidman, 1985).

5. People commit suicide because of the way they feel.

There is substantial evidence that past and recent experiences of the person contribute to risk for suicide over and above the level of depression. For example, people who have had family members commit suicide are themselves at elevated risk for suicide (Kety, 1990), and young people in particular are more likely to commit suicide if a friend or classmate has recently committed suicide (Gould, 1990; Holinger et al., 1994). Well-publicized suicides often lead to clusters of suicides, inducing some people who have been considering suicide to act on their feelings (Coleman, 1987).

factors that differentiate these groups. This epidemiological approach has been the backbone of suicide research (Roy, 2000).

Epidemiological research has identified several factors associated with suicide risk, including age, sex, nationality, diagnosis, substance abuse, and past history of suicide attempts. The evidence indicates that these risk factors interact with one another (Young et al., 1994), and this interaction makes it even more difficult to predict suicide risk. Nevertheless, research has substantially improved prediction and has led to marginally more effective prevention strategies (Shneidman, 1993).

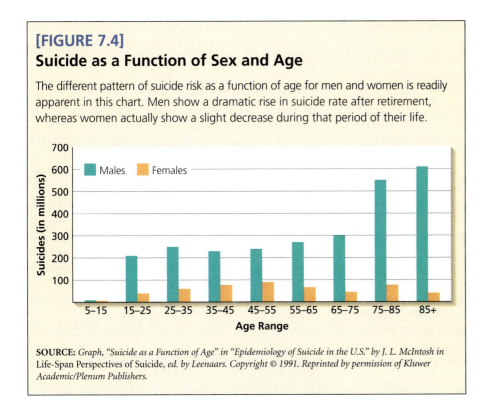

[FIGURE 7.4]

Suicide as a Function of Sex and Age

The different pattern of suicide risk as a function of age for men and women is readily apparent in this chart. Men show a dramatic rise in suicide rate after retirement, whereas women actually show a slight decrease during that period of their life.

SOURCE: *Graph, "Suicide as a Function of Age" in "Epidemiology of Suicide in the U.S." by J. L. McIntosh in Life-Span Perspectives of Suicide, ed. by Leenaars. Copyright © 1991. Reprinted by permission of Kluwer Academic/Plenum Publishers.*

The strongest predictor of suicide risk is a history of suicide attempts. The next most critical risk factors are the demographic variables of age and sex, as illustrated in Figure 7.4. Males are at higher risk than females, and this differential risk is found virtually everywhere in the world (Lester, 1996). Age is also a surprisingly strong predictor of suicide risk (McIntosh, 1992), at least for men. The risk of suicide for males is low in childhood, rises quickly during adolescence, remains stable throughout most of adulthood, and then rises again in old age (Holinger et al., 1994; McIntosh, 1991). In contrast, females tend to have relatively stable rates of suicide across the lifetime. It should be noted that this interaction between age and sex in determining risk for suicide is stronger for whites than for blacks (McIntosh, 1991). The risk for suicide among the young (those 15–24 years old) has risen dramatically in recent years, more than tripling between 1960 and 1990 (Holinger & Offer, 1991). The rates of suicide among the elderly also rose during this period, though much less dramatically (McIntosh, 1992).

Marital status and occupation are also strong predictors of risk for suicide. Divorced and widowed individuals are at higher risk than married and single people as illustrated in Figure 7.5 (Maris, 1997; McIntosh, 1991), although the pattern varies as a function of sex (Tsuang et al., 1992). For example, the death of a spouse increases the risk for suicide slightly in women but by 500% in men. People in certain occupations, such as psychologists, psychiatrists, physicians, lawyers, dentists, and police officers, are at especially elevated risk (Holmes & Rich, 1990; Stillion, 1985; Wekstein, 1979).

Suicide rates vary by ethnic status and nationality. For example, white Americans are more likely to commit suicide than black Americans. White males have historically committed suicide at more than twice the rate of black

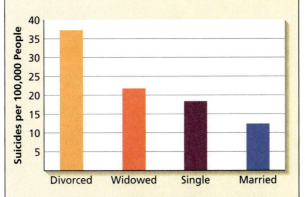

[FIGURE 7.5]

Suicide as a Function of Marital Status

Marital status affects the risk for suicide in both men and women. Being widowed or divorced increases risk for both men and women, but divorce appears to be more disruptive for females, whereas being widowed is more disruptive for males.

SOURCE: *Graph, "Suicide as a Function of Sex and Marital Status" in "Epidemiology of Suicide in the U.S." by J. L. McIntosh in Life-Span Perspectives of Suicide, ed. by Leenaars. Copyright © 1991. Reprinted by permission of Kluwer Academic/Plenum Publishers.*

males, although that gap has been narrowing as suicide rates for blacks have risen (McIntosh, 1991). The suicide rate in the United States and Canada is about 13 people per 100,000 per year. The rates in Denmark and Finland are about double that, and in Germany and Hungary the rates are almost 4 times higher. In contrast, the U.S. suicide rate is twice as high as that in Argentina, about 8 times higher than that in Mexico, and more than a 100 times higher than that in Egypt (Diekstra, 1990; Lester, 1996; WHO, 1988).

Substance abuse is also related to suicide. Alcoholics—particularly male alcoholics—are at high risk, especially if there is comorbid depression accompanying the alcoholism (Merrill et al., 1992). Furthermore, alcohol or drug use is often associated with suicide, perhaps because these substances lower inhibitions (Rogers, 1992).

What do all these demographic findings mean? By themselves, they mean little, but they do provide clues about what factors may be most relevant. You might want to inspect the demographic findings outlined in Table 7.6 and try your hand at generating hypotheses that could be tested with other research. For example, psychologists have a much higher suicide rate than people in general. Could this be due to unique stresses associated with that profession? Or could it have more to do with who decides to become a psychologist? Or does their greater exposure to suicide increase the likelihood of psychologists considering suicide? Could these reasons also explain the higher risk for police officers and dentists? As you work through the findings in Table 7.6, the same realization that strikes most

researchers who study suicide will probably strike you: Suicide is a complex phenomenon, and many factors can contribute to suicide risk (Roy, 2000).

Psychological Autopsies. Epidemiological studies provide valuable clues about factors that increase risk for suicide, but they do little to explain an individual suicide. To understand a specific suicide, professionals conduct a **psychological autopsy** of the case—carefully gathering information about the person, the events that led up to the suicide, and the way those events seem to have contributed to the final outcome (Shneidman et al., 1994). What invariably is found is that most suicides appear to be the result of a cascading series of events, rather than just a single event, and there often appear to have been many lost opportunities to reduce the risk for suicide in the individual. The following case history illustrates the complexity of such an analysis.

[TABLE 7.6] Interpreting Epidemiological Finding in Suicide

Try your hand at generating possible interpretations of the interesting epidemiological findings on suicide that are listed below. Ask yourself what other relationships should exist if your hypothesis is correct.

1. The rates of suicide among people in their late teens and in early adulthood have more than tripled in recent years.
2. The rates for females are much lower than for males, and the rates for black females are exceptionally low throughout the lifetime.
3. The rates of suicide are steady for females throughout the lifetime, but they rise sharply in males after about the age of 65.
4. Black males show a peak in suicide risk about age 30 and then decline before rising again at about retirement age. In contrast, white males exhibit a relatively steady rate of suicide across their adult years before showing a sharp upturn in risk after age 65.
5. Females showed a very stable rate of suicide from 1930 through 1990. In contrast, the rate of suicide in males dropped over 30% between 1930 and 1955, only to rise again from 1970 to 1990.

Unable to Live Up to Expectations

ROGER

By any reasonable standard, Roger was successful—a professor at a major university with an impressive publication record, excellent teaching skills, and the respect of students and colleagues. He also had a loving wife and two talented sons. He had several friends, including one close friend—a colleague who was almost a part of the family. Nevertheless, Roger felt inadequate, confiding to friends that he felt like a fraud and that his family would be better off without him.

During the last summer of his life, Roger grew increasingly depressed. His productivity fell dramatically, and he would disappear for hours. As the fall semester approached, he became more agitated, telling his wife that he could not face his students. On the Friday afternoon before classes were to begin, he received a phone call that greatly upset him, but his wife and friends never found out who called or what was said. He spent the entire day Saturday at his office but accomplished nothing. By late Saturday night he was in tears, unable to sleep, and unable to function. He left early Sunday morning without saying goodbye to his wife—something he never did. When she awoke and found him gone, she immediately became worried, and her worry turned to terror when she realized he had left his briefcase. She spent several hours looking for him before calling friends to help in the search. When he had not returned by nightfall, she expressed her belief that he must be dead because he would never leave his family worrying like that. His body was found the next morning about a block from where he once had worked, a single gunshot to the head. There was no note. The gun had been his father's—the only item that Roger

psychological autopsy An investigation conducted in an effort to understand a specific suicide by gathering information about the person, the events that led up to the suicide, and the way those events may have contributed to the final outcome.

had kept after his father's death two years earlier. The bullets had been purchased that morning from a nearby sporting goods store, just 10 minutes after it opened for business.

A psychological autopsy of Roger's suicide would begin by gathering as much information as possible on Roger, on his life, and on the events that preceded the suicide. It was clear that Roger was depressed, but he had been depressed before. Why did *this* depression push him over the edge? It is clear that he had low self-esteem. He thought his work was of little value and doubted that he could fulfill his professional duties. However, those feelings were not new either. He and his wife had always been close, and his family was everything to him, even when everything else seemed terrible. Somehow that made little difference this time. Of all the things he could have taken from his father's effects after his father's death, he chose a gun. Roger hated guns, never owned one, and so far as people knew had never fired one, although his father and his brother were both avid gun enthusiasts. There was no history of suicide in Roger's family or among his friends. As you will see, genetics appears to play a role in suicide, and learning about recent suicide attempts seems to increase the risk of suicide in those who might be contemplating it (Gould, 1990). Important clues in understanding what happened to Roger are missing because he was so withdrawn during the last two weeks of his life. Did something set him off, destroying what little sense of self-worth he still had? Who called on Friday? Was it something important or just a routine question from a student about his upcoming class? He certainly had some risk factors. He was white, male, and depressed. However, he also did not have other risk factors. He was healthy and middle-aged, with a stable family and no substance abuse. One could offer the simple answer that he was very depressed, but that answer ignores the obvious question of "Why now?"

The case of Roger is frustrating for someone interested in doing a psychological autopsy. The facts raise many questions but provide few answers. Most psychological autopsies are more fruitful because there is more information to analyze. But Roger was not one to share his feelings with other people. He had seen a therapist in the past, but not during the two years before his suicide. When he became depressed, he withdrew from people. His wife and children knew he was depressed, but his colleagues and friends had no idea. Even his wife did not know what was depressing him. There were no obvious traumatic events, such as a personal failure, in the months before his suicide. Finally, he left no note to explain his reasons and offer insights into his feelings.

One of the most salient clues in many psychological autopsies is the suicide note (Shneidman, 1973). These notes, which sometimes are written quickly and impulsively and sometimes are crafted for months in advance of the suicide, provide insights into people's thought processes as they ready themselves to die at their own hands. They often express anger, which suggests that the suicide may be partially motivated by the desire to hurt others and make them feel guilty. They often detail critical incidents, usually some recent failure that the person considers particularly shameful (Blumenthal, 1990). They often express a sense of hopelessness—a conviction that things will never improve. Some letters display badly distorted thinking, whereas other letters are impressive in that they lay out a very convincing argument for the suicide. By themselves, the letters mean little, but coupled with a thorough analysis of the person, his or her recent experiences, and the sources of available support, they can shed light on a person's agonizing decision to die.

One factor that seems to reduce the risk for suicide is social support. This phenomenon has been studied for over a century by sociologists and psychologists (Durkheim, 1897/1951). Many people who commit suicide have minimal social support or have recently been cut off from the primary social support, as is true of divorced or widowed men (Maris, 1997). Children, social responsibilities, and caring family and friends all seem to contribute to making life worthwhile—and therefore to making suicide less likely.

The best psychological predictor of suicide risk is the person's degree of hopelessness (Beck et al., 1985; Soloff et al., 2000). Hopelessness takes away a person's reason to go on. If the terrible situation that suicidal individuals find themselves in cannot be changed, then what is the point of continuing? If there is hope for a change, then there is a reason to wait for things to improve. Giving people a reason to be hopeful is a major strategy in suicide prevention (Shneidman, 1985, 1993).

Studying Genetic Factors. There is mounting evidence that genes play a role in suicide risk. Psychologists have long known that suicide tends to run in families, but either genes or environment could explain this finding. However, both twin and adoption studies suggest that genes play a stronger role than environment in influencing suicide risk (Roy et al., 1991; Wender et al., 1986). The evidence suggests that the genetic influences on suicide are independent of the genetic influences on disorders associated with suicide (Roy et al., 1999). That is, it is not merely that the genes increase risk for disorders with high suicide risk. Genetic vulnerability to suicide is unlikely to lead to suicide unless the person also has a psychiatric disorder or has experienced unusual stress (Roy et al., 1999). With the incredible recent advances in gene technology, investigators are now trying to identify specific genes that may contribute to suicide risk (Du et al., 1999). The results to date are promising, but many studies of specific genes in psychopathology have failed to be replicated. Therefore, it is wise to reserve judgment about the finding of specific suicide genes until later studies confirm it.

Evolutionary Impact

The fact that genes play a role in increasing risk for suicide raises an interesting question. How have those genes survived evolutionary pressures? There is no simple answer to this question. Part of the answer may lie in the fact that these genes seem to influence risk for suicide only when combined with severe stress or psychopathology (Roy et al., 1999). Furthermore, the majority of suicides occur in individuals who have survived most of their reproductive years, so the suicide has little effect on reproductive success. Therefore, the genes experience little negative selective pressure. However, that explanation would suggest only that the genes would be eliminated more slowly by evolution, not that they would survive. For genes that can contribute to the premature death of the individual to survive in the gene pool, they must provide some compensatory advantage. One might speculate, for example, that certain genes encode an almost impulsive, "take charge" response that can lead to suicide when one is depressed but increases leadership—and thus reproductive success—when one is not depressed. Another possible explanation is that one's survival may occasionally represent a drain on the survival and reproduction of relatives, who also carry one's genes. In such a situation, suicide decreases the person's reproductive potential but might increase the reproductive potential of family members, thus ensuring greater representation, in the next generation, of the genes that one and one's relatives shared. As speculative as this hypothesis seems, there is evidence to support it (Brown et al., 1999).

PHYSICIAN-ASSISTED SUICIDE

Perhaps one of the most controversial topics in medicine these days is **physician-assisted suicide,** in which the physician provides the person with the means to take his or her own life. The most vocal proponent of physician-assisted suicide is Jack Kevorkian, a retired pathologist. Kevorkian has argued for the rights of people to take their own lives and has provided specific individuals with the means to commit suicide, despite the fact that state law expressly prohibits such action. Kevorkian has argued primarily for suicide as an alternative to a slow and painful death from a terminal illness or as an alternative to a life that is not worthwhile because of severe physical limitations or pain.

The state of Oregon has recently enacted a law permitting physician-assisted suicide under some circumstances (Ganzini et al., 2001). The law is controversial, and it is still uncertain what impact it will have. Many worry that the availability of physician-assisted suicide will raise the possibility of future abuses. Certainly one could make the argument that people should have the right to decide how they will die. States routinely recognize so-called *living wills,* in which the person specifies in advance what medical procedures he or she authorizes in the event of specific medical

Jack Kevorkian has challenged the notion that suicide is always unreasonable by assisting those who are intent on suicide in their efforts. In the process, he has spurred debate on suicide and on the treatment of terminally ill patients.

conditions. For example, people may specify that they do not want to be kept alive by artificial means if there is either little chance of recovery or significant brain damage. Terminally ill individuals often request that they not be resuscitated if they experience a heart attack. However, there is a difference between allowing a person to die naturally and hastening that death. Some argue that the availability of suicide would exert pressure on some individuals to elect suicide to save their family the cost and pain of their continued treatment (Sherlock, 1983).

No one seems to argue that physician-assisted suicide should be available for people suffering from emotional disorders, such as depression. Unlike terminal illnesses, emotional disorders are often episodic or may respond to medications and/or psychotherapy. Almost 90% of suicides are committed by people with emotional disorders (Roy, 2000), and the right to physician-assisted suicide is not likely to be extended to these people.

SUICIDE PREVENTION

Given the finality of suicide and the fact that many people who commit suicide are suffering from treatable psychological disorders, it is not surprising that considerable effort is focused on suicide prevention. Mental health workers routinely assess suicide risk in their clients. Most major cities have suicide prevention hotlines. The phone numbers for these hotlines are usually listed on the first page of the telephone directory along with other emergency numbers. Volunteers from the community, who have been specifically trained to assess and intervene in crises, often staff these hotlines. These volunteers are backed up by professionals, such as psychologists and social workers, who are experts in the field of crisis intervention.

The key to successful suicide prevention is the identification of those at risk. For both the mental health professional who is meeting with a client and the crisis hotline volunteer who is talking to someone who has called, the task is to determine the degree of lethality or risk that the person represents. Much of this assessment relies on the demographic and diagnostic variables that are known to be predictive of risk. More detailed risk assessment focuses on the plan for suicide formulated by the person. People who are feeling suicidal but have not thought about how they might commit suicide are at relatively low risk. People with specific plans and the means to carry them out, such as

those who plan to shoot themselves and have a gun and ammunition readily available, are at much higher risk.

The methods used to reduce suicide risk often rely on connecting emotionally with the person contemplating suicide. The crisis hotline volunteer will talk with the person, often seeking to understand what brought her or him to the point of feeling hopeless. Most suicidal individuals harbor at least some ambivalence about killing themselves, and the professional or volunteer often tries to tap into that ambivalence. Many suicidal individuals feel that the situation is hopeless and that there is no other way out (Shneidman, 1985, 1987). Working with the person to identify other options—not necessarily desirable options, but other options nonetheless—often reduces the intense need to commit suicide immediately. Just acknowledging that suicide is still an option tomorrow may reduce the immediate pressure and allow the person to look at the wider range of possibilities.

Preventing suicide is both a science and an art. Scientific information about factors that contribute to suicide gives the practitioner—whether a professional or a volunteer—the tools to make critical decisions in interactions with suicidal individuals. However, connecting with people who are feeling so hopeless that they are considering suicide is still a very personal, one-on-one interaction. Sometimes you can do everything right, exactly by the book, and still not make the connection that will cause the person to reconsider. Such losses are devastating to the professional and the volunteer alike (Gitlin, 1999). However, the satisfaction of providing hope to someone who has lost all hope is an indescribable feeling.

Check Yourself 7.8

Suicide

1. How common is suicide?
2. What factors contribute to suicide risk?
3. What strategies are used in suicide prevention?

Ponder this . . . *Imagine that you are Roger, sitting on a tree stump with a gun in your hand contemplating your own suicide. Imagine what you must be feeling to have come to this point. Now use this speculation about the feelings that Roger probably had to formulate a way to talk to him about his situation and try to dissuade him from suicide.*

physician-assisted suicide The taking of one's own life with the assistance of a physician.

● SUMMARY

CONCEPTUALIZING MOODS AND MOOD DISORDERS

- Mood is a feeling of sadness or elation that is often a response to environmental events and can be a motivator of future behavior.
- Mood disorders are defined by excessive mood shifts, which affect the ability of the person to cope with normal everyday responsibilities.

DEPRESSIVE DISORDERS

- Major depression is a severe episodic depression that significantly disrupts functioning.
- Dysthymia is a chronic, almost traitlike depression. People with dysthymia occasionally develop a major depressive episode—a phenomenon known as double depression.
- Seasonal affective disorder, or SAD, is a depressive condition that tends to develop during the winter months and to remit by spring.

EXPLAINING DEPRESSION

- Three major neurotransmitters have been implicated in depression: serotonin, norepinephrine, and dopamine.
- Depressed individuals tend to show distinctive lateralized differences in brain functioning, although the patterns of such differences have proved to be more complicated than once was thought. Overall, the data suggest a right-hemisphere dysfunction.
- Genes clearly affect the risk for major depression.
- Evolutionary theories of depression focus on the impact of depression in helping the organism to give up on a fruitless course of action.
- Beck's cognitive model of depression emphasizes how cognitive style, which can be shaped by early learning, can affect the way in which people interpret events— and thus affect their mood.
- The behavioral model, which is now largely incorporated into the cognitive model, emphasizes how depressive behavior can maintain a depressive state by depriving the person of most sources of reinforcement.
- The learned helplessness model, originally developed from animal models, reflects the fact that exposure to a situation in which the organism cannot cope often results in a period during which the organism appears to give up and stops trying to cope. The reformulation of this model emphasizes how the attributions that a person makes for failures can affect the likelihood of a learned helplessness response.

- The hopelessness model suggests that specific attributional styles, coupled with negative life events, can lead to a specific kind of depression—hopelessness depression.
- The psychodynamic model, drawing on the similarity between grief and depression, emphasizes the role of loss or symbolic loss in the creation of a depressed state.

TREATING DEPRESSION

- Three classes of medications have proved effective in reducing depression: tricyclic antidepressants, MAO inhibitors, and selective serotonin reuptake inhibitors (SSRIs).
- Electroconvulsive therapy is also effective for treating depression and may even be preferred in some cases, such as when suicide risk is high or in the elderly.
- Phototherapy is usually effective in reducing the depression associated with seasonal affective disorder.
- Cognitive therapy seeks to sensitize clients to how their cognitions are shaping their mood and how they can change those cognitions.
- Behavioral therapy encourages clients to avoid the social isolation and restriction of activities that may be contributing to their depression.
- A largely psychodynamic therapy called interpersonal therapy, or IPT, seeks to strengthen those social relationships that provide the client with personal satisfaction.

BIPOLAR DISORDERS

- Bipolar disorder and cyclothymia are characterized by both depressed and manic or hypomanic periods.

EXPLAINING BIPOLAR DISORDERS

- Genes clearly play a strong role in bipolar disorder.
- There is evidence for the involvement of norepinephrine in bipolar disorder, although most scientists believe that other neurotransmitters are involved as well.
- Body dysregulation is clearly present in bipolar disorder, although it is not clear whether this is a cause or an effect of the disorder.
- Life stress appears to increase the risk for early episodes of mania in bipolar disorder, but it seems to have little impact on later episodes.
- The cognitive approach of the hopelessness model leads to an interesting prediction of who would be at risk for hypomania, a prediction that preliminary data support.

TREATING BIPOLAR DISORDERS

- The primary treatment for bipolar disorder for the last 50 years has been lithium, although it has recently been discovered that some antiseizure medications may also regulate the mood swings in bipolar individuals.
- Traditional psychotherapy is ineffective with bipolar disorder, although family therapy aimed at reducing expressed emotion shows some promise.

SUICIDE

- Suicide is surprisingly common, affecting about 1 person of 10,000 in any given year, but there are large variations across cultures.

- Many factors have been found to be associated with suicide risk, including sex, marital status, occupation, age, cultural background, genetic factors, social support, and a person's sense of hopelessness.
- Most major cities have established suicide hotlines to provide 24-hour counseling for those who might be considering suicide.

 ## KEY TERMS

affect   (167)
attribution   (182)
bipolar disorder   (168)
bipolar I disorder   (193)
bipolar II disorder   (193)
circadian rhythms   (176)
cognitive triad   (180)
cyclothymic disorder   (194)
depression   (168)
depressogenic   (170)
double depression   (169)
down regulation   (186)
dysthymic disorder   (169)
early morning awakening   (176)
functional brain asymmetry   (174)
hopelessness model   (183)
hypomania   (192)

interpersonal therapy, or IPT   (192)
learned helplessness model   (181)
major depression   (169)
mania   (168)
mood   (167)
mood disorder   (168)
phototherapy   (189)
physician-assisted suicide   (204)
postpartum depression   (172)
psychological autopsy   (202)
response desynchrony   (174)
seasonal affective disorder, or SAD   (171)
schemas   (180)
suicidal ideation   (200)
suicide   (199)
transcranial magnetic stimulation, or TMS   (190)
unipolar depression   (168)

 ## SUGGESTED READINGS

Jamison, K. R. (1992). *Touched with fire: Manic depressive illness and the artistic temperament.* New York: Free Press. This book has become a classic description of mood disorder and its impact on the lives of real people.

Johnson, S. L., Hayes, A. M., Field, T. M., Schneiderman, N., & McCabe, P. M. (Eds.). (2000). *Stress, coping, and depression.* Mahwah, NJ: Erlbaum. This volume provides an overview of several cutting-edge psychological theories of depression and its treatment.

Klein, D. F., & Wender, P. H. (1993). *Understanding depression: A complete guide to its diagnosis and treatment.* New York: Oxford University Press. Written by two eminent psychiatrists, this book provides a scholarly but readable look at depression and bipolar disorder. It does an especially good job of covering biological theories and treatments.

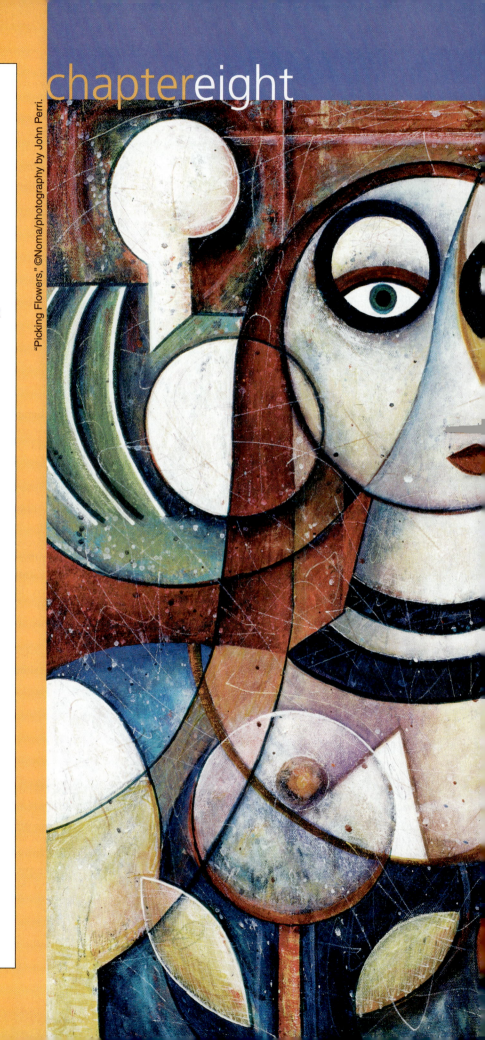

"Picking Flowers," ©Noma/photography by John Perri.

chaptereight

Anxiety Disorders

Unseen Terror

CONNIE

Connie's anxiety began during her freshman year in high school. At first it was a vague sense of doom, but it soon progressed to an overwhelming terror that would grip her without warning. Her heart would pound, her face would drip sweat, and she would literally shake. Her mind would race uncontrollably, and she thought she would go crazy. She saw no reason to be anxious, but that did little to comfort her. When the terror struck, she would drop whatever she was doing and run home to safety. She started cutting classes because she was so nervous. Within a month she stopped attending school altogether, but the attacks continued. She had them at the grocery store, a nearby shopping plaza, and a local fast-food hangout. She could not identify what was causing them, so with each attack she grew more wary of her surroundings. Eventually, she withdrew into her house as her only safe haven. Even at home the terror would occasionally grip her, but there was no place left for her to run.

Paralyzed by Doubt

BRIAN

A walk to the grocery store, just two blocks away, to pick up a few items for supper was an ordeal for Brian. The trip would take between 30 minutes and 2 hours, depending on how often he had to go back to make sure he had not dropped something. If he did not check . . . and recheck . . . and check again, his fear that something important would be lost forever would overwhelm him. In the store, he had to do his shopping in a certain order, and any deviation from that order forced him to put everything back and start the shopping ritual again from the beginning. Because the items had to be rung up in exactly the same order in which he selected them, he would space them carefully so that the checkout person would be fed one item at a time in the "correct" order. He had learned that some of the checkout personnel would oblige him, but some of the high school kids working the afternoon shift would deliberately take items out of order because they knew it upset him. Brian realized that his rituals were unreasonable and illogical, but he could not tolerate the anxiety he experienced if he deviated even a little from the routine.

A Casualty of War

JERRY

Jerry wasn't a war hero; he was just a soldier in an unpopular war. He put in his one year in Vietnam and then went home. The year was hell, and he prayed every day that he would make it home alive. Four of his friends did not, including three who were killed just a week before they were all scheduled to rotate home. In a sense, he did not make it home either. He still has nightmares about the firefights, the blood, the screaming, and the death. Even when he is awake, he experiences frequent flashbacks of his buddies dying. The fear triggered by these nightmares and flashbacks is as intense as it was in the jungles of Vietnam. When the fear gets too bad, Jerry drinks himself into oblivion. His friends have long since deserted him, saying he changed. He is a regular at the VA hospital, where he has been treated for alcohol toxicity, severe depression, and two suicide attempts—one that left him with a shattered leg and a two ruptured disks in his back.

Connie, Brian, and Jerry all suffer from severe anxiety that overwhelms their ability to cope. The patterns of anxiety differ, but the detrimental effects are the same. Things that were once easy for them have become impossible. Connie cannot bring herself to go to class or to go out with her friends. Even the most basic tasks take Brian hours because of his constant need to check details and perform rituals. Jerry cannot go a day without reliving his fear. His constant irritability, which sometimes borders on rage, has prevented him from holding a job or maintaining friendships. The lives of all of these people were devastated by something they could not see or touch—their own anxiety.

THE NATURE OF ANXIETY

Anxiety is an uncomfortable feeling of apprehension. Its intensity can range from the mild discomfort you may feel when you first meet someone to the sheer terror experienced by Connie. Anxiety is as much a part of life as breathing, and it serves a critical function: It motivates behavior. For example, people avoid dangerous situations, drive carefully in bad weather, and prepare for an uncertain future—all because such behavior makes them less anxious. But when anxiety is too intense, functioning deteriorates. If you have ever panicked on an exam or become so anxious when introduced to an attractive person that you sounded like a blithering idiot, you can appreciate this effect. When anxiety consistently interferes with, rather than facilitates, functioning, it is considered a symptom of an **anxiety disorder.**

People often think of anxiety as a single response. However, psychologists recognize that anxiety is composed of three distinct elements: a behavioral response, a physiological reaction, and an internal psychological experience or feeling (Lang, 1985). For example, Connie's anxiety is evident because she avoids situations (the behavioral response); experiences accelerated heart rate, sweating, shaking, and a nervous stomach (the physiological response); and feels afraid (the psychological experience). Connie and Jerry were most aware of their psychological experience. Brian, on the other hand, was aware of both his psychological experience and his behavior, because his behavior caused him considerable embarrassment. Often these three elements occur together, but it is not uncommon to see one or more of them occur without the other(s). For a while, for example, Connie attended school (and thus maintained her

customary behavior) even though she experienced both the physiological arousal and the feeling of fear that characterized her anxiety.

When people get too anxious, their performance declines. They tense up, and their fine motor behavior is disrupted. Their minds may race, and they find themselves unable to think clearly. They become more irritable and less patient and thus are unable to solve problems they could easily solve when less upset. What happens when people are not anxious enough? Imagine you have a project due in two days—a project that will take at least a week to complete successfully—and you are not a bit worried that you haven't begun it yet. An attitude like this could easily cost you your job or that good grade you were expecting. These examples illustrate the extremes of the relationship between anxiety and performance. When people are too anxious or not anxious enough, they perform poorly. A person's best performance occurs at an anxiety level somewhere between these extremes. This concept is expressed in a more general manner by the Yerkes-Dodson Law (Teigen, 1994; Yerkes & Dodson, 1908), which is illustrated in Figure 8.1. According to the **Yerkes-Dodson Law,** as arousal increases, performance increases, but only up to a point. Once the optimal point of arousal is exceeded, performance rapidly deteriorates with additional arousal. Anxiety is one type of arousal. The overwhelming anxiety that Connie experienced prevented her from doing everyday tasks, such as attending school, going to the store, and hanging out with her friends. Brian's anxiety prevented him from trusting his senses when he started to wonder whether he had dropped something. Jerry's anxiety made him so irritable and distracted

anxiety An uncomfortable feeling of apprehension.

anxiety disorder A condition in which anxiety consistently interferes with, rather than facilitates, functioning.

Yerkes-Dodson Law As arousal increases, performance increases, but only up to a point.

neuroses A broad class of nonpsychotic conditions characterized by unwarranted anxiety as well as other clinical features; the term is no longer used in the DSM.

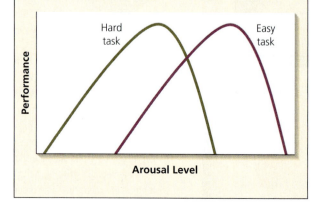

[FIGURE 8.1]
The Yerkes-Dodson Law

The Yerkes-Dodson Law suggests that the relationship between arousal and performance is positive for a while but then becomes negative once one passes an optimal performance level. Furthermore, the anxiety level at which optimal performance is achieved varies depending on the difficulty of the task.

that he could not contend with normal social demands or concentrate on his work.

Figure 8.1 also illustrates another important principle of performance and arousal. The optimal arousal level varies depending on the difficulty of the task. For easy tasks, people not only can tolerate higher arousal but also tend to perform better at higher arousal levels. On difficult tasks, the optimal point of arousal is much lower. For example, the pressure of a baseball tournament often overwhelms Little League baseball players, many of whom are still honing their skills. In contrast, major league players, who have mastered the sport, often give their best performance in the pressure-filled playoffs. The pros perform well despite the high anxiety—and perhaps in part because of it. When overwhelmed by anxiety, Connie was unable to handle the complex social tasks demanded of her in school but could still perform the much simpler task of running home.

The conceptualization of anxiety disorders has changed considerably over the past 40 years. In DSM-II (APA, 1968), most of the current anxiety disorders were classified as neuroses. **Neuroses** represented a broad class of nonpsychotic conditions that were characterized by unwarranted anxiety as well as by other clinical features. Freud argued that the unifying theme for each of these neuroses was the underlying anxiety—anxiety that he believed was often repressed by the person and therefore not always apparent in the disorder. The term *neurosis* was dropped

starting with DSM-III (APA, 1980), and the neurotic disorders were divided among three categories: anxiety disorders (covered in this chapter), somatoform disorders (covered in Chapter 9), and dissociative disorders (covered in Chapter 15). These disorders are now grouped on the basis of similar symptomatology rather than in terms of the previously hypothesized, but never established, underlying association with anxiety.

Evolutionary Impact

No other behavioral element has more evolutionary significance than anxiety. Anxiety motivates survival behavior so effectively that it is hard to imagine how a species without anxiety could survive. It is the human ability to think hypothetically about the future—a great evolutionary triumph—that is the primary source of most human anxiety (Liddell, 1950). People are typically anxious about things that are not in front of them. They worry about what might happen, what danger may lurk around the next corner, or what things they might screw up. They make predictions about the future by evaluating their experiences as well as what they have observed happening to others. The anxiety that people experience today motivates the behavior necessary to make future danger less likely or to prepare them for danger that they cannot avoid. The remarkable success of human beings

Fear and anxiety are normal experiences that protect us from danger. Even this experienced steel worker needs to retain a healthy respect for the danger, because he is just a single gust of wind away from death.

as a species is due in large part to this intellectual capacity and to the motivating effect of anxiety.

Yet the driving force behind evolution is environmental change—the world changes, and species must either adapt or die. With the exception of the environmental catastrophe (apparently the earth's colliding with a huge asteroid) that wiped out the dinosaurs, there has never been a period of more dramatic environmental change. Today, the change is the result of the incredible social and technological advances implemented by human beings. People no longer need to grow their own food. Therefore, they are free to pursue other tasks. People have become specialists, creating technological wonders that were unimaginable just a few generations ago. Today's world is considerably more complicated than that which our ancestors faced just 20 generations ago. Today, people are more likely to live in or near cities, operating machines, computers, and telephones. They meet and deal with strangers many times a day. Surviving in today's world means getting and keeping a good job, adjusting to technological changes that occur at an ever increasing pace, and doing it all while appearing cool and collected. But the 20 generations in which many of these changes occurred are just the blink of an eye in evolutionary terms, so people are dealing with this infinitely more complex world with a body and mind only slightly different from those of the Middle Ages. In fact, humans have probably evolved little in the thousand generations that represent all of recorded history (Nesse & Williams, 1994). The typical level of anxiety that may have been optimal when life was simpler may now be pathological in that it is too high for optimal performance in today's complex world.

The current DSM (APA, 2000) recognizes seven distinct anxiety disorders: generalized anxiety disorder, panic disorder, obsessive-compulsive disorder, specific phobias, social phobias, acute stress disorder, and posttraumatic stress disorder. This chapter will describe each of these disorders, the factors that contribute to them, and the major treatment approaches.

Check Yourself 8.1

The Nature of Anxiety

1. What is anxiety? What are anxiety disorders?
2. What impact does anxiety have on performance?
3. What is the evolutionary significance of anxiety?

Ponder this . . . *Consider a scenario wherein humans evolved without anxiety. What impact would this lack of anxiety have had on human behavior?*

GENERALIZED ANXIETY DISORDER

Generalized anxiety disorder (GAD) is a syndrome characterized by excessive worry. Everyone worries at times—some more than others. Such worries are often productive in that they motivate people to prepare for every eventuality. What is different in people with GAD? One difference is that the worries in GAD do not seem to stop. Often people with GAD worry about the same issues over and over with no apparent resolution. For an individual to qualify for the diagnosis of GAD, the worrying has to involve something other than concern about another psychiatric condition, such as worrying about having panic attacks. Most people with GAD report that the worrying has gone on for years. They report many of the same worries as other people, such as job security, health, relationships, and getting things done on time, but the worries are more constant and intense. The worrying is often accompanied by such symptoms as restlessness, muscle tension, difficulty concentrating, disturbed sleep, irritability, and emotional fatigue (APA, 2000). Symptoms common in other anxiety disorders, such as heart palpitations, are less common in GAD (Brown et al., 1992; Marten et al., 1993). People with GAD find it difficult to control the worrying and it often distracts them so much that it affects their functioning (Borkovec & Inz, 1990). GAD tends to be chronic, although the intensity of the symptoms waxes and wanes, depending on the level of stress. This pattern is clearly evident in the case of David.

Endless Worries

David worried constantly about everything. Would he keep his job? Would the football team win the big game? Did his customers like him? Would his car break down? Would his girlfriend dump him? This last worry seemed justified, because in a recent argument, she had told him that if he didn't stop worrying about every little thing, she would leave to protect her own sanity. In the two weeks since this argument, David had been reasonably successful at keeping his worries to himself, but he doubted that he could continue hiding them indefinitely.

David traced his worrying back to early childhood. An only child, David suffered until the age of 11 from severe asthma attacks, two of which required hospitalization. David worried constantly about asthma attacks. In grade school and high school, he worried so much about his homework that he had difficulty sleeping. And that was nothing compared with his worrying about social interactions. Everything he said and did socially would bother him, sometimes for weeks. He told his therapist about a dozen events from high school that he was still worrying about over 15 years later. His worrying had worsened in the last year, which he attributed to a new job and problems with his girl-

generalized anxiety disorder (GAD) A syndrome characterized by excessive worry.

friend. He also reported two periods when the worrying was noticeably better: during his last two years of college and during a three-year period in his late twenties. He had felt in control of his life during those two periods, although he did not know why.

———————————————————————————————●

David illustrates many of the characteristics of GAD. His worrying has gone on for years, although the intensity has waxed and waned. He worries about many things, and the worries don't stop. He tries to hide his worries, but their intensity affects his behavior to the point that his girlfriend threatens to leave him. Clearly, the worrying not only is making his life miserable but also is negatively affecting the people around him.

Generalized anxiety disorder afflicts about 5% of the population at some point during their lifetimes, and it is about twice as common in women as in men (Blazer et al., 1991a, 1991b; Horwath & Weissman, 2000; Wittchen et al., 1994). Most people who develop GAD symptoms do so early in life, and the symptoms tend to be chronic (Barlow, 2002). Most do not seek treatment, which is surprising given the intensity of the symptoms and their chronicity. Little is known about cultural differences in GAD (Neal & Turner, 1991). Hollifield et al. (1990) found higher rates of GAD in an African village than in the United States, but just as in the United States, females were almost twice as likely as males to have GAD.

GAD is one of the more controversial anxiety disorders. Some psychologists have suggested that GAD is a personality style and therefore should be diagnosed on Axis II (Brown et al., 1994). GAD is often comorbid with other disorders, especially mood and psychotic disorders (Brown & Barlow, 1992; Wittchen et al., 1994). That is, these disorders occur in individuals with GAD more frequently than would be expected to occur by chance. Between 80 and 90% of people with GAD qualify for another psychiatric diagnosis sometime during their lives, which is one of the highest comorbidity rates of all mental disorders. These data have led some to argue that GAD is better conceptualized as either a nonspecific risk factor for psychopathology or a common symptom of many disorders, rather than as a disorder in its own right (Wittchen et al., 1994). However, the lifetime comorbidity data can be misleading. Many people with GAD who also have comorbid conditions have periods when only the GAD symptoms are present. Furthermore, recent data suggest that there are a set of anxiety symptoms, such as restlessness and muscle tension, that differentiate GAD from other psychiatric conditions (Brown et al., 1992; Joormann & Stoeber, 1999; Marten et al., 1993). Nonetheless, GAD remains controversial, in part because it is a difficult disorder to diagnose reliably.

CAUSES OF GAD

It is not entirely clear what causes GAD, although considerable progress has been made in understanding this disorder in the last decade. This section will review evidence for genetic, biological, cognitive, and psychodynamic influences.

Genetic Influences. Genes appear to play a modest role in increasing risk for GAD. Let's look at the genetic data in more detail, because they raise some interesting issues.

Examining the Evidence

In one of the first genetic studies of GAD, Noyes et al. (1987) found that relatives of people with GAD were about 5 times more likely to qualify for a diagnosis of GAD than relatives in a comparison sample. This study is interesting in that these investigators also included a second comparison sample of people with panic disorder and *their* relatives. This strategy enabled them to see whether the genetic factor(s) contributing to GAD also contributed to other anxiety disorders. They found an increased risk for GAD only in families with a member who had GAD, not in families with a member who had panic disorder, which implied some specificity for the genetic risk factor(s) that contribute to GAD. However, more recent research suggests that there is a modest overlap in the genetic influence for GAD and panic disorder (Chantarujikapong et al., 2001; Scherrer et al., 2000). Of course, family studies do not rule out the possibility that environment accounted for the increased risk in these families. Kendler (Kendler, 1996; Kendler et al., 1992a) used a twin study paradigm to evaluate genetic contributions independent of environmental elements. Their data suggested a modest genetic contribution to GAD and further implied that the same genes that contribute to GAD also contribute to depression (Ballenger et al., 2001). More recent twin studies confirm the earlier finding of a modest genetic contribution to GAD (Hettema et al., 2001b; Scherrer et al., 2000).

Biological Influences. Knowing that genes play a role in GAD does little to explain how the disorder develops and how it is maintained. Tom Borkovec and his colleagues (Borkovec et al., 1991; Borkovec & Hu, 1990; Borkovec et al., 1998) have proposed a theory of generalized anxiety that integrates what is known about the physiological functioning and the symptom pattern in people with GAD. Anxiety is both a physiological response and a psychological experience (Lang, 1985). We associate an accelerated heart rate, muscle tension, and sweatiness with anxiety, and those features accompany most anxiety. However, people with GAD show a distinctive pattern of excessive muscle tension, but not the other responses of the sympathetic nervous system that are normally associated with anxiety, such as accelerated heart rate (Borkovec & Hu,

1990; Hoehn-Saric et al., 1989; Thayer et al., 2000). Those who exhibit this pattern of muscle tension are called **autonomic restrictors,** and most people with GAD fall into this category. Despite their constant worrying, people with GAD do not experience the pronounced physiological arousal normally associated with anxiety. Borkovec suggests that these people are engaging in intense cognitive activity (the worrying) but that somehow they avoid the more complete experience of anxiety. He argues that they avoid visualizing the source of the worry and thus never experience the worry with sufficient vividness to trigger autonomic arousal. Consistent with this hypothesis is the fact that EEGs from people with GAD reveal intense activity in the left frontal lobes, but much less activity on the right side of the brain (Borkovec & Hu, 1990). The activation of the left frontal lobes suggests excessive processing of verbal material, whereas the limited activity in the right hemisphere suggests little or no visualization. Borkovec argues that, in effect, people with GAD are so busy worrying (a cognitive activity), that they do not have the resources to actually experience the anxiety. Because they do not experience the anxiety, they never really confront it and therefore are never able to overcome it. As we will see shortly, exposure to anxiety-arousing stimuli is a critical treatment element (Barlow & Craske, 2000; Craske et al., 2002; Craske & Barlow, 2001). Imagining the fearful stimuli is one type of exposure, but the effectiveness of imaginal exposure depends on the ability of clients to visualize the feared object (Lang et al., 1983). People with GAD appear to worry, but they rarely visualize what they are worrying about and therefore fail to desensitize to the objects of their worry. In effect, they worry excessively because the normal mechanism that decreases worrying in others—desensitization due to repeated exposure to the anxiety-producing thoughts—is not operating.

It is hard to imagine that one could worry constantly and yet not be anxious. The fact that we all worry gives us the illusion that we know what people with GAD experience. However, no one can know what other people are experiencing. We have to rely on what they say, how they appear, how they behave, and on the occasional laboratory study of their physiological responding. Their behavior looks and sounds like the experience we know as worrying, so both they and we call it that. But there may be subtle differences between their worrying and the worrying of other people. For example, their worrying may be more mechanical and automatic and thus less likely to trigger the problem-solving strategies that others employ to reduce the root cause of a particular worry.

There is another way of looking at the curious nature of the anxiety experienced in GAD. Remember that genetic studies suggest that GAD and major depression share genetic influences. Also remember from Chapter 7 that virtually everyone with depression shows anxiety and that the anxiety often precedes the onset of depression. Barlow (2002) interpreted this finding as signaling a change in cognitive interpretation from feeling the need to be on guard about a potential danger (anxiety) to questioning one's ability to handle the potential danger (depression). That may well be the case, but it is also possible that a shared biological influence contributes to each disorder. This influence might be responsible for short-circuiting normal anxiety, making it less effective at resolving the problem that brought it on, as Borkovec argues, and thus contributing to its persistence. That same influence might short-circuit mood regulation, thus increasing the risk of depression. This speculative hypothesis illustrates how the same set of data can be interpreted in different ways, thus generating different lines of research. Until more is learned about the link between GAD and major depression, little more than speculation can be offered (Brown, 1997).

Cognitive Influences. Borkovec's theory explains why the worrying in GAD does not go away, but it does not explain where the worries come from in the first place. Why do everyday experiences trigger worrying so much more readily in people with GAD than in other individuals? The answer may lie in the way these people process information. Beck and his colleagues (1985) noted that people with GAD appear to have numerous automatic thoughts, such as "I will never be able to succeed," that seem to fuel the anxiety in GAD. Furthermore, people with GAD often dwell on such themes as injury, death, failure, and loss of control—a tendency that could easily increase anxiety. Of course, it is difficult to know the direction of causation. Do these automatic thoughts and images increase the anxiety? Or are they the result of the excessive anxiety that characterizes GAD? Probably both propositions are true. The thoughts increase anxiety, and this increased anxiety increases the intensity of these anxiety-producing thoughts, thus creating a vicious circle.

Other cognitive factors also affect GAD. For example, people with GAD are much more sensitive to threat cues than people without the disorder (MacLeod & Mathews, 1991; Mathews, 1993). Their attention is drawn to such cues, whereas most people defend against such exposure to threat. This process appears to occur in the first few milliseconds after the stimulus is presented, long before people are aware of this shift in their focus. Such an attentional processing style may appear to provide convincing evidence that the world is dangerous. This tendency is enhanced because people with GAD tend to perceive ambiguous stimuli as threatening more frequently than other individuals do (MacLeod & Cohen, 1993). Again, it is not clear whether these attentional biases are a cause or an effect of GAD. Nevertheless, they do increase anxiety, thus contributing to the chronic nature of this disorder.

autonomic restrictors A pattern of excessive muscle tension, but no other autonomic responses, when anxious.

Psychodynamic Influences. Psychodynamic theory attributes the anxiety in GAD to unconscious conflicts between the id and the ego. That is, the worries in GAD are thought to be a displacement of anxiety over unconscious id impulses onto a variety of other targets. For example, people who are anxious about personally unacceptable sexual desires that they have may instead experience that anxiety as worry about getting their work done correctly. This is a harder theory to test than, say, Borkovec's theory. For example, how could you establish that unconscious id impulses exist, and how would you show that a given worry represents a displacement of those id impulses? In contrast, Borkovec was able to use psychophysiological measures to document differences in the processing of worries (the EEG data) and the emotional response to the worries (the heart rate and muscle tension data). Furthermore, he was able to tie these elements into a model that explained why the worrying would not stop, and, as we will see in the next section, he translated his ideas into an effective treatment strategy. This is why Borkovec's model has largely replaced the classic psychodynamic explanations for most GAD researchers.

TREATING GAD

Several treatments for GAD have been developed, ranging from classic psychoanalysis to medications to several forms of cognitive-behavioral therapy.

Medications. The most common treatment for GAD is anxiolytic medication, such as the benzodiazepines. **Anxiolytic** is another name for "antianxiety." The early benzodiazepines included diazapam (Valium) and chlordiazepoxide (Librium), which were at one time the most widely prescribed drugs in the United States and much of the Western world (Solomon & Hart, 1978). More powerful drugs, known as high-potency benzodiazepines, have largely replaced Valium and Librium. This class of drugs includes alprazolam (Xanax), clonazepam (Klonopin), and lorazepam (Ativan). Although these drugs are widely used for treatment of the anxiety associated with GAD, the research supporting their effectiveness is mixed at best (Barlow, 2002; Davidson, 2001; Klein et al., 1985; Solomon & Hart, 1978).

Benzodiazepines are central nervous system depressants. They provide symptom relief from anxiety, but they also impair thinking and motor performance and, in high doses, can induce sleep (PDR, 2002). They reduce anxiety, but the anxiety usually returns, sometimes with a vengeance, whenever the drugs are discontinued (Rickels et al., 1990). Because anxiety rebounds when the drug is withdrawn, many people feel dependent on the drug, and some describe themselves as addicted. The chronic use of these medications for treating GAD has been decreasing, partly

because they tend to be ineffective when used in this manner (Craske et al., 1992; Davidson, 2001). Instead, doctors now encourage people with GAD to take these drugs only when the anxiety is unusually severe. This strategy minimizes dependence and the negative side effects noted previously and, if anything, seems to make the drugs more effective (Ballenger, 2000).

Psychological Treatments. Several psychological treatments have been developed for GAD, but most lack demonstrated effectiveness. Traditionally, therapists used such insight-oriented treatments as psychoanalytic and client-centered therapies. Psychoanalytic approaches focus on unconscious conflicts between id impulses and the ego, whereas client-centered approaches focus on both conscious and unconscious factors behind the anxiety. The effectiveness of these approaches for GAD was modest, and they were typically long-term and costly. Insight-oriented therapies have gradually been replaced by cognitive and behavioral therapies that teach clients alternative strategies for handling their anxiety.

Given that the primary symptom of GAD is excessive worry, it is not surprising that several cognitive treatments have been developed. The rational-emotive therapy developed by Ellis (Dryden & Ellis, 2001; Ellis, 1977) is one such approach. Ellis argues that people hold irrational beliefs about the world and their place in the world. These beliefs are implicit statements or rules that are typically unstated and therefore unchallenged. An example is "I must find the perfect solution to every problem." These irrational beliefs fuel the worrying in GAD. The person is unable to accept that perfect solutions are rare and usually unnecessary. Instead, the person persists in the fruitless task of trying to find perfect solutions and is therefore unable to break the worry cycle. Ellis trains clients to recognize these often implicit, irrational beliefs and then to challenge them explicitly by making counterstatements, such as "Solutions do not have to be perfect."

Aaron Beck developed another cognitive approach (Beck et al., 1974, 1985; DeRubeis et al., 2001). Beck focused on the impact of automatic thoughts on feelings and behavior. Once automatic thoughts become associated with certain worries, they are triggered whenever those worries occur. The automatic thoughts that contribute to GAD include "What if I am wrong?" and "Nothing seems to work." The effect is like throwing gasoline on a fire: The worries are amplified to an unreasonable level. Challenging these automatic thoughts can reduce their impact and decrease the level of anxiety and worry (Barlow et al., 1992; Sanderson et al., 1994). For example, people who are thinking "Nothing seems to work" might replace this thought with "What I have tried so far has not worked." This rephrasing leads naturally to a more productive search for alternative solutions.

Borkovec and his colleagues have applied what they learned about the nature of the worry in GAD to devise a treatment approach that shows considerable promise

anxiolytic Antianxiety.

(Borkovec & Costello, 1993; Borkovec & Ruscio, 2001). As we noted earlier, their research suggested that people with GAD worry excessively but do not confront the worries by fully experiencing them. They proposed a treatment that encourages such confrontation. Clients are asked to think steadily about the things that worry them until they experience significant anxiety. This approach is usually combined with relaxation to help clients manage the anxiety they trigger with such exposure. This approach not only reduces GAD symptoms (Borkovec & Costello, 1993) but also reduces the symptoms of disorders that are often comorbid with GAD, such as specific phobias and depression (Borkovec et al., 1995). It is not clear why these comorbid conditions also improve. Perhaps clients are generalizing the anxiety reduction skills to other problems, or perhaps the excess anxiety that was part of GAD was fueling these symptoms—and hence the symptoms disappeared once excess anxiety was eliminated.

Craske and her colleagues (Craske, 1999; Craske et al., 1992) have combined many of the elements described above into a comprehensive treatment protocol for GAD. Their approach incorporates the direct exposure advocated by Borkovec, some of the cognitive elements of Beck and Ellis, relaxation techniques, and general anxiety management training. This kind of hybrid treatment is becoming increasingly common as researchers assemble all the available knowledge about effective treatment into a single package.

Check Yourself 8.2

Generalized Anxiety Disorder

1. What is the defining characteristic of generalized anxiety disorder?
2. How common are other psychiatric disorders in individuals with a GAD diagnosis?
3. What is the key component of Borkovec's theory of GAD?
4. What treatments are available for GAD?

Ponder this . . . *Would you expect that a chimpanzee could suffer from something like GAD? What about a dog? a rat? an earthworm? What is the logic behind your speculations?*

PANIC DISORDER AND AGORAPHOBIA

Panic disorder is characterized by recurrent, unexpected attacks of overwhelming fear, coupled with anxiety about having more such attacks. These **panic attacks** may include

[TABLE 8.1] Symptoms of a Panic Attack

Listed below are the symptoms that define a panic attack. At least 4 of these 13 symptoms must be present for the attack to qualify as a panic attack.

1. Palpitations, pounding heart, or accelerated heart rate
2. Sweating
3. Trembling or shaking
4. Sensations of shortness of breath or smothering
5. Feeling of choking
6. Chest pain or discomfort
7. Nausea or abdominal distress
8. Feeling dizzy, unsteady, light-headed, or faint
9. Derealization (feeling of unreality) or depersonalization (being detached from oneself)
10. Fear of losing control or going crazy
11. Fear of dying
12. Paresthesias (numbness or tingling sensations)
13. Chills or hot flashes

SOURCE: *Reprinted with permission from the* Diagnostic and Statistical Manual of Mental Disorders, *4th ed., text revision. Copyright © 2000 American Psychiatric Association.*

any or all of the symptoms listed in Table 8.1. A person must experience at least four of these symptoms for the event to qualify as a panic attack (APA, 2000), and most panic attacks easily meet this criterion.

Most panic attacks occur during the day, but a small number occur during the night. One might expect that these **nocturnal panic attacks** would be triggered by dreams, but that is not the case. Nocturnal panic attacks occur during deep sleep; they almost never occur during REM sleep (Barlow, 2002). Because most deep sleep occurs early in the sleep cycle, most nocturnal panic attacks occur in the first three hours after a person goes to bed. In contrast, most REM sleep occurs later in the sleep cycle, so most nightmares are experienced in the hours just before the person's normal awakening.

Evolutionary Impact

A panic attack is the body's alarm response—that is, it prepares the organism to deal with acute danger. The

panic disorder A disorder characterized by recurrent, unexpected attacks of overwhelming fear, coupled with anxiety about having more such attacks.

panic attack An unexpected attack of overwhelming fear.

nocturnal panic attack A panic attack that occurs during sleep.

agoraphobia The avoidance of certain situations because of a fear of having panic attacks.

term *fight or flight syndrome* is often used to describe panic attacks, although a better term would be *flight or fight syndrome,* because the first instinct is to flee. A panic attack is essentially a fear response, the same kind of response that would occur if one were in a life-or-death situation (Barlow, 2002). It mobilizes the body for rapid flight to escape a life-threatening situation; the organism is literally preparing to run for its life. The muscles tense, creating a tight feeling in the chest and neck that may be experienced as difficulty in breathing or as a choking sensation. This muscle tension may also create a shaky feeling. However, this muscle tension has survival value. It decreases the reaction time and provides the organism, whether an animal or a human being, with a much faster first couple of steps in flight, which could be the difference between escaping and falling victim to a predator. The heart starts to beat faster and harder in anticipation of the strong demand the muscles will make for oxygen if the organism has to flee. The palms and face begin to sweat, turning parts of the body into the functional equivalent of an automobile radiator, prepared to dissipate the heat generated by muscle activity. All of this activity would clearly increase the chances of survival in a life-or-death situation, which is probably why virtually every vertebrate has the response. But when all of this activity occurs for no apparent reason, it can feel as though one is either dying or going crazy—sensations often reported by people who have had panic attacks (Barlow & Craske, 2000; Craske et al., 2002). It is common for people with panic disorder to go to an emergency room at least once,

convinced that they are having a heart attack when what they are actually experiencing is panic (Barlow, 2002). Connie, whom we met in one of the cases that opened the chapter, visited the emergency room twice when her panic attacks were so severe that she thought she was dying.

To appreciate how frightening a panic attack can be, imagine being mugged by someone who puts a gun to your head. The intense, overwhelming fear that you are likely to experience in such a situation is comparable to a full-blown panic attack. Now imagine such fear gripping you for no apparent reason in a variety of situations. Imagine worrying about what you might do if you were overwhelmed by such fear in a public situation. Would you lose control and run away screaming? Would you pass out? Would you say or do something terribly inappropriate? If you can imagine these situations vividly, you will have a good idea what it is like to experience a panic attack and why people go to great lengths to avoid situations in which they might occur.

Panic attacks are only one element of a panic disorder. In addition to the attacks, there is a secondary anxiety—the fear of having more attacks. This secondary anxiety is often the more critical problem. It is the driving force behind the avoidance of certain situations, known as **agoraphobia,** that is so common in panic disorder. This withdrawal reduces the anxiety and thus negatively reinforces the agoraphobia—that is, agoraphobia becomes more likely because it reduces the aversive state of intense anxiety. Some of these aspects of panic disorder are illustrated by the case of John.

Nature has equipped organisms well for survival. The "fight or flight" response provides a nearly instantaneous mobilization of the organism to help it survive this kind of life-or-death situation.

A Delicate Balance Is Lost

Panic was nothing new to John. He had experienced regular panic attacks since early adolescence. With every attack, his heart would race and pound, he would physically shake, he would gasp for breath, and he would desperately want to run away. For 40 years he had dealt with it, although the fear never really left him. The panic attacks were more common in social settings, so he avoided these whenever possible. Nevertheless, he had been married for over 30 years, had raised three children, and had worked for a local manufacturing firm since he left high school. Although a valued employee, he had turned down several promotions because the additional responsibilities would have included attending meetings that would have triggered panic attacks.

John maintained a delicate balance with the help of antianxiety medication, pushing himself hard enough to be able to work, but not so hard that the anxiety would overwhelm him. However, it all came apart one mild November day, when he had one of his worst panic attacks ever while at work. His whole body shook so hard that even his co-workers thought he was dying. His co-workers took him to the nurse's office immediately, where the nurse confirmed a heart rate of over 150 beats a minute. She called an ambulance, fearing that he was having a heart attack. Although it felt like a panic attack to John, he had never experienced one this intense, so he did not hesitate to go to the hospital. After an extensive series of tests over three days, John was cleared to return to work, but within an hour after returning, he had another massive panic attack. He left work immediately, calling the nurse's office from home to explain what had happened. John's anxiety was now so intense that he was afraid to leave his home and was unable to return to work.

The pattern of anxiety that John experiences is very different from GAD. He worries, but he worries almost exclusively about having more panic attacks and losing control. His fear of having more attacks prevents him from leading a normal life. He avoids situations in which he has had attacks before or from which he would be unable to escape if he were to have a panic attack.

There are two types of panic attacks: cued and uncued. *Cued panic attacks* are responses to specific objects or situations, whereas *uncued panic attacks* occur at unpredictable times. People describe uncued panic attacks as coming "out of the blue." Cued panic attacks can occur with many anxiety disorders, whereas uncued panic attacks rarely occur outside of panic disorder (APA, 2000). Their unpredictability makes uncued panic attacks more frightening (Craske et al., 1995).

Between 2 and 3% of the population will qualify for a diagnosis of panic disorder sometime during their lifetimes (APA, 2000; Barlow, 2002; Horwath & Weissman, 2000), although the rates are slightly lower in Mexican Americans (Eaton et al., 1991). Panic disorder is 2 to 3 times more common in women than in men (Katerndahl & Realini,

1993; Eaton & Keyl, 1995) and is found around the world. In some cultures, panic attacks are experienced as magical events, sometimes thought to be the result of witchcraft, but in most Western cultures, the most common experience is a feeling that one is dying or going crazy (APA, 2000). Most cases of panic disorder develop during late adolescence or early adulthood (APA, 2000; Barlow, 2002). Even without treatment, the panic may subside for a while, only to return later (Barlow, 2002). However, panic disorder tends to be rather chronic without treatment (Ehlers, 1995).

There was no panic disorder diagnosis until publication of DSM-III (APA, 1980). Of course, panic disorder existed before its official recognition in the diagnostic manual, but mental health professionals often misinterpreted it. The panic attacks, which are one of the defining characteristics of panic disorder, were referred to as anxiety attacks. Although panic attacks feel like anxiety, they are really a different phenomenon. Panic and anxiety are generated in different regions of the brain and serve different purposes. Panic is the "fight or flight" response that prepares the body for immediate action, whereas anxiety is the sense of apprehension that places the organism on alert and prompts advanced organisms such as humans to plan for potential problems that may occur later.

If the "fight or flight" response of a panic attack is so valuable, why does it feel so terrible? Perhaps the major reason is that a panic attack is a false alarm. There is no danger, so the attack feels alien, as though one's body or mind were out of control. This feeling of being out of control is a critical element in panic disorder. A smoke detector provides a good analogy. Smoke detectors sample the air and respond with a loud alarm if smoke is detected, but this is not a foolproof process. A smoke detector sometimes sounds a false alarm—going off when there is no fire. One way to reduce false alarms is to reduce the sensitivity of the detector, but doing so increases the risk that the unit will fail to detect a real fire. The same is true of panic attacks. The human brain may be infinitely more complex than a smoke detector, but it serves a similar function with respect to danger—taking in information and deciding whether danger is present. Having the body fail to respond to a real danger is a much more serious problem than an occasional, unnecessary panic attack.

Figure 8.2 illustrates the hypothetical situation that the brain faces in assessing the risk of danger. Rarely is real danger completely obvious. Sometimes the evidence is unmistakable; sometimes there is no sign of danger; most often the evidence that danger exists is somewhere between these extremes. Furthermore, the situation is just as complex when there is no danger; at times it is obvious that there is no danger, but often there are things in the environment that suggest danger may be present. The curves in Figure 8.2 illustrate this situation graphically. Each curve represents the level of evidence suggesting danger for situations that either are or are not dangerous. Note that these curves overlap, which is almost always the case in the real

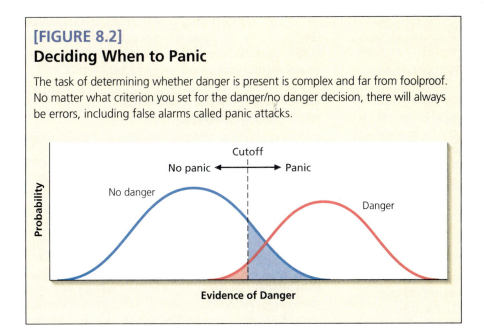

[FIGURE 8.2]

Deciding When to Panic

The task of determining whether danger is present is complex and far from foolproof. No matter what criterion you set for the danger/no danger decision, there will always be errors, including false alarms called panic attacks.

world. In this region of overlap, the organism may react unnecessarily (a false alarm) or may fail to react in a truly dangerous situation (a miss). As long as the curves overlap, there is no criterion for responding that will avoid these errors. If you slide the criterion for responding to the right to avoid false alarms, you increase the risk of misses. As we will see later, the situation is likely to be more complex in people with panic disorder. They typically experience their panic attacks as dangerous, and therefore any sign that a panic attack is possible is interpreted as a danger signal. This process distorts the "No Danger" curve by extending the right tail, thus increasing the overlap and the likelihood of false alarms. Even in people who do not have panic disorder, the situation is dynamic and the criterion is likely to be affected by the situation. If there is reason to believe that danger is probable, the organism is likely to (1) scan more for signs of danger and (2) set the criterion for the "flight or fight" response a bit lower just to be safe. Both of these actions increase the likelihood of a false alarm. We will consider examples of all of these elements when we discuss the causes of panic disorder.

Panic attacks, at least cued panic attacks, are actually rather common. Some studies have suggested that up to a third of young adults in the United States report experiencing a panic attack in any given year (Asmundson & Norton, 1993; Whittal et al., 1994), but few of those people develop panic disorder. Most people who have a panic attack are able to explain it away by saying things like "I should not have had those last two cups of coffee" or "I must be wound up too tight" or "I overreacted." It would be more difficult to explain away an uncued panic attack. Perhaps the strategy of dismissing the panic attack reduces the secondary anxiety—the fear of impending panic attacks—that separates people who develop panic disorder from those who have panic attacks but never develop panic disorder.

Evolutionary Impact

Panic disorder is often accompanied by agoraphobia. Agoraphobia is often thought of as a fear of open spaces, but the literal translation is "fear of the marketplace." Diagnostically, agoraphobia refers to both (1) the anxiety about going into situations or places where panic may occur and where escape may be difficult or embarrassing and (2) the avoidance of those situations or places. It is a natural response to what feels like a life-threatening situation. Some people also experience a fear of open spaces, which on the surface seems puzzling. However, from an evolutionary perspective, either being trapped in a small space *or* being exposed in the open was dangerous for early primates, who had to deal daily with threats from predators (Nesse, 1988).

An individual with agoraphobia may avoid a variety of situations. Crowded places are often avoided because the individual fears losing control in front of so many people. Shopping malls and large grocery stores are particularly problematic, because in addition to there being many people around, escape can often be difficult or embarrassing. It could be a considerable distance to the nearest exit in a shopping mall, and leaving your shopping cart while standing in the checkout line will likely call attention to you. Planes and trains are problematic because they are usually crowded and escape is often impossible. The pilot is unlikely to pull over at 30,000 feet to let off a nervous passenger. For agoraphobic individuals, the fear of flying has nothing to do with dreading a crash. They are more fearful having no escape in the event of a panic attack on the plane (McNally & Louro, 1992). Long bridges and limited-access highways, such as interstate highways, are often avoided because of the possibility of being trapped in traffic with no way to escape. Any situation in which the individual has experienced panic in the past can produce enough fear to trigger agoraphobic avoidance.

Between 30 and 50% of individuals diagnosed with panic disorder in a community sample show significant agoraphobic avoidance, and the figure is even higher in clinical samples (APA, 2000). This may be because the restrictions on everyday life associated with agoraphobia increase the likelihood of seeking treatment in individuals who have panic disorder. Women are much more likely than men to suffer from agoraphobia—and not just because women have higher rates of panic disorder (Barlow, 2002). With severe agoraphobia, in which the person is effectively housebound, women outnumber men nearly 4 to 1. The usual explanation for this finding is that it is more acceptable for women to withdraw from feared situations, whereas men are often expected to challenge the fear. Perhaps because withdrawal is less accepted for males, men with panic disorder are more likely to turn to alcohol abuse, which may serve as a self-medication strategy (McNally, 1996).

Evolutionary Impact

Not all avoidance of fearful objects or situations is agoraphobia. Avoidance of situations that produce intense fear is a natural survival instinct. Fear is a normal response to danger, and danger is something that people should generally avoid if they want to live a long and healthy life. No one would consider it unusual to avoid climbing up the side of tall buildings. Such activity is inherently dangerous, not to mention illegal. Avoiding such behavior is prudent and not at all symptomatic of a disorder. In fact, one could argue that engaging in such activities is more pathological than avoiding them. But what about skydiving? Skydiving is less dangerous than climbing up the sides of tall buildings, and a lot more people do it. Still, most people consider sky diving potentially dangerous (which of course it is) and would choose to avoid it. Again, such avoidance is not agoraphobia. Professionals generally do not consider avoidance a symptom of agoraphobia until relatively safe situations are avoided. Those suffering from agoraphobia do not avoid relatively safe places out of a fear of danger, but rather out of a fear of fear. They fear panic itself and are unsure that they can handle a panic attack in public.

Agoraphobia can become severe and can totally disrupt one's normal life (Taylor & Arnow, 1988). Some individuals start by avoiding a few situations in which they have had panic attacks, such as school, a particular store, or the like. Gradually, however, the avoidance generalizes until they avoid virtually every situation in which panic *might* occur. In some rare cases, people with agoraphobia become completely housebound, unable to leave their homes or immediate neighborhoods, even for medical emergencies (Barlow, 2002). Treatment for such individuals must start with house calls because the person is initially unable to come into the office.

CAUSES OF PANIC DISORDER AND AGORAPHOBIA

Recent research has provided considerable insight into the factors that may increase the risk for panic disorder and agoraphobia. This section covers biological, genetic, and psychological variables that contribute to panic disorder. In addition, we will examine a research strategy—provoking panic in the laboratory—that has been a particularly effective way of studying the biological and psychological factors contributing to panic and the way these factors interact.

Biological Factors. Much of the credit for initiating the modern conceptualization of panic goes to Donald Klein (Klein, 1964; Klein & Fink, 1962), who observed that people with panic disorder responded positively to the antidepressant medication imipramine. In contrast, panic disorder did not respond well to the benzodiazepine medications used to treat GAD. Furthermore, GAD did not respond well to the antidepressant medications that eased panic symptoms. All of these observations led Klein to conclude that panic was somehow different from anxiety. At the time of these discoveries, there was no official diagnostic recognition of panic disorder, there was no recognition that panic was not just intense anxiety, and little was known about the physiological mechanisms of either anxiety or panic.

Recognizing that panic is distinct from anxiety was a major breakthrough in the effort to understand panic disorder. Because the antidepressant drugs that reduced the panic symptoms were known to affect the neurotransmitter norepinephrine, this substance became the focus of considerable research. Drugs that stimulate norepinephrine functioning, such as yohimbine, were found to trigger panic attacks reliably in people with panic disorder and occasionally even in people without the disorder (Barlow, 2002). Furthermore, drugs that inhibit norepinephrine activity, such as clonidine, reduced the symptoms of panic (Uhde et al., 1985). Taken together, these data clearly implicate the neurotransmitter norepinephrine in panic disorder.

Other researchers focused on the **locus coeruleus,** which is in the brain stem, as the probable trigger for panic attacks because (1) its neurons are heavily influenced by norepinephrine and (2) it has direct connections to the limbic system, which regulates many emotional reactions. The locus coeruleus, with its connections to the limbic system, could explain both the panic attacks and the secondary anxiety that is so common in panic disorder (Gorman et al.,

locus coeruleus   An area of the brain stem that may trigger panic attacks.

1989). These key brain regions are illustrated in Figure 8.3. Furthermore, stimulation of the locus coeruleus in monkeys produces a response that appears very similar to a panic attack in humans (Redmond, 1977).

Genetic Factors. Given the evidence for a biological mechanism for panic, one might anticipate that genetic factors play a role. Indeed, the available evidence is consistent with this expectation. Crowe et al. (1983) found that panic disorder was 10 times more likely in families with a member who has panic disorder than in comparison families. There was no increase in the risk for GAD in the families wherein panic disorder occurred, a result consistent with Klein's (1964) contention that GAD and panic disorder are different phenomena. Furthermore, several twin studies of panic disorder suggest a substantial genetic contribution (Hettema et al., 2001a).

Psychological Factors. Given that panic attacks are relatively common (Asmundson & Norton, 1993; Whittal et al., 1994) and that most people who have panic attacks do not develop panic disorder, one might ask what factors predispose people to develop panic disorder. One possibility is that the panic attacks are more intense or different in nature in those who develop panic disorder than in those who are able to dismiss an occasional panic attack. This is an interesting speculation, but not an easy one to test scientifically. Scientists could study the degree of physiological arousal during a panic, but this would not tap the critical psychological experience. People who develop panic disorder may simply be more frightened by the panic without being more physiologically aroused.

A more fruitful area of speculation is the hypothesis that there are personality, or traitlike, variables that make some individuals more prone to panic disorder. Three variables have been hypothesized to predispose people to panic disorder: a tendency to fear panic attacks (Goldstein & Chambless, 1978), a tendency to overinterpret unusual body sensations (Clark, 1986), and a tendency to respond with fear to anxiety symptoms in general (McNally, 1994).

The first predisposition hypothesis focuses on a tendency to fear panic attacks, which is often referred to as "fear of fear." This model suggests that people with panic grow so afraid of experiencing additional panic attacks that they become hypervigilant about their physiological functioning, searching for any clue of an impending panic attack. Any physiological experience that resembles a panic symptom is responded to fearfully—so fearfully, in fact, that the person may actually trigger a panic attack. In this model, the panic disorder is the result of a random panic attack, which is sufficient to set off this hypervigilant response, which in turn sets off additional panic attacks.

David Clark (1986) suggested the second predisposition hypothesis, that people who develop panic disorder

[FIGURE 8.3]
Neurophysiological Mechanisms for Panic and Anxiety

The complex behavior associated with panic disorder results from the actions of several different brain mechanisms. Panic attacks are triggered in the locus coeruleus, the secondary anxiety is generated in the limbic system, and the goal-directed avoidance behavior is mediated by the frontal lobes of the cerebral cortex.

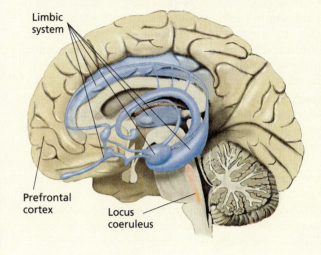

tend to make catastrophic misinterpretations of unexpected or unusual body sensations. For example, a person may notice that his or her heart is racing and assume that this means he or she is having a heart attack. People's hearts race whenever they have a high aerobic demand—that is, a need to supply more oxygen to muscles and organs. A racing heart in such situations is a sign of a healthy cardiovascular system. However, Clark argued that some people misinterpret this normal sensation as a sign of an impending heart attack and that this catastrophic misinterpretation is sufficient to trigger a panic attack. People are rarely aware of their catastrophic misinterpretations; rather, these misinterpretations are automatic thoughts that are typically just outside the person's awareness (Beck et al., 1985). Supporting Clark's hypothesis is the fact that people with panic disorder rarely think about danger when they are challenging their fears. For example, people with an agoraphobic fear of driving do not think about crashing when they drive on the expressway. Instead, they focus mostly on their own physiological sensations and how well they are handling them (Williams et al., 1997).

The third predisposition hypothesis focuses on the tendency to respond fearfully to symptoms of anxiety, which is called **anxiety sensitivity** (McNally, 1992; Reiss & McNally,

anxiety sensitivity   A tendency to respond fearfully to symptoms of anxiety.

1985; Schmidt et al., 1997). McNally and his colleagues hypothesized that anxiety sensitivity was different from the trait anxiety that characterizes GAD, although there is disagreement on this point (Lilienfeld, 1996; McNally, 1996). A high level of anxiety sensitivity may predispose an individual to overreact to a panic attack, interpreting the symptoms as dangerous and thus triggering avoidance responses (Clark, 1988). This may in turn trigger a hypervigilance to physiological sensations associated with panic (Chambless et al., 1984). This hypersensitivity to physiological sensations may cause people to interpret normal physiological events as indicators of an impending panic (Barlow & Craske, 2000; Craske et al., 2002) and may, in the process, trigger a panic attack. There have been recent efforts to understand anxiety sensitivity in terms of broad personality characteristics, some of which are known to have genetic and biological underpinnings (Lilienfeld, 1997). This kind of information may eventually help scientists to understand how genetic factors shape psychological factors, which in turn shape one's predisposition to conditions such as panic disorder.

All of these psychological explanations for panic disorder agree on one point: The reaction to the panic attack is what makes future panic attacks more likely. Whether it is being hypervigilant to body changes, making catastrophic misinterpretations of paniclike feelings, or being inherently sensitive to the sensations of anxiety, the person overreacts, thus increasing anxiety and increasing the likelihood of further panic attacks. Remember that most people who have panic attacks never develop panic disorder. Without the overreaction, panic attacks are just momentary uncomfortable feelings that are quickly forgotten.

Agoraphobia is learned and maintained through reinforcement (Barlow, 2002). The intense fear of a panic attack prompts one to flee, and this retreat decreases the fear. Any behavior that decreases an unpleasant feeling is reinforcing and thus is more likely to be repeated. This process is called escape. In time, however, the mere thought of entering a situation in which such unpleasant feelings as fear are possible will lead to avoidance. Here the process is more complex. With avoidance, the individual is no longer escaping the fearful situation but, rather, is escaping the anxiety about entering that situation. The decision to avoid the risk reduces that anxiety and thus is reinforcing as well. These two learning models are illustrated in Figure 8.4.

Avoidance behavior is particularly problematic because it reduces the opportunities for corrective feedback (Barlow & Craske, 2000; Craske et al., 2002). It is a bit like the story of the man who wore a foul-smelling pendant to ward off vampires. When told that there were no vampires around, he would always respond, "See how well it works!" However, to determine whether his pendant really worked, he would have to be willing not to wear it occasionally and see whether vampires appeared. As long as people with agoraphobia avoid certain situations, they never find out whether they are now able to control their emotions in those situations.

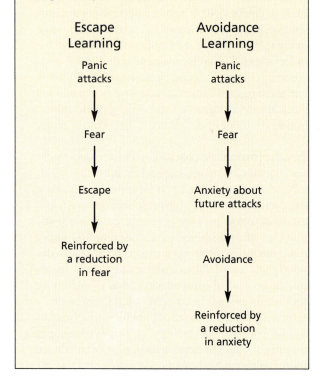

[FIGURE 8.4]

Escape and Avoidance Learning in Panic Disorder

These models of the learning of escape and avoidance in panic suggest that escape is reinforced by a reduction in the fear associated with panic, whereas avoidance is motivated by a reduction in the secondary anxiety about having future panic attacks.

Escape Learning

Panic attacks
↓
Fear
↓
Escape
↓
Reinforced by a reduction in fear

Avoidance Learning

Panic attacks
↓
Fear
↓
Anxiety about future attacks
↓
Avoidance
↓
Reinforced by a reduction in anxiety

Provoking Panic in the Laboratory. One of the most significant developments in panic disorder research was the discovery of chemical substances that trigger panic attacks in panic-prone individuals. People with panic can readily identify some of these substances. For example, they often reduce caffeine intake because it makes them jumpy and more likely to have a panic attack (Barlow, 2002; Barlow & Craske, 2002; Craske et al., 2000). In addition to caffeine, adrenaline (Breggin, 1964; van Zijderveld et al., 1999), yohimbine (Charney et al., 1984; Sallee et al., 2000), sodium lactate (Maddock, 2001; Pitts & McClure, 1967), and carbon dioxide (Barlow, 2002) can also trigger panic attacks in individuals who are panic-prone.

The ability to provoke a panic attack enables researchers to study both the physiology and the psychology of these attacks in the laboratory. Many people who suffer from panic disorder are committed enough to helping in the effort to understand panic that they volunteer to have researchers provoke a panic attack while sophisticated monitoring is performed. Identifying the precise time course of a panic attack, the variability in attacks among individuals and within the same individual, and the relationship between these elements and the experience of the individual all provide insight into the attack and generate ideas about how to cope with or prevent future ones.

The fact that so many different biological procedures successfully provoke panic in the laboratory raises the question of whether there is some common underlying mechanism. It may be that the common underlying mechanism is not biological but psychological. Clark's (1986) cognitive model of panic, in which he suggests that panic attacks are produced by the catastrophic misinterpretations of unexpected or unusual bodily sensations, might provide the underlying mechanism. Clark's model would also explain why such medical conditions as mitral valve prolapse, hypoglycemia, vestibular dysfunction, asthma, and hyperthyroidism are all found more frequently in people with panic disorder than in the general population (McNally, 1994). These conditions, like the procedures used to trigger panic in the laboratory, are all associated with unusual or unpredictable bodily sensations. Ironically, the wealth and diversity of biological triggers may offer some of the best evidence for a psychological mechanism for panic—the catastrophic misinterpretation of these experiences as dangerous.

Reliable methods for triggering panic attacks in the laboratory can also be used to evaluate the effectiveness of treatments. For example, medications that have been shown to block panic in the lab, such as alprazolam, are also effective at blocking panic in the real world (Sanderson et al., 1994). Psychological treatments can be tested in this manner as well. Let's look at one such study.

Examining the Evidence

Sanderson et al. (1989) tested the notion that feeling in control may be a critical component in the treatment of panic. After all, feeling out of control is one the most terrifying aspects of a panic attack. These investigators had people with panic disorder breathe an air mixture that contained 5.5% carbon dioxide, which is normally sufficient to trigger panic in panic-prone individuals. In a clever manipulation, they included a control knob that participants were told would allow them to decrease the carbon dioxide level, but only when the signal light next to the knob was illuminated. The participants were urged to use the knob only if necessary. In truth, the control knob did nothing. Half of the participants had the signal light on during the testing session, giving them an illusion of control over their situation; the other half did not. The illusion of control had a powerful effect. Participants who thought they had control over the CO_2 level experienced significantly fewer and less intense panic attacks during the testing period and less subjective anxiety. Without the

ability to provoke panic in the laboratory, this critically important factor, a sense of being in control, could not have been discovered.

Identifying which substances trigger panic has contributed in many ways to the understanding of panic disorder. For example, each substance provides clues about possible mechanisms for panic attacks in the real world. If a given substance, such as sodium lactate, is known to have a particular effect on the body, such as raising the sodium bicarbonate levels and triggering hyperventilation, scientists can speculate about how these actions could trigger panic. Of course, the body is incredibly complex, and each change in body chemistry leads to dozens of other changes. Narrowing the search to one or two critical actions is risky, because there is always the chance that an overlooked process may initiate a series of events that eventually lead to a panic attack. Years of research have provided considerable insight into the many possible triggers for panic attacks (Barlow, 2002). Of course, showing that panic can be triggered in the lab via a particular procedure does not prove that this is the mechanism that precipitates panic in the real world. Nevertheless, this research has provided insights that have enhanced both biological and psychological treatment.

The history of research and theorizing on the mechanisms underlying panic disorder illustrate how much can be achieved through the sophisticated integration of behavioral and biological information (Barlow, 2002; Gorman et al., 1989). The complexity of panic disorder is gradually being unraveled through systematic, theory-driven research.

TREATING PANIC DISORDER AND AGORAPHOBIA

Two approaches—medications and cognitive-behavioral therapy—have shown promise in the treatment of panic disorder.

Medications. Several categories of drugs have demonstrated modest effectiveness for the treatment of panic disorder. Donald Klein's early research with imipramine, one of the early antidepressant medications, demonstrated that panic could be controlled with medications not normally effective for anxiety (Klein, 1964; Klein & Fink, 1962). It is interesting that imipramine seems to block the action of sodium lactate, a substance that will normally trigger a panic attack in panic-prone people (Aronson, 1987). The newer antidepressant medications—the SSRIs, such as Prozac and Paxil—are also effective in reducing the frequency of panic attacks (Coplan et al., 1997; Otto et al., 2001). The SSRIs have fewer side effects than imipramine. A third class of antidepressant drugs—the MAO inhibitors—is also occasionally used for the treatment of panic (Silberman, 1999). Although effective, these are not usually the treatment of choice because of the severely restrictive diet one must observe when taking them.

Even though the so-called antidepressant medications are effective in reducing panic, antianxiety drugs are still commonly used for treating panic disorder, especially the newer high-potency benzodiazepines, such as alprazolam (Xanax) and clonazepam (Klonopin). These medications reduce the anxiety associated with panic disorder while reducing the frequency of panic attacks and agoraphobic avoidance. In one study, half of the people taking alprazolam were panic-free at the end of 8 weeks (Ballenger et al., 1988). However, high-potency benzodiazepines have a serious drawback. They are effective only while the person is taking them, and the anxiety and panic tend to return when these medications are discontinued. In fact, if these drugs are discontinued too quickly, the anxiety and panic can be worse than before treatment (Fyer et al., 1987; Noyes et al., 1991; Rickels et al., 1990). The shorter the half-life of a drug, the more rapidly it leaves the body when the drug is discontinued. When a person discontinues alprazolam, which has a short half-life, the therapeutic effect is lost

Panic attacks can happen to anyone, including fictional mob boss Tony Soprano.

almost immediately. In fact, many people who take alprazolam know when it is time to take their next pill because the therapeutic effect has worn off by the time that the next pill is scheduled. Medications with a longer half-life, such as clonazepam, leave the body more slowly, so withdrawal from the medication is less abrupt. To counteract the problem of withdrawal effects, gradual withdrawal from drugs such as alprazolam is recommended (Fyer et al., 1987).

The current standards for drug treatment of panic encourage the use of the SSRIs or the MAO inhibitors as the primary treatment option (Papp, 2000). Unlike benzodiazepines, these drugs have little potential for abuse and rarely produce an anxiety rebound when discontinued. The benzodiazepines may be used for immediate symptom relief in those individuals who are experiencing enormous anxiety because of uncontrolled panic attacks. However, they are generally used for only a few weeks until other medications, such as the SSRIs, start to take effect. The benzodiazepines may also be used in those rare cases when a person is unresponsive to other medication options.

Cognitive-Behavioral Therapy. The most effective psychological treatment for panic disorder and agoraphobia is a cognitive-behavioral approach that relies on several distinct elements. The first element involves teaching the person about panic, emphasizing that although panic is uncomfortable, it is not dangerous (Clark, 1986, 1988). Because many people experience their panic attacks as dangerous, convinced that they are dying or going insane, this message of the benign nature of panic is critical. Second, clients are trained to use such anxiety reduction techniques as diaphragmatic breathing and progressive muscle relaxation (Barlow & Craske, 2000; Craske et al., 2002). **Diaphragmatic breathing** involves taking exceptionally deep breaths; this increases the level of oxygen in the blood, which in turn reduces many of the physiological symptoms of anxiety and panic (Clark et al., 1985; McNally, 1994). **Progressive muscle relaxation** is a technique for relaxing the muscles of the body one muscle group at a time, which makes the client feel less anxious (Bernstein et al., 2000). A third element involves such cognitive techniques as distraction, labeling the anxiety and panic as safe, and reevaluating the likelihood that the anxiety will drive the person to do something embarrassing (Barlow, 1991; Beck, 1988; Clark, 1988; Taylor, 2000). All of these techniques have the effect of reducing the tendency of the anxiety to spiral out of control (Barlow & Craske, 2000; Craske et al., 2002).

diaphragmatic breathing Taking exceptionally deep breaths to increase the level of oxygen in the blood and reduce many of the physiological symptoms of anxiety and panic.

progressive muscle relaxation A technique for relaxing the muscles of the body one muscle group at a time, which makes the individual feel less anxious.

The therapist then moves on to the fourth element, directing the client through a series of gradual-exposure exercises. The client is encouraged to approach situations that have caused anxiety in the past—situations that the client has been avoiding. These exposure exercises teach clients to tolerate their anxiety, to manage it more effectively, and eventually to master the anxiety (Barlow & Craske, 2000; Craske et al., 2002). Exposure seems to be critical in this process. The gradual exposure to such previously frightening situations as crowded stores desensitizes the client to the cues that trigger the anxiety.

A common phenomenon in agoraphobia is the "safe person." People with severe agoraphobia may be able to go out if someone they trust—their safe person—accompanies them. Although this is perhaps an improvement over not going out at all, it distorts and strains normal relationships. The safe person can be a useful adjunct in behavioral therapy, providing a bridge to new challenges for the client (Carter et al., 1995), but successful treatment of agoraphobia requires that clients eventually confront their fears by themselves.

Some programs also desensitize clients to internal cues, primarily physiological cues (Barlow & Craske, 2000; Craske et al., 2002). As we noted earlier, people with panic disorder often become acutely sensitive to their own physiological reactions (Street et al., 1989). It is as though they are constantly searching for any sign that their panic is about to return. Such perfectly normal sensations as an irregular heartbeat, sweating, breathlessness, and dizziness from physical exertion create anxiety and can trigger panic. Having clients deliberately and repeatedly create these sensations gradually desensitizes them to the point where these sensations no longer trigger panic and anxiety (Craske et al., 2002). For example, running in place for a brief period is sufficient to produce breathlessness in most people. Such breathlessness may lead some people with panic disorder to become fearful and may even trigger panic attacks. However, with repeated exposure, usually orchestrated gradually to avoid triggering actual panic attacks, the person learns to accept those breathless feelings as normal and safe.

Although effective problem-focused treatment for panic disorder is available, the therapist must still recognize that each client is an individual and that factors other than the panic may require therapeutic attention (Craske et al., 2002). Some clients, for example, may experience significant depression or other disorders. These comorbid disorders may increase suicidal ideation, as discussed in the nearby Modern Myths box. Other clients may not have the kind of supportive environment that facilitates gradual exposure. Still other clients may have significant disincentives for getting better, such as having to return to a job they hate. Skilled clinicians can address all of these issues

MODERN Myths

Only Depressed Individuals Commit Suicide

Most people associate suicide with depression, and certainly suicide is a serious risk in depressed individuals. However, suicide is common in other individuals as well, including people with panic disorder. In an epidemiological study of over 18,000 adults drawn from five U.S. communities, the suicide risk for people with panic disorder was nearly 20%—2.5 times higher than for people with psychiatric disorders in general and 18 times higher than for people with no psychiatric disorder (Weissman et al., 1989). Although striking, these figures are difficult to interpret because people with panic disorder often qualify for other diagnoses, including depression. The helpless, out-of-control feeling associated with panic often produces depression. Because the risk of suicide in depression is high, it may be that the secondary depression in panic disorder accounts for elevated risk of suicide. However, Johnson et al. (1990) found that in 7% of uncomplicated panic cases—cases with no other diagnoses—the individual attempted suicide. In comparison, the suicide rate for depressed individuals is about 8%. However, the data on this issue have been inconsistent (McNally, 1994).

Friedman et al. (1992) found that the increased risk for suicide in people with panic disorder is due largely to comorbidity with borderline personality disorder. Frequent emotional swings, self-destructive behavior, and a high risk for suicide attempts characterize borderline personality disorder, which will be discussed in more detail in Chapter 12. Friedman et al. found that in people with panic disorder, 25% of those who also had borderline personality disorder and 2% of those without borderline personality disorder had attempted suicide. Although the story is clearly complicated, the moral is clear. Because suicide is common in people with panic disorder, a thorough evaluation, including identification of other psychiatric conditions, is critical in any treatment program.

within the context of using proven treatment techniques (Barlow, 2001; McFall, 2000).

Check Yourself 8.3

Panic Disorder and Agoraphobia

1. Why is a panic attack referred to as the body's "fight or flight" response?

2. What is the distinction between cued and uncued panic attacks?

3. What is the most serious secondary problem associated with panic disorder?

4. What three hypotheses have been proposed to explain the fact that some people seem to be predisposed to develop panic disorder?

5. What treatments have proved effective in reducing the symptoms of panic disorder?

Ponder this . . . *Provoking panic in the laboratory, where it can be carefully studied, has contributed significantly to the understanding of panic disorder. However, as is true of many laboratory studies, the experience in the lab may be fundamentally different from the "same" experience in the real world. How would laboratory-provoked panic differ from naturally occurring panic? How might these differences threaten the validity of conclusions drawn from studies in the lab?*

OBSESSIVE-COMPULSIVE DISORDER

Obsessive-compulsive disorder (**OCD**) is characterized by strong, unwanted thoughts that create significant anxiety. These thoughts and the anxiety they produce often drive repetitive behavior that is excessive, is utterly unnecessary, and sometimes seems foolish to the person. For example, a person might think that his or her action in closing the

---

obsessive-compulsive disorder (OCD) A disorder characterized by strong, unwanted thoughts that create significant anxiety and often drive repetitive behavior that is excessive, is unnecessary, and sometimes seems foolish to the person.

obsessions Unwanted thoughts that an individual cannot control.

compulsions The behaviors that an individual with obsessive-compulsive disorder feels compelled to perform.

rituals Another term used for compulsions, because the behaviors involved must be performed repeatedly and (usually) in a very specific manner.

---

door was "not right" and that family members would get sick because of it. In response, the person opens and closes the door several more times until it feels "right." In this case, the feeling of "right" and "not right" is vague and personal, and the individual is rarely able to say how the door has to be closed to feel "right."

The unwanted thoughts that the individual cannot control are called **obsessions.** The behaviors that the individual feels compelled to perform are called **compulsions.** The compulsions are often described as **rituals** because they must be performed repeatedly and usually in a very specific manner. Brian—whom we met in one of the cases that opened the chapter—illustrates how disruptive to life such obsessions and compulsions can be. The obsessions seem to create anxiety, and the compulsions seem to reduce the anxiety, at least temporarily. But the obsessive thoughts and the accompanying anxiety quickly return, and then the compulsive behavior must be repeated. The compulsive behavior often becomes so automatic that there is little indication of anxiety in the person with OCD, which may make one wonder why OCD is classified as an anxiety disorder. However, if anything prevents the person from performing the compulsive rituals, the anxiety skyrockets. Brian's reaction when the high school students rang up his groceries out of the order he had set up bordered on panic. Although his reaction embarrassed him terribly, Brian simply could not control its intensity.

Until quite recently, the base rate of OCD was dramatically underestimated, even by professionals. Psychiatric textbooks from 40 years ago talked about OCD as a rare disorder almost never seen in traditional practice (Horwath & Weissman, 2000). Even 20 years ago, professionals believed that OCD was rare (APA, 1980). More recent data suggest that 2 to 3% of the population suffer from OCD at some point during their lives, and these rates are similar across many cultures (APA, 2000; Horwath & Weissman, 2000; Stein et al., 1997b). Furthermore, OCD was formerly considered rare in children. Once again, recent data paint a different picture, suggesting that it is about as common in children as is adults (Piacentini & Bergman, 2000). Did OCD suddenly increase in frequency, or were original estimates of OCD inaccurate? It appears that original estimates were inaccurate because many people hid their symptoms (Nemiah & Uhde, 1989). And because many people with OCD are able to function well in society in spite of their symptoms, most did not seek professional treatment. Now that OCD is receiving more coverage in the popular press (see, for example, Fischman, 2000, *U. S. News and World Report;* Dowling, 2001, *People;* Rosen, 1997, *Ladies' Home Journal;* and Bridge, 1997, *Mademoiselle*), much of it sympathetic toward the affected person, it is perhaps becoming more acceptable to acknowledge experiencing symptoms of OCD.

OCD is about as common in adult men as in adult women, although childhood-onset OCD may be more common in males (APA, 2000; Piacentini & Bergman,

2000). Curiously, only half of adults with OCD marry (Nemiah & Uhde, 1989), a figure that is well below baseline. It may be that the symptoms of OCD interfere with social relationships, or it may be that the tendency of individuals with OCD to be secretive about their symptoms undermines the trust building so critical in a relationship.

Any thought could be obsessive and any behavior could be compulsive, but certain thoughts and behaviors are more common than others in OCD. For example, a person who obsesses about contamination may wash repeatedly, sometimes 50 or more times in a single day. Such people are referred to as "washers." OCD "checkers" fear that something will happen, such as a break-in, if they forget to do something, such as checking the locks. The fears and reactions of washers and checkers are understandable, but washing until your skin literally falls off or taking 90 minutes to be sure the house is locked securely before leaving for work each morning is clearly unreasonable and excessive. Interestingly, females are more likely to show washing compulsions, males to show checking compulsions. Other compulsions are less understandable. For example, counting rituals may drive a person always to do things in pairs or triplets, always to select the third choice and never the first or second, or to count to a specific number each time an obsessive thought occurs. These rituals seem silly to other people, and people with OCD are usually well aware of how silly the rituals are. Nevertheless, they find it nearly impossible to stop performing the rituals, although they are often able to hide them. They suffer in silence, always worried that someone will uncover their "secret." The compulsions shown by people with OCD may vary over the course of the illness; an individual may be primarily a checker at one point, may be a washer at another point, and may engage in other compulsions, such as counting, at still another point (Steketee, 1999; Steketee & White, 1990). Many of these symptoms are illustrated in the case of Laura.

Was She Right?

LAURA

Laura's obsessions started in early adulthood. They were mild at first, but by the age of 30 they seemed to rule her life. She knew it was silly, but she obsessed about "catching cancer." A college-educated social worker, who ironically worked for a mental health agency, she knew that cancer was not contagious. Nevertheless, she never opened the windows on the south side of her house because the neighbor on that side had been treated for cancer. She avoided people with cancer, and if she could not avoid them, she washed thoroughly after spending time with them. Laura had other rituals as well. She checked the doors and windows at home as often as ten times an hour to make sure they were locked. She had several magical rituals involving numbers. For example, at the store, she had to choose the second item on the shelf—never the first or the third. If there was only a single item left, the store shelf might as well have been empty, because she would

not buy it. Curiously, when she shopped with her niece, she could allow her niece to select any item. Of course this made no sense, and she knew it. After years of practice, she had learned to perform each of these compulsions in a manner that hid them from her co-workers and most of her friends. But sometimes life plays cruel jokes. Two years after successful behavioral treatment for her OCD, Laura was diagnosed with cancer. Detected early, the cancer was treated successfully, but the OCD symptoms returned with a vengeance. Shortly after surgery and chemotherapy, she reentered behavior therapy and in a matter of weeks was able to bring the compulsions back under control.

Although both obsessions and compulsions are present in most individuals with OCD, some people exhibit just obsessions or just compulsions (Steketee, 1993, 1999). Sometimes the compulsions are difficult to spot because the behavior is not visible. For example, people may have a compulsion to repeat a phrase silently three times whenever they think a particular thought. Even though these actions are not observable, they are still behavior—that is, an activity designed to reduce anxiety—and they are clearly compulsions.

OCD can be harder on the affected person than some psychotic disorders. People with psychotic disorders often do not realize that their thinking and actions are bizarre. Psychotic symptoms are usually **ego syntonic,** which means that the behavior feels normal to the person. People with OCD are usually well aware of the unreasonableness of their feelings and actions. Their symptoms are **ego dystonic,** which means that the behavior feels alien and abnormal to them. Therefore, people with OCD often hide their symptoms, sometimes even from their closest friends and family.

Finally, there is controversy about whether body dysmorphic disorder, a condition categorized under somatoform disorders, is actually a subtype of obsessive-compulsive disorder (Guggenheim, 2000; Phillips, 1996; Simeon et al., 1995). Body dysmorphic disorder is characterized by unrealistic and obsessive preoccupation with one's physical appearance. This disorder and the evidence that it may be a subtype of OCD will be discussed in Chapter 9.

CAUSES OF OCD

Three broad classes of hypotheses about the cause(s) of OCD have been offered: psychodynamic, biological, and cognitive/behavioral. Each is covered in this section.

Psychodynamic Factors. Early conceptualizations of obsessive-compulsive disorder were almost exclusively psychodynamic (Rado, 1959). Freud (1917/1963) believed

ego syntonic   Behavior that feels normal to the person performing it.

ego dystonic   Behavior that feels alien and abnormal to the person performing it.

that OCD represented a retreat to the anal stage of development because of oedipal conflicts during the phallic stage (Gabbard, 2000). Individuals who remained fixated in the anal stage would attempt to control their anxiety with defense mechanisms characteristic of that stage. Freud argued that some obsessive-compulsive individuals used reaction formation to transform unacceptable thoughts and feelings into safer thoughts. For example, parents who harbor aggressive thoughts about their children might become obsessively protective, sometimes to the point of smothering their children. Other people with OCD might use the defense mechanism of displacement, substituting one thought or behavior for another that is too anxiety-producing. For example, an aggressive thought might be converted into a focus on counting things or checking locks. The occasional magical elements and beliefs found in OCD were considered evidence of regression to earlier levels of development. More recent psychodynamic approaches focus more on the sense of helplessness experienced by those with OCD (Horney, 1937; Salzman, 1968). Unfortunately, these conceptualizations did not lead to effective and affordable treatments and so have been replaced by biological and behavioral explanations for the disorder (Steketee, 1993; Welkowitz, 2000).

Biological Factors. Genes clearly play a role in OCD. The rates of OCD in the family members of people with OCD are 5 to 10 times higher than in the general population (Pauls et al., 1995; Steketee & White, 1990), and the rates in identical twins of people with OCD are more than 20 times higher than in the general population (Rasmussen & Tsuang, 1986). Furthermore, OCD is often found in people who have Tourette's syndrome, a disorder that is known to have a genetic component (Pauls et al., 1995). As you will see shortly, the relationship of OCD and Tourette's syndrome provides valuable clues about the biological factors that contribute to OCD.

Several lines of research suggest that neurological mechanisms play a part in OCD. The nearby Advances box describes some of the research methods that have contributed to this understanding. People with OCD show dysregulation in several brain regions, including the orbitofrontal cortex, the caudate nuclei of the basal ganglia, and the anterior cingulate. These brain regions, which are illustrated in Figure 8.5, form a critical circuit that filters impulses from the frontal cortex and determines which of these impulses will be passed on to the thalamus to be translated into action. It is hypothesized that the failure to filter repetitive impulses properly results in the obsessive

---

[FIGURE 8.5]

Neurophysiological Mechanisms for Obsessive-Compulsive Disorder

The orbital frontal cortex and basil ganglia are the brain structures most often implicated in OCD. Increased metabolic activity has been found in both of these brain regions in people with OCD. In addition, the caudate nucleus may be smaller in people with OCD.

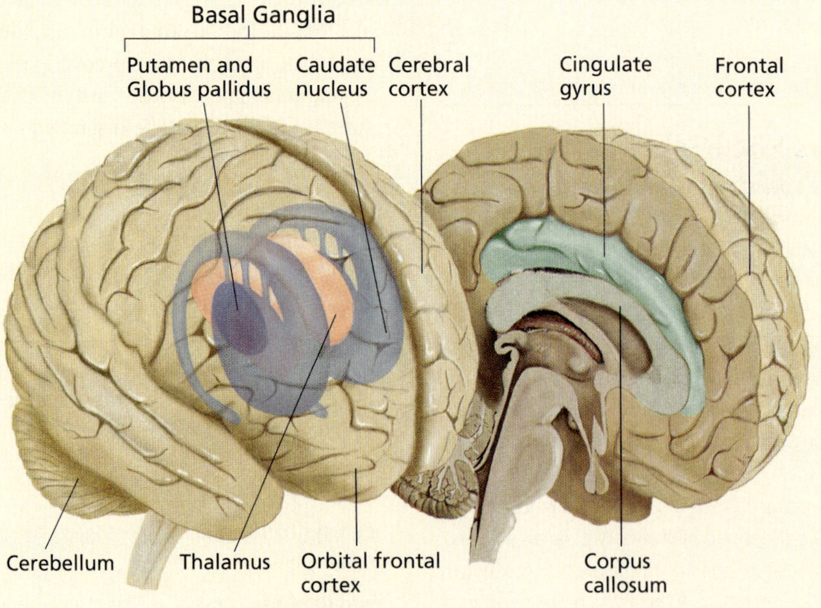

ADVANCES

A window on the brains of people with OCD

Scientists have come a long way in expanding their understanding of brain mechanisms for many types of psychopathology, including OCD. This progress has been fueled by two factors: (1) an increasingly sophisticated understanding of how the brain works in general and (2) the ability to look into a functioning brain to see both structural detail and, more recently, operational detail. The Advances box in Chapter 2 introduced the procedures now available to scientists for imaging both the structure and the functioning of the brain. Here we will see how these procedures have been used to study psychopathology, especially OCD.

The current understanding of brain functioning is based on over 100 years of studying relationships between brain and behavior. It is this understanding, not just the new imaging techniques, that has fueled the recent advances. However, the new imaging techniques have provided tools never before available. The high-quality, detailed images offered by CAT scans and MRIs have led to an explosive growth in the understanding of the role of specific brain mechanisms in complex behavior. These techniques have contributed to the understanding of psychopathology, but not so much as one might expect because structural abnormalities are

rare in psychopathology. There are exceptions, however. For example, Robinson et al. (1995) found that the caudate nucleus was significantly smaller in people with OCD than in those with no psychiatric disorder, although there was no difference in the size of the prefrontal cortex. These brain regions had been implicated previously in OCD.

The advent of the PET scan provided the first real window on the brain of individuals with most forms of psychopathology. These techniques enable researchers to detect abnormal brain functioning. For example, Rauch et al. (2001) used PET scans to show abnormal functioning in the right caudate nucleus, the left anterior cingulate cortex, and both the right and the left orbitofrontal cortex during obsessions in people with OCD. Other research showed that the abnormal functioning in these regions decreased after successful treatment (Baxter et al., 1992; Schwartz et al., 1996). Rauch et al. (2001) found that activation in a particular region of the cingulate cortex was predictive of who would benefit from a cingulotomy.

Even newer technology promises to increase the understanding of OCD and many other forms of psychopathology. The functional MRI (fMRI) is able to produce images of brain activity with greater time resolution than does the PET scan. That is, the

fMRI can identify brain activity that occurs for brief periods of time, whereas the PET scan can identify only activity that continues for several minutes. Adler et al. (2000), using fMRIs, found activation in the orbitofrontal, superior frontal, and dorsolateral prefrontal cortex; in the anterior, medial, and lateral temporal cortex; and in the right anterior cingulate during obsessions, relative to periods when the individual was not obsessing. This newest technology will eventually allow scientists to watch a complex behavior, such as an OCD obsession, develop as one brain region after another is activated.

Brain imaging has contributed significantly to the study of psychopathology. However, the effectiveness of these new tools depends on how well scientific theories and past research focus the attention of brain researchers. The brain is an incredibly complex organ. Trying to find specific pathologies in the brain associated with a particular psychopathology is like looking for a needle in the haystack. The needle is much easier to find if you know about where to look in the haystack. By understanding how the normal brain works, scientists can make educated guesses about what parts are likely to be dysfunctional in a given disorder.

thoughts and compulsive behaviors of OCD. PET studies (Baxter et al., 1987) suggest an overactivation of the orbitofrontal cortex and the basal ganglia in people with OCD, compared to those without the disorder. Abnormalities in the anterior cingulate were found as well (Insel, 1992). Successful drug treatment decreases the overactivation in these regions (Swedo et al., 1992), and provoking symptoms in people with OCD increases activation of these regions (Rauch et al., 1994). Consistent with the findings of excessive activation in the frontal cortex are deficits in cog-

nitive functioning that are normally associated with frontal cortex dysfunction (Cox et al., 1989; Head et al., 1989), although some studies have failed to find these deficits (Insel et al., 1983).

Another line of evidence implicating the basal ganglia is the fact that OCD is often associated with other disorders that are characterized by a dysfunction in the basal ganglia. For example, genetic vulnerability to OCD appears to be greater in relatives of individuals with Tourette's syndrome (Comings & Comings, 1987), which is known to involve the basal ganglia (Rapoport & Wise, 1988). People with **Tourette's syndrome** experience uncontrolled tics and other movements and may uncontrollably blurt out obscenities and other embarrassing things. Tourette's syndrome is diagnosed more frequently in families that have one or more individuals with OCD, and OCD and Tourette's are comorbid more frequently than one would expect by chance. OCD is also often comorbid with two other medical disorders associated with basal ganglia dysfunction: Sydenham's chorea (Swedo et al., 1989) and encephalitis lethargica (Schilder, 1938). Sydenham's chorea, like Tourette's syndrome, is characterized by motor tics apparently related to basal ganglia dysfunction. OCD and OCD-like symptoms are found frequently in people with Sydenham's chorea, whereas people with tic disorders that are not associated with basal ganglia dysfunction, such as those triggered by rheumatic fever, do not show this increased risk for OCD. All of these data suggest the importance of the basal ganglia and the orbital frontal cortex in OCD, although the exact mechanism by which such dysfunctions may lead to OCD symptoms is still a matter of speculation.

Indirect evidence suggests that the neurotransmitter serotonin plays a role in OCD, although the exact nature of that role is unclear. The primary evidence comes from the effectiveness of SSRI drugs, which are known to increase the level of available serotonin in the synapse by blocking its reuptake (Hoehn-Saric et al., 1991; Perse et al., 1987; Stanley & Turner, 1995; Tollefson et al., 1994). However, the data on the serotonin hypothesis are not entirely consistent. For example, Zohar et al. (1987) found that giving a serotonin agonist—a drug that increases the availability of serotonin—produced a short-term increase in OCD symptoms in people with OCD. Although this may seem to contradict the drug treatment findings that increasing serotonin decreased symptoms, there may be an explanation. The drugs that reduce OCD symptoms do not have an immediate impact on symptoms. Instead, they may take several months to work. This time course suggests that they are having their impact by decreasing the sensitivity of neurons to serotonin—a process called down regulation, which you learned about in Chapter 7. In other words, it may be excessive sensitivity to serotonin, rather than a deficit in the amount of serotonin, that characterizes OCD.

Cognitive and Behavioral Factors. Several psychological explanations for OCD symptoms have been offered. The cognitive perspective examines the thought processes of people with OCD and how these processes differ from those of people who don't have OCD. People with OCD often engage in black-and-white thinking (Steketee & White, 1990), seeing things in extremes, especially when there is potential risk. People with contamination fears, for example, appear to want an iron-clad guarantee that there is absolutely no risk of disease if they do not engage in their cleaning rituals. Of course, nothing in life is that clear-cut.

The reassurance that is acceptable to most people who do not have OCD—that the risk of disease is low—is insufficient to relieve the anxiety of people with OCD.

Many people with OCD exhibit magical thinking, believing that their thoughts or actions can lead to specific consequences (Jenike et al., 1986; Riggs & Foa, 1993). For example, one person believed that a loved one would die if he did not repeat a specific phrase whenever he turned on a light. Most people with OCD realize that such magical beliefs are irrational. However, some individuals with OCD believe that their obsessive thoughts, even grossly unreasonable thoughts like the one just described, are rational and reasonable (Kozak & Foa, 1994). What is striking is that even when magical beliefs are recognized as irrational, the person with OCD cannot dismiss them. The earlier case study of Laura illustrates this point. She was well aware that it made no sense that only the second object on the shelf was safe, but she could not use this reasoning to dismiss her obsessive thoughts or abandon her compulsive behavior of selecting only the second item.

Other evidence indicates that basic cognitive functions may be disrupted in OCD and that this disruption may account for some of the symptoms. For example, Kenneth Sher and his colleagues have found memory deficits (Sher et al., 1989) in compulsive checkers and in nonclinical checkers (college students who scored high on an OCD index; Sher et al., 1983, 1984). One might expect such deficits, because people with OCD often report being unsure that they checked everything. Sher et al. (1989) also found that OCD checkers reported less vivid imagery—that is, they could not clearly visualize what they had previously checked. This may account for their poor memory performance and their need to check again, but other explanations are possible. For example, excessive anxiety reduces performance on many tasks, including memory tasks. In addition, although the memory deficits may explain checking behavior, they do not explain other symptoms of OCD, such as washing compulsions. Furthermore, there are millions of people with memory deficits that result from brain damage or old age, yet few show OCD. Therefore, it seems unlikely that memory deficits alone account for OCD.

Behavioral theories have emphasized Mowrer's (1947) classic **two-process theory of avoidance learning,** which proposes that the anxiety that accompanies obsessive thoughts is initially the result of associations between the

....

Tourette's syndrome A disorder characterized by uncontrolled tics and other movements that may include blurting out obscenities and other embarrassing things.

two-process theory of avoidance learning Mowrer's theory that the anxiety in OCD is generated by the obsession due to its association with fearful stimuli and the compulsions are negatively reinforced by a reduction in anxiety.

obsessive thought and an already anxiety-producing thought. For example, people might imagine a vicious assault by a burglar when they are thinking about checking to see that the doors are locked. The anxiety associated with this image becomes associated with the related thought of needing to check the locks. Once this process is initiated, a second process is implemented. The anxious person with OCD, like all anxious people, seeks to reduce the anxiety and finds that checking the locks achieves that goal. In other words, the compulsive behavior is negatively reinforced. In time, checking becomes so automatic that it is initiated as soon as the obsessive thought occurs, sometimes even before the anxiety develops. The person essentially avoids the intense anxiety instead of waiting for it to arise.

Mowrer's two-process theory does a nice job of explaining the development and maintenance of compulsive symptoms, but it is less effective at explaining why the obsessions develop in the first place. Why do some people form the associations that make the obsessions so anxiety-arousing, whereas others do not? Despite this shortcoming, the two-process model does provide the basis for an effective treatment, as we will see in the next section.

Evolutionary Impact

Could the symptoms of OCD have survival value? Endless checking, counting, or washing would certainly interfere with everyday life, so OCD itself probably has little survival value. But could OCD represent a disruption of normal mechanisms that do have survival value? Is obsessional thinking, for example, found in an adaptive form outside of OCD? Anyone who has obsessed about a new love, a stupid mistake, or a critical upcoming event can attest to the fact that not all obsessions are OCD. These obsessive thoughts and the anxiety they produce motivate effective action, and once such action is completed, the obsessive thoughts decrease. Assuming that one's judgment about the importance of the situation is accurate, such a system enhances effective planning and action.

Compulsive behaviors can also have survival value, although it depends on the nature of the compulsions. There is probably little survival value in compulsively tapping your knee, but there may be survival value in compulsively checking for predators. As noted earlier, in theory any behavior could become a compulsion, but a small number of behaviors account for the majority of compulsions (Steketee, 1993). People seem to be prepared to develop these more common compulsions, which include cleaning, checking, and magical rituals. Cleaning can reduce the chance of disease and infection; checking can reduce a variety of risks from accidents or attacks by predators; magical rituals probably do little objectively to increase survival, but subjectively they may decrease anxiety that is interfering with performance. Magical rituals of all kinds increase during periods when people feel that they have little control over their lives, such as during an economic recession (McCann & Stewin, 1984, Padgett & Jorgenson, 1982). Magical rituals are also more common in people whose lives involve uncertainty, such as professional athletes (Zusne & Jones, 1989) and primitive tribes that depend on fishing in dangerous waters (Malinowski, 1954).

Both obsessions and compulsions can have potential survival value, but in OCD the intensity and persistence of these experiences go well beyond the adaptive. The normal regulatory mechanisms for these thought and behavioral processes seem to be distorted, creating obsessive thoughts that keep coming back, no matter what the person does, and forcing the endless repetition of behaviors. It may be that the real problem in OCD is not the obsessions and compulsions but, rather, malfunctioning of the regulatory mechanisms that keep these valuable behaviors in check. Better understanding of the normal regulatory mechanisms will certainly help scientists to understand the dysregulation that defines OCD.

TREATING OCD

Three treatment approaches have proved effective in treating OCD. They include medication, behavior therapy, and (as a last resort) psychosurgery.

Medications. The first medication used widely for the treatment of OCD was clomipramine (Anafranil). Clomipramine is a tricyclic antidepressant, which in high doses reduces OCD symptoms (Insel et al., 1981; Jenike et al., 1989). Clomipramine is still used today, but such SSRIs as fluoxetine (Prozac) and fluvoxamine (Luvox) have largely replaced it. The SSRIs tend to be about as effective as clomipramine and usually produce fewer side effects (Hoehn-Saric et al., 1991; Papp, 2000; Perse et al., 1987; Stanley & Turner, 1995; Tollefson et al., 1994). The effectiveness of SSRIs is one of the pieces of evidence for the serotonin hypothesis of OCD. The majority of people with OCD respond positively to an SSRI, exhibiting clinically significant improvement in their symptoms and associated distress (Papp, 2000; Stanley & Turner, 1995). Furthermore, continuing to take SSRIs after the symptoms are under reasonable control decreases the chance of a relapse (Romano et al., 2001). However, not every person responds to every SSRI, and some people who fail to respond to one SSRI show a positive treatment response to another. Clearly, much remains to be learned about the psychopharmacology of these drugs and the neurochemistry of OCD.

Behavior Therapy. Although traditional psychotherapies are ineffective in treating OCD (Black, 1974; Steketee, 1993), a specific behavior therapy—exposure with response prevention—has demonstrated considerable value in reducing obsessive-compulsive symptoms (Foa & Goldstein,

1978; Rachman et al., 1971; Riggs & Foa, 1993; Steketee, 1993). This therapy is based on the two-process model of Mowrer. In **exposure with response prevention,** pioneered by Victor Meyer, clients are asked to challenge the symptoms by first putting themselves in situations in which their obsessions are likely to occur (the exposure) and then blocking their compulsions (the response prevention). For example, clients with a contamination obsession may be asked to hold objects that they believe are contaminated without immediately washing to remove the feeling of contamination. Clients are in control of both the exposure and the response prevention. The therapist simply coaches them and then encourages them to perform additional exposures as homework assignments (Steketee, 1993). This treatment can be carried out at whatever pace is tolerated, although there is evidence that intense exposure is the most efficient approach (Rabavilas et al., 1976; Steketee, 1993, 1999). It is critical that the exposure be maintained until the anxiety decreases. If the person gives in, perhaps by washing to remove the feeling of contamination, the symptoms will

In exposure with response prevention, clients expose themselves to the obsessive thoughts and the anxiety these thoughts generate and avoid performing the kind of compulsive behavior illustrated here to neutralize the thoughts.

persist (Steketee, 1993, 1999). In general, the more a person gives in to OCD symptoms, the stronger the symptoms become, and the more a person resists the symptoms, the weaker they become.

Recently, there has been increased interest in using cognitive therapy or cognitive therapy combined with behavior therapy to treat OCD. Early efforts to use cognitive therapy to reduce obsessions and the distress from the obsessions were ineffective (Steketee, 1993), but recent studies suggest that cognitive therapy can reduce OCD symptoms and has the added advantage that it also reduces the depression so common in OCD (Cottraux et al., 2001). People with OCD cannot simply tell themselves to ignore their obsessions and not be bothered by them; it just doesn't work. However, a different cognitive strategy shows promise—a habituation approach to obsessions (Rachman & Hodgson, 1980). In this approach, the client is encouraged to obsess repeatedly in an effort to reduce, through habituation, the strong emotional responses that the obsessions provoke. A person who wanted to check all the doors and windows would be encouraged to continue to obsess about checking without either trying to block the obsessions or turning them off by checking. The treatment is almost indistinguishable from exposure with response prevention, although the conceptual rationale, as presented to the client, focuses on habituating to the obsessions rather than on discovering that the fear is unwarranted. Other cognitive therapists have argued that people with OCD tend to believe that their obsessions and the anxiety they produce are unbearable (Clark & Purdon, 1993) and that this belief exacerbates their anxiety and fuels the desperate efforts to reduce that anxiety through compulsive behavior. These therapists emphasize that the exposure teaches the client that the anxiety is not unbearable. Again, this approach changes the treatment specifics very little; only the rationale presented to the client differs. It is clear that exposure and the prevention of the compulsions are critical to the success of the treatment (Steketee, 1993, 1999).

Behavior therapy and medication are often combined in the treatment of OCD (Griest, 1992). Many clients report that behavior therapy is easier when they are taking medication. The general assumption in the treatment community is that using both treatments increases the likelihood that the person will improve, even though the research data suggest that adding medication to behavior therapy does not improve clinical outcome (Foa & Franklin, 2001).

exposure with response prevention Putting oneself in situations in which one's obsessions are likely to occur (the exposure) and then blocking one's compulsions (the response prevention).

phobias Unreasonable fears of specific objects, places, or situations.

specific phobia An intense and unwarranted fear of a specific object or situation.

Psychosurgery. Psychosurgery is a treatment reserved for the most severe cases of OCD that fail to respond to medications or behavior therapy. It involves neurosurgical procedures to destroy specific regions of the brain thought to be critical in maintaining the OCD symptoms, such as the anterior cingulate or the connections between the frontal lobe and the thalamus (Papp, 2000). In both cases, the intent is to destroy connections that are thought to be dysfunctional. Early results of these surgical procedures are promising (Ballantine et al., 1987; Irle et al., 1998). These experimental procedures are now being performed without scalpels, using microwaves that are focused precisely on a specific brain structure, sparing the critical tissue all around the offending structure (Spangler et al., 1996).

OCD can be terribly disruptive to a person's life, but with modern treatment the prognosis is good. The following autobiographical account illustrates how a person's life can be brought back on track with appropriate treatment.

Overcoming OCD

OCD controlled my every move. From the time I was in elementary school, I exhibited a few odd behaviors. I remember spending two days locked in my room organizing my closet—lightest to darkest, with corresponding hanger colors, and by clothing type. Or after I learned how to type: From that point on, every word I heard or spoke was being typed by my fingers. I'm sure most people can relate to strange compulsions. When mine began to interfere with my life, I needed help. I would go for days without sleep—afraid that if I fell asleep, someone in my family might die. I would get up several times in the middle of the night to check on them and make sure they were okay. Then I began to obsess over self-control. I feared that I might unknowingly violently harm someone I loved or myself. I hid all of the scissors in the house out of fear that I might wake up and kill myself. I wasn't suicidal, but the irrational fears overwhelmed me. Eventually, I lost the ability to function. The obsessions would make me ask everyone close to me to reassure me that I was ok. But I wasn't.

Two years later, I'm doing great. I take Zoloft daily with no side effects. I went through behavioral therapy and have learned how to control my thoughts. When I'm stressed, it may get worse; but I can finally sleep at night.

Check Yourself 8.4

Obsessive-Compulsive Disorder

1. What is the distinction between obsessions and compulsions?
2. How common is OCD?

3. What biological factors have been implicated in OCD?
4. On what classic theory is the behavioral treatment of OCD based?
5. What biological treatments are effective with OCD?
6. What psychological treatments are effective with OCD?

Ponder this . . . *Obsessing about important matters can have value, so what is the crucial distinction between useful obsessions and obsessions that are maladaptive?*

PHOBIAS

The word *phobia* comes from the Greek word for "fear." **Phobias** are unreasonable fears of specific objects, places, or situations—fears so intense that they interfere with the person's functioning. The key word in this definition is *unreasonable.* Having a healthy fear of poisonous snakes is not unreasonable; having the same intense fear of a 10-inch garter snake is. In theory one can develop a phobia of almost anything. That fact is illustrated in the proliferation of terms to describe hundreds of phobias; a few of these terms are listed in Table 8.2 on page 234. Unlike the anxiety in GAD, the anxiety associated with phobias tends to be triggered only by the specific object or situation that is feared. The DSM makes the distinction between specific phobias, social phobias, and agoraphobia. Agoraphobia was covered in the section on panic disorder. This section covers specific and social phobias.

SPECIFIC PHOBIAS

A **specific phobia** is an intense and unwarranted fear of a specific object or situation. In contrast to most other anxiety disorders, the fear is circumscribed, and functioning outside of the area of the phobia is usually unaffected. However, when the individual is confronted by the feared object or situation, the anxiety can be overwhelming, creating a sense of danger and sometimes triggering a panic attack. Consequently, individuals with phobias avoid situations in which they could come into contact with their phobic stimulus. That certainly was the case with Eleanor.

Every Bridge Was Too Far

Eleanor could not remember a time when she was not afraid of crossing a bridge. Her mother told her that the fear began when she was about 8 years old, after she observed young boys jumping

[TABLE 8.2] A Phobia for All Seasons and All Reasons

There is a name for almost every conceivable phobia. Listed below are a few examples. The DSM does not use these names but instead focuses on the two broad classes of social and specific phobias.

achluophobia	darkness, night	hypsophobia	heights
acrophobia	heights	kakorrhaphiophobia	failure
ailurophobia	cats	maieusiophobia	childbirth, pregnancy
androphobia	men (sex with men)	mechanophobia	machinery
antlophobia	floods	megalophobia	large objects
astraphobia	thunderstorms, lightning	molysmophobia	contamination, infection
ballistophobia	missiles, projectiles	necrophobia	dead bodies, cadavers, death
belonephobia	pins, needles, sharp objects	noctiphobia	night
bibliophobia	books	ochlophobia	crowds
brontophobia	thunder	ombrophobia	rain
cardiophobia	heart disease	ophidiophobia	snakes, reptiles
chionophobia	snow	ophthalmophobia	being stared at
chrematophobia	money	ornithophobia	birds
claustrophobia	enclosed spaces	phagophobia	eating
climacophobia	staircases, climbing	phasmophobia	ghosts
demonia	demons	phobophobia	developing a phobia
dysmorphophobia	deformity	pyrophobia	fire
eisoptrophobia	mirrors	rhypophobia	filth, dirt
emetophobia	vomiting	satanophobia	devils
genophobia	sex	spectrophobia	mirrors
graphophobia	writing	syphilophobia	syphilis
gynephobia	women	thanatophobia	death, dying
heliophobia	sunlight, the sun	traumatophobia	injury
hematophobia (hemophobia)	blood, bleeding	trichophobia	hair
		triskaidekaphobia	the number 13
homilophobia	sermons	vaccinophobia	vaccination
hydrophobia	water	xenophobia	strangers
hypnophobia	sleep	zoophobia	animals

SOURCE: *Adapted from J. D. Maser. "List of Phobias." In* Anxiety and the Anxiety Disorders, *edited by A. H. Tuma & J. D. Maser. (Hillsdale, NJ: Erlbaum, 1985.)*

off a nearby bridge into the river below. Still, Eleanor did not know what caused her fear; she just knew that it refused to go away. For most of her 45 years, she had experienced terror whenever she had to cross a bridge, and she would go to incredible lengths to avoid such crossings or to cross on the shortest bridge possible. For 8 years, her best friend had lived just over 2 miles away, but she regularly drove 40 miles out of her way to avoid crossing a long bridge.

Eleanor's entire life was shaped by her fear of bridges. She once confided to a friend that she used sex to keep her boyfriend satisfied with hanging around the house, because going out in the river town where they lived would almost certainly mean crossing bridges. Yet in spite of this debilitating fear, Eleanor led a rather normal life. She raised two daughters and worked part-time as a decorator. She always had friends, and her friends considered her one of the most

caring people they knew. Most knew about her fear and were willing to be accommodating.

Although any object or situation can become a phobic stimulus, a relatively small number of stimuli account for most of the specific phobias. Snake and animal phobias are common, especially in childhood (Muris et al., 1999; Ollendick & King, 1991). Environmental situations, such as heights, storms, and water, can be phobic stimuli, as can flying, crossing a bridge, and going through a tunnel. To qualify for a diagnosis of specific phobia, the phobia must be "marked and persistent" and "excessive or unreasonable" (from DSM-IV-TR criteria; APA, 2000, p. 449). These criteria are somewhat vague, so it is difficult to get precise estimates of the prevalence of specific phobias. Lifetime prevalence rates of approximately 10% are typically reported, although the rate depends on the criteria used and the number of possible phobias surveyed (APA, 2000). Children tend to experience more phobias than adults. Because fears are common in children, the diagnosis of a specific phobia is made only if the phobia results in clinically significant impairment (APA, 2000). Culture can also make a difference (Brown et al., 1990). Fear of magic or spirits, which is relatively rare in Western adults, is much more common in cultures in which magic and spirits are readily accepted (APA, 2000). Women are 2 to 9 times more likely than men to report specific phobias, although there is an interesting exception. Women just barely outnumber men in **blood-injection-injury phobias** (APA, 2000), which entail a fear of getting an injection or of having blood drawn.

Evolutionary Impact

The blood-injection-injury phobia is particularly interesting for several reasons (Öst, 1992). Unlike most other specific phobias, this phobia is often associated with fainting (Thyer et al., 1985). Whenever people experience a puncture wound that causes bleeding, the cardiovascular system responds by dropping the blood pressure to minimize the loss of blood—a reflex known as **vasovagal syncope** (Öst, 1992). This response has significant survival value under the right circumstances, because it minimizes the risk of bleeding to death. In some individuals, that drop in blood pressure can be significant enough to cause the person to pass out. This tendency to overrespond physiologically to bleeding has a strong genetic component (Öst, 1992). Some individuals generalize the syncope response to the mere sight of blood, either their own or that of others. Of course, passing out can be rather embarrassing for the person, thus creating a potential social phobia.

The intensity of the syncope response is generally consistent within the individual but shows wide variability among people. When one sees such wide variability for a genetically determined trait, it usually suggests that the evolutionary advantage or disadvantage depends on the environment and that there is enough environmental variability to support wide individual differences. Consider, from an evolutionary perspective, the advantage or disadvantage of a strong syncope response. If you fall off a small cliff and puncture yourself in the fall, momentarily losing consciousness to avoid excessive blood loss and possible death seems like a good trade-off. But what if a predator has managed to inflict a significant wound. In this situation, the last thing you want to do is risk passing out to avoid blood loss, because losing consciousness would guarantee that you would be someone's lunch. Thus a strong syncope response would be advantageous in some situations and disadvantageous in others.

SOCIAL PHOBIAS

We are all routinely evaluated in social situations. Such evaluations invariably create anxiety, but for some people the intensity of that anxiety is overwhelming. When the anxiety of being evaluated in a social situation reaches this level, it is called a **social phobia,** which is also called social anxiety disorder. The most common social phobia is a fear of public speaking. Up to 20% of the public reports significant fear of public speaking, although only a portion of those individuals would meet the intensity criterion for a social phobia. Meeting new people, talking with authority figures, performing in front of people, engaging in conversation, dating, eating in front of people, and using public restrooms are other common social phobias. Most people experience significant anxiety in just one or two of these situations, although a few socially phobic individuals experience anxiety in nearly all social situations. These latter individuals are said to suffer from a **generalized social phobia** (APA, 2000). Sometimes just thinking about those situations is sufficient to trigger extensive anxiety. It is not uncommon for the anxiety to reach the level of a full-blown

Fear of public speaking is by far the most common social phobia, affecting almost 20% of U. S. adults.

---

blood-injection-injury phobia   A fear of getting an injection or having blood drawn.

vasovagal syncope   A reflex reaction to a puncture wound: the cardiovascular system drops the blood pressure to minimize the loss of blood.

social phobia   A disorder in which the anxiety of being evaluated in a social situation is overwhelming.

generalized social phobia   Overwhelming anxiety experienced in nearly all social situations.

panic attack, although unlike the attacks in panic disorder, the panic occurs only in the feared social situations. The lifetime prevalence of generalized social phobia is 1 to 2% (Horwath & Weissman, 2000). Social phobias are often so intense that people make life decisions on the basis of their desire to avoid feared social situations, even at considerable cost to their careers or social lives. That is clearly what happened to Jim.

Some People Need More Privacy

Jim could not use public restrooms for most of his adult life because of his intense anxiety. Consequently, his social life was restricted to a few family outings and to whatever he could do in five hours or less (the length of time he could go without needing to use a bathroom). His whole life was planned around finding a private restroom, which usually meant that he had to stay close to home. For the first 20 years of his adult life he avoided dating, even though he was comfortable with women, enjoyed their company, craved intimacy, and was attractive to women. However, a simple dinner and a movie would strain his bladder to the breaking point. His workday was structured around taking a lunch break, when he would go home to use the bathroom. The hardest part was trying to hide his problem from others. He often feared that people would figure out why he behaved the way he did and would laugh at him for having such a "silly problem."

Jim's situation is an excellent example of how debilitating a single social phobia can be. His social life, work life, and family life were completely shaped and severely limited by his inability to use public restrooms. Furthermore, his inability to handle this phobia had a devastating effect on his morale and self-esteem.

Social phobias are relatively common, affecting between 3% and 13% of the population (APA, 2000; Horwath & Weissman, 2000). The wide range in prevalence estimates for this disorder reflects the disagreement among professionals about how severe the anxiety should be to qualify for a social phobia diagnosis. Social phobias are about twice as common in women as in men (Schneier et al., 1992) and can be either short-lived or chronic. Jim's fear of using public restrooms is a good example of a chronic social phobia. Even in chronic phobias, the intensity of symptoms ebbs and flows, depending on life circumstances and life stress. For example, fear of public speaking may be more intense when people are in school, where public speaking may be required, but may decrease once people obtain jobs that do not require public speaking. The anxiety inflicted by social phobias can be terribly debilitating, because it often leads to avoidance of such critical opportunities as education and leadership positions. The more chronic cases tend to develop during high school, but later onset, often following a traumatic incident, is also common (APA, 2000).

CAUSES OF SPECIFIC PHOBIAS

A variety of explanations have been offered to explain specific phobias. No explanation seems to account for all the data, and it is likely that phobias can develop and be maintained in more than one way. This section will review the genetic, psychodynamic, and behavioral explanations for specific phobias.

Genetic Factors. Genes influence risk for specific phobias (Kendler et al., 1992b), although the strength of their influence is much less than for the psychiatric disorders discussed so far in this text (schizophrenia, mood disorders, panic disorder, and OCD). There is a stronger genetic component for the blood-injection-injury phobia than for most other specific phobias (Neale et al., 1994).

Psychodynamic Factors. Freud believed that fears could be displaced from one situation to another, thus creating a phobia that had no obvious cause. His best-known phobic client was Little Hans, a young boy who developed an intense fear of horses (Freud, 1909). His mother reported to Freud that a few weeks before the fear developed, Hans had been playing with his penis and that he had asked his mother to touch his penis. Hans's mother sharply scolded the lad, emphasizing that his behavior was inappropriate and threatening to cut off his penis if he did not stop it. Freud believed that this interaction set the stage for the later phobia of horses. He argued that Hans experienced intense anxiety about the threat of castration, began to fear castration, and then displaced those intense fears onto the horse. Freud argued that Hans displaced his anxiety because it was less terrifying to fear horses than to fear castration. However, it is difficult to test this hypothesis scientifically. Furthermore, Freud's explanation also ignored the fact that a horse frightened Hans shortly before the phobia of horses developed. A behaviorist would argue that Hans's frightening experience with a horse is a more parsimonious, or economical, explanation for the phobia than the explanation offered by Freud.

Behavioral Factors. In some cases, specific phobias are learned through a process called classical conditioning. Recall from Chapter 3 that classical conditioning involves the pairing of two stimuli—one that produces a specific response and one that does not. When two such stimuli consistently occur together, the response produced by the first stimulus will soon be produced by the second stimulus. Watson and Raynor (1920) demonstrated this phenomenon with their own case study of Little Albert. They conditioned a fear of rabbits by pairing the presence of rabbits with a loud and frightening sound. Albert's conditioned fear of rabbits generalized to other white fury creatures, such as a white rat. In theory, any fear could be conditioned in this manner. For example, being chased by a big dog as a child or being on a particularly turbulent

Little Albert was perhaps the most famous phobic. Watson and Raynor (1920) classically conditioned fear of rabbits in Albert by making a loud noise whenever Albert played with the rabbit.

airline flight—both frightening experiences—might create a dog phobia or a fear of flying. But learning need not always be direct. It is not uncommon for children to learn to fear many of the same things their parents fear by observing the obvious distress their parents exhibit when near the feared stimulus. In fact, pets can learn some of their owners' fears. For example, if you show fear of thunderstorms, your dog or cat may well pick up on that fear and develop its own (Coren, 1994). Animals also learn from other animals. Mineka and her colleagues showed that monkeys can learn fears by observing the fearful responses of other monkeys (Mineka et al., 1984) and that this process is very similar to observational learning in human beings (Mineka & Cook, 1993).

There are many specific phobias for which it is impossible to identify a traumatic event, either experienced or observed, to account for the fear. Rachman (1977) proposed a third method by which phobias can be learned—through the transmission of information or misinformation. For example, if you have been told that spiders can bite and that many of them are deadly, you might well develop a fear of spiders without ever experiencing a spider bite or observing one in others.

Evolutionary Impact

There is also evidence for a phenomenon called **preparedness,** in which some fears are learned more readily than others (Seligman, 1971). For example, people learn to fear snakes more quickly and easily than to fear flowers (Cook et al., 1986; Hugdahl et al., 1977). Other species, such as monkeys, also show preparedness in their fear learning (Mineka et al., 1984). It is almost as

though the brain is wired to recognize certain stimuli as more inherently dangerous than other stimuli and is therefore prepared to activate fear at the slightest provocation (Seligman, 1971). Being prepared to learn realistic fears of dangerous objects quickly would give an organism considerable evolutionary advantage.

That phobias can be learned has been demonstrated in the laboratory many times. Whether this is the process by which most phobias develop in the real world is less clear. At least some evidence suggests that it is not. DiNardo et al. (1988) found that only half of the people they studied who had a dog phobia could report a traumatic event involving a dog. Even more interesting, half of their controls—people who had no dog phobia—remembered at least one traumatic incident involving a dog. Learning theories of phobic disorders cannot by themselves explain these puzzling data.

Many behaviorists believe that the two-factor theory, described earlier in this chapter, is the best model for understanding phobias. The two-factor theory suggests different processes for the acquisition and maintenance of phobias. The argument is that fears are learned initially through association with traumatic events—a form of classical conditioning. Once learned, the fear is maintained through operant conditioning—that is, the person is reinforced for escape or avoidance behavior by a reduction in anxiety.

Neither the psychodynamic nor the behavioral model provides an adequate explanation of what causes phobias, and genetics appears to play a rather minor role. There is some evidence that people may be prepared to learn to fear some things more readily than other things. Some fears are clearly learned, but other fears seem to develop without learning. The best interpretation of the current data on specific phobias is that there are likely to be multiple ways in which such fears develop, and the cause(s) for at least some phobias remain a mystery.

CAUSES OF SOCIAL PHOBIAS

Conceptually, specific phobias and social phobias are similar in that both are fears. In practice, however, social phobias are harder to explain because they involve more complex stimuli. Social situations are more diverse and unpredictable than the objects of most specific phobias, and the social situation invariably makes specific performance demands. Hence it would not be surprising to find that many of the factors that contribute to specific phobias also contribute to social phobias, but one would expect other factors to play a role as well.

Social phobias tend to run in families, but it is not clear whether genes, environment, or both account for this tendency (APA, 2000). Twin studies suggest that genes contribute, especially to the more generalized social phobias (Kendler et al., 1992a). These more generalized social phobias are traitlike and may overlap with other diagnoses,

preparedness   A phenomenon that makes some fears more readily learned than others.

such as avoidant personality disorder (see Chapter 12). Like some specific phobias, the more limited social phobias, such as fear of eating in a restaurant, often develop after a particularly embarrassing incident in which the individual's anxiety in a social situation was obvious and debilitating. This suggests that some social phobias may be classically conditioned. Other social phobias do not appear to stem from such traumatic events. There is evidence that individuals with generalized social phobia are more prone to blush when anxious—a response that is very noticeable in social situations and can lead to further embarrassment (APA, 2000; Gerlach et al., 2001). It also appears that some of the anxiety experienced by socially phobic individuals may be justified in that such individuals are less socially skilled and more socially awkward in many situations (van Dam-Baggen & Kraaimaat, 2000). To make matters worse, socially phobic individuals overestimate the likelihood of embarrassing situations, such as getting flustered when they are introduced to someone (Foa et al., 1996). This tendency increases the person's sense of threat in a social situation, thus contributing to excess anxiety (Woody, 1996).

Evolutionary Impact

To understand social phobias, it is helpful to view them from an evolutionary perspective. Individuals are caught between two drives in their day-to-day social functioning. People are social animals by nature, and their survival and prosperity depend on cooperation (Aronson, 1999). But at the same time, they are competitive creatures, competing with others for territory, resources, and access to suitable mates. Given these sometimes mutually exclusive drives, people often feel uncertain about the best course of action, so it is little wonder that they are often self-conscious about their public performances. Social phobias represent excessive anxiety about performing in public, whether that performance involves giving a speech, eating a meal, or interacting with someone you have just met. Such anxiety is often reasonable, given the importance of people's many day-to-day public "performances." Nevertheless, when the anxiety becomes excessive, it clearly interferes with performance.

Increases in social anxiety and social phobias would be expected from an evolutionary perspective. In today's world, people are required to engage in frequent public performances that have a significant impact on the quality and success of their lives. Whether they are presenting their ideas to others, trying to be charming and witty with a stranger, or just eating with appropriate grace, people are being judged—and they are usually well aware of that fact. This dramatic increase in social demands is a relatively recent phenomenon created by the increased population density and the more complex social structure of modern societies. Given these rapid changes, it is surprising how well most people manage their social anxiety.

TREATING PHOBIAS

The key element in the treatment of phobias is exposure; people must face down their anxiety in order to overcome it. This can be difficult, but when it is done properly, the anxiety is manageable. This section describes two exposure-based treatments that have proved effective with phobias: systematic desensitization and flooding. The final section addresses the specific treatment strategies used with social phobias.

Systematic Desensitization. One of the first truly effective treatments for an emotional problem was systematic desensitization. This technique combines relaxation with a gradual exposure to the feared objects or situations (Wolpe, 1958). Initially, this exposure was done through imagining the situation, **imaginal exposure.** More recently, the emphasis has been on actual exposure to the feared stimuli, **in vivo exposure.** The in vivo exposure overcomes a serious problem found in imaginal exposure—the fact that some people are unable to imagine situations with sufficient vividness to produce the desensitization (Antony & Barlow, 2002; Lang et al., 1983).

The therapist begins systematic desensitization by helping clients construct a hierarchy of their fears. Table 8.3 lists a typical hierarchy for a client with a fear of flying. After teaching the client progressive muscle relaxation, the therapist has the person begin the exposure, starting with the easiest item in the hierarchy. The exposure increases the person's anxiety, but the progressive muscle relaxation is sufficient to control this increased anxiety. The items of the hierarchy may be imagined, experienced in real life, or some combination of the two. For example, the person may be asked to go through the fear-of-flying hierarchy at an airport, where the first few items are real and the items that involve actual boarding and flying are performed in imagination. Clients are able to imagine flying more vividly at a busy airport than in the psychologist's office, although the security measures that have recently been imposed make such in vivo exposure impractical. The pace of the exposure depends on the person's progress, and the exposure usually has to be repeated several times before the anxiety is reduced to acceptable levels. Nevertheless, systematic desensitization is a remarkably effective treatment for most people (Antony & Barlow, 2002; Chambless & Ollendick, 2001).

Flooding. An alternative to the gradual-exposure approach of systematic desensitization is flooding. **Flooding** involves intense and prolonged exposure to the feared

imaginal exposure An exposure to a feared object or situation through imagining the object or situation.

in vivo exposure An actual exposure to a feared object or situation.

[TABLE 8.3]   A Desensitization Hierarchy for a Flying Phobia

A desensitization hierarchy moves in graded steps from items that trigger little anxiety to items that trigger intense anxiety. The therapist has the client imagine an item until the item no longer produces significant anxiety. Then the therapist moves on to the next item. The following hierarchy, for example, might be used to treat a flying phobia.

1. It is a month before the plane trip, and you call to make a reservation.
2. A week before the trip, you start to plan what you will take with you.
3. The night before the trip, you are packing your clothes and cannot stop worrying about the trip and how you will handle your anxiety.
4. You arise early for the trip after a restless night. You are so anxious that you are sweating.
5. On the way to the airport, you can feel your heart start to pound.
6. As you check your bags, your palms are sweating and you begin to wonder whether you can go through with it.
7. As they start the boarding process, you watch the people get in line to board the plane, and you feel like a lamb being led to slaughter.
8. As you take your seat in the plane, you feel as though you are about to lose control.
9. When the door of the plane shuts, you start to feel closed in. You now know that it is too late to get off the plane.
10. As the plane starts to taxi, your mind goes blank. You cannot hear the flight attendants. You think to yourself, "If flying is so safe, why do they need to take so much time to discuss emergency procedures?"
11. As the plane takes off, you feel pinned into your seat, totally unable to run to safety.

There is some truth to this approach, or at least it feels that way to people in treatment for anxiety. The key to reducing anxiety is exposure—that is, challenging the fear by facing it and learning to handle the anxiety.

"SEE, MY INTENSIVE-STRESS THERAPY REALLY WORKS. YOU ARE NO LONGER CONCERNED WITH YOUR MINOR ANXIETIES."

SOURCE: *By permission of Sidney Harris,* http://www.ScienceCartoonsPlus.com

treatment prematurely. The "exposure with response prevention" treatment for obsessive-compulsive disorder, discussed earlier in this chapter, is essentially a flooding procedure (Steketee, 1993).

Social Skills Training. In some ways, the treatment of social phobia is similar to the treatment of any phobia. The key element is exposure to the feared situation(s). However, there is an additional element in social phobias that must be addressed if the treatment is to be successful. Performing ineffectively in social situations can have significant negative consequences, and those consequences need to be avoided. Therefore, before using exposure with a socially phobic client, it is important that the therapist assess the level of skill the client has in dealing with the feared social situation. Sometimes the social phobia is a realistic fear of not being able to deal with specific social demands (Hofmann & Barlow, 2002; Hope & Heimberg, 1993; Turner et al., 1994). Clients should also be trained to camouflage their anxiety, because showing excessive anxiety in many social situations may lower their status among peers. Finally, cognitive elements are often included to manage the intense sensitivity that socially phobic individuals develop to the real and imagined impressions of others (Foa et al., 1996; Hofmann & Barlow, 2002). This hypersensitivity to the impact that one's actions have on others can feed the social phobia by providing numerous cues suggesting inadequate performance, which can distract individuals enough to decrease their performance. The case of Linda illustrates many of these treatment elements.

stimulus. Such intense and lengthy exposure is extremely uncomfortable, but if the person tolerates the discomfort, the anxiety diminishes (Crow et al., 1972; Saigh, 1998). For example, someone who is afraid of heights may go out on a roof and stay there until the anxiety subsides. The exposure is usually done in vivo, but it is possible to use imaginal exposure. There is even a variation of flooding, termed **implosive therapy,** that uses imaginal exposure to psychoanalytic anxiety themes, such as castration anxiety (Stampfl & Levis, 1967). Flooding is an effective treatment for phobias, but it is emotionally draining (Crow et al., 1972). It also can increase the anxiety if the person stops

flooding   Intense and prolonged exposure to a feared stimulus.

implosive therapy   A variation of flooding that uses imaginal exposure to psychoanalytic anxiety themes.

Getting Help Quickly

LINDA

Linda developed her fear of public speaking in graduate school during a routine class presentation. It was the worst moment of her life. A normally confident speaker, Linda was literally shaking as she tried to get through a presentation. Her mind was racing and she had no idea what she was saying. She had never experienced anything like it before, and she had no idea why she was experiencing it now. Linda had been a near-straight-A student from grade school through college, and she expected that trend to continue through graduate school. Her presentations were always the best in the class, but this one was one of the worst.

After class Linda started to think about the two other talks she was scheduled to give in classes that semester, the teaching assistant position she had accepted for the spring semester, and the teaching position she had just applied for. After two days of worrying and not sleeping, she stopped by to talk with her professor, who referred her to the Student Counseling Center for an evaluation. The center referred her to an Anxiety Disorders Clinic on campus, where Linda joined a group of three other students with intense fear of public speaking in a ten-session group treatment program. The program taught her how to manage her anxiety and to fear it less. She sharpened her public speaking skills and rebuilt her confidence. She practiced giving talks to the group, controlling and hiding her anxiety, and connecting with her audience. Her next class presentation, about halfway through the treatment program, was nerve-wracking, but it went well. The TA position that she had dreaded turned out to be a godsend. Twice a week she stood in front of 30 students, presenting material and answering their questions. By the end of the semester, her discomfort when speaking before groups was history.

The quick and effective group treatment that Linda received prevented the public speaking phobia from taking over her life. In the month before she started treatment, she had noticed that her phobia was generalizing to the point where she experienced anxiety talking in groups as small as five people. There is no telling how debilitating the social phobia might have become without treatment. The group treatment format is being used increasingly often for treating social phobias. It not only facilitates rehearsal of skills but also provides group members with needed social support (Turk et al., 2001).

Check Yourself 8.5

Specific and Social Phobias

1. What is the distinction between specific and social phobias?
2. How common are phobias?
3. What is unique about the blood-injection-injury phobia?

4. What theories have been proposed to explain phobias, and how strong is the evidence for those theories?
5. What are the best treatment approaches for phobias?

Ponder this . . . *From an evolutionary perspective, the survival value of the vasovagal syncope response depends on how the person received the puncture wound—whether from a predator or by accident. Given that humans rarely encounter predators in today's technological world, what would you predict will happen to the syncope response in humans over the next 10,000 generations?*

ACUTE AND POSTTRAUMATIC STRESS DISORDERS

Living a Nightmare

JANICE

Janice was just 17, a college freshman living away from home for the first time. On a mild November night, while walking home from her campus job, she was dragged into the bushes, raped, sodomized, and severely beaten by a man wearing a ski mask and carrying a knife. The last thing he said to her was "You're lucky I'm letting you live." Dazed and bleeding badly, she wandered for a couple of blocks before another student found her and summoned police and an ambulance. In the emergency ward, Janice shook violently as she tried to answer questions from the female officer. She tried to relax as the doctor treated her injuries and gathered evidence for later prosecution, but the best she could do was "zone out." Her sister met her at the hospital, and a police officer drove them both home.

The powerful sedative that the doctor had given Janice made her incredibly drowsy, but she could not fall asleep until nearly dawn. Her sleep that first night was fitful. She awoke screaming three times from nightmares, finally falling asleep in her sister's arms. Most of the next two days were spent talking to the police and the district attorney, her doctor, a rape counselor, and a dentist who did some emergency repairs on two teeth that had been broken in the attack. Her parents then took her home to recover from her ordeal. Over the next two weeks, she had nightmares almost every night, was afraid to go out, and could not concentrate. She would be crying one minute and screaming in anger the next. Although greatly relieved when the police caught her attacker, she still feared facing him in court. Fortunately for Janice, the police obtained a quick confession, and the DA negotiated a guilty plea.

Within a couple of weeks, Janice's bruised face started looking better, and she was less self-conscious about going out. She forced herself to see friends, go to a movie, and visit the library. She received tremendous support from her family and friends during this period. Her nightmares gradually decreased in frequency. By Christmas, she had decided that she was not going to let the attack prevent her from living. She contacted the university in early January and arranged to return for the spring semester. Less than ten weeks after the attack, she was back in school determined to pick up her life where she had left off. There are still emotional scars, but the nightmares, the jumpiness, and the constant fear are gone.

Life can be a hassle some days, but it is rare that people actually have to look death in the face the way Janice did. She faced a trauma of a lifetime, and it took an emotional and physical toll on her. When people face such trauma, it changes them—sometimes for the better but often for the worse. There are two anxiety disorders—acute stress disorder and posttraumatic stress disorder (PTSD)—that represent changes for the worse. Both are covered in this section.

ACUTE STRESS DISORDER

An **acute stress disorder** is an immediate and short-term physical and emotional reaction to an overwhelming and

Life-threatening traumas like those pictured here can result in either acute stress disorder or posttraumatic stress disorder. In fact, just witnessing such events can result in psychological trauma.

potentially life-threatening trauma. Its symptoms include emotional numbing; feeling in a daze; **derealization,** which is a feeling that the situation is not real; **depersonalization,** which is a feeling that you are watching yourself experience life instead of experiencing it directly; and selective amnesia for specific events associated with the trauma. The trauma is frequently relived in flashbacks and nightmares, although the person often makes a concerted effort to avoid such recollections. **Flashbacks** are vivid feelings of reliving the trauma. The person is also hyperaroused, easily agitated, irritable, jumpy, and restless. Janice experienced all of these symptoms in the first few weeks after her attack. For the diagnosis of acute stress disorder to apply, the symptoms must be experienced for a minimum of two days and a maximum of four weeks and must begin within four weeks of the trauma (APA, 2000). If the symptoms are delayed or last longer than four weeks, the diagnosis of posttraumatic stress disorder is used. Although Janice recovered quickly given the severity of her trauma, the symptoms lasted long enough to warrant first an acute stress disorder diagnosis and later a diagnosis of posttraumatic stress disorder.

The likelihood of experiencing an acute stress disorder depends on the severity of the trauma (APA, 2000; Bryant & Harvey, 1999). An acute stress disorder is very likely to appear following the type of assault experienced by Janice but is much less likely to appear following a near-miss traffic accident. Stress disorders can be induced by many types of stressors, including torture (Başoğlu & Mineka, 1992), physical and psychological abuse (Astin et al., 1995), sexual abuse (McLeer et al., 1988), sexual assault (Valentiner et al., 1996), combat or risk of combat (King et al., 1995; Litz et al., 1997), such natural disasters as earthquakes (Pratap et al., 1996), and even motor vehicle accidents (Buckley et al., 1996). Under some circumstances, it may be possible to develop a stress disorder without a significant stressor (Scott & Stradling, 1994), although such cases do not technically qualify for a diagnosis because the DSM diagnostic criteria require the presence of a potentially life-threatening trauma.

POSTTRAUMATIC STRESS DISORDER

Posttraumatic stress disorder (PTSD) is the more long-term response to potentially life-threatening situations.

acute stress disorder   An immediate and short-term physical and emotional reaction to an overwhelming and potentially life-threatening trauma.

derealization   The feeling that a situation is not real.

depersonalization   The feeling that you are watching yourself experience life instead of experiencing it directly.

flashbacks   Vivid feelings of reliving a trauma.

posttraumatic stress disorder (PTSD)   A long-term dysfunctional response to potentially life-threatening situations.

The symptoms are similar to those of acute stress disorder, but they can last for months or years. For example, fully a third of World War II POWs still qualified for a PTSD diagnosis 40 years after their release (Speed et al., 1989). People with PTSD re-experience the trauma through intrusive thoughts, nightmares, or flashbacks—all of which generate intense distress. They often try, usually without success, to avoid things that remind them of the trauma. They may experience a sense of detachment, a restricted range of affect, and a sense that there is nothing in their future. Finally, people with PTSD are often hyperaroused, with an exaggerated startle response, difficulty sleeping, intense irritability, and **hypervigilance,** which is a feeling of constantly being on guard. They are often prone to angry outbursts. This hyperarousal may continue for 20 years or more (Orr et al., 1995). It is little wonder that people suffering from PTSD find it difficult to function in day-to-day situations (Foy, 1992; McNally, 1999). They seem to live in their own private emotional hell, unable to escape and resume the task of living their lives. Not surprisingly, substance abuse is common in people with PTSD, especially male combat veterans (Jacobsen et al., 2001; Sipprelle, 1992).

Jerry—one of the cases that opened this chapter—showed all of these classic symptoms of PTSD years after returning from Vietnam. His friends said that Vietnam changed him, and indeed it did. Always jumpy and irritable, he spends his days trying not to think of the hell he experienced in Vietnam. In contrast, Linda responded well to the support of friends, family, and her counselor. In a matter of a few weeks she was able to put her trauma largely behind her, although the memory remained. These two cases illustrate the extremes of PTSD.

PTSD is more common than was once believed. Studies have suggested that approximately 2% of the population qualifies for a PTSD diagnosis at any given time (Stein et al., 1997a) and that approximately 8% will suffer from PTSD at some time during their lives (APA, 2000; Breslau, 2001; Horwath & Weissman, 2000). PTSD occurs twice as often in women than in men (Kessler et al., 1995). Among those who have been exposed to a potentially life-threatening trauma, such as combat veterans or people who have survived a volcanic eruption, estimated prevalence rates range from 3 to 58% (APA, 1994; Keane & Barlow, 2002). It is too early to tell how many of the survivors of the attack on the World Trade Center of September 11, 2001, will experience significant PTSD symptoms, although it is safe to say it will be a substantial number. The high rate of PTSD symptoms in individuals exposed to significant trauma impresses most people. Some have even suggested that PTSD may be a normal response to an abnormally severe stressor (McNally, 1999). However, the fact that many people faced with the same life-threatening situa-

tion recover quickly from their trauma and appear to go on to lead normal lives suggests that individual differences are important in determining the long-term recovery from trauma.

Many people associate PTSD with combat situations, in part because this disorder was first recognized in soldiers (Baskir & Strauss, 1981; Keane & Barlow, 2002). Terms such as *shell shock* and *combat fatigue* emphasized the early belief that this condition was associated primarily with combat. There is no question that firsthand experience with combat can take an emotional toll. If you have seen the film *Saving Private Ryan,* you can begin to appreciate what soldiers experience in combat. However, any life-threatening situation is capable of producing PTSD. In the last few years, PTSD research has focused more on assault victims and victims of natural and man-made disasters (Keane & Barlow, 2002). Life-threatening events need not be directly experienced to produce PTSD. Simply observing such an event or having a loved one experience it appears to be sufficient to produce PTSD in some individuals. For example, the September 11 attacks on the World Trade Center and the Pentagon are likely to produce PTSD symptoms in some individuals who were hundreds of miles away. However, most people who experience life-threatening trauma do not develop PTSD (Foy, 1992), an observation that suggests that PTSD is more than just an automatic response to a devastating experience.

CAUSES OF STRESS DISORDERS

Stress disorders are caused by traumatic or life-threatening events, as illustrated in the case of Janice, but are other factors also involved? Perhaps anyone would have responded as strongly as Janice when faced with a trauma as severe as a brutal rape. Research shows that 80% of women who have been raped develop PTSD, although many eventually recover, as Janice did (Breslau et al., 1991). However, many people survive trauma, sometimes even severe trauma, without exhibiting the symptoms of acute stress disorder or PTSD. Why do some people respond to a trauma with significant and prolonged stress symptoms, whereas others do not? The nature of the trauma and the biological and psychological characteristics of the victim differentiate those who do from those who do not develop a stress disorder.

Nature of the Trauma. The severity of the trauma plays a significant role in determining the likelihood of PTSD (Foy et al., 1984; March, 1993; McNally, 1999). Foy and his colleagues found that both the amount of combat exposure and its intensity affected the likelihood of PTSD symptoms occurring in Vietnam soldiers. Furthermore, prisoners of war during World War II were found to have a 3 times higher rate of PTSD than combat veterans who were never prisoners (Sutker et al., 1993). Similar patterns have been found for other stresses, such as sexual assaults (Valentiner et al., 1996). However, some veterans with com-

....

hypervigilance The feeling of constantly being on guard.

bat exposure comparable to that of those who developed PTSD handled the stress of combat without developing symptoms. This suggests that the intensity and duration of the trauma are not the only causal factors in PTSD.

The nature of the trauma is both a physical reality and an individual experience. Research with torture victims suggests that the perspective of the victim not only affects the impact that the torture has but also changes the experience of the torture (Başoğlu & Mineka, 1992). These factors are discussed in the nearby Focus box. The research on the psychological impact of torture illustrates how integrating the information provided by victims with a sophisticated understanding of the research on stress and stress reactions can provide unique insights into a more general problem— posttraumatic stress disorder.

Biological Factors. Genes also influence risk for PTSD. A history of anxiety disorders in one's family increases the risk of experiencing PTSD when one is faced with a significant trauma (Davidson et al., 1985). In fact, a history of any psychiatric disorder increases the risk of PTSD in response to a trauma (Davidson et al., 1991;

FOCUS   Studying the psychological effects of torture

Studying psychopathology is difficult because one cannot ethically experiment with people's lives. Nowhere is that more true than with PTSD, which involves exposure to potentially life-threatening trauma. Instead, one can carefully study those who have faced such trauma and integrate these observations with other research.

That is the strategy employed by Başoğlu and Mineka (1992) in their study of victims of state-sponsored torture (Amnesty International, 1984). Not surprisingly, many of the survivors of such torture show signs of PTSD. Başoğlu and Mineka interviewed torture survivors about their experiences and integrated this information with over 25 years of stress research. The stress research provided insights into the processes that may contribute to PTSD in these torture victims. Stress is known to have its greatest impact when it is unpredictable and uncontrollable (Başoğlu & Mineka, 1992; Mineka & Henderson, 1985). People can prepare themselves to handle predictable and/or controllable stressors. Even the illusion of control reduces stress levels (Sanderson et al., 1989).

The impact of predictability and controllability on response to torture is amply illustrated in the reports of torture victims (Stover & Nightingale, 1985). Victims are typically isolated from the outside world and from other prisoners, both to reduce the moral support they might receive and to minimize the exchange of information that might enhance predictability. Typically, a variety of torture methods are used, and these methods are selected randomly to decrease predictability. The length of sessions and the timing of sessions are also varied. It is common for the torturer to pretend a session is over and then moments later resume the torture to catch the victim off guard. Victims are often blindfolded so that they cannot see where the next attack will come from, and torturers routinely feign attacks to decease predictability further. Victims are often subjected to mock executions—a threat that is very real because summary executions are not uncommon in countries that use torture. The impact of these strategies on victims mirrors the findings from experimental research on stress.

Many victims of torture developed an understanding of these principles. They communicated with other prisoners any way they could, sometimes just by knocking on the walls of their cells to say they were alive. Even before arrest, politically active groups formed tight-knit organizations so that members who were arrested would know that the group was aware of their plight and was doing everything possible to free them. Prisoners often increased their sense of control over their torture by deliberately challenging their captors, even though this behavior inevitably led to immediate reprisals. Such actions frustrated their torturers and were a satisfying way for prisoners to gain a sense of control and restore morale. Interestingly, political prisoners survived torture better than nonpolitical prisoners, even though the severity and duration of the torture were often greater for political prisoners. Political prisoners were better prepared emotionally to cope with the impact of their confinement and torture (Başoğlu et al., 1996; McNally, 1999). They were generally brighter, more committed to a cause, and better organized, and they enjoyed greater social support from peers than did nonpolitical prisoners.

Başoğlu and Mineka (1992) found that the factors that increase the impact of torture and the techniques that victims use to minimize its impact are consistent with stress research. This converging evidence increases confidence in the conclusions drawn from working with survivors of torture. Understanding the impact of torture improves the treatment of its victims. Furthermore, such information can be used to prepare potential victims, such as soldiers who may be captured, to handle the stress better.

Hodgins et al., 2001; McFarlane, 1988). More recent evidence suggests an interesting interaction between psychiatric risk factors and sex: Anxiety disorders were a risk factor for PTSD in men but not women, and mood disorders were a risk factor for women but not men (Dierker & Merikangas, 2001). Evidence from twin studies suggests that genes influence risk for PTSD (Chantarujikapong et al., 2001; True et al., 1993; Xian et al., 2000), although the nature of these genetic factors is complex. For example, some of the genetic influence for PTSD overlaps the genetic influence for drug and alcohol abuse (Xian et al., 2000). Furthermore, the genetic influences for PTSD overlap those for several anxiety disorders (Chantarujikapong et al., 2001). These findings suggest that genetic factors not yet identified may predispose people to many anxiety disorders and that the form of the disorder that one shows may depend on other genetic factors or environmental influences (Barlow, 2002; Smoller et al., 2000).

PTSD is characterized by physical symptoms, such as excessive autonomic arousal, that suggest a physiological dysfunction. There is evidence for the involvement of several systems in PTSD: the endogenous opioid system, which regulates pain (Wolf et al., 1991); the noradrenergic system, which regulates arousal (Southwick et al., 1994); the sleep regulation system (Lipper et al., 1989; March, 1990); and the hypothalamic-pituitary-adrenal (HPA) axis, which regulates stress reactions (Yehuda et al., 1991, 1995). People with PTSD often show insensitivity to pain at times and hypersensitivity at other times. These states seem to correlate with abnormal levels of the opioids that normally control pain. The dysregulation of the noradrenergic system increases arousal and can even trigger panic attacks in people with PTSD (Southwick et al., 1994). Sleep cycles are often dramatically disturbed in PTSD. Not only do people with PTSD have difficulty falling asleep, but their sleep is often disrupted, including REM sleep (Clum et al., 2001; Lavie, 2001). Finally, the dysregulation in the HPA axis results in an excessive release of glucocorticoids, which suppress immune and metabolic functions. Such suppression is reasonable as a response to a short-term stressor but creates serious problems when the suppression is prolonged. These findings provide interesting clues to the physiological pathology of PTSD, but scientists do not yet know whether these phenomena are part of the cause of the PTSD symptomatology or a secondary effect of that pathology.

Psychological Factors. People deal with traumas within the context of their past experiences and general coping strategies. Those variables influence how well a person copes. Some experiences and strategies increase coping effectiveness, whereas others decrease it. For example, individuals who experience severe traumatic events, such as childhood physical abuse, are at increased risk for PTSD when faced as adults with a new life-threatening trauma (Bremner et al., 1995). Severe traumas may weaken adap-

tive capacity, thus creating a diathesis for PTSD. This makes conceptual sense, but some traumas could strengthen adaptive capacity. For example, Seligman (1992) suggests that exposure to *moderate* stressors may actually increase people's adaptive capacity by giving them practice in dealing with stress and the negative feelings associated with it. Years earlier a similar notion was advanced by Gray (1982), who referred to the concept as "toughening up." Although Seligman argued from a learning perspective and Gray from a physiological perspective, both suggested that experience with mild traumas may inoculate people, reducing their risk from later, more severe trauma.

By far the most critical psychological variable affecting the likelihood of stress-related symptoms is the level of social support available (Boscarino, 1995; Carroll et al., 1985; Tucker et al., 2000). Social support buffers people against the effects of stress. Sometimes the level of social support is a function of the situation. For example, people who take a new job and move away from friends and family lose day-to-day social support until new friendships are developed. Social support is often a function of how strong a support network the individual has established prior to the trauma. Friends and family are the most typical sources of support, but counselors and members of the clergy may also provide support. Community agencies often provide short-term counseling or support groups for people who have experienced trauma, as a way of speeding recovery (Dutton, 1992).

Evolutionary Impact

It is hard to imagine that something as debilitating and disruptive as PTSD could have evolved. Surely the negative impact that this disorder has on people should have led to the elimination of whatever genes contribute to it through a process of natural selection. But natural selection does not select genes for the comfort of the organism (Nesse & Williams, 1994). Natural selection favors genes that contribute to survival and, as a consequence, to reproductive success.

Nothing could be more critical to survival than responding successfully to a life-threatening event. Learning quickly to avoid the dangerous situation would enhance survival. Given that such life-threatening events as attacks by predators might happen again, a prolonged state of heightened arousal would enhance survival. Vivid memories of the threat (flashbacks and nightmares) could help maintain the arousal. Such constant arousal might take an emotional and physical toll, but those affected would survive long enough to reproduce or nurture dependent offspring. Hence their genes would survive as well.

The world in which such natural selection took place was quite different from today's world. Long life expectancy and relative day-to-day safety are very recent achievements of human beings. Without weapons, without protective and defendable domiciles, and without the advantage of living in organized groups, most species, including early humans, were subject to frequent attacks by predators. The PTSD that disrupts functioning in the complex world of today may well have enhanced survival in the simpler—and much more dangerous—world of a hundred thousand years ago.

TREATING STRESS DISORDERS

The treatment of stress disorders, especially acute stress disorder, often focuses on attenuating symptoms with medications. Antianxiety drugs can reduce the restlessness and minimize the arousal symptoms, whereas antidepressant drugs not only relieve the depressive symptoms so common in PTSD but may also minimize the flashbacks and nightmares (Marmar et al., 1994; Papp, 2000). Sleep aids can provide the critical rest needed to maintain adequate coping resources. Effective pharmacological treatment of these debilitating symptoms reduces drug abuse and alcohol abuse, which are often attempts at self-medication.

Once the disruptive physiological symptoms of PTSD are controlled, treatment focuses on a combination of exposure and rethinking of the experience. Both of these elements require considerable support to be effective (Carroll et al., 1985; Foa & Franklin, 2001). Therefore, treatment is commonly conducted in groups, in which all of the members of the group have had similar traumatic experiences. The therapy deals with specific issues, which may vary from one traumatic situation to another. For example, battered women often must first deal with the issue of

safety, because many of them continue to live in fear of their boyfriend, spouse, or ex-spouse (Bell & Goodman, 2001; Dutton, 1992). For some people, reliving the trauma in the supportive environment of therapy enables them to attenuate their strong emotional responses to the memories and gives them an opportunity to rethink the trauma. Traumatic events create classically conditioned emotional responses to the stimuli that surround the event (Foy et al., 1987; Wirtz & Harrell, 1987). For example, a woman who is assaulted and raped in a park on a hot summer day may experience anxiety whenever she is near that park, and the anxious response may generalize to other parks. She may also experience anxiety whenever it is hot. Hot days and park settings are not signs of danger, but she responds to them as such because they were associated with her attack and have thus become classically conditioned fear-producing stimuli. Re-experiencing the stimuli surrounding the trauma in a less threatening environment encourages the extinction of these strong negative feelings and restores people's sense of control over their emotions. They gradually desensitize to the stimuli that trigger their PTSD symptoms.

PTSD is often difficult to treat. Although the affected people are clearly suffering, they can be so worn out emotionally that it is difficult for them to commit themselves to treatment. Furthermore, substance abuse, which is common in individuals with PTSD (Meisler, 1999; Sipprelle, 1992), complicates treatment. This was especially true for Vietnam combat veterans, who also had the added problem of being alienated from a country that disparaged their efforts and sacrifices in Vietnam and from a government

Talking about the trauma can often be helpful for victims of PTSD, but often family and friends tire of hearing about it. Support groups, consisting of others who have experienced similar traumas, provide the opportunity to share experiences and feelings.

Supportive interventions with sexual assault victims can often attenuate the severity of stress-related symptoms and speed the process of psychological recovery. Many communities have set up programs to provide such immediate support to victims.

that refused for many years to acknowledge their problems (Horne, 1981; Wong & Cook, 1992).

Most treatment efforts made from a psychological perspective are geared to helping the person come to grips with the trauma to avoid a more chronic course. For example, supportive counseling for sexual assault victims usually focuses on strengthening emotional supports, reducing the guilt, fear, and shame associated with the attack, and helping people return to normal activities as soon as possible (Golding et al., 1989; Rauch et al., 2001). These efforts can often reduce the likelihood of a prolonged stress response.

PTSD symptoms often improve in the supportive therapy just described, but there is disagreement on the mechanism underlying this improvement. The behavioral perspective emphasizes a desensitization process, but a humanistic or existential perspective interprets the process as extracting meaning from the traumatic event (Greening, 1997; Horowitz, 1986). Extracting meaning is a vague concept but is one with which you probably have personal familiarity. People often experience setbacks or traumas in life—setbacks that they feel have contributed to their personal growth. Janoff-Bulman (1995) has argued that the severe trauma that precipitates PTSD temporarily overcomes this natural rebound phenomenon, leaving people feeling vulnerable, helpless, and uncertain. With time and a supportive environment, people can reinterpret even severe trauma, finding meaning in the experience and then letting the memory of the trauma rest. This is an interesting hypothesis, though a difficult one to distinguish from the desensitization hypothesis just described. However, it does suggest specific approaches to take during supportive therapy for PTSD—approaches that tend to be viewed by

clients as enormously relevant. People often spend considerable energy during the healing process trying to reinterpret their traumatic experience in a way that will give meaning to it (Dutton, 1992). They may, for example, start to think of the trauma as a way to test their resolve, strengthen their character, or stimulate them to build more extensive support networks. In this way, they translate the trauma into a growth experience.

In the last several years, a new treatment approach has been proposed for PTSD: **eye movement desensitization and reprocessing,** or **EMDR** (Shapiro, 1989, 1995). This procedure involves imaginal exposure to the traumatic event while the person engages in a prescribed series of eye movements. It is argued that the eye movements facilitate a reprocessing of the trauma, thus leading to rapid healing (Shapiro, 1995). There is evidence that this procedure reduces PTSD symptoms (Wilson et al., 1995, 1997, 2001), although there is considerable controversy about the mechanism behind its effectiveness (Lohr et al., 1998; Keane & Barlow, 2002). For example, it appears that the eye movements for which the treatment is named are not necessary to achieving symptom reduction. Therefore, it is not clear whether EMDR is simply a variation on exposure and desensitization (Foa & Meadows, 1997; Lohr et al., 1998) or is a procedure that utilizes an entirely different treatment mechanism (Shapiro, 1997).

eye movement desensitization and reprocessing (EMDR)   A procedure that involves imaginal exposure to a traumatic event while the person engages in a prescribed series of eye movements.

Check Yourself 8.6

Acute and Posttraumatic Stress Disorders

1. How important is the stressor in acute and posttraumatic stress disorders?
2. How long can the PTSD symptoms last?
3. What are the symptoms of a stress disorder?
4. What biological systems are disrupted in PTSD?
5. What treatment strategies are used for PTSD?

Ponder this . . . *What would be the evolutionary advantage of being hyperaroused and vigilant for a long period of time following a trauma? What would be the disadvantages? Has this balance shifted in today's world compared to the world in which our species evolved?*

GENDER DIFFERENCES

You may have noticed as you read this chapter that women outnumber men for many—though not all—of the anxiety disorders. You may remember from the previous chapters that depression is twice as common in women as in men but that schizophrenia occurs as often in men as in women, although it tends to develop earlier in men. You will learn in later chapters that there are a number of disorders in which there is no sex difference or men greatly outnumber women. Such information on gender differences, coupled with other information, can provide significant clues about what variables influence the development and maintenance of a disorder. Whether one likes it or not, the data suggest that men and women have different cultural experiences and are treated differently by parents, teachers, and peers (Archer, 1996; Segall et al., 1990). Therefore, sex differences could have a sociocultural origin. Of course, there are also many biological differences between men and women, so biology could account for observed sex differences as well. Other information, such as cross-cultural studies, may help researchers to disentangle these competing hypotheses.

Which anxiety disorders show the greatest gender differences? Panic disorder is diagnosed twice as often in women as in men, and agoraphobia is diagnosed 3 times as often in women (APA, 2000). Women also outnumber men for specific phobias, although the ratio of women to men varies dramatically from one phobia to another. For example, fear of storms is 5 times more common in women than in men, whereas fear of heights and fear of injections are only slightly more common in women (Agras et al., 1969). Stress-related disorders are twice as common in women as in men, although this difference may be attributable in part to the greater frequency of sexual assaults experienced by women (Kessler et al., 1995). In contrast, social phobias are more common in men than in women, at least in clinical

settings, and generalized anxiety disorder is about equally common in men and women in clinical settings, although it is more common in women than in men in the general population (APA, 2000). Finally, OCD is equally common in adult men and women, but boys with this diagnosis substantially outnumber girls (APA, 2000).

What do these gender differences indicate? There is no one simple answer to this question. Some have argued that women are more likely than men to admit to a problem and seek appropriate treatment. The evidence offered for this position is that women seek treatment in outpatient clinics twice as often as men, although the rates of pathology are roughly similar for men and women. However, GAD is more common in women in the general population but more common in men in clinical populations (APA, 2000). In other words, men with GAD seek treatment at a higher rate than women with this disorder. The same appears to be true for social phobia (APA, 2000). Therefore, it seems unlikely that women show higher rates of many anxiety disorders than men simply because they seek treatment more readily. Furthermore, there are now excellent epidemiological studies of psychopathology that have sampled the general population, rather than relying on clinical samples (Kessler et al., 1995).

Evolutionary Impact

A critical issue to keep in mind is that anxiety is not a weakness; it is a critically important factor in survival. Sometimes people are required to perform in spite of their anxiety, but in many cases, there is little advantage to challenging anxiety and there may be considerable disadvantage. Avoiding dangerous situations has an evolutionary advantage for both men and women, although one might argue that the traditional caregiver roles of women increased the stakes for them. Women who avoided danger tended to increase not only their own longevity but also the longevity of their children, who often accompanied them. Therefore, their avoidance of danger was probably more fruitful from the perspective of natural selection. The disorders that are most closely associated with recognizing danger or risk (GAD, panic disorder, and PTSD) and with avoiding the risk (agoraphobia and specific phobias) show the largest female-to-male ratios. In contrast, anxiety disorders that are only weakly associated with identifying and avoiding risk (OCD, blood-injection-injury phobia, and social phobia) affect approximately equal numbers of males and females.

Social psychology has traditionally explained gender differences in terms of socialization (Yoder, 1999), although evolutionary arguments often explain the data better (Archer, 1996). An evolutionary argument provides a reasonable explanation for the relative rates of anxiety disorders in men and women. However, this question is far from resolved. There needs to be much more cross-cultural research on anxiety disorders. Evolutionary arguments should hold across a wide range of cultures. There are currently not enough data either to challenge the evolutionary position or to provide strong support.

Check Yourself 8.7

Gender Differences

1. What anxiety disorders show the greatest gender differences in the rates of the disorder?

2. What anxiety disorders show the least gender differences in the rates of the disorder?

3. Describe the evolutionary argument for gender differences in anxiety disorders.

Ponder this . . . *The socialization argument for gender differences suggests that men and women behave differently because they are treated differently from childhood on. Is this argument incompatible with the evolutionary argument?*

● SUMMARY

THE NATURE OF ANXIETY

● Anxiety is as much a part of life as breathing—and just as important to survival. Anxiety warns people to be careful in potentially dangerous situations, and it motivates action to reduce risks. As critical as anxiety is to survival, however, excessive anxiety can disrupt day-to-day functioning.

GENERALIZED ANXIETY DISORDER

● Generalized anxiety disorder is characterized by excessive worrying. The worrying is accompanied by some signs of physiological arousal, such as muscle tension, but does not include all of the physiological symptoms of anxiety.

● Genetic factors have been implicated in GAD. Although it is often treated with anxiolytic (antianxiety) medications, the treatment of choice for GAD is an exposure-based treatment that challenges clients to confront emotionally, rather than just think about, the objects of their worry.

PANIC DISORDER AND AGORAPHOBIA

● Frequent panic attacks and a pervasive fear of having more such panic attacks characterize panic disorder. The fear of additional panic attacks often restricts the person's mobility, leading to agoraphobic avoidance.

● Genetic factors play a role in panic, and specific brain triggering mechanisms, such as the locus coeruleus, have been implicated in panic attacks.

● Both antidepressant and anxiolytic medications attenuate panic symptoms, but symptoms often return after the drugs are withdrawn. Cognitive-behavioral treatment shows the greatest promise for long-term relief of panic symptoms.

OBSESSIVE-COMPULSIVE DISORDER

● Obsessive-compulsive disorder involves unwanted thoughts that create anxiety (the obsessions) and be-

havioral responses that reduce the anxiety (the compulsions). Once thought to be rare, OCD is now known to affect 2 to 3% of the population.

● Genes influence risk for OCD, and specific brain regions have been implicated, including the orbitofrontal cortex, the basal ganglia, and the anterior cingulate.

● Both medications and behavior therapy are effective in reducing the symptoms of OCD.

PHOBIAS

● Phobias are intense fears of specific objects, places, or situations. A phobia can develop to any object, place, or situation, although fear of certain objects, such as snakes, is learned especially readily.

● Some phobias have little impact on day-to-day life, but others severely disrupt a person's life. People with a public-speaking phobia, for example, may turn down jobs and promotions because of their fear of public speaking.

● Specific phobias respond well to a behavioral therapy called systematic desensitization or to a more intense treatment called flooding. Social phobias may require specific skills training.

ACUTE AND POSTTRAUMATIC STRESS DISORDERS

● Any potentially life-threatening situation may result in an acute stress disorder. An acute stress disorder is a psychological and physiological response that many, but not all, individuals experience when faced with overwhelming threat.

● An acute stress disorder that continues beyond a month qualifies as a posttraumatic stress disorder (PTSD). PTSD is characterized by approach (flashback and nightmares) and avoidance (emotional numbing and physical avoidance) reactions, as well as hyperarousal.

- PTSD can be difficult to treat. Support groups have been used with war veterans and victims of physical and sexual assault. Early intervention and a strong support network minimize the chance of PTSD developing.

GENDER DIFFERENCES

- Many, but not all, anxiety disorders show gender differences. Significantly more women than men exhibit panic disorder, agoraphobia, and most phobias, whereas OCD, GAD, and blood-injection-injury phobias occur at roughly equal rates in men and women. An evolutionary argument is consistent with this pattern of different rates for anxiety disorders in men and women.

KEY TERMS

acute stress disorder   (241)
agoraphobia   (217)
anxiety   (210)
anxiety disorder   (210)
anxiety sensitivity   (221)
anxiolytic   (215)
autonomic restrictors   (214)
blood-injection-injury phobia   (235)
compulsions   (226)
depersonalization   (241)
derealization   (241)
diaphragmatic breathing   (224)
ego dystonic   (227)
ego syntonic   (227)
exposure with response prevention   (232)
eye movement desensitization and reprocessing, or EMDR   (246)
flashbacks   (241)
flooding   (238)
generalized anxiety disorder, or GAD   (212)
generalized social phobia   (235)
hypervigilance   (242)

imaginal exposure   (238)
implosive therapy   (239)
in vivo exposure   (238)
locus coeruleus   (220)
neuroses   (211)
nocturnal panic attack   (216)
obsessions   (226)
obsessive-compulsive disorder, or OCD   (226)
panic attack   (216)
panic disorder   (216)
phobias   (233)
posttraumatic stress disorder, or PTSD   (241)
preparedness   (237)
progressive muscle relaxation   (224)
rituals   (226)
specific phobia   (233)
social phobia   (235)
Tourette's syndrome   (230)
two-process theory of avoidance learning   (230)
vasovagal syncope   (235)
Yerkes-Dodson Law   (210)

SUGGESTED READINGS

Barlow, D. H. (2002). *Anxiety and its disorders: The nature and treatment of anxiety and panic* (2nd ed.). New York: Guilford. This book is considered the bible of anxiety disorders.

Borkovec, T. D., & Inz, J. (1990). The nature of worry in generalized anxiety disorder: A predominance of thought activity. *Behavior Research and Therapy, 28,* 153–158. This is perhaps the most influential theory of generalized anxiety disorder.

Gorman, J. M., Liebowitz, M. R., Fyer, A. J., & Stein, J. A. (1989). Neuroanatomical hypothesis for panic disorder. *American Journal of Psychiatry, 146,* 148–161. This is an excellent example of a sophisticated, multiperspective look at an anxiety disorder.

McNally, R. J. (1994). *Panic disorder: A critical analysis.* New York: Guilford. An outstanding review of the research and theorizing on panic disorder and agoraphobia, written by one of the finest scholars in the field.

Nesse, R. M., & Williams, G. (1994). *Why we get sick: The new science of Darwinian medicine.* New York: New York Times Books. A great overview of the evolutionary perspective on health, including psychological health.

Steketee, G., & White, K. (1990). *When once is not enough.* Oakland, CA: New Harbinger Publications. This book was written for people with OCD and their loved ones. It is a readable presentation of what is known about OCD and its treatment.

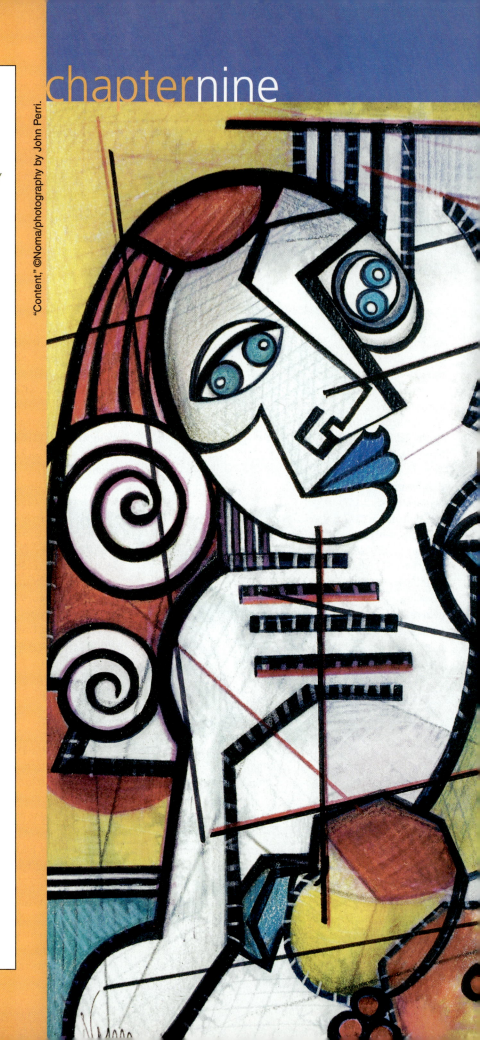

"Content," ©Noma/photography by John Perri.

chapternine

Stress, Health, and Somatoform Disorders

Absolutely Driven

TITO

At the age of 47, with three kids and a wife, a thriving business, and more success than he could ever have imagined, Tito still felt driven to achieve more. However, after he suffered two heart attacks in three years, his doctors told him that if he did not change his lifestyle, he was unlikely to survive to retirement. There were always long hours, pressing deadlines, and critical decisions to make. The construction company he had founded now employed almost 300 people, and it was his job to keep it running smoothly. At ages 20 and 30 and 40, the long hours had not bothered him, but now they took a toll. His irritability—always a part of his character—grew more pronounced with each passing year. He tried to watch his diet, to lose weight, and to get more exercise, but he refused to cut down on his hours or to hire someone to take over some of the management responsibilities. His doctor called him a ticking time bomb. Tito could hear the ticking too, but to him it was the clock that marked time faster than he could get the work done.

Finally Able to Quit

MARVIN

Marvin started smoking in his early twenties while serving in the Pacific theater during World War II. An excellent athlete before the war, he had always avoided smoking out of concern that it would affect his endurance. However, he found that smoking helped relieve the stress of being combat-ready, and by the time the war ended, he was smoking one to two packs a day. He tried to quit after returning to civilian life but was unable to do so. In fact, he tried to quit more than a dozen times, over the course of 25 years, without success. For much of that time, he was smoking two to three packs per day, so just cutting down was terribly uncomfortable. Even a health scare in his mid-forties, when a suspicious mark showed up on a lung X-ray, failed to induce him to stop. A blockage of the circulation in one leg, due primarily to diabetes but significantly exacerbated by his smoking, finally gave him the motivation he needed. The doctor told him that unless he controlled his blood sugar better and stopped smoking, he would probably lose the leg within a year.

It Really Wasn't Vanity

CAROLYN

It started when Carolyn noticed a few stray hairs on her pillow. She started inspecting her hair more carefully, and soon she was seeing hair specialists to alleviate the "thinning" problem. The more the specialists told her that her hair was normal, the more obsessed she became. She would spend an hour a day just checking her hair and up to 2 hours styling it to hide the "thinning." Within a year, she was spending 4 to 6 hours a day on her hair, wearing a wig to hide her real hair, and refusing to go out. She began seeking reassurance from her husband about her hair and would cry uncontrollably whenever he refused to give it to her. She then turned to her two teenage sons for reassurance, again tearfully begging them to tell her she looked all right. She refused to allow her sons to have friends over because she did not want their friends to see her hair. Yet her hair was perfectly normal; no one would have noticed anything wrong with it—no one, that is, except Carolyn.

I t has been said that if you have your health, you have everything. That is probably an overstatement, but it rings true for anyone who has had to deal with significant health problems. The many factors that contribute to health include genes, exposure to infections and toxic agents, behavior, the availability of appropriate medical care, and just plain luck. Traditional wisdom suggests that health problems can be classified as either physical or psychological. A case of the flu is an example of a physical problem, and depression is an example of a psychological problem. If you have accepted this traditional wisdom, you may be surprised by the content of this chapter. There is a fine line between the so-called physical and the so-called psychological disorders, and it is a line that is frequently crossed. Physical processes contribute to psychological disorders, and psychological processes contribute to physical disorders.

This chapter covers several health-related topics. It begins by addressing the role of stress on one's functioning and health. The chapter then addresses **stress-related disorders**—that is, physical disorders that are either caused or exacerbated by chronic stress. In the DSM, these disorders fall in the category of *psychological factors affecting medical conditions*. There follows a section on behavioral medicine, a rapidly growing area of psychology that is making significant contribution to the health care of individuals. Somatoform disorders are also covered. **Somatoform disorders** are psychological disorders that appear on the surface to be physical disorders but for which there is no identifiable physical basis. Note that psychological factors contribute to both stress-related and somatoform disorders. The distinction is that there is a clear indication of a physical abnormality in stress-related disorders, whereas somatoform disorders are characterized by physical symptoms that appear not to be the result of a physical disorder. The chapter ends with a discussion of physical disorders that can create psychological symptomatology.

People think of physical health and emotional health as very different, but they are often intertwined.

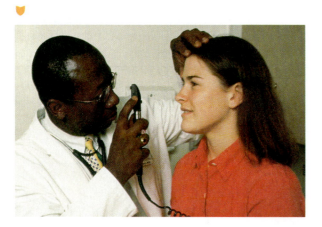

STRESS AND ITS IMPACT ON HUMAN FUNCTIONING

Stress is a fact of life, and, contrary to popular belief, it is not always bad. **Stress** is both a physiological and a psychological reaction to situations that demand adaptation. Although it is uncomfortable, stress facilitates and motivates adaptation. This section discusses the physiology of the stress response, the many ways in which stress can be measured, and the impact that chronic stress has on the immune system. It closes with a brief discussion of stress management strategies.

PHYSIOLOGY OF STRESS

The concept of stress and its relationship to psychological and physiological variables is so much a part of modern thinking that most people think it has been around for centuries. In fact, the concept is relatively new, dating back to the pioneering work of Hans Selye (1936). Like several critical concepts in psychology, Selye's work on stress was an almost accidental outgrowth of other research. In studying the effects of substances on the physiological functioning of rats, Selye noticed that his control group in one study showed evidence of deterioration—specifically, stomach ulcers and damage to the immune system. This control group was simply receiving injections of saline (salt water), which should not have been toxic. After conducting a series of studies, Selye determined that the injection itself, rather than the contents of the injection, was responsible for the deterioration. Furthermore, Selye discovered that many experiences, such as electric shock or being forced to swim in pool of water from which escape was impossible, could lead to the same deterioration. At the time, there was not even a generally accepted term for the common element that each of these experiences shared. Selye borrowed a term from engineering—*stress*—to refer to these experiences and the animals' reactions to them.

Selye's research focused on prolonged stress. The body is capable of handling intermittent stress with few long-term negative consequences. However, Selye noted that when faced with prolonged stress, the body appears to go

stress-related disorders   Physical disorders that are either caused or exacerbated by chronic stress.

somatoform disorders   Psychological disorders that appear on the surface to be physical disorders but for which there is no identifiable physical basis.

stress   Both a physiological and a psychological reaction to situations that demand adaptation.

general adaptation syndrome (GAS)   The three phases that a body goes through when faced with prolonged stress: alarm, resistance, and exhaustion.

Hans Selye discovered that the experience of repeatedly being handled and given injections of saline solution was sufficient to change the behavior and physiology of laboratory rats. He used the term *stress* to refer to these adverse experiences.

through three phases—alarm, resistance, and exhaustion—which he collectively referred to as the **general adaptation syndrome,** or **GAS.** These phases are illustrated in Figure 9.1. During the *alarm reaction,* the organism recognizes the stress and begins to respond to it. This initial response is mediated primarily by the central nervous system, which monitors the environment and reacts quickly to danger or other stimuli. The *resistance phase* involves adapting to the stress by mobilizing the body's resources for coping. This

resistance phase is mediated both by sympathetic nervous system activity and by a variety of hormones. Finally, if the stress lasts too long, the organism succumbs to fatigue in what is termed the *exhaustion phase,* and permanent damage or even death may result. Figure 9.1 illustrates that effective resistance to a stressor does not begin immediately, nor does it last forever. Yet the survival of the organism may depend on a rapid mobilization of resources during the alarm stage and on the ability to resolve the stressful situation or remove oneself from it before exhaustion sets in.

Although stress responses are initially mediated by the nervous system, longer-term stress responses are driven by the endocrine system. Remember from Chapter 4 that the endocrine system utilizes chemicals called hormones, which are secreted by endocrine glands throughout the body. These hormones circulate through the body via the bloodstream. Hormones coordinate dozens of individual organs in responding to specific situations. The situation may be as benign as being sexually aroused or as critical as being in fear of one's life. The alarm reaction triggers the hypothalamus to release a hormone called *corticotropin-releasing factor,* or *CRF,* which stimulates the pituitary gland to secrete ACTH (adrenocorticotropic hormone), which in turn stimulates the cortex of the adrenal gland. The adrenal cortex releases several hormones that are of great significance in cardiovascular disease, including *aldosterone,* which affects blood pressure. Also released is *cortisol,* which activates critical organ systems to respond to stressors in a coordinated and effective manner. The specific organs in this chain of actions are referred to as the

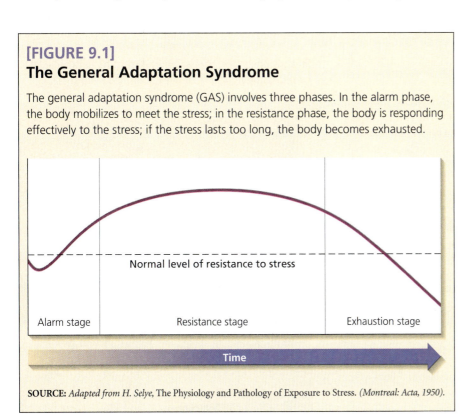

[FIGURE 9.1]
The General Adaptation Syndrome

The general adaptation syndrome (GAS) involves three phases. In the alarm phase, the body mobilizes to meet the stress; in the resistance phase, the body is responding effectively to the stress; if the stress lasts too long, the body becomes exhausted.

Normal level of resistance to stress

Alarm stage   Resistance stage   Exhaustion stage

Time

SOURCE: *Adapted from H. Selye,* The Physiology and Pathology of Exposure to Stress. *(Montreal: Acta, 1950).*

[FIGURE 9.2]
The HPA Axis

The HPA axis consists of the hypothalamus, the pituitary gland, and the adrenal cortex. When stressed, the hypothalamus secretes CRF, which in turn stimulates the adrenal cortex. The adrenal cortex secretes cortisol and other stress-related hormones, which activate the body to deal with stress.

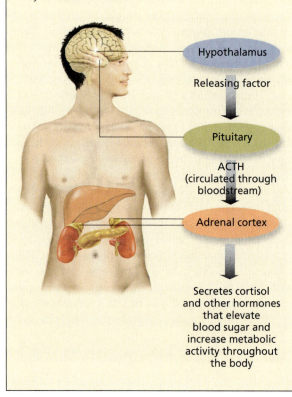

Hypothalamus

Releasing factor

Pituitary

ACTH
(circulated through bloodstream)

Adrenal cortex

Secretes cortisol and other hormones that elevate blood sugar and increase metabolic activity throughout the body

HPA axis (hypothalamus-pituitary-adrenal), as shown in Figure 9.2. The hippocampus inhibits the release of key stress hormones, thus dampening the hormonal response to stress and eventually bringing the system back into balance following a stressful situation.

Evolutionary Impact

This physiological stress system, like virtually every other neurological system, operates via a delicate balance between stimulation and inhibition. Threatening events stimulate the physiological stress response, which is gradually inhibited by other physiological systems, provided that the stressful situation has subsided. It has served organisms well for millions of years, but main-

HPA axis The three organs involved in a chain of actions when a body is stimulated by stress: the hypothalamus, the pituitary gland, and the adrenal cortex.

taining the balance is dependent on the health of the entire system. The major inhibitory influence—the hippocampus—can actually be damaged by prolonged exposure to stress hormones, which upsets this balance (Virgin et al., 1991). The result is a stress system that tends not to shut down, even when the stressor is gone. Organisms clearly evolved to deal with occasional stressful situations that are typically handled in a matter of minutes or hours, such as risk from predators or a forest fire. The system is designed to turn on quickly through central and autonomic nervous system activity, to be reinforced through hormonal action that coordinates a broad-based physiological response, and then to shut down rather quickly and reset for the next stressor. Today, however, many people are subjected to chronic stresses, resulting in chronic and excessive levels of such hormones as cortisol. The modern 24/7/365 world creates the psychological equivalent of a constant crisis. Single working parents are especially stressed. When not working, they must try to meet the constant demands of children, with no partner to relieve them when the demands start to take a toll. Can people deal with such a world with bodies that evolved over millions of years to deal with a very different environment? This is an area in which cross-cultural studies will be especially valuable, because these relatively recent environmental changes have not occurred everywhere. In fact, such anthropological studies are already under way (Stinson, 2000). There are many Polynesian and African tribal cultures in which the rise and fall of the sun do more to shape the individual's life than cell phones and e-mails. Contrasting them with technological cultures may provide valu-

Stress is uncomfortable and may disrupt functioning, but people usually perform better under moderate stress.

able insights, although one must be careful in such research. The stresses are clearly different in different cultures, but each culture has its own stresses. The tribal cultures may not be hassled with phone calls, but their next meal may be less certain than in Western cultures.

MEASURING STRESS

What is stress? The answer to this question is far from simple, although on the surface it seems simple. You would probably have little difficulty identifying things in your life that you find stressful. Most measures of stress take this very approach; they define stress in terms of the frequency and severity of recent stressful events.

The first stress measure—the *Social Readjustment Rating Scale*—identified events that people rated as stressful and obtained stress ratings for each event (Holmes & Rahe, 1967). Selected items and their stress ratings are illustrated in Figure 9.3. Note three things about this list: (1) There is quite a range of items and levels of stress, from the death of

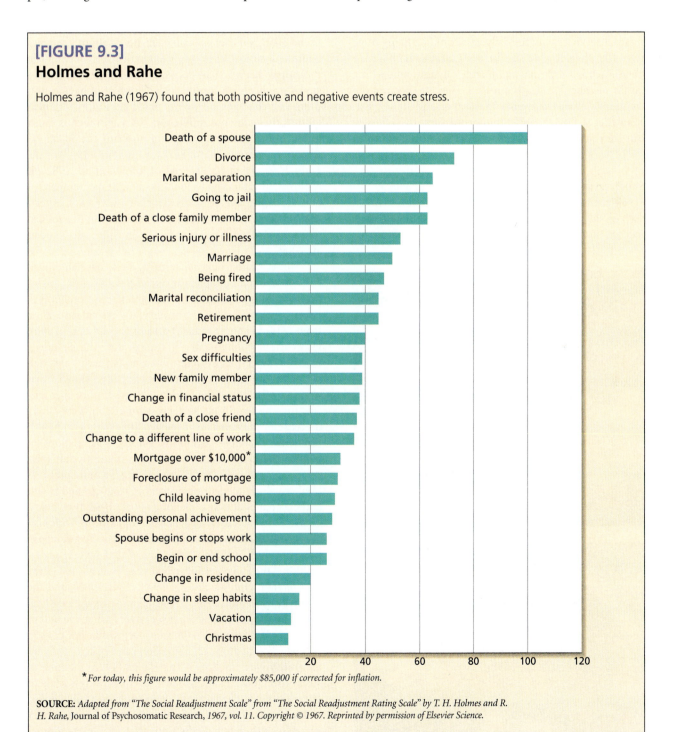

[FIGURE 9.3]

Holmes and Rahe

Holmes and Rahe (1967) found that both positive and negative events create stress.

* For today, this figure would be approximately $85,000 if corrected for inflation.

SOURCE: *Adapted from "The Social Readjustment Scale" from "The Social Readjustment Rating Scale" by T. H. Holmes and R. H. Rahe,* Journal of Psychosomatic Research, *1967, vol. 11. Copyright © 1967. Reprinted by permission of Elsevier Science.*

a spouse to a vacation. (2) Some of the items, such as getting married and having a new family member, are surprising. These are supposed to be happy events, and most people implicitly equate stress with negative events. Nevertheless, these joyful events are also stressful because they force people to adapt. Getting married or having a child is stressful, even if it is what you have wanted for years. (3) The events on the list are relatively infrequent. Most occur just once or twice a year, and many occur only once or twice in a lifetime.

The stressful events in Holmes and Rahe's list are clearly stressful, but they represent only one class of stressful events. What about the daily hassles of life? Being stuck in traffic when you are late for work, dealing with a rude person while shopping, and having an argument with a family member are clearly stressful. They also occur more frequently than the events in Holmes and Rahe's list. Kanner et al. (1981) sought to measure these daily *hassles,* but they added an interesting element to their hassles

Stress can come from many sources. Holmes and Rahe (1967) focused on the major stressors in a person's life, such as getting married. In contrast, Kanner et al. (1981) focused on the everyday hassles of life, such as traffic jams.

measure—the measurement of positive daily experiences, which they called *uplifts.* Examples of uplifts include being complimented, completing a big job, and affectionate contact with people who are important to you. The logic of measuring uplifting experiences is that these experiences may compensate for the presence of hassles, thus reducing the overall level of perceived stress.

A third approach to the measurement of stress recognizes that the level of stress associated with an event is a function of many variables (Brown & Harris, 1978). For example, the psychological impact of a pregnancy depends on many factors. A 16-year-old high school girl whose boyfriend "dumped" her as soon as he heard about her pregnancy will almost surely react differently from a couple in their early 30s who had decided to start their family and stopped using birth control with the intent of having children. Just checking off events that a person experiences ignores these obvious differences. This approach is much more time-consuming than administering the *Social Readjustment Rating Scale* of Holmes and Rahe (1967) or the *Daily Hassles and Uplifts Scale* of Kanner et al. (1981). It requires an interview to identify the critical details that determine the level of stress associated with each experience. However, the extra effort associated with this refined measure of stress appears to be worthwhile (McQuaid et al., 2000).

These approaches to measuring stress have all proved their value. For example, the *Social Readjustment Rating Scale* shows a consistent, though weak, relationship between stress and risk for a variety of physical disorders, from colds to cancer to heart attacks (Scully et al., 2000). However, a problem arises in interpreting these studies, because they typically determined health status through self-reports. Watson and Pennebaker (1989) showed that *negative affectivity*—the tendency to experience such uncomfortable emotions as depression and anxiety—may increase both reports of negative life events and health problems. Therefore, part of this already weak relationship may be due to the confounding effect of negative affectivity. The *Hassles and Uplifts Scale* shows a bit more promise, predicting marital distress (Harper et al., 2000) and health and occupational status (DeLongis et al., 1988; Ivancevich, 1986). However, the *Daily Hassles and Uplifts Scale* also accounted for only a small portion of risk. For example, Maybery and Graham (2001) found that several scales, including the *Perceived Stress Scale* (Cohen et al., 1983), the *Satisfaction with Life Scale* (Diener et al., 1985), and the *Positive and Negative Affect Scale* (Watson et al., 1988), all added additional predictive power over and above that of the *Daily Hassles and Uplifts Scale.* Depressive episodes in people who are prone to depression can be predicted very accurately with the Brown and Harris (1978) measure of stress (McQuaid et al., 2000). Clearly, no single scale of stress works in all situations. There are at least half a dozen scales in current use. As you will see later, stress is a complex variable, with subtle distinctions that are clearly important in predicting risk for such negative consequences as health problems.

STRESS AND THE IMMUNE SYSTEM

Stress adapts the body to environmental demands by reassigning available coping resources. Activation of the sympathetic nervous system during stress tends to inhibit the parasympathetic nervous system and the physiological functions it controls (see Chapter 4 for details). This reassignment of resources enhances immediate coping but also has costs. In this section, you will see how stress compromises the immune system and therefore increases the risk for physical disorders.

Common Colds. A widespread but erroneous belief is that one can get a cold from getting a chill. In fact, viruses cause colds, although the physiological stress of being chilled may weaken the body's natural defenses. There are thousands of cold viruses, and new ones develop all the time. Each is capable of producing an infection and the typical symptoms of a cold. To prevent exposure to cold

Stress can depress the immune system, making one more likely to get a cold or other infection.

viruses, one would have to live virtually in a bubble. Yet some people tend to get more colds than others. How is it possible to stay healthy when your roommate has a cold? There are probably many reasons, but one is that a person's level of stress affects the risk for developing the symptoms of a cold. Let's look at the research on this issue.

Examining the Evidence

How can one test the hypothesis that stress increases vulnerability for colds? It has long been known that colds are more common in those under stress (Steptoe & Wardle, 1994), but this observation merely reflects the correlation between the variables of illness and stress level, and it is impossible to determine causation from a correlation alone. The stress may have contributed to the cold; the cold may have intensified the stress; or another variable, such as a physiological imbalance, may have contributed to both.

The ideal study would experimentally manipulate the relevant variables—exposure to the virus and level of stress. In a classic experiment, one of these variables was manipulated and the second variable was measured. Cohen et al. (1991) deliberately exposed 394 healthy volunteers to one of five common cold viruses, and a control group of 26 individuals were exposed to a placebo (no virus). The cold viruses were blown up the volunteers' noses in a mist at a low dose to simulate the exposure one might receive from being in close proximity to someone who had a cold. The volunteers were then isolated in apartments to prevent additional exposure. Of the participants exposed to a cold virus, 82% became infected (the cold viruses replicated within the person's body), and 38% developed such traditional cold symptoms as a sore throat, a runny nose, and chest congestion. These are clearly two separate steps: (1) contracting the virus when exposed and (2) developing symptoms if the virus is contracted. Cohen et al. (1991) discovered that stress during the past two months predicted which people were most likely to contract the virus when exposed. Furthermore, stress levels predicted who among those who contracted the virus developed cold symptoms. This finding has been replicated several times (e.g., Stone et al., 1992).

Cohen et al. (1993) examined the recent stressful experiences of their participants in more detail and found that "stress" was more complex than one might think. They measured stress with several different instruments, each of which captured a different aspect. One instrument measured the frequency of stressful life events, a second measured perceived level of stress, and a third measured negative affect. They found that high scores on each instrument predicted risk for cold symptoms when exposed to cold viruses, but with some interesting twists. Specifically, the number of recent stressful life events predicted who would develop cold symptoms if infected with the virus, but not who would become infected with the virus. In contrast, the level of perceived stress and the level of negative affect predicted who would become infected, but not who among the infected individuals would develop cold symptoms. It is not at all clear why this curious pattern of findings exists. These different measures of stress may be capturing different aspects of the stress effects. If nothing else, these findings indicate that the relationship between stress and illness is complex and subtle and will take considerable research to untangle.

The complexity of the findings on stress and viral infection should convince you of two things. First, stress appears to play a role in moderating risk for infections such as colds, but this relationship is complex and involves more than just the level of stress. Second, scientists are only beginning to understand the processes involved, and much more research is needed. An exciting new field—psychoneuroimmunology—is seeking to address these various questions. The nearby Advances box describes some of the work in this area.

AIDS. **Acquired immune deficiency syndrome,** or **AIDS,** is a deadly disease that weakens the immune system to the point that the person can no longer fight off infections. The result is a series of ever more deadly opportunistic infections that eventually lead to death. The human immunodeficiency virus, or HIV, is the cause of AIDS. Although there is presently no cure for AIDS, modern treatments extend the lives of people with HIV infection. Nevertheless, the best "treatment" for the disorder is to prevent the infection in the first place, a topic that will be covered later in this chapter.

What role can stress play in the course of AIDS? One might think that it would have little effect, given the natural virulence of the disease, yet the evidence suggests otherwise. Stress affects immune functioning and thus the progression of AIDS (Kennedy, 2000). Consequently, moderating the level of stress is critical. Social support can moderate some of the negative impact of stress (Kennedy, 2000), as

can cognitive stress management (Lutgendorf et al., 1997; Schneiderman et al., 1992). Supportive friends always lighten the load when people are feeling overwhelmed. Identifying and challenging faulty beliefs, such as "I should never let this illness get me down," often reduces stress. A simple exercise program can reduce stress and thus slow the progression of AIDS (Schneiderman et al., 1992). Finally, people with AIDS who feel in control of their own treatment typically report experiencing less stress (Suarez & Reese, 2000).

Cancer. After learning that stress adversely affects resistance to diseases as diverse as the common cold and AIDS, you perhaps will not be surprised to find out that stress affects cancer as well. Of course, having cancer is immensely stressful. Although there have been substantial improvements in cancer treatment, especially when it is detected early (Rubens & Coleman, 1999), most people associate cancer with high mortality and therefore worry about survival. Furthermore, cancer treatments are stressful—they often make people sick and uncomfortable, sometimes dramatically so. What, then, is the role of stress and other psychological variables in cancer?

Cohen et al. (2000) demonstrated a mechanism by which stress may increase risk for cancer. To understand the mechanism, however, you have to understand how cancers begin. Cancers are the result of a mutation in a cell that causes the cell to grow and multiply at excessively high rates. Such mutations can be caused by a number of factors, including chance, but most often the mutations are the result of exposure to **carcinogenic agents**—substances that tend to trigger cancer mutations. Normally, the conversion of a normal cell into a cancer cell requires two mutations. Mutated cells are normally destroyed by the body's immune system before they can experience a second mutation and become cancerous. However, Cohen et al. (2000) found that stress decreased the efficiency of this immune system response, which could increase the risk for cancer in anyone who is exposed to carcinogenic agents. They evaluated medical students halfway through a five-day exam period and then again three weeks later after a vacation. They took blood samples at each testing and measured the capacity to repair damaged cells. Not surprisingly, the medical students reported significantly more stress during the exam period than after a three-week vacation. More important, the students' immune systems repaired damaged cells much more slowly during the stressful exam period than during the vacation.

Although stress has been linked to risk for cancer, there are few studies of the impact of stress during cancer treatment. One of the best studies found no relationship between (1) the frequency and intensity of stressful life events in the five years prior to diagnosis and (2) survival rates for women with breast cancer (Maunsell et al., 2001). This is an area that cries out for an experimental study. For example, few people with cancer currently receive stress management

Acquired immune deficiency syndrome (AIDS)   A deadly disease that weakens the immune system to the point where the person can no longer fight off infections.

carcinogenic agents   Substances that tend to trigger cancer mutations.

psychoneuroimmunology   The study of the effects that behavior has on the immune system.

ADVANCES   Psychoneuroimmunology

Psychoneuroimmunology is the study of the effects that behavior has on the immune system (Kiecolt-Glaser et al., 2002) as a consequence of the reciprocal interactions among the nervous, endocrine, and immune systems (Cohen & Kinney, 2001). It is a relatively new field, with roots going back two decades (Ader, 1981). Textbooks tend to organize and simplify nature by, for example, breaking down complex systems into discrete parts. For example, you learned about the central and autonomic nervous systems in Chapter 4 but were warned that these are really one coordinated system. Even when systems can be clearly separated, such as the endocrine and nervous systems, their operations are so closely coordinated that they often work as a unit.

Evolutionary Impact ——

The human body was not assembled like an automobile, with individual parts designed separately and then attached to create the finished product. It evolved over millions of years. What difference does this fact make? In evolution, every new element has to work in harmony with existing elements or the organism will be flawed and thus less likely to pass on its genes. Evolution favors harmonious interactions among systems. Furthermore, systems do not just show up fully formed, like a fuel injection system for a car. They have to evolve over hundreds of millennia.

They evolve faster if they do not have to be built from scratch, which is one reason why nature borrows existing structures and systems and adapts them to new uses. For example, it is unlikely that nature evolved a "reader" for the brain—a specialized part of the brain devoted exclusively to decoding and comprehending the squiggly marks your eyes are focused on right now. It is more likely that the recognition of letters is based on already existing "form perception units" in the brain, that the organization of letters into words employs already existing organizational units, and that interpreting the meaning of those words uses slightly adapted advanced processing capabilities.

Psychoneuroimmunology seeks to identify the interactions among systems and to understand how they overlap and why they interact. The earliest findings that stress affects the immune system were surprising. Now the data on the effects of stress on the immune system are overwhelming (Cohen & Kinney, 2001). Neurological and endocrine responses to stress clearly affect many aspects of immune system function, but other evidence suggests that the immune system also affects both the nervous and endocrine systems (Felten et al., 1991). If understanding the workings of the nervous system or immune system is the scientific equivalent of putting together 1000-piece puzzles, then

understanding their interactions with one another is more like putting together a million-piece puzzle. It will take decades of additional research. The focus can be narrowed by concentrating on interactions that make evolutionary sense—that is, interactions based on borrowing critical components and adapting them to new purposes. Existing species, with their wide variety of system capabilities, provide fragments of evolutionary history to guide such an educated guessing game. Understanding the interactions among these systems could provide far more effective ways of managing stress without hindering immune system functioning.

It is a safe bet that technological development, population growth, and environmental problems will increase stress. Humans will continue to evolve, but the evolutionary process is slow. On the other hand, infectious agents are locked in an evolutionary arms race with humans. Their survival depends on developing ways to defeat our immune systems, and our survival depends on our immune systems adapting rapidly enough to handle these new infectious agents. The survival of humans may well depend on our understanding the functioning of the immune system well enough to bolster its defenses artificially when humans fall behind infectious agents in this evolutionary struggle.

services during treatment. Randomly assigning people with cancer to standard treatment or to standard treatment supplemented with stress management and then following both groups for a few years would provide valuable information about the possible value of stress management in recovery from cancer.

STRESS MANAGEMENT

Given that stress increases the risk for some diseases, speeds the progression of others, and reduces the normal functioning of the immune system, managing stress effectively is important. Stress management programs typically combine several effective elements into a comprehensive package, including (1) physiological methods to reduce arousal, (2) cognitive strategies to minimize the stress experienced in specific situations, (3) behavioral strategies to minimize the stress, and (4) strategies to provide external buffers against the stress.

Physiological Strategies. Stress is both a psychological and a physiological experience. It is characterized by sympathetic nervous system activity, which increases heart rate, muscle tension, facial flushing, and sweating. Two strategies to dampen these physiological responses are often taught to individuals as part of an overall stress management program. The first is **progressive muscle relaxation,** which involves relaxing the muscles of the body, one group at a time (Bernstein & Borkovec, 1973; Bernstein et al., 2000; Jacobson, 1939). It is no accident that people use terms such as *tense* and *relaxed* to refer to their level of anxiety or stress. When one is anxious or stressed, the muscles of the body tense. The progressive muscle relaxation procedure directly relaxes those muscles, leaving the person feeling more relaxed and less stressed. The second physiological stress management procedure is **diaphragmatic breathing,** which is deep breathing that involves the diaphragm. Diaphragmatic breathing is essentially overbreathing— breathing more than is necessary to meet the aerobic demands of the body. The excess breathing increases the level of oxygen in the blood, which in turn slows the heart rate and relaxes the muscles. Both progressive muscle relaxation and diaphragmatic breathing are effective strategies for attenuating the physiological responses that are a part of stress. When combined with other components, these techniques are effective in stress management.

Biofeedback is a technique that utilizes sensors and electronic transformation to provide people with accurate information about such body states as muscle tension, heart rate, and blood pressure. This information is presumed to be helpful in learning to control these body states. Biofeedback practitioners found that their greatest success was obtained when working with muscle training rather than with responses of autonomically controlled activity, such as cardiac and vascular responses. For example, to help people learn relaxation skills, biofeedback instruments might provide a client with feedback in the form of an

With practice, people can learn to calm themselves, thus reducing their stress.

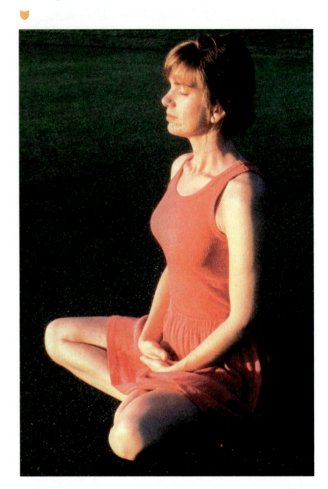

auditory signal whose pitch was directly related to the client's level of muscle tension. As the client's muscles relaxed, the auditory signal would decrease in pitch to indicate progress. Biofeedback is often successful in such applications, but it appears to add little to simpler techniques, such as progressive muscle relaxation and diaphragmatic breathing (Schwartz & Olson, 1995). Hence its use in stress management programs has declined in the past decade, although it is still used as an adjunct to physical therapy in the rehabilitation of stroke victims or accident victims who have lost partial use of large muscles.

Cognitive Strategies. Although it may not always be obvious, the way people interpret and respond to events has considerable impact on how much stress they experience (McLean & Woody, 2001). For example, it is common to have more to do in a given period of time than one can possibly get done, and such situations are stressful. How stressful people find such periods depends on how they react. If they tell themselves they *must* do everything, the stress will be intense. It will be even more intense if they imagine severe consequences for their failure to get everything done,

---

progressive muscle relaxation   A strategy, used in an overall stress management program, that involves relaxing the muscles of the body, one group at a time.

diaphragmatic breathing   Deep breathing that involves the diaphragm; a technique used in stress management.

biofeedback   A technique that utilizes sensors and electronic transformation to provide people with accurate information about such body states as muscle tension, heart rate, and blood pressure.

such as being fired. If, on the other hand, they recognize that they cannot complete everything in the time available, set priorities, work on the top priorities first, and take steps to delegate other items or negotiate extensions, their stress will be more manageable.

Note that cognitive strategies do not attempt to eliminate stress (Curwen et al., 2000). Convincing yourself that it does not matter how good a job you do at work may temporarily reduce your stress, but you are likely to experience considerably more stress after you are fired for poor work performance. Stress is a reality of life; it is not evil and is not even problematic unless it becomes excessive. The cognitive perspective seeks to prevent stress from becoming excessive.

Behavioral Strategies. Behavioral strategies seek to minimize stress by either changing the situation or changing the way the situation is handled. For example, setting priorities and delegating work to others are behavioral strategies to decrease stress. Behavioral strategies can include learning to do things more efficiently, solving ongoing problems that produce stress, and avoiding situations that create stress. There are several ways to increase efficiency, such as using appropriate technology, improving your skills in handling problems, and rearranging your schedule to allow more time. If certain people or activities produce stress and you have options, you may want to associate with other people or engage in other activities. If watching your favorite team on TV drives you nuts because it is playing badly this season, you might stop watching the games. It is sometimes even appropriate to consider making major changes in your life, such as job changes or changes in relationships.

Stress Buffering. Although stress is an inevitable part of life, there are ways of buffering yourself from its negative effects. Supportive relationships are an important buffer (Larose & Bernier, 2001). Sometimes it helps just to talk about stresses with someone who is willing to listen and understand. Periods away from stress for recuperation can also be an effective stress-buffering technique. These may include periodic vacations, but they may also include something as simple as an hour to relax before going to bed. Exercise, reading, or getting together with friends can dissipate stress and distract people from the sources of their stress (Davis et al., 2000). Adequate sleep is important; everyday stressors that can be handled easily when one is well rested may feel insurmountable when one is too tired to cope.

No single stress management strategy works in every situation. However, the combination of physiological, cognitive, and behavioral strategies, coupled with the effective use of social support to buffer one from the more severe effects of stress, can dramatically improve the response of most people to stressful situations. For some acute stressors, one may want to consider the short-term use of mild

The support of others may not eliminate stressors, but it does make them easier to face.

anxiolytic drugs, such as *Xanax* or *Valium* (Thom et al., 2000). These are usually not the treatment of choice, but for people with poor stress management skills who are faced with an overwhelming stressor, they may provide a bridge until other stress management strategies can be learned and implemented. This might be necessary, for example, when a person is faced with an overwhelming loss, such as the tragic death of a close family member or friend.

Check Yourself 9.1

Stress and Its Impact on Human Functioning

1. What are the stages of the general adaptation syndrome?
2. Cite three ways in which stress has been measured.
3. How does stress affect the immune system?
4. How can stress be managed?

Ponder this . . . *Stress, like many psychological and physiological responses, is a double-edged sword—sometimes helpful and sometimes harmful. The world has changed dramatically from the world in which the stress response evolved. What impact have these changes had on the effectiveness of the stress response described by Hans Selye?*

PSYCHOLOGICAL FACTORS THAT AFFECT MEDICAL CONDITIONS

As you learned in the previous section, stress affects many physical disorders, including some that people do not normally associate with stress, such as AIDS, cancer, and the common cold. There are specific disorders that have a long history of association with stress. These conditions were once called **psychosomatic disorders,** which are physical (somatic) disorders with a significant psychological contribution, usually stress. The more modern term for this category is **psychophysiological disorders.** The DSM refers to these disorders as *psychological factors affecting medical conditions.* The stress-related disorders covered in this section typically are coded as medical conditions on Axis III. This section covers three broad categories of stress-related disorders: gastrointestinal disorders, cardiovascular disorders, and headaches.

GASTROINTESTINAL

The gastrointestinal system is the body's digestive system. It includes everything from the saliva-generating glands in the mouth that facilitate swallowing, to the esophagus that delivers the food to the stomach, and the intestines and bowels, which extract the nutrients and remove the nonnutritive elements as waste. This system is critical to survival. Without food and the nutrients it provides, organisms would quickly die. Stress can disrupt the normal functioning of the gastrointestinal system, as anyone who has responded to a stressful situation with an upset stomach or diarrhea can attest. This section discusses ulcers and irritable bowel syndrome, two gastrointestinal disorders that are exacerbated by stress.

Ulcers. Ulcers are lesions or holes that gastric juices have burned into the wall of either the stomach or the duodenum (the upper portion of the intestine). Ulcers of the stomach are called *gastric ulcers,* and ulcers of the duodenum are called *peptic ulcers.* Ulcers can be painful, may cause vomiting, and can be life-threatening when they bleed. They were once thought to be primarily the result of stress (Hernandez & Glavin, 1990), but more recent research suggests that many factors contribute to ulcers besides stress, including weakness in the lining of the stomach or intestines, excessive production of gastric acids, and a specific bacterial infection called *helicobacter pylori* (Thagard, 1999).

....

psychosomatic disorders Older term for physical (somatic) disorders that have a significant psychological component, usually stress.

psychophysiological disorders The modern term for psychosomatic disorders.

ulcers Lesions or holes that gastric juices have burned into the wall of either the stomach or the duodenum (the upper portion of the intestine).

irritable bowel syndrome (IBS) The rapid and sometimes unpredictable onset of intense cramps and diarrhea.

coronary heart disease Heart disease caused by blockages to the blood vessels that feed the heart muscles.

Irritable Bowel Syndrome. Irritable bowel syndrome, or **IBS,** is characterized by a rapid and sometimes unpredictable onset of intense cramps and diarrhea. Its lifetime prevalence is estimated at 20%, and it is twice as common in women than in men (Naliboff et al., 2000). Interestingly, 40% of people with a severe mood disorder and 60% with dysthymia have IBS (Masand et al., 1997), although in nearly every case, the onset of the IBS preceded the onset of the mood disorder (Dewsnap et al., 1996). The rates of IBS are also substantially elevated in alcohol abuse or dependence (Masand et al., 1998), posttraumatic stress disorder (Irwin et al., 1996), panic disorder (Kaplan et al., 1996), and generalized anxiety disorder (Tollefson et al., 1991) and in those who have been sexually abused (Walker et al., 1993). Although it is typically thought of as a disorder of adulthood, recent evidence suggests that the symptoms of IBS often first appear in childhood (Burke et al., 1999). The autonomic nervous system has been implicated in IBS, and there are gender differences in autonomic nervous system functioning that may contribute to the different rates of this disorder in men and women (Naliboff et al., 2000). Those who seek treatment for IBS report elevated stress. This finding might suggest that stress is a cause. However, most people with IBS do not seek treatment, and those individuals that do not seek treatment do not report elevated stress (Drossman, 1994). In other words, stress is associated with seeking treatment for IBS rather than with IBS itself.

CARDIOVASCULAR

The cardiovascular system consists of the heart and lungs, as well as the arteries, veins, and capillaries that move blood throughout the body. Two cardiovascular diseases, coronary heart disease and essential hypertension, have traditionally been considered stress-related disorders.

Coronary Heart Disease. Coronary heart disease involves blockages to the blood vessels that feed the heart muscles. The blood that is pumped by the heart to the rest of the body simply passes through the heart, providing no benefit to the muscles of the heart. The coronary arteries supply the blood the heart muscles need. Coronary heart disease actually represents a range of disorders. At the mild end is *angina pectoris,* which is severe chest pain due to a partial blockage of a coronary artery. *Coronary occlusion* is a near total blockage of a coronary artery. Occlusions often result in destruction of heart muscle, which is called a *myocardial infarction* or, more commonly, a *heart attack.* In the United States, coronary heart disease is the leading cause of death for people over 40 (Blanchard, 1994). Nearly 150,000 people under the age of 65 and 650,000 people over the age of 65 die of coronary heart disease every year—one American a minute (Anderson et al., 1997; Blanchard, 1994). Nearly 80% of people under the age of 65 who have a heart attack die from it (American Heart Association,

2001). Coronary heart disease is more common in men than in women, although this difference seems to be narrowing. The rates are much higher in middle-age men than in middle-age women, but after menopause, the rates rise dramatically for women, eventually reaching the rates for men (American Heart Association, 2001). The rates are nearly 50% higher in black Americans than in white Americans (Anderson et al., 1997).

The racial differences in heart disease are substantial, and one might be tempted to attribute them primarily to genetic differences. However, the data on this question are complicated and somewhat confusing. For example, the risk of coronary disease varies dramatically among ethnic subgroups of African Americans. Fang et al. (1996) showed that substantial differences in risk exist as a function of the early cultural experiences of blacks as defined by where the person was born. Furthermore, there are very different rates of coronary heart disease in African American and African Caribbean blacks, despite the fact that these groups are very similar in genetic heritage (Zoratti, 1998). Some have suggested that these subcultural differences may be due to differences in nutritional history (Zoratti, 1998).

Several factors are known to increase risk for coronary heart disease, including being overweight and sedentary, smoking, and having a poor diet, high cholesterol, and a family history of heart disease. Several of these biological risk factors—diet, exercise, smoking—are behaviors that, in theory, can be changed to enhance health. Such changes will be discussed in the "Behavioral Medicine" section of this chapter.

Stress increases the risk for heart attacks, especially in people who have other risk factors for coronary heart disease. For example, Massing and Angermeyer (1985) inspected the distribution of fatal heart attacks across the days of the week. One might expect that heart attacks would occur randomly across the week, but heart attacks in men 25 to 55 years old were more common on Mondays and Saturdays—the days on which the men transitioned from work to leisure activities, and vice versa. Both Mondays and Saturdays are likely to be marked by more stress. Mondays represent back-to-work days, with the stresses stemming from the demands of work. Saturdays are the start of the weekend, during which people who are relatively sedentary during the week exert themselves doing yard work and engaging in recreational activities.

One of the more interesting factors associated with risk for coronary heart disease is the Type A behavior pattern (Friedman & Rosenman, 1959, 1974). **Type A behav-**

The key component of Type A personality is hostility, which is strongly associated with increased risk for coronary heart disease.

ior includes intense competitiveness, a constant feeling of time pressure, impatience, high activity level, aggressiveness, and hostility. Tito, whom we met at the beginning of this chapter, showed many of these characteristics, which may have contributed to his heart attacks. People without these traits are said to exhibit **Type B behavior.** These terms have developed popular meanings: "hard-driving" and "laid back," respectively. However, these popular meanings are an oversimplification at best. The research on Type A behavior is a classic example of construct validation (see Chapter 6). Therefore, this research will be covered in some detail.

Examining the Evidence

The observations of Friedman and Rosenman that their cardiology patients frequently exhibited the hard-driving traits that they labeled Type A were a critical first step in the recognition and later validation of this construct. However, their ideas would never have become the staple of textbooks that they are today if the work had stopped there. They had observed what appeared to be a tendency for apparently healthy, vigorous men who were driven and successful to be struck

---

Type A behavior   Behavior that includes feelings of intense competitiveness, constant time pressure, impatience, high activity level, aggressiveness, and hostility.

Type B behavior   People without Type A traits are said to exhibit Type B behavior.

by heart attacks. Was this observation correct? Were these people really at risk?

The first large-scale test of the hypothesis was the *Western Collaborative Group Study* (Rosenman et al., 1975). This was a prospective study that followed over 3000 men, aged 39 to 59, for more than 8 years. Each participant was categorized as Type A or Type B on the basis of his reported behavior and a structured interview, and each participant was evaluated on such risk factors as family history of heart disease, smoking history, and cholesterol level. Men with Type A personalities were found to be twice as likely as men with Type B personalities to develop coronary heart disease, and this finding was independent of other known risk factors. This study provided strong support for the hypothesis that Type A personality was associated with risk for coronary heart disease. Several other studies conducted at about the same time produced similar results, but later studies showed a much weaker correlation between the Type A personality and risk for coronary heart disease (Appels, 1996). What happened? Were the original studies wrong, or did something change? Cultures and normative behavior do change over time, and such changes could account for the change in the predictive validity of the Type A behavior pattern (Appels, 1996). Another possibility is that the Type A behavior pattern was only a crude estimate of the factor that actually predicted risk for heart disease.

The Type A behavior pattern originally contained several different characteristics (hard-driving, impatient, time-conscious, irritable, hostile). A reasonable question is whether all of these behaviors, or only some of them, predict risk for heart disease. Research suggests that hostility is by far the most critical component in predicting risk for heart disease (Dembroski & Costa, 1987; Williams, 1996). Hostility includes such behaviors as road rage, getting angry while waiting in line, and expressing cynicism. When one of the largest studies of risk for coronary heart disease was reanalyzed, the hostility component, but none of the other components of the Type A pattern, was found to predict heart disease (Dembroski et al., 1989). Hostility has been postulated as a mediator to explain the large differences between men and women in risk for coronary heart disease, because men tend to show more overt hostility than women (Stoney & Engebretson, 1994). The concept of hostility, like the concept of the Type A personality, is also heterogeneous. Recent evidence suggests that expressed anger—that is, yelling at others in anger—is more predictive of coronary heart disease than other subtypes of hostility (McDermott et al., 2001). This is exactly the opposite of popular wisdom, which suggests that it is more healthful to express anger than to hold it in.

What is it about hostility that contributes to risk for heart disease? This question is far from answered, but one possible biological mechanism has been identified. Several studies have found that people with high levels of hostility show increased sympathetically mediated physiological reactivity, such as increased heart rate, in response to interpersonal conflict (Suarez et al., 1998; Williams, 1996). Furthermore, in their everyday lives, hostile people show evidence of sympathetic nervous system hyperreactivity (Szczepanski et al., 1997) and parasympathetic hyporeactivity (Fukudo et al., 1992). That is, they respond more strongly to stressful situations and relax more slowly when the stress has passed. Finally, there is evidence that hostile individuals may also engage in behaviors that increase risk for coronary heart disease; these include eating in a manner that increases both weight and cholesterol level, as well as smoking and drinking more (Siegler et al., 1992). Such a combination of factors could easily account for the increased risk for coronary heart disease (Williams, 1996).

Cultural factors also play a role in risk for coronary heart disease, although the exact nature of this role is not always clear. Figure 9.4 shows the mortality rates for coronary heart disease in persons 55 to 64 years old in 21 countries. Even a cursory glance reveals that something important is going on here. The mortality rates vary dramatically from one country to the next, even between countries that share a border. Is it diet, genes, medical treatment, or lifestyle that accounts for these findings? Probably all of these factors contribute. However, some of the aspects of the Type A personality style, applied on a national level, may play a role. Specifically, Appels (1996) correlated the mortality rates shown in Figure 9.4 with average Need for Achievement scores for these countries. *Need for Achievement* represents the degree to which people strive to accomplish specific personal goals and judge their worth by the success they achieve in reaching those goals. In other words, it is similar to the hard-driving facet of the Type A behavior pattern. Appels found that the average Need for Achievement scores of the countries could explain 35% of the variability in mortality rates across countries. However, there is another way of looking at this finding. The Need for Achievement measure focuses on individual goals, so the scores are higher in countries that encourage individual achievement than in countries that stress collectivistic cultural goals. These cultural differences are associated with dozens of other differences, from diet to exercise to income to medical philosophy and care, any one of which could account for different rates of coronary heart disease. Again, one must be careful in interpreting such correlational data, because multiple interpretations are possible.

[FIGURE 9.4]

Coronary Heart Disease Around the World

The death rate from coronary heart disease in people between 55 and 64 varies dramatically from country to country, some countries showing rates 5 times higher than other countries. This graph shows the number of deaths per 100,000 people per year.

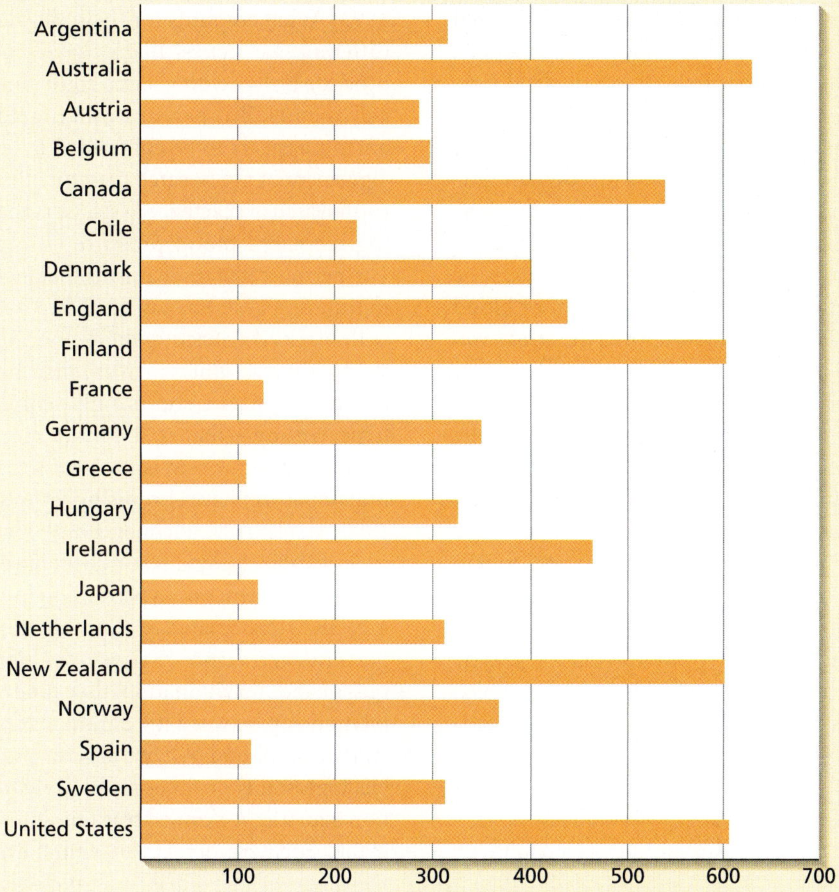

Horizontal bar chart of deaths per 100,000 people per year by country. The x-axis ranges from 100 to 700 in increments of 100. Countries listed from top to bottom: Argentina, Australia, Austria, Belgium, Canada, Chile, Denmark, England, Finland, France, Germany, Greece, Hungary, Ireland, Japan, Netherlands, New Zealand, Norway, Spain, Sweden, United States.

Essential Hypertension. **Hypertension** is the technical term for elevated blood pressure, and **essential hypertension,** also called primary hypertension, is elevated blood pressure for which no physical cause can be found. Note that hypertension should not be confused with the psychological meaning of *tension.* Psychological tension often has little or no impact on blood pressure. Hypertension usually produces few if any symptoms, yet it increases the risk for heart attacks, strokes, and kidney disease. This is why hypertension is often called the silent killer. Hypertension affects about 20% of the adult population (Johnston, 1997).

To understand blood pressure and hypertension, you need to know a little about the functioning of the heart and circulatory system. The heartbeat forces blood into the arteries, which are flexible tubes that stretch from the force of the pumping blood. The maximum pressure in the arteries occurs just after the blood is forced out of the heart, and this pressure is called the *systolic blood pressure.* This is the higher of the two numbers that define your blood pressure. After the heartbeat, the flexible walls of

hypertension   The technical term for elevated blood pressure.

essential hypertension   Elevated blood pressure for which no physical cause can be found. Also called *primary hypertension.*

the arteries begin to return to their normal position, essentially serving as a secondary pump to push the blood farther down the arteries. This is comparable to a balloon pushing the air out as it deflates. As the arteries contract, the pressure drops. The lowest pressure occurs just before the next heartbeat, and this pressure is called the *diastolic blood pressure.* This is the smaller of the two blood pressure numbers. A typical blood pressure is about 120/80 (this is read "120 over 80"). Blood pressures that exceed 140/90 increase the risk for a variety of medical disorders. Low blood pressure generally carries fewer medical risks than high blood pressure.

Many things can contribute to elevated blood pressure. As one ages, the walls of the arteries lose some of their flexibility, especially if plaque builds up on the inside of the arteries because of excessive levels of cholesterol. This build-up increases the systolic blood pressure and decreases the efficiency of blood flow. Increasing the amount of blood pumped by each beat of the heart—termed the *stroke volume*—or decreasing the volume available in the blood vessels by constricting them increases blood pressure. Both of these effects occur when the person is physiologically aroused. Obesity decreases the volume of the blood vessels by squeezing them. Increases in the amount of blood in the circulatory system increase pressure. Excessive salt intake can increase blood pressure by increasing fluid retention in a subset of people who are sensitive to salt. Both genes and hormones contribute to the regulation of blood pressure. In fact, blood pressure is a very complex balance, and its regulation depends on dozens of variables, some of which may interact. This is one reason why it is difficult to regulate blood pressure with a single medication, although high blood pressure can nearly always be brought under reasonable control with the right medication. There are several types of medication available for treating hypertension, but each has side effects. A doctor should evaluate each case to select the best medication for a given person.

Hypertension affects nearly twice as many black Americans as whites (Anderson et al., 1993; Fray & Douglas, 1993). What accounts for these elevated rates? Could it be differences in genes? Blacks have higher rates of certain other disorders with genetic contributions, such as sickle-cell anemia. But perhaps other factors contribute. The answer appears to be complex. There is almost universal agreement in the research literature that blacks have greater cardiovascular reactivity to stressors than do whites, including increased blood pressure (Anderson et al., 1993). Furthermore, the mechanisms that increase blood pressure in response to stress may be different in blacks and whites, with blacks constricting their blood vessels in response to stress, whereas whites increase their heart rate. The degree of reactivity to stressors is highly correlated with degree of hypertension—that is, the more reactive an individual's cardiovascular system is to a stressor, the more likely that individual will have chronic hypertension (McAdoo et al., 1990; McNeilly & Zeichner, 1989). However, there may be other factors. Several researchers have argued that the increased prevalence of hypertension in blacks may be due to excessive stress related to a combination of socioeconomic pressures and racism (Krieger et al., 1998). In regard to the racism and discrimination, they note that there is a strong relationship between the darkness of a black person's skin and the likelihood of hypertension and that a dark-skinned black person is 11 times more likely to report discrimination than a light-skinned black person (Klonoff & Landrine, 2000). Furthermore, experimental evidence suggests that the threat of racial discrimination temporarily increases blood pressure in African Americans (Blascovich et al., 2001). Because they are correlational, these data do not prove that the chronic stress associated with racial discrimination *causes* hypertension, but it is a reasonable hypothesis that merits further study.

HEADACHES

Everyone has an occasional headache, but some people experience frequent and severe headaches. There are dozens of conditions, most of them physical, that can cause chronic headaches, and some of these conditions are dangerous if left untreated (Silberstein et al., 2001a). That is why it is best to consult a doctor if you are experiencing chronic and severe headaches. Two types of headaches have strong environmental contributions. **Tension headaches** are due

Hypertension—often called the silent killer—affects 20% of all adults but nearly 40% of African American adults.

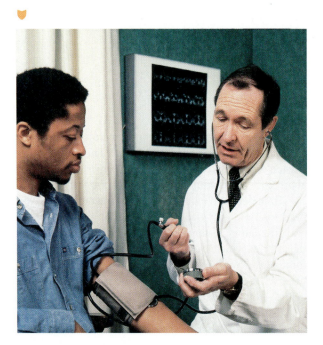

tension headaches Headaches due to excessive muscle tension in the neck and face.

to excessive muscle tension in the neck and face. They are experienced as a dull ache, pressure, or tight sensation and are usually a response to periods of excessive stress. This most common form of headache affects nearly 80% of people at some point in their life and about 40% of people in any given year. About 12% of people experience 14 or more tension headaches per year (Solomon & Newman, 2001). **Migraine headaches** are due to dilation of blood vessels in the brain. They produce pounding headaches that are often lateralized to one side of the head and that often induce nausea and vomiting. Many migraines are preceded by an *aura,* which includes visual or other sensory disturbances. About 12% of adults experience a migraine in any given year, and migraines are 3 times more common in women than in men (Silberstein et al., 2001b).

Although both tension headaches and migraine headaches respond to environmental stressors, there are genetic predisposing factors, especially for migraine headaches (Ferrari & Haan, 2001). Tremendous advances have been made over the past two decades in understanding the underlying physiological processes that trigger headaches. The primary process for tension headaches is simple muscle tension that gradually builds to the point where the facial muscles spasm, which causes the pain. These headaches are usually associated with stress that lasts several hours and requires considerable mental concentration. However, muscle tension alone cannot account for these headaches, because EMG studies have found that there is no difference between tension headache sufferers and comparison individuals on the level of muscle tension (Solomon & Newman, 2001). Attention clearly plays a role; the pain of the tension headache often decreases if the person is distracted by such activities as carrying on a conversation.

The physiology of migraine headaches is complex and well beyond what could be covered here (Silberstein et al., 2001b). It also appears that there may be several mechanisms that are capable of triggering these headaches, including environmental exposure and withdrawal from substances. For example, nitroglycerine (the active ingredient in dynamite) expands blood vessels and often causes migraine headaches. Nitroglycerine is often used to treat angina that results from restricted blood flow to heart muscles. Rapid withdrawal from high levels of caffeine can also trigger migraines. Birth control pills may trigger migraines in some women, although discontinuation of birth control pills is more likely to trigger a migraine (Silberstein, 2001). Stress can also trigger migraines, but not in the way you might expect. Unlike tension headaches, which are likely to occur during the stressful period, migraines are likely to occur shortly after the stressful period ends. They are essentially a rebound phenomenon, in which the rapid withdrawal of stress hormones triggers a dilation of blood vessels in and around the brain (Silberstein et al., 2001b).

TREATING STRESS-RELATED DISORDERS

Stress-related disorders are, first and foremost, physical disorders. Regardless of what factors contributed to it, a bleeding ulcer, is potentially life-threatening if not treated promptly. Some stress-related disorders, such as migraine headaches, can be treated and sometimes even prevented with medication. To the extent that stress contributes to the disorder, stress management packages are instituted as appropriate. In fact, such psychological interventions may be the best way to prevent stress-related disorders. Lifestyle changes, such as increasing one's exercise, stopping smoking, or eating a healthier diet, may also reduce the likelihood of stress-related disorders. These broad lifestyle changes are not easy. Assisting in such changes has become the focus of a relatively new discipline, behavioral medicine, which is the focus of the next section.

Check Yourself 9.2

Psychological Factors That Affect Medical Conditions

1. What factors besides stress can contribute to ulcers?
2. What is Type A behavior, what relationship does it have to coronary heart disease, and what is the most critical component of Type A behavior?
3. What is the distinction between hypertension and essential hypertension?

Ponder this . . .   *Black Americans have nearly twice the rate of coronary heart disease as white Americans and they show different patterns of cardiac response to stress. Could these differences reflect different evolutionary histories, and, if so, what factors might be involved?*

BEHAVIORAL MEDICINE

What is the single most commonly recommended treatment for health problems? Is it surgery, medications, or something exotic like acupuncture? The answer is "none of the above." The single treatment most commonly advocated for health problems is changing one's behavior (Jonas, 2000). Behavior has an enormous impact on the risk for many diseases. Lose some weight; give up smoking; reduce your stress; eat better; get more rest; monitor your blood sugar more carefully; get more exercise; avoid foods high in fat, cholesterol, or sugar; drink less alcohol; never have unprotected sex. Each time a doctor advises a patient to change

migraine headaches   Headaches due to dilation of blood vessels in the brain.

behavior, the doctor is practicing **behavioral medicine**—that is, using psychological techniques to facilitate changes in behavior. Giving advice is just one of many psychological techniques, and it is a technique that is rarely effective. If it were effective, there would be very few smokers, very few obese people, and very few people with poor diets.

Are patients ignoring the good advice of their doctors, or is something else happening? Probably something else is happening. Changing behavior is difficult, and most people need help to make such changes. That is where the specialist in behavioral medicine comes in. Such specialists are usually psychologists who are trained to facilitate the behavioral changes that promote better health or adaptation to chronic medical problems. This section begins with a review of several common behaviors that compromise health and then outlines strategies that have successfully addressed these problem behaviors. The section closes with a discussion of behavioral strategies that minimize medical complications and maximize life satisfaction in individuals who have a chronic disease.

HEALTH-COMPROMISING BEHAVIORS

Few people make only healthful choices for themselves. That extra piece of cheesecake is probably not good for either one's diet or one's cholesterol. But some choices have a greater negative impact than others. This section briefly reviews four behaviors that are known to have a significant impact on health: smoking, drinking, poor diet, and limited exercise. Smoking and drinking are also discussed in Chapter 14.

Smoking. Anyone who has smoked knows that cigarettes are addictive; that is, people experience significant withdrawal symptoms when trying to stop. Cigarette manufacturers have long known this fact, although until recently most have denied it (Cohen, 2000). More precisely, it is the nicotine in cigarettes that is addictive. Unfortunately, cigarettes deliver more than just a shot of nicotine to the smoker. More than 1200 chemical substances are contained in tobacco products, and the smoker ingests these with each puff. Many are known to be toxic. For example, the level of hydrogen cyanide in smoke is 160 times higher and the level of carbon monoxide 840 times higher than the maximum recommended levels (Gold, 1995). The EPA estimates that smoking causes more than 400,000 premature deaths a year in smokers and at least another 3000 in nonsmokers as a result of second-hand smoke. To put that into perspective, it is 4 times as many premature deaths as are caused by alcohol and 10 times as many as are caused by car accidents. A third of all cancer deaths are associated with smoking. Smoking is one of the few items routinely taken into

Many health problems can be prevented if one leads a healthful lifestyle. Smoking, excessive drinking, lack of exercise, and poor diet all contribute to higher risk for health problems.

account when life insurance premiums are computed. Smokers pay significantly more for life insurance because they die significantly younger than nonsmokers. Smoking is clearly unhealthful, and yet it is estimated that 40 to 50 million Americans smoke (Anthony & Echeagaray-Wagner, 2000). Marvin, whose case was described at the beginning of this chapter, was a heavy smoker most of his life and was unable to quit for years even though the habit threatened his health.

Drinking. Moderate drinking appears to have few health consequences unless there is a complicating medical condition, such as diabetes. Moderate drinking may even have some cardiovascular health benefits (Brenner et al., 2001). However, excessive drinking has significant health consequences, including increased risk for damage to the gastrointestinal, cardiovascular, cerebrovascular, and nervous systems (Schuckit, 2000). The brain and liver are most vulnerable to heavy alcohol consumption. Alcohol, like nicotine, is an addictive substance. Consequently, heavy drinkers can easily find themselves unable to stop drinking or even to cut down.

behavioral medicine The use of psychological techniques to facilitate changes in behavior.

Evolutionary Impact

Poor Diet. Throughout evolution, the most common dietary problem was starvation. In certain regions of the world, starvation is still a reality. However, in most developed countries, the problem now is excessive eating, especially eating of foods high in sugars and fats. This is because foods that are high in sugars and fats taste good. Sugars and fats are a valuable part of a normal diet, but they are not readily available in many naturally occurring foods. To ensure that these vital elements are consumed when available, organisms evolved taste preferences for them (Brown & Konner, 1987). In this age of processed foods, with food manufacturers competing for your business, it is in their best interest to make their products as tasty as possible. Hence many processed foods rely heavily on fats and sugars to make them flavorful—and the amounts of fats and sugars far exceed what occurs naturally in foods. Furthermore, when people get used to foods so high in fat and sugar, foods without such flavor enhancers taste bland and unappealing. Humans are not the only organisms affected by such diets. Laboratory rats maintain a steady weight on the normal nutritionally balanced rat food used in labs. However, when rats are given a choice between that food and food with sugar and fat content similar to that in processed foods, they overwhelmingly prefer the latter, and their weight (along with their bodies) quickly balloons (Smith et al., 1998). In the modern era of processed foods, one can no longer rely on taste preferences that have been shaped across millions of years of evolution to guide food choices.

Limited Exercise. In addition to excessive calorie intake, many people today do not get adequate exercise. Evolution shaped human beings for the rigors of hunting and gathering, but modern life demands little intense activity. In fact, jobs are becoming ever more sedentary. More than ever before, people sit at computers, behind a wheel, or at a desk. Long workdays leave people fatigued—fatigue that is more emotional than physical, but fatigue nonetheless. Flopping down in front of the TV is a popular way to unwind after a long day. Getting limited exercise is a lot like eating a high-fat, high-sugar diet. If you eat such a diet, your desire for healthful food decreases. If you do not exercise for a while, you quickly get out of shape, and exercise becomes uncomfortable, even painful. Yet exercise is a critical component in a health maintenance program. It is also a critical component in any weight control program.

PROMOTING HEALTHFUL BEHAVIOR

Promoting healthful behavior is not a trivial task. Exercise is hard work, especially if you are out of shape. The pain is almost immediate, and the benefits take weeks, months, or even years to see. Rich food usually tastes better than food that is good for you, and the negative consequences of eating too much rich food are considerably delayed. Smoking relaxes a person immediately, whereas most of the negative health consequences of smoking are delayed by years. The timing of the consequences of behavior is important; the more immediate the consequences, the more effective they are in shaping behavior. The primary goal of behavioral medicine is to change behavior to a more healthful lifestyle (Elder, 2001; Jonas, 2000).

The key to changing behavior is to motivate people to make changes and to modify the environment to make changes more likely to occur. For example, "eating healthy" is easier if you have a goal, such as looking better, feeling better, or being healthier. But it is harder to eat healthy if your cupboards are filled with tasty, high-calorie snacks or if most of your meals are eaten on the run from fast-food outlets. Reducing temptations helps; increasing rewards for healthful eating helps even more; and making the rewards immediate probably helps the most. This final point is one of the reasons why support groups are so popular with

A healthful lifestyle has a number of long-term rewards. The difficult task is to begin. Exercise is at first uncomfortable for people who are out of shape, but it helps those who exercise regularly feel great.

many programs designed to change behavior (Fletcher, 2001; Jason et al., 1995; Westphal & Smith, 1996). A support group provides each of the group's members with immediate reinforcement for positive behavior.

Behavioral medicine specialists have addressed all of the lifestyle issues that are related to better health. For example, behavioral programs have been developed to help people stop smoking (Bolman et al., 2002), and other programs have been developed to encourage young people to not take up smoking (Freestone et al., 2001). Similarly, programs to help people reduce their drinking or stop drinking are becoming increasingly more effective (Krystal et al., 2001; Liddle et al., 2001). Programs to encourage healthful eating have had modest success (Wardle et al., 2001). Unlike the fad diets beloved by magazines, these programs seek to promote new, sustainable eating patterns that will serve a person for a lifetime (Baranowski & Hetherington, 2001). Exercise is also important in a healthful lifestyle (King et al., 2002). Encouraging exercise involves finding the right combination of activities that provide inherent reinforcement and can be integrated into a busy life. The exercise program that is right for one person may not be right for another. Some people love the camaraderie of working out at the gym; others prefer to exercise at home. Exercise need not even be designed as exercise. Walking up stairs instead of taking the elevator is just as effective as using a Stairmaster at the gym. The key to all of these programs is to tailor them to the needs and interests of the person. Furthermore, programs must be flexible and varied. People easily tire of a single routine. (Imagine eating your favorite food, and *only* your favorite food, for the next 30 days. After 30 straight days, it is not likely to be your favorite food anymore.) Hence variety should be worked into both healthful eating and exercise programs.

AIDS PREVENTION

Much of behavioral medicine is devoted to prevention of disease, and nowhere is prevention more important than with AIDS. To date, there is no cure for this disease, so prevention is the only strategy that significantly reduces the number of deaths. Unlike virtually every other epidemic known, AIDS is entirely preventable if appropriate behavioral steps are taken. Groups at high risk for AIDS (male homosexuals and intravenous drug users) have been the focus of prevention efforts for years (Des Jarlais, 1999; Hart, 1996; McKay, 2000), but increasingly, attention has shifted to heterosexual interactions. One major prevention effort has focused on the proper use of condoms (McKay, 2000). A surprising number of sexually active young people do not know how to use condoms properly or even how to buy them (Baele et al., 2001).

One would think that the best way to increase safe sex would be to scare sexually active people by warning them of the potential consequences of unprotected sex. However, such scare tactics make most people defensive, increase

their denial of the risk, and thus reduce the likelihood that they will take appropriate precautions (Blumberg, 2000). Because the risk of HIV transmission in heterosexual encounters is greater for females than for males, more effort at education and prevention has been aimed at females (O'Leary, 2000). Although AIDS prevention has had some success, it appears that each new generation has to learn the lessons of the previous generation. Until a vaccine is developed or a cure is found, prevention will remain a major component in the war on AIDS and on the HIV virus responsible for the disorder.

REDUCING CORONARY RISK

You learned earlier in the chapter that Type A behavior, or, more accurately, the hostility component of Type A behavior, is associated with risk for coronary heart disease. This behavior pattern is also associated with elevated risk for a second heart attack, and the mortality rate for second heart attacks is higher than that for first heart attacks (Johnston, 1997). Therefore, changing the lifestyle and behavior of those individuals with a Type A behavior pattern has the potential to reduce mortality by preventing a second heart attack. Research on coronary heart disease has addressed two questions. The first is whether it is possible to change such behavior. Many professionals believe that Type A behavior is a personality trait, and personality traits are difficult or impossible to modify. The second question is whether the changes reduce the risk of further heart problems (Levenkron & Moore, 1988).

The largest single study to evaluate the treatment of Type A behavior was the Recurrent Coronary Prevention Project (Friedman et al., 1982). Men who had experienced a heart attack and who showed Type A behavior were counseled on what to modify in their lifestyle to reduce the risk of future heart attacks. For example, they were encouraged to talk and work more slowly, to delegate work to others, to take more time to relax, to reduce the time pressure in their days, and to decrease their overt hostility. Although these changes were often difficult to implement, change did occur. The key seemed to be to convince these men, most of whom were hard-driving executives, that the pressure-packed days and fierce, hostile competitiveness were not critical to business success (Friedman & Ulmer, 1984). Did these changes make a difference in risk for a second heart attack? Friedman et al. (1984) found that the rate of second heart attacks was cut in half for those receiving this treatment, compared with those who received the traditional coronary counseling of the era. Other investigators have demonstrated the feasibility of such treatment programs for individuals with Type A behavior who have had a heart attack (Burrel et al., 1986; Mendes de Leon et al., 1991). This study was conducted before other research demonstrated that it was only the hostility component of Type A behavior that predicted coronary heart disease. Hence the broad focus on changing the entire Type A behavior pattern.

Type A behavior pattern also appears to be responsive to environmental demands. People classified as Type A while working often qualify as Type B within a year after they retire (Howard et al., 1986). This finding suggests that the demands of the workplace interact with personality variables to create the Type A behavior pattern.

ADJUSTING TO CHRONIC DISEASE

Most health care dollars are spent on the management of such chronic diseases as diabetes, heart and lung diseases, AIDS, arthritis, Alzheimer's disease, and neurological disorders. For the most part, these conditions are never cured but, rather, must be managed. The effective management of chronic diseases requires a partnership among patients, their families, and their doctors. Some diseases, such as diabetes and arthritis, require specific actions on the part of the patient, who often must follow specific regimens in order to avoid medical complications (Bishop et al., 1998; Scott & Hochberg, 1998). Other diseases, such as AIDS and Alzheimer's, require effective management to make affected people comfortable and to extend their lives and functioning as long as possible (Folkman & Chesney, 1995; Lawlor, 1995).

With a disorder such as diabetes, the emotional well-being of those affected is significantly related to how well they follow the regime required to maintain good health (Landis, 1996). In general, feeling in control of their illness is critical (Macrodimitris & Endler, 2001). Emphasizing such practices as monitoring one's own blood sugar and adjusting one's diet in response to minor changes in blood sugar can enhance one's sense of control and therefore improve one's morale. However, other factors, such as the degree of social support, are also critical predictors of health outcomes in people who are diabetic (Glasgow et al., 2000).

Although the most common form of diabetes (Type II diabetes) develops in later adulthood, some people develop the disorder in childhood (Type I diabetes). Adjusting to the strict regimens required to maintain reasonable blood sugar levels is particularly difficult and draining for children (Kovacs et al., 1990). It also can affect the other children in the family, sometimes creating considerable family tension (Safyer et al., 1993). Brief family therapy can reduce some of the stress experienced by affected children, siblings, and parents. More important, such therapy can reduce the medical complications by producing better medical compliance (Wysocki et al., 2000).

Adjusting to a life-threatening chronic illness presents a whole host of problems for both the people with the disease and their loved ones. Cancer is perhaps the most studied of all life-threatening diseases. Without question, cancer creates enormous stress for both patients and their families (Koocher & Pollin, 2001). The stress on parents when a child is diagnosed with cancer is especially severe (Hoekstra-Weebers et al., 2001). Adjusting to having one's life turned upside down by learning that one has a life-threatening disease is usually a multistep process. Most people receive considerable support from friends, family, and professionals at the time of diagnosis, but the level of support often diminishes over time. This is especially true for parents of children diagnosed with cancer (Hoekstra-Weebers et al., 2001). Coping with having cancer is more than just an emotional issue; the effectiveness with which people cope often affects their odds of survival (Faller et al., 1999).

Adapting to cancer entails more than just accepting that one has a life-threatening illness. The treatments for cancer can be very uncomfortable, repeated treatments are usually required, and many individuals develop varying levels of anxiety about the treatments. For example, severe illness and nausea are common side effects of chemotherapy, and the level of anxiety that one has about the nausea is predictive of both the degree of the nausea in future chemotherapy sessions and the level of adaptation to the cancer (Blasco et al., 2000). Both cognitive and behavioral interventions, such as redirecting one's attention or using progressive relaxation, can significantly reduce the distress associated with cancer treatment (Roscoe et al., 2000). Sometimes interventions as simple as adjusting one's diet

Staying healthy with a chronic disease such as diabetes requires discipline as one carries out all the behaviors necessary to maintain one's health. With diabetes, that includes checking one's blood sugar, giving oneself regular insulin shots, and eating a proper diet.

during chemotherapy can significantly reduce nausea during chemotherapy (Cassileth, 1999).

Facing a life-threatening illness is not always devastating. Virtually everyone is shaken emotionally by the initial diagnosis of cancer, yet some people are able to reestablish their premorbid level of emotional functioning rapidly. Support from family and friends is clearly important (Ben-Zur, 2001), as is the premorbid personality of the person diagnosed with cancer (Scheier & Carver, 2001). Cognitive therapy can also help people to reestablish emotional equilibrium (Lepore, 2001). For example, Classen et al. (2001) found that supportive group therapy significantly reduced the level of distress in women with breast cancer. Furthermore, dealing with cancer may even present a growth opportunity. For example, Cordova et al. (2001) found that breast cancer survivors showed more positive psychological growth during treatment and during the two years following treatment than a sample of age- and education-matched women. The survivors reported better relationships with friends and family, more satisfaction with life, and a greater sense of spirituality.

Of course, life-threatening illnesses sometimes take lives. Dealing with being terminally ill or with having a friend or family member who is terminally ill is difficult. An interesting thing happens when it becomes clear that an individual is terminally ill. At some point, the people who have been caring for the individual and his or her family pass the care on to other specialists. For example, the treating doctors may make a referral to a *hospice*, an organization that provides supportive care during the last few weeks of a person's life. The behavioral medicine specialist often refers the case to a member of the clergy to provide spiritual support if the person is religious. The concern changes from maintaining an optimistic outlook to dealing with the emotional trauma of facing one's own death (Strang & Strang, 2001). The prospect of death creates all kinds of emotional crises, from loneliness (Rokach, 2000) to fear of dying (Ackerman & Oliver, 1997) to dealing with physical pain (Fishman, 1992). Yet many people are able to deal with all of these issues, to accept the inevitability of their own death, and to die peacefully surrounded by friends and family (Corr et al., 2000).

Check Yourself 9.3

Behavioral Medicine

1. Name several behaviors that compromise health.

2. What is the most challenging problem in promoting healthful behavior?

3. Does reducing Type A behavior reduce risk for second heart attacks?

4. How can specialists in behavioral medicine help those people who are diagnosed with cancer?

Ponder this . . . Research indicates that Type A behavior can be modified in people who have had a heart attack and that such modification reduces the risk of a second heart attack. Would the same treatment be as effective or as cost-effective if it were applied to people who have never had a heart attack? What are your reasons for your position?

SOMATOFORM DISORDERS

Somatoform disorders are characterized by the presence of physical symptoms that suggest a medical condition but for which no evidence of a medical cause can be found. These disorders are sometimes confused with psychosomatic (or psychophysiological) disorders, in which there is clearly a medical problem, such as an ulcer, but psychological factors are presumed to have contributed to it. For a condition to qualify as a somatoform disorder, the symptoms cannot be better explained either by substance use or by another psychiatric disorder. For example, acute alcohol intoxication can create a variety of physical symptoms, such as dizziness and gastrointestinal distress, and panic attacks often produce heart palpitations or tingling sensations. However, these symptoms are better explained by these disorders and therefore do not qualify as symptoms of somatoform disorders. Finally, some people do not imagine symptoms but, rather, make them up. These are recognized in DSM under two categories—malingering and factitious disorder. Both are discussed in the nearby Focus box. The DSM recognizes seven somatoform disorders, which are summarized in Table 9.1 on page 273. This section will cover five of them: somatization disorder, conversion disorder, pain disorder, hypochondriasis, and body dysmorphic disorder.

SOMATIZATION DISORDER

Somatization disorder is characterized by a pervasive and recurring pattern of reports of multiple physical symptoms

---

somatization disorder   A disorder characterized by a pervasive and recurring pattern of reports of multiple physical symptoms for which no adequate physical cause can be found.

malingering   Falsely presenting one or more physical or psychological disorders for personal gain.

factitious disorder   A disorder characterized by feigning symptoms, deliberately distorting objective measures of symptoms, or doing things that might produce actual symptoms in order to assume the sick role.

Munchausen syndrome   Factitious disorder with physical symptoms.

Munchausen syndrome by proxy   A disorder characterized by the deliberate creation of physical disorders in another person in order to get sympathy and support from others.

FOCUS   Malingering and factitious disorders

There is an important distinction between somatoform disorders and two other disorders recognized by the DSM. People with somatoform disorders *believe* that they have one or more medical problems, despite the fact that the evidence suggests otherwise. In contrast, **malingering** is falsely presenting one or more physical or psychological disorders for personal gain. For example, feigning illness or injury may enable the person to avoid work or other responsibilities or to profit through a lawsuit or insurance settlement. Another disorder, **factitious disorder,** is characterized by feigning symptoms, deliberately distorting objective measures of symptoms, or doing things that might produce actual symptoms. The distinction between malingering and factitious disorder has to do with motivation. In malingering, the person is motivated by personal gain or

the avoidance of responsibility. In factitious disorders, the person is motivated by a desire to take on the patient role, apparently because of the extra attention it provides. Factitious disorders with physical symptoms are called **Munchausen syndrome,** although this is not the terminology used by the DSM.

Perhaps the most frightening of factitious disorders is **Munchausen syndrome by proxy**—a disorder characterized by the deliberate creation of physical disorders in *another person* in order to get sympathy and support from others (Ayoub et al., 2000). Typically, it is a parent who deliberately makes a child ill. Rarely is the intent to hurt the victim, but nevertheless, 10 to 30% of the victims die from the symptoms (Von Burg & Hibbard, 1995). Parents with a sick child often get considerable attention, support, and encouragement. It appears that people with Munchausen

syndrome by proxy become virtually addicted to such support and will do anything to get more, including making their children sick. A particularly gruesome case involved a 9-year-old girl from Florida, whose mysterious ailments led to over 200 hospitalizations and 40 operations (Katel & Beck, 1996). It appeared that most of her medical problems were the result of actions by her mother, who did not stop until the legal authorities got involved. The psychiatric community views this disorder as an extreme form of factitious disorder in someone who is sufficiently narcissistic to be willing to hurt a family member just to gain attention. In contrast, the legal community views it as a dangerous form of child abuse (Feldman & Lasher, 1999; Naegele & Clark, 2001). The public simply expresses outrage at such callous actions by a parent.

[TABLE 9.1]   Somatoform Disorders

The DSM recognizes seven somatoform disorders. For each diagnosis, the symptoms must be clinically significant in that they cause considerable distress to the person, result in a disruption in functioning, or both. They also must *not* be the result of a general medical condition, use of one or more substances, or another psychiatric disorder.

Somatization disorder is characterized by multiple clinically significant physical complaints that begin before age 30 and tend to recur. These symptoms are not intentionally feigned and are not the result of a medical condition. The terms *hysteria* and *Briquet's syndrome* are also used to describe this disorder.

Undifferentiated somatoform disorder is characterized by one or more physical complaints that last at least six months and are not the result of a physical disorder. This diagnosis is often used when individuals fall just short of meeting the criteria for somatization disorder.

Conversion disorder is characterized by motor and sensory symptoms that are not the result of a medical condition.

Pain disorder is characterized by persistent reports of significant pain, in one or more body locations, that does not have a physical cause. This diagnosis is not used if the pain is vaginal and is associated with sexual intercourse.

Hypochondriasis is characterized by a preoccupation with, or fear of having, a specific serious disease on the basis of a misinterpretation of one or more bodily sensations or symptoms. Disconfirming medical tests do *not* relieve the person's anxiety or conviction that he or she has the disease.

Body dysmorphic disorder is characterized by a preoccupation with either an imagined or an exaggerated defect in appearance. This diagnosis is not made for individuals who are concerned primarily with body size. The term *dysmorphophobia* was used previously to describe this condition.

Somatoform disorder not otherwise specified is characterized by one or more somatoform symptoms that are not sufficient to qualify the individual for another somatoform diagnosis.

SOURCE: *Adapted from American Psychiatric Association, DSM-IV-TR. (Washington, DC: APA, 2000).*

for which no adequate physical cause can be found. This pattern starts before the age of 30 and typically lasts for many years (APA, 2000). To qualify for the diagnosis, at least four symptom domains must be included in the somatic complaints—pain and gastrointestinal, sexual, and pseudoneurological symptoms—which are summarized in Table 9.2. The requirement that these four separate symptom domains be represented decreases the chance that someone with an undiagnosed physical disorder will be mistakenly given a somatization disorder diagnosis, because it is rare for any one physical disorder to generate so many different physical symptoms. The case of Julia illustrates many of the features and consequences of somatization disorder.

JULIA

Constant Suffering

It started when she was 17. Her first symptom was excruciating back pain. X-rays detected nothing, and a chiropractor could do little for her. A series of stomach problems her senior year caused her to miss so much school that she was unable to graduate with her high school class. Again, an exhaustive series of tests found nothing. Joint pain, first in her knees and later in her elbows, restricted her mobility during her early twenties. Her menstrual period was never regular and was often associated with such severe pain that she would be forced into bed rest for a week or more each month. By her mid twenties, Julia started suffering from periodic dizziness and blurred vision, but again, exhaustive testing could find nothing wrong. The back pain returned in her late twenties but was found to be the result of moderately severe endometriosis, which was surgically corrected. Throughout her twenties, crushing headaches, abdominal pain, and painful urination plagued her. She averaged 20 or more doctor visits a year and thousands of dollars in tests, which almost never revealed anything of consequence. Her friends and co-workers called her a hypochondriac; some actually ridiculed her for her constant physical complaints. She was fired four times before age 30 because of her excessive absences, and two boyfriends left her because they could no longer tolerate her preoccupation with her health.

Julia's case is not unusual for someone with somatization disorder. Barely 30 years old, she has been to the doctor more than most families would in a lifetime. She has lost jobs and friends because of her constant physical complaints, and her doctor is so tired of Julia's visits that she borders on being abusive at times. Nonetheless, Julia's physical symptoms continue unabated. As soon as one test comes back negative, another problem develops that requires more testing. Julia's case also illustrates another point. Even amid this barrage of physical symptoms that appear to have no medical cause, there can be physical symptoms that indicate the presence of a disorder. In Julia's case, it was endometriosis—an abnormal tissue growth in the pelvic cavity—which probably went undetected longer than it otherwise might have because her other complaints

[TABLE 9.2] Symptoms Required for Somatization Disorder

Somatization disorder is characterized by the report of multiple physical symptoms over years or decades. The diagnosis requires symptoms in each of four categories.

Pain symptoms. There must be a history of diverse pain complaints involving at least four different sites. These may include the head, abdomen, back, joints, extremities, chest, and rectum and pain during menstruation, sexual intercourse, or urination.

Gastrointestinal symptoms. There must be a history of at least two gastrointestinal complaints that are not pain-related. These may include nausea, bloating, vomiting (unless it is part of pregnancy), diarrhea, and intolerance of several different foods.

Sexual symptoms. There must be a history of at least one sexual or reproductive symptom that is not pain-related. Such symptoms may include sexual indifference, erectile or ejaculatory dysfunction, irregular menses, excessive menstrual bleeding, and vomiting throughout pregnancy.

Pseudoneurological symptoms. There must be a history of at least one neurological symptom that is not pain-related. Such symptoms may include impaired coordination or balance, paralysis or localized weakness, difficulty swallowing or lump in the throat, loss of voice, difficulty urinating, hallucinations, loss of touch or pain sensations, double vision, blindness, deafness, seizures, amnesia, and loss of consciousness.

SOURCE: *Adapted from American Psychiatric Association, DSM-IV-TR. (Washington, DC: APA, 2000).*

had doctors looking for other disorders. Follow-up studies of individuals with such a pattern of multiple complaints find that there is a larger than expected occurrence of actual disorders that are later diagnosed (Lecompte, 1987). Often, the diagnosis was missed because the wide variety of physical complaints prevented doctors from identifying a specific problem. The diagnosis of many medical conditions relies more on the pattern of symptoms and the history of those symptoms over time than on a specific definitive diagnostic test. If two particular symptoms might indicate the presence of a disorder, but the patient is telling the doctor about a dozen or more symptoms over several months, it is easy for the doctor to miss the critical symptom pattern amid the "noise" of so many physical complaints.

Somatization disorder is much more common in women than in men, although there are interesting cultural variations in sex ratios. For example, high rates of somatization disorder are found in both Greek and Puerto Rican men (APA, 2000; Shrout et al., 1992). This finding suggests that cultural factors influence at least some cases of the disorder. The rates of the disorder vary dramatically from sam-

....

chronic fatigue syndrome (CFS) A disease characterized by a dramatic loss of energy; pain in the joints, muscles, throat, or head; and significant depression following a period of exertion.

ple to sample, with lifetime prevalence rates between 0.2% and 2% in women and less than 0.2% in men (APA, 2000; Narrow et al., 2002; Rief et al., 2001). The disorder tends to be chronic, lasting years but varying in intensity over time. Somatization disorder is found in 10 to 20% of the first-degree female relatives of women with somatization disorder, a rate about 10 times higher than one would expect by chance (APA, 2000; Guze, 1993). Curiously, the first-degree male relatives of women with somatization disorder do not show an increased risk for somatization disorder, but they do show an increased risk for antisocial personality disorder and substance use disorders (these are covered in Chapters 12 and 14, respectively). Because it is unlikely that a single environment could shape somatization disorder in

women *and* antisocial personality disorder in men, these data suggest that shared genetic factors may account for this relationship (Lilienfeld, 1992; Lilienfeld & Hess, 2001).

Having symptoms for which doctors cannot find a cause is not by itself an indication of somatization disorder. Many diseases have yet to be identified or are of such recent origin that they are not readily identified. When the disease creates dramatic and obvious symptoms, such as extensive swelling or tissue destruction, few people question its physical reality even if a firm diagnosis cannot be made. However, not every disorder shows such obvious symptoms. There is a puzzling disorder, or perhaps a set of disorders, called chronic fatigue syndrome, which is discussed in the nearby Focus box. This disorder has generated considerable

FOCUS   Chronic fatigue syndrome

Perhaps one of the most controversial diagnoses in medicine today is a condition called **chronic fatigue syndrome,** or **CFS.** Chronic fatigue syndrome is characterized by a dramatic loss of energy; pain in the joints, muscles, throat, or head; and significant depression following a period of exertion. Although its principal symptom is profound fatigue, the fatigue does not appear to be the result of normal exertion and is rarely improved by a period of rest. CFS affects between 2 and 5 million Americans, and the majority of sufferers are women (Tuck & Wallace, 2000). These symptoms overlap two other disorders—*fibromyalgia* and *multiple chemical sensitivity*—which leads some doctors to suspect that they may be variations of the same disorder (Natelson, 2001). The controversy surrounding this disorder concerns whether it is primarily physical or psychological. There is evidence that similar symptoms can be caused by a virus—specifically, the Epstein-Barr virus (Straus et al. 1985)—and there is speculation about other possible physical causes, including immune system dysfunctions (Visser et al., 2000) and exposure to toxins (Abbey & Garfinkel, 1991). More recent data suggest unusually low lev-

els of the stress hormone cortisol in people with CFS (Cleare et al., 2001). Many Gulf War veterans showed similar symptoms, known as the Gulf War syndrome, which increased suspicions that environmental toxins are involved in at least some cases (Kippen et al., 1999). To date, however, the cause of the vast majority of CFS cases remains a mystery.

What makes CFS so interesting is that it is remarkably similar to a condition called *neurasthenia,* which was widely reported in the mid-1800s (Abbey & Garfinkle, 1991). As in the case of CFS, no physical cause was ever found for neurasthenia, and many doctors attributed the symptoms to the increasing stress and pressure of the time. With both disorders, women outnumbered men, and during both periods, there were unique additional stressors being placed on women. These facts have led some to speculate that CFS is a variation of depression—essentially a shutdown of physical and emotional productivity in the face of chronic, unrelenting stress. Depression, which is typically considered a psychological disorder, clearly includes such physical symptoms as fatigue, inability to concentrate, and appetite and sleep disturbance. Perhaps it should not be surprising that preliminary evidence suggests

that the SSRIs used to treat depression can sometimes improve the symptoms of CFS (Goodnick & Sandoval, 1993). One certainly cannot yet rule out this hypothesis, but one cannot rule out the physical disorder hypothesis either.

The controversy about the cause(s) of CFS persists. Some doctors strongly believe it is psychological, whereas others believe it is due to unknown physical causes (Wessely, 2001). The majority of people suffering from the disorder believe that it is physical and find it hard to believe that such potent physical symptoms could simply be imagined (Wray, 1997). They often feel that doctors who dismiss their symptoms as psychological are blaming them for having a disorder that medicine does not yet understand (Twombly, 1994). Until something definitive is discovered, this controversy is likely to continue. Until then, some lessons can be learned from the content of this chapter. No disorder is exclusively physiological or psychological. Physiological factors can affect primarily psychological disorders, and vice versa. Disorders that are primarily psychological in origin are no less real than disorders that are primarily physiological in origin. Psychological disorders can be just as painful and just as debilitating as physiological disorders.

controversy. There are doctors on both sides of the issue of whether it is a physical or a psychological disorder.

CONVERSION DISORDER

A **conversion disorder** is typically characterized by the report of a single symptom that usually represents a motor and/or sensory dysfunction. For example, the person may report the paralysis of one hand or a loss of feeling in a foot or a part of the face. There is no evidence of a physical cause for the symptom, and in many cases, the symptom does not even make physiological sense. For example, the way the nerves innervate the arm and hand makes it impossible for just the hand to be paralyzed without other dysfunctions being present farther up the arm.

Conversion disorders were more common in an earlier era. Many of the people treated by Freud presented with conversion disorders (Crimlisk & Ron, 1999). In fact, it was Freud who first coined the term, arguing that the physical symptoms his patients reported were actually psychological symptoms that had been converted into a physical manifestation. Freud could have simply concluded that these people did not have a physical disorder and just sent them on their way. If he had, his name would not be the household word it is today. Instead, he hypothesized that even though there was no obvious physical cause, that there was probably some other cause for these puzzling symptoms. Because his patients did not seem to be feigning the symptoms, Freud hypothesized that an unconscious psychological process was behind them.

Conversion disorders now are rare. The estimated prevalence rates vary from 1 in 200 to 1 in 10,000 (Martin & Yutzy, 1996). These cases account for approximately 3% of the people in outpatient therapy and for between 1 and 14% of those in inpatient medical settings (APA, 2000). Conversion symptoms are up to 10 times more frequent in women than in men (APA, 2000; Martin & Yutzy, 1996). Most develop these symptoms between the ages of 10 and 35 (APA, 2000). Onset is usually rapid, and duration is usually short (typically less than two weeks). There may be a single episode, but episodes often reoccur. The nature of the conversion symptom is predictive of outcome. Rapid onset

of symptoms in the face of a clearly identifiable stressor is generally associated with good prognosis (APA, 2000). Prognosis is also better if the primary conversion symptom is paralysis, loss of speech, or blindness (Hafeiz, 1980).

The rate of conversion symptoms has been dropping as the medical sophistication of the population has increased. Conversion disorders are now more likely to be found in rural settings or developing countries, in individuals of lower socioeconomic status, and in people who are relatively naïve about medical and psychological disorders (APA, 2000). Curiously, symptoms are much more common on the left than on the right side of the body, especially in women (Galin et al., 1977). A few women with conversion disorders eventually qualify for a diagnosis of somatization disorder (APA, 2000). When conversion disorders are found in men, they are most often precipitated by an accident or a military action. Finally, there is a relationship between conversion disorder and antisocial personality disorder in men, but not in women (APA, 2000).

PAIN DISORDER

As the name implies, **pain disorders** are characterized by prominent pain symptoms that cause significant distress and interfere with social, occupational, or other role expectations. This diagnosis is applied only when psychological factors are presumed to be a significant contributor to the intensity of the pain and to the interference with daily functioning that it causes. The diagnosis can be applied even when a physical cause is present, provided that the physical cause is unlikely to account for the level of pain reported. If it is believed that the pain is due primarily or exclusively to a physical cause, the diagnosis of pain disorder should not be made (APA, 2000).

Evolutionary Impact

Pain is a critical factor in survival. It tells the organism when something is wrong and encourages appropriate action, such as avoiding, until healing occurs, the use of a limb that has been injured or broken. Pain is also a part of the immune system response to infection. Whether you have a bad case of the flu or an infected wound, you experience significant pain, and that pain motivates you to minimize activity and gives the immune system time to heal the body. In the modern world, pain encourages people to seek help from their doctor, dentist, or other health practitioner. Thus pain, like anxiety, generally motivates behavior that is in the best interest of the organism. However, pain not associated with a physical disorder may motivate inappropriate behavior, just as excessive anxiety can motivate inappropriate avoidance behavior. Furthermore, pain is a subjective experience—that is, it is an internal event that is not directly observable by others. One can see expressions of pain and can witness avoidance behavior associated with pain, such as

---

conversion disorder A disorder typically characterized by the report of a single symptom, usually representing a motor or sensory dysfunction.

pain disorders Disorders characterized by prominent pain symptoms that cause significant distress and interfere with social, occupational, or other role expectations.

hypochondriasis A disorder characterized by an unwarranted and inaccurate belief, based on the misinterpretation of one or more bodily sensations, that one has a disease.

body dysmorphic disorder (BDD) A disorder characterized by a preoccupation with an imagined or minor defect in one's appearance.

limping, but the intensity of the pain itself can only be guessed at. Are people who appear to be more sensitive to pain actually feeling more pain, or are they just more distressed by the pain they feel? No one knows. Unless there is reason to believe that the person may be feigning pain—as might be the case if someone wanted to defraud another person in a lawsuit over an accident—it makes sense to assume that the pain is real and that it is a function of both physical and psychological factors.

All pain involves psychological factors in that attention to pain increases pain. Have you ever had a bad tension headache? If you are distracted from the pain by a conversation, you may find that the pain decreases significantly. Even when there is a clear physiological reason for pain, the intensity of the pain is affected by such psychological variables as attention and anxiety.

HYPOCHONDRIASIS

Hypochondriasis is characterized by an unwarranted and inaccurate belief, based on a misinterpretation of one or more bodily sensations, that one has a disease. For example, bad cramps and excessive gas may prompt someone to conclude that he or she has colorectal cancer. People with hypochondriasis rarely accept negative medical tests; instead, they continue to believe that they have the disease and that the doctors were unable to detect it. This definition is at odds with the popular notion of what a hypochondriac is like, as discussed in the nearby Modern Myths box.

The prevalence of hypochondriasis in the general population is estimated at 1 to 5%, although it is more common (estimated at 2 to 7%) among those visiting primary-care physicians (APA, 2000). Although the data are not always consistent, it appears that hypochondriasis is found in men and women at approximately equal rates (Eminson et al., 1996). Onset is usually in early adulthood, although later onset is possible. The course tends to be chronic—so chronic that hypochondriasis is almost a personality trait (Tyrer et al., 1999). In fact, some have argued that it should be classified as a personality disorder (Layne et al., 1999). The chronic concern for one's health becomes a central feature of the person's life and may affect many aspects of daily functioning. It is not unusual for hypochondriacs to check repeatedly for signs of the feared disease or to spend inordinate amounts of time discussing their concerns with other people. Offering a wealth of medical information on virtually every known disease, the Internet may inadvertently feed hypochondriacal tendencies. People concerned with their health can find information that may validate their suspicions, no matter what those suspicions are.

BODY DYSMORPHIC DISORDER

Body dysmorphic disorder, or **BDD**, is characterized by a preoccupation with a defect in one's appearance—a defect that either is imagined or is so minimal that most people would not even notice it. Carolyn, who was one of the cases that opened this chapter, suffered from body dysmorphic disorder. She believed that her hair was thinning. Her hair was naturally fine, but it was well within normal range.

MODERN Myths

Hypochondriasis VERSUS Somatization Disorder

Most people think that hypochondriacs are people who believe they have every illness under the sun. In fact, that popular description applies more to people with somatization disorder than to people with hypochondriasis. People with somatization disorder complain about multiple symptoms and visit the doctor constantly to be checked out for one problem after another. In contrast, people with hypochondriasis are typically concerned about a single, very serious disease, such as cancer or AIDS, which they continue to worry about even when medical tests rule out the possibility that they have it.

There are similarities and differences between somatization disorder and hypochondriasis. The typical age of onset for both is early adulthood. In fact, the DSM criteria require that the onset of somatization disorder be before the age of 30. This age criterion makes it clear that the multiple somatic complaints associated with normal aging are not a part of the disorder. Both are chronic conditions that often last a lifetime, although they both wax and wane depending on stress level. However, whereas somatization disorder is found almost exclusively in women, hypochondriasis tends to occur about equally in men and women. It is not likely that the popular but incorrect use of the term *hypochondriac* will disappear. Calling a person a hypochondriac, even if it is a misstatement, is a lot easier than referring to the person as having a somatization disorder. Just don't be misled by (and try not to indulge in) the imprecision of popular jargon.

People with body dysmorphic disorder believe unreasonably that there is something terribly wrong with the way they look, and they often try desperately to hide these perceived imperfections.

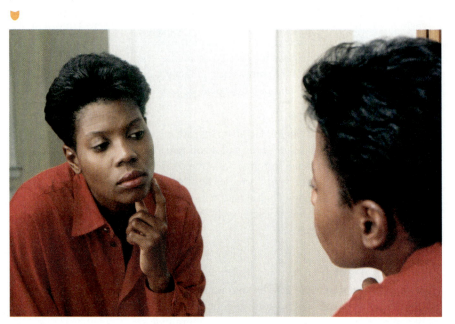

Nevertheless, she spent the better part of the day obsessing about her hair and trying to correct the problem by styling her hair differently. On bad days, she would be in tears most of the day. Even on good days, she could not leave the house without wearing a wig or spending several hours trying to get her hair just right. That meant she could not work, could barely handle weekly trips to the grocery store, and was unable to pick up her children after school. Clearly, Carolyn's BDD caused significant distress and interfered with her normal functioning.

The rate of BDD in the general population is unknown. Rates between 5 and 40% are reported in outpatient clinics that treat anxiety and depression (APA, 2000). One might think that the rates would be even higher in dermatology and cosmetic surgery clinics, but the data suggest that only 6 to 15% of people in such centers qualify for the diagnosis of body dysmorphic disorder (Phillips, 1996). The reason for this surprising finding is unclear. Perhaps the psychological distress is so strong that it, instead of the imagined physical defect, becomes the primary treatment focus. Perhaps dermatology and cosmetic surgery professionals discourage people with BDD by telling them that medical treatment is unwarranted. Perhaps many people with BDD instinctively know that no medical procedure will ease their discomfort. Surgical corrections of imagined physical defects rarely relieve the anxiety of people with BDD (Veale, 2000), which may be one reason why some people with BDD undergo repeated cosmetic surgeries.

Onset of BDD is usually in adolescence or even childhood, and the course is chronic (APA, 2000). It is rare for the person with BDD to be free of symptoms, although the symptoms wax and wane depending on the level of stress.

External pressures to look attractive can exacerbate symptoms, although such pressures are rarely the primary cause of the symptoms (APA, 2000; Phillips, 1996). Men and women seem equally likely to develop BDD.

BDD is included in the somatoform category in the DSM because of the focus on perceived physical imperfections. However, many professionals believe it is really a subtype of obsessive-compulsive disorder (Phillips, 1996). If one were to categorize BDD on the basis of symptoms, it could be conceptualized as either a somatoform or an anxiety disorder. It clearly has many of the features of obsessive-compulsive disorder, including obsessing about one's appearance and compulsively trying to improve one's appearance. Carolyn spent hours engaging in these activities every day. Furthermore, when the compulsive behavior is prevented, the individual typically experiences considerable anxiety. However, categorizing solely on the basis of similar symptoms is a scientifically weak approach. You learned in Chapter 6 that a diagnosis is a construct and that multiple lines of evidence are necessary to establish the validity of a construct. For example, if BDD is a subtype of obsessive-compulsive disorder, you might expect similar family histories, course, response to treatment, and response to laboratory measures in people with these two disorders. What do the data show on these dimensions?

Examining the Evidence

If BDD is a subtype of OCD, these two disorders should co-occur—that is, we would expect other OCD symptoms in someone with BDD. Phillips (1996) reports that 24% of people with BDD also qualified for a diagnosis of OCD and that another 5% had a history of OCD but did not meet criteria for that diagnosis at the time of the interview. That association is 10 times higher than we would expect if these two disorders were independent of each other. Of course, disorders may co-occur without being variations of the same disorder. The same study found that 57% of the individuals with body dysmorphic disorder had major depression and that 26% had social phobia. These high co-occurrence rates may be due to some shared etiological factors, but they may also represent reactions to the BDD symptoms. For example, the social phobia may develop because people with BDD are afraid of being around people because of the way they think they look. Secondary depression is common in many disorders. The frustration of having to deal with the intense, uncontrollable symptoms of BDD may leave people discouraged and depressed.

One can look at the co-occurrence issue from the opposite perspective as well: How many individuals with other disorders also qualify for a BDD diagnosis? Several studies that have examined this question for OCD found co-occurrence rates for BDD ranging from 8% to 37% and averaging 22% (Phillips, 1996). In contrast, only 8% of people with major depression and 11% of people with a social phobia qualified for a BDD diagnosis (Phillips, 1996). The overall pattern of OCD/BDD co-occurrence suggests not that it is the result of one disorder being secondary to the other but, rather, that these two disorders share something, such as genetic predisposing factors. However, the family history data of individuals with BDD does not suggest a genetic or environmental link to OCD. Only 4% of those with BDD had first-degree relatives with OCD (Phillips, 1996). However, the patterns of family history for other disorders are remarkably similar in people with OCD and BDD.

What other similarities between OCD and BDD might suggest that they represent variations of a single process? The two disorders show similar patterns of obsessions, compulsions, anxiety, and depression (McKay et al., 1997). Age of onset and symptom severity are comparable in these two disorders (Simeon et al., 1995). They respond to similar medications—specifically, the SSRIs (Hollander, 1991). They are characterized by similar patterns of memory deficits (Deckersbach et al., 2000) and by similar variations in the density of serotonin receptors in the brain (Marazziti et al., 1999). These data are consistent with the hypothesis that there may be shared etiological factors in BDD and OCD, but most of these variables are nonspecific. For example, high levels of anxiety and depression characterize many disorders

besides BDD, and the SSRIs are effective in treating at least a dozen disorders. Nevertheless, this impressive collection of similarities, coupled with the other data, suggest that the disorders may be variations of a single underlying condition.

There are also some interesting differences between OCD and BDD. People with OCD tend to have more insight into their disorder than those with BDD—that is, they recognize that their preoccupations are unreasonable (McKay et al., 1997; Simeon et al., 1995). Carolyn was absolutely convinced that her hair was ugly, despite repeated reassurances from friends, family, and hair care professionals. Although such lack of insight occasionally occurs with OCD, it is rare (Kozak & Foa, 1994).

BDD also overlaps another disorder—delusional disorder, somatic type. Unlike the BDD/OCD overlap, where there is a question about whether BDD is a subtype of OCD, the diagnosis of delusional disorder is typically used to indicate that the body image distortions in BDD have reached a delusional level (APA, 2000).

CAUSES OF SOMATOFORM DISORDERS

There are plenty of theories about what causes somatoform disorders. Some proposed causes are no longer taken seriously. For example, the ancient Greeks believed that hysterical disorders, such as conversion disorder, somatization disorder, and pain disorder, occurred only in women and were due to the uterus of a sexually unfulfilled woman wandering through the body. Wherever the uterus lodged, it produced a physical symptom! Modern theories are less obviously incorrect, but no current theory explains these disorders well. Nevertheless, this section will briefly review the major theories, including the psychodynamic, behavioral, cognitive, sociocultural, and biological perspectives.

Psychodynamic Perspective. No group has studied somatoform disorders more than psychoanalytic theorists. Freud was one of the few nineteenth-century physicians who took conversion disorders seriously, actively seeking both the cause and effective treatments (Crimlisk & Ron, 1999). He proposed that the physical symptoms were a manifestation of an underlying psychological conflict. Because his clients with conversion disorder were all female, he hypothesized that its origins involved a unique aspect of female psychological development—specifically, the phallic stage of development for the girl (about age 3 to 5). During this period, the girl begins to experience her first sexual feelings toward men, which are initially directed at her father—a process called the *Electra complex*. She quickly realizes, however, that she cannot compete with her mother and therefore represses these sexual feelings. Freud speculated that if this Electra complex is not resolved, events that trigger sexual feelings in adulthood will lead to additional efforts to hide those feelings, thus creating the conditions that foster the development of conversion symptoms. Freud believed that the conversion symptoms were the woman's effort to hide, even from herself, the sexual feelings that she found abhorrent. One problem with this explanation is that although most people with conversion disorder are women, men *do* qualify for the diagnosis. Modern psychoanalytic theorists therefore downplay the role of the Electra complex in shaping conversion symptoms. Instead, they focused on generic unconscious conflicts that arouse such anxiety that the individual must translate them into something less threatening, such as a physical symptom (Merskey, 1995). Unfortunately, these are difficult theories to study scientifically, so there are few supportive data.

Behavioral Perspective. The behavioral perspective focuses on the consequences of having a disorder. If those consequences are positive, such as enabling the person to avoid unwanted responsibilities or providing the person with supportive attention, they will reinforce the symptomatic behavior. Such an outcome is referred to as **secondary gain**—that is, the pathology is being maintained by the positive reinforcement it produces as a secondary effect. Freud actually used these behavioral principles in his theory, arguing that the reduction in anxiety that resulted from the conversion of a psychologically distressing feeling into a physical symptom was what motivated the conversion process. He also noted that the symptoms of conversion disorder often had secondary gain in that his clients could avoid activities that they disliked. Nevertheless, the data in support of the behavioral perspective are inconclusive. Although some individuals may experience some secondary gain from their symptoms, such as avoidance of work obligations, others experience significant aversive consequences, such as skepticism and hostility from family and even doctors.

Cognitive Perspective. Could the way one thinks affect the likelihood of somatoform symptoms? There are many theorists who believe so. People with hypochondriasis, somatization disorder, and conversion disorder all experience physical sensations that they misinterpret as signs of one or more physical disorders. Everyone experiences occasional aches and pains, fatigue, cramping, or unexplained arousal. Most people ignore these symptoms as normal unless they persist. However, if one focuses on them, as people with somatoform disorders do, the perceived intensity of the symptoms increases. Furthermore, if one is convinced that the feelings are signs of an illness,

anxiety increases, which intensifies the whole experience (Salkovskis & Warwick, 2001).

Is there independent evidence that people with somatoform disorders are especially sensitive to illness-related material? This can be evaluated using the Emotional Stroop Test (Williams et al., 1996), which is a variation of the Stroop Color Word test in which the task is to name, as quickly as possible, the colors in which words are printed. Sample lists are shown in Figure 9.5. Some sets of words are emotionally neutral, whereas others include a mixture of neutral and target words. Target words are words suspected of being emotionally charged for a group of individuals. For example, target words for people with somatoform disorder might include *sick, disease, symptom, pain, death, surgery,* and so on. If people have a special sensitivity to the target words, they will be distracted more readily by the

---

[FIGURE 9.5]
Emotional Stroop Test

In the Emotional Stroop Test, people name the color in which each word in a list is printed. The assumption is that people will be slower to do this task when the list contains words that have special significance for the person. In this example, the emotional list contains several words related to illness, and it is hypothesized that people with somatoform disorders will be especially sensitive to these words.

Neutral List	Emotional List
Salad	Sick
Play	Play
Rock	Rock
Intelligence	Disease
Chimney	Chimney
Printer	Symptom
Joy	Pain
House	House
Walk	Walk
Smile	Smile
Friend	Death
Woman	Woman
Doorway	Surgery
Handle	Handle

---

secondary gain A secondary effect that yields positive reinforcement and thus maintains the pathology that produces it.

words themselves and will thus take longer to name the colors from lists that contain such words. That is exactly what happens when illness-related target words are given to people with somatoform disorders (Hitchcock & Mathews, 1992), and this result suggests that these people are especially sensitive to the target words.

Sociocultural Perspective. The sociocultural perspective focuses on both family and cultural influences. For example, it has long been recognized that individuals with hypochondriasis or somatization disorder have histories that include excessive illness in their families while they were growing up, which may have sensitized these individuals to health issues (Kellner, 1991). Furthermore, people with somatoform disorders often report the same symptoms reported by family members. To be concerned about having a disease that one or more family members has had is reasonable, because many diseases run in families. However, excessive concern can lead to the vicious circle described earlier. Furthermore, this family pattern suggests the possibility that individuals learn to be afraid of illnesses and thus show these exaggerated health concerns.

Another sociocultural issue involves conversion disorders, which are much less common today than they once were and are most often reported by people who are unsophisticated about medical issues (Binzer & Kullgren, 1996). These findings are generally undisputed, but there is considerable dispute over their interpretation. Could they reflect changing cultural attitudes? Could conversion disorders represent culturally acceptable ways of responding to stress, but only in some cultures? A recent study of an indigenous group in Colombia found an epidemic of conversion symptoms during a particularly stressful period for the group (Anonymous et al., 1998). Was this simply an acceptable way for group members in this culture to say they were overwhelmed? Some professionals have gone so far as to suggest that chronic fatigue syndrome is the conversion disorder for industrialized nations, although there is considerable controversy around that speculation (Taylor et al., 2001).

Biological Perspective. With the exception of somatization disorder, very little is known about the biology of somatoform disorders. There are no studies of genetic influences on either hypochondriasis or conversion disorder. There is evidence that pain disorders run in families, but this does not establish that genes are responsible (Chaturvedi, 1987).

Much more is known about the biology of somatization disorder. For example, family, twin, and adoption studies all suggest that somatization disorder has a genetic component, which appears to be shared with antisocial personality disorder (Guze, 1993; Lilienfeld, 1992). Antisocial personality disorder (Chapter 12) is characterized by a pervasive pattern of disregard for the rights of others,

and on the surface it looks very different from somatization disorder.

Somatization disorder is also the only somatoform disorder for which there is a viable biological theory. That theory is based in part on the genetic evidence linking somatization disorder and antisocial personality disorder. Lilienfeld (1992) postulated that these two disorders may share a neurologically based disinhibition—that is, both groups tend to be behaviorally impulsive. The brain mechanisms associated with this behavioral inhibition process are well known (Fowles, 1993, 2000). They include the orbital frontal cortex, the hippocampus, and the septal area of the brain. These areas are disrupted in both somatization disorder and antisocial personality disorder, which suggests that there might a biological underpinning for these disorders (Lilienfeld, 1992).

How could a single neurological problem result is such dramatically different symptoms? Many believe that this basic biological process interacts with other processes, either biological or sociocultural, to shape the specific symptom pattern. It is well known that males show more aggressiveness than females (Maccoby & Jacklin, 1974; Geen, 1990), and this finding holds for many species (Gray & Buffery, 1971; Alcock, 2001). Females tend to show more dependency than males, although this sex difference is not nearly so consistent as that for aggression (Lazarus & Monat, 1979). Lilienfeld (1992) speculated that these sex differences, coupled with the normal socialization processes that differ for men and women, account for the differential symptom patterns exhibited in somatization disorder and antisocial personality disorder despite their shared biological underpinnings.

Review of the Theories. Although research has been conducted to address the issue of what causes various somatoform disorders, the quality and quantity of that research are nowhere near the level of research on other disorders, such as mood disorders. Somatoform disorders were among the first psychological disorders to be studied, going back to the pioneering work of Freud. Nevertheless, they have garnered only a fraction of the research effort devoted to other disorders, as indicated by the number of empirical research studies published in the last 20 years. In a sense, little has changed since the time of Freud. People with these disorders were of little interest to medicine at the time; Freud was one of the few people who took them seriously and tried to understand what caused them. Perhaps a subtle bias against people with such symptoms still discourages researchers from making a career studying these disorders.

However, there may be another reason. There are more case histories with speculations about internal dynamics published for people with somatoform disorders than for any other class of disorders other than dissociative disorders (Chapter 15). Many of these papers discuss constructs that cannot be independently measured, so these theories cannot be scientifically evaluated. But things may be changing. The definitions of these disorders have been clarified in recent editions of the DSM, which facilitates their construct validation (see Chapter 6). In the last ten years, many traditional construct validation studies have been undertaken, including epidemiological, genetic, cognitive processing, and treatment studies. These basic studies have helped refine diagnoses in other diagnostic categories, and there is every reason to believe that they will, in time, do the same for somatoform disorders.

TREATING SOMATOFORM DISORDERS

There is virtually no controlled research on the treatment of somatoform disorders. Therefore, the treatments discussed in this section are largely based on common wisdom, with occasional empirically supported elements. The treatment approaches differ by condition, but share many features. This section begins by discussing the necessary medical treatments and then the psychological strategies that have been used. The use of medications is discussed briefly. Finally, because the treatment of BDD is different from the treatment of other somatoform disorders, a separate section is devoted to BDD.

Ruling Out Physical Disorders. When physical symptoms are present, the most reasonable expectation is that a physical problem is responsible. You would certainly not be pleased with your doctor if she or he routinely assumed that your physical complaints indicated a psychological problem and therefore did not conduct a physical examination or run appropriate medical tests. Looking for a physical cause when the presenting complaint includes physical symptoms should always be the first step. However, doctors who treat people with somatization disorders often encounter such a long history of reported symptoms that prove to have no physical cause that they may come to expect that all such symptoms are part of the somatization disorder. That is problematic, because the only way to rule out a physical cause is to test for it and have the test come back negative. Remember the case of Julia, who was introduced in the somatization disorder section. Julia had undergone hundreds of tests that came back negative over nearly 15 years. Nevertheless, her doctor appropriately took her symptoms seriously each time she reported them, asking additional questions and following up with reasonable tests. The result is that she correctly diagnosed Julia's endometriosis and made the appropriate referral.

Providing Clients with Alternatives. A variety of psychological approaches have been tried for the treatment of somatoform disorders, although with few exceptions, these approaches have not been subjected to rigorous evaluation. All of the treatment approaches have one thing in common: They attempt to give clients alternative ways of looking at their symptoms. This section focuses on strategies for handling trauma-related symptoms, psychological distress from the symptoms, and behavioral problems that arise from the symptoms.

Whenever somatoform symptoms appear to be related to a traumatic event, as might be the case with a conversion disorder, the clinical focus is the trauma. This strategy dates back to the early work of Freud (Crimlisk & Ron, 1999). The rationale for this approach is that the symptoms are presumably a reaction to the trauma, so interpreting the trauma in a more psychological manner will reduce the likelihood of experiencing the physical symptoms. Any trauma has the potential to produce psychological consequences, as you learned in Chapter 8. Helping clients to develop insight into their response to the trauma, showing them alternative ways to deal with the distress from the trauma, and providing support during the normal healing process following a trauma are all appropriate strategies. That having been said, most of these strategies are taken as a matter of faith, because so little controlled research on their efficacy has been conducted.

Regardless of whether there is a trauma associated with somatoform disorders, there is usually considerable distress about the symptoms and their consequences. For example, not only do people with somatization disorder experience anxiety from their constant fears of disease, but they usually experience negative consequences from the reactions of doctors, family members, and employers to the unending physical complaints. The standard stress management strategies discussed earlier in this chapter can be effective in reducing this distress. Because there is evidence that increased stress may worsen somatoform disorders, these strategies may reduce somatoform symptoms as well. Individuals with somatoform disorders often show little insight into their symptoms, but they rarely have to be convinced that they are under stress. Consequently, they often readily accept this approach. Cognitive-behavioral therapy, one of the few approaches that has been systematically evaluated, shows promise (Warwick et al., 1996; Warwick & Salkovskis, 2001). For example, Warwick et al. (1996) taught clients with hypochondriasis to challenge their beliefs that they had a serious illness. These researchers also showed that the severity of symptoms increased and decreased depending on how strongly the client concentrated on them. This approach provided clients with an alternative explanation for their symptoms—specifically, that the symptoms were partly controlled by the amount of attention paid to them.

Family therapy has been employed with some somatoform disorders, usually with the focus on how family members respond to the person with the somatoform disorder and on what benefits, if any, the person derives from the symptoms (McDaniel & Speice, 2001). Hypnosis has also been suggested for the treatment of conversion disorders (Chaves, 1996; Mander, 1998), although no controlled studies of hypnosis have been published. Some conversion disorders respond to physical rehabilitation, which essentially treats the disorder as though it were real but gives the person the expectation that it will respond to physical therapy (Deaton, 1998). Using such treatment when it is not justified by a physical disorder is essentially a placebo, so any improvement is probably due to the power of suggestion.

Finally, there are significant behavioral consequences associated with somatoform disorders, such as alienating friends and family by constantly complaining and seeking reassurance. Furthermore, the typical client with a somatoform disorder uses an incredible amount of medical services, which cost the person, the insurance company, or both a great deal of money. Most treatments of somatoform disorders attempt to reduce this excessive seeking of reassurance and medical care. Warwick et al. (1996) demonstrated that direct efforts to reduce such behavior, based on cognitive-behavioral approaches, were effective. Presumably, the natural positive consequences (improved relations and decreased costs) maintain such behavioral changes once they occur, although such data are not yet available.

Medications. Medications are not often used as a major treatment for somatoform disorder, although it is not uncommon to use them to treat symptomatically the anxiety and depression that are often present. In addition, low doses of the antidepressant imipramine (Tofranil) reduce the pain and distress often reported by individuals with somatoform disorders (Phillip & Fickinger, 1993).

Treating BDD. Because BDD so strongly resembles OCD, you will not be surprised to learn that the treatment procedures are very similar for these two disorders. The two treatment strategies most commonly used are (1) the behavioral strategy of exposure with response prevention and (2) medication. Because both have been discussed in Chapter 8, they will be reviewed only briefly here.

BDD is most often treated with one of the SSRIs, usually with a good treatment response (Phillips et al., 1998). Medication is the preferred treatment because individuals with BDD often show little insight into their disorder. As a consequence, it is difficult to convince them to undergo exposure. It is common to utilize cognitive therapy to increase insight as part of exposure therapy. The exposure for Carolyn involved venturing out in public. The response prevention involved avoiding the hours of grooming and not wearing the wig she used to hide her real hair. The exposure was done gradually, starting with chores in her backyard, where only a few neighbors could see her. She then drove her children to school, went to the store and the doctor's office, and finally attended a party with her husband. The hierarchy was arranged to increase gradually the number of people who saw her and, consequently, the pressure on her to look her best.

Check Yourself 9.4

Somatoform Disorders

1. What is the difference between psychosomatic disorders and somatoform disorders?
2. What is the difference between somatization disorder and conversion disorder?
3. Which somatoform disorder is best understood biologically?
4. What is the first step in treating a somatoform disorder?

Ponder this . . .   *Most people with somatoform disorders receive little positive reinforcement and are frequently ridiculed for their constant health complaints. Normally, such aversive consequences would lead to a rapid decrease in the behavior. What must be happening to make the somatoform symptoms so resistant to extinction?*

PSYCHOFORM DISORDERS

The DSM recognizes somatoform disorders, which are psychological disorders that appear on the surface to be physical disorders. There is also the opposite class of conditions—physical disorders that appear on the surface to be psychological disorders. These disorders might be called psychoform. **Psychoform disorder** is not a DSM category; in fact, it is not a standard term. There is no term for these disorders, despite the fact that they deserve attention.

Optimal treatment of any disorder requires accurate diagnosis. Treating a client for anxiety and depression when the symptoms are due to failure of the adrenal gland to produce sufficient cortisol is unlikely to help. Furthermore, failure to recognize and screen for some physical disorders may result in the disease process reaching a point where successful treatment is no longer possible. Mental health professionals cannot be as knowledgeable about physical disorders as physicians, but they do need a basic understanding of what to watch for and a willingness to encourage a medical evaluation whenever there is a concern about an undiagnosed physical problem (Morrison, 1997). This section begins with a brief review of physical disorders that can produce psychological symptoms, with a special focus on disorders whose early symptoms may be primarily psychological in nature. It then reviews several common medications that can produce psychological side effects.

psychoform disorder   A physical disorder that appears on the surface to be a psychological disorder.

PHYSICAL DISORDERS

Most experienced therapists have sufficient background concerning psychological disorders to make a reasoned guess about a client's diagnosis after just a few minutes of conversation with the client. Most disorders present themselves as reasonably consistent syndromes, with certain symptoms likely to be recognized and reported immediately by the client. For example, people with panic disorder are likely to mention panic attacks and a pervasive fear of more such attacks and to exhibit avoidance when asked a general question about the problem. A few confirming questions about the nature of the attacks and the course of the symptoms are sufficient to confirm that the person qualifies for a diagnosis of panic disorder. However, such limited questioning is not sufficient for a diagnostic work-up because there may well be other problems. For example, severe panic often makes people feel helpless and thus can trigger feelings of depression. The anxiety associated with panic may drive the person to seek relief through alcohol or drug abuse in an attempt to self-medicate. The high levels of anxiety associated with panic can also exacerbate numerous preexisting problems, such as sexual dysfunctions, relationship problems, phobias, impulse control problems, and mood disorders. Finally, it is entirely possible to have multiple disorders that are unrelated to one another. Just as it is possible to have both cancer and a broken leg, it is possible to have both panic disorder and a social phobia or a gambling problem. A good assessment not only must obtain details about the primary presenting complaint but also should screen for a variety of related and unrelated psychological disorders.

Just as it is important to screen for a wide range of psychological disorders, it is valuable to screen for possible physical disorders as well. This screening should focus on both physical disorders that have already been diagnosed and physical disorders that may exist but have yet to come to the attention of medical personnel. Table 9.3 lists a few of the many physical disorders that can produce psychological symptoms, along with both the psychological and the physical symptoms usually associated with them. One does not have to ask about every imaginable symptom to screen for possible physical disorders. Rather, all that is necessary is to inquire about changes in clients' health, about physical problems they may be having, and about such physical symptoms as fatigue, pain, dizziness, and difficulty in concentrating. If such symptoms are reported, detailed information should be obtained about the nature of the symptoms, their course, and the degree of distress they are causing. When doubt exists, clients should be referred for a medical evaluation. It is not the responsibility of the psychologist to diagnose a physical disorder. However, it is the psychologist's responsibility to screen for possible physical disorders and make appropriate referrals when necessary. Even psychiatrists, who are trained as physicians, should refer clients to doctors with specialized expertise.

MEDICATION EFFECTS

Medications can do wonders—sometimes saving lives, often improving health, and occasionally reversing medical problems. However, medications can also cause a variety of side effects. Table 9.4 on page 286 lists some common medications, along with the psychological side effects that they can cause. Psychologists should routinely obtain a list of the medications that clients are taking. Information on all medications, including possible side effects, can be obtained from the *Physician's Desk Reference,* or PDR. If some of the psychological symptoms could be the result of medications, clients should be encouraged to talk with their doctors about alternatives. Sometimes just a change in dosage or a change in when the medications are taken is sufficient to eliminate the symptoms.

Check Yourself 9.5

Psychoform Disorders

1. How would one screen for psychoform disorders?
2. What steps should therapists take in evaluating their clients for possible medication effects?

Ponder this . . . *One might think of somatoform and psychoform disorders as essentially opposite phenomena. However, from a diagnostic and referral perspective, they represent different challenges. Can you explain why?*

[TABLE 9.3] Physical Disorders with Psychological Symptoms

Listed here are a few medical disorders that may produce psychological symptoms.

DISORDER	PSYCHOLOGICAL SYMPTOMS	PHYSICAL SYMPTOMS
Brain tumor	Loss of memory, cognitive decline, personality change, depression, dissociation, psychosis, dementia	Headache, vomiting, dizziness, lateralized perceptual disturbances or deficits, seizures
Cancer	Depression, anxiety, suicidal ideation, delirium, symptoms of PTSD	Physical weakness, pain, loss of weight, general fatigue (varies depending on the type and location of the cancer)
Cardiac arrhythmias	Anxiety, delirium	Palpitations, fatigue, dizziness, feeling faint
Cerebrovascular accident	A variety of cognitive disorders, personality change, depression and/or mania, psychosis	Lateralized perceptual deficits, difficulty identifying objects and their use, memory losses, difficulty in using or understanding language, difficulty in carrying out everyday tasks
Congestive heart failure	Anxiety, panic attacks, insomnia, depression, delirium	Shortness of breath, extreme fatigue, weakness, swelling or coldness in the extremities, bluish cast to the face or extremities
Fibromyalgia	Chronic fatigue, depression, anxiety	Muscle pain, stiffness, tenderness in the muscles and joints
Huntington's disease	Depression, psychosis, personality change, dementia	Shaking motions in limbs, uncoordinated and ticlike motions, inarticulate speech
Hyperparathyroidism	Personality change, depression, suicidal ideation, anxiety, delirium, psychosis	Weakness, fatigue, appetite loss, nausea, vomiting, constipation, thirst, abdominal or muscle pain
Hypoparathyroidism	Irritability, depression, anxiety, paranoid ideas, delirium, dementia	Numbness and tingling, seizures, spasms of the face or extremities
Liver failure	Irritability, depression, delirium	A yellowish cast to the skin, weakness, fatigue, appetite loss, red palms, easy bruising, tremor, coordination problems
Lupus	Severe depression, delirium, dementia, psychosis	Muscle and joint pain, rash, fatigue, fever, appetite and weight loss, nausea, diarrhea, cough, painful breathing, weakness, pale complexion
Lyme disease	Depression, psychosis, anxiety, some mild cognitive symptoms	Headache, fever, chills, pains, fatigue, loss of energy and interest, stiff neck, paralysis, arthritis
Multiple sclerosis	Depression, mania, sudden emotionality, cognitive impairment, dementia	Weakness, visual problems, incontinence, trouble walking, fatigue, burning or prickling sensations
Parkinson's disease	Depression, anxiety, dementia	Tremor, muscle rigidity, decrease in mobility, difficulty walking
Pneumonia	Delirium, anxiety, panic attacks	Fever, cough, chest pain
Pulmonary thrombosis	Anxiety, delirium	Faintness, shortness of breath, chest pain, coughing up blood
Rheumatoid arthritis	Depression	Fatigue, weakness, weight loss, swollen and painful joints
Sleep apnea	Insomnia, daytime drowsiness, depression, irritability, poor concentration	Severe snoring or gasping for breath while sleeping, morning headache
Syphilis	Fatigue, personality change, mood disorder, psychosis, dementia	Genital ulcers or rash, multiple neurological symptoms

SOURCE: *Adapted from "Physical Problems with Psychological Symptoms" from* When Psychological Problems Mask Medical Disorders: A Guide for Psychotherapists *by J. Morrison. Copyright © 1997. Reprinted by permission of The Guilford Press.*

[TABLE 9.4] **Medications That Can Produce Psychological Symptoms**

Listed below are just a few of the drugs that can cause psychological side effects.

DRUG	USED TO TREAT	PSYCHOLOGICAL SIDE EFFECTS
Pemoline (Cylert)	ADHD	Hallucinations, mild depression
Valproic acid (Depakene)	Seizure disorder	Hallucinations
Terazosin HCl (Hytrin)	Enlargement of the prostrate	Depression, sleepiness, impotence
Betaxolol HCl (Betoptic)	Lowering pressure in the eye in people with glaucoma	Depression
Metoprolol succinate (Toprol-XL)	Hypertension	Depression, mental confusion
Metaproternol sulfate (Alupent)	Bronchial asthma	Nervousness
Hydralazine HCl (Apresoline)	Hypertension	Psychosis
Fluoxetine HCl (Prozac)	Depression and some anxiety disorders	Anxiety, nervousness, insomnia
Amantadine HCl (Symmetrel)	Influenza A virus	Anxiety, hallucinations, confusion, anorexia
Molindone HCl (Moban)	Psychotic disorders	Depression, hyperactivity, euphoria
Sumatriptan succinate (Imitrex)	Migraine headaches	Anxiety
Bisoprolol fumarate and hydrochlorthiazide (Ziac)	Hypertension	Insomnia, loss of libido, impotence
Ofloxacin (Floxin)	Infections	Anxiety, depression, sleep disorders, euphoria, hallucinations, mental confusion

SOURCE: *Adapted from the* Physician's Desk Reference, *56th ed. (Montvale, NJ: Medical Economics Data Production Company, 2002).*

 ## SUMMARY

STRESS AND ITS IMPACT ON HUMAN FUNCTIONING

- Hans Selye's pioneering work on stress identified three phase to a stress response—the alarm reaction, resistance, and exhaustion—which collectively make up the general adaptation syndrome (GAS). These responses are controlled by a combination of brain mechanisms and endocrine glands.

- Three primary methods have been used to measure stress. One counts major life stressors, a second counts everyday hassles, and a third identifies stressors but seeks specific details to determine how stressful they are likely to be for a given individual.

- Stress decreases the efficiency of the immune system and, consequently, increases risk for such disorders as the common cold, AIDS, and cancer.

- Stress can be managed with physiological, cognitive, and behavioral techniques. In addition, supportive relationships and proper rest and relaxation can buffer people against the effects of stress.

PSYCHOLOGICAL FACTORS THAT AFFECT MEDICAL CONDITIONS

- Psychosomatic, or psychophysiological, disorders are physical disorders that are due at least in part to psychological stress. The current DSM category for these disorders is psychological factors affecting medical conditions.

- Two gastrointestinal disorders (ulcers and irritable bowel syndrome) and two cardiovascular diseases (coronary heart disease and essential hypertension) are considered stress-related.

- The Type A personality is associated with increased risk for coronary heart disease, but the component of hostility is the best predictor of heart disease. The Type A behavior pattern can be modified, and such modification does decrease the risk of heart disease.

- Both tension and migraine headaches are related to stress, although genetic predisposing factors also play a role.

- Treating stress-related disorders begins by treating the physical symptoms, but stress management skills may prevent further problems.

BEHAVIORAL MEDICINE

- Behavioral medicine involves using psychological techniques to facilitate such behavior changes as stopping smoking, eating a better diet, and getting more exercise. It is also concerned with preventing AIDS, reducing coronary heart disease, and helping people adjust to chronic diseases.

SOMATOFORM DISORDERS

- Somatoform disorders appear to be physical disorders, but no physical dysfunction can be found. Included are somatization disorder, conversion disorder, pain disorder, hypochondriasis, and body dysmorphic disorder.

- Body dysmorphic disorder has many of the features of obsessive-compulsive disorder, and a substantial body of evidence suggests that it may be a variation of OCD.

- Both psychodynamic and behavioral perspectives recognize that secondary gain may contribute to somatoform disorders, and the cognitive perspective assumes an excessive sensitivity to illness-related stimuli. The sociocultural perspective argues that people with somatoform disorders learn to play the sick role. Genes influence risk for one somatoform disorder, somatization disorder.

- Treating somatoform disorders starts with ruling out physical causes. Supportive, cognitive, behavioral, and family therapies are used to give people with these disorders ways of handling the stress that is presumed to underlie the disorder. Body dysmorphic disorder is treated with the same procedures as OCD.

PSYCHOFORM DISORDERS

- Psychoform disorders are physical disorders that appear to be psychological disorders. Therapists should routinely screen for physical disorders and for medication side effects.

 KEY TERMS

acquired immune deficiency syndrome, or AIDS   (258)
behavioral medicine   (268)
biofeedback   (260)
body dysmorphic disorder, or BDD   (277)
carcinogenic agents   (258)
chronic fatigue syndrome, or CFS   (275)
conversion disorder   (276)
coronary heart disease   (262)
diaphragmatic breathing   (260)
essential hypertension   (265)
factitious disorder   (273)
general adaptation syndrome, or GAS   (253)
HPA axis   (254)
hypertension   (265)
hypochondriasis   (277)
irritable bowel syndrome, or IBS   (262)
malingering   (273)
migraine headaches   (267)

Munchausen syndrome   (273)
Munchausen syndrome by proxy   (273)
pain disorders   (276)
progressive muscle relaxation   (260)
psychoform disorder   (283)
psychoneuroimmunology   (259)
psychophysiological disorders   (262)
psychosomatic disorders   (262)
secondary gain   (280)
somatization disorder   (272)
somatoform disorders   (252)
stress   (252)
stress-related disorders   (252)
tension headaches   (266)
Type A behavior   (263)
Type B behavior   (263)
ulcers   (262)

 SUGGESTED READINGS

Morrison, J. (1997). *When psychological problems mask medical disorders: A guide for psychotherapists.* New York: Guilford. An encyclopedic list of physical disorders that might present as psychological disorders.

Phillips, K. A. (1996). *The broken mirror: Understanding and treating body dysmorphic disorder.* New York: Oxford University Press. A fascinating account of body dysmorphic disorder by the leading authority. It is filled with case examples.

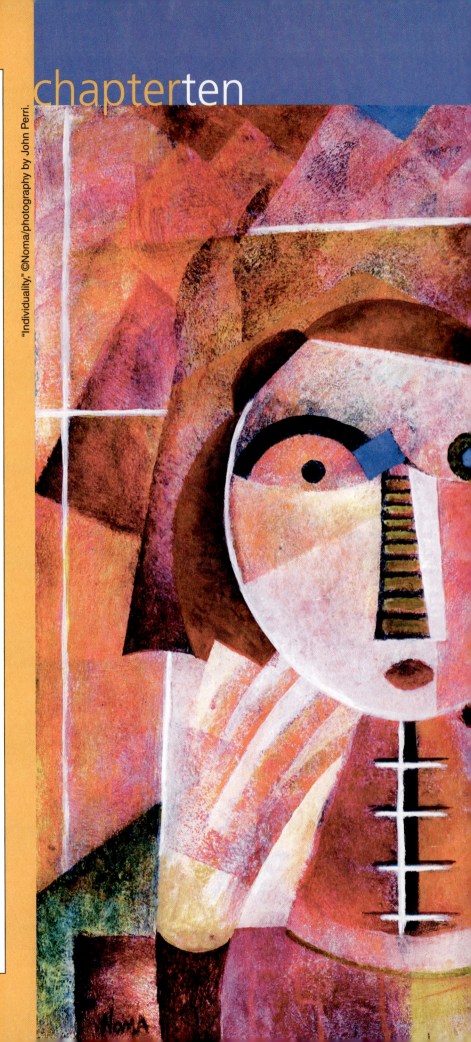

chapter**ten**

"Individuality," ©Noma/photography by John Perri.

10

Eating and Sleep Disorders

ARLENE
Wasting Away

Arlene was only 13 when she started dieting. Slightly overweight in grade school, she felt that she needed to lose weight to be more popular. The oldest of four kids and a solid student, she was a parent's dream. By her freshman year in high school, she started to blossom into a beautiful young woman. No longer overweight, she was now the recipient of constant attention from boys in her class. But she still felt fat, and so she continued to watch her weight. She would pick at her food, often eating no more than a fraction of what was on her plate. Her parents encouraged her to eat more, but Arlene argued that she was eating more than enough. In time, she started taking her meals to her room, where she could dispose of most of them in a plastic bag and return a nearly empty plate to please her mother. She continued to lose weight. By the time she dropped below 100 pounds on her 5-foot-7-inch frame, it was very noticeable. Her face was gaunt, and her arms and legs looked emaciated. Yet she still felt fat and continued to diet. On those rare occasions when she did eat, she would take powerful laxatives or exercise until she dropped. Not realizing how little Arlene was really eating, her parents had her doctor run a series of tests to determine the reason for the weight loss—all of them negative. And still Arlene continued to feel fat.

MICHELLE
A Hidden Problem

At 21, Michelle appeared to have it all. A successful college student with a 3.74 GPA, several good friends, a supportive family, and a loving boyfriend, Michelle had a great future ahead of her. However, Michelle had a secret that none of her friends or family members knew about. Two or three times a week, she would be overcome by an urge to eat . . . and eat . . . and eat. She might consume an entire bag of potato chips, cookies by the handful, ice cream a half gallon at a time, and anything else she could find. She would eat until she felt she was ready to burst, and then in a flood of guilt and shame, she would force herself to vomit. She selected an apartment with a private bathroom so that she could hide this behavior. She avoided keeping a lot of food around the house because the temptation was overwhelming. Nevertheless, the urge to eat would grow so strong that she felt compelled to go out and buy enough food for five people. She had gotten into the habit of buying food from three different markets during her binges so that it would be less obvious to the clerks what she was doing.

TYLER
A Self-Fulfilling Prophecy

Tyler could hardly keep his eyes open most of the day, yet no sooner did he lie down to sleep than he would wake right up. This went on night after night for months. He would try to bury his head under the pillow, to watch TV or read, even to count sheep—all to no avail. He would be so tired he could not keep his eyes open, yet sleep refused to come. All night long he would watch the clock tick away the hours. If he slept two hours a night, he was lucky. The sleep problem had started 8 months before, when he was under tremendous pressure at work and his son was having a problem in school. He had been too wound up to sleep then, so he had often paced a good part of the night. That was behind him now, but he could not get back to a normal sleep cycle.

Evolutionary Impact

There are few things more important to one's health and functioning than eating and sleeping. One might think that these behaviors could not be more automatic, given their critical importance to survival. At one level, that is true. Babies are born with suckling reflexes that are triggered within minutes of their first contact with their mother's breast. Sleeping and eating make up the majority of a baby's life and almost half of an adult's life. As we will see, these body functions are controlled automatically at several levels, but they are also responsive to psychological factors. For example, mood and anxiety disorders may either increase or decrease both appetite and sleepiness. When eating or sleep is disrupted by psychological disorders, the eating or sleep disorder is said to be *secondary*—that is, it is the result of the primary diagnostic condition. This chapter will focus on eating and sleep disorders that are themselves *primary disorders*—that is, they are the principal problem and not the result of some other psychological or medical condition.

The eating disorders of Arlene and Michelle are primary disorders that have had a devastating effect on these young women, potentially threatening the life of Arlene and compromising the health of both. Tyler's sleep disorder is also primary. It may have initially been due to stress, but now it has taken on a life of its own. He is now so tired that there is no joy in his life. He drags himself through each day, hoping that the sleep his body so desperately needs will come that night. In the meantime, the quality of his work has decreased, his concentration is almost nonexistent, and he has barely avoided two traffic accidents because he dozed off while driving. This chapter will discuss these and other eating and sleep disorders.

EATING DISORDERS

Of all the disorders covered in this text, none is more common among college students than eating disorders. You probably know someone with an eating disorder, perhaps well enough to appreciate how disruptive it can be. You probably know several people with eating disorders but don't realize it. Many battle eating disorders privately, sharing their struggle with very few people. You may even have battled an eating disorder yourself. If this is a disorder that hits close to home, I hope that this chapter will provide the information, perspectives, and encouragement you may need to deal with it in yourself, a family member, or a friend.

Eating disorders are characterized by severe disruptions in eating behavior that affect physical, psychological, and social functioning (APA, 2000). They can become life-threatening, and they often create health problems, disrupt

normal physiological functioning, and interfere with family and other social relationships. Depression is common in people with eating disorders (Keel et al., 2001). Most people try to hide their eating disorders from friends and family, suffering significant loss of self-esteem in the process (McFarlane et al., 2001). Both Arlene and Michelle tried to hide their eating patterns, although her severe weight loss made it impossible for Arlene to hide her disorder.

This section covers two eating disorders, anorexia nervosa and bulimia nervosa. The DSM also includes in an appendix another eating disorder, *binge-eating disorder*. The DSM lists potential disorders in an appendix if there are insufficient data to warrant including them in the current manual, but there is sufficient interest and information to encourage further study. Binge-eating disorder will be briefly covered in the section on bulimia. Table 10.1 summarizes the diagnostic criteria for the DSM eating disorders, including three eating disorders of childhood—pica, rumination disorder, and feeding disorder of infancy and early childhood—which will not be covered in this chapter.

ANOREXIA NERVOSA

Anorexia nervosa, often simply referred to as anorexia, is characterized by a refusal to consume and digest enough calories to maintain a normal weight (APA, 2000). Consequently, there is significant weight loss, sometimes so severe that medical complications result (Hewitt et al., 2001). The weight criterion for this diagnosis is 15% below normal weight, so if normal weight for a person is 120 pounds, a weight of 102 pounds (18 below normal) would meet this criterion. However, some people are naturally thin, and for them a weight that is 85% of normal for their height may be normal for them. Thus weight is only one of four diagnostic criteria for this disorder. The other three are (1) an intense fear of gaining weight or being fat, even when severely underweight, (2) body distortions that involve feeling fat even though one's weight is normal to severely below normal, and (3) loss of at least three menstrual cycles in women who are past puberty (APA, 2000). The DSM distinguishes two subtypes of anorexia. **Restrict-**

---

eating disorders   Disorders characterized by severe disruptions in eating behavior, which affect physical, psychological, and social functioning.

anorexia nervosa   A disease characterized by refusal to consume and digest enough calories to maintain a normal weight.

restricting type anorexia   A subtype of anorexia that includes individuals who use only dieting to lose weight.

binge-eating/purging type anorexia   A subtype of anorexia that includes individuals who regularly binge-eat, purge, or both.

purging   The use of vomiting, diuretics, laxatives, or enemas as methods of minimizing the caloric impact of food.

[TABLE 10.1]   DSM Diagnostic Criteria for Eating Disorders

Listed below are the diagnostic criteria for the DSM eating disorders.

Anorexia Nervosa

1. Refusal to maintain body weight that is at least 85% of normal weight for the person's height and age.
2. Intense fear of gaining weight or becoming fat, even in someone who is underweight.
3. Tendency to see oneself incorrectly as fat or to deny the seriousness of one's weight loss or to have one's self-image unduly influenced by one's weight or body shape.
4. In females who have reached puberty, at least three consecutive menstrual periods have been missed because of the excessive weight loss.

Bulimia Nervosa

1. Recurrent episodes of binge eating that feel out of control to the individual.
2. Recurrent inappropriate compensatory behavior to avoid the consequences of the binge, such as purging, fasting, or excessive exercise.
3. The binge eating and compensatory behavior must occur at least twice a week for three months.
4. One's sense of self is unduly influenced by weight or body shape.
5. The person does not qualify for a diagnosis of anorexia nervosa.

Binge-Eating Disorder

1. Recurrent episodes of binge eating.
2. The binge eating should include at least three of the following: (a) rapid eating; (b) eating past comfortably full; (c) heavy eating when not hungry; (d) eating alone because of embarrassment about how much is being eaten; and (e) feeling disgusted, depressed, or guilty about the eating.
3. Significant distress over the binge eating.
4. Occurs at least two days per week for six months.
5. Does not include compensatory behavior, such as purging.

Pica

1. Consistently eating nonnutritive substances, such as dirt, for at least one month.
2. This behavior is developmentally inappropriate.
3. The behavior is not part of a culturally sanctioned activity.
4. If the eating behavior is part of another mental disorder, such as mental retardation, it should be diagnosed only if it is so severe that it requires independent clinical attention.

Rumination Disorder

1. Repeated regurgitation and rechewing of food that lasts at least one month.
2. The regurgitation is not due to a medical problem.
3. The regurgitation must not be exclusively a part of another eating disorder. When it is part of a disorder such as mental retardation, the diagnosis should be made only if the problem is so severe that it requires independent clinical attention.

Feeding Disorder of Infancy or Early Childhood

1. A persistent failure to eat adequately, which lasts at least one month and results in a significant weight loss or in failure to gain weight.
2. The condition is not due to a medical problem.
3. The condition is not due to another medical disorder or to lack of food.
4. The condition develops before the age of 6.

ing type anorexia includes individuals who simply diet to lose weight. **Binge-eating/purging type anorexia** includes individuals who regularly binge-eat, purge, or both. **Purging** refers to the use of vomiting, diuretics, laxatives, or enemas as methods of minimizing the caloric impact of food.

Weight loss can be so severe in anorexia that hospitalization is required for medical stabilization. Of those who require hospitalization, nearly 10% eventually die from complications associated with the weight loss (APA, 2000). Overall, between 5% and 8% of all people with anorexia die from complications associated with the disorder (Espie, 2002; Moller-Madsen et al., 1996).

The severe loss of weight associated with anorexia can lead to several medical problems (Halmi, 2000). Blood pressure is often low, which can make people feel faint if they stand up too quickly. Heart rate also slows, as does the output of the thyroid. There is a reduction of cortocotropin-releasing hormone in response to stress. If binge-eating is also present, there is likely to be an electrolyte imbalance, which can affect the normal electrical activity of the heart. All of these medical problems decrease once the person with anorexia starts to eat normally and puts on at least a minimal amount of weight. Purging, especially in someone who is severely underweight, can create more severe situations, such as extreme lethargy and muscle weakness. Some of these complications can be life-threatening, such as irregular heart rates that may precipitate cardiac arrest.

Women with anorexia outnumber men nearly 10 to 1 (APA, 2000; Woodside & Kennedy, 1995). Approximately

Although it is hard to imagine, people with anorexia can be this thin and still be convinced that they are fat.

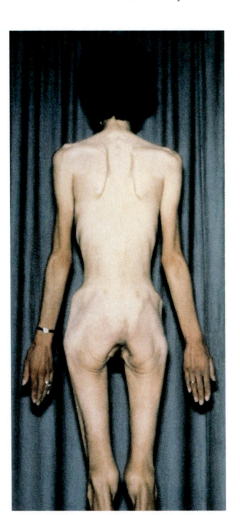

1 woman in every 200 qualifies for the diagnosis at some point during her life. Many more women show significant weight loss but do not meet the other criteria for a diagnosis of anorexia. For example, they may continue to experience menstrual periods, although the periods may be less regular than found in women of normal weight. Anorexia typically begins in mid- to late adolescence and almost never develops after the age of 40 (Bulik, 1998; Garfinkel et al., 1995). There is no single course for the disorder. Some individuals experience a single episode after which eating is normal or nearly normal. A more common course is to have intermittent episodes of anorexia, with normal eating and weight gain between episodes. Onset is more likely during stressful periods, and life stress appears to be a precipitating factor in relapse (Bennett & Cooper, 1999).

Arlene's situation is typical. She started dieting in her teens and was clearly anorexic by her junior year in high school. By age 16, her menstrual periods had stopped because of her severe weight loss. Although she looked emaciated, she felt fat, and no amount of dieting could change that feeling. She was trying so hard to be perfect for everyone, but she could no longer hear her friends telling her that she was going too far—much too far.

BULIMIA NERVOSA

Bulimia nervosa, or bulimia for short, is characterized by frequent binge eating followed by compensatory behavior to maintain weight. The most common compensatory behavior is purging, but excessive exercise and fasting are also used. The binges typically last an hour or two and are well in excess of what most people would eat in such a period. Michelle would often consume a bag of cookies, half a gallon of ice cream, and several candy bars in a single binge. Binges frequently include such high-calorie, easily digestible foods. To qualify for the diagnosis, the binges must occur on average at least twice a week for at least three months, and the self-worth of the person must be unduly influenced by body shape or weight. Compensatory behaviors may include vomiting, diuretics, laxatives, enemas, prolonged fasting, and excessive exercise. If a person meets diagnostic criteria for both anorexia and bulimia, only the anorexia diagnosis should be applied.

The estimated lifetime prevalence for bulimia is 1 to 3%, and about 90% of affected individuals are women (APA, 2000; Bushnell et al., 1990; Kendler et al., 1991). The rate of bulimia is especially high in college women, affecting about 1 in 15 (Cooley & Toray, 2001; Schlundt & Johnson, 1990). The disorder typically begins in late adolescence or early adulthood, often during a period of dieting (Stice,

bulimia nervosa   A disease characterized by frequent binge eating followed by compensatory behavior to maintain weight.

2001). The course may be chronic or intermittent (Keel & Mitchell, 1997). The severity and frequency of the bingeing tend to decrease with age (APA, 2000). Cross-sectional data suggest that the prevalence of bulimia is increasing. For example, Bushnell et al. (1990) found a lifetime prevalence of 1.6% in 18 to 44-year-old women but a prevalence rate three times higher in the 18–24 subgroup.

Michelle's binges were typically triggered by incidents that decreased her already shaky self-esteem. For example, a critical remark by a classmate, a lower grade than she expected, or someone ignoring her would be devastating, and she would feel compelled to binge. The binges were unsatisfying, but at least they removed momentarily the feelings of failure, although these were replaced moments later by intense shame for having binged. With her head over the toilet, forcing herself to vomit, she would cry uncontrollably—the guilt and the shame setting herself up for the next incident.

The binge eating, and especially the purging, create a variety of medical risks (Halmi, 2000). For example, individuals who frequently purge often show electrolyte imbalances, kidney and stomach problems, and dental problems.

Lady Diana, the late Princess of Wales, struggled with bulimia most of her public life. Under intense pressure and scrutiny, she strove to both look and act the part of a princess.

The constant exposure to stomach acids from the frequent vomiting can damage the hard enamel of teeth (Stege et al., 1982). Purging can also create disruptions in the heart rate and may even precipitate cardiac arrest (Halmi, 2000). EKG abnormalities are common, especially elevated heart rates. In rare instances, there can be an acute dilation of the stomach in someone who purges frequently. Using *ipecac*—a substance sold in drug stores to induce vomiting in children who have swallowed poison—dramatically increases the risk of cardiac failure.

Check Yourself 10.1

Types of Eating Disorders

1. Define the term *anorexia* nervosa.
2. Define the term *bulimia* nervosa.
3. What demographic group has the highest rate of eating disorders?

Ponder this . . .   *The most striking aspect of eating disorders is that they are about 10 times more likely to occur in women than men. Speculate about the possible reasons for this finding.*

CAUSES OF EATING DISORDERS

The exact causes of eating disorders are unknown, but biological, cultural, and psychological factors probably combine to increase risk. This section begins by outlining evolutionary mechanisms that control eating. Then the evidence for genetic, cultural, and psychological contributions is reviewed.

EVOLUTIONARY FACTORS
Evolutionary Impact

It is interesting to look at eating disorders from an evolutionary perspective. Anyone who has dieted is well aware of one of its effects—you become very hungry. Hunger is a critical drive because eating is absolutely necessary to survival, and hunger generally increases the longer a person goes without eating. One of the greatest threats to survival in the evolutionary past was from starvation, which was common before recent advances in agriculture and transportation (de Waal, 1997). Unfortunately, starvation still occurs all too frequently in Third World countries, especially during periods of war and political upheaval, as illustrated recently in Afghanistan, Somalia, and Ethiopia (Diamond, 1999). Accordingly, many species evolved mechanisms to deal with starvation. One such mechanism is to slow the metabolism when food is in short supply so that the organism will survive as long as possible. Natural famines end as weather conditions turn more favorable, and individuals that survive to the end of the famine are rewarded by (1) having new sources of food and (2) encountering less competition for the food because so many others have died. One consequence of this metabolism-slowing mechanism is that people who go on rigid diets often find that weight loss quickly plateaus. Less stringent diets, especially if they include increased exercise, tend to reduce this effect and therefore are more successful in the long run (Berg, 1998).

Nature also prepared organisms to deal with occasional famine by providing a storage mechanism for food. *Fat cells* store nutrients, which can be used by the body during famines. Although the current trend is to disdain fat cells, in the evolutionary past, organisms with a moderate amount of fat tended to survive longer when food was in short supply than organisms without such fat. When organisms are hungry, perhaps because of a famine, they gorge themselves when food is available,

thus storing the food as fat until the next available meal. It has been argued that the chronic dieting that often precedes the development of bulimia sets people up for binge eating, thus precipitating the cycle that becomes bulimia nervosa.

The hypothesis that dieting predisposes one to bulimia is called the **dietary restraint hypothesis.** Dietary restraint is the conscious effort to reduce one's caloric intake significantly. As a conscious effort, it represents a psychological process affected by many psychological variables. For example, it is well documented that societal pressure can influence dietary restraint. Furthermore, other psychological processes disrupt dietary restraint. For example, breaking a diet makes people who have been restraining their eating more likely to binge (Herman & Polivy, 1975; Polivy & Herman, 2002). This has typically been interpreted as a cognitive reaction: "I've already wrecked my diet, so I might as well just eat what I want." However, you can also look at this same process from a physiological perspective. The human body cannot tell the difference between intense dieting and famine, so radical dieting triggers *famine survival mechanisms*. The binge eating of bulimia is one such mechanism, and it is also occasionally found in people with anorexia. The constant feeling of hunger

In evolutionary history, the risk surrounding eating was not having enough to eat. Consequently, mechanisms evolved to ease the effects of starvation by (1) storing food as fat and (2) slowing metabolism in times of famine. These mechanisms backfire when people go on strict diets. The body interprets the diet as starvation and slows metabolism, making a more extreme diet necessary if the individual is to continue to lose weight. Furthermore, food becomes an incredible temptation, because consuming food and storing it as fat promote survival when periodic famines occur.

during diets is another. The obsession with food often found in people with anorexia is yet another. Research on the effects of prolonged starvation conducted on volunteers during World War II shows that all of these mechanisms are routinely evoked after a prolonged period without adequate nourishment (Keys et al., 1950). This theory could be invoked to account for the dramatic increase in bulimia over the past several decades by arguing that the recent obsession with thinness led to the excessive dieting that triggered episodes of bingeing. It is less effective in explaining anorexia, because it cannot account for the fact that the voluntary starvation that is central in anorexia continues in spite of the natural body mechanisms that regulate eating.

GENETIC FACTORS

Genes clearly play a role in eating disorders, although the exact nature of this role is unclear (Kaye et al., 2000a; Klump et al., 2001a). Kendler et al. (1991) found that 23% of female monozygotic twins were concordant for bulimia, whereas the concordance rate for dizygotic female twins was 9%. The difference between MZ and DZ concordance suggests a moderately strong genetic contribution, but the fact that less than a quarter of the identical twins of a person with bulimia also have bulimia suggests that environmental variables play a substantial role. An even stronger genetic contribution was found in twin studies of anorexia (Klump et al., 2001b; Wade et al., 2000). Efforts are now under way to identify specific genes that contribute to anorexia, although no such gene has yet been identified (Kaye et al., 2000b). Furthermore, some researchers doubt that single genes will be found, believing instead that many gene combinations contribute to eating disorders (Kipman et al., 1999). And although the evidence for a genetic contribution to eating disorders appears to be strong, not everyone agrees. Fairburn et al. (1999) noted that the heritability estimates for anorexia and bulimia vary widely from study to study. Such wide variability in heritability estimates suggests that the strength of genetic contributions may vary from one subgroup to another. These authors do not deny that genes play a role, but they argue that psychological and environmental factors need to be considered seriously in any model of eating disorders. Furthermore, there may be some subgroups in whom psychological or environmental factors are the primary contributor to an eating disorder.

There is considerable evidence of a genetic relationship between eating disorders and mood disorders. Let's look at those data more closely.

dietary restraint hypothesis   The hypothesis that dieting predisposes one to bulimia.

Examining the Evidence

It has long been recognized that depression is common in people with eating disorders, but why is this the case? One possibility is that anorexia and depression share some genetic predisposing factors. Major depression is present more frequently in first-degree relatives of people with anorexia than one would expect by chance, and it is often found in family members who do not themselves show eating disorders (Gershon et al., 1984; Hudson et al., 1983; Nagel & Jones, 1992). A similar relationship between bulimia and depression has been found (Hudson et al., 1983; Stern et al., 1984). More recent data suggest that depression is overrepresented in families of people with both anorexia (Wade et al., 2000) and bulimia (Walters et al., 1992) and that the elevated risk appears to result from shared genetic factors rather than shared environmental factors. Finally, there is evidence for increased risk of bipolar disorder in people with bulimia (Shisslak et al., 1991), although it is not clear whether this comorbidity of bulimia and bipolar disorder reflects shared genetic factors or some other relationship, such as mood swings influencing eating. Collectively, these data indicate a probable genetic overlap between mood disorders, especially depression, and eating disorders. But determining the nature of that overlap will have to await more sophisticated research.

BIOLOGICAL FACTORS

Until recently, the research on eating disorders largely ignored biological factors, which is unfortunate because there is a substantial animal literature on eating that might have provided new insights into the phenomenon of eating disorders. Increasingly, however, there is a recognition that biological factors are involved and that these factors interact with the other variables that contribute to eating disorders (Ferguson & Pigott, 2000).

Several neurotransmitters have been implicated in eating disorders, including norepinephrine, serotonin, and dopamine. Serotonin and norepinephrine regulate appetitive behaviors, such as eating. Specifically, serotonin inhibits eating behaviors and norepinephrine activates them (Ferguson & Pigott, 2000). Individuals with bulimia show reduced central and peripheral norepinephrine activity, which is thought to be the result of a down regulation of this system (Pirke, 1996). Remember from Chapter 7 that down regulation is an adjustment in the sensitivity of receptor systems in neurons as a response to excessively high or low levels of a given neurotransmitter. There is substantial evidence for a dysregulation of the serotonin system in bulimia as well; people with bulimia show lower serotonin activity levels than age- and sex-matched controls during bulimic periods, but higher activity levels than controls during periods of remission (Kaye et al., 1998). You may remember from Chapters 7 and 8 that serotonin has been implicated in depression and obsessive-compulsive disorders, which may partially explain the high prevalence of mood disorders and obsessive-compulsive features found in bulimia.

There is also evidence of neuropeptide dysregulation in eating disorders. Neuropeptides are hormonelike substances that can act as neurotransmitters. People with both anorexia and bulimia show dysregulation in growth hormones and fluid balance as well as autonomic instability and reduction in metabolic functioning (Kaye, 1992). Furthermore, they show neuropeptide concentrations that are typical of a starvation state (Casper et al., 1988). Although many of these findings may be a result of the eating disorder, rather than a cause, there is reason to believe that some may be risk factors for eating disorders, because neuropeptides play a significant role in modulating food intake. Clearly, this is an area that could benefit from additional research.

CULTURAL FACTORS

The epidemiological data for bulimia show several interesting trends. Bulimia has been found to exist in every industrialized country that has been studied and to have roughly the same lifetime prevalence (APA, 2000; Szmukler & Patton, 1995). Like anorexia, bulimia is 10 times more common in women than in men (Woodside & Kennedy, 1995). However, unlike anorexia, the prevalence rates of bulimia appear to have increased rapidly over the past 40 or 50 years (Bushnell et al., 1990; Gordon, 2000). Bulimia, like anorexia, is more common in subcultures in which the feminine ideal is thin (Rieger et al., 2001). For example, it is more common in white than in black women (Crago et al., 1996; Osvold & Sodowsky, 1993). Blacks tend to have fewer concerns about weight than do whites, and their self-esteem is less dependent on their weight (Crago et al., 1996).

It is clear how an obsession with thinness can contribute to anorexia, but how does it contribute to bulimia? Women who develop bulimia are often upwardly mobile and strongly interested in meeting cultural expectations, including the expectation that they be thin (Silverstein & Perlick, 1995). College students (Drewnowski et al., 1988) and students in private high schools (Lesar et al., 2001) are such upwardly mobile groups, and both groups show high rates of bulimia. Interestingly, the "upwardly mobile and ambitious" variable is predictive across cultures. That is, both white *and* black college students are at increased risk for bulimia compared with individuals who are not in college (Crago et al., 1996). The feminine ideal of thinness may also contribute to bulimia in another way. The majority of women with bulimia start bingeing after a period of intense dieting (Brewerton et al., 2000), which may have created the physiologically driven need to binge. Women diet to be thin because the culture implies that they will be more attractive if they are thin. There is some truth to that idea in current Western cultures, but this is not a universal phenomenon, as discussed in the nearby Focus box.

Societal Pressure. What cultural factors have been implicated in eating disorders? The factor most often cited is a fascination—some would say an obsession—with thinness. The pressure to be thin is applied almost exclusively to women, which may explain why eating disorders are found primarily in women. Thinness is also highly valued in the gay community, which may explain why almost half of the men with eating disorders are either homosexual or bisexual (Carlat et al., 1997). A quick glance at the covers of women's magazines, such as *Glamour* and *Cosmopolitan,* or of men's magazines, such as *Playboy,* will illustrate how thin current fashion models tend to be. However, this trend is relatively recent. The first *Playboy* centerfold was Marilyn Monroe, who by modern standards for models would be considered overweight. Yet in the 1950s, Marilyn Monroe's figure and weight were considered not only normal but also very attractive and desirable. Ever since 1960, the average weight of *Playboy* centerfold models and Miss America pageant contestants has been gradually decreasing (Garner et al., 1980; Wiseman et al., 1992). In fact, almost two-thirds of *Playboy* centerfolds and Miss America contestants meet the weight criterion for anorexia, being at least 15% below normal body weight (Wiseman et al., 1992). The last 20 years have also seen a trend toward portraying in magazine ads more men who are muscular and partially unclothed (Pope et al., 2001). It will be interesting to see whether this trend will eventually inflict on men the same pressure to live up to a specific body ideal that women have experienced for 40 years. There is already some suggestive evidence that more males are insecure with their bodies than was once the case and that they are turning to weight training to improve muscle tone (Olivardia, 2001).

It is not only the images of attractive women and men that have been changing. The interest in dieting and exercise—the two primary ways of controlling weight—has increased dramatically over the last two to three decades, as indicated by the number of articles appearing in popular women's magazines (Wiseman et al., 1992). To date, no such dramatic increase has occurred in magazines aimed at male audiences, which tend to be focused on activities rather than on such personal attributes as weight and fitness. This increased focus on diet and exercise is not entirely bad; eating well and getting enough exercise are important parts of a healthful lifestyle. However, the combination of the image of attractive women portrayed in the media as thin—sometimes very thin—and the constant focus on dieting and exercise may well impart the message that such excessive thinness is the goal. Who is most likely to be

FOCUS Attractiveness and cultural style

In modern Western cultures, thin women are in. That is a style, and styles come in and out of fashion. In the 1920s, the style for women was also slim, as exemplified by the "flappers" of the era. In the 1950s, a more voluptuous look was the vogue. Sociologists and anthropologists are interested in the factors that contribute to such styles. That issue is not addressed in this box. Instead, we will consider the issue of whether there are universal elements that contribute to the attractiveness of individuals.

Evolutionary Impact

Being physically attractive has value in that it enhances one's ability to attract a mate. Of course, it is only one of many variables that makes one person attractive to another, but few people doubt that it affects the individual's success in finding mates. Some features appear to be universally attractive across cultures, and these features often are indicators of health (Buss, 1994). For example, *bilateral symmetry*—the degree to which the right side and left side of the body are perfect mirror images—is universally considered attractive in both men and women across cultures. Injuries and diseases often reduce symmetry. Muscular development in men is generally attractive, although not necessarily the excessive muscular development of body builders. Muscle development is partly a function of the testosterone level, which also contributes to male fertility. In women, thinness is not universally accepted as attractive, but an appropriate ratio of waist to hips is (Buss, 1994). This characteristic is associated with two factors. The first is health. Many diseases distend the stomach, thus affecting this ratio. The second is age. On average, younger women have smaller waists compared to their hips. In women especially, fertility is governed by age, younger women being significantly more fertile than older women. Thus, even though there are cultural overlays to what people consider physically attractive in the opposite sex, there also appear to be some universals, and most of these universals are indicators of health and fertility. This would make sense from an evolutionary perspective.

Ideas about feminine beauty change, much as fashions change. What was considered attractive in the 1950s differs from what is considered attractive today. However, the genes that influence weight regulation could not possibly change as quickly as these trends. Thus society exerts on women enormous pressure to live up to what is for most an impossible ideal.

affected by such messages? It is the young, ambitious person who wants to be successful and therefore is looking for guidance about societal expectations. Perhaps it is no accident that upwardly mobile women in high school and college are the most likely to be affected by these messages.

Let's look at the evidence that contemporary women perceive thinness as critical to female physical attractiveness.

Examining the Evidence

In a classic study, Fallon and Rozin (1985) asked college students to rate (1) their body shape, (2) the body shape they thought was most attractive to the opposite sex, and (3) their ideal body shape, using the visual scales created by Stunkard et al. (1980). These scales—separate ones for men and women—are illustrated in Figure 10.1. The students were also asked to indicate the body shape that they found most attractive in the opposite sex. For men, there were almost no differences among the ideal, attractive, and actual body shapes reported, but women showed substantial differences in their ratings. They consistently rated their actual body shape as significantly larger than either their ideal or the shape that they thought would be most attractive to men. Neither men nor women were particularly good at predicting what body shape was most desirable to the opposite sex. Women felt that men wanted them to be thinner than men actually wanted, and men felt that women wanted them to be more muscular than women actually wanted. Both of these distortions probably were influenced by media portrayals of "ideal" men and women (Katzman & Lee, 1997).

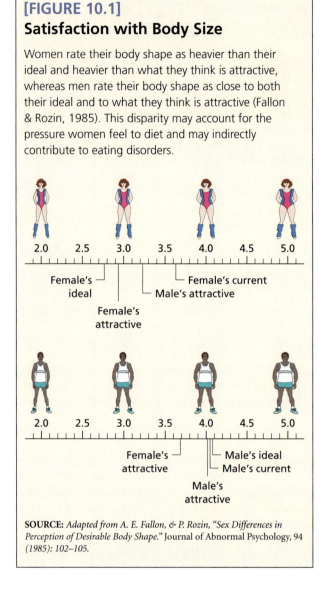

[FIGURE 10.1]
Satisfaction with Body Size

Women rate their body shape as heavier than their ideal and heavier than what they think is attractive, whereas men rate their body shape as close to both their ideal and to what they think is attractive (Fallon & Rozin, 1985). This disparity may account for the pressure women feel to diet and may indirectly contribute to eating disorders.

SOURCE: *Adapted from A. E. Fallon, & P. Rozin, "Sex Differences in Perception of Desirable Body Shape."* Journal of Abnormal Psychology, 94 *(1985): 102–105.*

Eating disorders are especially common in young people who are involved in certain sports or activities. For example, dancers often value a slim figure, and thus many diet or exercise excessively to maintain that figure (Neumaerker et al., 2000); curiously, the same is not true for gymnasts (Smolak et al., 2000). Male wrestlers are often pressured to stay in a particular weight category and therefore diet excessively and/or use diuretics and laxatives to lose weight just before a weigh-in. Recent pressure on NFL linemen to stay under a certain weight or risk team fines has led to a variety of abuses in the name of meeting those target goals. Such eating patterns in athletes can lead to significant medical problems (Yates, 1999). The greatest risk of eating disorders was recently found to occur in athletes competing at an elite level—that is, athletes who were the most competitive in their sports (Smolak et al., 2000). Perhaps for those athletes, the small advantage associated with weight control was worth the risks associated with

eating problems. However, the good news is that for the majority of athletes competing in high school, college, and intramural leagues, there was no increase in risk for eating disorders. In fact, there was actually a decrease in risk in these athletes (Smolak et al., 2000).

Family Environment. Does the family environment affect the risk for eating disorders? Early theories of anorexia emphasized this concept, and there are data in support of it. For example, in sisters discordant for anorexia, there was a higher level of parental expectation and a greater likelihood of sexual abuse in the sister who developed anorexia than in the unaffected sister (Karwautz et al., 2001). In addition, the sister with anorexia perceived more maternal control, had fewer friends and boyfriends, and was more antagonistic toward family members than the unaffected sister (Murphy et al., 2000). Interpreting such findings is difficult. For example, more perceived maternal control may reflect an environmental variable (mother actually being more controlling) or a personality variable (daughter feeling more controlled). Another problem with these findings is that they are not specific to eating disorders but, rather, are found in many disorders. A recent study of identical twins discordant for bulimia found that the twin with bulimia reported less self-esteem, less parental warmth, and more maternal overprotection (Wade et al., 2001). But again, these findings may represent the perceptions of the affected individuals rather than the reality of their lives as they were growing up.

PSYCHOLOGICAL FACTORS

Several psychological variables have been implicated in eating disorders. Karwautz et al. (2001) found that girls with anorexia showed more perfectionism, more negative self-evaluation, and more extreme compliance than their sisters who did not develop anorexia. Control and sexuality are also major themes in the lives of people with eating disorders (Haas & Clopton, 2001). In anorexia, the person demonstrates control by deciding what will and will not be consumed. In bulimia, the person loses control by bingeing but regains it by purging. Binges are often precipitated by events that decrease a person's sense of control, such as criticism or failure. People with anorexia frequently come from backgrounds that include a strict, puritanical attitude toward female sexuality (Richter, 2001). Many theorists believe that the extreme starvation associated with anorexia represents an attempt by a young woman to avoid being sexual. Her emaciated form hides such secondary sexual characteristics as breasts, and the starvation actually stops ovulation. Sexuality in bulimia is viewed as an impulsive activity, much like a binge, with the goal of providing a certain degree of comfort (Richter, 2001). These speculations about control and sexuality are widely accepted by many who work with eating disorders, but they are difficult to establish scientifically. Nevertheless, many people struggling with eating disorders find that these concepts help them to come to grips with their problem (Gordon, 2000).

Eating disorders are increasing in frequency and represent a significant threat to the well-being of young women. Understanding these disorders is the first step to effective treatment and, eventually, effective prevention. Research over the past three decades has substantially increased the scientific understanding of these disorders and has dramatically improved treatment. Nevertheless, much remains to be done. The focus in the future needs to be on prevention, which is an area that has received surprisingly little attention to date but that has tremendous potential (Robert-McComb, 2001). The nearby Advances box illustrates one approach to prevention.

It is common for people with anorexia or bulimia to see themselves as fat, even when that clearly is not the case.

Check Yourself 10.2

Causes of Eating Disorders

1. How do genes affect eating disorders?
2. What sociocultural factors may be contributing to eating disorders?
3. What psychological variables have been implicated in anorexia?

Ponder this . . . *Besides breathing, nothing is more important to survival than eating. Therefore, it is puzzling that eating disorders exist. Given the evidence for a genetic contribution, one might expect natural selection to have weeded out these disorders by now. Why might natural selection not yet have eliminated these disorders?*

ADVANCES   Studying eating disorders prospectively

Prospective studies are likely to shed light on the psychological and developmental variables that contribute to eating disorders. By following people longitudinally and observing who develops eating disorders and what variables predict their development, one can build a powerful understanding of a disorder, which can form a basis for prevention. Killen et al. (1994) followed nearly a thousand adolescent girls for over three years. Of their sample of teenage girls, 4% developed eating disorders during the study. A simple scale, focused on concern about weight, dieting history, and feelings of being fat (see Table 10.2), identified those at greatest risk for eating disorders.

Killen (1996) then evaluated a prevention program designed to educate young women (aged 11–13) about weight. For example, weight gain is a normal part of sexual maturation, when a woman's body fills out and takes on such secondary sexual characteristics as breasts and broader hips. Furthermore, excessive calorie restriction during this period can actually enhance long-term weight gain by increasing the supply of fat storage cells. Half of the girls in this study received this educational intervention, and the other half did not. The program reduced concern about weight, especially in those girls who were initially most concerned about their weight. These promising results indicate that simple interventions may significantly reduce risk for eating disorders.

Identifying young women at greatest risk for the eating disorders simplifies the task of prevention, making it possible to focus prevention efforts on those people most in need. The *McKnight Risk Factor Survey* was

[TABLE 10.2]   Measuring Concern About Weight

Killen (1996) found that this simple five-item scale of weight concerns was an effective predictor of who among adolescent girls would develop eating disorders. Girls who showed excessive concerns about weight on this scale were at risk for eating disorders.

1. How much more or less do you feel you worry about your weight and body shape than other girls your age?
   a) I worry a lot less than other girls
   b) I worry a little less than other girls
   c) I worry about the same as other girls
   d) I worry a little more than other girls
   e) I worry a lot more than other girls
2. How afraid are you of gaining three pounds?
   a) Not afraid of gaining
   b) Slightly afraid of gaining
   c) Moderately afraid of gaining
   d) Very afraid of gaining
   e) Terrified of gaining
3. When was the last time you went on a diet?
   a) I've never been on a diet
   b) I was on a diet about one year ago
   c) I was on a diet about six months ago
   d) I was on a diet about three months ago
   e) I was on a diet about one month ago
   f) I was on a diet less than a month ago
   g) I'm now on a diet
4. How important is your weight to you?
   a) My weight is not important compared to other things in my life
   b) My weight is a little more important than some other things
   c) My weight is more important than most, but not all, things in my life
   d) My weight is the most important thing in my life
5. Do you ever feel fat?
   a) Never
   b) Rarely
   c) Sometimes
   d) Often
   e) Always

SOURCE: *"Measuring Concern About Weight" by J. K. Killen from* The Developmental Psychopathology of Eating Disorders: Implications for Research, Prevention, and Treatment, *ed. by L. Smolak, M. P. Levine, & R. Streigel-Moore. Copyright © 1996. Published by Lawrence Erlbaum Associates, Inc. Reprinted by permission of Copyright Clearance Center.*

designed to assess simultaneously several potential risk factors for eating disorders. This survey has demonstrated adequate test-retest and internal consistency reliability (Shisslak et al., 1999). Only time will tell whether this broader approach to identifying people at risk for eating disorders will be more effective than the simple scale used by Killen et al. (1994). Other recent work has focused on the question of why some girls have

excessive weight concern, whereas others do not. Peer pressure and TV and magazine exposure appear to play critical roles in the development of this attitude (Taylor et al., 1998). Clearly, researchers have increasingly turned their attention to understanding and modifying dysfunctional attitudes and beliefs that contribute to eating disorders, with an eye to prevention.

TREATING EATING DISORDERS

Eating disorders have always been considered difficult to treat. However, in the last two decades, promising new treatments have been developed. The treatment approaches differ somewhat for anorexia and bulimia, although they share critical elements. This review will be organized along two broad dimensions: biological treatments and psychological treatments.

BIOLOGICAL TREATMENTS

Two biological interventions are used frequently in the treatment of eating disorders. Medical stabilization is used whenever the weight loss in anorexia becomes severe, and medications have been used for both anorexia and bulimia.

Medical Stabilization. Medical stabilization utilizes hospitalization and acute treatment strategies to decrease the immediate medical threats from excessive weight loss. The goals of such hospitalization are to treat potentially life-threatening health problems, such as an irregular heartbeat or hypotension (low blood pressure). The cause of the medical problems—the massive weight loss—is addressed via an intensive feeding program, which may include both intravenous feeding and a behavioral program of normal eating under close supervision (Watson et al., 2000). There is often close monitoring of what is consumed and what is expelled to prevent the person from discarding food or purging later. The goal of this acute treatment is not to restore normal eating; such a short hospitalization is unlikely to achieve that. Rather, the goal is to stabilize existing medical problems and to have the person get a sufficient amount of nourishment to decrease the likelihood of further medical complications.

The advent of managed care has had profound effects on the treatment of people with anorexia. In the mid-1980s, the average hospitalization for anorexia was about five months; by 1998, it had been reduced to a little over three weeks—just enough time to manage the acute medical crisis, but rarely enough to normalize eating behavior (Wiseman et al., 2001).

Medications. One might suspect that, given the many biological mechanisms involved in the regulation of eating, medications would be an effective treatment for eating disorders. Recent data support this notion. For example, amisulpiride facilitates weight gain in severe cases of anorexia, although it has no impact on such variables as fear of weight gain and body image disturbance (Ruggiero et al., 2001). It has long been recognized that one of the undesirable side effects of some of the SSRIs is weight gain. Hence, the idea of using these drugs to facilitate weight gain in people with anorexia makes intuitive sense (Harvey & Bouwer, 2000). A double-blind study showed that fluoxetine (Prozac) was effective in increasing weight in people with anorexia and in reducing relapse over a one-year period (Kaye et al., 2001). Fluoxetine was also found to be effective in reducing the frequency of binges and purges in women with bulimia when the drug was combined with a comprehensive inpatient treatment program (Strober et al., 1999) or a self-help manual (Mitchell et al., 2001). However, relapse is common unless medication is combined with behavior therapy to help individuals to develop critical coping skills (Ferguson & Pigott, 2000). One might suspect that the treatment efficacy of fluoxetine in bulimia is due to a reduction in the depression that often accompanies bulimia. People with bulimia often report that they binge more when depressed. However, Goldstein et al. (1999) found that fluoxetine reduced bingeing and purging in people with bulimia regardless of levels of depression. Furthermore, fluoxetine is effective with those individuals who have not responded to psychotherapy, so it gives treatment specialists another option (Walsh et al., 2000).

PSYCHOLOGICAL TREATMENTS

The psychological treatment of choice for bulimia has been *cognitive-behavioral therapy,* or CBT (Porzelius et al., 1999). CBT also shows promise for the treatment of anorexia, although the research on anorexia lags behind that on bulimia (Porzelius et al., 1999; Whittal & Zaretsky, 1996). CBT has largely replaced eating disorder treatments that focused on either family dynamics (Minuchin et al., 1978) or self-esteem (Bruch, 1986; Wooley & Kearney-Cooke, 1986). However, *interpersonal therapy,* or IPT—a dynamically based treatment that also contains behavioral elements (see Chapter 7)—shows considerable promise.

Fairburn (Carter & Fairburn, 1998; Fairburn, 1984) pioneered a cognitive-behavioral treatment for bulimia that relies on a combination of education, behavior change, and modification of dysfunctional attitudes and thoughts. For example, most people with bulimia view purging as a way of eliminating the excessive calories of a binge and thus undoing the damage. However, vomiting, laxatives, and enemas are relatively ineffective in eliminating the calories consumed during a binge, and they create such potentially serious health hazards as electrolyte imbalance (Mitchell, 1986). This information about the ineffectiveness and dangers of purging forces people with bulimia to confront the bingeing that triggers the purging. The treatment also addresses the consequences of dieting, explaining how rigid diets are ineffective in maintaining weight loss because of changes in metabolism. Furthermore, severely restrictive diets set people up for binges; such diets are experienced as starvation, so people on them have overpowering urges to gorge themselves whenever food is available. Clients are encouraged to eat more frequently, up to six times a day, but to eat small portions. Because most bingeing is done privately, clients are encouraged to avoid being alone for long periods and to structure their lives so that others are around to provide social support (Rorty et al., 1999).

The unique element of the cognitive-behavioral approach to bulimia is its focus on modifying dysfunctional attitudes and thoughts. For example, people with bulimia often associate self-worth with body shape and size. In fact, this is so prevalent that it is one of the defining criteria in the DSM (APA, 2000). Clients are taught to challenge those ideas by recognizing that their worth is defined by countless factors and that the most important factors involve how they behave, not how they look.

Let's look at some of the outcome research on the treatment of bulimia.

Examining the Evidence

Fairburn et al. (1993) compared behavioral, cognitive-behavioral, and interpersonal therapy approaches to the treatment of bulimia. The cognitive-behavioral approach was described earlier in this section. The behavioral approach emphasized the learning of new eating habits, and the interpersonal therapy emphasized improvement of current interpersonal functioning. All of the treatments were effective in reducing bingeing, but the cognitive-behavioral treatment was clearly superior at the end of treatment. However, an interesting pattern developed over the following six years (see Figure 10.2). Those who received behavioral therapy lost 50% of the initial gain from treatment during that follow-up period, whereas those who received cognitive-behavioral therapy maintained their gains throughout the follow-up period (Fairburn et al., 1995). Those who received interpersonal therapy showed modest gains by the end of therapy, but they continued to improve during the follow-up period until their outcome exceeded that of the cognitive-behavioral group at the six-year follow-up. In other words, behavior therapy produced rapid gains that were not maintained, cognitive-behavioral therapy produced rapid gains that were maintained, and interpersonal therapy produced slow gains, but those who received this treatment continued to show improvement long after therapy was discontinued. A reasonable conclusion is that the combination of cognitive-behavioral and interpersonal therapy is likely to produce rapid gains and may also provide clients with skills that facilitate further gains after treatment is completed.

Another approach, *dialectical behavior therapy,* is also effective in treating bulimia (Safer et al., 2001). It was developed by Marsha Linehan to treat the emotional volatility and impulsive behavior so common in borderline personality disorder (see Chapter 12). People with bulimia often report such emotional volatility, and the binges are typi-

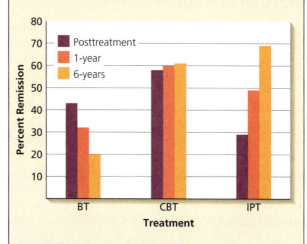

[FIGURE 10.2]
Treating Bulimia

Behavior therapy, cognitive-behavioral therapy, and interpersonal therapy were all effective in reducing bingeing in people, but the follow-up data suggest important differences. Whereas the gains were maintained by cognitive-behavioral therapy and improvement continued even after interpersonal therapy, about half the gains from behavior therapy were lost over time.

SOURCE: *"Treating Bulimia" from "A Cognitive-Behavioral Treatment for Bulimia" (pp. 160–162) by C. G. Fairburn in* Handbook of Psychotherapy for Anorexia and Bulimia, *ed. by Garner & Garfield. Copyright © 1995. Reprinted by permission of The Guilford Press.*

cally impulsive acts that later cause the person to feel considerable regret. Safer et al. (2001) found that people who received a 20-week program of dialectical behavior therapy were significantly less likely to binge or purge than people who were waiting to start therapy. However, there were no other control groups in this study, so it is unclear how this approach compares with other treatments.

What is the mechanism behind successful behavioral and cognitive-behavioral therapy for bulimia? One possible mechanism is that controlled exposure to food and to the thought of food changes its impact on the person. Carter et al. (2001) found that people who had been treated successfully for bulimia showed a decrease in both behavioral and physiological reactivity to high-calorie foods. Specifically, they experienced weaker urges to binge and less heart rate and blood pressure response to the sight of high-calorie food. Interestingly, treatment did not affect salivary reactivity—that is, how much the person salivated in response to the sight or smell of food. Salivation is an indication of how desirable the food is to the person. Thus treatment did not decrease the desirability of food, although it did change some of the behavioral and physiological reactivity that may have mediated the binge eating.

Treating anorexia has proved more difficult than treating bulimia. One problem is that the often dramatic loss of weight creates immediate health problems that must be managed first. Medically stabilizing affected individuals is the easiest part of the treatment. In fact, inpatient programs have become quite adept at handling this task (Hsu, 1990). Unfortunately, success in this first stage of treatment is virtually uncorrelated with long-term treatment success (Hsu, 1988). Long-term success depends on changing the attitudes and beliefs of people with anorexia, who believe that (1) they are fat and (2) they must be thin. The traditional treatment approach with anorexia is family therapy. The affected person is nearly always a young woman, typically in her teens, who in most cases is well behaved and cooperative (Bruch, 2001). The assumption is that the anorexia represents a distortion of a desire to be a "good girl" and live up to the expectations of her parents. Alternatively, the eating disorder may be a way of revolting against the "good girl" persona—that is, doing something of which her parents do not approve. These speculations are difficult to test, but they can form the basis for a family intervention, which can then be evaluated.

Check Yourself 10.3

Treating Eating Disorders

1. Why is medical stabilization so critical in anorexia?
2. What medication shows promise in reducing bingeing and purging in bulimia?
3. What psychological treatment produces the largest initial gains in the treatment of bulimia? What treatment produces the most improvement after treatment ends?

Ponder this . . . *Obsession with thinness is a recent phenomenon. As long as this obsession continues, young girls are likely to be at risk for eating disorders. What would it take for the culture to reduce this obsession? What people are most likely to be influential in such a change?*

SLEEP DISORDERS

Sleep is an active recuperative process during which people are physically inactive and relatively unaware of their surroundings. It is critical to survival, yet it still is not fully understood (Dement & Vaughan, 1999). Almost everyone has experienced how easily sleep can be disrupted by stress, pain, or anxiety. However, these disruptions are normally brief, and most people return to a reasonable sleeping

pattern in a few days. Although some sleep problems are clearly the result of either a physical or a psychiatric disorder, others are disorders in their own right. Furthermore, all sleep disorders are known to affect psychological functioning. Remember how you felt after pulling an all-nighter to get ready for an exam? Perhaps you got through the exam running on adrenaline. However, if you are like most people, you crashed afterwards, too tired to think straight. Chronic sleep deprivation, which is common with many sleep disorders, can leave you feeling like that all the time. Let's look at data on sleep deprivation more closely.

Examining the Evidence

Tyler (1955) investigated the effects of severe sleep deprivation by having 350 people stay awake for 112 straight hours. Virtually all showed significant deterioration in psychological functioning, and 7 showed such psychotic symptoms as hallucinations and delusions. Fortunately, all recovered after a prolonged period of sleep. Without sleep, a person's neurological and behavioral functioning quickly deteriorates (Baranski et al., 1998; Jeong et al., 2001). There is also evidence that chronic sleep deprivation may precipitate psychological disorders in people who are predisposed to them (Brauchi & West, 1959) and may even play a role in such disorders as sudden infant death syndrome (Simpson, 2001). Furthermore, recent evidence suggests that sleep disturbances precede the onset of several disorders, including bipolar disorder (Dilsaver et al., 1999) and major depression (Perlis et al., 1997). Even when sleep disorders are clearly biologically caused, correcting them reduces the risk of other psychiatric disorders (Dahloef et al., 2000). Furthermore, if sleep deprivation is severe enough, the organism dies (Rechtschaffen et al., 1989). Finally, sleep deprivation is associated with increased risk for a variety of disorders, including cancer (Wingard & Berkman, 1983).

To understand sleep disorders, you have to know a bit about sleep. Therefore, this section begins with a quick primer on the topic. It then covers sleep disorders under two broad categories: dyssomnias and parasomnias. Not covered in this section are sleep disturbances that are secondary to other medical or psychiatric conditions, such as the sleep disturbances associated with mood or anxiety disorders (Ware & Morin, 1997).

NATURE OF SLEEP

Evolutionary Impact

At the beginning of the twentieth century, before electric lights were widely available, the average adult slept

---

sleep An active recuperative process during which people are physically inactive and relatively unaware of their surroundings.

approximately 10 hours per night. Today, the average adult sleeps 6.7 hours per night, and the average college student sleeps 6.1 hours (Maas, 2002). It is highly unlikely that the physiological need for sleep decreased by 40% in less than a century. Rather, 43% of adults and well over half of college students are sleep deprived. What are the implications of being sleep deprived? College students are often walking zombies, getting less than two-thirds of the sleep they need. Such sleep deprivation decreases cognitive alertness, clouds thinking and judgment, and interacts with other variables. For example, the debilitating effects of alcohol are much more dramatic in people who are sleep deprived than in well-rested individuals (Fairclough & Graham, 1999).

Although sleep appears to be a passive activity, it definitely is not (Hirshkowitz et al., 1997). The brain remains active during sleep. Sleep clearly has an impact on organisms; they function more effectively with sleep than without. In addition, sleep enhances functioning not normally associated with sleep, such as stabilization of long-term memories (Idzikowski, 1984). Nevertheless, the exact function of sleep is still not clearly understood (Hirshkowitz et al., 1997).

The wide variety of sleep patterns found in the animal kingdom suggests that there is more than one way to meet sleep needs and maintain a level of safety. For example, when human beings sleep, the entire brain is involved. This is true of most mammals. However, for many birds, reptiles, and aquatic species, only half of the brain is asleep at any one time (Rattenborg et al., 2000). This seems like such an obvious solution to the problem that one has to wonder why all species did not evolve such sleep patterns. One possibility is that the advantage of a complete brain sleep might outweigh the disadvantages of being unaware of the immediate surroundings. One sleep activity that has been hypothesized to have survival advantages is dreaming, especially if dreaming focuses on rehearsal for handling dangerous situations (Revonsuo, 2000). Furthermore, typical dream content shows a strong bias toward negative and threatening situations and feelings (Domhoff, 1999), and traumatic events increase this bias (Nader, 1996). Humans currently experience relatively few dreams of an intensely traumatic nature, although the number of such dreams rises dramatically when a person has recently been exposed to a trauma (Mellman, 2000). In the evolutionary past, life expectancies for humans and their ancestors were much shorter, the number of dangers was much higher, and therefore the rate of traumatic exposure to life-threatening situations was much higher. Traumatic dreams—essentially nightmares—might help the organism to prepare mentally for the next dangerous encounter, thus providing a small survival advantage. Of course, this advantage could be offset by the risks associated with being unconscious, although some have speculated that these risks may not be great. In fact, some have argued that sleep and the limited activity associated with sleep conserve energy and reduce exposure to predators, provided that the organism selects a site that provides reasonable safety (Anderson, 1998). Whatever the role of sleep, it must be critical to survival or it would not be so universal.

Although sleep appears on the surface to be a passive activity, the brain remains active. The mechanisms by which sleep produces its restorative effects are still largely unknown.

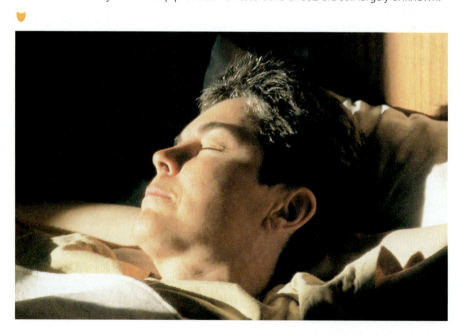

[FIGURE 10.3]
Brain Wave Patterns for Different Stages of Sleep

The stages of sleep are identified by changes in brain wave activity. Deep sleep is characterized by high-amplitude, slow waves.

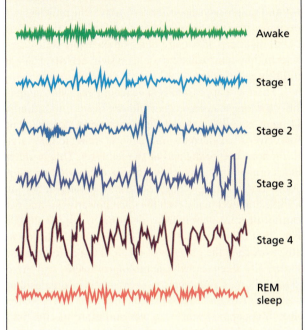

Awake

Stage 1

Stage 2

Stage 3

Stage 4

REM sleep

Most people think of sleep as a consistent period of unconsciousness during which restorative processes are ongoing. However, sleep is more complex than that. Sleep specialists identify several distinct stages of sleep, which represent the depth of sleep defined by how difficult it is to awaken the person. Each stage is characterized by a specific pattern of brain, muscle, and eye movement activity. Figure 10.3 illustrates the typical brain wave patterns for each stage of sleep. Stage 1 sleep is the lightest sleep—between wakefulness and sleep. The body relaxes, and slow rolling eye movements are common. Stages 2 through 4 are characterized by relaxed muscular activity and no eye movement; these stages represent progressively deeper levels of sleep. The stages are differentiated by changes in brain wave activity, the deeper stages of sleep being characterized by slower brain waves. After a period of deep stage 4 sleep, the person moves back through lighter sleep into a period of rapid eye movement sleep, or **REM sleep,** during which dreaming takes place. REM sleep is often referred to as *paradoxical sleep,* because the person is very resistant to awakening, but the more rapid brain wave pattern suggests light sleep. During REM sleep, the body is virtually paralyzed, the eyes dart back and forth, and brain wave activity is more varied and complex than during other stages of sleep. Figure 10.4 illustrates a typical sleep pattern for a young adult. The person moves from wakefulness to deep sleep and then back into lighter sleep before entering a REM

REM sleep   A sleep period of rapid eye movement, during which dreaming takes place.

[FIGURE 10.4]
Sleep Patterns

Sleep is not a unitary process. The individual goes through several stages repeatedly during a typical night's sleep. Most of deep sleep occurs early in the sleep cycle, whereas most REM sleep occurs later.

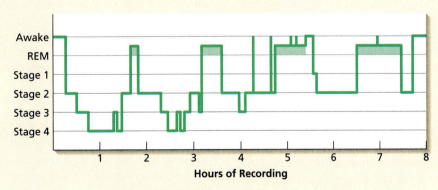

SOURCE: *Graph from p. 23, "The Basics of Sleep" by M. Hirshkowitz in* Understanding Sleep, *ed. by M. R. Pressman & W. C. Orr. Copyright © 1997 by the American Psychological Association. Reprinted with permission.*

period. There are four to six such sleep cycles during a typical night's sleep. Over the course of the night, the person spends increasing amounts of time in REM sleep and decreasing amounts of time in deep sleep.

REM sleep is not unique to human beings. It is found in virtually all mammals. It is known to be associated with dreams in humans, because humans can be awakened during REM and asked what they were experiencing. It is not clear whether it is also associated with dreaming in animals for the obvious reason that animals cannot report their subjective experiences. Children show higher percentages of REM sleep than adults, and fetuses in utero show very high percentages of REM sleep. It is hard to imagine that a fetus could be dreaming as we know it during REM sleep, given that the fetus has no experience with the outside world. REM is a convenient marker of when a person is dreaming, but that fact raises interesting questions. Why don't humans dream without REM, and why don't humans have REM without dreaming? Why are these two divergent behaviors linked? This is one of those intriguing questions for which no adequate answer exists—at least not yet.

Evolutionary Impact

Sleep also raises several interesting issues from an evolutionary perspective. First, given that sleep makes the organism more vulnerable to a variety of risks, such as attacks by predators, this risk must be balanced by survival benefits for sleep to become so universal. But what are those benefits? A second question involves the pattern of sleep. A night's sleep is like a series of naps, each lasting about 60 to 90 minutes. There are differences between the cycles. For example, early cycles include more deep sleep, and later cycles include more REM sleep. Could this be a remnant of the evolutionary history of humans? Were ancestors of humans more inclined to take short naps, thereby limiting their vulnerability to short periods? Scouting an area for potential danger before sleeping would be advantageous, but a safe area would remain safe for only a short time because predators are often on the move. Humans are capable even today of functioning for prolonged periods on multiple short naps. Thomas Edison was alleged to have lived on such naps for years (Newton, 1987). Many animals adopt this style in the wild. For example, rats will sleep for short periods, awaken and check out their surroundings, and then fall back to sleep if everything appears safe (Borbély, 1986). With protective shelter and the security of being a part of a group, humans have been largely able to abandon this need to check periodically for danger. Perhaps that is why most humans sleep through the night, although no one knows. What *is* known is that sleeping through the night appears to have given humans the opportunity to modify sleep from a series of very similar naps to a prolonged period of sleep, in which the later cycles have much higher percentages of REM sleep.

Although the exact purpose of sleep is still a matter of debate, there is considerable information about the mechanisms by which sleep is regulated. Sleep involves a change in the balance of the autonomic nervous system so that parasympathetic activity is dominant. The frontal portion of the hypothalamus and the preoptic area of the frontal lobe are involved in regulating this transition to parasympathetic activity (Hirshkowitz et al., 1997; Parmeggiani, 1994). This process slows the heart, relaxes the muscles, and decreases blood pressure, all of which facilitate the process of falling asleep. If you are upset or excited, a state characterized by sympathetic nervous system activity, you are unlikely to fall asleep.

There also appears to be a *drive* for sleep, which intensifies the longer a person goes without sleep (Carskadon & Dement, 1981). You almost certainly have felt the effects of this drive as you burn the midnight oil trying to get everything done before the end of the semester. This is much like a hunger drive, which intensifies the longer a person goes without eating. Stimulants may hold sleep at bay for a while, but eventually even the most powerful stimulants cannot prevent people from sleeping (Caldwell, 2001). Note that the purpose of sleep is not to reduce this drive any more than the purpose of eating is to reduce hunger. Eating and sleep serve basic biological needs, and these drives—hunger and sleepiness—motivate the organism to engage in activities that satisfy these drives. The drive for sleep is apparently more complex and more specific than was once believed. For example, if someone is deprived of REM sleep by constantly being awakened as soon as the rapid eye movements of this stage begin, but is not awakened during any other stage of sleep, the person will report feeling sleepy (Nykamp et al., 1998). However, upon then falling asleep, the person spends an unusually large amount of time in REM sleep—a phenomenon known as **REM rebound** (Dement, 1960). In other words, the drive for sleep may feel homogeneous (just feeling tired), but the body is apparently able to tell what specific sleep elements the person needs at the moment.

Sleep is also regulated by circadian rhythms. The term *circadian* comes from two Latin words, *circa* and *dian*, which mean "approximately" and "day," respectively. Therefore, a circadian rhythm is the normal daily body rhythm. The body maintains an internal clock in the suprachiasmatic nucleus of the brain to organize these circadian

REM rebound   An unusually large amount of time in REM sleep following a period of REM deprivation.

dyssomnias   Disorders characterized either by difficulty initiating and maintaining sleep or by excessive sleep.

primary insomnia   A disorder, not due to another physical or psychological disorder, characterized by difficulty in initiating sleep or in maintaining sleep long enough to allow the person to feel rested and refreshed in the morning.

[FIGURE 10.5]
Temperature Changes Across the Day

The body's core temperature is one of several functions that are controlled as part of the circadian rhythm. It reaches its maximum in the late afternoon and its minimum in the very early morning. The body temperature tends to be correlated with sleep in that people feel most sleepy when their core body temperature is low.

SOURCE: *Graph from p. 37, "The Basics of Biological Rhythms" by S. S. Campbell in* Understanding Sleep, *ed. by M. R. Pressman & W. C. Orr. Copyright © 1997 by the American Psychological Association. Reprinted with permission.*

rhythms, although this clock is imprecise (Sleep Research Society, 1993). The length of the "day," as measured by this internal clock, varies from person to person and usually is somewhere between 24 and 26 hours (Moore-Ede et al., 1982). Fortunately, the clock is reset each day by the sun, which keeps it synchronized with the actual daylight period. The circadian rhythm affects many aspects of body functioning, including body temperature. As body temperature falls, the person tends to get sleepy. The body temper-

ature generally starts to rise again just before the normal time to awaken. This change over the course of a day is illustrated in Figure 10.5, which shows the plot of core body temperature for a person across a 36-hour period.

A dysregulation in any of the mechanisms that regulate sleep can contribute to a sleep disorder. Furthermore, psychological factors can also contribute to sleep problems. Before we discuss the causes of sleep disorders, each of the sleep disorders in the DSM will be described.

Occasional insomnia is common, especially during stressful periods. It may leave people tired the next day, but it typically has little impact on functioning. However, more chronic insomnia can significantly affect one's daytime functioning.

DYSSOMNIAS

Dyssomnias are disorders characterized either by difficulty initiating and maintaining sleep or by excessive sleep. They not only affect sleep but also typically undermine the performance of the individual when awake. The dyssomnias covered in this section are primary insomnia, primary hypersomnia, narcolepsy, breathing-related sleep disorders, and circadian rhythm sleep disorders.

Primary Insomnia. Primary insomnia is characterized by a difficulty in initiating sleep or in maintaining it long enough to allow the person to feel rested and refreshed in the morning. The modifier *primary* is used to indicate that this diagnosis should not be used if the insomnia is due to substance abuse or another medical or psychiatric condition, including another sleep disorder. To qualify for the diagnosis of primary insomnia, the sleep problems must last at least a month, because occasional disruption of sleep is common, and they must cause clinically significant distress or impairment during waking hours. Tyler, whom we met at the beginning of the chapter, suffered from primary insomnia. His insomnia had been going on for months. As a result, he was so sleepy during the day that he found it almost impossible to function.

There are few epidemiological studies of insomnia. The available data suggest that from one-third to one-half of adults complain of experiencing insomnia in the last year, although fewer than 10% and perhaps as few as 1% actually qualify for the diagnosis of primary insomnia (APA, 2000). Primary insomnia is most common in the elderly, affecting almost a quarter of people over age 65 (APA, 2000; Scharf & Jennings, 1990), although in many cases the insomnia may be due to the everyday aches and pains associated with aging (Bootzin et al., 1996; Lichstein et al., 2001). About 20% of people who seek treatment at sleep clinics for chronic insomnia qualify for the diagnosis of primary insomnia. The remaining 80% have another sleep disorder or their insomnia is a result of another medical or psychiatric condition (Espie, 2002; Morin, 1993). Insomnia is more common in women than in men and tends to increase with age (Fichten et al., 2000). Complaints of insomnia are especially frequent in elderly women, although sleep studies suggest that elderly men are more likely to have sleep problems that are physiologically detectable (APA, 2000; Sternbach, 1998). Tyler's insomnia began during a stressful period but then took on a life of its own. Long after the stress had subsided, Tyler was walking the floors at night, unable to get the sleep his body so desperately needed.

Primary Hypersomnia.

Primary hypersomnia is characterized by excessive sleep, which may include either sleeping for unusually long periods or taking frequent naps during the day. To qualify for the diagnosis, the excessive sleep should be an almost daily occurrence for at least a month, should cause clinically significant distress or dys-

---

primary hypersomnia A disorder, not due to another physical or psychological disorder, characterized by excessive sleep, which may include either sleeping for unusually long periods or taking frequent naps during the day.

narcolepsy A disorder characterized by repeated irresistible attacks of sleep.

cataplexy A loss of muscle tone so dramatic that the person may collapse onto the floor during a narcoleptic episode.

breathing-related sleep disorders Disorders characterized by disruptions in normal breathing during sleep, which disturb the quality of the sleep and leave the person feeling excessively sleepy during the day.

function, and should not be due to another medical, psychiatric, or substance use disorder.

The prevalence of hypersomnia in the general population is unknown. Between 0.5 and 5% of adults complain of daytime sleepiness, although it is unclear how many would meet criteria for primary hypersomnia (APA, 2000). Approximately 5% to 10% of cases seen in sleep clinics qualify for this diagnosis. Primary hypersomnia typically begins in late adolescence or early adulthood and then gradually intensifies. It is often chronic, affecting the person for a lifetime. There is an intermittent form of hypersomnia called *Kleine-Levin syndrome.* This disorder usually shows a sudden onset and typically lasts from a few days to a few weeks. Compulsive overeating, impulsive behaviors, irritability, and hypersexuality often accompany it. Symptoms of other psychiatric disorders may also be present, such as depression and thought disorder (Masi et al., 2000). Kleine-Levin syndrome develops in early adulthood and usually decreases in intensity by middle age.

Narcolepsy.

Narcolepsy is characterized by repeated irresistible attacks of sleep. Essentially, the person falls asleep instantly, sometimes in mid-sentence. These sleep attacks often occur in response to strong emotional arousal. Many narcoleptic episodes include **cataplexy**—a loss of muscle tone so dramatic that the person may collapse onto the floor. During these rapid attacks of sleep, the person often goes immediately into REM sleep, rather than going through the normal sleep stages leading up to REM sleep. Furthermore, about one-third of affected people experience vivid dreamlike images that occur either just before falling asleep (*hypnogogic hallucinations*) or just after awakening (*hypnopompic hallucinations*). Approximately one-third to one-half of people with narcolepsy also experience paralysis either just before or just after awakening. These dramatic symptoms occur on rare occasions in people without sleep disorders. For example, approximately 10% of adults experience occasional hypnogogic or hypnopompic hallucinations, and nearly half report rare occurrences of paralysis on first awakening (APA, 2000). The hallucinations and paralysis that occur in narcolepsy probably result from the rapid onset of REM sleep—so rapid that the person is virtually awake. The hallucinations probably feel dreamlike because they are fragments of dreams. These very unusual experiences are thought to be the basis for some of the reports of alien abductions (French, 2001). The hallucinatory phenomena, coupled with the paralysis, can produce a powerful sensation of being taken against one's will. Consistent with this hypothesis is the fact that a significant proportion of people who report alien abductions say that they were abducted from their beds at night.

The prevalence rate of narcolepsy in the adult population is somewhere between 1 and 8 people in 5000, and the disorder is equally common in men and women (APA, 2000). The first sign of narcolepsy is typically intense daytime sleepiness, which usually is first noticed in late adolescence or early adulthood, although milder sleepiness may have been present for years (APA, 2000). The more dramatic symptoms of narcolepsy, such as cataplexy, may not develop until many months or even years later, or they may never develop.

Breathing-Related Sleep Disorders. **Breathing-related sleep disorders** are characterized by disruptions in normal breathing during sleep, which disturb the quality of the sleep and leave the person feeling excessively sleepy during the day (APA, 2000). As with all sleep disorders, the diagnosis should not be made if the sleep problem is better accounted for by another medical or psychiatric disorder or by substance abuse. The nature of the breathing difficulty may vary from person to person. The most common breathing-related sleep disorder are **sleep apneas,** in which the person stops breathing for a time during sleep. The result is that the blood oxygen level gradually drops until the person awakens with a start and begins to breathe again. The person is usually unaware of this process and typically does not remember the repeated awakenings. However, the frequent awakenings prevent normal sleep, especially the deep sleep and REM sleep that are restorative, and therefore leave the person feeling tired and unrefreshed on awakening (Bardwell et al., 2000). In fact, most people with sleep apneas visit sleep clinics with the complaint of daytime sleepiness (Orr, 1997). Someone who sleeps with the affected person is likely to report intermittent loud snoring and/or dramatic startle movements throughout the night, which often disrupt the partner's sleep. Careful observation also indicates that the loud snoring and startle movements

Loud snoring can disrupt the sleep of one's bed partner. The snoring may also indicate breathing problems that can lead to obstructive sleep apneas.

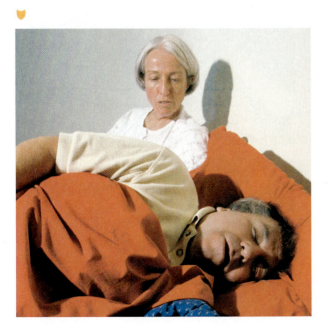

are preceded by periods of 20 to 30 seconds of silence. Some of these features are illustrated in the case history of Harry.

HARRY

Sleep But No Rest

Harry was 57, had been married for almost 35 years, and was thinking about retirement. However, for the last two years he had barely been able to drag himself through the day. He attributed some of his problem to being 50 pounds overweight and badly out of shape, but there was clearly something else. His doctor ran him through a series of tests but found nothing wrong. When Harry mentioned that he woke up every morning feeling like he had not had a moment's sleep, his doctor referred him to a sleep clinic for evaluation. Harry's description of his problem and his wife's description of his unbelievably loud snoring and gasping made the doctors suspect a sleep apnea, which was confirmed by monitoring his sleep in the laboratory.

A distinction is made between obstructive and central sleep apneas. **Obstructive sleep apneas** are caused by an intermittent blockage of the upper airways during sleep. The person continues to try to breathe but is unable to take in air because of the blockage. In contrast, **central sleep apneas** involve intermittent cessation of breathing—that is, the lungs stop working for a time. Obstructive sleep apneas are by far the most common form of apnea (Orr, 1997), and the most common risk factor for obstructive apneas is excessive weight (Sloan & Shapiro, 1995; Stoohs et al., 1993).

Obstructive sleep apneas affect between 1% and 10% of adults, whereas central sleep apneas affect fewer than 1% (APA, 2000; Partinen & Telakivi, 1992). Obstructive sleep apneas are most common in middle-aged, overweight males and in children with enlarged tonsils. Both central and obstructive apneas increase with age and, in fact, may be part of the normal aging process (Lichstein et al., 1999). Men outnumber women approximately 3 to 1 in obstructive sleep apneas. Men also outnumber women in central sleep apneas, although the prevalence rates are similar for men and women by age 50. There are no sex differences in the rates of sleep apneas in children (APA, 2000).

sleep apneas   The most common forms of breathing-related sleep disorders, in which the person stops breathing for a time during sleep.

obstructive sleep apneas   Apneas caused by intermittent blockages of the upper airways during sleep.

central sleep apneas   Apneas involving intermittent cessation of breathing—that is, periods when the lungs stop working for a time.

Circadian Rhythm Sleep Disorders. **Circadian rhythm sleep disorders** are characterized by a persistent or recurrent mismatch of the person's sleep-wake cycle and the demands from the environment for a sleep-wake cycle. For example, a person who is consistently unable to sleep until 4 A.M., but has to awaken at 7 A.M. for work, will not obtain sufficient sleep. The result is significant daytime sleepiness that causes distress or clinically significant impairment in functioning. The DSM recognizes three subtypes of circadian rhythm sleep disorders: delayed sleep phase type, jet lag type, and shift work type. These are described in Table 10.3.

Evolutionary Impact

Note that two of the circadian rhythm disorders are the result of the impact of modern technology and culture on human beings. Jet travel across several times zones and a 24/7 modern world can significantly disrupt the circadian rhythms that regulate body functioning. Humans evolved in a far more dependable world, in which each day began with the rising of the sun. This is a classic example of an evolutionary mechanism challenged beyond its limits by dramatic and rapid changes in the environment. It is not likely that humans will return to slower transportation or that shift work will be elimi-

nated. In fact, companies routinely conduct business around the globe, where it is always daytime somewhere (Maher, 2000). It is also unlikely that evolution will catch up with these rapid changes. Therefore, one can safely predict that circadian rhythm sleep disturbances will increase in frequency. A better understanding of the process by which circadian rhythms are regulated may lead to procedures that minimize the problems or that

Things that disrupt circadian rhythms, such as shift work and flying across several time zones, can have pronounced effects on sleep patterns and on the quality of sleep.

[TABLE 10.3] Circadian Rhythm Sleep Disorder Subtypes

The DSM recognizes three subtypes of circadian rhythm sleep disorders.

Delayed Sleep Phase Type

In this type, individuals are unable to adjust their circadian and sleep cycles to coincide with the demands of the environment. In this case, the shift in the circadian cycle is stable and may persist for years.

Jet Lag Type

In this type, the circadian rhythm no longer matches the day-night cycle because of travel across several time zones. The result is difficulty in sleeping at normal times and an experience of sleepiness during the day. The severity of this disruption depends on how many time zones the person crosses in a short period and on the direction of the travel. Generally, traveling west is easier than traveling east.

Shift Work Type

In this type, people's circadian rhythms are mismatched with their work schedule. For example, the circadian rhythm may suggest that it is time to sleep, but the person is scheduled to work the night shift. Shift work is especially disruptive when the person is constantly changed from one shift to another. Even a steady night shift can be disruptive. Night shift workers often report shorter sleep periods than other workers, with more disruption of their sleep—and therefore more sleepiness.

help individuals to normalize their functioning more quickly when it is disrupted. Unfortunately, such information has not often been used effectively. For example, it has long been recognized that the disruption of functioning caused by rotating shifts can be minimized by planning shift changes in such a way that when the changes occur, the workers always work one shift later rather than one shift earlier (Czeisler & Allan, 1988). Nevertheless, many companies fail to utilize this information, instead assigning workers to shifts in a nearly random manner.

The delayed sleep phase type of circadian rhythm sleep disorder is most common in late adolescence or early adulthood, with prevalence rates as high as 7% reported in such groups (APA, 2000). The prevalence rates in adults vary dramatically from one study to another, with rates between 0.1% and 4% being reported (Billiard et al., 1987; Coren, 1994; Nakatani et al., 2000). Circadian rhythm sleep disorders are common among shift workers, with as many as 60% of night-shift workers reporting significant sleep problems (APA, 2000). Jet lag type circadian rhythm disorders are common, although the severity of the impact varies from person to person. In general, the normal circadian rhythm readjusts to the new time zone within a few days, and the adjustment is typically easier in traveling west than in traveling east. This is because most people's internal circadian clock naturally runs a little longer than 24 hours, thus making it easier to adjust to a day that is artificially longer because of the jet travel than to one that is artificially shorter.

PARASOMNIAS

Parasomnias represent abnormal behavior or physiological responding that occurs during sleep or during the transitions into and out of sleep. The DSM recognizes three parasomnias: nightmare disorder, sleep terror disorder, and sleepwalking disorder.

....

circadian rhythm sleep disorders Disorders characterized by a persistent or recurrent mismatch of the person's sleep-wake cycle and the demands from the environment for a sleep-wake cycle.

parasomnias Abnormal behavior or physiological responding that occurs during sleep or during the transitions into or out of sleep.

nightmare disorder A disorder characterized by frequent awakenings due to frightening dreams (nightmares), with detailed recall of the content of the dreams.

sleep terror disorder A disorder characterized by abrupt awakening from sleep, often with a terrified scream.

sleepwalking disorder A disorder characterized by complex motor behavior during sleep, such as getting up and walking around.

Nightmare Disorder. **Nightmare disorder** is characterized by frequent awakenings due to frightening dreams (nightmares), with detailed recall of the content of the dreams. The nightmares cause significant distress, disrupt sleep, and impair daytime functioning. This diagnosis should not be made if the nightmares are better accounted for by another disorder, such as posttraumatic stress disorder.

Nearly 50% of children experience at least occasional nightmares that are severe enough to disturb their parents (Rosen et al., 1996). Nightmares are less common in adults than in children, although up to half of adults report experiencing at least occasional nightmares (Zadra & Donderi, 2000). Approximately 1 in 30 young adults reports frequent nightmares (Blanes et al., 1993).

Sleep Terror Disorder. **Sleep terror disorder** is characterized by abrupt awakening from sleep, often with a terrified scream. However, unlike the case with nightmares, people with sleep terrors do not orient quickly to where they are, so the terrifying feeling may continue for several minutes. People with night terrors are difficult to comfort and reassure. They usually report no dream content to account for their night terrors, and night terrors do not occur during REM sleep. They typically show signs of intense autonomic arousal, including racing heart, rapid breathing, and sweating. Some of these features are illustrated in the case history of Paul.

Terror in the Night

PAUL

It all started when Paul was six. Once or twice a week, in the middle of the night, he would start screaming as though he were being murdered. His parents would run to his room to find him sitting bolt upright, sweating profusely, and terrified, with screaming that would not stop. He was virtually unresponsive to their efforts to calm him. He could never tell his parents what he was afraid of. He did not seem to be dreaming, nor did he seem to be afraid of anything specific in the room, and he usually had no recollection of the incident the next morning.

There is little information on the prevalence of sleep terror disorder in the general population. It is more common in children than in adults (Hublin et al., 1999). Childhood onset is usually between 4 and 15, adult onset in the twenties (APA, 2000). Boys outnumber girls, but in adulthood there is no sex difference in prevalence. In children, sleep terrors typically cease during adolescence (Ware & Orr, 1992), whereas the course is often chronic and intermittent in adults (Hublin et al., 1999).

Sleepwalking Disorder. **Sleepwalking disorder** is characterized by complex motor behavior during sleep, such as getting up and walking around. However, to qualify for the sleepwalking disorder diagnosis, the sleepwalking must cause clinically significant distress for the person. The type of sleepwalking behavior can vary, but most often it is routine. For example, the person may get up and go to the bathroom or walk downstairs or outside. The person may talk or eat during the episode and, on rare occasions, may operate complex machinery. Sleepwalking in children may include inappropriate behavior, such as urinating on the floor. Occasionally, sleepwalkers are injured because they run into or trip over things. Often the person returns to bed with no recollection of the activity the next morning. On other occasions, people may wake up during the sleepwalking activity, understandably confused about where they are and how they got there. If awakened by someone else, the sleepwalker is likely to be confused, but no other problem is likely to occur, as discussed in the nearby Modern Myths box.

In most cases, sleepwalking does not cause the clinically significant distress necessary for a sleepwalking disorder diagnosis. Hence the prevalence of this disorder is low. However, sleepwalking is not uncommon. Between 10% and 30% of children have had at least one known sleepwalking episode, and about 2% sleepwalk frequently. Somewhere between 1% and 7% of adults report at least occasional sleepwalking, and about 1 in 200 adults sleepwalks

frequently (APA, 2000; Ohayon et al., 1999). It is likely that these figures are underestimates because, by definition, people who sleepwalk have no recollection of the sleepwalking the next morning. Therefore, people who live alone may sleepwalk with little evidence of the experience, except perhaps things being slightly rearranged the next morning.

Check Yourself 10.4

Types of Sleep Disorders

1. What differentiates the different sleep stages?
2. When do dreams occur?
3. In what age group is primary insomnia most prevalent?
4. What is the most common form of sleep apnea, and what risk factor is most closely associated with this form?
5. What is the distinction between nightmare disorder and sleep terror disorder?

Ponder this . . . *What arguments can be made that obstructive sleep apnea is likely to have been rare in evolutionary history?*

MODERN Myths

Sleepwalking

There is probably no sleep disorder for which there are more misconceptions than sleepwalking. Perhaps it is the zombielike state of someone carrying out behavior while sleepwalking, or perhaps it is the idea that the person appears to be out of control. Whatever the reason for the myths, let's take a minute to debunk a few.

Waking someone from sleepwalking is dangerous for the sleepwalker. Being awakened entails no risk to the person who is sleepwalking. People who are sleepwalking are likely to show surprise when awakened, because they have no awareness of their sleepwalking and therefore

believe they are in bed sleeping. Awakening them may lead to puzzlement about what is happening, but nothing more.

Waking someone from sleepwalking may be dangerous to you. Waking someone who is sleepwalking is no more dangerous than waking someone who is sleeping. Some people wake up gently when touched or spoken to, whereas others wake up with a startle. These same differences are found in people sleepwalking, although in general the sleepwalking person is often a bit harder to awaken.

Sleepwalkers are dangerous to others. This myth may be due to the way a sleepwalker looks when sleep-

walking—like a zombie from a 1960s movie. Sleepwalkers are not under the control of some menacing agent. They are simply asleep, and it is odd to see a person who is asleep doing things that are normally done when awake.

Sleepwalkers are dangerous to themselves. There is actually some truth to this one. Sleepwalkers are not dangerous to themselves because they will do things that they would not normally do while awake, such as jump out of a window, but they may hurt themselves by tripping over things or running into things because they have minimal awareness of their surroundings.

CAUSES OF SLEEP DISORDERS

Because there are many ways in which sleep can be disordered, you should not be surprised to learn that there are also many factors that can disrupt sleep. This section discusses the causes of sleep disorders.

DYSSOMNIAS

There is no one cause for all dyssomnias. In fact, there is probably no one cause for any given dyssomnia. Like most psychological disorders, biological diatheses probably interact with environmental events to trigger a sleep disorder. Some sleep disorders, such as narcolepsy, are influenced by genes (Mignot, 1998). Others, such as most cases of insomnia, appear to have little genetic contribution (Parkes & Lock, 1989). However, even in disorders with moderately strong genetic influences, environment plays an important role, as indicated by the fact that only 30% of the identical twins of people with narcolepsy develop narcolepsy.

Other biological factors besides genes increase risk for sleep disorders. As we noted earlier, obesity increases the risk for obstructive sleep apneas (Grunstein et al., 1995; Winkelman, 2001), as can the shape and size of airways and such natural obstructions as tonsils. Health problems, especially those that involve pain or discomfort, increase the risk of insomnia (Roberts et al., 1999). Biological factors also contribute to some sleep disorders, although the primary problem is environmental. For example, jet lag and shift work (environmental factors) can trigger a circadian rhythm sleep disorder because of the interaction between the environment and the biological rhythms that regulate sleep.

Psychological factors also play a major role in many sleep disorders. This section focuses on insomnia because more is known about the psychological variables that contribute to this dyssomnia than about those that contribute to any other sleep disorder. Insomnia is a common response to a variety of environmental events, including a hot, humid night without air conditioning, excessive noise, sore muscles from overexertion, a stressful day, or persistent worries. Such insomnia tends to be transient and disappears when the bedroom cools, the noise stops, the muscles heal, the days grow less stressful, or the sources of worry subside. More persistent insomnia is usually the result of a multitude of variables.

Most cases of primary insomnia start out as occasional episodes of the transient insomnia just described (Morin, 1993). The responses to this occasional insomnia can either increase or decrease the likelihood of later insomnia. For example, sleep is one of those things you just have to let happen; it is not something you make happen by trying harder. If you are not sleeping and you try harder to sleep, you will simply get aroused, which decreases the likelihood of sleep. Watching the clock tick away the hours will frustrate some-

one who is trying to sleep, again creating arousal and thus blocking sleep. Going to bed early because you feel you need the sleep will do nothing to help you sleep if you are not sleepy. Most people with insomnia are overly concerned with sleep and feel that a full night's sleep is more important than it really is (Morin, 1993). As a consequence, they tend to stay in bed trying to sleep even when they are not sleepy. In time, the negative experience of not being able to sleep makes the very process of going to bed aversive.

Many people with insomnia respond in ways that exacerbate the problem, largely because they do not understand the process of sleep well enough to make better choices. For example, they may sleep late or take a nap in the afternoon if they could not fall asleep the night before. When their usual bedtime rolls around, they are not tired because they have gotten enough sleep by sleeping in or napping. Consequently, they spend another restless night, unable to fall asleep when they think they should, becoming more frustrated, and repeating the cycle of the night before. Others resort to self-medication strategies, such as having a couple of drinks before retiring. Alcohol may help a person relax and thus may help initiate sleep, but it wears off in a few hours, leaving one restless and unable to sleep well (Janowsky et al., 1987). Furthermore, alcohol decreases the amount of REM sleep (Roehrs & Roth, 1997).

Some people unknowingly promote insomnia through their choice of late-night activities. For example, vigorous or exciting activities increase sympathetic arousal, which decreases the likelihood of sleep until parasympathetic arousal can take over. Such activities include watching scary movies, having argumentative discussions with others, working out, and studying intensely. Sex to the point of orgasm is typically not a problem, but without orgasmic release, the excess arousal may inhibit sleep. Eating a lot just before bed or consuming such stimulants as coffee, chocolate, or caffeinated soft drinks may also interfere with sleep.

Cognitive interpretations of occasional insomnia can create scenarios that promote future insomnia. For example, believing that getting a good night's sleep is absolutely critical can put so much pressure on a person that sleep is impossible. Feeling that the night's sleep is ruined because one does not fall asleep quickly is likely to increase frustration and thus interfere with sleep. Interpreting a few nights of sleep difficulties as a sign that one will never be able to sleep again clearly sets up a situation in which the anxiety about sleeping in future nights prevents sleep. All of these elements are addressed in the behavioral treatment of insomnia (Bootzin & Rider, 1997; Morin, 1993).

PARASOMNIAS

Much less is known about parasomnias. It is even difficult to determine the prevalence of some parasomnias, such as sleepwalking and night terrors, because the affected person is often unaware of experiencing them.

Occasional nightmares are relatively common, especially in children (Rosen et al., 1996). More frequent nightmares are often associated with specific psychopathology, such as posttraumatic stress disorder. Evaluations of people suffering from PTSD found no difference in brain or eye movement patterns associated with nightmares, but nightmare sufferers tended to awaken more during the night, apart from awakenings from nightmares (Woodward et al., 2000). It is not clear whether this finding is unique to nightmares in PTSD or applies to all nightmare sufferers. Nightmares are more common in people who show psychopathology on self-report measures, but little in the way of overt psychopathology (Berquier & Ashton, 1992; Levin, 1998; Levin & Raulin, 1991; Ohayon et al., 1997). The reason for this interesting finding is unclear. It may be that people who experience psychopathological processes, but who maintain normal functioning while awake, are unable to compensate for the pathological processes when asleep and thus experience frequent disturbing dreams. However, this is speculative.

There is a large psychoanalytic literature on dreams, dating back to Freud's classic book *The Interpretation of Dreams* (1900). However, there is little psychodynamic study of nightmares per se. Hartman (1984) suggested that frequent nightmare sufferers have thin or permeable ego boundaries, which means that they have difficulty distinguishing reality from their thoughts, feelings, and fantasies. The same mechanisms have been hypothesized to predispose people to such forms of psychopathology as schizophrenia (Blatt & Wild, 1976). This is more of a descriptive theory than an explanatory one, because there is no way to discern how permeable ego boundaries are, independently of the presence of such symptoms as thought disturbance or nightmares.

Almost nothing is known about the causes of sleep terrors. They are more common in children than in adults (Hublin et al., 1999), which suggests that developmental processes may be involved and that once a certain level of biological maturity is reached, the sleep terrors decrease or disappear. However, no one knows what processes might be involved. Sleep terrors run in families (Mindell, 1993), but it is not known whether this finding reflects a genetic contribution.

Genetic factors appear to play a role in sleepwalking (Abe et al., 1984), although environmental factors have also been implicated. Stress, mood and anxiety disorders, significant sleep deprivation, medical conditions, and shift work are all associated with sleepwalking (Ohayon et al., 1999). With many of these variables, it is difficult to determine the direction of causation. For example, do mood and anxiety disorders predispose to sleepwalking, or does sleepwalking increase risk for mood and anxiety disorders, or does another factor increase risk for both? Other variables appear easier to evaluate. For example, it seems unlikely that sleepwalking increases the amount of shift work a person does. Even here, however, it is not clear how shift work affects the person or contributes to sleepwalking. There is some evidence of brain abnormalities in many people who sleepwalk—specifically, intermittent epilepticlike activity in the temporal lobes during sleep (Atay & Karacan, 2000). Treatment with antiseizure drugs is sufficient to eliminate sleepwalking in individuals with these abnormal brain patterns.

Check Yourself 10.5

Causes of Sleep Disorders

1. What three factors contribute to primary insomnia?
2. What process is presumed to be involved in sleep terrors?
3. Which parasomnia is known to have a genetic influence?

Ponder this . . .   *Given what is known about the factors that contribute to primary insomnia, what personality characteristics would you expect to be associated with this disorder?*

TREATING SLEEP DISORDERS

Suffering from a sleep disorder has an enormous impact on a person's life. Feeling tired constantly, being unable to concentrate or to be productive, and feeling helpless to achieve something that others take for granted is frustrating and depressing. People who suffer from a sleep disorder want to know how to correct it. Treating a sleep disorder, however, requires knowing exactly what is wrong. Therefore, treatment always begins with assessment. This section describes the typical assessment strategies for sleep disorders before turning to current treatments.

ASSESSING SLEEP DISORDERS

The assessment of sleep problems utilizes two general strategies. The first is a clinical interview, which often includes a self-report sleep log. The second is a sleep study, in which the person is monitored during sleep.

Clinical Interview. Most people are referred to sleep clinics by their doctors after they complain of difficulty sleeping or of feeling fatigued during most of the day. The sleep specialist begins the assessment with a clinical interview. The nature of the interview varies, depending on

sleep hygiene The manner in which one prepares for, obtains, and maintains normal sleep.

whether the primary complaint is insomnia or daytime tiredness.

When insomnia is the primary complaint, the sleep specialist starts by obtaining a history of the problem. When did it start? How did it progress? What was going on before it started? How has the person reacted to the insomnia? Such questions often highlight critical elements that need to be addressed in treatment. The interview also covers sleep habits. When do you go to bed? What do you do before you go to bed? How do you try to fall asleep? What do you do if you are unable to fall asleep? Do you wake up during the night? These questions identify aspects of behavior that are referred to as **sleep hygiene**—that is, the manner in which one prepares for, obtains, and maintains normal sleep.

The interview is usually supplemented with a sleep log, which records critical details of sleep and variables that may be enhancing or disturbing sleep. For example, sleep logs include the times at which one goes to bed, falls asleep, and awakens, as well as how refreshed one feels in the morning. Other variables, such as what one eats and drinks, when one is exposed to sunlight, how much and when one exercises, and one's general performance during the day are recorded. These variables are usually recorded for at least a two-week period so that information is available for both weekdays and weekends (Spielman & Glovinsky, 1997). These sleep logs are often cleverly designed so that all of this information can be easily recorded, as illustrated in Figure 10.6.

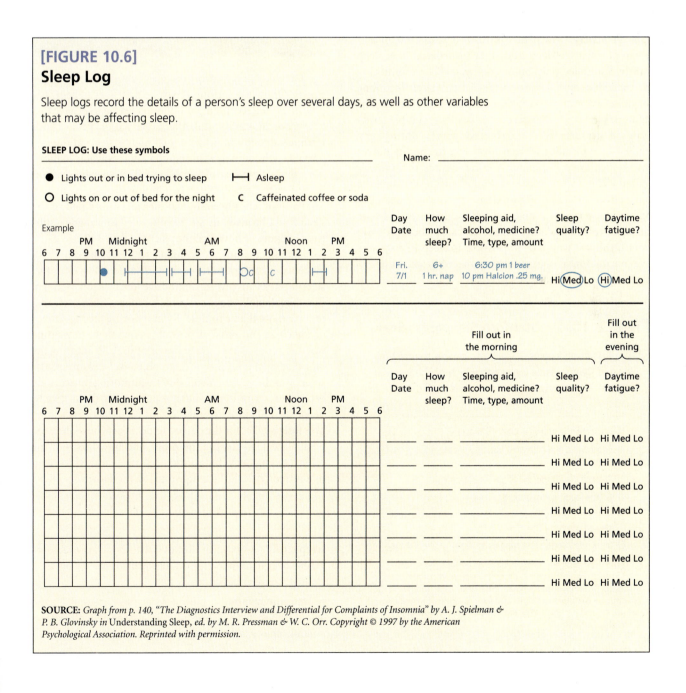

[FIGURE 10.6]
Sleep Log

Sleep logs record the details of a person's sleep over several days, as well as other variables that may be affecting sleep.

SOURCE: *Graph from p. 140, "The Diagnostics Interview and Differential for Complaints of Insomnia" by A. J. Spielman & P. B. Glovinsky in* Understanding Sleep, *ed. by M. R. Pressman & W. C. Orr. Copyright © 1997 by the American Psychological Association. Reprinted with permission.*

When the primary complaint is daytime sleepiness, it is critical to obtain information on exactly what that means. Sleepiness is a subjective experience and therefore is difficult to verify. The most effective way to identify a person's level of sleepiness is to identify the situations in which that person has fallen asleep (White & Mitler, 1997). If a person falls asleep while reading a book or watching a movie at home, this shows some level of sleepiness. However, if the person falls asleep while driving (being awakened when the car hits the rumble strips on the side of the road) or while eating a meal, this is evidence for a much stronger level of sleepiness. Sleepiness can also be quantified via such self-report measures as the Stanford Sleepiness Scale (Hoddes et al., 1973), which is shown in Table 10.4. And it can be measured objectively by timing how long it takes a person to fall asleep (Mitler et al., 1979; Thorpy, 1992).

Sleep Study. When there is reason to suspect significant sleep problems, a sleep study may be ordered. The **sleep study,** also called **polysomnography,** involves monitoring an individual during one or more nights of sleep, recording both behavior and a variety of physiological indices. The term *polysomnography* refers to the fact that multiple physiological measures (*poly*) are recorded (*graphy*) during sleep (*somno*). Typically, the sleep study records bodily movements, heart rate, respiration, eye movements, brain waves, blood oxygen level, muscle tone, and airflow through the nose (Ancoli-Israel, 1997). Modern sleep labs feed all of this information into a computer. Most modern sleep labs are set up to resemble a bedroom rather than a laboratory. You might think it would be impossible to sleep in a strange room with dozens of electrodes connected to you, but most individuals are able to get a nearly normal night's sleep in

The use of polysomnography to monitor physiological changes that occur while one sleeps has greatly improved both the scientific understanding of sleep and the diagnosis of specific sleep problems.

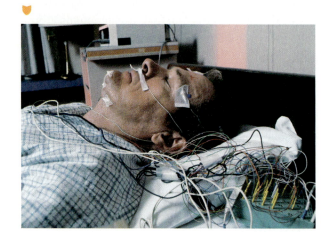

the lab. On rare occasions, it may be necessary to bring the person in for a second night if there is reason to believe that the first night was atypical. Alternatively, if the person finds it impossible to obtain a normal night's sleep in the lab, portable polysomnographic equipment is available to monitor a limited number of variables while the person sleeps at home (Ancoli-Israel, 1997). In addition to objective behavioral and psychophysiological measures obtained in the sleep study, individuals are usually asked to provide a subjective report of how well they slept (Allen, 1997).

The sleep study is invaluable in providing definitive evidence for several serious sleep disorders. For example, sleep apneas involve a distinctive respiration pattern: Breathing literally stops for periods ranging from a few seconds to more than a minute. By monitoring the movement of the chest and nasal airflow, it is possible to determine whether the apnea is obstructive or central. Monitoring the blood oxygen level provides an objective measure of the severity of the apnea (Allen, 1997). Monitoring muscle tone can detect movements that are potentially disruptive to sleep. The EEG provides markers for sleep stages, indicating how long it takes for the person to fall asleep, how often the person awakens during the night, and how much of the night's sleep is devoted to the deep sleep and REM sleep that are so critical to feeling rested in the morning.

[TABLE 10.4] Stanford Sleepiness Scale

The Stanford Sleepiness Scale asks people to rate their level of sleepiness by indicating which of the following statements most closely describes how they feel.

(1) Feeling active and vital, alert, wide awake

(2) Functioning at a high level, but not at peak; able to concentrate

(3) Relaxed, awake, not at full alertness, responsive

(4) A little foggy, not at peak, let down

(5) Fogginess, beginning to lose interest in remaining awake, slowed down

(6) Sleepiness, prefer to be lying down, fighting sleep, woozy

(7) Almost in reverie, sleep-onset soon, hard to stay awake

SOURCE: *"The Standford Sleepiness Scale" from "Quantification of Sleepiness: A New Approach" by E. Hoddes et al., in* Psychophysiology, *Vol. 10, 1973. Copyright © 1973. Reprinted with the permission of Cambridge University Press.*

sleep study   A study that involves monitoring an individual during one or more nights of sleep, recording both behavior and a variety of physiological indices.

polysomnography   Another term for a sleep study; this term reflects the fact that multiple physiological measures (*poly*) are recorded (*graphy*) during sleep (*somno*).

TREATMENT PROGRAMS

As with all disorders, the nature of the treatment varies depending on the specific disorder, complicating factors, or both. This discussion of treatment strategies divides the approaches into biological and behavioral manipulations, although in some cases it is advantageous to combine them.

Biological Manipulations. The biological manipulation that most people think of when they think of treating sleep problems is the use of sleeping pills, which are called **hypnotics.** Note that the term *hypnotics* has nothing to do with hypnosis but, rather, refers to the fact that the drugs induce sleep. Hypnotics range from mild over-the-counter remedies that make people drowsy to powerful prescription drugs that virtually knock people out. The hypnotics most commonly used today are benzodiazepines—drugs in the same class as those used for the treatment of acute anxiety (Roehrs & Roth, 1997). Hypnotics are generally ineffective for the chronic treatment of insomnia. They tend to lose their ability to induce sleep after only a few nights, and there is significant rebound insomnia when the person stops taking them (Roehrs & Roth, 1997). Nevertheless, they can be effective for the occasional night of insomnia or for someone who is having difficulty sleeping because of a recent trauma. Pain medications, such as codeine, also have hypnotic effects, but they are not used for the treatment of insomnia per se. Serious pain disrupts sleep, and the treatment of acute pain can increase the likelihood of sleep. However, the chronic use of such medications may actually disrupt sleep (Bliwise, 1997).

Sleep apneas require special treatment strategies—both medical and behavioral. Sometimes, all it takes is for the person to lose some weight, which can decrease the intensity of an obstructive apnea enough so that no other treatment is necessary (Saskin, 1997). Other strategies that may reduce an obstructive sleep apnea include decreasing the use of alcohol, sedatives, and narcotics, all of which decrease muscle tone in the upper airways and thus increase the likelihood of obstructions during sleep (Saskin, 1997). Changing one's sleeping position can also make a difference. Obstructions are more common when people sleep on their backs (Cartwright, 1984). Using a dental device that shifts the lower jaw forward expands the airway and thus minimizes obstructions (Schmidt-Nowara et al., 1991). In more extreme cases, surgical interventions can widen the airway or remove potential obstructions, such as the tonsils and adenoids (Saskin, 1997). A less dramatic, but very effective, treatment is the continuous positive airway pressure (CPAP) device (Sullivan et al., 1981). This portable device, which is about the size of a shoebox, produces a positive airflow through a mask that the person wears over

The CPAP (continuous positive air pressure) machine can prevent obstructions that restrict breathing during sleep, thereby allowing people with obstructive sleep apneas to sleep normally and to awaken refreshed.

the nose and mouth. This pressure prevents obstructions. People who use a CPAP machine say it is like breathing with an 80 mile-an-hour wind in your face, but they quickly adjust to it. The CPAP machine makes a remarkable difference in the quality of sleep in people with obstructive sleep apneas (Saskin, 1997). Nevertheless, some people find that the mask makes them feel claustrophobic and therefore avoid using it (Kribbs, 1997).

The use of bright lights helps to regulate circadian rhythm sleep disorders caused by jet lag or shift work (Zisapel, 2001). For example, a combination of extremely bright lights at work for those working the night shift and very dark bedrooms during the day when the person was sleeping helped to normalize sleep for people on the night shift (Czeisler et al., 1990). Sitting in front of light boxes that put out light nearly as bright as the sun just before reporting for the night shift reduces sleepiness at work (Eastman, 1987, 1990). Such light boxes also facilitate adjustment to jet lag (Czeisler et al., 1986), although awakening at dawn and going for a walk in the morning sun accomplishes the same thing.

Psychological Manipulations. Psychological manipulations have proved to be most effective for insomnia (Bootzin & Rider, 1997; Morin, 1993). A variety of behavioral techniques are typically combined into an overall treatment protocol. Although insomnia may be caused by a variety of physical or psychiatric disorders, most insomnia is due to ineffective sleep habits, ill-advised compensatory strategies, and an inability to relax enough to allow oneself to fall asleep. This section will cover sleep hygiene information, stimulus control strategies, sleep restriction, relaxation techniques, and cognitive approaches to insomnia.

You learned earlier in this chapter that the term *sleep hygiene* refers to the manner in which one prepares for and

hypnotics   Sleeping pills.

maintains sleep. Many cases of insomnia are due primarily to poor sleep hygiene—that is, to doing things that decrease the likelihood of falling asleep in a reasonable period of time, maintaining sleep long enough to leave a person refreshed in the morning, or both. Most people realize, for example, that caffeine can interfere with sleep, but few people realize how much nicotine and alcohol interfere with sleep. Nicotine may make a person feel relaxed, but it is actually a mild stimulant and thus can make it more difficult to fall asleep. Alcohol makes people feel relaxed and therefore may help one fall asleep, but it disrupts the quality of the sleep. Irregular sleeping hours and daytime naps can disrupt sleep schedules, thus making it difficult to sleep. Having a regular sleep schedule is increasingly important as one ages (Bliwise, 1997; Espie, 2002). Educating people about these variables and convincing them to change counterproductive behaviors can make a significant contribution to better sleep. These sleep hygiene rules are summarized in Table 10.5.

[TABLE 10.5] Sleep Hygiene

The term *sleep hygiene* refers to the manner in which people sleep and the way they prepare for sleep. Many sleep problems can be corrected simply by changing the way a person approaches sleep. Listed below are some guidelines that may improve sleep.

1. Avoid consuming caffeine during the evening because of its stimulant effects.

2. Avoid smoking just before falling asleep or when you wake up during the night, because nicotine is a mild stimulant.

3. Do not use alcohol as a sleep aid. As a central nervous system depressant, it may help you fall asleep, but it often causes people to awaken during the night, and it decreases the restfulness of sleep.

4. Vigorous exercise during the day may facilitate sleep, but vigorous exercise in the evening is likely to increase arousal and therefore inhibit sleep.

5. A comfortable environment contributes to sleep. If there is too much noise, use earplugs or a white-noise machine to mask it. Maintain a comfortable temperature. Most people sleep better if the room is kept reasonably dark.

6. Do not stay in bed if you are not tired. You cannot force yourself to fall asleep. Get up, read or watch TV, and wait until you feel tired before returning to bed.

7. If you are having trouble sleeping, do not watch the clock. Doing so will only add to your anxiety. Turn the clock around so that you cannot see what time it is.

8. Do not rely on sleep medications. They quickly lose effectiveness if they are used every night. They should be used only for occasional bouts of sleeplessness.

SOURCE: *Adapted from "Sleep Hygiene" from* Insomnia: Psychological Assessment and Management *by C. M. Morin. Copyright © 1993. Reprinted by permission of The Guilford Press.*

One of the most consistent problems reported by people with insomnia is the frustration they feel when they are lying in bed and unable to sleep. They watch the clock, try to relax by reading a book or watching TV, and worry about not sleeping. A few nights of this routine and people develop anticipatory anxiety about being able to sleep (Bootzin et al., 1991). This is where *stimulus control* strategies come in. For one to be able to sleep consistently when one goes to bed, the bed must be associated with sleep. If one stays in bed while unable to sleep, tossing and turning and becoming increasingly frustrated, it will not be long before the bed is associated with not sleeping instead of with sleeping. Sleep specialists recommend that people with insomnia use their bed for sleeping and avoid such activities as reading and watching TV. If you want to read or watch TV, do so in the living room until you feel ready to fall asleep. If you cannot fall asleep after a reasonable period of time, leave the bed and wait until you feel sleepy. Consistently following these simple rules prevents the development of an association between the bedroom and not sleeping and thus promotes better, more consistent sleep.

Sleep restriction is one of those techniques that appears counterproductive, although evidence suggests that it works well (Dashevsky & Kramer, 1998; Friedman et al., 1991; Wohlgemuth & Edinger, 2000). It involves reducing

Worrying and sleeping are often mutually exclusive. When sleep does not come, it is not uncommon for people's thoughts to start to feel out of control.

the amount of time allowed in bed to match the current amount of sleep time (Spielman et al., 1987). For example, if the person normally goes to bed at 11 P.M. and awakens at 7 A.M. but usually is unable to fall asleep until 2 A.M., sleep restriction would have the person not go to bed until 2 A.M. The rationale is that insomniacs tend to try to catch up on sleep they missed by going to bed earlier, often when they are not tired and therefore are unlikely to fall asleep. If the person has been sleeping only 5 hours, as in this example, the sleep restriction will have them in bed for only 5 hours. Usually, the person is dead tired by the agreed-upon bedtime and therefore falls asleep quickly. Over time, the bedtime can be moved up, provided that the person is clearly tired and ready to sleep. Although this is a generally effective technique, most people with insomnia require only education about sleep hygiene (Friedman et al., 2000).

Another effective tool for treating insomnia is *progressive relaxation therapy* (Bernstein et al., 2000; Morin, 1993). This technique involves the relaxation of muscles, one muscle group at a time. Sleep involves gradual reduction in arousal, and progressive relaxation facilitates such changes. In fact, a common problem in training many people with anxiety disorders in using progressive relaxation is that they often fall asleep while doing the relaxation exercises.

It is common for people with insomnia to hold dysfunctional beliefs about sleep. For example, if one is having difficulty falling asleep, exaggerating the consequences of not sleeping is likely to upset one enough to block any possibility of sleep (Morin, 1993). Not sleeping may be unpleasant and frustrating, but one can certainly function reasonably well the next day. People miss sleep all the time and are still able to function. As long as the sleep deprivation does not last too long, people can easily adjust to it. Accepting this premise reduces the pressure to fall asleep—pressure that nearly always backfires. Table 10.6 lists some faulty beliefs that may contribute to insomnia, along with alternative interpretations of the phenomena these beliefs address.

Although much has been learned about sleep over the past 50 years, in many ways it remains a mystery. The increasing demands of life, the movement away from a 9-to-5 workday, and the complex world in which many people now live all conspire to make obtaining adequate sleep a problem. Increases in obesity contribute to some sleep problems, such as obstructive sleep apneas. The more that is understood about the basic processes of sleep, the more scientists can help people adjust to the demands of an ever-changing and increasingly demanding world.

Check Yourself 10.6

Treating Sleep Disorders

1. What is sleep hygiene?

[TABLE 10.6]   Faulty Beliefs Contributing to Insomnia

Listed below are several common faulty beliefs associated with insomnia (Morin, 1993).

Loss of control: Many people with insomnia view it as a personal loss of control. A less damaging interpretation is that difficulty sleeping is due to a stressful day or to having a lot on one's mind, which is a transient event rather than a personal failure.

Attributing all daytime problems to the insomnia: Attributing every mistake during the day to sleep problems increases the pressure on a person to get sleep, which is counterproductive. People make mistakes because no one is perfect. Not sleeping may contribute to some mistakes, but it is never true that all mistakes are due to lack of sleep.

Evolutionary Impact _____

Unrealistic expectations: Many people have unrealistic beliefs about sleep, such as that one has to have eight hours of sleep a night or that few people experience sleepless nights. Such beliefs fuel anxiety when one cannot sleep. Accepting that the body regulates sleep, and that when one really needs sleep the body will promote it, removes much of this unnecessary pressure. Evolution prepared organisms to sleep when necessary but also to forgo sleep when sleeping would be ill advised. Humans still maintain this flexibility, even though the world is more structured today because of the invention of clocks.

Rumination, magnification, catastrophizing, overgeneralizing, etc.: These common errors (introduced in Chapter 4) occur in many psychological disorders, including insomnia. Losing a night's sleep will not destroy one's chance of success the next day (catastrophizing), and it does not mean that one will never be able to sleep again (overgeneralizing). Sleeping less than one would like is not the same as not sleeping at all (magnification), and worrying all day about sleeping (rumination) is not an effective strategy to promote sleep that night. Sleep specialists routinely probe for such cognitive errors and help people to challenge them as part of the treatment of insomnia.

---

2. What role do clinical interviews, sleep logs, and polysomnography play in the assessment of sleep disorders?

3. What biological treatment is most common for insomnia?

4. What is the logic behind sleep restriction as a treatment for insomnia?

Ponder this . . .   *Primary prevention seeks to avoid problems by using an intervention directed at the entire population. How might a primary-prevention program for insomnia be implemented?*

SUMMARY

EATING DISORDERS

- Anorexia nervosa is characterized by a refusal to consume and digest enough calories to maintain normal weight.

- Bulimia nervosa is characterized by frequent binge eating followed by compensatory behavior, such as vomiting, to prevent weight gain.

CAUSES OF EATING DISORDERS

- Cultural factors, such as pressure on women to be thin, appear to contribute to eating disorders. This pressure leads to dieting, which gets out of control in anorexia. Constant dieting fosters intense urges to binge on high-calorie food when it is available, thereby contributing to bulimia.

- Both genes and environment contribute to eating disorders.

- People who develop anorexia tend to be perfectionistic and compliant, to have a negative self-image, and to have fewer friends and more hostility than people from the same family who do not develop anorexia.

- Such themes as control and sexuality are central to many theories of eating disorders, although these theories are difficult to test scientifically.

TREATING EATING DISORDERS

- Hospitalization can medically stabilize people with anorexia who have lost excessive weight.

- Prozac promotes weight gain in anorexia and reduces the frequency of bingeing and purging in bulimia.

- Cognitive-behavioral therapy has been the treatment of choice for bulimia, although recent evidence suggests that interpersonal therapy (IPT) may be more effective over time. Dialectical behavior therapy is also effective for bulimia. The psychological treatment of anorexia has proved to be more difficult than the treatment of bulimia.

SLEEP DISORDERS

- Sleep is a complex activity that is controlled by parasympathetic nervous system activity, circadian rhythms, and a drive for sleep that increases with lack of sleep.

- Dyssomnias are disorders of initiating and maintaining sleep or of excessive sleep. Parasomnias involve abnormal behavioral or physiological responding during sleep.

- Primary insomnia is characterized by a difficulty in falling or staying asleep. In contrast, primary hypersomnia is characterized by excessive sleep. Narcolepsy is characterized by irresistible attacks of sleep. Breathing-related sleep disorders are characterized by disruptions in breathing during sleep. Finally, circadian rhythm sleep disorders are characterized by an inability to sleep during the time normally allotted for sleep.

- Nightmare disorder is characterized by frequent nightmares severe enough to awaken the person and cause significant distress. In contrast, sleep terror disorder involves an intense fear response during sleep that is not related to dream activity. Finally, sleepwalking disorder is characterized by complex motor behavior that occurs during sleep.

CAUSES OF SLEEP DISORDERS

- Genes play a role in some dyssomnias, but environment is also relevant. Obesity increases risk for obstructive sleep apneas. Health problems can contribute to insomnia. Environmental factors, such as jet lag or shift work, contribute to circadian rhythm disorders.

- Psychological factors contribute significantly to primary insomnia. Poor sleep habits, engaging in stimulating activities before going to bed, and dysfunctional cognitions about sleep and insomnia may also contribute to the maintenance of insomnia.

TREATING SLEEP DISORDERS

- The treatment of sleep disorders always begins with a thorough assessment, which may include a clinical interview, a sleep log, and a sleep study.

- If used intermittently, hypnotics are effective in promoting sleep. Many physical disorders interfere with sleep, and their effective management improves sleep. Light therapy is effective in resetting the internal biological clock that regulates circadian rhythms.

- Cognitive-behavioral therapy is often the most effective treatment for insomnia. It involves training people in proper sleep hygiene, using appropriate stimulus control strategies, sometimes restricting sleep, using relaxation techniques, and identifying and changing dysfunctional cognitions about sleep.

KEY TERMS

anorexia nervosa (290)
binge-eating/purging type anorexia (291)
breathing-related sleep disorders (309)
bulimia nervosa (292)
cataplexy (308)
central sleep apneas (309)
circadian rhythm sleep disorders (310)
dietary restraint hypothesis (294)
dyssomnias (307)
eating disorders (290)
hypnotics (317)
narcolepsy (308)
nightmare disorder (311)
obstructive sleep apneas (309)

parasomnias (311)
polysomnography (316)
primary hypersomnia (308)
primary insomnia (307)
purging (291)
REM rebound (306)
REM sleep (305)
restricting type anorexia (290)
sleep (303)
sleep apneas (309)
sleep hygiene (315)
sleep study (316)
sleep terror disorder (311)
sleepwalking disorder (311)

 SUGGESTED READINGS

Gordon, R. A. (2000). *Eating disorders: Anatomy of a social epidemic.* Malden, MA: Blackwell. A provocative book about the range and impact of eating disorders in our culture.

Maas, J. B. (1999). *Power sleep: The revolutionary program that prepares your mind for peak performance.* New York: HarperCollins. A very readable primer on sleep and its effect on functioning.

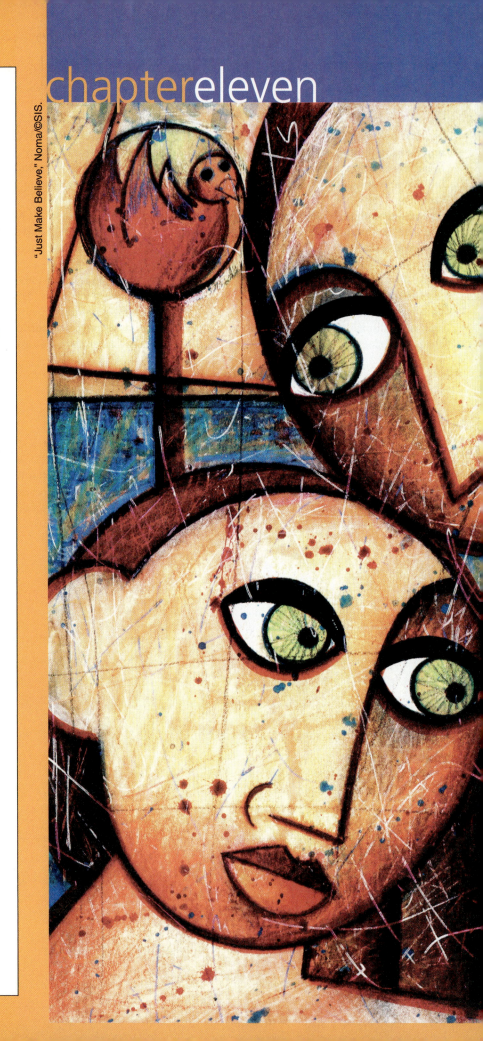

"Just Make Believe," Noma/©SIS.

chaptereleven

Sexual and Gender Identity Disorders

TERRY

Hopelessly Unable to Perform

Terry was bright and hardworking but was socially shy and terribly uncomfortable around girls. A year ago, an attractive but obviously inebriated classmate (Leslie) had flirted with him at a school dance, eventually convincing him to accompany her to her car, where they both drank heavily. Terry had fantasized about Leslie for months, but he had never even kissed a girl, and so he had little idea what to do in the backseat of Leslie's car. He was both excited and terrified. More important, he was distressed by his lack of sexual arousal and was mortified when Leslie asked what was wrong. In desperation, he bolted from the car, mumbling an apology. Terry obsessed about the events of that evening for weeks, avoiding contact with Leslie. Finally, Leslie approached him and they talked. Over the next couple of months, they talked frequently in class, and eventually Terry asked her out. It was several dates before he kissed her and several more before they started petting. Months later, Terry and Leslie were petting on the couch in her living room when Leslie suggested that they go upstairs. Her parents were gone for the weekend, and the house was theirs. As Leslie sat on the edge of the bed, she reached into a drawer and removed a condom. Terry could feel the blood drain from what seemed like his entire body. Even after half an hour of foreplay, Terry's penis was unresponsive. Leslie did everything she could to excite him but to no avail. As Terry broke down in tears, she lovingly tried to comfort him, but for Terry, his world was collapsing.

CHARLES

Trapped in the Wrong Body

It had been a difficult decision, but Charles, age 29, was about to become Charlene. It had simply become too painful to continue to live as a male when he felt so certain that he was really a female. For the last 18 months, he had been living as a female. The hormone injections had transformed his body, and two female friends had taught him how to dress as a woman and how to apply makeup. He had chosen to isolate himself from most of his friends during this transition. He knew it would be difficult to tell them. How would they react? What would they think? Some would understand, but many would not. Some would accept him as a woman, but he had no idea how many. In another month, he would undergo surgery to remove his penis and replace it with something that looked like a vagina. He knew that he could never be a real woman anatomically or be able to have children. Right now he just wanted to be able to live as the woman he was sure he was inside.

JENÁE

Pleasure Was Pain

Jenáe's idea of sexual pleasure would have terrified most women. She enjoyed being bound, gagged, and physically hurt. It was a craving—a craving that could never be fully satisfied. It drove her to travel hundreds of miles to clubs in distant cities, where like-minded people engaged in such activities. No one from her hometown knew her at these clubs, so her professional career would not be jeopardized. If her schedule did not permit one of these trips, she would use clothespins, needles, and clamps to give herself the intense pain she needed. Her hope was that in one of these clubs she would meet someone—a decent guy who understood and accepted her need for sexual pain. She had given up on finding such a person in her hometown. Some of her boyfriends had been willing to try bondage games, but when she had asked them to hurt her, each one had backed off.

Jenáe traced her interest in masochism back to "cowboy and Indian" games she played as a child. On one occasion, she was captured and tied to a tree. One of the boys briefly fondled her and pinched her arms and legs to "torture information out of her." She found herself shaking violently, scaring her captors into releasing her. Years later she realized that she probably had an orgasm without knowing what it was. Her adolescent sexual fantasies were almost exclusively of bondage and sexual torture, always by a masked man who would come to love her for the pain she endured. She did not really want to be kidnapped and abused; she wanted it to be a game played with someone who loved her. But after years of trying to find that person, she had all but given up.

T
erry, Charles, and Jenáe are all experiencing sexual problems—problems that cause them embarrassment or worse. Terry is suffering from a **sexual dysfunction,** impairment in either the ability or the desire to function sexually. Charles is experiencing a **gender identity disorder,** which involves a strong desire to be, or an insistence that one is, the opposite sex, coupled with a persistent discomfort about one's own sex. Finally, Jenáe has a **paraphilia,** a disorder characterized by intense sexually arousing fantasies, urges, or behaviors involving nonhuman objects or the suffering and humiliation of oneself, one's partner, or nonconsenting individuals. This chapter covers these sexual disorders and several others. The chapter begins with an overview of human sexuality. This is followed by a discussion of sexual dysfunctions, gender identity disorder, and paraphilias. The chapter ends with a discussion of rape.

HUMAN SEXUALITY

Sexuality is critical to the survival of one's genes. Sexual intercourse creates the embryo that grows into a human being. There are few things in life that generate as much inherent interest as sex. Yet in spite of this intense interest,

Advertisers use sexuality and the promise of sexuality to hype their products, because most people respond positively to sexual images. The notion is that the pairing of a positive stimulus (sex) and a formerly neutral stimulus (the product) will condition a positive response to the product.

many people are incredibly naïve about sexuality, obtaining much of their information from such unreliable sources as TV and movies. The assumption is that sex is natural and therefore "just happens." But it didn't happen for Terry, one of the cases that opened this chapter. This section introduces the broad topic of human sexuality, and the remainder of the chapter covers various aberrations in sexual behavior.

EVOLUTIONARY SIGNIFICANCE
Evolutionary Impact

Many species reproduce sexually. One advantage of sexual reproduction is that it results in offspring that are unique combinations of the genes donated by their parents, and thus increases genetic variability. A second advantage of sexual mating is that the enjoyment associated with sex helps cement a strong pair bond between lovers—a bond strong enough to last for years, providing the partnership that facilitates raising offspring.

Because sexuality serves the purpose of passing on genes to the next generation, it has been subjected to the most direct and intense of evolutionary pressures. The likelihood of one's genes being passed to the next generation depends entirely on the effectiveness of one's mating strategies. The optimal strategy for passing on one's genes is different for males and females (Buss, 1994). For example, human females have considerably more resources inherently tied up in reproduction than do males, and they have more limited reproductive capacity. Each child is fertilized in the female's body and must be carried for 9 months before another child can be conceived. In contrast, it is theoretically possible for a male to impregnate hundreds of females in that same period. Consequently, women need to be selective about the quality of the males who father their children if they want their genes to have the best chance of survival. Historically, a good choice might have been a strong male, because genes for strength increase the likelihood of his offspring's survival. That may be one of the reasons why men are larger and stronger than women: They have been selectively bred for strength by the historical preferences of females for physically strong mates (Thornhill & Palmer, 2000). However, the physical im-

sexual dysfunction   Impairment in either the ability or the desire to function sexually.

gender identity disorder   A disorder characterized by a strong desire to be, or an insistence that one is, the opposite sex, coupled with a persistent discomfort about one's own sex.

paraphilia   One of several disorders characterized by intense sexually arousing fantasies, urges, or behaviors involving nonhuman objects or the suffering and humiliation of oneself, one's partner, or nonconsenting individuals.

maturity of human infants at birth and their years of youthful vulnerability means that their survival depends on an extended period of nurturance and protection. Both males and females have a stake in choosing a mate with the temperament to provide this nurturance. Therefore, females prefer males who are strong and powerful *and* who show a willingness to share their resources. Males prefer females who appear to have the qualities that would make them good mothers—fertility, vigor, and a caring attitude (Buss, 1994).

There is a good chance that you reacted to the previous paragraph with raised eyebrows, or perhaps even a smirk. "Hey," you say, "that is *not* what I look for in a potential mate." Well, that may be how you feel, but our distant ancestors who showed preferences for these qualities probably were more successful than others in passing their genes to the next generation. If they had consistently chosen unwisely, their genes would have long since died out. Whether we like it or not, we carry the genetically influenced drives that led to greater reproductive success. As you will see in this chapter, that fact has implications for the variability in human sexuality seen today. Of course, human evolution has taken people well beyond primal drives, as intellectual capacity has afforded people more options for adaptive success. Buss (1994) found that both males and females prefer mates who are kind and intelligent. The physically strong male who could successfully defend his family from predators may be less well adapted to the modern world than the smart, hard-working male who can obtain and hold lucrative jobs. Furthermore, women are no longer confined to the home raising children. They are often economic providers for their families. The pace of modern social and technological development far exceeds the current pace of evolution. Social norms, which can react more quickly than evolutionary changes, provide people with guidance on acceptable behavior in these rapidly changing times.

BALANCING DRIVES AND SOCIAL NORMS

Drives that have been shaped through millions of years of natural selection influence many human behaviors. Social norms provide guidance when drives give confusing and/or contradictory cues. For example, social norms help guide teenagers on appropriate sexual behavior when sexual hormones might otherwise overwhelm their good sense. Studying social norms across cultures yields clues about what drives are present. For instance, when hundreds of cultures independently develop social norms that show remarkable consistency of purpose, those norms may well have been shaped by human drives or may represent a necessary modification to redirect human drives (Lumsden & Wilson, 1985). An example of such a consistent social norm is the *incest*

taboo, which strongly discourages sex among close family members. Of course, other factors, such as communication among cultures, may also have contributed to this cross-cultural consistency.

Some have argued that social norms may be a product of evolutionary development in that they heavily influence survival and social functioning and thus are likely to be affected by natural selection (Wilson, 1975, 1978). This perspective, called *sociobiology,* has merit. Humans are clearly social creatures, and many genes contribute to the social nature of our species. Social norms may well reflect genetic influences rather than being solely the product of culture.

Many social norms provide a reinforcement of human drives. For example, the optimal strategy for having "high-quality" offspring is to find a "high-quality" mate and make a mutual commitment to bond for the purpose of having and raising a family. Courtship rituals, marriage ceremonies, and laws define this process. These customs and legal constraints smooth a natural process of pair bonding, but clearly they are not the motivation behind pair bonding. The overwhelming feeling of falling in love with someone is the mechanism behind the pair-bonding drive. Such powerful negative feelings as jealousy are reminders that bonding drives are strong and that a threat to a pair bond stimulates primal responses. This is not to say that only two-parent families can provide the nurturing environment that fosters the development of children but merely that it is easier for a couple working together as a team to achieve this goal.

Evolutionary Impact

Other social norms limit actions that might occur if left unchecked. For example, powerful males in many species are able to mate with a nearly unlimited number of females. Although a few cultures have allowed such polygamy, most cultures explicitly forbid it. Why would that happen? Given the strong drive to mate, allowing a few powerful males to control a disproportionate share of females for mating would probably result in significant conflict among males for the limited number of available females. In a species whose success is built on social cooperation, such infighting would have significant negative consequences. This is only one of many social norms that appear to be aimed at conflict reduction. However, this social norm has the additional advantage of promoting the monogamous pair bond, which provides stable two-parent families. Such families are probably at least as important as the quality of genes in affecting the growth and development of offspring.

Social norms provide guidelines for behavior, but rarely are they sufficient to control behavior. For example, the traditional marriage vow says "'til death do us part," yet divorce laws exist. The law says that it is illegal to engage in extramarital sex, yet adultery occurs more frequently than most people want to admit, and by and large, those laws are ignored or are enforced rarely. The law says that punishment for rape or child abuse should be handled by the state, yet family members have powerful urges to take the law into their own hands. Understanding why people feel the way they do about sexual matters and why societal norms address these issues will provide insights into the diverse topics covered in this chapter.

CULTURAL DIVERSITY AND SEXUALITY

Evolutionary Impact

Sexuality plays a role in every culture. However, what is considered *normal* can vary dramatically from one culture to another. For example, you learned in Chapter 1 that some Polynesian cultures expect parents to initiate their children into sex (Danielsson, 1956). In most Western cultures, such activity is condemned. Most cultures prohibit marriages with close relatives, which prevents problems associated with inbreeding. Yet some cultures have promoted inbreeding among their royalty, usually with severe genetic consequences. Close family marriages tend to make negative genetic traits more likely to emerge, because most such traits are recessive and their expression requires two doses of the gene. Royal families that engaged in generations of inbreeding tended to show such traits frequently because of the concentration of these relatively rare recessive genes in a single breeding population. How did nature handle inbreeding before cultures regulated the process? Look at the often strained relationships between parents and their teenagers and you will see evidence of nature's solution. Most communal species—that is, species that live in close-knit communities—show strained relationships between parents and their offspring around puberty. In many species, this antagonism results in the offspring leaving and joining another community group, thereby reducing inbreeding. However, in today's complex world, teenagers are frequently ill equipped to leave their parents and make it on their own, a circumstance that creates tension with no easy solution.

Cultural expectations can affect the classification of many sexual behaviors. Take something that is noncontroversial in that it is encouraged in every culture: sexual intercourse within marriage. There are dramatic differences among cultures in the average frequency of sexual intercourse, which ranges from a few times a year to a few times a day (Hofstede, 1998). A person's frequency of sexual intercourse could be normal in some cultures, abnormally low in others, and abnormally high in some others. Such sexual variations as homosexuality are readily accepted in some cultures but not in others. Furthermore, the level of

acceptance within a culture may change over time. For example, homosexuality has become more acceptable in many Western cultures in the last few decades, as discussed in the nearbly Modern Myths box. Sexuality is such an important part of one's being that sexual success and cultural acceptability of one's sexual behavior significantly affect one's self-esteem.

This chapter covers several areas of human sexuality, addressing many of the evolutionary and cultural issues outlined in this section. Many of the topics covered are controversial, the subject of strongly held—and widely divergent—opinions. This chapter will help give you the information and perspective you need to judge for yourself. In the next section, we will examine impairment in sexual functioning.

Check Yourself 11.1

Human Sexuality

1. What are two advantages of sexual reproduction in humans?
2. From an evolutionary perspective, what is the purpose of falling in love?
3. What is the role of cultural norms regarding sexuality?

Ponder this . . .   *What could be the evolutionary significance of sexual jealousy?*

SEXUAL DYSFUNCTION

Sexual dysfunction is an inability to perform such normal and expected functions as sexual intercourse. The diagnosis of any sexual dysfunction requires three elements:

1. A specific sexual performance problem.
2. The problem causes significant personal distress or interpersonal difficulties.
3. The problem cannot be better explained by another Axis I disorder by drug effects, or by the impact of a medical disorder. (APA, 2000)

Sexual dysfunctions occur in both heterosexual and homosexual individuals and in every culture and every social class. The DSM divides sexual dysfunctions into four broad

homosexuality   A preference for sexual contact with one's own sex.

ego dystonic homosexuality   A homosexual orientation that is so uncomfortable for the person that he or she wishes to become heterosexual.

MODERN Myths

Homosexuality Is a Choice

Heterosexuals often view **homosexuality,** a preference for sexual contact with one's own sex, as a conscious choice, but the evidence suggests otherwise. Most people with a homosexual orientation are aware of their sexual preferences by puberty. In most cases, they choose to hide their preferences because they perceive, often correctly, a strong negative societal bias against homosexuals (Herek, 2000). Furthermore, there is increasing evidence that genetic factors probably contribute to a homosexual orientation (Bailey et al., 1999, 2000).

Homosexuality is not a sexual disorder and therefore is not included in the DSM. However, it was included in the DSM until 1973. In that year, the membership of the American Psychiatric Association, which publishes the DSM, accepted a recommendation of the Nomenclature Committee to replace the diagnosis of homosexuality with the diagnosis of "sexual orientation disturbance." This new diagnosis was to be applied to people with a homosexual orientation *only* if they were disturbed by their sexual orientation. DSM-III (APA, 1980) changed the label again to **ego dystonic homosexuality**—a homosexual orientation that is uncomfortable enough for the person that he or she wishes to become heterosexual. This diagnosis focused on the discomfort with one's homosexual orientation, not on the orientation itself. However, it made no conceptual sense to define homosexuality as normal but to define distress about one's homosexuality as a problem. By that logic, there should have been a companion diagnosis of ego dystonic heterosexuality! Therefore, DSM-III-R (APA, 1987) dropped the diagnosis. Even so, considerable controversy still surrounds homosexuality.

Why did these changes in the diagnostic system occur? The answer is far from simple. Certainly, there was considerable pressure from gay rights groups and others to reconsider the diagnosis, but pressure alone probably would not have led to the changes. A new attitude of acceptance of diversity evolved during the 1960s and 1970s—an attitude that continues to this day. The argument was based on the civil rights movement, in which activists proclaimed that it was wrong to judge people in terms of factors out of their control, such as skin color. But not everyone accepted that a homosexual orientation was something that a person could not control (Herman, 1997). In that respect, removing homosexuality from the list of psychiatric disorders was a necessary first step to decreasing this prejudicial climate and allowing people with a homosexual orientation to express themselves in a climate of acceptance and safety. We are painfully reminded that society has not yet reached that ideal of acceptance when we hear about a man being dragged to his death because he was black or a college student being beaten to death because he was homosexual.

Evolutionary Impact —

Should homosexuality be considered abnormal from an evolutionary perspective? After all, the reproductive success of humans depends on heterosexual mating. Clearly, from that perspective, homosexual couples would be less "reproductively fit," so genes contributing to the disorder should decrease in frequency. Why, then, didn't homosexuality disappear long ago? It could be that genetics plays no role, although the data suggest otherwise (Bailey et al., 1999, 2000). It could be that some people who carry the relevant genes do not express them because of other factors; hence those genes are not subjected to negative selective pressures. Finally, some people with homosexual inclinations choose to marry and have children (Isay, 1998; Matteson, 1999), which of course would minimize any negative selective pressure. This is not an easy problem, and that is why debate continues to this day.

---

categories: sexual desire disorders, sexual arousal disorders, orgasmic disorders, and sexual pain disorders. Table 11.1 on page 328 summarizes the disorders covered in this section, and Figure 11.1 on page 328 shows the prevalence of these classes of disorders. You may be surprised by how common these disorders are: Between 8% and 25% of adults suffer from any given disorder, and many people qualify for a diagnosis of more than one sexual dysfunc-tion (APA, 2000). Before covering these disorders, we will discuss the pioneering work of Masters and Johnson on human sexual functioning.

HUMAN SEXUAL RESPONSE

Masters and Johnson (1965) studied human sexual functioning in volunteers who engaged in sexual activity while

[TABLE 11.1] Sexual Dysfunctions

The DSM classifies sexual dysfunctions under four broad classes as shown here.

Sexual Desire Disorders

Hypoactive sexual desire disorder—characterized by a serious deficiency in, or total lack of, sexual fantasy and desire.

Sexual aversion disorder—characterized by a general distaste for, and avoidance of, genital contact with a sexual partner.

Sexual Arousal Disorders

Female sexual arousal disorder—characterized by an inability to achieve or maintain adequate lubrication of the vagina to allow comfortable intercourse.

Male erectile disorder—characterized by a persistent or recurrent inability to attain or maintain an adequate erection.

Orgasmic Disorders

Female orgasmic disorder—characterized by either a failure or a significant delay in achieving orgasm in a woman who is able to achieve normal sexual arousal.

Male orgasmic disorder—characterized by either a failure or a significant delay in achieving orgasm in a man who is able to achieve and maintain an erection.

Premature ejaculation—characterized by an onset of orgasm in a male after limited sexual stimulation and typically before or shortly after penetration of his partner.

Sexual Pain Disorders

Dyspareunia—characterized by the experience of genital pain during intercourse.

Vaginismus—characterized by a persistent and recurrent tightening of the muscle in the outer portion of the vagina in response to any penetration.

[FIGURE 11.1]
Prevalence of Sexual Dysfunctions

Laumann et al. (1999) found that 43% of women and 31% of men reported having a sexual dysfunction. The breakdown by category is shown here.

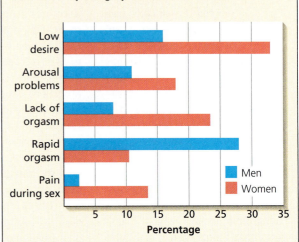

SOURCE: *"Prevalence of Sexual Dysfunction" from "Sexual Dysfunction in the U.S.: Prevalence & Predictors" (pp. 537–544) by E. O. Laumann, A. Paik, & R. C. Rosen,* Journal of the American Medical Association. *Copyright © 1999. Reprinted by permission of the American Medical Association.*

being observed and monitored with special equipment, and this research dramatically increased scientific understanding of human sexuality. They observed that people go through four stages in a sexual encounter—excitement, plateau, orgasm, and resolution—which are illustrated in

excitement stage Physiological changes during a sexual encounter, such as genital swelling and vaginal lubrication.

plateau stage A relatively steady state of sexual arousal.

orgasm A physiological release characterized by involuntary pelvic muscular contractions and intense sexual pleasure.

resolution A relaxed sense of well-being following the intense release of orgasm.

refractory period For men, the period following orgasm during which another orgasm is impossible.

appetitive stage Stage of the human sexual response that Kaplan suggested be added before excitement; involves an increase in sexual desire.

Figure 11.2. The **excitement stage** is characterized by such physiological changes as genital swelling and vaginal lubrication. The **plateau stage** is a relatively steady state of sexual arousal. The **orgasm** is characterized by a physiological release, with involuntary pelvic contractions and intense sexual pleasure. Finally, **resolution** involves a relaxed sense of well-being following the intense release of the orgasm. This basic pattern is similar for both males and females: a rapid rise in excitement, a plateau that may last a short time or a longer time depending on the level of stimulation, a very rapid rise to orgasm, and then the resolution. Following orgasm, men have a **refractory period** during which another orgasm is impossible. This refractory period lengthens with each successive orgasm. In contrast, women are capable of multiple orgasms, as shown in curve A in the top figure. Women may also experience a rapid orgasm and resolution (curve C) or a long plateau without orgasm and a very gradual resolution (curve B). Kaplan (1974) suggested adding a stage before excitement called the **appetitive stage,** which involves an increase in sexual desire. Three of these stages—appetitive, excitement, and orgasm—form broad classes for the current DSM sexual dysfunction disorders. A fourth broad class—sexual pain disorders—rounds out the group of sexual dysfunctions covered in this chapter.

ASSESSING SEXUAL FUNCTIONING

The key to the diagnosis and treatment of any disorder is a thorough and accurate assessment of the problem. Assess-

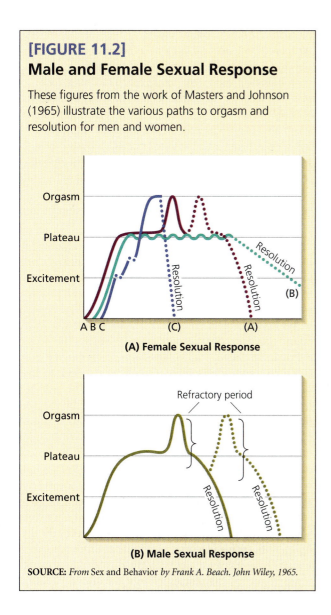

[FIGURE 11.2]

Male and Female Sexual Response

These figures from the work of Masters and Johnson (1965) illustrate the various paths to orgasm and resolution for men and women.

(A) Female Sexual Response

(B) Male Sexual Response

SOURCE: *From* Sex and Behavior *by Frank A. Beach. John Wiley, 1965.*

ing sexual disorders poses some unique challenges, which are addressed in this section. At a minimum, assessing sexual dysfunctions should include an interview and medical examination, but some diagnostic assessments may require specialized psychophysiological assessment of sexual functioning.

Interview. The core assessment tool in all of psychopathology is the diagnostic interview. However, interviewing people about sexual problems poses a special problem. Most people are especially sensitive about their sexuality, and many are too embarrassed to discuss critical details. Without such details, no diagnostic determination is possible. From the groundbreaking work of Kinsey more than 50 years ago, professionals have recognized that the style of interviewing is critical in getting accurate information about a person's sexuality (Kinsey et al., 1948, 1953). The interviewer has to set the tone by being clearly comfortable talking about sexuality, must react to the individual

in a manner that is completely accepting and supportive, and must take steps to decrease the anxiety and embarrassment of the client.

A diagnostic interview for sexual dysfunction is no different from any other diagnostic interview in terms of coverage. The interview should identify the problem, when the problem is most severe, when and how the problem started, how it is affecting the person's life, and what factors might be contributing to the problem, such as relationship difficulties. Information about health problems and medications should be routinely gathered, because medical factors can contribute to sexual dysfunctions. Some information is best gathered in interviews. However, many people are more comfortable providing information by answering questionnaires, so most sex clinics use such questionnaires extensively (Bach et al., 2001).

Medical Examination. Although medical information is routinely gathered in the diagnostic interview, a specific medical examination is often necessary to identify potential physical problems or to rule out physical causes. Sometimes the person's primary-care physician can conduct the examination, but often it is advisable that the individual be examined by someone with specific expertise in sexual dysfunction, because such specialists know exactly what to look for. As you will learn shortly, there are many medical conditions that can contribute to a sexual dysfunction. It is not uncommon for undiagnosed medical problems, such as hypertension or diabetes, to be discovered in the context of a medical examination for a sexual dysfunction (Mulhall, 2000). Furthermore, some sexual dysfunctions, especially those associated with painful intercourse, are nearly always medical problems (Graziottin, 2001).

Psychophysiological Assessment. Psychophysiological assessment is not routinely used in the diagnosis of sexual disorders, but it can be used and is often available in sex clinics. Such assessment is used more frequently in research on sexual disorders and sexual functioning (Weisberg et al., 2001). Psychophysiological measures can provide objective assessment of autonomic arousal in response to sexual stimuli. Specialized measures can provide more specific information about sexual arousal. For example, the **penile plethysmograph** measures the swelling of the penis in response to sexual arousal (Broderick, 1998). Sexual arousal in women is measured with a **vaginal photoplethysmograph,** which measures the increase in blood flow in the vagina in response to sexual arousal (Everaerd et al., 2000). Clients are typically shown, via a plastic model

penile plethysmograph   A device that measures the swelling of the penis in response to sexual arousal.

vaginal photoplethysmograph   A device that measures the increase in blood flow in the vagina in response to sexual arousal.

of the penis or vagina, how to attach these devices, and then they attach them in private. The use of such devices provides an objective measure of the physiological elements of sexual arousal, which are not always well correlated with the psychological experience of sexual arousal (Weisberg et al., 2001).

SEXUAL DESIRE DISORDERS

Sexual desire disorders, as the name implies, are characterized by a deficiency in the desire for sexual activity. Two sexual desire disorders are included in the DSM: hypoactive sexual desire disorder and sexual aversion disorder.

Hypoactive Sexual Desire Disorder. **Hypoactive sexual desire disorder** is characterized by a serious deficiency in, or a total lack of, sexual fantasy and desire. This loss of interest in sex can cause significant personal distress or create interpersonal difficulties, such as straining a marital relationship (APA, 2000). Hypoactive sexual desire disorder is often associated with problems in sexual arousal or orgasm. In such cases, the decrease in sexual desire may be due to the lack of sexual gratification stemming from these other problems. However, some people with low sexual desire can become sexually aroused and reach orgasm in a normal fashion, which suggests that sexual desire can be independent of sexual enjoyment. The case of Rosalie illustrates how disruptive this disorder can be.

The Honeymoon Is Over

ROSALIE

Rosalie and Carlos had been married for nearly 15 years and had had three children when they stopped having sexual relations because Rosalie was no longer interested in sex. Early in their marriage, she and Carlos had enjoyed a wonderfully satisfying sex life, but over the years, Rosalie's interest had been gradually decreasing. For nearly five years, she would make love with her husband every two or three weeks, but mostly out of duty. Two years ago, he stopped initiating sex and they stopped having intercourse. For a while, they continued to be supportive and loving to one another, but gradually Carlos became increasingly resentful. A year ago, he had an affair with a woman from work, blaming Rosalie for driving him to seek sex elsewhere. For the last several months, they have slept in separate bedrooms and have barely talked. Rosalie wants to please her husband and loves him deeply, but she has no desire to have sexual relations with him or with anyone else.

The experience of Rosalie and Carlos is repeated in many households. One or both partners simply lose interest in sex. Sometimes the impact on the relationship is minimal. More often, the impact is negative. Hypoactive sexual desire disorder is surprisingly common and appears to be increasing in frequency (Laumann et al., 1994; Spector & Carey, 1990), especially among males (LoPiccolo & Friedman, 1988). Studies have found rates ranging from 17% in a community sample (Osborn et al., 1988) to 55% in sex therapy clinics (Bancroft & Coles, 1976). Affected females outnumber males 4 to 1 and tend to be younger than affected males (Segraves & Segraves, 1991). Almost half of the people with hypoactive sexual desire disorder qualify for another sexual dysfunction, usually an arousal or an orgasmic disorder (Segraves & Segraves, 1991). People with this disorder are often depressed and anxious (Apt et al., 1993; Donahey & Carroll, 1993) and have elevated rates of marital conflict (Beck, 1995), but it is unclear whether these problems are a cause or an effect of the disorder. Both men and women with this disorder report few sexual fantasies, yet males with the disorder masturbate more frequently than males without the disorder (Nutter & Condron, 1983, 1985).

Sexual Aversion Disorder. **Sexual aversion disorder** is characterized by a general distaste for, and avoidance of, genital contact with a sexual partner. The aversion is so strong that it can trigger panic attacks if sexual contact is likely. Needless to say, sexual partners tend to take it personally when sexual contact with them is experienced as aversive. Consequently, relationship difficulties are a common secondary problem with this disorder. People with this disorder may use a variety of strategies to avoid sex, such as

The absence of sexual desire in a partner can be very frustrating. Many partners find it hard to believe that love can be independent of such sexual attraction.

sexual desire disorders Disorders characterized by a deficiency in the desire for sexual activity.

hypoactive sexual desire A disorder characterized by a serious deficiency in, or a total lack of, sexual fantasy and desire.

sexual aversion disorder A disorder characterized by a general distaste for, and avoidance of, genital contact with a sexual partner.

going to bed early, traveling, or being excessively involved with work or other activities.

SEXUAL AROUSAL DISORDERS

Sexual arousal disorders involve a dysfunction in one or more aspects of the psychological excitement or physiological preparatory responses that occur in the early stages of sex. There are two sexual arousal disorders recognized by the DSM: female sexual arousal disorder and male erectile disorder.

Female Sexual Arousal Disorder. **Female sexual arousal disorder** is characterized by an inability to achieve or maintain adequate lubrication and swelling of the vagina to allow comfortable sexual intercourse. Female sexual arousal disorder is often associated with a sexual desire disorder, a female orgasmic disorder, or both. The term *frigidity* was once used to designate female sexual arousal disorder, but like many ill-conceived diagnostic terms, it has taken on pejorative overtones and has been replaced.

Male Erectile Disorder. **Male erectile disorder** is characterized by a persistent or recurrent inability to attain or maintain an adequate erection. Some men are totally unable to obtain an erection, whereas others obtain an erection but are unable to maintain it long enough for sexual penetration. Still others are able to maintain an erection long enough for penetration but lose it during intercourse before either partner can reach orgasm. Most men with erectile dysfunction can maintain an erection long enough when masturbating to achieve orgasm, perhaps because masturbation provides more direct stimulation of the penis. Male erectile disorder is strongly related to age; older men are much more likely to suffer from it than younger men, as shown in Figure 11.3. Half of all 40- to 70-year-old men experience at least intermittent erectile dysfunction (Feldman et al., 1994). The risk is highest in men of retirement age or older. The case of Josh typifies this disorder.

The Spirit Is There

JOSH

Josh and Sheila have been happily married for nearly 25 years. For most of that time, their sex life has been satisfactory, although neither would say that it was incredible. Both are successful professionals in demanding careers. As a consequence, two or three weeks would sometimes pass between the times they made love because one or the other was working late or too tired even to consider it. About 5 years ago, Josh started having occasional problems maintaining an erection. He found it embarrassing but attributed it to fatigue and stress. Within a year, he could rarely get an erection when he and Sheila made love, although he could occasionally get an erection and an orgasm through masturbation. At first, he and Sheila

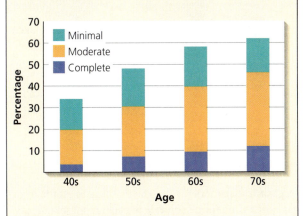

[FIGURE 11.3]
Prevalence of Erectile Dysfunction by Age

Erectile dysfunction is relatively rare in young men, but from middle age on it is rather common, affecting about one-third of men in their forties and two-thirds in their seventies.

SOURCE: *"Prevalence of Erectile Dysfunction by Age"* in *"Impotence and Its Medical and Psychosocial Correlates"* (pp. 54–61) by H. A. Feldman, Journal of Urology, *151, 1994. Copyright © 1994. Reprinted by permission of Lippincott, Williams & Wilkins.*

would patiently try to bring him to full arousal, but in time, both found the process distressing. Josh was embarrassed, and Sheila did not want to frustrate him even more. Their relationship continues to be strong even though their sex life has dwindled to almost nothing. Sex was never the most critical aspect of their marriage, but now it has become just a memory.

Josh's case is more typical of male erectile dysfunction than the case of Terry presented at the beginning of the chapter. Josh was in his late forties—a high-risk age for erectile dysfunction—when he started experiencing difficulty maintaining an erection, whereas Terry was in his teens. The relatively high prevalence of erectile problems is illustrated by the success of the new drug sildenafil citrate, which is better known by its brand name of Viagra.

sexual arousal disorders   Disorders that involve a dysfunction in one or more aspects of the psychological excitement or physiological preparatory responses that occur in the early stages of sex.

female sexual arousal disorder   A disorder characterized by an inability to achieve or maintain adequate lubrication and swelling of the vagina to allow comfortable sexual intercourse.

male erectile disorder   A disorder characterized by a persistent or recurrent inability to attain or maintain an adequate erection.

One of the most heavily promoted pills on the market, Viagra, makes it possible for many men with erectile problems to function normally. Taken an hour before sexual intercourse, Viagra enhances the normal penile erection when a male is sexually aroused.

ORGASMIC DISORDERS

Orgasmic disorders involve the inability to attain an orgasm in a time frame suitable for achieving sexual satisfaction by both partners. The DSM recognizes three such disorders: female orgasmic disorder, male orgasmic disorder, and premature ejaculation.

Female Orgasmic Disorder. **Female orgasmic disorder** is characterized by either inability to achieve or significant delay in achieving orgasm in a woman who is able to achieve normal sexual arousal. This is often a judgment call, because many factors affect the length of time needed to reach orgasm, including the woman's age, her sexual experience, and the amount and type of sexual stimulation. Orgasmic responsiveness in women generally increases with increased sexual experience. Consequently, female orgasmic disorder is more common in younger women and is rare in women who have had a period of normal orgasmic functioning, unless there is a traumatic sexual experience or a serious relationship conflict (APA, 2000). About 20% of women qualify for this diagnosis, and it is the most

orgasmic disorders Disorders that involve the inability to attain an orgasm in a time frame suitable for achieving sexual satisfaction by both partners.

female orgasmic disorder A disorder characterized by either failure to achieve or significant delay in achieving an orgasm in a woman who is able to achieve normal sexual arousal.

male orgasmic disorder A disorder characterized by either failure to achieve or a significant delay in achieving orgasm in a male who is able to achieve and maintain an erection.

premature ejaculation The onset of orgasm in a male with little sexual stimulation and typically before or shortly after penetration of his partner.

common reason why women seek treatment in sex therapy clinics (Laumann et al., 1994; Spector & Carey, 1990).

Male Orgasmic Disorder. **Male orgasmic disorder** involves either inability to achieve or significant delay in achieving orgasm in a male who is able to achieve and maintain an erection. A common report from such males is that the initial penetration and thrusting in his partner's vagina is pleasurable and arousing but that the experience quickly deteriorates to the point of feeling like work instead of pleasure. Both males and females can, and sometimes do, fake orgasms, and they may be especially likely to do so when there is an orgasmic disorder. However, a female orgasm is not a prerequisite for pregnancy, whereas a male orgasm usually is. Consequently, it is not uncommon for couples to seek treatment for infertility when the real problem is the failure of the male to ejaculate. Male orgasmic disorder affects 3% to 8% of clinical populations (Spector & Carey, 1990). Base rates in the general population are not available. It occurs more frequently among homosexual men, affecting 10% to 15% of these men (Wilensky & Myers, 1987).

Premature Ejaculation. **Premature ejaculation** is characterized by an onset of orgasm in a male with little sexual stimulation and typically before or shortly after penetration of his partner. To qualify for diagnosis as a disorder, the premature ejaculation must be persistent and recurrent, because unusual or novel sexual stimulation may be sufficiently arousing to cause an early ejaculation. It is common for the male affected with this disorder to be able to delay ejaculation considerably longer when engaged in self-masturbation than when engaged in either intercourse or mutual masturbation with a partner (APA, 2000).

There are no fixed criteria for defining premature ejaculation, just as there are no fixed criteria for defining a delayed orgasm in an orgasmic disorder. Except at the extremes (extremely quick male orgasm or extremely slow female orgasm), it is a judgment call when the male reaches a climax before his partner can achieve orgasm (Rosen & Leiblum, 1995). Is it a female orgasmic disorder or premature ejaculation? Consequently, many sex therapists treat it as a couple problem—the couple is unable to make love in a manner that is mutually satisfying (Kaplan, 1987a).

Premature ejaculation is common, affecting 25% to 40% of males sometime during their lives (Spector & Carey, 1990; St. Lawrence & Madakasira, 1992). Recent evidence suggests that there is a meaningful distinction between those males who have a chronic problem with premature ejaculation and those who experience the problem intermittently (Cooper et al., 1993). Men with chronic premature ejaculation tend to be younger, with a high sex drive and considerable sexual anxiety. Although it has been suggested that chronic premature ejaculation may be due to excessive penile sensitivity, the data on this hypothesis have been inconsistent (Faniullaci et al., 1988; Rowland et al.,

1993). In contrast, those men with intermittent premature ejaculation tend to have a history of erectile dysfunction.

Evolutionary Impact

It has been hypothesized that premature ejaculation, which is rather common in young males but less common in more mature males, may be a nonadaptive by-product of an evolutionary adaptation (Nesse & Williams, 1994). Young males in many species are rarely able to challenge dominant males successfully for the sexual attention of available women, so they are usually unable to establish the pair bonds that normally provide sexual access. However, by completing sexual intercourse quickly, young males are able to have sex and escape before being challenged by the dominant males in the group. However, this speculative hypothesis will require considerably stronger scientific evidence before it can be accepted. Scientists simply do not know why premature ejaculation is so common in young men.

SEXUAL PAIN DISORDERS

Sexual pain disorders are characterized by the experience of vaginal or penile discomfort during sexual intercourse. The DSM recognizes two sexual pain disorders: dyspareunia and vaginismus.

Dyspareunia. **Dyspareunia** refers to the experience of genital pain during intercourse. It can occur in either women or men, but it is more common in women (Bancroft, 1989; Steege, 1984). Approximately 10% to 15% of women in community samples report experiencing painful intercourse (Laumann et al., 1994; Rosen et al., 1993). Women often report both surface pain during the initial insertion of the penis and deep pain during the thrusting phase of intercourse (APA, 2000). The experience of such pain in one of the most sensitive parts of the body often leads to avoidance of sexual activity.

Vaginismus. **Vaginismus** is characterized by a persistent and recurrent involuntary tightening of the muscle in the outer portion of the vagina in response to penetration. The penetration may include sexual intercourse but can also include the insertion of a speculum during a gynecological exam or even the insertion of a tampon. The degree of tightening varies dramatically from one woman to the next. In some women, the tightening is mild and produces only slight discomfort. In other women, the tightening is so extreme that penetration of any kind is impossible. Vaginismus is reported in about 15% of all women who seek help at sex therapy clinics (Spector & Carey, 1990). Clinicians distinguish primary from secondary vaginismus. In primary vaginismus, any insertion is difficult or impossible, whereas in secondary vaginismus, some insertions, such as a tampon, are possible.

Check Yourself 11.2

Sexual Dysfunction

1. How is the term *sexual dysfunction* defined?
2. What are the four broad categories of sexual dysfunctions?
3. What is the most common sexual dysfunction, accounting for half of the cases in sex therapy clinics?
4. Which sexual dysfunction occurs primarily in young men? Which occurs primarily in older men?
5. Which sexual pain disorder do both men and women experience?

Ponder this . . .   *Which sexual dysfunctions would be most likely to encounter the greatest negative selection pressure if genes contributed to the dysfunction?*

CAUSES OF SEXUAL DYSFUNCTION

Asking what causes sexual dysfunctions is a bit like asking what causes wars. It depends on the war or the dysfunction. Traditionally, sexual dysfunction has been attributed to psychological factors, although physiological and sociocultural factors may play significant roles in many disorders. For any given individual, it is likely that several factors contribute to a sexual dysfunction. This section reviews the factors thought to be important contributors to the four broad classes of sexual dysfunctions.

SEXUAL DESIRE DISORDERS

Sexual behavior begins with sexual desire, but sometimes this most basic response is inhibited. Some people develop sexual desire disorders at puberty, but more commonly people develop them in adulthood following a period of significant psychological distress. The disorder can be either episodic or continuous. The episodic pattern is often associated with relationship difficulties, whereby sexual desire decreases during times of marital distress. This pattern is consistent with early psychodynamic theorizing that underlying psychological problems may account for sexual dysfunctions. Sexual desire disorders are also increasing in

....

sexual pain disorders   The experience of vaginal or penile discomfort during sexual intercourse.

dyspareunia   The experience of genital pain during intercourse.

vaginismus   A persistent and recurrent tightening of the muscle in the outer portion of the vagina in response to penetration.

frequency, at least among men (LoPiccolo & Friedman, 1988), although women who qualify for the diagnosis still outnumber men 4 to 1 (Beck, 1995). For years, the cliché response for women who did not desire sexual intercourse was "Not tonight, honey, I have a headache," but soon this may be an equal-opportunity cliché, with men as likely to utter it as women. Everyday hassles also significantly affect sexual desire in both men and women (Avery-Clark, 1986; Morokoff & Gillilland, 1993). The more hassled people feel, the less likely they are to feel sexual. What is the impact of longer work days, less job security, pagers, cell phones, and faxes on a person's stress level and on the resultant sexual desire? Sex typically depends on having time to be together in safety and comfort. It used to be that the biggest worry a couple had was whether they would wake the kids or the phone would ring. Now it is whether they will get an urgent page or e-mail. In a world that has become increasingly stressful, changes in the level of sexual desire may be an early warning that stress has reached a level that is clearly affecting the most basic of functions.

Other theories have also been advanced to explain sexual desire disorders (Beck, 1995). Kaplan (1977, 1979) and Barlow (1986) argued that the negative emotions of anxiety and anger interfere with the development of normal sexual desire. Studies of people with normal sexual desire confirm that anxiety and anger can reduce sexual desire and may even reduce sexual arousal (Beck & Bozman, 1995; Bozman & Beck, 1991). Changes in hormone secretion are a major contributor to loss of sexual desire in men, whereas the evidence for women has been inconsistent, with some studies finding hormonal differences and others not (Bancroft, 1988; Sherwin, 1988; Wincze & Carey, 1991). Perhaps the natural variability in hormonal levels in women over the course of their menstrual cycle masks subtle hormonal problems that may contribute to this disorder. A variety of drugs are known to affect sexual desire, including drugs to treat hypertension (Inderal, Aldomet), anxiety and depression (Valium, Xanax, Nardil, Prozac, Luvox, Paxil, etc.), psychosis, glaucoma, and cancer (Beck, 1995). The use of many of these drugs is increasing, especially among people of middle age and older.

Little is known about the causes of sexual aversion disorder, but they appear to be psychological rather than physiological. Women with the disorder show normal sexual responses in the laboratory when exposed to sexually arousing stimuli, so physiological factors are unlikely to be the primary culprit (Kaplan, 1997). Sexual abuse and assault can lead to sexual aversion disorder (van Berlo & Ensink, 2000). Even a panic disorder could lead to sexual aversion, because sexual arousal could be interpreted as paniclike, and therefore be experienced as dangerous by someone with an active panic disorder (Kaplan, 1987b).

Sociocultural factors can also play a role in sexual desire disorders. For example, some individuals are raised in a climate that regards sexuality as negative, sometimes to the point of viewing it as evil. Not surprisingly, people raised in such environments develop a negative view of sex, which is called *erotophobia* (Leiblum, 2000). Such views may color all of a person's sexual life but are more likely to interact with other events, creating, under the right circumstances, a genuine aversion to sex. A history of sexual trauma, either childhood sexual abuse or sexual assault, can dramatically affect one's desire for sexual contact (Berman et al., 2001).

SEXUAL AROUSAL DISORDERS

Many factors—physical, psychological, and sociocultural—contribute to sexual arousal disorders. The term *frigidity*, once used to describe arousal disorders in women, suggests that the woman is cold and uncaring, which is not supported by data. The term *frigidity* also implies an exclusively psychological origin, whereas the best available evidence suggests that physiological factors probably play a larger role than psychological factors (Anderson & Cyranowski, 1995). For example, diabetes or the effects of drugs for such conditions as hypertension or depression can interfere with sexual arousal in women (Hulter et al., 1998; Rothschild, 2000).

Several factors contribute to erectile problems. For example, chronic health problems such as diabetes can produce erectile problems (Melman et al., 1988), although technically the DSM diagnosis of erectile disorder should not be given if the erectile problems are due to medical conditions. Drugs and alcohol can also significantly inhibit sexual responding, including erections. Such psychological and interpersonal factors as relationship difficulties and job stress have also been associated with erectile problems (Ackerman & Carey, 1995). The case of Terry, which opened this chapter, illustrates how anxiety and alcohol can combine to inhibit sexual arousal and erection, leading in Terry's case to terrible shame and distress (Farkas & Rosen, 1976; Perelman, 1994).

ORGASMIC DISORDERS

Female orgasmic disorder is relatively common, especially in younger women. The majority of women with this disorder can be sexually aroused but are unable to trigger orgasmic release (APA, 2000). There is evidence that women need to learn to experience sexual release. Unlike men, women typically reach their sexual prime—that is, the time when they are most responsive sexually—in their thirties, although the timing depends on their level of sexual experience. Furthermore, women with more masturbatory experience are much *less* likely to have an orgasmic disorder (Kinsey et al., 1953). Biological and psychological factors may also be involved. For example, low levels of sympathetic arousal disrupt the sexual arousal of women with an orgasmic disorder, whereas the same arousal levels enhance sexual functioning in other women (Meston & Gorzalka, 1996; Meston et al., 1997). This is a physiological response that would have psychological consequences. A woman with an orgasmic disorder is likely to worry about whether she will be able to climax, thus increasing her sympathetic arousal and inhibiting the orgasm. Finally, sexual experiences and attitudes may well affect orgasmic release. For example, if a woman is raised to view sex as somehow improper, she may find it impossible to relax enough to permit orgasm.

Such medical conditions as multiple sclerosis and spinal cord injuries and such medications as antipsychotic drugs and antiadrenergic drugs can result in male orgasmic dysfunction (Rosen, 1991; Rosen & Leiblum, 1995). In addition, such psychological factors as lack of sexual desire or arousal, fear of impregnating the woman, and performance anxiety are related to male orgasmic disorder (Apfelbaum, 1989; Zgourides & Warren, 1989).

Premature ejaculation appears to have many causes (Metz & Prior, 2000). Excessive anxiety is often present (Dunn et al., 1999), although it is not clear whether this is a cause or an effect. Excessive penile sensitivity may be responsible (Rowland et al., 1996). The most dramatic finding regarding premature ejaculation is that it is primarily a problem of young men. Whether this is due to an oversensitivity that gradually decreases or to some other factor, such as anxiety, is unclear. The explanation may be as simple as inexperience; a younger male may simply not yet have learned to adjust the stimulation he receives during the sexual encounter to allow his partner to achieve arousal at the same rate that he does.

SEXUAL PAIN DISORDERS

Most people suffering from sexual pain disorders seek treatment from their physician first, which is a reasonable choice given that several physical disorders can cause pain during sex. Technically, this diagnosis is not applied if the pain is due to a medical or psychiatric condition. This requirement is parallel to the diagnostic criteria for other sexual dysfunctions. The origin of this exclusion dates back to the time when sexual dysfunctions were thought to be psychogenic—that is, due to psychological factors. However, the vast majority of dyspareunia cases are due to medical factors, many of which can be corrected (Leiblum, 2000)

In contrast to dyspareunia, psychological and sociocultural factors appear to play a significant role in vaginismus. Factors associated with vaginismus include sexual abuse and trauma, sexual fears, and a negative psychosexual upbringing that may increase sexual guilt (Becker et al., 1986; Leiblum, 2000; Leiblum et al., 1989).

Check Yourself 11.3

Causes of Sexual Dysfunction

1. What are some of the biological factors that contribute to sexual dysfunctions?

2. What are some of the psychological factors that contribute to sexual dysfunctions?

3. What are some of the sociocultural factors that contribute to sexual dysfunctions?

Ponder this . . . *Given that day-to-day stress may decrease sexual desire, how might a young couple maintain an active and fulfilling sex life in the face of multiple demands on their time and energy?*

TREATING SEXUAL DYSFUNCTION

The discussion of psychological treatments for sexual dysfunction is divided into historical and modern approaches, because in the 1970s there was a dramatic shift in philosophy and procedures (Masters & Johnson, 1970). Several newer biological treatments are also discussed in this section.

HISTORICAL PSYCHOLOGICAL TREATMENTS

The early conceptualizations of sexual dysfunction were primarily psychodynamic, which is hardly surprising, given the emphasis that Freud placed on sexuality (Freud, 1963). Sexual dysfunction was presumed to be the result of unconscious processes, ineffective defense mechanisms, distortion of normal psychological processes, or some combination of these factors (Fenichel, 1945). Because the presumed source of psychological energy—the libido—was sexual in nature, it was natural to assume that psychological problems might manifest themselves as a sexual dysfunction. The treatment of choice was psychoanalytic therapy, in which the goal was to understand the symbolic significance of the sexual dysfunction, help the client develop insight into the psychological processes that created the dysfunction, and use that insight to overcome the dysfunction. Psychoanalytic treatment of sexual dysfunction was long and was generally ineffective (Wincze & Carey, 1991). Although psychological mechanisms like those hypothesized by psychodynamic therapists probably account for some aspects of sexual functioning and sexual dysfunction, there are many other contributing factors that need to be addressed. Nevertheless, professionals should always assess psychological factors that may contribute to a sexual dysfunction as part of any thorough clinical evaluation (Kaplan, 1987a). For example, sexual trauma early in life may predispose an individual to sexual dysfunction, and difficulties in a current relationship may contribute to sexual problems experienced by a couple (Laumann et al., 1994).

MODERN PSYCHOLOGICAL TREATMENTS

Modern treatments for sexual dysfunctions owe a tremendous debt to the pioneering research of Masters and

The research of Masters and Johnson on the physiology and psychology of human sexual response provided the rationale for the modern psychological treatment of sexual dysfunction.

Johnson (1970). Building on their earlier work on human sexual responding (Masters & Johnson, 1966), they introduced a reconceptualization of sexual dysfunction that emphasized the many ways in which complex sexual behavior can be disrupted. Their treatment approach was more direct and more comprehensive than the traditional psychodynamic approach it replaced. Rather than focusing on how the dysfunction might have developed, the Masters and Johnson strategy was to focus on how it was being maintained. The treatment approach relied on research on the physiology of sex as well as on such behavioral techniques as shaping.

The Masters and Johnson clinic in St. Louis was the place to go for treatment of sexual dysfunctions in the 1970s and 1980s. Couples would fly in for three-week programs, stay in nearby motels, and work every day with their therapist on their sexual problems. Masters and Johnson worked with couples because the problems were conceptualized as couple problems. The techniques varied with the clinical problem, but each approach tended to include four elements: education, communication, anxiety management, and specific techniques to address specific dysfunctions.

Education. You would think that something as critical to the survival of a person's genes as sex would require no training or special information, and in one respect, it doesn't: Sexual desires generally do come naturally. However, human sexuality is far more than just sex. It involves a complex social interaction with significant consequences. Most people are interested in learning about sexuality, but often the source of such information is far from authoritative. Consequently, the subject is characterized by a lack of

crucial information and by considerable misinformation as well. This lack of accurate information can often result in performance inadequacies. Furthermore, the social expectations concerning sex—reinforced by everything from literary classics to pornography to romance novels—demand far more than the mere transfer of sperm into the vagina to induce pregnancy.

Modern sex therapists thoroughly assess the sexual behavior of couples, looking both for gaps in information and for misinformation that may contribute to sexual dysfunction (Leiblum & Rosen, 2000). Many people know more about how their car or computer works than about the mechanisms underlying sexual responsivity. Sometimes all the couple needs is accurate information to correct a potential problem. For example, alcohol may lower inhibitions and therefore put some people in the mood for sex, but alcohol is a central nervous system depressant, which in higher doses can significantly interfere with sexual functioning (Charlton & Quatman, 1997). Physical and emotional fatigue, medications, and such negative emotions as anger can also interfere with performance. Understanding the sexual needs of your partner is critical if the goal is to achieve mutual satisfaction. Your partner's arousal may be slower or faster than yours, and coordinating arousal requires considerable information about how to modulate both your arousal and that of your partner. Sex therapists often deal with all of these issues in the treatment of sexual dysfunction in couples (Kaplan, 1987a; Leiblum & Rosen, 2000).

Communication. The key to solving many sexual problems is the accurate communication of information and feelings between partners. For example, if one person is aroused by specific actions but that information is not conveyed to his or her partner, it is unlikely that the partner will be able to satisfy the person consistently. Many of the exercises used in treating sexual dysfunction are designed to improve sexual communication. For example, Masters and Johnson (1970) use an exercise called **sensate focus,** which involves physical caresses and touching designed to produce pleasurable sensations, but not necessarily sexual arousal. As part of this exercise, couples are encouraged to communicate, both verbally and nonverbally, what stimulation is most pleasurable. Such communication is difficult for some people because it feels somehow improper. Others mistakenly assume that such communication is unnecessary between people who are in love. Sex therapists encourage open discussions of sexual desires and preferences as a way to improve the sex life of their clients (Rosen & Leiblum, 1995).

sensate focus An exercise that involves physical caresses and touching designed to produce pleasurable sensations, but not necessarily sexual arousal.

Anxiety Management. Anxiety contributes to a variety of sexual disorders (Leiblum & Rosen, 2000; Rosen & Leiblum, 1995). Furthermore, anxiety-based sexual problems can become self-fulfilling prophecies. For example, suppose a man experiences an episode of erectile dysfunction similar to Terry's (one of the cases that opened this chapter). Regardless of the reason for the original problem, he is likely to be embarrassed and anxious about obtaining an erection in his next sexual encounter. Terry was mortified and therefore was extremely anxious during later sexual encounters. His anxiety almost certainly inhibited his performance, thus increasing his anxiety still more. This kind of vicious circle can contribute to a variety of sexual dysfunctions.

Recognizing the importance of performance anxiety in many sexual problems, Masters and Johnson (1970) begin their treatment of couples with the sensate focus exercises described earlier. Couples are specifically asked not to engage in sexual intercourse or even sexual behavior in order to minimize performance anxiety during these initial exercises. More explicit sexual exercises are introduced gradually to provide an opportunity to dispel anxiety that might be contributing to the problems.

Specific Techniques. The major advance in the treatment of sexual dysfunctions is the focus on specific techniques to deal with specific behavioral deficits. This is a dramatic change from the psychoanalytic approach, in which the goal was to provide symptom reduction through insight. The newer techniques often rely on gradual exposure to the problem, with bridging exercises designed to bring the person from marginally functional to fully functional. For example, most people who suffer from orgasmic difficulties are able to achieve orgasm through **masturbation**—that is, through manual self-stimulation or direct partner stimulation of the penis or clitoris. A procedure called **guided masturbation** is used to treat female orgasmic disorder. This procedure teaches the woman and her partner how, through masturbation, to achieve sufficient arousal for her to reach orgasm. Often the woman is encouraged to use a vibrator to increase the intensity of the manual stimulation and hence facilitate arousal. A more recent advance is the *Eros clitoral therapy device,* which increases arousal and pleasurable sensations with a gentle vacuum pump that increases blood flow in the clitoral region. Once the woman is able to experience orgasms consistently through masturbation, the therapist instructs the couple on how to introduce sexual intercourse gradually into their sexual activity until they can reach sexual satisfaction through intercourse alone (Kaplan, 1987a; Morokoff & LoPiccolo, 1986; Rosen & Leiblum, 1995).

Several specific treatment techniques exist—more than could be covered in this section. For example, two techniques have proved successful for the treatment of premature ejaculation. Masters and Johnson (1970) used the **squeeze technique,** in which the penis is squeezed near its head just as the male approaches orgasm. The effect is to cause the penis momentarily to lose its erection and inhibit the orgasm. Repeating this process gradually teaches the man greater ejaculatory control. The **stop-start technique** involves sexual stimulation until just before orgasm, at which point the stimulation is stopped until the orgasmic urge decreases (Kaplan, 1987a). Like the squeeze technique, this procedure is repeated until the male has developed sufficient ejaculatory control.

Such complex disorders as vaginismus require a series of techniques (Kaplan, 1987a). With vaginismus, the goal is to decrease the strength of the vaginal spasm that prevents penetration. A shaping procedure is used in which the woman begins by gently observing her vagina in a mirror while slowly massaging it. When comfortable with this level of stimulation, she gradually inserts her fingertip and later her entire finger, trying to maintain the relaxed and sexually aroused state that had been induced by the previous manual stimulation of the outside of her vagina. Over time, a tampon, a small vibrator, or her partner's finger is used to provide penetration, all while the woman seeks to maintain relaxed sexual arousal. By the time penile penetration is attempted, the strength of the vaginal spasm has been dramatically reduced.

Masters and Johnson argued that sexual dysfunctions were specific problems that could be addressed with specific treatment approaches. However, modern sex therapists have broadened this conceptualization, arguing that one has to take into account the general quality of the couple's overall relationship, not just their sexual relationship (Rosen & Leiblum, 1995). Problems in a relationship often spill over into the bedroom, and ignoring such problems would virtually guarantee treatment failure. In a sense, this perspective integrates some of the ideas of the original psychodynamic perspective with the concepts introduced by Masters and Johnson. Today, highly trained specialists in the treatment of sexual disorders use specialized techniques to improve the sexual functioning of their clients, but they also address nonsexual aspects of their clients' relationship.

masturbation   Manual self-stimulation or direct partner stimulation of the penis or clitoris.

guided masturbation   A procedure that teaches the woman and her partner how to achieve sufficient arousal through masturbation to reach orgasm.

squeeze technique   A technique for delaying male orgasm in which the penis is squeezed near its head just as the male approaches orgasm.

stop-start technique   A technique for delaying male orgasm in which sexual stimulation is stopped just before orgasm, until the orgasmic urge decreases.

BIOLOGICAL TREATMENTS

Physiological factors clearly contribute to many sexual dysfunctions (Rosen & Leiblum, 1995), and therefore physiological elements are a necessary part of treatment. Some examples of effective physiological treatments are the use of vasoactive drugs to treat erectile disorder, the use of SSRIs (selective serotonin reuptake inhibitors) to treat premature ejaculation, and surgical procedures to reduce dyspareunia in women and severe erectile dysfunction in men. Vasoactive drugs affect the vascular actions that lead to penile erection (Virag et al., 1984). The SSRIs are believed to slow ejaculation by increasing alpha-adrenergic tone, although there is controversy about the exact mechanism of action (Assalian, 1994; Rosen & Leiblum, 1995). Such medical problems as hymeneal scarring and pelvic inflammatory disease can contribute to dyspareunia in women and can often be corrected surgically (Steege & Ling, 1993). In severe erectile dysfunction, surgical implants are used; these can be either semirigid or inflatable with a small pump (Carson et al., 2000). Occasionally, these medical approaches are sufficient, although they are often combined with the psychological approaches described earlier to obtain optimal improvement in functioning.

Viagra is an effective treatment for erectile problems in many men. Not all men who use Viagra would qualify for the diagnosis of erectile disorder, even though they may be experiencing erectile problems. Remember that the diagnosis of any sexual dysfunction in the DSM requires that the person with the dysfunction (1) be significantly distressed by the problem and (2) not be experiencing the dysfunction because of medication effects or a medical condition. Regardless of the diagnosis, Viagra has improved the sex lives of hundreds of thousands of couples (Berman & Berman, 2000). Of course, Viagra is not for everyone. For example, men with significant cardiovascular disease should not use it (PDR, 2002).

Check Yourself 11.4

Treating Sexual Dysfunction

1. What was the treatment of choice for sexual dysfunctions prior to the pioneering work of Masters and Johnson?
2. What four elements are central to the Masters and Johnson treatment approach?
3. Cite two techniques used for the treatment of premature ejaculation.

Ponder this . . .   *Some sexual dysfunctions seem to be related to a sexual trauma. How might you creatively treat a case of vaginismus in a woman who was raped and still remembers the rape vividly? You can also draw on the material from Chapter 8 on anxiety disorders.*

GENDER IDENTITY DISORDER

The diagnosis of gender identity disorder is made when a person feels as though he or she is trapped inside the body of the opposite sex and experiences significant distress from this feeling. This disorder involves far more than being uncomfortable with the social roles of one's sex. People with this disorder are uncomfortable with their biological sex and often want to change it. One of the cases that opened this chapter, Charles, was an example of gender identity disorder. From the time he was a child, Charles felt that he was a woman mistakenly placed in a man's body. He was not delusional; he knew he was male. Nevertheless, he felt like he was a woman. He suffered considerable ridicule as a child because he did not want to play male games, instead preferring to play with his sister and her friends—a pattern that is common with this disorder.

Gender identity disorder is apparent even in children (APA, 2000). A young boy with this disorder typically prefers games and activities that are more stereotypically female. For example, he may prefer to play house not as the father of the household, but rather as the mother, and is more likely to play with dolls than with toy soldiers. He avoids the aggressive play typical of other boys his age and even avoids nonaggressive toys preferred by boys, such as toy trucks and cars. The identification as a woman carries over into other areas. It is not uncommon for the boy to assert that he intends to grow up to be a woman. He may insist on sitting on the toilet to urinate and will often hide his penis while doing this by pushing it between his legs (APA, 2000). He may also express disgust for his penis, saying he wants it replaced with a vagina.

The young girl with gender identity disorder shows a similar pattern of cross-gender preferences and activities (APA, 2000). She may refuse to wear a dress and may even refuse to attend events in which dresses are expected. She may dress and act so much like a boy that she is mistaken for a boy. She typically plays with boys, playing the games that boys prefer in much the same way that boys do. This is much more than just being a tomboy, however. A tomboy may prefer the activities of boys, but she feels like a girl and expects to grow into a woman. A girl with gender identity disorder feels like a boy, expects to grow into a man, and may even express the idea that she will soon be growing a penis (APA, 2000). Her behavior may even extend into the bathroom, where she may show a marked preference for standing while urinating.

Gender identity disorder typically begins between the ages of two and four and usually comes to the attention of professionals about the time the child starts school (APA, 2000). At that age, the parents begin to worry that their child is not "growing out of this phase." The boys affected greatly outnumber the girls at this age, although this may be partly because there is less tolerance in our society for cross-gender behavior in boys than in girls. The majority of children who develop gender identity disorder no longer show symptoms by adolescence (APA, 2000). It is not clear whether the feelings subside or the children learn to redirect or ignore those feelings because of their social consequences. By late adolescence, about 75% of boys in whom gender identity disorder persists develop a homosexual or bisexual orientation, although most consider their sexual activities with men to be heterosexual (APA, 2000). It is less clear what happens developmentally to girls because detailed studies have not been conducted. Girls with gender identity disorder are harder to study, because the behaviors associated with this disorder are more widely tolerated in girls than in boys, so girls are less likely to be followed by professionals throughout their development.

The early onset and the pervasive feeling of being a member of the opposite sex suggest that something biological may underlie this puzzling disorder. How do people know as children what sex they are and how they should behave? From the time they are very young, boys and girls behave differently (Marini, 1988). Boys prefer roughhouse activities and competitive games, whereas girls prefer social interactions and less aggressive games. The strength of the individual's conviction in gender identity disorder can be appreciated if you consider that (1) the feeling of being the wrong sex starts very early in life, (2) for some people it remains stable throughout life, and (3) it can be so intense that some adults with gender identity disorder undergo surgery to change their physical characteristics and hence become able to live life as the sex they want.

Surgical procedures can dramatically transform how an individual looks, although clearly one's genes and internal organs cannot be altered. In other words, a man who is surgically transformed into a woman will not be able to conceive a child, and a woman transformed into a man cannot impregnate another woman. However, modern

Dr. Richard Raskin, who was both a tennis professional and a physician, decided to take the very public step of having himself transformed surgically into a woman— Renée Richards.

surgical procedures and hormone injections can produce individuals who can pass easily, even when naked, for the opposite sex. The surgical procedure is generally easier, less expensive, and more satisfactory for men who desire to be women than for women who desire to be men. For example, the penis produced in the operation to transform females will not become erect on its own, and the individual must rely on a pump mechanism.

Few people with gender identity disorder take the drastic step of surgically changing their bodies to look like the opposite sex. It is estimated that about 1 in 30,000 males and 1 in 100,000 females seek such surgery (APA, 2000). These estimates are from European countries, where such operations are more readily accepted and where surgical procedures for sex transformation were pioneered. It is difficult to obtain accurate figures in countries like the United States, where acceptance for such surgery is low.

If people with gender identity disorder feel that they are the wrong sex, whom do they find sexually attractive? Most males and virtually all females with this disorder are attracted to members of their own biological sex (Blanchard, 1992), although most would argue that they are not gay. Because a male with gender identity disorder feels like a female, and a female so affected feels like a male, it only seems natural that both prefer members of their own sex.

The sex reassignment surgery mentioned earlier is the most common treatment, although the high cost puts it out of reach of many people. However, when such surgery is done, it is usually successful in that the people who undergo it feel better about themselves and do not regret their decision to change their sex (Blanchard, 1985; Green & Fleming, 1990). However, the best adjustment following sex reassignment surgery occurs in individuals who were well adjusted before surgery. Therefore, it is common to evaluate candidates psychologically prior to surgery and to discourage those with a poor psychological adjustment from undergoing this procedure.

Treatments to change the feelings of individuals with gender identity disorder are rarely effective (Arndt, 1991), although there have been a few case studies of effective treatment. Barlow et al. (1973) used an intensive and comprehensive behavioral and cognitive-behavioral program to change the gender identity of a young man. They worked with him to shape new, more masculine mannerisms and speech, used classical conditioning to increase sexual arousal to women and aversive conditioning to decrease sexual arousal to men. They also used social skills training to improve his social interactions with women. After six months of intensive work, the client had reached the point where he thought of himself as a man, behaved like a man, and found women attractive. Furthermore, most of these changes were maintained over the next five years (Barlow et al., 1979). Although this is a pretty impressive accomplishment, the intensity of this program makes it impractical for most people with gender identity disorder. Furthermore, it

is only a single case, so one must be cautious about assuming this program would work for others.

Check Yourself 11.5

Gender Identity Disorder

1. How is gender identity disorder different from homosexuality?
2. At what age does gender identity disorder first appear?
3. What is the typical treatment for gender identity disorder?

Ponder this . . . *What is the best evidence that one's sexual identification and one's sexual orientation have different biological mechanisms?*

PARAPHILIAS

Paraphilias are characterized by recurrent and intense fantasies, urges, or behaviors that involve objects, nonconsenting partners, or physical pain and humiliation. The DSM lists a variety of paraphilias, which are summarized in Table 11.2. In each case, the urge, sexual fantasy, or behavior has to be powerful and to last for at least six months before it qualifies for a diagnosis. The individual also has to suffer clinically significant distress or impairment in social, occupational, or other important areas of functioning in order to be diagnosable—with one notable exception. The exception is the diagnosis of pedophilia, which in the latest DSM (APA, 2000) can be made on the basis of behavior alone, with no need to document clinically significant distress. **Pedophilia** involves sexual urges or activities with a prepubescent child. Even though diagnosis does not generally require behavior, it is important to distinguish behavior from urges. Certainly, people would respond differently to an individual who experienced urges to have sexual relations with children, but successfully resisted them, than to an individual who routinely gave in to those urges and actively pursued sexual activity with children.

There is considerable variability within the category of paraphilias. Some paraphilias, such as fetishes, are typically private and usually hurt no one. Other paraphilias, such as pedophilia, can produce terrible consequences for other people. It is important to distinguish between normal sexual fantasies and paraphilias, which cause significant distress or social dysfunction. Reliable data on the frequency of sexual fantasies are hard to obtain because many of these

pedophilia   Sexual urges toward or activities with a prepubescent child.

[TABLE 11.2] Paraphilias

Listed below are the definitions for several paraphilias.

Exhibitionism—Obtaining sexual gratification by exposing one's genitals to a stranger, usually someone of the opposite sex.

Voyeurism—Obtaining sexual gratification by unobtrusively watching someone undress or engage in sexual activity.

Fetishism—Obtaining sexual gratification primarily or exclusively from contact with an object, such as women's shoes, panties, or rubber clothing.

Transvestic fetishism—Obtaining sexual gratification by dressing in clothing of the opposite sex, especially undergarments.

Frotteurism—Obtaining sexual gratification by touching or rubbing against someone, usually in a crowded place.

Pedophilia—Obtaining sexual gratification through sexual contact with children.

Sexual sadism—Obtaining sexual gratification by inflicting pain or humiliation on one's partner.

Sexual masochism—Obtaining sexual gratification by receiving pain or humiliation from one's partner.

Necrophilia—Obtaining sexual gratification through sexual contact with corpses.

Zoophilia—Obtaining sexual gratification through sexual contact with animals.

Partialism—Being particularly aroused by just a single part of the body, such as feet.

Coprophilia—Obtaining sexual gratification through contact with feces.

Urophilia—Obtaining sexual gratification through contact with urine.

Klismaphilia—Obtaining sexual gratification through the use of enemas.

Telephone scatologia—Making repeated obscene phone calls for sexual gratification.

The popularity of fetish films, magazines, and products in adult bookstores attests to the fact that enough people are interested in such material to make marketing it profitable.

exhibitionism, voyeurism, fetishism, transvestic fetishism, frotteurism, pedophilia, and sexual sadism and masochism. Some less common paraphilias are also defined but are not discussed.

EXHIBITIONISM

Exhibitionism involves obtaining sexual gratification from exposing one's genitals to a stranger. There is rarely sexual activity beyond the exposure. The sexual gratification appears to come from the expected surprise, shock, or sexual arousal of the victim. Exhibitionism is against the law. When caught, many exhibitionists argue that they were just urinating outside because they could not find a convenient restroom. Exhibitionism generally develops early, usually during adolescence or early adulthood (APA, 2000; Murphy, 1997). Onset after 40 is rare (Murphy, 1997). Many of these characteristics are illustrated in the case history of Fernando.

fantasies are embarrassing to the people who harbor them. Nevertheless, fantasies once thought to be rare are apparently more common than most people realized (Byrne & Osland, 2000). The large market in pornographic material related to paraphilias suggests that these are not rare fantasies (Linz & Malamuth, 1993). Increasingly, people with paraphilias are attracted to the Internet, where they can find pictures, stories, and movies depicting their sexual desires and can discuss their interests anonymously with hundreds or thousands of people with similar interests (Leiblum, 1997).

People with paraphilias are rarely seen in clinical settings (APA, 2000). Paraphilias that have potential legal consequences, such as voyeurism, exhibitionism, and pedophilia, are more likely to be seen in a clinical sample, but even these cases are uncommon. Paraphilias are much more common in men than in women, with the exception of sexual masochism (APA, 2000; Arndt, 1991; Laws & O'Donohue, 1997). This section covers the paraphilias of

Driven to Expose Himself

To look at him, you would never know that every cop in the precinct knew of Fernando and his "exploits." To put it bluntly, Fernando was a flasher. About twice a month an uncontrollable

exhibitionism Obtaining sexual gratification from exposing one's genitals to a stranger.

urge would come over him, and he would roam the streets or ride buses looking for targets. His favorite targets were older women or high school girls. He never wore the traditional trench coat of the exhibitionist, and at 22, he did not look like the stereotype of a dirty old man. His method was either to urinate on the street or to masturbate on the bus in full view of his target, hoping to shock her. Once or twice a year, the police would knock on his door because someone had complained. They would take him to the station and hold him for an hour or two, but they always let him go with a warning. Fernando wished he could control his exhibitionism, but the urges always returned and he could never resist them.

Most exhibitionists are male and most victims are female or children (MacDonald, 1973; Murphy, 1997), although there are a few rare cases of female exhibitionists (Freund, 1990; Grob, 1985). More than half of exhibitionists are married, and there appears to be no difference in education, intelligence, or occupation between exhibitionists and other males (Blair & Lanyon, 1981). The base rate of exhibitionism is unknown (Murphy, 1997). Judging by the number of women who report being victimized, it is probably not rare, although it may be that a small number of exhibitionists account for a large number of the reported incidents. Roughly a third of college women and almost half of middle-aged women have experienced at least one episode of a man exposing himself (Cox & MacMahon, 1978; Gittleson et al., 1978). Fewer than 20% of exhibitionist incidents are reported (Cox & Maletzky, 1980).

VOYEURISM

Voyeurism involves attempts to observe unsuspecting people who are naked, undressing, or engaged in sexual activity. The terms *peeping Toms* and *peepers* are sometimes used to describe voyeurs; the first is a reference to the shopkeeper named Tom who watched Lady Godiva ride naked through the streets. Voyeurs want to observe activity that is normally private (dressing, bathing, sexual activity) without the knowledge and consent of the individual(s) being watched. They typically report experiencing little satisfaction from observing strip shows or pornographic movies, apparently because the "victims" are both aware of being observed and willing to be observed (Kaplan & Krueger, 1997). The sexual gratification derived from voyeurism appears to be in the act of looking; rarely is there a desire for actual sexual contact. Voyeurs may fantasize about contact with the people they observe, but they are seldom motivated to seek such contact. Masturbation, either during the voyeuristic activity or while remembering it later, is common. Voyeurism typically begins during early adolescence and is

voyeurism Obtaining sexual gratification from observing unsuspecting people who are naked, undressing, or engaged in sexual activity.

remarkably stable over a lifetime (APA, 2000). In severe cases, voyeurism is the exclusive sexual activity of the individual, but many voyeurs appear to be normal in every other way. These characteristics are illustrated in the case of Matt.

Always an Eye Out

MATT

Matt could not remember a time when he was not a voyeur. He would peep into his family's bathroom in his early teens while his mother or sister was taking a bath. He bought a pair of binoculars in early high school so that he could look into several nearby houses from his attic windows. By late high school, he would wander nearby neighborhoods, looking for windows to peep in. An honors student, he was terrified of getting caught but could not stop himself. Even as an adult, he had a strong desire to spy on unsuspecting women. Married with two children, he selected as his den the room that provided the best view of five different houses in the neighborhood. He thought seriously of installing hidden surveillance equipment in some rental property he owned, but he decided the risk was too great. When his desire to peep was high, he tried several "diversionary tactics," such as making love to his wife or visiting a local strip club, but these strategies never worked. For a while, he found that peep cameras on the Internet satisfied his craving, but that worked only for a couple of months. At age 46, he still sat in his pitch black den at midnight one or two nights a week, his camera and telephoto lens mounted on a tripod in front of him, hoping that one of his neighbors' wives or older daughters would undress without bothering to pull the shade.

The prevalence of voyeurism is unknown and would be difficult to determine because most voyeurs are secretive about their activities (Kaplan & Krueger, 1997). Arrest records are of little value because most voyeurs are not caught, and when they *are* caught, they are charged with offenses like trespassing or loitering. Most voyeurs appear to be male (Finkelhor, 1986). The compulsive nature of voyeurism has led some to speculate that it might be a variation of OCD (Rinehart & McCabe, 1998). Drugs that are effective with OCD have shown some promise in treating voyeurism, although no controlled clinical trials have been conducted (Abouesh & Clayton, 1999; Emmanuel et al., 1991). Voyeurs who come into contact with law enforcement, which is of course a biased sample, have above average risk for other paraphilias, come disproportionately from dysfunctional families, and show poor social and sexual skills and low self-esteem (Abel et al., 1985; Bradford et al., 1992). However, most of the people in forensic samples were identified *because* they had committed some other sexual offense, so it is not surprising to find comorbidity in such a sample. Furthermore, such forensic samples are probably biased in several ways, so one should not accept these clinical descriptions too readily.

FETISHISM

A **fetish** is a fascination with an object—usually a nonliving object—from which the individual receives sexual gratification through contact or fantasy. The contact may include handling, rubbing, or smelling the object. Typical fetish objects are women's undergarments, stockings, shoes or boots, and leather or rubber clothing. In severe cases, the fetish can become essential for sexual gratification. When primary gratification comes from wearing the articles, the diagnosis is transvestic fetishism, which is discussed in the next section. Fetishism usually begins by adolescence and is remarkably stable over time (APA, 2000). Most societies tolerate fetishists, provided that they do not infringe on the rights of others (Mason, 1997). Fetishism rarely results in hospitalization (Chalkley & Powell, 1983). However, if the fetishist seeks to add to his collection of women's under-wear or shoes by breaking into homes, legal authorities quickly become involved. The following news item, re-printed by permission from the *Peoria Journal Star*, illus-trates how a fetish can create legal difficulties. Although the person's name appeared in the article, his last name is deleted in the version below.

It Won't Play in Peoria

Joseph had a fetish for women's underwear, which would have been harmless enough had he just ordered them through catalogs. Instead, he broke into homes to steal them.

Man avoids panty trial with plea—He's given 10-year prison term on burglary counts

The Morton panty pilferer won't be striking again for a while. Joseph C., 34, of Marquette Heights was sentenced to 10 years in prison Monday on two counts of burglary and to 6 years in prison on a felony charge of criminal damage to property. Tazewell County Circuit Court Judge Michael Brandt ordered the sentences to run concurrent to each other and consecutively with a case out of Ford County. Mr. C. was on parole on a Ford County burglary conviction when he was arrested in 1999 for stealing women's panties from a laundry room at a Morton apartment complex.

Mr. C. pleaded guilty to the panties charges Monday—the day his jury trial was scheduled to begin. . . . On Oct. 1, the apartment manager told police that after learning of the stolen underwear, maintenance workers found several pairs in the furnace rooms of several buildings at the complex. The workers also discovered holes in several doors from the laundry rooms into the furnace rooms and holes in the walls. Later, more holes in the drywall were found, and more underwear was found in a crawl space by a laundry room. Surveillance equipment was installed in one of the buildings. On Nov. 14, the surveillance alarm was triggered and police arrested Mr. C. exiting the building. Mr. C. admitted entering the apartment complex, taking clean underwear from dryers and damaging the doors, according to court records.

Source: "Man Avoids Panty Trial with Plea" from Peoria Journal Star, May 16, 2000. Copyright © 2000. Reprinted with permission of Journal Star.

Approximately 11% of males and 6% of females report some experience with a fetish (Janus & Janus, 1993). Unlike Joseph, most people who have a fetish do not come to the attention of authorities. It is generally believed that patho-logical fetishism—that is, experiencing sexual arousal only in response to fetish objects—is rare (Chalkley & Powell, 1983; Mason, 1997), but fetishistic fantasies are common (Gosselin & Wilson, 1980). There is a large and profitable industry that caters to traditional fetish wear, including stores such as Victoria's Secret and Frederick's of Hollywood in mainstream retail malls. The difference between this activity and pathological fetishism is that the outfits are designed to spice up one's sex life, rather than to be the dominant part of it. The overwhelming majority of fetish-ists are males, although an occasional female fetishist has been reported (Greenacre, 1996).

TRANSVESTIC FETISHISM

Transvestic fetishism involves receiving sexual gratification from cross-dressing—that is, wearing the garments typi-cally worn by members of the opposite sex. Transvestites are almost exclusively males who dress in women's clothing, especially intimate clothing such as undergarments (Zucker & Blanchard, 1997). This is deceptive, however, because cross-dressing in females is so widely accepted that it is almost not recognized (Janus & Janus, 1993). There is tremendous variability in how dramatic the transvestic fetishism behavior is. Some transvestites wear only certain garments, such as women's panties, and wear the garments only in the privacy of their homes. Others wear one or more women's garments under their clothes on a regular basis. Still others wear outer as well as inner garments, sometimes completing the transformation with a wig, make-up, and carefully studied female mannerisms. Many cities have a considerable subculture of transvestic fetish-ists, with cross-dressers getting together regularly to show off their attire and even staging galas to raise money for local charities. In most reported cases, the cross-dressing began in adolescence and continued into adulthood (Zucker & Blanchard, 1997). In many cases, the strength of the transvestic fetishism waxes and wanes across adult-hood, increasing in intensity during periods of stress. The case of Bill illustrates many of these features.

fetish   A fascination with an object—usually nonliving—from which the individual receives sexual gratification through contact or fantasy.

transvestic fetishism   Receiving sexual gratification from wearing the garments—especially the undergarments—typically worn by members of the opposite sex.

Dressing in His Mother's Clothes

BILL

Bill started dressing in his mother's undergarments at about age 12, four years after his parents divorced. His mother caught him on several occasions, but her admonitions had little impact on his behavior. Her attempt to stop the cross-dressing by putting a lock on her bedroom door also failed. Bill masturbated while wearing his mother's panties, often putting them back in the drawer with the semen stains still on them. He also wore his mother's lipstick. Other than the cross-dressing, Bill appeared to be a normal teenager. (Adapted from Zucker and Blanchard, 1997.)

Most transvestites are heterosexual and cross-dress for the sexual arousal they experience from the cross-dressing per se, not because they want to attract a sexual partner, as might be the case for a homosexual drag queen. When not cross-dressing, transvestites look and behave normally, typically hiding their cross-dressing. Cross-dressing is reported by 6% of males and 3% of females (Janus & Janus, 1993). Transvestites almost never show the effeminate behaviors that are common in many gay men (Chung & Harmon, 1994; Doorn et al., 1994), and their occupational and social functioning are typically unaffected by the cross-dressing (Person & Ovesey, 1978). Except for the embarrassment that many men would feel if their secret were revealed, there is so little evidence for dysfunction in transvestites that some researchers have questioned whether it should be considered a disorder (Zucker & Blanchard, 1997).

Is this a caring person or a sexual predator? If it is hard for an adult to tell just by looking, imagine how hard it is for a child. Yet parents must educate children about strangers so that they can avoid potentially dangerous situations.

FROTTEURISM

Frotteurism involves sexually touching or rubbing against someone, often in such crowded locales as subways and elevators. The man often rubs his penis against a woman or fondles her breasts or buttocks. Virtually all of the people with this disorder are young men, most between the ages of 15 and 25. Frotteurism declines dramatically after age 25 (APA, 2000). Little is known about frotteurism or about the people who qualify for this diagnosis.

PEDOPHILIA

Few topics generate more intense feelings than childhood sexual abuse. This section will cover pedophilia and a subset of pedophilia—incest.

Pedophilia. Pedophilia involves sexual urges toward or activity with a prepubescent child, usually under the age of 13. To qualify for the diagnosis, the perpetrator must be over the age of 16 and must be at least 5 years older than the victim. This disorder usually begins during adolescence, although a few people report that their sexual interest in children did not begin until middle age (APA, 2000). DSM-IV required that the urges or activity cause clinically significant distress for the perpetrator in order to meet diagnostic criteria (APA, 1994). This definition excluded any child molesters for whom the molestation was ego syntonic—that is, molesters whose behavior was not upsetting to themselves. Many child molesters rationalize their activity as providing the child with useful information about sexu-

FOCUS   Politics, ratings, and sexual abuse

Science is never conducted in a vacuum, but sometimes the political realities of the real world make it quite uncomfortable to conduct science in an objective manner. Take the example of Bruce Rind, Philip Tromovitch, and Robert Bauserman, who published a review of the research literature on the long-term psychological consequences of childhood sexual abuse (Rind et al., 1998). They reviewed 59 studies of college students who reported being sexually abused as children in an effort to synthesize the findings into a coherent understanding of this question. They found that the majority of people who had been abused sexually as children showed no severe psychological problems as adults, although psychological problems of a less severe nature were common. However, most of those who reported being sexually abused as children also reported a variety of other mistreatment, making it unclear whether the long-term consequences were due to the abuse, to this other mistreatment, or to some combination of these factors. This should have

been good news, because it indicates that the victims of such abuse are generally able to recover from its negative effects and to lead productive lives. However, what these researchers got for their scientific efforts was nothing short of character assassination and widespread condemnation.

The controversy was fueled when Dr. Laura Schlessinger reported on the study and condemned it on her radio show and in a published newspaper article (Schlessinger, 1999). Journalists and commentators from around the country picked up on the study, reporting its findings in newspapers, on the radio, and on television. Even the U.S. Congress got into the debate. After a discussion of the findings, Congress voted overwhelmingly to condemn the study as bad science. It is unlikely that many of the representatives who voted for this condemnation ever read the article—and even more unlikely that they had the training to evaluate its scientific merit. None of that mattered in the heat of political correctness. Suggesting that the long-term psychological consequences of childhood

sexual abuse may not be so negative as many believed was condemned by some as an endorsement of child sexual abuse, although no one who had actually read the article could have missed the authors' explicit statement that their findings do not justify or condone childhood sexual abuse.

This is an example of a disagreement on a critically important matter—the possible psychological consequences of child sexual abuse—being reduced to name calling. It raises critical issues about how science and society handle difficult and controversial findings (Lilienfeld, 2002). It is obvious that most of the people who expressed strong negative opinions did not read the article in question carefully. You may find it informative to read both the article, which was published in the *Psychological Bulletin* (volume 124, pages 22–53), and Dr. Laura's condemnation of it, which was published by United Press Syndicate in several newspapers on April 18, 1999. Her article is readily available on the Internet. Make your own decision on this controversial topic.

---

ality, and these molesters would not qualify for the diagnosis of pedophilia under the DSM-IV criteria. The newest version of the DSM (DSM-IV-TR; APA, 2000) requires only that the urges cause clinically significant distress *or* that the person act on his or her urges. Thus it includes everyone who would be described as a child molester. This change in the DSM was not without its critics, many of whom argued that it redefined this specific paraphilia to placate judges and attorneys rather than on the basis of scientific theory and evidence. These critics argue that child molestation is a crime, whereas pedophilia is a disorder, and the two do not have to be synonymous.

Most pedophiles are male, although their victims may be either male or female. The rate of pedophilia is

difficult to ascertain, in part because it is dramatically underreported (Marshall, 1997). About 12% of men and 17% of women report having been sexually touched as children (Laumann et al., 1994). The American Humane Association's National Reporting Study (1988) estimated that there are 300,000 incidents of child sexual abuse in the United States every year. Almost 80% of the victims are female, and over 80% of the perpetrators are male. A government-funded research project in Canada found that about one-third of males and over half of females reported that they had been sexually abused at least once as a child (Committee on Sexual Offenses Against Children and Youths, 1984).

The long-term consequences of being sexually abused as a child are hotly debated. No one argues that the long-term consequences of sexual abuse are positive, but there is some question about how negative the consequences are (Rind et al., 1998). The nearby Focus box illustrates how controversial this topic has become.

---

frotteurism   Sexually touching or rubbing against someone, often in such crowded places as subways and elevators.

Evolutionary Impact

Incest. **Incest** is considered a subtype of pedophilia in which members of the victim's family commit the sexual abuse. Virtually every society has had some form of incest prohibition. The exact origins of these incest prohibitions are unknown, but two theories have been proposed. Anthropologists suggest that the incest taboo encourages people to form relationships outside their immediate family, thus promoting the formation of larger cultural groups. Such larger groups are more conducive to the expansion of knowledge. A second theory suggests that the incest taboo serves a valuable evolutionary function. Many common genetic disorders are the result of single recessive genes. If two carriers of the gene mate, 25% of their children, on average, will develop the disorder. However, the likelihood of two carriers mating is low unless they are closely related. Perhaps incest taboos, which predate recorded history, were established because our ancestors observed that the offspring of matings of close relatives were often diseased, deformed, or dysfunctional. The moralistic tone of the taboos may have reflected beliefs that God was punishing the parents for wrongdoing.

Although incest is a subtype of pedophilia, there are differences between men who molest unrelated children and men who molest relatives. The most striking has to do with sexual object preference and sexual arousal. Whereas men who molest nonrelatives prefer young children and are sexually aroused by young children, most incest perpetrators prefer older children and are more sexually aroused by young women than by children (Freund et al., 1982; Hanson et al., 1994; Marshall et al., 1986; Quinsey et al., 1979). Furthermore, many incest perpetrators report feeling entitled to having sex with their own children (Hanson et al., 1994). The case study of Jack illustrates some of these characteristics.

Remorseful or Fearful?

JACK

Jack claimed to be a 54-year-old father of four daughters and grandfather of seven who was a respected businessperson in a nearby community. However, the therapist noted that Jack was inconsistent about the details, which suggested that he was lying to protect his identity. He said he had come to therapy at the insistence of his daughters for treatment of his incestuous behavior toward his grandchildren. Jack was seen several years before the advent of

....

incest A subtype of pedophilia in which members of the victim's family commit the sexual abuse.

mandatory reporting laws, which require professionals to report all cases of suspected child abuse. Nevertheless, he was terrified that the therapist would report him to the authorities. He later confided that he routinely parked several miles from the clinic and took a bus or cab to protect his identity.

Jack admitted that he had abused two of his four daughters. Two weeks before his first contact with the clinic, Jack was caught by two of his daughters sexually abusing his 11-year-old granddaughter. A family conference was called. According to Jack, his wife and two of his daughters had no idea that he had sexually abused two of his children and that he was capable of abusing his own grandchildren. The two abused daughters, who had remained silent to protect their father, now wanted to go to the police. Jack's wife pleaded with them not to, but everyone agreed that if Jack did not seek therapy, legal action should be taken.

Jack was a difficult client. He talked constantly about his guilt, but his counselor grew increasingly skeptical, believing that Jack was more interested in protecting himself than in confronting the impact of his actions. Jack's fear of being discovered made it increasingly difficult for him to discuss things openly, perhaps because he feared that the therapist would learn enough to identify him to the authorities. The more he discussed his abuse of his daughters, the more he intellectualized the action, refusing to accept responsibility. Six months into therapy, Jack summoned the courage to apologize to his oldest daughter, whom he had abused for eight years. Her reaction shocked him. He had expected her to hug him and say that all was forgiven. Instead, she told him that she hated him for what he had done and for the hypocritical manner in which he behaved. In the first therapy session after this confrontation, Jack was stoic; in the second session, he was deeply depressed, crying uncontrollably; in the third session, he did not want to talk about the abuse or his family. There was no fourth session. Jack never returned.

The case of Jack and his family illustrates several common themes in incest. The first is that it often continues until the perpetrator is confronted. A second is that family members often hide it. Both the reaction of Jack's wife (begging her daughters not to turn their father in) and the fact that the abused daughters kept the abuse to themselves are common. The therapist wanted Jack to understand how his behavior affected his family, so he encouraged Jack to talk with the daughters he abused. This conversation was devastating for Jack because it was probably the first time he had had to confront the negative impact of his abuse. Whether the experience was a turning point for Jack is unknown.

Jack's case would have been handled much differently today. Therapists are required to report such incidents as soon as they hear of them. Seeing a client like Jack under the arrangement described above is now professionally unacceptable. The ultimatum from Jack's family that he seek treatment or face the police would have been irrelevant. His first contact with a treatment professional would have led to reporting of the case and to an investigation, which in Jack's case would probably have resulted in legal action. The reporting laws have almost certainly saved many children from abuse by identifying abusing adults earlier, but they may also have had the unintended effect of making it harder for some abusers to seek treatment for fear of legal consequences.

SEXUAL SADISM AND MASOCHISM

Sexual sadism involves sexual gratification from inflicting physical pain and/or humiliation on another person. **Sexual masochism** involves sexual gratification in response to being subjected to physical pain and/or humiliation. The two are obviously complementary in that people with either of these orientations often get together to engage in **S&M**—short for sadism and masochism. Most S&M activities are mild and ritualistic, with clearly understood limits (Baumeister & Butler, 1997). Although most S&M enthusiasts have a preferred role, many are willing to switch roles and can derive pleasure from either role. Many proponents of sadomasochistic behavior are comfortable with their sexual lifestyle and are otherwise unremarkable in their daily lives (Moser & Levitt, 1987). Their level of comfort precludes the diagnosis of either sexual masochism or sexual sadism, because both diagnoses require a significant degree of personal distress, a disruption in the person's functioning, or both.

Quite a range of activities are included in S&M, as illustrated in Figure 11.4 on page 348. With most devotees, the intensity of these activities is mild, and they are generally a part of foreplay. In only a minority of cases are the activities more intense (Baumeister & Butler, 1997). Most sadists and masochists are careful to avoid injury (Lee, 1983; Scott, 1983). Loss of control and humiliation are often central themes in S&M activity (Baumeister & Butler, 1997), but the loss of control is more symbolic than real. Most masochists have well-scripted ideas of what they want and will quickly end a relationship with a partner who

Sadomasochistic activity is widespread enough that shops all over the country—and on the Internet—cater to enthusiasts.

exceeds those guidelines (Lee, 1983). A dominatrix—a woman who caters to the desires of masochists—can be found in most large cities through advertisements placed in underground newspapers or on the Internet. Such activity is legal, even when money is exchanged, provided that sexual activity is not included (Smith & Cox, 1983).

It is not clear how prevalent sadism and masochism are. Kinsey et al. (1953) reported that 3% to 12% of females and 10% to 20% of males acknowledged being aroused by sadomasochistic themes, and more recent data confirm these figures (Janus & Janus, 1993). Masochism is the only paraphilia in which women are well represented (APA, 2000). The case of Jenáe, one of those that opened this chapter, illustrates how strong the desire for S&M activity can be. A professional, Jenáe drove hundreds of miles to S&M clubs so as not to endanger her local reputation. The case of Jerry and Jenny illustrates that S&M activity can coexist with otherwise traditional activities and concerns.

A Traditional Nontraditional Marriage

Jerry and Jenny had been dating for almost seven months before they discovered their shared interest in S&M fantasies. During a playful bout of lovemaking, Jerry took Jenny over his knee threatening to give her a spanking. Jenny dared him to, and so he did. When Jenny threatened to spank Jerry in retaliation, he told her to go ahead. They both agreed that their lovemaking that night was more passionate than ever. Over the next several months, they experimented with a number of sadomasochistic fantasies that included bondage, paddling, forced masturbation, and verbal abuse.

A year after their first experiments with S&M, they were married in a traditional church ceremony. When they entered therapy, they had been married for just over three years. S&M was a major part of their sex lives, and both agreed that it met their sexual and emotional needs. Jenny was concerned, however, because Jerry wanted her to take on an increasingly abusive dominant role during their "love games," as they called them. Jerry also wanted to experiment with other couples who were into S&M, whereas Jenny was uncomfortable with the idea. Neither Jerry nor Jenny wanted to stop their S&M games, although both recognized the unusual nature of their love life. What they wanted from their therapist was help in resolving their differences in this area and in how they handled their finances. For them, it was just a matter of negotiating an arrangement they could both live with.

sexual sadism   Sexual gratification from inflicting physical pain and/or humiliation on another person.

sexual masochism   Sexual gratification in response to being subjected to physical pain and/or humiliation.

S&M   Sadism and masochism.

[FIGURE 11.4]

Sexual Interests of S&M Enthuasiasts

Shown here is the wide range of activities engaged in by those who enjoy S&M.

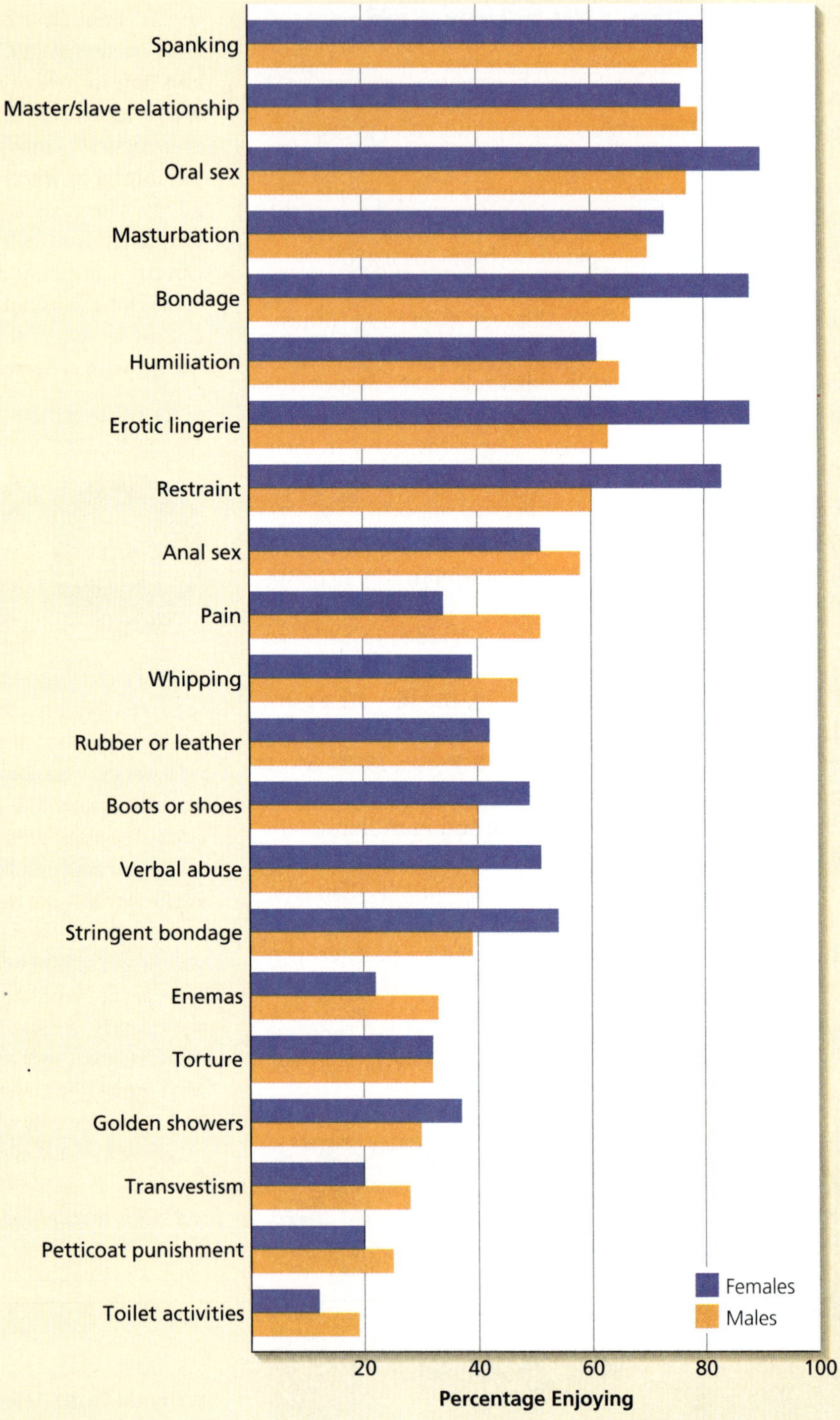

Females
Males

Percentage Enjoying

SOURCE: *"S & M Activities" from "On the Prevalence and Roles of Females in the Sadomasochistic Subculture: Report of an Empirical Study" by N. Breslow et al., Archives of Sexual Behavior, 14, 1985. Copyright © 1985. Reprinted by permission of Kluwer Academic/Plenum Publishers.*

One type of masochistic behavior—called **hypoxyphilia**—can be quite dangerous. It involves momentarily cutting off oxygen to the brain as a way to heighten sexual sensations during masturbation. This is accomplished through strangulation, use of plastic bags, masks, chest compression, or chemical means. At least 500 people die from hypoxyphilia each year in the United States alone (O'Halloran & Dietz, 1993).

At one time, sadomasochistic fantasies and behavior were thought to be a sign of deep-seated pathology. No less an authority on public values than Ann Landers proclaimed it "sick, sick, sick" (Cowan, 1982). Today, there is more of a recognition that for the vast majority of S&M enthusiasts, these are harmless sexual games played among consenting adults. As a consequence, there is more tolerance, perhaps even acceptance, of this and other paraphilias involving consenting adults (Baumeister & Butler, 1997). However, this acceptance does not extend to paraphilias that involve nonconsenting individuals. Voyeurism, exhibitionism, and frotteurism are much less accepted, and sexual exploitation of children continues to be universally condemned.

ADDITIONAL PARAPHILIAS

There are several paraphilias that are less common and are therefore grouped in the DSM under the category of paraphilias not otherwise specified (NOS). **Necrophilia** involves obtaining sexual gratification through sexual contact with corpses. **Zoophilia** involves sexual activity with animals. Some individuals derive sexual satisfaction from just a single part of their partner's body, such as the hands or feet—a paraphilia known as **partialism.** Some individuals obtain sexual gratification through contact with feces (**coprophilia**), through contact with urine (**urophilia**), or through the use of enemas (**klismaphilia**). Someone who makes repeated obscene phone calls would be diagnosed with **telephone scatologia.**

A condition that is not currently included in the paraphilias has received considerable attention lately. That condition is **sexual addiction,** which is defined as engaging in sexual behavior that the person feels unable to control and continues to exhibit despite significant negative consequences (Goodman, 1998). The nearby discusses this condition.

Check Yourself 11.6

Paraphilias

1. How interesting would most voyeurs find the activities of a strip club?
2. What is the distinction between fetishism and transvestic fetishism?
3. How are pedophiles that molest nonrelatives different from perpetrators of incest?
4. Which paraphilias is the public more willing to tolerate and why?

Ponder this . . . *With the exception of masochism, paraphilias are almost exclusively found in men. What factors might account for this very uneven sex distribution?*

CAUSES OF PARAPHILIAS

It is not clear what factors contribute to paraphilias, although several hypotheses have been suggested. For example, Freund et al. (1997) speculated that several paraphilias make up what they call courtship disorders. They describe four phases of normal courtship: (1) a finding phase in which people identify potential mates, (2) an affiliative phase in which people exchange glances and verbal overtures, (3) a tactile phase in which physical contact is made, and (4) a copulatory phase in which sexual intercourse occurs (Freund, 1990; Freund et al., 1983, 1984). Courtship disorders are hypothesized to be pathological versions of each of these phases, in which the individual is assumed to lack the social skills to achieve these courtship goals in a normal manner. Voyeurism represents the finding phase, exhibitionism the affiliative phase, frotteurism the tactile phase, and rape the copulatory phase. If this theory is correct, *all* men who engage in these paraphilias should be single with little successful dating experience, and that clearly

---

hypoxyphilia   A type of masochistic behavior that involves momentarily cutting off oxygen to the brain as a way to heighten sexual sensations during masturbation.

necrophilia   Obtaining sexual gratification through sexual contact with corpses.

zoophilia   Sexual activity with animals.

partialism   A paraphilia in which one derives sexual satisfaction from just a single part of one's partner's body, such as the hands or feet.

coprophilia   Sexual gratification through contact with feces.

urophilia   Sexual gratification through contact with urine.

klismaphilia   Sexual gratification through the use of enemas.

telephone scatologia   A disorder characterized by making repeated obscene phone calls.

sexual addiction   Engaging in sexual behavior that the person feels unable to control and continues to engage in despite significant negative consequences.

FOCUS Sexual addiction

Sexual addiction is similar to the paraphilias covered in this chapter as well as to such impulse control disorders as pathological gambling. The term *sexual addiction* has been part of the psychoanalytic literature for more than a century. Fenichel (1945) included sexual addiction in his class of addictions that did not require drugs. Freud (1892–1899) argued that sexual addiction was the underlying process from which all other addictions derived.

The concept of sexual addiction raises critical questions about the general mechanisms behind addictions, as well as about the characteristics of sexual activity that can make it addictive. Few people would dispute that sex is enjoyable under the right circumstances, just as eating food is enjoyable, especially when one is hungry. It has to be enjoyable for organisms to devote the energy needed to arrange it and to engage in it. But what makes activities like sex and eating enjoyable? Furthermore, why don't people engage in sex and eating all the time? To answer the first question, one must first consider the second. You probably already know the reason why you do not eat all the time. You get "full" and are no longer interested in eating. The process is called **satiation**—the reduction in the intensity of a drive when the needs

met by that drive have been satisfied. People gradually become satiated as they eat, and that satiation eventually decreases their desire to eat. With hunger, satiation is controlled primarily by the hypothalamus. Damaging the medial hypothalamus in rats prevents satiation, and therefore the rats continue to eat until they are three times normal size (Teitelbaum, 1961). However, studies with humans suggest that there is also a psychological component to satiation and that the nature of the stimulus can also affect satiation. It is well known that people who eat while engaged in other activities, such as watching TV, often eat past the point of satiation (Epstein et al., 1997). That is one reason why many diet programs discourage people from eating while distracted by other activities. The distraction prevents people from realizing that they have eaten enough and thus contributes to overeating. Variety also affects satiation, which is amply demonstrated by how readily we can find room for dessert even if we felt stuffed after we finished the main course. Do the same principles apply to sexuality? Are there brain mechanisms that account for hyperactive sexual desire and activity? Do psychological factors also contribute?

There is little evidence to support a specific biological cause of sexual addiction, although researchers may

not be looking in the right places (Goodman, 1998). There have been numerous attempts to link sexual addiction to other known disorders, such as OCD (Goldsmith et al., 1998; Hollander, 1993), mood disorders (Kafka & Prentky, 1992; McElroy et al., 1992), and impulse control disorders (Carnes, 2001b; Hollander & Rosen, 2000; McElroy et al., 1992). The assumption is that the biological mechanisms involved in these disorders may contribute to sexual addiction, although the research is too preliminary to support strong conclusions.

Psychological factors appear to be related to sexual addiction. For example, about 30% of men and 65% of women with sexual addiction reported being sexually abused as children (Carnes, 2001a; Kafka & Prentky, 1994)—rates much higher than reported by people without sexual addiction. Could such abuse create insatiable psychological needs for sexual closeness or disrupt the normal sexual-satiety mechanisms? Alternatively, could the sex drive of the sexually abusive parent and the sexual addiction of the offspring be due to a shared genetic factor? Sex is obviously reinforcing, so the question should be not why some people are addicted to sex but why everyone is not addicted. Clearly, more research is needed to understand this intriguing condition.

is not the case. It may be that some males engage in these so-called courtship disorders because of social inadequacies that prevent normal courtship, but this clearly does not explain all instances of these disorders.

The psychodynamic explanation of paraphilias argues that men who are insecure in their own sexuality resort to

paraphilias as a safer way to experience their sexual urges. For example, exhibitionists are presumed to be driven by castration anxiety to expose their genitals in an effort to reassure themselves of their manhood. Such men were assumed to be shy, inhibited, and nonassertive, which is exactly what early studies found (Blair & Lanyon, 1981). However, most of these early studies of exhibitionists were flawed because of their failure to use standardized assessment procedures and appropriate sampling strategies (Murphy, 1997). More recent and better-controlled studies suggest that there are few differences between exhibitionists

satiation The reduction in the intensity of a drive when the needs that that drive functions to meet have been satisfied.

and nonexhibitionists except for a tendency for exhibitionists to be slightly more likely to have engaged in impulsive and illegal activity (Smukler & Schiebel, 1975). Although psychodynamic explanations of paraphilias have not stood up well to data, this perspective is one of the few that has tried to explain the large discrepancy in rates of paraphilias between men and women.

The behavioral explanation relies on classical conditioning as the mechanism behind most paraphilias. For example, a young boy might be sexually aroused by a picture in a magazine and masturbate to it. Secondary features in the picture, such as underwear, shoes, boots, etc., could thus become sexually arousing by themselves as a consequence of the repeated pairing with the sexual feelings created by the masturbation. Let's look at some evidence relevant to this hypothesis

Examining the Evidence

Rachman and Hodgson (1968) demonstrated decades ago that such conditioning was possible. They paired a slide of a pair of black knee-high boots (the conditioned stimulus) with a series of slides of scantily clad women (the unconditioned stimuli). Several different slides of women were used to maintain a high arousal response in the participants. Five males participated in the study, viewing in each trial the slide of the boots for 30 seconds, followed immediately by a 10-second presentation of one of the scantily clad women. After a brief period, during which the participants did math problems to distract them, another trial was initiated. Trials were continued until conditioning occurred. Rather than rely on self-report, these investigators measured arousal with a penile plethysmograph, which measured changes in penile volume—a fairly accurate indicator of sexual arousal in young men. They found that they could reliably condition a sexual response in all of the participants in 20 to 45 trials. Furthermore, three of the five participants showed evidence of generalization to other stimuli (brown boots, black high-heel shoes). The conditioning took only between 30 and 60 minutes to achieve. It did not last long, extinguishing in 10 to 50 trials in which the unconditioned stimuli of the scantily clad women were not presented with the slide of the boots. But nevertheless, this study clearly demonstrated that sexual arousal to a fetish object could be easily conditioned under the right circumstances.

Showing that conditioning is possible is a long way from showing that it accounts for most, or even many, of the paraphilias. Some individuals do remember events that

might be the original source for a classically conditioned paraphilia, but given the inherent unreliability of memory for events from the distant past, such evidence should be viewed skeptically. The behavioral explanation also does not explain why paraphilias are found almost exclusively in men. There is no reason to expect that the same conditioning would not occur in women as well.

Any explanation of paraphilias has to address the fact that men dramatically outnumber women in virtually every diagnosis. It is unclear why this is so, but several explanations have been offered (Mason, 1997). Kinsey et al. (1953) attributed the larger number of male fetishists to males being more easily conditioned by their sexual experiences and the various objects that were associated with them. Gosselin and Wilson (1980) argued that most fetish objects are visual and that men tend to be more sensitive to visual stimuli. Flor-Henry (1987) suggested that brain differences due to the impact of testosterone might account for this difference. However, the fact is that no one really knows why males are more likely than females to develop fetishes (Hunter & Mathews, 1997).

One reason that so little is known about paraphilias and their causes is that little research on the question has been conducted. One exception is pedophilia, which is so upsetting to people that it has appropriately garnered the lion's share of research. Let's look at some of that research.

Examining the Evidence

Finkelhor (1984) suggested that pedophiles lack empathy for their victims, and there is evidence to support this hypothesis. However, Fernandez et al. (1999) found that although pedophiles lacked empathy for their victims, they showed more empathy toward the victims of other pedophiles and appeared to have normal empathy for all other children. These data suggest that the lack of empathy shown by pedophiles for their victims is more likely to be the result of a defensive rationalization than of a basic deficit in empathy per se. Many pedophiles convince themselves that their actions do not hurt children and may even provide these children with a positive introduction to sexuality (Maletzky, 1998).

There are many other proposed explanations for pedophilia. Pedophiles report frequent sexual fantasies involving children, although it appears, on the basis of their self-reports, that these fantasies have not always preceded the first offense (Abel et al., 1987; Marshall et al., 1991). The popular wisdom is that child abusers were sexually abused as children (Marshall, 1997). The data on this question vary dramatically, with between 0% and 67% of pedophiles reporting being sexually abused as children. However, these data are suspect for two reasons. The first is that they rely solely on the self-report of the pedophile. The second is that the self-reports come, for the most part, from pedophiles who have been apprehended, so such a report might be considered an extenuating circumstance that could result in a shorter sentence. Although there have been efforts to identify subtypes of pedophiles (Knight, 1988, 1989, 1999), as yet there is no consensus on how to subdivide this group. Nevertheless, most experts acknowledge that pedophiles are heterogeneous (Marshall, 1997). It is likely that many factors can contribute to pedophilia, including personality variables, learning history, sexual trauma, and neurochemical/endocrine influences.

Father/daughter incest, a subset of pedophilia, has also received research attention. There is a growing consensus that such behavior is far more common than was once believed (Finkelhor, 1979; Kuehnle et al., 2000). In a classic study of the topic, Gebhard et al. (1965) found that a majority of the fathers in their sample were strongly moralistic in their beliefs. It is tempting to interpret this observation, but such correlational data are always ambiguous. Perhaps those most inclined to feel incestuous impulses attempt to control them with a strong commitment to moral values. Alternatively, an overly strong commitment to moral values may create a state of sexual starvation that can lead to inappropriate sexual behavior. The role of the mother in father/daughter incest families has also been studied. Finkelhor (1979) speculated that the mother is around less in such families, thus eliminating a possible constraint on the behavior of fathers inclined to incest. Certainly, the mother is affected by the abuse once she becomes aware of it, especially if she feels powerless to stop it (Strand, 2000).

Very little is known about most paraphilias, and conducting research in the area is difficult. Most people who engage in these behaviors do so privately, and many hide their activities. Those who have been studied, such as convicted sex offenders, are almost certainly a biased sample of the target population. Except for those paraphilias that harm others, such as pedophilia, little research is being done and not much research is likely to be done in the near future.

Check Yourself 11.7

Causes of Paraphilias

1. What paraphilias are included in the concept of courtship disorders?

2. What is the behavioral explanation for paraphilias?

3. What critical feature of paraphilias has yet to be explained and will have to be explained by any viable theory of these disorders?

Ponder this . . .   *Why is it so difficult to study paraphilias scientifically?*

TREATING PARAPHILIAS

Few people seek treatment for paraphilias on their own. Most are court referred or are adolescents who are brought into treatment by their parents (Junginger, 1997). This is dramatically different from sexual dysfunctions, in which clients seek treatment. Most people in treatment for paraphilias are motivated to modify behaviors that have become legally problematic, and it is not clear that they would be so motivated if it were not for the legal implications. Consequently, there is little research on whether paraphilias can be modified in the vast majority of people with them. Nevertheless, both psychological and medical treatments for paraphilias are available.

PSYCHOLOGICAL APPROACHES

Two general psychological approaches have demonstrated effectiveness with legally problematic paraphilias: cognitive-behavioral therapy and aversive therapy (Maletzky, 1998). The cognitive-behavioral approach focuses on challenging the distorted perceptions of men whose paraphilias affect others, as do exhibitionism, voyeurism, frotteurism, and pedophilia. These men often believe that their actions are harmless or even helpful. For example, voyeurs commonly assume that no harm is done because their victims are unaware of being watched. They fail to realize the trauma their actions could have if the victims discovered they were being watched. Some sexual offenders lack the social skills necessary to achieve sexual satisfaction in socially acceptable ways. Using behavior therapy to provide those skills may reduce the compulsion to engage in paraphilias (McFall, 1990).

A second psychological treatment for paraphilias employs aversive strategies to decrease the sexual arousal that drives paraphilic behavior. The earliest approaches paired electric shock with pictures of the arousing stimuli to make those stimuli aversive. This approach has largely been replaced with **assisted covert sensitization** (Maletzky,

assisted covert desensitization   A treatment approach in which the person is asked to imagine exposure to the arousing stimuli and, while imagining that exposure, to imagine the potential aversive consequences, such as arrest, social embarrassment, or being assaulted by a victim or a family member of a victim.

1998). In this approach, the person is asked to imagine exposure to the arousing stimuli and, while imagining that exposure, to imagine the potential aversive consequences, such as arrest, social embarrassment, or being assaulted by a victim or a family member of a victim. This pairing of the thought of aversive real-life consequences with the sexually arousing stimuli is reinforced by pairing with a foul odor, which is more effective than electric shock in enhancing this aversive conditioning. Of course, aversive conditioning is controversial—all the more so because most of the people who are seeking treatment for paraphilias are there because treatment has been mandated by the courts. Nonetheless, for those who are motivated to change their behavior, this is a strategy with demonstrated effectiveness.

BIOLOGICAL APPROACHES

Two biological treatment approaches show promise with paraphilias: antiandrogen therapy and antidepressant therapy (Krueger & Kaplan, 1997). The antiandrogen approach uses drugs that reduce the level of testosterone, the male sexual hormone. Reducing this hormone decreases sexual arousal and thus decreases the intensity of paraphilias that are driven by such sexual arousal (Bradford, 1985; Bradford & Pawlak, 1993; Cooper, 1986). Although generally effective, this approach decreases sex drive and can produce such side effects as weight gain, migraine headaches, leg cramps, hypertension, gastrointestinal problems, gallstones, and diabetes.

SSRIs have also shown promise in the treatment of paraphilias (Kafka, 1991; Kruesi et al., 1992). The logic of using SSRIs to treat paraphilias is that many paraphilias have an obsessive-compulsive quality (Krueger & Kaplan, 1997), and SSRIs are effective in treating OCD. Treating paraphilias with SSRIs has the added advantage that these drugs often lower sex drive (Krueger & Kaplan, 1997).

For individuals with paraphilias who want to change their behavior, several approaches are effective. However, most people with paraphilias are apparently unmotivated to change, and with at least some of the paraphilias, there is no societal need for the person to change. There is a growing tolerance of paraphilias that involve consenting adults, and this makes treatment less of an issue. However, when the rights of others are in conflict with the sexual urges of individuals, there will continue to be a demand to treat or incarcerate the offender.

Check Yourself 11.8

Treating Paraphilias

1. What psychological treatments are effective with paraphilias?
2. What medical treatments are effective with paraphilias?

3. What nontreatment issues complicate the treatment of paraphilias?

Ponder this . . . *What are the ethical, professional, and personal implications of court-mandated treatment for a paraphilia?*

RAPE

Rape involves sexual intercourse with a nonconsenting partner. The law distinguishes two types of rape. **Forcible rape** involves sexual intercourse with an adult, coerced through violence or the threat of violence. **Statutory rape** involves sexual intercourse between an adult and a minor, who legally cannot give consent.

Rape unfortunately is not rare; approximately one in every five adult women has been raped (Kilpatrick et al., 1992), and this rate is much higher in some other countries, such as New Zealand (Feehan et al., 2001). Almost 80% of rapes are not reported to authorities (Bachman, 1998). Rape is an experience that leaves significant emotional scars. Between 30% and 90% of women in clinical settings report being raped or sexually assaulted (Beebe et al., 1994; Root, 1991; Saunders et al., 1989; Stone & Archer, 1990). This overrepresentation of sexual assault victims in clinical settings suggests that the assault may (1) contribute to psychological problems or (2) reduce psychological coping mechanisms needed to handle day-to-day stresses.

Although many people think of rape as an event that involves a stranger dragging the victim into the bushes, over 80% of rapes are committed by someone the victim knows, as illustrated in Figure 11.5 on page 354 (Hudson & Ward, 1997; Jackson & Petretic-Jackson, 1996). Such rapes are referred to as **acquaintance rape** or **date rape.** Many date rapes begin with consensual kissing and petting but become rape when the woman decides that she has gone as far as she wishes and her partner refuses to listen to her clear statements that she wants to stop. However, other date rapes are premeditated and involve the use of the so-called date-rape drug Rohypnol. Rohypnol causes the victim to pass out and later to have little memory of what happened. It is colorless and odorless and therefore can be slipped into a drink without the victim noticing its presence. The use of Rohypnol became so widespread in the mid-1990s that a

rape   Sexual intercourse with a nonconsenting partner.

forcible rape   Sexual intercourse with an adult, coerced through violence or the threat of violence.

statutory rape   Sexual intercourse between an adult and a minor, who legally cannot give consent.

acquaintance rape or **date rape**   Rape committed by someone the victim knows.

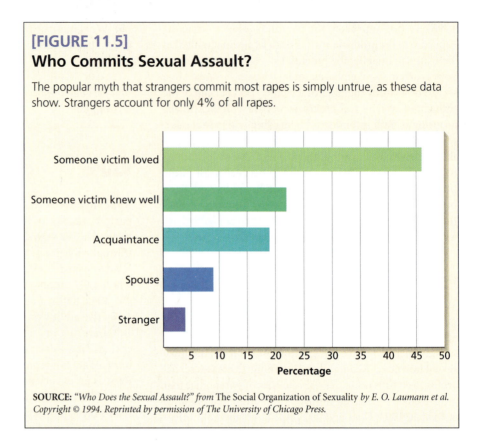

[FIGURE 11.5]

Who Commits Sexual Assault?

The popular myth that strangers commit most rapes is simply untrue, as these data show. Strangers account for only 4% of all rapes.

SOURCE: *"Who Does the Sexual Assault?" from* The Social Organization of Sexuality *by E. O. Laumann et al. Copyright © 1994. Reprinted by permission of The University of Chicago Press.*

federal law was passed adding 20 years to a rape sentence if Rohypnol was used. Rohypnol is used less frequently now, having been largely replaced by GHB (gamma hydroxybutyrate), which produces similar incapacitating effects. Date rape has become such a problem that some universities have instituted informational programs to reduce its frequency. Initial assessments of these programs suggest that they may be effective but that one-shot programs have little long-term impact on either the potential rapists or their potential victims (Lonsway & Kothari, 2000; Shultz et al., 2000).

THE VICTIM

Anyone can be raped. However, most rape victims are young adult women (Thornhill & Palmer, 2000). Women who are alone are vulnerable and are therefore more likely than accompanied women to be raped. Rapists apparently evaluate the risk of being caught and select victims and circumstances in which risk is relatively low (Thornhill & Palmer, 2000). This means that rape prevention programs that provide an escort to accompany young women to their cars or homes can be especially effective.

Most coercive sexual behavior is perpetrated by someone known to the victim. Only 1 in 25 rapes is committed by a stranger. A far more common situation is date rape—sexual behavior that starts out consensual and then becomes coercive.

Forcible rape is a devastating experience, both for victims and for their families (Foa & Rothbaum, 1998). The response during the rape is sheer terror, as the victim realizes that she has lost control and may lose her life. Her impulse may be to fight back, but too much resistance could escalate the violence. Some victims experience a rape-induced paralysis, during which fear renders them unable to move.

The trauma does not end with the rape. Most rape victims show acute stress reactions, including heightened arousal, constant fear, nightmares and flashbacks, and a serious disruption in their ability to function in day-to-day situations. At two weeks after being raped, 94% of victims meet symptom criteria for posttraumatic stress disorder (Rothbaum et al., 1992). For about half, these symptoms dissipate in the first two months following the rape, but as Figure 11.6 illustrates, many women continue to show significant PTSD symptomatology long after the rape. In addition, many women develop fears, depression, alcohol abuse, and/or aversion to sexual contact after the rape (Larimer et al., 1999; Nishith et al., 2001).

Other issues further complicate a rape. There is the possibility of pregnancy and of sexually transmitted infections, including AIDS. To make matters worse, it takes weeks to obtain a reliable assessment of pregnancy and months to obtain a reliable assessment of HIV infection. The victim often has to deal with police, hospital personnel, and family and friends. Although police are more sensitive to the feelings of rape victims than in the past (Brown & King, 1998), they are nevertheless focused on (1) establishing whether a crime has been committed and (2) gathering the information they need to capture and convict the perpetrator. They are in a rush to acquire this information, because apprehending a suspect grows less likely as time passes. In addition, the family is not always supportive (Thornhill & Palmer, 2000). The victim's report of being raped is sometimes met with distrust, especially if she was not injured (Jones et al., 1998). This very hurtful response from relatives, especially the woman's husband or partner, may be a vestige of human evolutionary history, as discussed in the nearby Advances box. Regardless, these additional stressors add to the already horrendous experience of rape.

Acquaintance rape creates a different series of feelings for the victim. Acquaintance rape is generally less violent than stranger rape (Ullman & Seigel, 1993), but the victim is clearly aware that she has lost control over her sexual choices. More than 75% of victims of acquaintance rape eventually reinterpret the experience and define it as something other than rape (Wilson & Leith, 2001). This reinterpretation can be problematic, because the person who commits an acquaintance rape is likely to repeat that behavior (Gidycz & Layman, 1996).

Several treatment approaches have been used to reduce the psychological trauma associated with rape. Some of these were discussed in Chapter 8 under the treatment of PTSD. However, there are some treatment elements that are unique to rape. By far the most commonly used treatment is crisis intervention, which is usually implemented within days or even hours after the rape (O'Sullivan &

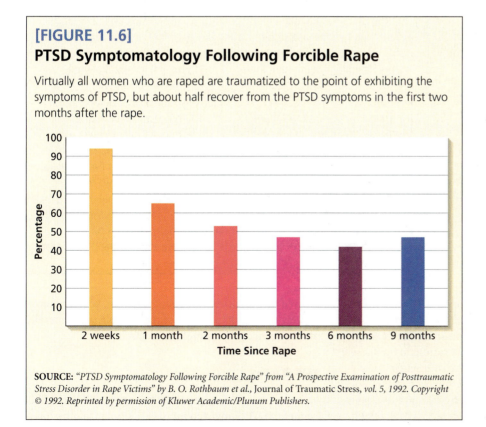

[FIGURE 11.6]

PTSD Symptomatology Following Forcible Rape

Virtually all women who are raped are traumatized to the point of exhibiting the symptoms of PTSD, but about half recover from the PTSD symptoms in the first two months after the rape.

SOURCE: *"PTSD Symptomatology Following Forcible Rape" from "A Prospective Examination of Posttraumatic Stress Disorder in Rape Victims" by B. O. Rothbaum et al.,* Journal of Traumatic Stress, *vol. 5, 1992. Copyright © 1992. Reprinted by permission of Kluwer Academic/Plunum Publishers.*

ADVANCES   Rape from an evolutionary perspective

Evolutionary Impact

It is difficult to look at the horrors of rape objectively, and yet advances in understanding and preventing rape will probably come from such objective analyses. In a provocative and controversial book, Randy Thornhill and Craig Palmer (2000) suggest that the failure to look at rape from an evolutionary perspective is one of the reasons why current theories of rape have not led to effective interventions. They argue that an evolutionary perspective provides clear explanations for many of the most puzzling questions associated with rape, including the following*:

▶ Why are males the rapists and females (usually) the victims?
▶ Why is rape a horrendous experience for the victim?
▶ Why does the mental trauma of rape vary with the victim's age and marital status and with the types of sex acts?
▶ Why does the mental trauma of rape vary with the degree of visible physical injuries to the victim, but not in the direction one might expect?
▶ Why do young males rape more than older males?
▶ Why do rapists select young women more often than older women and girls?

Adapted from A Natural History of Rape: Biological Bases of Sexual Coercion *(pp. 2–3) by R. Thornhill and C. T. Palmer. Copyright © 2000. Reprinted by permission of The MIT Press.*

▶ Why are people (especially husbands) often suspicious of an individual's claim to have been raped?
▶ Why is rape often treated as a crime against a victim's husband?
▶ Why does rape exist in many, but not all, species?
▶ How can rape be prevented?

Thornhill and Palmer (2000) argue that an evolutionary approach to studying rape may open new avenues of investigation. This approach worked well for the study of child abuse: Some 20 years of research had produced evidence for dozens of factors related to child abuse, but an evolutionary perspective led immediately to one factor that was a more powerful predictor than all the rest put together—that is, abuse is most often inflicted by nonbiological parents or caregivers.

The psychological distress experienced by rape victims depends on many variables, and most are predicted by evolutionary theory (Thornhill & Palmer, 2000). For example, women in their reproductive years (12 to 44) report more psychological distress when raped than either young girls or older women (Thornhill & Thornhill, 1990a, 1990c). Furthermore, greater physical force is typically used in the rape of reproductive-age women than in that of younger or older women. Both

of these outcomes are predicted by evolutionary theory, because women of reproductive age are expected (by the theory) to fight harder to protect their reproductive choices, and men who rape such women are expected to fight harder because of the greater chance of inseminating their victim (Thornhill & Thornhill, 1990c). The degree of physical force predicts psychological trauma from a rape, but in the direction opposite to what most people expect. The greater the physical force, the *less* trauma reported by rape victims (McCahill et al., 1979). This may be because rape victims who are seriously beaten receive more emotional support and because people are less likely to suggest that such victims acquiesced to the rape. Finally, married women report more distress from being raped than unmarried women (Thornhill & Thornhill, 1990a), and women raped by a stranger report more distress than those raped by a family member or friend (Thornhill & Thornhill, 1990b).

The underlying principle in many rape crisis programs is that rape is not about sex but is rather about power over women (Donat & D'Emilio, 1998). However, the evolutionary perspective suggests that rape *is* about sex. If it were about power, physical assaults would make more sense. A physical assault takes less time and therefore exposes the perpetrator

Carlton, 2001). Crisis intervention provides a combination of supportive listening and information designed to reduce the impact of the immediate trauma and minimize long-term consequences (Bell, 1995). The rationale for these programs is that immediate supportive counseling is likely to have the greatest impact on rape victims, although recent evidence suggests that there may be an advantage to delaying this intervention slightly. For example, Foa et al. (1995)

showed that an active treatment program, begun approximately two weeks after the sexual assault, was generally more effective than immediate treatment.

THE RAPIST

Most rapists are men, generally young men (Thornhill & Palmer, 2000). Convicted rapists are similar to other pristo less risk, and if the perpetrator is caught, the punishment is less severe. However, de Waal (2000) argues that both of these perspectives are flawed; rape is not about power alone or sex alone, and it is foolish to try to oversimplify this complex behavior.

Like any theory, the evolutionary theory of rape has strengths and weaknesses. One strength is that it explains many types of data with a single theory, and such parsimony is rare in science. For example, husbands or partners are often surprisingly unsupportive of the victim, especially if she was not seriously injured. Thornhill and Palmer argue that sexual partners may subconsciously question the faithfulness of the rape victim. Blaming the husband or partner for not being supportive is unlikely to create anything other than ill will. But if the therapist works with husbands or partners to help them understand that their often puzzling emotional response may be a vestige of their evolutionary history, this may be sufficient to turn these feelings around so that the victim can get the emotional support that she needs.

However, the theory falls short in other areas. For example, most rapes go unreported, so basing conclusions on reported rapes is dangerous. Coyne and Berry (2000) note that survey data suggest that rapes may be more common in prepubescent girls than in young women, which clearly contradicts the evolutionary theory. Furthermore, homosexual rape cannot be explained at all by the theory, because there is no chance of reproduction from such rapes. de Waal (2000) notes that Thornhill and Palmer do not even address the two most critical elements of the theory—whether men who rape are genetically different from those who do not rape and whether rape is an effective reproductive strategy. Other data can be explained with multiple theories. For example, the fact that rapes of women of reproductive age tend to be more violent could easily be explained by the fact that young women are stronger and more physically fit than young girls or older women and thus could fight harder, which would escalate the violence. Finally, some of the suggestions that follow from this theory would not be acceptable to most people. For example, Thornhill and Palmer suggest that women dress less provocatively when out in public, arguing that looking sexually appealing may trigger impulses in those marginal men who may be prone to rape. Some cultures advocate just such measures. However, most people in our culture would find this suggestion silly or offensive.

Looking at rape from an evolutionary perspective is about as politically incorrect as one can get, but being politically incorrect is not the same as being wrong. The worry that many people voice is that the evolutionary perspective is just another way to justify the rape of women by men. That argument is a straw man; it has never been true, and no evolutionary theorist has ever made that argument. The goal in studying rape, whether one approaches it from a feminist perspective, a behavioral perspective, or an evolutionary perspective, is to understand its causes and consequences so that rapes can be reduced and women who are raped can receive effective treatment to avoid long-term emotional scarring. The feminist perspective on rape has dramatically increased awareness and led to some effective programs. However, the feminist perspective simply cannot answer some of the questions listed above, or the answers it proposes do not fit the facts. A different perspective, even a politically incorrect one, may be able to suggest new, more effective approaches. Feminists probably were right when they suggested that the answer involved looking at societal values (Koss & Cleveland, 1997). Combining this insight with the insights from an evolutionary perspective could provide the blueprint for real progress in rape prevention. It is rare that any one theory explains everything, but new theories can provide new insights, which can in turn lead to real advances.

oners on many dimensions. They tend to be high school dropouts from lower social classes with an unstable employment history (Hudson & Ward, 1997). Their social competence and psychiatric histories are similar to those of other inmates, but they tend to be less assertive (Hudson & Ward, 1997; Stermac & Quinsey, 1986).

The reasons why men rape have been debated for years (Muehlenhard & Kimes, 1999). The best answer is that the reason may be different for each rapist. Prentky and Knight (1991) found that rapists tended to differ on several dimensions. Some of the more critical dimensions were (1) whether the motivation for rape is primarily sexual or primarily aggressive, (2) how impulsive the rape is, and (3) how sadistic the rapist is. It is clear that rape is a sexual act for some men, whereas it is an aggressive act for others. About 70% of convicted rapists qualify for a substance abuse diagnosis and 35% are clinically depressed, although it is unclear whether these factors contribute to the rape (Hillbrand et al., 1990). Many rapists have a past history of exhibitionism (Longo & Groth, 1983), and 10% of exhibitionists either have attempted to rape or have had a strong desire to rape (Gebhard et al., 1965). Let's look at some interesting research on this issue.

Examining the Evidence

Conducting research on why men rape is inherently difficult. The classic study of Abel et al. (1977) provided one of the first clues. They found that convicted rapists were equally aroused by descriptions of consensual sex and of rape, whereas most men were aroused only by accounts of consensual sex. Arousal was measured with a *penile plethysmograph*—a device that monitors changes in the size of the penis that correspond to changes in the degree of sexual arousal. This finding has been replicated several times (Barbaree et al., 1979; Lalumiere & Quinsey, 1994; Quinsey et al., 1984), although at least one study failed to find the effect (Murphy et al., 1984). Could this pattern of arousal increase the probability that a man will rape? It might, but don't forget that convicted rapists are not a random sample of rapists; most rapes are not reported and therefore most rapists are not convicted. Convicted rapists may be more violent, less careful, or less convincing to juries than those rapists who are not caught, charged, and convicted. To be more confident that specific arousal patterns could contribute to rape, it is important to show other lines of evidence for this effect.

Bernat et al. (1999) investigated arousal patterns of college men who had been selected on the basis of their self-reported experiences and attitudes toward sex. The selection measures included the *Sexual Experiences Survey* and the *Calloused Sexual Beliefs Scale*. The Sexual Experiences Survey included items such as "I have had sexual intercourse with a woman when she did not want to by using some degree of physical force (e.g., twisting her arm, holding her down, etc.)." The Calloused Sexual Beliefs Scale used forced-choice items, in which the participant was asked to chose the item that best described his feelings. For example, one item might give the following two choices: "Get a woman drunk, high, or hot and she will let you do whatever you want" or "It is gross and unfair to use alcohol or drugs to convince a woman to have sex."

Participants listened to two sexual interactions—one consensual and one a date rape—both of which had been prepared using actors. The consensual-sex scenario featured a man and a woman engaged in an obviously mutually desired sexual interaction, whereas the date-rape scenario featured a man gradually increasing the level of coercion for sex while the woman clearly expresses her desire to stop. The date-rape scenario was divided into five sections for the purpose of analysis: (1) consensual sex, (2) mild verbal pressure, (3) moderate verbal pressure, (4) verbal threats, and (5) force. The consensual-sex scenario was similarly divided into five sections that ranged from initial petting to intercourse. Figure 11.7 indicates what was found. Both groups show increasing arousal to the audiotaped sexual scenario as the level of sexual activity increases. Both groups show less arousal to the

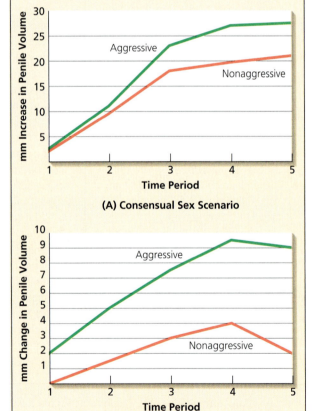

[FIGURE 11.7]
Role of Sexual Aggressiveness

Sexually aggressive males show slightly more sexual arousal than nonaggressive males in response to a consensual-sex scenario, but much more arousal than nonaggressive men in response to a date-rape scenario. Furthermore, the aggressive males fail to inhibit arousal when physical force is used.

(A) Consensual Sex Scenario

(B) Date Rape Scenario

SOURCE: *"Role of Sexual Aggressiveness" from "Sexually Aggressive and Nonaggressive Men: Sexual Arousal and Judgments in Response to Acquaintance Rape and Consensual Analogues" by J. A. Bernat, K. S. Calhoun, & H. E. Adams,* Journal of Abnormal Psychology, *vol. 108, 1999. Copyright © 1999 by the American Psychological Association. Reprinted with permission.*

date-rape scenario than to the consensual-sex scenario, but the sexually aggressive men show more arousal throughout the date-rape scenario than the nonaggressive men, especially in the final section in which physical force is introduced. These data suggest that men who describe themselves as more sexually aggressive show generally stronger sexual arousal to both consensual and nonconsensual scenarios and that when force is introduced, their sexual arousal is not inhibited as it is for sexually nonaggressive men, a finding consistent with earlier research (Lohr et al., 1997; Tescavage, 1999).

These investigators then subdivided the sexually aggressive men on the basis of their scores on the Calloused Sexual Beliefs Scale. Figure 11.8 shows the results of this breakdown. The most interesting finding here was in the date-rape scenario, in which the level of callousness in the sexually aggressive men was associated with large differences in arousal. Such research provides insights into the mechanisms that may predispose some men to rape. Not just a high sex drive but also attitudinal factors contribute. Other research suggests that situational variables may also contribute. For example, Bernat et al. (1998) found that belief that the couple had consumed alcohol acted as a permissive cue for sexually aggressive men but not for sexually nonaggressive men—that is, only sexually aggressive men considered force more justifiable if the couple had been drinking.

[FIGURE 11.8]
Role of Callous Sexual Beliefs

Sexually aggressive men who also have calloused sexual beliefs show the greatest sexual arousal in response to the date-rape scenario. Presumably, they would be the most likely to commit a date rape.

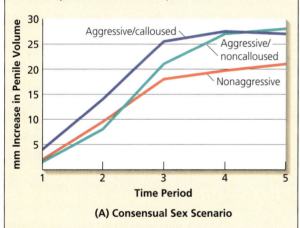

(A) Consensual Sex Scenario

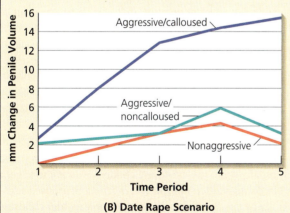

(B) Date Rape Scenario

SOURCE: *"Role of Callous Sexual Beliefs"* from *"Sexually Aggressive and Nonaggressive Men: Sexual Arousal and Judgments in Response to Acquaintance Rape and Consensual Analogues"* by J. A. Bernat, K. S. Calhoun, & H. E. Adams, *Journal of Abnormal Psychology, vol. 108, 1999. Copyright © 1999 by the American Psychological Association. Reprinted with permission.*

Preventing rapes can be addressed from several perspectives. One can seek to capture rapists and either imprison them or treat them to reduce the risk of future rape. One can modify laws to increase their deterrent value. One can develop other deterrents, such as a national DNA databank of sex offenders to provide positive identification of repeat rapists. Finally, as discussed in the previous section, one can decrease the opportunity for rape by increasing security for those most vulnerable to rape. This section will deal with efforts aimed at the rapist.

Treating rapists is difficult at best, and its effectiveness is questionable. Biological treatments to reduce sex drive, coupled with cognitive therapy to challenge rape impulses, appear to be the best approach, showing a modest reduction in recidivism in convicted rapists (Hanson & Bussiere, 1998). However, most rapists deny responsibility for their crime even when the evidence is overwhelming (Ward et al., 1997). Furthermore, they often lack empathy for their victims (Rice et al., 1994). Many show signs of antisocial personality disorder, which will be covered in Chapter 12. People who deny their responsibility and are unable to grasp the devastating consequences that their actions have had on others are not good candidates for treatment. However, young men commit most rapes (Thornhill & Palmer, 2000), and therefore time behind bars may be as effective a treatment as any other program. Men who may have had a high propensity to rape at age 25 are less likely to rape at age 40. Finally, the actions of most rapists suggest that they are concerned about the risks associated with their behavior, so increasing those risks may decrease the frequency of rape. Aggressive and effective legal enforcement of existing laws, increased surveillance to decrease the vulnerability of individual women, and supportive environments to facilitate the cooperation of victims in apprehending and prosecuting rapists would probably go a long way toward decreasing the risk of rape. Realistically, however, rape has been around much longer than recorded history. There have always been consequences to the rapists, who in an earlier time might well be killed in vengeance by relatives of the victim. Yet rape persists. Rape is not an invention of modern society, although perhaps modern society is better equipped than any other generation to make a difference.

Check Yourself 11.9

Rape

1. Define forcible rape, statutory rape, and acquaintance rape.

2. Who is most likely to rape, and who is most likely to be raped?

3. What factors predict sexual arousal in response to a date-rape scenario?

Ponder this . . . *How could the evolutionary explanation of rape contribute to the design of rape prevention programs?*

SUMMARY

HUMAN SEXUALITY

- Human sexuality is critical to the perpetuation of one's genes. Males and females have probably evolved different sexual behaviors because the optimal strategy for passing on one's genes is different in men and women. Evolutionary sexual drives are modified by cultural norms and prohibitions.

SEXUAL DYSFUNCTION

- The work of Masters and Johnson on human sexuality helped to identify specific sexual dysfunctions and to pave the way for effective behavioral treatments.
- Sexual desire disorders, characterized by a deficiency in the desire for sexual contact, include hypoactive sexual desire and sexual aversion disorder.
- The sexual arousal disorders reflect problems in the preparatory aspects of a sexual response. Included in this category are female arousal disorder and male erectile disorder.
- Orgasmic disorders are characterized by an inability to obtain an orgasm from a reasonable level and amount of sexual stimulation. Included in this category are female orgasmic disorder, male orgasmic disorder, and premature ejaculation.
- Sexual pain disorders involve genital pain during sexual intercourse. Included in this category are dyspareunia and vaginismus.

CAUSES OF SEXUAL DYSFUNCTION

- Sexual trauma, relationship problems, drugs, health problems, and such negative emotions as anger and anxiety can cause desire and arousal problems. Medical problems, drugs, and excessive sensitivity to sympathetic arousal can cause orgasmic disorders. Premature ejaculation may simply be due to excessive sensitivity of the penis. Most pain disorders are the result of medical problems, many of which can be corrected surgically.

TREATING SEXUAL DYSFUNCTION

- Prior to Masters and Johnson, sexual dysfunctions were treated with insight-oriented therapy. The current approach is to treat the dysfunction directly with behavior therapy and information. Specific techniques have been developed to treat each of the sexual dysfunctions. Modern sex therapists also address nonsexual relationship problems.

GENDER IDENTITY DISORDER

- Gender identity disorder involves feeling as though one is a member of the opposite sex and wanting to be the other sex. It usually develops in the first four years of life and can remain very stable. Some adults with this disorder undergo sex reassignment surgery to change their physical appearance.

PARAPHILIAS

- Paraphilias involve obtaining sexual gratification from an unusual source or activity. To qualify for the diagnosis, the person must experience significant distress or impairment from the activity. Included under the category of paraphilias are exhibitionism, voyeurism, fetishism, transvestic fetishism, frotteurism, pedophilia, sexual sadism, and sexual masochism. There is also a category of less common paraphilias, which is listed in the DSM as paraphilias NOS (not otherwise specified). Most people with paraphilias are men.
- Pedophiles tend to be sexually aroused by children and usually try to molest young children who are strangers. In contrast, incest perpetrators are more aroused sexually by young adults and tend to molest older children.

CAUSES OF PARAPHILIAS

- Very little is known about the causes of paraphilias. Psychodynamic and behavioral explanations clearly fall short in accounting for all paraphilias. The most striking issue that any theory of paraphilias must address is why most people with these disorders are men.

TREATING PARAPHILIAS

- There is a question of whether most paraphilic activity needs to be treated if it includes only consenting adults. For those paraphilias that do require treatment, cognitive-behavioral approaches and aversive conditioning hold some promise, as does drug treatment with antiandogen or antidepressant medications.

RAPE

- Rape includes forcible rape, statutory rape, and acquaintance rape. Men commit most rapes, and women are usually the victims. The impact of rape on the victim can be devastating. Most women meet the symptom requirements for PTSD in the first two weeks after a rape, and about half of rape victims still meet those criteria after several months.

 ## KEY TERMS

acquaintance rape or date rape   (353)
appetitive stage   (328)
assisted covert desensitization   (352)
coprophilia   (349)
dyspareunia   (333)
ego dystonic homosexuality   (327)
excitement stage   (328)
exhibitionism   (341)
female orgasmic disorder   (332)
female sexual arousal disorder   (331)
fetish   (343)
forcible rape (353)
frotteurism   (344)
gender identity disorder   (324)
guided masturbation   (337)
homosexuality   (327)
hypoactive sexual desire disorder   (330)
hypoxyphilia   (349)
incest   (346)
klismaphilia   (349)
male erectile disorder   (331)
male orgasmic disorder   (332)
masturbation   (337)
necrophilia   (349)
orgasm   (328)
orgasmic disorders   (332)
paraphilia   (324)
partialism   (349)

pedophilia   (340)
penile plethysmograph   (329)
plateau stage   (328)
premature ejaculation   (332)
rape   (353)
resolution   (328)
refractory period   (328)
S&M   (347)
satiation   (350)
sensate focus   (336)
sexual addiction   (349)
sexual aversion disorder   (330)
sexual arousal disorders   (331)
sexual desire disorders   (330)
sexual dysfunction   (324)
sexual masochism   (347)
sexual pain disorders   (333)
sexual sadism   (347)
squeeze technique   (337)
statutory rape   (353)
stop-start technique   (337)
telephone scatologia   (349)
transvestic fetishism   (343)
urophilia   (349)
vaginal photoplethysmograph   (329)
vaginismus   (333)
voyeurism   (342)
zoophilia   (349)

 ## SUGGESTED READINGS

Leiblum, S. R., & Rosen, R. C. (Eds.). (2000). *Principles and practice of sex therapy* (3rd ed.). New York: Guilford. This book is an authoritative manual of the current treatment approaches for sexual disorders.

Rosen, R. C., & Leiblum, S. R. (1995). *Case studies in sex therapy.* New York: Guilford. This book provides numerous case examples of the treatment of sexual disorders.

Thornhill, R., & Palmer, C. T. (2000). *A natural history of rape: Biological bases of sexual coercion.* Cambridge, MA: M.I.T. Press. This is a provocative review of what social scientists know about rape, interpreted from an evolutionary perspective.

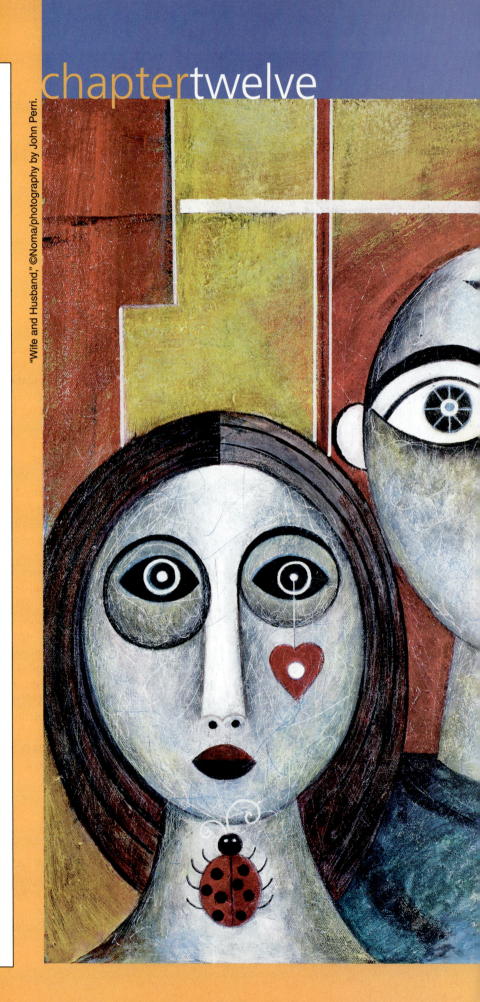

"Wife and Husband," ©Noma/photography by John Perri.

Personality Disorders

A Broken Record

DOMINIC

Dominic was a successful businessman and a recognized leader in his industry. At the age of 36, he had worked for three different companies, engineering impressive turnarounds in their profit picture. Yet the people at each company that he left were more relieved than saddened by his departure. Dominic had a well-deserved reputation for being difficult. The people who knew him best described him as moody and unpredictable, but people who had just met him had a completely different impression. They saw him as warm, caring, and incredibly astute, with a dynamic personality and an ability to win friends. These apparent contradictions would make sense if you observed Dominic's interactions over a few months. He would enter a new relationship with energy, charm, and a wonderful sense of relief that he had finally found the person or the company that did not engage in the backbiting hostility he had experienced in the past. It never took long for people to warm up to him, to feel close, and to want to interact with him, but it also did not take long for those things to change. One day Dominic would come in upset at someone for some small thing that he or she had done. The person would apologize, feeling confident that this was just a minor problem that would never resurface. However, in a few days or weeks there would be another problem, and Dominic's anger and self-righteousness would be stronger. People would find themselves walking on eggshells, not sure which Dominic would show up. In time, people either actively avoided Dominic or were openly hostile to him. Eventually, Dominic would move on to get away from all the hostile people around him, but each time, the pattern repeated itself in an uncannily similar fashion.

Always on a Stage

BONITA

Bonita was once described by an acquaintance as a human pinball at a party. She would move from person to person, making quick small talk while clearly looking for someone else to talk to. She was always nice, sometimes excessively so. She would give big hugs to everyone, dramatically saying how wonderful each acquaintance looked, before moving on to someone else. There was nothing about her to dislike, although one could just as easily say that there was little about her to like. She just seemed shallow, almost a caricature of a person. If you shared something about yourself, you had the feeling that she missed the point even when she said the right things. She was moderately successful as a sales associate in a local department store, where her friendly style was very effective. She had a boyfriend, and in fact they had talked about marriage. Yet after dating for three years, neither one knew how the other felt about such issues as abortion, poverty, education, and children. In fact, her boyfriend once remarked that he knew more about her younger sister, whom he had met only twice.

Always Puzzled

MIKE

At the age of 45, Mike felt like a failure, and by many standards he was. Although he had earned a professional degree, he had never been employed for more than three years with any one firm. He had dated only one woman more than once—a relationship that lasted about two months before she moved to another city. He had a few friends but often felt as though his friends were pushing him away. Given that he was talented, hard-working, and incredibly persistent and that he wanted a wife and a family more than anything, one would think that his life would be easy, but it was not.

A five-minute conversation with Mike would leave you with the impression that he was rather odd. You would not be able to put your finger on what bothered you, but you clearly would feel uneasy. Perhaps it was his laugh, which had a rather strange quality, or the tone of his voice, which at times was perfectly normal and at other times had a mocking tone. Perhaps it was his posture and handshake, which were rigid and stilted and yet somehow limp and lifeless. He was a nice person, and yet your instinct would tell you to keep your distance. The more you got to know Mike, the more wonderment you would feel that this bright, educated person often had no idea how to behave in social situations. He seemed to be oblivious to the feelings of others—not that he was malicious, but rather that he was unable to imagine how others would respond.

A lthough Dominic, Bonita, and Mike are all successful in some aspects of their lives, each seems unable to build the social relationships that most other people develop. You may recognize people you know in these descriptions above, although perhaps their symptoms are not so extreme. It is the extreme and persistent nature of the behavior that makes each of these patterns problematic. Each of these people would qualify for a personality disorder diagnosis. **Personality disorders** are characterized by pervasive and inflexible patterns of emotional reaction and behavior that interfere with an individual's functioning. The DSM lists six general criteria for a personality disorder diagnosis:

1. There is an enduring pattern of inner experience and behavior that deviates markedly from the expectations of the individual's culture.
2. This pattern is inflexible and pervasive across a broad range of personal and social situations.
3. It leads to clinically significant distress or impairment in social, occupational, or other important areas of functioning.
4. It is stable and of long duration, and its onset can be traced back at least to adolescence or early adulthood.
5. It is not better accounted for as a manifestation or consequence of another mental disorder.
6. It is not due to substance abuse or to a medical condition.

Dominic, Bonita, and Mike meet these criteria. Each shows significant pathology that disrupts interpersonal functioning and causes distress. Furthermore, in each case the pathology has been present for most of the person's adult life and does not seem to be secondary to another psychological or medical problem.

Unlike most of the other disorders covered in this text, personality disorders are coded on Axis II. **Axis II diagnoses** can be thought of as persistent characteristics that affect the individual's clinical functioning or response to

treatment. Although disruptive, they are often not as severe as Axis I disorders, and most people who qualify for Axis II disorders are able to carry on despite the pathology.

This chapter begins with a discussion of personality, personality disorders, and the structure of Axis II. It then covers the currently recognized personality disorders, which are grouped in the DSM into three clusters. Numerous case descriptions are included to illustrate these disorders. Finally, the chapter closes with a discussion of several unresolved issues and questions pertaining to the diagnosis and treatment of personality disorders.

THE CONCEPT OF PERSONALITY DISORDERS

Most people tend to think of personality as something that a person has. For example, people say things like "She has a lot of personality" or "His personality is obnoxious" or, more specifically, "She is aggressive" or "He is caring." But what is personality? **Personality** is a set of internal predispositions that affects the way people behave in different settings and at different times. But people do not always behave consistently across time and situations (Mischel, 1968). Rather, people are often responsive to the demands of the situations, adjusting their behavior to situational constraints.

PERSONALITY TRAITS AND DIMENSIONS

Personality traits are specific behavioral tendencies. For example, if you say that people are aggressive, you are saying that they tend to behave aggressively. Traits are inferred from observations of a person's behavior across a wide variety of situations. Consequently, they are descriptive entities only and should not be used to explain behavior, because to do so would be circular. It would be inferring the existence of a trait from behavior and then explaining the behavior by attributing it to this trait. Modern trait theorists are interested in the variables that underlie personality traits, and they recognize that most traits are really the result of multiple influences.

It is unfortunate that the fields of personality disorders and personality have remained rather independent of one another, because these research areas should be natu-

personality disorders   Pervasive and inflexible patterns of emotional reaction and behavior that interfere with an individual's functioning.

Axis II diagnoses   Persistent characteristics that affect the individual's clinical functioning or response to treatment.

personality   A set of internal predispositions that affects the way people behave in different settings and at different times.

personality traits   Specific behavioral tendencies.

rally synergistic, feeding each other in productive ways. It is helpful to understand some basic principles of personality theory as a lens for viewing the current theories of personality disorders. Personality theories have had an increasingly important impact on theories of personality disorder (Millon, 1996).

If you go painstakingly through the dictionary, identifying every word that describes a personality trait, you will be surprised to find that there are thousands (Wiggins, 1973), clearly far too many to study in any comprehensive way. Personality theorists have dealt with this problem by searching for a small number of underlying **trait dimensions** that can account for many, or even most, personality traits. Trait dimensions are underlying characteristics on which traits can be ordered. For example, the traits of kind, courageous, hopeful, mean, barbaric, helpful, understanding, driven, and hurtful can be organized along the dimension of social desirability, in which courageous, hopeful, helpful, and understanding would be near the socially desirable end of this dimension, and mean, barbaric, and hurtful would be on the socially undesirable end. A trait such as driven would be near the middle on this dimension because it can be either socially desirable or undesirable, depending on the situation.

Many personality theorists have proposed the existence of trait dimensions. For example, Cattell (1950) identified 16 personality dimensions, which form the basis of a current psychological inventory—the 16-PF (or 16 personality factors)—which was introduced in Chapter 2. In contrast, Eysenck (1947) suggested two dimensions: extraversion and neuroticism. **Neuroticism** is essentially a dimension of emotional stability. People high on this dimension show considerable emotional *instability*. **Extraversion** is the level of sociability. An extraverted person is more outgoing, tends to be more fun-loving, and is more open and affectionate with other people. In contrast, **introversion**—the other end of the extraversion dimension—is a tendency to be more socially retiring,

sober, and reserved. This model is illustrated in Figure 12.1. Eysenck later added a third dimension that he called **psychoticism.** This label was an unfortunate choice, because the dimension actually assesses such traits as callousness, lack of empathy, vindictiveness, and impulsivity, rather than the characteristics one normally associates with psychosis, such as thought disorder and delusional thinking.

[FIGURE 12.1]
Eysenck's Two-Dimensional Model

Eysenck's two-dimensional personality model (Eysenck & Eysenck, 1985) organizes personality traits according to how they fall on the two critical dimensions of introversion/extraversion and neuroticism (essentially a measure of emotional stability).

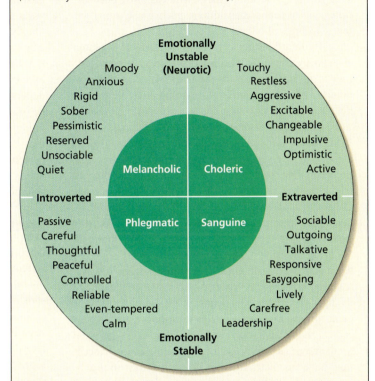

SOURCE: *"Eysenck's Two-Dimensional Model" (p. 448) from* Personality and Individual Differences *by H. J. Eysenck & M. W. Eysenck. Copyright © 1985. Reprinted by permission of Kluwer Academic/Plenum Publishers.*

trait dimensions   Underlying dimensions on which personality traits can be ordered.

neuroticism   A trait dimension of emotional instability.

extraversion   A tendency to be outgoing, fun-loving, and open and affectionate with people.

introversion   A tendency to be socially retiring, sober, and reserved.

psychoticism   A tendency to be callous, lacking in empathy, vindictive, and impulsive.

Evolutionary Impact

Millon (1990) approached the problem of classifying personality disorders from an evolutionary perspective, postulating the existence of three dimensions—pleasure-pain, active-passive, self-other—which he argued would define clinically relevant personality distinctions. People high on the pleasure end of the pleasure-pain dimension are influenced more by pleasure or the promise of pleasure, whereas those closer to the pain end of that dimension are influenced by the desire to avoid uncomfortable situations. People high on the active end of the active-passive dimension try to shape their environment to meet their needs, whereas those nearer the passive end of that dimension tend to react to the environment rather than shaping it. Finally, people high on the self end of the self-other dimension tend to view the world from an egocentric perspective, seeing what is relevant to them, whereas those near the other end of that dimension are particularly sensitive to the feelings of others.

Millon did not select these dimensions by looking at the currently recognized personality disorders; rather, he proposed them on the basis of what was known about the biological mechanisms that affect behavior. Yet combinations of these dimensions describe recognized personality disorders rather well (Millon & Davis, 1995). For example, antisocial personality disorder, which will be discussed later in the chapter, represents preoccupation with seeking pleasure, an active approach to the environment, and a self-centered perspective. Other combinations of these dimensions describe other personality disorders, and some combinations describe personality styles that are not in the diagnostic manual. Studying these hypothetical personality styles, some of them clearly not pathological, provides insights into the underlying biological processes that make up personality and may explain why personality disorders survived evolutionary pressures. The evolutionary pressure on each of these biologically mediated dimensions depends on their average survival value. For example, a self-focus may have survival value generally but may be much less valuable, perhaps even detrimental, if there is also passivity. Such a combination would produce individuals who tend to obsess excessively about how they feel rather than carrying out necessary survival tasks. The survival value of any personality characteristic for an individual depends on what other characteristics are present. Thus, some combinations may be harmful, whereas others are either benign or beneficial.

How do these dimensional models of personality apply to personality disorders? That is the topic of the next section.

CATEGORICAL VERSUS DIMENSIONAL

The tradition in diagnosis is to assume the existence of categories. This tradition is based on a disease model in which one either has or does not have a specific disease, such as a virus. Some disorders probably are categorical. However, there is considerable debate about whether categories or dimensions best describe personality disorders (Millon, 1996; Millon & Davis, 1999). A few examples will illustrate the distinction between categories and dimensions. Pregnancy is a category—you are pregnant or not; there is no

such thing as being a little bit pregnant. In contrast, height is a dimension—height varies continuously from very short to very tall.

Earlier editions of the diagnostic manual presented the traditional categorical model of personality disorders; more recent editions used the categorical model but acknowledged that dimensional models may be more appropriate in some cases (APA, 1994, 2000). If one were to hazard a guess about the nature of personality disorders on the basis of existing research on personality, it would be that genes play a substantial role in the formation of the disorders and that the disorders are likely to be dimensional. Of course, each disorder would be different. Some disorders, such as dependent personality disorder, may be dimensional, with people varying widely in degree of dependent behavior. Other disorders, such as schizotypal personality disorder, may be categorical. As we saw in Chapter 5, schizotypal personality disorder is a schizophrenic spectrum disorder, which means that it appears to share the same underlying genetic predisposition as schizophrenia.

DISTINCTION BETWEEN AXIS I AND AXIS II

Personality disorders were introduced into the diagnostic system as a group distinct from other psychiatric disorders in DSM-III (APA, 1980), although many of the current personality disorders were listed in earlier versions of the DSM (Millon & Davis, 1995). Axis II disorders include the personality disorders discussed in this chapter and mental retardation (see Chapter 13). There are two rationales for separating personality disorders from other psychiatric disorders. The first is that Axis II disorders are more chronic, often remaining stable throughout the individual's adult life. The second is that many people experience a series of Axis I disorders that appear to be caused, in part, by a consistent pattern of ineffective behavior—the personality disorder. In most cases, this ineffective pattern of behavior is ego syntonic (that is, it feels natural and right for the person), although, as you will see, there are exceptions. In contrast, most, but not all, psychiatric disorders are ego dystonic (that is, they feel uncomfortable and alien to the person). This is one of the reasons why people with personality disorders rarely come to therapy because of their personality disorders. Instead, they enter therapy because of one or more Axis I conditions, such as major depression or panic disorder. Nevertheless, about half of all individuals who seek outpatient psychotherapy suffer from one or more personality disorders (Cloninger & Svrakic, 2000).

Relationships to Specific Axis I Disorders. You will see shortly that several personality disorders are associated with one or more Axis I disorders. For example, schizotypal, paranoid, and possibly schizoid personality disorders are part of the schizophrenic spectrum. In this case, the relationship appears to be due to shared genetic factors. In other cases, however, there is no evidence of shared genetic factors and yet certain personality disorders show consistent relationships to specific Axis I disorders. These observed relationships can provide clues about the etiologies of both the personality disorder and the related Axis I disorder. For example, if major depression occurs frequently in people with a specific personality disorder, one might consider whether the two disorders share etiological factors or whether something about the personality disorder predisposes the individual to depression.

Current Structure of Axis II. The DSM recognizes ten personality disorders, divided into three clusters, as well as a general category for personality disorders that do not meet criteria for any specific diagnosis. In addition, two potential personality disorders—depressive personality disorder and passive-aggressive personality disorder—are included in an appendix. Including potential disorders in an appendix is the mechanism that the DSM committee employs to encourage research on disorders that may be included in future editions. Table 12.1 lists the currently recognized personality disorders. To complete the Axis II

[TABLE 12.1]   DSM Axis II Disorders

The Axis II disorders include the following personality disorders and mental retardation.

Cluster A Personality Disorders (Odd/Eccentric)
Paranoid personality disorder
Schizoid personality disorder
Schizotypal personality disorder

Cluster B Personality Disorders (Dramatic/Erratic)
Antisocial personality disorder
Borderline personality disorder
Histrionic personality disorder
Narcissistic personality disorder

Cluster C Personality Disorders (Anxious/Fearful)
Avoidant personality disorder
Dependent personality disorder
Obsessive-compulsive personality disorder

Personality Disorder Not Otherwise Specified

Personality Disorders Under Consideration
Depressive personality disorder
Passive-aggressive personality disorder

Mental Retardation
Mild mental retardation
Moderate mental retardation
Severe mental retardation
Profound mental retardation

disorders, Table 12.1 also lists the mental retardation disorders. The personality clusters into which the DSM divides the personality disorders are named A, B, and C, and are also associated with the general descriptors odd/eccentric, dramatic/erratic, and anxious/fearful, respectively. These cluster descriptors were included in the earlier versions of the DSM but have been deleted from the more recent versions. These descriptors provided a crude way of categorizing the personality disorders in terms of behavioral similarity. However, there is little evidence to support these clusters as overarching categories that represent underlying similarities (Millon, 1996).

The list of personality disorders gives the impression of order, when in fact there is little. Research shows that people who qualify for one personality disorder are likely to qualify for several (Dahl, 1986; Timmerman & Emmelkamp, 2001; Widiger et al., 1986). How one interprets the tremendous overlap in personality disorders depends on one's perspective. For example, some argue that personality disorders are comorbid with other personality disorders because they all share underlying predisposing factors (Millon, 1996). Others argue that such massive overlap suggests that the classification system fails to recognize critical distinctions (Tyrer, 1995). This argument assumes that the way the current disorders are identified by a cluster of similar symptoms does not effectively represent the underlying mechanisms that shape personality disorders.

The next three sections describe the personality disorders and give an overview of the research on each disorder. In some cases, such as schizotypal and antisocial personality disorder, considerable research has been conducted. In other cases, research has been minimal or has relied almost exclusively on case studies.

Check Yourself 12.1

The Concept of Personality Disorders

1. What are personality disorders?
2. What is the logic of coding personality disorders on a separate axis from psychiatric disorders?
3. Are personality disorders categorical or dimensional?
4. What is included on Axis II?

Ponder this . . .   *How could a personality disorder lead to the development of one or more Axis I disorders?*

CLUSTER A DISORDERS

Cluster A—the odd/eccentric cluster—includes paranoid, schizoid, and schizotypal personality disorders.

PARANOID PERSONALITY DISORDER

The defining characteristic of **paranoid personality disorder** is a pervasive distrust and suspicion of other people and their motives. The paranoia rarely reaches the level seen in delusional disorder or in paranoid schizophrenia. Those disorders include psychotic delusions, in which the person strongly holds unfounded and unreasonable beliefs. Nevertheless, the paranoia is significant and can be disruptive to the functioning of the individual, as illustrated in the case of Charissa.

Trusting Was So Hard

Charissa kept her distance from people for many reasons. Most of the people she knew had disappointed her, used her, or talked about her behind her back. She could not tolerate such deception, and if a person lied to her, she never spoke to him or her again. It seemed to Charissa that everyone was lying to her, that she was constantly the butt of jokes, and that people were always trying to con her in one way or another. Her occasional outbursts at work defending herself from such behavior raised eyebrows but never changed the way people behaved, with one exception. Now people did not just talk about her behind her back; some told her to her face that she was paranoid and crazy.

The case of Charissa illustrates the pervasive nature of the distrust often found in paranoid personality disorder, as well as the impact that it has on the individual's behavior. Charissa has no real friends and few acquaintances, both because of her feelings toward people and because of the way she reacts to them. This case also illustrates how some feelings, and the behaviors that those feelings generate, can breed self-fulfilling prophecies. Charissa's behavior increased the likelihood of the very thing she suspected—people talking about her behind her back.

There may occasionally be a basis for the distrust experienced by people with paranoid personality disorder, but most reasonable observers would see the distrust as extreme and unwarranted. It is common for people with this disorder to brood excessively about the loyalty of friends or colleagues. They are often reluctant to confide in others, perhaps because people frequently challenge their ideas, just as Charissa was challenged. When challenged, people with paranoid personality disorders often add the person who challenged them to the ever-increasing group of people who cannot be trusted. Such paranoia can have a devastating impact on people's social lives. They become increasingly isolated as more and more people challenge

paranoid personality disorder Characterized by a pervasive distrust and suspicion of other people and their motives.

the legitimacy of their beliefs. They typically become sensitive to small slights, which would go unnoticed or be easily forgiven by others, bearing grudges that can last for months or years. As a result, they are constantly disappointed with relationships.

Paranoid personality disorder is more prevalent in males in clinical populations (Bernstein et al., 1995; Reich, 1987), although the sex distribution in the general population is unknown. The prevalence in clinical populations has been estimated to be between 15% and 30%, with a median of about 18% (Bernstein et al., 1993a). One might imagine that this personality style would contribute to social isolation and relatively persistent stress, perhaps accounting for some, if not all, of the increased prevalence in clinical settings. The best estimate of the prevalence of paranoid personality disorder in the general population is 1% to 3% (Bernstein et al., 1993a; Drake & Vaillant, 1985). Paranoid personality disorder is found more commonly in relatives of people with schizophrenia (Baron et al., 1985; Kendler et al., 1993) and of people with delusional disorder, persecutory type (Kendler et al., 1985).

Paranoid personality disorder has been described vividly and in remarkably similar ways throughout history. The earliest of these accounts date back more than 2000 years to the writings of Theophrastus, and they include some excellent descriptions by Kraepelin (1904) and Schneider (1923). Few personality disorders have been so clearly and consistently recognized over the ages (Tyrer, 1995). Paranoid personality disorder is a part of the schizophrenic spectrum (Kety et al., 1968; Siever & Davis, 1991). It overlaps with schizotypal personality disorder so heavily that they almost appear to be the same disorder (Bernstein et al., 1995). It also overlaps heavily with borderline and avoidant personality disorders and to a lesser extent with histrionic, antisocial, and dependent personality disorders (Bernstein et al., 1995). It has long been recognized that some individuals with schizophrenia have a premorbid paranoid personality style (Kraepelin, 1921), although more recent evidence suggests that this personality style may also precede delusional disorders (Herbert & Jacobson, 1967). You may remember from Chapter 5 that the evidence suggests that schizophrenia and delusional disorders are distinct and share little genetic overlap. Therefore, it would appear that paranoid personality disorder is heterogeneous—that is, there is more than one underlying genetic mechanism.

Paranoid personality disorder is found more frequently in certain populations, such as prisoners, refugees, immigrants, the elderly, and the hearing-impaired (Bernstein et al., 1995). In each of these cases, it can be argued that there is something about the environment that increases the likelihood of paranoia. For example, prisoners need to be ever watchful, given that assaults in prisons are common. The hearing-impaired often are unable to hear what others are saying and, therefore, are unable to disconfirm suspicions that others might be talking about them. Whether the increased paranoia in these groups represents paranoid personality disorder as defined by the DSM is unclear. It may be more reasonable to assume that these paranoid feelings are a normal reaction to a difficult situation.

The Stanford prison experiment (Haney et al., 1973) illustrates how the environment can create paranoia in individuals not normally prone to such feelings. These investigators had college students play the roles of prisoners and guards in a study to determine the impact of social roles on behavior. They converted part of the psychology building to something resembling a prison and randomly assigned participants to either guard or prisoner roles. Those in the prisoner roles were actually picked up at their homes by police officers in a squad car and treated as any prisoner would be treated. All of the participants were screened prior to the study to be sure that everyone participating was physically and emotionally healthy. This study, which had been planned to last two weeks, was ended early because the action got out of hand. The prisoners developed intense paranoia about the guards, and vice versa. If normal college students can develop significant paranoia in a short-term role-play of prison life, one can only imagine what a real prison environment could do to a person. Therefore, it is wise to take a person's situation into account when diagnosing paranoid personality disorder. If there is not evidence for paranoia across a range of situations and the paranoia is seen only in a situation that might generate paranoid feelings in almost anyone, the diagnosis is probably not warranted.

SCHIZOID PERSONALITY DISORDER

Individuals with **schizoid personality disorder** show a pervasive pattern of detachment from social relationships and an apparent lack of interest in such relationships. They are often viewed as loners who prefer solitary activities. They may show emotional blunting or flattening and little zest for life. The schizoid individual simply does not seem to get the same rewards from social interactions that others do. Even physical contact, including sexual intercourse, appears to be less pleasurable and less valued by people with this disorder. In other words, they tend to show mild forms of the negative symptoms of schizophrenia (Kalus et al., 1995). In contrast, people with paranoid and schizotypal personality disorder tend to show mild forms of the positive symptoms of schizophrenia, such as delusions and unusual thoughts.

The issue of how best to delineate schizoid personality disorder has been debated for the last 20 years. The DSM committee has tinkered with the diagnostic criteria in an effort to identify a more homogeneous group of individuals, hoping to differentiate schizoid from avoidant personality disorder and dysthymic disorder (Kalus et al., 1995). Schizoid individuals, unlike avoidant individuals, appear to restrict social relationships out of lack of interest instead of social anxiety. Although clearly anhedonic, schizoid individuals do not experience the other depressive features that characterize dysthymia. Yet even with these efforts by the DSM committee, there is still considerable debate about the appropriate boundaries of this disorder (Kalus et al., 1995).

Bleuler (1924), who coined the term *schizophrenia*, also coined the term *schizoid*. He argued that schizoid individuals tended to turn inward and away from the outside world. Although people with schizoid personality disorder appear to be indifferent to the outside world, there are some who have argued that their outside indifference hides an inner sensitivity (Wolff & Chick, 1980). Modern conceptualizations of schizoid personality disorder suggest an asexuality—that is, a lack of interest in sex. It is clear that people with this diagnosis tend to engage in little sexual contact with others, but early data challenge the idea that there is a lack of interest in sex. Terry and Rennie (1938), for example, noted that schizoid individuals often engaged in compulsive masturbation and harbored perverse sexual fantasies.

Prevalence estimates for schizoid personality disorder range from 0.5% to 7%, with an average around 2% (Drake & Vaillant, 1985; Zimmerman & Coryell, 1989, 1990). The rates in clinical populations also have a wide range, depending on the make-up of the clinical samples, but average around 8% (Kalus et al., 1995). Schizoid personality disorder overlaps heavily with schizotypal and avoidant personality disorders, perhaps in part because of the similarity in the diagnostic criteria (Kalus et al., 1995). Given the name of this personality disorder (schizoid) and its heavy overlap with schizotypal personality disorder, one might think that schizoid personality disorder would be included in the schizophrenic spectrum. However, the data on this issue have been inconsistent (Baron et al., 1985). When there are no schizotypal features present, the schizoid individual is best thought of as *not* being within the schizophrenic spectrum.

Individuals with schizoid personality disorders often make choices about their lives that work for them and are therefore able to function at a reasonable level with little apparent distress. They show emotional blunting and social avoidance. This pattern is sometimes found in people who develop a chronic form of schizophrenia, with a predominant negative symptom pattern and a poor prognosis (Chapman & Chapman, 1973). One might speculate that the social withdrawal and emotional blunting characteristic of schizoid personality disorder may be, for some individuals, an effective defense against the more disorganized cognitive state of schizophrenia. Social interactions can often be intense, and intense emotion is known to increase cognitive disorganization in those individuals who are prone to such disorganization (Millon & Davis, 1999). If the genetic loading for schizophrenia is not too strong, these individuals can lead stable, uneventful lives. However, in those

....

schizoid personality disorder   Characterized by a pervasive pattern of detachment from social relationships and an apparent lack of interest in such relationships.

individuals with strong genetic loading, the likelihood of developing schizophrenia is likely to be high.

SCHIZOTYPAL PERSONALITY DISORDER

The defining feature of **schizotypal personality disorder** is an oddness in thought, perception, and social interactions. Individuals with this disorder may report unusual perceptual experiences, including body image distortion, and may report odd beliefs or magical thinking (Meehl, 1964). There may be some of the suspiciousness found in paranoid individuals, but this is rarely a central feature. There may also be **ideas of reference**—the sense that an unrelated event is somehow uniquely linked to the person, which results in drawing conclusions that others would consider bizarre. For example, schizotypal individuals may interpret another person's actions as directed at them when, in fact, the actions had nothing to do with them. These individuals are often socially anxious and ineffective, probably because of their unusual ideas and occasional odd behavior. Like those with schizoid personality disorder, they usually have few

The title character in the movie *Taxi Driver*, which also starred Jodie Foster, showed many symptoms of schizotypal personality disorder, including unusual ideas, suspiciousness, social inappropriateness, and grandiosity. This fictional character apparently struck a resonant cord with John Hinckley, whose psychotic thinking and obsessional love for Jodie Foster led him to attempt to assassinate President Reagan.

friends beyond their own family. However, unlike schizoid individuals, who often appear indifferent to social relationships, individuals with schizotypal personality disorder typically desire such relationships but often are unable to form or maintain them.

Mike, who was one of the cases that opened this chapter, illustrates many of these features. He was bright and capable, but his odd behavior made it impossible for him to function adequately in social situations, thus holding him back both professionally and personally. If you got to know him well, you would be struck by his unusual ideas about people and by his inability to predict how others would react to his behavior. For example, Mike could not understand how a potential employer—a very formal woman in her fifties—would be offended by a blatantly sexist joke. He thought she would find it hilarious. On another occasion, he interpreted a series of statements made by a co-worker as indicating a homosexual orientation, even though the statements had nothing to do with sexual orientation. When he mentioned to a colleague his belief that the co-worker was homosexual, he was met with an incredulous look and a "you can't be serious" reply. Even when he correctly read the motives and interests of people, he often could not respond in a reasonable manner. For example, he usually recognized the irritation he engendered in people but often reacted in ways that only increased their irritation. He would be inappropriately assertive at times and passive at times when assertiveness was needed. This behavior led to many social and professional failures, eventually leaving Mike thoroughly discouraged.

Schizotypal personality disorder is the most recently adopted disorder in the odd/eccentric cluster (Siever et al., 1995), and it is the only personality disorder defined by its genetic relationship to an Axis I disorder—namely, schizophrenia (Kendler et al., 1993; Kety et al., 1968; Torgersen, 1994). People with schizotypal personality disorder show elevated risk for schizophrenia (Fenton & McGlashan, 1989), but, interestingly, they also show elevated risk for mania and depression (McGlashan, 1983). Approximately 3% of the general population qualifies for a diagnosis of schizotypal personality disorder (APA, 2000).

The diagnostic category of schizotypal personality disorder was heavily influenced by the work of Paul Meehl, who hypothesized a genetic diathesis for schizophrenia. Meehl's (1962, 1964, 1990) description of people with this diathesis closely resembles the current criteria for the

schizotypal personality disorder   An oddness in thought, perception, and social interactions.

ideas of reference   The sense that an unrelated event is somehow uniquely linked to oneself, which results in drawing conclusions that others would consider bizarre.

psychometric instruments   Psychological tests designed to measure the level of a specific psychological trait, such as anhedonia.

schizotypal personality disorder. His description also closely resembles the old concept of borderline schizophrenia—a condition thought to be on the border between psychosis and neurosis. This group of disorders was tremendously interesting to researchers in the 1950s and 1960s (Gunderson & Singer, 1975). Meehl was struck that a portion of this group appeared to be similar, though less extreme in their symptomatology, to people with schizophrenia. Furthermore, they showed elevated risk for developing schizophrenia. In contrast, Otto Kernberg (1967, 1977), noting that most people in this borderline schizophrenia group never developed a psychotic disorder, argued that the concept of borderline schizophrenia was misleading. He suggested dropping the word *schizophrenia* and advocated using a term such as *borderline, borderline states,* or *borderline personality* instead. Kernberg's ideas led to the development of the borderline personality disorder diagnosis. The criteria for schizotypal and borderline personality disorder were written specifically to differentiate the subtypes defined by Meehl and Kernberg, respectively—subtypes that were to be carved out of the heterogeneous group previously described as exhibiting borderline schizophrenia (Raulin & Brenner, 1993). Examining the diagnostic criteria for schizotypal and borderline personality disorders would lead one to expect little overlap. However, there is considerable overlap; individuals who qualify for one diagnosis have a 50% or higher probability of qualifying for the other (Serban et al., 1987; Siever et al., 1995).

Meehl's (1962, 1990) delineation of the concept of schizotypy laid the foundation for efforts to quantify schizotypic traits. Many of the schizotypic traits he defined have been translated into psychological instruments, which have formed the basis for the behavioral high-risk paradigm introduced in Chapter 6 (Chapman et al., 1978a). **Psychometric instruments** are psychological tests designed to measure the level of a specific psychological trait, such as anhedonia. Psychometric instruments

provide an alternative way of studying personality disorders, as discussed in the nearby Advances box. This research using the psychometric approach is proceeding independently of much of the research on Axis II disorders, but it is yielding useful insights that will probably inform future revisions of the diagnostic manual.

TREATING CLUSTER A DISORDERS

The disorders in the odd/eccentric cluster all have significant impact on social functioning. The evidence of risk for serious Axis I disorders, such as schizophrenia, delusional disorder, and severe mood disorders, suggests the importance of interventions that improve functioning and reduce the risk of psychiatric deterioration. Unfortunately, there are no controlled studies of the psychological treatment of these personality disorders, although there is discussion of the problem in the psychoanalytic literature (this is the only therapeutic orientation that has made a significant effort to understand and treat these difficult disorders). However, case study data suggest that the traditional psychoanalytic treatments not only are ineffective but also tend to precipitate psychiatric deterioration (Frosch, 1983; Hoch & Polatin, 1949; Knight, 1954). It appears that the strain of traditional psychoanalytic therapy, in which clients must confront their own contributions to emotional problems, is more than many of these individuals can tolerate. A more effective approach appears to be supportive therapy that seeks to enhance reality testing and improve the individual's understanding of, and engagement in, social activities (Stone, 1985).

Check Yourself 12.2

Cluster A Disorders

1. What is the defining characteristic of paranoid personality disorder?
2. What is the relationship between paranoid and schizotypal personality disorders?
3. What is the defining characteristic of schizoid personality disorder?
4. What is the primary distinction between avoidant and schizoid personality disorders?
5. What is the defining characteristic of schizotypal personality disorder?
6. What is the relationship between borderline and schizotypal personality disorders?

Ponder this . . .   *If schizotypal personality disorder shares the same genes as schizophrenia, how could the study of schizotypal individuals advance our understanding of the developmental course of schizophrenia?*

Paul Meehl not only proposed the leading diathesis-stress theory of schizophrenia but also influenced the definition of schizotypal personality disorder.

ADVANCES | Psychometric determination of personality disorders

Given the controversy regarding the best way to conceptualize personality disorders, it is not surprising that multiple approaches exist. The DSM provides one way of defining personality disorders, but it is conceptualized as a categorical system, and many theorists doubt that most personality disorders are categories. Although the DSM pays lip service to the possibility that personality disorders could be dimensional, the diagnoses are still operationalized as categories. In contrast, dimensions are typically measured on scales using psychological measures. This strategy of using a score on a psychological measure is referred to as a *psychometric approach*. There are several scales that use this psychometric approach to measure symptoms thought to be critical in the diagnosis of personality disorders. Some were developed just for that purpose; others were originally developed for another purpose but are now recognized as relevant to the task of diagnosing personality disorders; still others preceded the introduction of Axis II and remain a viable alternative to the DSM.

In Chapter 6, you learned about a behavioral high-risk approach developed by the Chapmans and their students (Chapman et al., 1978a). This approach used psychometric mea-

sures of traits hypothesized to be characteristic of people genetically at risk for schizophrenia (Meehl, 1962, 1964). They included such measures as anhedonia (Chapman et al., 1976), perceptual aberration (Chapman et al., 1978b), magical ideation (Eckblad & Chapman, 1983), social fear (Raulin & Wee, 1984), and cognitive slippage (Miers & Raulin, 1985). Although these scales were all developed because they tapped traits thought to indicate risk for schizophrenia, they are not necessarily symptoms of schizotypal personality disorder. For example, the Social Fear Scale taps a symptom that is central to avoidant personality disorder, and the Social Anhedonia Scale taps a central symptom of schizoid personality disorder. The Magical Ideation, Perceptual Aberration, and Cognitive Slippage Scales tap symptoms of schizotypal personality disorder. With such highly reliable independent measures of these specific symptoms, researchers can investigate the relationship of these symptoms more precisely. For example, if these scales measure characteristics of a categorical diagnosis, predictable mathematical relationships should exist (Waller & Meehl, 1998), and this provides researchers with a method to test the hypothesis that the diagnosis is categorical as opposed to dimensional.

The relationships between the scales and other variables provides critical clues that will help refine the diagnostic categories or dimensions.

Another approach is to operationalize the existing personality disorders as psychometric scales that provide a dimensional rating of how similar the person is to each personality disorder. Loranger and his colleagues (1987) took this approach in developing the *Personality Disorder Examination*. This measure offered a mechanism for obtaining standardized information that could be used to provide either the traditional diagnosis or a dimensional score. One advantage of such dimensional scores is that they can be graphed in much the same way as MMPI profiles (see Chapter 2). Researchers quickly discovered that a small number of MMPI profile patterns accounted for the vast majority of clients, which certainly suggests an underlying structure (Greene, 1991). The same may hold for personality disorders.

Finally, you will learn shortly about an effort to quantify the degree of psychopathy in individuals with a measure called the *Psychopathy Checklist* (Hare, 1991). Researchers use this diagnostic instrument almost as often as the DSM criteria.

CLUSTER B DISORDERS

Cluster B—the dramatic/erratic cluster— includes antisocial, borderline, histrionic, and narcissistic personality disorders.

ANTISOCIAL PERSONALITY DISORDER

Without question, the most widely studied personality disorder is antisocial personality disorder. The defining characteristic of **antisocial personality disorder** is a pervasive

pattern of disregard for the rights of others. The terms **psychopathy**[1] and **sociopathy,** which are generally used interchangeably, have also been used to describe this group of people, although, as you will see, the concepts of psychopa-

---

[1]The terms *psychopathy* and *psychopathology* are often confused. *Psychopathy* is the specific pathology shown by the psychopath or sociopath and overlaps the current antisocial personality disorder. *Psychopathology* is a general term that includes all forms of psychological pathology.

thy and antisocial personality disorder as defined in the DSM are not synonymous.

Detailed descriptions of people who show disregard for the rights of others have been around for almost 200 years. For example, Benjamin Rush (1812), an early proponent of psychiatric diagnosis and treatment, wrote vividly about these individuals in his psychiatric textbook. However, psychiatrist Hervey Cleckley's (1941) description of psychopaths has had the greatest impact on the field. He described them as experiencing few genuine emotions and engaging in impulsive and manipulative behavior. Emotions such as love, guilt, and shame may appear to be obvious concepts, but they are difficult to define behaviorally. Consequently, the current diagnostic system relies on more objective criteria, such as unlawful behavior, repeated lying, impulsivity, fistfights or assaults, and inconsistent work and financial histories. These factors are easier to document than the concept proposed by Cleckley, which focuses more heavily on emotional experiences. It is more difficult to assess emotional experiences than behavior, and therefore it is harder to obtain adequate interrater reliability. Nevertheless, some have argued that the current diagnostic system sacrifices validity for the sake of reliability by excluding emotional experiences in the diagnostic criteria for antisocial personality disorder (Hare & Hart, 1995).

Building on the work of Cleckley, Hare and his colleagues developed the *Psychopathy Checklist—Revised* (PCL-R, Hare, 1991; Hare et al., 1991). This checklist is a reliable and valid measure that comprises variables thought by many to be critical in defining psychopaths, including glibness, superficial charm, grandiose sense of self-worth, and a lack of empathy and guilt. Table 12.2 lists the items of the PCL-R. The PCL-R is used almost as often as the DSM criteria in psychological research, which perhaps reflects the belief by researchers that it captures the essence of this disorder more precisely. One of the reasons why the DSM did not employ the more detailed and complex criteria of the PCL-R is that this approach is more time-consuming and requires more training than applying the brief DSM criteria (Hare & Hart, 1995).

You might expect to find that individuals with antisocial personality disorder are overrepresented in prison populations because their attitudes and behaviors often get them into trouble with the law. In fact, this is true (Hare, 1980, 1983); people with antisocial personality disorder are several times more common in prisons than one would expect by chance. However, many people in prison do not qualify for the diagnosis of antisocial personality disorder, and many people who have this disorder never go to prison. This issue is addressed in the nearby Modern Myths box.

The base rate of antisocial personality disorder in the general population is about 3% in males and 1% in females (APA, 2000), although more than half of male prisoners qualify for the diagnosis (Hare, 1980, 1983). Prevalence rates vary slightly across cultures, but antisocial personality appears to be found in all cultures (Cooke, 1996; Cooke &

[TABLE 12.2] Psychopathy Checklist–Revised

The Psychopathy Checklist–Revised (PCL-R) represents an alternative diagnostic approach to the DSM definition of antisocial personality disorder. The PCL-R assesses antisocial personality in a manner much closer to the original definition of psychopathy.

1. Glibness and superficial charm
2. Grandiose sense of self-worth
3. Need for stimulation and a proneness to avoid boredom
4. Pathological lying
5. Conning or manipulative
6. Lack of remorse or guilt
7. Shallow affect
8. Callous and lacking empathy
9. Parasitic lifestyle
10. Poor behavioral controls
11. Promiscuous sexual behavior
12. Early behavioral problems
13. Lack of realistic, long-term goals
14. Impulsivity
15. Irresponsibility
16. Failure to accept responsibility for one's actions
17. Many short-term marital relationships
18. Juvenile delinquency
19. Revocation of conditional release from legal system
20. Criminal versatility

SOURCE: *"The Items of the Psychopathy Checklist–Revised"* from The Mask of Insanity *by Cleckley. Copyright © 1941. Reprinted by permission of Mr. Wm. A. Dolan for the Estate.*

Michie, 1999). Antisocial personality disorder is also overrepresented in clinical settings, especially in substance abuse treatment (APA, 2000; Pelissier & O'Neil, 2000). Both twin studies and adoption studies indicate that there is a significant genetic component to antisocial personality disorder (Cadoret & Stewart, 1991; Lyons et al., 1995). Considerable effort was made, in preparing the most recent revision of the DSM, to modify diagnostic criteria to reduce the high rates of comorbidity of antisocial personality disorder and substance abuse disorders—that is, the high frequency of people qualifying for both diagnoses (Widiger & Corbitt, 1995). However, one might argue that the effort to

antisocial personality disorder Characterized by a pervasive pattern of disregard for the rights of others.

psychopathy A term used to describe a pattern of antisocial personality traits.

sociopathy A term used to describe a pattern of antisocial personality traits.

MODERN Myths

All Criminals ARE Psychopaths

The traditional concept of psychopathy (Cleckley, 1941) and the modern concept of antisocial personality disorder (APA, 2000) are heavily overrepresented in prison populations (Hare, 1980, 1983). However, not all criminals are psychopaths and not all psychopaths are criminals. There are many ways in which one can become a criminal, a fact that is universally recognized by sociologists, psychologists, and cultural anthropologists (Cooke, 1996). This is very clear in the study of delinquent behavior. One can engage in criminal behavior (1) because it is effective at achieving one's goals, and one is unconcerned about consequences or (2) because it is reinforced by the approval of friends and family. Psychopaths tend to engage in criminal behavior for the first reason, whereas many delinquents tend to engage in criminal behavior for the second reason. Therefore, it

should not be surprising that the onset of delinquent and criminal behavior occurs earlier in psychopaths (Hinshaw, 1994; Moffitt, 1993) and is generally driven by personal desires instead of social pressure. Psychopaths typically engage in more criminal behavior of all types—both violent and nonviolent (Porter et al., 2001). In contrast, nonpsychopathic delinquents tend to begin engaging in criminal behavior during adolescence, largely in response to peer pressure from friends. For those delinquents who engage in illegal activity because of peer pressure, one might expect that such activity will decrease once they get past adolescence and are less susceptible to such pressure. However, if they already have a criminal record, difficulty in obtaining honest employment may increase the likelihood of criminal activity. Hence it is possible to become a career criminal even without psychopathic tendencies.

On the other side of the equation are psychopathic individuals who manage to avoid serious trouble with the law. They may not always follow the law, but they stay within reasonable limits and may reduce their risk of being punished for ignoring the law by being socially productive and useful. There may even be occupations in which such flexibility is advantageous (Lykken, 1995). An undercover cop or a spy has to take incredible risks, lie convincingly about his or her identity and purpose, and control anxiety well enough to function in a demanding environment. Most people could not tolerate the stress of such risk, nor could they pull off such elaborate lies without it being obvious that they were lying. The people who *can* have some of the temperamental characteristics of a psychopath, even if they are for the most part law-abiding.

reduce this comorbidity may have been misguided, because people with antisocial personality disorder may be genuinely more prone to substance abuse than other individuals (Lilienfeld et al., 1994; Meehl, 1971).

Given the low base rate of psychopathy in the general population and the high base rate in prison populations, it is perhaps understandable that much of the research on this disorder has been done on prison populations. However, it is instructive to see how psychopathic tendencies shape a person's behavior in nonprison settings. Let's look at some of this research.

Examining the Evidence

Widom (1977) recruited people from the general population with newspaper advertisements for "adventurous carefree individuals who have led exciting impulsive lives" (p. 675). This is a clever way of presenting the characteristics of psychopathy in a socially accept-

able manner. Widom was not interested in identifying psychopaths so much as in identifying individuals with emotional tendencies similar to those of psychopaths. However, the people who responded to her ad were behaviorally similar to psychopaths identified in clinical and forensic settings. Nearly half had been in outpatient therapy, and about a fifth had been inpatients. About a third had attempted suicide. Although 74% had been arrested, most had not been convicted. About half had been in jail, but only a quarter had spent more than two weeks in jail.

Individuals with psychopathic characteristics can also be found in rather selective populations, as Sutker and Allain (1983) discovered. They used the MMPI to identify what they called adaptive sociopaths. Just over 2% of the medical students that they interviewed showed such traits. Despite doing well in medical school, these individuals showed many sociopathic characteristics. About half of Sutker and Allain's sample had repeated sexual intercourse in casual relation-

Ted Bundy killed at least 36 women during his lifetime, and the number is probably higher. A classic psychopath, Bundy experienced little anxiety and remorse. He was able to lure victims with an innocent charm, which at times came close to fooling police. Bundy was finally caught, tried, convicted, and executed.

ships, two-thirds chronically ignored rules, and almost half admitted starting fights. Most had been arrested, although none had been convicted. Their desire to be successful in a demanding profession appeared to motivate these "adaptive sociopaths" to stay within acceptable social boundaries most of the time, though clearly not all the time. Studies like these indicate that people with psychopathic characteristics are not always driven to crime, although they often do flout traditional values. Studying such samples, in addition to the more traditional prison samples, provides a more balanced picture of psychopathic individuals and of how specific emotional response patterns in these people can shape their behavior patterns.

Arousal and Learning. Psychopathic individuals show distinctive physiological characteristics that may help explain their pattern of behavior. For example, they are underaroused physiologically, which has led some to suggest that the impulsive, sometimes dangerous, and often

illegal activity they engage in may be an effort to increase their arousal to a more comfortable level (Raine, 1989).

People tend to have an optimal level of arousal. This principle was covered in Chapter 8, when the Yerkes-Dodson Law was presented (Figure 8.1). This law states that performance is poor when arousal is too low, improves as arousal increases, and then dramatically declines as arousal exceeds the optimal level. Our earlier discussion of the Yerkes-Dodson Law focused on the dramatic decline in performance that occurs when arousal passes the optimal level, which is often noted in people with anxiety disorders. However, individuals affected by antisocial personality disorder are chronically underaroused, so our interest focuses on the lower end of the Yerkes-Dodson curve. When people are at their optimal level of arousal, they are comfortable, stimulated, and content. If arousal is too high, they find themselves anxious, irritable, and eager to withdraw from the situation. If it is too low, they find themselves bored, frustrated, and craving more excitement. The argument is that antisocial personality disorder may be characterized by a chronic boredom that is primarily physiological. This boredom increases the likelihood of the impulsive and irresponsible behavior often exhibited by such individuals.

The underarousal found in psychopathic individuals may be due primarily to a dramatically reduced fear response. In a classic study, Lykken (1957) found that individuals with psychopathic traits were consistently slower at learning to avoid punishment than individuals without such traits, presumably because they were constitutionally unable to experience the fear that the threat of punishment creates in other people. This finding has been replicated many times in a variety of settings (see Lykken, 1995). Don Fowles (Fowles, 1980; Fowles & Missel, 1994) has explained this finding by hypothesizing that the **behavioral inhibition system (BIS)** is deficient in psychopaths. The behavioral inhibition system is the neurological mechanism underlying the psychological experience of anxiety and fear (Gray, 1982; Gray & McNaughton, 1996). It is part of a complex motivational system that modulates behavior. The BIS is responsible for **passive avoidance learning**—that is, learning to avoid anxiety-producing situations by avoiding behaviors that will produce those situations. Most people refrain from impulsive and dangerous actions because they have learned that such actions often produce significant negative consequences. Fowles argues that this learning is deficient in psychopathy because the neurological mechanism that drives it is deficient. Interestingly, psychopaths are not deficient in their ability to learn to achieve rewards.

behavioral inhibition system (BIS) The neurological mechanism underlying the psychological experience of anxiety and fear.

passive avoidance learning Learning to avoid anxiety-producing situations by avoiding behaviors that will create those situations.

In fact, they are rather good at it. This suggests that the complementary system—the **behavioral activation system (BAS)**—is normal, or possibly even a bit overactive, in psychopaths (Fowles, 1980). The behavioral activation system is the neurological mechanism underlying reward and pleasure (Gray, 1982). This physiological model explains the performance of psychopaths in both laboratory and real-world settings. It is an excellent example of bridging the gap between behavior and physiology to understand the process more thoroughly.

Evolutionary Impact

Evolutionary Perspective. The behavior of individuals with antisocial personality disorder raises an interesting evolutionary question. The ability to exploit others without guilt often confers obvious advantages. It is much easier to take resources from someone who is weaker than to expend energy to garner the resources on one's own. In recent evolutionary history, humans have developed laws and created such authorities as police and courts to protect people from this sort of exploitation. The cost of exploiting others is that it prevents the building of strong supportive relationships. The exploited will shun those who have used them and may band together with others to provide protection or seek revenge. Hence, sociopathic individuals have to move constantly on to new relationships as their exploitive behavior poisons existing relationships. Examine the sociopathic traits in Table 12.2. Note that several of them could easily result from antisocial behavior. For example, many short-term marital relationships may reflect the dissatisfaction of partners with being exploited. Other sociopathic traits could be the result of an unusual amount of practice. Those who are constantly forced to move on to new relationships may well develop unusually good social skills in meeting people and making good impressions and thus may seem charming to those they first meet. Of course, it is easier to be charming when one's anxiety level is low, and most psychopaths experience little anxiety. Looking at these symptoms from an evolutionary perspective provides a unique way of rethinking the pattern of symptoms and provides some exciting hypotheses for further study.

Thinking about antisocial personality disorder from an evolutionary perspective also raises a number of fascinating questions. One question has to do with the process of parenting. Human beings are helpless at birth and remain relatively helpless for years. Their survival depends on appropriate parental care. The psychopathic individual, who is usually a male, is not temperamentally suited for such long-term care. Perhaps the frequent casual sexual encounters and the multiple short-term marriages that are typical in such individuals are ways to ensure the survival of one's genes when one is not committed to the long-term parenting of one's offspring.

Another issue involves the question of why psychopathy is not more common than it is. The exploitive nature of psychopaths has obvious advantages. Are there disadvantages that decrease the viability of the psychopath? Are there systemwide processes that affect viability? This is a difficult question to address, but there are speculations that might shed some light on these issues. Anyone who has studied sociology will be impressed by how critical social cooperation is to the long-term success of human beings. From the earliest days of hunter-gatherers to the modern technological world of today, the ability of humans to band together, pooling their skills and resources, has led to achievements that would have been impossible had they acted individually. Thus there are clear advantages to *not* being sociopathic: Cooperation with others enhances survival. Developing psychological mechanisms, such as guilt, that encourage individuals to maintain prosocial behavior when faced with situations in which antisocial behavior provides immediate gains would be critical to fostering this clear advantage.

Looking at the question from a systemwide perspective provides other useful insights. The effectiveness of the exploitive behavior of the psychopath rests on a high base rate of nonexploitive behavior in the culture. If there are too many psychopaths, others expect to be hoodwinked, and hence are unlikely to be trusting victims. When the environment has few psychopaths, people are likely to drop their defensive guard, thus making it easier for someone to exploit them (Mealey, 1995). Thus the selective advantage of genes that promote psychopathic personalities depends on the base rate of psychopathy in the population. This hypothesis is difficult to test in an evolutionary model because the fossilized bones of distant ancestors rarely leave clues about antisocial tendencies. However, comparing current subcultures that vary on the base rates of psychopathic behavior can provide a test of the hypothesis. The ability of psychopaths to con their victims should be inversely proportional to the base rate of psychopathy in the subculture.

Antisocial personality disorder is only one of several psychiatric disorders that include a significant impulsivity component. The DSM recognizes an entire category of impulse control disorders, which are briefly described in the nearby Focus box.

BORDERLINE PERSONALITY DISORDER

The defining characteristic of **borderline personality disorder (BPD)** is a pervasive pattern of unstable and intense relationships. The term *stable instability* has been used to capture this characteristic. People with BPD frequently find themselves in intense, wonderful relationships that turn terribly sour at some point, often breaking up painfully and dramatically. The relationships may be with professional colleagues, friends, or lovers. Generally speaking, the more intense the relationship, the more likely it is to collapse. For example, a relationship with a lover is more likely to collapse than a relationship with an acquaintance. Dominic, whom we met at the beginning of this chapter, showed this distinctive pattern. Not only did his professional relationships consistently deteriorate, but his personal relationships always turned hostile as well. He had been married twice, the longest marriage lasting 20 months, and he had endured half a dozen other painful breakups since college. What is striking about this pattern is that Dominic appeared to be certain that the problems always rested with his colleagues, his wives, or his girlfriends—never with himself.

Clinical Features. The DSM lists several characteristics of individuals with BPD, including the unstable and intense relationship pattern described above. Other characteristics include identity disturbance, tendency to show frantic efforts to avoid abandonment, impulsivity, recurrent suicidal gestures or threats, self-mutilation, affective instability, chronic feelings of emptiness, inappropriately intense anger, and transient, stress-related paranoid ideation or severe dissociative symptoms. People with BPD also tend to split, although this is not one of the diagnostic criteria. **Splitting** is a psychodynamic concept that refers to seeing objects, such as family members, jobs, or therapists, as either all good or all bad. This splitting may account for some of the volatile relationships of people with BPD, because they tend to categorize formerly good objects as bad if they find a single flaw. Thus a minor problem with a friend or colleague may lead to a complete loss of trust for that person, often forever.

Dominic's history of unstable relationships was largely due to his splitting. He viewed his previous employers and lovers as horrible and his current employers and lovers as perfect. However, the perfect relationships always deteriorated just like past relationships. Dominic's style was to break off strained relationships, often in an angry, hostile manner, rather than waiting for someone to ask him to leave. But he also showed several positive traits often found in individuals with BPD. In order to be a part of a disintegrating relationship, you have to be *in* a relationship. What is often missed in the typical portrayal of borderline individuals is that they are often remarkably adept at establishing new relationships after old ones fail. Dominic showed

The character played by Winona Ryder in the movie *Girl Interrupted* showed the intense, unstable personal relationships typical of borderline personality disorder.

the ability to move easily to new companies whenever he became dissatisfied with his current company. He was able to do this in spite of the fact that he was very well known in his industry—both for his talent and for his temperamental personality. However, he never had trouble convincing the next company that the company environment, and not his own actions, was responsible for his previous problems.

The estimated prevalence of borderline personality disorder is 2% in the general population, 10% in outpatient mental health clinics, and up to 20% in inpatient settings (APA, 2000; Dahl, 1995). The risk of BPD is five times higher in families of individuals with this disorder. Borderline personality disorder overlaps heavily with other personality disorders, especially antisocial, avoidant, and schizotypal personality disorders (Gunderson et al., 1995). Underlying cognitive and perceptual problems affect up to 75% of individuals with BPD (Gunderson et al., 1995). Although brief psychotic episodes are considered to be a diagnostic indicator of borderline personality disorder, they are actually about three times more likely to occur in individuals with schizotypal personality disorder (Dahl, 1986).

Etiology. The hypotheses that have been advanced to explain borderline personality disorder include biological, diathesis-stress, cultural, and psychodynamic models. Genes clearly play a role in increasing risk for BPD (Baron et al., 1985). Biologically, the focus has been on the impulsive behavior found in these individuals. Whether they reflect a dramatic reversal of feelings or suicidal ideation in response to feelings of abandonment, these impulsive actions are stronger than those found in other individuals. The frontal lobes of the brain are thought to be responsible for impulsive behavior, so the search for biological mechanisms for BPD has been focused there. Two lines of research

---

behavioral activation system (BAS)   The neurological mechanism underlying reward and pleasure.

borderline personality disorder (BPD)   Characterized by a pervasive pattern of unstable and intense relationships.

splitting   A psychodynamic term for the process of seeing objects, such as family members, jobs, or therapists, as either all good or all bad.

FOCUS Impulse control disorders

People with antisocial personality disorder may behave impulsively, caring little about the consequences of their behavior. As you have learned, their impulsive behavior may be due to an insensitivity to aversive consequences. Other individuals behave impulsively, and their impulsive behavior may be driven by different mechanisms. The DSM recognizes a broad class of *impulse control disorders,* each of which is characterized by problematic behavior that the individual feels helpless to control.

Intermittent Explosive Disorder. Intermittent explosive disorder is characterized by discrete episodes of aggressive and/or assaultive behavior, which may include screaming, physical threats, assaults, or significant and deliberate destruction of property. The diagnosis should not be used if the aggressive behavior is part of such disorders as antisocial personality disorder, borderline personality disorder, conduct disorder, attention-deficit/hyperactivity disorder, or a manic or psychotic episode. People with this disorder describe intense aggressive impulses that drive the anger and assaultive behavior. Psychophysiological and neuropsychological studies suggest that a brain dysfunction may contribute to the disorder.

Kleptomania. Kleptomania is characterized by impulsive stealing of objects that are not needed by the individual or that have little financial value to the individual. There is a rising tension or pressure to steal before the theft, and a reduction in this tension follows the theft. This resembles the emotional course of OCD, in which obsessions raise anxiety and compulsions lower it. This diagnosis is used only when other causes of

the behavior are excluded, such as anger or revenge, conduct disorder, mania, or antisocial personality disorder. Kleptomania is more common in females but is generally rare. Less than 5% of shoplifting is the result of kleptomania (APA, 2000).

Pyromania. Pyromania is characterized by multiple incidents of deliberate fire setting. Like kleptomania, there is usually a tension just before the fire setting, and the tension is relieved after the fire is set. People with pyromania tend to be fascinated with fires. They will watch neighborhood fires or even monitor police-band radios to be alerted to fires. They may join volunteer fire departments or become professional fire fighters. Again, this diagnosis is made only when such other potential explanations as vengeance, monetary gain, and psychotic symptomatology have been ruled out. Pyromania is more prevalent in males, although it is generally rare. It occurs more frequently in children than in adults. Most fire setting is not associated with pyromania.

Pathological Gambling. Pathological gambling is characterized by persistent and maladaptive gambling that significantly interferes with one's personal and family functioning. Such pathological gambling may be on the rise, with the increasingly ready access to casinos, bingo games, state lotteries, and Internet gambling. It is now estimated that 1% to 3% of the adult population suffers from pathological gambling (APA, 2000), and gambling is becoming more common in adolescents (Winters et al., 1993). What seems to drive pathological gambling is the adrenaline rush associated with the possibility of winning. In that respect, gambling is like an addiction to pleasure-producing drugs, and it is

sometimes referred to as an addiction. It is not unusual for people with pathological gambling to play until they have no more money and no more access to money. If they have credit cards available, they may well withdraw up to the limit to continue the gambling. Such behavior often leads to significant financial difficulties and strains personal relationships, especially with those who share the gambler's financial resources, such as a spouse.

Trichotillomania. Trichotillomania is characterized by a persistent pulling of one's hair until there is a significant and noticeable hair loss. The person may pull hair from any site of the body, but most often hair is pulled from the scalp, eyelashes, and eyebrows. Sometimes, the person will attempt to hide the hair pulling by pulling from sites not normally visible, such as pubic areas. At times, the pulling will be precipitated by an aroused state, much as in kleptomania or pyromania. However, much of the time, the hair pulling is done without thinking, while the person is relaxed or distracted by reading or watching television. There is evidence that trichotillomania may be related to OCD (Christenson & MacKenzie, 1995). Hair pulling is rarely driven by anxiety from obsessive thoughts, but there is considerable anxiety when the person tries to resist pulling, just as in OCD. Furthermore, exposure with response prevention, which is an effective treatment for OCD, is also effective with trichotillomania. Trichotillomania is a relatively rare condition, affecting less than 1% of the population. It is more common in women than in men, although in children it is equally common in boys and in girls (APA, 2000).

implicate the frontal lobes. The first is that there is reduced activity in the frontal lobes of people with BPD compared to other people (Goyer et al., 1994). The second is that people with BPD score lower than other people on tests of frontal lobe functioning, although their general level of intellectual functioning is comparable (van Reekum et al., 1993). Furthermore, there is indirect evidence that the neurotransmitter serotonin may be implicated in BPD; drugs that increase the level of this neurotransmitter tend to reduce the level of anger and impulsive behavior (Hollander et al., 1994).

Marsha Linehan (1987) has been the strongest proponent of a diathesis-stress theory of borderline personality disorder. She posited the existence of a genetic diathesis that increases the level of emotional volatility. In those individuals who experience "invalidating events" during childhood, this diathesis can lead to the development of BPD. What are invalidating events? According to Linehan, an invalidating event involves having one's needs, feelings, or communication consistently ignored. Any form of childhood abuse would qualify as an invalidating event, and childhood abuse is more common in individuals with BPD than in people without personality disorders (Atlas, 1995; Spoont, 1996; Wagner & Linehan, 1997). These findings of childhood abuse link borderline personality disorder to two other disorders that are associated with trauma. The first is dissociative identity disorder (covered in Chapter 15). People with borderline personality disorder do show occasional dissociative symptoms, although not nearly so strongly as individuals with dissociative identity disorder. The second is posttraumatic stress disorder (covered in Chapter 8). PTSD is a response to a severe psychological trauma. It often includes significant emotional volatility, although other symptoms of PTSD (such as an increased startle response) are not found in BPD (APA, 2000). The similarity in symptoms and histories has led some to speculate that borderline personality disorder is a variation on PTSD, in which the traumatic event took place in childhood but continues to affect the person well into adulthood (Gunderson & Sabo, 1993).

Sociocultural factors have been implicated in BPD as well. This theory postulates that the stress of rapid cultural changes increases the loss of identity and can precipitate borderline personality disorder in those who might be predisposed to it (Paris, 1991). This theory might explain the apparent increase in the rate of BPD (Millon, 1990).

Finally, Kernberg (1985) has advanced a psychodynamic explanation of BPD that addresses some of the questions that the other models leave unanswered. Kernberg's proposal comes from the object relations perspective of psychodynamic theory, which assumes that the way people behave in adulthood is heavily influenced by the social relationships they developed during their formative years. Kernberg believes that problems with these early relationships predispose people to emotional and interpersonal instability as adults. He views the splitting of objects as a defensive response invoked to deal with this emotional upheaval, although others view splitting differently, as shown in the nearby Focus box. Of course, abuse during childhood would constitute a significant disruption in the normal formation of object relations, but Kernberg argues that more subtle behaviors can also lead to the development of borderline personality disorder. For example, separation from parents during part of development or a high level of hostility and a low level of care by parents may be sufficient to disrupt the development of normal object relationships and thus precipitate BPD (Paris et al., 1994; Patrick et al., 1994).

The problem with many of these theories is that they rely on data that are suspect. For example, the abuse histories and the accounts of poor parenting are typically based on self-report. The very tendency of people with BPD to split objects—to see them as all good or all bad—could easily distort those self-reports. Many of these individuals are estranged from their parents and so are likely to see their parents as deficient in many ways. Reports of separation from parents are more objective and thus less likely to be influenced by such biases. Nevertheless, the consistency of these findings suggests the need for further, more methodologically sound research.

HISTRIONIC PERSONALITY DISORDER

Individuals with **histrionic personality disorder** typically show excessive emotionality and an attention-seeking behavior pattern. They seem to want to be the center of attention and typically exhibit considerable distress when they are not, often behaving in a dramatic fashion that draws attention to them. This behavior is typically excessive, appearing to be almost a caricature of normal social behavior. At times, these individuals may be sexually provocative and seductive. They tend to have superficial relationships. For example, it is common for them to describe people they have known for years in vague, nonspecific terms. It is as though they do not recognize the complexity of individuals and therefore are unable to describe them. You would appreciate why this might be the case if you observed such individuals interacting with people. In a gathering, they often chat with one person after another, typically engaging in small talk only, and are easily distracted by someone else entering the room. They often behave as though they were "on stage"; their behavior, their conversation, and their emotionality all appear to be excessive, as though they were trying to project to an audience several rows back. Bonita, who was one of the cases that opened this chapter, illustrates many of these characteristics.

The interesting aspect of this disorder is that the one thing that histrionic individuals need the most—attention

histrionic personality disorder   Characterized by excessive emotionality and an attention-seeking behavior pattern.

FOCUS Symptom or defense?

Sometimes the meaning of a trait depends on how you look at it and in what populations it is studied. Take a concept that is perhaps one of the most widely recognized psychodynamic contributions to the understanding of people with BPD—the concept of splitting. Splitting is the tendency to view the world in black and white. People who show splitting divide people into good and bad, good people being perfect and bad people being worthless. Furthermore, splitting may take the form of seeing a formerly "good" person as "bad" if that person does one thing wrong. Breuer and Freud (1895/1955) used the term initially to describe a failure to integrate all aspects of the ego. The person splits off from consciousness feelings and ideas that cannot be integrated with existing feelings. Fairbairn (1944/1955) hypothesized that such splitting could be an active defense mechanism that reduces a person's anxiety about ambivalent

feelings by keeping the negative and positive feelings separate. Kernberg (1967) recognized that people with borderline personality disorder tend to utilize this defense in an exaggerated manner—almost a caricature of Fairbairn's splitting. It is this definition of splitting—the extreme tendency to see people as all good or all bad—that survives. You would be hard pressed to find any substantial article on borderline personality disorder, regardless of the theoretical orientation of the writer, that does not make mention of splitting. Therapists experienced with borderline clients are well aware that the high praise the client lavishes on the quality of clinical care may change in a heartbeat.

The modern conceptualization of splitting in clients with BPD is remarkably similar to the concept of ambivalence introduced by Bleuler (Raulin & Brenner, 1993). Bleuler's (1911/1950) definition of ambivalence was different from the modern dictionary defi-

nition. He described it as the tendency to have simultaneous positive and negative feelings toward the same object at the same time, often without apparent awareness of those opposite feelings. For example, a person might love a rose for its beauty and at the same time hate a rose for its thorns, without ever integrating these divergent feelings toward the same object (loving the beauty of the rose but respecting the fact that the thorns can be painful). The common notion of ambivalence today no longer includes the idea of being unaware of the divergent feelings, probably because few people ever experience the intense ambivalence that Bleuler argued was a central symptom of schizophrenia.

Bleuler (1911/1950) argued that schizophrenic ambivalence was a result of the same processes that caused thought disorder in schizophrenia—specifically, a breakdown in the ability to maintain the normal associations that enable people to

---

and approval—is often difficult for them to receive. Certainly the dramatic style commands attention, but this attention is often negative. Histrionic individuals are often viewed as shallow and flighty. It is common for them to have many acquaintances but few friends, and their friends often describe them in unflattering terms. Their excessively dramatic tone often antagonizes people. This exaggerated display of emotion is also apparent in other realms. For example, physical symptoms are often described dramatically—so dramatically, in fact, that few people take the symptoms seriously. It is perhaps not surprising that histrionic traits are often found in individuals with somatization or conversion disorders (covered in Chapter 9). People with these disorders often present their symptoms in a dramatic and flamboyant manner. In addition, suicidal gestures in response to apparently minor provocations are common (APA, 2000).

The base rate of histrionic personality disorder is 2%–3% in the general population and 10%–15% in clinical populations (APA, 2000). Like most personality disorders, histrionic personality disorder tends to be comorbid with

other Axis II disorders, especially borderline and antisocial personality disorders (Pfohl, 1995).

Many of the people studied by Freud early in his career showed a classic histrionic personality as well as conversion symptoms. Conversion symptoms are physical symptoms for which no physical cause is apparent and that appear to have a psychological cause. Not all individuals with histrionic personality disorder show conversion symptoms, but many people with conversion symptoms show a histrionic personality pattern (APA, 2000). The term *hysteria* has traditionally been associated with females, although males can show histrionic personality disorder as well. Because the stereotypically histrionic person is often thought of as female, some have raised significant concerns about a gender bias in the diagnosis of this disorder (Pfohl, 1995). Let's look at some of the evidence on this question.

narcissistic personality disorder   Characterized by a pervasive pattern of acting grandiose, having a constant need for admiration, and appearing to lack empathy for others.

form an integrated perspective on the world. In sharp contrast, Kernberg (1967, 1977) maintained that the splitting found in people with BPD was a primitive defense against more severe psychological deterioration. Remember that the modern concept of borderline personality disorder is a refinement of the concept of borderline schizophrenia (Gunderson & Singer, 1975), which includes those individuals thought to be on the border between psychosis and neurosis. It now seems clear that these two outstanding theorists were talking about the same behavior but were interpreting the behavior in dramatically different ways. Who was correct? Perhaps both were correct. It may well be that in people with the extreme psychological deterioration found in schizophrenia, ambivalence is just another indication of an underlying disordered process. Those who are at risk for schizophrenia would be likely to show a similar process, though

probably not so extreme. The process of splitting often creates traumatic breakups in relationships, but it may be that such immediate breakups are less stressful in the long run than the possibility of being caught in a long-term dysfunctional relationship. Hence the splitting in people with BPD defends their ego by avoiding the potential of overwhelming stress. A process such as ambivalence may be dysfunctional when carried to an extreme but functional in other situations. Of course, this is a speculative hypothesis, but dozens of predictions from this brief bit of speculation could be tested with the right observations. That is what science brings to the table: a way to separate speculations that are unfounded from those that have merit.

Evolutionary Impact —

There is another point to consider here. The functionality of a characteristic from an evolutionary

perspective is determined primarily by its impact on the individual, not by its impact on surrounding people, although there are exceptions. For example, behavior that alienates potential mates may limit reproductive success. People with BPD are often difficult to deal with. Being easy to deal with may improve one's chance of survival by increasing the likelihood of developing and maintaining a social support network, which is probably why most people make a concerted effort to smooth their social relationships. However, such an advantage may come at too high an emotional price for people with BPD, who could experience significant emotional distress if forced to maintain smooth relationships with people they have grown to hate.

Examining the Evidence

Is there a gender bias in the diagnosis of histrionic personality disorder? Reich (1987) found that when formal diagnostic criteria and decision rules are used, males clients are as likely as female clients to qualify for a diagnosis of histrionic personality disorder. However, most clinicians do not use such formal criteria for diagnosis, so subtle biases may have a significant impact on their diagnosis. This bias was clearly illustrated in a study by Ford and Widiger (1989), who presented identical clinical descriptions of a person but identified the person as male to some clinicians and as female to others. They found that the stated sex of the client did not affect the number of histrionic traits that were identified during a diagnostic work-up but that it did affect the diagnosis. This fictitious client was more likely to be given a histrionic personality disorder diagnosis when identified as a

female than when identified as a male. One reason for having clearly delineated behavioral criteria for diagnosis is to avoid such biases, which can creep into the work of even the most well-intentioned professionals. The evidence suggests that the diagnostic criteria for histrionic personality disorder work well and manage to avoid bias, but only when they are used systematically (Pfohl, 1995).

NARCISSISTIC PERSONALITY DISORDER

People with **narcissistic personality disorder** are grandiose, have a constant need for admiration, and appear to lack empathy for others. They often view themselves in unrealistic terms, seeing themselves as more attractive, more interesting, or more talented than they really are. These individuals rarely come into treatment unless their unrealistic views of themselves are challenged, at which point they may experience depression and anxiety.

Because people with narcissistic personality disorder feel they are special, they expect be treated as special. They believe that people with their special talents should not associate with individuals who do not themselves possess special talents. They appear pretentious, self-centered, and are downright obnoxious at times. They often insist on having the best of everything. This extends to the best services as well as the best goods. They need the admiration of others and experience considerable distress when that need is not met. There is often a sense of entitlement, which demonstrates itself in the way narcissistic people deal with others. They appear to believe that their work is more important than the work of others and that people should understand this and give way. They often exploit others and typically will not get involved in a relationship unless it advances their personal agenda. It is perhaps not surprising, given this pattern of behavior, that narcissistic individuals rarely have empathy toward others. In fact, they sometimes appear to be oblivious to the feelings of others. These features are illustrated by the case of Jermaine.

be interpreted that way. But he said that he was simply trying to get his point across to his boss. He had expected to get his job back on appeal, but the appeals board sided with his boss, pointing out that Jermaine had received numerous warnings over the past ten years. In fact, Jermaine alone had received more warnings during that period than the rest of the staff in his department put together (over 110 people).

Jermaine dealt with his therapist much as he dealt with his co-workers. Near the end of this first session, the therapist asked Jermaine how he could be of help. Jermaine was puzzled by the question and responded angrily, suggesting that the therapist was "clueless." The therapist noted that Jermaine obviously was suffering from the things that had happened to him and that there was considerable uncertainty right now in his life. Jermaine disagreed with this analysis, arguing that there was little uncertainty in his life. His supervisor clearly had screwed him. He was a first-rate employee, a leader in his field who was widely recognized as such, and would have no difficulty finding another job. The therapist asked again how he could be of help, but this time the therapist added that he was sure Jermaine had the strength of character to bounce back from the recent setbacks. Jermaine agreed with this analysis, saying that what he needed from therapy was support while he mobilized his efforts to turn the situation around.

Unappreciated and Envied

JERMAINE

Jermaine came into therapy just a few weeks after being fired from his job. He talked bitterly about the people he worked for, especially the supervisor who fired him, saying his firing was unjustified and motivated by envy. He acknowledged that he often had difficulties working with other people, primarily because he did not respect the quality of their work. He said that he was fired for insubordination for refusing to follow a direct order and admitted that his behavior could

Jermaine genuinely seemed to believe that he was special. He was talented, but not nearly so talented as he thought. He was also oblivious to how he came across to others. His reaction to his therapist's question about how he could help is typical. Jermaine could not believe that the therapist would treat him as just another client. He calmed down only after the therapist stroked his ego by expressing confidence in Jermaine's resilience.

The word *narcissistic* derives from the legend of Narcissus, who in Greek mythology fell in love with his own reflection in a pool.

Unlike many of the personality disorders, narcissistic personality disorder was not a part of the diagnostic system before the publication of DSM-III. It was included primarily because of the widespread usage of the term by psychodynamic theorists (Gunderson et al., 1995). Freud (1914/1957) used the term *narcissism* to refer to the self-focus typical of infants. He believed that infants had little awareness of the world as being separate from their own experience of it. However, Freud recognized that narcissism was also found in adults to varying degrees and under specific circumstances. Reich (1933/1972) and Horney (1937) later acknowledged that some individuals show strong and persistent narcissistic tendencies. However, it was Kernberg (1976) and Kohut (1971) who provided the extensive theoretical underpinnings of pathological narcissism, and their work became the foundation for the DSM diagnosis of narcissistic personality disorder.

Somewhere between 2% and 16% of people who seek psychological treatment qualify for this diagnosis (Dahl, 1986; Frances et al., 1984; Zanarini et al., 1987). The base rate in the general population is about 1% (Zimmerman & Coryell, 1990). Although systematically compiled data are not available, the extensive references to narcissistic personality in the psychoanalytic case literature suggest that the base rate in outpatient dynamic therapy is considerably higher than the figures just quoted (Gunderson et al., 1995). Over 80% of people with narcissistic personality disorder qualify for diagnosis of at least one other personality disorder, most often in the dramatic/erratic cluster (Widiger et al., 1987). Jermaine showed characteristics of both borderline and histrionic personality disorders, in addition to the obvious narcissistic features.

TREATING CLUSTER B DISORDERS

This section covers the treatment of cluster B personality disorders, including antisocial, borderline, histrionic, and narcissistic personality disorders.

Treating Antisocial Personality Disorder. There is general agreement in the clinical literature that treatments for antisocial personality disorder tend to be ineffective, especially for those individuals who fit into the traditional psychopathic category (Millon, 1996). However, there is a tendency for the dramatic antisocial behavior, such as promiscuity and crime, to decrease naturally after age 30 (Cloninger & Svrakic, 2000; Moffitt, 1993). When individuals with antisocial personality disorder are caught and convicted of crimes, evidence of psychopathic characteristics often results in more severe sentences. Because there is little evidence that more severe sentences are a deterrent for these individuals, the primary justification seems to be that society needs to be protected from those who might be inclined to prey on others.

Treatments for antisocial behavior have focused on children, with the implicit assumption that such conditions are more mutable in children (Moffitt, 1993). Research suggests that adolescent delinquent behavior can be classified into two categories (Moffitt, 1993). Some delinquent behavior is carried out by groups of adolescents, in which the group provides heavy peer reinforcement for the behavior. These *socialized delinquents* can often be influenced positively by efforts to connect them to different peer groups although recent evidence suggests that such group treatments must be carefully constructed and monitored or delinquent symptoms will get worse rather than better (Dishion et al., 1999). In contrast, there is a smaller group of delinquents whose behavior is less dependent on the reinforcement of peers. These *unsocialized delinquents* are less responsive to treatment and are more likely to qualify for a diagnosis of antisocial personality disorder as adults. This group is also more likely to show the lack of empathy and resultant cruelty that may be a precursor to later violent antisocial behavior, such as cruelty to animals and other children (Moffitt et al., 1989). Although effective treatment for this unsocialized group of delinquents has not been promising to date, the possibility of making an impact on this group warrants continued effort. The cost to society of a single individual with antisocial personality disorder justifies considerable research on prevention through early intervention.

Children who show attention-deficit/hyperactivity disorder (ADHD) are at risk for developing antisocial personality disorder as adults if there are any antisocial features present during childhood (Lilienfeld & Waldman, 1990; Moffitt, 1990). ADHD, which will be covered in Chapter 13, is characterized by excessive energy and serious deficits in maintaining attention. Children with ADHD show disruptive behavior, poor school performance, difficulty in interacting with peers, and eventual social isolation from peers. Although drugs are often used as the primary treatment for ADHD, behavior therapy can be helpful, especially intensive all-day programs that focus on building social skills (Pelham & Gnagy, 1999; Pelham & Waschbusch, 1999). Such interventions reduce the social isolation that may cut such children off from peer interactions and peer influence. Peer expectations have strong influences on children, and strengthening peer interaction may provide powerful prosocial developmental influences. The data on whether these positive treatment effects translate into a reduction in antisocial behavior are not yet in, but this is a promising avenue of research for the subgroup of people who show an antisocial personality pattern and comorbid ADHD.

Although antisocial personality disorder may be difficult to treat, it is too early to write this group off. There is clear evidence that not all people who show the personality traits associated with antisocial personality disorder get in to serious trouble with the law or routinely violate the rights of others, although they may skirt the law and be less

Research indicates that some delinquent behavior is motivated by strong social pressure from one's peer group. In contrast, children who engage in delinquent behavior on their own are often motivated by drives that will eventually qualify them for the diagnosis of antisocial personality disorder.

sensitive to the feelings of others than most people (Babiak, 1995; Sutker & Allain, 1983; Widom, 1977). Furthermore, the recognition that these individuals are deficient in behavioral inhibition, but not in behavioral activation, suggests a mechanism for intervention that may be fruitful in some instances. For example, emphasizing the rewards that can be obtained via prosocial behavior may provide a mechanism for these individuals to fit into society despite their pattern of emotional responses. Unfortunately, the normal response to children who display antisocial behavior is to emphasize punishment, and research suggests that these individuals are generally insensitive to such interventions (Lykken, 1957, 1995).

Treating Borderline Personality Disorder.
There is a substantial literature on the treatment of borderline clients, much of it in a psychodynamic tradition (Kernberg, 1967, 1977, 1996). Unfortunately, most of this literature is difficult to assess because there is no specified treatment focus that can be systematically evaluated. Many practitioners choose to administer intensive psychoanalytic treatment, but such intensive and demanding treatment often triggers primitive defense mechanisms, strong transference, brief periods of psychological regression, and even occasional brief psychotic episodes (Gabbard, 2000).

Borderline individuals are often difficult clients—so much so that the term *borderline* is sometimes used inappropriately to describe almost any difficult client. It is not uncommon for borderline clients to start therapy by berating the approach and sincerity of their previous therapists (seeing them as all bad) and praising the current therapist's every word and action (seeing him or her as all good). However, the current therapist invariably does something that upsets the client and thus joins the ranks of bad therapists. In addition, borderline individuals react badly to anything that feels like abandonment, including such insignificant things as the therapist making a comment that the client interprets as critical or canceling a session because of illness. The response may include anger, paranoid ideation, and suicidal threats or gestures.

An alternative to the psychodynamic treatment approach for borderline personality disorder is a behavioral approach developed by Marsha Linehan (1993) and known as **dialectical behavior therapy (DBT)**. The cornerstone of this approach is the belief that individuals with borderline personality disorder are unable to tolerate strong negative emotions and hence engage in a variety of self-destructive and self-defeating behaviors in response to intermittent

....

dialectical behavior therapy (DBT) The combining of several cognitive and behavioral techniques to target problem thoughts and behaviors common in borderline personality disorder, such as suicidal ideation, self-mutilation, aggressive physical and social responses to people, and substance abuse.

strong negative feelings. Dialectical behavior therapy combines several cognitive and behavioral techniques to target problem thoughts and behaviors, such as suicidal ideation, self-mutilation, aggressive physical and social responses to people, and substance abuse. The client is trained to recognize and accept negative emotions, to avoid reflexive reactions to those negative emotions, and to use a variety of techniques to manage negative feelings and reduce the likelihood of interpersonal stress. This focused therapy has shown promise in controlled studies, achieving reductions in all targeted negative behaviors (Linehan et al., 1994, 2001). This is a substantial improvement over traditional therapy, but even after successful therapy, these clients still experience more emotional disruption and problem behaviors than most people.

Selective serotonin uptake inhibitors, such as Prozac, can also reduce borderline symptoms (Fornari & Pelcovitz, 2000). Serotonin is a critical component in the behavioral inhibition system, which appears to be dysfunctional in borderline individuals (Hollander et al., 1994). Of course, such drugs as Prozac are often prescribed for people with BPD because they are seeking treatment for depression. But several studies have suggested that Prozac may also reduce such symptoms as impulsive aggression (Fornari & Pelcovitz, 2000).

Treating Histrionic and Narcissistic Personality Disorders.   For the two remaining personality disorders in the dramatic/erratic cluster—histrionic personality disorder and narcissistic personality disorder—there is almost no research evidence to support a treatment approach. The majority of theoretical and treatment articles for both histrionic (Bornstein, 1999) and narcissistic personality disorder (Auerbach, 1993) are in the psychoanalytic tradition. Although there is a substantial literature of case reports of individuals who qualify for these disorders, there are no published controlled studies. In fairness, it should be noted that these are not disorders that clients typically recognize as problematic or for which they seek treatment. When these people come to the attention of treatment professionals, they typically present with a complex combination of Axis I and Axis II disorders, so controlled treatment trials would be exceedingly difficult to carry out.

Check Yourself 12.3

Cluster B Disorders

1. How does the antisocial personality disorder differ from Cleckley's psychopathy?

2. Explain how differences in physiological functioning in people with antisocial personality disorder affect their learning and behavior.

3. What is the defining characteristic of borderline personality disorder?

4. What is the defining characteristic of histrionic personality disorder?

5. What are the defining characteristics of narcissistic personality disorder?

6. How treatable is antisocial personality disorder?

7. What is the only empirically-supported treatment for borderline personality disorder?

Ponder this . . .   *What would it be like to work for a boss who qualified for a diagnosis of borderline personality disorder? What would be your best strategy to avoid problems with this boss?*

CLUSTER C DISORDERS

Cluster C—the anxious/fearful cluster—is covered in this section. This cluster includes avoidant, dependent, and obsessive-compulsive personality disorders.

AVOIDANT PERSONALITY DISORDER

Individuals with **avoidant personality disorder** often show a pervasive pattern of shyness, social inhibition, and hypersensitivity to negative evaluation. They actively avoid social situations and often respond to negative feedback by withdrawing even more. They tend to have low self-esteem, seeing themselves as incapable and undesirable. Consequently, they rarely take social risks, which makes it hard for them to meet new people. Unlike most personality disorders, avoidant personality disorder is consistently ego dystonic. The case of Roberta illustrates this personality disorder.

Finding a Comfortable Niche

ROBERTA

Roberta has worked the last six years on the night shift of a janitorial firm. This is not the kind of job she dreamed of in college, but at least it's a comfortable job. She quit her last several jobs abruptly after being criticized for her work. Her supervisor has been generally supportive, and Roberta feels that he likes her. She doesn't enjoy working the night shift but welcomes the fact that there are few people around. Roberta has a reasonable relationship with the three people she works with, although she rarely talks to them more than five minutes in an entire shift. She has no other friends that she sees on a regular basis. She lives alone in an apartment a few blocks from her parents, and she has two older brothers whom she sees occasionally.

avoidant personality disorder   Characterized by a pervasive pattern of shyness, social inhibition, and hypersensitivity to negative evaluation.

However, for all practical purposes, her social life is restricted to a visit to her parents two or three times a week. She is discouraged by this limited social life but is much too uncomfortable to risk getting involved with other people. She would love to marry, but she hasn't gone on a date in almost ten years. She is so fearful of the reactions of men that she rarely talks with them for more than a few seconds.

Roberta illustrates the key features of avoidant personality disorder. She is socially isolated, but unlike people with schizoid personality disorder, she does not *want* to be socially isolated. However, she is so fearful of negative evaluation in social situations that she is willing to live the life of a virtual hermit. Her social skills are weak because she has had so little practice, but they are not so bad that she could not socialize. Nevertheless, because she cannot be assured that she will always make a positive impression, she prefers to make no impression at all.

The diagnostic category of avoidant personality disorder grew out of the biosocial learning theory of Millon (1969). Millon argued that the best way to understand personality disorders is to understand what reinforcers have the greatest impact on the person, where they come from, and the strategies that the person uses to obtain them. For example, does the person seem more interested in trying to obtain rewards or in trying to avoid punishments? The expected behavioral pattern would differ dramatically depending on which of these was most prominent. Someone interested primarily in rewards would take greater risks, would be less discouraged by failures, and would learn little from failures. In contrast, someone interested primarily in avoiding punishment would avoid risks, would be devastated by failures, and would rarely repeat behaviors that resulted in failures. Most of the traditional personality

Some people just prefer to be alone; others are simply too fearful of social encounters to engage in social activities. Schizoid individuals are indifferent to social interactions and therefore isolate themselves. In contrast, avoidant individuals isolate themselves out of fear.

disorders—those that were recognized in earlier diagnostic manuals—can be easily represented in Millon's model. However, the model also predicted other combinations, one of which corresponded to avoidant personality disorder. According to Millon (1969, 1990, 1996), avoidant personality disorder is characterized by a focus on avoiding aversive experience rather than on obtaining positive reinforcers. These people take an active approach to achieving this goal by systematically withdrawing from social situations. Their style limits their access to the social reinforcers that drive the behavior of most other people.

There is some debate about whether there is a meaningful distinction between the Axis I diagnosis of social phobia (generalized type) and avoidant personality disorder (Millon & Martinez, 1995). Most social phobias tend to be specific to certain situations. For example, a person might be anxious in a dating or public-speaking situation but be reasonably comfortable when having a conversation with friends. Some socially phobic individuals, however, are anxious in virtually all social situations. Such individuals typically qualify for the diagnoses of both social phobia (generalized type) and avoidant personality disorder. Although it is possible for generalized social phobics to force themselves to engage in social activity despite their anxiety, and thus disqualifying themselves from the avoidant personality disorder diagnosis, this rarely happens.

The prevalence of avoidant personality disorder is approximately 0.5% to 1.0% in the general population and about 10% in clinical samples (APA, 2000; Millon & Martinez, 1995). There has been little research on this disorder and, unlike narcissistic personality disorder, little coverage in the clinical literature.

DEPENDENT PERSONALITY DISORDER

The defining characteristic of **dependent personality disorder** is clinging behavior coupled with a fear of separation. People with this disorder often ask for advice, sometimes requesting advice from many people before making a decision. At times it appears that they are unwilling to make any decision on their own. They appear to doubt their capacity to care for themselves adequately. Consequently, they are often desperate to maintain relationships in order to ensure that someone will be there to care for them. Because of their excessive dependence and their lack of self-confidence, individuals with dependent personality disorder often have difficulty initiating projects. And once they do start projects, they often have difficulty continuing them without the support of others. However, they can function well if they are in a supportive environment, as illustrated in the following case study.

dependent personality disorder Characterized by a pervasive pattern of clinging behavior coupled with a fear of separation.

Alone and Lost

RICK

Rick was a 25-year-old graduate student in a competitive program. He had been married for several years to a woman who was completing a medical degree. Rick was functioning well as a graduate student, showing considerable promise. He frequently asked other students for advice, but no one saw it as a problem. His work was always of high quality, and when people asked for *his* advice, he was happy to oblige. Those who knew him considered him a good friend, a valued colleague, and a promising student. All that changed, however, when his wife filed for divorce. Almost overnight, his apparent self-confidence disappeared, and Rick found it increasingly impossible to make decisions. Even the most mundane decisions, like what to have for lunch, required consultation with a half-dozen or more people. He was unable to handle his research job and was forced to resign the position. It became virtually impossible for him to write papers. He struggled with the loss of his marriage, realizing that his excessive dependency on his wife finally drove her to end the relationship. Over the next 18 months, he was briefly involved in two relationships, but his new partners also backed out because they felt smothered by his excessive dependence.

It is easy to empathize with Rick, whose life seemed to collapse once the supportive relationship with his wife ended. If you did not know about the nature of their relationship, you might be inclined to attribute his indecisiveness following the breakup to depression. Clearly, Rick was depressed, but his indecisiveness existed long before the breakup. His wife had provided the guidance that he felt he desperately needed, and he was lost without her. When they were married, he would ask her advice a hundred or more times a day. He turned control over to her in virtually every aspect of his life, from mundane things, like what socks to wear, to important things, like how to handle disagreements with colleagues. He could do nothing without first checking with her, which in time became such a burden to her that she initiated a divorce. She had fulfilled his dependence needs so well that most of his colleagues saw little of this side of Rick's personality—that is, until she left him. When he found another woman three years later who was comfortable with his dependence, he was able to get right back on track.

The history of the concept of dependence is interesting, especially when viewed from a Western perspective. It is rooted in the psychodynamic concept that humans seek to achieve their goals through the cooperation of others (Hirschfeld et al., 1995). Dependency begins in infancy, when children are incapable of doing anything for themselves. It continues into adulthood, when people recognize that they are stronger as groups than as individuals. The nature and healthiness of the dependence relationship is presumably a function of the first dependent relationship with the child's primary caregiver (Bowlby, 1969). Optimal

functioning is a delicate balance between dependence and independence, although in Western cultures independence is often glorified and dependence vilified. It is probably no accident that the DSM lists a dependent personality disorder but no independent personality disorder. A high level of independence may characterize antisocial and schizoid personality disorders, but the independence in these disorders is secondary to other factors.

Dependent personality disorder is one of the most frequently reported in clinical settings (APA, 2000), which is perhaps not surprising given that the nature of the symptoms might well drive individuals to seek professional help. No figures are available for the prevalence in the general population. Dependent personality disorder has been especially controversial because of the presumed gender bias in its diagnosis (Brown, 1986). The data suggest that when no formal diagnostic procedures are used, dependent personality disorder is diagnosed more frequently in women than in men (Kass et al., 1983), although the ratio of women to men drops when formalized procedures are used that precisely follow the guidelines of the DSM (Reich, 1987). Like histrionic personality disorder, it appears that subtle biases can creep into the diagnosis of dependent personality disorder when clinicians rely more on their gut feelings than on the specific criteria spelled out in the diagnostic manual. It is worth emphasizing that a difference in the rates of a disorder is not by itself an indication of bias in the diagnostic system (Widiger & Spitzer, 1991). There may be excellent reasons for sex differences, and often a sex difference in the risk for a disorder provides researchers with clues about the factors that contribute to the disorder.

OBSESSIVE-COMPULSIVE PERSONALITY DISORDER

The defining feature of **obsessive-compulsive personality disorder** is a preoccupation with orderliness, perfectionism, and control, often to the extent of reducing the person's flexibility and efficiency. People with this disorder are preoccupied with details, rules, organization, and schedules, even when these factors are no longer contributing to the person's goals. Often individuals will show such extreme perfectionism that they are unable to complete tasks. Some individuals with obsessive-compulsive personality disorder work considerable overtime because of their work style, leaving little time for leisure. They may be excessively conscientious and inflexible on moral issues, sometimes to the extreme found in paranoid individuals. They may hoard things, saving anything and everything, regardless of its value. They tend to treat their money as they treat other objects, hoarding it for future needs. Finally, they can be

obsessive-compulsive personality disorder   Characterized by a preoccupation with orderliness, perfectionism, and control that often reduces a person's flexibility and efficiency.

stubborn and rigid, convinced that their way is the only correct way. Consequently, they often have difficulty working with other people. Several of these characteristics are illustrated in the following case study.

Too Inflexible to Function

MARY

Mary was pleasant enough, but she often got on people's nerves. It wasn't that her behavior was malicious; quite the opposite. Mary always wanted to please. She worked hard to make everything work properly. The only problem was that for her, there was only one way to do things—her way. Every day was filled with routines. Her desk was always perfectly ordered; her clothes were always perfectly pressed. Every task she was given at work was neatly organized before she did anything. However, despite all her effort, she accomplished little. Every detail of every task had to be done a certain way. She drove others nuts, because she would insist on redoing everything unless it was done her way. As hard as Mary worked, she was in danger of losing her job because no one wanted to work with her and she couldn't get things done on her own.

Note how pervasive Mary's obsessive attention to detail had become and that it affected many areas of her life, including her interactions with co-workers. If her obsessiveness were just a bit less extreme, she could function fine, perhaps even developing a reputation of being a detail-oriented person. Note that obsessive-compulsive disorder and obsessive-compulsive personality disorder both include ritualistic behavior. However, these are different disorders, and well-trained clinicians can easily distinguish between them by the intensity and characteristics of the symptoms (APA, 2000). For example, most of the behaviors that people with obsessive-compulsive personality disorder perform are ego syntonic, whereas most compulsions in OCD are ego dystonic. Furthermore, the exhibited behaviors differ in nature. The typical behaviors of obsessive-compulsive personality disorder involve organizational details, whereas OCD behaviors are true compulsions, which are clearly aimed at reducing the anxiety from the obsessions. There is a slightly increased risk for obsessive-compulsive disorder in individuals with obsessive-compulsive personality disorder, but the increased risk is much less than the similarity in the diagnostic labels might lead one to expect (Diaferia et al., 1997), and most people with OCD do not have obsessive-compulsive personality disorder (Pollack, 1979, 1987). The confusion caused by the similarity of names for these disorders has prompted calls to rename this personality disorder. The *International Classification of Diseases* diagnostic manual uses the term *anankastic personality disorder*, although this label is not used in the DSM, which adheres to the general principle that the label for a disorder should be generally descriptive of the symptom pattern (Pfohl & Blum, 1995).

This may have a humorous tone, but people with obsessive-compulsive personality may indeed be well suited for some types of work. However, when the obsessions interfere with functioning, the person may qualify for a diagnosis of obsessive-compulsive personality disorder.

"SEE—IT'S NOT IMPOSSIBLE FOR AN OBSESSIVE-COMPULSIVE TO GET A RESPONSIBLE JOB."

SOURCE: *By permission of Sidney Harris,* http://www.ScienceCartoonsPlus.com.

The base rates of obsessive-compulsive personality disorder are approximately 1% in the general population and 3%–10% in clinical populations, and it is twice as common in men than in women (APA, 2000). There is substantial overlap between this personality disorder and several other personality disorders, including avoidant, histrionic, borderline, and paranoid personality disorders (Pfohl & Blum, 1995). It is somewhat surprising that there is an overlap between borderline and obsessive-compulsive personality disorders. The borderline individual is normally conceptualized as being emotionally volatile, whereas the obsessive-compulsive individual is normally thought of as being emotionally rigid and controlled. This surprising overlap, averaging about 40% (Pfohl, 1995), may provide some tantalizing clues about the internal dynamics of individuals who show the rigidity characteristic of obsessive-compulsive disorder. Could it be that their rigid perfectionism is a defense against powerful internal emotions? This question has yet to be resolved.

TREATING CLUSTER C DISORDERS

There is little or no controlled research on the treatment of the personality disorders in the anxious/fearful cluster. Two of these disorders bear a strong resemblance to Axis I disorders. Avoidant personality disorder has extensive overlap with generalized social phobia, and obsessive-compulsive personality disorder has some overlap with obsessive-compulsive disorder. Consequently, the clinical literature, which consists primarily of case studies rather than controlled treatment studies, often suggests the use of the treatment approaches found to be effective for these Axis I conditions. That would include social skills training coupled with anxiety management tools for avoidant personality disorder and exposure with response prevention for obsessive-compulsive personality disorder (see Chapter 8 for details of these treatment approaches).

Check Yourself 12.4

Cluster C Disorders

1. What is the defining characteristic of avoidant personality disorder?
2. What Axis I disorder shares many characteristics with avoidant personality disorder?
3. What is the defining characteristic of dependent personality disorder?
4. How pathological is dependency?
5. What is the defining characteristic of obsessive-compulsive personality disorder?
6. How does obsessive-compulsive personality disorder differ from OCD?

Ponder this . . .   *What kind of work would be ideal for someone with obsessive-compulsive personality disorder? What kind of work would not be good for someone with this disorder?*

ISSUES AND UNANSWERED QUESTIONS

This closing section outlines several unresolved issues regarding personality disorders. It begins with a discussion of treatment issues, before addressing the most critical treatment issue: Can personality be reshaped? The topic then shifts from treatment to prevention of Axis I disorders in people with a personality disorder. The final section raises conceptual issues that psychopathology researchers must resolve in order to bring Axis II to the next level of diagnostic efficiency and validity.

TREATMENT DILEMMAS

The treatment of personality disorders raises several interesting issues. The first is that many people with a personality disorder find the disorder ego syntonic, and therefore they do not seek treatment. A second issue is that, by definition, these disorders are difficult to treat. They are defined as chronic and inflexible behavior patterns, so achieving significant change may be impossible. A third issue is that most people with personality disorders who seek treatment are seeking treatment for an Axis I condition, such as de-

pression or panic disorder. They are far more interested in relieving those symptoms than in changing their personality. Finally, although much has been written about therapy with people who have a personality disorder, there have been few controlled treatment studies. Perhaps for these reasons, there has been little concerted effort at treating personality disorders. Some disorders are known to be particularly difficult to treat, such as antisocial personality disorder (Millon, 1996). Others, such as schizoid personality disorder, have relatively little impact either on the individual or on society, so there is little incentive to develop treatments.

CAN PERSONALITY BE RESHAPED?

A central question when one considers the issue of treating personality disorders is how much personality can be modified. There is extensive evidence that genes play a role in shaping personality—a much stronger role than was once believed (Bouchard et al., 1990; Lykken et al., 1992; Segal, 1999). In contrast, the evidence for childhood experiences as a determinant of personality is generally weak (Seligman, 1990). In an adult client, both of these variables are fixed; you cannot change people's genes or their developmental history. So how much can one change personality, especially the rigid personality characteristics found in personality disorders? The answer to that question is still unknown, but the successes to date provide some interesting clues.

The only personality disorder for which there is a treatment with solid scientific evidence for its effectiveness is borderline personality disorder, for which dialectical behavior therapy has proved effective. However, this treatment approach only manages behaviors; it does not change underlying behavioral tendencies. The client continues to experience emotional fluctuations, but various strategies are used to attenuate the impact of these mood fluctuations on both social and occupational functioning.

There are those who argue that personality can be reshaped with drugs. In the controversial book *Listening to Prozac,* Kramer (1993) maintained that Prozac can do more than just relieve psychiatric symptoms. He argued for using drugs like Prozac to reshape people's outlook, emotional responses, and behavior in ways that improve their lives. The controversy surrounding this book mirrors the controversy of the 1960s, when people such as Timothy Leary, a Harvard psychology professor, was encouraging young people to use drugs like LSD to "expand their minds." Whether Prozac or any other drug can reshape personality is far from established. Furthermore, the wisdom of trying to reshape personality with drugs is likely to engender lively debate for some time to come.

PREVENTION OF FUTURE PSYCHOPATHOLOGY

Because most people with personality disorders do not seek treatment for their personality problems, the clinician does not have a mandate to try to change the person's personality. Even if that were possible, the real goal is to change the things the client wants changed and to reduce the risk of those problems returning. Knowing how Axis II disorders are related to risk for specific Axis I disorders can be immensely valuable in treatment planning. It can suggest areas in which preventive measures may significantly reduce risk. Many treatment procedures, such as cognitive-behavioral therapy, can easily be generalized to the treatment of other symptoms. If those other symptoms develop, the client can use cognitive-behavioral techniques to address them. However, devising more powerful preventive interventions will rest on an understanding of the developmental course of a disorder and of the means by which a specific personality disorder increases risk for a given Axis I disorder. The field barely pays lip service to this concept now, and no systematic study has been devoted to it. Understanding it will be one of the ultimate goals of research into personality disorders, but this effort will have to wait for researchers to address some of the core conceptual issues, which are discussed in the next section.

THE FUTURE OF AXIS II

The implementation of Axis II in DSM-III was a significant advance in diagnostic thinking. For the first time there was recognition of a distinction between the episodic emotional disturbances of Axis I, which are normally ego dystonic, and the chronic, generally ego syntonic disturbances of Axis II. Unfortunately, the promise of this new distinction is far from being fully realized (Bernstein et al., 1993b). The most basic issues, such as whether these personality variables are best conceptualized as categorical disorders or as a series of overlapping dimensions, have yet to be adequately addressed. Some of the more widely studied personality disorders, such as schizotypal and antisocial personality disorders, were intensively investigated before the development of Axis II and are frequently operationalized in research by procedures different from the DSM diagnostic criteria. For other Axis II disorders, there is virtually no controlled research on which to base theories or treatment decisions. Nevertheless, there are signs that personality disorders are being taken more seriously by psychopathology researchers. The question before researchers now is what needs to be done to revitalize this research area.

Clarifying the Conceptual Model. The disorders in the current Axis II are a heterogeneous collection of chronic disorders that were no different from other Axis I disorders, some that have been known for centuries and others just recently recognized. Most were first written about as disorders, with vivid descriptions of the prototypical case—that is, the average person in the diagnostic class. Yet the most basic issues have yet to be addressed adequately. For example, are these disorders better conceptualized as categories or as dimensions? Perhaps some are categorical and others dimensional. Some people have tried to address this issue, but their work has apparently had little impact on the field (Grove & Tellegen, 1991; Harris et al., 1994; Lenzenweger, 1999; Trull et al., 1990). The sophistication of the empirical work on diagnostic criteria is less than what is typically seen for Axis I disorders. Current diagnostic criteria are still being selected largely on the basis of clinician judgments, rather than on the basis of the value of the criteria in enhancing the validity of the diagnosis (Livesley, 1995). Remember from the discussion of construct validation in Chapter 6 that the object is to tinker with diagnostic criteria, or when necessary completely overhaul the criteria, using data such as the reliability and predictive validity of the diagnosis as the index of whether the new diagnostic criteria are superior to the old (Raulin & Lilienfeld, 1999; Robins & Guze, 1970). If, for example, a new set of criteria more accurately predicts both response to treatment and performance on laboratory measures, then it is assumed that the new criteria have greater validity than the old. This hard-nosed scientific approach to personality disorders may lead to a refinement of several current personality disorders. However, with other personality disorders, researchers might be better off scrapping the historical diagnoses and developing new, more carefully validated diagnostic entities. Some researchers are suggesting that a theory-driven reformulation of the concept of personality disorders would provide a set of diagnoses with much higher validity than that of the current set of personality disorders (Millon, 1996).

Dealing with the Problem of Comorbidity. Everyone recognizes that comorbidity is an issue in personality disorders. People who meet the criteria for one personality disorder usually meet the criteria for several (Dahl, 1986; Widiger et al., 1986). Some argue that this is a problem and that it should be addressed by modifying the criteria to reduce the overlap. This argument rests on the implicit assumption that there are separate and distinct disorders. However, this assumption does not imply that there should not be overlap in disorders. For example, the diagnosis of AIDS is based on an HIV+ blood test and on the presence of such opportunistic diseases as tuberculosis or Kaposi's sarcoma—a normally rare malignant tumor that occurs frequently in people who have AIDS. These conditions clearly overlap, yet conceptually they are separate and distinct disorders, each with well-understood etiologies and courses. The overlap does not indicate an error in the diagnostic process but, rather, indicates legitimate shared etiological features and processes. Similarly, the overlap in personality disorders may be perfectly legitimate, because several personality disorders may share common underlying factors or dimensions. In this model, the task is to verify that factors are shared by obtaining independent measures of those factors and developing sophisticated theories of how those factors contribute to the disorder.

Understanding the Contributions of Biology and Environment.

The research on Axis II disorders needs to adopt a more developmental psychopathology approach (Millon & Davis, 1999). Specifically, researchers need to ask how biological variables predispose people to specific behavior under specific conditions, how this behavior can affect future behavior, and how these various factors combine to produce personality disorders. Meehl's (1962, 1990) model of schizotypy is one example of this approach, and the model has triggered dozens of carefully designed studies of critical variables (Edell, 1995). Fowles's (1980) model of psychopathy is another example that seeks theoretically to link biology and behavior in ways that stimulate productive theorizing and critical research. It is reasonable to expect biological factors to interact with environmental factors. However, unless solid measures of these variables are available, as well as strong theory to suggest what interactions are most likely, the resulting research is likely to be disappointing.

Attacking the Disorders from a Developmental Perspective.

Personality disorders, like other disorders, are not likely to develop spontaneously. There may be strong genetic contributions, but those contributions will interact with the person's learning history to produce specific behavioral tendencies. The perspective that has probably contributed the most to the current understanding of personality disorders—the psychodynamic perspective—has emphasized the hypothesized developmental course for these disorders but has neglected the interaction with biology. Surely, no one would want to argue that all people have an equal risk for developing personality disorders. Furthermore, some of the more biological research on personality disorders has ignored developmental variables. The questions investigated should be "What factors predispose individuals to personality disorders, how do those factors contribute to the developmental course, how do environmental experiences interact to shape personality, and finally, why is it that these resulting behavior patterns remain so stable despite their obvious disadvantages?"

There is nothing unique about personality disorders that would prevent the kind of sophisticated research just described. It is worth noting that research on Axis I disorders also floundered for a while because researchers had not come to grips with these basic questions. Yet once they were addressed, the research led quickly to new insights—and often to better treatments. This could be an exciting time for research on personality disorders. There is no question about their clinical importance and the emotional toll they take on individuals and their friends, family, and co-workers. The next 20 years of research on personality and personality disorders could yield the kind of conceptual shift that Kraepelin produced with the introduction of differential diagnosis in the nineteenth century.

The incorporation of Axis II into DSM-III was a significant step forward in the overall conceptualization of personality and its impact on psychopathology. Its inclusion in the diagnostic manual has stimulated research, discussion, and debate, which eventually will enhance the scientific understanding of these disorders (Livesley, 1995) and may eventually improve treatment (Turkat, 1990).

Check Yourself 12.5

Issues and Unanswered Questions

1. Name three treatment dilemmas faced by therapists regarding Axis II disorders.
2. What is the only personality disorder for which there is a treatment that has been demonstrated to be effective?
3. What is the most basic conceptual issue still to be resolved regarding personality disorders?

Ponder this . . .   *How could researchers study the impact of early developmental events on later personality development? How difficult is it to study these variables without confounding them with other variables?*

SUMMARY

THE CONCEPT OF PERSONALITY DISORDERS

- Personality disorders are pervasive and inflexible patterns of emotional reaction and behavior that interfere with the interpersonal functioning of the individual. They are diagnosed on Axis II. Unlike most Axis I disorders, personality disorders tend to be ego syntonic.

- The fields of personality and personality disorders have operated independently of one another, although there is now some cross-fertilization. Personality theorists have been interested in identifying underlying dimensions of personality.

CLUSTER A DISORDERS

- The paranoid personality disorder is characterized by a pervasive distrust of people and their motives. It appears to have a genetic relationship to both schizophrenia and delusional disorders.

- The schizoid personality disorder is characterized by a pervasive pattern of detachment from social relationships and an apparent lack of interest in those relationships. It is not clear whether it is part of the schizophrenic spectrum.

- The schizotypal personality disorder is characterized by oddness in thought, perception, and social interactions. This disorder shares a genetic diathesis with schizophrenia.

- The clinical wisdom is that people with disorders in the odd/eccentric cluster tend not to respond to traditional psychodynamic treatment and may even deteriorate. A more supportive therapy is recommended.

CLUSTER B DISORDERS

- Antisocial personality disorder is characterized by a pervasive pattern of disregard for the rights of others. These individuals are underaroused, which may account for their reduced anxiety and their impulsive behavior. They experience a deficit in their behavioral inhibition system, which causes deficits in learning to avoid punishment, but not deficits in learning to obtain rewards.

- Borderline personality disorder is characterized by a pervasive pattern of unstable and intense relationships.

- Histrionic personality disorder is characterized by excessive emotionality and attention-seeking behavior.

- Narcissistic personality disorder is characterized by grandiosity, a constant need for admiration, and an apparent lack of empathy for others.

- Antisocial personality disorder is difficult to treat, although there may be more optimism if treatment is begun during childhood. Some common comorbid conditions, such as ADHD, may warrant treatment. The treatment of choice for borderline personality disorder is dialectical behavior therapy. There is very little controlled research on treatment for histrionic and narcissistic personality disorders.

CLUSTER C DISORDERS

- Avoidant personality disorder is characterized by a pervasive pattern of shyness, social inhibition, and hypersensitivity to negative evaluations. Unlike schizoid personality disorder, the social isolation of avoidant personality disorder is motivated by social anxiety.

- Dependent personality disorder is characterized by clinging behavior and a fear of separation.

- Obsessive-compulsive personality disorder is characterized by a preoccupation with orderliness, perfectionism, and control. Although there are similarities between obsessive-compulsive personality disorder and OCD, well-trained clinicians can easily distinguish between them.

- There is very little controlled research on the treatment of Cluster C personality disorders.

ISSUES AND UNANSWERED QUESTIONS

- Most people with Axis II disorders seek treatment only when they have an Axis I disorder and usually are not interested in changing their personality.

- There is little evidence to suggest that it is possible to reshape personality. Therefore, treatment needs to focus on managing the impact that the personality disorder has on the person's behavior rather than on changing the person completely.

- For research on Axis II disorders to make progress, researchers need to be more explicit about their conceptual model, to account for the excessive comorbidity among these disorders, and integrate both biological factors and environmental influences within a developmental framework.

KEY TERMS

antisocial personality disorder   (372)
avoidant personality disorder   (385)
Axis II diagnoses   (364)
behavioral activation system, or BAS   (376)
behavioral inhibition system, or BIS   (375)
borderline personality disorder   (376)
dependent personality disorder   (386)
dialectical behavior therapy, or DBT   (384)
extraversion   (365)
histrionic personality disorder   (379)
ideas of reference   (370)
introversion   (365)
narcissistic personality disorder   (381)
neuroticism   (365)

obsessive-compulsive personality disorder   (387)
paranoid personality disorder   (368)
passive avoidance learning   (375)
personality   (364)
personality disorders   (364)
personality traits   (364)
psychometric instruments   (371)
psychopathy   (372)
psychoticism   (365)
schizoid personality disorder   (369)
schizotypal personality disorder   (370)
sociopathy   (372)
splitting   (377)
trait dimensions   (365)

SUGGESTED READINGS

Millon, T. (1996). *Disorders of personality: DSM-IV and beyond* (2nd ed.). New York: Wiley. This is considered the definitive book on personality disorders.

chapterthirteen

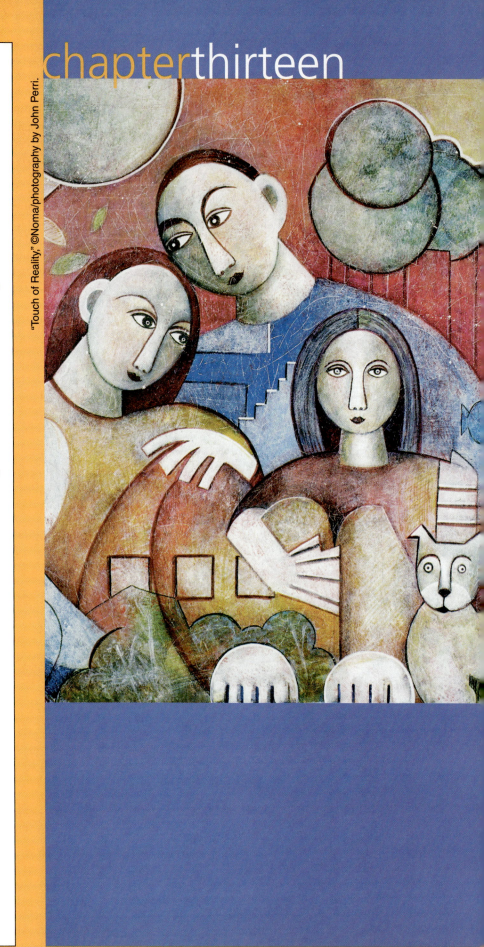

"Touch of Reality," ©Noma/photography by John Perri.

Disorders First Apparent in Childhood

More Than a Handful

DONALD

Donald was a challenge from the time he first started to crawl. He got into everything and never stopped moving. Now, at nine years of age, Donald's boundless energy and poor judgment constantly create problems. In school he finds it impossible to sit still, often getting up without permission and wandering around the room. On the playground he tries to join one game after another, although he is usually rebuffed because he never follows through. His fellow students mostly shun him, not because they dislike him but because they can never count on him. Medication helps to control his behavior, but even with the medication, he finds it difficult to concentrate. Clearly a very bright boy, he still gets D's and F's in school because of his inconsistency. His parents often find him impossible to handle. If they turn their backs for even a minute, he wanders off. At the age of four, he wandered away from home and was found four hours later happily playing in a public fountain in the middle of a busy street.

In a World of His Own

NATHAN

On a good day, Nathan might respond to his name and might be able to play for a few minutes with his parents. More often he plays by himself, doing things over and over. His favorite game is watching the toilet flush—something that he could do for hours if his parents let him. At other times he pounds his head against the wall, apparently oblivious to the pain it must be causing. Barely able to talk, he is more likely to repeat verbatim the things that he hears. When he talks, it is usually in one- or two-word sentences, such as "Hungry," "Me want," and "Where dad?" He spends eight hours a day,

five days a week, in a special program at a psychiatric hospital 40 miles from his home. The program has increased his functioning, added considerably to his communication skills, and decreased his occasional self-destructive behavior.

Finding Her Niche

ADRIAN

Adrian was diagnosed with moderate mental retardation. She attended a special school and lived at home until just before her parents died, at which point she was placed in a state institution. She did poorly in the institution. Her parents had spoiled her, so her reaction to the institution was to be demanding and confrontational. The psychiatrist put her on strong medication to calm her and, when that did not work, increased the dose and then increased it again. Over a period of ten years, her functioning deteriorated and her disruptive behavior increased. She was also becoming increasingly intolerant of the medication, until the side effects were so severe that she spent most of the day in a fetal position. At that point, her brother challenged her treatment in court, forcing the state to place her in a group home, to reduce her medications dramatically, and to provide psychological rehabilitation. Six years, two group homes, and three daytime rehabilitation programs later, Adrian is doing much better. The neurological symptoms from the years of overmedication have decreased, her outbursts are less frequent, and she is finally finding things in life that she really enjoys.

The psychological problems discussed in earlier chapters primarily affect adults. But psychopathology is not limited to adults, and the psychopathology found in children is often severe and disabling. It is important to note that the DSM does not have a category of childhood disorders but, rather, has a category of *disorders first evident in childhood.* The reason for this subtle distinction is that many disorders of childhood continue into adulthood, others show residual effects, and many disrupt critical development, thus affecting a person throughout adulthood. For example, Donald's inability to focus his attention is severely disrupting both his academic and his social development. Nathan's severe symptoms disrupt every aspect of his development, which almost certainly will mean that he will require some form of care throughout his life. Adrian's mental retardation affects every aspect of her development. Now in her forties, she still requires constant supervision. She will never hold a real job, is unlikely to be able to live in unsupervised housing, and will always be a ward of the state.

This chapter is divided into four sections. The first covers disorders characterized by disruptive behavior—that is, behavior that disrupts the people who are around the child. The second section covers functional and learning disorders—that is, disorders in basic functioning, from eating, to communication, to learning, to elimination of wastes. This group of disorders is too extensive to cover in its entirety, but this chapter discusses a brief sampling. The chapter also covers autistic disorder, a severe mental disorder that strikes in the first year or two of life and concludes with mental retardation.

DISRUPTIVE BEHAVIOR DISORDERS

Disruptive behavior is any behavior that interferes with the day-to-day functioning of other people. This section addresses two types of disruptive behavior in children: attention-deficit/hyperactivity disorder and conduct disorder.

ATTENTION-DEFICIT/ HYPERACTIVITY DISORDER

The defining characteristics of **attention-deficit/hyperactivity disorder (ADHD)** are inattention and excessive activity or impulsivity. Donald, who was one of the cases that opened the chapter, showed many such symptoms. For example, he could never follow through on games with other kids because his attention would quickly be drawn to other activities. His attentional problems were even more severe in the classroom, where he found it impossible to focus on a task for more than a few minutes. On a vacation to Disney World, he took off, going on rides and talking with strangers for the better part of two hours before

park security located him. His parents were so distressed that they returned from their vacation two days early. Examples of the full range of ADHD symptoms are listed in Table 13.1. These symptoms are usually evident even before the onset of school, but they typically become more relevant once a child starts school, because they are so disruptive in a structured school setting. To qualify for the diagnosis, these symptoms must be present in at least two different settings (school, home, play, etc.) and must contribute to clinically significant impairment in social, academic, or occupational functioning (APA, 2000). Most often, ADHD contributes to impairment in all of these areas (Casat et al., 2001). The DSM distinguishes three subtypes of ADHD: ADHD, predominantly inattentive type; ADHD, predominantly hyperactive-impulsive type; and ADHD, combined type. These subtype designations were introduced in DSM-IV. Previously, both inattention and hyperactivity/impulsiveness were required for the diagnosis. Research suggests that these subtypes may be different disorders, with different etiologies, although it is too soon to say for certain (Carlson & Mann, 2002; Milich et al., 2001). The research presented in this section applies primarily to the combined-type subgroup, which represents the vast majority of people with this diagnosis (APA, 2000). Many people know ADHD by

[TABLE 13.1] Symptoms of ADHD

Inattention Symptoms (minimum of six required for diagnosis)

◆ Lack of attention to detail; makes many careless mistakes

◆ Frequent difficulty in sustaining attention on tasks

◆ Often appears not to listen when spoken to directly

◆ Often fails to follow through on instructions or complete tasks

◆ Often has difficulty in organizing tasks and activities

◆ Avoids or dislikes tasks that require sustained mental effort

◆ Often loses things necessary for tasks or activities

◆ Is often easily distracted by extraneous stimuli

◆ Is often forgetful in daily activities

Hyperactivity/Impulsivity Symptoms (minimum of six required for diagnosis)

◆ Often fidgets or squirms in seat

◆ Often leaves seat in settings in which such behavior is inappropriate, such as a classroom

◆ Often runs about or climbs excessively when such behavior is inappropriate

◆ Often has difficulty in playing quietly

◆ Is often "on the go" or acts as if "driven by a motor"

◆ Often talks excessively

◆ Often blurts out answers before questions are completed

◆ Often has difficulty awaiting turn

◆ Often disrupts or intrudes on others, such as by barging into a conversation

SOURCE: *Reprinted with permission from the* Diagnostic and Statistical Manual of Mental Disorders, *Fourth Edition, Text Revision. Copyright © 2000 American Psychiatric Association.*

attention-deficit/hyperactivity disorder (ADHD)
Characterized by inattention and excessive activity or impulsivity.

an earlier diagnostic label, such as *attention deficit disorder (ADD)* or *hyperactivity.*

There is considerable heterogeneity in the symptom patterns found in people with ADHD (Quinlan, 2000). To complicate diagnosis further, several psychiatric disorders are overrepresented in people who carry an ADHD diagnosis, including mood disorders (Spencer et al., 2000), anxiety disorders (Tannock, 2000), learning disorders (Stevenson, 2001; Tannock & Brown, 2000), substance use disorders (Wilens et al., 2000), antisocial personality disorder (Martens, 2000), and neurologically based disorders (Comings, 2000; Denckla, 2000). It is unclear why so many different conditions are comorbid with ADHD. Some, such as substance use disorders, may be secondary to the impulsive behavior that characterizes ADHD. Others, such as learning disorders, may share common neurological underpinnings. More research on these questions is urgently needed.

The prevalence of ADHD depends on the age of the child. Approximately 5% of school-age children meet criteria for this disorder (APA, 2000), but that figure drops as children mature. The hyperactivity symptoms tend to decrease by adolescence (Weiss et al., 1971), but impulsivity tends to remain (Weiss & Hechtman, 1993). Adults with ADHD complain less of attentional problems, but this may be because adults select jobs and activities that require little sustained attention (Weiss et al., 1999). ADHD is more common in boys than in girls by a ratio of from 2:1 to 9:1, depending on the subtype of ADHD (APA, 2000).

Traditionally, people have thought of ADHD as a disorder that affects children and adolescents, but what happens when these children grow into adults? Do the symptoms disappear or moderate? How do the developmental and academic problems from childhood and adolescence affect the adult? These questions are receiving more attention now than they received just a few years ago (Weiss et al., 1999). Let's look at this issue.

Examining the Evidence

The gross restlessness associated with ADHD in children decreases as people with this disorder mature (Weiss & Hechtman, 1993), although adults with ADHD still report feeling restless. Unlike children who cannot sit still, adults are able to conform to most social constraints. They can sit through meetings, remain seated on airplanes, and focus their attention well enough to complete tasks. The behavioral changes are dramatic enough that many no longer qualify for the diagnosis of ADHD. Only 30% of children with ADHD still meet criteria for the disorder by late adolescence, and fewer than 10% meet these criteria by their mid-twenties (Mannuzza et al., 1993, 1998). However, ADHD continues to leave scars. For example, about a quarter of people with ADHD fail to complete high school, a figure that is much higher than comparison groups (Mannuzza et al., 1997). Interestingly, about a fifth of children with ADHD develop antisocial personality disorder as adults, and the rate of crime in this group is especially high (Weiss et al.,

The inability to focus attention and the impulsive behavior of children with ADHD create numerous problems in school settings, because the child is unable to conform to classroom expectations.

1985; Mannuzza et al., 1998). Virtually all of the children who have ADHD and who develop antisocial personality disorder as adults showed antisocial tendencies as children. Drug abuse is more common in adults with ADHD, although it is far more common in those who develop antisocial personality disorder than in those who do not (Weiss et al., 1999). Although not every adult who was diagnosed with ADHD as a child has difficulties in adulthood, these people qualify for more psychiatric disorders, have more suicide attempts, have greater difficulty in finding and holding jobs, have more traffic accidents, and report less self-esteem than unaffected adults (Barkley et al., 1996; Hechtman et al., 1980).

Causes. What causes ADHD? This is a complex question. Research suggests that genes contribute significantly to ADHD (Faraone et al., 2000; Hudziak, 2000). Interestingly, there appear to be separate genetic contributions to the inattention and the hyperactivity/impulsivity dimensions of ADHD, although these factors are strongly correlated (Hudziak et al., 1998). Most intriguing, when one breaks down the cases on either the inattention dimension or the hyperactivity/impulsivity dimension into mild, moderate, and severe categories, the twin data suggest that these severity categories may represent different disorders (Hudziak et al., 1998). For example, those people with moderate levels of inattention have twins with a greater risk for moderate inattention, but not a greater risk for mild or severe levels of inattention; this result suggests that different genes contribute to the different levels of ADHD (Hudziak, 2000). Finally, family studies that have grouped children with ADHD according to the presence of comorbid disorders suggest that (1) there may be meaningful subgroups of children with ADHD and (2) at least some of the genes that predispose children to develop ADHD may also predispose people to other disorders, such as depression (Faraone & Biederman, 1997), bipolar disorder (Faraone et al., 1997), and learning disorders (Seidman et al., 2001). To summarize these complicated findings, the inattention and hyperactivity symptoms of ADHD have separate genetic contributors, ADHD is genetically heterogeneous, and the various genes that increase risk for ADHD also contribute to other forms of psychopathology.

Professionals have long suspected that subtle brain damage was a major contributor to ADHD. In fact, at one point *minimal brain damage,* or *MBD,* was the diagnostic term applied to the people now diagnosed as having ADHD. At the time, there was no direct evidence of brain damage, but the high comorbidity of ADHD with learning disorders suggested that subtle brain abnormalities might be involved. More recent evidence suggests that brain abnormalities do exist. For example, children with ADHD have a slightly smaller total brain volume than unaffected children, and many have a significantly smaller cerebellum (Rapoport et al., 2001). Finally, there is evidence of abnormalities in the basal ganglia—a brain structure that serves as a switching station for information from other regions of the brain (Kalat, 2001). There is also evidence of dysregulation in several other brain regions, including the prefrontal cortex, locus coeruleus, cerebellum, and amygdala-septo-hippocampal system (Castellanos, 1999).

Perhaps the most influential theory of ADHD is Russell Barkley's (1997, 2001) *behavioral inhibition model.* Barkley argues that the primary deficit in ADHD is a diminished capacity to inhibit behavior and exercise self-control, which results in such inappropriate behavior as getting up and walking around a classroom during class. He believes that the underlying deficit is one of **executive functioning**—that is, those self-directed behaviors that regulate and coordinate actions to achieve goals. Executive function resides primarily in the frontal lobes of the brain; hence Barkley's behavioral inhibition model is consistent with other evidence for frontal lobe dysfunction in ADHD (Giedd et al., 2001). It also explains dozens of findings from classroom and laboratory studies of children with ADHD (Barkley, 1997). It is one of the few attempts to provide an integrative theory of ADHD. This area of research has been largely atheoretical—that is, not much effort has been made to develop explanations for the phenomenon. The result is that although a tremendous number of facts that have been discovered about ADHD from individual studies, there has been no way to organize them. Barkley's model provides such organization. It posits an underlying neurological dysfunction, primarily in the frontal lobes, that leads to a deficit in executive functioning that prevents or delays the development of behavioral inhibition and self-control. The poor behavioral inhibition results in both impulsive behavior and an inability to maintain focused attention, thus explaining both of the primary symptoms of ADHD with a single mechanism. Although a major step forward, Barkley's behavioral inhibition model has been criticized for glossing over critical mechanisms (Nigg, 2001). However, this kind of healthy scientific debate will likely enhance our understanding of ADHD.

Evolutionary Impact

Not everyone agrees that brain mechanisms are involved in ADHD (Baumeister & Hawkins, 2001). However, a fair reading of the research suggests that brain mechanisms are involved in many, if not most, cases of ADHD but that different brain mechanisms may be involved in different cases. Like the genetic research, brain research suggests that ADHD is a heterogeneous disorder. But the involvement of brain mechanisms does not necessarily

executive functioning Those self-directed behaviors that regulate and coordinate actions to achieve goals.

imply pathology. Jaak Panksepp (1998) has suggested that the real problem in ADHD is that the intensive regimentation of the modern classroom, coupled with decreased time for active rough-and-tumble play, leaves children who have high needs for such activities unable to satisfy those needs and therefore unable to pay attention in the classroom. This is an evolutionary hypothesis in that it suggests that the real problem has been a change in environment, which now penalizes certain children who, in another era or under different circumstances, would have functioned normally. It might also explain the rapid and dramatic increase in ADHD over the past century.

Could Panksepp's hypothesis about ADHD be correct? Several findings are consistent with it. For example, despite decades-old claims that neurological damage is responsible for ADHD, there is little evidence of significant brain abnormalities. There are small differences in the frontal lobes, but they appear to be the extreme of a normal distribution rather than uniquely pathological (Castellanos et al., 1996). Behaviorally, ADHD children often look like the extreme of children in their playfulness and limited ability to focus on classroom activity. They often function reasonably well in nonclassroom settings that do not require the constant attention and impulse control demanded in the classroom (Barkley, 1997). In fact, most children with ADHD are not diagnosed until they start school, despite the fact that their high energy levels are apparent from an early age (APA, 2000). Could the traits associated with ADHD have been adaptive in an earlier era? Impulsive individuals with rapidly shifting attention may have made better hunters, and the so-called distractibility associated with ADHD might well be beneficial in an environment with multiple predators, because shifting attention constantly would increase the likelihood of detecting such danger (Panksepp, 1998). Similar arguments could be made for each of the other characteristics of ADHD. Perhaps these natural variations in temperament, though adaptive in some environments, are especially maladaptive in the modern classroom. Perhaps there just are not sufficient outlets for children whose temperament demands high activity. Boys have always engaged in more rough-and-tumble play, and boys dramatically outnumber girls in the diagnosis of ADHD.

Barkley (1997) has argued that the frontal lobes are critical in long-term planning and that the ability to engage in such planning requires considerable development and maturation. Some children may simply develop this ability more slowly. Viewing the symptoms of ADHD as problematic and controlling them with drugs may deny the child the opportunity to develop neurological and behavioral controls for this impulsive and rambunctious activity. Perhaps providing these children with reasonable outlets for their energies and allowing normal developmental processes to regulate the behav-

ior in time would be more effective. The concern raised by many teachers is that accepting such rough-and-tumble and impulsive behavior as normal will lead to the children's becoming more wild and uncontrollable. However, animal studies suggest just the opposite; animals with tendencies to engage in such behavior show more normal response and development if allowed the opportunity for such play (Panksepp et al., 1984). As you will see shortly, this evolutionary hypothesis has implications for treatment.

Perhaps one of the most controversial hypotheses regarding ADHD is the suggestion that it is the result of dietary elements—specifically, additives and food colorings that are routinely included in modern processed foods. This hypothesis has led many parents to place children with ADHD on a special diet, called the Feingold diet, to eliminate the food additives. However, there is no evidence that this diet reduces ADHD symptoms or that these substances increase ADHD symptoms (Rapoport & Castellanos, 1996). More recently, another dietary treatment has been proposed—specifically, a diet high in omega-3 fatty acids (Stoll, 2001). This diet is known to decrease risk for heart disease, although the evidence that it may be helpful in treating ADHD is weak at best. One must hope that this diet will not become a large-scale treatment approach like the Feingold diet until hard evidence of its effectiveness is available. Because parents of children with ADHD are often overwhelmed with the management of their children, they are easy targets for programs that are heavily promoted but not adequately researched.

Psychological factors also play a significant role in shaping, maintaining, and possibly even producing some of the symptoms of ADHD. At the very least, psychological factors enhance the problems associated with ADHD (Barkley, 1998). The manner in which teachers, parents, and peers respond to the behavior of children with ADHD will either increase or decrease the severity of symptoms. Furthermore, the negative way in which others react to these children contributes to a significant loss of self-esteem (Treuting & Hinshaw, 2001).

Treatment. There is no treatment that cures ADHD. Rather, treatment should be thought of as managing the symptoms so that the child can experience the normal social and academic development so critical to success in adulthood. Two treatment strategies have dominated the field: stimulant medications and behavioral therapies (Pelham & Gnagy, 1999).

The use of stimulant medications to treat a disorder characterized by hyperactivity may seem like a contradiction, but in fact, these medications are often effective. The most widely used medication for ADHD is methylphenidate (Ritalin). Chemically similar to amphetamines, Ritalin increases arousal and therefore increases the ability of

This may look like play, but it is one of the best ways to improve the functioning of children with ADHD. Most such children have terrible social relationships because they are unable to meet the expectations of play situations. Teaching children with ADHD how to play games is often helpful in improving social interactions and increasing self-esteem.

children with ADHD to focus their attention. Dozens of controlled studies over the last two decades, some of them double-blind studies, have clearly established the short-term effectiveness of Ritalin (Mehta et al., 2001). However, once the drug wears off, the symptoms of ADHD return immediately (Greenhill, 2001). Clearly, stimulant medications are not a cure for ADHD, but they do permit some children to function better. Nevertheless, many people question the wisdom of using stimulant medication to treat children with ADHD (Greene & Ablon, 2001; Harwood & Beutler, 2001).

The use of stimulant medication with children raises several issues, and drug companies are increasing the controversy by attempting to market drugs like Ritalin directly to the public rather than through prescribing doctors (Novak, 2001). One issue is the possible side effects of the chronic use of such medications. Stimulants are known to affect growth hormones (PDR, 2002), so doctors often encourage parents to use the stimulant drugs to help their child function better in school but to minimize use of the drugs after school and on weekends. Drug holidays—that

is, not taking the drugs for a few days or weeks—are also encouraged, as well as periodically checking to see whether a lower dose is effective (Greenhill, 2001). Most negative side effects of drugs are dose-dependent. Therefore, using the lowest dose possible reduces the risk of side effects. Some have expressed concern about possible unknown risks from the chronic use of stimulants over several years (DeGrandpre, 1999). Although it appears that such risks are low, there has not been enough experience with these drugs over long time periods to rule it out completely. Finally, although the use of stimulant medications improves the functioning of most children with ADHD, it almost certainly masks underlying problem(s). Given the strong evidence that ADHD is heterogeneous, it is unlikely that one drug could treat so many different underlying causes (Denney, 2001). The task facing researchers now is to identify which treatments are most effective for a given child by identifying predictors of treatment effectiveness (Whalen, 2001).

A second strategy in the management of problem behaviors in ADHD is behavior therapy (Turchiano, 2000). The goal of behavior therapy is to show the child ways of effectively handling the many tasks demanded of children every day. For example, many children with ADHD have severely strained relationships with peers and parents because of their inappropriate behavior. Teaching the child effective socialization skills, reinforcing improved behavior until the natural reinforcements from the environment take over, and then showing parents and teachers ways to foster and maintain the treatment gains are all necessary to progress. Contrary to popular belief, children with ADHD are responsive to the consequences of their behavior (Carlson & Tamm, 2000). Behavior therapy typically employs a variety of techniques, including progressive relaxation to reduce arousal, contingency management to increase desirable behaviors and decrease undesirable ones, training in social skills to improve the children's social functioning, and cognitive therapy to increase awareness of internal motivations and the responses of others to their behavior (Abikoff & Hechtman, 1996).

The behavioral treatment of ADHD need not always focus on the child. Sonuga-Barke et al. (2001) showed that training parents in behavior management can significantly improve the functioning of preschoolers with ADHD. Successful treatment with behavior therapy, stimulant medication, or both reduces both parental and family stress and thus improves parenting behavior (Wells et al., 2000).

One of the most recent and best-controlled treatment studies was the National Institute of Mental Health–sponsored Multimodal Treatment Study, which compared stimulant-drug treatment to both behavior therapy and the combination of behavior therapy and drug treatment. This study found that drug therapy was significantly better at controlling inattention and hyperactivity and that the addition of behavior therapy to drug therapy added little to the treatment (Jensen et al., 2001). However, the combination of behavior therapy and stimulant medications was more effective than either treatment alone for improving social skills, academic performance, child-parent relations, oppositional behavior, anxiety, and depression. One of the strongest criticisms of this study was that the behavioral treatment was not intensive enough to have a significant impact on the child. Pelham and his associates have experimented with intensive summer treatment programs for children with ADHD. These programs typically last several weeks, meet five days a week, and include up to eight hours of programmed activities each day. Such programs are designed to be fun for the children. The focus is on games and activities, with behavioral treatment skillfully woven into the entire program. When *this* intensive behavioral treatment was combined with stimulant medications, the combination was consistently superior to medication alone in decreasing ADHD symptoms and improving the functioning of the child (Pelham et al., 2000).

Evolutionary Impact

The evolutionary hypothesis for ADHD has implications for treatment. Remember that it suggests that children with this diagnosis are simply those with higher needs for rough-and-tumble play and with more impulsive temperaments. It suggests an alternative treatment that has not received sufficient attention (Panksepp, 1998). Specifically, could giving children with ADHD more opportunity for the rough-and-tumble play that they need or reducing the demand for quiet attention in the classroom enable children with ADHD to function in school and to develop the neurological and behavioral constraints to manage their high energy level? Right now, there is no answer to this question. But it is worth noting that the behavioral program that shows the greatest promise relies heavily on intensive activity and sports and seeks to shape attentional processes within this context (Pelham et al., 2000). It does not exclusively reinforce attentive classroom behavior but rather provides healthful outlets for the energy of children with ADHD.

Stimulant medications increase arousal and thus improve the ability of children with ADHD to cope with their symptoms. In contrast, behavior therapy is targeted to specific symptoms or problem behaviors. Ultimately, the goal is to provide the right combination of treatments for each child—a combination that is effective and represents the least risk and/or cost (Whalen, 2001). Some headway is now being made on this issue, although much more needs to be done. For example, behavior therapy appears to be

especially effective in those children with ADHD who also have a comorbid anxiety disorder (Multimodal Treatment Study of ADHD, 1999). Additional research of this type is likely to improve the delivery of services to affected children. Encouraging energetic exercise and play in ADHD children may decrease their inattention in the classroom and decrease the need for high doses of stimulant medication, although this hypothesis has not yet been adequately tested.

CONDUCT DISORDER

Conduct disorder is characterized by a pervasive pattern of behavior that reflects a basic lack of respect for the rights of others and consistent violations of rules or norms. Table 13.2 presents several examples of such behavior. In order to qualify for this diagnosis, the child's behavior must be severe enough to cause clinically significant impairment in social, occupational, or academic functioning. This pattern of behavior may develop even before the child starts school or may become apparent only during adolescence (Shaw et al., 2001). You may have noticed that the behaviors listed in Table 13.2 are similar to the behaviors that define antisocial personality disorder, which was covered in Chapter 12. Personality disorder diagnoses are *not* made until at

[TABLE 13.2] Conduct Disorder Symptoms

Aggression to People or Animals
- Often bullies, threatens, or intimidates others
- Often initiates physical fights
- Has used dangerous weapons in fights
- Has been physically cruel to people
- Has been physically cruel to animals
- Has stolen while confronting a victim (e.g., mugging)
- Has forced someone into sexual activity

Destruction of Property
- Has deliberately set fires with intention to destroy property
- Has destroyed property deliberately in other ways than fire setting

Deceitfulness or Theft
- Has broken into someone else's house, building, or car
- Often lies to obtain goods or favors or to avoid responsibility
- Has stolen costly items without confronting the victim (e.g., shoplifting)

Serious Violations of Rules
- Often stays out late at night against parents' wishes before age 13
- Has run away from home overnight at least twice
- Is often truant from school starting before age 13

SOURCE: *Reprinted with permission from the* Diagnostic and Statistical Manual of Mental Disorders, *Fourth Edition, Text Revision. Copyright © 2000 American Psychiatric Association.*

conduct disorder A pervasive pattern of behavior that is characterized by a basic lack of respect for the rights of others and by consistent violations of rules or norms.

least early adulthood, because one's personality is still forming until then. The conduct disorder diagnosis provides a diagnostic option to acknowledge antisocial behaviors in a child, without giving the child a diagnosis that is, by definition, stable throughout the lifetime. Many children who qualify for a diagnosis of conduct disorder also qualify for a diagnosis of antisocial personality disorder in adulthood (Langbehn & Cadoret, 2001). However, some children who display delinquent behavior that could qualify them for a conduct disorder diagnosis do not develop the stable antisocial pattern in adulthood (Biederman et al., 2001; Loeber et al., 2000).

There is also a related disorder—**oppositional defiant disorder**—which is characterized by a pattern of negativistic, hostile, and defiant behaviors. Because such oppositional behaviors are common in teenagers, the DSM cautions against making this diagnosis unless the behavior is persistent. It is not uncommon for oppositional defiant disorder to develop later into conduct disorder, perhaps because these disorders may share genetic factors (Simonoff, 2001). Many professionals believe that oppositional defiant disorder is a milder form of conduct disorder.

The DSM makes two distinctions regarding conduct disorder. The first is whether the onset is during childhood or adolescence. The second is whether the symptoms are mild, moderate, or severe. Mild symptoms include lying, shoplifting, and truancy—behaviors that usually do not hurt others directly. Moderate symptoms include burglary and vandalism—symptoms that affect others, but not necessarily in a severe manner. Severe symptoms include physical cruelty, muggings, breaking and entering, and rape—behaviors that physically and psychologically harm others. Typically, less severe behaviors develop first. Those who develop severe symptoms at a young age often go on to qualify for antisocial personality disorder (APA, 2000). Males outnumber females, and the pattern of symptoms varies by sex. For example, males are more likely to engage in aggressive behaviors, such as fighting, vandalism, and school discipline problems. Females are more likely to engage in less aggressive behaviors, such as lying, truancy, drug use, and prostitution. The prevalence rates depend on the setting. Rates have ranged from 1% to 10% (APA, 2000). Prevalence rates are higher in urban settings, especially inner-city neighborhoods, than in rural settings (Pliszka et al., 2000), and these rates appear to be rising (Tiet et al., 2001). Conduct disorder is one of the most frequent reasons for the placement of children in either inpatient or outpatient treatment centers (Malone, 2000).

Causes. There is no single factor that accounts for all cases of conduct disorder. Brain dysfunction is found in at least some children with conduct disorder (Teichner &

Golden, 2000). Verbal deficits are the neuropsychological deficit most consistently found in conduct disorder, but deficits in visuospacial processing, sensory processing, motor processing, and organization have also been found. This constellation of neuropsychological findings does not suggest any particular localized deficit but, rather, suggests generalized poor neurological performance.

Neurochemical and hormonal factors may also contribute to conduct disorder. The neurotransmitter serotonin shows a dysregulation in children with conduct disorder—that is, serotonin activity fluctuates for no obvious reason. This is especially true in those who show a propensity for violence (Unis et al., 1997). Furthermore, SSRI drugs decrease aggression in individuals with conduct disorder (Cherek & Lane, 1999). Those individuals with conduct disorder who are especially aggressive also show a stronger cortisol response to a stressor than those with conduct disorder who are not aggressive or those without conduct disorder (Soloff et al., 2000). These findings of abnormal serotonin and cortisol levels are recent, and to date there is no agreement about how to interpret them.

Genes increase the risk for conduct disorder, especially in those cases in which the person qualifies for the diagnosis of antisocial personality disorder in adulthood (Goldstein et al., 2001; Slutske et al., 1998). However, most theorists emphasize how genes and environment interact in shaping the behaviors of conduct disorder (Simonoff, 2001). Genes may make a child prone to aggressive and impulsive behavior, but whether those tendencies are enhanced or attenuated depends on the consistency of discipline in the home and on the degree of nurturance (Frick et al., 1999; Kilgore et al., 2000).

Early theories suggested that the parents of children with conduct disorder failed to provide a strong sense of right and wrong during the children's formative years (Hoffman, 1970). These early theories may have had intuitive appeal, but the situation is apparently much more complicated than that. Children are influenced in many ways. For example, psychologists have known for decades that aggressiveness can be increased through modeling, such as by watching violence on TV (Bandura & Walters, 1963), and the evidence for this effect has been accumulating (Huesmann, 1997). There is little doubt that virtually all children are subjected to an ever-widening array of violent images, and this influence should not be overlooked. However, it is important to recognize that most children do not develop conduct disorder in spite of their exposure to such material, an observation that again emphasizes the interaction of environment and genetics in shaping conduct disorder.

Treatment. Several treatment approaches have been used with conduct disorder. There is considerable interest in finding effective treatments because some people with conduct disorder will develop antisocial personality disorder. The hope is that early intervention with these chil-

---

oppositional defiant disorder   Characterized by a pattern of negativistic, hostile, and defiant behaviors.

dren can reduce this number. This section will describe cognitive-behavioral approaches, family interventions, and drug treatment.

Cognitive-behavior therapy has been used extensively with conduct disorder and is probably one of the best-studied treatment approaches (Mpofu & Crystal, 2001). The goal is to encourage prosocial behavior and to teach problem-solving skills, social perspective taking, and moral reasoning (Herbert, 1998). Such treatment is most effective if applied early, before the child has developed a lifestyle and friendship pattern that helps to maintain antisocial behavior (Sanders, 1996). The cognitive-behavioral approach focuses on the core symptoms of conduct disorder as they play out in real-life situations. For example, every child is teased or provoked occasionally. Children with conduct disorder tend to respond to such teasing with verbal and physical aggression. Teaching the child alternative strategies for stopping this teasing will reduce the incidence of aggression, decrease the social isolation that such aggression can produce, and increase the child's sense of control over the situation.

Although cognitive-behavioral therapy is effective, interventions that include the other family members appear to be the most promising (Carr, 2000). Of course, not every family is willing to participate, and some parents are unable to be consistent with a program. Nevertheless, if the parents are cooperative, they should definitely be included in the treatment (Sholevar, 2001). Family therapy typically employs a combination of the cognitive-behavioral approaches just described for the child and training in effective parenting and discipline. Cognitive-behavioral techniques, such as social skills training, are much more effective when done within a family context (Taylor et al., 1999). Unfortunately, dropout rates are considerably higher in family therapy than in therapy focused on the child alone, perhaps because it is the parents who decide whether to continue therapy, and family therapy puts more pressure on parents to change their behavior (Luk et al., 2001). One particularly innovative program uses videotapes of vignettes to train both the child and the parents in more effective ways of handling difficult situations (Webster-Stratton, 1996). These vignettes have the advantage of engaging both the parents and the child, and they model effective behavior.

Several medications have been used to treat conduct disorder. For example, antipsychotic, antianxiety, and antidepressant drugs have all been used to reduce the aggressiveness so common in conduct disorder (Campbell et al., 1999; Fava, 1997). The antidepressants, especially the SSRIs, have the greatest impact (Cherek & Lane, 1999). Drug treatment of conduct disorder is complicated by the fact that comorbid disorders are common (Kruesi & Lelio, 1996). To date, there have been few studies that take comorbid conditions into account, so it is unclear which drug is most likely to be effective for a given person with conduct disorder. Although drug treatments have been used with conduct disorder, drugs are rarely the treatment of choice. The

drugs simply mask problems, which usually return once the drugs are withdrawn. Combining medication with psychological techniques provides both short-term management of problems and long-term behavioral changes in the child.

Check Yourself 13.1

Disruptive Behavior Disorders

1. What group is most likely to qualify for a diagnosis of ADHD?
2. What factors contribute to ADHD?
3. What are the two most common treatment approaches for ADHD?
4. What are the defining characteristics of conduct disorder?

Ponder this . . .   *The evolutionary perspective on ADHD suggests that a modern school system's demands for attention, compliance, and self-control are too much for some children to handle. If this argument has merit, what school adaptations might help children with ADHD to function better and learn to their full potential?*

FUNCTIONAL AND LEARNING DISORDERS

Functional disorders involve difficulties in performing one or more tasks. Unlike the disorders covered so far in this chapter, functional disorders affect children in more narrow ways but nonetheless create significant distress for children and their parents. **Learning disorders** are characterized by significant deficits in reading, mathematics, or written expression (APA, 2000). This section will review both functional and learning disorders under three headings: elimination disorders, communication disorders, and learning disorders.

ELIMINATION DISORDERS

Elimination disorders are disruptions or developmental delays in control of the elimination of bodily wastes, such as

....

functional disorders   Difficulties in performing one or more tasks.

learning disorders   Significant deficits in reading, mathematics, or written expression.

elimination disorders   Disruptions or developmental delays in control of the elimination of bodily wastes (urine and feces).

urine and feces. There are two elimination disorders recognized by the DSM: enuresis and encopresis.

Enuresis. **Enuresis** is characterized by persistent voiding of urine, most often during the night, in children who are at least five years old. The voiding may be voluntary or involuntary, although the vast majority of cases are involuntary (APA, 2000). To qualify for the diagnosis, the wetting must occur at least twice a week for three consecutive weeks or must cause clinically significant distress. For many bed-wetting children, the fear of bed-wetting prevents normal social activities, such as going to camp or sleeping over at a friend's house.

Enuresis appears to be a developmental delay, and most children with enuresis grow out of it. Figure 13.1 shows how the rate of enuresis drops steadily from age 5 through age 15. It may be that some children are simply slower at developing bladder control, especially when they are sleeping. Alternatively, children with nocturnal enuresis may either sleep too soundly or be less aware of signals that indicate that their bladder is full. Enuresis is more common in boys than in girls (Rona et al., 1997). Genes may play a role; 75% of children with enuresis have at least one first-degree relative who also has enuresis, although it is possible that environment, and not genes, account for this finding (APA, 2000; von Gontard, 1998). Coexisting psychopathology in children with enuresis is common (Swadi, 1996), although it is not clear whether this is a cause or an effect of the enuresis. For example, increased anxiety may disrupt bladder control, but it is equally likely that not having adequate bladder control when other children of the same age do may be a source of significant anxiety.

Although most children with enuresis grow out of the disorder, approximately 1% have problems with bed-wetting that continue into adulthood (APA, 2000). One might think that such an embarrassing problem would create other psychiatric problems, but the evidence suggests otherwise. A 13-year follow-up of young adults with enuresis showed that they had a lower frequency of personality and mood disorders and higher global functioning than a matched group of controls (Brieger et al., 2001).

There is an effective treatment for enuresis that has been around for decades (Christophersen & Mortweet, 2001). It is a simple system that employs a pad placed under the sheet, as illustrated in Figure 13.2. When water hits the

enuresis Characterized by persistent voiding of urine, most often during the night, in children who are at least five years old.

encopresis Characterized by the repeated passage of feces into such inappropriate places as one's clothes or the floor.

communication disorders Deficits in the ability to understand or express verbal messages at an age-appropriate level.

[FIGURE 13.1]
Prevalence of Enuresis by Age

Enuresis is common in young children but drops steadily in prevalence as children age. This leads many professionals to suspect that most cases of enuresis represent a developmental delay.

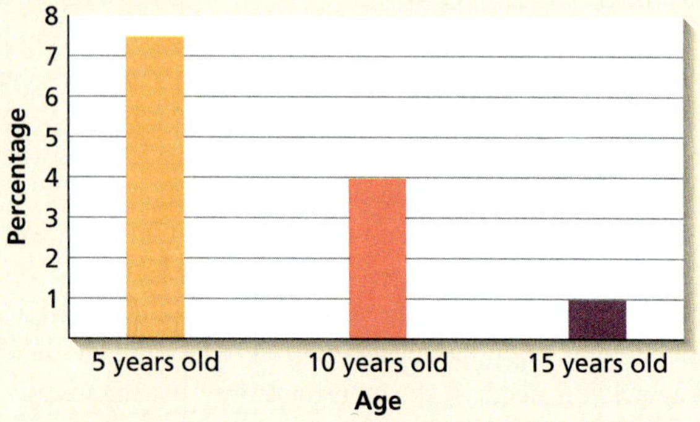

SOURCE: *Reprinted with permission from the* Diagnostic and Statistical Manual of Mental Disorders, *Fourth Edition, Text Revision. Copyright © 2000 American Psychiatric Association.*

[FIGURE 13.2]
Treating Enuresis Behaviorally

This simple device has proved to be an effective treatment for enuresis. A pad is placed under the mattress sheet. The pad has a series of electrical circuits that are completed if urine touches the pad, which then sets off an alarm that awakens the child. This safe device teaches children to sense when their bladders are full, enabling them to awaken before they void their bladders.

pad, it completes a circuit that sets off an alarm to awaken the child. This allows the child to go to the bathroom before the bed is severely wet. More important, the alarm seems to increase the child's ability to detect a full bladder and to awaken before wetting the bed. This warning system is the most effective treatment for enuresis, although programs to train children to enhance urinary retention and education programs for parents about the factors contributing to enuresis show modest effectiveness (Murphy & Carr, 2000).

Encopresis. Encopresis is characterized by the repeated passage of feces into such inappropriate places as one's clothes or the floor. Because a certain level of development is necessary to control bowel functions, the diagnosis is never made before the age of four. If the child is mentally retarded, the diagnosis is not made until a mental age of four is reached. Encopresis affects approximately 1% of five-year-olds and is more common in males than in females (APA, 2000).

The treatment of encopresis combines several elements, including medical management if necessary and behavior therapy aimed at shaping and maintaining toilet routines (Murphy & Carr, 2000). Typically, parents manage the behavior therapy under the supervision of a therapist. Many cases of encopresis are due to problems in control of the sphincter muscle, which opens and closes the anus. When such problems are detected, programs to train or strengthen the control of this muscle are often effective (Griffiths & Livingstone, 1998; Griffiths & Watson, 1999).

COMMUNICATION DISORDERS

Communication disorders are characterized by deficits in the ability to understand or express verbal messages at an age-appropriate level. In the case of mentally retarded children, the deficits must be worse than what one would expect given the mental age of the child. Several communication disorders are described in the DSM, including expressive language disorder, mixed receptive-expressive language disorder, phonological disorders, stuttering, and selective mutism. These disorders are briefly summarized in Table 13.3 on page 406. Many of these diagnostic categories are relatively new additions to the DSM. Consequently, little is known about the cause(s) or the best treatment for some of these disorders.

Some communication disorders have been recognized for decades. Stuttering, for example, has been studied extensively at almost every level—genetic, physiological, emotional, and behavioral. Effective treatments, such as speech training to mask many of the more dramatic stuttering

Communication is a critical skill, and being unable to communicate effectively creates numerous problems for children. Many children with selective mutism actually have an undiagnosed speech disorder, and their mutism may be due to embarrassment about not being able to speak clearly.

[TABLE 13.3] Communication Disorders

DISORDER	PREVALENCE	SYMPTOMS	CAUSE(S)
Expressive language disorder	10%–15% of children under 3; 3%–5% of school-age children	Significant impairment in the ability to express oneself verbally that is well beyond what would be expected given the person's nonverbal IQ or level of receptive language development	Most often a developmental delay, especially in bilingual households (Crutchley, 2000); strong genetic component (Tomblin & Buckwalter, 1998)
Mixed expressive-receptive language disorder	5% of preschoolers; 3% of school-age children	Deficits in both receptive and expressive language—that is, the child has difficulty both in understanding verbal communication and in expressing himself or herself verbally	Runs in families, but not clear whether this is due to genetic influences (APA, 2000); little else is known about this disorder
Phonological Disorder	2% at age 7; 0.5% at age 17	Failure to use developmentally expected speech sounds, such as saying "kable" instead of "table"; severity can range from being difficult to understand to being completely incomprehensible	Possible developmental delay; more common in males than in females and more common in children raised in bilingual families than in children raised in single-language families (Holm et al., 1999); runs in families, but it is not clear whether genes are responsible (APA, 2000); possibly immature level of perceptual processing of auditory speech (Watson & Hewlett, 1998)
Stuttering	1%–5%	Disruption in the normal fluency and time patterning of speech sounds severe enough to interfere with academic, occupational, or social functioning	Three times more common in boys than in girls; strong evidence for genetic influence (Felsenfeld et al., 2000; Yairi, 1999); tends to co-occur with phonological disorder and expressive language disorder (APA, 2000)
Selective mutism	<1%	A persistent failure to speak in situations in which speaking is expected, which affects social or academic performance and is not due to lack of knowledge or a language problem	Unclear; once assumed to be due to anxiety (Anstendig, 1998), but there is recent evidence that undiagnosed speech disorders may contribute (Cleator & Hand, 2001)

symptoms, are now available (Silverman, 1996). Other disorders, such as mixed expressive-receptive language disorder, have not been widely studied and therefore are not well understood. Disorders such as phonological disorder fall somewhere in between. Some research has been conducted on possible causes (Watson & Hewlett, 1998) and treatments (Beattie, 2001; Howell et al., 1993), but overall, this is an area badly in need of more research.

With the possible exception of stuttering, communication disorders have been considered developmental delays, because many children grow out of the problem by adolescence. However, it is now clear that these language problems continue in a significant proportion of individuals and that academic training is significantly disrupted even in those who eventually grow out of the problem.

expressive language disorder Significant impairment in the ability to express oneself verbally that is well beyond what would be expected given the person's nonverbal IQ or level of receptive language development.

mixed receptive-expressive language disorder Deficit in both receptive and expressive language.

phonological disorder Failure to use developmentally expected speech sounds, such as saying "kable" instead of "table."

stuttering Disruption in the normal fluency and time patterning of speech sounds severe enough to interfere with academic, occupational, or social functioning.

selective mutism A persistent failure to speak in situations in which speaking is expected, which affects social or academic performance and is not due to lack of knowledge or to a language problem.

LEARNING DISORDERS

Learning disorders involve significant deficits in reading, mathematics, or written expression, with performance that is well below developmental norms, the child's level of schooling, or the child's IQ. These disorders are specific deficits in a narrow cognitive realm and should be diagnosed on the basis of individually administered tests of academic skills. Approximately 5% of students in American schools qualify for one or more learning disorders. Table 13.4 summarizes the DSM learning disorders. This section focuses on reading disorder because it is the only learning disorder on which significant research has been conducted.

[TABLE 13.4] Learning Disorders

DISORDER	PREVALENCE	SYMPTOMS	CAUSES
Reading disorder (dyslexia)	4% of school-children (60%–80% male)	Substantially lower levels of reading speed and/or comprehension than one would expect on the basis of the child's age, education, and IQ	Substantial genetic influences (APA, 2000; Plomin, 2001; Wadsworth et al., 2000), although it is genetically heterogeneous (Raskind et al., 2000)
Mathematics disorder	1% of school-children	Substantially lower computational and mathematical reasoning skills than one would expect on the basis of the child's age, education, and IQ	Very little is known about mathematics disorder, which is often overlooked in children because there is such a wide range of mathematical ability (O'Hare et al., 1991)
Disorder of written expression	Unknown	Substantially lower levels of writing ability than one would expect on the basis of the child's age, education, and IQ; may be manifested as terrible handwriting, serious problems in copying text, or difficulty in remembering letter sequences in words	Very little is known about this disorder or the factors that might contribute to it

Until recently, there was little interest in learning disorders, with the exception of dyslexia. **Dyslexia** is another name for *reading disorder.* Dyslexia has long been recognized as a specific problem that is independent of the general level of cognitive development and potential. In fact, there are descriptions of dyslexia that date back at least to the seventeenth century (Anderson & Meier-Hedde, 2001). Genes are known to play a substantial role in dyslexia (APA, 2000; Plomin, 2001), although dyslexia is clearly genetically heterogeneous (Raskind et al., 2000). Interestingly, even though affected males outnumber females, evidence from twin studies suggests that the strength of the genetic component for dyslexia is comparable in men and women (Wadsworth et al., 2000). In the last few years, substantial progress has been made in understanding the genetics and neurobiology of reading disorders, and some specialists in this area believe that breakthroughs are just around the corner (Grigorenko, 2001). By contrast, little is known about either mathematics disorder or disorder of written expression, although what is known about how brain damage affects mathematical skills in adults may help shed light on mathematics disorder in children.

The primary treatment for learning disorders is intensive educational interventions designed to give the child additional practice, more detailed tracking of progress, and specific exercises to overcome specific deficits (Swanson et al., 1999). There is general agreement that the earlier a learning disorder is detected and the sooner children are placed in such programs, the better the prognosis (Hurford, 1998).

Dyslexia is clearly not a single problem. Some children have difficulty in recognizing individual letters, whereas

The most common learning disorder in children involves reading. Because most of learning is based on reading, if left untreated this learning disorder can significantly disrupt the child's education.

reading disorder   Substantially lower levels of reading speed and/or comprehension than would be expected on the basis of the child's age, education, and IQ.

dyslexia   Another name for *reading disorder.*

mathematics disorder   Substantially lower computational and mathematical reasoning skills than would be expected on the basis of the child's age, education, and IQ.

disorder of written expression   Substantially lower levels of writing ability than would be expected on the basis of the child's age, education, and IQ.

others have difficulty in associating sounds with letters or words (Seymour & Evans, 1999). Neuropsychological studies of children with dyslexia have provided numerous insights into the mechanisms behind the problems, and these insights have often been incorporated into the treatment exercises (Habib, 2000; Rourke, 1991). However, some have argued that the neuropsychological treatment methods have relied too heavily on research on the effects of brain damage and thus fail to take into account the difference between developmental disabilities and acquired deficits, which may have entirely different causal mechanisms (Basso & Marangolo, 2000). For example, the cognitive processes that prevent children from developing reading skills may be different from the reading processes that are lost as a consequence of specific brain damage.

Bakker (1990) has proposed an interesting model that suggests that early reading skills are based on right-hemisphere processing but that as reading skills advance, processing shifts to the left hemisphere. The rationale is that the most basic reading skills are form recognition skills—that is, the child has to recognize individual letters and later words and associate them with sounds and concepts already learned (objects, actions, and so on). Once this form recognition skill becomes automatic, the child needs to learn the more complex skills of organizing and remembering concepts, anticipating words to reduce workload during reading, and picking up subtle distinctions in written material, such as time and subject/object distinctions. Bakker (1990) argues that the left hemisphere more effectively carries out these analytical skills. This model suggests a two-stage treatment for students with reading problems. The first is to drill students on the form recognition task of letter and word recognition. Once this skill is mastered, the student is given training in interpreting words in context and anticipating which words will come later in a sentence. These treatment techniques show promise (Goldstein & Obrzut, 2001), but it is unclear whether their effectiveness is due to the specific interventions or to the general intensity and repetition that is a part of this approach (Dryer et al., 1999).

Check Yourself 13.2

Functional Disorders

1. What is the difference between enuresis and encopresis?
2. Define the term *communication disorders*.
3. What are learning disorders?

Ponder this . . . How much impact would an untreated learning disorder have on an individual throughout that individual's lifetime?

AUTISTIC DISORDER

Autistic disorder is a dramatic and disheartening disorder, primarily because it affects very young children and has such a poor prognosis. It is the best known of the **pervasive developmental disorders,** which are characterized by severe disruptions in social interaction and communication skills. In addition, pervasive developmental disorders may include unusual or deficient interests in the outside world, limited activities, and pronounced stereotypic behavior, such as repeatedly performing actions that serve no purpose. Table 13.5 lists the pervasive developmental disorders recognized by the DSM. This section will focus almost exclusively on autistic disorder.

SYMPTOMS AND COURSE

Autistic disorder is characterized by markedly abnormal or significantly delayed development in both social functioning and communications. The social dysfunction is apparent in the first three years of life and typically includes a general failure to engage in appropriate reciprocal social interactions. For example, children may show grossly inappropriate facial expressions, body postures, gestures, and eye contact, which make what little social contact that these children have seem bizarre. In fact, one of the early theories about the cause of autism—a theory that proved to be wrong—was that these children were using this bizarre behavior as a way to avoid social communication (Arieti, 1959). In addition to the bizarre aspects of social communication, children with autistic disorder seem unable to form relationships on the basis of shared interests and are unable achieve normal social and emotional reciprocity. In other words, they do not share their feelings or thoughts in response to others sharing their feelings or thoughts, or they do not listen to others' feelings after sharing some of their own.

Nathan, who was one of the cases that opened this chapter, exhibited many of these features. He showed no interest in any of the people around him. His facial expres-

pervasive developmental disorders   Disorders characterized by severe disruptions in social interaction and communication skills.

autistic disorder   Markedly abnormal or significantly delayed development in both social functioning and communications.

Rett's disorder   Disruption of normal head growth, between 5 and 48 months, which leads to significant brain dysfunction, mental retardation, and significant loss of functional abilities.

childhood disintegrative disorder   A significant regression in multiple areas of functioning after a period of at least two years of apparently normal development and functioning.

Asperger's disorder   A severe and sustained impairment in social interactions and the development of restricted and repetitive patterns of behavior and activities.

[TABLE 13.5] Pervasive Developmental Disorders

Listed below are brief descriptions of the pervasive developmental disorders.

Autistic disorder. This disorder is characterized by markedly abnormal or impaired development in social skills and communication, coupled with a very restricted repertoire of activities and interests. These abnormalities are apparent early, usually before the age of three, and the course is chronic. The majority of these children grow into adults who are incapable of living independently. Autistic disorder affects approximately 5 in 10,000 people and is four to five times more common in boys than in girls.

Rett's disorder. This disorder is characterized by normal prenatal and perinatal physical, social, and cognitive development. Somewhere between 5 and 48 months, normal development is disrupted by a deceleration of head growth, which leads to significant brain dysfunction, mental retardation, and significant loss of functional abilities. This very rare disorder has only been reported in girls.

Childhood disintegrative disorder. This disorder is characterized by a significant regression in multiple areas of functioning following a period of at least two years of apparently normal development and functioning. The areas affected may include expressive and receptive language, social skills, bowel and bladder control, play, and motor skills. In addition, specific abnormalities in functioning develop that are similar to those found in autistic disorder or Asperger's disorder. This condition is very rare and appears to affect boys more frequently than girls.

Asperger's disorder. This disorder is characterized both by a severe and sustained impairment in social interactions and by the development of restricted and repetitive patterns of behavior and activities. The social interactions often are characterized by significant disruption in such nonverbal communication as eye contact, facial expressions, and body language. In contrast to autistic disorder, language and cognitive development are normal. It is unclear how common this disorder is, though it is five times more common in boys than in girls. Many people with the disorder may be seen as socially naïve or eccentric but may function well enough never to be diagnosed.

Pervasive developmental disorder not otherwise specified. This disorder, which is sometimes referred to as atypical autism, is characterized by a pervasive impairment in one or more areas of social, language, and cognitive development but does not meet *all* of the criteria for one of the other pervasive developmental disorders.

SOURCE: *Reprinted with permission from the* Diagnostic and Statistical Manual of Mental Disorders, *Fourth Edition, Text Revision. Copyright ©️ 2000 American Psychiatric Association.*

sions were animated but could only be described as strange, and the animation appeared to be unconnected to any aspect of his surroundings. Until an intensive treatment program was implemented, he had no functional speech and showed little interest in communicating with other people. He would spend countless hours engaging in mindless stereotypic behavior, such as flushing the toilet, twirling objects, or shaking his hands a few inches in front of his face. He also engaged in an activity that is not part of the diagnostic criteria for autism but that occasionally is found in such children: self-destructive behavior. Specifically, he would forcefully pound his head against the wall, often doing significant damage to himself.

Many professionals believe that Asperger's disorder, or Asperger syndrome, is a milder version of autism, because Asperger's is characterized by the social deficits but not the severe communication deficits found in autism. The nearby Focus box discusses the evidence for this position and illustrates with a case example how powerfully such social deficits can affect one's life.

Language deficits are prominent in autism. Many children with autism are unable to develop any functional use of language without intensive programs (Harris, 1998). Their only use of language may be to repeat words or phrases they hear. When they do use language, it is often idiosyncratic. For example, they may develop words and even a crude grammar that does not correspond to normal usage. Not surprisingly, such deficits interfere with normal social interactions.

Some children with autism show remarkable talents in narrow areas, such as lightning-fast mathematical calculations, impressive memory, calendar calculations, or musical ability (Rimland, 1978). For example, they might be able to multiply five-digit numbers instantaneously, flawlessly remember lists of hundreds of unrelated words, instantly tell you the day of the week for any date, or reproduce the notes of a single instrument from listening to an orchestra play. What is striking is that these remarkable abilities do not translate into anything useful (Prior & Ozonoff, 1998). The autistic child who can remember hundreds of random words may still be unable to communicate. This pattern led Pring et al. (1995) to suggest that the problem in autism is impairment *not* of basic processing but of the ability to derive meaningful ideas from the wealth of information in the world. It is interesting that those autistic children who show such remarkable abilities often lose them if treatment is successful at reducing autistic symptoms (Rimland, 1978).

Autistic disorder is rare, affecting approximately 5 people in 10,000, and it is four to five times more common in boys than in girls (APA, 2000). Most children with autistic disorder are not formally diagnosed until about age two or three. However, the social and communication deficits are apparent much earlier. Many parents report being concerned about the social withdrawal starting during their child's first year of life, although some children show apparently normal development for a year or two (APA, 2000). The course is variable. Some children show improvement as they start to attend school, getting involved more in social interactions with peers, but others do not. Adolescence is another period in which some children with autistic disorder show modest improvement, whereas others show marked deterioration (APA, 2000). The best prognostic indicators are intellectual ability and acquisition of the functional use of language. Those children with autistic disorder who are bright appear to be able to compensate for

FOCUS Are there degrees of autism?

I s there a milder form of autism? Many people in the field believe that Asperger's disorder is such a milder form. What is their evidence? Both monozygotic co-twins and siblings of children with autistic disorder have elevated rates of Asperger's disorder (Bailey et al., 1995; Bolton et al., 1994), an observation that suggests a genetic link. Asperger's disorder is characterized by the deficits in social interactions and some of the stereotypic behaviors that are found in autism, but without the severe language deficits. In fact, many children with Asperger's disorder do quite well in school, which sometimes misleads parents and teachers into believing that these children's behavioral and social problems are willful and deliberate (APA, 2000). Such individuals experience lifelong social problems because of their inability to understand and respond to social situations. These deficits are amply illustrated in the case history of William.

WILLIAM

Trying Without Success

William was the oldest of two children, with an IQ of around 150. His parents were both professionals. He had always done well in school, but he never really fit in. Shy and retiring, he often sat on the sidelines in social situations. He had friends in high school, but his friendships were with people who essentially took him under their wing, rather than real reciprocal relationships. It was not that he wasn't caring. Quite the contrary, he would do anything for his friends. It was just that he couldn't understand other people's perspectives, so he frequently irritated friends and family. For example, after getting into some legal difficulties, he failed to show up for a court hearing because he wanted to visit out-of-town friends. He believed that the hearing did not require his presence, which was true, but he failed to appreciate his parents' reaction to his failing to show. In another incident, he took a problematic situation at school and made it much worse by discussing it cavalierly with the dean, which led to his suspension. It was not just these major issues that created problems for William. He often had no idea how to behave in everyday situations. He could not carry on conversations because he never knew what to say. When he did say things, his comments were often so far off the topic that he simply got puzzled looks from people. At times, he was viewed as trying too hard to be friendly; at other times, he was viewed as aloof and arrogant. These were never his intentions, but he could not appreciate how his behavior would be viewed by others. His behavior, which was almost always well intentioned, created one social crisis after another—and sometimes created legal and academic crises as well.

William's case illustrates how pervasive and devastating Asperger's disorder can be. Incredibly bright and motivated, he nevertheless seemed destined for failure. Perhaps if he had not been so bright, others would have judged his social behavior more generously. However, most people viewed his consistently inappropriate social behavior as deliberate rather than as an unintended result of social incompetence. William's constant social failures created a sense of helplessness and, sometimes, severe depression. Therapy gave him some useful compensatory skills but could not improve his ability to understand the perspectives of others. Consequently, as a way to protect him from his disability, both his therapist and his parents focused more on helping him to find an occupation that would demand less of him socially.

---

some of their deficits and thus are able to function to a degree in a social environment (Harris & Handleman, 2000). Those children who learn to use language have a much better chance of independent or semi-independent functioning than those children who do not (Harris, 1998). However, even in those autistic children who show the greatest recovery, significant social and communication deficits remain apparent in adulthood (Church et al., 2000).

CAUSES OF AUTISTIC DISORDER

Leo Kanner (1943), a Harvard psychiatrist, was the first to recognize the existence of autistic disorder. He noted a small group of very young children who showed social and communication deficits as well as peculiar behavior. To refer to this syndrome he used the term *autism*, a term that was originally used by Bleuler (1911/1950) to describe the tendency of people with schizophrenia to have unusual ideas and thoughts that they fail to self-correct through social interaction. Autism is complex and puzzling. Consequently, there are a wide variety of theories about its cause(s). In this section we will look at several.

Family Influences. One of the earliest theories of autism, and one of the most controversial, was the theory that the social withdrawal was a response to the child's parents. For example, Kanner noted that many autistic children had successful fathers who seemed to behave in strange or odd ways with their children (Volkmar & Lord, 1998). Other professionals noticed oddness—even a coldness—in the child's parents and concluded that the parents may well have been a major influence in the development of autism. Bruno Bettelheim (1967) was struck by the similarity of autistic behavior to the psychological numbing so often found in survivors of Nazi concentration camps. Speculating that such a dramatic response must be due to a dramatic situation, he looked for evidence of such situations in the histories of these children. Finding none, but seeing an emotional coldness in many of the parents of autistic children, he speculated that autism was a response to this parental style.

The idea that psychopathology, including autism, was caused by parents was consistent with the zeitgeist of the era. Psychodynamic formulations emphasized the role of development in psychopathology, and parents are the central figure in a child's development. Fromm-Reichman's (1948) schizophrenogenic mother hypothesis was widely accepted during this era (see Chapter 6). There are three problems, however, with the theory that autism results from some aspect of parenting. The first is that the dramatic symptoms of autism would suggest that there must be a dramatic cause, and the *informal* observations of Kanner, Bettelheim, and later investigators of parents being cold and/or odd do not seem sufficient to cause such dramatic symptoms. The second is that *systematic* studies of parents who have an autistic child suggest that they are not different from other parents (Cantwell et al., 1979) or that the differences are small and as likely to be due to shared genetic influences as the cause of the child's autism (Piven, 2002). The third is that many of these same parents raised children who turned out to be perfectly normal. It seems unlikely that a parental characteristic sufficiently intense to create autism in one child could have no affect on other children raised by the same parents.

Even if the parents of autistic children were aloof, the focus on parents as a potential cause of autistic disorder blinds people to an equally plausible—some would say more plausible—interpretation of the same data. Could the coldness and odd social aspects of parents be a result, rather than a cause, of the autism in their children? We saw in Chapter 6 that whenever two things are correlated, there are three possible interpretations. Even if you accept the early observations that parents of children with autism were emotionally cold, it does not follow that their coldness caused the autism. It may be that the coldness in the parents represented an emotional numbing due to the stress of having a child with autism. However, there is yet another possibility. A third variable may have accounted for both the autism and the parental style. Parents and their offspring share 50% of their genes. To the extent that genes contribute to autism, it is conceivable that both the child's dramatic symptoms and the parents' much less dramatic emotional style may be due to shared genetic influences.

Perceptual and Cognitive Influences. What could be behind the three central symptoms of autism—social withdrawal, communication deficits, and repetitive behavior? Can one better understand these symptoms by identifying other psychological variables that are associated with them? This section addresses this question by looking at several possible underlying factors that may contribute to the symptoms of autism.

There are several deficits in autistic disorder that are significant, but they are not good candidates as underlying causes because they are found in other disorders. Included in this category are being oversensitive to some stimuli while being undersensitive to other stimuli (Prior & Ozonoff, 1998), developmental delays in sensory processing (Losche, 1990), deficits in imitation skills (Prior et al., 1975), and sensorimotor deficits (Damasio & Mauer, 1978; DeMyer et al., 1981; Manjiviona & Prior, 1995). However, other psychological deficits seem more promising. Let's look at some of them.

Examining the Evidence

Children with autism show an unusual pattern of attentional problems. They are more likely to be *excessively attentive,* whereas children who are retarded or have ADHD tend to be inattentive (Casey et al., 1993; Lovaas et al., 1979). They also show interesting and unique patterns of cognitive deficits, including severe deficits in language, imitation, abstract reasoning, sequencing, organization, and planning skills, but little or no deficit in visuospacial skills, eye-hand coordination, and rote memory (Green et al., 1995; Lincoln et al., 1995). In fact, they do *better* than controls on reading single words and spelling, while doing much worse on reading comprehension (Minshew et al., 1994). Like the attentional problems, this pattern is different from that seen in other children with reading problems, who usually have the greatest difficulty in identifying individual words. Could this be another critical clue about the unique factors that contribute to autism?

Children with autistic disorder usually have excellent rote memory, a fact that was first noted by Kanner (1943). They can list an incredible number of facts, although they rarely understand the significance of those facts. They can also remember random lists of words as easily as they remember the same words in meaningful sentences (Hermelin & Frith, 1971). This suggests that they do not process the meaning of words, although they can apparently process and remember the actual words just fine. No wonder they find it difficult to communicate; for them, words have little meaning other than rote associations with actions, and the order of the words apparently adds little information for them. Their tendency to echo words mindlessly may be a crude attempt to communicate, but it clearly is ineffective.

Could the deficit in processing words account for the social deficits and stereotypic movements of autism? Certainly, communication deficits would hinder social relationships, but children with autistic disorder often show social relationship problems in the first few months of life, long before verbal communication develops. These children are not typically cuddly and do not respond to being picked up by an adult (Kanner, 1943; Prior & Ozonoff, 1998). As children with autism age, social contacts can range from complete social nonresponsiveness to active, but ineffective and inappropriate, attempts to socialize. These children seem unable to understand another person's perspective and rarely make attempts to help others to understand their perspective. For example, children as young as 12 months will draw others into their social interactions by pointing at things that interest them. Children with autistic disorder rarely develop this behavior (Mundy & Sigman, 1989). Even higher-functioning autistic individuals have difficulty understanding the perspective of others, which often means that they are confused and frustrated by social interactions (Sigman et al., 1992).

Children with autism are generally nonresponsive to emotional cues from a very young age (Hobson, 1989). They tend to ignore emotional expressions in others (Sigman et al., 1992), and they are also remarkably ineffective at sorting faces on the basis of emotional cues (Weeks & Hobson, 1987). Obviously, such deficits would hinder normal social relationships. Are these deficits related to any of the other deficits documented in autism? Interestingly, verbal deficits are highly correlated with these emotional recognition deficits, which suggests that they may share underlying factors (Serra et al., 1995). The still unanswered question is "What is shared?"

A picture is emerging of children who are unbelievably insensitive to nonverbal emotional communication and unable to process language in a way that reflects an understanding of its meaning and its value in sharing ideas. Somehow, these divergent deficits are linked in that they are highly correlated in these children. These children seem to lack the natural ability to share a perspective with others during social interaction and, perhaps because of that, never develop the ability to understand another person's perspective. Even otherwise high-functioning people with autistic disorder have great difficulty in taking another person's perspective into account in their social interactions, a deficit that creates frustration and leads to consistently inappropriate social behavior. This was illustrated in the case of William (see Focus box on page 410).

Even very young children appreciate the need to communicate their interests to others. This child is pointing at the bubble, communicating to his mother what is going on in his mind. Children with autistic disorder do not engage in this type of social communication.

Evolutionary Impact

The devastating symptoms of autistic disorder raise several important questions about general human functioning. Human beings are social creatures, and much of the success of humans is due to that social nature. The cooperation and specialization of effort that social interactions permit has promoted advances from the times of early hunter-gatherers to the modern societies of today. But social communication is not restricted to human beings. If you have pets, you know that you can read their mood and that they can read yours in that they adjust their behavior according to your mood. If you are sad, your dog may try to comfort you, and if you are angry, your dog is likely to hide. The ability to respond to others on the basis of emotional cues has survival value and hence should be favored by natural selection. One would think that this skill must be enormously complex and therefore controlled by hundreds of different genes and biological mechanisms working together. But the impressive degree to which it is disrupted in autistic disorder makes one wonder just how fragile it is.

In autistic disorder, there is a strong relationship between the deficits in emotional recognition and in verbal communication. This finding raises an intriguing, although clearly speculative, hypothesis. Could it be that the functional use of language, not just the ability to recognize and remember words, "borrows" some or all of the mechanisms used to recognize the emotions of others? Natural selection often borrows existing mechanisms, reshaping them with a few minor changes or additions to serve other purposes. For example, the behavioral response to depression is apparently mediated by mechanisms borrowed from the immune system

(Konsman et al., 2000; Leonard, 2001a, 2001b). The finding of such a close relationship between communication and emotional receptivity in autism may suggest research that could eventually clarify the mechanisms behind both of these critical behaviors and provide insights into their behavioral evolution.

Genetic Contributions. Scientists now know that autistic disorder has one of the strongest genetic components of any psychiatric disorder, although until recently they believed that genes contributed little. The early family studies suggested a weak genetic influence (Hanson & Gottesman, 1976). However, these early data were misleading. Studying the genetic contributions for rare disorders like autism is difficult. For example, the rate of autism in the general population is approximately 1 in 2000 people. The rate of same-sex twin births is 1 in 120 births (Plomin et al., 1990), and being a twin is independent of having autism. Therefore, only 1 in 240,000 births will be that of same-sex twins in which at least one twin is autistic—just over 1000 potential twin pairs in the entire United States. Imagine how difficult it is to find such rare events for research. Consequently, early genetic studies used the family study approach, in which the risk of autism in first-degree relatives of children with autism was determined.

It may not be immediately obvious, but the family approach, which already suffers from the problem of confounding genetic and environmental influences, has a much more serious problem in the case of autism. Who are the first-degree relatives of autistic children? They include the parents, full siblings, and offspring. Autism is such a devastating disorder that virtually no one with the disorder becomes a parent. This means that the affected child's parents would not have the disorder and there would be no offspring from the affected person to evaluate. What about the siblings? If one is studying a disorder with adult onset, looking at siblings is helpful. However, the devastating nature of autism, coupled with its onset shortly after birth, almost certainly affects the decision of parents whether to have more children. The demands of raising an autistic child and the uncertainty of whether other offspring will develop autism typically leads parents to decide not to have additional children. The result is that parents have children until they have a child who is autistic and then decide not to have more children. Therefore, most families have only one autistic child, an observation that led researchers inaccurately to conclude that autism did not run in families and so did not have a genetic component.

The current twin study data, which took years to collect, suggest just the opposite. Twin studies, unlike family studies, are not affected by parental decisions not to have more children after having an autistic child. Therefore, they give a less biased indication of the degree of genetic risk. Twin studies indicate a genetic component for autism that is stronger than that found in any other psychiatric disorder

(Szatmari & Jones, 1998). The estimated heritability index for autism based on these twin studies is 0.90—that is, 90% of risk is due to genes (Smalley et al., 1988). Autism is genetically heterogeneous; more than one genetic abnormality can produce the disorder (Szatmari & Jones, 1998). Numerous efforts have been made to isolate individual genes, so far with little success. These studies are becoming increasingly sophisticated as information from the human genome project is incorporated. It is possible that major breakthroughs will occur in the near future. In addition, there is evidence that viral infections during pregnancy may occasionally produce autism (Garrow et al., 1984).

Evolutionary Impact

There is an issue with autism for which there currently is no good answer. Given that (1) autism has a strong genetic influence and (2) it is a disorder that is devastating to functioning, one must predict that there would be a rapid drop in gene frequency over generations because those with the disorder do not reproduce. However, if anything, the data suggest that the rates may be rising (Powell et al., 2000). Why, then, has the disorder not disappeared? Several explanations are possible, but most are too complex to describe fully here. In general, they fall into one of three categories: (1) The rates are falling, but the data are insufficient for us to detect the decline or changes in diagnostic criteria are masking the decline. (2) The rates are falling but are falling slowly because most of the people with the genes never develop autism. (3) The rates are remaining stable because some of the carriers of the genes are enjoying a selective advantage to offset the obvious selective disadvantage of having autism. Why autism has persisted remains a mystery, but exploring this question may well shed light on the nature of autism and therefore merits continued research.

Biological Abnormalities. With a disorder as severe as autism and a 0.90 heritability index, one has to suspect that there are significant biological problems underlying the symptoms. Over 75% of children with autistic disorder show significant neurological abnormalities, including abnormal reflexes and muscle tone, perceptual and motor coordination problems, and movement and posture problems (Poustka, 1998). Interestingly, people with Asperger's disorder have the same degree of motor coordination problems as people with autism (Ghaziuddin et al., 1994). An early study suggested that birth complications were more common in children who developed autistic disorder (Lobascher et al., 1970). However, the diagnostic criteria used in that early study were imprecise compared with modern studies. Furthermore, birth complications in that study were invariably preceded by complications during the course of the pregnancy, so abnormalities may have been present throughout gestation (Gillberg & Gillberg, 1983). More recent research suggests that genes are more important than birth complications in increasing risk for autism (Poustka, 1998).

One of the most consistent neurobiological findings with autism is an increased risk of seizures and abnormal EEGs; fully 50% of autistic children have EEG abnormalities (Tsai et al., 1985). Interestingly, these abnormalities are found throughout the brain, which implies that no single brain region is involved (Minshew, 1991). The rate of seizure disorders in autistic children is around 25%—50 times higher than that in unaffected children (Volkmar & Nelson, 1990). Seizure disorders are most common in those autistic children who showed the highest degree of mental retardation (Tuchman et al., 1991).

Early postmortem studies suggest abnormalities in the cerebellum of people with autism (Ritvo et al., 1986), and these findings have been confirmed with more recent MRI studies (Hashimoto et al., 1995). The abnormal cerebellum is consistent with animal models. Socially deprived monkeys in some of Harry Harlow's early studies showed abnormal cerebellar functioning as well as the rocking motion that is so common in children with autistic disorder (Michael & Zumpe, 1998). This finding raises an interesting question. Harlow's monkeys were experimentally deprived of social contact, whereas children with autistic disorder "voluntarily" restrict social contact. Could it be that social stimulation is necessary for normal development of the cerebellum? If so, the cerebellar damage in autistic children may be an effect of the disorder rather than a cause. There is currently insufficient information to answer this question.

Children with autistic disorder also show greater brain weight, head size, and brain volume as measured with an MRI than control children (Bailey et al., 1993; Piven et al., 1995). These findings suggest an excessive number of neurons. It is not clear why this is so, but human brains always start out with more neurons than are necessary, and unused neurons are pruned in the first years of life. Perhaps this pruning process is disrupted in autism. Multiple brain abnormalities, affecting several brain regions, have been found in postmortem studies (Bauman & Kemper, 1994), and many of these postmortem findings have been confirmed with MRI and CAT scan studies (Poustka, 1998). The large number of documented abnormalities, the variability in those abnormalities, and the weak relationship that most abnormalities have to behavioral functioning suggests that the biological underpinnings of autistic disorder are complex and still far from understood.

Serotonin has been implicated in at least some cases of autism. Approximately 25% of children with autism show elevated levels of serotonin in the blood plasma and urine (Cook, 1990). Some have speculated that this excess serotonin had a negative impact on brain development, thus leading to the brain abnormalities described earlier (Buznikov, 1984). However, there is currently little evidence to support this speculative hypothesis. The studies of serotonin level and functioning in autism have been confusing and contradictory (Poustka, 1998). Again, this is an area for further research, especially given its possible implications for drug treatment.

TREATING AUTISTIC DISORDER

There is no cure for autistic disorder. Most people with the disorder continue to show significant symptoms into adulthood, and many require institutional care throughout their lives. Nevertheless, treatment can reduce symptoms, enhance functioning, and increase the level of independence for people with autistic disorder. Both behavioral and drug treatments have been used with autistic disorder.

Behavioral Treatment.   The most common form of treatment for autism is intensive behavior therapy. These programs, which were pioneered by O. Ivar Lovaas (Lovaas et al., 1966), seek to address the individual deficits and pathological behavior so common in autism. For example, most children with autism have little or no language skills and are generally socially unresponsive. Furthermore, they may show uncontrolled outbursts—essentially temper tantrums—and sometimes severe self-destructive behavior (Stein & Niehaus, 2001). The self-destructive behavior may include head banging—that is, pounding one's own head against a wall or solid surface or hitting oneself repeatedly in the head with a fist or other object. The head banging may be severe enough to risk brain damage. The programs that Lovass and his colleagues developed use behavioral principles to reduce undesirable behavior and to shape such desirable behavior as speaking and responding to the speech of others.

Most behavioral programs rely on positive reinforcement and use as little punishment as possible. However, it is common to have periods in which interfering behavior occurs, such as persistent inattention or temper tantrums.

O. Ivar Lovass pioneered the behavioral treatment of autism. His programs trained children to use language and interact socially.

Normally, these can be extinguished by ignoring the behavior, but the process is slow. Imagine trying to look away and completely ignore someone screaming and pounding just a few feet away, offering them praise and a food reward the instant they stop the tantrum, and then going on to the next learning presentation a few seconds later as though nothing had happened.

If extinction does not work or is working too slowly, the therapist may decide to use punishment. Punishment usually involves social sanctions, such as telling the child that his or her behavior was bad. However, autistic children are insensitive to social interactions, which means that the therapist must exaggerate the response. The word "No" may have to be virtually screamed to get the child's attention, and the facial expression of dissatisfaction must be exaggerated as well. A brief explanation that focuses on the behavior that is expected must be given. Seconds later, when the child responds appropriately, a broad smile and a cheerful "good job" are necessary. Showing anger rather than this controlled reinforcement stifles progress. Feeling anger will render any therapist ineffective or worse.

The earliest behavioral treatment programs were conducted within institutions, with a focus on treating the child. However, it quickly became apparent that it was critical to involve families if treatment gains were to be maintained (Lovaas et al., 1973). Families are now routinely included in the treatment of their autistic children (Harris, 1989). The task of raising a child with autistic disorder is demanding. Understanding the best ways of managing problem behavior, enhancing adaptive skills, and supporting a child who often feels overwhelmed by the demands of the world is critical to both long-term success and the emotional well-being of parents (Gill & Harris, 1991).

The behavioral programs pioneered by Lovaas have come a long way in the last 35 years (Harris, 1998). The focus remains on developing language and social skills and on reducing aggressive and self-destructive behavior. However, the techniques have changed in response to research. For example, there has been a shift from teaching language skills in a highly structured hospital setting to doing as much of the training as possible in natural settings because that enhances generalization (Harris, 1975; McGee et al., 1983). More effort is directed to encouraging natural speech than to emphasizing correctness in the speech. Koegel et al. (1988) found that encouraging any speech, regardless of its quality, was more effective in the long term. Others found that lengthening the time delay before an adult spoke increased spontaneous speech in children with autism (Charlop et al., 1985).

Advances also have been made in increasing socialization skills in children with autism (Harris, 1998). Early treatment focused on language development, paying less attention to socialization, on the assumption that these children would naturally socialize once they had the ability to communicate, but that assumption was wrong. Whereas most people learn social skills through observation and

The self-destructive behavior associated with autism can be so severe that it threatens the health of the child, and therefore the child must be protected. In this case, the child is wearing a helmet to protect his head when he bangs it against the wall.

trial and error, children with autistic disorder require detailed and often painstaking training to reach even minimal levels of social competence (Harris, 1998). Such training is most effective if it is conducted in a natural environment. For example, some researchers build training around games (Coe et al., 1990). Peer modeling of appropriate social interactions is also effective, although the child with autism learns more slowly from such modeling than unaffected children (Odom & Strain, 1986).

One of the most controversial aspects of the early work of Lovaas was the use of punishment to decrease dangerous behavior (Cohen, 1998). The punishment used was electric shock, typically administered immediately upon the child's beginning an episode of self-destructive behavior, such as head banging. Although painful, the shocks were actually less painful than the self-destructive behavior they were designed to stop. Punishment proved effective, and it created an atmosphere in which positive behaviors could be established (Harris et al., 1991; Lovaas, 1989). However, more recent research suggests that such punishment is unnecessary (Harris, 1998). For example, Durand and Carr (1991) found that focusing on training the child to engage in alternative activities, such as games and social interactions, is often sufficient to reduce self-destructive and other acting-out behavior.

Drug Treatment. Several medications are used to treat autism, although there is currently no medication that is recognized as the treatment of choice (McDougle, 1998). The medications used most affect serotonin, dopamine, and norepinephrine.

Two factors led doctors to suspect that drugs that affected serotonin would be useful in the treatment of autistic disorder. First, serotonin levels are abnormal in people with this disorder. Second, one of the defining characteristics of autistic disorder is a pattern of stereotypic behavior that is similar to obsessive-compulsive symptomatology. Drugs that affect serotonin levels, especially the SSRIs, have demonstrated their effectiveness in treating OCD. Several SSRIs have been tested in the treatment of autistic disorder, including fenfluramine (Pondimin), fluvoxamine (Luvox), fluoxetine (Prozac), sertraline (Zoloft), and paroxetine (Paxil). Two other drugs known to affect serotonin have also been evaluated: clomipramine (Anafranil) and buspirone (BuSpar). The quality of these drug studies varies dramatically, and the ideal of a double-blind, controlled trial has been more the exception than the rule. These drugs reduce both aggressive and compulsive behavior and increase social behavior (McDougle, 1998). However, their effects are modest at best.

Another class of drugs that shows promise is neuroleptic medications, which have a primary effect on the neurotransmitter dopamine. These are drugs normally used to treat schizophrenia and other psychotic disorders. The rationale for using these drugs is weaker than that for the SSRIs. Specifically, there is some evidence that dopamine metabolism may be disrupted in some people with autistic disorder (Gillberg et al., 1983), and the symptoms of autism are somewhat similar to some of the symptoms of schizophrenia. Haloperidol (Haldol) has been shown to reduce social withdrawal, compulsive behavior, hyperactivity, anger, and volatile moods in children with autistic disorder (Anderson et al., 1984). Unfortunately, such side effects as excessive sedation and increased irritability were common. A newer atypical neuroleptic, risperidone (Risperdal), also shows promise in treating adults with the disorder (McDougle et al., 1995). Risperidone affects both dopamine and serotonin levels in the brain.

Finally, two drugs that exert their primary effect on norepinephrine show promise. Interestingly, the biological evidence implicating norepinephrine in autistic disorder is equivocal at best (Gillberg et al., 1983; Lake et al., 1977). Nevertheless, the beta blocker propranolol (Inderal) re-

duces aggression and increased socialization in autistic adults (Ratey et al., 1987). In addition, clonidine (Catapres) produces modest improvement in inattention, impulsivity, and hyperactivity in children with autistic disorder (Jaselskis et al, 1992).

The use of medications to treat symptoms of autistic disorder is common, but the evidence for their effectiveness is weak. Furthermore, no medication is effective for all people with autistic disorder. This should not be surprising, given the evidence that autism is heterogeneous. At best, these medications reduce some specific symptoms, but they do not represent a cure.

Long-Term Prognosis. When it comes to long-term prognosis with autistic disorder, there is both good news and bad news. The bad news is that, in general, the prognosis is not very good. Most children with autism do not grow up to live independently and hold a job (Howlin & Goode, 1998). However, the good news is that the prognosis has been steadily improving over the last several decades (Howlin, 1997). This is illustrated in a review of published studies by Howlin (1997), which is briefly discussed here.

Examining the Evidence

Howlin (1997) used 1980 as a dividing point and compiled outcome variables from all published studies of autism before and after that date. The main findings are illustrated in Figure 13.3. These data nicely illustrate where the most impressive gains have been made and what areas continue to be problems. For example, the number of adults with autism who qualify for an overall competence rating of good or fair has nearly doubled. However, despite enormous efforts, there are only modest gains in the functional use of language. There have been dramatic increases in employment and independent living and a dramatic decrease in the number requiring hospitalization. However, only one in four adults with autism can work, and the majority of them are working at menial jobs. Only one in nine can live independently. Most live with family or in group homes in the community. The dramatic drop in the number of people living in hospital settings is the most impressive change, although part of this change is due simply to the movement away from chronic hospitalization to less restrictive treatment options.

There have been no revolutionary advances in either the understanding or the treatment of autism since it was first defined by Kanner (1943). However, steady progress has been made, which has translated into improved outcomes for many people. Intervention programs now start

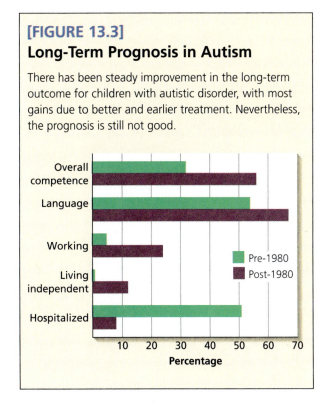

[FIGURE 13.3]

Long-Term Prognosis in Autism

There has been steady improvement in the long-term outcome for children with autistic disorder, with most gains due to better and earlier treatment. Nevertheless, the prognosis is still not good.

earlier, and earlier intervention is generally more effective (Howlin & Goode, 1998). Programs to train these children in the functional use of language have been gradually improving, and more effort has been focused on increasing their socialization skills and sociability (Harris, 1998). Medications help with the management of some of the more disruptive symptoms but clearly are ineffective by themselves. Yet even with these efforts, it is extremely rare for a child with autism to grow into an adult who does not show significant residual symptomatology.

Check Yourself 13.3

Autistic Disorder

1. What are the defining characteristics of autistic disorder?
2. Children with autistic disorder show many symptoms that are found in other disorders, but what symptoms are unique to autism?
3. What treatments are used with autistic disorder?

Ponder this . . .   *It is difficult to imagine a child with autistic disorder surviving without extensive support. What is the evolutionary impact of current efforts to treat and care for people with this devastating disorder?*

MENTAL RETARDATION

Mental retardation is characterized by significant intellectual and functional deficits that begin before the age of 18. Like personality disorders, mental retardation is diagnosed on Axis II, because it is a stable aspect of the individual. This section begins by describing the diagnostic criteria for mental retardation. It then examines some of the causes before concluding with a discussion of treatment and prevention strategies.

DIAGNOSING MENTAL RETARDATION

There are two functional criteria that one must meet to qualify for a diagnosis of mental retardation: sufficiently low IQ and significant social and functional deficits. These factors are highly correlated, but nevertheless, both must be present for the diagnosis.

Intellectual Deficits. Intelligence is a collection of adaptive skills that facilitate functioning in a complex world. Note two things about this definition: (1) Intelligence is a *collection* of skills. Being very good at just one skill, while being poor at most others, does not qualify as intelligence. (2) Intelligence matters because it affects functioning. Intelligence is typically measured as an intelligence quotient (IQ) score, as we saw in Chapter 2.

The distribution of scores on a typical IQ test approximates a bell-shaped curve. However, it is believed that the IQ curve is really two curves. The larger curve shown in Figure 13.4 on page 418 represents the distribution of IQ scores for the general population, whereas the smaller curve, with a much lower mean IQ, represents that subgroup of individuals hypothesized to have a severe physical disorder that results in dramatically lowered intelligence (Zigler, 1967). IQ scores below 70 represent one of the two criteria for a diagnosis of mental retardation. Between 2% and 3% of the population scores below 70. Those whose low scores simply represent the low end of the IQ distribution are said to have **cultural-familial mental retardation.** This group represents about 2% of the general population and usually qualifies for a diagnosis of mild mental retardation. Those in the smaller curve, with much lower IQs due to severe physical disorders, are said to suffer from **organic mental retardation.** This group represents approximately 0.5% to 1% of the population (King et al., 2000).

mental retardation   Characterized by significant intellectual and functional deficits that begin before the age of 18.

cultural-familial mental retardation   Mild mental retardation exhibited by those whose low IQ scores simply represent the low end of the IQ distribution.

organic mental retardation   Significant mental retardation due to a severe physical disorder.

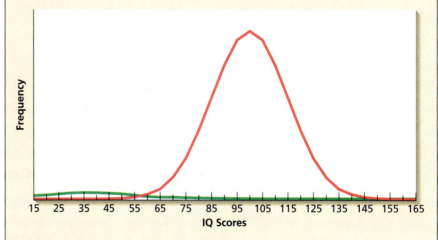

[FIGURE 13.4]
IQ Distribution

The distribution of IQ scores is generally bell-shaped, but there is a separate group with very low IQ scores that represent severe retardation resulting from physical disorders, such as Down syndrome. The result is a distribution that is nearly normal, but with a slight excess of people with low IQ scores.

SOURCE: *"IQ Distribution" from "Familial Mental Retardation: A Continuing Dilemma" by E. Zigler, Science, 155, 292, 1967. Copyright © 1967 by American Association for the Advancement of Science. Reprinted by permission.*

Social and Functional Deficits. To qualify for a diagnosis of mental retardation, an individual must have, in addition to a low IQ, demonstrated deficits in at least two areas of adaptive functioning, which include communication, self-care, home living, interpersonal skills, use of community resources, self-direction, functional academic skills, work, leisure, health, and safety. Retarded individuals normally show deficits in several of these areas. The case of Aaron illustrates some of these deficits in adaptive functioning.

Doing His Best

AARON

At 48 years old, Aaron had lived with his parents his entire life. In his hometown of 500 people, everyone knew him, liked him, and watched out for him. He had a paper route, although he could not handle collections because he did not understand money. Instead, his customers put money in an envelope, which he picked up each week. His father would then update his books on the basis of the collections. Aaron was outgoing, but he was just as likely to strike up an intimate conversation with a stranger as with a close family friend. For example, he might tell someone whom he had just met at the town diner about his father's prostate problems and the surgery that was contemplated. He was allowed to roam around town, but his parents had set limits on how far he could go because he got lost easily. He was strictly forbidden to go into the woods; twice he had gotten lost in the woods that surrounded this little town. He had never been able to handle school, but he did receive several years of home tutoring. He could not do math or read a book, but he learned to recognize the names of baseball players and to read their statistics in the paper. In fact, he could quote virtually any statistic for any player, although he did not understand what the numbers meant.

Aaron illustrates several functional deficits: He is unable to perform even the most basic academic tasks, is socially inappropriate at times, and he is unable to recognize such risks as getting lost in a new place. With tremendously supportive parents and a small town that served almost as an extended family, Aaron has done well. With his parents rapidly aging, his care will now fall on an older sister, who lives in a large city. It remains to be seen whether Aaron, now nearly 50, will be able to adapt.

Just as IQ tests provide a standardized measure of intellectual performance, there are also standardized measures of adaptive functioning. The two most widely used are the Vineland Adaptive Behavior Scale (Sparrow et al., 1984) and the Adaptive Behavior Scale (Nihira et al., 1975). The advantage of these standardized measures over a more subjective impression of adaptive functioning is that they systematically evaluate a wide range of adaptive behaviors, from self-care skills, to basic memory functions, to social skills, to planning skills, to insight and learning from experience.

Levels of Retardation. The DSM defines four levels of mental retardation: mild, moderate, severe, and profound. Remember that although these levels are defined in terms of IQ, the diagnosis also requires significant social or functional deficits.

Mild mental retardation represents an IQ of 50–55 to approximately 70. Approximately 1 person in 50 qualifies for this diagnosis (APA, 2000). People with mild mental retardation are often able to benefit from intensive educational effort, learning to read and write and do basic computations. They may appear normal during preschool years and may develop the level of social and communicative skills expected of such young children. Once they start school, however, their intellectual difficulties become more apparent, and they quickly fall behind their peers. With hard work, they can usually reach the level of an average sixth-grader by their late teens and are often able to develop sufficient social and occupational skills to be marginally employable. However, they may continue to require supervision and guidance, especially when under stress. With appropriate support, they can live reasonably independent lives in the community.

Moderate mental retardation represents an IQ from 35–40 to approximately 50–55. About 1 person in 400 qualifies for this diagnosis (APA, 2000). It was once believed that people with moderate mental retardation could not benefit from educational programs but could be trained to take care of themselves and handle menial tasks. However, with appropriate educational programs, many can reach the level of the average second-grader (Baroff & Olley, 1999; Hodapp & Zigler, 1999). People with this level of retardation are able to develop communication skills and can often take care of many of their basic needs, but most require supervision and reminders of what should be done. They also can benefit from social skills training (Matson & Hammer, 1996), but even with such training, they have serious difficulties in interpreting social situations, which makes it hard for them to function socially. Most are able to be modestly productive at unskilled or semi-skilled work in

a sheltered workshop. Their level of productivity is typically low, but the satisfaction associated with earning a paycheck can be an enormous boost to their self-esteem (Wehmeyer & Bolding, 1999). Most are able to live in community residential settings under close supervision.

Severe mental retardation represents an IQ from 20–25 to approximately 35–40. About 1 person in 1000 qualifies for this diagnosis (APA, 2000). People with this level of mental retardation normally do not acquire communication skills without specific and intensive clinical interventions (Baroff & Olley, 1999). Even basic self-care skills, such as brushing one's teeth, require considerable training and constant supervision. Many are able to live in community residences, but they normally require constant supervision and protective oversight.

Profound mental retardation represents an IQ below approximately 20–25. Approximately 1 person in 3000 qualifies for this diagnosis (APA, 2000). The majority of people in this category have a serious physical disorder that accounts for their retardation. Consequently, they often have multiple physical problems and significant sensorimotor impairment. Most are unable to manage even the most basic self-care tasks without constant oversight, although some learn to do simple tasks under one-on-one supervision.

CAUSES OF MENTAL RETARDATION

This section begins with a discussion of the many ways in which organic mental retardation can develop, including chromosomal and genetic abnormalities, pregnancy and birth complications, and environmental toxins. **Chromosomal abnormalities** occur when disruption in the formation of eggs or sperm results in an embryo with either an abnormal number of chromosomes or damaged chromosomes. In contrast, **genetic abnormalities** are typically due to single genes that affect development and functioning. The section ends with a discussion of cultural-familial mental retardation.

Evolutionary Impact

Chromosomal Abnormalities. Human genes are carried on 23 pairs of chromosomes—46 in all—with each parent contributing half of the chromosomes to a fertilized egg. With the exception of the X and Y chromosomes, which determine the sex of the child, the chromosomes from each parent are similar in make-up. The process of dividing the set of 46 chromosomes into the 23 that constitute either sperm cells or egg cells is far from foolproof. As many as 5% of pregnancies involve a chromosomal abnormality, and 90% of these are miscarried (Smith et al., 1978). Miscarriage is essentially natural selection at work even before birth. Most fetuses with a chromosomal abnormality are not viable—that is, they have no chance of survival—and even in the

---

mild mental retardation   Characterized by an IQ of 50–55 to approximately 70.

moderate mental retardation   Characterized by an IQ from 35–40 to approximately 50–55.

severe mental retardation   Characterized by an IQ from 20–25 to approximately 35–40.

profound mental retardation   Characterized by an IQ below approximately 20–25.

chromosomal abnormalities   A disruption in the formation of eggs or sperm that results in an embryo with either an abnormal number of chromosomes or damaged chromosomes.

genetic abnormalities   Abnormalities typically due to single genes that affect brain development and functioning.

protected environment of the womb, they are unable to function well enough to survive to birth.

Several chromosomal abnormalities do not affect the viability of the fetus sufficiently to produce a spontaneous abortion. Nevertheless, they affect the developing offspring in significant ways, such as impairing neurological and cognitive development. Two common chromosomal abnormalities—Down syndrome and fragile-X syndrome—result in mental retardation. Table 13.6 lists several other chromosomal abnormalities often associated with mental retardation or specific cognitive deficits.

An extra chromosome 21 characterizes **Down syndrome,** which was first described by British physician Langdon Down 150 years ago. Down syndrome is the leading cause of organic mental retardation (King et al., 2000). It occurs approximately once in every 1000 births, although the rate varies dramatically with the age of the mother. For example, only 1 in every 2500 births have this abnormality when the mother is under 30, but the figure is 1 in 80 when the mother is over 40 and is 1 in 32 when the mother is over 45 (King et al., 2000).

People with Down syndrome typically have moderate to severe mental retardation and several distinctive characteristics, including short stature, upward slanting eyes, a wide and flat nasal bridge, a large tongue coupled with a smaller than normal mouth, and short, stubby fingers. In addition, they often have thyroid abnormalities, congenital heart problems, and occasional blockages of the intestinal tract. Because of these health problems, the infant mortality rate in this group is almost 15%. Until recently, heart problems prevented children with Down syndrome from living

Down syndrome, which is the result of having three chromosome 21, can lead to mental retardation and a host of physical problems. However, with proper care, most people with this disorder lead meaningful and productive lives.

past 30, but modern medical advances often make it possible to manage these heart problems. Now that people with Down syndrome are living longer, another problem has been recognized: People with this disorder develop an Alzheimer's-like disease by middle age (Dalton & Janicki, 1999; Friedman & Brown, 2001).

The second most common cause of organic mental retardation is **fragile-X syndrome,** which is characterized by a broken X chromosome. It affects 1 in 1000 males and 1 in 3000 females (Dykens et al., 1988; King et al., 2000). Females with fragile-X syndrome typically show mild mental retardation, and males typically show moderate to severe mental retardation (King et al., 2000). Females are probably

[TABLE 13.6] Other Chromosomal Abnormalities

Listed below are a few of the more common chromosomal abnormalities that are often associated with mental retardation.

DISORDER	ABNORMALITY	CHARACTERISTICS
Down syndrome	Three instead of two copies of chromosome 21	Moderate to severe mental retardation; short stature; distinctive facial features, including upward-slanting eyes, flat nasal bridge, and large tongue; serious medical problems, including abnormal thyroid functioning, heart problems, and intestinal blockages; Alzheimer's-like neuropathy in adulthood
Fragile-X syndrome	A broken X chromosome	Mild mental retardation in females; moderate to severe mental retardation in males; distinctive physical features, including long face, large ears, arched palate, and short stature; mitral valve prolapse; visual gaze problems
Turner's syndrome	A single X chromosome and no Y chromosome	Mental retardation is more common in this disorder than in the general population, although most are not significantly retarded
Klinefelter's syndrome	Two X chromosomes and one Y chromosome	Phenotypically male; small testes; occasionally mild mental retardation

less affected because they have at least one intact X chromosome, whereas males have none and therefore lack the blueprint for the protein synthesis controlled by the DNA on the X chromosome. As in Down syndrome, people with fragile-X syndrome typically show a constellation of distinctive physical features, including a long face and large ears, short stature, and a high arched palate. Heart problems (specifically mitral valve prolapse) are common. In addition, people with fragile-X syndrome often have difficulty in focusing both eyes simultaneously on an object, and males often show such autisticlike symptoms as language delay, echolalia, self-injurious behavior, perseveration, and poor eye contact (King et al., 2000).

Genetic Abnormalities.

Genetic abnormalities can result in a major disruption of functioning, including mental retardation. This section covers the disorders PKU and Hunter, Hurler, Lesch-Nyhan, and Rubinstein-Taybi syndromes.

The most common genetic abnormality resulting in mental retardation is **phenylketonuria, or PKU,** which is caused by a recessive gene on chromosome 12. It occurs in approximately 1 in 11,500 births (King et al., 2000). People with PKU lack a critical enzyme that breaks down phenylalanine, and the resulting build-up of phenylalanine in the body produces brain damage. Phenylalanine is a substance that is found in many kinds of foods and beverages, so it is naturally introduced into the body when one eats or drinks. To appreciate how common phenylalanine is, look on the side of a can of Coke or Diet Coke, and you will see the warning PHENYLKETONURICS: CONTAINS PHENYLALANINE. Thousands of food products carry this warning. Children with PKU are normal at birth because there has been no toxic build-up of phenylalanine. However, if the condition is not diagnosed and their diet is not restricted to virtually eliminate the intake of phenylalanine, the resulting brain damage can lead to severe retardation. Such diets are extremely limiting but are critical to the neurological health of affected individuals.

At least a half-dozen known genetic disorders can result in mental retardation (King et al., 2000). Fortunately, they are all rare. Hunter syndrome is caused by an X-linked recessive gene that affects 1 in 100,000 newborns. Affected individuals typically have coarse faces with a flat nasal bridge and flared nostrils, hearing loss, enlarged liver and spleen, joint stiffness, recurrent infections, growth retardation, and cardiovascular abnormalities. Both hyperactivity and retardation are apparent by age 2. Hurler syndrome is caused by an autosomal recessive gene that affects 1 in 100,000 newborns. Short stature, coarse facial features, recurrent respiratory symptoms, moderate to severe mental retardation, and death usually by age 10 are typical for individuals with this disorder. Lesch-Nyhan syndrome is caused by a recessive gene that affects approximately 1 in about 25,000 newborns. Individuals with this disorder are uncoordinated, with persistent jerky movements, often experience liver failure, and show severe self-biting behavior, aggression, and mild to moderate mental retardation. Rubinstein-Taybi syndrome is believed to be caused by an autosomal dominant gene that affects 1 in 250,000 newborns. Affected individuals have short stature and a small head, broad thumbs and big toes, frequent bone fractures, feeding difficulties in infancy, congenital heart disease, seizures, and mild mental retardation, with greater deficits on verbal as compared to performance IQ.

Pregnancy and Birth Complications.

The rapidly developing fetus is especially vulnerable to stressors. In addition, the birth process itself is stressful and can be dangerous if complications develop. This section covers factors during pregnancy and delivery that can lead to mental retardation.

It is estimated that 300,000 children each year are born to women who are taking drugs or drinking alcohol during pregnancy (Stevens & Price, 1992). The toxic impact of drugs on the developing fetus is one of the most significant sources of preventable mental retardation. **Fetal alcohol syndrome** is a condition that affects newborns whose mothers drank heavily during pregnancy. It will be covered in more detail in Chapter 14 on substance-related disorders. The rates of fetal alcohol syndrome are difficult to determine, because the syndrome is detectable at birth only in infants exposed to very large quantities of alcohol during gestation (Baroff & Olley, 1999). The best estimate is that 3 in 10,000 newborns suffer from the disorder, although there are wide variations in rates depending on the culture. Hispanics and whites show rates closer to 1 in 10,000, whereas blacks show rates of 6 in 10,000 (NIAAA, 1991). However, the higher rate in blacks is more a function of a biological susceptibility to fetal alcohol syndrome than of differences in the rate of alcohol abuse during pregnancy (Sokol et al., 1986). Other groups show much higher rates of fetal alcohol syndrome that are due largely to higher rates of alcohol abuse during pregnancy. For example, the rate is 10 in 10,000 among Native Americans in the Southwest (May et al., 1989) and is 120 in 10,000 (over 1%) in an isolated Canadian Indian population in British Columbia (Robinson et al., 1987). However, the rates are not elevated in all groups of Native Americans. For example, the rates in Navajo and Pueblo Indians are comparable to that in European Americans—about 1 in 10,000 (May et al. 1989).

Down syndrome   A disorder that occurs when the individual has an extra chromosome 21.

fragile-X syndrome   A disorder caused by a broken X chromosome.

phenylketonuria (PKU)   Retardation caused by a recessive gene on chromosome 12.

fetal alcohol syndrome   A condition that affects newborns whose mothers drank heavily during pregnancy.

Exposure to other drugs, such as cocaine, opiates, and marijuana, may increase the risk for behavioral problems and mental retardation, but the effects are generally small (Coles, 1993; Coles et al., 1999; Menkes, 1995). Smoking tobacco during pregnancy does increase risk for mental retardation in newborns, although the effect may be due to the fact that smoking increases the risk for pregnancy complications that can interfere with brain development (Graham, 1992).

Therapeutic drugs used during pregnancy can also contribute to an increased risk for mental retardation. The greatest risk is with drugs used to treat epilepsy and/or bipolar disorder, such as Dilantin, phenobarbital, valproate, and carbamazepine (Hanson et al., 1976). Because mothers with severe epilepsy or bipolar disorder often require such drugs to control their symptoms, it is hard to avoid the risk. However, careful monitoring of the blood levels of these drugs can reduce the risk substantially (Gaily & Granstrom, 1988). In addition, the anticoagulant coumadin (Warfarin) and the acne drug isotretinoin (Accutane) pose risks to the fetus, which may include retardation (Benke, 1984; Hall et al, 1980). Accutane is not a problem when it is applied topically but is a problem when ingested. Clearly, pregnant women and women considering becoming pregnant should consult with their doctors about any medications they are taking.

Radiation used to treat cancer has disastrous effects on a developing embryo (Menkes, 1995), resulting in significantly reduced brain size and mental retardation (Rugh, 1958). However, the much lower doses of radiation associated with diagnostic X-rays pose little risk (Menkes, 1995).

Infections during pregnancy can have significant consequences for the long-term health of the child. The viral infection rubella (German measles) often has little impact on the mother but devastating consequences for the fetus. Although not every fetus is affected, those that are have a high probability of spontaneous abortion. Those that survive may be retarded, sometimes profoundly so (Chess et al., 1971; Cooper, 1968). Taxoplasmosis, which is caused by a protozoan infection, is similar to rubella in that it has little effect on the mother but serious effects on the fetus, including severe to profound mental retardation (Menkes, 1995). If the mother has syphilis, the disease is normally transmitted to the fetus sometime between the fourth and seventh months of pregnancy. Syphilis causes subtle neurological problems in the newborn, which show up as intellectual impairment as the child matures (Hutchinson & Sandall, 1995). HIV infection can be passed from mother to fetus, the baby being born HIV+ (Crocker, 1992). Fortunately, almost 70% of these children show a gradual reduction in the HIV virus during the first few years of life. For those who do not, however, the HIV virus can cause significant brain damage, severe retardation, and death (Belman et al., 1988).

The fetus is at especially high risk for brain damage during delivery. Any physical damage to the head because of the position of the fetus in the birth canal or any cutting off of the blood supply to the brain during delivery may result in significant brain damage and mental retardation. A common complication is the umbilical cord wrapping around the neck of the infant, essentially choking the baby during delivery (Machin et al., 2000).

Environmental Toxins. Many substances are toxic to the human brain, especially the developing brain of a young child. Fortunately, most such substances are rare, and therefore few children are exposed to them. However, two toxins—lead and mercury—are sufficiently common in many environments to pose significant risk to children.

It is estimated that 3 to 4 million American children have blood lead levels high enough to be toxic to the brain (Needleman, 1992). Lead is present in the environment from many sources, although recent awareness of the problem has reduced the number of such sources. For example, most gasoline sold in the United States no longer contains lead. Until the 1960s, virtually all gasoline contained lead, so the exhaust emitted lead into the air. Water pipes in the nineteenth century were often made of lead, and some older water systems still have occasional lead-contaminated piping in their systems. Many paints from earlier eras contained lead. Older buildings may have layers of paint flaking off the walls, much of it containing lead. Toddlers often pick up and eat such paint chips and thus receive toxic levels of lead (Berney, 1993). Lead-based paints were used extensively for painting bridges, so special precautions are now used when sanding the bridges for repainting to avoid lead contamination of the soil and ground water. Batteries, especially car batteries, often contain lead and other toxic substances. Consequently, there is a substantial effort to recycle them rather than allowing them to go into

Many older houses still have layers of paint that contain substantial amounts of lead. When the paint peels, as in this room, it makes a tempting target for toddlers, who like to explore new things with their mouths. Lead poisoning is still a major contributor to brain damage in children.

landfills. Despite these efforts, lead poisoning is the most common preventable health problem for children today (Chang, 1999).

High levels of lead are clearly toxic (Lane & Kemper, 2001), but even low levels are toxic and may reduce cognitive performance (Hawk et al., 1986; Phelps, 1999). These reductions in performance are rarely dramatic enough to create mental retardation unless the child's IQ is already low. Nevertheless, they represent a significant risk for any exposed child.

Mercury is also highly toxic to the brain and is capable of producing mental retardation if the level of exposure is high enough (Myers & Davidson, 1998). Fortunately, the risks of mercury poisoning have been known for many years, and for the most part, exposure to mercury is rare. However, mercury can accumulate in the food chain if there has been contamination. For example, fish (especially swordfish, salmon, and tuna) can store mercury that contaminates lakes, streams, or oceans.

Cultural-Familial Mental Retardation. Most people with mental retardation do not have the kind of specific biological abnormality that characterizes organic mental retardation. They either represent the low end of the distribution of intelligence or have low intellectual development because of a severely deficient environment.

There is a distribution of intelligence in the general population, with most people having IQs in the middle range (about 70% fall between 85 and 115). The extreme low scores in this distribution are in the range of mental retardation. The people with these intelligence scores are said to have cultural-familial mental retardation; that is, their mental retardation is due to the genetic and/or environmental effects of the family, *not* to physical abnormalities. They are usually in the mild mental retardation range and are often capable of functioning adequately in a supportive environment. It is estimated that 60% of known genes have an impact on the development and functioning of the brain, and most also affect other organ systems (Shore, 1997). Determining how each of these genes affects brain development, to say nothing of how each interacts with other genes, is well beyond current technological capability.

Genes contribute substantially to intelligence. In fact, the heritability index for intelligence is .60–.80 (Mackintosh, 1998). Does this mean that intelligence and mental retardation are predominantly due to genes? The answer is yes. Does this mean that environment generally plays a lesser role than genes? The answer is again yes. Does this mean that environment is unimportant? The answer is no, as you will see shortly. The heritability index is perhaps the most widely misunderstood statistic in all of psychology, as discussed in the nearby Modern Myths box.

Although genes play a substantial role in many cases of cultural-familial mental retardation, extreme environmental situations can also produce such retardation. Most brain development is dependent on the appropriate stimulation during critical periods (Ramey et al., 1998). If a child does not receive adequate experiences to stimulate specific brain regions at the time that those brain regions are developing, that part of the child's brain will never develop adequately, no matter how much stimulation is provided later. Therefore, it should not be surprising that severe stimulus deprivation during early development is likely to have profound consequences for intellectual development. Most children are fortunate enough to grow up in an environment that provides at least minimal stimulation, but some children are raised in households in which the level of stimulation is insufficient to allow normal cognitive development. For example, parents who are unusually poor, have low intellectual ability, or are not motivated to spend time with their children may fail to provide adequate stimulation for their children during critical periods in their development (Ramey et al., 1996).

TREATING AND PREVENTING MENTAL RETARDATION

Treating mental retardation does not mean reversing it; such reversals are currently impossible. Instead, treating mental retardation involves helping retarded individuals to achieve as much as they can and to enhance their quality of life. This section begins by reviewing the history of institutionalization and then addresses three current treatment approaches: residential treatment, rehabilitation, and special education. The section ends with a discussion of prevention strategies.

Institutionalization. Until the nineteenth century, families took care of mentally retarded children (Baroff & Olley, 1999). Those children with severe and profound mental retardation rarely survived past childhood as a consequence of multiple physical problems. The ones who did survive were typically mildly retarded and would often contribute to the family business or farm. By the later part of the nineteenth century, the state began to take responsibility for the care of severely retarded individuals. Special institutions were built, staffs were hired and trained, and families were encouraged to accept these programs as the best alternative for their retarded children. Like the mental hospitals constructed in the same era, most of these institutions were on the edge of town or in the country, away from population centers. These locations were selected in part to isolate the mentally retarded from the rest of society.

Although state institutions were created with the best of intentions, many were underfunded, improperly staffed, and poorly managed. Managing moderately to profoundly retarded individuals, helping them to develop to their full potential, and providing a satisfying living environment demand considerable patience, expertise, and resources. Overworked and underpaid staffs were rarely able to handle

MODERN Myths

Misunderstanding Heritability

There is probably no concept that is more consistently misunderstood than heritability. Heritability, which is often written as h^2, is defined as the proportion of variability in a trait that is due to genetic factors. Variability is an index of the degree of differences among people. If people are very similar, the variability is low; if people differ considerably, the variability is high. If h^2 is 0.80, that means that 80% of the variability in the trait is due to genes; by extension, the remaining 20% is due to environment. The total of all the sources of variability is always 100%, or 1.00 if expressed as a proportion. This scenario is illustrated in column A in Figure 13.5. In this graphical illustration, the height of the lower portion of the bar is the heritability index—the proportion of variability that is due to genes.

Most people *incorrectly* assume that the heritability index indicates how much impact genes and environment *can have* on the *trait*. What it actually shows is how much impact genes and environment *currently*

[FIGURE 13.5]
Heritability Index

The heritability index is the proportion of the total variability of a trait that is due to the effects of genes. In this graph, the heritability index is the height of the lower portion of the bar.

have on the *variability in the trait.* Confused? At first glance this distinction appears to be no more than semantic, but it isn't. Some examples will help to illustrate the concept. The number of legs that a person has is strongly determined by genes. In fact,

the general features of the human body are all genetically determined. It is an extremely rare genetic event that might cause a person to be born with something other than two legs. Environmental events, such as traffic accidents, affect the number of legs

---

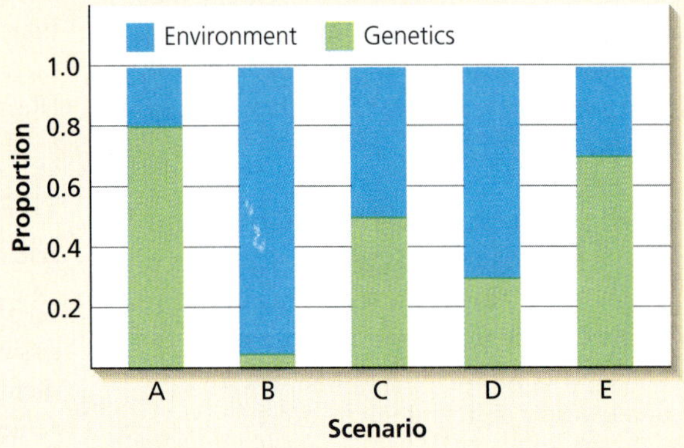

the behavioral problems posed by many of the residents. The relative isolation of the institutions probably made it easier for legislatures gradually to reduce expenditures, thus squeezing the programs more. By the 1950s, many programs began to rely on medications for the management of behavioral problems. Television and magazine exposés in the 1960s brought the deplorable conditions of some state institutions to light, forcing a rethinking of the approach and leading to changes that continue to this day (Baroff & Olley, 1999). The result of this rethinking was a dramatic and rapid shift from large state institutions to smaller, residential settings, a trend that reduced the populations in the large institutions from nearly 200,000 in 1967 to 68,000 (out of a much larger national population) in 1994 (Rothholz & Massey, 1996). The courts also stimulated many of these changes by affirming that mentally retarded individuals have specific rights (Baroff & Olley, 1999).

One of the people described at the beginning of this chapter, Adrian, spent over 10 years in a state institution. After living with her parents for 20 years, she adapted poorly to the structure and demands of an institutional environment. Her physical needs for clothing, shelter, and food were met, and the staff tried valiantly to engage her in recreational and educational programs. However, her temper tantrums increased in frequency and intensity, and medications proved ineffective. The failure of the institution to meet Adrian's needs was a serious problem—a problem that was much more pervasive in institutional settings than the occasional mismanaged institution featured in the exposés of the era.

Residential Treatment. Residential treatment involves housing and treating mentally retarded individuals in community residences that resemble a family living a person has only infrequently, but much more frequently than genetic events. Hence we might conclude that because genes always produce two-legged people, and because environment only rarely produces a loss of one or more limbs, the heritability of the trait "number of legs" should be close to 1.00—that is, this trait is almost entirely genetically determined. In actuality, however, the heritability index for this case is near zero, even though that may seem counterintuitive. The reason is that there is almost no variability in the genes that determine the number of legs a person has. Therefore, whether someone has two legs, one leg, or no legs is due almost entirely to environmental factors, such as accidents. This situation is illustrated in Column B of Figure 13.5. In other words, the heritability index does not indicate how much genes contribute to a trait; it indicates only how much *the variability in the trait* is due to *variability in genes*.

As if that weren't enough, heritability also does not indicate how much the environment *could* affect a trait. Suppose, for example, that genes and the environment each accounted for 50% of the variability in the scores on IQ tests and that the primary environmental factor accounting for the variability in IQ scores was the quality of the preschool environment. This scenario is illustrated in column C of Figure 13.5. What would happen if someone devised a wonderfully stimulating environment that dramatically increased the IQ of preschoolers? If this revolutionary program were applied to 10% of the population, those 10% would show dramatic increases in IQ, which would increase the variability in IQ score but, more important, would increase the variability in IQ scores that was *due to the environment.* Those fortunate enough to have participated in the program would have higher IQ scores, and the others would not. This would lower the heritability index as shown in column D of Figure 13.5. If the initial success of this program prompted a commitment to apply the program to everyone, then everyone would benefit and there would be *less* variability due to environment, because the most critical element of the environment—this program—was being applied to everyone. The result is shown in column E of Figure 13.5. In other words, as you start to apply the program to only a few people, the variability in the environment increases, but as the program is applied to more and more people, the variability in the environment starts to decrease, because everyone is now being treated the same. The variability of the genes remains unchanged, but the relative impact of the genes, compared with the environment, changes as the environmental situation changes.

Why would anyone develop such a counterintuitive index of heritability? Actually, the index usually works fine, because both the gene pool and the environment tend to change slowly. Therefore, heritability indices are reasonably stable indicators of how much of the current variability in a trait is due to genetic factors. Just remember that high heritability does *not* mean that environment cannot affect the distribution of a trait in the population.

environment. They live in houses called **group homes** with a small number of other retarded individuals and are involved in community activities. For example, they go to movies, amusement parks, churches, and other attractions. This residential treatment approach is currently the dominant model for the treatment of the mentally retarded (Baroff & Olley, 1999). Centralized state institutions still exist, and for people with severe and profound retardation, such centralized programs are often necessary.

residential treatment   The housing and treatment of mentally retarded individuals in community residences that resemble a family living environment.

group homes   Houses where a small number of retarded individuals live and are involved in community activities.

The goal of residential treatment is to provide humane and effective treatment in a setting that maximizes integration into the community. A secondary goal is to reduce stigmatization by increasing exposure of the public to the mentally retarded. The proposal to open a residential home for retarded individuals is often met with community opposition, referred to as NIMBY or "not in my backyard" (Wilmoth et al., 1987). However, thousands of residential treatment homes have opened over the past 20 years, and the general success of these homes and the minimal problems they have caused to neighbors may be decreasing this reaction. Laws have generally supported the right of agencies to open group homes, so neighbors have limited veto power. Nevertheless, most agencies are sensitive to this issue and work hard to court the good will of people living close to their group homes (Goldstein et al., 1989).

The philosophy of treatment and rehabilitation for the mentally retarded has changed dramatically over the past half-century. At one time, the mentally retarded were housed in institutions; today, most live in group homes in the community.

Rehabilitation. Rehabilitation comprises the set of programs designed to help individuals with mental retardation reach their full potential. For example, residential treatment usually includes specific programs to teach responsibility for household chores, such as vacuuming, watering plants, and preparing meals. These are genuine treatment programs, not just ways to get the residents to do some of the household work. It generally requires more time and effort by staff to train and supervise residents in such tasks than it would take to just do the tasks. Most retarded individuals are also involved in day rehabilitation programs or sheltered workshops. **Day rehabilitation programs** are comprehensive programs that individually tailor their treatment to the needs of the individual. Typical programs include social skills training, educational efforts, social activities in both the center and the community, work training, and behavior modification for problem behaviors.

Sheltered workshops are programs for the employment of mentally retarded individuals. These programs contract with companies to provide specific work, design methods to train and supervise retarded individuals to do

the work, and then pay them on the basis of their level of productivity. The work may involve packing sponges into a bag that is then heat-sealed or placing items onto a display card that is then shrink-wrapped. Local companies sometimes go out of their way to create useful contracts for local sheltered workshops. The fees for the work are set to be comparable to the costs for doing the same work in another way—either by machine or by an alternative labor force. Therefore, out of necessity, these programs are exempted from minimum-wage requirements because the level of productivity of most retarded individuals could not support such a wage. Even though the wage may be low, it is an important part of the sheltered workshop program in that it is a significant motivator for participants and often a great source of personal pride.

The ideal goal of day rehabilitation programs and sheltered workshops is to prepare participants to compete for work in the real world. This goal is unrealistic for many participants, but some are able to develop the work habits and skills to qualify for outside work. Again, because of concerted efforts by agencies, many employers are willing to provide competitive jobs to those graduates of the sheltered workshops who are ready for that level of responsibility.

Aaron, whom we discussed earlier in the chapter, was able to handle a paper route on his own. His parents trained him to deliver the papers appropriately and to collect regularly from his customers. They also provided the supervision to make sure that the work continued to be done well, although Aaron was very responsible and required little supervision. Aaron's father later taught him how to make a sales pitch to nonsubscribers. Perhaps because Aaron and his parents were so well liked, he was able to increase circulation of the local newspaper substantially, which made hiring Aaron a good business decision. In contrast, Adrian could not work in a competitive environment, even though her level of retardation was less than Aaron's. However, she did benefit from a rehabilitation program that included a sheltered workshop. Her disruptive behavior decreased, her paycheck improved her morale, and her social skills were enhanced.

Special Education. Special education is any school-based program that is designed to meet the unique learning needs of one or more students. For example, students who are unable to learn specific material at the same pace as other students must be provided with a program of study that is tailored to their learning difficulties and designed to provide maximum learning given the abilities or disabilities of the person. This may include smaller classes with more individualized teacher attention, teachers with special training in teaching the mentally retarded, or special tutorial programs to supplement the standard curriculum. Like many of the programs to benefit people with mental retardation, special-education programs did not become universally available until federal mandates were handed down. Beginning with the Education for All Handicapped

---

rehabilitation   The set of programs designed to help individuals with mental retardation reach their full potential.

day rehabilitation programs   Comprehensive programs that individually tailor their treatment to the needs of the individual.

sheltered workshops   Programs for the employment of mentally retarded individuals.

special education   Any school-based program that is designed to meet the unique learning needs of one or more students.

eugenics   The science of selective breeding.

Children Act of 1975 (Public Law 94-142), the federal government codified the educational rights of the mentally retarded. Federal and state governments have recognized that many school districts do not have the financial resources to meet the needs of all their students. Therefore, federal and state funds are often, but not always, given to school districts to pay for the programs that are mandated (Hartman, 1992).

Preventing Mental Retardation. Not all mental retardation is preventable, but given its impact, prevention efforts are important. This discussion will focus on three prevention strategies: genetic counseling, adequate prenatal care, and reducing environmental toxins.

Genetic counseling often has a bad reputation because of inappropriate comparisons with eugenics. **Eugenics** is the science of selective breeding, and it was the rationale that Nazi dictator Adolf Hitler used for exterminating millions of people that he considered inferior. In contrast to the forced sterilization and mass murder of the Third Reich, genetic counseling leaves decisions about reproduction entirely to parents. The goal is to provide parents with information on which to base their decisions about having children. For example, some disorders, such as PKU, are the result of a known genetic abnormality. If a couple has a child with PKU and neither parent has the disorder, both must be carriers of the PKU gene. Therefore, the probability of their having another affected child is 1 in 4. With that information, a couple can make an informed decision about whether they want to risk having another child with such a severe disorder.

There is another level of genetic counseling, but it benefits only parents who are willing to abort a fetus. It is possible to obtain cells from the placenta—a procedure called *amniocentesis*—and inspect the cell's chromosomes for abnormalities. The extra chromosome of Down syndrome is easily identified with this method (Ormond, 1997). Because the risk of chromosomal abnormalities increases with the age of the parents, especially the age of the mother, doctors often recommend this procedure for women over 40. The technology is just beginning to be developed to the level of identifying specific genes, and the technology is

ADVANCES   Evaluating specific genes

The advances that have occurred in genetics over the past couple of decades have been incredible, and the coming decade is likely to dwarf past accomplishments. It is now possible to detect the genes that contribute to PKU (Acosta et al., 2001) and Huntington's disease (Daniel, 2000). Given the tremendous advances in mapping the human genome, it is only a matter of time before genes associated with other psychiatric disorders are discovered. What may not be immediately obvious is that the ability to map the human genome will enable scientists to zero in on the genetic basis of disorders that are the result of multiple genes. With previous technology, it was virtually impossible to identify the genes contributing to polygenic disorders. That is likely to change within your lifetime.

These advances may be a boon to medical science, but there are potential costs. For example, if one can detect the presence of genes that contribute to serious disorders, could insurance companies use that information to deny coverage to some people or charge them higher rates? Insurance companies already charge higher premiums for people who are known to have higher risks, such as smokers. What would happen if genetic factors that contribute to diseases such as Alzheimer's could be identified? Would what one paid for insurance be based on genetic test data?

Genetic information may help couples make decisions about having children, but the information will certainly not make the decisions easier. If genetic testing determines, for example, that the risk in a certain couple's offspring will be 6 times higher than the average for heart disease, 3 times higher for depression, and 12 times higher for Alzheimer's, should the couple decide not to have children? It is unlikely that similar statistics will be available for how likely the child will be to grow into a happy, productive individual, make contributions to the community, or raise healthy children. The early genetic information will almost certainly focus on known pathology. Would the parents of Vincent van Gogh or Isaac Newton, both of whom suffered from emotional disorders, have decided against having children because the risks were too high? What about the first generation exposed to this genetic technology? Genetic testing would tell them only what genes they already have. Would you want to know that you have, for example, an 80% chance of developing Alzheimer's by age 75? How would that affect your retirement planning and your enjoyment of life in general?

Like all advances in technology, genetic technology creates both opportunities and problems. Like cloning, which is currently the subject of vigorous debate, these new advances will be debated extensively, just as they should be.

likely to advance substantially in the next few years, given the tremendous advances in the field of molecular genetics. The PKU gene can already be identified in a fetus (Acosta et al., 2001). The nearby Advances box describes some of the recent work in this area and its potential consequences.

The health of pregnant women dramatically affects the fetus. For that reason, pregnant women need to receive good prenatal health care, and they should be informed about the risks to their children of certain behaviors, such as drug use. Proper health care during pregnancy can prevent many problems (Ivonov & Flynn, 1999). For example, infections such as syphilis can be treated early in the pregnancy before they are transmitted to the fetus (Menkes, 1995).

There will always be toxins in water, air, and food. Contrary to popular belief, not all toxins are human-made. Many occur naturally and can build up in the water supply or food chain. Nevertheless, the modern industrialized world has dramatically increased the concentration of such toxins, often to dangerously high levels. There is a growing awareness of this problem, and systematic efforts are being made to reduce contamination (Enzer & Heard, 2000). However, these are not easy issues to address. The government has enacted laws requiring industrial polluters to

reduce pollution and to clean up polluted sites (such as refineries, steel mills, and even local gas stations) before they can be sold. This approach seems reasonable because it assigns responsibility most often to the people who were originally responsible for the problem, and it provides financial incentives to avoid polluting the environment.

Although it is not always economically feasible to remove all toxins from the environment, it clearly is feasible to reduce the introduction of toxins. For example, lead-based paint is rarely used now, and gasoline no longer contains lead. Manufacturers know that introducing lead into the environment creates legal liabilities that they do not want. Gas stations now have sophisticated monitors to detect leaks, and their tanks are designed to last longer. These steps make the world a somewhat safer place.

The most effective way of preventing cultural-familial retardation is to focus on enriching the early lives of children who might otherwise experience an environment with little social, perceptual, and cognitive stimulation (Ramey et al., 1998). The earlier the intervention in the child's life, the more helpful it is and the longer-lasting the results (Campbell & Ramey, 1994), presumably because the intervention provides the stimulation necessary for

[FIGURE 13.6]
Impact of Early-Life Deprivation

The model proposed by Ramey and Ramey (1998) suggests that deficits in early life experiences affect the developmental course for a child and lead to large differences in cognitive and social deficits in adulthood, because these early deficits change the entire trajectory of development.

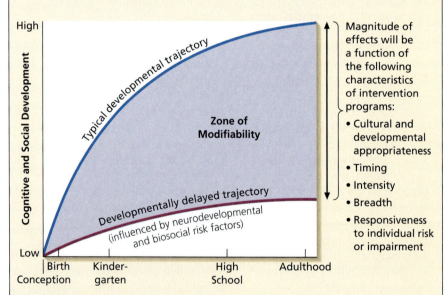

SOURCE: *Graph, "Impact of Early Life Deprivation" (p. 12) from "Early Intervention and Early Experience" by C. T. Ramey and S. L. Ramey, American Psychologist, 53, 1998. Copyright © 1998 by the American Psychological Association. Reprinted by permission.*

normal brain development. This model suggests that deficits in experience can change the entire trajectory of cognitive development, as shown in Figure 13.6. Head Start programs were an attempt to provide critical stimulation in an effort to avoid these early deficits. Unfortunately, many of these programs focused on children who were of almost school age and therefore were well past most of the critical periods for brain development. Also, Head Start programs targeted children solely on the basis of family income, which research has shown is less predictive of intellectual development than is the level of stimulation in the household (Ramey et al., 1998). The programs that have been most effective in increasing the intellectual development of children and in maintaining the gains are those that (1) begin when children are very young, (2) are intensive (up to several hours per day several days per week), (3) provide the experience directly to the children rather than indirectly through parent training, (4) are broad in their focus rather than focusing on a single cognitive skill, (5) are tailored to individual children, and (6) seek to continue intellectual stimulation after the program ends (Ramey et al., 1998).

Check Yourself 13.4

Mental Retardation

1. What three criteria must be met for a diagnosis of mental retardation?
2. Distinguish between cultural-familial and organic mental retardation.
3. What is the cause of Down syndrome and which children are most at risk?
4. What toxin is still a major contributor to brain damage and mental retardation?
5. What is the goal of current treatment programs for the mentally retarded?

Ponder this . . .   *What effect would you expect mental retardation to have on survival? Would you expect that effect be stronger or weaker today than it was 5000 years ago?*

SUMMARY

DISRUPTIVE BEHAVIOR DISORDERS

- Attention-deficit/hyperactivity disorder is characterized by attentional problems, hyperactivity/impulsivity, or both. It affects about 5% of school-age children and is more common in boys than in girls. Although the dramatic symptoms of ADHD decrease with age, some people continue to show symptoms into adulthood. ADHD interferes with school and social activities.

- Genes contribute to several of the symptoms of ADHD, and the disorder is genetically heterogeneous. Subtle brain abnormalities may also contribute. Although it was once believed that food additives contributed to ADHD, data do not support that hypothesis. Psychological factors can increase or decrease the ADHD symptoms.

- The most common treatment for ADHD is stimulant medication, which produces short-term decreases in the symptoms but is controversial. Behavioral therapy is also helpful, particularly if it is an intensive program designed to teach social skills and show the children better ways to manage their energy levels.

- Conduct disorder is characterized by a pervasive lack of respect for the rights of others. Both genes and environment contribute. Several treatment options show promise for reducing the severity of conduct disorder.

FUNCTIONAL AND LEARNING DISORDERS

- Enuresis is characterized by the involuntary voiding of urine, usually while asleep. Encopresis is the inappropriate voiding of feces. Both appear to be developmental delays. Enuresis is most often treated with a device that awakens the child as soon as nocturnal urination begins.

- Communication disorders are characterized by deficits in understanding or expressing oneself verbally. With the exception of stuttering, communication disorders appear to be developmental delays.

- Learning disorders involve significant deficits in reading, mathematics, or written expression. The best understood is reading disorder, also called dyslexia, which is

a heterogeneous disorder with a strong genetic component. Intensive educational interventions can improve the reading skills of people with dyslexia.

AUTISTIC DISORDER

- Autistic disorder is the best known of the pervasive developmental disorders. It is characterized by severe disruptions in social and communication skills. Although it was once believed to be a response to emotional coldness in parents, scientists now know that there is a strong genetic component to autism. Neurological deficits are common in people with autism, and there is suggestive evidence that serotonin may be involved in at least some cases of autism.

- Autism is most often treated with intensive behavioral programs focused on the primary symptoms: communication deficits and social deficits. A variety of medications have been used to reduce specific symptoms, but none are cures.

MENTAL RETARDATION

- The diagnosis of mental retardation requires a low IQ coupled with significant functional deficits, which must be present before age 18. The DSM recognizes four levels of mental retardation: mild, moderate, severe, and profound.

- Cultural-familial mental retardation represents the low end of the normal IQ distribution and affects 2% of the population. Organic mental retardation is due to biological causes and affects 0.5% of the population. Chromosomal abnormalities, genetic abnormalities, pregnancy and birth complications, and exposure to toxins can all lead to organic mental retardation.

- For nearly a hundred years, most mentally retarded individuals were treated in institutions. Now most are treated in residential settings, most treatment being geared to integrating the retarded individual into the community.

KEY TERMS

Asperger's disorder (409)
attention-deficit/hyperactivity disorder, or ADHD (396)
autistic disorder (408)
childhood disintegrative disorder (409)
chromosomal abnormalities (419)
communication disorders (405)
conduct disorder (401)
cultural-familial mental retardation (417)
day rehabilitation programs (426)
disorder of written expression (407)
Down syndrome (420)
dyslexia (407)
elimination disorders (403)
encopresis (405)
enuresis (404)
eugenics (427)
executive functioning (398)
expressive language disorder (406)
fetal alcohol syndrome (421)
fragile-X syndrome (420)
functional disorders (403)
genetic abnormalities (419)

group homes (425)
learning disorders (403)
mathematics disorder (407)
mental retardation (417)
mild mental retardation (419)
mixed receptive-expressive language disorder (406)
moderate mental retardation (419)
oppositional defiant disorder (402)
organic mental retardation (417)
pervasive developmental disorders (408)
phenelketonuria, or PKU (421)
phonological disorder (406)
profound mental retardation (419)
reading disorder (407)
rehabilitation (426)
residential treatment (424)
Rett's disorder (409)
selective mutism (406)
severe mental retardation (419)
sheltered workshops (426)
special education (426)
stuttering (406)

SUGGESTED READINGS

Baroff, G. S., & Olley, J. G. (1999). *Mental retardation: Nature, cause, and management* (3rd ed.). Philadelphia: Brunner/Mazel. This is a readable and scholarly presentation of the causes and treatments of mental retardation.

DeGrandpre, R. (1999). *Ritalin nation.* New York: Norton. This provocative reexamination of a culture and its dependence on drugs challenges the notion that every child with a short attention span needs a powerful stimulant in order to function. Although a bit overstated in places, it is thought-provoking and raises legitimate issues.

Hurford, D. M. (1998). *To read or not to read: Answers to all your questions about dyslexia.* New York: Scribner/ Simon & Schuster. This book describes the nature of dyslexia and outlines the treatment options that are currently available.

chapterfourteen

"Grapes," ©Noma/photography by John Perri.

14

Substance-Related Disorders

One for the Road

PATRICE Patrice was 59, but she looked more like 75, in part because she was dying of cirrhosis of the liver. Married with three grown children, she did not fit the popular image of an alcoholic. She had been an office manager, a PTA president, and an active participant in community affairs. She never had a DWI because she never drove when she drank. But her moods were unpredictable when she was drinking, and this often created tension within her family and among close friends. She never drank before 5 P.M., but would consume between 8 and 15 beers or mixed drinks every evening, drinking until she could not walk a straight line or talk without slurring her words. She barely ate during the day because the calories in the alcohol had already created a weight problem. Her husband used to drink with her in the evening, but now he rarely drinks and stays out of the house until she goes to bed. Now, with a life expectancy measured in weeks, Patrice has started violating her hard and fast rule of never drinking before 5 P.M.

Going Down

TYRONE Tyrone was a successful stockbroker who worked 70-hour weeks. He had been told that he could not get addicted to cocaine if he snorted it only on weekends, and for 18 months that seemed to be true. But gradually he found an excuse to party occasionally during the week. Then he started snorting just a little at work for an energy boost. He worked hard and played hard, and he felt his life was good. However, within two years of his first experiments with cocaine, Tyrone was clearly addicted. He no longer took the cocaine just for pleasure or for an energy boost. Rather, he took it to prevent crashing—a deep feeling of pain and depression that followed each use. He was hooked, but he was still employed, he was still making good money, and he never resorted to stealing or dealing drugs to pay for his habit. Although he made a half-hearted attempt to kick the habit by enrolling in an outpatient program, he quickly stopped attending. But when the stock market softened, his six-figure salary was cut in half, his luxury car was repossessed, and he felt compelled to push more aggressively with his existing accounts to increase commissions. His firm fired him after receiving complaints, and no other brokerage would touch him. At 29 he had no job, no money, and a drug habit he could not kick.

More Pain

SANDRA She should have died, but the seatbelt and air bag saved her life. It took two hours for the rescue crew to cut her out of the car. Two years and 12 operations later, she still could not walk without a cane, but at least she could walk again. Now she carried an additional burden—addiction to the pain medication that had gotten her through the nightmare.

The accident shattered both of Sandra's legs. The doctors could not even count the number of breaks. In the first few days, not even a morphine drip could stop the pain. Each surgery renewed the agony, as the doctors painstakingly reassembled her leg bones. In the weeks between the surgeries, the doctors gave Sandra codeine to use when the pain was bad. However, if she waited until it got bad, she would be in agony for hours, so she started taking the pain pills to prevent the pain. Soon the prescription from her surgeon would not last the month, so she sought a prescription from her general practitioner as well. He reluctantly gave her a prescription for a week's supply, saying that her surgeon should be responsible for the pain management. The second prescription triggered the state's computer that monitors controlled substances such as painkillers, and Sandra was forced to face her addiction.

The histories of Patrice, Tyrone, and Sandra illustrate both the positive and the negative aspects of drugs. It could be argued that each of them benefited, at least for a while, from the use of a substance. Patrice found that alcohol relaxed her when she was young, that it was associated with wonderful parties with her friends, and that it gave her the confidence to extend herself socially. But 40 years later, it had seriously compromised her health. Tyrone found that cocaine produced an incredible high, unlike any he had experienced. It increased his energy and boosted his confidence. But within three years, it cost him everything—his job, his home, his friends. Sandra was not looking for confidence or pleasure. She just wanted to escape unbearable pain, and a narcotic drug gave her some blessed relief as surgeons rebuilt her legs. Pain is a terrible thing—something one starts to dread after a while. Sandra's fear of pain prompted her to overmedicate until she could no longer control her use of painkillers. In each of these cases, use of a substance became abuse of the substance, at which point any positive benefits that might have existed were lost. What is somewhat unusual about these cases is that each involves the abuse of a single drug.

Drugs are much more a part of today's culture than most people realize, as illustrated in Figure 14.1. The coffee that many people are convinced they need in the morning to get going contains a drug—caffeine. Caffeine is also found in a variety of other substances, from chocolate to soft drinks. The nicotine in cigarettes and the alcohol in beer and wine are both drugs. People routinely take drugs to ease uncomfortable feelings, such as stuffy heads, muscle aches, and motion sickness. Every drugstore has hundreds

Two widely used drugs, alcohol and nicotine, have been part of the social scene for many years, but a popular new option—the coffee bar—provides a setting for those who want to socialize and meet people but do not want to drink or to breathe second-hand smoke. Even this option, however, includes a drug: caffeine.

[FIGURE 14.1]
Drug Use in the United States

Drug use is common in the United States, but as this figure illustrates, the drugs that most people associate with abuse (cocaine and heroin) are much less of a problem than drugs such as alcohol and nicotine.

Drug	Percent Using Regularly
Alcohol	
Cigarettes	
Marijuana	
Cocaine	
Hallucinogens	
Crack	
Heroin	

Percent Using Regularly: 10 20 30 40 50 60

SOURCE: *Adapted from NIDA.* National Household Survey on Drug Abuse: Population Estimates 1995. *(Washington, D.C.: Department of Health and Human Services, 1996.)*

of drugs, from over-the-counter remedies to powerful and sometimes dangerous prescription drugs. Thus when people speak of the "drug culture," they may be talking about more than just a few homeless addicts. It may not be that great a leap from using an over-the-counter or prescription drug to modify every unpleasant feeling to using street drugs to produce a pleasant high or relieve an overpowering sense of self-doubt.

This chapter discusses substance abuse and dependence, the factors that contribute to these problems, and the strategies that have been used to treat and prevent them. It opens with a discussion of the addiction process, clarifying the distinction between abuse and dependence and classifying the most widely abused drugs. We then discuss specific classes of drugs: sedatives, narcotics, stimulants, and hallucinogens. Each section describes the drugs' effects, the pharmacological mechanisms underlying those effects, and the short- and long-term consequences of using the drugs. The single most widely abused drug—alcohol—is covered in greater detail because it is an excellent exemplar of drug abuse. The chapter concludes with a discussion of the theories of drug addiction and the treatment approaches currently in use.

ABUSE AND DEPENDENCE

Evolutionary Impact

There is nothing wrong with wanting to feel good. Human beings are hedonic creatures who seek pleasurable experiences and avoid situations that produce unpleasant sensations. Pleasure as a motivator of behavior has proved to be an enormous evolutionary success. Specific brain centers produce pleasure when stimulated, reinforcing those behaviors that produce the stimulation. Other centers produce alertness, enhancing a person's sense of control. Still other centers produce such unpleasant experiences as pain. Human beings have discovered that these centers can be manipulated chemically. This chemical manipulation overwhelms the delicate balance that evolved over millions of years, often leading to abuse and dependence on these chemicals. Ingesting a substance is reinforcing if it produces a pleasant experience or reduces an unpleasant one. So what is the problem? The problem is that some substances damage the body, rob the person of the ability to stop using the substance, or interfere with a person's functioning.

DEFINING ABUSE AND DEPENDENCE

The DSM makes a distinction between substance dependence and substance abuse. The term *substance dependence* refers to what most people think of as addiction. The dic-

tionary defines **addiction** as a dependence on a substance to the extent that discontinuation causes significant discomfort or trauma. The DSM is more specific. It defines **substance dependence** as a maladaptive pattern of substance use, leading to clinically significant impairment or distress, as manifested by three or more of the following seven symptoms, occurring at any time in the same 12-month period.

- ▶ **Tolerance,** as defined by either of the following:
  - A need for markedly increased amounts of the substance in order to achieve intoxication or desired effects
  - Markedly diminished effect with continued use of the same amount of the substance
- ▶ **Withdrawal,** as manifested by either of the following:
  - The characteristic withdrawal syndrome for the substance (for example, the cravings and jitteriness experienced when one stops smoking)
  - Taking the same substance (or a closely related substance) to relieve or avoid withdrawal symptoms
- ▶ The substance is often taken in larger amounts or over a longer period than was intended.
- ▶ There is a persistent desire or unsuccessful efforts to cut down or control substance use.
- ▶ A great deal of time is spent in activities necessary to obtain the substance, use the substance, or recover from its effects.
- ▶ Important social, occupational, or recreational activities are given up or reduced because of substance use.
- ▶ The substance use is continued despite knowledge of having a persistent or recurrent physical or psychological problem that is likely to have been caused or exacerbated by the substance.   **(APA, 2000, page 197)**

The tolerance and withdrawal effects typically indicate a physiological dependence on the substance—that is, the body has become so accustomed to the drug that it cannot function well without it. The process involves a gradual increase in tolerance with continued use of a drug, which forces the person to take more of the drug to get the same

---

addiction   Dependence on a substance to the extent that discontinuation causes significant discomfort or trauma.

substance dependence   A maladaptive pattern of substance use, leading to clinically significant impairment or distress.

tolerance   A condition that develops over the course of use of a subtance wherein the individual needs markedly increased amounts of the substance to achieve intoxication or desired effects, or experiences a markedly diminished effect with continued use of the same amount of the substance.

withdrawal   Period during which an addict or substance abuser either stops using a drug or uses less than customary. Unpleasant withdrawal symptoms result, which the user may avoid by resuming use of the same (or a closely related) substance.

effect. As the body becomes more tolerant of the drug, it becomes less tolerant of not having the drug, which is what produces the withdrawal effects. Drugs differ on how quickly this process proceeds and on how easily one can become dependent. Some drugs, such as heroine, produce dependence rapidly, whereas other drugs, such as alcohol, produce dependence much more slowly.

The DSM recognizes levels of substance misuse. Less severe than substance dependence is the category of **substance abuse,** which is defined as a maladaptive pattern of substance use leading to clinically significant impairment or distress, as manifested by one or more of the following four symptoms. These symptoms must occur within a 12-month period, and the person must not meet requirements for the diagnosis of substance dependence.

► Recurrent substance use resulting in a failure to fulfill major role obligations at work, school, or home

► Recurrent substance use in situations in which it is physically hazardous

► Recurrent substance-related legal problems

► Continued substance use despite having persistent or recurrent social or interpersonal problems caused by, or exacerbated by, the effects of the substance   (**APA, 2000, page 199**)

The concept of addiction has been largely replaced by the modern concepts of substance dependence and substance abuse. These concepts recognize that a person's psychological and social functioning can be significantly affected by the chronic use of substances, even though there may be no physiological addiction. Furthermore, some drugs that produce a strong addiction, such as nicotine, may have minimal effects on a person's day-to-day functioning, whereas other drugs that produce little physiological addiction, such as marijuana, may have a major impact on a person's functioning.

One problem with the concept of addiction is the fact that treatment professionals have expanded it into many other areas. The term *psychological addiction* is used to refer to any behavior that people engage in repeatedly and feel unable to control. Entire books have been written on such phenomena as gambling addiction (Castellani, 2000), sexual addiction (Goodman, 1998), and addictive shopping (Kottler, 1999). These so-called psychological addictions may or may not share underlying mechanisms with the substance dependence problems discussed in this chapter. The surface similarities of the symptoms—repeating a behavior that has significant negative consequences and being unable to resist the behavior—are not sufficient to

substance abuse A maladaptive pattern of substance use leading to clinically significant impairment or distress.

sedatives Drugs that tend to calm or relax an individual.

The conventional image of addiction is the down-and-out person shooting up in a place like this. However, this is only one face of addiction.

establish that they share an underlying mechanism. These same surface characteristics are found in the compulsive behavior of OCD (see Chapter 8), so it is not surprising that terms like *compulsive gambling* and *compulsive shopping* are also used to describe such behavior. But these terms imply a similarity to other disorders that may not exist. Scientists clearly know much less about these behaviors than about the substance abuse and dependence behaviors covered in this chapter. Of these behavioral addictions, the DSM recognizes only pathological gambling, which is included under the heading of impulse control disorders (see the Focus box on page 378 in Chapter 12).

CLASSIFYING DRUGS

Drugs are classified on the basis of their general impact on the individual. This chapter covers sedatives, narcotics, stimulants, and hallucinogens.

Sedatives. The term **sedative** is applied to any drug that tends to calm or relax an individual. This broad definition includes anxiolytic and hypnotic drugs. Anxiolytic drugs, such as the benzodiazepines introduced in Chapter 8, reduce anxiety and are used primarily for the treatment of anxiety disorders. **Hypnotic drugs** are used to induce sleep (*not* hypnosis, as one might think from the name). By far the most widely used sedative in the world is alcohol, which has both anxiolytic and hypnotic effects. Barbiturates also have both anxiolytic and hypnotic properties. Technically, narcotics are hypnotic drugs, but they are addressed separately in this chapter because they behave differently from the other drugs in the sedative category. Nicotine, the active ingredient in cigarettes, has both sedative and stimulant properties. This makes it difficult to classify, but in this text, nicotine is included in the stimulant category.

Narcotics. The word **narcotic** is derived from the Greek word *narco*, which means "stupor or stuporous state." Narcotics are drugs that produce a reversible suppression of the central nervous system, thereby rendering the person stuporous and insensitive to pain. Such narcotic drugs as morphine and codeine are routinely used in medicine for the short-term treatment of severe pain, but they are only 2 of nearly 20 narcotics in medical use today (Jaffe & Jaffe, 2000). Narcotics also can be abused. The most widely abused narcotic is **heroin,** a highly addictive derivative of morphine. Morphine, codeine, and heroin are all derived from opium, which comes from poppy flowers, and hence are referred to as **opiates.** Synthetic versions of opiates, which are created in the laboratory, are called **opioids.** Many people believe incorrectly that the word *narcotic* refers to all illicit drugs, rather than to the narrow range of drugs defined here.

. . . .

hypnotic drugs   Drugs used to induce sleep.

narcotics   Drugs that produce a reversible suppression of the central nervous system, thereby rendering the person stuporous and insensitive to pain.

heroin   A highly addictive derivative of morphine.

opiates   Drugs that are derived from opium, such as morphine, codeine, and heroin.

opioids   Synthetic opiates created in the laboratory.

stimulants   Drugs that arouse the central and/or autonomic nervous systems, thereby increasing a person's energy and alertness.

hallucinogens   A broad, heterogeneous class of drugs that alter one's perceptions and awareness, thus producing a strange and surrealistic image of the world.

psychedelics   Hallucinogenic drugs that highlight the perception of bright, distorted colors and shapes.

polydrug abusers   Those who abuse more than one drug (the majority of drug users).

Stimulants. **Stimulants** are drugs that arouse the central and/or autonomic nervous system, thereby increasing a person's energy and alertness. A mild stimulant familiar to most people is caffeine, the active ingredient in coffee and several soft drinks. Although caffeine may seem like an innocuous stimulant, and for most people it is, excessive amounts of caffeine make people jumpy, nervous, and quite uncomfortable. Furthermore, people accustomed to regular doses of caffeine experience considerable discomfort in the form of severe headaches if they abruptly stop getting their regular caffeine fix. More powerful stimulants, such as amphetamines and cocaine, dramatically increase energy and alertness and can give a person a sense of control and power. However, they also have powerful withdrawal effects, which can leave the individual nonfunctional and craving more of the drug. Nicotine is a mild stimulant that also has sedative characteristics.

Hallucinogens. **Hallucinogens** are a broad, heterogeneous class of drugs that were first widely used in the 1960s and 1970s as part of a general counterculture movement. They alter one's perceptions and awareness, thus producing a strange and surrealistic image of the world. The term *hallucinogens* highlights these extreme perceptual distortions. These drugs are also referred to as **psychedelics,** a term that highlights the perception of bright, distorted colors and shapes popularized in the psychedelic art of the 1960s and 1970s. This chapter discusses marijuana, LSD, mescaline, psilocybin, and PCP.

Table 14.1 on page 438 lists the most commonly used and abused drugs. With the exception of caffeine, all of these drugs will be covered in this chapter. Although each of these drugs will be discussed separately, the majority of drug abusers are **polydrug abusers**—that is, they abuse more than one drug (Winstock et al., 2001). For example, a typical user might abuse cocaine, marijuana, alcohol, and tobacco, each of which may lead to dependence.

Check Yourself 14.1

Abuse and Dependence

1. What is substance dependence?
2. What is substance abuse?
3. What are the four broad categories of drugs that are discussed in this chapter?

Ponder this . . .   *Much of substance abuse and dependence is motivated, at least initially, by hedonic drives. What impact would you expect natural selection to have on drug dependence, given the powerful negative impact of such dependence?*

[TABLE 14.1] Commonly Abused Drugs

SEDATIVES	
Alcohol	A central nervous system depressant that is a by-product of the fermentation of fruits or grains
Barbiturates	Synthetic drugs that were once widely used for the treatment of anxiety and sleep problems
Anxiolytics	Drugs that are manufactured and sold for the treatment of anxiety
NARCOTICS	
Morphine/ codeine	Opium-based drugs derived from the poppy flower that are used medically to treat severe pain
Heroin	A derivative of morphine that is the most widely abused opiate
STIMULANTS	
Caffeine	A stimulant that is the active ingredient in coffee and many soft drinks
Nicotine	The addictive element in tobacco products. Nicotine is hard to classify because it has both sedative and stimulant qualities.
Amphetamines	Synthetic stimulants that were once widely used as energy enhancers or as diet pills
Cocaine	A powerful stimulant drug derived from the coca plant, which also has pain-relieving qualities when applied topically
Ecstasy	A modern amphetamine drug that has become popular among young people during music marathons called raves.
HALLUCINOGENS	
Marijuana/ hashish	Drugs that are made from the crushed leaves and flowers of the hemp plant and produce a relaxed intoxication
LSD	A synthetic drug that produces vivid visual distortions
PCP (angel dust)	A synthetic drug that can cause severe paranoia and violent behavior

SEDATIVES

Sedatives are drugs that calm or relax people. Some, like alcohol, are used socially, whereas others, like barbiturates and benzodiazepines, are used medically.

ALCOHOL

Alcohol, the most widely used addictive drug, is consumed regularly by over half the U.S. population (NIDA, 1996). Many people who drink alcohol do so responsibly, but a disturbing percentage drink to excess. The popular term for

a person who drinks excessively is *alcoholic;* **alcoholism** is an imprecise term that includes both alcohol abuse and alcohol dependence. Approximately 20% of males and 8% of females qualify for a diagnosis of alcohol dependence sometime during their lives (Kessler et al., 1994). In any given year, 10% of U.S. adults qualify for a diagnosis of alcohol abuse (Narrow et al., 2002). Remember that alcohol dependence, like dependence on any drug, involves a physiological dependence, an inability to control one's drinking, or both. These figures are frightening when one considers the health consequences of heavy drinking, such as cirrhosis of the liver, increased risk for heart disease and stroke, and progressive damage to the neurons of the brain. Alcohol and driving are a deadly combination that accounts for 40% of all traffic deaths (NHTSA, 2001). The abuse figures are even higher at colleges, where 50% of males and 40% of females regularly engage in binge drinking—that is, consuming more than four or five drinks in a single session (Jones et al., 2001; Wechsler et al., 1994, 1998). Binge drinking is also growing rapidly among female college students (Morse, 2002). Nearly a third of high school seniors report regular binge drinking (D'Amico et al., 2001; NIAAA, 1997). Although alcohol abuse and dependence have generally been higher for men, at least in the United States, the rates for women are rapidly catching up. Binge drinking carries additional risks for young women. Remember from Chapter 11 that women are more likely to be sexually victimized if they have been drinking (Emmers-Sommer & Allen, 1999; George et al., 2000). Alcohol may be one of the most widely used substances in society, but there is still considerable misunderstanding in the general public about its effects, as illustrated in the nearby Modern Myths box. The information in the remainder of this section will dispel some of those myths.

Evolutionary Impact

There are several interesting cultural differences in alcohol abuse and dependence, some of which may be due to differences in recent evolutionary history. For example, some Native American groups, though not all, have especially elevated risk for alcoholism (Frank et al., 2000). Unlike Europeans and European immigrants, most Native American cultures were exposed to alcohol for the first time just a few hundred years ago. Hence little evolutionary pressure shaped adaptation to the harmful effects of alcohol abuse (Nesse & Williams, 1994). The fact that isolated populations are often unusually sensitive to the effects of alcohol suggests two things: (1) Genes influence response to alcohol. (2) Ex-

alcoholism A popular, though imprecise, term for drinking excessively and habitually. The term comprises both alcohol abuse and dependence.

MODERN Myths

Alcohol AND Alcoholism

Alcohol is a stimulant. This myth is probably based on the initial effects of alcohol on a party: to liven it up. This effect is due to the release of inhibitions. Alcohol actually depresses nervous system functioning and thus activity level—a fact that is obvious if you observe people who have consumed large quantities of alcohol.

Alcohol promotes sleep. People who have been drinking may find it easier to fall asleep, but their sleep will be disrupted, resulting in a less restful experience for the same amount of sleep. Moreover, alcohol withdrawal further disrupts sleep.

Drinking coffee can sober one up. If you believe old movies, this appears to be true. But although coffee increases alertness, it does not counteract the intoxicating effects of alcohol. The sobering-up process involves the breakdown of alcohol, and caffeine has no effect on the rate of this breakdown. Furthermore, caffeine may increase risk by stimulating activity, some of which may be dangerous. Finally, caffeine, like alcohol, is a diuretic. Consequently, it increases the dehydration that is a major contributor to the hangover.

One cannot become dependent on alcohol in the same way as to heroin. This myth is actually partly true, depending on how you look at it. Dependence occurs faster, with less exposure, for drugs like heroin. Nevertheless, with sufficient exposure to alcohol, physiological dependence is likely to develop. There are individual differences in how quickly such dependence develops, and some people are more prone than others to become dependent on alcohol.

A person who drinks only beer will never become an alcoholic. Alcohol is alcohol, regardless of its source. If one consumes enough alcohol over a long enough period, dependence is likely. This myth is probably fueled by the fact that tolerance develops quickly with alcohol, and therefore it takes more to achieve the same psychological impact. Beer drinkers often start to drink hard liquor, because the sheer volume of beer needed to achieve the desired level of intoxication becomes prohibitive as tolerance develops.

Alcohol is less dangerous than other drugs. Again, this myth is partly true. Alcohol is less dangerous than some drugs, but other drugs, such as marijuana, are less dangerous than alcohol. Heavy alcohol consumption damages vital organ systems.

The brain damage associated with alcoholism occurs only in those who drink for a lifetime. This myth looks true on the surface, for brain damage is not apparent in a 25-year-old heavy drinker. This is because the brain is wired in such a way that it is remarkably stable in the face of neuron death, at least until the number of damaged neurons reaches a critical level. The results of heavy drinking early in life are not apparent until late adulthood, when the additional neuronal damage from early drinking results in premature deterioration of cognitive functions.

Problem drinking during college is just a phase that one grows out of. It is true that many people who were problem drinkers early in life, such as President George W. Bush, are able to reduce their alcohol consumption dramatically after college. However, many find themselves dependent on alcohol by the time they graduate or drop out of school. Some people are more genetically prone than others to developing alcohol dependence from heavy exposure in college.

Everyone drinks. This may seem true, but it isn't. In the United States, about half of women and a quarter of men do not drink at all. In some Muslim cultures, virtually no one drinks.

cessive sensitivity to alcohol probably affects survival and/or reproduction, because it is selected out in populations in which alcohol use is common, but not in populations without such use. The rates of alcohol abuse and dependence vary widely across countries, as illustrated in Figure 14.2 on page 440. Furthermore, there are interesting patterns of alcohol abuse within cultures. For example, in the United States, alcohol abuse among whites and Latinos is most common during late teens and early adulthood, but among blacks it is most common during middle age.

Alcohol abuse and dependence will be covered more extensively in this chapter because alcohol is an excellent exemplar of abuse and because it is the most widely abused drug by far. Our coverage begins with a discussion of the

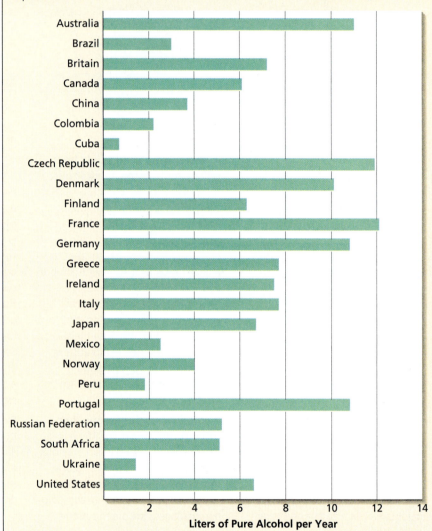

[FIGURE 14.2]

Cross-Cultural Differences in Per Capita Alcohol Consumption

There are large cross-cultural differences in the rate of consumption of alcohol. Not surprisingly, these differences tend to parallel the rates of alcohol abuse and dependence.

SOURCE: *"Cross-Cultural Differences in Alcohol Consumption" from "Drinking Patterns" by E. Goddard et al., The Alcohol Report, ed. by M. Plant and D. Cameron. Copyright © 2000. Reprinted by permission of Free Association Books, UK.*

typical course for alcohol abuse and dependence, followed by a discussion of both the short-term and the long-term effects of heavy alcohol use. The short-term effects consist of the impact that alcohol has on the individual during the first few minutes to the first few hours after consumption. These intoxication effects include the metabolic, behavioral, and expectancy effects. The long-term effects consist of the impact that alcohol has on the individual over months or years. They include physiological addiction as well as physical and psychological deterioration.

Course. The only thing that can be said for certain about the course of alcohol abuse and dependence is that one has to start drinking and to engage in a period of alcohol abuse in order to become dependent on alcohol. It was once be-

metabolic effects The physiological impact of a drug.

blood alcohol level (BAL) The percentage of alcohol in the bloodstream.

lieved that all people who developed alcohol abuse followed the same course (Jellinek, 1952). This belief was based on data from 2000 chronic alcoholics in Alcoholics Anonymous (AA). However, more recent data suggest that the course varies dramatically from person to person. Some people start drinking early, proceed to abusive drinking in a matter of months, and are dependent on alcohol before the age of 20. Others begin drinking socially, perhaps in college, become used to heavy drinking, and eventually become dependent. Still others have periods of heavy drinking, interspersed with periods of light to moderate drinking, which continue for years before dependence develops. In general, women tend to become dependent on alcohol at a later age than men, but when they do become dependent, they often do so more quickly than men (Mezzich et al., 1994). The peak age of onset of alcohol dependence is between 25 and 40 (Schuckit, 2000), but alcohol dependence can occur in children and the elderly (Gurnack et al., 2002). As you will see, many things can shape the typical course. Those with a strong genetic predisposition to alcohol dependence tend to develop the dependence at a young age (Cloninger et al., 1996). Males tend to develop alcohol dependence at a younger age than women because heavy social drinking is more common in young men than in young women (Chermack et al., 2000).

Metabolic Effects. The term **metabolic effects** refers to the physiological impact of the drug. Alcohol is initially absorbed into the bloodstream primarily though the small intestines. This absorption is rapid, especially if the stomach is empty, which is one reason why you feel the effects of alcohol more quickly if you have not eaten for a while. Alcohol's metabolic impact is complex and varies with the level of alcohol consumed, the size of the individual, and the time since alcohol consumption stopped. The **blood alcohol level,** or **BAL,** quantifies the level of alcohol in a person's system. It is the percentage of alcohol in the bloodstream. The BAL is a function of the amount the person drinks and of the person's weight, because weight is roughly correlated with volume of blood. The BAL is often assessed with a Breathalyzer—a device that determines BAL by analyzing the alcohol content of one's breath. However, the most accurate BAL figures are based on blood samples.

There are subtle sex differences in alcohol metabolism that affect intoxication level and long-term consequences of drinking. Women tend to have higher BAL levels and

Alcohol is one of the most widely used recreational drugs in the Western world. Except for the brief period of Prohibition in the United States, it has been legal to manufacture, sell, and consume alcohol, provided that the consumer is of legal drinking age.

The most critical short-term effects of alcohol include a reduction in inhibitions, loss of coordination, increased reaction time, and loss of ability to think and reason. All of these effects contribute to dramatically impaired driving.

higher levels of intoxication for a given amount of alcohol, even when the amount of alcohol is adjusted for the differences in body size (Mumenthaler et al., 1999). For example, you might expect that three drinks in a 100-pound woman would produce the same BAL as six drinks in a 200-pound man, but those three drinks actually produce a higher BAL—and greater intoxication—in the woman.

Alcohol is a **central nervous system depressant**—that is, it slows and disrupts the operation of the central nervous system. Its impact on functioning depends on the BAL, which is a function of the amount consumed and the amount of time the liver has had to oxidize, or break down,

....

central nervous system depressant   A drug that slows and disrupts the operation of the central nervous system.

congeners   By-products of the fermentation process by which alcohol is produced from fruits or grains.

expectancy effects   Changes in behavior that are due not to the specific effects of alcohol but, rather, to the expectations that people hold about how alcohol will affect them.

balanced placebo design   A research design that independently manipulates two factors (consumption of a substance and belief that one has consumed the substance).

the alcohol (Ehrig & Li, 1995). The liver oxidizes alcohol at a constant rate of 0.5 ounce an hour (Schuckit, 2000). That is equivalent to 1.0 ounce of hard liquor, one 4-ounce glass of wine, or one 12-ounce beer. The alcohol content of a beverage is quantified in terms of "proof," which is double the percentage of alcohol. Thus pure alcohol is 200 proof, hard liquor is 80–100 proof (40%–50% alcohol), wine is 25 proof, and beer is 6 to 10 proof. When a person drinks steadily, consuming one drink an hour, the level of intoxication remains low. When that pace is exceeded, the BAL rises accordingly.

Evolutionary Impact

The physiological effects of alcohol vary with ethnic origin, and these differences are probably due largely to genetic factors. For example, many people from Asian cultures display a high level of facial flushing (turning red) at moderate levels of alcohol consumption, a response that is rare in Europeans (Wolf, 1972; Yamashita et al., 1995). This effect does not appear to be the result of other variables, such as diet or setting, because the difference is also present in Americans of European and Asian ancestry (Wilson et al., 1978; Wolf, 1973). Some American Indians also show this facial flushing at rates higher than Americans of European ancestry (Wolf, 1973). Differences among ethnic groups on such physiological responses to alcohol could indicate differences in basic metabolic reactions that may increase or decrease the risk for alcohol abuse. For example, approximately 10% of Asians lack a critical enzyme that breaks down harmful by-products produced by the liver during the oxidation of alcohol. The result is that as little as a single drink can induce powerful flushing, dramatically reduced blood pressure, and vomiting (Schuckit, 2000). This response to alcohol is generally more common in women than in men, which may help explain the generally lower rates of alcoholism in Asian women compared to Asian men (Chermack et al., 2000). Not surprisingly, these individuals quickly learn to abstain and therefore almost never develop alcohol abuse or dependence.

Some metabolic effects of alcohol are delayed, as anyone who has experienced a hangover can attest. The hangover is really a collection of physiological symptoms that result from the dehydrating effects of alcohol and the impact of the congeners found in most alcoholic beverages (Swift & Davidson, 1998; Wiese et al., 2000). **Congeners** are by-products of the fermentation process that produces alcohol from fruits or grains. Generally speaking, darker-colored and more flavorful alcoholic beverages contain more congeners than light-colored and less flavorful alcohol. For example, brandy and whiskey have more congeners than vodka, and red wine has more than white wine. The immune system attacks these congeners as though they were invading bodies, releasing small molecules called cytokines. These cytokines produce the nausea, headache, diarrhea, muscle pain, and weakness associated with a hangover. Fortunately, the immune system is more efficient at eliminating congeners than flu viruses; otherwise, hangovers would last a week as the flu does (Wiese et al., 2000).

Behavioral Impact.   The impact that drinking has on behavior depends on the BAL, as illustrated in Figure 14.3. The initial experience when one starts to drink is a reduction in anxiety and stress, which is due to the inhibition of those components of the nervous system that

[FIGURE 14.3]
Impact of Alcohol Level

The impact of alcohol on behavior depends on the level of alcohol in the blood. The effects can range from pleasant relaxation to death. Drinking more does not increase the strength of a given feeling. Instead, drinking more produces different sensations as the central nervous system is increasingly depressed by the alcohol.

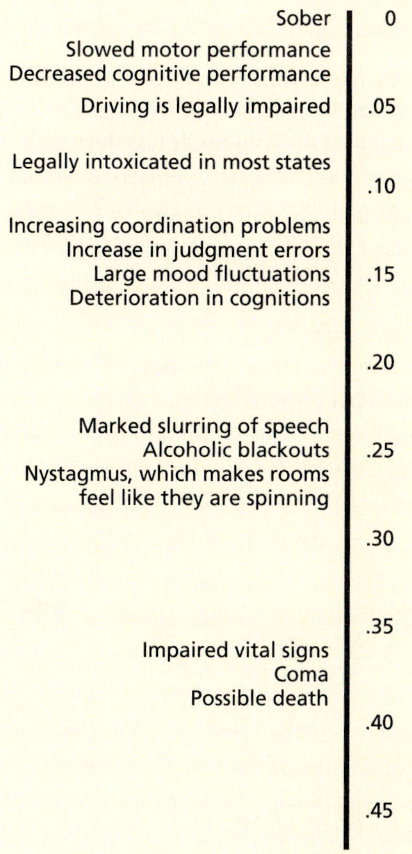

Sober	0
Slowed motor performance	
Decreased cognitive performance	
Driving is legally impaired	.05
Legally intoxicated in most states	
	.10
Increasing coordination problems	
Increase in judgment errors	
Large mood fluctuations	.15
Deterioration in cognitions	
	.20
Marked slurring of speech	
Alcoholic blackouts	.25
Nystagmus, which makes rooms feel like they are spinning	
	.30
	.35
Impaired vital signs	
Coma	
Possible death	
	.40
	.45

SOURCE: *From "Alcohol-related Disorders" by M. A. Schuckit in* Kaplan & Sadock's Comprehensive Textbook of Psychiatry, *7th ed., by B. I. Sadock and V. A. Sadock. Copyright © 2000. Reprinted by Lippincott, Williams & Wilkins.*

normally produce such feelings. It is this initial effect on emotions that gives alcohol its reputation as a drug that relaxes people. However, with increased levels of alcohol consumption, the impact on the central nervous system intensifies: Reaction time is slowed, coordination is impaired, and thought processes are inhibited. Depending on the level of alcohol consumed, people may be unable to catch something thrown to them, walk a straight line, stand up, or even recite the alphabet. At BAL levels around .40%, the person lapses into unconsciousness and may even enter a coma or die. About once every two years, a U.S. college student dies of alcohol intoxication from excessive drinking due to peer pressure or as part of fraternity hazing. Patrice, who was one of the cases that introduced the chapter, routinely drank to the point of slurring her words and being unable to walk a straight line. She often bumped into things, accidents that she attributed to awkwardness but that in fact were caused by her drinking. She rarely bumped into things when she was not drinking. With higher consumption, sensitivity to pain is dramatically reduced. Patrice often found deep bruises that she could not account for. Most likely, she injured herself with one of her "little accidents" while drinking. However, because she was so drunk, she did not recognize the seriousness of the injury when it occurred; she was quite literally feeling no pain.

Expectancy Effects.   **Expectancy effects** are changes in behavior that are due not to the specific effects of alcohol but, rather, to people's expectations about how alcohol will affect them. You might ask how researchers can separate expectancy effects from pharmacological effects. In the real world these two effects are confounded—that is, they occur together. When people drink, they experience both the pharmacological and the expectancy effects. However, these effects can be separated in the laboratory with a research design known as the **balanced placebo design,** which cleverly manipulates these two factors independently (Marlatt et al., 1973). This is accomplished by giving half of the participants alcohol and the other half a nonalcoholic beverage. However, through an ingenious deception, half of the people receiving alcohol are led to believe that they are not receiving alcohol, and half of the people who are not receiving alcohol are led to believe they are receiving alcohol. This research design creates four cells in what is called a 2 × 2 factorial design (see Table 14.2 on page 444). Let's examine this research in more detail.

Examining the Evidence

How do you pull off the elaborate deception of the balanced placebo design? Participants are told that they will be randomly assigned to either the alcohol or the placebo (no alcohol) condition, and each participant selects a card for the random assignment to the

[TABLE 14.2] The Balanced Placebo Design

The balanced placebo design involves four conditions to which participants are assigned. In the cells labeled A and D, participants receive what they believe they are receiving (alcohol and no alcohol, respectively). In the cells labeled B and C, the expectation and the actual situation are different from one another. The participants in cell B receive alcohol, but they believe they are just drinking tonic water. The participants in cell C believe they are receiving alcohol, but in reality they receive none.

ACTUALLY RECEIVE	BELIEVE THEY ARE RECEIVING	
	Alcohol	**No Alcohol**
Alcohol	A	B
No Alcohol	C	D

drinking conditions. The drawing is rigged, however. There *was* a random assignment, but it was done before the participant arrived, and it was to the four conditions shown in Table 14.2, not just to the two conditions (drinking and not drinking) that the participants expected. The researcher mixes the beverages as participants watch. The drinking condition uses vodka and tonic, and the nondrinking condition uses just tonic. In the two conditions in which expectations and reality are the same, the drinks are mixed normally. The other two conditions involve deception. In the condition in which the participants are getting alcohol but think they are getting just tonic, the researcher fills the glass with tonic. However, unbeknownst to participants, the "tonic" was previously spiked with vodka. In the condition in which participants believe they are getting alcohol but in fact are not, the researcher mixes the drink in front of participants, measuring the "vodka" from a new bottle and then adding the tonic. The "vodka" in this condition is distilled water. The bottle was filled earlier with water, sealed with a machine to look just as though it were new, and sealed with a state tax stamp to make it look entirely authentic. Vodka is used because it is almost tasteless and the tonic (or sometimes orange juice) hides the taste effectively. The deception is done so well that virtually every participant is fooled.

What patterns of results might be expected? Refer to Table 14.2. If it is the pharmacology of alcohol that affects behavior, then the two top cells (A and B) should be affected, because the people in those cells are receiving alcohol. If expectations account for the so-called effects of alcohol, then the left two cells (A and C) should be affected, because people in those cells believe they are drinking alcohol.

What do researchers find? Table 14.3 presents the results of one of the first studies to use this design—a study that tested the "loss of control" theory of alcoholism (Marlatt et al., 1973). This theory suggested that ingestion of one drink is sufficient to set off uncontrollable drinking in an alcoholic (Jellinek, 1960). Marlatt and his colleagues tested this hypothesis by recruiting alcoholics who were still drinking regularly and asking them to participate in a study of taste sensitivity. The participants' task was to rate three drinks on several dimensions. Depending on the condition, participants were told that they would be rating either three brands of vodka or three brands of tonic water. In actuality, the design included the four cells shown in Table 14.2. The dependent measure was the amount of the beverages consumed by each participant during the bogus "taste test." The mean number of ounces consumed by the alcoholics in each condition is shown in the top part of Table 14.3. The results are clear: The effect of uncontrolled drinking is *not* a function of alcohol consumption but, rather, is a function of the expectation that alcohol is being consumed. Alcoholics drank twice as much if they thought they were drinking alcohol, regardless of whether they really were. Marlatt and his colleagues ran this same study on a group of social drinkers—people who drank regularly with friends but rarely to excess. The social drinkers showed a strikingly different pattern, consuming more when they thought they were drinking tonic. Do these findings suggest that alcoholism does not have a biological component and that alcoholics really can drink and stop whenever they want? Not at all! What they show is that expectations play a large role in the failure of people who abuse alcohol to control their drinking once they have started. This information is critical if one is to develop effective treatments.

Alcohol expectancies have been studied extensively over the years. Expectancy effects account for increased sociability between men and women in a dating situation (Abbey et al., 2000), increased sexual arousal and sexual aggression (Seto & Barbaree, 1995), reduced anxiety in social situations (de Boar et al., 1993, 1994), increased creativity (Lapp et al., 1994), increased expression of racial prejudice (Reeves & Nagoshi, 1993), increased interpersonal aggression (Lang & Sibrel, 1989), and even decreased motor steadiness (Laberg & Loeberg, 1989). Hull and Bond (1986) provide an excellent review of some of the earlier studies of alcohol expectancies. The balanced placebo design has also been used to investigate the impact

[TABLE 14.3] Results of Marlatt et al. (1973)

These are the results from an early balanced placebo study that examined the hypothesis that alcoholics are physiologically unable to drink without losing control of their drinking. Two groups were tested: non-abstinent alcoholics and social drinkers. The values reported are the average number of ounces consumed during a sham taste test.

RESULTS FROM ALCOHOLIC PARTICIPANTS

ACTUALLY RECEIVE	BELIEVE THEY ARE RECEIVING	
	Alcohol	No Alcohol
Alcohol	22.13	10.25
No Alcohol	23.87	10.94

RESULTS FROM SOCIAL DRINKERS

ACTUALLY RECEIVE	BELIEVE THEY ARE RECEIVING	
	Alcohol	No Alcohol
Alcohol	9.31	14.62
No Alcohol	5.94	14.44

SOURCE: *"Loss of Control Drinking in Alcoholics: An Experimental Analogue"* by G. A. Marlatt et al., Journal of Abnormal Psychology, *1973, vol. 81. Copyright © 1973 by the American Psychological Association. Reprinted with permission.*

of other drugs, such as nicotine, on behavior (Gottlieb et al., 1987).

Physiological Addiction. The first time one drinks, the most obvious experience is intoxication, which may be characterized by an initial loss of inhibitions, loss of coordination, and eventually "blacking out" if one drinks enough. Alcohol-induced blackouts are not the same as passing out; the intoxicated person continues to function but, after sobering up, has no recollection of his or her actions. If this is the person's first experience with alcohol, little alcohol is required to trigger these effects. However, with repeated exposure, people build tolerance and become able to consume more alcohol before they experience intoxication. Tolerance is part of the addiction process. The body becomes accustomed to the alcohol and thus does not respond so strongly to it. Because drinkers typically drink for the express purpose of experiencing the intoxicating effects of the alcohol, they increase their intake to overcome the tolerance that has developed and obtain those effects.

Prolonged heavy drinking can lead to an intense rebound phenomenon called **delirium tremens,** or the **DTs.** The DTs are not a response to a week or two of heavy drinking but rather to years of heavy drinking, followed by an abrupt cessation of the drinking. They may include vivid visual and tactile hallucinations, such as feeling like bugs and snakes are crawling all over you. People with the DTs will also be feverish, terrified, and delirious (Schuckit, 2000). Although the DTs are relatively rare, months or years of heavy drinking does produce withdrawal symptoms when the drinking stops. Such withdrawal resembles a case of the flu, with headache, chills, body aches, and mild to moderate depression, and it can include seizures, which are known colloquially as "rum fits" (Schuckit, 2000).

Physical Deterioration. The chronic heavy use of alcohol can damage the gastrointestinal, cardiovascular, cerebrovascular, and nervous systems, especially the liver and the brain. Furthermore, alcohol abuse is associated with birth defects in infants born to drinking mothers and with higher rates of several cancers (Schuckit, 2000).

Chronic alcohol consumption stresses the entire gastrointestinal system, including the liver, pancreas, esophagus, and stomach. The liver breaks down alcohol, but the chronic stressing of the liver with heavy drinking may lead to **cirrhosis**—a condition that involves a stiffening of the blood vessels of the liver, thus reducing its effectiveness (Maher, 1997). People cannot survive without a functioning liver, so cirrhosis is a terminal disease unless a liver transplant can be performed. It is estimated that 26,000 people a year die in the United States from cirrhosis and that up to 90% of these deaths are due to excessive alcohol use (de la Vega et al., 2001; Du Four et al., 1993). Approximately 15% of alcoholics develop cirrhosis (Schuckit, 2000). Another 15% develop severe inflammation of the pancreas, which often results in acute illness and hospitalization. In some such cases the pancreas is permanently damaged, resulting in diabetes. Finally, heavy alcohol consumption often causes severe inflammation of the esophagus and stomach, which can induce vomiting and bleeding (Schuckit, 2000). If not treated promptly, the bleeding can be life-threatening.

Unlike most cells, neurons typically do not regenerate, and the neurons in the brain are dying steadily almost from birth. Heavy alcohol consumption increases the rate of neuronal death. The heavily interconnected nature of the brain makes it incredibly resilient to a loss of neurons,

delirium tremens (the DTs)   An intense rebound phenomenon brought on, after years of heavy drinking, by an abrupt cessation of the drinking. The DTs may include vivid visual and tactile hallucinations and feelings of fever, terror, or deliriousness.

cirrhosis   A stiffening of the blood vessels of the liver, thus reducing its effectiveness.

but only up to a point (Rumelhart, 1997; Rumelhart et al., 1986). At some point, the neuronal loss hits a critical level, and cognitive functioning deteriorates rapidly with additional loss—a process known as *senile dementia.* Because of the accelerated neuronal loss in alcoholics, this cognitive decline occurs earlier in their lives (Parsons, 1998). However, most alcoholics never reach senility because the toxic effects of alcohol on other organ systems shorten their lives considerably.

The neuronal damage associated with alcoholism also affects peripheral nerves, causing numbness in the hands or feet and loss of balance. This damage is a result of both the toxicity of some of the metabolites of alcohol and the vitamin deficiencies that are common in alcoholics because of poor diet (Schuckit, 2000). Alcohol contains considerable calories, so most alcoholics do not have an adequate appetite. Consequently, they fail to eat the kind of balanced diet needed to deliver essential vitamins and nutrients. These vitamin deficiencies can also affect the central nervous system, leading to two neurological disorders: Wernicke's encephalopathy and Korsakoff's syndrome. Uncontrolled facial movements, tics, and paralysis of facial muscles characterize *Wernicke's encephalopathy.* It usually remits quickly when the affected person is given vitamin supplements. Significant memory and learning problems characterize *Korsakoff's syndrome.* The memory problems include difficulties both in remembering things from the past and in forming new memories. In 50%–70% of cases of Korsakoff's syndrome, these deficits are irreversible (Schuckit, 2000).

Alcoholics often suffer from other life-threatening conditions. Heavy drinking can dramatically increase blood pressure as well as elevate LDL cholesterol (the "bad" cholesterol), thus increasing risk for heart attacks and strokes. In very high concentrations, alcohol is toxic to heart muscles (Schuckit, 2000). Furthermore, many types of cancers are common in alcoholics, especially cancers of the head, neck, esophagus, stomach, colon, liver, and lungs. Exactly what brings about this increased cancer risk is still unknown, but it is presumed that suppression of the immune system by the heavy alcohol use plays a role (Schuckit, 2000).

Heavy alcohol consumption inflicts significant physiological problems on the fetus of an alcoholic mother. **Fetal alcohol syndrome** is a condition in which the baby is born with birth defects that result from the mother's heavy alcohol consumption during pregnancy. Some of the birth defects are visible, such as facial and limb abnormalities. Others are less visible but every bit as critical, such as lifelong cognitive deficits (Allison, 1994). Fetal alcohol syndrome is the third leading cause of birth defects and the

---

fetal alcohol syndrome A condition in which a baby is born with birth defects that are the result of heavy alcohol consumption by the mother during pregnancy.

Heavy drinking during pregnancy carries serious risks for the fetus. Fetal alcohol syndrome is the leading cause of mental retardation in the United States and the third leading cause of birth defects.

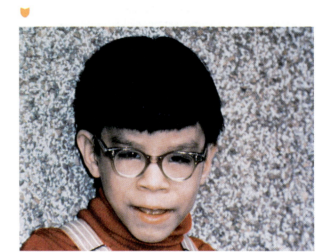

leading preventable cause of mental retardation in the United States (Kaemingk & Paquette, 1999; NIAAA, 1990). Furthermore, fetal alcohol syndrome is related to the later development of psychiatric problems. For example, Famy et al. (1998) found that 72% of adults with fetal alcohol syndrome had received psychiatric treatment, including treatment for drug and alcohol abuse (60%), depression (44%), and psychosis (40%). (It should be noted that this increased risk for alcohol and drug abuse may be due to genetic influences shared by the drinking mother and her offspring and therefore may not be part of the fetal alcohol syndrome per se.) Although it is clear that heavy drinking during pregnancy poses a greater risk to the fetus than light drinking, even light drinking may be risky (Raskin, 1993). Therefore, most doctors encourage women to abstain from drinking during pregnancy.

Psychological Deterioration. Alcohol abuse takes a toll on one's psychological functioning and on the stability of one's social relationships. Alcohol abuse is associated with both depression and excessive anxiety, although the direction of causation is unclear (APA, 2000). People who tend to be anxious or depressed may drink as a form of self-medication. Alternatively, heavy alcohol consumption may increase anxiety and depression. Most likely, both effects are present. Alcohol abuse also decreases one's energy level because it disrupts sleep (Roehrs & Roth, 1997).

Alcohol abuse affects functioning in a variety of ways. It is associated with unsafe sexual behavior (O'Hare, 2001; Strunin & Hingson, 1993), traffic accidents (del Rio et al., 2001; NHTSA, 1994), crime (Collins & Messerschmidt, 1993; Martin et al., 2001), and child abuse (Harter & Taylor, 2000), although these associations are not necessarily causal. For example, it is possible that heavy drinking and crime are due to a third variable, such as the presence of antisocial personality disorder or general impulsivity (Forrest, 1994; Jorm et al., 2000). The direct and indirect costs attributed to alcohol abuse in 1990—costs that include medical expenses, treatment costs, and lost productivity—were estimated at $99 billion for the United States alone (Hogan, 1993).

Often the most serious psychological consequence of chronic alcohol abuse is the strain it imposes on relationships (Jacob & Johnson, 1999; Robitschek & Kashubeck, 1999). Heavy drinkers may behave erratically, creating strains in their relationships and sometimes triggering domestic violence (Kantor, 1993; Testa & Leonard, 2001). The strains can affect both the spouse or partner and the children, including infant children who may suffer abuse or neglect (Eiden et al., 1999). Furthermore, the effects on children may last a lifetime (Jaeger et al., 2000; Moser & Jacob, 1997). Heavy drinking is also associated with excessive sick days at work, low productivity because of hangovers, and dramatic drops in productivity if the drinking starts to occur during working hours (McFarlin & Fals-Stewart, 2002; Moore et al., 2000). Finally, the problems associated with alcohol abuse take a personal toll on the individual, decreasing self-esteem and support from friends and family.

BARBITURATES

Developed in the 1930s, **barbiturates** are synthetic sedatives. Once widely used for calming patients or as sleeping pills, they were quickly replaced for anxiety relief because of their strong sedating effects. Like alcohol, they relax in low doses and induce sleep in higher doses. In very high doses they are lethal, and moderate to high doses significantly affect decision making, problem solving, motor coordination, and reaction time (Pickworth et al., 1997). These effects are much stronger when barbiturates are combined with alcohol, and this combination is potentially lethal (Ciraulo & Sarid-Segal, 2000). Chronic use leads to both physiological and psychological dependence. The physiological dependence includes an increase in tolerance, but unfortunately, the tolerance to the lethal effects of the drugs develops slowly, thus increasing the risk of accidental overdose (Ciraulo & Sarid-Segal, 2000).

When barbiturates were readily prescribed, the most common pathway to dependence was an extended use of these drugs for sleep or anxiety management. This is rare now, because more effective and less dangerous drugs have largely replaced barbiturates. Although these drugs can also lead to dependence, dependence requires several months of steady use to develop. Today, the more likely pathway to dependence is for polydrug abusers to purchase barbiturates on the street, but even this is less frequent than it once was, which may be one of the reasons why it is now relatively rare to see individuals in treatment for barbiturate dependence (Ciraulo & Sarid-Segal, 2000).

BENZODIAZEPINES

Benzodiazepines are antianxiety drugs. The early benzodiazepines were Valium and Librium—terms that became household words in the 1960s and 1970s because of these drugs' heavy use at that time. At one point, Valium was the most widely prescribed drug in America, with most of the prescriptions written by general practitioners to calm anxiety. Use peaked between 1973 and 1975, when approximately 87 million prescriptions for benzodiazepines were written each year (Ciraulo & Sarid-Segal, 2000). At the time, these drugs were viewed as safe and not habit-forming. Valium and Librium have been largely replaced by high-potency benzodiazepines, such as Xanax and Klonopin. Although they are still widely used for the treatment of anxiety, routine prescriptions for these drugs for anyone complaining of anxiety have decreased dramatically.

Abuse of benzodiazepines is possible, but it is not so serious a problem as that of other drugs covered in this chapter (Ciraulo & Sarid-Segal, 2000). They rarely are used for recreational purposes, and even if they were, people would be unlikely to become dependent on them. Like the barbiturates, benzodiazepines tend to become habit-forming only when they are taken in large quantities over prolonged periods. Consequently, abuse is more likely to develop in people with chronic anxiety who have taken these medications in high doses for years. The reinforcing properties of these drugs come both from the negative reinforcement associated with rapid anxiety reduction and from the punishment associated with not taking the drug (a rapid return of the anxiety). People with relatively low anxiety are much less susceptible to these reinforcing effects and thus are less likely to become dependent on these drugs. Those with the shortest half-life, such as Xanax and Ativan, have the greatest risk for dependence (Malcom et al., 1993). These drugs enter and leave the body most quickly, thus providing immediate effects. Abuse of benzodiazepines in people without anxiety disorders is nearly always a part of a polydrug abuse pattern (Busto et al., 1996).

Most sedatives, including the benzodiazepines, affect $GABA_A$ receptors. GABA is normally an inhibitory neurotransmitter—that is, it reduces or slows neurological activity. When these drugs bind to the GABA receptor, they increase the ability of these receptors to be stimulated by GABA, thus increasing GABA inhibition and calming the part of the nervous system that produces anxiety. It is interesting to note that those at genetic risk for alcohol dependence are also at risk for benzodiazapine dependence. This suggests that GABA receptors may play a critical role in both benzodiazapine and alcohol dependence (Ciraulo et al., 1988, 1989, 1996).

....

barbiturates   Synthetic sedatives developed in the 1930s.

Check Yourself 14.2

Sedatives

1. What is the distinction between the pharmacological effects and the expectancy effects of alcohol?
2. What physiological systems are damaged by excessive alcohol consumption?
3. What is fetal alcohol syndrome?
4. What were the original medical uses of barbiturates?
5. Who is most likely to abuse anxiolytics?

Ponder this . . .   *How could one use information on the pattern of alcohol abuse across cultures to improve alcohol abuse prevention programs?*

NARCOTICS

Narcotics are a medical godsend for the treatment of pain. However, they can be abused. Both the medicinal and the pleasurable aspects of narcotics have been known for thousands of years. Today, several countries in Southeast Asia and the Middle East derive a significant portion of their gross national product from the growing of opium-producing poppies (Bewley-Taylor, 1999). This section will focus on heroin because it is by far the most heavily abused narcotic.

Opiates were legal in the United States until the passage of the Harrison Act of 1914, despite the fact that their addictive properties had been known since the 1700s (Jaffe & Jaffe, 2000). The most widely abused opiate, heroin, is typically injected, although such alternative forms of administration as snorting and smoking are becoming more popular. The drug can be injected directly into a vein, which is called *mainlining,* or just under the skin, which is called *skin-popping.* It is estimated that 600,000 to 800,000 people in the United States use opiates, mostly heroin, and that 2,000,000 people have used opiates illicitly at some time during their lives (Jaffe & Jaffe, 2000). After falling for years, the rate of heroin abuse began to rise in the 1990s, especially among high school students, who reported lifetime rates of heroin use of 2.8% in 1975, 0.9% in 1991, and 2.1% in 1997 (Jaffe & Jaffe, 2000).

Heroin produces rapid and intense euphoria, known as the *rush,* shortly after injection. This euphoria lasts about a minute and is enormously reinforcing. It is followed by four to six hours of relaxed lethargy. For those who have become addicted, this lethargic period is followed by cravings for more heroin, which is part of the physiological withdrawal. The intensity of withdrawal symptoms varies dramatically from person to person. In some people, the withdrawal simply involves cravings, whereas others experience dysphoria, irritability, restlessness, and severe muscle aches. In contrast to alcohol and barbiturate withdrawal, withdrawal from opiates is *not* life-threatening in healthy adults. The intensity of the withdrawal symptoms depends on the typical level of previous heroin use, how continuously it has been used, and how abruptly its use is terminated (Jaffe & Jaffe, 2000).

Heroin dependence can take over one's life. It is common for dependent individuals to engage constantly in theft or prostitution to support their habit, living for nothing other than the drug. Productivity drops dramatically as the person gets high, lies around lethargically, and then goes out to do whatever is necessary to get more of the drug. Sharing needles is common among heroin addicts and is a significant cause of HIV infection. Overdoses are relatively common with heroin, and they can be life-threatening. Disease, a dangerous lifestyle, and the risk of overdose all conspire to shorten the life expectancy of heroin addicts considerably (Sanchez-Carbonell & Seus, 2000; Staples, 1990).

One can look at the process of dependence on opiates from both a psychological and a physiological perspective. From a psychological perspective, there is a rapid and powerful positive reinforcer—the rush—as well as a prolonged pleasant feeling. The timing and intensity of the positive reinforcement lead to rapid learning of drug-taking behavior. Furthermore, as dependence develops, intense withdrawal symptoms negatively reinforce continued drug use. From a physiological perspective, opiates affect a brain region known as the ventral tegmentum, which is a critical part of the brain's natural reward system (Bozarth, 1986). The involvement in this region probably accounts for the euphoric rush experienced immediately after an injection of heroin. The powerful stimulation that heroin provides to these reward centers causes a down regulation or changing of the sensitivity of these cells, which no doubt contributes to the well-known withdrawal symptoms of heroin (Terenius & O'Brien, 1992).

Check Yourself 14.3

Narcotics

1. What is the principal medical use for narcotics?
2. What is the most widely abused opiate, and what are its effects?
3. What factors affect the strength of withdrawal symptoms for narcotics?

Ponder this . . .   *Pain is one of the most aversive experiences in life, so being able to control pain is critical. Why would natural selection favor the existence of pain?*

nicotine   The active ingredient in cigarettes.

STIMULANTS

The most commonly used stimulant by far is caffeine, but it is a mild stimulant with little potential for abuse. The second most widely used is nicotine, a mild stimulant that simultaneously relaxes people. This section covers nicotine and two more powerful stimulants, amphetamines and cocaine, that have serious abuse potential.

NICOTINE

Nicotine is the active ingredient in cigarettes. Despite claims made by some tobacco industry executives, it is unquestionably an addictive substance (NIDA, 2001). The addictive nature of cigarettes is hardly news to anyone who has tried to quit smoking. Since 1964, the official position of the Surgeon General of the United States has been that smoking is dangerous to one's health. Figure 14.4 illustrates how dangerous smoking is. Note that smoking kills more than four times as many people each year as alcohol abuse and over eight times as many people as traffic accidents. Cigarettes kill more people than all other drugs—legal and illegal—combined (Gold, 1995; NIDA, 2001). The Centers for Disease Control estimates that smokers lose, on average, 7 minutes of life for every cigarette they smoke. That is over a month of living lost for every year that one indulges a 1-pack-a-day habit. It is not the nicotine that kills; nicotine is just the substance that keeps people smoking. As the industry's own memos indicate, cigarettes are the delivery mech-

You do not always have to buy cigarettes to be a smoker. Breathing second-hand smoke can carry significant health risks, and those risks are especially high for young children.

anism for nicotine (Toufexis, 1994). Unfortunately, cigarettes are also the delivery mechanism for an estimated 1200 other chemicals, nearly all of them harmful. For example, the level of hydrogen cyanide in smoke is 160 times higher, and that of carbon monoxide 840 times higher, than the maximum recommended levels (Gold, 1995).

The dangers do not stop with the smoker. The Environmental Protection Agency (EPA) classifies secondhand smoke as a Group A carcinogen—that is, it causes cancer in humans. The EPA estimates that secondhand smoke causes over 3000 deaths a year from lung cancer and between 8000 and 26,000 new cases of pediatric asthma each year. Other research suggests that secondhand smoke causes ten times as much heart disease as lung disease, which makes it the third leading cause of preventable death, behind only active smoking and alcohol (Gold, 1995). It is no wonder that laws are increasingly restricting when and where people can smoke. Nevertheless, an estimated 57 million Americans smoke, and another 8 million use smokeless tobacco (NIDA, 2001).

How addicting is nicotine? It is not easy to quantify the strength of an addiction, although one can get an idea by watching the behavior of drug users. Smokers do not appear to experience, nor do they report, a rush similar to that delivered by drugs such as heroin and cocaine. Nor do they experience significant tension reduction, as with alcohol, although there is one exception. You can often tell the smokers from the nonsmokers after a long meeting because they are the ones who go straight outside for a cigarette. They are clearly experiencing uncomfortable withdrawal effects, and a cigarette reduces the tension created by

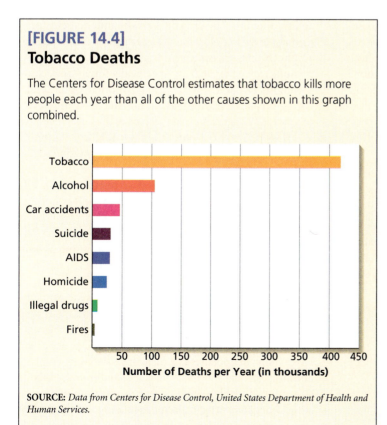

[FIGURE 14.4]
Tobacco Deaths

The Centers for Disease Control estimates that tobacco kills more people each year than all of the other causes shown in this graph combined.

Number of Deaths per Year (in thousands)

Categories (top to bottom): Tobacco, Alcohol, Car accidents, Suicide, AIDS, Homicide, Illegal drugs, Fires. X-axis: 50, 100, 150, 200, 250, 300, 350, 400, 450.

SOURCE: *Data from Centers for Disease Control, United States Department of Health and Human Services.*

these effects. The distress experienced while trying to quit smoking is one of the biggest reasons why most people fail to kick the habit on the first few tries. On the other hand, smokers do not resort to stealing to support their habit, as is common for other addictive drugs, although this may be due to the relatively low cost of cigarettes. And if given an unlimited supply of cigarettes, they do not smoke at the expense of all other activities, which often happens with other drugs. By and large, smoking does not interfere with a smoker's productivity, provided that smokers can get their nicotine "fix" on a fairly regular basis.

The mechanisms of dependence for nicotine are much more complicated than for drugs such as cocaine and heroin. This is because nicotine-responsive sites are spread throughout the central and peripheral nervous systems and even in some muscles. The impact of nicotine is different at each of these sites, which accounts for the complex and sometimes contradictory effects from smoking (Gold, 1995). The primary source of the dependence on nicotine is the fact that it stimulates neuropathways associated with reward (Rosencrans & Karan, 1993). The intensity of the stimulation of these reward centers is much less than with drugs such as cocaine and heroin. Nevertheless, the subtle pleasure associated with smoking is primarily biological and is more than sufficient to lead to dependence. In addition, nicotine is a stimulant, increasing one's energy level and activity. These effects are mediated by the action of nicotine on dopamine receptors, which modulate activity level (Damaj & Martin, 1993). Nicotine influences an entire range of neurobehavioral systems, including the levels of epinephrine, norepinephrine, endorphins, adrenocorticotropic hormones, and cortisol (Gold, 1995). Probably the single most critical element in making these subtle effects so highly addictive is the delivery system. Smoking nicotine, just like smoking other drugs, produces a nearly instantaneous effect on the brain. Obtaining the same level of nicotine from either the patch or nicotine gum is not nearly so addicting (Pomerleau, 1992).

AMPHETAMINES

Amphetamines, known on the street as "speed," are synthetic stimulants. They increase energy and alertness. Several amphetamines have been widely used for years, including amphetamine (Benzedrine), dextroamphetamine (Dexedrine), and methamphetamine (Methedrine). Amphetamines were first synthesized in the 1930s and were originally used to treat asthma, although it was not long before other potential uses were recognized. For example,

....

amphetamines Synthetic stimulants that increase energy and alertness. Also known as speed.

Ecstasy The name of two new amphetamines—MDA (methylenedioxyamphetamine) and MDMA (methylenedioxymethamphetamine).

they increase metabolism and decrease appetite, which made them a natural as a diet pill. They increase alertness and endurance, which made them popular with long-haul truckers and others who often had to go on little sleep. At one time, prescriptions for such uses were easy to obtain from a doctor. These casual medical uses have decreased substantially, yet many people still buy amphetamines from the corner drug dealer for these purposes (Weaver & Schnoll, 1999). The lifetime prevalence of amphetamine dependence in the United States —that is, the percentage of people dependent on amphetamines at some point during their lifetime—is estimated to be as high as 2% (Anthony et al., 1995), and 4.5% of adults report having used amphetamines sometime during their adult lives (NHSDA, 1997).

Ecstasy is the name applied to two new amphetamines—MDA (methylenedioxyamphetamine) and MDMA (methylenedioxymethamphetamine)—which are the most popular of the so-called designer drugs (Jaffe, 2000b). These drugs have been a part of the music scene since the 1990s and are commonly used during all-night parties called raves. Users swear that Ecstasy enhances their awareness of the music, increases insight and sensitivity, and improves the quality of sexual relationships. These claims are similar to those made for the psychedelics of the 1960s— claims that proved to be unfounded. Ecstasy use entails significant risks, including accidental overdose and death (Climko et al., 1987). It also can affect brain functioning in a way that impairs memory (Reneman et al., 2000).

Amphetamines used medically were produced as capsules and taken orally. They are still used that way medically and are often sold by drug dealers who obtain their stocks through diversion of legitimate pharmaceuticals. However, amphetamines are easily synthesized in makeshift labs, so manufacture of these drugs specifically for abuse is common. They can be injected as a liquid or prepared for smoking—a preparation known as "crank." Injection and smoking lead to stronger and faster responses than oral ingestion and thus increase the potential for addiction. Amphetamines can be very addictive; in fact, amphetamine addictions develop more quickly with fewer exposures to the drug than do cocaine addictions (Castro et al., 2000). Tolerance increases rapidly for amphetamines. It is not uncommon for chronic users to be taking several times their original dose to produce the same subjective effects. Unfortunately, physiological tolerance develops much more slowly, which means that accidental overdose is a real danger to new users of the drugs (Brauer et al., 1996).

The stimulant effects of amphetamines are immediately obvious to new users. The decrease in appetite is often barely noticed at first, although those who take amphetamines for that purpose are usually well aware of the suppression of appetite. The rush associated with amphetamines is strongest if the drug is injected into the bloodstream or smoked. In high doses, amphetamines produce several negative effects, including anxiety, sleep disturbances, mood disorders, sexual dysfunction, and psychosis

(Wyatt & Ziedonis, 1998). The psychosis produced by excessive use of amphetamines is often indistinguishable from paranoid schizophrenia, which is one reason why a screen for amphetamines is routine when an acutely paranoid individual is brought into the Emergency Room. Amphetamine psychosis is responsive to antipsychotic medication (Jaffe, 2000b).

Amphetamines trigger the release of dopamine, which probably accounts for their mood-elevating effects and pleasurable sensations. In addition, amphetamines trigger the release of norepinephrine, which affects many body systems, including the cardiovascular system. This norepinephrine release probably accounts for the increase in endurance and energy. The excess dopamine in the synapse leads to down regulation of receptors to make them less sensitive to the massive amounts of dopamine. This down regulation accounts for the rapid tolerance to the subjective effects of amphetamines and for the powerful anhedonia and dysphoria experienced during withdrawal (Jaffe, 2000b).

COCAINE

Cocaine is a drug extracted from coca shrubs, which grow in the highlands of the Andes Mountains in South America. A powerful stimulant with broad effects on the nervous system, it is occasionally used to relieve pain when applied topically. But for the most part, cocaine is a massive cash crop—grown, harvested, refined, and delivered by international drug cartels to millions of addicted users, the vast majority of whom live in the United States (Bewley-Taylor, 1999). Although the dangers of cocaine use are now clear, they have not always been so. For example, Freud once touted the therapeutic benefits of cocaine and even became addicted himself (Gay, 1988). Cocaine was also the active ingredient in the original formula for Coca Cola, although it was dropped from the formula for coke just two years after the beverage was introduced in 1903.

Cocaine enhances alertness and increases energy. It blocks the reuptake of dopamine, which is the major neurotransmitter in the pleasure center of the brain, thereby producing an overall pleasurable sensation (Volkow et al., 1997). In addition, there are increases in self-confidence, well-being, and sexual desire. Cocaine also affects other organ systems. For example, it constricts blood vessels, and in high doses this constriction can be life-threatening. The vasoconstriction can rob heart muscles of oxygen and cause blood pressure to spike to dangerously high levels (Jaffe, 2000a). This vasoconstriction is probably what killed Len Bias, a University of Maryland basketball star who died of

Once used largely by the wealthy, cocaine is now one of the more heavily abused drugs in the United States, behind only alcohol, nicotine, and marijuana.

cardiac failure shortly after ingesting cocaine. As with many drugs, tolerance for cocaine develops over time, and more of the drug is needed to obtain the same subjective effect. Unlike many drugs, however, cocaine also produces **sensitization** effects, which means that with repeated administration, smaller doses can achieve results that previously required larger doses. Because of this sensitization, repeated use of cocaine can result in seizures that would not have been triggered initially. Cocaine may also produce psychotic symptoms with prolonged use, especially in those with a past history of psychosis (Jaffe, 2000a).

Cocaine can be taken by injection, inhalation through the nose (snorting), smoking, or ingestion. A highly addictive form of cocaine is crack, which is typically smoked. Its name derives from the fact that the white, chalky material tends to crackle as it is being smoked. Crack is particularly potent because the body absorbs it rapidly, producing a rush similar to that experienced with heroin. Injecting cocaine or smoking crack typically leads the most rapidly to addiction, although any method of delivery can lead to addiction if cocaine is used repeatedly. That is what Tyrone, one of the cases who opened this chapter, discovered. Tyrone thought he could use cocaine occasionally without becoming addicted, but he gradually started using it more until he was hooked and his job was in jeopardy. Withdrawal from cocaine produces a depressive state, a temporary loss of capacity for pleasure, and severe fatigue. The cravings for more cocaine, which can be unbelievably intense, do not appear to be a part of the withdrawal process. Rather, they seem to result from long-term changes in the brain's chemistry (Jaffe, 2000a).

The popularity of cocaine has skyrocketed in recent years, and with it a variety of problems associated with the drug. In the early 1960s, cocaine was almost unheard of. It

- -

cocaine   A stimulant drug extracted from coca shrubs.

sensitization   An effect observed with some drugs when, with repeated administration, smaller doses of the drug can achieve results that previously required larger doses.

is estimated that only a few thousand people in the United States had even tried it. By the mid-1990s, the government estimated that as many as 21 million people had tried cocaine and that as many as 1.5 million were addicted (SAMHSA, 1996). That figure is down substantially from the estimated 5.7 million Americans who were regular users in 1985 (NIDA, 1999). The lifetime prevalence of cocaine dependence has been estimated to be 3% (Anthony et al., 1995; NIDA, 1999). These figures are frighteningly high when one considers how difficult it is to treat cocaine dependence. The powerful reinforcing qualities of the drug are sufficient in many cases to entice even casual initial users into repeated exposure, which often leads to dependence. The ready availability of cocaine, especially to young people, coupled with its powerful addictive properties, makes cocaine one of the most dangerous of the abused drugs.

Check Yourself 14.4

Stimulants

1. What is the addictive element in cigarettes?
2. What were some of the early medical uses for amphetamines?
3. What impact does cocaine have on the brain?
4. What impact does the method of consumption have on the effect of amphetamines and cocaine?

Ponder this . . .   *One would think that stimulant drugs should simply provide a psychological lift and not lend themselves to abuse. Why do you think these drugs turn out to be so addictive and so disruptive to normal functioning?*

HALLUCINOGENS

Hallucinogens became popular during the 1960s, and all produce perceptual distortions and hallucinations. It is worth noting that the hallucinations from these drugs tend to be visual and wildly distorted, whereas the hallucinations reported in such disorders as schizophrenia tend to be auditory—usually undistorted voices. This section covers several hallucinogenic drugs, including marijuana, LSD, mescaline, psilocybin, and PCP. Though all of these drugs have abuse potential, they typically produce less tolerance and physiological dependence than most of the other drugs covered in this chapter.

MARIJUANA

Marijuana is made from the crushed leaves and flowers of the hemp plant. It is most often smoked, usually in hand-rolled cigarettes called *joints*. It can also be consumed in other ways, such as baking it into foods or making a tea

from it. **Hashish** is made from the resin found in the tops of hemp plants. Hashish is stronger than marijuana, and it is typically smoked in a special pipe. Both belong to a family of drugs produced from the hemp plant, called **cannabis.**

The history of marijuana is interesting. The hemp plant was originally grown in the United States for its fibers, which were used in the manufacture of rope. In the 1800s, medicinal properties of the resin from the hemp plant were discovered, so this resin was sold commercially for such conditions as rheumatism and depression. At the time, marijuana was legal and was rarely used recreationally. It did not become a popular recreational drug until prohibition, when the manufacture and consumption of alcohol were banned. Marijuana was declared illegal by federal law in 1937. Much of the impetus behind this law was publicity about the impact of marijuana on behavior, especially criminal behavior, but most of these claims were untrue. Misinformation has been the norm ever since, on both sides of the issue. Those opposed to marijuana have typically exaggerated the risks, whereas those in favor of marijuana have typically minimized them. The controversy surrounding marijuana has led to some puzzling policies. For example, doctors routinely prescribe narcotics to control pain and can use cocaine as a topical anesthetic, but they are prohibited from prescribing marijuana when it is medically appropriate. Marijuana can dramatically reduce the nausea that often accompanies chemotherapy and is effective in treating glaucoma—an eye disease in which the pressure inside the eye builds to destructive levels.

Although marijuana use dates back 5000 or more years, its popularity in the United States is relatively recent. Until the 1960s, its use was confined largely to jazz musicians and members of minority groups (MacFadden & Woody, 2000). Starting in the 1960s, marijuana became the drug of choice among college students, and its availability has spread throughout the culture since that time. It is difficult to estimate the number of marijuana users and the amount of marijuana consumed, because it is an illegal drug without the controlled distribution channels of drugs such as nicotine and alcohol. Kandel et al. (1986) found that almost 75% of 25-year-olds admitted to having at least tried marijuana, and over 15% reported having used it more than 1000 times. Bobashev and Anthony (1998) found that more than a third of the people in their large national survey reported having used marijuana in the past, 8% reported having used it in the previous year, and 5% reported having used it in the previous month. The difference between these two studies is probably due to the

---

marijuana   A hallucinogen made from the crushed leaves and flowers of the hemp plant.

hashish   A hallucinogen made from the resin found in the tops of hemp plants.

cannabis   A family of drugs derived from the hemp plant.

Hemp Fest is an annual program that travels around the country bringing together those who advocate the legalization of marijuana.

age ranges of those questioned. The participants in the Kandel et al. study would have been of college age in 1980, whereas the participants in the Bobashev and Anthony study represented people of a wide range of ages, many of whom attended college before the rapid rise in the popularity of marijuana. It is estimated that there are between 200 and 300 million regular users of marijuana worldwide (MacFadden & Woody, 2000). Even a former United States president acknowledged trying marijuana,

although he claimed he did not inhale. Marijuana use in the United States peaked around 1980, although current usage is still high (Kandel, 2000; NIDA, 1996). Although widespread use started among college students, use quickly moved to high school students, as shown in Figure 14.5. The trend lately has been for kids to begin using marijuana at younger ages. For example, 15% of eighth-graders, 30% of tenth-graders, and nearly 40% of twelfth-graders recently reported using marijuana in the past year (Swan, 1995).

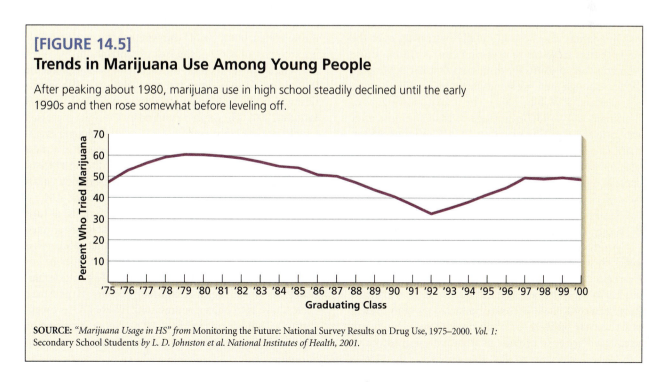

[FIGURE 14.5]

Trends in Marijuana Use Among Young People

After peaking about 1980, marijuana use in high school steadily declined until the early 1990s and then rose somewhat before leveling off.

SOURCE: *"Marijuana Usage in HS" from* Monitoring the Future: National Survey Results on Drug Use, 1975–2000. *Vol. 1:* Secondary School Students *by L. D. Johnston et al. National Institutes of Health, 2001.*

There are interesting sex and ethnic differences in the pattern of marijuana usage (MacFadden & Woody, 2000). Among regular users, males outnumber females 2 to 1 in those 26 and older, but there are no sex differences among regular users in younger people (ages 12 to 17). In the 17–34 age group, whites report higher lifetime usage of marijuana than blacks or Hispanics, but in the 35-and-over age group, there are no differences between whites and blacks. In the 18–25 age group, rates of usage are similar across educational levels, except for lower rates of current use in college graduates. In the 26-to-34 age group, amount of current usage is negatively correlated with level of education—that is, the more education, the less likely the person is to use marijuana currently. Finally, across all age groups, current users of marijuana are more likely to use other drugs—both legal, such as alcohol and cigarettes, and illegal, such as cocaine and hallucinogens (MacFadden & Woody, 2000). This finding has often been used to suggest that marijuana is a stepping stone to the abuse of other drugs. There are two problems with this argument. The first is that most people who experiment with or use marijuana regularly do not go on to regular use of other drugs. Logically, to draw even tentative conclusions, one must evaluate both the positive occurrences (people who start with marijuana and go on to use hard drugs) and the negative occurrences (people who start with marijuana and do *not* go on to use hard drugs). The second problem is that there may be another variable that leads to abuse of many substances. For example, some people like to "live on the edge," and their polydrug use is just one indication of that temperament.

The active ingredient in marijuana and hashish is THC (Δ_9-tetrahydrocannabinol). The level of THC (and therefore the level of intoxication) is much higher for hashish than for marijuana. It is believed that the level of THC in marijuana has also been gradually increasing over the years thanks to selective breeding efforts among those who grow hemp plants for drug sale (Zimmer & Morgan, 1995), although there are some who question this assertion (MacFadden & Woody, 2000). The intoxication effects of marijuana are rapid, beginning less than a minute after smoking and reaching a peak in 20 to 30 minutes. When marijuana is ingested, intoxication begins in about 30 minutes and does not reach its peak for 2 or 3 hours. Cannabis-specific receptors in the brain have been discovered, and naturally occurring substances—called *anandamides,* from the Sanskrit word for "bliss"—use these sites (MacFadden & Woody, 2000).

Studying the short-term effects of marijuana use is generally easier than studying the long-term effects. Short-term effects have been explored in some well-designed studies in which the amount and quality of the marijuana have been controlled. There are no such long-term studies, and there are unlikely to be any, because no researcher or agency will agree to provide pharmaceutical-grade mari-

juana for extended periods of time to determine the long-term effects on the body. Consequently, the long-term studies have had to rely on existing samples of marijuana users and nonusers, and these groups nearly always differ on other variables that might confound the results (Wert & Raulin, 1986a). For example, most heavy marijuana users drink alcohol, and many use other drugs as well. Alcohol is known to have long-term health consequences, including central nervous system effects. There are also preexisting group differences between marijuana users and nonusers on such variables as education, occupation, and motivation, any of which could affect health and performance.

There is general agreement that the acute intoxication effects of marijuana disrupt cognitive and motor functioning much as alcohol does. In many states, driving under the influence of marijuana is treated in much the same way as driving under the influence of alcohol. However, there is no clear way of quantifying the degree of marijuana intoxication. The BAL is highly correlated with the degree of alcohol intoxication, whereas with marijuana, the level of THC in the bloodstream is poorly correlated with intoxication. The THC level rises very rapidly after the smoking of marijuana, when there are few intoxication effects, and is much lower later, when the intoxication is maximal (MacFadden & Woody, 2000).

Cognitive and psychomotor tasks are significantly affected by marijuana intoxication (Peterson, 1980). Especially hard hit is memory, which can be disrupted for some time after the immediate intoxication (Millsaps et al., 1994). The mechanism for these memory problems may be dramatic changes in the functioning of the amygdala (Jones, 1980). Heavy use of marijuana is associated with increased apathy and decreased motivation, although there is controversy about how to interpret this finding. Many heavy marijuana users do appear to be apathetic and unmotivated, but it is not clear whether the marijuana use is a cause or an effect of the lack of motivation.

The short-term physiological effects of marijuana use include an elevated heart rate and dilation of blood vessels, which often produces facial flushing (MacFadden & Woody, 2000). The oxygen demand by the heart increases, which decreases exercise tolerance—that is, people smoking marijuana fatigue more quickly from exercise. If there is any blockage of the arteries that supply the heart tissue with blood and oxygen, there is an increased risk of a heart attack. Because marijuana contains more tar and respiratory irritants than tobacco, there can be short-term lung irritation, and it is reasonable to expect that long-term use could lead to the kind of lung problems that tobacco has been documented to cause. Marijuana affects sperm production, leading to lower sperm counts and greater numbers of abnormal sperm cells. Subtle changes in menstrual cycles have also been documented. There are few well-controlled studies on the effects of marijuana smoking on developing fetuses, because most mothers who use marijuana during pregnancy also use alcohol, cigarettes, and other illicit drugs. The research that has been done suggests that there is no evidence for a general loss of intellectual functioning following neonatal exposure to marijuana, but subtle attentional and perceptual deficits are found that persist in the child for years (Fried & Smith, 2001). However, given what is already known about the physiological effects of marijuana, it would be unethical to conduct the kind of experimental study of neonatal exposure to marijuana that would provide clear answers to this question.

The long-term effects of marijuana have been inherently difficult to study, and there has been considerable controversy about how to interpret the available studies. An early study (Campbell et al., 1971) reported that marijuana users showed cerebral atrophy, but this study was fatally flawed. Furthermore, two sophisticated and well-controlled studies found no such atrophy (Co et al., 1977; Kuehnle et al., 1977). In retrospect, it hardly seemed likely that marijuana caused cerebral atrophy; given the widespread use of marijuana at the time of the Campbell et al. study, if they had been correct, hospitals and nursing homes would have been filled to overflowing with marijuana users (Wert & Raulin, 1986a). Over two dozen better-designed studies suggest that the long-term neurological effects of marijuana smoking by adults are minimal and are certainly less than the known effects of chronic alcohol use (Wert & Raulin, 1986b).

PSYCHEDELIC DRUGS

Several hallucinogenic drugs became popular during the 1960s and 1970s, including LSD (*d-lysergic acid dimethylamide*), mescaline, psilocybin, and PCP. A Swiss chemist named Albert Hofmann, synthesized **LSD** in 1943. In the process, he discovered quite by accident that it produced potent distortions in perceptions. **Mescaline** is the active ingredient in the peyote cactus. Native tribes in the desert Southwest of the United States consumed peyote as part of their religious rituals for hundreds of years prior to the discovery of mescaline. **Psilocybin** is the active ingredient in the *Psilocybin mexicana* mushroom. Similarly to peyote, the *Psilocybin mexicana* mushroom played a central role in the religious ceremonies of ancient Aztec tribes and more modern Mexican Indian tribes. **PCP** (*phencyclidine*), also known as **angel dust,** is often incorrectly included in this general class of psychedelics, primarily because it became popular during the same era. PCP is quite dangerous: It can cause severe paranoia, coma, and even death. Despite these hazards, it was once a popular drug, and its use has recently been increasing (NIDA, 1996; Weiss & Millman, 1998). Some drug dealers mix PCP with marijuana to give the marijuana more of a "kick." Although they are chemically different, all of these hallucinogenic substances momentarily disrupt the chemistry of the brain so that affected individuals experience significant distortions in their thought and perceptual processes.

The use of LSD and other psychedelics during the 1960s was encouraged by the proclamations of a Harvard psychology professor, Dr. Timothy Leary, who experimented with some of these substances to see whether their use could reduce the rate of recidivism of prisoners. As part of these studies, Leary experimented on himself to see what effects the drugs had. He became convinced, like many others centuries earlier, that the drugs represented a pathway to a higher plane of consciousness. LSD was the most popular of the psychedelics, in part because it could be manufactured easily and inexpensively. Its use peaked in the late 1960s, dropped off by the early 1980s, and began to increase again in the early 1990s (Ivis & Adlaf, 1999; NIDA, 1982, 1996).

Hallucinogenic drugs have been around for centuries and will probably continue to be around for centuries to come. Once based on naturally occurring substances in plants, they now are produced in chemistry labs. Their purpose, however, remains unchanged. The majority of people who use these drugs seek a consciousness-expanding experience—something that will enable them to experience the world or their religious beliefs in a more intimate and intense manner. This desire for enhanced awareness is a reasonable goal. It is not clear, however, whether drugs can help people achieve it.

Check Yourself 14.5

Psychedelics and Hallucinogens

1. When did marijuana become a widely abused drug?
2. How do the long-term neurological effects of marijuana compare with the long-term effects of alcohol?
3. How were hallucinogenic drugs used centuries ago?

Ponder this ... *The popularity of hallucinogenic drugs has waxed and waned over the years, but each new generation seems to rediscover them. What do you think is the appeal of these drugs for young people, especially college students? Why do you think that each generation, after experimenting with these drugs, seems to lose interest?*

LSD Synthesized from *d*-lysergic acid dimethylamide, this drug produces potent distortions in perception.

mescaline The active ingredient in the peyote cactus.

psilocybin The active ingredient in the mushroom *Psilocybin mexicana*.

PCP, or angel dust A dangerous drug (phencyclidine) that can cause severe paranoia, coma, and even death.

THEORIES OF DRUG ABUSE

Virtually everyone working in the field of drug abuse and dependence recognizes that many factors contribute to drug abuse and that these factors may vary from person to person. Therefore, no single theory will explain drug abuse and dependence. Several theories have been advanced, and the major theories will be covered in this section. To understand drug dependence, one has to divide the process of dependence into stages. The *initiation stage* involves the individual's first exposure to the substance and early experiences with it. The *addiction stage* occurs later, when the person feels he or she has lost control of the drug usage; not every user, however, becomes dependent (Goode, 1999). Finally, the *treatment stage* involves efforts to overcome the dependency. As you will see, some factors contribute heavily to one stage but play only peripheral roles in other stages. This section reviews the contributions to addiction in the initiation and addiction stages. Contributions to the treatment stage are covered in the section that follows. This section begins with a discussion of genetic factors that contribute to alcoholism, followed by a review of biological, psychological, and sociocultural influences on drug abuse and dependence.

GENETIC INFLUENCES

Genes influence so much of human behavior that it should not be surprising that they also contribute to risk for drug abuse and dependence. Much of this section will be devoted to genetic influences on alcohol abuse and dependence, because much more is known about this area than about other types of drug dependence. Furthermore, it is much easier to find people who abuse alcohol primarily, whereas most people who abuse the other drugs covered in this chapter are actually polydrug abusers. The genetic risk factors for polydrug abuse are likely to be personality characteristics that predispose people to seek thrills and discount risks (Duaux et al., 2000). We will first discuss genetic influences on alcohol abuse and then turn to genetic influences on other forms of drug abuse.

Alcohol Abuse. There is no question that genes play a role in alcohol abuse and dependence. That said, the role played by genes has proved to be complex and difficult to unravel. The best generalization one could make on the basis of current data is that there are probably several genetic mechanisms that predispose people to alcoholism. Genes appear to have a stronger influence for males than for females. However, some forms of alcohol dependence seem to have little genetic influence (Jacob & Johnson, 1999). Finally, no matter how strong the genetic influence, alcohol dependence can develop only if the person starts to drink. Let's look at the data supporting each of these generalizations.

Examining the Evidence

That alcoholism runs in families has been recognized for millennia (Hesselbrock, 1995). About 25% of first-degree male relatives (fathers, brothers, and sons) of an alcoholic are alcoholics themselves (Goodwin, 1976), and 80% of alcoholics have at least one first-degree or second-degree relative who is an alcoholic (Hesselbrock et al., 1992). These data are not sufficient to demonstrate a genetic influence, because either genes or family environment could yield this pattern. However, twin studies uniformly support the notion that genes play a role in risk for alcohol dependence, revealing concordance rates near 30% in monozygotic twins and 12% in dizygotic twins (Hesselbrock, 1995; Kaji, 1960). But the picture is more complex than these average figures suggest. Males show higher concordance rates for alcohol dependence for both MZ and DZ twins (Pickens et al., 1991), although both males and females show a high MZ/DZ ratio suggestive of genetic influence. Nevertheless, these data suggest that genes play a stronger role in risk for alcohol dependence in males than in females (McGue, 1999). Furthermore, although genes appear to influence risk for alcohol *abuse* in males, there is no evidence from twin studies that they influence risk in females (Pickens et al., 1991). This pattern is consistent in both black and white Americans (Caldwell & Gottesman, 1991), although unfortunately, there is very little information available from other cultures.

Adoption studies confirm a genetic contribution to alcoholism, in addition to providing tantalizing clues about the heterogeneous nature of this disorder. For example, Goodwin et al. (1973) found that the adopted-away sons of alcoholics had higher rates of alcoholism (18%) than the adopted-away sons of non-alcoholics (5%), clearly indicating that genes influence risk. A parallel study with women showed no evidence of heritability of alcoholism, but 90% of this female sample were abstainers or light drinkers (Goodwin et al., 1977). This reinforces a point made earlier: Alcohol dependence will not develop without a period of heavy exposure to alcohol. Goodwin also found something interesting in his sample of male adoptees. Whereas genes played a strong role in risk for alcohol dependence, it was the environment, not genes, that played the strongest role in risk for alcohol abuse (Goodwin et al., 1973). It appears that one learns to abuse alcohol, but it takes a particular genetic make-up to develop a physiological dependence.

Swedish adoption studies uncovered evidence of subtypes of alcoholism. Cloninger et al. (1981) noted two distinct groups in their sample—one that developed after age 25 and another that developed in the late teens or early adulthood. There was a strong genetic influence on the latter but much less genetic influence on the former. They named these subtypes Type I and Type II alcoholism, respectively. The rates of Type I alcoholism are roughly equal in men and women, whereas the majority of Type II alcoholics are male. Bohman et al. (1981) added a detail not formerly noted: evidence for a mother/daughter transmission of alcoholism. For daughters, having an alcoholic mother increased risk for alcoholism fourfold, but having an alcoholic father had no effect on the daughter's risk for alcoholism. In a reanalysis of the data, Bohman et al. (1987) found that their families could be divided into three groups. In the largest group, genetic and environmental factors contributed to alcoholism for both males and females. In another group, males showed a highly heritable form of alcoholism, and females showed somatization disorder but rarely showed alcoholism. In a third group, males showed heritability for both alcoholism and antisocial traits, including violent behavior, whereas females showed strong heritability for somatization disorder. You may remember that this genetic relationship between antisocial behavior and somatization disorder was discussed in Chapter 9. These genetic studies highlight the heterogeneity of alcoholism and the importance of taking into account these diverse research results.

Other Drug Abuse. In contrast to the extensive genetic research on alcohol abuse and dependence, there is surprisingly little genetic research on other drug abuse. Admittedly, this is a more difficult area to study. The majority of other drugs are illegal, so people are less likely to be candid about their drug use. Furthermore, many people who abuse other drugs are polydrug abusers, which makes it hard to identify factors specific to one type of drug abuse. The phenomenon of polydrug abuse has convinced many researchers that any genetic influences that exist are probably general, affecting risk for many types of drug abuse (Duaux, 2000).

The first step in any addiction process is the initial exposure to the potentially addictive drug. The second step is the repeated exposure required for the physiological dependence to develop. What factors contribute to these behaviors? One of the strongest predictors of risk for drug abuse and dependence is the presence of antisocial personality disorder (Forrest, 1994; King et al., 2001), and antisocial behavior is known to have a genetic influence (Cadoret & Stewart, 1991; Langbehn & Cadoret, 2001; Lyons et al., 1995). As we saw in Chapter 12, antisocial personality disorder is characterized by impulsivity, sensation seeking, and insensitivity to potential aversive consequences

of one's actions. It would be difficult to imagine a constellation more conducive to the initial exposure to drugs, the repeated exposure to obtain gratification, and the willingness to dismiss negative consequences. However, not all drug abusers qualify for the diagnosis of antisocial personality disorder. What other factors can predispose someone to become addicted to substances? There are several that seem to be relevant. They will be discussed in the section on psychological influence, because it is not clear whether these factors have a genetic influence.

BIOLOGICAL INFLUENCES

The biological contributors to the addiction process have their greatest impact at the addiction stage, when the body is reacting to the substance and readjusting to the point where it becomes increasingly difficult to live comfortably without the substance. These physiological changes continue to affect people during the treatment stage, when they create terribly uncomfortable feelings for days after the drugs are stopped and cravings for weeks or months.

Powerful drugs, such as heroin and cocaine, cause dramatic changes in the functioning of the brain and other organ systems, which is the basis for their psychological impact on the individual. However, the human body is a delicately balanced instrument, which responds to changes in the environment with adaptations designed to maintain homeostasis—that is, a functional balance in which organ systems operate within relatively narrow boundaries. These homeostatic adaptations enable humans to adapt their physiological functioning to a variety of changing environments. Adaptations to repeated drug use decrease the sensitivity of the body to the drug, thereby increasing tolerance. Furthermore, once the body has adjusted to the presence of high levels of a drug, there is another adjustment required when the drug is withdrawn—an adjustment that is often painful because it represents a swing in the opposite direction from the one produced by the drug. Instead of a pleasant high, or rush, the person experiences a painful "low" and intense discomfort during withdrawal.

The exact mechanism by which these changes take place varies from one drug to another. Furthermore, some drugs produce dependence rapidly, whereas with others considerable exposure is necessary for dependence to occur. Not every drug has the biological and psychological potential for dependence. To lead to dependence, the drug must produce a substantial change in the brain's chemistry and functioning and must do so without killing the person. Most drugs that produce dramatic changes in brain and body functioning are life-threatening. There are millions of chemical substances, but few have these characteristics and therefore have serious abuse potential. The changes also have to produce a rewarding psychological experience, or the drug is unlikely to be ingested again. Dependence cannot occur without repeated exposure, and the exposures must occur in close temporal proximity so that the body is forced to adapt to the drug. The drugs most likely to prompt frequent exposure are drugs that produce an intense high and an immediate rebound low, thereby creating a craving for more. However, drugs without those characteristics can also produce a strong physiological dependence if there is sufficient repeated exposure. Nicotine, for example, does not initially produce that kind of response, and therefore some people can limit their smoking to Saturday night at the bar for years without becoming dependent. However, once someone starts to smoke regularly, the physiological addiction process will start to take place. As anyone who has tried to quit smoking knows, nicotine dependence can be powerful, even though the psychological effect of smoking may be small compared with that of such drugs as heroin and cocaine.

There is more known about the biological mechanisms behind alcohol abuse. People who are prone to develop alcoholism may respond differently to alcohol, showing more tolerance from the outset and being less likely to develop hangovers (Schuckit & Smith, 1996). Such a finding suggests that alcohol metabolism may be different in those most vulnerable to alcohol dependence. Tsai et al. (1995) has suggested that this finding and others may be the result of a disturbance in the glutaminergic system. Glutamate is a neurotransmitter that provides fast transmission in the centers of the brain associated with arousal. However, it is also involved in memory functioning, neuronal growth and degeneration, and adaptations of synapses to maintain homeostasis. Alcohol has its greatest impact on the glutaminergic system, so differences in the sensitivity of this system to the effects of alcohol may account for differences in risk for alcoholism. It would be premature to say that this is the biological mechanism underlying differences in risk for alcoholism, but it is a promising lead.

Evolutionary Impact

Looking at the incredible impact that drug dependence has on the individual, one can't help but wonder about the evolutionary origin and the evolutionary impact of such dependence. When an animal is given ready access to such a powerful drug as cocaine or heroin, the animal will continuously do whatever it takes to obtain the drug, even at the expense of such critical survival behaviors as eating. People dependent on drugs will violate reciprocal social contracts with other people by lying, cheating, and stealing to obtain more drugs. Millions of burglaries are committed each year by a small group of drug-dependent individuals who need immediate cash to feed their habit (Cantor, 1999). These people are surviving, but all of their efforts are geared toward getting more drugs, rather than toward the broader goals that lead to reproduction and raising a family, such as getting and holding a job, courting, and so on.

What are the evolutionary consequences of such actions? It depends on the base rate of the abuse and on a variety of other factors. For example, at one extreme cocaine will have no effect on natural selection if no one uses cocaine. At the other extreme, if everyone uses cocaine, perhaps because it becomes a central part of the food chain through some bizarre twist of events, it will have an enormous impact on natural selection. Most individuals in this scenario will experience a dramatic drop in reproductive rate as a result of their cocaine consumption. Only those individuals who tend not to respond to the cocaine will be able to function at a sufficiently high level to maintain a high reproductive rate. Such "thought experiments" illustrate a key principle of natural selection: Negative selective pressure is proportional to exposure to the deleterious agent. However, one does not have to rely on thought experiments. You may remember from our discussion of alcoholism that those populations with a long history of alcohol use, such as Northern Europeans, have greater tolerance for alcohol and a less dramatic response to it than those populations with little historical exposure to alcohol, such as many Native American groups (Wolf, 1973). Some drugs, such as alcohol and tobacco, have been a part of some cultures long enough to have had an impact on natural selection. However, the impact is likely to have been subtle, because neither of these drugs so incapacitates people as to have a dramatic effect on their reproductive rates. Both of these drugs increase life-threatening illnesses, but for the most part, those increases are not significant until people are in their forties or fifties, well after their most fertile period. On the other hand, drugs such as cocaine and heroin, if they were to become widely used, would exert tremendous selective pressure because of their powerful effects on functioning and the increased mortality rates they cause.

PSYCHOLOGICAL INFLUENCES

Psychological variables contribute at all stages of the addiction process, including the addiction stage itself, which some people have incorrectly assumed to be a purely physiological phenomenon. Psychological variables contribute to the willingness to experiment with drugs. Other psychological variables contribute to the willingness to take the difficult steps that must be taken to break the drug dependence during the treatment stage. Psychological variables may also contribute to the emotional impact of the drug.

Behavioral Perspective. The behavioral perspective on addiction argues that any behavior that produces a pleasant state or reduces an aversive state will be reinforced. Under the right circumstances, the drugs covered in this chapter produce one or both of these effects. For example, modest amounts of alcohol reduce inhibitions and produce a mild euphoria, although larger amounts of alcohol may undo those effects. Individual users may differ substantially in how reinforcing they find the effects of a specific drug. For example, some people dislike even mild intoxication because it makes them feel out of control. Others find it pleasant, relaxing, and thoroughly enjoyable.

Alcohol can reduce an unpleasant state of anxiety and, in high doses, makes people emotionally numb, thus blocking any unpleasant state. The idea that this effect accounts for drug addiction is referred to as the **tension-reduction hypothesis** (Kushner & Sher, 1993; Mann et al., 1987; Pollack et al., 1988). Although the evidence that tension reduction is a major contributor to drug addiction is weak—that is, most drug users do not seem to fit this profile—there probably is a subgroup of people who use drugs in this manner (Cox & Klinger, 1987). However, alcohol can also produce a variety of aversive states. The hangover the next day can be excruciatingly uncomfortable. One's behavior when drunk can be a source of embarrassment. The long-term health consequences associated with heavy alcohol use not only are life-threatening but also significantly reduce the quality of one's life. One would think that such a balance of positive and negative effects would dramatically favor controlled drinking to obtain most of the benefits and avoid most of the aversive consequences. The problem is that the effectiveness of a reinforcer depends on both the strength of the reinforcer and the timing of its delivery. In general, immediate reinforcers are more effective in altering behavior. Therefore, in the initiation stage, the reinforcing properties of alcohol generally favor consumption, because the positive effects occur immediately and the negative effects are delayed, sometimes for years. There are also reinforcing elements present in this initiation stage in the form of social influences, which will be discussed in the next section.

During the addiction stage, when the physiological dependence on a drug develops, the reinforcing elements from the initiation stage may continue to operate, but additional factors are present. For example, avoiding the drug becomes aversive because withdrawal symptoms essentially punish such efforts. Using the drug may be producing a variety of aversive situations at home; for example, family problems may be intensified by the abuse. In theory, these problems could punish drug use, but in many cases, they are used instead as excuses for more drug use (Margolis & Zweben, 1998).

One problem with the behavioral perspective is that it does not address the question of why some people become drug dependent and others do not. There may be different learning histories, but often two people can grow up in the same community, attend the same school, and even live in the same house and still differ in their drug use. Individual differences in sensitivity to alcohol and to the reinforcing

properties of drinking may account for those differences in alcohol use. We noted some of the potential biological factors when we examined genetic influences. Psychological factors may also contribute. For example, alcohol abuse is more common in certain personality disorders, especially in antisocial and borderline personality disorders and to a lesser extent in paranoid and avoidant personality disorders (Morgenstern et al., 1997). It is also more common in people with certain Axis I disorders, including mood disorders, anxiety disorders, schizophrenia, and ADHD (Andersson et al., 1997; APA, 2000). Certain individual characteristics are associated with increased risk for alcoholism. These include sensation seeking (a need to have new experiences constantly), stronger reactivity to the threat of punishment, and a greater impact of alcohol on the cardiovascular system (Finn et al., 1992). Clearly, there may be more than one path to alcoholism—and probably to most forms of drug abuse.

Psychodynamic Perspective. Psychodynamic theorists offer a different interpretation of these data. Instead of examining the co-occurrence of drug dependence and other disorders and the relationship between various personality traits and the development of drug dependence, they seek a common underlying theme to explain these associations (Thombs, 1999). For example, Wurmser (1974, 1978) argued that two conditions are necessary for the development of substance abuse and dependence. The first is an "addictive search," which he defined as a constant and impulsive craving for pleasurable or exciting activities. The second is an "adventurous entrance" to chemicals, which simply means that you have to try a drug to become addicted to it. All the experts on drug and alcohol abuse, regardless of their orientation, agree with this second point. Wurmser (1974, 1978) argues that without the addictive search component, however, exposure to drugs or alcohol will not result in addiction. This idea suggests a line of research—specifically, identifying the key elements of an addictive personality and the factors that contribute to it.

Other Psychological Variables. Given the public service announcements about the hazards of drug abuse, it is hard to imagine that anyone is unaware of the risks. However, it is probably not so much the awareness of the risks that is the critical variable but, rather, the perceived level of risk and the concern that one has about it. For example, becoming dependent on heroin poses a significant risk to one's long-term career aspirations. However, the impact of such a potential risk may be different for a professional with a six-figure income and a high school dropout earning the minimum wage. Furthermore, one would expect that young people would discount risks more than older people. Young people tend to feel invincible (Wills et al., 1999). This feeling of invincibility contributes to many different kinds of risk taking (Tursz, 1997), including experimentation with drugs (Adlaf & Smart, 1983).

....

tension-reduction hypothesis   The idea that drug addiction occurs because drugs can make people emotionally numb, thus blocking any unpleasant state.

Cigarette smoking has been glamorized for decades by cigarette company advertisements. Increasingly, the antismoking forces are using the same technique to challenge these glamorous images of smokers.

Finally, psychological factors have an impact on how readily someone can recover from a period of addiction. Those who are most likely to recover are those who can form supportive relationships with others and draw strength from them (Landau et al., 2000). They are also people who have reason to believe that they could have a satisfying life if only they could break the addictions that are controlling them (Irving et al., 1998). These are difficult concepts to operationalize and measure, so there are limited data to support these contentions. Nevertheless, treatment specialists take these principles almost as a matter of faith and, in the treatment process, seek to enhance both supportive relationships and hope for the future. More than

in any other area of psychological treatment, professionals in the addiction field include a number of former clients, who often believe that their experience and their success can enhance treatment outcome (White, 2000a, 2000b). This does not occur in the treatment of other disorders, such as schizophrenia, mood disorders, or anxiety disorders. Whatever is behind it, this phenomenon has shaped the treatments for drug addiction in significant ways.

SOCIOCULTURAL INFLUENCES

Sociocultural contributors have their greatest impact in the initiation and treatment stages of the addiction process. In the initiation stage, these variables affect the likelihood that someone will have access to the substance, will choose to experiment with it, and will continue to use the substance long enough for the physiological process of addiction to begin to occur. For example, the ready availability of alcohol in some cultures contributes to increased rates of alcoholism, because it virtually ensures that people will be exposed to alcohol during the initiation stage. In the treatment stage, sociocultural factors shape an environment that either supports the individual's difficult efforts to stop the substance use or discourages attempts to stop. Sociocultural factors can be divided into two broad categories. The first involves influences from immediate peers and the general culture. The second involves influences from family members.

The expectations and behavioral norms of a culture can exert a significant impact on the likelihood of drug use. For example, having friends who smoke is a powerful predictor of whether you will smoke (Killen et al., 1997). Even the state in which you live is associated with your risk for starting to smoke; in general, smoking is substantially higher in states that grow tobacco (Males, 1999). Smoking is more common among high school students who are getting poor grades and have more behavioral problems (Sussman et al., 1990). Heroin addiction is more likely in the lower socioeconomic classes (Kleinman, 1979), although it occurs in the middle and upper classes as well (Friedman & Alicea, 1995). In contrast, cocaine is used more frequently than heroin in middle and upper-middle classes (Sterk-Elifson, 1996). College students heavily abuse some drugs, such as alcohol and marijuana, but rarely abuse other drugs, such as heroin (Rivers & Shore, 1997). Gang members are far more likely to abuse heroin than are

Settings dramatically affect the consumption of alcohol. Many college campuses are notorious for the level of alcohol consumption on or near campus. Fully 50% of male and 40% of female college students regularly engage in binge drinking, and a significant portion of those individuals go on to develop alcohol dependence.

college students (Moore, 1994). Blacks are more likely than whites to abuse heroin and crack cocaine, but whites are more likely than blacks to abuse other drugs (Friedman & Ali, 1998). The norms of the cultural groups contribute significantly to the pattern of drug abuse observed within the group.

Cross-cultural studies suggest wide variations in the rate of alcohol consumption. Europe and countries with historical ties to Europe, such as the United States, Canada, New Zealand, Argentina, and Chile, have much higher rates of alcohol consumption than the rest of the world (Barry, 1995). Ethnicity and family history were the two variables that were most predictive of the outcomes in a 33-year prospective study of alcoholism (Vaillant, 1995). It is unlikely that ethnicity and family history caused the outcomes. Rather, differences associated with these variables, such as poverty, stress, or attitudes toward substance use, are more likely to be the causal agents. In this monumental study of how alcoholism develops, Vaillant (1995) found that alcohol problems were highest in Irish Americans, Native Americans, and those of Northern European decent and were lowest in Jews, Italians, and those of Southern European descent. In treatment populations in the United States, African Americans and Latinos are slightly overrepresented relative to their population size, and Asian Americans are underrepresented (NIAAA, 1997).

Ethnicity is only one sociocultural variable that predicts the level of drug abuse. For example, it has been known for decades that age, sex, and social status predict alcohol abuse (Cahalan, 1970). Young people, especially college students, are more likely to be heavy drinkers. Forty percent of college students consume five or more drinks in a single sitting in any given two-week period (Johnston et al., 1992; Wechsler et al., 1994), and 33% report that they drink for the express purpose of getting drunk (Jones et al., 2001; Wechsler & Isaac, 1992). The rates are especially high among college students who belong to a fraternity or sorority (Cashin et al., 1998), illustrating again how dramatically role expectations can affect behavior. In general, males are more likely than females to be problem drinkers. Although problem drinkers are found in every social class, the lower social classes are overrepresented (APA, 2000). Few people question these data, yet some argue that the cause of alcoholism is entirely biological and that social factors are irrelevant (Milam & Ketcham, 1983). Biology clearly plays a role, but it would be shortsighted to assume that these cultural variables are irrelevant. If nothing else, these cultural variables influence the exposure to alcohol necessary to trigger any biological predisposition to alcoholism.

When looking at family influences, one has to be especially careful about drawing conclusions. If both parents and their children abuse drugs, the children may have learned to abuse drugs from their parents. However, a shared genetic factor may also account for this finding. Several family variables are predictive of drug use in children. Let's take a closer look at them.

Examining the Evidence

Malkus (1994) found that family size, the quality of the relationship between parents, the number of parents present in the home, and birth order were predictive of drug abuse. Piercy et al. (1991) found that the level of family cohesion, the quality of the communication between children and the mother, and the style of discipline were predictive of risk for drug abuse. Jessor and Jessor (1977) found that mothers who were religious, conventional, and traditional were less likely to have children who abused alcohol or drugs than were mothers who de-emphasized religion and traditional social values. Barnes (1990) found that parents who drank excessively were more likely to have children who abused alcohol. Kandel and Andrews (1987) found that the quality of the relationship between parents and their teenagers was significantly related to the likelihood of drug and alcohol abuse. Fawzy et al. (1987) found that children from families whose father either was a professional or occupied a leadership position, such as a foreman, were less likely to be involved in drug abuse. At least two studies found that older siblings appeared to influence the substance abuse patterns of younger siblings (Brook et al., 1983; Needle et al., 1986). Of course, all of these findings are correlational by nature—that is, none of these variables was experimentally manipulated—so one must be cautious in drawing causal conclusions. For example, it may be that drug-using children disrupt family cohesion rather than that poor family cohesion influences children to experiment with drugs. Nevertheless, these findings suggest some interesting theories about what factors may contribute to drug and alcohol abuse in young people.

When adults start families of their own, their drinking can have significant effects on the family. Those involved in the treatment of alcoholism have addressed this issue extensively. Specifically, they have focused on how a family can contribute to an alcoholism problem in family members by making excuses for their drinking, protecting them from the natural consequences of their drinking, or behaving in ways that give them an excuse to drink. This process is referred to in popular psychology as **codependency,** which means that family members, although not dependent on alcohol themselves, contribute to the alcohol problem of their family member. The concept of codependency is con-

troversial. Some have argued that there is little evidence to support it and that it amounts to shifting the blame from those who are drinking excessively to the people around them (Tavris, 1992). Nevertheless, as we shall see in the next section, family therapy is often included in the treatment of alcoholism to address these issues of codependency.

Check Yourself 14.6

Theories of Drug Abuse

1. How does the genetic contribution to alcoholism vary by sex?
2. What biological process underlies tolerance and withdrawal symptoms?
3. What factors are predictive of experimentation with drugs?
4. What sociocultural factors have been shown to affect smoking?
5. In the 33-year follow-up study of Vaillant (1995), what two factors emerged as the most critical in predicting alcohol abuse?

Ponder this . . . *Because no drug is addictive for an individual if the individual never tries it, an effective prevention strategy would be to reduce drug experimentation. How might one discourage high school students from experimenting with drugs?*

TREATING DRUG ABUSE

The cost of drug abuse, in both human terms and dollars, is enormous. This section will discuss the most commonly used treatments for drug abuse and dependence. Probably the best-known drug intervention is Alcoholics Anonymous, or AA. AA deserves credit as one of the first successful attempts to reclaim the lives of people addicted to drugs—in this case, alcohol. It ushered in a new era in which a concerted effort was made to understand drug dependence and treat it effectively. However, AA is only one of many available treatments. This section covers the wide range of treatment options now available for alcohol and drug dependence. The section begins with an overview of biological treatments and then outlines the most common psychological and sociocultural interventions. It closes with a brief look at treatment alternatives that have yet to receive widespread acceptance.

BIOLOGICAL TREATMENTS

Three biological approaches to the treatment of drug abuse will be covered in this section: detoxification, medications, and drug substitution.

codependency The actions of family members of a drug-dependent individual that inadvertently encourages or supports continued drug dependence.

Alcoholics Anonymous, a mutual-help group, argues strongly that alcoholism is a disease that cannot be overcome without the help of both a higher power and other people.

Detoxification. **Detoxification** is the process of withdrawing the addicted individual from drugs and their effects. Most addictive drugs produce significant withdrawal effects, which are uncomfortable and sometimes life-threatening. The medical management of these withdrawal effects reduces the risk, decreases the discomfort, and probably increases the willingness of addicted individuals to commit their efforts to treatment.

The detoxification process varies across drugs. It can utilize either a rapid or a gradual withdrawal from the substance, although the former strategy is generally preferred. With some drugs, such as marijuana, the detoxification process is barely noticed because the physical withdrawal symptoms are mild (MacFadden & Woody, 2000). With other drugs, such as cocaine, the withdrawal symptoms are uncomfortable but not dangerous, so little medical management is required (Jaffe, 2000a). Still other drugs, such as heroin, produce potentially dangerous withdrawal symptoms (Jaffe & Jaffe, 2000). In the case of heroin withdrawal, drugs are typically prescribed to minimize the most severe symptoms. For example, clonidine reduces such withdrawal symptoms as muscle aches, lethargy, insomnia, restlessness, and craving for more heroin. A new technique for heroin detoxification—an ultrarapid detoxification—is becoming more popular. Heroin addicts who stop taking heroin do not experience rapid detoxification because the

drug's effects wear off slowly. However, administering an opiate antagonist makes the withdrawal virtually instantaneous, and the withdrawal symptoms last for hours instead of days. However, this rapid withdrawal creates intense withdrawal symptoms, which must be managed with a combination of drugs, sometimes including several hours of anesthesia (Brewer, 1997; Jaffe & Jaffe, 2000).

For some drugs, the preferred method of withdrawal is gradual. One such case is nicotine, where smokers may use nicotine gum, the patch, or smoking filters to reduce the amount of nicotine in their systems gradually (Hughes, 2000; NIDA, 2001). Using the patch or another source of nicotine instead of cigarettes decreases the immediate health risks that smoking poses, and the amount of nicotine is then gradually reduced to minimize cravings. This gradual approach is also used for other potentially addictive drugs, such as some benzodiazepines (Ciraulo & Sarid-Segal, 2000). For example, Xanax, a high-potency benzodiazepine with a short half-life, is habit-forming. Its short half-life translates into a rapid reduction in anxiety but also into a quick return of anxiety as it wears off, rendering anxious people desperate for their next pill. Reducing the dosage gradually is usually sufficient to wean the person from Xanax or similar medications without excessive stress.

Medications are often used to minimize withdrawal symptoms. For example, benzodiazepines can reduce the discomfort and anxiety associated with withdrawal from such drugs as narcotics and alcohol (Jaffe & Jaffe, 2000). Individuals who have successfully undergone withdrawal from cocaine often experience prolonged periods of depression, which can be treated with traditional antidepressants (Jaffe, 2000a). It is still a matter of debate whether the depression that commonly follows cocaine withdrawal is really an extension of a premorbid depression that the person was self-medicating with cocaine or a depression created by the cocaine (Kreek & Koob, 1998).

Medications. Medications can be used to enhance treatment of drug dependence in several ways. For example, medications can either make drinking aversive or decrease the pleasure associated with drinking. The best-known drug treatment for alcohol dependence is disulfiram, better known as Antabuse. **Antabuse** is a drug that blocks the normal metabolism of alcohol and creates noxious byproducts that induce vomiting whenever the person drinks. Although it was once touted as the best treatment available for alcohol dependence, the results from controlled studies

detoxification   The process of withdrawing an addicted individual from drugs and their effects.

Antabuse   The best-known drug treatment for alcohol dependence, which blocks the normal metabolism of alcohol and creates noxious by-products that induce vomiting whenever the person drinks. Also known as disulfiram.

of Antabuse have been unimpressive (Fuller et al., 1986). It is generally effective only in highly motivated people, who typically respond to any treatment. Furthermore, the dropout rate is high. People who want to drink simply stop taking their Antabuse (Schuckit, 2000).

Two other medications show promise for the treatment of alcoholism. Naltrexone decreased both alcohol cravings and relapse in two small-scale studies (Volpicelli et al., 1995, 1997). However, like Antabuse, naltrexone is effective only for those individuals who continue to take it. A second promising medication—acamprosate (Campral)—is currently available only in Europe (Schuckit, 2000). The exact mechanism behind acamprosate's effectiveness is still unknown, but it is believed that the drug reduces the craving for alcohol by affecting the GABA inhibitory system.

Medications are available for many drug addictions. Naltrexone and naloxone are narcotic antagonists—that is, they block the effects of such narcotics as heroin. They are used in the treatment of morphine and heroin addiction, essentially blocking the effects of these drugs and thus reducing their reinforcing value. The hope is that without the reinforcing value of the drug, drug use will gradually extinguish (Jaffe & Jaffe, 2000). However, in controlled trials, most individuals simply stop taking these drugs (Cornish et al., 1997). A more promising approach is to use partial antagonists, which inhibit but do not completely block the action of narcotics. The partial antagonist buprenorphine has shown considerable promise in controlled trials for the treatment of narcotic addiction (Johnson et al., 1992).

Drug Substitution. Drug substitution is a treatment strategy that involves switching a person addicted to one drug to another, less problematic drug. The best-known drug substitution treatment is **methadone maintenance,** which involves substituting the synthetic opioid methadone for the natural opiate heroin. Methadone is no less addictive than heroin, but systematic administration of methadone in a medical setting reduces most of the secondary risks of heroin addiction, and it is more effective at reducing these risks than simply providing heroin to users in a medical setting (Jaffe & Jaffe, 2000). For example, heroin sold on the street typically contains numerous contaminants, some of which are toxic. The strength of the heroin also varies considerably from one supplier to the next, which increases the risk of accidental overdose. Finally, many heroin addicts share needles with other addicts, dramatically increasing their risk of contracting

such diseases as AIDS. Although methadone maintenance reduces secondary risks and the criminal activities engaged in to finance a heroin habit (Payte, 1989; Jaffe & Jaffe, 2000), it was not without its critics (Cornish et al., 2001). It is simply substituting one addiction for another. Methadone is actually harder to withdraw from than heroin, because although they tend to be less severe, the withdrawal symptoms last nearly twice as long (Kleber, 1981; Strain et al., 1999). Furthermore, methadone is not completely risk-free, especially for the fetus of a mother on methadone maintenance (Jansson et al., 1997). Nevertheless, methadone maintenance programs are considered a major improvement over heroin dependence (Yoast et al., 2001).

PSYCHOLOGICAL TREATMENTS

A variety of psychological treatments have been tried for drug dependence. In general, traditional insight-oriented therapies have proved to be of little value, at least in the early stages of drug treatment (Cornish et al., 2001). Instead, the psychological treatments that have proved most effective with drug addiction have focused on the dependence itself and on the psychological barriers to overcoming it. These psychological treatments are normally combined with one or more biological treatments. However, many of the traditional psychotherapy concepts, such as the relationship between client and therapist, appear to be as important in the treatment of drug addiction as in traditional psychotherapy (Miller, 2000). This section reviews behavioral therapies, a cognitive-behavioral approach called relapse prevention, and an approach unique to the treatment of alcohol abuse—controlled drinking.

Behavioral Therapies. Behavior therapy seeks to modify the situations that trigger drug use or the reinforcers for drug use and/or abstinence. The situations that signal that a behavior will be rewarded, or at least not punished, are called discriminative stimuli. The discriminative stimuli for drug use vary across individuals, but the places where people used drugs and the people with whom they used them are often discriminative stimuli for drug use. Avoiding those situations and those people increases the likelihood that an individual will be able to resist drug use. Certain feelings, such as frustration or fear, can also be discriminative stimuli for drug use. To the extent that people can avoid situations that trigger such feelings, it will be easier for them to resist drugs. However, sometimes that is impossible, in which case the person must be taught to recognize when the potential for drug use is high and must be especially vigilant during those periods.

Behavioral self-control training seeks to sensitize the person to the cues that trigger drug use and teach strategies that can be employed to resist drug use (Miller et al., 1992; Miller & Heather, 1998; Walters, 2000). For example, recognizing that certain situations trigger cravings for drugs can lead to a conscious effort to avoid those situations.

---

methadone maintenance   The best-known drug substitution treatment, which involves substituting the synthetic opioid methadone for the natural opiate heroin.

behavioral self-control training   Training that seeks to sensitize a person to the cues that trigger drug use and teaches strategies to resist drug use.

Essentially, this is using the behavior strategy just discussed, but the elements are internalized so that people can administer the treatment on their own. Although behavioral self-control training has been applied primarily to the treatment of alcoholism, variations on this theme have been applied with other addictions.

Another behavioral strategy, called **contingency management,** seeks to make reinforcers contingent on drug avoidance. This strategy is generally used during intensive treatment programs, in which even basic privileges are under the control of the program. Such contingency programs are more effective, at least in the short run, than supportive therapy (Azrin et al., 1996). Theoretically, such contingencies already exist in the environment, but those contingencies are often either too delayed or too intermittent to be effective in shaping behavior. For example, loss of a job, loss of friends, and loss of status are serious contingencies, but because those consequences often do not occur until months or years after the start of the drug use, they have little impact on this behavior. In contrast, small privileges, such as television, evenings out, and special meals, that are contingent on drug abstinence and are granted quickly have more impact on behavior.

Relapse Prevention. **Relapse prevention** comprises strategies designed to reduce the likelihood that a slip in a person's resolve to control his or her drug use will lead to relapse (Marlatt & Gordon, 1985). Few people who are drug dependent are able to stop using and never go back to using drugs. The drug cravings can be intense, and the individual may lack the skills to deal with life's problems without resorting to drug use.

The key issue with relapse is the tendency to "give up" once one has used drugs again after a period of abstinence. There are many reasons for this tendency. For example, there is the common notion that in alcoholics, a single drink can trigger an overwhelming and uncontrollable urge to drink more. The Marlatt et al. (1973) study reported earlier in this chapter challenged that assumption by showing that it was not the alcohol that triggered additional drinking but, rather, the drinker's expectations about the effects of alcohol. Nevertheless, this expectation can easily fuel the belief that "Now I've gone over the cliff, and hitting the bottom is inevitable."

The key elements in relapse prevention are the cognitive challenge of that belief and specific behavioral strategies to (1) remove oneself as quickly as possible from the setting and (2) seek the support necessary to resist the urge to use drugs. Taking drugs is called a slip, not a relapse. If it is a relapse, then there is no reason to keep struggling because you have already lost. If it is a slip, then you can catch yourself before it becomes a full-fledged relapse. These may seem like trivial semantic differences, but they can make a considerable difference in long-term outcome (Parks et al., 2001), as illustrated in the case of Phil.

Fighting the Tendency to Give Up

Phil had gone through treatment for his heavy drinking four times in the last five years, and each time he had returned to drinking. This time he was determined to stay away from the booze, and he felt that he had finally learned the way to make that happen. In the past, he would slip and have a beer, perhaps while watching a football game with friends. That single beer would eat at him as he criticized himself for being a wimp. By the time someone asked if he was ready for another, he had given up on sobriety and would usually drink himself into a stupor. Within a couple of weeks, he was drinking every day, just like before treatment. This time around, his therapist recognized that the most effective strategy to prevent a relapse was to turn down the first drink. The therapist role-played with Phil how to refuse a drink gracefully until Phil felt comfortable handling this problem. The next time his neighbor handed him an unopened beer, he started to open it but caught himself. He turned to his neighbor and said, "If it is all right with you, I think I'll have a Coke instead." With a smile, his neighbor returned the beer to the cooler and pulled out a soda, asking, "Will Pepsi do?" Feeling good that he had turned this potential slip around, Phil smiled. "Of course!"

Controlled Drinking. A major controversy in the treatment of alcoholism is whether the goal should be abstinence or controlled drinking. **Controlled drinking** means that the individual occasionally drinks but does so responsibly and does not drink to the point of intoxication. For decades, the popular wisdom among treatment professionals, especially those committed to the AA approach, was that the only reasonable goal for alcoholics was abstinence, because alcoholics could not control their drinking. Like many strongly held beliefs, this one seemed to be impervious to the influence of data. For example, Davies (1962) found that 7 out of 93 alcoholics in a long-term follow-up study showed a pattern of normal drinking. Granted, that is only 8% of his sample, but it is more than enough to refute the general proposition that *no* alcoholic is capable of controlled drinking. How well does controlled drinking work?

....

contingency management   A behavioral strategy that seeks to make reinforcers contingent on drug avoidance.

relapse prevention   Strategies designed to reduce the likelihood that a slip in a person's resolve to control his or her drug use will lead to relapse.

controlled drinking   Strategy whereby a person with alcohol dependence drinks occasionally but does so responsibly and does not drink to the point of intoxication.

Examining the Evidence

The controlled-drinking controversy came to a head following the publication of several articles describing a controlled-drinking treatment program developed by Mark and Linda Sobell (Sobell & Sobell, 1973, 1976, 1978). Teaching alcoholics to control their drinking was at least as effective, and in some ways more effective, than teaching them abstinence. Pendery et al. (1982) interviewed some of the participants in the Sobells' study several years later and came to startlingly different conclusions. They found that most participants in the controlled-drinking group of the Sobells' study "failed from the outset to drink safely. The majority were rehospitalized for alcoholism treatment within a year after their discharge from the research project" (p. 169). However, Pendery et al. did not interview the participants in the abstinence group, who also showed high rates of relapse. Nevertheless, these investigators went so far as to accuse the Sobells of scientific fraud (*New York Times,* June 28, 1982). Accusing a scientist of scientific fraud is *the* most serious charge that one can make, and it triggered a series of investigations by an independent blue-ribbon panel convened by the Addiction Research Foundation, where the research was conducted; the United States National Institutes of Health, which funded the research; and the United States Congress. These investigations completely exonerated the Sobells of scientific misconduct, noting that their conclusions were supported by their data and that their data were collected in a manner consistent with the best scientific methodology (Marlatt, 1983).

The Sobells' study was an experiment, with alcoholics randomly assigned to a controlled-drinking or an abstinence treatment group. In contrast, the Pendery et al. (1982) group chose to look only at the controlled-drinking group and failed to examine the control group. Ignoring the control group was at the very least a scientific blunder, and it could also be interpreted less kindly as a distortion of the Sobell study. Furthermore, Pendery et al. relied almost exclusively on the retrospective reports of the people they interviewed, whereas the Sobells followed their participants prospectively, gathering information on functioning as it occurred. As you learned in Chapter 6, retrospective data are much weaker than prospective data because they are nearly always distorted by normal memory biases. Nevertheless, the controversy remains, and some people are still unwilling to accept that controlled drinking may be a reasonable treatment goal for some alcoholics.

The Pendery et al. (1982) study did highlight an important problem in the treatment of alcoholism: The majority of people treated are not problem-free even after successful treatment. More recent research on the controlled-drinking approach has suggested that a variety of strategies can enhance controlled drinking, such as having the person wait for several minutes between drinks to allow time to evaluate the costs and benefits of drinking (Sobell & Sobell, 1993). Another issue that has since emerged is that controlled drinking may be appropriate for some alcoholics but not for others (Larimer et al., 1998). There may well be a subset of alcoholics who are constitutionally unable to achieve control in their drinking, and for them abstinence is indeed the best treatment approach. Just as most theorists believe that there are several risk factors for alcoholism and several ways in which alcoholism may develop, treatment specialists now believe that the best treatment approach for one person may not be the best for another (Kalman et al., 2000).

SOCIOCULTURAL TREATMENTS

Sociocultural treatments focus on the environmental variables that may contribute to addictions. This section will cover mutual-help groups, residential treatment, and environmental manipulations.

Mutual-Help Groups. Mutual-help groups are groups of affected individuals who meet regularly to provide members with guidance and support as they struggle with their problem. Perhaps the best-known mutual-help group for alcoholism (in fact, the best-known treatment for alcoholism) is **AA,** or **Alcoholics Anonymous.** Two recovered alcoholics founded AA in 1935, and it has become by far the largest mutual-help group (Raphael, 2000). It has over 2 million members and over 70,000 individual chapters. Each chapter is a loose-knit group of recovered and recovering alcoholics who meet on a regular basis to provide support and help to one another. Anyone is welcome to attend meetings, and most large cities have a phone number that people can dial to learn the time and location of meetings throughout the area. Part of the logic of a mutual-help group such as AA is that, when one has been a heavy user of substances like alcohol, one's friends are likely to be fellow drinkers. It is hard enough to stop drinking, but it is even harder to do so when either the people you associate with continue to drink or you feel that you have to disown all of your friends and rebuild

....

mutual-help groups   Groups of affected individuals who meet regularly to provide members with guidance and support as they struggle with their problem.

Alcoholics Anonymous (AA)   The largest mutual-help group, founded by two recovered alcoholics in 1935.

your life on your own. AA provides the support and fellowship of a group of people who have decided not to drink—support that is absolutely critical during the first few months of abstinence.

The philosophy of AA is spelled out in the 12 steps of the AA program, which rest heavily on a strong belief in the need to rely on the help of a higher power, such as God. Of course, AA may not be for everyone (Oakes et al., 2000). However, many people who have battled against alcoholism swear by the support and strength they have received through AA. A much smaller group with the same goal but a narrower clientele is Women for Sobriety. The mutual-help philosophy has been extended to two additional groups designed to serve the needs of family members of alcoholics. Al-Anon is a group for family members of alcoholics. The meetings are devoted to discussing the actions of the alcoholic family members and the best ways to help them. Alateen is a similar organization designed for the teenage children of alcoholic parents. ACoA (Adult Children of Alcoholics) is a group devoted to helping people who have grown up in a household with an alcoholic deal with emotional scars from the experience. All of these groups share a common goal, but there are vast differences in their underlying philosophies (Humphreys & Kaskutas, 1995). For example, AA stresses the need to give oneself over to a higher power, whereas Women for Sobriety stresses the importance of self-reliance.

Until recently, there was little research data on the effectiveness of AA. In fact, the organization was hostile to establishment researchers, perhaps because of the considerable skepticism that treatment professionals expressed early in the history of the organization. Recent research found that AA was about as effective as either cognitive-behavioral treatment or a combination of AA and cognitive-behavioral treatment in helping people to stop drinking and keeping them sober over a one-year period (Ouimette et al., 1997). On some measures, such as the proportion of people remaining abstinent after one year, AA was more effective. These encouraging data support the previous claims of AA. However, not all of the data on AA have been as supportive. Kownacki and Shadish (1999) reviewed the results of 12 controlled studies of alcoholism treatment and found that people in AA were no more likely to be alcohol-free at 12 months than people in other treatments or in no treatment. The dropout rate for AA is high, which complicates the comparison of this approach with other approaches. Those who stay with AA generally do well, but they are probably more motivated than those who drop out, and more motivated people tend to do well in virtually any treatment.

A variety of mutual-help groups have sprung up for other drug-dependent individuals, most based closely on the AA model (Miller, 1995). Two of the more widely available are Narcotics Anonymous, or NA, and Cocaine Anonymous. Like AA, these organizations provide long-term support to people fighting addiction to drugs. Members meet regularly and are available 24 hours a day to help talk fellow members through a crisis that might result in a relapse.

Community Residential Treatment Programs.

The concept of community residential treatment of drug and alcohol abuse is an outgrowth of the community mental health movement of the 1960s. The idea is that treatment should be provided in the least restrictive setting possible and, whenever possible, in the community in which the person lives. Furthermore, community-based treatment has the advantage of being closer to the normal lifestyle of the individual, so treatment gains are more likely to generalize to the everyday situation in which the person lives. Many of the current residential treatment programs were outgrowths of mutual-help groups, such as Phoenix House and Daytop Village (Landry, 1994). They provide a level of support and care somewhere between hospitalization and the traditional mutual-help group. By providing a therapeutic community, these organizations allow people to rebuild their lives gradually, thus making the transition back into the community easier (Landry, 1994). This is one area of treatment in which more research is critically needed (Lamb et al., 1998).

Environmental Manipulations.

Treatment is normally focused on the individual, but that need not be the case. For example, drugs such as alcohol and nicotine are legal and readily available. Like any consumer good, they are subject to economic laws—that is, they are price sensitive. Cigarettes that sell well at $2.50 a pack might be somewhat less popular if the price were $5.00 or $10.00 a pack. That is the logic of proposing dramatically increased taxes on products like cigarettes. In the United States, the current tax on cigarettes is just over 50¢ a pack, whereas European countries have taxes that range from $1.50 to $4.00 per pack (Gold, 1995). It is estimated that increasing the taxes on cigarettes to $5.00 a pack, essentially tripling the price, would cut cigarette consumption by 40%. Such a hypothetical tax increase would increase the cost of a pack-a-day habit by almost $2000 per year. Who would be most affected by such an increase? Those affected most would be the ones who make the least money, and that would include most teenagers. Most smokers started smoking during adolescence. With higher cigarette taxes, teenagers would have to give up the equivalent of prime seats at a major concert every other week to support their habit. Given that quitting is very hard for many people, preventing young people from starting to smoke is likely to reduce the overall number of smokers substantially.

Given the tremendous personal and societal costs of alcoholism, prevention is a highly desirable approach. Unfortunately, there has been little research on prevention. Both primary-prevention and secondary-prevention efforts are possible. To refresh your memory of concepts covered in Chapter 4, primary prevention involves applying a program to all members of a group without making any effort to identify who might be at greatest risk for a disorder. Secondary prevention involves focusing a program on those individuals known to be at elevated risk for the disorder.

Primary prevention of alcoholism is geared toward encouraging responsible drinking. Remember that even in those who may be genetically predisposed, alcoholism cannot develop unless there is a period of excessive alcohol consumption. Therefore, restraining drinking to moderate levels should dramatically reduce alcohol dependence. From 1920 to 1933 the United States government tried an

One way to prevent the use of drugs is to use law enforcement officers to cut off the supply. However, the U.S. experience with Prohibition demonstrated that legal attempts to cut off supply rarely work if demand remains high.

experiment in abstinence via enactment of the Eighteenth Amendment to the Constitution. Prohibition failed dismally, however, because many adults did not want to give up social drinking. Less extreme—and possibly more effective—approaches have relied on public service announcements that encourage responsible drinking. The "Know when to say when" ads that have run for the last several years are examples. In this case, the ads are sponsored by the alcohol industry. Other ads are focused less on moderate drinking and more on responsible drinking. The "Friends don't let friends drive drunk" ads fall into this category. Ads run in the 1970s focused on being a responsible host, emphasizing the importance of not pushing alcohol on guests and of having nonalcoholic alternatives at parties. A variety of school programs have also been designed to educate students about alcohol. Unfortunately, the effectiveness of these programs has rarely been evaluated.

Secondary-prevention programs target at-risk populations. Two particular at-risk populations for alcoholism are (1) offspring of alcoholic parents and (2) college students. Many therapists who work with alcoholic adults make it a point to meet at least once with family members, including children, to provide information about risk for alcoholism (Nye et al., 1999). Such interventions are informal, and we know little about their effectiveness, but at least they are a first step. Numerous universities have undertaken to educate students about the risk of alcohol and to encourage responsible drinking (Larimer et al., 1998). Often, these efforts are initiated or intensified after a particularly tragic alcohol-related incident, as illustrated in the well-publicized case history of Scott.

One Too Many

SCOTT

Scott was a talented and popular student—a freshman at M.I.T. But in September of 1997, his life ended because he drank beyond his limit while attending a fraternity function. With a BAL of 0.41%, he was already in a deep coma by the time the ambulance got him to the hospital. Three days later he died (Dabek, 1997). This tragedy prompted an immediate response. The Interfraternity Council unanimously passed a resolution canceling all fraternity events that would have served alcohol. M.I.T. president Charles M. Vest commissioned an investigation into the incident, examining both the immediate and the underlying causes. The Boston police looked into possible criminal responsibility for Scott's death. Within days, Dr. Vest announced a series of sweeping changes, which included plans to restrict the use of alcohol on campus, construction of more on-campus housing so that students, especially freshmen, would not be routinely living in fraternity housing, and the inauguration of a student/faculty seminar, headed by a Nobel laureate, on the problems of alcohol abuse on campus (Lane, 1997). These changes came too late to save Scott, but his name lives on in a scholarship endowed by the university.

Whether the steps taken by M.I.T. will discourage the kind of excessive drinking that led to Scott's death, and in the process discourage the kind of excessive drinking that can result in alcohol dependence in some students, is yet to be seen. Dozens of other universities have also examined their own drinking policies to determine what can be done to reduce the risks. Parties and drinking have been a part of college for a long time. It is unlikely that the functional equivalent of prohibition on campus will ever occur. Nevertheless, small reductions in the rate of alcohol abuse may be sufficient to reduce the number of students who go on to develop alcohol dependence.

Marlatt and his colleagues demonstrated that a brief intervention could significantly reduce alcohol abuse in college students. Let's look at their research more closely.

Examining the Evidence

Marlatt et al. (1998) implemented a brief, personalized intervention for college freshmen designed to motivate students to control their problem drinking. They obtained information from students about their drinking habits during the first trimester of college. Then they selected students who appeared to be problem drinkers, randomly assigning them to a treatment group or a control group. During the second trimester, the students in the treatment group were asked to track their drinking for two weeks prior to coming in for a feedback interview based on the information they provided earlier in the school year. The feedback interview was actually designed to provide motivational information about the student's drinking history, about the risks of excessive alcohol consumption, and about the effects of alcohol. The interviewers specifically avoided confrontations, which might have made students defensive. Instead, they sought to provide information that was individually tailored to the student's reported drinking pattern and how it compared to other students, allowing each student to draw his or her own conclusions. The investigators were able to contact 88% of their 456 participants six months, one year, and two years later to assess drinking history. They found that the drinking habits of those students who were given this motivational interview showed significantly less alcohol abuse than the drinking habits of the control sample of problem drinkers who did not receive the interview. Furthermore, this pattern showed stronger effects as time progressed. That is, the difference between these groups was larger at the one-year and two-year follow-ups than at the six-month follow-up. The treatment group still showed significantly more problem drinking than the typical college student, but the level of problem drinking was cut in half by the brief interview and

feedback session. This outcome certainly suggests that it is both practically and economically feasible to reduce problem drinking in college with a targeted intervention.

Prevention efforts have also been directed to general drug abuse. The government has been committed to producing public service announcements about the dangers of drugs and about programs available for those who are experiencing a drug problem. Some of these programs have been rather effective, whereas others have been less so (Wiliszowski et al., 1998). Some of these ads are memorable. In one, the announcer holds up an egg and says, "This is your brain." Smashing the egg in a frying pan, he adds, "This is your brain on drugs." And, as the egg sizzles and fries, he adds, "Any questions?" A recent ad, first aired during the 2002 Super Bowl, sought to capitalize on the increased patriotism following the attacks of September 11, 2001. It pointed out that drug proceeds fund many terrorist activities. It is not yet clear whether this approach will be effective. Other ad campaigns have been less memorable, but possibly more successful. For example, the ads

The best method of prevention is to decrease demand by teaching young children about the dangers of drugs. Parents can often influence their children's choices about drugs. Talking about drugs with your children is not easy, but there are resources available to help.

that tell parents that they really can influence their children's drug use has potential, because children do respond to consistent and supportive messages from parents. Government sources have produced pamphlets to help parents talk with their children about drugs. Not all the efforts have been directed at illicit drugs. Since the first "surgeon general's report" on smoking was issued in 1964, the government has sought to discourage smoking in a variety of ways. Some of these efforts have made a big difference, whereas others can only be described as failures, as discussed in the nearby Focus box.

Not every environmental intervention has proved to be successful. One of the best-known drug prevention programs is DARE, or Drug Abuse Resistance Education. The DARE program teaches children about drugs and seeks to provide them with the skills and attitudes that are thought to be necessary in resisting peer pressure to experiment with drugs. This program has been widely implemented across the country and has enjoyed widespread support from parents (Donnermeyer, 2000) and educators (Donnermeyer, 1998). The problem is that it is not particularly effective (Lynam et al., 1999). Students exposed to the program are

FOCUS · Government antismoking efforts

One of the most important government health initiatives of this century was the publication in 1964 of the surgeon general's report on smoking. This report called into question the tobacco industry's claims that smoking was safe. This was an eye opener for most Americans, who up until then had obtained their information about smoking from commercials, several of which included doctors extolling the health benefits of certain cigarette brands.

The early government efforts to discourage smoking involved mandating the inclusion of a warning label on each pack and funding and disseminating research on the potential risks of smoking. However, the surgeon general under President Reagan, C. Everett Koop, spearheaded a campaign to establish a "smoke-free society by 2000." Under his leadership, the risks of second-hand smoke led to increased regulations about where one could smoke. Smoking was banned in many public buildings, on domestic airline flights, and in designated sections of restaurants. Dr. Koop even suggested that smoking should be banned wherever children are present because of the unique risk that second-hand smoke holds for children. Under Dr. Koop's leadership, the rate of smoking dropped

significantly, the largest drop being among teenagers. There were still many smokers, but attitudes toward smoking had changed, and the credibility of the tobacco industry had been seriously challenged.

The more recent antismoking efforts under the Clinton administration provide a perfect example of how programs can easily backfire (Males, 1999). Whereas Koop was engaged in an all-out war on smoking, the Clinton administration focused almost exclusively on youth smoking, accepting that adults have a right to decide for themselves whether they will smoke. Sales to minors were banned, and the bans were enforced with sting operations designed to identify retailers who were selling to youths. Even the tobacco industry got behind this effort to keep cigarettes out of the hands of teenagers. Young people were portrayed as foolish pawns of tobacco industry advertising and peer pressure. Advertising aimed at youths, such as the infamous Joe Camel ads, were attacked and eventually banned. The results of these efforts were clear: Smoking generally increased, and it increased most sharply among teenagers (Males, 1999).

What went wrong? A social psychologist could easily have predicted the results of these efforts. Teenagers are striving to be adults, with the

rights and privileges that adults enjoy. When the official policy is that adults can decide whether they are going to smoke, many teens will seek to smoke as a right of passage into adulthood. Furthermore, portraying teens as immature and foolish is hardly an effective way to gain their respect and influence their behavior. Telling them that Joe Camel tricked them into smoking is insulting. Despite claims to the contrary, the data on advertising and rates of smoking among youth clearly demonstrate that advertising does *not* particularly influence young people. Between 1975 and 1992, the advertising budget for cigarettes increased over 300%, while the rate of teenage smoking fell 30%. Joe Camel was introduced in 1988 and appeared to have little effect on youth smoking. Advertising budgets began to fall in 1993 because of the Clinton administration's antismoking initiatives, and youth smoking rates immediately started climbing sharply. Good intentions, such as wanting to curb teenage smoking, do not ensure that a program will work. Teens were smoking less on their own, before any focused government effort to "discourage" teenage smoking. The recent efforts to curb teen smoking simply backfired.

no more or less likely than others to abuse drugs 10 years later. Nevertheless, DARE remains popular. There is no question that the program is well-meaning and that on paper it sounds like a great idea. However, the experience with DARE illustrates how important it is to evaluate programs for effectiveness early in order to prevent large expenditures for programs of questionable value.

OTHER TREATMENT ALTERNATIVES

Most treatments for drug abuse share the same basic idea—to prevent or stop the abuse—but there are exceptions to this model. For example, methadone maintenance does not attempt to stop the addiction to heroin but seeks to substitute for it addiction to a synthetic narcotic. The point is to provide ready access to this alternative substance in a clinic to avoid the secondary problems of infections, overdose, and crime to support addiction. This principle of reducing secondary problems is called **harm reduction.** Although it is not incompatible with efforts to reduce drug abuse through treatment or prevention, the harm reduction philosophy is often viewed as encouraging or condoning drug abuse (Reuter & MacCoun, 1995). Consequently, there is considerable resistance to the approach. For example, needle exchange programs designed to reduce the transmission of HIV infection are effectively blocked in most of the United States by laws designed to make drug abuse more difficult, such as requiring a prescription for purchasing needles (MacCoun, 1998). Yet such needle exchange programs clearly decrease risk of HIV infection.

Most treatment or prevention programs are evaluated in terms of the rate of drug abuse. This sets up an essentially dichotomous criterion with just two outcomes: The individual is simply either a user or a nonuser. The harm reduction philosophy recognizes that although all drug abuse may be problematic, a heavy drug user is creating more harm than a light drug user. Therefore, efforts to reduce or control consumption reduce the harmful consequences of drug use. The controlled-drinking approach that we discussed earlier follows this model. If extended to other drugs, this philosophy would argue that reducing or preventing the heavy use of drugs that is characteristic of addiction would reduce the total harm associated with drug abuse. Casual drug users are at much lower risk for disease

and other health consequences of heavy drug use, and they are much less likely to resort to crime to maintain their habit. Can such reductions be achieved? That is an empirical question, but merely asking it is considered almost heresy in today's politically charged environment surrounding drug abuse policy (MacCoun, 1998).

It is hard to argue against the position that the world would be better if there was no drug abuse. However, it is equally hard to argue against the position that reducing the harm associated with drug abuse is a worthwhile objective. Yet many would argue against this latter proposition by maintaining that reducing the harm of drug abuse increases its likelihood. This is a legitimate concern that should be included in the empirical evaluation of any harm reduction program. For example, does providing clean needles in exchange for used needles increase the number of people who abuse drugs? This question is no more difficult to answer than the question of whether the needle exchange reduces the prevalence of HIV transmission. Some harm reduction policies may prove to be counterproductive. But it would be a real mistake to ignore these approaches, which have the potential of reducing some of the problems associated with drug abuse.

Check Yourself 14.7

Treating Drug Abuse

1. Describe the biological treatments for drug abuse and dependence.
2. What psychological approaches are effective in treating alcoholism?
3. How can environmental interventions reduce drug abuse?
4. What is the controversy regarding controlled drinking as a treatment goal?
5. Describe the philosophy behind AA.
6. Explain the principle of harm reduction.

Ponder this . . .   *Given the tremendous social costs of drug abuse, effective treatment and prevention are critical. Focusing on prevention, brainstorm ways in which one could prevent specific types of drug abuse. Concentrate on how you would evaluate a prevention program to see whether it is effective.*

---

harm reduction   The principle of reducing the secondary problems spawned by substance abuse, such as infections, overdosing, and commission of crimes to support the habit.

SUMMARY

SUBSTANCE ABUSE AND DEPENDENCE

- Substance dependence is characterized by at least three of the following: tolerance, withdrawal, excessive use, desire to reduce consumption, large blocks of time consumed by the substance use, role dysfunctions, and continued use despite recurrent substance-related problems.

- One or more of the following defines substance abuse: failures to meet role obligations as a consequence of the substance use, use in physically hazardous situations, legal problems due to use of the substance, and continued use despite recurrent substance-related problems.

- Abused drugs include sedatives, narcotics, stimulants, and hallucinogens.

SEDATIVES

- In the United States, 20% of males and 8% of females qualify for the diagnosis of alcohol dependence. The rates are especially high in college students. There are substantial ethnic differences in the rates of alcohol abuse and dependence.

- Alcohol is a central nervous system depressant. At low BAL levels, alcohol releases inhibitions and reduces anxiety, but at high levels, it disrupts coordination and reaction time and can even lead to death. Many of the presumed effects of alcohol appear to be the result of expectations concerning how alcohol affects people rather than direct effects of alcohol.

- The chronic heavy use of alcohol can damage the gastrointestinal, cardiovascular, cerebrovascular, and nervous systems. In pregnant mothers, it can cause severe and permanent damage to a fetus. Finally, it can disrupt and even destroy relationships.

- Barbiturates are synthetic sedatives that were once used extensively to calm individuals or as sleeping pills. They are used less frequently now because they can be addictive, because the risk of accidental overdose is high, and because less hazardous prescription drugs have been developed.

- Those being treated for anxiety may abuse benzodiazepines.

NARCOTICS

- Narcotics are drugs that are derived from the poppy flower and that induce sleep and ease pain. The most widely abused narcotics are heroin and morphine. Narcotics produce a rush, followed by a prolonged period of pleasant lethargy. Withdrawal symptoms can be quite unpleasant.

STIMULANTS

- Stimulants arouse the central and autonomic nervous systems, thereby making the person more alert and energized.

- Nicotine is a complex drug that does not fit neatly into any one class. It is delivered through smoking cigarettes, which makes it one of the most dangerous drugs, accounting for more deaths than all other drugs combined.

- Amphetamines are synthetic stimulants that were initially used to fight off drowsiness and to curb appetite.

- Cocaine is a widely abused stimulant that can be snorted, injected, or smoked. It is most addictive when it is injected or is smoked as a white powder called crack.

HALLUCINOGENS

- Marijuana was the drug of choice among college students during the 1960s and 1970s and is still widely abused. It produces rapid intoxication, which lasts a few hours. It is less toxic to the CNS than alcohol.

- Psychedelics (LSD, mescaline, PCP, and psilocybin) became popular during the counterculture movement of the 1960s. Use of these drugs had been dropping for years but has recently started to increase again.

THEORIES OF DRUG ABUSE

- Genes play a role in alcoholism, although their role is stronger in men than in women. Alcoholism is genetically heterogeneous. Even among those genetically predisposed to alcoholism, there must be a period of heavy alcohol use to trigger dependence. Several sociocultural factors have been implicated in alcoholism, including ethnicity, age, sex, and social class.

- Addictive drugs disturb the homeostasis of the body and trigger compensatory responses that result in tolerance and withdrawal symptoms.

- Any factor that contributes to either trying drugs or finding them reinforcing increases the likelihood that there will be sufficient exposure to cause addiction.

- A variety of sociocultural factors are associated with drug abuse, especially cultural, peer, and family influences.

TREATING DRUG ABUSE

- Biological treatments for drug addiction include detoxification, drug treatment for withdrawal effects, and drug substitution.

- Behavioral therapy, relapse prevention, and controlled-drinking approaches have demonstrated their effectiveness with drug abuse, usually in conjunction with biological treatments.

- Sociocultural approaches have focused on mutual-help groups (such as AA) and community residential treatment programs. Government programs have also attempted to reduce drug abuse through education and prevention.

- The controversial area of harm reduction seeks to find ways to minimize the negative consequences of drug abuse.

 ## KEY TERMS

addiction　(435)
Alcoholics Anonymous, or AA　(466)
alcoholism　(438)
amphetamines　(450)
Antabuse　(463)
balanced placebo design　(443)
barbiturates　(447)
behavioral self-control training　(464)
blood alcohol level, or BAL　(441)
cannabis　(452)
central nervous system depressant　(442)
cirrhosis　(445)
cocaine　(451)
codependency　(462)
congeners　(442)
contingency management　(465)
controlled drinking　(465)
delirium tremens, or the DTs　(445)
detoxification　(463)
expectancy effects　(443)
Ecstasy　(450)
fetal alcohol syndrome　(446)
hallucinogens　(437)
harm reduction　(471)
hashish　(452)

heroin　(437)
hypnotic drugs　(437)
LSD　(455)
marijuana　(452)
mescaline　(455)
metabolic effects　(441)
methadone maintenance　(464)
mutual-help groups　(466)
narcotics　(437)
nicotine　(449)
opiates　(437)
opioids　(437)
PCP, or angel dust　(455)
polydrug abusers　(437)
psilocybin　(455)
psychedelics　(437)
relapse prevention　(465)
sedatives　(436)
sensitization　(451)
stimulants　(437)
substance abuse　(436)
substance dependence　(435)
tension-reduction hypothesis　(459)
tolerance　(435)
withdrawal　(435)

 ## SUGGESTED READINGS

Males, M. A. (1999). *Smoked: Why Joe Camel is still smiling.* Monroe, ME: Common Courage Press. This paperback argues that the tobacco industry is winning the fight against antismoking forces, despite its recent losses in court.

Regan, C. (2001). *Intoxicating minds: How drugs work.* New York: Columbia University Press. This is a readable description of how drugs affect the brain and behavior.

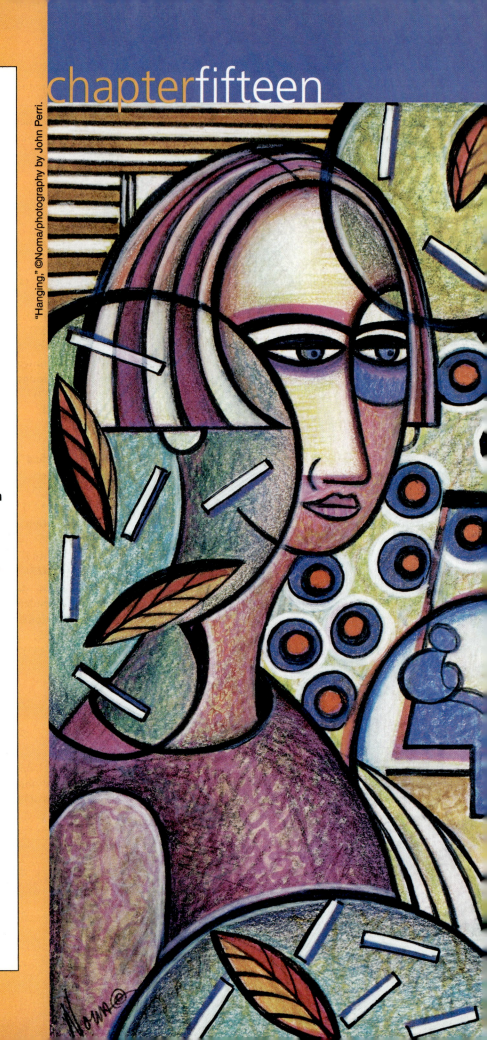

"Hanging," ©Noma/photography by John Perri.

chapterfifteen

Cognitive and Dissociative Disorders

A Devastating Accident

DARRYL

Darryl had worked in construction for almost 20 years. It had always provided his family with a great living until, at the age of 37, he was struck at work by a wooden pole that had fallen three floors. The blow broke his neck, and the doctors thought that he would be paralyzed. Fortunately, the doctors were able to stabilize his spine sufficiently to avoid paralysis. However, it soon became clear that Darryl had sustained other injuries, including damage to his brain. He had difficulty remembering things, and he could no longer interpret diagrams. In frustration, he threw his daughter's new tricycle against the basement wall after three hours of unsuccessful efforts to assemble it. Destroying his daughter's present was only one of several violent outbursts after his accident—outbursts that became so frequent that his wife sought a separation, then a divorce, then sole custody of their children, and finally a restraining order. Although Darryl previously had been mild-mannered and loving, since the accident he was a different person.

A Shell of His Former Self

BURT

Burt was a successful businessman, a loving father and husband, and an active community leader. He retired early, intending to travel the country with his wife, but he soon settled into a routine of having breakfast with his retired friends, playing a little golf, watching TV, and reading. His wife and son noticed he was a bit forgetful and moody, but they attributed it to his diabetes. However, the symptoms worsened until he was diagnosed with Alzheimer's disease at age 74 and a year later required nursing home care. During the first few months at the nursing home, he would lose control and scream at his wife, who spent several hours at his side every day. Ten minutes later he would cry uncontrollably, realizing what he had done and believing that his wife could never forgive him. His confusion intensified to the point where he would get lost in the nursing home, a relatively small, one-story building. He would forget to dress before going to meals and could not remember the names of the staff. By this time, he rarely knew what day of the week or even what month it was. Often he failed to recognize his wife of over 45 years. The last few months of his life, he had no idea who anyone was. By the time he died quietly in his sleep, he could no longer take care of even his basic needs.

Battling Inner Demons

JAMIE

It did not happen often, but when it did, it always shocked her therapist. Jamie, who generally was passive and weepy, would suddenly bolt upright and express her anger at what she had been forced to endure. The first time lasted only a few seconds, leaving her therapist stunned and Jamie confused by his expression. It was not until the third such transformation that this forceful side of Jamie introduced herself as Paula. Whereas Jamie was passive, Paula was bold and aggressive. Paula seemed to know everything there was to know about Jamie, but Jamie apparently knew nothing about Paula, including the fact that Paula existed. Paula told Jamie's therapist that she rarely introduced herself to people, preferring to do her thing and leave, letting Jamie take the blame.

This chapter covers both cognitive and dissociative disorders. **Cognitive disorders** are characterized by dysfunctions of thought and memory that are known to be the result of specific damage to the brain. For example, a person may be confused and unable to think clearly or unable to remember such basic information as the name of a loved one. **Dissociative disorders** are characterized by an emotional and/or cognitive separation from one's core identity. For example, people who have been subjected to severe stress may be unable to remember elements of the stressful situation and, in extreme cases, may not even remember who they are.

No organ of the body is more complex or more critical to human functioning than the brain. It controls not only thought and behavior but also perception, memory, emotion, and the complex behavioral patterns that make up personality. When it operates properly, it is an incredible wonder of nature. When it does not, it can have devastating effects on individuals and their families. Darryl's brain was damaged in an industrial accident. On the surface, it looked as though little had changed, but his wife noticed personality changes so dramatic that she could no longer live with him or even trust him with their children. A terrible disease destroyed Burt's brain—and destroyed Burt in the process. All that remained was a shell that could breathe but could no longer think or feel. Jamie showed a very different constellation of symptoms. Her brain was apparently intact, but her personality and sense of identity were not. She appeared to have two distinct personalities—one that was shy and helpless and a second that was brash and assertive. This chapter covers three cognitive disorders (delirium, dementia, and amnestic disorders) and four dissociative disorders (depersonalization disorder, dissociative amnesia, dissociative fugue, and dissociative identity disorder).

DELIRIUM

The DSM defines three patterns of brain dysfunctions: delirium, dementia, and amnestic disorders. They represent neurological syndromes with biological causes that are diagnosed on Axis III. Remember from Chapter 2 that Axis III is used to code medical conditions. This section covers delirium, and the next two sections cover dementia and amnestic disorders, respectively. However, this section begins with a brief overview of the brain and brain functioning.

cognitive disorders Characterized by dysfunctions of thought and memory that are known to be the result of specific damage to the brain.

dissociative disorders Characterized by emotional and/or cognitive separation from one's core identity.

THE BRAIN
Evolutionary Impact

The human brain is perhaps the single most impressive evolutionary achievement. Weighing about as much as a notebook computer, it packs more memory, computational power, flexibility, and usefulness than even the fastest supercomputer in existence. The brain is often compared to the computer because both take input, make computations, access memory, and produce output. But comparing the human brain and the modern computer leaves one more impressed with the differences than with the similarities, as shown in Table 15.1.

One thing that the brain has in common with computers is that different parts perform different operations. Consequently, damage to a specific part of the brain is usually associated with a specific pattern of functional deficits. We first discussed this concept in Chapter 4. For example, the control of motor activities is in the frontal lobe. Furthermore, the control of the right side of the body is on the left side of the brain, and vice versa. Therefore, if someone is paralyzed on the right side of the body, one can infer that the brain damage occurred in the left frontal lobe.

Some infections are toxic to brain tissue, causing considerable brain damage. High fevers can cause delirium and, if not controlled quickly, may cause brain damage.

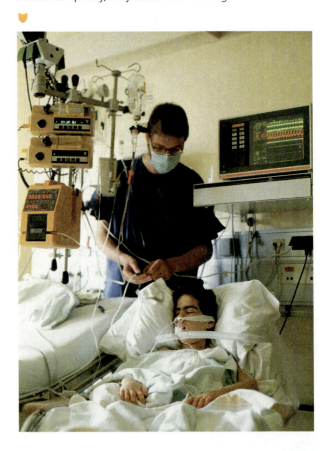

[TABLE 15.1] The Computer versus the Brain

The human brain and the computer are often compared, but as the following comparison shows, they really are substantially different.

FACTOR	THE BRAIN	THE COMPUTER
Composition	Living tissue (mostly water)	Silicone (mostly sand)
Speed of operation	Relatively slow and not getting any faster	Very fast and doubling in speed every 18 months
Color	Gray with a lot of white matter for contrast	Beige or black, although a few now sport bright colors
Method of operation	Parallel processing (computing thousands of aspects of a problem separately for optimal performance)	Serial processing (doing one thing at a time, but doing it very fast), although some specialized computers have been programmed to do parallel processing of complex problems
Type of processing	Stochastic (does not always come up with the same answer to the same question)	Deterministic (always produces the same answer to the same question, or at least that is what it is supposed to do)
What happens when there is not enough time to find the best solution?	The person acts when an action is required, although it may not always be an optimal choice.	Nothing
Computational performance	Can add two 1-digit numbers in about a second	Measured in billions of operations per second
Memory performance	Extensive and flexible, but not always dependable; on the other hand, it does not have a hard drive that crashes, losing everything in the process	Remembers everything but is subject to catastrophic failures from which recovery is difficult or impossible; upgradeable and expandable
Recognition	Remarkably efficient and flexible; can accurately recognize words spoken by people with a variety of accents; can read handwriting regardless of the person's style; can recognize a person even if basic features, such as a hairstyle, are changed.	Unless you are an alphanumeric character coded as zeros and ones, rather poor recognition; it took over 40 years of research to get reasonably accurate recognition of voice and handwriting; facial recognition is improving, and it has been taught to recognize eyeballs and fingerprints well
Problem-solving ability	Flexible, adaptable, with a wide range of functioning; tendency to recognize poor solutions	Narrow, focused, fast; if not programmed carefully, it is perfectly happy with a ridiculous solution
Operating temperature	−40° F to +120° F	+30° F to +100° F
Resistance to damage	Able to withstand loss of random neurons for years with only a small loss in performance; cushioned better against damage while operating than the computer was in the shipping box	Subject to catastrophic failure from impact, moisture, or temperature extremes
Response to specific damage	Loss of specific functioning; emotional reaction is likely; efforts at compensation; repair impossible	It stops dead; bad component can be replaced—even upgraded
Reproduction	Sex; the new unit is never identical to earlier units	Factory assembled, sometimes by robots; each unit is manufactured to precise specifications
Emotional capacity	A mechanism for changing either the focus of the brain or the capacity of the body	Hal (from *2001: A Space Odyssey*) notwithstanding, computers have no equivalent of emotional arousal

Figure 15.1 on pages 478 and 479 illustrates about a dozen critical brain regions and lists the disability likely to be associated with damage to each.

delirium   Dramatic and widespread disruption in normal cognitive functioning.

SYMPTOMS OF DELIRIUM

Delirium is characterized by dramatic and widespread disruption in normal cognitive functioning. There is typically a loss of ability to focus attention, think clearly and rationally, perceive surroundings accurately, form new memories, and recall existing memories. There may even

[FIGURE 15.1]
Brain/Behavior Relationships

Many of the functions of the brain are localized to specific regions as shown in this figure and table.

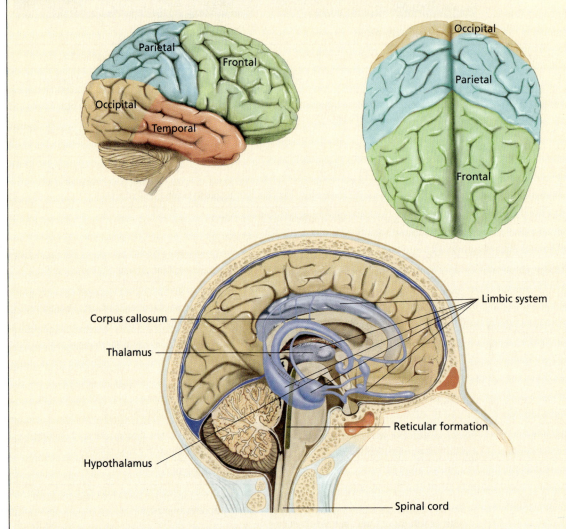

SOURCE: *Fig. 16-1 & Table 16-1 (pp. 574–575) from* Psychological Testing and Assessment: An Introduction to Tests and Measurement *by R. J. Cohen. Copyright © 1992. Reprinted by permission of The McGraw-Hill Companies.*

be psychotic symptomatology, such as hallucinations. The delirious person is typically agitated, sometimes to the point of being assaultive. Some of these features can be seen in the case of Rhonda.

It Wasn't Just a Bump

RHONDA

It was like something out of a slapstick comedy. Carrying a basket of clothes up the hardwood steps, Rhonda slipped on a sock that had fallen from the basket and tumbled down half a flight of stairs. Her knee and ankle took a beating, and she hit the back of her head on the floor. Her mother took her to the emergency room, where she was X-rayed and sent home with instructions to put ice on the knee and ankle. Four hours later, her headache intensified, she started talking nonsense, and she became agitated. Her mother called the ER to report the change and was told to bring her in immediately. By the time they reached the hospital 15 minutes later, Rhonda was completely incoherent. The nurses rushed her into X-ray, but before the X-ray could be developed, Rhonda had a seizure. She was rushed into surgery, where the neurosurgeon took one look at the X-ray and immediately drilled a hole near the back of her head to relieve the pressure from the bleeding.

[FIGURE 15.1]
Continued

SITE	CHARACTERISTIC
Temporal lobes	These lobes contain auditory reception areas as well as certain areas for the processing of visual information. Damage to the temporal lobe may affect sound discrimination, recognition, and comprehension; music appreciation; voice recognition; and auditory or visual memory storage.
Occipital lobes	These lobes contain visual reception areas. Damage to this area could result in blindness to all or part of the visual field or deficits in object recognition, visual scanning, visual integration of symbols into wholes, and recall of visual imagery.
Patietal lobes	These lobes contain reception areas for the sense of touch and for the sense of bodily position. Damage to this area may result in deficits in the sense of touch, disorganization, and distorted self-perception.
Frontal lobes	These lobes are involved in ordering information and sorting stimuli. Concentration and attention, abstract-thinking ability, concept-formation ability, foresight, problem-solving ability, speech, as well as gross and fine motor ability may be affected by damage to the frontal lobes.
Thalamus	The thalamus is a kind of communications relay station for all sensory information being transmitted to the cerebral cortex. Damage to the thalamus may result in altered states of arousal, memory defects, speech deficits, apathy, and disorientation.
Hypothalamus	The hypothalamus is involved in the regulation of bodily functions such as eating, drinking, body temperature, sexual behavior, and emotion. It is sensitive to changes in environment that call for a "fight or flight" response from the organism. Damage to it may elicit a variety of symptoms ranging from uncontrolled eating or drinking to mild alterations of mood states.
Reticular formation	In the core of the brain stem, the reticular formation contains fibers en route to and from the cortex. Because stimulation to this area can cause a sleeping organism to awaken and cause an awake organism to become even more alert, it is sometimes referred to as the *reticular activating system*. Damage to this area can cause the organism to sleep for long periods of time.
Limbic system	Composed of the amygdala, the cingulate cortex, the hippocampus, and the septal areas of the brain, the limbic system plays an integral part in the expression of emotions. Damage to this area may profoundly affect emotional behavior.
Spinal cord	Many reflexes necessary for survival (such as withdrawing from a hot surface) are carried out at the level of the spinal cord. In addition to its role in reflex activity, the spinal cord plays an integral part in the coordination of motor movements. Spinal cord injuries may result in various degrees of paralysis or other motor difficulties.

Although delirium can occur in anyone, including young adults like Rhonda, it is most common in elderly individuals who have been hospitalized for medical conditions; in fact, it affects between 10% and 15% of this group (APA, 2000). Whether the elderly are more susceptible to delirium because of their age and the cumulative effect of neuronal loss over a lifetime, or whether the diseases that are likely to lead to hospitalization in this age group are more likely to cause delirium is still a matter of debate (Aiken, 1995). Delirium is also common in young children with high fevers (104°F and above). In the case of Rhonda, the delirium was caused by a *subdural hematoma*—that is, the fall ruptured a blood vessel in the membrane that cov-

ers the brain, and the bleeding was putting pressure on the brain. Draining the blood relieved that pressure before brain damage occurred, and consequently, Rhonda made a complete recovery.

CAUSES OF DELIRIUM

In most cases, delirium is due to some form of metabolic disturbance. It is usually a temporary condition, but it can lead to permanent dysfunction, including death. Delirium usually develops rapidly—over hours or at most days. It represents a complete breakdown of the functioning of the central nervous system. It is not unusual for someone in a delirious state to slip into a coma. Delirium may be caused by a number of conditions, such as head injuries, substance abuse or withdrawal, infections, metabolic disorders, fluid or electrolyte imbalances, postoperative states, a vitamin B_1 deficiency, liver or kidney disease, or excessive pressure on the brain. These are all medical conditions—some temporary and others permanent. In some cases, such as drug intoxication, drug withdrawal, and postoperative states, the conditions resolve themselves. In other cases, the cause can be diagnosed and treated, such as with infections, vitamin B_1 deficiency, and pressure on the brain.

TREATING AND PREVENTING DELIRIUM

Treating delirium involves diagnosing its cause and taking the appropriate medical action. For example, someone who is delirious after spending an afternoon playing golf in hot weather is most likely to be suffering from dehydration or sunstroke. Cooling the body and replacing critical body fluids and salts often reduces the delirium quickly. In general, treating delirium rapidly is important, because many of the processes that cause it can also cause permanent brain damage if left untreated (Noback et al., 1991).

Delirium in hospitalized elderly individuals is often due to such a preventable condition as dehydration or sleep deprivation (APA, 2000). These problems are less common in younger people who are hospitalized, but the elderly are more prone to such problems and therefore require more careful medical management to prevent them. Research has shown that an aggressive effort to manage such complicating factors in older hospitalized individuals can significantly reduce delirium (Inouye et al., 1999).

Anyone can become delirious under the right circumstances. Understanding those circumstances can lead to better management of one's health. Although delirium is usually reversible, it nevertheless indicates that a person's brain does not have the balance necessary for normal functioning. For example, delirium can be the result of acute intoxication or withdrawal from prolonged use of certain intoxicating substances, such as alcohol. Vitamin deficien-

cies caused by poor diet in substance abusers can also trigger delirium, as in the case of Korsakoff's syndrome (see Chapter 14). The obvious preventative strategy is to reduce excessive consumption and take steps to ensure proper nutrition even in those who continue their substance abuse. Some delirium may not be preventable but can be managed. For example, the delirium common after surgery is due to the combination of anesthesia and the intense pain of surgery. The anesthesia will wear off quickly, but until it does, patients are monitored carefully to prevent harm. Effective pain management can further reduce the delirium.

Check Yourself 15.1

Delirium

1. What is delirium and what causes it?
2. How does one treat delirium?

Ponder this . . . *At one level, the brain is an incredibly effective and versatile computer, but at another level, it falls short. For example, would you tolerate a computer that gave different answers each time you asked a given question? Looking at Table 15.1, consider what things computer engineers might learn from the operation of the brain and how that information might improve electronic computer functioning.*

DEMENTIA

Dementia is characterized by multiple cognitive deficits that are due to one or more medical problems. There is nearly always memory impairment, but there are likely to be other symptoms, such as aphasia, apraxia, agnosia, and a disturbance in executive functioning. **Aphasia** is a deficit in the ability to understand or use language. For example, the person may experience serious difficulties in finding the right word to express an idea or, in severe cases, may not be able to use language at all. **Apraxia** is a deficit in the ability to carry out familiar activities or use familiar objects. For example, the person may not be able to copy simple figures or use such familiar objects as a door key. **Agnosia** is a deficit in sensory perception and recognition. For example, the person may be unable to recognize objects by feel or even by sight. Finally, **executive functioning** is the coordination of behavior to achieve a goal. For example, making dinner requires a series of steps that must be coordinated. The steps must be completed in a specific order and with a specific timing. Putting the dinner in the oven does little good if one has forgotten to turn the oven on.

dementia Multiple cognitive deficits that are due to one or more medical problems.

aphasia A deficit in the ability to understand or use language.

apraxia A deficit in the ability to carry out familiar activities or to use familiar objects.

agnosia A deficit in sensory perception and recognition.

executive functioning The coordination of behavior to achieve a goal.

presenile dementia Dementia at an early age brought on by disease processes that accelerate the natural death of brain cells.

Alzheimer's disease A progressive and terminal presenile dementia.

Dementia is usually the result of generalized brain deterioration due either to natural causes, such as aging, or to a degenerative disease, such as Alzheimer's. Unlike delirium, which tends to have a dramatic and rapid onset, dementia often has a slow, barely perceptible onset. There follows a gradual decline in cognitive abilities, often to the point where the person is unable to function.

Evolutionary Impact

In theory at least, dementia is the inevitable fate of anyone who lives long enough—a process known as *senile dementia* or *senility.* The gradual death of brain cells that everyone experiences over a lifetime eventually causes rapid cognitive decline. Virtually all of those few people healthy enough to reach the age of 100 show dementia, and in most it is severe (Powell, 1994). Of course, many people die long before their brains deteriorate to this point. However, some people show dementia earlier than expected as a result of disease processes that accelerate the natural death of brain cells. These conditions are called **presenile dementias.** You might wonder why brain cells are not replaced, given that skin and blood cells are replaced every few weeks. Skin and blood cells are essentially commodities—that is, they are all alike. In contrast, neurons and their connections to other neurons are modified as the result of experience, so to replace them would be to lose the information that is coded in these modifications. It would be equivalent to getting a new hard drive on your computer every few weeks, but never being able to transfer the old information to the new hard drive. The ability to learn from experience and retain that learning for years provides an organism with substantial selective advantage in the struggle to survive. Therefore, what has evolved is a stable brain, with a massive interconnection of neurons. The interconnection of neurons makes the brain capable of functioning despite steady losses of neurons over a person's lifetime.

This section covers Alzheimer's disease, other causes of dementia, treatment for dementia, and its prevention.

DEMENTIA OF THE ALZHEIMER'S TYPE

The most common presenile dementia is **Alzheimer's disease,** which was first described by the German physician Alois Alzheimer in 1907. Alzheimer's disease is a progressive and terminal illness that accounts for roughly half of all the dementias in developed countries (Jacques & Jackson, 2000; Muir, 1997). Although Alzheimer's is a presenile dementia, it still occurs in older people. The rate of Alzheimer's in the population is increasing, largely because people are living longer and therefore are living well into the age when the risk is greatest. Figure 15.2 illustrates the dramatic rise in the number of elderly people—those people at greatest risk for Alzheimer's.

Although Alzheimer's may occasionally develop in middle-aged people, it is most likely to develop in the elderly. The rates rise dramatically with increasing age. For example, less than 1% of 65-year-olds have the disease, whereas the rates are 12%, 22%, and 38% at ages 85, 90, and 95, respectively (APA, 2000). However, more recent data suggest that the incidence of Alzheimer's disease

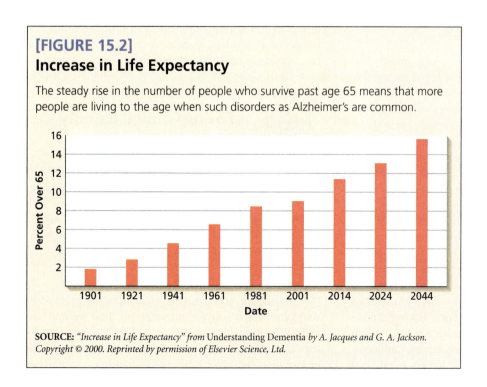

[FIGURE 15.2]

Increase in Life Expectancy

The steady rise in the number of people who survive past age 65 means that more people are living to the age when such disorders as Alzheimer's are common.

SOURCE: *"Increase in Life Expectancy" from* Understanding Dementia *by A. Jacques and G. A. Jackson. Copyright © 2000. Reprinted by permission of Elsevier Science, Ltd.*

No one, even former presidents, is immune from the ravages of Alzheimer's disease. President Reagan's willingness to make his condition public soon after the diagnosis helped to reduce the stigma and social isolation that many families feel when a member has Alzheimer's.

plateaus and may even drop slightly for people in their 90s, perhaps because the majority of people at risk for the disease have already developed it and died by then (Miech et al., 2002). It is estimated that the prevalence of Alzheimer's in developed countries will nearly triple in the next 50 years because of the aging of the population (Katzman & Fox, 1999). It is more common in women than men, and this difference is not due solely to the fact that women tend to live longer than men. At each age group, the rates for women are about 20% greater than the rates for men (APA, 2000). Alzheimer's is also more common in blacks than in whites (Baker, 2000; Froehlich et al., 2001). It is the most common cause of dementia in Great Britain, North America, and Scandinavia, whereas vascular dementia (to be covered in the next section) accounts for the majority of dementia in Japan (Jorm, 1991) and in African Americans (Farrer, 2001; Froehlich et al., 2001). The estimated annual cost for the care of those with Alzheimer's is $112 billion in the United States, $3.4 billion in Canada, $4.7 billion in England, $12 billion in France, and $52 billion in Italy, and those costs are expected to double or triple in the next 50 years (Katzman & Fox, 1999).

Symptoms and Course. It is easy to overlook the early stages of Alzheimer's, because the symptoms are just exaggerations of normal aging. Mild memory problems and attentional lapses are typically the first symptoms. Later, language problems, especially difficulty finding words, become more common—that is, people may consistently have trouble remembering the word they want to use. These symptoms gradually increase in both frequency and intensity until people forget critical information, such as appointments, directions, and the names of people close to them. By this point, the ability to carry out basic tasks, such as fixing a simple meal, cleaning the house, or finding one's way to the store, may be severely compromised. Most people with Alzheimer's eventually are unable to care for themselves and become more than their families can handle, thus requiring nursing home care (Knopman et al., 1999). There are often personality changes, which may include hypersexuality, paranoia, and aggression (Miesen, 1999). Burt, who was one of the cases that opened this chapter, initially showed subtle symptoms that were barely noticed. By the time he required nursing home care, he was showing dramatic personality changes and rapid cognitive decline.

Several psychological measures can be used to quantify the decline in cognitive functioning, but the one used most often is the mental status examination. The **mental status examination** consists of a series of observations and questions that probe a person's level of functioning. Table 15.2 summarizes the elements of a typical mental status examination. It is semi-standardized in that there is a list of variables that are to be assessed, but the exact manner in which they are assessed varies. Rather than provide a score, the physician or psychologist provides a brief description of the person in a narrative, as in the following evaluation of a nursing home patient's mental status.

Losing Ground Rapidly

CLARA

Patient's dress is sloppy; grooming incomplete. Sitting quietly in a daze. Oriented to person, but not place or time. Moderately depressed and anxious. Ideas of reference, but no delusions or hallucinations. Speech is slowed and vacuous. Generally unresponsive to questions and unable to concentrate. Affect is blunted. Information, computations, and serial sevens are poor. Unable to remember objects or recent events. Insight is poor. Judgment is fair.

As you can see, many of the comments are understandable even to a layperson, whereas others seem to be a code. What this physician noticed is that Clara was not taking care of herself; as people become more demented, their grooming deteriorates. Clara was also unresponsive to her

[TABLE 15.2] The Mental Status Examination

The Mental Status Examination is a measure of mental functioning and awareness. Although not formally standardized, most mental status examinations touch on most of the following items.

Observations (some possible descriptions are given in parentheses)

Dress (disheveled, inappropriate, flamboyant)

Grooming (properly bathed, hair combed, teeth brushed)

Demeanor (apathetic, impulsive, anxious, suspicious)

Mood (sad, angry, irritable, jocular)

Affect (blunted, flat, labile, unresponsive)

Speech and language (mute, stuttering, pressured, slowed, fluid aphasia, echolalia)

Psychomotor behavior (slowed, stereotypic movements, compulsions, hyperactive, gait abnormalities)

Neuropsychiatric Evaluation

Thought form (tangential, flight of ideas, loose associations)

Thought content (delusions, obsessions, intrusive ideas, derealization)

Perception (hallucinations, illusions)

Mental Functioning

Orientation (person, place, and time)

Attention (alertness, arousal, concentration)

Language (reading, comprehension, repetition, speaking)

Calculations (arithmetic, serial sevens)

Information

Abstraction (similarities {In what way are an apple and a banana alike?}, proverbs {What does this saying mean? "Let sleeping dogs lie."})

Visuospacial (copying figures, drawing simple figures, recognizing objects)

Judgment and insight

---

environment. She could give her name (oriented to person) but did not know where she was or what day of the week it was (not oriented to place or time). She displayed signs of depression and anxiety in her facial expressions, her tone of voice, and the content of her speech. She had a vague feeling that people were talking about her (ideas of reference) but denied experiencing hallucinations or delusions. She talked unusually slowly, and she did not seem to be saying anything of consequence. For example, her response to the question "What do you think about the weather?" was "It all depends on how you look at it. It is better when one knows how it should be." Besides being nonresponsive to the question, these two sentences communicate nothing. This kind of vacuous speech is common during later stages of dementia. Clara appeared distracted in that she asked the doctor to repeat questions several times. However, to interpret this as a psychological symptom, one has to rule out hearing problems, which are common in the elderly (Kreeger et al., 1995). Clara showed little emotion. She did not know such simple facts as who the president was or how many days there are in a year (information was poor), nor could she do simple arithmetic (12 + 8; 9 – 6) or the more complicated counting backwards by 7 from 100 (serial sevens). She also could not remember three objects, even after the doctor repeated them several times for her, nor could she remember what she had had for breakfast. She apparently had little idea that her cognitive skills had dramatically deteriorated (poor insight). Finally, the doctor estimated that her judgment was fair, suggesting that he felt that Clara was unlikely to do things that could be harmful. Frankly, however, this is as much a guess as anything, because Clara was unable to provide sufficient information on which to make such a determination. This woman raised three kids and just four years earlier managed a 12-person office but now she barely knows her own name.

This brief mental status examination of Clara illustrates many of the characteristics of Alzheimer's dementia. Clara's cognitive abilities have been deteriorating for about five years. Initially she was well aware of her cognitive decline, but her insight decreased as her cognitive decline worsened. She now has little awareness of what is happening to her or even of where she is. Her grooming has deteriorated dramatically over the past year. Grooming problems also occur in severe psychiatric disorders, such as schizophrenia. Nevertheless, they are a good indication of the severity of dementia. It is impossible to know a person's thoughts, but the fact that Clara stares blankly into space for extended periods, almost never initiates a conversation, and can talk with someone for several minutes without saying anything other than clichés suggests that she no longer has meaningful thoughts that she wishes to communicate to others. In the next few months, she will probably become virtually mute, and her facial expressions will suggest that she is almost totally unresponsive to the environment. This is a terrible thing for a loved one to watch; it is essentially death in slow motion.

Causes. Scientists have discovered the proximal cause of the cognitive deterioration in Alzheimer's, although it is less clear what the distal cause is. The brain cells of people who have Alzheimer's are destroyed by a combination of neurofibrillary tangles and senile plaques. **Neurofibrillary tangles** are proteins that are so called because they are twisted

· ·

mental status examination   A series of observations and questions that probe a person's level of functioning.

neurofibrillary tangles   Tangles of proteins that form in neurons as people age. Their formation in excessive numbers contributes to the destruction of brain cells in Alzheimer's disease.

Alzheimer's disease attacks and destroys neurons. The neurofibrillary tangles (blue-green formations) and senile plaques (black disks) responsible for this accelerated neuron death are shown here.

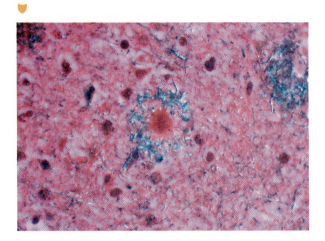

into something that looks like a tangled mess. They form normally in neurons as one ages, but in Alzheimer's disease the number of such tangles is extreme. **Senile plaques** are β-amyloid protein deposits that resemble disks. They form between neurons and interfere with neuronal communication, thus increasing the likelihood that affected neurons will die. Senile plaques are also a normal part of aging, but the rate of formation of these plaques in Alzheimer's disease is several times higher than normal. The neurofibrillary tangles and senile plaques do not appear to form randomly in the brain but, rather, are overrepresented in the hippocampus and those regions of the cerebral cortex most involved in thought processes (Murialdo et al., 2000). This distribution accounts for the dramatic memory losses that occur while such functions as walking remain relatively intact. Brain regions associated with movement—the motor cortex, cerebellum, and sensory and motor pathways—are less affected (Lavretsky et al., 1998). Traditionally, the definitive diagnosis of Alzheimer's has had to await an autopsy to determine whether these tangles and plaques were present. However, a diagnosis based on the combination of symptoms of dementia, especially prominent memory losses, and a ruling out of other likely causes of the dementia is remarkably accurate (Burns, 1991; Gearing et al., 1995).

Although the tangles and plaques are the fingerprint of Alzheimer's, the real question is why these destructive deposits form. The answer to this question has proved elusive. There is probably more than one cause for these deposits. A single dominant gene on any one of three different chromosomes (1, 14, and 21) appears capable of triggering early-onset Alzheimer's (Henderson, 1999).

senile plaques β-amyloid protein deposits, resembling disks, that form between neurons and interfere with neuronal communication.

However, the early-onset form of Alzheimer's, which usually develops in middle age, is rare and clearly does not represent the majority of Alzheimer's cases. These relatively rare genes appear not to be involved in late-onset Alzheimer's, which develops after the age of 60. The late-onset variation is apparently polygenic, although one gene has been highlighted as a significant contributor. That gene is on chromosome 19. It encodes for a protein—apolipoprotein E—that is critical in the repair of neurons (Poirier, 1994). A variation of this gene, called ε4, dramatically increases risk for Alzheimer's (Strittmatter et al., 1993), especially in women (Payami et al., 1996).

Genes clearly play a role in risk for Alzheimer's, but psychological factors and other biological factors also affect risk. For example, the female hormone estrogen appears to decrease the risk of Alzheimer's in women (Henderson, 1999). Women with later onset of menopause and women who receive estrogen replacement therapy after menopause are less likely to develop Alzheimer's or they develop it later. Furthermore, estrogen replacement therapy for women who have been diagnosed with Alzheimer's reduces the cognitive symptoms, especially memory loss (Henderson et al., 1996).

There is an interesting relationship between Alzheimer's disease and Down syndrome. Down syndrome is the result of a chromosomal abnormality—specifically, there are three instead of two chromosomes 21. Until recently, the life expectancy of people with Down syndrome was short because of multiple health problems. With modern medical advances, these people are living longer, and consequently another problem has surfaced. Virtually everyone with Down syndrome who survives to age 40 develops Alzheimer's disease (Mann & Esiri, 1989). It is believed that a gene on chromosome 21 that encodes for the amyloid precursor protein (APP) is responsible for the early development of Alzheimer's in those with Down syndrome (Mayeux, 1999). Having a triple dose of this APP gene results in an increase in amyloid production and thus an increased build-up of the senile plaques in the brain (Scheuner et al., 1996). Although this mechanism for Alzheimer's-like brain deterioration is clearly different from that for most cases of Alzheimer's, it provides a way of understanding at least one of the possible mechanisms behind this devastating disorder.

Education and cognitive activity in early adulthood are both predictors of who will eventually develop Alzheimer's. The reason for this interesting relationship is unclear, but several studies have shed some light on the question.

Examining the Evidence

Alzheimer's is twice as likely to develop in people who have less than an eighth-grade education than in those with more education (Stern et al., 1994), although not every study has found this relationship (Cobb et al., 1995). How should one interpret this finding? It is conceivable that the factors associated with Alzheimer's affect cognitive functioning early and thus reduce school performance and increase the likelihood of the individual's dropping out of school (Mayeux, 1999). Perhaps consistent with this idea is the research of Snowden et al. (1996), who found that people with high linguistic ability were less likely than people with low linguistic ability to develop Alzheimer's. Snowden et al. (1996) analyzed the autobiographical essays written by nuns just before they took their final vows, a half-century before any of them developed Alzheimer's. The quality of the writing proved to be a potent predictor of who would eventually develop this disease. Alternatively, it may be that other factors contribute to risk—factors that are related to education level. For example, people with more education tend to "eat healthier" and to get better medical care, and they are less likely to be engaged in occupations that bring them into regular contact with toxic substances. Factors such as these could account for the relationship between level of education and risk for Alzheimer's, although at this point no one knows. However, Evans et al. (1997) have argued that education, and the cognitive growth associated with such education, contributes to synaptic growth and thus may reduce the risk of cognitive dysfunction for such neuro-degenerative diseases as Alzheimer's—essentially a "use it or lose it" model of brain functioning. This interesting hypothesis would be difficult to test scientifically, because the level of cognitive activity throughout one's life is often correlated with cognitive ability. Should you resolve to exercise your brain more in an effort to prevent Alzheimer's? The current data do not support this action, but it is unlikely to hurt, and it probably has other benefits even if it doesn't reduce risk for Alzheimer's.

Evolutionary Impact

Anyone who has watched the steady progression of Alzheimer's will have little difficulty appreciating how the disorder disrupts functioning until the person is virtually vegetative. You might wonder why such a devastating illness with genetic predisposing factors has not been eliminated by natural selection. The answer is clear. There is virtually no natural selection pressure on a disorder like Alzheimer's, because it rarely affects individuals until they are well past reproductive age. Yet somehow that answer is not satisfying. Is there a reason why the processes that eventually lead to Alzheimer's developed? Could they have had a selective advantage at one time? The answer to both questions is maybe. Any gene that provides a selective advantage early in life will be favored by natural selection even if it provides a selective disadvantage later in life (Nesse & Williams, 1994; Buss, 1999). To date, there is no evidence for such early selective advantage, but scientists have only recently isolated some of the genes that contribute to Alzheimer's and have not yet studied the question of selective advantage. Rapaport (1988, 1990) noted that those portions of the brain most severely affected by Alzheimer's are the same areas that have undergone the most rapid evolutionary development and that there appears to be no comparable disease in nonhumans. Therefore, he proposed that the mechanism that facilitated the rapid evolution of certain regions of the human brain may be contributing to the disease processes that attack these unique areas. This interesting hypothesis is rather speculative and in need of more supportive data. However, it has the advantage of explaining why Alzheimer's disease tends to damage specific brain regions, while leaving others spared, and why it appears to be unique to humans.

OTHER CAUSES OF DEMENTIA

Several conditions besides Alzheimer's cause the generalized brain damage that produces dementia. This section will discuss some of the more common causes of brain damage, including head injuries, tumors, strokes, substance abuse, infections, and presenile dementias other than Alzheimer's disease.

Evolutionary Impact

Head Injuries. The brain is a delicate instrument encased in a rigid protective structure—the skull—that protects it from shock. However, it is not nearly so shock resistant as the brains of apes. The rapid evolutionary development of the human brain, which provides extensive selective advantage, also resulted in a thinner, more fragile skull (Nesse & Williams, 1994). When the human skull is subjected to enough force, significant brain damage results. Such damage is referred to as a **traumatic brain injury,** or **TBI.** TBIs are the leading cause of death in people under the age of 44 (Wu et al., 2000). Serious head injuries often produce functional disabilities, such as motor weakness or language problems. Darryl, who was one of the cases that opened the chapter, showed both language and memory difficulties. He also showed dramatic personality changes, which are common with serious head injuries (O'Shanick & O'Shanick, 1994). Severe head injuries can cause dementia (Erlanger et al., 1999) and tend to increase the risk for such disorders as Alzheimer's (Plassman et al., 2000). This increased risk

traumatic brain injury (TBI)   Brain damage that is caused by a blow to the skull.

probably occurs not because the head injury exacerbated the disease process but because the disease process is more disruptive to the functioning of an already compromised brain.

Tumors and Strokes. **Tumors** are growths that damage surrounding tissue. The type of neurological symptoms experienced as a result of a tumor depends on the tumor's location, type, and growth rate. Because many functions in the brain are localized, a tumor in the right parietal lobe, for example, produces dramatically different symptoms than one in the left temporal lobe. The multiple brain tumors that occur when a cancer in another part of the body metastasizes often cause dementia. The diffuse brain damage caused by such a massive assault on the brain can lead to rapid cognitive deterioration. Tumors outside of the brain can also affect brain functioning. For example, tumors that develop in the meninges—membranes that cover the brain—exert pressure on the brain. If such pressure is prolonged because the tumor is not identified and removed quickly, it can result in permanent damage of that portion of the brain.

Evolutionary Impact

The rate at which a tumor grows affects the type of symptoms seen for a given area of brain damage. You might think that if area X in the brain is damaged, then one should automatically see the symptoms associated with damage to area X. However, the brain compensates for gradual dysfunctions, and if the process is gradual enough, the compensation may be sufficient to maintain satisfactory performance. Perceptual processes are especially effective at adapting to neurological damage. Perhaps perception is so critical to survival that natural selection favored organisms that had the ability to invoke backup systems when critical perceptual systems failed. Whatever the reason, this phenomenon has been well documented (Lezak, 1995). More advanced cognitive functions, such as memory and reasoning, do not adapt to brain damage so quickly, if they adapt at all. This is one of the reasons why people with Alzheimer's show massive cognitive declines while showing few difficulties in perceptual processing.

Strokes, which are also known as **cerebrovascular accidents (CVAs),** represent a blockage or rupture of a

tumors Growths that damage surrounding tissue.

strokes, or cerebrovascular accidents (CVAs) A blockage or rupture of a blood vessel in the brain, which deprives the portion of the brain serviced by that blood vessel of oxygen.

vascular dementia Deteriorating cognitive functioning brought on by damage to a portion of the brain after multiple small strokes.

blood vessel in the brain, which deprives the portion of the brain serviced by that blood vessel of oxygen. The result is that the brain tissue dies and the functions served by that brain area are lost. Blockages of blood vessels may be partial and temporary. When such blockages occur, the person experiences transient, but often dramatic, symptoms. Such transient symptoms may indicate significant risk for a major stroke, because the material that briefly lodged in a blood vessel is likely to lodge in another blood vessel within a short period of time (hours or days).

Multiple small strokes throughout the brain sometimes produce what is called **vascular dementia.** Each stroke is so small that it is almost unnoticed, but a portion of the brain is decommissioned with each stroke, and eventually the damage becomes clear as the cognitive functioning of the person dramatically deteriorates. Whereas the effects of a major stroke are easy to discern, vascular dementia may be superficially similar to Alzheimer's dementia, although neurological testing can often differentiate between them (APA, 2000). In general, Alzheimer's produces a more gradual onset of dementia, whereas vascular dementia is more characterized by abrupt worsening of symptoms after periods of stable cognitive performance. For example, neurological reflexes are often impaired in vascular dementia, whereas such impairment is rarely present in Alzheimer's. Vascular dementia is somewhat more common in men than in women, but it is much less common than Alzheimer's, at least in the United States (APA, 2000).

Strokes are one of the more preventable causes of brain damage because factors such as high blood pressure and high cholesterol can dramatically increase the risk of blockage or breakage in the delicate blood vessels that supply the brain. These factors tend to increase in significance as a person ages, so regular physicals are more important as people age. This is especially true for blacks, who have a high risk for hypertension and therefore a high risk for stroke (Hyman et al., 2000). However, even young people can experience strokes. Drugs such as cocaine can trigger strokes in vulnerable people. One would be vulnerable if a blood vessel were not perfectly formed, perhaps having a section that is a bit thin. Such a situation would be undetectable until a spike in blood pressure stretched the vessel beyond the breaking point. Cocaine and similar drugs cause such blood pressure spikes (Tolat et al., 2000).

Substance Abuse. Substance abuse may lead to brain damage in three ways: (1) People under the influence of substances tend to have more accidents that include head trauma. (2) Many substances are directly toxic to the brain, so chronic use of them can result in significant brain deterioration. (3) Chronic substance use is associated with such factors as poor diet, which can compromise neurological functioning.

People who are intoxicated do not need to get behind the wheel of a car to put themselves at risk for head injury.

Heavy drinking may not appear to damage the brain, but it does. Heavy drinkers who live long enough typically develop dementia much earlier than friends who drink moderately.

The intoxication may decrease balance, thus increasing the risk of a fall. Other substances increase people's willingness to take risks, thereby putting them in situations in which injury is more likely. Some substances do both, increasing risk by decreasing judgment *and* coordination.

Alcohol abuse carries with it the risk for early dementia due to the toxic effects of alcohol on the brain (Schuckit, 2000). This condition is related to significant cerebral atrophy that is primarily the result of two factors—the direct toxic effects of alcohol and the chronic vitamin deficiencies associated with alcohol dependence. Both were discussed in Chapter 14.

Infections. Infections are also capable of damaging brain tissue. Some infections, such as encephalitis, are directly toxic to the brain. Other infections change the environment of the brain in ways that indirectly damage it. For example, excessively high fevers (105°F and above) are capable of damaging the brain, especially in children (Edmondson, 2000). With early diagnosis and aggressive treatment, it is possible to minimize the risk of brain damage from most infections. For example, general paresis represents the terminal stage of the venereal disease syphilis. In the early twentieth century, this disease filled more psychiatric hospital beds than any other psychiatric disorder. Today, syphilis is easily detected and treated, essentially eliminating general paresis.

The human immunodeficiency virus (HIV), which causes AIDS, can cause dementia as well. Scientists began to recognize the impact that AIDS had on emotional and cognitive functioning in the mid-1980s (Caine & Lyness, 2000). Before that, individuals with AIDS often died quickly from opportunistic infections long before cognitive symptoms developed. AIDS compromises brain functioning, causing substantial dementia and even psychotic symptoms—referred to as the **AIDS dementia complex** (Lipkin, 2000). Most of the brain damage from AIDS is subcortical,

adversely affecting memory, concentration, and motor skills. The person often becomes apathetic and withdrawn. It is only later that the cognitive symptoms of dementia develop (Caine & Lyness, 2000). HIV infections appear to damage the brain through multiple processes, some of which are not yet well understood (Grant & Atkinson, 2000). The HIV virus is directly toxic to neurons, but it can also cause encephalitis or meningitis—infections that seriously damage brain tissue.

Other Presenile Dementias. Although Alzheimer's is by far the most common cause of presenile dementias, there are other disorders in this category. **Pick's disease** is a relatively rare neuro-degenerative disorder that primarily attacks the frontal and temporal lobes of the brain (Wu et al., 2000). Its early symptoms include personality changes, emotional blunting, and a reduction in social functioning. In time the individual shows either extreme apathy or intense agitation, and only later do the more obvious signs of cognitive deterioration become apparent. This disorder usually strikes people in their fifties (APA, 2000).

Creutzfeldt-Jakob disease and **bovine spongiform encephalopathy** (better known as **mad cow disease**) are both caused by an infectious agent called a *prion* (Caine &

AIDS dementia complex   Substantial dementia and even psychotic symptoms caused by AIDS.

Pick's disease   A relatively rare neuro-degenerative disorder that primarily attacks the frontal and temporal lobes of the brain.

Creutzfeldt-Jakob disease   A disease typically transmitted through tissue transplants and caused by prions, which are subviral proteins capable of replication.

bovine spongiform encephalopathy, or mad cow disease   A disease that is transmitted through eating infected meat and is caused by prions, which are subviral proteins capable of replication.

Lyness, 2000). Prions are subviral proteins that are capable of replication. Creutzfeldt-Jakob disease is typically transmitted through tissue transplants, whereas mad cow disease is transmitted through eating infected meat. The prions that cause Creutzfeldt-Jakob disease can incubate in the body for decades before the onset of symptoms, but once symptoms develop, death usually follows within six months to two years (Caine & Lyness, 2000). The incubation period for mad cow disease is estimated to be 13 years, but once symptoms start, the pattern is similar to that seen in Creutzfeldt-Jacob disease. Both diseases produce significant dementia in addition to such neuromuscular symptoms as twitching and loss of coordination. Genes contribute to risk for Creutzfeldt-Jakob disease (Caine & Lyness, 2000). Fortunately, Creutzfeldt-Jakob disease is rare, affecting approximately 1 in 1 million people. However, there is serious concern that the rate of mad cow disease may be much higher, and given the long incubation period, there could be many people who already have the disorder, but no symptoms yet.

Huntington's disease is an inherited disorder that involves a gradual degeneration of brain tissue, which causes spasmodic twitching and progressive cognitive deterioration starting around age 40. There are also dramatic cognitive and personality changes that initially resemble schizophrenia. It is a terminal illness that usually leads to death within 13 to 15 years after symptoms first appear. It is caused by a dominant gene on chromosome 4, and it affects about 1 in 20,000 people (Daniel et al., 2000). Unfortunately, until recently, the late onset made it impossible for people to know whether they carried the gene until they had already had children. This situation created some difficult personal decisions for people who had a family history of Huntington's disease, because half of the children of an affected individual will develop the disorder. Yet they had to decide whether to have children without knowing whether they themselves were carriers. It is now possible to identify, even in a fetus, whether an individual carries the Huntington's gene (Daniel et al., 2000). But people with a family history still have the painful decision of whether to be tested. Would you want to know in your twenties that you would die in your fifties from Huntington's disease?

Parkinson's disease, first described by James Parkinson in 1817, is a slowly degenerative neurological disorder that is primarily characterized by tremors, unsteadiness, and muscle rigidity. In about 40% of cases, there is also a slow

Huntington's disease An inherited disorder that involves a gradual degeneration of brain tissue, which causes spasmodic twitching and progressive cognitive deterioration starting around age 40.

Parkinson's disease A slowly degenerative neurological disorder that is characterized primarily by tremors, unsteadiness, and muscle rigidity.

Muhammad Ali is one of many people who suffers from the effects of Parkinson's disease. His once forceful moves are now replaced by a shaky tentativeness due to the impact of the disease.

onset of dementia (APA, 2000). Typical onset is between 50 and 60, but onset as early as 30 is possible. Severe disability usually takes about 10 years to develop. Muhammad Ali has suffered from Parkinson's for years, and the actor Michael J. Fox also suffers from the disorder. Parkinson's disease results from degeneration of subcortical structures, primarily structures that use dopamine and, to a lesser extent, serotonin as their primary neurotransmitters (Caine & Lyness, 2000).

TREATING AND PREVENTING DEMENTIA

The nature of treatment and prevention strategies for dementias varies depending on the cause. Few dementias can be reversed, but treating the pathological process that is contributing can slow some dementias. Other dementias are untreatable in that the destructive process cannot be slowed or reversed. For such dementias, it makes more sense to focus efforts on prevention. This section begins by discussing the various treatment strategies and then turns to the topic of prevention.

Surgical and Other Medical Interventions.
Very few brain disorders can be surgically corrected. Surgical procedures are reserved for correcting problems that, if left uncorrected, could result in significant brain damage. These include vascular insufficiency due to blockage of the major arteries supplying the brain and removal of tumors that may be putting pressure on the brain.

The carotid arteries—one on each side of the neck—provide the critical blood supply to the brain. Any blockage of that blood supply results in cognitive symptoms, and a prolonged blockage can result in loss of brain tissue. Furthermore, reduced blood flow to the brain weakens blood vessels in the brain and thus increases the chance of later strokes. Surgical procedures can open clogged arteries sufficiently to permit an adequate blood flow to the brain again.

Some tumors can be surgically removed, thus relieving the pressure that they may be exerting on adjacent brain tissue. Such surgery can be delicate, depending on the tumor's location. It is not unusual for such surgery to be conducted under local anesthesia so that nearby regions of the brain can be electrically stimulated to verify the locations of critical brain functions. A small electrical signal is applied to the brain tissue, and the physical response is observed or the patient reports his or her psychological experience. This brain mapping requires patients to be conscious because they must inform the surgeon of their subjective experiences in response to the stimulation. Incidentally, there are no pain receptors in the brain, so brain stimulation is painless. The local anesthesia is to deaden pain receptors in the scalp and skull so that the surgeon can access the brain. By mapping critical regions of the brain in this manner, the surgeon can avoid damaging areas that control important functions.

Not all tumors are operable. For example, when a cancer metastasizes, there may be hundreds of small tumors growing throughout the brain. The only reasonable treatments for such a condition are radiation and/or chemotherapy. Such treatments can slow the onset of the dementia, although when cancers reach this stage, they are very difficult to stop (Cappuzzo et al., 2000).

Rehabilitation. Rehabilitation consists of a wide range of compensatory training techniques designed to maximize the functioning of individuals after neurological damage (Prigatano, 1999). Although rehabilitation can be provided to anyone, it tends to be used only with those whose neurological condition is stable. This means that it is rarely used with individuals who have such degenerative conditions as Alzheimer's.

The rationale behind neurological rehabilitation is that most complex tasks can be performed in more than one way. Therefore, it is possible to bypass functions that are lost to brain damage by teaching the person to rely more on intact functions or on external aids (Dougherty & Radomski, 1993). For example, most people rely on their memory to coordinate the multiple demands of a busy life. They may make lists occasionally, such as grocery lists, but they probably rely on lists infrequently. Because some brain injuries dramatically compromise memory, people with those injuries cannot rely on their memory. Instead, they must find alternatives. An organizational program that employs lists of tasks—essentially an external memory—may enable such people to function adequately. Of course, individuals must be trained to remember to use the list and to have the resources available with them to add to the list whenever necessary. An alternative is to avoid the need to remember tasks by attempting to do as many things as possible as soon as the need becomes apparent. Still another alternative is to reduce the need to remember most tasks by

developing a system that allows people to scan their environment systematically for tasks that may need their attention; thus they need not remember tasks that will be rediscovered with a routine scan. Such rehabilitation requires a thorough understanding of the abilities and disabilities of the person and a fair amount of creativity to find alternative procedures.

Treating Alzheimer's. Alzheimer's is a progressive disease that eventually leads to death (Burns, 1992). Treating it, therefore, does not mean reversing the deterioration or even arresting it (Abusamra, 1998). Instead, treatment involves slowing the process (Moore, 1998) and minimizing uncomfortable symptoms as they appear (Schneider, 2000; Turnbull, 1998). Traditionally, doctors have provided emotional support, management of symptoms via medication, and nursing care to keep people reasonably healthy and comfortable as they grow increasingly less able to care for themselves. Behavioral programs can sometimes be helpful in dealing with such problem behaviors as hypersexuality and aggressiveness, which are common in Alzheimer's (Lancaster et al., 1998). For most individuals with Alzheimer's, however, there comes a point when the care needed exceeds the ability of family members to provide it, and at this point, nursing home care is necessary (Colerick & George, 1986; Lancaster, 1998; Lieberman & Fisher, 2001). Recent efforts have attempted to find drugs that can slow the brain's deterioration and the cognitive decline that results.

Examining the Evidence

There has been considerable interest in the role of acetylcholine in Alzheimer's. There is a disproportionate loss of cholinergic cell bodies in Alzheimer's, which has led to treatment efforts either to stimulate the production of acetylcholine or to inhibit its breakdown in people with Alzheimer's. In general, the efforts to stimulate the production of acetylcholine have been ineffective (Schneider, 2000). More effective have been drugs that slow the normal breakdown of acetylcholine in the synapses between neurons. One of the earliest such drugs was physostigmine (Synapton), which showed a modest ability to improve cognitive functioning for a few hours in people with Alzheimer's. In recent years, several new drugs have been introduced, and others are in the testing stage (Schneider, 2000). For example, tacrine is a central-acting agent that inhibits the breakdown of acetylcholine. In clinical trials, it has improved cognitive functioning in people with Alzheimer's (Francis et al., 1999) and slowed the course of the disorder (Giacobini, 2000). The mechanism for the slowing of the course of Alzheimer's appears to be a blocking of the damaging action of the senile plaques (Xiao et al., 2000). Other drugs that have showed promise in early testing are donepezil, rivastigmine, and galantamine (Stahl, 2000). Donepezil is often the treatment of choice because among these drugs, it is the least toxic to the liver (Doody et al., 2001). Drugs that affect nicotine receptors in the brain have also been investigated. Simulating nicotine receptors enhances attention and improves concentration in healthy adults (Schneider, 2000), and there is modest evidence that stimulating nicotine receptors may attenuate cognitive symptoms in Alzheimer's (White & Levin, 1999). However, there is no evidence for the claim that smoking may reduce the risk for Alzheimer's (Brayne, 2000).

Several new drug treatments for Alzheimer's are under study. None of these drugs is a cure for the disorder, but several show promise for improving functioning, and some may even slow the process. Coupling this technology with earlier detection could decrease the prevalence of Alzheimer's. The technology for early detection has been gradually improving. Efforts are now under way to develop both PET scan (Sihver et al., 2000) and neuropsychological detection methods (Petersen et al., 2001). There is even work being done on developing a blood test to detect the β-amyloid protein that forms the senile plagues in Alzheimer's (DeMatttos et al., 2002). One or more of these methods may enable doctors to detect Alzheimer's years before any significant cognitive decline, thus permitting interventions that may significantly slow the disease.

Alzheimer's is a disease that affects more than the person afflicted by it. Family members experience an increasingly heavy responsibility while they struggle to provide care (Donaldson & Burns, 1999; Zarit et al., 1985). In fact, the stress of coping with a deteriorating family member is one of the primary reasons for placement in a nursing home (Colerick & George, 1986). Even after people are admitted to nursing homes, the emotional stress on their loved ones continues. Depression is common in family caretakers of people with Alzheimer's (Buckwalter et al., 1999). Treatment programs are increasingly recognizing that care must be extended to family members (Cox, 1998; Zarit et al., 1985). In addition, efforts are now being made to provide emotional support to nursing home staff members, who have the incredibly demanding job of caring for these individuals (Lancaster et al., 1998).

Preventing Dementia. Given that dementia is usually irreversible, preventing it whenever possible is critical. Some sources of dementia, such as Alzheimer's, are currently not preventable, although some recent work offers hope. For example, we saw earlier that estrogen treatments in women might delay or prevent the onset of Alzheimer's

symptoms (Henderson, 1999). Other evidence suggests that anti-inflammatory drugs, such as those used to treat arthritis, may delay the onset of Alzheimer's symptoms (Kawas, 1999).

Other sources of dementia are more preventable. For example, head injuries account for a number of dementia cases. Anything that reduces head injuries or minimizes the damage they cause—including things like safer cars, air bags, and better-constructed highways—could reduce dementia. The chronic abuse of such substances as alcohol can also lead to dementia. Therefore, alcoholism prevention and treatment programs are also prevention programs for dementia. Strokes can produce dementia, so public service campaigns to enhance awareness of the dangers of hypertension may reduce strokes and the resulting dementia. In other words, there are already dozens of dementia prevention programs that are labeled as prevention or treatment programs for other conditions.

Check Yourself 15.2

Dementia

1. What is the typical course of Alzheimer's disease?
2. What factors contribute to Alzheimer's disease?
3. Besides Alzheimer's, what other disorders can lead to dementia?
4. How is Alzheimer's disease treated?

Ponder this . . . *It may soon be possible to determine the degree of risk that a person has for developing Alzheimer's disease. What will be the personal and social-policy implications if such technology becomes routinely available?*

AMNESTIC DISORDERS

Amnestic disorders are characterized by a persistent disturbance in memory, which may be due either to the physiological effects of a general medical condition or to the effects of a substance or toxin. People with these disorders are impaired in their ability to learn new information, to recall previously learned information, or both. These memory disturbances are separate from the general decline in mental functioning that characterizes dementia, The memory deficits may be generalized but are more likely to be in specific domains, such as visuospatial memory or verbal

....

amnestic disorders Disorders characterized by a persistent disturbance in memory, which may be due either to the physiological effects of a general medical condition or to the effects of a substance or toxin.

memory. Visuospacial memory is the ability to remember where things are in space. For example, is the light switch to the left or the right of the door as you enter? Verbal memory is the ability to remember words and ideas. For example, after reading a short story, can you relate the plot accurately? The memory deficits are more likely to affect more recent memories than memories from the remote past. For example, a person might remember a high school dance but be unable to remember who stopped by to visit yesterday. Some of these characteristics are illustrated in the case history of Aman.

A Breath Away from Dying

AMAN

Aman did not remember collapsing onto the kitchen floor, and he certainly was surprised when he woke up in the hospital. All he could remember is that he had stopped on his way home to pick up a pizza. The portable heater that he had used on this unusually cold winter night had nearly killed him with its output of carbon monoxide. Had it not run out of fuel, it probably would have killed him. Over the next few days, his strength gradually returned, but his cloudy memory did not improve. More important, he now was finding it difficult to remember day-to-day events. He was able to recognize his doctor, but no matter how many times the doctor gave his name, Aman could not remember it.

———————————————●

The case of Aman illustrates the rapid onset of some amnestic disorders. He experienced loss of memory for the events just prior to his carbon monoxide poisoning, weakening of memory for relatively recent events, and considerable difficulty in forming new memories. Several conditions can lead to amnestic disorder; they include stroke, head injury, and exposure to specific neurotoxins, such as the carbon monoxide that occasioned Aman's amnestic disorder. Each of these conditions leads to an abrupt onset. Depending on the specific situation, amnestic symptoms may continue indefinitely or may improve with time. There are also situations that lead to a gradual onset of amnestic disorder; they include prolonged exposure to neurotoxins, extended periods of substance abuse, and sustained nutritional deficiencies. Chronic alcohol abuse, and the nutritional deficiencies that result (Korsakoff's syndrome), are common sources of amnestic symptomatology (Caine & Lyness, 2000; Fadda & Rossetti, 1998). Intermittent blockages of the cerebrovascular network that supplies blood to the brain can cause brief periods of amnestic symptoms, which will reoccur if further blockages develop and may become permanent if the blockage weakens the blood vessel enough to cause it to rupture.

The parts of the brain most consistently implicated in amnestic disorders are the thalamus and the hippocampus. The thalamus is a midbrain structure that acts as a relay station between other parts of the brain. It is critical to the formation of memories; damage to the thalamus severely affects memory performance in animals (Celerier et al., 2000). The hippocampus regulates both emotion and learning. Because many individuals with amnestic disorders have focal lesions, the study of memory performance in amnestic and nonamnestic individuals has yielded insights into both the mechanisms behind amnestic disorders and the brain processes that contribute to memory (Reinvang, 1998; Schacter et al., 1998).

Treatment for amnestic disorder depends on the cause of the disorder. For example, with Korsakoff's syndrome, the treatment is to give vitamin supplements. However, most amnestic disorders are due to brain damage that cannot be reversed. Hence, treatment usually involves rehabilitation. Over the last 20 years, a variety of cognitive rehabilitation techniques have been developed (Kashima, 1999). These usually involve teaching affected individuals to employ strategies for working around their memory deficits or to rely on aspects of their memory that are not impaired.

Check Yourself 15.3

Amnestic Disorders

1. Define amnestic disorders. What can cause them?
2. How are amnestic disorders treated?

Ponder this . . . *People with amnestic disorders may not be able to remember past events, but they will still be able to remember how to drive a car. Why do you think that some memories are more vulnerable to disruption than others?*

DISSOCIATIVE DISORDERS

Have you ever had the momentary feeling that you were living a dream? Things somehow do not seem real. It is as though you are watching yourself acting out a role. That feeling is a mild form of dissociation—something that virtually everyone feels occasionally. Under stressful conditions, the dissociation can increase in frequency and intensity, and if it becomes strong enough, it might qualify as a dissociative disorder. Dissociative disorders are among the most puzzling of psychological disorders. They are characterized by a disruption in the normal integrative functions of consciousness, memory, identity, and perception. In other words, people with dissociative disorders are unable to access one or more of these critical functions at will. The process of **dissociation**—separating emotionally and/or

....

dissociation Emotional and/or cognitive separation from one's core identity.

cognitively from one's core identity—is not rare, but the degree of dissociation found in dissociative disorders is well outside the range of what most people experience. Do these dissociations represent a breakdown of normal cognitive functioning or, as hypothesized over a hundred years ago, a defense against overwhelming anxiety? These questions are still unanswered, although these mysteries are gradually being unraveled. This section provides a clinical description of the four dissociative disorders: depersonalization disorder, dissociative amnesia, dissociative fugue, and dissociative identity disorder. Subsequent sections discuss causes, treatments, and several controversies.

DEPERSONALIZATION DISORDER

Depersonalization is a feeling of detachment or estrangement from oneself. For example, people may feel as though they are living a dream, are just going through the motions of life, or are separated from their bodies and watching themselves behave. **Depersonalization disorder** is characterized by these feelings of detachment, which may be either persistent or recurrent. Unlike people with schizophrenia who may believe that such feelings are reality, the individual realizes that the depersonalization is only a feeling. For the individual to qualify for the diagnosis, the feelings must cause clinically significant distress or interfere with functioning and must be independent of other psychiatric disorders. For example, depersonalization is common in acute stress disorder, but if the person has recently faced a life-threatening experience, only the diagnosis of acute stress disorder should be used. Depersonalization is also common in panic disorder, social phobia, and schizophrenia and should not be diagnosed if it appears to be a part of these disorders (APA, 2000). Almost 40% of people hospitalized for psychiatric disorders show significant depersonalization, although few qualify for the diagnosis of depersonalization disorder because the depersonalization is clearly secondary to other psychiatric disorders. The case history of Carol illustrates some of the features of depersonalization disorder.

Going Through the Motions

CAROL

Carol had taught school for nearly 25 years. Perhaps she was burning out. Perhaps it was the loss of both of her parents in the last two years. Perhaps she had just run out of energy. Whatever it was, life no longer had meaning for her. She felt detached from her day-to-day actions. She watched herself plug through her day without feeling any connection to her actions. She did what was expected but got nothing emotionally in return. She felt like a zombie. She showed emotion but felt none. At first she thought she might be depressed, even though she did not feel depressed. She talked to her doctor, who assured her that she showed little evidence of depression. Yet each day was the same—get up, do what is expected, and go to bed.

She hated her life and wondered how much longer she had to endure it. She wanted to feel like she was living her life again, rather than just watching it go by.

The prevalence of depersonalization disorder in the general public is unknown. However, depersonalization symptoms are a relatively common reaction to stress, affecting about half of the adult population at least once (APA, 2000). This disorder is relatively common in adolescents and young adults and is also common in occupational burnout (Collins, 2000), which may well explain some of Carol's symptoms.

DISSOCIATIVE AMNESIA

The hallmark of **dissociative amnesia** is a loss of autobiographical memory—that is, memory about one's own life experiences. The memory loss is psychologically mediated and not due to a head injury or other physiological dysfunction. This amnesia is typically a response to a traumatic event, and it is usually the traumatic event itself that is "forgotten." To qualify for the diagnosis of dissociative amnesia, the information forgotten must be too extensive to have been lost as the result of simple forgetfulness, must not be better explained by another disorder, and must cause significant distress or functional disturbance in the individual. Most people with dissociative amnesia spontaneously recover the "forgotten" material. The pattern of amnesia may vary from one individual to another. Table 15.3 describes five patterns that may occur. Localized and selective amnesia are the most common (APA, 2000).

Dissociative amnesia can occur at any age. The prevalence is unknown, and there is currently considerable controversy about its existence. Some believe that it is common

....

depersonalization   A feeling of detachment or estrangement from oneself.

depersonalization disorder   Characterized by feelings of detachment, which may be either persistent or recurrent.

dissociative amnesia   A loss of autobiographical memory.

dissociative fugue   The sudden moving away from one's home, coupled with amnesia for one's past.

localized amnesia   A failure to recall events during a specific period of time, usually following a traumatic event.

selective amnesia   Ability to recall some, but not all, events during a specified time period.

generalized amnesia   A failure to recall anything about one's life.

continuous amnesia   An inability to remember anything from a specified time period up to the present time.

systematized amnesia   An inability to remember any items in a particular conceptual category.

[TABLE 15.3] Types of Dissociative Amnesia

Localized amnesia	These people fail to recall events during a specific period of time, usually following a traumatic event. For example, a witness to a fatal accident may not remember the accident or anything that happened in the first few hours or days after the accident. Short-term localized amnesia is a common side effect of ECT.
Selective amnesia	These people can recall some, but not all, events during a specified time period. For example, a soldier may remember some events from his or her combat service but be unable to recall other events.
Generalized amnesia	These people fail to recall anything about their lives. Although a common feature in movie plots, generalized amnesia is very rare.
Continuous amnesia	These people are unable to remember anything from a specified time period up to the present time.
Systematized amnesia	These people are unable to remember any items in a particular conceptual category. For example, a person may be unable to remember anything having to do with employment at a particular company.

when childhood sexual abuse occurs (Bass & Davis, 1988, 1994), although others doubt these claims (Loftus & Ketchum, 1994; Loftus & Polage, 1999). This topic will be covered near the end of the chapter.

DISSOCIATIVE FUGUE

The primary disturbance in **dissociative fugue** is a sudden moving away from one's home, coupled with amnesia for one's past. Fugue is from the Latin *fuga*, which means "flight." People with fugue may be confused about their identity or may assume another identity. For the individual to qualify for this diagnosis, these symptoms must not be better explained by another disorder and must cause significant distress or disruption in functioning. Some of the features of fugue are illustrated in the case history of Brad.

In the film *Nurse Betty,* Renée Zellweger plays a character who experiences dissociative fugue after witnessing the brutal killing of her husband.

did not recognize the man or even his own name. Brad had been going by the name John. He had no idea what his real name was or where he was from. He had awakened in a motel on the edge of this small town six months earlier with $400 in his pocket, a set of keys he did not recognize, and no memory of his past, although a tan line suggested that he had recently worn a wedding ring. He worked odd jobs for a while before taking the convenience store job, hoping that his memory would eventually return. But his memory did not return, so he had settled into a new life in this quiet town—a life he had grown to enjoy. Thus it was with mixed feelings that he searched the eyes of this man who said his real name was Brad and that his wife had never given up hope that he was still alive.

Stripped of His Identity

BRAD

It happened by chance. A former co-worker spotted Brad at a convenience market in a small Oregon town. Brad, who had been working at the convenience market for almost four months,

Brad had abruptly moved 400 miles from his home, apparently hitchhiking most of the way. He had left shortly after he and his wife had received a foreclosure notice. His business was failing, his mother had died recently, and he had had to put his dog to sleep because he could not afford the vet bills for surgery to remove a tumor. He knew he had lost his identity, so he quietly took on another identity and began a new life. Some cases of fugue last for months or longer, as in Brad's case. Others last only a few hours (APA, 2000). Brad's case illustrates an interesting aspect of dissociative fugue. He strongly suspected that he had been married because he could see signs that he had worn a wedding ring. He should have known that people would be looking for him. He probably could have discovered who he was in a matter of days if he had gone to the authorities and enlisted their help. He did none of that. Although they may not have been deliberately chosen for the purpose, his actions suggest that he did *not* want to find out who he was and to return to his former life.

The prevalence of dissociative fugue in the general population is estimated at 1 in 500, although exact figures are not available. It is believed that the rate may increase during times of widespread trauma, such as an earthquake or a war (APA, 2000). The expression of dissociative fugue may be shaped by cultural factors. For example, a syndrome that exists in Malaysia, called "amok," includes a sudden onset of high activity, a trancelike state, and running to the point of exhaustion, followed by sleep and amnesia for the entire event. It is unclear whether this is a cultural variation of dissociative fugue or another disorder. The common phrase *running amok* derives from this condition. The current DSM (APA, 2000) lists a potential new disorder in its appendix—dissociative trance disorder—which may better capture the "amok" syndrome just described.

DISSOCIATIVE IDENTITY DISORDER

Dissociative identity disorder (DID), formerly known as multiple personality disorder, is characterized by the presence of two or more distinct identities, or "personalities," that recurrently take control of the individual. The distinct identities are referred to as **alters,** which is short for *alternate personalities.* The primary or dominant personality is referred to as the host personality. Typically, the alters rotate taking control of the individual. When one alter is in control, the others may or may not be aware of what is going on. Those alters that are unaware of the actions of other alters experience lapses of time during which they cannot account for their actions. For the individual to qualify for this diagnosis, these disturbances must not be better accounted for by other disorders, such as substance abuse or

a general medical condition. For example, we saw in Chapter 14 that heavy drinking can lead to alcohol-induced blackouts, during which the person is conscious and functioning but the high level of intoxication interferes with the formation of memories. Consequently, the person has no recollection of what happened during these blackouts. Children often have imaginary playmates, which might suggest the presence of other identities. By itself, however, this is not evidence of DID (APA, 2000). There is considerable confusion about the nature of DID, which is addressed in the nearby Modern Myths box.

Dissociative identity disorder is relatively rare, although there has been a sharp rise in reported cases in recent years (Putnam, 1989; Ross, 1997). Some professionals argue that the rates may be as high as 1% in the general population and 5% among psychiatric inpatients (Ross, 1999), although few professionals believe the prevalence is that high (Rifkin et al., 1998). There are two divergent interpretations of this rise in reported cases. One group argues that there is now a greater awareness of the disorder and that, as a result, more people with the disorder are being recognized and properly diagnosed (Gleaves, 1996; Putnam, 1989; Ross, 1997). Another group argues that the diagnosis is being overused and that many of the diagnosed cases are **iatrogenic,** or unintentionally shaped or caused by the practitioner (Lilienfeld et al., 1999; Spanos, 1994). This view is especially prevalent among professionals in Europe (Casey, 2001). No one suggests that such shaping is done consciously, but, rather, that the professional is eager to understand the complexities of a challenging case in which the client is easily influenced by the therapist. A therapist's questions set up demand characteristics for clients, who often respond by believing that they actually experienced the things that are suggested by the questions. Wanting to be a "good client," the person eventually, but unconsciously, "acts out" the role of someone with dissociative identity disorder.

An example may help to illustrate how this might happen. About half of all people who are diagnosed with DID also qualify for the diagnosis of borderline personality disorder (APA, 2000), and the personality disorder is typically prominent when the person first enters therapy. As we saw in Chapter 12, borderline personality disorder is characterized by rapid and sometimes marked shifts in feelings, impulsivity, self-damaging behavior, and serious identity issues. The way a therapist phrases questions may shape how clients think about their symptoms. For example, asking, "What was it about their action that upset you?" focuses the person on the situation. In contrast, asking, "Was there a part of you that took what they said personally?" focuses the person more internally and implies the existence of separate and distinct psychological entities. Phrasing questions in this manner is encouraged by professionals who specialize in DID (Lilienfeld et al., 1999). When clients with borderline symptoms are puzzled by their own actions, the therapist might ask, "Might there be a part of

··

dissociative identity disorder (DID) The presence of two or more distinct identities or "personalities" that recurrently take control of the individual. Formerly known as multiple personality disorder.

alters Alternate personalities that are distinct.

iatrogenic Unintentionally shaped or caused by the practitioner.

MODERN Myths

Multiple Personality Disorder

The diagnosis of multiple personality disorder was replaced in DSM-IV with the current diagnosis of dissociative identity disorder. Multiple personality disorder has a long history of confusion and myth. You learned in Chapter 5 that multiple personality disorder, sometimes colloquially referred to as split personality, is not the same as schizophrenia. Here you will learn that it does not even involve multiple personalities.

The term *multiple personality disorder* became a household word through two books—*The Three Faces of Eve* (Thigpen & Cleckley, 1957) and *Sybil* (Schreiber, 1973)—both of which were made into movies. The movie portrayals in particular give the impression that the various identities of the lead characters were fully formed personalities. The truth is that the alters found in DID are often fragmented personalities that are unable to func-

tion in a complex social environment. It is often hard to determine exactly which personalities are present, and for many clients, hypnosis is necessary to bring out the personalities. Eve, whose real name was Chris Sizemore, actually had more than a dozen documented personalities, although it would have made confusing reading and an even more confusing movie to portray all of them.

There are other popular misconceptions about multiple personality disorder that belong in the category of modern urban myths. For example, claims that some personalities speak different languages, have different medical diseases, and have completely different physiological functioning are simply not supported. Documentation for these claims is nowhere to be found. It is hardly possible for one alter to have cancer or diabetes when others do not. There is some evidence for dif-

ferences in brain patterns depending on which alter is active (Cocker et al., 1994), but volunteers who are asked to simulate the disorder also produce different brain patterns for their simulated alters (Putnam et al., 1990). If anything, physiological data suggest that alters are not separate units of a person's consciousness. For example, Allen and Movius (2000) measured physiological indicators of recognition of material. The material was originally presented to one alter, and then the person was tested while another alter was in control. The data suggested that the other alter was physiologically responding in a way that implied recognition of the material. In short, the truth about DID is much less dramatic than some of the claims made in the popular press. If it were this dramatic, there would be less controversy about the nature of DID and the factors that contribute to its symptoms.

---

you with whom I haven't spoken who is doing these things?" When clients report self-mutilation, the therapist might ask, "Is it possible that it was a different part of 'you' that cut yourself?" These questions are clearly leading the

Chris Sizemore is the real Eve portrayed in the film, *The Three Faces of Eve*. After years of supportive therapy, she now leads a normal life as an artist, author, and frequent spokesperson for mental health issues.

client to reconceptualize the situation. The issue of whether DID is iatrogenic will be discussed in more detail later.

Most people with DID initially seek treatment for such problems as anxiety or depression (Putnam et al., 1986). Jamie, who was one of the cases that introduced the chapter, sought treatment for depression and for a general dissatisfaction with life. She was diagnosed with dysthymia, borderline personality disorder, and histrionic personality disorder. Substance abuse, especially alcohol abuse, is also common in individuals with DID (McDowell, 1999), although this was not the case for Jamie. The course of DID is unpredictable and varies considerably from person to person (Ross, 1997). There is often a considerable period of time—six or seven years on average—between the time when the client first seeks treatment and the time when the diagnosis of DID is first applied (APA, 2000; Gleaves, 1996). Jamie had seen three other therapists over the previous ten years, none of whom was aware of the alter named Paula. Jamie's therapist elected not to reinforce the presentation of Paula by Jamie, instead focusing on the family issues raised during

Paula's brief appearance in the therapy session. The personality of Paula never returned during the sessions, but Jamie made significant strides on these family issues over the next two months.

It is argued that clients with DID have little insight into what is happening and therefore are unable to provide therapists with the critical information necessary for diagnosis. Furthermore, many clients with insight report actively hiding their symptoms out of shame (Cohen et al., 1991). For some clients, DID is episodic, with alters typically appearing during times of stress and then disappearing at other times (Ross, 1997). For other clients, the course is more chronic, with alters coexisting for years. In general, the manifestations of DID become less dramatic as the person ages, and most affected individuals past the age of 40 show alters only during times of stress (APA, 2000). DID is diagnosed three to nine times more frequently in females than in males (APA, 2000). However, these figures may be misleading because women seek therapy, and thus receive a diagnosis, more frequently than men, and no epidemiological studies of DID have been conducted. DID runs in families, but there are no genetic studies of the disorder, in part because the prevalence is too low to make such studies feasible.

Check Yourself 15.4

Clinical Descriptions

1. Depersonalization is a common symptom of many disorders, but what features must be present for the individual to qualify for the diagnosis of depersonalization disorder?

2. What is the difference between dissociative amnesia and dissociative fugue?

3. What is the essential feature of dissociative identity disorder?

Ponder this . . . *Dissociation as a response to trauma hardly seems like a feature that would be favored by natural selection. A person who "zones out" following a traumatic event might be easy prey. What hidden value might there be to such dissociation?*

CAUSES OF DISSOCIATIVE DISORDERS

Two causal factors have been associated with dissociative disorders, especially DID: trauma and suggestibility. This section examines these factors and also discusses possible evolutionary contributions to dissociation.

It is common for people who undergo a trauma, such as the death of a loved one, to experience intermittent dissociation as they struggle to come to grips with the situation.

TRAUMA

Trauma can lead to dissociation in many people. It is common for people who have just had someone close to them die to feel as though everything is unreal—a feeling known as **derealization.** This feeling is likely to come and go. For example, a person may be overwhelmed by sorrow at one moment and feel as though it is all a bad dream the next moment. Trauma has also been implicated in each of the dissociative disorders, although the nature of the trauma and the reaction to it vary by disorder and among people. This section first reviews the evidence linking childhood abuse and DID and then discusses dissociation as a general response to trauma.

Abuse in Childhood and DID. In dissociative identity disorder, the key trauma appears to occur during childhood (Carlson et al., 1998; Chu, 1998). Kluft (1993) argues that the first signs of alters typically appear around the time of the trauma, as the child struggles to deal with the situation. These alters may be a coping mechanism whereby children remove themselves psychologically from abusive situations (Ross, 1997). Whatever the reason for the development of these alters, once they do develop, they continue even if the trauma decreases. This would explain why they persist even though they are more of a liability than an asset to the adult (Kluft, 1993).

How strong is the evidence of childhood abuse in DID? Dissociation is common in those who report histories of childhood physical and/or sexual abuse. Female psychiatric inpatients who report *either* physical or sexual abuse show twice as much dissociation as inpatients who report no abuse. Furthermore, inpatients who report *both* phys-

derealization   The intermittent feeling that everything is unreal.

Parents occasionally have to punish their children, but when punishment is abusive or when other forms of abuse are present, the child may be traumatized. Childhood abuse is frequently reported by people who later develop DID, although external evidence of the abuse is often lacking.

ical and sexual abuse report three times as much dissociation as inpatients who report no abuse (Chu, 1998). Over a dozen published studies have found significantly more dissociative symptoms in non-psychiatric-patient adults who report a history of abuse than in adults who do not report such a history (see Putnam & Carlson, 1998). Thus dissociative symptoms are clearly associated with a reported history of abuse. Over 90% of individuals who qualify for a diagnosis of DID report a childhood history of abuse, the vast majority reporting both physical and sexual abuse (Gleaves, 1996).

The weakness with most of these studies is that they rely almost exclusively on retrospective self-reports of abuse—that is, the clients are asked as adults about their experiences as children. Such retrospective reports are notoriously unreliable (Raulin & Lilienfeld, 1999). Furthermore, the reports themselves call into question their accuracy. For example, one-fourth of individuals with DID report remembering abuse that occurred before age three. The report of memories of abuse that occurred before age three calls into question the validity of all reports of abuse, because autobiographical memories are almost never accurate before the age of five (Fivush & Hudson, 1990). Clients who report such memories may well be misremembering other experiences. Furthermore, one-fourth report satanic abuse, sometimes including human sacrifices, but no evidence for satanic activity has ever been found (Bottoms et al., 1996; Mulhern, 1991). Consequently, it is critically important that there be external evidence of such abuse before we have confidence that the abuse really occurred. Such evidence does not currently exist (Lilienfeld et al., 1999), but it might include either (1) objective information to confirm retrospective self-reports or (2) prospective studies of abused children, in which abused children are

followed for years to determine the long-term effects of the abuse. There are currently no prospective studies of childhood abuse that show a risk for DID, although prospective studies of abused children are now under way (Widom & Morris, 1997).

One question that prospective studies might answer is why there is so little evidence of alters in children around the time of abuse. If, as has been speculated, the alters are formed during childhood to cope with the abuse, they should be apparent during childhood and not be detected for the first time decades later. The evidence for such alters in children is weak at best (Lilienfeld et al., 1999). It is possible that the development of DID takes years. If so, prospective studies might identify the elements of the developmental process that so far are unknown. These are not easy questions to answer. DID is apparently rare, even in children who have been abused. To identify enough abused children who will later develop DID will probably require very large samples that may need to be followed for 20 years or more. Furthermore, the handling of these children during the research must avoid the iatrogenic effects currently suspected by some scientists.

The central question, which has yet to be answered, is why children who are abused would develop DID instead of PTSD. For adults, the opposite is true; significant trauma leads often to PTSD but almost never to DID. Although scientists have learned much in the last two decades about stress and its effects on humans and other animals, there is still obviously much more to learn.

Dissociation and Trauma. If dissociation is a common response that many people experience when faced with a traumatic event, could dissociative disorders simply represent higher than average levels of dissociation? Dissociation is common in a variety of psychiatric disorders, some of which are triggered by trauma (Bremner et al., 1998). Could the dissociation in these diagnoses be intermediate between the normal dissociation experienced by many people and the extreme dissociation of dissociative disorders? Let's look at the data.

Examining the Evidence

The degree of dissociation is typically measured with a self-report inventory called the Dissociative Experiences Scale, or DES (Bernstein & Putnam, 1986; Carlson & Putnam, 1993). This scale includes 28 items that tap such dissociative symptoms as disturbance in awareness, memory, and identity. For example, one item reads, "Some people have the experience of finding new things among their belongings that they do not remember buying. Mark the line to show what percentage of the time this happens to you." The line for this, and for all other items, goes from 0% to 100%, and the score is the average percentage for the 28 items. As you can see in Figure 15.3a, the mean DES scores are highest in individuals with dissociative disorders, but they are also elevated in other diagnostic groups relative to non-psychiatric-patient controls. However, a problem with looking at only the mean scores is that doing so can hide information. A mean score can be elevated if either (1) most people in the group have slightly elevated scores or (2) a few people have dramatically elevated scores. Putnam et al. (1996) examined the DES scores of over 1500 people in a variety of diagnostic categories and found that the elevated means previously reported in nondissociative disorders were due to a small number of people who showed dramatically elevated levels of dissociation. Figure 15.3b shows the proportion of individuals in each diagnostic group who have significantly elevated scores on the DES (scores of 30 and above). Note that the dissociative disorders stand out more from the other disorders on this index than when mean scores are used, with the notable exception of PTSD (to be discussed shortly). In other words, severe dissociation is not common in these other disorders, but a few people with these diagnoses do show high levels of dissociation. Whether the elevated scores in these few individuals are due to a history of trauma or to some other cause is unknown, but this question certainly warrants further study.

The disorder with the most direct link to trauma is PTSD, which is characterized by hyperarousal, avoidance of the stressful situation, flashbacks, and nightmares. The avoidance may be behavioral, emotional, or cognitive (Carlson et al., 1998). Behavioral avoidance involves not going to places that are similar to those where the trauma occurred; emotional avoidance is an emotional numbing; cognitive avoidance is the attempted repression of a painful or anxiety-producing event. The emotional numbing and forgetting represent dissociation, which may explain why the level of dissociation in PTSD is comparable to the non-DID dissociative disorders, and only people with DID show a higher level of dissociation. Momentarily "forgetting" the details of a traumatic event or becoming emotionally numb is dissociative, but not nearly so dissociative as forming the functional equivalent of a separate personality.

Evolutionary Impact

The mechanisms underlying PTSD are better understood than the mechanisms underlying dissociation. Humans respond to significant trauma with complex physiological and psychological adaptations. The nature and intensity of these adaptations are a function of both personality characteristics and past experiences. Furthermore, the nature and timing of the trauma affect the likelihood and nature of the symptoms. For example, adult trauma, no matter how severe, does not appear to lead to DID. Finally, one's interpretation of and response to trauma may affect the long-term emotional consequences. Political prisoners subjected to torture have long known ways to protect their sanity in the face of such trauma (Başoğlu & Mineka, 1992). Natural selection almost certainly influenced biological adaptations to trauma, and many of those adaptations are clearly shared with other species (Bremner et al., 1995). For example, the heightened arousal following trauma in PTSD may well enhance the likelihood of survival because the source of the trauma, such as predators, may still be present. Whether psychological responses, such as dissociation, lead to a selective advantage is still an open question. Whereas the biological mechanisms behind PTSD have been delineated, it is less clear what biological mechanisms underlie dissociative disorders. Evidence suggests that the hippocampus and the medial portion (middle) of the temporal lobes may be involved in the switching of alters in DID (Tsai et al., 1999), but these data are preliminary and therefore should be interpreted cautiously.

SUGGESTIBILITY

Most people who experience severe trauma react with an acute stress disorder and many develop PTSD, but few develop a dissociative disorder. The obvious question is why. How do people who respond to stress with dissociation severe enough to lead to a dissociative disorder differ from those who do not? One hypothesis is that those who develop dissociative disorders are more capable of dissoci-

[FIGURE 15.3]
Mean DES Scores

The mean scores (top) on the Dissociative Experiences Scale suggest that moderate dissociation is common in many psychiatric disorders, but the percent with high scores (above 30, bottom) suggests that intense dissociation is common in only dissociative disorders and PTSD.

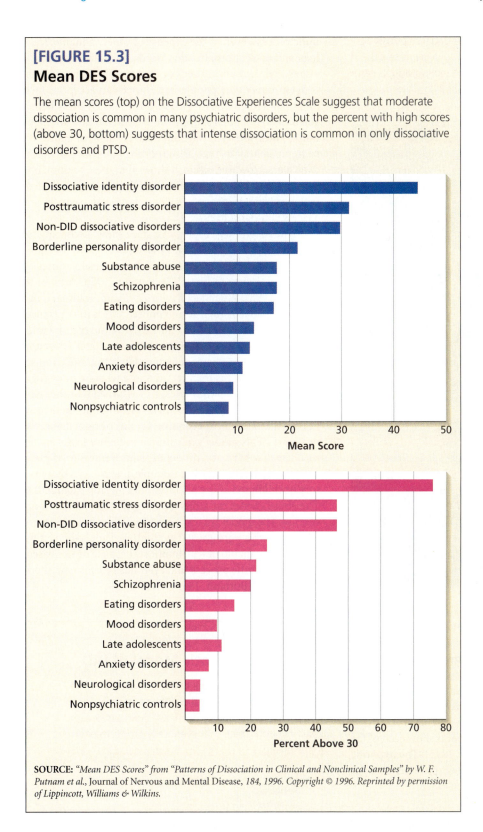

SOURCE: *"Mean DES Scores" from "Patterns of Dissociation in Clinical and Nonclinical Samples" by W. F. Putnam et al.,* Journal of Nervous and Mental Disease, *184, 1996. Copyright © 1996. Reprinted by permission of Lippincott, Williams & Wilkins.*

ation and that the relief from anxiety that dissociation produces reinforces the dissociation (Vermetten et al., 1998).

Suggestibility—the ease with which a person can accept an idea proposed by another person—is a personality trait that shows considerable variability among people. Those who are highly suggestible tend to have a rich fantasy life. Furthermore, they are more easily hypnotized and are able to respond more dramatically to hypnotic suggestions.

suggestibility   The ease with which a person can accept an idea proposed by another person.

Some of the things that people can do under hypnosis are impressive and may seem impossible. However, research shows that highly motivated unhypnotized individuals can match these feats.

Hypnosis is not the magical experience that is implied in movie or TV portrayals. It does not have the power to control unwilling victims. Rather, **hypnosis** represents a state of consciousness that involves focal concentration, a receptiveness to certain input, and a relative suspension of peripheral awareness (Spiegel & Spiegel, 1987). There is debate about whether hypnosis is a special process or a form of role-playing in which participants show each of the above characteristics (Kirsch & Lynn, 1995). The hypnotic state, called a trance, involves total absorption in the hyp-

hypnosis   A state of consciousness that involves focal concentration, a receptiveness to certain input, and a relative suspension of peripheral awareness.

autohypnotic model   The theory that DID may develop through the use of self-hypnosis as a defense against intense emotional trauma.

notic process, even at the expense of other thoughts, feelings, and perceptions. In other words, the individual blocks out everything but the focus of the hypnotic trance, which is presumably why people in a trance can accept as fact ideas that are obviously untrue, such as their body being stiff as a board. Such suggestions are often used with hypnotized individuals in stage shows to create what appear to be impossible tasks, such as supporting one's body between two chairs. However, research shows that these presumably impossible tasks are quite possible if the person is provided with sufficient motivation, such as a large cash payment for success (Putnam, 1999).

Not all hypnosis is part of a stage show. According to the **autohypnotic model** of DID, a select group of individuals can use self-hypnosis as a defense against intense emotional trauma (Kluft, 1984; Putnam, 1986; Putnam & Carlson, 1998). When faced with significant trauma, individuals capable of such self-hypnosis retreat into a trance that protects them emotionally during the trauma and may even provide amnesia for the trauma later (Putnam & Carlson, 1998). The people most likely to be able to use autohypnosis in this manner are those who are most suggestible in their everyday lives. It is assumed that the self-hypnotic state is transformed over time into the alters seen in DID, although the mechanism for this transformation is unknown. This model is illustrated in Figure 15.4.

The autohypnotic model explains a number of phenomena related to DID. For example, it explains why a history of childhood abuse is so common in people with DID. The abuse creates the stress that triggers the autohypnotic defense. The model also explains why DID is not present in all people who were abused as children. Unless the victim of abuse is capable of self-hypnosis because of increased suggestibility, the process that eventually forms new alters never begins (Putnam, 1997).

[FIGURE 15.4]

The Autohypnotic Model of DID

The autohypnotic model of DID suggests that the combination of repeated childhood trauma and a suggestible personality can lead, during trauma, to a self-hypnotic state that eventually produces alternate personalities.

Repeated trauma + Suggestible personality → Self-hypnotic state → Formation of alters

However, there are other aspects of DID that are not explained by this model. For example, why is only a history of *childhood* abuse associated with DID? One might expect that a prolonged period of wartime or political torture would be sufficient to trigger a dissociative escape into a self-hypnotic trance, yet there is little or no evidence for such a developmental course for DID. Such experiences undergone by adults leads to PTSD, which often includes dissociation, but not to DID. Is there something about childhood that adds a critical third element to the model in Figure 15.4? If so, what is it? Although no one has looked at this issue specifically, it appears that individuals with DID report physical and sexual abuse, usually by family members, but do not report other trauma, such as war-related trauma or even being severely bullied at school. Is there something unique about that kind of psychological trauma? Freyd et al. (2001) argue that the unique aspect of such trauma is that it involves betrayal of trust. Although an interesting idea, more research is needed before this theory can be accepted.

The auto-hypnotic model has two other critical flaws. One has already been mentioned: the lack of specificity about how alters develop from self-hypnotic states. The second is that there is little or no evidence of alters in people with DID until well into adulthood. Even in adulthood, the alters are not readily apparent because the diagnosis is rarely made when the person first seeks therapy (Gleaves, 1996).

Hypnosis, suggestibility, and dissociation have been associated with one another since the early writings of Freud and his colleagues on the topic (Breuer & Freud, 1893–1895/1955), as discussed in the nearby Focus box. Freud initially used hypnosis to help clients "remember" critical incidents from the past, but he later abandoned it because it seemed to elicit a large number of inaccurate memories. Hypnosis is still commonly used for bringing out alters during treatment of DID (deVito, 1993; Maldonado & Spiegel, 1998). Many clinicians who work with individuals with dissociative disorders regard hypnosis and dissociation as virtually identical processes (Putnam & Carlson, 1998).

AN EVOLUTIONARY DEFENSE MECHANISM

Evolutionary Impact

Nijenhuis and his colleagues in the Netherlands have proposed a fascinating evolutionary model to explain some of the symptoms associated with DID, and they have collected data in support of the theory (Nijenhuis et al., 1998a, 1998b). It has long been recognized that individuals with DID often show a variety of the somatic and behavioral symptoms (Ross et al., 1989), including changes in sensitivity to pain, changing taste and smell preferences, distorted visual perception, penile or vaginal pain, other pain, disturbed eating, gastrointestinal problems, motor freezing (being unable to move), excessive arousal, unexplained losses of consciousness, and changes in response to drugs, alcohol, and allergic reactions. These symptoms are not part of the diagnostic criteria for DID, but they occur in many people with this

 FOCUS   Dissociation and hysteria

Freud believed that traumatic events, especially during childhood, were significant contributors to many kinds of psychopathology, especially hysteria (Freud, 1896a/1962, 1896b/1962). Janet argued that there was a strong link between hysteria and dissociation. Hysteria is a personality pattern characterized by dramatic emotional displays, a caricature of feminine behavior, and social naïveté. It is also characterized by suggestibility and an increased susceptibility to hypnosis, which may help explain the link to dissociative disorders. This personality type has traditionally been associated with conversion disorders. However,

with the publication of DSM-III (APA, 1980), conversion disorders were placed in the category of somatoform disorders (see Chapter 9), and the dissociative disorders were accorded their own category.

Nemiah (1998) argues that these changes in the diagnostic system, which were motivated by a desire to define syndromes behaviorally in order to enhance interrater reliability, created a distinction between these disorders that does not exist naturally. Whether this assertion is true is an empirical question that has yet to be resolved. What is clear is that trauma, especially childhood trauma, is reported by people with both hysterical

disorders, such as conversion disorder (Loeb, 1997), and dissociative disorders, such as DID (Putnam & Carlson, 1998). Although modern psychopathology has not generally accepted psychodynamic interpretations, often because of the limited data supporting them, this may be an area in which some of the earliest observations of Freud and others offer clues to the developmental processes underlying both somatoform and dissociative disorders. Certainly it is worth entertaining the hypothesis that a common process—trauma—may, in combination with other factors, contribute to each of these disorders.

disorder. Several of these behaviors are also apparent in animals that have faced specific traumas (van der Kolk et al., 1985, 1989, 1994). Furthermore, the constellation of symptoms found in traumatized animals depends on the nature of the trauma, its intensity, and its duration (Bolles & Fanselow, 1980; Siegfried et al., 1990).

Given these similarities and the fact that childhood abuse is often reported by people with DID, Nijenhuis and his colleagues speculated that some of the symptoms commonly found in people with DID may be evolutionary adaptations that serve a protective function in traumatized animals. For example, motor freezing decreases the visibility of an animal to predators, and decreased sensitivity to pain permits flight even when the individual is hurt. Disturbed eating decreases risk because the animal is avoiding periods of vulnerability when seeking food, and excessive arousal shortens reaction time and therefore permits more rapid escape. Exactly what processes are most protective of the animal will depend on the situation. Some protect the animal that is in potential danger; others protect the animal that is facing an immediate threat; others allow rapid recovery from a dangerous situation.

Nijenhuis and his colleagues measured each of these somatic symptoms with a self-report scale in a group of 50 individuals with dissociative disorders (mostly DID) and a comparison group of people with other psychiatric disorders that were not dissociative in nature (mostly anxiety disorders and depression). They found that individuals with dissociative disorders showed significantly higher levels of all of the somatic and behavioral characteristics observed in traumatized animals, which suggests that these symptoms may well be part of a general response to trauma that exists in both animals and humans (Nijenhuis et al., 1998a). These data are summarized in Figure 15.5. Not all of the data imply continuity between humans' and other animals' responses to trauma. For example, for reasons that are unclear, humans sometimes show chronic pain in response to trauma, whereas animals tend to show pain only during the recuperative stage (Nijenhuis et al., 1998b). Taken together, these data support the idea that trauma affects somatic and behavioral systems and that these effects can apparently last for years. Given that these same effects are found in a variety of animals, the speculation that they are an evolutionary response that either serves a defensive function or aids in recuperation is plausible, although considerably more research is necessary.

Nijenjuis and his colleagues have argued that many of the features that co-occur with dissociation, such as freezing and diminished pain sensitivity, may be part of an evolutionary response to significant threat and trauma. These features are also apparent in animals that are terrified.

Check Yourself 15.5

Causes of Dissociative Disorders

1. What two factors have been proposed as contributing to dissociative disorders?
2. How strong is the evidence for childhood abuse as a risk factor for DID?
3. Describe the autohypnotic model of DID.
4. What elements, in addition to dissociation, do Nijenhuis and his colleagues suggest may be part of an evolutionary response to trauma?

Ponder this . . .   Brainstorm reasons why there might be little evidence of alters in childhood when the current evidence suggests that abuse in childhood contributes to the development of DID. For each speculation, what data would researchers need in order to confirm or disconfirm it?

TREATING DISSOCIATIVE DISORDERS

Unlike the disorders covered in earlier chapters, in which there is a general consensus on the most effective treatments, much less is known about the best ways to treat dis-

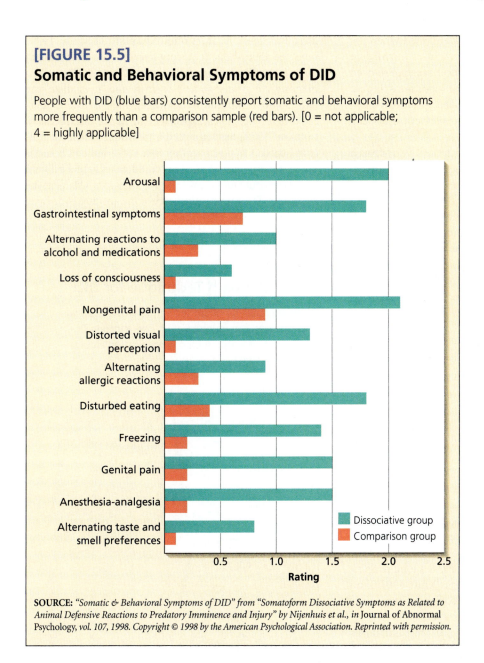

[FIGURE 15.5]

Somatic and Behavioral Symptoms of DID

People with DID (blue bars) consistently report somatic and behavioral symptoms more frequently than a comparison sample (red bars). [0 = not applicable; 4 = highly applicable]

SOURCE: *"Somatic & Behavioral Symptoms of DID" from "Somatoform Dissociative Symptoms as Related to Animal Defensive Reactions to Predatory Imminence and Injury" by Nijenhuis et al., in* Journal of Abnormal Psychology, *vol. 107, 1998. Copyright © 1998 by the American Psychological Association. Reprinted with permission.*

sociative disorders. There are probably many reasons for this, but the most important is that, because these are relatively rare disorders, there is little clinical experience and no controlled research on treatment.

TREATING DEPERSONALIZATION DISORDER

There are no controlled studies on the treatment of depersonalization disorder, although dozens of books offer suggestions regarding its treatment (Spiegel, 1996; Steinberg, 2000). Most advocate a combination of supportive therapy and insight-oriented therapy aimed at helping clients to recognize the source of their depersonalization and to reconnect with family, friends, work, and other aspects of their lives. If there is a history of abuse, it is discussed until

the person feels in control of the situation again. Medication may be used to treat specific symptoms, such as depression, but is rarely used to treat the depersonalization per se. Behavioral techniques, such as progressive relaxation, have been used with mixed results. Although many respond well to relaxation, almost 20% show a paradoxical increase in anxiety (Edinger, 1985).

TREATING DISSOCIATIVE AMNESIA AND FUGUE

Dissociative amnesia and fugue generally require little more than supportive therapy, because clients typically improve on their own (Spiegel, 1996). Dissociative fugue often requires couple or family counseling, because family members may feel that they were abandoned when the person with the fugue moved away without warning or explanation. Because individuals who have experienced one episode of dissociative amnesia or fugue are at higher risk for other episodes when stressed, preventive approaches, such as teaching stress management skills, can be helpful.

Macleod (1999) devised a clever preventive approach for a client who suffered from both severe PTSD and dissociative fugue. He had the client wear a locator beacon so that he could be found if he forgot who he was and wandered off. An interesting and unexpected side effect was that the client wandered off less frequently, apparently avoiding some of the fugue states he might have experienced. It is not clear why the frequency of fugues decreased. Perhaps the escape function of the fugue was lost when this client could be found in a matter of minutes via the locator beacon.

TREATING DID

Several suggestions on the best way to treat DID have been offered (Kluft & Fine, 1993), although there have been no adequately controlled treatment studies (Gleaves, 1996; Lilienfeld et al., 1999). There is general agreement that people with DID cannot function well with multiple alters operating, but there is disagreement about the best strategies for integrating them. Some argue that it is important to identify and map the alters in order to understand the underlying dynamics of the individual and help the person achieve a stable personality integration (Fine, 1993). Others argue that efforts to map alters may create additional alters, thus complicating the therapy (Spanos, 1994). There is general agreement that therapy is a long process, often requiring years of intensive work (Kluft, 1993), and that it is rare for people with DID to recover spontaneously (Spiegel, 1996).

Critical in the treatment of DID is the formation of a trusting relationship between client and therapist (Burton & Lane, 2001; Kluft, 1993). Such a relationship is not easy to form, because clients with DID have typically been in treatment for some time with little success, often have a history of strained relationships with professionals, and may be secretive about some of their symptoms. They may also have faced considerable skepticism from prior treatment professionals (Cohen et al., 1991). The traditional approach to treatment seeks first to identify each of the alters, then to help the client understand the role that each alter may be playing, and eventually to integrate the alters into a single, more functional personality (Kluft, 1993; van der Hart et al., 1998). Simply introducing all the alters to each other can be overwhelming. For example, if there are 10 alters, there may be 45 different introductions to make. Some therapists report cases with 100 or more alters (over 5000 different

introductions). At least one therapist (Acocella, 1999) reported 4500 alters, requiring over 10 million introductions. If an alter does not have a name, Ross (1997) recommends giving it one to help identify and "crystallize" the alter. Some communication between alters is done in therapy, often with the therapist serving as the intermediary. Putnam (1989) has suggested a technique called the bulletin board. A hypothetical version of the bulletin board is illustrated in Figure 15.6. This could be an actual bulletin board but could just as easily be a journal in which alters are encouraged to communicate with one another by leaving

[FIGURE 15.6]
Bulletin Board Technique for DID

Putnam's bulletin board technique provides a way for alters to communicate with one another. The presumption is that such communication among alters will facilitate fusion.

Julie – What did you do that Brad is so mad at me? Barb
—
I haven't seen Brad. Ask Cathy. Julie
—
Brad was being a jerk, so I put him in his place. Cathy

Who has the car keys? I had to take a cab because I couldn't find them. Julie

I am going out with Brad on Saturday. I really like him, so please, don't anyone screw it up for me. Barb

Barb,
Stop trying to block me. You are a wimp without me. Cathy
—
I am a jerk whenever you are in control. Barb

OK–who made an $89 purchase at Sears? What the heck did you buy? Barb notes. Hypnosis and sodium amobarbital (so-called truth serum) are often employed to help bring out the personalities and to help clients recover lost memories (de Vito, 1993; Kluft, 1993). However, it is important to note that sodium amobarbital, despite claims that it is a truth serum, does not produce consistently accurate reports (Piper, 1993). The eventual goal is the integration or *fusion* of the personalities. Although therapists discuss this goal straightforwardly with their clients, many clients are uncomfortable with it, or, more accurately, many alters are uncomfortable with it, expressing fear that such an integration will mean their death (Kluft, 1988). Fusion can take years, although some therapists report considerable success with it (Kluft, 1993). No controlled study of this approach, or of any other approach for that matter, has been conducted to date.

There is considerable controversy about the DID treatments just described. Many professionals believe that such treatment methods may exacerbate symptoms and may even inadvertently create symptoms. This issue will be discussed in the last section of the chapter.

Check Yourself 15.6

Treating Dissociative Disorders

1. Which dissociative disorders are most likely to improve spontaneously?
2. What does controlled research suggest about the treatment of DID?

Ponder this . . .   *Why do you think there is general agreement that treatment of DID must seek to minimize or eliminate the operation of multiple alters, despite the fact that there is strong disagreement about the cause of the disorder?*

CONTROVERSIES SURROUNDING DID

DID has been a controversial diagnosis almost from its inception. The idea that two or more separate identities could be contained within a single person is outside the experi-

ence of almost everyone, and therefore it is difficult for most people even to imagine. This section will review some of the controversies surrounding this disorder. A related issue—recovered memories in therapy—is also addressed.

COULD THERAPISTS INADVERTENTLY SHAPE DID?

Perhaps the single most controversial issue surrounding DID is the question of how much influence therapists have on the presentation of the symptoms. This issue was explored in a series of articles in the prestigious journal *Psychological Bulletin.*

Spanos (1994) proposed the **sociocognitive model of DID,** in which he argued that many of the dramatic symptoms of DID may be shaped by a combination of generally available information about the disorder and subtle differences in therapists' responses to client behavior. Vague statements suggesting the possibility of DID in a client may fascinate therapists, because this is a rare and unusual disorder. Could this increased interest in what clients are saying influence clients to say more along the same lines? Spanos thinks so. He suggests that the normal social reinforcement found in any interaction may contribute to the shaping of DID. What he asserted was that the symptoms of DID may be more parsimoniously explained by assuming a subtle shaping in therapy—part of an active effort to uncover new identities as a step toward an eventual cure. For example, the bulletin board technique described earlier clearly implies the existence of multiple identities and puts subtle pressure on clients to "produce" these identities. Spanos (1994) argued that a more effective treatment strategy would be to avoid reinforcing the report of multiple identities by essentially ignoring those reports and focusing on such issues as current functioning, depression, anxiety, and the way the clients respond to everyday stressors. Spanos did not suggest that clients are faking the disorder to please therapists or that either therapists or clients are aware of their influences on each other. He also did not claim that clients who had DID do not have emotional problems. The clinical literature clearly indicates that these clients have multiple psychological problems, function poorly in social and work environments, and have generally been in therapy for years prior to the diagnosis of DID (Gleaves, 1996). Let's look at the evidence relevant to this sociocognitive model of DID.

sociocognitive model of DID   A model proposed by Spanos, in which he argued that many of the dramatic symptoms of DID may be shaped by a combination of generally available information about the disorder and subtle differences in therapists' responses to client behavior.

Examining the Evidence

Spanos's sociocognitive model of DID has been the subject of considerable debate. Gleaves (1996) challenged both his assumptions and his conclusions, noting, for example, that people with DID are shy and unlikely to seek attention by displaying unusual symptoms. He also questioned Spanos's argument that people with DID receive special treatment, pointing out that most individuals with DID attract considerable skepticism about their symptoms from mainstream treatment professionals. He also challenged the contention that the procedures commonly used to treat DID could actually create symptoms, maintaining that there is no foundation for this claim. He noted that the goal of treatment was to help clients to understand that the alters *are* self-generated, not to convince clients that they represent real personalities. This common misunderstanding about the nature of DID was one of the reasons why researchers studying DID pushed for a change from the name *multiple personality disorder* to the name *dissociative identity disorder* (Kluft, 1988; Ross, 1990).

Gleaves (1996) addressed the iatrogenic issue in several ways. First, he noted that people with DID report a history of sexual abuse, which he argued should not exist if therapists created the disorder (Ross et al., 1991). He also noted that DID is apparently found in many cultures (Coons et al., 1991) and that it has been formally recognized for only 30 years (APA, 1980). He attributed the dramatic rise in DID cases to this formal diagnostic recognition, but the increase in DID cases predated DSM-III and actually began about the time that the book *Sybil* was published (Borch-Jacobsen, 1997). *Sybil* was also the first publication to suggest a link between child abuse and DID. Child abuse was not mentioned in the case histories published before *Sybil* was released (Borch-Jacobsen, 1997). Finally, Gleaves argued that the claim that the best way to treat people with DID is to ignore the manifestations of alters is called into question by the fact that most DID individuals are treated for years, without significant improvement, before the DID diagnosis is recognized.

Spanos died shortly after the publication of his paper in 1994 and so was unable to respond to Gleaves's commentary. However, a group of scholars did reply. Lilienfeld et al. (1999) began by clarifying the theory of role enactment, which hypothesizes that individuals adopt social roles on the basis of their own aspirations and the demand characteristics of the situation. The model does not imply that these roles are consciously adopted, and it certainly does not imply that individuals fake symptoms to please their therapists. Rather, it posits that all people are sensitive to the impact of their behavior on others and adjust their behavior accordingly. They also clarified that there was no debate about the existence of DID, only a question about the

factors responsible for the most dramatic symptom—the presentation of multiple personalities. Although accepting the reality of DID, Lilienfeld et al. (1999) noted that some of the supposedly unique aspects of the disorder are not so unique as had been claimed. For example, many people with DID have significant gaps in their memory for childhood events, but so do 20% of the general population (Read, 1997). They also point out that the data on the relationship between child abuse and DID is based exclusively on retrospective self-reports, nearly always without independent corroboration, and that, as noted earlier, many of the self-reports contain information that makes them suspect. Finally, Lilienfeld et al. (1999) note that there is no other DSM diagnosis in which an essential feature is "often or usually unobservable prior to treatment and . . . tends to emerge and become considerably more florid during treatment" (p. 512). This fact alone raises suspicions regarding iatrogenic effects. Questions about iatrogenic effects will continue until there is strong evidence that the multiple personalities exist prior to treatment.

These three papers are a good example of science at work—scholars, looking at a controversial issue from divergent perspectives, challenging ideas and conclusions, looking for points of agreement, and identifying areas in which research is needed to resolve critical theoretical issues. Scientific consensus on these issues has yet to be achieved, but there is agreement on some issues. For example, there is a group of people who show a constellation of symptoms that includes a strong tendency toward dissociation. Most of them report a history of childhood abuse, although it is unclear whether such abuse is a critical element in the formation of this disorder. There is still considerable debate about how and when the alters that define DID form, although Gleaves et al. (1999) reported preliminary data suggesting that they may have existed prior to therapy. However, those data are preliminary and lack the scientific rigor necessary to answer this question. Most agree that the pathology is disruptive to those suffering from it, that it interferes with many aspects of functioning, and that it is difficult to treat. Finally, little is known about the biological contributors to DID.

RECOVERED MEMORIES

An issue that is related to the controversies about DID, but extends beyond them, is the accuracy of recovered memories of abuse in childhood. It is relevant to the DID controversies because recovered-memory techniques are used to assess abuse histories in people with DID.

In the late 1980s, a provocative book entitled *The Courage to Heal* (Bass & Davis, 1988, 1994) was published. This combination treatise and self-help book was aimed primarily at women who had been experiencing emotional and relationship difficulties. It suggested that one's emotional difficulties could be the result of a past history of sexual abuse and that the memory of such abuse is often repressed because it is too painful. The book was widely read and cited, probably because it struck a responsive chord in many people. Therapists who had seen firsthand the negative impact of childhood abuse began to suspect that such abuse was more widespread than they had realized, and they began to encourage clients to search their minds for *repressed memories* of that abuse. These probing techniques often uncovered case after case of seemingly forgotten prior sexual abuse. Clients were suing relatives for abuse alleged to have occurred 20 or more years earlier, and even well-known public figures, such as Rosanne Barr, talked about recovering memories of earlier abuse.

Memory researcher Elizabeth Loftus and her colleagues (Loftus & Ketchum, 1994; Loftus & Polage, 1999) challenged the repressed-memory position on two grounds. The first was that there was little scientific evidence that memories of trauma could be repressed and then reliably recovered later. The second was that there was evidence that false memories could be unintentionally implanted through the techniques that were being employed by therapists. For example, Loftus demonstrated that one could easily implant, in either young children or adults, a memory of being lost in a mall as a child. Showing that such memories *can* be implanted does not of course show that a recovered memory *has* been implanted. However, the techniques used to implant such memories in the laboratory were virtually identical to those used by therapists to "recover" repressed memories, which certainly raises the possibility that these memories were created by the therapeutic process itself.

There is now scientific research that suggests that the use of recovered-memory techniques, rather than being therapeutic, tends to make clients worse. For example, clients with a diagnosis of DID and depression who recovered memories of sexual abuse during treatment showed a greater risk for suicide attempts after treatment than before, whereas a comparison group of depressed individuals showed a reduction in suicide attempts following treatment (Fetkewicz et al., 2000). However, not everyone agrees with these findings or believes that the recovered-memory techniques are problematic, arguing instead that this research is politically motivated and is essentially antifeminist (Gaarder, 2000). However, such arguments are also political and do nothing to refute the scientific evidence.

This controversy, like many in society, has made it into the courts, and in several cases, therapists who practiced the techniques for recovering repressed memories have been held liable for using questionable and harmful techniques (Appelbaum, 2001). Increasingly, courts are rejecting as unreliable the testimony of clients who, in the course of therapy, "recovered" memories of abuse (Gordon, 1998). No one is saying that therapists should not consider the very real problem of child sexual abuse in the treatment of clients, nor is anyone saying that no clients with such a history have repressed the memory of it. What is being challenged is the use of techniques that research shows are likely to create false memories—that is, memories that feel real but are not real—without regard to the welfare of clients and their families.

The issue remains contentious (Partlett & Nurcombe, 1998). A review of the published papers on this question quickly reveals the intensity of the feelings on both sides of the issue. Few debates on the scientific merits of divergent opinions have been marked by as much name calling, sometimes even in the titles of the articles (see, for example, Piper et al., 2000). In the meantime, everyone agrees that people are suffering needlessly, although they disagree on why. By and large, the argument has been between two groups. One is composed primarily of academic researchers—many of them memory researchers like Loftus—who argue that the claims for repressed memory are refuted by scientific evidence. The other group is composed of therapists who work with clients who have been abused and with other clients who they strongly suspect have been abused. One side argues that people's lives are being turned inside out by inadvertently implanted memories, whereas the other side argues that there is a systematic effort to prevent necessary treatment. Both sides have good intentions, but only one side buttresses its arguments with scientific data.

CAN DID BE FAKED?

One might wonder why anyone would want to fake DID. Under normal circumstances, there is little reason to fake such a disorder, but for those in legal difficulty, it may provide a way to escape the consequences of one's actions. That was the case for Kenneth Bianchi, better known as "the Hillside Strangler." Together with a relative, Bianchi abducted, brutally raped, and murdered ten women in the Los Angeles area in the late 1970s. Each was left naked along the hillsides that surround LA.

When Bianchi was finally caught, with overwhelming evidence against him, he continued to assert his innocence, which led his attorney to suspect the presence of psychiatric problems. The attorney brought in a psychologist to evaluate Bianchi. Bianchi was hypnotized and asked whether there was another part of himself who could speak with the psychologist conducting the examination. This deliberately vague question is often used by treatment experts to draw out alters in individuals suspected of having DID

The Hillside Strangler, Kenneth Bianchi, tried unsuccessfully to convince a jury that he suffered from DID. However, the prosecution's expert witness pointed out inconsistencies in Bianchi's account that discredited his contention.

(Putnam, 1989). Bianchi immediately responded with another personality named Steve, who readily confessed to all the murders and asserted that Kenneth knew nothing about any of them. On the basis of this finding, Bianchi's attorney argued that Bianchi was "not guilty by reason of insanity."

The prosecution bought none of it, and they brought in their own expert, Martin Orne (Orne et al., 1984). Orne interviewed Bianchi extensively, sometimes under hypnosis, and gathered information about Bianchi from those who knew him well. In testimony, he argued that if Bianchi had a true multiple personality disorder, then

▶ His alters should have been consistent over time.

▶ The nature of his alters should not be readily changed by social cues.

▶ He should respond to hypnosis in the same way that others respond.

▶ Those who knew him should be able to provide examples of sudden, inexplicable changes in behavior and identity and other evidence to corroborate his claimed intermittent amnesias.

Orne testified that Bianchi responded to a subtle, but untrue, suggestion that true multiple personalities always have at least three identities by producing another identity during a subsequent hypnosis session. In fact, Bianchi responded to a whole series of such suggestions over the long interview process. Furthermore, Bianchi's behavior under hypnosis was not the same as one typically finds with individuals who are truly hypnotized. For example, he showed little of the suggestibility that is common in hypnosis and more awareness of surrounding activity. Finally, there was absolutely no evidence in Bianchi's history of the kind of personality shifts, periods of amnesia, or other behaviors commonly reported in people with DID. Not a single acquaintance could recall such behavior prior to Bianchi's arrest. The prosecution also presented evidence that Bianchi had several psychiatric texts at his home, some of which discussed the symptoms of multiple personality disorder. They argued that Bianchi used this information to fake the disorder in an effort to avoid the death penalty.

Did Kenneth Bianchi attempt to fake multiple personality disorder to avoid the gas chamber? Probably. The jury certainly thought so. If he had been more sophisticated, could he have convinced the experts and a jury that he truly had multiple personality disorder? He might have, although juries are skeptical of psychiatric defenses (Simon, 1999). Does this case offer any evidence about the normal processes of DID? Definitely not. Bianchi was almost certainly malingering—that is, deliberately trying to fake a disorder for his own benefit. Even those who suggest an iatrogenic origin for some DID symptoms do not believe that most clients are actively malingering (Lilienfeld et al., 1999).

Check Yourself 15.7

Controversies Surrounding DID

1. What is the single most critical issue that must be addressed by those who argue that the multiple personalities of DID are not shaped by therapists?

2. What is the basic problem with the recovered-memory techniques used by some therapists?

Ponder this . . . *In criminal cases, defendants may have an incentive to fake a psychiatric disorder to avoid responsibility for a crime. Consequently, doctors must be skeptical of the symptoms being presented during such forensic assessments. However, such skepticism is not part of a normal diagnostic interview, because therapists assume that clients have little incentive to be dishonest about their experiences. What implications would the routine introduction of such skepticism on the part of the therapist have for the therapeutic relationship?*

SUMMARY

DELIRIUM

- Delirium is a widespread disruption in cognitive functioning. Identifying the physiological problems that are responsible and correcting them is the most effective treatment. Delirium can often be prevented by carefully monitoring and managing the variables likely to contribute to delirium.

DEMENTIA

- Dementia is a gradual deterioration of intellectual functioning, which typically develops over months or years. The most common cause of dementia is Alzheimer's disease. Other causes of dementia include head injuries, tumors, strokes, substance abuse, infections, and other presenile dementias.

- Surgical interventions are used to treat some neurological problems, such as tumors. Rehabilitation can help overcome functional deficits. Treating Alzheimer's involves trying to slow the progress of the disease, using medication for managing symptoms, and providing support.

AMNESTIC DISORDERS

- Amnestic disorders are characterized by a persistent memory disturbance due to a medical disorder or exposure to toxins. With the exception of Korsakoff's syndrome, which can be reversed with vitamin supple-

ments, treatment for amnestic disorders usually involves cognitive rehabilitation.

DISSOCIATIVE DISORDERS

- Depersonalization, a feeling of detachment or estrangement from oneself, is a common reaction to stress. When these feelings are persistent and distressing, the person may qualify for a diagnosis of depersonalization disorder.

- Dissociative amnesia and fugue both involve loss of autobiographical memory, but fugue also involves the person moving away and taking on a new identity.

- Dissociative identity disorder (DID) is characterized by the presentation of two or more alternate personalities, or alters.

CAUSES OF DISSOCIATIVE DISORDERS

- Trauma has long been associated with dissociative symptoms, and childhood trauma is commonly reported in DID.

- The autohypnotic model of DID argues that some individuals use self-hypnosis as a way of emotionally escaping abusive situations and that the hypnotic trance eventually becomes a distinct personality.

- The somatic and behavioral symptoms that occur with dissociation are also found in traumatized animals, which suggests that they may represent an evolutionary adaptation that facilitates emotional and physical recovery.

ers argue for ignoring alters and focusing on current problems.

TREATING DISSOCIATIVE DISORDERS

- Depersonalization disorder is usually treated with a combination of supportive therapy and insight-oriented therapy.
- Dissociative amnesia and fugue usually remit without treatment.
- Treating DID is a long process, and there is considerable debate about the best approach. Some argue for mapping the alters and then integrating them, whereas oth-

CONTROVERSIES SURROUNDING DID

- Some argue that well-meaning therapists may, through differential reinforcement, be shaping the presentation of alters in people with DID.
- Other therapists may inadvertently be implanting false memories of childhood abuse by using recovered-memory techniques.
- Although it is possible to fake DID, it is unlikely that one would, unless it was to avoid responsibility for a crime.

KEY TERMS

agnosia   (480)
AIDS dementia complex   (487)
alters   (494)
Alzheimer's disease   (481)
amnestic disorders   (490)
aphasia   (480)
apraxia   (480)
autohypnotic model   (500)
bovine spongiform encephalopathy,
   or mad cow disease   (487)
cognitive disorders   (476)
continuous amnesia   (493)
Creutzfeldt-Jakob disease   (487)
delirium   (477)
dementia   (480)
depersonalization   (492)
depersonalization disorder   (492)
derealization   (496)
dissociation   (491)
dissociative amnesia   (492)
dissociative disorders   (476)
dissociative fugue   (493)

dissociative identity disorder, or DID   (494)
executive functioning   (480)
generalized amnesia   (493)
Huntington's disease   (488)
hypnosis   (500)
iatrogenic   (494)
localized amnesia   (493)
mental status examination   (482)
neurofibrillary tangles   (483)
Parkinson's disease   (488)
Pick's disease   (487)
presenile dementia   (481)
selective amnesia   (493)
senile plaques   (484)
sociocognitive model of DID   (505)
strokes, or cerebrovascular accidents (CVAs)   (486)
suggestibility   (499)
systematized amnesia   (493)
traumatic brain injury, or TBI   (485)
tumors   (486)
vascular dementia   (486)

SUGGESTED READINGS ——————————————————

Acocella, J. (1999). *Creating hysteria: Women and multiple personality disorder.* San Francisco: Jossey-Bass. This book takes a hard look at the repressed-memory movement and its relationship to the diagnosis of DID.

Hamdy, R. C., Turnbull, J. M., Edwards, J., & Lancaster, M. M. (Eds.). (1998). Alzheimer's disease: A handbook for caregivers (3rd ed). St. Louis: Mosby. This volume includes chapters on every aspect of the diagnosis and treatment of Alzheimer's.

Loftus, E., & Ketcham, K. (1994). *The myth of repressed memory: False memories and allegations of sexual abuse.* New York: St. Martin's Press. This book outlines the memory research that calls into question the validity of recovered memories. It is an evenhanded and sensitive discussion of this very emotional and sometimes divisive topic.

"A Light Hole," by Noma & Jim Bliss/©SIS.

chaptersixteen

16

Contemporary Issues and Future Directions

Out of Control

JENNA

Jenna's psychosis had controlled her life for the last several years. She had been in and out of hospitals a dozen times starting at age 19. Her bizarre delusions prompted her to do one strange thing after another. She talked to herself and to the voices she heard constantly, walked the street night and day, and sometimes went for days without eating. She confronted people on the street with crazy questions like "When will the son of God come to save us?" The wild look in her eyes, the desperate tone of her voice, and the bizarreness of her questions often terrified people. Complaints led to the police picking her up several times, but each time she was released after a few hours. The police tried to take her to the local mental hospital, but she was always released after 48 hours because there were no grounds to hold her. Her family talked to the district attorney about forcing her into treatment. Her symptoms were much less severe when she was on medication, but each time she was released from the hospital she immediately stopped taking her medication.

Did He Mean It?

TRAVIS

To say that Travis was intense would be an understatement. His therapist found the first session with him unsettling. Travis had seen several therapists and spoke negatively of each—in fact, he spoke negatively of everyone. He had never been arrested, but had been in several shouting matches with neighbors, co-workers, and strangers on the highway. He admitted to following and harassing a woman who had cut in front of him on the highway. He did not back off until he saw her pick up her cell phone and make a call. A college graduate, he had been underemployed for the last several years, perhaps because his hostile attitude was apparent even in job interviews. He had been fired twice for engaging in fistfights. So when he detailed a feud between himself and a neighbor, his therapist knew that it could easily get out of hand. A war of words became increasingly contentious, the neighbor called the police on two occasions, and Travis was threatened with arrest. Thus it was not surprising when during a therapy session, in a heated discussion of a recent incident, Travis said, "If he calls the police one more time, I'll kill the son of a bitch."

Needing More Care

PATRICIA

Patricia was 48 and had never seen a psychologist or psychiatrist in her life, but now the depression was more than she could handle. A widow with three grown children, Pat lived by herself in a modest home in the suburbs. Her husband's death from cancer three years earlier had left her with lots of bills and very little life insurance to cover them, forcing her to declare bankruptcy. Her grief from losing her husband was intense, but with the help of her children, friends, and co-workers, she was able to handle it. However, starting about a year ago, a black cloud of depression settled over her. She tried to fight it, but to no avail. Her general practitioner gave her a prescription, which helped a little. But she found it increasingly difficult to keep up with the house or go to work. Her doctor referred her to a psychiatrist, who took over the medication management and referred her to a psychologist for cognitive-behavioral therapy. A different antidepressant medication seemed to work better, and Patricia was responding well to psychotherapy, slowly turning her life around. Her insurance company had authorized four initial sessions of psychotherapy and then four additional sessions after those were used. A request for additional psychotherapy sessions was denied because she was not immediately suicidal. The insurance company did not dispute the existence of Pat's depression but argued that given her current symptoms, the medication was a sufficient treatment.

T he first 15 chapters of this text were devoted to understanding psychopathology, which has led to significant treatment advances. But there are other issues to consider. For example, although psychopathology researchers seek to understand the disorder that so completely disrupts Jenna's life, therapists, judges, and family members are placed in the position of dealing today with her behavior and its consequences. The issue for the therapist seeing Travis is less the nature of his psychopathology and more the seriousness of his threat of violence. Finally, while Pat is struggling to overcome depression, she is forced into an adversarial relationship with her insurance company over whether the treatment she is receiving will be covered. Although none of these issues addresses the causes of psychopathology, they are critically important to those who suffer from it, as well as their family members and society at large. This chapter outlines legal, ethical, and practical issues surrounding the diagnosis and treatment of psychopathology. It ends with a brief look into the future of psychopathology research.

LEGAL ISSUES

There is always an inherent tension between the rights of people who suffer from psychopathology and the rights of the public. The odd behavior of those with severe psychopathology can be annoying and disruptive to others, and on rare occasions, it can pose a threat. You learned earlier in the text that mental hospitals and programs for the mentally retarded were once built well away from population centers, in part to isolate people with psychopathology. This unreasonable approach essentially punished people with psychological disorders for being different. As you will learn in this section, recent changes have tended to give more rights to people with psychopathology, limiting actions that would restrict their freedom unless there is evidence that they represent significant immediate risk.

Few laws govern the vast majority of interactions between therapists and clients. The therapist is required to be competent and may have to prove competence through licensure. Each state has its own licensure requirements for professionals. The client is expected to pay for the agreed upon services or risk legal action for collection. The same laws apply to a plumber hired by a homeowner to replace a hot water heater. However, there are several unique situations in the field of psychopathology that raise complex legal questions and place a legal burden on the therapist, the state, and other people involved (Schopp, 2001). This section addresses three such issues: civil commitment, criminal commitment, and the therapist's duty to warn.

Psychiatric hospitalization is not intended as punishment, but sometimes a person is committed to the hospital because she or he is deemed to be dangerous. With proper care, the risk can be reduced and the person can return to the community.

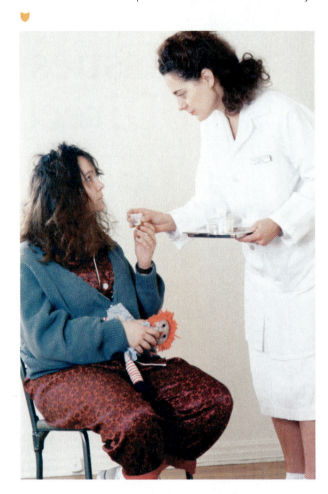

CIVIL COMMITMENT

The purpose of law is to balance the rights of individuals against the rights of society. This balance is always difficult, especially when the question of commitment is raised (Benditt, 2002). Most psychiatric hospitalizations are voluntary (Appelbaum et al., 1998; Lewis et al., 1994); those hospitalized, their families, and the doctors typically agree that hospitalization is the best option. It is generally in people's best interest to be voluntarily hospitalized, because under these circumstances they retain the right to change their mind and check out of the hospital. **Civil commitment** is the involuntary hospitalization of a person with a mental illness. When people are committed, a judge listens to evidence and decides that the person must be hospitalized. Traditionally, civil commitment is associated with hospitalization, but many states have developed

civil commitment   The involuntary hospitalization of a person with a mental illness.

statutes for outpatient commitment—requiring individuals to be in treatment, but not requiring them to be hospitalized (Reed, 2001).

Although there are subtle differences from state to state in the criteria used for commitment of someone with a severe mental disorder, the only acceptable criterion is posing a danger either to oneself or to others (Werth, 2001). All state laws governing civil commitment are based on the landmark Supreme Court ruling in *Addington v. Texas* (1979), which held that there must be clear and convincing evidence for both mental illness and dangerousness. In most cases, that involves a mental illness, such as schizophrenia, that dramatically distorts thought processes, leading to delusional beliefs that are likely to lead to violence or hallucinatory voices that actively incite the person to violence. Because males tend to be more aggressive than females, it is not surprising that the majority of individuals who are civilly committed are males who suffer from schizophrenia (Crisante & Love, 2001). One could be a danger to oneself by being suicidal, but the more common "danger to oneself" occurs in someone who is so psychotic that she or he is unable to take care of such basic needs as eating, sleeping, and minimal hygiene.

Only a judge can commit someone to a psychiatric hospital, and then only after a hearing has determined that the person meets criteria for commitment. Such hearings have to be requested by a responsible party, such as a relative, the police, or a mental health specialist. Mental health specialists tend to get involved when someone who is hospitalized on a voluntary basis seeks release, but the staff believes that the person is dangerous. In most states, professional hospital staff can block release or temporarily commit an individual deemed to be imminently dangerous if two physicians authorize the action—a process called a *2PC*. However, this is only a temporary step, and the person is entitled to a hearing before a judge at the earliest possible opportunity.

If there is sufficient reason to believe that the person might meet criteria for commitment, a judge will normally order a brief inpatient stay for an evaluation prior to a more formal commitment hearing. Most states require that anyone who is being considered for commitment have legal representation, and the state provides such representation for anyone who is unable to afford it. Many states also pay the costs of an independent psychiatric evaluation to protect the person's rights further. If the evidence supports commitment, the judge can order it. Once the person is deemed no longer to be dangerous, no matter how psychotic she or he may be, the law requires that the civil commitment be lifted (*United States v. DeBellis,* 1981). All commitments are periodically reviewed by the court to determine whether commitment is still legally justified (Schopp, 2001). More often, the professional staff treating the person determines that sufficient improvement has been made to justify either release or reclassification to a voluntary-admission status.

This section reviews the grounds for commitment and two issues that are intimately tied to commitment: the right to treatment and the right to refuse treatment.

Danger to Self or Others. As we have noted, the only justification for infringing on the civil rights of an individual with a mental disorder is that the person poses an imminent danger to self or others. Being psychotic, no matter how severe the psychosis, is insufficient. Being annoying to other people, no matter how severe the annoyance, is insufficient. Being potentially dangerous because delusional thinking may lead to unpredictable and dangerous behavior is insufficient. The person must engage in behavior that poses an immediate threat. This may include significant suicidal ideation in which lethality is judged to be high, an actual suicidal threat, aggressive and threatening behavior toward others, or a physical assault. However, as in most legal proceedings, the wording of the law typically leaves the judge a degree of discretion in the decision, and in most cases, there are conflicting opinions and information from professionals (Arrigo, 1996; Schopp, 2001).

These limited criteria for commitment were developed to protect the rights of mentally ill individuals not to be deprived of their freedom unless there is an immediate danger. This is certainly an improvement over a system that at one point allowed people to commit family members who were an "embarrassment" with little more than a doctor's approval (Benditt, 2002). However, one of the unintended side effects of this legislation is that most of the focus in commitment hearings is on the dangerousness, rather than on the therapeutic goals of the forced hospitalization (Winick, 2001).

Jenna, whom you met at the beginning of the chapter, illustrates some of these principles. She had been hospitalized repeatedly over a 10-year period. Most of her hospitalizations were voluntary. Typically her parents would beg her to admit herself, sometimes threatening to have her committed if she did not. Occasionally, she would stay in the hospital long enough to be stabilized; she would take her medications, and her functioning would improve. More often, she would check herself out in a few days, stop taking her medications immediately, and within a few weeks be as psychotic as she had been when she was admitted. However, each hospitalization provided her with decent meals, a safe place to sleep, and necessary medical care. She rarely stayed in the hospital long enough to reduce her psychotic symptoms. On three occasions, her behavior toward others was deemed aggressive enough to pose a threat, so the judge committed her. In each case, she was quickly stabilized with medication and supportive treatment. Then, because the doctors deemed her no longer dangerous, she was converted to a voluntary-admission status, and she soon requested a hospital release. In her case, she never required a long hospitalization for stabilization, and so she never returned to court for a follow-up hearing on her commitment. This process frustrated Jenna's parents to no end, because it seemed to them that as soon as she started receiving the treatment she so clearly needed, she was allowed to check herself out of the hospital. Again, this illustrates the inherent tensions in commitment laws, which are geared to protecting the public from danger while protecting the rights of individuals not to be incarcerated without cause; commitment laws are not designed to mandate treatment— even treatment that may be in the best interest of the individual.

The concept of danger to others has been applied recently to sexual predators, as described in the nearby Advances box. After you read about it, decide whether this is a valid application of the legal principle or whether society would be better served by specific changes in the laws governing these offenses.

A Right to Treatment. Most people take for granted that one can expect to receive treatment in a hospital, but that has not always been the case with mental hospitals. We saw in Chapter 1 that early asylums were little more than human warehouses and in Chapter 13 that early institutions for people with mental retardation were not much better. "Care" was interpreted as providing a place to live,

food to eat, and protective oversight. Treatment was by no means assured in such institutions (Baroff & Olley, 1999), although some institutions made great efforts to provide good care (Sheth & Imbroglia, 1999).

The right to treatment was established by *Wyatt v. Stickney* (1972), in which an Alabama court held that the only rationale for commitment of a person to a hospital was treatment. If the hospital was incapable of providing treatment or was unwilling to provide it, the individual could petition the court to overrule the commitment order. The judge argued in his decision that it was unreasonable to suspend the civil liberties of people with mental disorders by confining them to a psychiatric hospital unless there was some clear benefit to those who were being confined. Without an active and effective treatment program, the incarceration in a mental hospital was essentially punishment for crimes that had never been committed, which made it unconstitutional.

Wyatt v. Stickney was a landmark case because it was the first time that the courts attempted to establish minimal requirements for mental health services. The decision established several minimal criteria, some, such as minimal professional staffing levels, clearly relevant to the qual-

ADVANCES Sexual predators

The legal system has always rested on the premise that people are responsible for their actions and that they must pay for legal transgressions, either through forfeiture or incarceration. For example, if you are caught speeding, you will probably pay a fine, and if you rob a bank, you are likely to go to jail. Civil commitment laws violate this basic premise by permitting incarceration, in a hospital instead of a prison, for posing a *potential* threat rather than for committing a crime. Although there is considerable debate about the reasonableness of this exception (Schopp, 2001), it is the universal legal principle governing commitment.

Recent debate has centered on the legal fate of sexual predators, especially those who prey on children (Schlank & Bidelman, 2001). Three issues drive this debate. The first is that people who prey sexually on

other people do not usually change, as we saw in Chapter 11. The second is that such crimes are utterly abhorrent to most people, who want the perpetrators to be severely punished. There is little sympathy for the child abuser. The third is that people want to be protected from such individuals. The laws provide for a period of incarceration, depending on the crime. Most states have procedures to provide additional protection from sexual predators by making a list of their names and their whereabouts available to the public, often through the Internet, *after their release* (Schlank & Cohen, 1999).

Using the principles of civil commitment, many states routinely assess the potential risk to the population of releasing these offenders after their sentence has been served (La Fond, 2000). The U.S. Supreme Court opened the way for these hearings in their *Kansas v. Hendricks*

(1997) decision, which held that a violent sexual predator who suffers from a mental disorder can be involuntarily committed to a mental hospital even after serving a full term for the sexual offense. Although this ruling was hailed in some quarters as protecting the public from dangerous individuals, some mental health professionals have questioned whether evaluating sexual predators under this law represents a misuse of mental health laws (Janus, 2000). The issue is whether including sexual predators under this law is an end run around constitutional protections for the accused in an effort to protect the public. This ruling is likely to be debated extensively in the coming years, and new laws and new court decisions will clarify the limits of the *Kansas v. Hendricks* decision. It is certainly a dramatically different use of commitment laws from what we have seen before.

Dorothea Dix founded the Trenton Psychiatric Hospital in 1848. Unlike many of the hospitals of its era, it always has sought to provide quality care for the mentally ill.

ity of treatment, and others, such as the number of bathrooms and the size of the common area on a treatment unit, related to general quality of life. This was one of several court decisions in the 1960s through the 1980s that codified the right to quality care for people who were committed for psychiatric treatment. The impact was felt much more widely, however, because these rulings dictated that states provide treatment facilities with the financial resources to meet these minimal requirements (Marty & Chapin, 2000). Because the cost of treatment for severely and chronically mentally ill individuals is prohibitively expensive for all but the wealthiest people, the state provides the vast majority of such treatment.

A Right to Refuse Treatment. Not only does a person who is committed to a psychiatric hospital have a right to treatment, but that same person has a right to refuse treatment (Simon, 2001). Most often, the issue is the use of powerful antipsychotic medications, which can produce severe side effects and can sometimes be dangerous. The right to refuse treatment is similar to the right to refuse hospitalization in that it is not absolute; it is based on the assessment of the ability of the person to understand both the risks of treatment and the consequences of not receiving treatment. For example, if the decision to refuse treatment is based on psychotic delusions rather than on a reasonable assessment of the risks inherent in the treatment, the court may deem the person unable to make a reasoned decision and may mandate treatment. In many states, courts seek an independent evaluation of the person by someone not connected with the hospital to ascertain the person's competence to refuse treatment. The judge deciding the case often interviews the client in court and hears testimony

from several experts familiar with the person. If the treatment is successful in reducing the psychotic symptoms that were initially considered too severe to permit the person to make a rational choice, and the individual still wants to refuse treatment, the court is likely to accept the person's decision at that time.

There is an interesting paradox in the right to refuse treatment. In effect, the court has said that a person committed to the hospital has the right to refuse treatment that is likely to promote an early release. This might not be a wise decision on the part of the person, but the government does not have the authority to judge the wisdom of people's decisions. Imagine how you would feel if your decisions were being overruled by a government intent on protecting you from yourself. The right to refuse treatment also makes it clear that hospitalization and treatment are not synonymous and that hospitalization can sometimes be used solely for protection of the person or society, without treatment being required. Of course, there are many kinds of treatment. A person who refuses a particular drug treatment may be willing to try another drug or work with hospital staff on psychological interventions to improve functioning. Especially in cases of commitment, in which people have been deprived of the civil liberty of their freedom, the hospital staff has a professional obligation to provide services that are acceptable to the person and that are likely to improve psychiatric functioning to the point where discharge is possible.

CRIMINAL COMMITMENT

In contrast to civil commitment, which does not require that a crime has been committed, criminal commitment involves legal proceedings against someone who is accused of a crime. Two issues are relevant in criminal cases involving severe psychopathology: the insanity defense and competency to stand trial.

Insanity Defense. The insanity defense is probably the most controversial and most misunderstood legal issue in psychiatry. The **insanity defense,** often referred to as the *not guilty by reason of insanity* defense, is based on the premise that people cannot be held responsible for crimes if they did not understand the nature of their actions or were unable to control their actions. It is based on the legal principle that people have free will and choose their actions. Therefore, people should be held accountable for those actions *unless* they do not have the capacity for reason or choice. Actually, the exact definition of legal insanity has varied over the years as courts and legal scholars have struggled with this question. Table 16.1 summarizes the various definitions of insanity that have been used by the courts.

The legal concept of insanity is not the same as the common-sense notion of insanity, which is often thought of as synonymous with psychosis. Legal insanity is much narrower and is based on an entirely different set of assumptions from those that underlie psychological science. Whereas the legal definition of insanity rests on the concept of free will, psychological science rejects this concept, instead construing behavior as a product of antecedent factors that range from learning history to genes. Even Freud and Skinner agreed on this principle. This underlying difference in basic philosophy is the primary reason why legal insanity and the psychological definition of insanity are so different.

The concept of legal insanity has evolved over nearly two hundred years of jurisprudence. It dates back to the concept of the **irresistible impulse,** formulated in 1834, which states that people should not be held accountable for actions that they could not control. At roughly the same time in England, the **M'Naghten rule** was articulated in a murder trial; the defendant had killed the secretary to the Prime Minister because he believed God had commanded him to do so. The principle in the M'Naghten rule was that anyone who, because of a severe psychiatric disorder, did not understand the nature of an action, or whether the action was wrong, could not be held accountable for the crime. The M'Naghten rule focused more on the disordered thought processes, which could prevent a reasonable judgment about one's behavior, than on the strength of the impulse behind the behavior. It was also explicit about applying this concept only to defects that were the result of mental disease.

One or the other of these principles formed the basis for state laws on the insanity defense for over a century until the **Durham rule** (*Durham v. United States,* 1954),

[TABLE 16.1] Criteria for Insanity Defense

The various criteria for defining legal insanity, the date each was established, and the definition of each is listed below.

Irresistible Impulse	1834	This criterion defined insanity as a pathological impulse beyond the ability of the person to resist or avoid.
M'Naghten Rule	1843	This criterion defined insanity as a lack of understanding of the nature of one's action as a result of severe defects of reasoning. This rule also applied if the defect prevented the person from understanding that the behavior was wrong.
Durham Rule	1954	This criterion argued that a person was not responsible for behaviors that were the product of mental disease or defect.
American Law Institute Guidelines	1962	This criterion stated that a person could not be held responsible for a crime if, at the time of the crime, the person lacked "substantial capacity" to either appreciate the wrongfulness of the action or conform his or her actions to the requirements of law. The inability to understand the wrongfulness or the behavior or to control it had to be due to mental disease or defect, which had to be manifested in other ways besides the criminal activity.
Insanity Defense Reform Act	1984	This criterion defined insanity as an inability of a person to understand the nature of her or his crime as the result of a severe mental illness or defect. It also shifted the burden of proof to the defense. Finally, it changed the law so that the minimum period of incarceration was the sentence the person would have received if convicted. If the person recovered earlier, he or she would serve the remainder of the time in prison.
Guilty But Mentally Ill	1975	This criterion separates the question of guilt (Did the person do it?) from responsibility (Was the person sane at the time of the crime?). In that sense, the person is being held responsible for her or his actions. This criterion allows the usual sentence to be imposed, but the judge can decide whether the sentence will be served in a psychiatric facility or a prison.

Although people sometimes are led to believe that insanity defenses are get-out-of-jail-free cards, nothing could be further from the truth. Juries tend to be as skeptical of this defense as these judges.

"FRANKLY, I'M DUBIOUS ABOUT AMALGAMATED SMELTING AND REFINING PLEADING INNOCENT TO THEIR ANTI-TRUST VIOLATION DUE TO INSANITY."

SOURCE: *By permission of Sidney Harris,* http://www.ScienceCartoonsPlus.com.

which created a more general concept of legal insanity, defining it as any illegal act that was a product of mental disease or mental defect. The goal of this approach was to provide a flexible criterion that could be addressed in court via the testimony of expert witnesses. However, the problems associated with such a broad conceptualization, and the need to rely on psychiatric testimony that was often contradictory, led to a series of challenges. For example, the phrase "mental disease or mental defect" was so vague that it allowed considerable courtroom debate among mental health professionals about whether it applied to a given defendant. The **American Law Institute guidelines** were published in 1962 as an alternative to the Durham rule. They essentially combined the concept of irresistible impulse and the M'Naghten rule, defining legal insanity as either the inability to control one's actions or the inability to appreciate the wrongfulness or one's actions. They also clarified the concept of "mental disease or defect" that had been used in previous laws by specifically excluding what would now be called antisocial personality disorder.

The assassination attempt on President Reagan by John Hinckley, and the *not guilty by reason of insanity* verdict in the case, prompted the **Insanity Defense Reform Act,** which the United States Congress passed in 1984. This act made it harder to prove insanity and decreased the potential advantage of the insanity defense by fixing minimum periods of incarceration. The criteria for insanity were narrowed by eliminating the irresistible-impulse argu-

ment and requiring that the person be *unable* to appreciate the wrongfulness of an action as the result of a *severe* mental illness or defect. The words *unable* and *severe* represented more stringent requirements for insanity, but the biggest change in this law was that the burden of proof was shifted to the defense. In other words, the defense had to prove that the person was insane at the time of the crime, rather than just raising the possibility of insanity and forcing the prosecution to prove that the defendant was sane. The final provision of the Insanity Defense Reform Act eliminated the automatic release from a mental hospital if the person was later found no longer to present a danger. Instead, a defendant who recovered would be transferred from the mental hospital to a prison to serve the remainder of whatever the maximum sentence would have been for the crime. Ironically, in the case that inspired enactment of this law—John Hinckley's attempted assassination of Reagan—the defendant has already spent considerably more time in a maximum-security treatment facility than he would ever have spent in prison if he had been found guilty of attempted murder.

The Insanity Defense Reform Act applies to federal courts, although some states have adopted variations of this law. Several other states have adopted another principle— **guilty but mentally ill**—as an alternative. This verdict means that the person will be incarcerated for a period of time, but it acknowledges the presence of mental illness and

....

insanity defense A legal defense based on the premise that people cannot be held responsible for crimes if they did not understand the nature of their actions or were unable to control their actions.

irresistible impulse The concept that people should not be held accountable for actions that they could not control.

M'Naghten rule The principle that anyone who does not understand the nature of an action or whether the action was wrong, as the result of a severe psychiatric disorder, should not be held accountable for the crime.

Durham rule The definition of legal insanity as any illegal act that was a product of mental disease or mental defect.

American Law Institute guidelines Published in 1962 as an alternative to the Durham rule, they combined the irresistible-impulse principle and the M'Naghten rule, defining legal insanity as either the inability to control one's actions or the inability to appreciate the wrongfulness of one's actions.

Insanity Defense Reform Act Passed by Congress in 1984, this act defines legal insanity as existing when the person is *unable* to appreciate the wrongfulness of an action as the result of a *severe* mental illness or defect.

guilty but mentally ill A verdict that allows the person to be incarcerated for a period of time but also acknowledges the presence of mental illness and suggests the need for treatment during incarceration.

suggests the need for treatment during incarceration. In other words, it is a guilty verdict, so the defendant is being held responsible for his or her crime. In practice, the period of incarceration is about the same for guilty and guilty but mentally ill verdicts.

Note in Table 16.1 that most of the definitions of legal insanity use a phrase such as *due to mental disease or defect.* This phrase has two implications. The first is that defendants cannot claim not to be responsible for their actions because "they just didn't think about the consequences." That is not considered a valid defense. If someone runs another person off the road in anger, that person is responsible for his or her actions, regardless of whether he or she considered the implications of the actions, unless his or her failure to consider the implications was due to mental disease or defect. That criterion eliminates the popular notion of temporary insanity as a defense. The law does, however, take into account the intent of defendants in deciding the *level* of responsibility, making, for example, a distinction between manslaughter (no intent to kill) and murder (an intent to kill). But people who are capable of judging the rightness and wrongness of their actions are expected to do so. The second implication of the phrase *due to mental disease or defect* is that there are two ways in which one may be impaired in judgment: (1) as the result of a psychiatric disorder, such as schizophrenia, or (2) as a result of mental retardation or severe brain injury.

Controversy Surrounding the Insanity Defense. The reason for the changes in the definition of insanity over time is that no definition is entirely satisfactory. It is a difficult task to determine the state of mind of a defendant at the time of a crime. Note that a psychiatric diagnosis is not the criterion by which legal sanity is defined. People with schizophrenia or mental retardation may or may not be declared legally sane. Sanity in the legal sense is based not on a person's level of psychotic symptoms or IQ but, rather, on the person's ability to determine right from wrong and to control her or his actions. Of course, the degree of psychosis and mental retardation is correlated with this definition of insanity, but it is not a perfect correlation.

There has been a movement over the past 30 years to recognize that some people may not be responsible for their actions, that they deserve treatment rather than punishment, but that they represent a danger and should therefore be incarcerated for an extended period of time to protect the public (Edwards, 2001). Actually, this is not a dramatic change from previous philosophies and actions, but it has been more clearly articulated in the more recent definitions of insanity. For example, both the Insanity Defense Reform

Act and the *guilty but mentally ill* verdict specify that the person be incarcerated for a minimum term, regardless of whether the mental disease or defect improves. One reason for this change is the popular misconception, addressed in the nearby Modern Myths box, that the insanity defense was frequently being used by people to avoid responsibility and punishment (Silver et al., 1994).

Thomas Szasz has challenged the concept of the insanity defense on similar grounds to his challenge of the concept of mental illness (Szasz, 1961). Szasz (1963) argues that attributing criminal actions to mental illness may prematurely absolve people of responsibility for their actions. It reduces people's inclination to understand the reasons for a crime by essentially declaring it to be unreasonable—that is, committed by someone who was insane. Furthermore, the foundation for people's legal rights has always been the accompanying legal responsibilities. If mentally ill people are not considered legally responsible for their actions, what is the basis for granting them the legal rights associated with the civil commitment laws? He notes that the law makes a distinction between descriptive responsibility (the person did it) and ascriptive responsibility (the person is responsible for it). However, Szasz (1963) argues that this distinction is difficult to determine in practice and should be ignored. These provocative arguments about the insanity defense have generated considerable debate and controversy (Greenberg & Bailey, 1994). However, it is interesting to note that the most recent changes in the insanity defense implicitly increase one's level of responsibility for one's actions, even when legally insane, by requiring a minimum period of incarceration.

Another controversial issue surrounding legal insanity is capital punishment—specifically, whether it is reasonable to execute someone who meets the criteria for legal insanity. This issue was first raised by the case of Horace Kelly, who was convicted in California of a 1984 rape and triple murder and was sentenced to death. The issue of insanity was not raised at his trial, but his psychiatric condition deteriorated considerably while he was on death row. His attorneys argued that it would be unreasonable to execute someone who met the criteria for legal insanity at the time of execution (Dolan, 1999). A similar argument has recently been raised regarding the execution of people with mental retardation (Associated Press, 2002). These questions are far from legally resolved and will probably inspire considerable debate for some time to come. The recent case of Andrea Yates illustrates how psychiatric functioning, although it may not justify legal insanity, can contribute to a verdict by influencing the sentence. In her case, she was spared the death penalty, despite the heinousness of her crime of killing her five children, presumably because of the contribution that her mental state made to the crime.

Competency to Stand Trial. In order for a person to be tried for a criminal offense, he or she must be capable of understanding the charges and of helping his or her

---

competent to stand trial A declaration that a person is capable of understanding the charges and of helping his or her attorney in the preparation of his or her defense.

MODERN Myths

Not Guilty by Reason OF Insanity

Nearly 90% of the general public believes that the insanity defense is used too much and that it allows many guilty people to go free (Pasewark & Seidenzahl, 1979). The views of legislators are similar (Pasewark & Pantle, 1979). The actual figures are nowhere near what people believe (Silver et al., 1994). For example, the public believes that over a third of felony cases involve insanity pleas, when the actual number is fewer than 1%. The public believes that almost half of all insanity pleas are successful, when the actual number is about 25%. The public believes that half of those who successfully plead insanity are released, when the actual figure is 15%, and most of those involve minor offenses that would not have resulted in prison time anyway. Finally, the public believes that most people who are found not guilty by reason of insanity are likely to spend little time in the hospital, when in truth, they spend on average 50% more time confined in the hospital than they would have spent in prison if they had been found guilty.

The misconceptions may stem from strong public responses to cases wherein the insanity defense was used. For example, in 1981 John Hinckley attempted to assassinate President Ronald Reagan in the psychotic belief that this action would impress the actress Jodie Foster, with whom Hinckley had become obsessed. Hinckley was found not guilty by reason of insanity after a widely publicized trial, but the verdict outraged many and led to the Insanity Defense Reform Act. Many believed that Hinckley got away with murder, or at least attempted murder. The fact is that Hinckley has been held in a maximum-security psychiatric hospital for over 20 years and is unlikely to be released any time soon. Had he pled guilty to attempted murder, he would probably have spent less time in prison and, by law, would have had to be released at the end of his term.

A more recent case—that of Andrea Yates—illustrates how difficult it is to convince a jury of legal insanity. Yates killed each of her five children, ages 6 months to 7 years, by drowning them in the bathtub. At her trial, there was no question that she was mentally disturbed and had been for some time. There was little question that her mental disturbance contributed to her systematic murder of her children. Yet she was found to be legally sane, was convicted of the crime, and was sentenced to life in prison (Ahearn, 2002). However, she was not given the death penalty, perhaps because the jury felt that her level of culpability did not warrant execution.

It is difficult to prove legal insanity. All the experts agreed that Andrea Yates was mentally ill when she killed her five children, but they disagreed on whether she was legally insane. The jury decided that she did not meet the criteria for legal insanity and therefore found her guilty.

attorney in the preparation of the case. In other words, the person must be deemed **competent to stand trial.** The United States Supreme Court first articulated this standard in 1960 (*Dusky v. United States*), and it has remained the standard since that time. The issue of competency is independent of the issue of sanity at the time of the crime. The defendant may have been legally sane during the crime but may not be sane enough to meet criteria for competency to stand trial, or the defendant may have been legally insane during the crime but may later be sane enough to be competent to stand trial. Adam is typical of the kind of person who is found incompetent to stand trial.

Creating Another Mess

ADAM

Police picked up Adam for allegedly breaking over $5,000 worth of merchandise at a local furniture store after being asked to leave. Adam was homeless, and it was cold outside. He had lived on the streets for several years, except for a few brief periods during which he was hospitalized for psychiatric problems. The police who transported him to the station noted that he appeared to be hallucinating—carrying on a running conversation with some unseen individual. After a brief stay in the holding center, he was arraigned, with a public defender assigned to his case. His attorney asked the judge to order a psychiatric evaluation, because she had found her client incoherent in their brief conversation before the arraignment. Adam was transported to the local psychiatric center for the evaluation, which determined that he suffered from chronic undifferentiated schizophrenia, that he was unable to understand the charge against him, and that he could not communicate about the charge sufficiently to help with his defense. With no objection from the district attorney, Adam was remanded to the psychiatric center for treatment until such time as he was competent to stand trial.

If a defendant is found to be incompetent to stand trial, the trial is postponed *until* the client is able to understand the charges and aid in the defense. The defendant is *not* released but, rather, is typically held for treatment and is returned for trial only when the psychosis has decreased to the point where trial may proceed. This protects the public from people whose psychiatric illness or mental retardation makes them potentially dangerous, judging on the basis of their past history, and provides critically needed treatment for such defendants. This is a far more common outcome than being found not guilty by reason of insanity (Steadman, 1979). Many of these defendants never return for trial because they remain incompetent, although Adam is likely to return because his symptoms have typically waxed and waned over time. However, this procedure should never be used as a backdoor way to incarcerate someone who may be guilty of a crime, but against whom there is a weak case. The courts have held that the person found incompetent must be periodically reevaluated and that after a reasonable period of time, the defendant must either be released, be found competent to stand trial and be tried, or be subjected to civil commitment procedures (*Jackson v. Indiana*, 1972). The standard

The law holds that people cannot be tried for crimes unless they are capable of understanding the charges and of assisting in their own defense.

for civil commitment requires that the person pose an immediate threat to self or others, so many people who are incompetent to stand trial will eventually be released because they do not meet the stricter criterion. However, it would be a mistake to assume that these people "beat the rap" by avoiding standing trial, because they often spend more time in the hospital than they would have spent in jail if they had been found guilty (Arrigo, 2000).

A THERAPIST'S DUTY TO WARN

Commitment laws are based on the state's obligation to balance the rights of individuals against the rights of society. Is there a parallel responsibility for therapists? Normally, a therapist's primary responsibility is to her or his clients, and one of those responsibilities is to maintain the confidentiality of the therapeutic exchange. However, as with most legal principles, this is not an absolute. In the landmark case *Tarasoff v. Regents of the University of California* (1974, 1976), a California court held that it is the responsibility of therapists to warn potential victims when there is a reasonable expectation that one of their clients poses a significant risk to a specific person. In 1969 Tatiana Tarasoff was killed by Prosenjit Poddar, a graduate student at the University of California, after she rejected his romantic advances. Mr. Poddar was being treated at the University Health Center at the time of the murder and had been diagnosed with paranoid schizophrenia. In his last therapy session before the murder, Mr. Poddar suggested that he intended to kill Ms. Tarasoff. His therapist did not take this statement as an idle threat. In fact, the therapist chose to violate the client's normal expectation of confidentiality and spoke to the campus police. The police in turn talked with Mr. Poddar, informing him that they knew of his threat against Ms. Tarasoff. Mr. Poddar assured the police that the threat was made in anger and that he had no intention of hurting her. Unfortunately, just a few weeks later, he killed Ms. Tarasoff after failing repeatedly to contact her.

The suit against the university, the University Health Center, and the campus police argued that Ms. Tarasoff should have been warned of the danger from Mr. Poddar, given the specific threat made during therapy. The court agreed, and in doing so, set up a principle called the **duty to warn,** which states that therapists are required to warn potential victims of specific threats made by a client in a therapy session. As with many legal decisions, later cases clarified the circumstances that trigger this responsibility. For example, in *Thompson v. County of Alameda* (1980), the court found that the responsibility to warn applies only when there is a specific threat against a specific person or persons. Over the past two decades, many states have broadened the concept from a duty to warn to a duty to protect. The duty to protect concept gives therapists more latitude in their response to a threat, provided that the actions taken are sufficient to safeguard the well-being of threatened individuals. For example, taking steps to com-mit a psychotic individual who poses a threat would meet the duty-to-protect standard without requiring a specific warning to the threatened individual.

How would the duty-to-warn principle be applied for the therapist seeing Travis, who was one of the cases that opened this chapter? There is no question that Travis had a history of aggressive behavior, including fistfights, although there was no history of life-threatening assaultive behavior. He made a specific threat to a specific person, although one could argue "I'm going to kill the son of a bitch" might be just a generic statement of aggressive intent rather than a specific threat. What would you do if you were the therapist? Would a judge or jury hold the therapist responsible if no warning were given and Travis later killed his neighbor? In this case, after consulting with two colleagues and his attorney, the therapist did call the police and warn the neighbor. Travis threatened to sue for breach of confidentiality but was told by attorneys that he had been warned, in the consent form he signed before beginning therapy, of the therapist's duty to warn and that his words constituted a specific threat. Consequently, he did not have a case against the therapist. This case illustrates the fact that therapists can be caught between competing rules. The foresight of this therapist in spelling out limitations to confidentiality in a consent form that every client signs before therapy begins, coupled with his obtaining and documenting advice from colleagues and his attorney before acting, probably avoided a potential lawsuit. More important, his actions in this case may have saved a life.

Check Yourself 16.1

Legal Issues

1. What are the primary criteria for civil commitment?
2. What is the difference between the insanity defense and incompetency to stand trial?
3. When is a therapist required to warn someone about a potential danger?

Ponder this . . .   *The role of the justice system is to balance the rights of people. In dealing with people who have mental problems, the goal is to preserve as many of their rights as possible without allowing them to infringe significantly on the rights of others. Using this as a guideline, what ethical issues apply when dealing with an emotionally disturbed child who is extremely disruptive in the classroom?*

duty to warn   The principle that therapists are required to warn potential victims of specific threats made by a client in a therapy session.

ETHICAL ISSUES

Every profession is governed by a set of ethical principles designed to guide the activities of those in the profession (Gardner et al., 2001). In the field of abnormal psychology, there are two primary areas in which ethical principles are applied: treatment and research. There are also ethical principles associated with teaching and other functions of psychologists, but because these are not unique to the field of psychopathology, they will not be covered in this section. The current ethical guidelines for psychologists are available on the Web site of the American Psychological Association (**www.apa.org**), and the major ethical principles on which these guidelines are based are summarized in Table 16.2.

ETHICAL ISSUES IN TREATMENT

Therapists have a responsibility to their clients that involves providing appropriate and professional care and protecting the interests of the clients. This section addresses many, but not all, of these professional responsibilities, including confidentiality, competence, record keeping, clarifying who is considered the client, and treating clients when no empirically supported treatment exists. Each professional group (psychiatrists, social workers, etc.) has its own set of ethical guidelines, although the principles underlying these guidelines are similar across disciplines. Because of space limitations, we will focus on the ethical guidelines for psychologists.

Confidentiality. In general, the therapeutic interaction is a protected relationship, which means that the information provided to the therapist is confidential. Therapists should not share information about clients with anyone, including other professionals, unless the client has given them explicit permission to do so in writing. However, there are exceptions to this rule, and it is the responsibility of the therapist to inform clients of these exceptions before therapy starts. You learned about one such exception earlier in this chapter—the Tarasoff rule on the duty to warn. State statues dictate other exceptions. For example, in all 50 states, therapists and other professionals are required to report, to a designated state agency, information that might reasonably lead them to conclude that child abuse may be occurring (Kalichman, 1999). The abuse need not be by the client. For example, if a client describes abuse or suspected abuse by a spouse or sibling, it must be reported.

It is common for professionals who are working with the same client to share information about their treatment of the client. This information is usually shared through letters or brief summary forms, although it could also be communicated over the phone or in face-to-face conversations. This exchange of information is desirable but is permissible only if the client has given written authorization. It is often helpful for therapists to seek professional advice

[TABLE 16.2] APA Ethical Principles

The American Psychological Association's ethical guidelines cover every aspect of professional conduct. Listed here are the principles on which these ethical guidelines are based.

Principle A: Competence

Psychologists strive to maintain the highest standards of competence, and they recognize and respect the limits of their competence, providing only those services that they are qualified to provide.

Principle B: Integrity

Psychologists promote the integrity of their discipline by being honest, fair, and respectful of others. They do not make false, misleading, or deceptive statements about their qualifications or services.

Principle C: Professional and Scientific Responsibility

Psychologists clarify their professional roles and obligations and accept responsibility for their actions. They coordinate their efforts with other professionals to serve the best interests of their clients. Psychologists are concerned about both their own ethical conduct and the ethical conduct of other psychologists.

Principle D: Respect for People's Rights and Dignity

Psychologists respect the rights, dignity, privacy, confidentiality, and autonomy of all people. They strive to eliminate cultural and other biases in their professional work.

Principle E: Concern for Others' Welfare

Psychologists are concerned with the welfare of others, and they strive in their professional interactions to avoid doing anything that threatens the welfare of another. Psychologists are sensitive to the difference in power between themselves and others, and they never exploit that power differential in their professional relationships.

Principle F: Social Responsibility

Psychologists have a responsibility both to their community and to the society in which they live, and they should use psychological principles to enhance human welfare and reduce human suffering. They are encouraged to donate some portion of their professional time to this cause.

SOURCE: *"Ethical Principles of Psychologists and Code of Conduct,"* 1992, from http://www.apa.org. *Copyright © 1992 by the American Psychological Association. Reprinted with permission.*

on a case from colleagues. In fact, the ethical guidelines encourage such exchanges, especially if there is a question about an ethical issue. During such exchanges, however, the therapist should avoid providing information that could reasonably permit the colleague to identify the client.

Psychologists are permitted to use case information for educational purposes, provided that the confidentiality of the client is maintained. About 70% of the case material in this textbook was drawn from cases seen or supervised by the author. The other cases were drawn from published sources or from the caseloads of colleagues. In each case, the name was changed, and any such identifying information as occupation or nonessential details of the person's background was modified to protect the identity of the client. The client might recognize her or his case, even though some details had been changed, but no one else should be able to identify the person. Special care needs to be taken to protect the confidentiality of clients when cases are presented to an audience that is likely to include someone who knows the client.

It is the client who has the right of confidentiality, not the therapist. Clients have a right to discuss anything they want about the therapist or therapy sessions. Clients also have the right to waive their confidentiality. For example, a client may agree to meet with a group of professionals as part of a case presentation or may consent to be taped for instructional purposes. However, the therapist should be especially careful not to put pressure on the client or to influence the client's decision, keeping in mind that clients may feel an obligation to cooperate with such an enterprise even though they may not really wish to be involved.

Competence. The ethical guidelines state that psychologists should practice within their areas of competence and that such competence is defined by a combination of education, training, and experience. It would be unethical, for example, to conduct a neuropsychological assessment if one did not have the requisite background to do the assessment. For something as complex as neuropsychological assessment, competence usually requires formal education, specific training, and a reasonable level of experience. Until such qualifications are achieved, a person should practice, in that area, only under the supervision of a qualified professional. Other areas may require less formal training for a person to achieve professional competence. For example, someone trained in cognitive-behavioral therapy can achieve competence in a new cognitive-behavioral treatment protocol through systematic self-study and reading, continuing-education training programs, or supervision from a qualified person. General familiarity with cognitive-behavioral interventions will enable a therapist to generalize and apply variations of those methods to new problems. Competence also involves a familiarity with cultural, gender, and other individual differences and of how those differences affect the psychologist's work. For example, it would be unethical to ignore the cultural values of a client during the planning and execution of a treatment program.

The ethical guidelines state explicitly that psychologists are expected to remain current in their field by keeping up to date on current research and professional information relevant to their work. It is not adequate to earn a Ph.D. and then spend an entire career using just the information acquired in graduate school. You saw in Chapter 15 that professionals have been held accountable by courts for being unaware of memory research that would have caused them to question the validity of the recovered-memory techniques they were using (Brown et al., 1998; Corelli et al., 1997). Not only must psychologists be aware of current research relevant to their work, but their professional judgments must be based on such work.

Records. Clinical psychologists, like other health care providers, are expected to maintain appropriate records of client contact to facilitate and document treatment. These records should be sufficient to provide a basis for treatment decisions and treatment monitoring. If there is a reasonable expectation that the records may become part of a legal action, the therapist has an additional duty to keep sufficiently detailed and accurate records to meet the needs both of therapy and of a judicial action. Some records are created for insurance companies, which use them to decide whether additional services are covered under the policy. Those records should accurately reflect what is happening in therapy and why.

Who Is the Client? Asking who the client is may seem silly if you envision psychologists as people who meet one-on-one with adult clients in their offices. However, psychologists provide services to a wide variety of clients in a wide variety of settings. For example, school psychologists assess learning problems in students. Is the client the child, the child's parents, or the school? In this context, the word *client* does not necessarily apply to the person being seen but, rather, to the person or institution to which the psychologist has primary responsibility. In other words, if the interests of the parties involved differ, whose interests should take precedence? The ethical guidelines do not give clear answers, but they encourage psychologists to avoid multiple roles and to clarify their roles whenever there might be ambiguity. For example, a 16-year-old normally does not have the same right to confidentiality that an adult has, and therefore parents could ask about therapy sessions. However, some therapists ask parents to grant their child such confidentiality, within certain limits, to facilitate therapy. The limits may exclude information on suicidal ideation, criminal activity, or whatever areas on which all parties mutually agree. It is especially important to clarify roles if it is expected that the case may involve legal action.

What If No Treatment Exists? Throughout this text, the various treatment options for disorders have been described, often with the research that supports the effectiveness of these treatment options. For every disorder, there was a time when no empirically supported treatment existed, and even now, for some disorders (such as antisocial personality disorder) there is no reasonably effective treatment.

It is certainly legitimate to experiment with new procedures. Without such experimentation, none of the current treatments would have been developed. However, clients must be informed that the procedure being used is experimental. If there is another procedure that has been shown to be effective, clients should be told that before they are

Therapists should always clarify what their role will be. When treating a child, does the therapist have primary responsibility to the child or to the child's parent(s), who brought the child into therapy?

asked to undergo the experimental procedure. Most often, an experimental procedure is tried after an empirically supported procedure has not worked. *Empirically supported* simply means that the procedure has been shown to be at least better than a placebo, and there is no guarantee that the treatment will work for any given client. The clinician also has a responsibility to design experimental procedures on the basis of the best available scientific information, not just hunches. The science of psychology provides information and theories about human functioning on which plausible treatments can be based.

ETHICAL ISSUES IN RESEARCH

The APA specifies ethical principles that govern the research process. These principles apply to all psychological research, but some principles are especially important in research on psychopathology.

Ethical Constraints on Research Design. All research raises ethical issues, but psychopathology research raises more issues than most other research. Many scientifically relevant research studies will never be conducted, because they are ethically unacceptable. For example, say a researcher believes that child abuse increases risk for dissociative identity disorder (Chapter 15). The strongest way to test this hypothesis would be an experiment in which the researcher manipulated the amount of abuse that children receive. Of course, that design is completely unacceptable; even stating it here for the purpose of illustration is repugnant. Dozens of theories of psychopathology are experimentally untestable because of ethical constraints, so re-

searchers are forced to evaluate these hypotheses through indirect means, as discussed in Chapter 6. Despite these ethical constraints, research on psychopathology has led to significant breakthroughs in the understanding of several disorders and the factors that contribute to them.

By its very nature, psychopathology research involves sensitive issues—and therefore raises ethical concerns. The ethics of all research is judged on the basis of a risk/benefit analysis (Emanuel et al., 2000). Some risks are so extreme that no benefit justifies them. More often the risks are not that extreme and must be weighed against the benefits. For example, an uncomfortable treatment procedure, such as exposure therapy for anxiety, may be justified if the person is significantly handicapped by the current anxiety, if the treatment has a reasonable chance of succeeding, and if no other treatments exist. These are all judgment calls, which is one reason why research plans are routinely evaluated by outside bodies called **Institutional Review Boards (IRBs)**. These IRBs evaluate the ethical appropriateness of studies, with an eye to protecting the welfare of study participants. Most universities, hospitals, and research institutes have their own IRB, and all research must be reviewed by it before any data are collected.

Treatment studies pose a unique ethical challenge. Unlike most psychopathology research, in which experimental manipulation is often unethical, the random assign-

· ·

Institutional Review Boards (IRBs) An appointed group of people who evaluate the ethical appropriateness of studies with an eye to protecting the welfare of study participants.

ment of participants in a treatment study is both ethical and desirable. The ethical issues in treatment research involve what conditions to include. Is it ethical to include a **placebo control group**—one that receives an inert treatment with no active treatment elements? Many argue that such controls are unethical because they effectively deny people treatment in the name of research (La Vaque & Rossiter, 2001). But not including a placebo renders it very difficult to interpret findings (Fritze & Moeller, 2001). The way this ethical dilemma is handled is that most studies include a placebo control group, but those given the placebo are typically offered other treatment at the end of the study (National Academies of Sciences and Engineering and Institute of Medicine, 1995). It is also not unheard of for a study to be terminated prematurely, so that all participants can benefit, if it becomes clear early in the study that the experimental treatment is effective.

Informed Consent. The primary safeguard in any research project is **informed consent,** which means that the research participants agree to participate in the study only after they have been given an adequate description of the project, what is involved, what risks might exist, and what benefits they can expect. Many journals now routinely refuse to publish research unless the author attests to the fact that appropriate informed consent was obtained from all participants (Ilgen & Bell, 2001). Informed consent gives people a choice whether to participate, but it does not remove the researchers' responsibility to operate ethically and professionally in every aspect of the research. As part of the informed consent, participants should be told that they have the right not only not to participate at all but also to cease participating at any point.

On rare occasions, deception is included in a research study of psychopathology. The use of deception runs counter to the principle of informed consent, so one might expect that deception is unethical. But the principle of

One of the most critical ethical safeguards in research is informed consent. Every research subject has the right to decide, after being fully informed about the study, whether to participate.

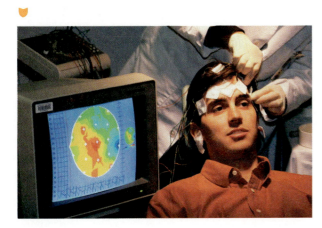

informed consent is not absolute, and deception may be ethically justified under the right conditions. However, deception cannot be used if it entails significant risk for participants, and it should not be used if the research question could be answered adequately via nondeceptive procedures. Chapter 8 described a study that employed deception to answer a question that could not be answered in any other way. Sanderson et al. (1989) exposed people with panic disorder to CO_2, which normally triggers panic attacks in people with the disorder. They were told that a knob controlled the flow of the CO_2, but only when a light was on. Half were exposed to the CO_2 with the light on and half without the light on. In truth, the knob did nothing, regardless of whether the light was on. Thus these researchers were testing the effect of an "illusion of control" on panic, and they found that this illusion of control significantly reduced panic attacks. This finding had enormous significance for the cognitive-behavioral treatment of panic, and it could not have been discovered without the deception. Similarly, the many balanced placebo studies of the pharmacological and expectancy effects of alcohol all involve deception (see Chapter 14).

Vulnerable Populations. In addition to the ethical constraints on research designs, ethical issues are raised by the nature of the people studied in psychopathology research. Many, though not all, people with psychopathology are sensitive to outside stressors. Procedures that may seem innocuous to others may create anxiety, frustration, or worse in those struggling with one or more psychiatric disorders. It is the responsibility of researchers to use procedures that do not stress participants too much, to monitor the response of participants, and to discontinue procedures that are excessively upsetting.

People with dementia or psychosis represent another vulnerable population. Severe dementia or psychosis may make informed consent impossible, so consent must come from those family members or others who are entrusted with power of attorney. In addition, weighing the risks and benefits of research on dementia is difficult (Karlawish & Casarett, 2001). With a terminal illness, such as Alzheimer's, is any risk acceptable given the alternative of not acting? Should one discount health risks of experimental drugs because participants are likely to die of the disease in a matter of months? What about pain and other aversive consequences? These are not trivial issues, and in the case of dementia, participants are generally unable to voice their feelings about them.

placebo control group   In a study, a group that receives an inert treatment with no active treatment elements.

informed consent   The principle that research participants can agree to participate in a study only after they have been given an adequate description of the project, of what is involved, of what risks might exist, and of what benefits they can expect.

The use of children in research raises several ethical issues. By law they are unable to give consent, so someone else must consent to the research (King & Churchill, 2000). Normally that will be parents, but in some instances it will be another responsible party. Although children cannot give legal consent, they can give **assent**—their simple, non-legal agreement to participate in the study ("nonlegal" in the sense that it does not constitute legal consent, which still must be obtained from parents or another responsible party). Children have the right to refuse to participate or to withdraw from a study at any time, even if their parents consented to their participation.

The federal government now mandates that children be included in government-funded research unless the researcher can justify excluding children on scientific or ethical grounds. Past research often failed to include children, and consequently, too little is known about health and psychological issues in children (**www.nih.gov**). Of course, it is legitimate to exclude children from some studies. For example, children would not be included in a study of Alzheimer's disease. But studies of anxiety and depression, both of which occur in children, now often include children. This mandate, based primarily on the principle that all segments of the population should be represented in research funded by taxpayers, may eventually yield a scientific bonanza. Including children in studies of psychopathology increases investigators' opportunities to study the developmental course of disorders, or at least highlights potentially important developmental issues that could be addressed in later research. The same government mandates apply to including both sexes and culturally diverse populations in government-funded research. Again, including such individuals in research samples enables researchers to identify cultural and gender influences that might otherwise be overlooked. This practice not only provides information on how relevant the findings are to various subsets of the population, such as women or Hispanics, but also alerts researchers to possible cultural influences that they might miss if they studied a more culturally homogeneous sample.

Some of the most important research with children is also the most ethically sensitive. For example, the abuse and maltreatment of children are a major concern. There are heated debates about the extent of the problem (Oates, 1996) and about the ability of children to report accurately the events associated with such abuse (Eisen et al., 2002). But how do you evaluate such issues scientifically? Johnson (2000) discusses some of the challenges in ethically studying the ability of children to report abusive behavior. He used videotapes of simulated parent-child interactions, some of which contained abusive content. He was inter-

ested in how accurately the children could report what occurred on the videotapes. The central issue is how graphic one can ethically make the content. If the content is too graphic, the research probably crosses an ethical boundary, because it could be too upsetting for the child. However, if the content is too bland, the research will fail to yield any useful information about the reliability of children's reports of abusive behavior. Society needs to know about such reliability in order to guide investigations of alleged abuse. It is a difficult task to balance the rights of children to be free of abuse and the rights of accused adults not to be convicted on the basis of possibly unreliable evidence.

Confidentiality. Every research participant has a right to expect confidentiality. However, in much research, because of the innocuous nature of the data collected, little damage would be done if confidentiality were breached. That is almost never the case in psychopathology research, in which the nature of the information gathered is nearly always sensitive. For example, most psychopathology research obtains information about a person's functioning—information that could be embarrassing to the person if it were released. In fact, some information could potentially affect the person's employment, insurability, or relationships. Even relatively innocuous data are often associated with sensitive diagnostic information. For example, one might be studying the eye tracking performance of people with and without the diagnosis of schizophrenia, as Holzman and his colleagues (Holzman, 2000) have done. The record of one's eye movements is not terribly sensitive, but the fact that the participants were selected because they had a psychiatric disorder or had a relative with such a disorder *is* sensitive information.

The confidentiality of data is maintained through a combination of procedures. The data should be stored in a secure location, to which only authorized people have access. Whenever possible, the data also should be coded so that identifying information is stored separately from other sensitive information. Giving each participant a number code and using only that code to identify each piece of data is routine in psychopathology research. The key to the number code is usually stored in a separate location, which has only the code numbers and names of participants.

Check Yourself 16.2

Ethical Issues

1. How does a professional develop the competence required to administer a specific treatment ethically?
2. How should a treatment specialist proceed when faced with a clinical problem for which no treatment is known to be effective?
3. What is informed consent?

---

assent Nonlegal agreement to participate in a study. A child, for example, may give assent, but legal consent must be given by the child's parent or other responsible adult.

4. How are the ethical responsibilities of researchers complicated by working with people who are experiencing one or more psychological disorders?

Ponder this . . .   _One problem with ethical principles is that situations are often complex, bringing more than one ethical principle into play. Suppose you are the therapist for a client who expresses intense suicidal ideation during the therapy session and then walks out of the session saying he has had enough. What is the ethical and professional thing to do?_

PRACTICAL ISSUES

There are several practical issues associated with psychopathology, including the delivery of treatment services, alternative treatment settings, and public attitudes.

MENTAL HEALTH CARE DELIVERY

Anyone who has experienced a psychological disorder, either personally or in a friend or family member, is acutely aware how important it is to have effective and affordable treatments. This section addresses three issues surrounding treatment: the development of effective treatments, the dissemination of such treatments to professionals, and insurance coverage for treatment.

Developing Effective Treatments. The last several years have witnessed great advances in the understanding and treatment of psychological disorders (Millon et al., 1999). Many factors contributed to these advances. The first is that the diagnostic manual has refined the criteria for diagnoses on the basis of increasingly sophisticated construct validation studies (First et al., 1990; Spitzer & Wakefield, 1999). The intent was to define more homogeneous groups, in which the people are similar enough that they are likely to respond to the same treatment. The second is that there is more interest in developing procedures that are tailored to specific disorders (Barlow, 2001).

As you have learned in this text, the majority of effective treatments are biological, behavioral, or cognitive-behavioral, although other approaches are sometimes useful (Barlow, 2001). However, many of the recently developed psychological treatments take into consideration information about biological aspects of a person's functioning. For example, the most widely used treatment for panic disorder recognizes that high levels of anxiety increase the sensitivity of the biological trigger, so anxiety management techniques are included as part of the treatment (Craske & Barlow, 2001). It is likely that the treatments of the future will incorporate a sophisticated understanding of the disorder from multiple perspectives.

Disseminating Effective Treatments. Developing effective treatments is only the first of three steps necessary to bring treatments to affected people. The second step is the training of mental health practitioners in the latest and most effective techniques. Physicians typically obtain their information about new drugs from representatives of the companies that manufacture them. The drug companies have a financial incentive to bring such information to the attention of doctors. Although this system is far from perfect, few doctors can (or want to) avoid hearing about new medications through such channels. The doctors also receive free samples of the medications, which they can give to their patients who are not responding well to existing medications. Furthermore, the basic information on all drugs is readily available from a single source— the _Physician's Desk Reference (PDR)_—which provides basic descriptive information on every drug on the market. Every physician's office has this reference source, and many now have this manual on a computer or hand-held personal organizer. In addition, every state requires physicians to complete continuing-education programs. For psychiatrists, such courses might focus on diagnosis and treatment, with a heavy emphasis on selecting the most effective medications with the fewest side effects.

Unfortunately, many of the mechanisms by which treatment information is disseminated to physicians are less readily available to psychologists, social workers, and other nonphysician mental health professionals. Unlike medications, psychological treatments are not covered by patents, so there is little profit motive to drive the dissemination of information about a new treatment. In addition, not all states require that psychologists and other nonphysician mental health professionals receive continuing education. Even those states that do require continuing education do not typically evaluate the scientific merit of the continuing-education programs accepted. Furthermore, it is all too common for graduate training programs for mental health professionals to teach treatment methods for which there is little evidence to support their effectiveness, while ignoring treatments that have been clearly shown to be effective. The result is that many mental health professionals are not well informed about the newest and best treatments—a situation that is both regrettable and inexcusable.

Finally, the nature of psychotherapy is such that most clients have little basis for comparison. Although it may be trendy in some circles to discuss your psychotherapy with colleagues and friends, most people are rather secretive about their treatment, because some stigma continues to be associated with psychological problems. The result is that few clients have the type of information necessary to engage in comparison shopping—one of the most effective ways of ensuring quality in the products and services one selects. However, an alternative mechanism is sometimes available. For example, a group called the OC Foundation was formed to empower clients by making information about obsessive-compulsive disorder and effective treatments for OCD available to people with the disorder. It is perhaps not an accident that this empowerment option was first

FOCUS Empirically supported treatments

One of the most significant movements in clinical psychology has been the focus on **empirically supported treatments,** which are treatments for specific forms of psychopathology that have demonstrated their effectiveness in controlled research trials. This movement was not a part of early clinical psychology. The treatment philosophies behind early therapeutic methods were not consistent with it. For example, most humanistic and existential therapists argued that trying to measure therapeutic change would oversimplify human beings, reducing them to a collection of symptoms. Psychodynamic therapists argued that because underlying pathologies could be represented by a variety of symptoms, reducing one symptom without focusing on the underlying causes was counterproductive.

Three factors contributed to the movement toward empirical validation as the norm for psychological treatments, and two people deserve particular credit for making it happen. The first factor was the development of a diagnostic system that had sufficient detail and clarity to stimulate the process of construct validation. Psychiatrist Robert Spitzer spearheaded the efforts that led to this diagnostic improvement, and he has continued to shape improvements in the diagnostic system.

The second factor was the push within psychology to emphasize that successful psychological treatment often varies by diagnosis. Psychologist David Barlow (1985) emphasized this point with the publication of the *Clinical Handbook of Psychological Disorders,* which included chapters by research clinicians detailing the most successful treatments for specific disorders. This handbook has been updated twice, each time providing therapists with a single source of information about optimal treatment approaches for common disorders (Barlow, 1993, 2001). Later, as president of the Clinical Psychology Division of the American Psychological Association, Dr. Barlow initiated the effort to compile a list of effective psychological treatments for specific psychopathology (Barlow, 1996). This list is now routinely updated on the basis of new research (Chambless & Ollendick, 2001). Table 16.3 gives just a sampling of disorders and the psychological treatments that are effective in treating them.

The third factor that has contributed to the movement toward empirically supported treatments is the pressure applied by the insurance industry to reduce the costs of psychological treatment by using the most effective treatments available. This has not always meant emphasizing the best psychological treat-

ments. In many cases, the push has been to utilize medication as the most cost-effective treatment, discouraging or denying psychological treatments that are equally or more efficacious (Robison, 2002). However, many insurance companies evaluated the reasonableness of treatment plans submitted by mental health care professionals against the scientific evidence for effectiveness, and they authorized additional treatment sessions only for treatment plans supported by scientific data (King, 1999). The insurance companies may have been more interested in controlling cost than in promoting optimal psychological treatment, but the effect of their efforts was to exert pressure to utilize treatments that had been shown to work.

This is an exciting era for treatment research. Improvements in treatment are occurring for most psychological disorders. Furthermore, high-quality treatment research is contributing valuable data that psychopathology researchers can use to refine diagnoses further. The people who benefit most are those who suffer from psychological disorders, because many now have effective treatment options available and the promise of even more effective options in the future.

developed for people with OCD. The symptoms of OCD are difficult to understand unless one suffers from them. Consequently, support groups for people who have OCD have been common for years. It was only a small leap from providing support to providing information—and another small leap from providing word-of-mouth connections among members of different support groups to a more for-

mal newsletter shared with group leaders and later with individual members. Of course, the Internet makes it possible to share information very easily, and the OC Foundation has its own Web site (**www.ocfoundation.org**). The up-to-date and authoritative information provided to members by the OC Foundation gives people the information they need to select practitioners most likely to help.

The Internet and other outlets provide extensive information about almost any imaginable topic. The problem isn't finding information but finding authoritative information. There is a need for authoritative information

empirically supported treatments Treatments the effectiveness of which have been demonstrated in controlled research trials.

[TABLE 16.3]   Empirically Supported Treatments

Listed below is a sampling of disorders, each followed by psychological treatments for which there is strong support, in the form of *at least two* controlled studies, for their effectiveness.

Anxiety and Stress
Cognitive-behavioral therapy
Exposure

GAD
Applied relaxation
Cognitive-behavioral therapy

OCD
Exposure with response prevention

Panic Disorder
Applied relaxation
Cognitive-behavioral therapy
Exposure

PTSD
Exposure
Stress inoculation

Social Anxiety/Phobia
Cognitive-behavioral therapy
Exposure

Specific Phobia
Exposure

Alcohol Abuse and Dependence
Community reinforcement
Motivational interviewing
Behavior modification + Antabuse

Major Depression
Behavior therapy
Cognitive-behavioral therapy
Interpersonal therapy

Anorexia
Behavior therapy
Cognitive-behavioral therapy

Bulimia
Cognitive-behavioral therapy
Interpersonal therapy

Erectile Dysfunction
Behavior therapy
Cognitive-behavioral therapy

Vaginismus
Behavior therapy

Marital Discord
Behavioral marital therapy

Borderline Personality Disorder
Dialectical behavior therapy

Schizophrenia
Behavior therapy (token economy)
Behavioral family therapy
Social-learning programs
Social skills training
Supportive long-term family therapy

SOURCE: *"Empirically-Supported Treatments"* from *"Empirically Supported Psychological Interventions: Controversies and Evidence"* by D. L. Chambless & T. H. Ollendick, Annual Review of Psychology, vol. 52, 2001. Copyright © 2001 by Annual Reviews. Reprinted by permission of Annual Reviews, www.AnnualReviews.org.

about the range of treatment options so that consumers can make informed decisions and ask service providers hard questions about their treatment approaches. This is essentially the *Consumer Reports* model of educating the public about available treatment options. Division 12 of the American Psychological Association—the Clinical Psychology Division—instituted an initiative in the 1990s to publish a list of empirically supported psychological treatments for various psychological disorders. The nearby Focus box describes the history of this initiative. The list is regularly updated on the basis of new research (Chambless

& Ollendick, 2001). This list does not make recommendations about what is the best treatment for a disorder, which could stifle innovation and development of new treatments. Instead, it simply lists, for a given disorder, the available treatments for which there is at least some evidence of effectiveness.

The empirically supported treatment movement is a major initiative in clinical psychology, and it is surprising that a discipline built on scientific research took so long to embrace such a movement. There is a long history of treatments for psychopathology that were used extensively, sometimes for decades, without scientific evidence for their effectiveness. You learned about some of these treatments, such as lobotomies and recovered-memory therapy, in the pages of this text. These are particularly egregious treatments, because they clearly do more harm than good, yet well-meaning people employed them confidently in the absence of any evidence for their effectiveness. There are other therapies, such as traditional psychoanalysis, that may be effective but for which little or no controlled research has documented that effectiveness. The human cost of psychopathology is so enormous that one would want to use the best available treatments.

Managed Care and Psychological Treatment.

For better or worse, managed care has become a routine part of the health insurance environment. **Managed care** is a process by which insurance companies, or their designated representatives, gather information about the medical or psychological condition of people in treatment and work with the treating professionals to decide what services will be covered under the insurance. The primary impetus for managed care was the runaway cost of health care (Shaffer, 2001). Like many initiatives, managed care has experienced considerable growing pains. Some companies realized such substantial cost savings with early initiatives that they continued to restrict services to reduce costs still further. Of course, those companies operated in a competitive environment, so if their efforts to cut costs became too excessive, they tended to lose customers to other companies that provided more coverage or imposed less restriction on how the coverage could be used. Therapists are concerned about managed care because many believe that the restriction of therapy services often deprives clients of optimal care for psychological disorders (Moran, 2000).

Patricia, whom you met at the beginning of the chapter, learned about managed care only after she was denied additional psychotherapy sessions for her depression. Although she and her therapist argued that she needed additional sessions, her company insisted that the sessions she completed and the medication she was taking were sufficient. Not accepting this position, Patricia chose to pay for additional sessions out of pocket, but she made it a point to tell her insurance company that she would be switching to another insurance carrier at her next opportunity. Such situations are not uncommon with managed care, although many mental health professionals are learning to handle managed care companies more effectively (Davis & Meier, 2001).

It is unclear what the future of health insurance will hold. It is unlikely that insurance companies will go back

....

managed care A system in which insurance companies, or their designated representatives, gather information about the medical or psychological condition of people in treatment and work with the treating professionals to decide what services will be covered under the insurance.

to allowing subscribers and their doctors to make all of the decisions about what procedures will be performed (Chambliss, 2000). The management of health care services saves money and thus allows insurance carriers to provide coverage at a lower cost (*The Economist,* January 19, 2002). Throughout most of the history of managed care, insurance companies were exempted from legal responsibility for their decisions under federal law (*Health Management Technology,* 2000). It seems likely that such protection will not continue, so insurance companies are moving toward clearly articulated and defensible policies that define the limits of their coverage. Before managed care, insurance companies controlled costs with co-payments and with fixed policy limits. It was assumed that if a person had to pay 25% of the cost of a procedure, for example, the person would question the need for the procedure and would avoid excessive expenses out of self-interest. The marketplace will ultimately decide the nature of health insurance. Insurers will provide what people want and can afford and, within those constraints, will fashion products with features that make the policies attractive.

DEINSTITUTIONALIZATION

The concept of deinstitutionalization came up in our discussion of the history of psychopathology in Chapter 1. Deinstitutionalization was the movement to replace traditional hospital treatment of severe psychopathology with community-based treatment programs (Honkonen et al., 1999). It was based on the idea that institutional living tended to decrease adaptive living skills, thus making it difficult for individuals who had been hospitalized for long periods to reintegrate into the community after their release. Unfortunately, the process of moving people out of the hospital occurred more quickly than the process of developing effective community treatment, so the result was often that many individuals with severe mental illness ended up on the street, unable to care for themselves and unable to obtain the treatment promised (Lamb & Weinberger, 2001). There have been thoughtful analyses of the problems of providing community care, but these have not always influenced the policy makers and politicians who fund programs (Rochefort, 1997). Not everyone agrees that deinstitutionalization has been a failure. Leff (2001) argues that many of the elements of community-based treatment blend into the community so effectively that most people fail to see it. In contrast, the occasional mentally ill homeless person tends to be clearly visible. These two situations give the false impression that deinstitutionalization has completely failed, when in fact it has improved treatment for many people with serious mental illness.

Because there are many advantages to deinstitutionalization, the concept should not be dropped simply because it has not always worked as planned. Most people with severe mental illness who have been hospitalized for extended periods experience significant difficulties adjust-

Homelessness remains a problem, and many of those who are homeless suffer from one or more mental disorders. As deinstitutionalization moves more people out of mental hospitals, community support is needed to avoid problems like homelessness.

ing to the community, but most make the adjustment and are able to function at higher levels in community settings than in hospital settings (Newton et al., 2001). This difficulty in initial adjustment probably accounts for the increase in suicide risk during the first year of living in the community, a risk that is especially elevated for men (Hansen et al., 2001). The cost of not providing adequate treatment for people with severe mental illness can be very high. A recent study found that people with schizophrenia who receive no treatment are 12 to 16 times more likely to kill someone than people in the general population (Erb et al., 2001). Providing adequate treatment dramatically reduces this homicide risk.

The term *deinstitutionalization* implies moving people out of the institution, and when the policy was first implemented, that is exactly what happened. But deinstitutionalization has been around long enough that there is a new generation of people with severe mental illness who have never been institutionalized (Pepper et al., 2001). These individuals appear to be doing well in community care, and they have avoided the need for the substantial reha-

bilitation that was necessary to prepare the previous generation of people with severe mental illness to return to the community.

Deinstitutionalization is here to stay. The courts have mandated that mental health treatment be provided in the least restrictive environment possible (Baroff & Olley, 1999). This mandate forces policy makers to develop community programs. There is a movement in many states toward privatization of services (Hudson et al., 1992). The groups providing the services are nearly always not-for-profit organizations that provide services on a competitive basis, most often funded by the state. In most cases, these agencies have been able to provide quality service for less money than state programs, and the increase in the number of such programs gives people a choice. The competition among agencies can stimulate improvement in programs as well as cost reductions. Not everyone agrees that these programs are desirable (Dumont, 1996; Paulson, 1988). But the pace of this movement is increasing, and families of people with mental health problems seem to appreciate the improvement in services and the greater choices available (Savella et al., 2000).

PUBLIC ATTITUDES ABOUT PSYCHOPATHOLOGY

You learned in Chapter 1 that psychopathology has sometimes in the past been viewed as a sign of demonic possession. Few people believe that today, but one does not have to look far to find evidence that people with psychopathology make other people uncomfortable. Although attitudes are gradually changing, there is still considerable stigma associated with psychopathology. The stigma appears to result from three factors: the belief that some psychopathology can be controlled, the disruptive effect that psychopathology can have on others, and the fear that people with psychopathology are dangerous.

Some forms of psychopathology are viewed almost as character flaws, in that people seem to think that the symptoms can be controlled through sheer force of will. This attitude is especially common for anxiety and mood disorders, but it is also often directed at paraphilias, eating disorders, substance abuse, and some personality disorders. For example, it is not uncommon to hear people with panic disorder being exhorted to just tell themselves that there is nothing to fear. The less tactful person may say something more hurtful, such as "Don't be a baby." People with OCD often hear "Just tell yourself you don't have to do it." People with PTSD or major depression are often told to "just snap out of it." These statements, whether well-meaning or not, imply that affected people could overcome their problems by simply trying harder, that they are just overreacting to their experiences, or that they are too weak to handle everyday problems. That view is both naïve and uninformed.

There are probably many reasons why people think of mental disorders as different from physical disorders, but few of these reasons are valid. For example, genes often contribute substantially to both mental and physical disorders. The strength of the genetic influence is roughly comparable for diabetes, major depression, and panic disorder, yet few people would expect someone with diabetes to will her or his pancreas to put out more insulin. Furthermore, environment often plays as substantial a role in physical disorders as in mental disorders. Building a support network can decrease the risk for many psychological disorders, but maintaining a reasonable weight, getting regular exercise, and eating a balanced diet does the same for many physical disorders. Again, the problem is that people continue to think of the psychological and the physical elements of a person as though they were separate entities, instead of simply different perspectives on the person.

Some forms of psychopathology disrupt the lives of others. For example, a mentally retarded individual is likely to move slowly and awkwardly, to engage another in a conversation that would normally be considered inappropriate, or to do things that others find upsetting, such as eating without proper manners. A depressed individual or someone with panic disorder may refuse to engage in activities, thus depriving a friend or partner of companionship. Someone with dementia or paranoia may make unfounded accusations. Children with ADHD may disrupt an entire classroom. These are real effects, and they can be annoying, but they are almost never deliberate. In general, people who engage in such actions either are unaware of their implications or are unable to control them. Sometimes the behaviors are embarrassing to others. For example, if an obviously retarded individual comes up to a total stranger, admiring his watch and asking to see it, the stranger is often shocked, perceives the request as unreasonable, and does not know how to respond. A friend who is forcefully told by a depressed individual to "leave me alone" often feels the same puzzlement.

There is no doubt that people with psychopathology can disrupt the lives of other people and that not everyone is able to handle such disruptions gracefully, but this problem is not unique to psychopathology. Some people are unable to talk to their friends who are terminally ill or even to visit them in the hospital. Some can visit, but they insist on talking about things other than the friend's medical condition. Yet the discomfort that people feel when confronting the impending death of a loved one can be overcome as one grows more accustomed to dealing with death. The same can be said for most of the discomfort that people experience when dealing with psychopathology.

Finally, many people interpret the unusual behavior found in severe mental disorders as an indication of dangerousness. Although some people with mental disorders are dangerous (Monahan & Steadman, 2001), the vast majority are not (Penn et al., 1999). For example, less than 15% of people with schizophrenia assault another person prior to admission (Monahan, 1993). They may be unpredictable or lack the social skills to handle routine prob-

Public attitudes about mental illness and mental retardation continue to interfere with efforts to integrate affected individuals into the community. Proposals for residential treatment facilities often encounter public opposition.

lems without getting upset, but that is not by itself a sign of dangerousness.

The fear that people have of those with mental disorders, coupled with the vestiges of stigma that remain, often makes people unwilling to consider having mentally disturbed individuals as neighbors. You learned about this problem—which is referred to as NIMBY, or Not in My Backyard—in Chapter 13. This attitude is the single greatest obstacle to the reintegration of people with mental and emotional disturbances back into the community. Early psychiatric hospitals and institutions for the mentally retarded were often built in the countryside to isolate those affected from the rest of society. But these people have done nothing to deserve such isolation. Most are not dangerous, and for the few who might be dangerous, steps are routinely taken to protect the public.

Check Yourself 16.3

Practical Issues

1. Why is it generally easier for physicians to find out about new drug treatments than for psychologists to find out about new psychotherapies?

2. What step did the Clinical Psychology Division of the APA take to disseminate information about effective psychological treatments?

3. Why will the move away from institutionalization continue?

Ponder this . . . *Imagine that you are teaching high school. What could you do to help reduce the stigma associated with psychopathology?*

FUTURE DIRECTIONS

Predicting the future of a field developing as rapidly as psychopathology is risky. New research technologies, improved understanding of basic psychological and neurological processes, and plenty of rigorous research have created an explosion of information about why and how psychopathology develops, how it is maintained, and how it can be more effectively treated. This explosion of research is the work of a surprisingly small group of gifted and dedicated people. Look over the references in this textbook, and you will be impressed by how often certain names reappear. Perhaps 300 people account for over half of all published psychopathology research. This section outlines some of the recent advances and the directions that psychopathology research is now taking.

NEW TECHNOLOGY

Science should not be driven by technology; technology should be driven by science. By itself, technology is a toy, but coupled with the theories of science, it can be used to answer questions that were unanswerable in previous generations. Psychology is in a unique position to benefit from research being done in various disciplines, and this is already happening in the field of cognitive neuroscience. You saw many examples throughout the text of cognitive neuroscience perspectives improving our scientific understanding of various forms of psychopathology. Three technological developments hold great promise for psychopathology research: brain imaging, the human genome project, and tagging drugs.

Brain Imaging. Chapter 1 introduced the remarkable brain-imaging tools now available to researchers, and the fruits of this technology have been featured throughout the text. But the future holds even greater promise. The ability to link thoughts, feelings, and actions to specific brain activity will yield insights into emotional functioning and psychopathology that are hard even to imagine now.

Early imaging equipment was purchased by hospitals and universities, and it was used for both clinical diagnosis and research. The economics of that arrangement nearly always meant that research was shortchanged. The majority of structural imaging equipment is still in hospitals, but increasingly the imaging equipment serves as the touchstone for a team of researchers, which concentrates broad expertise into a coordinated research effort. An outstanding example of this model is the W. M. Keck Laboratory for Functional Brain Imaging and Behavior at the University of Wisconsin, which opened in 2001. This laboratory brings together experts in diverse fields to address basic questions about the relationships between brain and behavior. With equipment at the cutting edge and a support staff of engineers and physicists capable of moving the technology even further, this team is breaking new ground every day. For example, it is working on developing methods of using PET scans to track specific molecules in the brain during everyday functioning. This is likely to become the model of imaging research in the twenty-first century.

Human Genome Initiative. You have learned throughout this text that genes play a significant role in many psychological disorders. In fact, genes are a major contributing factor for many of the disorders covered in this text. Yet almost nothing is now known about which genes are involved. The human genome project may change that. As we noted earlier, this project has mapped every human gene. This map does not tell what each gene does, but it dramatically increases the likelihood of identifying individual genes that contribute to specific disorders. Most of the genetic influences in psychopathology are polygenic, so uncovering such complex mechanisms will not be easy. But as recently as 10 years ago, identifying several genes that contribute to a psychological disorder was unthinkable. Today, it is imaginable. Tomorrow, it may be reality.

Being able to identify specific genes will enable researchers to tackle another critical issue, gene expression—that is, whether a gene will contribute to functioning. There is increasing evidence that mechanisms exist for turning genes on and off and that some of those mechanisms may be environmental events (LaBuda & Grigorenko, 1999). For example, Walker (2002) has argued that the dramatic increase in the production of sex hormones around puberty increases the expression of genes that influence risk for schizophrenia. It is impossible to study gene expression unless one can identify the presence of specific genes independent of the traits that they influence.

Tagging Drugs. When you take a drug, it circulates throughout your body, but that circulation is almost never optimal. The brain pathologies associated with most disorders are localized to one or two primary brain structures,

The human genome project, which mapped the location of all human genes, will usher in the next generation of genetic studies—studies that promise a level of understanding never before possible.

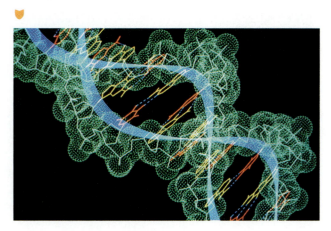

but medications that have a positive impact on those structures also affect other structures, and these secondary effects are nearly always undesirable. For example, some neuroleptic medications used to treat schizophrenia produce Parkinson's-like symptoms, because they affect dopamine transmission in motor regions of the brain.

Researchers and doctors have dreamt of the ability to place specific medications in specific locations to obtain exactly the desired effect without creating the myriad of side effects so common with powerful medications. Animal researchers have achieved this goal mechanically by implanting micro-cannulae (tiny tubes) that deliver chemicals into the brains of functioning animals (Kanarek et al., 2001). The techniques for such implantation have been refined to the point where these tubes can be surgically and permanently implanted without causing significant brain damage or discomfort to the animal. Hence, researchers can provide specific drugs to specific brain regions and observe their impact on behavior. Giving drugs systemically—that is, allowing them to circulate naturally throughout the body—produces different effects than delivering drugs to specific brain regions.

The micro-cannula technique is an incredibly powerful research paradigm, but it is impractical for the treatment of psychopathology. However, a technique under study in the treatment of cancer may someday provide a practical method for delivering specific drugs to specific brain locations. The technique is called tagging, and it involves attaching drugs to carriers that find their way to specific locations. In cancer treatment, the idea is to tag the poisons used in chemotherapy so that they have a greater affinity for the cancerous tumors than for other body tissue. All body tissues absorb the chemotherapy poisons, but rapidly growing tissues, such as cancerous tissue, absorb more and thus die more readily. However, it is quite a challenge to give the person just enough poison to kill the tumors, but not so much that it kills the person or damages critical organs. This drug-tagging technology, once developed, could be modified to deliver other medications to where they would do the most good. Tagging could potentially provide more specific and effective treatments for various psychological disorders, without producing significant side effects.

DEVELOPMENTAL MODELS

Perhaps the single most important change in psychopathology research in the last two decades has been the shift in attention to developmental processes in psychopathology. You learned about diathesis-stress models of psychopathology in Chapter 1, and all subsequent chapters have included this concept. People do not inherit disorders; they inherit predispositions to develop disorders. These dispositions sometimes interact with environmental events, triggering psychopathology. To understand such interactions, researchers must study the developmental course of psychiatric disorders.

Most of the research reported in this text is basic construct validation research. It is designed to identify and refine the criteria for diagnosing specific disorders, to identify the nature of disorders and their correlates, and to detect clues about their causes. This basic research is critical, but researchers can take this process only so far. Eventually, investigators must focus on how the disorder develops, using current research to identify critical areas to study in longitudinal work.

Such longitudinal studies have begun for some disorders, such as schizophrenia and depression. These early studies have used high-risk paradigms. Longitudinal studies for other disorders may be premature, because there are too many basic questions that still need to be answered. Without this basic information, it is difficult to make reasoned judgments about what factors are most likely to be relevant and, therefore, are worth measuring in a longitudinal study. The developmental course of most disorders is likely to be complex, and scientists may never understand all of the factors that may contribute to the onset of a given disorder. For example, some factors may be relevant only if they occur in a specific temporal sequence. You learned about a physical disorder for which this was true in Chapter 9. Cancers develop after a series of two mutations affect a single cell, causing it to turn cancerous. Scientists could never have discovered this biological mechanism without a lengthy series of studies that yielded an ever more sophisticated understanding of cancer. As in all of science, findings build on other findings, raising new questions that can then be addressed in later studies. It is the nature of such work to move from one platform to

The guide cannula implanted in this rat's brain allows researchers to deliver neurotransmitter agonists and antagonists to specific brain regions or to measure chemical activity in specific brain regions with a process called microdialysis. The cannula is the tiny tube in the middle of the mound of dental cement. The larger piece of metal is glued to the outside of the skull to hold connecting tubes in place to avoid discomfort for the animals during testing.

another. For example, epidemiological data provided hints about possible carcinogenic agents. Exposure in cell cultures confirmed the damaging effect of those agents. However, scientists needed to go back to studying people, instead of cell cultures, to identify the role of the immune system. Each of these studies represents a different perspective on the cancer process. This emphasizes a point we noted previously: The most sophisticated understanding of psychopathology will come from research that moves freely from one perspective to another to obtain the best possible view of each component of the developmental process.

Prevention is a natural outgrowth of understanding the developmental course of a disorder. Most psychological disorders are likely to have complex developmental courses, which may offer multiple places and ways to intervene. The proper intervention, delivered at the proper time, could reduce the risk for the disorder. For example, the armed services often use experiential training to prepare soldiers for the kind of extreme treatment that they might receive as prisoners of war. The hope is that such training will inoculate soldiers against the disruptive effects of such treatment, thereby reducing the likelihood that they will "crack" and suffer stress-related disorders. But imagine what could be done if a more specific understanding of the developmental process for a disorder like PTSD were available. What biological processes does a stressor disrupt? What causes them to reach the point of biological dysregulation that accounts for many of the symptoms of PTSD? Could people be trained to regulate their exposure to inevitable trauma so as to avoid this more lasting biological dysregulation? Could biological interventions in the first few hours or days following exposure normalize the biological dysregulation? Are there optimal ways of inoculating oneself from the toxic effects of trauma? Could psychological exercises provide a stabilizing influence or enhance skills that could be called on in case of a trauma?

Evolutionary Impact

Nature, through the process of natural selection, equipped people to deal with many of the stresses of life, but natural selection does not necessarily optimize adaptation, especially in the rapidly changing world in which we now live. Natural selection builds adaptive mechanisms on the basis of what is available. It lacks intentional design and therefore may be far from optimal. However, it may provide building blocks that can be used to create amazing adaptive strategies. The more that scientists learn about human functioning, the more tools will be available to study and treat psychopathology.

UNDERSTANDING MECHANISMS

Over the past century, huge strides have been made in understanding human functioning, but we still have a long way to go. As you have learned throughout this text, the ability to study the biological underpinnings of human behavior has dramatically increased our understanding of behavior and of the many factors that contribute to it. Scientists need to move away from a simplistic form of biological reductionism and recognize that simultaneously conceptualizing human behavior at several levels will be more fruitful. However, real understanding cannot be achieved without including the biological level, because humans are complex biological creatures.

Two unifying themes have tied together the material in this textbook. The first is that the road to understanding abnormal behavior must rest on a solid scientific footing. The second is that many forms of psychopathology can be better understood from an evolutionary perspective. The term *abnormal* implies a defect, which may be the case for some forms of psychopathology, but not for all. For example, the primary feature of anxiety disorders—anxiety—is critical to survival. Most anxiety is not pathological, and even anxiety that is now considered pathological may have been adaptive in an earlier era. Anxiety disorders did not just suddenly materialize. That simply does not happen in evolution. There may not have been a grand design behind evolution but, nevertheless, it follows design principles. What are those principles and how can they help scientists to zero in on the mechanisms behind a disorder? Although this question is enormously broad, some basic principles can be addressed in the limited space available here.

One principle is that evolution operates by modifying organisms, not by designing them from scratch. Systems are "borrowed" and used in different ways after minor additions or modifications are made. For example, recent evidence suggests that some of the mechanisms behind depressive symptomatology were borrowed from the immune system (Konsman et al., 2000; Leonard, 2001a, 2001b). When an individual is sick, the immune system fights off the infection in several ways and, by creating enormous fatigue and dramatically decreasing interest in normally pleasurable activities, encourages the person to cooperate with these disease-fighting efforts. Those symptoms also characterize depression, and the evidence suggests that they are triggered by the same biological mechanisms. These exciting findings offer an entirely new way of looking at depression. They raise new questions and suggest places where investigators should look to find the answers. Throughout this text, the evolutionary perspective was used to reconceptualize psychopathology, to recognize that it once may have been adaptive, and to help illustrate how the environment determines how effective a given class of behavior will be. This example, linking the biological underpinnings of the immune system and depression, illustrates how evolutionary perspectives can guide the search for underlying biological mechanisms of abnormal behavior.

<u>Check Yourself 16.4</u>

Future Directions

1. What is drug tagging, and how might it be helpful in treating psychopathology?

2. What area of psychopathology research is receiving more attention today than ever before?

3. How can evolutionary models help researchers focus on underlying mechanisms for psychopathology?

Ponder this . . . *Imagine the satisfaction of discovering something about a particular psychopathology that improves the treatment of millions of people. Imagine the satisfaction of helping someone to control or eliminate psychopathology using the most advanced methods available. There are some wonderfully satisfying research and professional careers in this field for those willing to commit themselves to being the best.*

THE HUMAN TOLL

How can you measure the human toll of psychopathology? How can you quantify suffering, embarrassment, and lost dreams? The entire purpose of this text and of the field it represents is to understand processes that have the potential to undo people's lives. The human toll comes from three sources: the impact of psychopathology itself, the stigma associated with it, and the reaction of the affected person.

The goal of this text has been to introduce you to the range of psychopathology, its nature, and its impact on the people who suffer from it. The descriptions and case studies were designed to give you a sense of what each disorder is like and what it would feel like to struggle with the disorder. You may have noticed that most of the case studies provided more information than would have been necessary just to illustrate each disorder. We wanted you to know something about these people besides their symptoms, to understand that the symptoms are superimposed on a person's longstanding pattern of functioning, and to appreciate the courage, fear, and frustration involved when psychopathology disrupts people's lives and dreams. Symptoms do not define a person; they merely affect a person. The vast majority of the people featured in the brief case histories of this text survived their psychopathology, and many triumphed over it. All of them struggled, both against the pathology and against their own discouragement. Psychopathology disrupts life, but it need not end it. In the past 25

years, there have been marked improvements in treatment, and there is every reason to believe that such improvements will continue.

Stigma can destroy a person's will to recover more effectively than any psychopathology. It is born of misunderstanding, ignorance, and an unwillingness to accept people as they are. There is no question that psychopathology continues to carry considerable stigma, although dramatic strides in combatting that uninformed attitude have been made over the past few decades for some disorders. Sympathetic magazine and newspaper articles, enlightened television and movie portrayals, and the willingness of increasing numbers of people in high-visibility positions to discuss their struggles with psychopathology have given hope to those who have struggled in silence for years. People often have no more control over whether they will develop a psychiatric disorder than over what color their skin will be, although with some disorders, such as substance abuse, personal decisions clearly do affect risk for psychopathology. Most psychopathology is not a moral weakness any more than it is a sign of demonic possession.

Finally, throughout the text, the population base rate of each disorder was presented. Most were low, generally less than 2% or 3%, although a few were considerably higher. Some of you have experienced psychopathology firsthand, and if so, you may have felt alone as you read about a disorder that you knew all too well. You were not alone. A substantial portion of the population will experience one or more forms of psychopathology at some point during their lifetime (Kessler et al., 1994; Narrow et al., 2002). What is the likelihood that you know someone—perhaps a family member or close friend—with a psychological disorder? It is a virtual certainty, although you may not realize it because many people hide psychopathology out of embarrassment. If you are one of those people who knows firsthand the impact that anxiety, depression, eating disorders, or any one of the 250+ diagnostic conditions in the DSM, I hope that the information in this text gave you reason for hope. There will probably always be psychopathology. We ask a lot of ourselves as we struggle to overcome the challenges of a world that is thousands of times more complex than the one in which humans evolved. However, the human spirit has proved itself enormously resilient. Furthermore, the intellectual talents and tenacity of researchers seem clearly up to the task of eventually unraveling the mysteries of psychopathology. It is no accident that this text has emphasized scientific approaches to the study of psychopathology. The human toll is so great that it is unreasonable to use anything but the best available strategies to understand these disorders and find effective treatments.

SUMMARY

LEGAL ISSUES

- Civil commitment refers to the involuntary hospitalization of a person, although some states now permit outpatient commitment as an alternative. Civil commitment is permitted only if the person is mentally ill and poses a danger to self or others. People who are committed have a right to receive adequate treatment, and they have a right to refuse treatment.

- The insanity defense rests on the principle that people should not be held responsible for behavior that they cannot control or do not realize is wrong. Several criteria for defining insanity and specifying the consequences of an insanity defense have been proposed.

- Defendants cannot be tried for a crime unless they are competent to stand trial; they must be able to understand the charges and to assist in their own defense.

- Courts have held that therapists have a duty to warn (or protect) potential victims if their clients voice a specific threat to a specific individual during therapy.

ETHICAL ISSUES

- There are several ethical issues associated with psychological treatment. Therapists are obliged not to violate client confidentiality and to practice within their area(s) of expertise, maintain adequate records, clarify their responsibilities to clients, and clearly label unvalidated treatments as experimental.

- All research in psychopathology demands special attention to the welfare of participants. Participants must give informed consent. The sensitive nature of data in psychopathology research also makes the issue of confidentiality important.

PRACTICAL ISSUES

- Three treatment issues are especially important; developing effective treatments, disseminating them to treatment professionals, and covering the costs of treatment through insurance or other means.

- The process of deinstitutionalization will continue because treatment must be provided in the least restrictive environment possible. This means that more people with psychopathology will be living in the community. However, the stigma and misconceptions that are still prevalent often affect the way people with mental illness are treated by the community.

FUTURE DIRECTIONS

- Researchers are, or will soon be, using such technology as brain imaging, gene identification, and drug tagging to understand psychopathology better.

- There is an increasing interest in understanding the developmental processes and the underlying mechanisms of psychopathology.

THE HUMAN TOLL

- Psychopathology takes a tremendous human toll, and the best reason for studying it scientifically is to reduce that toll in every possible way.

 KEY TERMS

American Law Institute guidelines   (519)
assent   (528)
civil commitment   (514)
competent to stand trial   (521)
Durham rule   (518)
duty to warn   (523)
empirically supported treatments   (530)
guilty but mentally ill   (519)

informed consent   (527)
insanity defense   (518)
Insanity Defense Reform Act   (519)
Institutional Review Boards, or IRBs   (526)
irresistible impulse   (518)
managed care   (532)
M'Naghten rule   (518)
placebo control group   (527)

 SUGGESTED READINGS

Schopp, R. F. (2001). *Competence, condemnation, and commitment: An integrated theory of mental health law.* Washington, DC: American Psychological Association.

This provocative book examines several legal issues surrounding psychopathology.

Check Yourself Answers

CHAPTER 1

1.1.1   Evolution is driven by natural selection.

1.1.2   The factors that contribute to adaptation are genetic makeup, physical condition, learning and reasoning, and socialization.

1.2.1   Abnormality can be defined as statistically unusual behavior, as socially unacceptable behavior, as dysfunctional behavior, or as personally distressing behavior.

1.2.2   The harmful-dysfunction approach of Wakefield defines abnormality in terms of twin criteria: (1) whether the behavior is harmful as judged by society and (2) whether the harmful behavior is the result of a system not performing as it evolved to perform.

1.3.1   The early Greeks were the first to attribute disease to natural causes. For example, Hippocrates argued that health was due to a proper balance of four basic body substances (yellow bile, black bile, blood, and phlegm).

1.3.2   During the Middle Ages, mental illness was believed to be the result of possession by the devil.

1.3.3   Asylums were a major improvement over the treatment that people with mental illness received when mental illness was believed to be the result of possession by the devil. However, early asylums were little more than human warehouses, which did little to preserve the dignity of the people confined to them.

1.3.4   Early reforms removed the chains from people in asylums and encouraged staff to treat each person in the asylum with respect. In the United States, people with mental illness were moved from jails to treatment centers.

1.4.1   A psychiatrist has an M.D. degree and can prescribe medications. A psychologist has a Ph.D. degree and provides psychological treatment.

1.4.2   A psychiatric nurse has a degree in nursing and experience in working with people with mental illness. A nurse practitioner has a nursing degree and advanced medical training and, therefore, is allowed to prescribe medications.

CHAPTER 2

2.1.1   The current diagnostic system in use in the United States is DSM-IV-TR (*Diagnostic and Statistical Manual of Mental Disorders*, 4th edition, text revision).

2.1.2   Axis I lists psychiatric disorders; Axis II lists personality disorders or mental retardation; Axis III lists relevant medical disorders; Axis IV lists recent stressors; Axis V rates the global functioning level of the person.

2.1.3   The three types of reliability are interrater, test-retest, and internal consistency reliability. Interrater reliability is most relevant to diagnosis.

2.1.4   The current diagnostic system, as well as each edition from DSM-III on, defines disorders in terms of clearly observable symptoms. This has increased interrater reliability and stimulated considerable research.

2.2.1   Structured interviews have specifically worded questions and clear rules to determine what questions should be asked. Semi-structured interviews cover a clearly defined content area, but the order of the questions and the exact wording are up to the professional. Unstructured interviews have no clearly defined topics to cover but, rather, are shaped by the information that is learned during the interview.

2.2.2   Binet developed the IQ test as a standardized way of identifying children with intellectual deficits severe enough to warrant special schooling.

2.2.3   The Minnesota Multiphasic Personality Inventory (MMPI) is the most commonly used objective psychological test.

2.3.1   People tend to behave differently when they know they are being observed. This effect is reduced when the behavioral observation is less obvious to participants.

2.3.2   Role-playing makes it possible to assess behavior in situations that are unlikely to occur very frequently in the natural environment.

2.4.1 Structural brain abnormalities are changes in brain structure or connections that are visible. In contrast, functional brain abnormalities are not visible but rather represent deficient operation of a brain structure.

2.4.2 An MRI uses magnetic fields to obtain a picture of the structure of a brain, whereas an fMRI uses the same technology to obtain pictures of the operation and activity level of various parts of the brain.

2.4.3 Psychophysiological techniques measure physiological arousal by monitoring organ systems—the heart, for example, or the sweat glands on the palms of the hands—that increase their activity during such arousal. Psychophysiological monitoring of the electrical activity of the brain gives insights into what is happening in the brain and indicates where that activity is occurring.

CHAPTER 3

3.1.1 The two principles that underlie the psychodynamic perspective are that behavior is the result of complex internal deliberation and that much of this internal deliberation is unconscious.

3.1.2 According to Freud, personality includes the id, ego, and superego.

3.1.3 The five stages of psychosexual development are the oral, anal, phallic, latency, and genital stages.

3.1.4 A healthy defense protects the ego from anxiety without interfering with performance, whereas primitive defenses stimulate dysfunctional behavior.

3.1.5 The neo-analytic approaches of Erikson and Kohut focus on socialization rather than sexuality.

3.2.1 Behaviorism focused exclusively on observable events.

3.2.2 Classical conditioning focuses on shifting the control of behavior from one stimulus to another, whereas instrumental conditioning focuses on how the consequences of behavior affect the likelihood of its occurring in the future.

3.2.3 Negative reinforcement involves the removal of an aversive stimulus following a behavior, whereas punishment involves the presentation of an aversive stimulus following a behavior. Negative reinforcement increases, whereas punishment decreases, the likelihood of recurrence of the behavior that precedes it.

3.2.4 Behavioral therapies include systematic desensitization, aversive conditioning, and contingency management.

3.3.1 Rogers is often considered the father of the humanistic perspective. He argued that people develop normally if they are in a supportive environment.

3.3.2 Maslow's hierarchy of needs is based on the principle that people cannot satisfy certain needs until more basic needs have been satisfied.

3.3.3 The basic premise of the existential perspective is that people are responsible for finding meaning in their lives and for making their own choices.

3.4.1 Each argued for a single underlying cause of all psychopathology.

3.4.2 The diathesis-stress model suggests that predisposing factors interact with environmental events to trigger psychopathology.

CHAPTER 4

4.1.1 Mendelian inheritance is the transmission of a genetic trait via a single gene. Polygenic inheritance is genetic transmission via multiple genes. Emergenic inheritance involves multiple genes in the particular combination necessary for transmission.

4.1.2 Chemicals called neurotransmitters are released into the synapse by the axon terminal of one cell and stimulate the dendrite of the next cell.

4.1.3 The parietal, occipital, and temporal lobes of the cerebral cortex are involved in perceptual processing of information.

4.1.4 The sympathetic nervous system tends to arouse organs in a coordinated manner, whereas the parasympathetic nervous system acts individually on organs and tends to have a calming effect.

4.1.5 Medications are the most frequently used biological treatment.

4.2.1 They both tend to be automatic and unconscious, and they both affect feelings and behaviors.

4.2.2 Rescorla showed that pairing the CS and the US did not result in conditioning if the US occurred at other times when the CS was not present. Conditioning appears to occur only if the CS is predictive of the US occurring.

4.2.3 Modeling allows the individual to learn contingencies without having to experience the negative, and sometimes life-threatening, consequences of actions.

4.2.4 Modern cognitive-behavioral treatments tend to package individual elements into packages called treatment protocols that are geared to the treatment of specific disorders.

4.3.1 Cognitive psychologists study human perceptual and thought processes.

4.3.2 Declarative memory is memory of events; procedural memory includes memories of how to do things. Procedural memory is more likely to be spared if a person suffers brain damage.

4.3.3 Flashbulb memories are the vivid recollections that people have of important events in their lives. However, like all memories, flashbulb memories are subject to distortion over time and so cannot be completely trusted.

4.3.4 Automatic processing involves doing things that do not require conscious attention, whereas controlled processing does require such attention.

4.4.1 Social class is defined by a person's education and occupation. Schizophrenia is far more common in the lowest social class than in the middle and upper social classes.

4.4.2 Cultural factors can increase or decrease the risk for certain forms of psychopathology and can influence the nature of symptoms seen in a given form of psychopathology.

4.4.3 Primary prevention is applied to all people in a population, whereas secondary prevention is applied only to those people thought to be at risk for a disorder.

4.5.1 The process of natural selection drives evolution.

4.5.2 Genes shape such behaviors as social cooperation, affiliation, and parenting. Each of these behaviors can contribute to one's survival or to the survival of one's offspring.

4.5.3 Humans have changed the world so dramatically and so quickly that there has been no time for human beings to evolve to meet these new demands.

4.5.4 Proximal causes are the most immediate causes of a situation, whereas distal causes are earlier events that may have created the environment that led to the situation.

CHAPTER 5

5.1.1 Approximately 1% of people develops schizophrenia during their lifetime.

5.1.2 Positive symptoms are clearly deviant behaviors, whereas negative symptoms are deficit symptoms—the lack of normal behaviors.

5.1.3 Delusions are beliefs that are not objectively true and would not be accepted as reasonable within a person's culture.

5.1.4 Auditory hallucinations are most common in schizophrenia.

5.1.5 The negative symptoms of schizophrenia include anhedonia, avolition, alogia, asociality, and flat affect.

5.1.6 The three phases of schizophrenia are the prodromal, active, and residual phases.

5.2.1 Disorganized schizophrenia typically has the most dramatic symptoms.

5.2.2 Paranoid schizophrenia tends to have the least thought disorder.

5.2.3 Residual schizophrenia consists of the milder symptom pattern that occurs between active episodes of schizophrenia.

5.3.1 The best evidence that both genes and environment contribute to schizophrenia is the fact that the concordance rate for identical twins is about 50%—well above the concordance rate for fraternal twins and well below 100%.

5.3.2 Dopamine has been strongly implicated in schizophrenia.

5.3.3 Both expressed emotion and affective style predict relapse in schizophrenia.

5.3.4 Thought disorder and communication deviance are independent concepts.

5.3.5 Schizophrenia appears to disrupt functioning and thus both interferes with upward social mobility and results in "downward drift" into the lower social classes.

5.4.1 The most common treatment for schizophrenia is antipsychotic medication.

5.4.2 Behavioral and cognitive approaches are promising treatments for schizophrenia.

5.4.3 Hospitalization is used to (1) protect the individual and others, (2) stabilize the individual, and (3) rehabilitate the individual.

5.5.1 Delusional disorders are characterized by stable delusions but by few of the other symptoms of schizophrenia.

5.5.2 The best treatments for delusional disorders are the atypical antipsychotics.

5.5.3 Schizoaffective disorder is characterized by symptoms of both schizophrenia and a mood disorder, such as bipolar disorder or major depression.

CHAPTER 6

6.1.1 Constructs are ideas about things that cannot be directly observed but can be studied by observing their effects.

6.1.2 There are two steps to the process of construct validation: (1) deriving predictions from the construct and (2) doing research to see whether those predictions are accurate.

6.2.1 The finding that people with manic depression responded well to lithium led to a refinement of criteria for the diagnosis of schizophrenia.

6.2.2 General paresis, amphetamine intoxication, and niacin deficiency can all cause psychotic symptoms similar to those found in schizophrenia.

6.3.1 The process of validating a psychological measure is the same as construct validation: (1) identifying the characteristics that the scale should theoretically have and (2) gathering data to see whether the scale has those characteristics.

6.3.2 Test-retest reliability is relevant if the construct being measured is theoretically stable. Internal consistency reliability is relevant if the construct being measured is theoretically traitlike.

6.4.1 Meehl hypothesized that schizotaxia represented a disruption in the functioning of individual neurons.

6.4.2 The best evidence that discordant identical twins of people with schizophrenia also carry the genetic risk factor for schizophrenia is that the risk in their offspring is identical to the risk in the offspring of the affected co-twin.

6.4.3 Modern diathesis-stress models emphasize that there are likely to be several diatheses and several stresses contributing to a disorder.

6.5.1 Case studies are rich sources of hypotheses for other research studies.

6.5.2 Experiments are the most powerful research strategies.

6.5.3   The most critical issue to consider in comparing groups that differ on diagnosis is that those groups are likely to differ on other variables as well.

6.5.4   Prospective studies follow people over time to see who develops a disorder and then look at the factors that predict the development of the disorder. In contrast, retrospective studies look into the histories of people who have developed a disorder to see what factors predict its development.

6.5.5   Genetic high-risk studies select participants on the basis of their being genetically related to someone with the disorder, whereas behavioral high-risk studies select people on the basis of behavioral characteristics or traits.

6.6.1   The underlying causes are likely to be subtle and pervasive. Anything not subtle would already have been discovered, and anything not pervasive is unlikely to have the enormous impact necessary to create such dramatic symptoms.

6.6.2   A marker exists before the symptoms develop, continues after the symptoms subside, and is assumed to be related to the diathesis.

6.6.3   The earliest stages of perceptual processing—the so-called preattentive processing stages—are the ones that are disrupted in schizophrenia.

6.6.4   People with schizophrenia are unable to follow moving objects smoothly with their eyes. Nicotine reduces this dysfunction.

6.7.1   The family study approach does not control for the confounding of genes and environment.

6.7.2   The proband in twin studies is diagnosed with schizophrenia and has a same-sex twin.

6.7.3   The two evolutionary mysteries surrounding schizophrenia are why it is not disappearing and why it developed in the first place.

6.8.1   People with schizophrenia who show predominantly positive symptoms show excessive left-brain activity, whereas those who show predominantly negative symptoms show decreased left-brain activity.

6.8.2   Agonists enhance the activity of the neurotransmitter, whereas antagonists inhibit or block the activity.

6.8.3   Treatments can be effective for many reasons, often reducing symptoms without affecting the underlying cause.

6.9.1   The environmental hypotheses that have supporting data are expressed emotion, affective style, and communication deviance.

6.9.2   The schizophrenogenic mother hypothesis is refuted by three lines of evidence: (1) Most siblings of people with schizophrenia do not develop schizophrenia. (2) Most mothers of people who develop schizophrenia do not show the alleged schizophrenogenic traits. (3) Schizophrenogenic traits are as common in families that do not have a child who develops schizophrenia as in families that do.

CHAPTER 7

7.1.1   Mood disorders have been around throughout recorded history.

7.1.2   Mood changes are triggered by environmental events, although there are large individual differences in the degree of mood swings experienced.

7.2.1   The three depressive disorders are major depression, dysthymic disorder, and seasonal affective disorder, or SAD. Major depression involves episodes of intense depression with normal periods intervening between episodes. Dysthymia is a chronic, low-level depressive affect that resembles a personality trait. Seasonal affective disorder is a depression that routinely develops in early to mid-winter and continues until spring.

7.2.2   Depressive symptoms include depressed mood, feelings of worthlessness or excessive guilt, loss of interest or pleasure in activities, change in appetite, sleep disturbance, physical agitation or slowing of motor activity, loss of energy, difficulty concentrating or thinking, and suicidal thoughts.

7.2.3   Double depression is a condition in which a person with dysthymia develops a major depression.

7.2.4   SAD occurs during winter months in higher latitudes (farther north in the Northern Hemisphere). The evidence suggests that the length of the day is the critical triggering variable.

7.2.5   Postpartum depression is a major depressive episode that occurs within a few weeks after a woman gives birth to her child.

7.2.6   There are differences in the depressive symptoms in childhood and adult depression, which are probably due to differences in the level of cognitive and emotional development. Also, unlike adult depression, the rate of depression in boys and girls is equal.

7.3.1   The primary neurotransmitters implicated in depression are serotonin, norepinephrine, and dopamine.

7.3.2   There are substantial differences in the MZ vs. DZ concordance rates for major depression, and evidence from adoption studies also suggests a genetic component to risk.

7.3.3   The cognitive errors described by Beck as central in depression are arbitrary inference, selective abstraction, overgeneralization, magnification or minimization, and personalization.

7.3.4   The learned helplessness model was initially based on animal research.

7.3.5   Attributions for failure that are internal, global, and stable are most likely to lead to depression.

7.3.6   The learned helplessness model focuses on the stress factor (the situation in which the person is helpless), whereas the hopelessness model focuses on the cognitive diathesis (the tendency to make attributions that create depression).

7.4.1   Medication is the most widely used biological treatment for depression.

7.4.2   Tricyclic antidepressants and MAO inhibitors affect both norepinephrine and serotonin, and the SSRIs affect primarily serotonin.

7.4.3   Scientists still do not know the mechanism by which ECT reduces depression.

7.4.4   Seasonal affective disorder responds to phototherapy.

7.4.5   The primary goal of cognitive therapy is to increase the client's awareness of cognitions that may be decreasing self-esteem and to challenge those cognitions.

7.4.6   IPT helps clients appreciate the importance of interpersonal relationships in meeting personal goals and seeks to foster such relationships.

7.5.1   The principal difference is that the mood swings are less severe in cyclothymia than in bipolar disorder.

7.5.2   The diagnosis of bipolar I disorder requires at least one manic episode, whereas the bipolar II diagnosis is made when the person has experienced one or more depressive episodes and a hypomanic episode but no manic episode.

7.5.3   The gender ratio is about 1:1 for both bipolar disorder and cyclothymia.

7.5.4   Both twin and adoption studies offer strong evidence for genetic factors in bipolar disorder.

7.6.1   There is a strong genetic contribution to risk for bipolar disorder.

7.6.2   There is some evidence for a prefrontal cortex dysfunction in bipolar disorder.

7.6.3   Stress can trigger manic episodes in some, but not all, people who are prone to develop manic episodes.

7.7.1   The primary treatment for mania is medications—especially lithium, but also some antiseizure drugs.

7.7.2   Traditional psychotherapy has little impact on mania, but it may be important between episodes in helping clients repair damage done as a result of their manic behavior.

7.7.3   Family therapy for bipolar disorder focuses on reducing expressed emotion in the family as a way of reducing the likelihood of relapse.

7.8.1   At least 30,000 people a year commit suicide in the United States and nearly a million worldwide, although there are large cultural differences in suicide rates.

7.8.2   Many factors contribute to suicide risk, including marital status, occupation, age, culture, clinical diagnosis, genetic factors, degree of social support, and degree of hopelessness.

7.8.3   Suicide prevention begins with accurate assessment of risk and includes interventions designed to connect with the suicidal person and give that person a reason to be hopeful about the future.

CHAPTER 8

8.1.1   Anxiety is an uncomfortable feeling of apprehension that motivates behavior. Anxiety that is consistently too high or occurs in inappropriate situations may suggest an anxiety disorder.

8.1.2   Anxiety tends to improve performance up to a point, but increases in anxiety beyond that point dramatically reduce performance. The optimal level of anxiety depends on the difficulty of the task. The optimal level is high for easy tasks but low for difficult tasks.

8.1.3   Anxiety motivates behavior that reduces risk of danger. Because humans can imagine future possibilities and experience anxiety about what might happen, anxiety also motivates preparatory behavior.

8.2.1   The defining characteristic of GAD is excessive worry.

8.2.2   GAD is usually accompanied by another disorder; almost 90% of people with GAD qualify for at least one other psychiatric diagnosis.

8.2.3   Borkovec believes that the worrying in GAD is a cognitive activity but that it does not qualify as anxiety because it does not include such autonomic components as accelerated heart rate.

8.2.4   GAD may be treated with anxiolytic medications or with cognitive therapy.

8.3.1   The actions associated with a panic attack are preparatory responses for flight from danger and, when flight is impossible, fighting for one's life.

8.3.2   Cued panic attacks are predictable fear responses to specific stimuli. In contrast, uncued panic attacks occur at unpredictable times.

8.3.3   Agoraphobia is the most serious consequence of panic disorder.

8.3.4   The three predisposition hypotheses are a tendency to fear panic attacks, a tendency to make catastrophic misinterpretations of physical sensations associated with panic, and a tendency to be fearful of anxiety symptoms in general (a phenomenon termed anxiety sensitivity).

8.3.5   Both medications and psychological treatments have been shown to be effective for panic disorder. Benzodiazepines and SSRIs are both effective medications. The most effective psychological treatment is a cognitive-behavioral approach that combines education, anxiety control techniques, and gradual exposure to feared situations.

8.4.1   Obsessions are unwanted thoughts that the person cannot control. Compulsions are behaviors that the person feels compelled to perform, usually because the behaviors momentarily reduce the anxiety created by the obsessive thoughts.

8.4.2   OCD affects about 2% to 3% of the population, occurs at about the same rate in children and adults, and shows similar rates across cultures.

8.4.3   Genes substantially influence risk for OCD. Two neurotransmitters (norepinephrine and serotonin) and several brain regions (orbitofrontal cortex, basil ganglia, and anterior cingulate) have been implicated in OCD.

8.4.4   Behavioral treatment of OCD is based on the two-process theory of avoidance learning, which suggests that the anxiety produced by the obsessions is learned by association and that the compulsions are reinforced by a reduction in this anxiety.

8.4.5   The primary medical treatment for OCD is medication—specifically, SSRIs or clomipramine. Only as a last resort is psychosurgery considered.

8.4.6   The only effective psychotherapy approach is exposure with response prevention, although cognitive elements are often included.

8.5.1   A specific phobia is a fear of an object or a nonsocial situation, such as flying. A social phobia is a fear of being judged negatively in a social situation.

8.5.2   There is controversy about the prevalence of phobias because diagnostic criteria are not always clear. Lifetime prevalence for specific phobias is probably around 10%. Phobias are generally more common in women than in men, although there are some exceptions (such as blood-injection-injury phobias).

8.5.3   Only blood-injection-injury phobia is associated with fainting.

8.5.4   Genes have a modest influence on the risk for phobias. Freud hypothesized that phobias were a displacement of anxiety from one object to another. The behavioral model proposes that phobias are learned through classical conditioning or observational learning.

8.5.5   Specific phobias are usually treated with systematic desensitization or flooding. Social phobias may require social skills training in addition to exposure.

8.6.1   The diagnosis of acute stress disorder or posttraumatic stress disorder cannot be made unless the person has experienced a significant stressor, even if all the symptoms are present. Evidence suggests that the likelihood of PTSD is proportional to the strength of the stressor.

8.6.2   PTSD symptoms can go on for decades, although for many individuals, the symptoms gradually fade with time.

8.6.3   The symptoms of an acute stress disorder can include emotional numbing, feeling in a daze, derealization, and depersonalization. Both acute and posttraumatic stress disorders may include flashbacks and nightmares, avoidance, and hyperarousal.

8.6.4   The biological systems disrupted in PTSD include the endogenous opioid system, the noradrenergic system, the sleep regulation system, and the HPA axis.

8.6.5   Medications are sometimes used to attenuate such stress-related symptoms as hyperarousal and sleep difficulties. Supportive therapy, often in groups, is used to treat PTSD. The supportive therapy allows for desensitization and for a reinterpretation of the trauma to provide meaning for the victim. A newer treatment, EMDR, shows promise, although there is controversy about the mechanism behind its effectiveness.

8.7.1   The anxiety disorders that show the greatest gender differences in the rates of the disorder (more women than men are affected) are panic disorder, agoraphobia, GAD, specific phobias, and PTSD.

8.7.2   The anxiety disorders that show the least gender differences in the rates of the disorder are OCD and blood-injection-injury phobias.

8.7.3   The evolutionary argument for the differences between men and women in the rates of anxiety disorders suggests that her role in taking care of offspring puts a larger premium on the woman's recognition and avoidance of risk, because it enhances survivability for both the mother and her offspring.

CHAPTER 9

9.1.1   The three stages of the general adaptation syndrome are the alarm reaction, the resistance phase, and the exhaustion phase.

9.1.2   Holmes and Rahe (1967) measured stress in terms of major life events, whereas Kanner et al. (1981) measured stress in terms of daily hassles. Brown and Harris (1978) focused on major life events but rated each event in terms of the details of the situation.

9.1.3   Stress decreases the efficiency of the immune system, making the person more susceptible to diseases ranging from the common cold to cancer.

9.1.4   Stress can be controlled with physiological, cognitive, and behavioral strategies, as well as via the use of social support.

9.2.1   The factors, besides stress, that can contribute to ulcers include a weakness in the lining of the stomach, excess production of gastric juices, and bacterial infection.

9.2.2   Type A is a behavior pattern characterized by intense competitiveness, feeling pressured, impatience, a high activity level, aggressiveness, and hostility. People who exhibit Type A behavior are prone to coronary heart disease, but hostility is the best predictor of who will develop heart disease.

9.2.3   Hypertension is chronically elevated blood pressure, and essential hypertension is chronically elevated blood pressure for which there is no obvious physical cause.

9.3.1   Some of the most common health-compromising behaviors are smoking, drinking, eating a poor diet, and getting little exercise.

9.3.2   The most challenging problem in promoting healthful behavior is that unhealthful behaviors are usually reinforced immediately, whereas the reinforcement for healthful behavior is often considerably delayed.

9.3.3   Type A behavior can be modified, and reducing it substantially reduces the risk of a second heart attack.

9.3.4   Behavioral medicine specialists help people with cancer to deal with having a life-threatening disease, with the discomfort of treatment, and with returning to their life after intensive treatment. Behavioral medicine specialists may also help people with terminal illnesses to deal with their upcoming death, although hospice workers and/or members of the clergy often handle this responsibility.

9.4.1   Psychosomatic disorders are physical disorders that are due in part to psychological distress. In contrast, somatoform disorders are psychological disorders that only appear to be physical disorders.

9.4.2   Somatization disorder is characterized by reports of multiple symptoms, whereas conversion disorder typically involves a single symptom.

9.4.3   Somatization disorder is the only somatoform disorder for which significant biological information is available.

9.4.4   One should begin treatment of somatoform disorders by ruling out medical disorders.

9.5.1   One can screen for possible physical disorders by asking clients about changes in their physical health, physical problems they have been having, or annoying physical symptoms such as fatigue, pain, and dizziness.

9.5.2   Therapists should routinely ask clients for a list of all medications they are taking and should then consult the PDR to learn about the possible side effects of any medications unfamiliar to them.

CHAPTER 10

10.1.1 Anorexia nervosa is characterized by a deliberate loss of weight, sometimes to dangerously low levels, a fear of being fat, a distorted sense of one's own body size, and (in women) a disruption in the menstrual cycle.

10.1.2 Bulimia nervosa is characterized by recurrent episodes of binge eating, compensatory behaviors to prevent weight gain, and excessive reliance on body shape and size for self-worth.

10.1.3 Anorexia and bulimia are most likely to occur in young women.

10.2.1 Both genes and environment contribute to eating disorders. The genes that predispose to eating disorders may also predispose to mood disorders.

10.2.2 The primary sociocultural factor contributing to eating disorders is a cultural pressure on women to be thin. Women with anorexia strive to achieve this ideal, and women with bulimia often try to diet excessively to be thin but are overcome by urges to eat when food is available.

10.2.3 Women who are perfectionistic, have a negative self-evaluation, and are extremely compliant appear to be at heightened risk for anorexia. A history of sexual abuse and high parental expectations may also increase risk.

10.3.1 The weight loss in anorexia is often so extreme that life-threatening medical complications are possible.

10.3.2 Fluoxetine (Prozac) is effective in the treatment of bulimia.

10.3.3 CBT produces the largest initial improvement in treating bulimia, but IPT yields the greatest gains after therapy is completed.

10.4.1 Sleep stages are differentiated by brain wave activity, deeper sleep being characterized by slower brain waves.

10.4.2 Dreams occur during REM sleep.

10.4.3 Primary insomnia is most common in the elderly.

10.4.4 The most common form of sleep apnea is obstructive sleep apnea, and the risk factor most strongly associated with it is obesity.

10.4.5 Nightmare disorder is characterized by frightening dreams, whereas sleep terror disorder is characterized by terrifying feelings that occur at night but not during dreams.

10.5.1 Trying too hard to sleep, making poor choices about sleeping and late night activities, and cognitive misinterpretations of the situation that increase anxiety and thus make sleep more difficult often contribute to primary insomnia.

10.5.2 Because sleep terrors are found primarily in children, a developmental process may be involved.

10.5.3 Genetic influences have been documented for sleepwalking disorder.

10.6.1 Sleep hygiene is the manner in which one prepares for, obtains, and maintains normal sleep.

10.6.2 Interviews provide information about the individual's sleep problems and their history; sleep logs record critical details of sleep and associated variables; polysomnography records information on actual sleep performance.

10.6.3 Hypnotic drugs are the most common biological treatment for insomnia.

10.6.4 The logic behind sleep restriction is that people with insomnia often try to catch up on their sleep by going to bed when they are not tired. Consequently, they often get upset because they are not able to sleep and thus promote more insomnia.

CHAPTER 11

11.1.1 Sexual reproduction creates greater genetic variability within a species, thereby increasing the odds that some members will survive when strong selective pressures appear. In addition, sex is inherently pleasurable and hence encourages strong emotional bonding in couples.

11.1.2 "Falling in love" is nature's way of forming the pair bond so critical in conceiving and raising children.

11.1.3 Cultural norms serve many functions. First, they codify and regulate behaviors. Second, they clarify societal expectations. Third, they can be modified more quickly than evolutionary changes when the need arises.

11.2.1 Sexual dysfunction is the inability to perform a normal sexual activity.

11.2.2 The four broad categories of sexual dysfunctions are (1) sexual desire disorders, (2) sexual arousal disorders, (3) orgasmic disorders, and (4) sexual pain disorders.

11.2.3 Hypoactive sexual desire disorder is the most common sexual dysfunction seen in sex therapy clinics, and its prevalence appears to be increasing.

11.2.4 Premature ejaculation is most common in young males, whereas male erectile dysfunction is most common in older males.

11.2.5 Both men and women can experience dyspareunia.

11.3.1 Such biological factors as hormonal changes, medications, diseases, hypertension, excessive sensitivity to sympathetic arousal, injuries, and genital scarring can contribute to sexual dysfunctions.

11.3.2 Such psychological factors as anxiety, anger, guilt, stress, relationship problems, sexual trauma, and sexual inexperience can contribute to sexual dysfunctions.

11.3.3 Such sociocultural factors as an upbringing that fosters sexual fears or negative sexual attitudes and a history of sexual trauma or threat of trauma can contribute to sexual dysfunctions.

11.4.1 The treatment of choice for sexual dysfunctions prior to Masters and Johnson was psychoanalytic psychotherapy.

11.4.2 The four elements in the Masters and Johnson treatment approach are education, communication, anxiety management, and specific techniques for specific disorders.

11.4.3 Two techniques that have proved effective for the treatment of premature ejaculation are the squeeze technique and the stop-start technique.

11.5.1 Homosexuality is characterized by a preference for same-sex sexual partners, whereas gender identity disorder is characterized by a desire to be a member of the opposite sex.

11.5.2 Gender identity disorder usually becomes apparent between two and four years of age.

11.5.3 The typical treatment of gender identity disorder is sex transformation therapy.

11.6.1 Voyeurs are excited by watching the sexual or other private activity of unwilling victims. Watching someone undress in a strip club would not particularly appeal to voyeurs.

11.6.2 Unlike the fetishist, who might be content just to hold and feel such objects as women's clothing, the transvestic fetishist desires to wear the clothing to obtain sexual arousal.

11.6.3 Pedophiles who sexually abuse nonrelatives tend to prefer young children and tend to be aroused by young children. In contrast, incest perpetrators tend to prefer older children and are more likely to be sexually aroused by young adults than by young children.

11.6.4 The public is becoming more tolerant of paraphilias that involve only consenting adults, such as fetishism, transvestic fetishism, and sadomasochism.

11.7.1 "Courtship disorders" include voyeurism, exhibitionism, frotteurism, and rape.

11.7.2 The behavioral explanation assumes that paraphilias are classically conditioned.

11.7.3 Any theory of paraphilias will have to explain why males dramatically outnumber females.

11.8.1 Both cognitive-behavioral therapy and aversive therapy are effective in reducing the intensity of a paraphilia. Cognitive-behavioral therapy seeks to change the self-serving attributions that may reduce guilt or to provide the person with social skills that may make it easier to achieve sexual gratification in appropriate ways. An aversive technique known as assisted covert sensitization is administered to increase the aversiveness of the paraphilia and thus make it easier to resist.

11.8.2 The two medication approaches that are effective in reducing the strength of paraphilias are reducing the level of testosterone and using SSRIs.

11.8.3 The most significant nontreatment issue for paraphilias is that most people seek treatment because of legal pressure, which may well affect their motivation. Also, it is not clear that there is any reason to change a behavior that is practiced only between consenting adults.

11.9.1 Forcible rape involves coerced sexual intercourse with an adult. Statutory rape involves sexual intercourse between an adult and a minor, who cannot legally give consent. Acquaintance rape involves sexual intercourse that was coerced by someone the victim knew.

11.9.2 Most rapists are young men, and most victims are young women.

11.9.3 The factors that predict sexual arousal in response to a date-rape scenario are sexual aggressiveness and callous sexual beliefs, which interact with one another.

CHAPTER 12

12.1.1 Personality disorders consist of pervasive and inflexible patterns of behavior that interfere with a person's social functioning.

12.1.2 Personality disorders are more chronic and ego syntonic than Axis I disorders.

12.1.3 The DSM describes the personality disorders as though they are categorical but acknowledges that they may be dimensional. It may be that some personality disorders are categorical and others are dimensional.

12.1.4 Axis II includes ten personality disorders and mental retardation.

12.2.1 The defining characteristic of paranoid personality disorder is a pervasive distrust of people and their motives.

12.2.2 Both paranoid and schizotypal personality disorder are in the schizophrenic spectrum. These diagnoses overlap so extensively that some have argued that they may represent a single disorder.

12.2.3 The defining characteristic of schizoid personality disorder is a pervasive pattern of detachment from social relationships and an apparent lack of interest in such relationships.

12.2.4 Although both avoidant and schizoid personality disorders involve a detachment from social relationships, the detachment is due in schizoid individuals to a lack of interest and in avoidant individuals to overwhelming anxiety.

12.2.5 The defining characteristic of schizotypal personality disorder is an oddness in thought, perception, and social interactions.

12.2.6 Both borderline and schizotypal personality disorders were carved out of the heterogeneous group referred to as borderline schizophrenia. Kernberg was impressed with how most of these people never developed psychosis, whereas Meehl was impressed that many appeared to be at risk for schizophrenia. Both were right. Kernberg's ideas influenced the borderline diagnosis, whereas Meehl's ideas influenced the schizotypal diagnosis.

12.3.1   Cleckley defined psychopathy in terms of emotional experience (loveless and guiltless), whereas the DSM defined antisocial personality disorder in terms of such behaviors as lying, fighting, unlawful activity, and inconsistent work and financial histories.

12.3.2   People with psychopathy show a deficiency in behavioral inhibition, an anxiety-based system that facilitates learning to reduce the likelihood of punishment. Consequently, they are less able to avoid behaviors that are punished, although they are quite effective at learning to obtain rewards.

12.3.3   The defining characteristic of borderline personality disorder is a pervasive pattern of unstable and intense relationships.

12.3.4   The defining characteristic of histrionic personality disorder is a display of excessive emotionality and attention-seeking behavior.

12.3.5   The defining characteristics of narcissistic personality disorder are grandiosity, a constant need for admiration, and an apparent lack of empathy.

12.3.6   Antisocial personality disorder does not respond well to treatment, although children with signs of this disorder may benefit from treatment.

12.3.7   The only empirically-supported treatment for BPD is dialectical behavior therapy.

12.4.1   The defining characteristic of avoidant personality disorder is a pervasive pattern of shyness, social inhibition, and hypersensitivity to negative evaluation.

12.4.2   Avoidant personality disorder shares features with generalized social phobia.

12.4.3   The defining characteristic of dependent personality disorder is excessive clinging behavior coupled with a fear of separation.

12.4.4   Although dependence is viewed negatively in Western cultures, a balance of dependent and independent behavior is critical to mature adult functioning.

12.4.5   The defining characteristic of obsessive-compulsive personality disorder is a preoccupation with orderliness, perfectionism, and control.

12.4.6   The symptoms of OCPD are usually ego syntonic, whereas OCD symptoms are usually ego dystonic. Furthermore, OCPD symptoms are focused on issues such as orderliness, whereas OCD symptoms are focused on performing compulsive rituals that reduce the anxiety generated by the obsessions.

12.5.1   The three treatment dilemmas faced by therapist treating an Axis II disorder are (1) that the disorder is often ego syntonic, (2) that personality disorders are chronic, and (3) that the client is usually seeking therapy for an Axis I disorder.

12.5.2   The only personality disorder for which treatment that has been demonstrated to be effective is borderline personality disorder.

12.5.3   Researchers have still not resolved the issue of whether specific personality disorders represent categories or dimensions.

CHAPTER 13

13.1.1   ADHD is most common in school-age boys.

13.1.2   Several factors contribute to ADHD, including genes, neurological deficits, and reinforcement contingencies. However, ADHD is clearly heterogeneous.

13.1.3   The two most common treatments for ADHD are stimulant medications and behavior therapy.

13.1.4   The defining characteristics of conduct disorder are a pervasive disregard for the rights of others and consistent violation of rules or norms.

13.2.1   Enuresis involves the inappropriate voiding of urine, most often while sleeping, whereas encopresis involves the inappropriate voiding of feces.

13.2.2   Communication disorders involve deficits in the ability to express or understand verbal communication.

13.2.3   Learning disorders involve impairment of selective cognitive skills, such as deficits in reading, math, or writing.

13.3.1   Autistic disorder is characterized by markedly abnormal social functioning, deficient communication, and stereotypic behavior.

13.3.2   The symptoms that are relatively unique to autistic disorder include (1) being oblivious to, and uninterested in, social communication; (2) showing unusually good attention and concentration, though not always with appropriate objects; (3) exceptional rote memory, but with an inability to use context to enhance memory; (4) insensitivity to emotional cues; and (5) inability to share a perspective with another person to facilitate communication.

13.3.3   Several medications have been used to decrease aggressiveness, hyperactivity, and lack of socialization in autistic disorder. However, these medications are only modestly effective. Behavioral therapy has been used with some success to improve communication, increase socialization, and decrease undesirable behaviors.

13.4.1   To qualify for a diagnosis of mental retardation, one must have an IQ below 70 and show deficits in adaptive functioning before age 18.

13.4.2   Organic mental retardation is due to a physical cause, whereas cultural-familial mental retardation has no known physical cause.

13.4.3   Down syndrome is caused by an extra chromosome 21. It is most likely to occur when the mother is over 40 years of age at conception.

13.4.4   Lead continues to be a significant contributor to mental retardation.

13.4.5   The goal of current treatment is to integrate mentally retarded people into the community and to help them to reach their full potential.

CHAPTER 14

14.1.1 Substance dependence is defined as involving three or more of the following: tolerance, withdrawal, excessive use, inability to stop, excessive effort to obtain the substance, reduction of normal role expectations as a result of substance use, and inability to stop despite the consequences.

14.1.2 Substance abuse includes one or more of the following: recurrent substance use that interferes with major role obligations, use in physically hazardous situations, legal problems resulting from use of the substance, and inability to stop despite recurrent problems due to the substance use.

14.1.3 This chapter covers sedatives, narcotics, stimulants, and hallucinogens.

14.2.1 Pharmacological effects of alcohol are due to the biological impact of this drug, whereas expectancy effects are due to the expectations that the person has about how alcohol changes behavior.

14.2.2 Excessive alcohol consumption damages the gastrointestinal, cardiovascular, cerebrovascular, and nervous systems.

14.2.3 Fetal alcohol syndrome may affect the fetus of a woman who drinks heavily during pregnancy. It is characterized by facial abnormalities and mental retardation.

14.2.4 Barbiturates were once used to calm individuals or as a sleep aid.

14.2.5 The person most likely to abuse anxiolytics is someone with considerable anxiety who has been prescribed these drugs to manage the anxiety.

14.3.1 Doctors use narcotics primarily to control pain.

14.3.2 Heroin is the most widely abused opiate. Heroin produces a brief rush of pleasure after injection, followed by 4 to 6 hours of relaxed lethargy.

14.3.3 The strength of withdrawal symptoms depends on the level of heroin use, on how continuously it has been used, and on how abruptly it is terminated.

14.4.1 The addictive component of cigarettes is nicotine.

14.4.2 Amphetamines were used to increase alertness and as a diet pill.

14.4.3 Cocaine blocks the reuptake of dopamine and, in the process, increases activity in the pleasure center of the brain.

14.4.4 Injecting the substance into the bloodstream or smoking it will result in faster absorption and a stronger psychological response.

14.5.1 Marijuana was rarely used or abused until the 1960s, when it became the drug of choice among college students.

14.5.2 Alcohol is more toxic to the brain than marijuana, and there is more evidence of cognitive decline from heavy drinking than from marijuana use.

14.5.3 Psychedelics have been used for centuries as part of religious ceremonies to enhance and expand the participants' consciousness.

14.6.1 Type I alcoholism develops later, has a weaker genetic contribution, and is equally common in men and women, whereas Type II alcoholism develops earlier, has a strong genetic component, and is much more common in men.

14.6.2 Both tolerance and withdrawal are the result of the body attempting to reach a state of homeostasis following a period of sustained drug use.

14.6.3 People with antisocial personality disorder, young people in general, and people who are impulsive are all likely to experiment with drugs.

14.6.4 Sociocultural factors that affect the rate of smoking include having friends who smoke, living in a state that has a high smoking rate, and being a problem student.

14.6.5 The two factors that predicted outcome in the Vaillant study were family history of alcoholism and ethnicity.

14.7.1 The biological treatments for drug dependence include detoxification, medication, and drug substitutions.

14.7.2 Behavioral therapy, relapse prevention, and controlled drinking are effective in the treatment of drug and alcohol dependence.

14.7.3 Changing costs by increasing taxes on cigarettes can reduce consumption and discourage people from smoking. Public service announcements can change attitudes and may change behavior in desired ways.

14.7.4 There are two controversies surrounding controlled drinking. The first is that many professionals and AA question whether controlled drinking is possible. The second is that some people have questioned the authenticity of data offered to support controlled drinking, although such concerns have proved to be unfounded.

14.7.5 AA is a mutual-help group, in which recovering alcoholics get together frequently to provide support for one another. It is based on 12 principles, which are outlined in the 12 steps of the program.

14.7.6 Harm reduction seeks to minimize the negative effects of drug abuse.

CHAPTER 15

15.1.1 Delirium is a widespread disruption of cognitive functioning that is usually due to a metabolic disturbance.

15.1.2 Treating delirium involves finding and correcting the physical problem.

15.2.1 People with Alzheimer's disease typically show first memory impairment, then personality changes, including hypersexuality, paranoia, and aggressiveness; and ultimately a complete loss of cognitive capacity.

15.2.2 Several genes increase risk for Alzheimer's, but high levels of cognitive activity may decrease risk. Neurofibrillary tangles and senile plaques kill the neurons.

15.2.3   Dementia can be caused by head injuries, tumors, strokes, substance abuse, infections, and presenile dementias.

15.2.4   No treatment will stop the degenerative process of Alzheimer's. Medications can treat symptoms and may slow the degenerative process. Providing emotional support and instruction in coping skills is critical.

15.3.1   Amnestic disorders are characterized by persistent memory problems caused by medical conditions or exposure to intoxicating or toxic substances.

15.3.2   The treatment of amnestic disorders depends on the cause. For Korsakoff's syndrome, the treatment is to give vitamin supplements. But for most amnestic disorders, cognitive rehabilitation is necessary.

15.4.1   The diagnosis of depersonalization disorder requires that the depersonalization cause clinically significant distress and/or impairment and that it not be better explained by another disorder.

15.4.2   Both dissociative amnesia and fugue involve a loss of biographical memory, but dissociative fugue also involves moving away from home and taking on a new identity.

15.4.3   The essential feature of DID is the presentation of two or more distinct identities, or alters, in the same person.

15.5.1   The two factors most consistently tied to DID are trauma and suggestibility.

15.5.2   Over 90% of individuals with DID report childhood abuse, but these reports are retrospective and therefore subject to numerous biases. Furthermore, some of the reports are suspicious in that the person reports remembering things that occurred when the individual would have been too young to remember them.

15.5.3   The autohypnotic model of DID suggests that those individuals who are capable of self-hypnosis may use hypnosis as a way of protecting themselves emotionally from abusive situations and that this self-hypnosis, in some unspecified way, leads to the formulation of alternate personalities.

15.5.4   Nijenhuis and his colleagues suggest that somatic and behavioral symptoms may represent a response to trauma that was shaped by natural selection.

15.6.1   The dissociative disorders most likely to improve spontaneously are dissociative amnesia and dissociative fugue.

15.6.2   Unfortunately, there are no controlled treatment studies for DID.

15.7.1   The best way to rule out iatrogenic effects in DID is to show clear evidence for the existence of alters prior to treatment.

15.7.2   The biggest problem with recovered-memory techniques is that laboratory evidence suggests that they are capable of implanting false memories.

CHAPTER 16

16.1.1   The primary criterion for civil commitment is that the person presents an imminent risk to self or others.

16.1.2   The issue in the insanity defense is whether the person was able to understand and control her or his actions at the time of the crime, whereas the issue in competency to stand trial is whether the person is able to understand the charges against him or her and to help in the defense.

16.1.3   A therapist has a duty to warn an individual if the therapist's client makes a specific threat of harm toward that individual.

16.2.1   A professional can develop competence in a given treatment through formal study, systematic self-study, continuing education, and/or supervision from another qualified professional.

16.2.2   When faced with a clinical problem for which there is no empirically supported treatment, a professional should inform the client of that fact, suggest an experimental treatment based on the best available scientific information, and proceed with that treatment only if the client consents.

16.2.3   Informed consent involves agreeing to participate in a research study after being fully informed about the study, including its risks.

16.2.4   The ethical responsibilities of researchers working with clinical problems are complicated, because some psychopathology may interfere with informed consent, there may be special risks (such as suicide), and the data are often sensitive.

16.3.1   The drug industry has a financial stake in informing doctors about new drugs, but there is no such financial stake for psychotherapies. Consequently, there are no sales reps to tell psychologists about new approaches.

16.3.2   The Clinical Psychology Division of the APA regularly publishes a list of empirically supported treatments and the level of validation for each of these treatments.

16.3.3   The courts have mandated that treatment must be delivered in the least restrictive environment possible, and for many people with psychopathology, that means that they should be treated in community settings.

16.4.1   Drug tagging may provide a mechanism to deliver effective medications for psychopathology to the specific brain regions that are dysfunctional.

16.4.2   Increasing attention is being paid to developmental models of psychopathology.

16.4.3   Because evolution proceeds by making small changes on existing mechanisms, it often "borrows" from already existing mechanisms. It is reasonable to expect that there will be overlap between psychological mechanisms that have evolved relatively recently and more primitive survival mechanisms.

Glossary

abnormal A term applied to people who consistently are unable to adapt and function effectively in a variety of conditions.

acquaintance rape, or **date rape** Rape committed by someone the victim knows.

Acquired immune deficiency syndrome (**AIDS**) A deadly disease that weakens the immune system to the point where the person can no longer fight off infections.

active phase of a disorder The period when symptoms are most pronounced.

acute stress disorder An immediate and short-term physical and emotional reaction to an overwhelming and potentially life-threatening trauma.

adaptive Behavior that produces positive outcomes.

addiction Dependence on a substance to the extent that discontinuation causes significant discomfort or trauma.

adoption studies Comparisons of the rates of a specified disorder in the biological and adopted relatives of people with the disorder who were adopted at birth.

affect The external expression of emotion.

affective style The tendency of one or more relatives to make critical or guilt-inducing statements to individuals with schizophrenia or to make repeated statements about what those individuals are thinking.

age of onset The age at which a disorder first develops.

agnosia A deficit in sensory perception and recognition.

agonists Drugs that enhance the activity of a neurotransmitter.

agoraphobia The avoidance of certain situations because of a fear of having panic attacks.

AIDS dementia complex Substantial dementia and even psychotic symptoms caused by AIDS.

Alcoholics Anonymous (**AA**) The largest mutual-help group, founded by two recovered alcoholics in 1935.

alcoholism A popular, though imprecise, term for drinking excessively and habitually. The term comprises both alcohol abuse and dependence.

alogia A negative thought disorder in which there is either a poverty of speech or a poverty of content to the speech.

alters Alternate personalities that are distinct.

Alzheimer's disease A progressive and terminal presenile dementia.

American Law Institute guidelines Published in 1962 as an alternative to the Durham rule, they combined the irresistible-impulse principle and the M'Naghten rule, defining legal insanity as either the inability to control one's actions or the inability to appreciate the wrongfulness of one's actions.

amnestic disorders Disorders characterized by a persistent disturbance in memory, which may be due either to the physiological effects of a general medical condition or to the effects of a substance or toxin.

amphetamines Synthetic stimulants that increase energy and alertness. Also known as speed.

anal stage The child's focus at 18–36 months is on the pleasure associated with controlling the retention and passing of feces.

anhedonia The inability to experience pleasure.

animal magnetism A theory that each person or animal emits a magnetic field and is affected by the magnetic fields of others.

anorexia nervosa A disease characterized by refusal to consume and digest enough calories to maintain a normal weight.

Antabuse The best-known drug treatment for alcohol dependence, which blocks the normal metabolism of alcohol and creates noxious by-products that induce vomiting whenever the person drinks. Also known as disulfiram.

antagonists Drugs that inhibit or block the activity of a neurotransmitter.

antipsychotic medications Drugs used to treat schizophrenia and other psychotic disorders.

antisocial personality disorder Characterized by a pervasive pattern of disregard for the rights of others.

anxiety An uncomfortable feeling of apprehension.

anxiety disorder A condition in which anxiety consistently interferes with, rather than facilitates, functioning.

anxiety sensitivity A tendency to respond fearfully to symptoms of anxiety.

anxiolytic Antianxiety.

aphasia A deficit in the ability to understand or use language.

appetitive stage Stage of the human sexual response that Kaplan suggested be added before excitement; involves an increase in sexual desire.

apraxia A deficit in the ability to carry out familiar activities or to use familiar objects.

asociality A lack of interest in social relations.

Asperger's disorder A severe and sustained impairment in social interactions and the development of restricted and repetitive patterns of behavior and activities.

assent Nonlegal agreement to participate in a study. A child, for example, may give assent, but legal consent must be given by the child's parent or other responsible adult.

assisted covert desensitization A treatment approach in which the person is asked to imagine exposure to the arousing stimuli and, while imagining that exposure, to imagine potential aversive consequences, such as arrest, social embarrassment, or being assaulted by a victim or a family member of a victim.

asylums Institutions for housing seriously disturbed people.

attention The process by which people focus on one thing while ignoring other things.

attention-deficit/hyperactivity disorder (**ADHD**) Characterized by inattention and excessive activity or impulsivity.

attribution A person's explanation for his or her behavior or the behavior of others.

atypical antipsychotics A new class of medications that show great promise for the treatment of schizophrenia.

autistic disorder Markedly abnormal or significantly delayed development in both social functioning and communications.

autohypnotic model The theory that DID may develop through the use of self-hypnosis as a defense against intense emotional trauma.

automatic thoughts Beck's term for thoughts that are triggered by the day's events.

autonomic nervous system Composed of the sympathetic and parasympathetic branches, this system links the central nervous system and the peripheral organs of the body.

autonomic restrictors A pattern of excessive muscle tension, but no other autonomic responses, when anxious.

aversive conditioning A counterconditioning strategy designed to increase negative affect to specific situations.

avoidant personality disorder Characterized by a pervasive pattern of shyness, social inhibition, and hypersensitivity to negative evaluation.

avolition Apathy or an energy deficit.

axes The distinct dimensions of a multiaxial diagnosis.

Axis II diagnoses Persistent characteristics that affect the individual's clinical functioning or response to treatment.

backward-masking task A visual test in which a simple target is presented for just a few milliseconds and is followed a few milliseconds later by a mask, which is another stimulus that appears in the same place.

balanced placebo design A research design that independently manipulates two factors (consumption of a substance and belief that one has consumed the substance).

balanced polymorphism A phenomenon in which genes with a negative impact on people are maintained in a population because they also have a positive impact.

barbiturates Synthetic sedatives developed in the 1930s.

base rate The frequency of a disorder in the population.

Beck's cognitive-behavioral therapy (CBT) Therapy in which the therapist explores daily events with the client, looking for instances in which automatic thoughts may be counterproductive.

behavioral activation system (BAS) The neurological mechanism underlying reward and pleasure.

behavioral assessment Observing the behavior of people in specified situations.

behavioral high-risk paradigm A study in which participants are selected, not on the basis of their genetic relationship to someone with a specified psychopathology, but on the basis of personality traits thought to be indicators of risk.

behavioral inhibition system (BIS) The neurological mechanism underlying the psychological experience of anxiety and fear.

behavioral medicine The use of psychological techniques to facilitate changes in behavior.

behavioral observation Watching and recording key aspects of a person's behavior.

behavioral self-control training Training that seeks to sensitize a person to the cues that trigger drug use and teaches strategies to resist drug use.

behaviorism The conviction that psychology can be scientific only if it restricts research to observable events. Behaviorism was focused mostly on learning principles.

binge-eating/purging type anorexia A subtype of anorexia that includes individuals who regularly binge-eat, purge, or both.

biofeedback A technique that utilizes sensors and electronic transformation to provide people with accurate information about such body states as muscle tension, heart rate, and blood pressure.

biological reductionism The belief that one can thoroughly understand human behavior just by understanding the biological mechanisms that underlie it.

bipolar disorder A pattern of mood fluctuations in which the mood is sometimes depressed and sometimes manic.

bipolar I disorder Diagnosis assigned when the individual has had at least one clear manic episode.

bipolar II disorder Diagnosis assigned when there is a history of major depressive episodes and at least one hypomanic episode, but no full manic episode.

blind Said of researchers who, in order to avoid potential bias, do not know the test scores of the people they interview.

blood alcohol level (BAL) The percentage of alcohol in the bloodstream.

blood-injection-injury phobia A fear of getting an injection or having blood drawn.

body dysmorphic disorder (BDD) A disorder characterized by a preoccupation with an imagined or minor defect in one's appearance.

borderline personality disorder (BPD) Characterized by a pervasive pattern of unstable and intense relationships.

bovine spongiform encephalopathy, or **mad cow disease** A disease that is transmitted through eating infected meat and is caused by prions, which are subviral proteins capable of replication.

brain stem The part of the brain that controls some of the most critical life functions. Damage to the brain stem usually results in immediate death.

breathing-related sleep disorders Disorders characterized by disruptions in normal breathing during sleep, which disturb the quality of the sleep and leave people feeling excessively sleepy during the day.

bulimia nervosa A disease characterized by frequent binge eating followed by compensatory behavior to maintain weight.

cannabis A family of drugs derived from the hemp plant.

carcinogenic agents Substances that tend to trigger cancer mutations.

case studies Careful evaluations of individuals.

cataplexy A loss of muscle tone so dramatic that the person may collapse onto the floor during a narcoleptic episode.

catatonia A psychomotor disturbance of movement and posture.

catatonic schizophrenia Schizophrenia characterized by catatonia—the psychomotor disturbance of movement and posture.

catatonic stupor A condition of being mute and apparently unaware of what is going on.

central nervous system depressant A drug that slows and disrupts the operation of the central nervous system.

central nervous system The brain and the spinal cord.

central sleep apneas Apneas involving intermittent cessation of breathing—that is, periods when the lungs stop working for a time.

cerebellum The part of the brain that controls fine motor coordination.

cerebral atrophy Loss of brain tissue.

cerebral cortex The part of the brain that processes perceptions, memories, and thoughts and also implements behavior.

childhood disintegrative disorder A significant regression in multiple areas of functioning after a period of at least two years of apparently normal development and functioning.

chromosomal abnormalities A disruption in the formation of eggs or sperm that results in an embryo with either an abnormal number of chromosomes or damaged chromosomes.

chronic fatigue syndrome (CFS) A disease characterized by a dramatic loss of energy; pain in the joints, muscles, throat, or head; and significant depression following a period of exertion.

circadian rhythm sleep disorders Disorders characterized by a persistent or recurrent mismatch of the person's sleep-wake cycle and the demands from the environment for a sleep-wake cycle.

circadian rhythms The normal pattern of biological changes that occur predictably throughout the day.

cirrhosis A stiffening of the blood vessels of the liver, thus reducing its effectiveness.

civil commitment The involuntary hospitalization of a person with a mental illness.

clang associations Ideas strung together on the basis of the sound of the words.

classical conditioning Credited to Pavlov, a process in which a response elicited *unconditionally* by one stimulus will in time be elicited by a second stimulus *on the condition that* the two stimuli consistently occur together.

client-centered therapy A supportive therapy designed to nourish the natural development of the client.

clinical course A specific pattern of changes in symptomatology over time.

clinical psychologists People with advanced training in psychology who apply the principles of psychology to understanding and treating emotional disturbance.

cocaine A stimulant drug extracted from coca shrubs.

codependency The actions of family members of a dug-dependent individual that inadvertently encourages or supports continued drug dependence.

cognitive-behavioral perspective A behavioral perspective that incorporates the realization that people's thoughts have a powerful impact on their behavior.

cognitive disorders Characterized by dysfunctions of thought and memory that are known to be the result of specific damage to the brain.

cognitive neuroscience perspective Looks at how people with a given disorder differ from other people in the way they perceive and think about the world and at how those differences may contribute to the onset or maintenance of a disorder.

cognitive psychologists Psychologists who study human perceptual and thought processes with the goal of understanding these processes and their limitations.

cognitive slippage A milder form of thought disorder.

cognitive triad The distortion of one's experiences, oneself, and one's future in ways that increase the likelihood of feeling depressed.

communication deviance The degree to which a relative's communication lacks clarity.

communication disorders Deficits in the ability to understand or express verbal messages at an age-appropriate level.

community psychology A field that focuses on understanding how social factors affect individual behavior, with an eye toward positive intervention.

comorbid conditions Diagnostic conditions that occur together in the same individual.

competent to stand trial A declaration that a person is capable of understanding the charges and of helping his or her attorney in the preparation of the defense.

compulsions The behaviors that an individual with obsessive-compulsive disorder feels compelled to perform.

computerized axial tomography (**CAT scan**) X-ray pictures used to view a person's body.

concordant Twin pairs who both have a specified disorder.

concurrent validity The relationship of a measure or diagnosis to some variable that is currently present.

conditioned response (**CR**) The response produced by a conditioned stimulus.

conditioned stimulus (**CS**) A neutral stimulus that later comes to elicit a response because it is repeatedly paired with an unconditioned stimulus.

conduct disorder A pervasive pattern of behavior that is characterized by a basic lack of respect for the rights of others and by consistent violations of rules or norms.

confounded variables Variables that vary together.

confounding variable Any variable, other than the variable of interest, on which research groups differ.

congeners By-products of the fermentation process by which alcohol is produced from fruits or grains.

construct validation Studying a construct.

constructs Ideas about things that cannot be directly observed.

content validity How well a test or measure covers the relevant content.

contingency management A behavioral strategy that seeks to make reinforcers contingent on drug avoidance.

continuous amnesia An inability to remember anything from a specified time period up to the present time.

Continuous Performance Test (**CPT**) A measure of attentional vigilance.

continuous reinforcement Reinforcement given for every response.

controlled drinking Strategy whereby a person with alcohol dependence drinks occasionally but does so responsibly and does not drink to the point of intoxication.

conversion disorder A somatoform disorder typically characterized by the report of a single symptom, usually representing a motor or sensory dysfunction.

coprophilia Sexual gratification through contact with feces.

coronary heart disease Heart disease caused by blockages to the blood vessels that feed the heart muscles.

correlational research Research that measures the relationship between variables.

counseling psychologists Psychologists trained to help people who have little psychopathology to make beneficial changes in their lives.

course The change in symptomatology of a disorder over time.

Creutzfeldt-Jakob disease A disease typically transmitted through tissue transplants and caused by prions, which are subviral proteins capable of replication.

criterion-related validities Validities concerned with the strength of the relationship between the measure or diagnosis and some criterion measure, such as school performance.

cross-sectional studies Studies in which groups are compared at one point in time.

cultural-familial mental retardation Mild mental retardation exhibited by those whose low IQ scores simply represent the low end of the IQ distribution.

culture The common expectations, experiences, and perspectives of a group of people living together.

cyclothymic disorder A chronic disorder characterized by frequent mood swings.

day rehabilitation programs Comprehensive programs that individually tailor their treatment to the needs of the individual.

declarative memories The memories of events.

defense mechanisms Strategies for reducing anxiety caused by thoughts, desires, or impulses.

deinstitutionalization An effort to limit hospitalization, based on the idea that institutional living tends to decrease a person's adaptive skills.

delirium Dramatic and widespread disruption in normal cognitive functioning.

delirium tremens (the **DTs**) An intense rebound phenomenon brought on, after years of heavy drinking, by an abrupt cessation of the drinking. The DTs may include vivid visual and tactile hallucinations and feelings of fever, terror, or deliriousness.

delusion of grandeur A belief that one is special or has special powers.

delusional disorders Characterized by dramatic and stable delusions but few other psychotic symptoms.

delusions Beliefs that are not objectively true, that would not be accepted as true within the person's culture, and that the person holds firmly in spite of contradictory evidence.

dementia Multiple cognitive deficits that are due to one or more medical problems.

denial Behaving as though things were different than they really are and refusing to acknowledge that reality, even to oneself.

dependent personality disorder Characterized by a pervasive pattern of clinging behavior coupled with a fear of separation.

dependent variable The variable that is measured to see whether the independent variable had an effect.

depersonalization A feeling of detachment or estrangement from oneself.

depersonalization disorder Characterized by feelings of detachment, which may be either persistent or recurrent.

depersonalization The feeling that you are watching yourself experience life instead of experiencing it directly.

depression A mood that is characterized by sadness and a loss of energy and enjoyment in life.

depressogenic Tending to create depression.

derealization The intermittent feeling that everything is unreal.

detoxification The process of withdrawing an addicted individual from drugs and their effects.

developmental models of psychopathology Cause-effect models that focus on how psychopathology develops over time.

Diagnostic and Statistical Manual of Mental Disorders (DSM) A compendium of diagnostic conditions and the criteria for each diagnosis.

dialectical behavior therapy (DBT) The combining of several cognitive and behavioral techniques to target problem thoughts and behaviors common in borderline personality disorder, such as suicidal ideation, self-mutilation, aggressive physical and social responses to people, and substance abuse.

diaphragmatic breathing Taking exceptionally deep breaths to increase the level of oxygen in the blood and reduce many of the physiological symptoms of anxiety and panic.

diathesis-stress model The theory that specific features—the diathesis—predispose people to specific psychopathology but that psychopathology develops only if triggered by sufficient life stresses.

dietary restraint hypothesis The hypothesis that dieting predisposes one to bulimia.

differential deficit research Studies in which people with schizophrenia are tested to see whether they do particularly poorly on one task compared with another.

differential diagnosis The process of determining the correct diagnosis when the superficial symptom pattern suggests several possible diagnoses.

differential research Research that compares already-existing groups.

discordant Twin pairs only one of whom has a specified disorder.

discrimination Essentially the opposite of generalization; occurs when people respond differently to two stimuli.

discriminative stimuli Stimuli that signal the availability of reinforcement.

disorder of written expression Substantially lower levels of writing ability than would be expected on the basis of the child's age, education, and IQ.

disorganized schizophrenia Schizophrenia characterized by disorganized speech or behavior and by flat or inappropriate affect.

displacement Taking unacceptable feelings toward one person and projecting them onto another person.

dissociation Emotional and/or cognitive separation from one's core identity.

dissociative amnesia A loss of autobiographical memory.

dissociative disorders Characterized by emotional and/or cognitive separation from one's core identity.

dissociative fugue The sudden moving away from one's home, coupled with amnesia for one's past.

dissociative identity disorder (DID) The presence of two or more distinct identities or "personalities" that recurrently take control of the individual. Formerly known as multiple personality disorder.

distal causes Remote factors that set up the conditions leading to an event.

dizygotic (DZ, or fraternal) twins A pair of twins who share 50% of their genes.

dominant gene A gene for which only a single dose is needed to obtain the trait that the gene specifies.

dopamine hypothesis The argument that in the brains of people with schizophrenia, there is either an excess of the neurotransmitter dopamine or, more likely, oversensitivity to dopamine.

double-bind hypothesis The discredited speculation that conflicting communications by a parent psychologically damage children.

double depression A condition characterized by occasional major depressive episodes in individuals who also suffer from the more chronic dysthymia.

down regulation A reduction in neurotransmitter sensitivity, in response to medication, to compensate for an excess of the neurotransmitter.

Down syndrome A disorder that occurs when the individual has an extra chromosome 21.

downward drift hypothesis The idea that schizophrenia makes it hard for people to achieve educationally and occupationally and that they therefore drift into lower social classes.

Durham rule The definition of legal insanity as any illegal act that was a product of mental disease or mental defect.

duty to warn The principle that therapists are required to warn potential victims of specific threats made by a client in a therapy session.

dyslexia Another name for *reading disorder*.

dyspareunia The experience of genital pain during intercourse.

dyssomnias Disorders characterized either by difficulty initiating and maintaining sleep or by excessive sleep.

dysthymic disorder A chronic, lower-level depression.

early morning awakening A depressive symptom that manifests itself when an individual awakens two to three hours before the normal wake-up time and finds it impossible to go back to sleep.

eating disorders Disorders characterized by severe disruptions in eating behavior, which affect physical, psychological, and social functioning.

Ecstasy The name of two new amphetamines—MDA (methylenedioxyamphetamine) and MDMA (methylenedioxymethamphetamine).

ego One's sense of self.

ego dystonic Behavior that feels alien and abnormal to the person performing it.

ego dystonic homosexuality A homosexual orientation that is so uncomfortable for the person that he or she wishes to become heterosexual.

ego psychology Erikson's theory that psychological development involves the maturation of the ego to handle social demands.

ego syntonic Behavior that feels normal to the person performing it.

Electra complex A girl's first sexual longings for another, in the person of her father.

electroconvulsive therapy (ECT) Producing a seizure in a person by passing an electric current through the brain. Also called *electroshock therapy*.

elimination disorders Disruptions or developmental delays in control of the elimination of bodily wastes (urine and feces).

emergenic traits Traits that result from specific *combinations* of characteristics, *all* of which must be present.

empirical approach to test development A test development technique that selects items based on their ability to differentiate people with and without a specified personality trait or diagnosis.

empirically supported treatments Treatments that have been demonstrated effective in controlled research trials.

empiricism Using observation to generate new knowledge.

encopresis Characterized by the repeated passage of feces into such inappropriate places as one's clothes or the floor.

endocrine system A variety of glands, each of which secretes one or more chemicals into the bloodstream.

enuresis Characterized by persistent voiding of urine, most often during the night, in children who are at least five years old.

essential hypertension Elevated blood pressure for which no physical cause can be found. Also called *primary hypertension*.

etiology The cause or causes of a disease or abnormality.

eugenics The science of selective breeding.

evolution The gradual changes in a species that occur across generations and are shaped by the environmental demands placed on that species.

evolutionary perspective Looks at how psychopathology evolves across generations, whether it was once adaptive, and what contributions the environment makes.

excitement stage Physiological changes during a sexual encounter, such as genital swelling and vaginal lubrication.

executive functioning Those self-directed behaviors that regulate and coordinate actions to achieve goals.

exhibitionism Obtaining sexual gratification from exposing one's genitals to a stranger.

existential perspective A belief that each person is responsible for finding meaning in life.

expectancy effects Changes in behavior that are due not to the specific effects of alcohol but, rather, to the expectations that people hold about how alcohol will affect them.

experimental research Studies in which participants are randomly assigned to one of two or more groups, each group is subjected to a particular treatment, and the groups are compared.

experimenter bias Occurs when a researcher expects a certain outcome and is inclined to interpret ambiguous responses as consistent with that expectation or ask questions in such a way as to elicit the expected result.

explicit memories Memories that people can recount because they are aware of them.

exposure with response prevention Putting oneself in situations in which one's obsessions are likely to occur (the exposure) and then blocking one's compulsions (the response prevention).

expressed emotion (**EE**) A family member's expression of hostile and critical comments directed at the person with psychopathology, coupled with an overinvolvement in the person's life.

expressive language disorder Significant impairment in the ability to express oneself verbally that is well beyond what would be expected given the person's nonverbal IQ or level of receptive language development.

extinction The process of "unlearning" a conditioned response so that the CS no longer produces the CR.

extraversion A tendency to be outgoing, fun-loving, and open and affectionate with people.

eye movement desensitization and reprocessing (**EMDR**) A procedure that involves imaginal exposure to a traumatic event while the person engages in a prescribed series of eye movements.

face validity The degree to which a test is measuring what it appears to measure.

factitious disorder A disorder characterized by feigning symptoms, deliberately distorting objective measures of symptoms, or doing things that might produce actual symptoms in order to assume the sick role.

false negatives Occur when one predicts that a situation, such as a diagnosis, does not exist, and the prediction is wrong. Also known as misses.

false positives Occur when one predicts a specific situation, such as a diagnosis, and the prediction is wrong. Also known as false alarms.

family studies Genetic studies designed to verify that a specific psychopathology runs in families.

family therapy A variation on traditional individual therapy, based on the belief that the dynamics of a family have powerful influences on individual members and that treating a psychological problem of one member without taking into account the impact of the family makes it difficult for any change to occur.

female orgasmic disorder A disorder characterized by either failure to achieve or significant delay in achieving an orgasm in a woman who is able to achieve normal sexual arousal.

female sexual arousal disorder A disorder characterized by an inability to achieve or maintain adequate lubrication and swelling of the vagina to allow comfortable sexual intercourse.

fetal alcohol syndrome A condition in which a baby is born with birth defects that are the result of heavy alcohol consumption by the mother during pregnancy.

fetish A fascination with an object—usually nonliving—from which the individual receives sexual gratification though contact or fantasy.

fight-or-flight response A complex survival reflex that mobilizes the body for defensive action in life-or-death situations.

fixated Stuck in a developmental stage because one's needs are not properly satisfied.

fixed delusional system Delusions that remain constant over time.

flashbacks Vivid feelings of reliving a trauma.

flashbulb memories Vivid memories of a critical event that are so clear they seem to be etched in one's mind forever.

flat or blunted affect A lack of emotional display.

flooding Intense and prolonged exposure to a feared stimulus.

forcible rape Sexual intercourse with an adult, coerced through violence or the threat of violence.

fragile-X syndrome A disorder caused by a broken X chromosome.

frotteurism Sexually touching or rubbing against someone, often in such crowded places as subways and elevators.

functional brain abnormalities Dysfunction in the brain that is not associated with some structural abnormality.

functional brain asymmetry A pattern of performance that indicates that one side of the brain is better than the other at a particular task.

functional disorders Difficulties in performing one or more tasks.

functional magnetic resonance imaging (**fMRI**) A way to measure changes in the activity level of various parts of the brain by measuring the magnetic properties of brain tissue.

gender identity disorder A disorder characterized by a strong desire to be, or an insistence that one is, the opposite sex, coupled with a persistent discomfort about one's own sex.

general adaptation syndrome (**GAS**) The three phases that a body goes through when faced with prolonged stress: alarm, resistance, and exhaustion.

general paresis Gradual destruction of brain tissue from the sexually transmitted disease syphilis.

general risk factors Factors such as reduced social support, psychological stress, and expressed emotion that may add to the risk of schizophrenia. Nevertheless, they are neither necessary nor sufficient to cause the disease, nor are they specific to a given disorder.

generalization Occurs when stimuli that have never been conditioned produce the same response as the CS because they are physically or functionally similar to the original CS.

generalized amnesia A failure to recall anything about one's life.

generalized anxiety disorder (**GAD**) A syndrome characterized by excessive worry.

generalized deficit The tendency of people with schizophrenia to do poorly on almost every task.

generalized social phobia Overwhelming anxiety experienced in nearly all social situations.

genetic abnormalities Abnormalities typically due to single genes that affect brain development and functioning.

genetic high-risk paradigm A study in which participants are selected on the basis of their genetic relationship to someone with a specified psychopathology.

genital stage Developmental stage in which the child's sexual interest is on sexual pleasure derived through one-on-one social/sexual relationships.

global assessment of functioning (GAF) A scale, utilized in the DSM, whereon the individual's overall clinical functioning is rated on a scale of 1 to 100.

group homes Houses where a small number of retarded individuals live and are involved in community activities.

guided masturbation A procedure that teaches the woman and her partner how to achieve sufficient arousal through masturbation to reach orgasm.

guilty but mentally ill A verdict that allows the person to be incarcerated for a period of time but also acknowledges the presence of mental illness and suggests the need for treatment during incarceration.

hallucinations Perceptual experiences that feel real although there is nothing there to perceive.

hallucinogens A broad, heterogeneous class of drugs that alter one's perceptions and awareness, thus producing a strange and surrealistic image of the world.

harm reduction The principle of reducing the secondary problems spawned by substance abuse, such as infections, overdosing, and commission of crimes to support the habit.

hashish A hallucinogen made from the resin found in the tops of hemp plants.

heroin A highly addictive derivative of morphine.

high-risk studies Prospective studies in which the people being followed are known to be at a higher than average risk for the disorder.

histrionic personality disorder Characterized by excessive emotionality and an attention-seeking behavior pattern.

homosexuality A preference for sexual contact with one's own sex.

hopelessness model The hypothesis that hopelessness depression results when people expect undesirable outcomes to occur and this expectation is confirmed by a series of negative events.

hormones The chemicals secreted by the glands of the endocrine system.

HPA axis The three organs involved in a chain of actions when a body is stimulated by stress: the hypothalamus, the pituitary gland, and the adrenal cortex.

humanistic perspective The view that humans are more capable than other animals and are uniquely aware of the world and of their role in it.

Huntington's disease An inherited disorder that involves a gradual degeneration of brain tissue, which causes spasmodic twitching and progressive cognitive deterioration starting around age 40.

hypertension The technical term for elevated blood pressure.

hypervigilance The feeling of constantly being on guard.

hypnosis A state of consciousness that involves focal concentration, a receptiveness to certain input, and a relative suspension of peripheral awareness.

hypnotic drugs Drugs used to induce sleep.

hypnotics Sleeping pills.

hypoactive sexual desire A disorder characterized by a serious deficiency in, or a total lack of, sexual fantasy and desire.

hypochondriasis A disorder characterized by an unwarranted and inaccurate belief, based on the misinterpretation of one or more bodily sensations, that one has a disease.

hypomania A less extreme level of mania, which may leave the person on the edge of control.

hypothesis A tentative statement about the relationship between things.

hypoxyphilia A type of masochistic behavior that involves momentarily cutting off oxygen to the brain as a way to heighten sexual sensations during masturbation.

iatrogenic Unintentionally shaped or caused by the practitioner.

id Basic drives, motives, and instincts.

ideas of reference The sense that an unrelated event is somehow uniquely linked to oneself, which results in drawing conclusions that others would consider bizarre.

imaginal exposure An exposure to a feared object or situation through imagining the object or situation.

implicit memories Memories that people are unaware of.

implosive therapy A variation of flooding that uses imaginal exposure to psychoanalytic anxiety themes.

in vivo exposure An actual exposure to a feared object or situation.

inappropriate affect Unusual and sometimes bizarre emotional responses.

incest A subtype of pedophilia in which members of the victim's family commit the sexual abuse.

incidence The percentage of new cases of a disorder that develop during a specified period.

independent variable The variable that defines the groups being studied.

individual differences The natural differences between human beings.

informed consent The principle that research participants can agree to participate in a study only after they have been given an adequate description of the project, of what is involved, of what risks might exist, and of what benefits they can expect.

insanity defense A legal defense based on the premise that people cannot be held responsible for crimes if they did not understand the nature of their actions or were unable to control their actions.

Insanity Defense Reform Act Passed by Congress in 1984, this act defines legal insanity as existing when the person is *unable* to appreciate the wrongfulness of an action as the result of a *severe* mental illness or defect.

Institutional Review Boards (IRBs) An appointed group of people who evaluate the ethical appropriateness of studies with an eye to protecting the welfare of study participants.

instrumental conditioning Sometimes called operant conditioning; based on the principle that behavior is modified by its consequences.

intelligence The ability to think and solve problems.

intelligence test, or **IQ test** A measure of the abilities believed to be at the core of intelligence. IQ is short for *intelligence quotient.*

intermittent reinforcement Reinforcement given for some, but not all responses.

internal consistency reliability The degree to which the items that make up a test all measure the same thing.

International Classification of Diseases (**ICD**) A manual similar to the DSM that lists physical and psychological disorders.

interpersonal therapy (**IPT**) A short-term neoanalytic approach that focuses on helping clients appreciate how their interpersonal interactions may be preventing them from achieving satisfying social relationships.

interrater reliability The degree to which professionals agree on a person's diagnosis.

introversion A tendency to be socially retiring, sober, and reserved.

irrational assumptions Ellis's term for distorted assumptions that people often hold about the world and themselves without being aware of it.

irresistible impulse The concept that people should not be held accountable for actions that they could not control.

irritable bowel syndrome (**IBS**) The rapid and sometimes unpredictable onset of intense cramps and diarrhea.

klismaphilia Sexual gratification through the use of enemas.

lack of insight Lack of awareness that one's experiences are unusual or abnormal.

latency period The child's sexual interest at 6–12 years appears to be minimal.

lateralization Differentiation of the functions of the left and right cerebral hemispheres.

learned helplessness model Seligman's proposal that depression results from being in aversive situations in which one has no control over the outcome.

learning Changing one's behavior to fit the needs of the situation better.

learning disorders Significant deficits in reading, mathematics, or written expression.

lifetime prevalence The percentage of the population that will experience a disorder sometime in their lifetime.

limbic system The subcortical structures of the brain that control emotional processing, learning, and memory.

localized amnesia A failure to recall events during a specific period of time, usually following a traumatic event.

locus ceruleus An area of the brain stem that may trigger panic attacks.

longitudinal studies Studies in which people are followed over time to observe changes in their clinical status.

loosening of associations Jumping from one topic to another, sometimes in mid-sentence; the most common form of thought disorder in schizophrenia.

LSD (*d*-lysergic acid dimethylamide) A synthesized drug that produces potent distortions in perception.

M'Naghten rule The principle that anyone who does not understand the nature of an action or whether the action was wrong, as the result of a severe psychiatric disorder, should not be held accountable for the crime.

magnetic resonance imaging (MRI) The use of a magnetic field to form images based on the varying magnetic properties of different body tissues.

major depression An intense form of depression that occurs in episodes.

maladaptive Behavior that produces negative outcomes.

male erectile disorder A disorder characterized by a persistent or recurrent inability to attain or maintain an adequate erection.

male orgasmic disorder A disorder characterized by either failure to achieve or a significant delay in achieving orgasm in a male who is able to achieve and maintain an erection.

malingering Falsely presenting one or more physical or psychological disorders for personal gain.

managed care A system in which insurance companies, or their designated representatives, gather information about the medical or psychological condition of people in treatment and work with the treating professionals to decide what services will be covered under the insurance.

mania A mood characterized by excessive energy, extreme confidence, euphoria, and irritability.

marijuana A hallucinogen made from the crushed leaves and flowers of the hemp plant.

marker A characteristic that is independent of the symptoms of the disorder, exists before the symptoms develop, and continues after the symptoms subside.

Maslow's hierarchy of needs A model reflecting awareness that self-actualization can be achieved only if more basic needs are met first.

masturbation Manual self-stimulation or direct partner stimulation of the penis or clitoris.

mathematics disorder Substantially lower computational and mathematical reasoning skills than would be expected on the basis of the child's age, education, and IQ.

memory The ability to encode information for later use.

memory biases The tendency to recall certain memories more readily than others.

Mendelian inheritance The mechanism of single-gene transmission, identified by Gregor Mendel.

mental retardation Characterized by significant intellectual and functional deficits that begin before the age of 18.

mental status examination A series of observations and questions that probe a person's level of functioning.

mescaline The active ingredient in the peyote cactus.

metabolic effects The physiological impact of a drug.

methadone maintenance The best-known drug substitution treatment, which involves substituting the synthetic opioid methadone for the natural opiate heroin.

midbrain structures The parts of the brain that regulate such body functions as hunger and thirst, generate emotions, and serve as a relay center for signals from other parts of the brain.

migraine headaches Headaches due to dilation of blood vessels in the brain.

mild mental retardation Characterized by an IQ of 50–55 to approximately 70.

Minnesota Multiphasic Personality Inventory (MMPI) The most widely used psychological test.

mismatch theory The theory that there is a mismatch between what humans have evolved to handle and what they are required to handle today.

mixed receptive-expressive language disorder Deficit in both receptive and expressive language.

modeling Learning from observing the consequences experienced by others. Also called *observational learning*.

moderate mental retardation Characterized by an IQ from 35–40 to approximately 50–55.

monozygotic (MZ, or identical) twins A pair of twins who share 100% of their genes.

mood A general emotional feeling that may vary gradually over time.

mood disorder A disorder characterized by mood shifts that are more dramatic, more frequent, or last longer than what is considered normal.

moral treatment Treating people in asylums with respect.

multiaxial diagnosis A diagnostic procedure that breaks diagnoses into several distinct dimensions.

Munchausen syndrome Factitious disorder with physical symptoms.

Munchausen syndrome by proxy A disorder characterized by the deliberate creation of physical disorders in another person in order to get sympathy and support from others.

mutual-help groups Groups of affected individuals who meet regularly to provide members with guidance and support as they struggle with their problem.

narcissistic personality disorder Characterized by a pervasive pattern of acting grandiose, having a constant need for admiration, and appearing to lack empathy for others.

narcolepsy A disorder characterized by repeated irresistible attacks of sleep.

narcotics Drugs that produce a reversible suppression of the central nervous system, thereby rendering the person stuporous and insensitive to pain.

natural selection The process whereby genetic traits that foster survival and reproduction increase in frequency across generations because the organisms that exhibit those traits survive longer and reproduce more successfully.

necrophilia Obtaining sexual gratification through sexual contact with corpses.

negative reinforcement The removal of an aversive stimulus to increase the likelihood of a desired behavior occurring again.

negative symptoms Deficit symptoms—that is, symptoms that represent a lack of normal functioning.

neologisms Made-up words.

neurodevelopmental hypothesis The theory that disruptions of normal development may increase the risk for schizophrenia.

neurofibrillary tangles Tangles of proteins that form in neurons as people age. Their formation in excessive numbers contributes to the destruction of brain cells in Alzheimer's disease.

neuron A specialized cell that makes up the nervous system.

neuropsychological tests Tests that measure detailed functioning in people in order to infer something about the functioning of their brains.

neuroses A broad class of nonpsychotic conditions characterized by unwarranted anxiety as well as other clinical features; the term is no longer used in the DSM.

neuroticism A trait dimension of emotional instability.

neurotransmitters Chemicals released from the axon terminals by the firing of a neuron.

nicotine The active ingredient in cigarettes.

nightmare disorder A disorder characterized by frequent awakenings due to frightening dreams (nightmares), with detailed recall of the content of the dreams.

nocturnal panic attack A panic attack that occurs during sleep.

nurse practitioners Nurses with advanced training in medicine.

object relations theory A recent psychodynamic development that focuses on social relationships as critical to psychological development and functioning.

objective psychological tests Tests in which the person selects, from a limited number of choices, the answer that seems most appropriate.

obsessions Unwanted thoughts that an individual cannot control.

obsessive-compulsive disorder (OCD) A disorder characterized by strong, unwanted thoughts that create significant anxiety and often drive repetitive behavior that is excessive, is unnecessary, and sometimes seems foolish to the person.

obsessive-compulsive personality disorder Characterized by a preoccupation with orderliness, perfectionism, and control that often reduces a person's flexibility and efficiency.

obstructive sleep apneas Apneas caused by intermittent blockages of the upper airways during sleep.

Oedipus complex A boy's first sexual longings for another, in the person of his mother.

operant conditioning Sometimes called instrumental conditioning; based on the principle that behavior is modified by its consequences.

operationalize To specify the procedures that one will follow to measure a variable.

opiates Drugs that are derived from opium, such as morphine, codeine, and heroin.

opioids Synthetic opiates created in the laboratory.

oppositional defiant disorder Characterized by a pattern of negativistic, hostile, and defiant behaviors.

oral stage The child's focus at 0–18 months is on oral pleasures, including eating and exploring the world with the mouth.

organic mental retardation Significant mental retardation due to a severe physical disorder.

orgasm A physiological release, with involuntary pelvic thrusting, ejaculation in the male, and intense sexual pleasure.

orgasmic disorders Disorders that involve the inability to attain an orgasm in a time frame suitable for achieving sexual satisfaction by both partners.

pain disorders Disorders characterized by prominent pain symptoms that cause significant distress and interfere with social, occupational, or other role expectations.

panic attack An unexpected attack of overwhelming fear.

panic disorder A disorder characterized by recurrent, unexpected attacks of overwhelming fear, coupled with anxiety about having more such attacks.

paradigm A research strategy that includes specific assumptions, research methods, and supporting data.

paranoid delusion A false belief that other people are plotting against one.

paranoid personality disorder Characterized by a pervasive distrust and suspicion of other people and their motives.

paranoid schizophrenia Schizophrenia characterized by fixed delusions of being persecuted.

paraphilia One of several disorders characterized by intense sexually arousing fantasies, urges, or behaviors involving nonhuman objects or the suffering and humiliation of oneself, one's partner, or nonconsenting individuals.

parasomnias Abnormal behavior or physiological responding that occurs during sleep or during the transitions into or out of sleep.

parasympathetic nervous system The nerves that tend to calm organs.

Parkinson's disease A slowly degenerative neurological disorder that is characterized by tremors, unsteadiness, and muscle rigidity.

parsimonious A theory that either offers a simple explanation for a phenomenon or explains several phenomena.

partialism A paraphilia in which one derives sexual satisfaction from just a single part of one's partner's body, such as the hands or feet.

passive avoidance learning Learning to avoid anxiety-producing situations by avoiding behaviors that will create those situations.

pastoral counselors Religious personnel (priests, ministers, rabbis) who are trained to address the emotional needs of the people in their ministry.

PCP, or **angel dust** A dangerous drug (phencyclidine) that can cause severe paranoia, coma, and even death.

pedophilia Sexual urges toward or activities with a prepubescent child.

penile plethysmograph A device that measures the swelling of the penis in response to sexual arousal.

perceptual biases The tendency to perceive some objects more readily than others.

personality A set of internal predispositions that affects the way people behave in different settings and at different times.

personality disorders Pervasive and inflexible patterns of emotional reaction and behavior that interfere with an individual's functioning.

personality inventories Psychological tests designed to assess a number of personality or diagnostic variables simultaneously.

personality traits Specific behavioral tendencies.

pervasive developmental disorders Disorders characterized by severe disruptions in social interaction and communication skills.

phallic stage The child's focus at 3–5 years is on his or her genitals.

phenylketonuria (PKU) Retardation caused by a recessive gene on chromosome 12.

phobias Unreasonable fears of specific objects, places, or situations.

phonological disorder Failure to use developmentally expected speech sounds, such as saying "kable" instead of "table."

phototherapy A treatment for SAD wherein the person spends approximately half an hour a day in front of a special light.

phrenology Obsolete field that attempted to relate people's personality traits to the bumps on their heads.

physician-assisted suicide The taking of one's own life with the assistance of a physician.

physiological perspective Looks at how physiological mechanisms affect behavior, including abnormal behavior.

Pick's disease A relatively rare neuro-degenerative disorder that primarily attacks the frontal and temporal lobes of the brain.

placebo control group In a study, a group that receives an inert treatment with no active treatment elements.

placebos Treatments that are effective solely because of the power of suggestion.

plateau stage A relatively steady state of sexual arousal.

polydrug abusers Those who abuse more than one drug (the majority of drug users).

polygenic Caused, or contributed to, by several genes.

polysomnography Another term for a sleep study; this term reflects the fact that multiple physiological measures (*poly*) are recorded (*graphy*) during sleep (*somno*).

positive reinforcement A positive reinforcer applied following a behavior to increase the likelihood of the desired behavior occurring again.

positive symptoms Clearly deviant behaviors, such as delusions, hallucinations, and thought disorder.

positron emission tomography (**PET scan**) A way to measure the relative activity of various parts of the brain by measuring the absorption of a harmless radioactive isotope into the cells of the brain.

postpartum depression A major depressive episode that occurs in a woman shortly after she gives birth.

posttraumatic stress disorder (**PTSD**) A long-term dysfunctional response to potentially life-threatening situations.

preattentive processing The way one organizes visual information in the first few milliseconds.

predictive validity The relationship of a measure or diagnosis to some future event.

prefrontal lobotomy A crude operation practiced in the 1940s that involved destroying portions of the frontal lobe.

premature ejaculation The onset of orgasm in a male with little sexual stimulation and typically before or shortly after penetration of his partner.

preparedness A phenomenon that makes some fears more readily learned than others.

prescription privileges The legal authority to prescribe medications, which has been extended in many states to nurse practitioners.

presenile dementia Dementia at an early age brought on by disease processes that accelerate the natural death of brain cells.

prevalence The percentage of the population afflicted with a disorder over a specified period.

primary hypersomnia A disorder, not due to another physical or psychological disorder, characterized by excessive sleep, which may include either sleeping for unusually long periods or taking frequent naps during the day.

primary insomnia A disorder, not due to another physical or psychological disorder, characterized by difficulty in initiating sleep or in maintaining sleep long enough to allow the person to feel rested and refreshed in the morning.

primary narcissism The level of functioning of a newborn.

primary prevention Preventive strategies applied to the entire population.

priming An enhancement in the likelihood of memory recall as a function of context.

probands People who have a specified disorder and are selected for a genetic study.

procedural memories Memories of how to do things.

prodromal phase The period before significant symptoms of a psychiatric disorder are apparent.

profound mental retardation Characterized by an IQ below approximately 20–25.

progressive muscle relaxation A strategy, used in an overall stress management program, that involves relaxing the muscles of the body, one group at a time.

progressive muscle relaxation A technique for relaxing the muscles of the body one muscle group at a time, which makes the individual feel less anxious.

projection Attributing one's own unacceptable feelings to another person.

projective tests Tests in which people are asked to respond to vague stimuli.

prospective study The longitudinal approach to following people over time to see if psychopathology develops.

proximal causes Those factors that are immediately responsible for an event.

psilocybin The active ingredient in the mushroom *Psilocybin mexicana*.

psychedelics Hallucinogenic drugs that produce perceptual distortions including bright, distorted colors and shapes.

psychiatric nurses Nurses who specialize in working with psychopathological populations.

psychiatric social workers People who usually have either a college degree or a Master's degree in social work, along with considerable field experience in working with psychopathology.

psychiatrists Physicians who have completed a specialized residency program in psychiatry.

psychoanalysis Early forms of psychodynamic therapy.

psychoanalyst, or **analyst** Someone who is trained in the delivery of psychodynamic psychotherapy.

psychodynamic theory The idea that behavior may be the end product of a long, often contentious and often unconscious discussion about how one should behave.

psychoform disorder A physical disorder that appears on the surface to be a psychological disorder.

psychological autopsy An investigation conducted in an effort to understand a specific suicide by gathering information about the person, the events that led up to the suicide, and the way those events may have contributed to the final outcome.

psychometric instruments Psychological tests designed to measure the level of a specific psychological trait, such as anhedonia.

psychoneuroimmunology The study of the effects that behavior has on the immune system.

psychopathology A range of disturbed behavior, including severe depression and anxiety, substance abuse, consistent emotional or behavioral overreactions to life stresses, and disruption in thought processes, emotional functioning, and behavior.

psychopathy A term used to describe a pattern of antisocial personality traits.

psychophysiological disorders The modern term for psychosomatic disorders.

psychophysiological techniques Measurements of the activity of body organs, including the brain, as the person is engaged in behavior.

psychosexual stages Five developmental periods identified by Freud. In each stage, the child has to resolve a sexual issue.

psychosocial stages of development Social developmental stages proposed by Erikson.

psychosomatic disorders Older term for physical (somatic) disorders that have a significant psychological component, usually stress.

psychosurgery The removal or modification of portions of the brain that are thought to be involved in creating a psychiatric disorder.

psychotherapy Nonmedical approach that helps clients understand their problems and develop the skills to manage them.

psychotic disorders Disorders so severe that the person has essentially lost touch with reality. Schizophrenia is classified as a psychotic disorder.

psychoticism A tendency to be callous, lacking in empathy, vindictive, and impulsive.

punctuated equilibrium The theory that evolution occurs rapidly at times when massive environmental changes affect natural selection.

punishment The application of an aversive stimulus after a behavior to decrease the likelihood of the behavior occurring again.

purging The use of vomiting, diuretics, laxatives, or enemas as methods of minimizing the caloric impact of food.

rape Sexual intercourse with a nonconsenting partner.

rational emotive behavior therapy (**REBT**) Therapy in which the therapist tries to help clients identify and then change their irrational assumptions.

rationalism The use of a system of logical inference to generate new knowledge.

rationalization Reinterpreting an unacceptable desire by creating an acceptable reason for that desire.

reaction formation Behaving in a manner that is opposite to the underlying, often repressed, feeling that one has.

reading disorder Substantially lower levels of reading speed and/or comprehension than would be expected on the basis of the child's age, education, and IQ.

recessive gene A gene for which a double dose is needed to obtain the trait that the gene specifies.

refractory period For men, the period following orgasm during which another orgasm is impossible.

regression A retreat to an earlier stage of development.

rehabilitation The set of programs designed to help individuals with mental retardation reach their full potential.

relapse prevention Strategies designed to reduce the likelihood that a slip in a person's resolve to control his or her drug use will lead to relapse.

reliability The degree of consistency in the diagnostic process or any other assessment situation.

REM rebound An unusually large amount of time in REM sleep following a period of REM deprivation.

REM sleep A sleep period of rapid eye movement, during which dreaming takes place.

repression A motivated forgetting in that thoughts that would create anxiety are prevented from reaching awareness.

residential treatment The housing and treatment of mentally retarded individuals in community residences that resemble a family living environment.

residual phase The period when the primary symptoms of the disorder have subsided but other symptoms may still be present.

residual schizophrenia The symptom patterns found in individuals with schizophrenia during periods of relative remission.

resolution A relaxed sense of well-being following the intense release of orgasm.

response cost The removal of a positive reinforcer; imposed to decrease behavior.

response desynchrony A situation in which some symptoms of a disorder are affected by medication but others are not.

restricting type anorexia A subtype of anorexia that includes individuals who use only dieting to lose weight.

retrospective study A study that looks into the history of people who develop a disorder to see what factors distinguish those who develop problems from those who do not.

Rett's disorder Disruption of normal head growth, between 5 and 48 months, which leads to significant brain dysfunction, mental retardation, and significant loss of functional abilities.

rituals Another term used for compulsions, because the behaviors involved must be performed repeatedly and (usually) in a very specific manner.

role-playing Behavioral assessment strategy that involves observing how people behave in imagined situations.

Rorschach Inkblot Test A test in which people are asked what a series of inkblots resemble.

S&M Sadism and masochism.

satiation The reduction in the intensity of a drive when the needs that that drive functions to meet have been satisfied.

schemas Cognitive structures, or attitudes, that form in childhood and thereafter serve to organize the individual's world.

schizoaffective disorder A controversial disorder involving a combination of schizophrenic symptoms and symptoms of either bipolar disorder or major depression.

schizoid personality disorder Characterized by a pervasive pattern of detachment from social relationships and an apparent lack of interest in such relationships.

schizophrenic spectrum disorders A group of disorders: schizoaffective, schizotypal personality, and paranoid personality disorders.

schizophrenogenic mother hypothesis The discredited speculation that schizophrenia can be attributed to psychologically toxic effects of the individual's parents, especially the mother.

schizotaxia An integrative neural deficit linked to a genetic risk factor for schizophrenia.

schizotypal personality disorder An oddness in thought, perception, and social interactions.

schizotypy A specific personality organization characterized by such traits as cognitive slippage, magical thinking, anhedonia, and disturbance in body image.

science The combined use of rationalism, to develop theories and derive predictions, and empiricism, to test the predictions.

seasonal affective disorder (SAD) Depression that develops consistently in late fall and continues until spring.

secondary gain A secondary effect that yields positive reinforcement and thus maintains the pathology that produces it.

secondary prevention Preventive strategies applied to groups that are known to be at risk, such as crisis interventions with rape victims.

sedatives Drugs that tend to calm or relax an individual.

selective amnesia Ability to recall some, but not all, events during a specified time period.

selective mutism A persistent failure to speak in situations in which speaking is expected, which affects social or academic performance and is not due to lack of knowledge or to a language problem.

self-actualization The process of fulfilling one's human potential.

self-psychology A perspective developed by Heinz Kohut that focuses on the individual's developing awareness of her or his identity.

semi-structured interviews Interviews that have a specific agenda but no strict format for what will be asked, how it will be asked, or in what order the questions will be asked.

senile plaques β-amyloid protein deposits, resembling disks, that form between neurons and interfere with neuronal communication.

sensate focus An exercise that involves physical caresses and touching designed to produce pleasurable sensations, but not necessarily sexual arousal.

sensitivity The probability that a person with a characteristic, such as a specific diagnosis, will be correctly identified as having that characteristic.

sensitization An effect observed with some drugs when, with repeated administration, smaller doses of the drug can achieve results that previously required larger doses.

severe mental retardation Characterized by an IQ from 20–25 to approximately 35–40.

sexual addiction Engaging in sexual behavior that the person feels unable to control and continues to engage in despite significant negative consequences.

sexual arousal disorders Disorders that involve a dysfunction in one or more aspects of the psychological excitement or physiological preparatory responses that occur in the early stages of sex.

sexual aversion disorder A disorder characterized by a general distaste for, and avoidance of, genital contact with a sexual partner.

sexual desire disorders Disorders characterized by a deficiency in the desire for sexual activity.

sexual dysfunction Impairment in either the ability or the desire to function sexually.

sexual masochism Sexual gratification in response to being subjected to physical pain and/or humiliation.

sexual pain disorders The experience of vaginal or penile discomfort during sexual intercourse.

sexual sadism Sexual gratification from inflicting physical pain and/or humiliation on another person.

sheltered workshops Programs for the employment of mentally retarded individuals.

signs External characteristics that often accompany a disorder.

sleep An active recuperative process during which people are physically inactive and relatively unaware of their surroundings.

sleep apneas The most common forms of breathing-related sleep disorders, in which the person stops breathing for a time during sleep.

sleep hygiene The manner in which one prepares for, obtains, and maintains normal sleep.

sleep study A study that involves monitoring an individual during one or more nights of sleep, recording both behavior and a variety of physiological indices.

sleep terror disorder A disorder characterized by abrupt awakening from sleep, often with a terrified scream.

sleepwalking disorder A disorder characterized by complex motor behavior during sleep, such as getting up and walking around.

smooth-pursuit eye movement (**SPEM**) Visually following a target as it moves.

social class A grouping of people on the basis of education level and occupation.

social phobia A disorder in which the anxiety of being evaluated in a social situation is overwhelming.

sociocognitive model of DID A model proposed by Spanos, in which he argued that many of the dramatic symptoms of DID may be shaped by a combination of generally available information about the disorder and subtle differences in therapists' responses to client behavior.

sociocultural perspective Looks at how institutions and cultural norms influence the likelihood of psychological disorders and shape the pattern of symptoms when those disorders develop.

sociopathy A term used to describe a pattern of antisocial personality traits.

somatization disorder A disorder characterized by a pervasive and recurring pattern of reports of multiple physical symptoms for which no adequate physical cause can be found.

somatoform disorders Psychological disorders that appear on the surface to be physical disorders but for which there is no identifiable physical basis.

span-of-apprehension test A test calling for a person to decide which target letter was included in an array of letters that is flashed briefly.

special education Any school-based program that is designed to meet the unique learning needs of one or more students.

specific phobia An intense and unwarranted fear of a specific object or situation.

specificity The probability that someone without a characteristic will be correctly identified as not having that characteristic.

splitting A psychodynamic term for the process of seeing objects, such as family members, jobs, or therapists, as either all good or all bad.

squeeze technique A technique for delaying male orgasm in which the penis is squeezed near its head just as the male approaches orgasm.

statutory rape Sexual intercourse between an adult and a minor, who legally cannot give consent.

stimulants Drugs that arouse the central and/or autonomic nervous systems, thereby increasing a person's energy and alertness.

stop-start technique A technique for delaying male orgasm in which sexual stimulation is stopped just before orgasm, until the orgasmic urge decreases.

stress Both a physiological and a psychological reaction to situations that demand adaptation.

stress-related disorders Physical disorders that are either caused or exacerbated by chronic stress.

strokes, or cerebrovascular accidents (**CVAs**) A blockage or rupture of a blood vessel in the brain, which deprives the portion of the brain serviced by that blood vessel of oxygen.

structural brain abnormalities Visible changes in the size and shape of brain areas.

structured interviews Formal interviews that incorporate precisely worded questions with rules for how the interviewer should select the questions to be asked.

stuttering Disruption in the normal fluency and time patterning of speech sounds severe enough to interfere with academic, occupational, or social functioning.

sublimation Channeling unacceptable impulses into socially appropriate activities.

substance abuse A maladaptive pattern of substance use leading to clinically significant impairment or distress.

substance dependence A maladaptive pattern of substance use, leading to clinically significant impairment or distress.

suggestibility The ease with which a person can accept an idea proposed by another person.

suicidal ideation The feeling of wanting to commit suicide.

suicide The deliberate taking of one's own life.

superego One's conscience and ego ideal—the image of what one wants to be.

sympathetic nervous system The nerves that tend to arouse such organs as the heart.

symptoms Internal experiences that are maladaptive, ineffective, or bizarre.

synapse The small gap between the axon terminal of one neuron and the dendrite of the next.

syndrome A cluster of symptoms. A person who shows one or two of these symptoms is likely to show the other symptoms in the cluster.

systematic desensitization A treatment that reduces anxiety to specific objects or situations via the person's gradual exposure to the feared stimulus while maintaining a relaxed state.

systematized amnesia An inability to remember any items in a particular conceptual category.

tardive dyskinesia Brain disorder caused by excessive use of neuroleptic medication, which is caracterized by abnormal, involuntary movements such as smacking of lips, sucking, and sideways jaw movements.

telephone scatologia A disorder characterized by making repeated obscene phone calls.

tension headaches Headaches due to excessive muscle tension in the neck and face.

tension-reduction hypothesis The idea that drug addiction occurs because drugs can make people emotionally numb, thus blocking any unpleasant state.

test-retest reliability How consistent a measure is over time.

Thematic Apperception Test (**TAT**) A test in which people are asked to tell stories based on pictures they are shown.

theories The detailed plans that connect constructs with one another and with scientific observations.

theory A statement about how one thinks something works.

thought disorder A disruption of normal cognitive functioning; the most dramatic and obvious symptom of schizophrenia.

token economy System in which clients who perform desired behaviors are given tokens as rewards that can be redeemed for goods or activities.

tolerance A condition that develops over the course of use of a substance wherein the individual needs markedly increased amounts of the substance to achieve intoxication or desired effects, or experiences a markedly diminished effect with continued use of the same amount of the substance.

Tourette's syndrome A disorder characterized by uncontrolled tics and other movements that may include blurting out obscenities and other embarrassing things.

trait dimensions Underlying dimensions on which personality traits can be ordered.

transcranial magnetic stimulation (**TMS**) A brain stimulation process that utilizes a magnetic field to treat depression.

transference relationship The client/therapist relationship.

transvestic fetishism Receiving sexual gratification from wearing the garments—especially the undergarments—typically worn by members of the opposite sex.

traumatic brain injury (**TBI**) Brain damage that is caused by a blow to the skull.

treatment protocols Treatment packages that combine specific elements to handle the range of symptoms shown by people with a particular disorder.

trephination The deliberate drilling of holes in the skull, perhaps as a way of treating individuals thought to be possessed. This procedure may be one of the earliest known treatments for abnormal behavior.

tumors Growths that damage surrounding tissue.

twin studies Comparisons of the risk of a specified disorder in the identical or fraternal co-twins of people with the disorder.

two-process theory of avoidance learning Mowrer's theory that the anxiety in OCD is generated by the obsession due to its association with fearful stimuli, and the compulsions are negatively reinforced by a reduction in anxiety.

Type A behavior Behavior that includes feelings of intense competitiveness, constant time pressure, impatience, high activity level, aggressiveness, and hostility.

Type B behavior People without Type A traits are said to exhibit Type B behavior.

ulcers Lesions or holes that gastric juices have burned into the wall of either the stomach or the duodenum (the upper portion of the intestine).

unconditional positive regard A nonjudgmental acceptance of the client's worth as a human being.

unconditioned response (UR) The response to an unconditioned stimulus.

unconditioned stimulus (US) A stimulus that produces a response without any need for conditioning.

unconscious Outside of conscious awareness.

undifferentiated schizophrenia A diagnosis used for people who meet the criteria for schizophrenia but do not clearly fit into the paranoid, catatonic, or disorganized subtype.

unipolar depression A disorder characterized by a pattern of serious depressive periods with no history of manic or hypomanic periods.

unstructured interviews Interviews in which the interviewer can ask any question and follow up on any answer.

urophilia Sexual gratification through contact with urine.

vaginal photoplethysmograph A device that measures the increase in blood flow in the vagina in response to sexual arousal.

vaginismus A persistent and recurrent tightening of the muscle in the outer portion of the vagina in response to penetration.

validity The property a test exhibits when the thing being measured is real and is related to critical variables.

variable Any characteristic that can take on different values.

vascular dementia Deteriorating cognitive functioning brought on by damage to a portion of the brain after multiple small strokes.

vasovagal syncope A reflex reaction to a puncture wound: the cardiovascular system drops the blood pressure to minimize the loss of blood.

voyeurism Obtaining sexual gratification from observing unsuspecting people who are naked, undressing, or engaged in sexual activity.

waxy flexibility A property of catatonic stupor, exhibited when a person's limbs can be moved by someone and he or she will maintain the new position.

withdrawal Period during which an addict or substance abuser either stops using a drug or uses less than customary. Unpleasant withdrawal symptoms result, which the user may avoid by resuming use of the same (or a closely related) substance.

word salad Associations so loose that the words seem random.

Yerkes-Dodson Law As arousal increases, performance increases, but only up to a point.

zoophilia Sexual activity with animals.

References

Abbey, A., Zawacki, T., & McAuslan, P. (2000). Alcohol's effects on sexual perception. *Journal of Studies on Alcohol, 61,* 688–697.

Abbey, S. E., & Garfinkel, P. E. (1991). Neurasthenia and chronic fatigue syndrome: The role of culture in the making of a diagnosis. *American Journal of Psychiatry, 148,* 1638–1646.

Abe, K., Amatomi, M., & Oda, N. (1984). Sleepwalking and recurrent sleeptalking in children of childhood sleepwalkers. *American Journal of Psychiatry, 141,* 800–801.

Abel, G. G., Barlow, D. H., Blanchard, E. B., & Guild, D. (1977). The components of rapists' sexual arousal. *Archives of General Psychiatry, 34,* 895–903.

Abel, G. G., Becker, J. V., Mittelman, M. S., Cunningham-Rather, J., Rouleau, J. L., & Murphy, W. D. (1987). Self-reported sex crimes of nonincarcerated paraphiliacs. *Journal of Interpersonal Violence, 2,* 3–25.

Abel, G. G., Mittelman, M. S., & Becker, J. V. (1985). Sexual offenders: Results of assessment and recommendations for treatment. In M. M. Ben-Aaron, S. I. Huckers, & C. D. Webster (Eds.), *Clinical criminology: Current concepts* (pp. 191–205). Toronto: M & M Graphics.

Abikoff, H. B., & Hechtman, L. (1996). Multimodal therapy and stimulants in the treatment of children with attention deficit hyperactivity disorder. In E. D. Hibbs & P. S. Jensen (Eds.), *Psychosocial treatments for child and adolescent disorders: Empirically based strategies for clinical practice* (pp. 341–369). Washington, DC: American Psychological Association.

Abouesh, A., & Clayton, A. (1999). Compulsive voyeurism and exhibitionism: A clinical response to paroxetine. *Archives of Sexual Behavior, 28,* 23–30.

Abramson, L. Y., Alloy, L. B., & Metalsky, G. I. (1995). Hopelessness depression. In G. Buchanan and M. Seligman (Eds.), *Explanatory style* (pp. 113–134). Hillsdale, NJ: Erlbaum.

Abramson, L. Y., Metalsky, G. I., & Alloy, L. B. (1989). Hopelessness depression: A theory-based subtype of depression. *Psychological Review, 96,* 358–372.

Abramson, L. Y., Seligman, M. E. P., & Teasdale, J. D. (1978). Learned helplessness in humans: Critique and reformulation. *Journal of Abnormal Psychology, 87,* 49–74.

Abusamra, L. C. (1998). General principles of management. In R. C. Hamdy, J. M. Turnbull, J. Edwards, & M. M. Lancaster (Eds.), *Alzheimer's disease: A handbook for caregivers* (3rd ed., pp. 143–149). St. Louis, MO: Mosby.

Ackerman, G. M., & Oliver, D. J. (1997). Psychosocial support in an outpatient clinic. *Palliative Medicine, 11,* 167–168.

Ackerman, M. D., & Carey, M. P. (1995). Psychology's role in the assessment of erectile dysfunction: Historical precedents, current knowledge, and methods. *Journal of Consulting and Clinical Psychology, 63,* 862–876.

Acocella, J. (1999). *Creating hysteria: Women and multiple personality disorder.* San Francisco: Jossey-Bass.

Acosta, A. X., Silva, W. A., Carvalho, T. M., & Zago, M. A. (2001). Ten novel mutations in the phenylalanine hydroxylase gene (PAH) observed in Brazilian patients with phenylketonuria. *Human Mutation, 17,* 77.

Addington v. Texas. (1979). 441 U.S. 418.

Ader, R. (Ed.). (1981). *Psychoneuroimmunology.* San Diego, CA: Academic Press.

Adlaf, E. M., & Smart, R. G. (1983). Risk-taking and drug-use behaviour: An examination. *Drug and Alcohol Dependence, 11,* 287–296.

Adler, C. M., McDonough-Ryan, P., Sax, K. W., Holland, S. K., Arndt, S., & Strakowski, S. M. (2000). fMRI of neuronal activation with symptom provocation in unmedicated patients with obsessive compulsive disorder. *Journal of Psychiatric Research, 34,* 317–324.

Adler, L. E., Hoffer, L. D., Wiser, A., & Freedman, R. (1993). Normalization of the auditory physiology by cigarette smoking in schizophrenia patients. *American Journal of Psychiatry, 150,* 1856–1861.

Adler, L. E., Olincy, A., Waldo, M., Harris, J. G., Griffith, J., Stevens, K., Flach, K., Nagamoto, H., Bickford, P., Leonard, S., & Freedman, R. (1998). Schizophrenia, sensory gating, and nicotinic receptors. *Schizophrenia Bulletin, 24,* 189–202.

Agras, W. S., Sylvester, D., & Oliveau, D. (1969). The epidemiology of common fears and phobias. *Comprehensive Psychiatry, 10,* 151–156.

Ahearn, L. (2002). Society must put children's safety first. *Newsday,* April 16, A35.

Aiken, L. R. (1995). *Aging: An introduction to gerontology.* Thousand Oaks, CA: Sage Publications.

Akiskal, H. S. (2000). Mood disorders: Clinical features. In B. I. Sadock & V. A. Sadock (Eds.), *Kaplan & Sadock's comprehensive textbook of psychiatry* (7th ed., pp. 1338–1377). Philadelphia: Lippincott Williams & Wilkins.

Alcock, J. (2001). *Animal behavior: An evolutionary approach* (7th ed.). Sunderland, MA: Sinauer Associates.

Allderidge, P. (1985). Bedlam: Fact or fiction? In W. H. Bynum, R. Porter, & M. Shepherd (Eds.), *The anatomy of madness*: Vol. II (pp. 17–33). London: Tavistock.

Allen, J. J., Iacono, W. G., Depue, R. A., & Arbisi, P. (1993). Regional electroencephalographic asymmetries in bipolar seasonal affective disorder before and after exposure to bright light. *Biological Psychiatry, 33,* 642–646.

Allen, J. J. B., & Movius, H. L. II. (2000). The objective assessment of amnesia in dissociative identity disorder using event-related potentials. *International Journal of Psychophysiology, 38,* 21–41.

Allen, R. P. (1997). The significance and interpretation of the polysomnogram. In M. R. Pressman & W. C. Orr (Eds.), *Understanding sleep: The evaluation and treatment of sleep disorders* (pp. 193–208). Washington, DC: American Psychological Association.

Allison, N. G. (1994). Fetal alcohol syndrome: Implications for psychologists. *Clinical Psychology Review, 14,* 91–111.

Alloy, L. B., & Abramson, L. Y. (1979). The judgment of contingency in depressed and nondepressed students: Sadder but wiser? *Journal of Experimental Psychology: General, 108,* 441–485.

Alloy, L. B., & Abramson, L. Y. (1988). Depressive realism: Four theoretical perspectives. In L. B. Alloy (Ed.), *Cognitive processes in depression* (pp. 223–265). New York: Guilford.

Alloy, L. B., Abramson, L. Y., Whitehouse, W. G., Hogan, M. E., Tashman, N. A., Steinberg, D. L., Rose, D. T., & Donovan, P. (1999a). Depressogenic cognitive styles: Predictive validity, information processing and personality characteristics, and developmental origins. *Behaviour Research and Therapy, 37,* 503–531.

Alloy, L. B., Reilly-Harrington, N. A., Fresco, D., Whitehouse, W. G., & Zechmeister, J. S. (1999b). Cognitive styles and life events in subsyndromal unipolar and bipolar disorders: Stability and prospective prediction of depressive and hypomanic mood swings. *Journal of Cognitive Psychotherapy: An International Quarterly, 13,* 21–40.

Alvidrez, J., & Azocar, F. (1999). Self-recognition of depression in public care women's clinic patients. *Journal of Women's Health and Gender-Based Medicine, 8,* 1063–1071.

American Heart Association. (1996). *1997 Heart and stroke statistical update.* AHA Publication 55-0524. Dallas, TX: National Center.

American Heart Association. (2001). 2001 heart and stroke statistics update (**www.americanheart.org/statistics/coronary.html**).

American Humane Association. (1988). *Highlights of official child neglect and abuse reporting, 1986.* Denver, CO: American Humane Association.

American Psychiatric Association. (1952). *Diagnostic and statistical manual of mental disorders.* Washington, DC: American Psychiatric Association.

American Psychiatric Association. (1968). *Diagnostic and statistical manual of mental disorders* (2nd ed.). Washington, DC: American Psychiatric Association.

American Psychiatric Association. (1980). *Diagnostic and statistical manual of mental disorders* (3rd ed.). Washington, DC: American Psychiatric Association.

American Psychiatric Association. (1987). *Diagnostic and statistical manual of mental disorders* (3rd ed., revised). Washington, DC: American Psychiatric Association.

American Psychiatric Association. (1994). *Diagnostic and statistical manual of mental disorders* (4th ed.). Washington, DC: American Psychiatric Association.

American Psychiatric Association. (2000). *Diagnostic and statistical manual of mental disorders* (4th ed., text revision). Washington, DC: American Psychiatric Association.

American Psychological Association. (1998). Ethics of research with human participants. Draft report being circulated for comment. Available at *www.apa.org.*

American Psychological Association. (1992). Ethical principles of psychologists. *American Psychologist, 45,* 390–395.

Amnesty International. (1984). Torture in the eighties. London: Amnesty International Publications.

Amos, A. (2000). A computational model of information processing in the frontal cortex and basal ganglia. *Journal of Cognitive Neuroscience, 12,* 505–519.

Ancoli-Israel, S. (1997). The polysomnogram. In M. R. Pressman & W. C. Orr (Eds.), *Understanding sleep: The evaluation and treatment of sleep disorders* (pp. 177–191). Washington, DC: American Psychological Association.

Andersen, B. L., & Cyranowski, J. M. (1995). Women's sexuality: Behaviors, responses, and individual differences. *Journal of Consulting and Clinical Psychology, 63,* 891–906.

Anderson, J. R. (1998). Sleep, sleeping sites, and sleep-related activities: Awakening to their significance. *American Journal of Primatology, 46,* 63–75.

Anderson, L., Campbell, M., Grega, D., Perry, R., Small, A., & Green, W. (1984). Haloperidol in the treatment of infantile autism: Effect on learning and behavioral symptoms. *American Journal of Psychiatry, 141,* 1195–1202.

Anderson, N. B., McNeilly, M., & Myers, H. (1993). A biopsychosocial model of race differences in vascular reactivity. In J. Blascovich & E. S. Katkin (Eds.), *Cardiovascular reactivity to psychological stress and disease* (pp. 83–108). Washington, DC: American Psychological Association.

Anderson, P. L., & Meier-Hedde, R. (2001). Early case reports of dyslexia in the United States and Europe. *Journal of Learning Disabilities, 34,* 9–21.

Anderson, R. N., Kochonk, K. D., & Murphy, S. L. (1997). A report of final mortality statistics, 1995. Monthly Vital Statistics Report, 45(11), Supplement 2 (DHHS publication 97–1120). Hyattsville, MD: National Center for Health Statistics.

Andersson, T., Magnusson, D., & Weinberg, P. (1997). Early aggressiveness and hyperactivity as indicators of adult alcohol problems and criminality: A prospective longitudinal study of male subjects. *Studies on Crime and Crime Prevention, 6,* 7–20.

Andreasen, N. C. (1980). Mania and creativity. In R. H. Belmaker & H. M. van Praag (Eds.), *Mania: An evolving concept.* New York: Spectrum.

Andreasen, N. C., & Olsen, S. A. (1982). Negative versus positive schizophrenia: Definition and validation. *Archives of General Psychiatry, 39,* 789–794.

Andreasen, N. C., Arndt, S., Alliger, R., Miller, D., & Flaum, M. (1995). Symptoms of schizophrenia: Methods, meanings, and mechanisms. *Archives of General Psychiatry, 52,* 341–351.

Andreasen, N. C., Nopoulos, P., O'Leary, D. S., Miller, D. D., Wassink, T., & Flaum, M. (1999). Defining the phenotype of schizophrenia: Cognitive dysmetria and its neural mechanisms. *Biological Psychiatry, 46,* 908–920.

Andreasen, N. C., Olsen, S. A., Dennert, J. W., & Smith, M. R. (1982). Ventricular enlargement in schizophrenia: Relationship to positive and negative symptoms. *American Journal of Psychiatry, 139,* 297–302.

Andreasen, N. C., Olsen, S. A., Flaum, M., Swayze, V. W., Tyrrell, G., & Arndt, S. (1990). Positive and negative symptoms in schizophrenia: A critical reappraisal. *Archives of General Psychiatry, 47,* 615–621.

Angrist, B., Lee, H. K., & Gershon, S. (1974). The antagonism of amphetamine-induced symptomatology by a neuroleptic. *American Journal of Psychiatry, 131,* 817–819.

Angst, J. (1997). Epidemiology of depression. In A. Honig & H. M. van Praag (Eds.), *Depression: Neurobiological, psychopathological and therapeutic advances* (pp. 17–29). New York: Wiley.

Anonymous, Rosselli, D., & Calderon, C. (1998). An epidemic of collective conversion and dissociation disorder in an indigenous group of Colombia: Its relation to cultural change. *Social Science and Medicine, 46,* 1425–1428.

Anstendig, K. D. (1998). Selective mutism: A review of the treatment literature by modality from 1980–1996. *Psychotherapy, 35,* 381–391.

Antelman, S. M., Caggiula, A. R., Kucinski, B. J., Fowler, H., Gershon, S., Edwards, D. J., Austin, M. C., Stiller, R., Kiss, S., & Kocan, D. (1998). The effects of lithium on a potential cycling model of bipolar disorder. *Progress in Neuro-Psychopharmacology & Biological Psychiatry, 22,* 495–510.

Anthony, J. C., & Echeagaray-Wagner, F. (2000). Epidemiologic analysis of alcohol and tobacco use. *Alcohol Health and Research World, 24,* 201–208.

Anthony, J. C., Arria, A. M., & Johnson, E. O. (1995). Epidemiological and public health issues for tobacco, alcohol, and other drugs. In J. M. Oldman and M. B. Riba (Eds.), *American Psychiatric Press Review of Psychiatry,* Vol. 14 (pp. 15–49). Washington, DC: American Psychiatric Press.

Antony, M. M., & Barlow, D. H. (2002). Specific phobias. In D. H. Barlow (Ed.), *Anxiety and its disorders: The nature and treatment of anxiety and panic* (2nd ed., pp. 380–417). New York: Guilford.

Apfelbaum, B. (1989). Retarded ejaculation: A much misunderstood syndrome. In S. R. Leiblum & R. C. Rosen (Eds.), *Principles and practice of sex therapy: Update for the 1990s* (pp. 168–206). New York: Guilford.

Appelbaum, B. C., Appelbaum, P. S., & Grisso, T. (1998). Competence to consent to voluntary psychiatric hospitalization: A test of a standard proposed by APA. *Psychiatric Services, 49,* 1193–1196.

Appelbaum, P. S. (2001). Third-party suits against therapists in recovered-memory cases. *Psychiatric Services, 52,* 27–28.

Appels, A. (1996). Personality factors and coronary heart disease. In K. Orth-Gomér & N. Schneiderman (Eds.), *Behavioral medicine approaches to cardiovascular disease prevention* (pp. 149–159). Mahwah, NJ: Erlbaum.

Apt, C., Hurlbert, D., & Powell, D. (1993). Men with hypoactive sexual desire disorder: The role of interpersonal dependency and assertiveness. *Journal of Sex Education and Therapy, 19,* 108–116.

Archer, J. (1996). Sex differences in social behavior: Are the social role and evolutionary explanations compatible? *American Psychologist, 51,* 909–917.

Arieti, S. (1959). *American handbook of psychiatry.* New York: Basic Books.

Arkin, R. M., Cooper, H. M., & Kolditz, T. A. (1980). A statistical review of the literature concerning the self-serving attribution bias in interpersonal influence situations. *Journal of Personality, 48,* 435–448.

Arndt, W. B., Jr. (1991). *Gender disorders and the paraphilias.* Madison, CT: International Universities Press.

Aronson, E. (1999). *The social animal* (8th ed.). New York: Worth.

Aronson, T. A. (1987). A naturalistic study of imipramine in panic disorder and agoraphobia. *American Journal of Psychiatry, 144,* 1014–1019.

Arrigo, B. A. (1996). *The contours of psychiatric justice: A postmodern critique of mental illness, criminal insanity, and the law.* New York: Garland.

Arrigo, B. A. (2000). *Introduction to forensic psychology: Issues and controversies in crime and justice.* San Diego, CA: Academic.

Asarnow, R. F., & MacCrimmon, D. J. (1978). Residual performance deficit in clinically remitted schizophrenics: A marker of schizophrenia? *Journal of Abnormal Psychology, 87,* 597–608.

Asarnow, R. F., Nuechterlein, K. H., & Marder, S. R. (1983). Span of apprehension performance, neuropsychological functioning, and indices of psychosis-proneness. *Journal of Nervous and Mental Disease, 171,* 662–669.

Asarnow, R. F., Steffy, R. A., MacCrimmon, D. J., & Cleghorn, J. M. (1977). An attentional assessment of foster children at risk for schizophrenia. *Journal of Abnormal Psychology, 86,* 267–275.

Asmundson, G. J. G., & Norton, G. R. (1993). Anxiety sensitivity and its relationship to spontaneous and cued panic attacks in college students. *Behavior Research and Therapy, 31,* 199–201.

Assalian, P. (1994). Premature ejaculation: Is it really psychogenic? *Journal of Sex Education and Therapy, 20,* 1–4.

Associated Press. (2002). Repair or repeal death penalty. *Newsday,* April 16, A19.

Astin, M. C., Ogland-Hand, S. M., Foy, D. W., & Coleman, E. M. (1995). Post-traumatic stress disorder and childhood abuse in battered women: Comparisons with maritally distressed women. *Journal of Consulting and Clinical Psychology, 63,* 308–312.

Atay, T., & Karacan, I. (2000). A retrospective study of sleepwalking in 22 patients: Clinical and polysomnographic findings. *Sleep and Hypnosis, 2,* 112–119.

Atherly, A. G., Girton, J. R., & McDonald, J. F. (1999). *The Science of Genetics.* Fort Worth, TX: Saunders.

Atlas, J. A. (1995). Association between history of abuse and borderline personality disorder for hospitalized adolescent girls. *Psychological Reports, 77,* 1346.

Auerbach, J. S. (1993). The origins of narcissism and narcissistic personality disorder: A theoretical and empirical reformulation. In J. M. Masling & R. F. Bornstein (Eds.), *Psychoanalytic perspectives on psychopathology* (pp. 43–110). Washington, DC: American Psychological Association.

Austen, M. L., & Wilson, G. V. (2001). Increased vagal tone during winter in subsyndromal seasonal affective disorder. *Biological Psychiatry, 50,* 28–34.

Avery, D. H., Eder, D. N., Bolte, M. A., Hellekson, C. J., Dunner, D. L., Vitiello, M. V., & Prinz, P. N. (2001). Dawn simulation and bright light in the treatment of SAD: A controlled study. *Biological Psychiatry, 50,* 205–216.

Avery, D., & Lubrano, A. (1979). Depression treated with imipramine and ECT: The DeCarolis study reconsidered. *American Journal of Psychiatry, 136,* 559–562.

Avery-Clark, C. (1986). Sexual dysfunction and disorder patterns of husbands of working and nonworking women. *Journal of Sex and Marital Therapy, 12,* 282–296.

Ayoub, C. C., Deutsch, R. M., & Kinscherff, R. (2000). Munchausen by proxy: Definitions, identification, and evaluation. In R. M. Reece (Ed.), *Treatment of child abuse: Common ground for mental health, medical, and legal practitioners* (pp. 213–226). Baltimore: Johns Hopkins University Press.

Azrin, N. H., Acierno, R., Kogan, E. S., Donohue, B., Besalel, V. A., & McMahon, P. T. (1996). Follow-up results of supportive versus behavior therapy for illicit drug use. *Behavior Research and Therapy, 34,* 41–46.

Baare, W. F. C., van Oel, C. J., Pol, H. E. H., Schnack, H. G., Durston, S., Sitskoorn, M. M., & Kahn, R. S. (2001). Volumes of brain structures in twins discordant for schizophrenia. *Archives of General Psychiatry, 58,* 33–40.

Babiak, P. (1995). Psychopathic manipulation in organizations: Pawns, patrons, and patsies. *Issues in Criminological and Legal Psychology, 24,* 12–17.

Bach, A. K., Wincze, J. P., & Barlow, D. H. (2001). Sexual dysfunction. In D. H. Barlow (Ed.), *Clinical handbook of psychological disorders* (3rd ed., pp. 562–608). New York: Guilford.

Bachman, R. (1998). The factors related to rape reporting behavior and arrest. *Criminal Justice and Behavior, 25,* 8–29.

Baele, J., Dusseldorp, E., & Maes, S. (2001). Condom use self-efficacy: Effect of intended and actual condom use in adolescents. *Journal of Adolescent Health, 28,* 421–431.

Bailey, A., Le Couteur, A., Gottesman, I., Bolton, P., Simonoff, E., Yuzda, E., & Rutter, M. (1995). Autism as a strongly genetic disorder: Evidence from a British twin study. *Psychological Medicine, 25,* 63–77.

Bailey, A., Luthert, P., Bolton, P., Le Couteur, A., Rutter, M., & Harding, B. (1993). Autism and megalencephaly. *Lancet, 341,* 1225–1226.

Bailey, J. M., Dunne, M. P., & Martin, N. G. (2000). Genetic and environmental influences on sexual orientation and its correlates in an Australian twin sample. *Journal of Personality and Social Psychology, 78,* 524–536.

Bailey, J. M., Pillard, R. C., Dawood, K., Miller, M. B., Farrer, L. A., Trivedi, S., & Murphy, R. L. (1999). A family history study of male sexual orientation using three independent samples. *Behavior Genetics, 29,* 79–86.

Bailine, S. H., Rifkin, A., Kayne, E., Selzer, J. A., Vital-Herne, J., Blieka, M., & Pollack, S. (2000). Comparison of bifrontal and bitemporal ECT for major depression. *American Journal of Psychiatry, 157,* 121–123.

Baker, F. M. (2000). Minority issues. In B. I. Sadock & V. A. Sadock (Eds.), *Kaplan & Sadock's comprehensive textbook of psychiatry* (7th ed., pp. 3164–3174). Philadelphia: Lippincott Williams & Wilkins.

Bakker, D. J. (1990). *Neuropsychological treatment of dyslexia* (trans. G. Spyer). New York: Oxford University Press.

Ballenger, J. C. (2000). Benzodiazepine receptor agonists and antagonists. In B. I. Sadock & V. A. Sadock (Eds.), *Kaplan & Sadock's comprehensive textbook of psychiatry* (7th ed., pp. 2317–2324). Philadelphia: Lippincott Williams & Wilkins.

Ballenger, J. C., Burrows, G. D., Dupont, R. L., Lesser, I. M., Noyes, R., Pecknold, J. C., Riskin, A., & Swinson, R. P. (1988). Alprazolam in panic disorder and agoraphobia: Results from a multicenter trial: I. Efficacy in short-term treatment. *Archives of General Psychiatry, 45,* 413–422.

Ballenger, J. C., Davidson, J. R. T., Lecrubier, Y., Nutt, D. J., Borkovec, T. D., Rickels, K., Stein, D. J., & Wittchen, H. (2001). Consensus statement on generalized anxiety disorder from the International Consensus Group on Depression and Anxiety. *Journal of Clinical Psychiatry, 62* (Supplement 11), 53–58.

Ballentine, H. T., Bouckoms, H. A., Thomas, E. K., & Giriunas, I. E. (1987). Treatment of psychiatric illness by stereotactic singulotomy. *Biological Psychiatry, 22,* 807–809.

Bancroft, J. (1988). Sexual desire and the brain. *Sexual and Marital Therapy, 3*, 11–29.

Bancroft, J. (1989). *Human sexuality and its problems.* New York: Churchill Livingstone.

Bancroft, J., & Coles, L. (1976). Three years experience in a sexual problems clinic. *British Medical Journal, 1*, 1575–1577.

Bandura, A. (1969). *Principles of behavior modification.* New York: Holt, Rinehart & Winston.

Bandura, A. (1973). *Aggression: A social learning analysis.* Englewood Cliffs, NJ: Prentice-Hall.

Bandura, A. (1976). *Social learning theory.* Englewood Cliffs, NJ: Prentice-Hall.

Bandura, A., & Walters, R. H. (1963). *Social learning and personality development.* New York: Holt.

Bandura, A., Ross, D., & Ross, S. (1963). Imitation of film-mediated aggressive models. *Journal of Abnormal and Social Psychology, 66*, 3–11.

Banyard, V. L., & Graham-Berman, S. A. (1998). Surviving poverty: Stress and coping in the lives of housed and homeless mothers. *American Journal of Orthopsychiatry, 68*, 479–489.

Baranowski, M. J., & Hetherington, M. M. (2001). Testing the efficacy of an eating disorder prevention program. *International Journal of Eating Disorders, 29*, 119–124.

Baranski, J. V., Cian, C., Esquivie, D., Pigeau, R. A., & Raphel, C. (1998). Modafinil during 64 hours of sleep deprivation: Dose-related effects on fatigue, alertness, and cognitive performance. *Military Psychology, 10*, 173–193.

Barbaree, H. E., Marshall, W. L., & Lanthier, R. D. (1979). Deviant sexual arousal in rapists. *Behavior Research and Therapy, 17*, 215–222.

Bardwell, W. A., Moore, P., Ancoli-Israel, S., & Dimsdale, J. E. (2000). Does obstructive sleep apnea confound sleep architecture findings in subjects with depressive symptoms? *Biological Psychiatry, 48*, 1001–1009.

Barkley, R. A. (1997). *ADHD and the nature of self-control.* New York: Guilford.

Barkley, R. A. (1998). *Attention-deficit hyperactivity disorder: A handbook for diagnosis and treatment* (2nd ed.). New York: Guilford.

Barkley, R. A. (2001). "Executive function and ADHD": Reply. *Journal of the American Academy of Child and Adolescent Psychiatry, 40*, 501–502.

Barkley, R. A., Murphy, K. R., & Kwasnik, M. A. (1996). Motor vehicle driving competencies and risks in teens and young adults with attention deficit hyperactivity disorder. *Paediatrics, 98*, 1089–1095.

Barlow, D. H. (Ed.). (1985). *Clinical handbook of psychological disorders: A step-by-step treatment manual.* New York: Guilford.

Barlow, D. H. (1986). Causes of sexual dysfunction: The role of anxiety and cognitive interference. *Journal of Consulting and Clinical Psychology, 54*, 140–148.

Barlow, D. H. (1991). Disorders of emotion. *Psychological Inquiry, 2*, 58–71.

Barlow, D. H. (Ed.). (1993). *Clinical handbook of psychological disorders: A step-by-step treatment manual* (2nd ed.). New York: Guilford.

Barlow, D. H. (1996). The effectiveness of psychotherapy: Science and policy. *Clinical Psychology: Science and Practice, 3*, 236–240.

Barlow, D. H. (Ed.). (2001). *Clinical handbook of psychological disorders* (3rd ed.). New York: Guilford.

Barlow, D. H. (2002). *Anxiety and its disorders: The nature and treatment of anxiety and panic* (2nd ed.). New York: Guilford.

Barlow, D. H., & Craske, M. G. (2000). *Mastery of your anxiety and panic: Client workbook for anxiety and panic (MAP-3).* San Antonio, TX: Graywind/Psychological Corp.

Barlow, D. H., Abel, G. G., & Blanchard, E. B. (1979). Gender identity changes in transsexuals. *Archives of General Psychiatry, 36*, 1001–1007.

Barlow, D. H., Rapee, R. M., & Brown, T. A. (1992). Behavioral treatment of generalized anxiety disorder. *Behavior Therapy, 23*, 551–570.

Barlow, D. H., Reynolds, E. J., & Agras, W. S. (1973). Gender identity change in a transsexual. *Archives of General Psychiatry, 29*, 569–576.

Barnes, G. M. (1990). Impact of the family on adolescent drinking patterns. In R. L. Collins, K. E. Leonard, B. A. Miller, & J. S. Searles (Eds.), *Alcohol and the family: Research and clinical perspectives* (pp. 137–161). New York: Guilford.

Baroff, G. S., & Olley, J. G. (1999). *Mental retardation: Nature, cause, and management* (3rd ed.). Philadelphia: Brunner/Mazel.

Baron, M., Gruen, R. S., & Romo-Gruen, J. M. (1992). Positive and negative symptoms: Relationship to familial transmission of schizophrenia. *British Journal of Psychiatry, 161*, 610–614.

Baron, M., Gruen, R., Rainer, J. D., Kanes, J., Asnis, L., & Lord, S. (1985). A family study of schizophrenic and normal control probands: Implications for the spectrum concept of schizotypy. *American Journal of Psychiatry, 142*, 447–454.

Barry, H. (1995). Naroll's analysis of alcohol problems. *Cross-Cultural Research: The Journal of Comparative Social Science, 29*, 58–69.

Barthell, C. N., & Holmes, D. S. (1968). High school yearbooks: A nonreactive measure of social isolation in graduates who later became schizophrenic. *Journal of Abnormal Psychology, 73*, 313–316.

Barzega, G., Maina, G., Venturello, S., & Bogetto, F. (2001). Dysthymic disorder: Clinical characteristics in relation to age at onset. *Journal of Affective Disorders, 66*, 39–46.

Baskir, L. M., & Strauss, W. A. (1981). The Vietnam generation. In A. D. Horne (Ed.), *The wounded generation: America after Vietnam* (pp. 5–15). Englewood Cliffs, NJ: Prentice-Hall.

Başoğlu, M., & Mineka, S. (1992). The role of uncontrollable and unpredictable stress in post-traumatic stress responses in torture survivors. In M. Başoğlu (Ed.), *Torture and its consequences* (pp. 183–225). London: Cambridge University Press.

Başoğlu, M., Paker, M., Ozmen, E., Tasdemir, O., Sahin, D., Ceyhanli, A., Incesu, C., & Sarimurat, N. (1996). Appraisal of self, social environment, and state authority as a possible mediator of posttraumatic stress disorder in tortured political activists. *Journal of Abnormal Psychology, 105*, 232–236.

Bass, E., & Davis, L. (1988). *The courage to heal: A guide for women survivors of sexual abuse.* New York: Harper & Row.

Bass, E., & Davis, L. (1994). *The courage to heal: A guide for women survivors of sexual abuse, featuring "Honoring the truth: A response to the Backlash"* (3rd rev. ed.). New York: HarperPerennial.

Basso, A., & Marangolo, P. (2000). Cognitive neuropsychological rehabilitation: The emperor's new clothes? *Neuropsychological Rehabilitation, 10*, 219–229.

Bateson, G., Jackson, D. D., Haley, J., & Weakland, J. (1956). Toward a theory of schizophrenia. *Behavioral Science, 1*, 251–264.

Bauman, M. L., & Kemper, T. L. (1994). Neuroanatomical observations of the brain in autism. In M. L. Bauman & T. L. Kemper (Eds.), *The neurobiology of autism* (pp. 119–145). Baltimore: Johns Hopkins University Press.

Baumeister, A. A., & Hawkins, M. F. (2001). Incoherence of neuroimaging studies of attention deficit/hyperactivity disorder. *Clinical Neuropharmacology, 24*, 2–10.

Baumeister, R. F., & Butler, J. L. (1997). Sexual masochism: Deviance without psychopathology. In D. R. Laws & W. O'Donohue (Eds.), *Sexual deviance: Theory, assessment, and treatment* (pp. 225–239). New York: Guilford.

Baxter, L. R., Jr., Phelps, J. M., Mazziotta, J. C., Guze, B. H., & Schwartz, J. M. (1987). Local cerebral glucose metabolic rates in obsessive-compulsive disorder: A comparison with rates in unipolar depression and normal controls. *Archives of General Psychiatry, 44*, 211–218.

Baxter, L. R., Schwatz, J. M., Bergman, K. S., Szuba, M. P., Guze, B. H., Mazziotta, J. C., Alazraki, A., Selin, C. E., Ferng, H., Munford, P., & Phelps, M. E. (1992). Caudate glucose metabolic rate changes with both drug and behavior therapy for obsessive-compulsive disorder. *Archives of General Psychiatry, 49*, 681–689.

Beardsley, T. (1996). Vital data. *Scientific American, 274*(3), 100–105.

Beattie, K. K. (2001). The effects of intensive computer-based language intervention on language functioning and reading achievement in language-impaired adolescents. *Dissertation Abstracts International, A (Humanities and Social Sciences), 61(8-A)*, 3116.

Beauclair, L., Radoi-Andraous, D., & Chouinard, G. (2000). Selective serotonin-noradrenaline reuptake inhibitors. In B. I. Sadock & V. A. Sadock (Eds.), *Kaplan & Sadock's comprehensive textbook of psychiatry* (7th ed., pp. 2427–2432). Philadelphia: Lippincott Williams & Wilkins.

Bebbington, P. E., Dunn, G., Jenkins, R., Lewis, G., Brugha, T., Farrell, M., & Meltzer, H. (1998). The influence of age and sex on the prevalence of depression conditions: Report from the National Survey of Psychiatric Morbidity. *Psychological Medicine, 28*, 9–19.

Beck, A. T. (1967). *Depression: Clinical experimental and theoretical aspects.* New York: Harper & Row.

Beck, A. T. (1976). *Cognitive therapy and the emotional disorders.* New York: International Universities Press.

Beck, A. T. (1988). Cognitive approaches to panic disorder: Theory and therapy. In S. Rachman & J. D. Maser (Eds.), *Panic: Psychological perspectives* (pp. 91–109). Hillsdale, NJ: Erlbaum.

Beck, A. T. (1993a). Cognitive approaches to stress. In P. M. Lehrer & R. L. Woolfolk (Eds.) *Principles and practice of stress management* (2nd ed.). New York: Guilford.

Beck, A. T. (1993b). Cognitive therapy: Past, present, and future. *Journal of Consulting & Clinical Psychology, 61*, 194–198.

Beck, A. T. (1999). A cognitive model for schizophrenia. Zubin Award Address to the annual convention of the Association for Research in Psychopathology, Montreal, Canada, November 19, 1999.

Beck, A. T., Emory, G., & Greenberg, R. L. (1985). *Anxiety disorders and phobia: A cognitive perspective.* New York: Basic Books.

Beck, A. T., Epstein, N., & Harrison, R. (1983). Cognitions, attitudes, and personality dimensions in depression. *British Journal of Cognitive Psychotherapy, 1*, 1–16.

Beck, A. T., Freeman, A., and Associates (1990). *Cognitive therapy of personality disorders.* New York: Guilford.

Beck, A. T., Laude, R., & Bohnert, M. (1974). Ideational components of anxiety neurosis. *Archives of General Psychiatry, 31*, 319–325.

Beck, A. T., Steer, R. A., Kovacs, M., & Garrison, B. (1985). Hopelessness and eventual suicide: A 10-year prospective study of patients hospitalized with suicidal ideation. *American Journal of Psychiatry, 142*, 559–563.

Beck, J. G. (1995). Hypoactive sexual desire disorder: An overview. *Journal of Consulting and Clinical Psychology, 63*, 919–927.

Beck, J. G., & Bozman, A. (1995). Gender differences in sexual desire: The effects of anger and anxiety. *Archives of Sexual Behavior, 24*, 595–612.

Becker, J. V., Skinner, L. J., Abel, G. G., & Cochon, J. (1986). Level of postassault sexual functioning in rape and incest victims. *Archives of Sexual Behavior, 15*, 37–49.

Becker, J. V., Skinner, L. J., Abel, G. G., & Treacy, E. C. (1982). The incidence and types of sexual dysfunctions in rape and incest victims. *Journal of Sex and Marital Therapy, 8*, 65–74.

Beckfield, D. F. (1985). Interpersonal competence among college men hypothesized to be at risk for schizophrenia. *Journal of Abnormal Psychology, 94*, 397–404.

Beebe, D. K., Gulledge, K. M., Lee, C. M., & Replogle, W. (1994). Prevalence of sexual assault among women patients seen in family practice clinics. *Family Practice Research Journal, 14*, 223–228.

Beers, C. (1970). A mind that found itself (rev. ed.). New York: Doubleday. (Originally published in 1908.)

Bell, J. L. (1995). Traumatic event debriefing: Service delivery designs and the role of social work. *Social Work, 40*, 36–43.

Bell, M. E., & Goodman, L. A. (2001). Supporting battered women involved with the court system: An evaluation of a law-based advocacy intervention. *Violence against women, 7*, 1377–1404

Bellack, A. S., & Mueser, K. T. (1993). Psychosocial treatments for schizophrenia. *Schizophrenia Bulletin, 19*, 317–336.

Belman, A. L., Diamond, G., Dickson, D., Horoupian, D., Llena, J., Lantos, G., & Rubinstein, A. (1988). Pediatric acquired immunodeficiency syndrome: Neurological syndromes. *American Journal of Diseases of Children, 142*, 29–35.

Benassi, V. A., Sweeney, P. D., & Dufour, C. L. (1988). Is there a relationship between locus of control orientation and depression? *Journal of Abnormal Psychology, 97*, 357–367.

Benditt, T. (2002). Mental illness and commitment. In J. M. Humber & R. F. Almeder (Eds.), *Mental illness and public health care: Biomedical ethics reviews. Contemporary issues in biomedicine, ethics, and society* (pp. 1–24). Totowa, NJ: Humana.

Benes, F. M., Sorensen, I., & Bird, E. D. (1991). Reduced neuronal size in posterior hippocampus of schizophrenic patients. *Schizophrenia Bulletin, 17*, 597–608.

Benke, P. J. (1984). The isotretinoin terntogen syndrome. *Journal of the American Medical Association, 251*, 3267–3269.

Bennett, D. A., & Cooper, C. L. (1999). Eating disturbance as a manifestation of the stress process: A review of the literature. *Stress Medicine, 15*, 167–182.

Ben-Zur, H. (2001). Your coping strategy and my distress: Inter-spouse perceptions of coping and adjustment among breast cancer patients and their spouses. *Families, Systems and Health, 19*, 83–94.

Berg, F. M. (1998). Is yo-yo dieting dangerous? In S. Nolen-Hoeksema (Ed.), *Clashing views on abnormal psychology: A Taking Sides custom reader* (pp. 156–174). Guilford, CT: Dushkin/McGraw-Hill.

Berman, K. F., & Weinberger, D. R. (1989). Schizophrenia: Brain structure and function. In H. I. Kaplan & B. J. Sadock (Eds.), *Comprehensive textbook of psychiatry* (5th ed., Vol. I, pp. 705–717). Baltimore: Williams & Wilkins.

Berman, L. A., & Berman, J. R. (2000). Viagra and beyond: Where sex educators and therapists fit in from a multidisciplinary perspective. *Journal of Sex Education and Therapy, 25*, 17–24.

Berman, L. A., Berman, J. R., Bruck, D., Pawar, R. V., & Goldstein, I. (2001). Pharmacotherapy or psychotherapy? Effective treatment for FSD related to unresolved childhood sexual abuse. *Journal of Sex and Marital Therapy, 27*, 421–525.

Bernat, J. A., Calhoun, K. S., & Adams, H. E. (1999). Sexually aggressive and nonaggressive men: Sexual arousal and judgments in response to acquaintance rape and consensual analogues. *Journal of Abnormal Psychology, 108*, 662–673.

Bernat, J. A., Calhoun, K. S., & Stolp, S. (1998). Sexually aggressive men's responses to a date rape analogue: Alcohol as a disinhibiting cue. *Journal of Sex Research, 35*, 41–348.

Berney, B. (1993). Round and round it goes: The epidemiology of childhood lead poisoning, 1950–1990. *Milbank Quarterly, 71*, 3–39.

Bernstein, D. A., & Borkovec, T. D. (1973). *Progressive relaxation training: A manual for the helping professions.* Champaign, IL: Research Press.

Bernstein, D. A., Borkovec, T. D., & Hazlett-Stevens, H. (2000). *New directions in progressive relaxation training: A guidebook for helping professionals.* Westport, CT: Praeger Publishers/Greenwood Publishing Group.

Bernstein, D. P., Cohen, P., Velez, C. N., Schwab-Stone, N., & Siever, L. (1993a). The prevalence and stability of the DSM-III-R personality disorders in a community-based survey of adolescents. *American Journal of Psychiatry, 150*, 1237–1243.

Bernstein, D. P., Useda, D., & Siever, L. J. (1993b). Review of the literature and recommendations for DSM-IV. *Journal of Personality Disorders, 7*, 53–62.

Bernstein, D. P., Useda, D., & Siever, L. J. (1995). Paranoid personality disorder. In W. J. Livesley (Ed.), *The DSM-IV personality disorders* (pp. 45–57). New York: Guilford.

Bernstein, E., & Putnam, F. (1986). Development, reliability, and validity of a dissociation scale. *Journal of Nervous and Mental Disease, 174*, 727–735.

Berquier, A., & Ashton, R. (1992). Characteristics of the frequent nightmare sufferer. *Journal of Abnormal Psychology, 101*, 246–250.

Berra, T. M. (1990). *Evolution and the myth of creationism: A basic guide to the facts in the evolution debate.* Palo Alto, CA: Stanford University Press.

Berrettini, W. H., & Pekkarinen, P. H. (1996). Molecular genetics of bipolar disorder. *Annals of Medicine, 28*, 191–194.

Bertelsen, B., Harvald, B., & Hauge, M. (1977). A Danish twin study of manic-depressive disorders. *British Journal of Psychiatry, 130,* 330–351.

Bettelheim, B. (1967). *The empty fortress.* New York: Free Press.

Bewley-Taylor, D. R. (1999). *The United States and international drug control, 1909–1997.* London: Pinter.

Beyer, S. (1998). Gender differences in causal attributions by college students of performance on course examinations. *Current Psychology: Developmental, Learning, Personality, Social, 17,* 346–358.

Bick, P. A., & Kinsbourne, M. (1987). Auditory hallucinations and sub-vocal speech in schizophrenic patients. *American Journal of Psychiatry, 144,* 222–225.

Biederman, J., Mick, E., Faraone, S. V., & Burback, M. (2001). Patterns of remission and symptom decline in conduct disorder: A four-year prospective study of an ADHD sample. *Journal of the American Academy of Child and Adolescent Psychiatry, 40,* 290–298.

Billiard, M., Alperovitch, A., Perot, C., & Jammes, A. (1987). Excessive daytime somnolence in young men: Prevalence and contributing factors. *Sleep, 10,* 297–305.

Binder, J. L., Strupp, H. H., & Henry, W. P. (1995). Psychodynamic therapies in practice: Time-limited dynamic psychotherapy. In B. M. Bongar & L. E. Beutler (Eds.), *Comprehensive textbook of psychotherapy: Theory and practice* (pp. 48–63). New York: Oxford University Press.

Binzer, M., & Kullgren, G. (1996). Conversion symptoms: What can we learn from previous studies? *Nordic Journal of Psychiatry, 50,* 143–152.

Bishop, D. B., Zimmerman, B. R., & Roesler, J. S. (1998). Diabetes. In R. C. Brownson, P. L. Remington, & J. R. Davis (Eds.), *Chronic disease: Epidemiology and control* (2nd ed., pp. 421–464). Washington, DC: American Public Health Association.

Black, A. (1974). The natural history of obsessional neurosis. In H. R. Beech (Ed.), *Obsessional states.* London: Metheuen.

Blackburn, I. M., Eunson, K. M., & Bishop, S. (1986). A two-year naturalistic follow-up of depressed patients treated with cognitive therapy, pharmacotherapy, and a combination of both. *Journal of Affective Disorders, 10,* 67–75.

Blair, C. D., & Lanyon, R. I. (1981). Exhibitionism: Etiology and treatment. *Psychological Bulletin, 89,* 439–463.

Blair, C., Freeman, C., & Cull, A. (1995). The families of anorexia nervosa and cystic fibrosis patients. *Psychological Medicine, 25,* 985–993.

Blair-West, G. W., Cantor, C. H., Mellsop, G. W., & Eyeson-Annon, M. L. (1999). Lifetime suicide risk in major depression: Sex and age determinants. *Journal of Affective Disorders, 55,* 171–178.

Blanchard, E. B. (1994). Behavioral medicine and health psychology. In A. E. Bergin & S. L. Garfield (Eds.), *Handbook of psychotherapy and behavior change* (4th ed., pp. 701–733). New York: Wiley.

Blanchard, R. (1985). Typology of male-to-female transsexualism. *Archives of Sexual Behavior, 14,* 247–261.

Blanchard, R. (1992). Nonmonotonic relation of autogynephilia and heterosexual attraction. *Journal of Abnormal Psychology, 101,* 271–276.

Blanes, T., Burgess, M., Marks, I. M., & Gill, M. (1993). Dream anxiety disorders (nightmares): A review. *Behavioural Psychotherapy, 21,* 37–43.

Blaney, P. H. (2000). Stress and depression: A personality-situation interaction approach. In S. L. Johnson, A. M. Hayes, T. M. Field, N. Schneiderman, & P. M. McCabe (Eds.), *Stress, coping, and depression* (pp. 89–116). Mahwah, NJ: Erlbaum.

Blasco, T., Pallares, C., Alonso, C., & Lopez, J. J. L. (2000). The role of anxiety and adaptation to illness in the intensity of postchemotherapy nausea in cancer patients. *Spanish Journal of Psychology, 3,* 47–52.

Blascovich, J., Spencer, S. J., Quinn, D., & Steele, C. (2001). African Americans and high blood pressure: The role of stereotype threat. *Psychological Science, 12,* 225–229.

Blatt, S. J. (1974). Levels of object representation in anaclitic and introjective depression. *Psychoanalytic Study of the Child, 29,* 107–157.

Blatt, S. J., & Wild, C. M. (1976). *Schizophrenia: A developmental analysis.* New York: Academic Press.

Blatt, S. J., Quinlan, D. M., Chevron, E. S., McDonald, C., & Zuroff, D. C. (1982). Dependency and self-criticism: Psychological dimensions of depression. *Journal of Consulting and Clinical Psychology, 50,* 113–124.

Blazer, D. G., George, L., & Hughes, D. (1991a). The epidemiology of anxiety disorders: An age comparison. In C. Salzman & B. Liebowitz (Eds.), *Anxiety disorders in the elderly* (pp. 17–30). New York: Springer.

Blazer, D. G., Hughes, D., George, L. K., Swartz, M., & Boyer, R. (1991b). Generalized anxiety disorder. In L. N. Robins & D. A. Regier (Eds.), *Psychiatric disorders in America* (pp. 180–203). New York: Free Press.

Blehar, M. C., & Rosenthal, N. E. (1989). Seasonal affective disorders and phototherapy: Report of a National Institute of Mental Health–Sponsored Workshop. *Archives of General Psychiatry, 46,* 469–474.

Bleuler, E. (1924). *Textbook of psychiatry* (Trans. A. A. Brill). New York: Macmillan.

Bleuler, E. (1950). The fundamental symptoms. In E. Bleuler (Ed.), *Dementia praecox; or the group of schizophrenias* (trans. J. Ziskin.). New York: International University Press. (Original work published 1911.)

Bliwise, D. L. (1997). Sleep and aging. In M. R. Pressman & W. C. Orr (Eds.), *Understanding sleep: The evaluation and treatment of sleep disorders* (pp. 441–464). Washington, DC: American Psychological Association.

Blumberg, H. P., Stern, E., Ricketts, S., Marinez, D., deAsis, J., White, T., Epstein, J., Isenberg, N., McBride, A., Kemperman, I, Emmerich, S., Dhawan, V., Eidenberg, D., Kocsis, J. H., & Silversweig, D. A. (1999). Rostral and orbital prefrontal cortex dysfunction in the manic state of bipolar disorder. *American Journal of Psychiatry, 156,* 1986–1988.

Blumberg, S. J. (2000). Guarding against threatening HIV prevention messages: An information-processing model. *Health Education and Behavior, 27,* 780–795.

Blumenthal, S. J. (1990). An overview and synopsis of risk factors, assessment, and treatment of suicidal patients over the life cycle. In S. J. Blumenthal & D. J. Kupfer (Eds.), Suicide over the life cycle: Risk factors, assessment, and treatment of suicidal patients. Washington, DC: American Psychiatric Press.

Bobashev, G. V., & Anthony, J. C. (1998). Clusters of marijuana use in the United States. *American Journal of Public Health, 148,* 1168–1173.

Bohman, M., Cloninger, C. R., Sigvardsson, S., & von Knorring, A. L. (1987). The genetics of alcoholism and related disorders. *Journal of Psychiatric Research, 21,* 447–452.

Bohman, M., Sigvardsson, S., & Cloninger, C. R. (1981). Maternal inheritance of alcohol abuse: Cross-fostering analysis of adopted women. *Archives of General Psychiatry, 38,* 965–969.

Bolles, R. C., & Fanselow, M. S. (1980). A perceptual-defensive-recuperative model of fear and pain. *Behavioral and Brain Sciences, 3,* 291–301.

Bolman, C., de Vries, H., & van Breukelen, G. (2002). Evaluation of a nurse-managed minimal-contact smoking cessation intervention for cardiac inpatients. *Health Education Research, 17,* 99–116.

Bolton, P., Macdonald, H., Pickles, A., Rios, P., Goode, S., Crowson, M., Bailey, A., & Rutter, M. (1994). A case-control family history study of autism. *Journal of Child Psychology and Psychiatry, 35,* 877–900.

Bootzin, R. R., & Rider, S. P. (1997). Behavioral techniques and biofeedback for insomnia. In M. R. Pressman & W. C. Orr (Eds.), *Understanding sleep: The evaluation and treatment of sleep disorders* (pp. 315–338). Washington, DC: American Psychological Association.

Bootzin, R. R., Epstein, D., & Wood, J. M. (1991). Stimulus control instructions. In P. J. Hauri (Ed.), *Case studies in insomnia* (pp. 19–28). New York: Plenum.

Bootzin, R. R., Epstein, D., Engle-Friedman, M., & Salvio, M. (1996). Sleep disturbances. In L. L. Carstensen, B. A. Edelstein & L. Dornbrand (Eds.), *The practical handbook of clinical gerontology* (pp. 398–420). Thousand Oaks, CA: Sage.

Borbély, A. (1986). *Secrets of sleep.* New York: Basic Books.

Borch-Jacobsen, M. (1997, April 24). Sybil—The making of a disease: An interview with Dr. Herbert Spiegel. *New York Review of Books.* Available on the Internet at www.nybooks.com.

Borkovec, T. D., & Costello, E. (1993). Efficacy of applied relaxation and cognitive-behavioral therapy in the treatment of generalized anxiety disorder. *Journal of Consulting and Clinical Psychology, 61,* 611–619.

Borkovec, T. D., & Hu, S. (1990). The effects of worry on cardiovascular response to phobic imagery. *Behaviour Research and Therapy, 28*, 69–73.

Borkovec, T. D., & Inz, J. (1990). The nature of worry in generalized anxiety disorder: A predominance of thought activity. *Behaviour Research and Therapy, 28*, 153–158.

Borkovec, T. D., & Ruscio, A. M. (2001). Psychotherapy for generalized anxiety disorder. *Journal of Clinical Psychiatry, 62* (Supplement 11), 37–42.

Borkovec, T. D., Abel, J. L., & Newman, H. (1995). Effects of psychotherapy on comorbid conditions in generalized anxiety disorder. *Journal of Consulting and Clinical Psychology, 63*, 479–483.

Borkovec, T. D., Ray, W. J., & Stoeber, J. (1998). Worry: A cognitive phenomenon intimately linked to affective, physiological, and interpersonal behavioral processes. *Cognitive Therapy and Research, 22*, 561–576.

Borkovec, T. D., Shadick, R., & Hopkins, M. (1991). The nature of normal and pathological worry. In R. M. Rapee & D. H. Barlow (Eds.), *Chronic anxiety, generalized anxiety disorder, and mixed anxiety depression.* New York: Guilford.

Bornstein, R. F. (1999). Criterion validity of objective and projective dependency tests: A meta-analytic assessment of behavioral prediction. *Psychological Assessment, 11*, 48–57.

Bornstein, R. F. (1999). Dependent and histrionic personality disorders. In T. Millon, P. H. Blaney, & R. D. Davis (Eds.), *Oxford textbook of psychopathology* (pp. 535–554). New York: Oxford University Press.

Boscarino, J. A. (1995). Posttraumatic stress and associated disorders among Vietnam veterans: The significance of combat exposure and social support. *Journal of Traumatic Stress, 8*, 317–336.

Bottoms, B. L., Shaver, P. R., & Goodman, G. S. (1996). An analysis of ritualistic and religion-related child abuse allegations. *Law and Human Behavior, 20*, 1–34.

Bouchard, T. J., Lykken, D. T., McGue, M., & Segal, N.L. (1990). Sources of human psychological differences: The Minnesota study of twins reared apart. *Science, 250*, 223–228.

Bowlby, J. (1969). *Attachment and loss*, Vol. 1. New York: Basic Books.

Bowlby, J. (1973). *Separation: Anxiety and anger. Psychology of attachment and loss* series (Vol. 3). New York: Basic Books.

Bowlby, J. (1980). *Attachment and loss*, Vol. 3: *Loss, sadness, and depression.* New York: Basic Books.

Bozarth, M. A. (1986). Neural basis of psychomotor stimulant and opiate reward: Evidence suggesting the involvement of a common dopaminergic system. *Behavioural Brain Research, 22*, 107–116.

Bozman, A., & Beck, J. G. (1991). Covariation of sexual desire and sexual arousal: The effects of anger and anxiety. *Archives of Sexual Behavior, 20*, 47–60.

Bradford, J. B., & Pawlak, A. (1993). Double-blind placebo crossover study of cyproterone acetate in the treatment of paraphilias. *Archives of Sexual Behavior, 22*, 383–402.

Bradford, J. B., Boulet, J., & Pawlak, A. (1992). The paraphilias: A multiplicity of deviant behaviors. *Canadian Journal of Psychiatry, 37*, 104–108.

Bradford, J. M. (1985). Organic treatments for the male sexual offender. *Behavioral Sciences and the Law, 3*, 355–375.

Bradley, G. W. (1978). Self-serving biases in the attribution process: A reexamination of the fact or fiction question. *Journal of Personality and Social Psychology, 36*, 56–71.

Brauchi, J. T., & West, L. J. (1959). Sleep deprivation. *Journal of the American Medical Association, 171*, 11–14.

Brauer, L. H., Ambre, J., & de Wit, H. (1996). Acute tolerance to subjective but not cardiovascular effects of *d*-amphetamine in normal, healthy men. *Journal of Clinical Psychopharmacology, 16*, 72–76.

Braver, T. S., Barch, D. M., & Cohen, J. D. (1999). Cognition and control in schizophrenia: A computational model of dopamine and prefrontal function. *Biological Psychiatry, 46*, 312–328.

Brayne, C. (2000). Smoking and the brain. *BMJ, 320* (April 22), 1087–1088.

Brebion, G., Amador, X., David, A., Malaspina, D., Sharif, Z., & Gorman, J. M. (2000). Positive symptomatology and source-monitoring failure in schizophrenia—An analysis of symptom-specific effects. *Psychiatry Research, 95*, 119–131.

Breggin, P. R. (1964). The psychophysiology of anxiety with a review of the literature concerning adrenaline. *Journal of Nervous and Mental Disease, 139*, 558–568.

Breggin, P. R. (1991). Shock treatment is not good for your brain. In P. R. Breggin (Ed.), *Toxic psychiatry* (pp. 184–215). New York: St. Martin's Press.

Bremner, J. D., Krystal, J. H., Putnam, F. W., Southwick, S. M., Marmar, C., Charney, D. S., & Mazure, C. M. (1998). Measurement of dissociative states with the Clinician-Administered Dissociative States Scale (CADSS). *Journal of Traumatic Stress, 11*, 125–136.

Bremner, J. D., Southwick, S. M., & Charney, D. S. (1995). Etiological factors in the development of posttraumatic stress disorder. In C. M. Mazur (Ed.), *Does stress cause psychiatric illness?* Washington, DC: American Psychiatric Association.

Brenner, H., Rothenbacher, D., Bode, G., Marz, W., Hoffmeister, A., & Koenig, W. (2001). Coronary heart disease risk reduction in a predominantly beer-drinking population. *Epidemiology, 12*, 390–395.

Breslau, N. (2001). The epidemiology of posttraumatic stress disorder: What is the extent of the problem? *Journal of Clinical Psychiatry, 62* (Supplement 17), 16–22.

Breslau, N., Davis, G. C., Andreski, P., & Peterson, E. (1991). Traumatic events and posttraumatic stress disorder in an urban population of young adults. *Archives of General Psychiatry, 48*, 216–222.

Breslow, N., Evans, L., & Langley, J. (1985). On the prevalence and roles of females in the sadomasochistic subculture: Report of an empirical study. *Archives of Sexual Behavior, 14*, 303–317.

Breuer, J., & Freud, S. (1893–1895/1955). Studies on hysteria (1893–1895). In *Standard edition of the complete works of Sigmund Freud*, Vol. 2 (pp. 1–319). London: Hogarth. (Trans. and ed. by J. Strachey.)

Breuer, J., & Freud, S. (1955). Unconscious ideas and ideas inadmissible to consciousness—Splitting of the mind. In J. Strachey (Ed.), *The standard edition of the complete psychological works of Sigmund Freud* (Vol. 2, pp. 222–239). London: Hogarth Press. (Original work published in 1895.)

Brewer, C. (1997). Ultra-rapid, antagonist-precipitated opiate detoxification under general anesthesia or sedation. *Addictive Biology, 2*, 291–295.

Brewerton, T. D., Dansky, B. S., Kilpatrick, D. G., & O'Neil, P. M. (2000). Which comes first in the pathogenesis of bulimia nervosa: Dieting or bingeing? *International Journal of Eating Disorders, 28*, 259–264.

Bridge, E. (1997, September). I couldn't stop myself. *Mademoiselle, 103*(9), 242.

Brieger, P., & Marneros, A. (1997). Dysthymia and cyclothymia: Historical origins and contemporary development. *Journal of Affective Disorders, 45*, 117–126.

Brieger, P., Sommer, S., Bloeink, R., & Marneros, A. (2001). What becomes of children hospitalized for enuresis? Results of a catch-up study. *European Psychiatry, 16*, 27–32.

Broderick, G. A. (1998). Evidence-based assessment of erectile dysfunction. *International Journal of Impotence Research, 10*, S64–S73.

Brook, J. S., Whiteman, M., Gordon, A. S., & Brenden, C. (1983). Older brother's influence on younger sibling's drug use. *Journal of Psychology, 114*, 83–90.

Brown, D. R., Eaton, W. W., & Sussman, L. (1990). Racial differences in prevalence of phobic disorders. *Journal of Nervous and Mental Disease, 178*, 434–441.

Brown, D., Scheflin, A. W., & Hammond, D. C. (1998). *Memory, trauma treatment, and the law.* New York: Norton.

Brown, G. W., & Harris, T. (1978). *Social origins of depression.* New York: Free Press.

Brown, J., & King, J. (1998). Gender differences in police officers' attitudes towards rape: Results of an exploratory study. *Psychology, Crime and Law, 4*, 265–279.

Brown, L. S. (1986). Gender role analysis: A neglected component of psychological assessment. *Psychotherapy, 23*, 243–248.

Brown, P. J., & Konner, M. (1987). An anthropological perspective on obesity. *Annals of the New York Academy of Sciences, 499*, 29–46.

Brown, R. M., Dahlen, E., Mills, C., Rick, J., Biblarz, A. (1999). Evaluation of an evolutionary model of self-preservation and self-destruction. *Suicide & Life-Threatening Behavior, 29*(1), 58–71.

Brown, T. A. (1997). The nature of generalized anxiety disorder and pathological worry: Current evidence and conceptual models. *Canadian Journal of Psychiatry, 42*, 817–825.

Brown, T. A., & Barlow, D. H. (1992). Comorbidity among anxiety disorders: Implications for treatment and DSM-IV. *Journal of Consulting and Clinical Psychology, 60*, 835–844.

Brown, T. A., Antony, M. M., & Barlow, D. H. (1992). Psychometric properties of the Penn State Worry Questionnaire in a clinical anxiety disorders sample. *Behaviour Research and Therapy, 30*, 33–37.

Brown, T. A., Barlow, D. H., & Liebowitz, M. R. (1994). The empirical basis of generalized anxiety disorder. *American Journal of Psychiatry, 151*, 1272–1280.

Brown, T. A., DiNardo, P. A., & Barlow, D. H. (1994). *Anxiety disorders interview schedule for DSM-IV*. Albany, NY: Graywind Publications.

Bruch, H. (1986). Anorexia nervosa: The therapeutic task. In K. D. Brownell & J. P. Foreyt (Eds.), *Handbook of eating disorders: Physiology, psychology, and treatment of obesity, anorexia, and bulimia* (pp. 328–332). New York: Basic Books.

Bruch, H. (2001). *The golden cage: The enigma of anorexia nervosa.* Cambridge, MA: Harvard University Press.

Bruder, G. E., Fong, R., Tenke, C. E., Leite, P., Towey, J. P., Steward, J. W., McGrath, P. J., & Quitkin, F. M. (1997a). Regional brain asymmetries in major depression with and without an anxiety disorder: A quantitative electroencephalographic study. *Biological Psychiatry, 41*, 939–948.

Bruder, G. E., Otto, M. W., McGrath, P. J., Stewart, J. W., et al. (1996). Dichotic listening before and after fluoxetine treatment for major depression: Relations of laterality to therapeutic response. *Neuropsychopharmacology, 15*, 171–179.

Bruder, G. E., Steward, J. W., Mercier, M. A., Agosti, V., Leite, P., Donovan, S., & Quitkin, F. M. (1997b). Outcome of cognitive-behavioral therapy for depression: Relationship to hemispheric dominance for verbal processing. *Journal of Abnormal Psychology, 106*, 138–144.

Bruder, G. E., Wexler, B. E., Steward, J. W., Price, L. H., & Quitkin, F. M. (1999). Perceptual asymmetry differences between major depression with or without a comorbid anxiety disorder: A dichotic listening study. *Journal of Abnormal Psychology, 108*, 233–239.

Brunell, L. F. (1985). Multimodal treatment of depression and obesity: The case of single Susan. In A. A. Lazarus (Ed.), *Casebook of multimodal therapy* (pp. 50–69). New York: Guilford.

Bryant, R. A., & Harvey, A. G. (1999). Acute stress disorder following motor vehicle accidents. In E. J. Hickling & E. B. Blanchard (Eds.), *The international handbook of road traffic accidents and psychological trauma: Current understanding, treatment and law* (pp. 29–42). New York: Elsevier Science.

Buckley, T. C., Blanchard, E. B., & Hickling, E. J. (1996). A prospective examination of delayed onset PTSD secondary to motor vehicle accidents. *Journal of Abnormal Psychology, 105*, 617–625.

Buckwalter, K. C., Gerdner, L., Kohout, F., Hall, G. R., Kelly, A., Richards, B., & Sime, M. (1999). A nursing intervention to decrease depression in family caregivers of persons with dementia. *Archives of Psychiatric Nursing, 13*, 80–88.

Bulik, C. M. (1998). Women and disordered eating. In S. E. Romans (Ed.), *Folding back the shadows: A perspective on women's mental health* (pp. 177–191). Dunedin, New Zealand: University of Otago Press.

Bunney, W. E., & Gerland, B. L. (1984). Lithium and its possible modes of action. In R. M. Post & J. C. Ballenger (Eds.), *Neurobiology of mood disorders, Vol 1: Frontiers of clinical neuroscience* (pp. 731–743). Baltimore: Williams & Wilkins.

Burke, P., Elliott, M., & Fleissner, R. (1999). Irritable bowel syndrome and recurrent abdominal pain: A comparative review. *Psychosomatics, 40*, 277–285.

Burns, A. (1991). Clinical diagnosis of Alzheimer's disease. *Dementia, 2*, 186–194.

Burns, A. (1992). Cause of death in dementia. *International Journal of Geriatric Psychiatry, 7*, 461–464.

Burrel, G., Sundin, O., Stroem, G., & Oehman, A. (1986). Heart and lifestyle: A Type A treatment program for myocardial infarction patients. *Scandinavian Journal of Behaviour Therapy, 15*, 87–93.

Burton, N., & Lane, R. C. (2001). The relational treatment of dissociative identity disorder. *Clinical Psychology Review, 21*, 301–320

Burton, T. M. (1991a). Antidepressant drug of Eli Lilly loses sales after attack by sect. *Wall Street Journal*, April 19, A-1.

Burton, T. M. (1991b). Scientologists fail to persuade FDA on Prozac. *Wall Street Journal*, August 2, B-1.

Bushnell, J. A., Wells, J. E., Hornblow, A. R., Oakley-Browne, M. A., & Joyce P. (1990). Prevalence of three bulimia syndromes in the general population. *Psychological Medicine, 20*, 671–680.

Buss, D. M. (1994). *The evolution of desire: Strategies of human mating.* New York: Basic Books.

Buss, D. M. (1999). *Evolutionary psychology: The new science of the mind.* Boston: Allyn & Bacon.

Bustillo, J., Keith, S. J., & Lauriello, J. (2000). Schizophrenia: Psychosocial treatment. In B. I. Sadock & V. A. Sadock (Eds.), *Kaplan and Sadock's comprehensive textbook of psychiatry* (7th ed., pp. 1210–1217). Baltimore: Lippincott Williams & Wilkins.

Busto, U. E., Romach, M. K., & Sellers, E. M. (1996). Multiple drug use and psychiatric comorbidity in patients admitted to the hospital with severe benzodiazepine dependence. *Journal of Clinical Psychopharmacology, 16*, 51–57.

Butcher, J. N. (1990). *MMPI-2 in psychological treatment.* New York: Oxford University Press.

Butler, G., & Mathews, A. (1983). Cognitive processes in anxiety. *Advances in Behaviour Research and Therapy, 5*, 51–62.

Butzlaff, R. L., & Hooley, J. M. (1998). Expressed emotion and psychiatric relapse. *Archives of General Psychiatry, 55*, 547–552.

Buysse, D. J., & Kupfer, D. J. (1993). Sleep disorders in depressive disorders. In J. J. Mann & D. J. Kupfer (Eds.), *Biology of depressive disorders, Part A: A systems perspective* (pp. 123–154). New York: Plenum Press.

Buznikov, G. A. (1984). The action of neurotransmitters and related substances on early embryogenesis. *Pharmacology and Therapeutics, 25*, 23–59.

Byrne, D., & Osland, J. A. (2000). Sexual fantasy and erotica/pornography: International and external imagery. In L. T. Szuchman & F. Mascarella (Eds.), *Psychological perspectives on human sexuality* (pp. 283–305). New York: Wiley.

Cade, J. F. J. (1949). Lithium salts in the treatment of psychotic excitement. *Medical Journal of Australia, 2*, 349–352. (Reprinted the *Australian & New Zealand Journal of Psychiatry, 33*, 619–622.)

Cadoret, R. J., & Stewart, M. A. (1991). An adoption study of attention deficit/aggression and their relationship to adult antisocial personality. *Archives of General Psychiatry, 47*, 73–82.

Cahalan, D. (1970). *Problem drinkers: A national survey.* San Francisco: Jossey-Bass.

Caine, E. D., & Lyness, J. M. (2000). Delirium, dementia, and amnestic and other cognitive disorders. In B. I. Sadock & V. A. Sadock (Eds.), *Kaplan & Sadock's comprehensive textbook of psychiatry* (7th ed., pp. 854–923). Philadelphia: Lippincott Williams & Wilkins.

Calabrese, J. R., Kimmel, S. E., Woyshville, M. J., Rapport, D. J., Faust, C. J., Thompson, P. A., & Meltzer, H. Y. (1996). Clozapine for treatment-refractory mania. *American Journal of Psychiatry, 153*, 759.

Caldwell, C. B., & Gottesman, I. I. (1991). Sex differences in the risk for alcoholism: A twin study. Paper presented at the 21st annual meeting of the Behavior Genetics Association, St. Louis, June.

Caldwell, J. A. (2001). Efficacy of stimulants for fatigue management: The effects of Provigil® and Dexedrine® on sleep-deprived aviators. *Psychology and Behaviour, 4*, 19–37.

Campbell, A. M. G., Evans, M., Thomson, J. L. G., & Williams, M. J. (1971). Cerebral atrophy in young cannabis smokers. *Lancet,* December 4, 1219–1224.

Campbell, F. A., & Ramey, C. T. (1994). Effects of early intervention on intellectual and academic achievement: A follow-up study of children from low-income families. *Child Development, 65*, 684–698.

Campbell, M., Cueva, J. E., & Adams, P. B. (1999). Pharmacotherapy of impulsive-aggressive behavior. In C. R. Cloninger (Ed.), *Personality and psychopathology* (pp. 431–455). Washington, DC: American Psychiatric Press.

Campbell, S. S. (1997). The basics of biological rhythms. In M. R. Pressman & W. C. Orr (Eds.), *Understanding sleep: The evaluation and treatment of sleep disorders* (pp. 35–56). Washington, DC: American Psychological Association.

Cancro, R., & Lehmann, H. E. (2000). Schizophrenia: Clinical features. In B. I. Sadock & V. A. Sadock (Eds.), *Kaplan and Sadock's comprehensive textbook of psychiatry* (7th ed., pp. 1169–1199). Baltimore: Lippincott Williams & Wilkins.

Canetto, S. S. (1997). Gender and suicidal behavior: Theories and evidence. In R. W. Maris, M. M. Silverman, & S. S. Canetto (Eds.), *Review of suicidology* (pp. 138–167). New York: Guilford.

Cannon, T. D., Barr, C. E., & Mednick, S. A. (1991). Genetic and perinatal factors in the etiology of schizophrenia. In E. F. Walker (Ed.), *Schizophrenia: A life-course developmental perspective* (pp. 9–31). San Diego: Academic Press.

Cannon, T. D., Mednick, S. A., & Parnas, J. (1993a). Antecedents of predominantly negative- and predominantly positive-symptom schizophrenia in a high-risk population. *Archives of General Psychiatry, 47*, 622–632.

Cannon, T. D., Mednick, S. A., Parnas, J., Schulsinger, F., Praestholm, J., & Vestergaard, A. (1993b). Developmental brain abnormalities in the offspring of schizophrenic mothers. I. Contributions of genetic and perinatal factors. *Archives of General Psychiatry, 50*, 551–564.

Cannon, T. D., Mednick, S. A., Parnas, J., Schulsinger, F., Praestholm, J., & Vestergaard, A. (1994). Developmental brain abnormalities in the offspring of schizophrenic mothers. II. Structural brain characteristics of schizophrenia and schizotypal personality disorder. *Archives of General Psychiatry, 51*, 955–962.

Cantor, D. (1999). Drug involvement among offender populations. In R. M. Bray & M. E. Marsden (Eds.), *Drug use in metropolitan America* (pp. 161–193). Thousand Oaks, CA: Sage.

Cantwell, D. P., Baker, L., & Rutter, M. (1979). Families of autistic and dysphasic children. I. Family life and interaction patterns. *Archives of General Psychiatry, 36*, 682–687.

Cappuzzo, F., Mazzoni, F., Maestri, A., DiStfano, A., Calandri, C., & Crino, L. (2000). Medical treatment of brain metastases from solid tumours. *Forum, 10*(2), 137–148.

Carlat, D. J., Camargo, C. A., Jr., & Herzog, D. B. (1997). Eating disorders in males: A report on 135 patients. *American Journal of Psychiatry, 154*, 1127–1132.

Carlson, C. L., & Mann, M. (2002). Sluggish cognitive tempo predicts a different pattern of impairment in the attention deficit hyperactivity disorder, predominantly inattentive type. *Journal of Community Psychology, 31*, 123–129.

Carlson, C. L., & Tamm, L. (2000). Responsiveness of children with attention deficit-hyperactivity disorder to reward and response cost: Differential impact on performance and motivation. *Journal of Consulting and Clinical Psychology, 68*, 73–83.

Carlson, E. B., & Putnam, F. W. (1993). An update on the dissociative experiences scale. *Dissociation, 6*, 16–27.

Carlson, E. B., Armstrong, J., Loewenstein, R., & Roth, D. (1998). Relationship between traumatic experiences and symptoms of posttraumatic stress, dissociation, and amnesia. In J. D. Bremmer & C. R.

Marmar (Eds.), *Trauma, memory, and dissociation* (pp. 205–227). Washington, DC: American Psychiatric Press.

Carlson, G. A., Bromet, E. J., & Sievers, S. (2000). Phenomenology and outcome of subjects with early- and adult-onset psychotic mania. *American Journal of Psychiatry, 157*, 213–219.

Carnes, P. (2001a). *Out of the shadows: Understanding sexual addictions* (2nd ed.). Minneapolis: CompCare.

Carnes, P. (2001b). *In the shadows of the net: Breaking free of compulsive online sexual behavior.* Center City, MN: Hazelden.

Carr, A. (2000). Evidence-based practice in family therapy and systemic consultation. I. Child-focused problems. *Journal of Family Therapy, 22*, 29–60.

Carroll, E. M., Rueger, D. B., Foy, D. W., & Donahoe, C. P. (1985). Vietnam combat veterans with posttraumatic stress disorder: Analysis of marital and cohabitating adjustment. *Journal of Abnormal Psychology, 94*, 329–337.

Carroll, M. E., & Overmier, J. B. (Eds.). (2001). *Animal research and human health: Advancing human welfare through behavioral science.* Washington, DC: American Psychological Association.

Carskadon, M. A., & Dement, W. C. (1981). Cumulative effects of sleep restriction on daytime sleepiness. *Psychophysiology, 18*, 107–113.

Carson, C. C., Mulcahy, J. J., & Govier, F. E. (2000). Efficacy, safety and patient satisfaction outcomes of the AMS 700CX inflatable penile prosthesis: Results of a long-term multicenter study. AMS 700CX Study Group. *Journal of Urology, 64*, 376–380.

Carter, F. A., Bulik, C. M., McIntosh, V. V., & Joyce, P. R. (2001). Changes in cue reactivity following treatment for bulimia nervosa. *International Journal of Eating Disorders, 29*, 336–344.

Carter, J. C., & Fairburn, C. G. (1998). Cognitive-behavioral self-help for binge eating disorder: A controlled effectiveness study. *Journal of Consulting and Clinical Psychology, 66*, 616–623.

Carter, M. M., Hollon, S. D., Carson, R., & Shelton, R. C. (1995). Effects of a safe person on induced distress following a biological challenge in panic disorder with agoraphobia. *Journal of Abnormal Psychology, 104*, 156–163.

Cartwright, R. D. (1984). Effects of sleep position on sleep apnea severity. *Sleep, 7*, 110–114.

Casat, C. D., Pearson, D. A., & Casat, J. P. (2001). Attention-deficit/hyperactivity disorder. In H. B. Vance & A. Pumariega (Eds.), *Clinical assessment of child and adolescent behavior* (pp. 263–306). New York: Wiley.

Casey, B. J., Gordon, C. T., Mannheim, G. B., & Rumsey, J. M. (1993). Dysfunctional attention in autistic savants. *Journal of Clinical and Experimental Neuropsychology, 15*, 933–946.

Casey, P. (2001). Multiple personality disorder. *Primary Care Psychiatry, 7*, 7–11.

Cashin, J. R., Presley, C. A., & Meilman, P. W. (1998). Alcohol use in the Greek system: Follow the leader? *Journal of Studies on Alcohol, 59*, 63–70.

Casper, R. C., Pandy, G. N., Jaspan, J. B., & Rubenstein, A. H. (1988). Hormone and metabolite plasma levels after oral glucose in bulimia and healthy controls. *Biological Psychiatry, 24*, 663–674.

Cassileth, B. R. (1999). Evaluating complementary and alternative therapies for cancer patients. *Ca: A Cancer Journal for Clinicians, 49*, 362–375.

Castellani, B. (2000). *Pathological gambling: The making of a medical problem.* Albany: State University of New York Press.

Castellanos, F. X. (1999). The psychobiology of attention-deficit/hyperactivity disorder. In H. C. Quay & A. E. Hogan (Eds.), *Handbook of disruptive behavior disorders* (pp. 179–198). New York: Kluwer Academic/Plenum Publishers.

Castellanos, F. X., Giedd, J. N., March, W. L., Hamburger, S. D., Vaituzis, A. C., Dickerstein, D. P., Sarfatti, S. E., Vauss, Y. C., Snell, J. W., Rajapakse, J. C., & Rapoport, J. L. (1996). Quantitative brain magnetic resonance imaging in attention-deficit hyperactivity disorder. *Archives of General Psychiatry, 53*, 607–616.

Castro, F. G., Barrington, E. H., Walton, M. A., & Rawson, R. A. (2000). Cocaine and methamphetamine: Differential addiction rates. *Psychology of Addictive Behaviors, 14*, 390–396.

Cattell, R. B. (1950). *Personality: A systematic, theoretical, and factual study.* New York: McGraw-Hill.

Ceci, S. J., & Roazzi, A. (1994). The effects of context on cognition: Postcards from Brazil. In R. J. Sternberg & R. K. Wagner (Eds.), *Minds in context: Interactionist perspectives on human intelligence* (pp. 74–101). New York: Cambridge University Press.

Celerier, A., Ognard, R., Decorte, L., & Beracochea, D. (2000). Deficits of spatial and non-spatial memory and of auditory fear conditioning following anterior thalamic lesions in mice: Comparison with chronic alcohol consumption. *European Journal of Neuroscience, 12*, 2575–2584.

Chalkley, A. J., & Powell, G. E. (1983). The clinical description of 48 cases of sexual fetishism. *British Journal of Psychiatry, 142*, 292–295.

Chambless, D. L., & Ollendick, T. H. (2001). Empirically supported psychological interventions: Controversies and evidence. *Annual Review of Psychology, 52*, 685–716.

Chambless, D. L., Bryan, A. D., Aiken, L. S., Steketee, G., & Hooley, J. M. (2001). Predicting expressed emotion: A study with families of obsessive-compulsive and agoraphobic outpatients. *Journal of Family Psychology, 15*, 225–240.

Chambless, D. L., Caputo, G. C., Bright, P., & Gallagher, R. (1984). Assessment of fear in agoraphobics: The body sensations questionnaire and the agoraphobic cognitions questionnaire. *Journal of Consulting and Clinical Psychology, 52*, 1090–1097.

Chambliss, C. H. (2000). *Psychotherapy and managed care: Reconciling research and reality.* Boston: Allyn & Bacon.

Chang, V. (1999). Lead abatement and prevention of developmental disabilities. *Journal of Intellectual and Developmental Disability, 24*, 161–168.

Chantarujikapong, S. I., Scherrer, J. F., Xian, H., Eisen, S. A., Lyons, M. J., Goldberg, J., Tsuang, M., & True, W. R. (2001). A twin study of generalized anxiety disorder symptoms, panic disorder symptoms and posttraumatic stress disorder in men. *Psychiatry Research, 103*, 133–146.

Chapman, J. P., & Chapman, L. J. (1987). Handedness of hypothetically psychosis-prone subjects. *Journal of Abnormal Psychology, 96*, 89–93.

Chapman, L. J., & Chapman, J. P. (1967). Genesis of popular but erroneous psychodiagnostic observations. *Journal of Abnormal Psychology, 72*, 193–204.

Chapman, L. J., & Chapman, J. P. (1969). Illusory correlation as an obstacle to the use of valid psychodiagnostic signs. *Journal of Abnormal Psychology, 74*, 271–280.

Chapman, L. J., & Chapman, J. P. (1973a). Disordered thought in schizophrenia. Englewood Cliffs, NJ: Prentice-Hall.

Chapman, L. J., & Chapman, J. P. (1973b). Problems in the measurement of cognitive deficit. *Psychological Bulletin, 79*, 380–385.

Chapman, L. J., & Chapman, J. P. (1980). Scales for rating psychotic and psychotic-like experiences as continua. *Schizophrenia Bulletin, 6*, 476–489.

Chapman, L. J., Chapman, J. P., & Raulin, M. L. (1976). Scales for physical and social anhedonia. *Journal of Abnormal Psychology, 85*, 374–382.

Chapman, L. J., Chapman, J. P., & Raulin, M. L. (1978b). Body-image aberration in schizophrenia. *Journal of Abnormal Psychology, 87*, 399–407.

Chapman, L. J., Chapman, J. P., Kwapil, T. R., Eckblad, M., & Zinser, M. C. (1994). Putatively psychosis-prone subjects ten years later. *Journal of Abnormal Psychology, 103*, 171–183.

Chapman, L. J., Chapman, J. P., Raulin, M. L., & Edell, W. S. (1978a). Schizotypy and thought disorder as a high risk approach to schizophrenia. In G. Serban (Ed.), *Cognitive defects in the development of mental illness* (pp. 353–360). New York: Brunner-Mazel.

Charlop, M. H., Schreibman, L., & Thibodeau, M. G. (1985). Increasing spontaneous verbal responding in autistic children using a time delay procedure. *Journal of Applied Behavior Analysis, 18*, 155–166.

Charlton, R. S., & Quatman, T. (1997). A therapist's guide to the physiology of sexual response. In R. S. Charlton & I. D. Yalom (Eds.), *Treating sexual disorders: The Jossey-Bass library of current clinical technique* (pp. 29–58). San Francisco: Jossey-Bass.

Charney, D. S., Heninger, G. R., & Breier, A. (1984). Noradrenergic function in panic attacks. *Archives of General Psychiatry, 41*, 751–763.

Chaturvedi, S. K. (1987). Family morbidity in chronic pain patients. *Pain, 30*, 159–168.

Chaves, J. F. (1996). Hypnotic strategies for somatoform disorders. In S. J. Lynn & I. Kirsch (Eds.), *Casebook of clinical hypnosis* (pp. 131–151). Washington, DC: American Psychological Association.

Cherek, D. R., & Lane, S. D. (1999). Effects of d,l-fenfluramine on aggressive and impulsive responding in adult males with history of conduct disorder. *Psychopharmacology, 146*, 473–481.

Chermack, S. T., Stoltenberg, S. F., Fuller, B. E., & Blow, F. C. (2000). Gender differences in the development of substance-related problems: The impact of family history of alcoholism, family history of violence and childhood conduct problems. *Journal of Studies on Alcohol, 61*, 845–852.

Chess, S., Korn, S., & Fernandez, P. B. (1971). *Psychiatric disorders in children with rubella.* New York: Brunner/Mazel.

Christenson, G. A., & MacKenzie, T. B. (1995). Trichotillomania, body dysmorphic disorder, and obsessive-compulsive disorder. *Journal of Clinical Psychiatry, 56*, 211–212.

Christophersen, E. R., & Mortweet, S. L. (2001). *Treatments that work with children: Empirically supported strategies for managing childhood problems.* Washington, DC: American Psychological Association.

Chu, J. A. (1998). Dissociative symptomatology in adult patients with histories of childhood physical and sexual abuse. In J. D. Bremmer & C. R. Marmar (Eds.), *Trauma, memory, and dissociation* (pp. 179–203). Washington, DC: American Psychiatric Press.

Chung, Y. B., & Harmon, L. W. (1994). The career interests and aspirations of gay men: How sex role orientation is related. *Journal of Vocational Behavior, 45*, 223–239.

Church, C., Alisanski, S., & Amanullah, S. (2000). The social, behavioral, and academic experiences of children with Asperger syndrome. *Focus on Autism and Other Developmental Disabilities, 15*, 12–20.

Ciarenello, A. L., & Ciaranello, R. D. (1995). The neurobiology of infantile autism. *Annual Review of Neuroscience, 18*, 101–128.

Ciraulo, D. A., & Sarid-Segal, O. (2000). Sedative-, hypnotic-, and anxiolytic-related abuse. In B. I. Sadock & V. A. Sadock (Eds.), *Kaplan & Sadock's comprehensive textbook of psychiatry* (7th ed., pp. 1071–1085). Philadelphia: Lippincott Williams & Wilkins.

Ciraulo, D. A., Barnhill, J. G., Ciraulo, A. M., Greenblatt, D. J., & Shader, R. I. (1989). Parental alcoholism as a risk factor in benzodiazepine abuse: A pilot study. *American Journal of Psychiatry, 146*, 1333–1335.

Ciraulo, D. A., Sands, B. F., & Shader, R. I. (1988). Critical review of liability for benzodiazepine abuse among alcoholics. *American Journal of Psychiatry, 145*, 1501–1506.

Ciraulo, D. A., Sarid-Segal, O., Knapp, C., Ciraulo, A. M., Greenblatt, D. J., & Shader, R. I. (1996). Liability to alprazolam abuse in daughters of alcoholics. *American Journal of Psychiatry, 153*, 956–958.

Clark, D. A. (1986). A cognitive approach to panic. *Behavior Research and Therapy, 24*, 461–470.

Clark, D. A., & Beck, A. T. (1999). *Scientific foundations of cognitive theory and therapy for depression.* New York: Wiley.

Clark, D. A., & Purdon, C. (1993). New perspectives for a cognitive theory of obsessions. *Australian Psychologist, 28*, 161–167.

Clark, D. M. (1986). A cognitive approach to panic. *Behaviour Research and Therapy, 24*, 461–470.

Clark, D. M. (1988). A cognitive model of panic attacks. In S. Rachman & J. D. Maser (Eds.), *Panic: Psychological perspectives* (pp. 71–89). Hillsdale, NJ: Erlbaum.

Clark, D. M., Salkovskis, P. M., & Chalkley, A. J. (1985). Respiratory control as a treatment for panic attacks. *Journal of Behaviour Therapy and Experimental Psychiatry, 16*, 23–30.

Classen, C., Butler, L. D., Koopman, C., Miller, E., DiMiceli, S., Giese-Davis, J., Fobair, P., Carlson, R. W., Kraemer, H. C., & Spiegel, D. (2001). Supportive-expressive group therapy and distress in patients with metastatic breast cancer. *Archives of General Psychiatry, 58*, 494–501.

Cleare, A. J., Blair, D., Chambers, S., & Wessely, S. (2001). Urinary free cortisol in chronic fatigue syndrome. *American Journal of Psychiatry, 158,* 641–643.

Cleator, H., & Hand, L. (2001). Selective mutism: How a successful speech and language assessment really is possible. *International Journal of Language and Communication Disorders, 36* (Supplement), 126–131.

Cleckley, H. (1941). *The mask of sanity.* St. Louis, MO: Mosby.

Climko, R. P., Roehrich, H., Sweeney, D. R., & Al-Razi, J. (1987). Ecstasy: A review of MDA and MDMA. *International Journal of Psychiatry in Medicine, 16,* 359–372.

Cloninger, C. R., & Svrakic, D. M. (2000). Personality disorders. In B. I. Sadock & V. A. Sadock (Eds.), *Kaplan & Sadock's comprehensive textbook of psychiatry* (7th ed., pp. 1723–1764). Philadelphia: Lippincott Williams & Wilkins.

Cloninger, C. R., Bohman, M., & Sigvardsson, S. (1981). Inheritance of alcohol abuse: Cross-fostering analysis of adopted men. *Archives of General Psychiatry, 38,* 861–868.

Cloninger, C. R., Sigvardsson, S., & Bohman, M. (1996). Type I and Type II alcoholism: An update. *Alcohol Health and Research World, 20,* 18–23.

Clum, G. A., Nishith, P., & Resick, P. A. (2001). Trauma-related sleep disturbance and self-reported physical health symptoms in treatment-seeking female rape victims. *Journal of Nervous and Mental Disease, 189,* 618–622.

Co, B. T., Goodwin, D. W., Gado, M., Mikhael, M., & Hill, S. Y. (1977). Absence of cerebral atrophy in chronic cannabis users. *Journal of the American Medical Association, 237,* 1229–1230.

Cobb, J. L., Wolf, P. A., Au, R., White, R., & D'Agostino, R. B. (1995). The effect of education on the incidence of dementia and Alzheimer's disease in the Framingham Study. *Neurology, 45,* 1707–1712.

Cocker, K. I., Edwards, G. A., Anderson, J. W., & Meares, R. A. (1994). Electrophysiological changes under hypnosis in multiple personality disorder: A two-case exploratory study. *Australian Journal of Clinical and Experimental Hypnosis, 22,* 165–176.

Coe, D., Matson, J., Fee, V., Manikam, R., & Linarello, C. (1990). Training nonverbal and verbal play skills to mentally retarded and autistic children. *Journal of Autism and Developmental Disorders, 20,* 177–187.

Cohen, B. M., Giller, E., & L., W. (1991). *Multiple personality disorder from the inside out.* Baltimore: Sidran Press.

Cohen, J. B. (2000). Playing to win: Marketing and public policy at odds over Joe Camel. *Journal of Public Policy and Marketing, 19*(2), 155–159.

Cohen, J. D., & Servan-Schreiber, D. (1992). Context, cortex, and dopamine: A connectionist approach to behavior and biology in schizophrenia. *Psychological Review, 99,* 45–77.

Cohen, J. D., & Servan-Schreiber, D. (1993). A theory of dopamine function and its role in cognitive deficits in schizophrenia. *Schizophrenia Bulletin, 19,* 85–104.

Cohen, L., Marshall, G. D., Jr., Cheng, L., Agarwal, S. K., & Wei, Q. (2000). DNA repair capacity in healthy medical students during and after exam stress. *Journal of Behavioral Medicine, 23,* 531–544.

Cohen, N., & Kinney, K. S. (2001). Exploring the phylogenetic history of neural–immune system interactions. In R. Ader, D. L. Felten, & N. Cohen (Eds.), *Psychoneuroimmunology* (3rd ed., pp. 21–54). San Diego: Academic Press.

Cohen, R. J., Swerdlik, M. E., & Smith, D. K. (1992). *Psychological testing and assessment: An introduction to tests and measurement* (2nd ed.). Mountain View, CA: Mayfield.

Cohen, S. (1998). *Targeting autism: What we know, don't know, and can do to help young children with autism and related disorders.* Berkeley: University of California Press.

Cohen, S., & Wills, T. A. (1985). Stress, social support, and the buffering process. *Psychological Bulletin, 98,* 310–357.

Cohen, S., Kamarck, T., & Mermelstein, R. (1983). A global measure of perceived stress. *Journal of Health and Social Behavior, 24,* 385–396.

Cohen, S., Tyrrell, D. A., & Smith, A. P. (1991). Psychological stress and susceptibility to the common cold. *New England Journal of Medicine, 325,* 606–612.

Cohen, S., Tyrrell, D. A., & Smith, A. P. (1993). Negative life events, perceived stress, negative affect, and susceptibility to the common cold. *Journal of Personality and Social Psychology, 64,* 131–140.

Coleman, L. (1987). *Suicide clusters.* Boston: Faber & Faber.

Colerick, E. J., & George, L. K. (1986). Predictors of institutionalization among caregivers of patients with Alzheimer's disease. *Journal of the American Geriatric Society, 34,* 493–498.

Coles, C. D. (1993). Saying "goodbye" to the "crack baby." *Neurotoxicology and Teratology, 15,* 290–292.

Coles, C. D., Bard, K. A., Platzman, K. A., & Lynch, M. E. (1999). Attentional response at eight weeks in prenatally drug-exposed and preterm infants. *Neurotoxicology and Teratology, 21,* 527–537.

Collins, J. J., & Messerschmidt, P. M. (1993). Epidemiology of alcohol-related violence. *Alcohol Health and Research World, 17,* 93–100.

Collins, V. A. (2000). A meta-analysis of burnout and occupational stress. *Dissertation Abstracts International:* Section B: *The Sciences & Engineering, 60*(9-B), 4942. (Available through University Microfilms International.)

Collison, M. (1993). Benefits for gay couples. *Chronicle of Higher Education, 40,* A17, November 3, 1993.

Comings, D. E. (2000). Attention-deficit/hyperactivity disorder with Tourette syndrome. In T. E. Brown (Ed.), *Attention deficit disorders and comorbidities in children, adolescents, and adults* (pp. 363–392). Washington, DC: American Psychiatric Press.

Comings, D. E., & Comings, B. G. (1987). Hereditary agoraphobia and obsessive-compulsive behavior in relatives of patients with Gilles de la Tourette's syndrome. *British Journal of Psychiatry, 151,* 195–199.

Committee on Sexual Offenses Against Children and Youths. (1984). *Report on the Committee on Sexual Offenses Against Children and Youths* (Badgley Report; Cat. No. J2-50/1984/E, Vols. 1–11, H74-13/1984-1E, Summary). Ottawa: Department of Supply and Services.

Cook, E. H. (1990). Autism: Review of neurochemical investigation. *Synapse, 6,* 292–308.

Cook, E. W., III, Hodes, R. L., & Lang, P. J. (1986). Preparedness and phobia: Effects of stimulus content on human visceral conditioning. *Journal of Abnormal Psychology, 95,* 195–207.

Cook, M., & Mineka, S. (1990). Selective Associations in the observational conditioning of fear in monkeys. *Journal of Experimental Psychology: Animal Behavioral Processes, 16,* 372–389.

Cook-Deegan, R. M. (1996). Bioethics and the federal government: Some implications for psychiatric genetics. In L. L. Hall (Ed.), *Genetics and mental illness: Evolving issues for research and society* (pp. 189–218). New York: Plenum.

Cooke, D. J. (1996). Psychopathic personality in different cultures: What do we know? What do we need to find out? *Journal of Personality Disorders, 10,* 23–40.

Cooke, D. J., & Michie, C. (1999). Psychopathy across cultures: North America and Scotland compared. *Journal of Abnormal Psychology, 108,* 58–68.

Cooley, E., & Toray, T. (2001). Disordered eating in college freshman women: A prospective study. *Journal of American College Health, 49,* 229–235.

Coons, P. M., Bowman, E. S., Kluft, R. P., & Milstein, V. (1991). The cross-cultural occurrence of MPD: Additional cases from a recent survey. *Dissociation, 4,* 124–128.

Cooper, A. J. (1986). Progestogens in the treatment of male sex offenders: A review. *Canadian Journal of Psychiatry, 31,* 73–79.

Cooper, A. J., Cernovsky, Z. Z., & Colussi, K. (1993). Some clinical and psychometric characteristics of primary and secondary premature ejaculators. *Journal of Sex and Marital Therapy, 19,* 276–288.

Cooper, J. E., Kendall, R. E., Gurland, B. J., Sharpe, L., Copeland, J. R. M., & Simon, R. (1972). *Psychiatric diagnosis in New York and London.* London: Oxford University Press.

Cooper, L. Z. (1968). Rubella: A preventable cause of birth defects. *Birth Defects. Original Article Series, 4,* 23–25.

Coplan, J. D., Papp, L. A., Pine, D., Martinez, J., Cooper, T., Rosenblum, L., Klein, D. F., & Gorman, J. M. (1997). Clinical improvement with fluoxetine therapy and noradrenergic function in patients with panic disorder. *Archives of General Psychiatry, 54,* 643.

Cordova, M. J., Cunningham, L. L. C., Carlson, C. R., & Andrykowski, M. A. (2001). Posttraumatic growth following breast cancer: A controlled comparison study. *Health Psychology, 20,* 176–185.

Corelli, T. B., Hoag, M. J., & Howell, R. J. (1997). Memory, repression, and child sexual abuse: Forensic implications for the mental health professional. *Journal of the American Academy of Psychiatry and the Law, 25,* 31–47.

Coren, S. (1994). *The intelligence of dogs: Canine consciousness and capabilities.* New York: Free Press.

Coren, S. (1994). The prevalence of self-reported sleep disturbances in young adults. *International Journal of Neuroscience, 79,* 67–73.

Cornblatt, B., Lenzenweger, M. F., Dworkin, R., & Erlenmeyer-Kimling, L. (1992). Childhood attentional dysfunction predicts social deficits in unaffected adults at risk for schizophrenia. *British Journal of Psychiatry, 161* (Suppl. 18), 59–64.

Cornelius, J. R., Salloum, I. M., Mezzich, J., Cornelius, M. D., Fabrega, H., Jr., Ehler, J. G., Ulrich, R. F., Thase, M. E., & Mann, J. J. (1995). Disproportionate suicidality in patients with comorbid major depression and alcoholism. *American Journal of Psychiatry, 152,* 358–364.

Cornish, J. W., McNicholas, L. F., & O'Brien, C. P. (2001). Treatment of substance-related disorders. In A. F. Schatzberg & C. B. Nemeroff (Eds.), *Essentials of clinical psychopharmacology* (pp. 519–538). Washington, DC: American Psychiatric Press.

Cornish, J. W., Metzger, D., Woody, G. E., Wilson, D., McLellan, A. T., Vandergrift, B., & O'Brien, C. P. (1997). Naltrexone pharmacotherapy for opioid dependent federal probationers. *Journal of Substance Abuse Treatment, 14,* 529–533.

Corr, C. A., Nabe, C. M., & Corr, D. M. (2000). *Death and dying, life and living* (3rd ed.). Belmont, CA: Wadsworth/Thomson Learning.

Cottraux, J., Note, I., Yao, S. N., Lafont, S., Note, B., Mollard, E., Bouvard, M., Sauteraud, A., Bourgeois, M., & Dartigues, J. (2001). A randomized controlled trial of cognitive therapy versus intensive behavior therapy in obsessive-compulsive disorder. *Psychotherapy and Psychosomatics, 70,* 288–297.

Courchesne, E. (1997). Brainstem, cerebellar, and limbic neuroanatomical abnormalities in autism. *Current Opinion in Neurobiology, 7,* 269–278.

Cowan, L. (1982). *Masochism: A Jungian view.* Dallas, TX: Spring.

Cox, C. S., Fedio, P., & Rapoport, J. L. (1989). Neuropsychological testing of obsessive-compulsive adolescents. In J. L. Rapoport (Ed.), *Obsessive-compulsive disorder in children and adolescents.* Washington, DC: American Psychiatric Press.

Cox, D. J., & MacMahon, B. (1978). Incidence of male exhibitionism in the United States as reported by victimized female college students. *National Journal of Law and Psychiatry, 1,* 453–457.

Cox, D. J., & Maletzky, B. M. (1980). Victims of exhibitionism. In D. J. Cox & R. J. Daitzman (Eds.), *Exhibitionism: Description, assessment, and treatment* (pp. 289–293). New York: Garland.

Cox, J. (1998). Social services. In R. C. Hamdy, J. M. Turnbull, J. Edwards, & M. M. Lancaster (Eds.), *Alzheimer's disease: A handbook for caregivers* (3rd ed., pp. 354–366). St. Louis, MO: Mosby.

Cox, W. M., & Klinger, E. (1987). Research on the personality correlates of alcohol use: Its impact on personality and motivational theory. *Drugs and Society, 1,* 61–83.

Coyne, J. A., & Berry, A. (2000). Rape as an adaptation. *Nature, 404,* 121–122.

Crago, M., Shisslak, C. M., & Estes, L. S. (1996). Eating disturbances among American minority groups: A review. *International Journal of Eating Disorders, 19,* 239–248.

Craighead, W. E., Evans, D. D., & Robins, C. J. (1992). Unipolar depression. In S. M. Turner, K. S. Calhoun, & H. E. Adams (Eds.), *Handbook of clinical behavior therapy* (2nd ed., pp. 99–116). New York: Wiley.

Craske, M. G. (1999). *Anxiety disorders: Psychological approaches to theory and treatment.* Boulder, CO: Westview Press.

Craske, M. G., & Barlow, D. H. (2001). Panic disorder and agoraphobia. In D. H. Barlow (Ed.), *Clinical Handbook of Psychological Disorders* (3rd ed., pp. 1–59). New York: Guilford.

Craske, M. G., Barlow, D. H., & Meadows, E. A. (2002). *Mastery of your anxiety and panic: Therapists' guide for anxiety, panics, and agoraphobia (MAP-3).* San Antonio, TX: Graywind/ Psychological Corporation.

Craske, M. G., Barlow, D. H., & O'Leary, T. A. (1992). *Mastery of your anxiety and worry.* Albany, NY: Graywind Publications.

Craske, M. G., Glover, D., & DeCola, J. (1995). Predicted versus unpredicted panic attacks: Acute versus general distress. *Journal of Abnormal Psychology, 104,* 214–223.

Crimlisk, H. L., & Ron, M. A. (1999). Conversion hysteria: History, diagnostic issues, and clinical practice. *Cognitive Neuropsychiatry, 4,* 165–180.

Crisanti, A. S., & Love, E. J. (2001). Characteristics of psychiatric inpatients detained under civil commitment legislation: A Canadian study. *International Journal of Law and Psychiatry, 24,* 399–410.

Crisp, A. (2001). The tendency to stigmatise. *British Journal of Psychiatry, 178,* 197–199.

Crocker, A. C. (1992). Human immunodeficiency virus. In M. D. Levine, W. B. Carey, & A. C. Crocker (Eds.), *Developmental-behavioral pediatrics* (pp. 271–275). Philadelphia: Saunders.

Crow, M. J., Marks, I. M., Agras, W. S., & Leitenberg, H. (1972). Time-limited desensitization implosion and shaping for phobic patients: A cross-over study. *Behaviour Research and Therapy, 10,* 319–328.

Crow, T. J. (1990). The continuum of psychosis and its genetic origins: The sixty-fifth Maudsley lecture. *British Journal of Psychiatry, 156,* 788–797.

Crowe, R. R., Noyes, R., Pauls, D. L., & Slymen, D. (1983). A family study of panic disorder. *Archives of General Psychiatry, 40,* 1065–1069.

Crutchley, A. (2000). Bilingual children in language units: Does having "well-informed" parents make a difference? *International Journal of Language and Communication Disorders, 35,* 65–81.

Csernansky, J. G., & Bardgett, M. E. (1998). Limbic-cortical neuronal damage and the pathophysiology of schizophrenia. *Schizophrenia Bulletin, 24,* 231–248.

Curwen, B., Palmer, S., & Ruddell, P. (2000). *Brief cognitive behaviour therapy.* Thousand Oaks, CA: Sage.

Czeisler, C. A., & Allan, J. S. (1988). Pathologies of the sleep-wake schedule. In R. L. Williams & I. Karacan (Eds.), *Sleep disorders: Diagnosis and treatment* (2nd ed., pp. 109–129). New York: Wiley.

Czeisler, C. A., Allan, J. S., Strogatz, S. H., Ronda, J. M., Sanchez, R., Rios, C. D., Freitag, W. D., Richardson, G. S., & Kronauer, R. E. (1986). Bright light resets the human circadian pacemaker independent of the timing of the sleep-wake cycle. *Science, 233,* 667–671.

Czeisler, C. A., Johnson, M. P., Duffy, J. F., Brown, E. N., Ronda, J. M., & Kronauer, R. E. (1990). Exposure to bright light and darkness to treat physiological maladaptation to night work. *New England Journal of Medicine, 322,* 1253–1259.

Dabek, F. (1997). Phi Gamma Delta freshman victim of alcohol poisoning. *The Vest, 117*(46), 1. **www-tech.mit.edu/V117/N46/alcohol.46n.html.**

Dadds, M. R., Schwartz, S., & Sanders, M. R. (1987). Marital discord and treatment outcome in behavioral treatment of child conduct disorders. *Journal of Consulting and Clinical Psychology, 55,* 396–403.

Dahl, A. (1986). Some aspects of the DSM-III personality disorders illustrated by a consecutive sample of hospitalized patients. *Acta Psychiatrica Scandinavica, 73,* 61–66.

Dahl, A. A. (1995). Commentary on borderline personality disorder. In W. J. Livesley (Ed.), *The DSM-IV personality disorders* (pp. 158–164). New York: Guilford.

Dahloef, P., Ejnell, H., Haellstroem, T., & Hedner, J. (2000). Surgical treatment of the sleep apnea syndrome reduces associated major depression. *International Journal of Behavioral Medicine, 7,* 73–88.

Dalton, A. J., & Janicki, M. P. (1999). Aging and dementia. In M. P. Janicki & A. J. Dalton (Eds.), *Dementia, aging, and intellectual disabilities: A handbook* (pp. 5–31). Philadelphia: Brunner/Mazel.

Damaj, M. I., & Martin, B. R. (1993). Is the dopaminergic system involved in the central effects of nicotine in mice? *Psychopharmacology, 111,* 106–108.

Damasio, A. R., & Maurer, R. G. (1978). A neurological model for childhood autism. *Archives of Neurology, 35,* 777–786.

D'Amico, E. J., Metrik, J., McCarthy, D. M., Frissell, K. C., Applebaum, M., & Brown, S. A. (2001). Progression into and out of binge drinking among high school students. *Psychology of Addictive Behaviors, 15,* 341–349.

Daniel, D. G., Egan, M. F., & Wolf, S. S. (2000). Neuropsychiatric aspects of movement disorders. In B. I. Sadock & V. A. Sadock (Eds.), *Kaplan & Sadock's comprehensive textbook of psychiatry* (7th ed., pp. 285–299). Philadelphia: Lippincott Williams & Wilkins.

Daniel, P. T. (2000). Dissecting the pathways to death. *Leukemia, 14,* 2035–2044.

Danielsson, B. (1956). *Love in the south seas.* New York: Reynal.

Darwin, C. (1859). *On the origin of species by means of natural selection, or the preservation of favored races in the struggle for life.* London: John Murray (New York: Modern Library, 1967).

Dashevsky, B. A., & Kramer, M. (1998). Behavioral treatment of chronic insomnia in psychiatrically ill patients. *Journal of Clinical Psychiatry, 59,* 693–699.

Davanloo, H. (1996). Management of tactical defenses in intensive short-term dynamic psychotherapy: Part II. Spectrum of tactical defenses. *International Journal of Short-Term Psychotherapy, 11,* 153–199.

Davidson, J. R. T. (2001). Pharmacotherapy of generalized anxiety disorder. *Journal of Clinical Psychiatry, 62* (Supplement 11), 46–50.

Davidson, J., Hughes, D., Blazer, D. G., & George, L. K. (1991). Posttraumatic stress disorder in the community: An epidemiological study. *Psychological Medicine, 21,* 713–721.

Davidson, J., Swartz, M., Storck, M., Krishnan, R. R., & Hammett, E. (1985). A diagnostic and family study of posttraumatic stress disorder. *American Journal of Psychiatry, 142,* 90–93.

Davidson, R. J. (1995). Cerebral asymmetry, emotion, and affective style. In R. J. Davidson & K. Hugdahl (Eds.), *Brain asymmetry.* Cambridge, MA: M.I.T. Press.

Davies, D. L. (1962). Normal drinking in recovered alcohol addicts. *Quarterly Journal of Studies on Alcohol, 23,* 94–104.

Davis, J. M., & Glassman, A. H. (1989). Antidepressant drugs. In H. I. Kaplan & B. J. Sadock (Eds.), *Comprehensive textbook of psychiatry* (5th ed., pp. 1627–1655). Baltimore: Williams & Wilkins.

Davis, J. M., Barter, J. T., & Kane, J. M. (1989). Antipsychotic drugs. In H. I. Kaplan & B. J. Sadock (Eds.), *Comprehensive textbook of psychiatry* (5th ed., Vol. II, pp. 1591–1626). Baltimore: Williams & Wilkins.

Davis, M., Eshelman, E. R., & McKay, M. (2000). The relaxation and stress reduction workbook (5th ed.). Oakland, CA: New Harbinger Publications.

Davis, R. D., & Millon, T. (1999). Models of personality and its disorders. In T. Millon, P. H. Blaney, & R. D. Davis (Eds.), *Oxford textbook of psychopathology* (pp. 485–522). New York: Oxford University Press.

Davis, S. R., & Meier, S. T. (2001). *The elements of managed care: A guide for helping professionals.* Belmont, CA: Brooks/Cole.

Dawson, D. A., & Grant, B. F. (1998). Family history of alcoholism and gender: Their combined effects on DSM-IV alcohol dependence and major depression. *Journal of Studies on Alcohol, 59,* 97–106.

de Boar, M. C., Schippers, G. M., & van der Staak, C. P. F. (1993). Alcohol and social anxiety in women and men: Pharmacological and expectancy effects. *Addictive Behaviors, 18,* 117–126.

de Boar, M. C., Schippers, G. M., & van der Staak, C. P. F. (1994). The effects of alcohol, expectancy, and alcohol beliefs on anxiety and self-disclosure in women: Do beliefs moderate alcohol effects? *Addictive Behaviors, 19,* 509–520.

de la Vega, M. J., Santolaria, F., Gonzalez-Reimers, E., Aleman, M. R., Milena, A., Martinez-Riera, A., & Gonzalez-Garcia, C. (2001). High prevalence of hyperhomocysteinemia in chronic alcoholism: The importance of the thermolabile form of the enzyme methylenetetrahydrofolate reductase (MTHFR). *Alcohol, 25,* 59–67.

de Waal, A. (1997). *Famine crimes : Politics and the disaster relief industry in Africa.* London: African Rights and International African Institute.

de Waal, F. B. M. (April 2, 2000). Survival of the rapist. *New York Times.* (Available at **http://reserve.libraries.psu.edu/wmnst/492/49208.htm**).

Deacon, T. W. (2000). Evolutionary perspectives on language and brain plasticity. *Journal of Communication Disorders, 33,* 273–291.

Deaton, A. V. (1998). Treating conversion disorders: Is a pediatric rehabilitation hospital the place? *Rehabilitation Psychology, 43,* 56–62.

Deckersbach, T., Savage, C. R., Phillips, K. A., Wilhelm, S., Buhlmann, U., Rauch, S. L., Baer, L., & Jenike, M. A. (2000). Characteristics of memory dysfunction in body dysmorphic disorder. *Journal of the International Neuropsychological Society, 6,* 673–681.

DeGrandpre, R. (1999). *Ritalin nation.* New York: Norton.

Delgado, P. L., Charney, D. S., Price, L. H., Aghajanian, G. K., Landis, H., & Heninger, G. R. (1990). Serotonin function and the mechanism of antidepressant action: Reversal of antidepressant-induced remission by rapid depletion of plasma tryptophan. *Archives of General Psychiatry, 47,* 411–418.

DeLongis, A., Folkman, S., & Lazarus, R. (1988). The impact of daily stress on health and mood: Psychological and social resources as mediators. *Journal of Personality and Social Psychology, 54,* 486–495.

del Rio, M. C., Gonzalez-Luque, J. C., & Alvarez, F. J. (2001). Alcohol-related problems and fitness to drive. *Alcohol and Alcoholism, 36,* 256–261.

DeMattos, R. B., Bales, K. R., Cummins, D. J., Paul, S. M., & Holzman, D. M. (2002). Brain to plasma amyloid-β efflux: A measure of brain Amyloid burden in a mouse model of Alzheimer's disease. *Science, 295,* 2264–2267.

Dembroski, T. M., & Costa, P. T., Jr. (1987). Coronary-prone behavior: Components of the Type A pattern and hostility. *Journal of Personality, 55,* 211–235.

Dembroski, T. M., MacDougall, J. M., Costa, P. T., Jr., & Grandits, G. A. (1989). Components of hostility as predictors of sudden death and myocardial infarction in the Multiple Risk Factor Intervention Trial. *Psychosomatic Medicine, 51,* 514–522.

Dement, W. C. (1960). The effects of dream deprivation. *Science, 131,* 1705–1707.

Dement, W. C., & Vaughan, C. (1999). *The promise of sleep.* New York: Dell.

DeMyer, M. K., Gilmor, R. L., Nendrie, H. C., DeMyer, W. E., Augustyn, G. T., & Jackson, R. K. (1988). Magnetic resonance brain images in schizophrenic and normal subjects: Influence of diagnosis and education. *Schizophrenia Bulletin, 14,* 21–37.

DeMyer, M. K., Hingtgen, J. N., & Jackson, R. K. (1981). Infantile autism reviewed: A decade of research. *Schizophrenia Bulletin, 7,* 388–451.

Denckla, M. B. (2000). Learning disabilities and attention-deficit/hyperactivity disorder in adults: Overlap with executive dysfunction. In T. E. Brown (Ed.), *Attention deficit disorders and comorbidities in children, adolescents, and adults* (pp. 297–318). Washington, DC: American Psychiatric Press.

Denney, C. B. (2001). Stimulant effects in attention deficit hyperactivity disorder: theoretical and empirical issues. *Journal of Clinical Child Psychology, 30,* 98–109.

Depression Guideline Panel. (1993, April). *Depression in primary care. Vol. 1: Detection and diagnosis* (AHCPR Publication No. 93-0550). Rockville, MD: U.S. Department of Health and Human Services.

Depue, R. A., Arbisi, P., Spoont, M. R., Leon, A., & Ainsworth, B. (1989). Dopamine functioning in the behavioral facilitation system and seasonal variation in behavior: Normal population and clinical studies. In N. E. Rosenthal & M. C. Blehar (Eds.), *Seasonal affective disorders and phototherapy* (pp. 230–259.). New York: Guilford.

Depue, R. A., Slater, J. F., Wolfstetter-Kausch, H., Klein, D., Goplerud, E., & Farr, D. (1981). A behavioral paradigm for identifying persons at risk of bipolar depressive disorder: A conceptual framework and five validation studies. *Journal of Abnormal Psychology, 90,* 381–437.

DeRubeis, R. J., Tang, T. Z., & Beck, A. T. (2001). Cognitive therapy. In K. S. Dobson (Ed.), *Handbook of cognitive-behavioral therapies* (2nd ed., pp. 349–392). New York: Guilford.

Des Jarlais, D. C. (1999). Preventing HIV infection among injection drug users: Intuitive and counter-intuitive findings. *Applied and Preventive Psychology, 8*, 63–70.

Dess, N. K. (2001). Eating, emotion, and the organization of behavior. In M. E. Carroll & J. B. Overmier (Eds.), *Animal research and human health: Advancing human welfare through behavioral science* (pp. 29–39). Washington, DC: American Psychological Association.

Detke, M. J., & Lucki, I. (1996). Detection of serotonergic and noradrenergic antidepressants in the rat forced-swimming test: The effects of water depth. *Behavior and Brain Research, 73*, 43–46.

deVito, R. A. (1993). The use of Amytal interviews in the treatment of an exceptionally complex case of multiple personality disorder. In R. P. Kluft & C. G. Fine (Eds.), *Clinical perspectives on multiple personality disorder* (pp. 227–240). Washington, DC: American Psychiatric Press.

Dewsnap, P., Gomborone, J., Libby, G., & Farthing, M. (1996). The prevalence of symptoms of irritable bowel syndrome among acute psychiatric inpatients with an affective diagnosis. *Psychosomatics, 37*, 385–389.

Diaferia, P., Bianchi, I., Bianchi, M. L., Cavedini, P., Eregovesi, S., & Bellodi, L. (1997). Relationship between obsessive-compulsive personality disorder and obsessive-compulsive disorder. *Comprehensive Psychiatry, 38*, 38–42.

Diamond, J. (1992). *The third chimpanzee: The evolution and future of the human animal.* New York: HarperCollins.

Diamond, J. (1999). War babies. In S. J. Ceci & W. M. Williams (Eds.), *The nature-nurture debate: The essential readings* (pp. 13–22). Malden, MA: Blackwell Publishers.

Diefendorf, A. R., & Dodge, R. (1908). An experimental study of the ocular reactions of the insane from photographic records. *Brain, 31*, 451–489.

Diehl, D. J., & Gershon, S. (1992). The role of dopamine in mood disorders. *Comprehensive Psychiatry, 33*, 115–120.

Diekstra, R. F. W. (1990). An international perspective on the epidemiology and prevention of suicide. In S. J. Blumenthal & D. K. Kupfer (Eds.), *Suicide over the life cycle.* Washington, DC: American Psychiatric Press.

Diener, E., Emmons, R. A., Larsen, R. J., & Griffin, S. (1985). The Satisfaction with Life Scale. *Journal of Personality Assessment, 49*, 71–75.

Dierker, L. C., & Merikangas, K. R. (2001). Familial psychiatric illness and posttraumatic stress disorder: Findings from a family study of substance abuse and anxiety disorders. *Journal of Clinical Psychiatry, 62*, 715–720.

Dilsaver, S. C., Chen, R., Shoaib, A. M., & Swann, A. C. (1999). Phenomenology of mania: Evidence for distinct depressed, dysphoric, and euphoric presentations. *American Journal of Psychiatry, 156*, 426–430.

DiNardo, P. A., Guzy, L. T., Jenkins, J. A., Bak, R. M., Tomasi, S. F., & Copeland, M. (1988). Etiology and maintenance of dog fears. *Behavior Research and Therapy, 26*, 241–244.

Doanne, J. A., Falloon, I. R. H., Goldstein, M. J., & Mintz, J. (1985). Parental affective style and the treatment of schizophrenia. *Archives of General Psychiatry, 42*, 34–42.

Docherty, N. M. (1995). Expressed emotion and language disturbance in parents of stable schizophrenia patients. *Schizophrenia Bulletin, 21*, 411–418.

Docherty, N. M., Gordinier, S. W., Hall, M. J., & Cutting, L. P. (1999). Communication disturbances in relatives beyond the age of risk for schizophrenia and their associations with symptoms in patients. *Schizophrenia Bulletin, 25*, 851–862.

Dolan, M. (1999). California and the West: Court to let killer appeal death penalty. *Los Angeles Times*, April 6, A, 3, Metro Desk.

Domhoff, G. W. (1999). New directions in the study of dream content using the Hall and Van de Castle coding system. *Dreaming, 9*, 115–137.

Donahey, K., & Carroll, R. (1993). Gender differences in factors associated with hypoactive sexual desire. *Journal of Sex and Marital Therapy, 19*, 25–40.

Donaldson, C., & Burns, A. (1999). Burden of Alzheimer's disease: Helping the patient and caregiver. *Journal of Geriatric Psychiatry and Neurology, 12*, 21–28.

Donat, P. L. N., & D'Emilio, J. (1998). A feminist redefinition of rape and sexual assault: Historical foundations and change. In M. E. Odem & J. Clay-Warner (Eds.), *Confronting rape and sexual assault* (pp. 35–49). Wilmington, DE: SR Books/Scholarly Resources.

Donnermeyer, J. F. (1998). Educator perceptions of the D.A.R.E. officer. *Journal of Alcohol and Drug Education, 44*, 1–17.

Donnermeyer, J. F. (2000). Parents' perceptions of a school-based prevention education program. *Journal of Drug Education, 30*, 325–342.

Doody, R. S., Dunn, J. K., Clark, C. M., Farlow, M., Foster, N. L., Liao, T., Gonzales, N., Lai, E., & Massman, P. (2001). Chronic donepezil treatment is associated with slowed cognitive decline in Alzheimer's disease. *Dementia and Geriatric Cognitive Disorders, 12*, 295–300.

Doorn, C. D., Poortinga, J., & Verschoor, A. M. (1994). Cross-gender identity in transvestites and male transsexuals. *Archives of Sexual Behavior, 23*, 185–201.

Dorpat, T. L., & Ripley, H. S. (1967). The relationship between attempted suicide and completed suicide. *Comparative Psychiatry, 8*, 74–79.

Dougherty, P. M., & Radomski, M. V. (1993). *The cognitive rehabilitation workbook: A dynamic assessment approach for adults with brain injury* (2nd ed.). Gaithersburg, MD: Aspen Publishers.

Dowling, C. G. (2001). Unhappy campers: One doctor's prescription for obsessive-compulsive disorder: Get down and dirty. *People,* October 22, 135.

Downhill, J. E., Jr., Buchsbaum, M. S., Hazlett, E. A., Barth, S., Roitman, S. L., Nunn, M., Lekarev, O., Wei, T., Shihabuddin, L., Mitropoulou, V., Silverman, J., & Siever, L. J. (2001). Temporal lobe volume determined by magnetic resonance imaging in schizotypal personality disorder and schizophrenia. *Schizophrenia Research, 48*, 187–199.

Drake, R., & Vaillant, G. (1985). A validity study of Axis II of DSM-III. *American Journal of Psychiatry, 142*, 533–558.

Drapalski, A. L., Rosse, R. B., Peebles, R. R., Schwartz, B. L., Marvel, C. L., & Deutsch, S. I. (2001). Topiramate improves deficit symptoms in a patient with schizophrenia when added to a stable regimen of antipsychotic medication. *Clinical Neuropharmacology, 24*, 290–294.

Drevets, W. C., Frank, E., Price, J. C., Kupfer, D. J., Holt, D., Greer, P. J., Huang, Y., Gautier, C., & Mathis, C. (1999). PET imaging of serotonin IA receptor binding in depression. *Biological Psychiatry, 46*, 1375–1387.

Drewnowski, A., Yee, D. K., & Krahn, D. D. (1988). Bulimia in college women: Incidence and recovery rates. *American Journal of Psychiatry, 145*, 753–755.

Drossman, D. A. (1994). Irritable bowel syndrome: The role of psychosocial factors. *Stress Medicine, 10*, 49–55.

Dryden, W., & Ellis, A. (2001). Rational emotive behavior therapy. In K. S. Dobson (Ed.), *Handbook of cognitive-behavioral therapies* (2nd ed., pp. 295–348). New York: Guilford.

Dryer, R., Beale, I. L., & Lambert, A. J. (1999). The balance model of dyslexia and remedial training: An evaluative study. *Journal of Learning Disabilities, 32*, 174–186.

Du Four, M. C., Stinson, F. S., & Cases, M. F. (1993). Trends in cirrhosis morbidity and mortality. *Seminars in Liver Disease, 13*, 109–125.

Du, L., Faludi, G., Palkovits, M., Demeter, E., Bakish, D., Lapierre, Y. D., Sotonyi, P., Hrdine, P. D. (1999). Frequency of long allele in serotonin transporter gene is increased in depressed suicide victims. *Biological Psychiatry, 46*, 196–201.

Duaux, E., Krebs, M. O., Loo, H., & Poirier, M. F. (2000). Genetic vulnerability to drug abuse. *European Psychiatry, 15*, 109–114.

Duffy, A., Grof, P., Grof, E., Zvolsky, P., & Alda, M. (1998). Evidence supporting the independent inheritance of primary affective disorders and primary alcoholism in the families of bipolar patients. *Journal of Affective Disorders, 50*, 91–96.

Dumont, M. P. (1996). Privatization and mental health in Massachusetts. *Smith College Studies in Social Work, 66*, 293–303.

Dunham, H. W. (1965). *Community and schizophrenia: An epidemiological analysis.* Detroit: Wayne State University Press.

Dunn, K. M., Croft, P. R., & Hackett, G. I. (1999). Association of sexual problems with social, psychological, and physical problems in men and women: A cross-sectional population survey. *Journal of Epidemiology and Community Health, 53,* 144–148.

Durand, V. M., & Carr, E. G. (1991). Functional communication training to reduce challenging behavior: Maintenance and application in new settings. *Journal of Applied Behavior Analysis, 24,* 251–264.

Durham v. United States. (1954). 214 F.2d, 862, 874–875 (D.C. Cir.).

Durkheim, E. (1951). *Suicide* (trans. J. A. Spaulding & G. Simpson). New York: Free Press. (Originally published in 1897, with second edition published in 1930.)

Dusky v. United States. (1960). 363 U.S. 402.

Dutton, M. A. (1992). Assessment and treatment of post-traumatic stress disorder among battered women. In D. W. Foy (Ed.), *Treating PTSD: Cognitive-behavioral strategies* (pp. 69–98). New York: Guilford.

Dworkin, R. H., Clark, S. C., Amador, X. F., & Gorman, J. M. (1996). Does affective blunting in schizophrenia reflect affective deficit or neuromotor dysfunction? *Schizophrenia Research, 20,* 301–306.

Dykens, E., Leckman, J., Paul, R., & Watson, M. (1988). Cognitive, behavioral, and adaptive functioning in fragile-X and non-fragile-X retarded men. *Journal of Autism and Developmental Disorders, 18,* 41–52.

Eastman, C. I. (1987). Bright light in work-sleep schedules for shift workers: Application of circadian rhythm principles. In L. Rensing, U. van der Heiden, & M. C. Mackey (Eds.), *Temporal disorder in human oscillatory systems* (pp. 176–185). New York: Springer-Verlag.

Eastman, C. I. (1990). Circadian rhythms and bright light: Recommendations for shift work. *Work and Stress, 4,* 245–260.

Eastman, C. I., Young, M. A., Fogg, L. F., Liu, L., & Meaden, P. M. (1998). Bright light treatment for winter depression: A placebo-controlled trial. *Archives of General Psychiatry, 55,* 883–889.

Eaton, W. W., & Keyl, P. M. (1995). The epidemiology of panic. In G. M. Asnis & H. M. van Praag (Eds.), *Panic disorder: Clinical, biological, and treatment aspects* (pp. 50–65). Oxford, England: Wiley.

Eaton, W. W., Dryman, A., & Weissman, M. M. (1991). Panic and phobia. In L. N. Robins & D. A. Regier (Eds.), *Psychiatric disorders in America: The epidemiological catchment area study* (pp. 155–179). New York: Free Press.

Eckblad, M., & Chapman, L. J. (1983). Magical ideation as an indicator of schizotypy. *Journal of Consulting and Clinical Psychology, 51,* 215–225.

Edell, W. S. (1995). The psychometric measurement of schizotypy using the Wisconsin scales of psychosis-proneness. In G. A. Miller (Ed.), *The behavioral high-risk paradigm in psychopathology* (pp. 3–46). New York: Springer.

Edinger, J. D. (1985). Relaxation and depersonalisation. *British Journal of Psychiatry, 146,* 103.

Edmondson, J. C. (2000). Neuropsychiatric aspects of child neurology. In B. I. Sadock & V. A. Sadock (Eds.), *Kaplan & Sadock's comprehensive textbook of psychiatry* (7th ed., pp. 359–373). Philadelphia: Lippincott Williams & Wilkins.

Edwards, C. N. (2001). *Responsibilities and dispensations: Behavior, science, and American justice.* Dover, MA: Four Oaks Press.

Egan, M. F., & Weinberger, D. R. (1997). Neurobiology of schizophrenia. *Current Opinion in Neurobiology, 7,* 701–707.

Ehlers, A. (1995). A 1-year prospective study of panic attacks: Clinical course and factors associated with maintenance. *Journal of Abnormal Psychology, 104,* 164–172.

Ehrig, T., & Li, T. (1995). Metabolism of alcohol and metabolic consequences. In B. Tabakoff & P. L. Hoffman (Eds.), *Biological aspects of alcoholism* (pp. 23–48). Seattle: Hogrefe & Huber.

Eiden, R. D., Chavez, F., & Leonard, K. E. (1999). Parent-infant interactions among families with alcoholic fathers. *Development and Psychopathology, 11,* 745–762.

Eisen, M. L., Quas, J. A., & Goodman, G. S. (Eds.). (2002). *Memory and suggestibility in the forensic interview.* Mahwah, NJ: Erlbaum.

Elder, J. P. (2001). *Behavior change and public health in the developing world.* Thousand Oaks, CA: Sage.

Elliot, M. (2001). Gender differences in causes of depression. *Women and Health, 33,* 163–177.

Ellis, A. (1962). *Reason and emotion in psychotherapy.* New York: Lyle Stuart.

Ellis, A. (1977). The basic clinical theory of rational-emotive therapy. In A. Ellis & R. Grieger (Eds.), *Handbook of rational-emotive therapy* (pp. 31–45). New York: Springer.

Ellis, A. (1991). The revised ABC's of rational-emotive therapy (RET). *Journal of Rational-Emotive and Cognitive-Behavioral Therapy, 9,* 139–172.

Ellis, A., & Dryden, W. (1987). *The practice of rational-emotive therapy (RET).* New York: Springer.

Emanuel, E. J., Wendler, D., & Grady, C. (2000). What makes clinical research ethical? *JAMA: Journal of the American Medical Association, 283,* 2701–2711.

Eminson, M., Benjamin, S., Shortall, A., & Woods, T. (1996). Physical symptoms and illness attitudes in adolescents: An epidemiological study. *Journal of Child Psychology and Psychiatry and Allied Disciplines, 37,* 519–528.

Emmanuel, N. P., Lydiard, R. B., & Ballenger, J. C. (1991). Fluoxetine treatment of voyeurism. *American Journal of Psychiatry, 148,* 950.

Emmers-Sommer, T. M., & Allen, M. (1999). Variables related to sexual coercion: A path analysis. *Journal of Social and Personal Relationships, 16,* 659–678.

Enzer, N. B., & Heard, A. L. (2000). Psychiatric prevention in children and adolescents. In B. I. Sadock & V. A. Sadock (Eds.), *Kaplan & Sadock's comprehensive textbook of psychiatry* (7th ed., pp. 2954–2961). Philadelphia: Lippincott Williams & Wilkins.

Epstein, L. H., Paluch, R., Smith, J. D., & Sayette, M. (1997). Allocation of attentional resources during habituation to food cues. *Psychophysiology, 34,* 59–64.

Erb, M., Hodgins, S., Freese, R., Mueller-Isberner, R., & Joeckel, D. (2001). Homicide and schizophrenia: Maybe treatment does have a preventive effect. *Criminal Behaviour and Mental Health, 11,* 6–26.

Erlanger, D. M., Kutner, K. C., Barth, J. T., & Barnes, R. (1999). Neuropsychology of sports-related head injury: Dementia pugilistica to post concussion syndrome. *Clinical Neuropsychologist, 13,* 193–209.

Erwin, E. (1978). *Behavior therapy: Scientific, philosophical, and moral foundations.* London: Cambridge University Press.

Espie, C. A. (2002). Insomnia: Conceptual issues in the development, persistence, and treatment of sleep disorder in adults. *Annual Review of Psychology, 53,* 215–243.

Evans, D. A., Hebert, L. E., Beckett, L. A., Scherr, P. A., Albert, M. S., Chown, M. J., Pilgrim, D. M., & Taylor, J. O. (1997). Education and other measures of socioeconomic status and risk of incident Alzheimer disease in a defined population of older persons. *Archives of Neurology, 54,* 1399–1405.

Everaerd, W., Laan, E. T. M., Roth, S., & van der Velde, J. (2000). Female sexuality. In L. T. Szuchman & F. Muscarella (Eds.), *Psychological perspectives on human sexuality* (pp. 101–146). New York: Wiley.

Evers, S., Hangst, K., & Pecuch, P. W. (2001). The impact of repetitive transcranial magnetic stimulation on pituitary hormone levels and cortisol in healthy subjects. *Journal of Affective Disorders, 66,* 83–88.

Exner, J. E., Jr. (1985). *A Rorschach workbook for the comprehensive system* (2nd ed.). Asheville, NC: Rorschach Workshops.

Exner, J. E., Jr. (1993). *The Rorschach: A comprehensive system, Vol. 1: Basic foundations* (3rd ed.). New York: Wiley.

Eysenck, H. J. (1947). *Dimensions of personality.* London: Routledge & Kegan Paul.

Eysenck, H. J., & Eysenck, M. W. (1985). *Personality and individual differences.* New York: Plenum.

Fadda, F. & Rossetti, Z. L. (1998). Chronic ethanol consumption: From neuroadaptation to neurodegeneration. *Progress in Neurobiology, 56,* 385–431.

Fairbairn, W. R. D. (1955). Endopsychic structure considered in terms of object-relationships. In W. R. D. Fairbairn (Ed.), *Psychoanalytic studies of the personality* (U.S. title: *An object relations theory of personality*). London: Tavistock. (Original work published in 1944).

Fairburn, C. G. (1984). A cognitive-behavioural treatment for bulimia. In D. M. Garner & P. E. Garfield (Eds.), *Handbook of psychotherapy for anorexia and bulimia* (pp. 160–192). New York: Guilford.

Fairburn, C. G., Cowen, P. J., & Harrison, P. J. (1999). Twin studies and the etiology of eating disorders. *International Journal of Eating Disorders, 26,* 349–358.

Fairburn, C. G., Jones, R., Peveler, R. C., Hope, R. A., & O'Connor, M. (1993). Psychotherapy and bulimia nervosa: The longer-term effects of interpersonal psychotherapy, behaviour therapy, and cognitive-behaviour therapy. *Archives of General Psychiatry, 50,* 419–428.

Fairburn, C. G., Noman, P. A., Welch, S. L., O'Connor, M., Doll, H., & Peveler, R. C. (1995). A prospective study of outcome in bulimia nervosa and the long-term effects of three psychological treatments. *Archives of General Psychiatry, 52,* 304–312.

Fairclough, S. H., & Graham, R. (1999). Impairment of driving performance caused by sleep deprivation or alcohol: A comparative study. *Human Factors, 41,* 118–128.

Faller, H., Buelzebruck, H., Drings, P., & Lang, H. (1999). Coping, distress, and survival among patients with lung cancer. *Archives of General Psychiatry, 56,* 756–762.

Fallon, A. E., & Rozin, P. (1985). Sex differences in perception of desirable body shape. *Journal of Abnormal Psychology, 94,* 102–105.

Falloon, I. R. H., Boyd, J. L., McGill, C. W., Razani, J., Moss, H. B., & Gilderman, A. M. (1982). Family management in the prevention of exacerbation of schizophrenia: A controlled study. *New England Journal of Medicine, 306,* 1437–1440.

Falloon, I. R. H., Boyd, J. L., McGill, C. W., Williamson, M., Razani, J., Moss, H. B., Gilderman, A. M., & Simpson, G. M. (1985). Family management in the prevention of morbidity of schizophrenia. *Archives of General Psychiatry, 42,* 887–896.

Famighetti, R. (1997). *The world almanac and book of facts.* Mahwah, NJ: World Almanac Books.

Famy, C., Streissguth, A. P., & Unis, A. S. (1998). Mental illness in adults with fetal alcohol syndrome or fetal alcohol effects. *American Journal of Psychiatry, 155,* 552–554.

Fang, J., Madhavan, S., & Alderman M. H. (1996). The association between birthplace and mortality from cardiovascular causes among black and white residents of New York City. *New England Journal of Medicine, 335,* 1545–1551.

Faniullaci, F., Colpi, G. M., Beretta, G., & Zanollo, A. (1988). Cortical evoked potentials in subjects with true premature ejaculation. *Andrologia, 20,* 326–330.

Faraone, S. V., & Biederman, J. (1997). Do attention deficit hyperactivity disorder and major depression share familial risk factors? *Journal of Nervous and Mental Disease, 185,* 533–541.

Faraone, S. V., Biederman, J., Mennin, D., Wozniak, J., & Spencer, T. (1997). Attention-deficit hyperactivity disorder with bipolar disorder: A familial subtype. *Journal of the American Academy of Child and Adolescent Psychiatry, 36,* 1378–1387.

Faraone, S. V., Biederman, J., Mick, E., Williamson, S., Wilens, T., Spencer, T., Weber, W., Jetton, J., Kraus, I., Pert, J., & Zallen, B. (2000). Family study of girls with attention deficit hyperactivity disorder. *American Journal of Psychiatry, 157,* 1077–1083.

Faravelli, C., Degl'Innocenti, B. G., Aiazzi, L., Incerpi, G., et al. (1990). Epidemiology of mood disorders: A community survey in Florence. *Journal of Affective Disorders, 20,* 135–141.

Farberow, N. L. (1994). Preparatory and prior suicidal behavior. In E. S. Shneidman, N. L. Farberow, & R. E. Litman (Eds.), *The psychology of suicide: A clinician's guide to evaluation and treatment* (rev. ed., pp. 55–86). Northvale, NJ: Jason Aronson.

Faris, R. E. L., & Dunham, H. W. (1939). *Mental disorders in urban areas: An ecological study of schizophrenia and other psychoses.* Chicago: University of Chicago Press.

Farkas, G. M., & Rosen, R. C. (1976). Effect of alcohol on elicited male sexual response. *Journal of Studies on Alcohol, 37,* 265–272.

Farrer, L. A. (2001). Intercontinental epidemiology of Alzheimer disease: A global approach to bad gene hunting. *JAMA: Journal of the American Medical Association, 285,* 796–799.

Fava, M. (1997). Psychopharmacologic treatment of pathologic aggression. *Psychiatric Clinics of North America, 20,* 427–451.

Fawzy, F. I., Coombs, R. H., Simon, J. M., & Bowman-Terrell, M. (1987). Family composition, socioeconomic status, and adolescent substance use. *Addictive Behaviors, 12,* 79–83.

Feehan, M., Nada-Raja, S., Martin, J. A., & Langley, J. D. (2001). The prevalence and correlates of psychological distress following physical and sexual assault in a young adult cohort. *Violence and Victims, 16,* 49–63.

Feldman, H. A., Goldstein, I., Hatzichristou, G., Krane, R. J., & McKinlay, J. B. (1994). Impotence and its medical and psychosocial correlates: Results of the Massachusetts male aging study. *Journal of Urology, 151,* 54–61.

Feldman, M. D., & Lasher, L. J. (1999). Munchausen by proxy: A misunderstood form of maltreatment. *Forensic Examiner, 8,* 25–29.

Fellin, P. (1989). Perspective on depression among black Americans. *Health and Social Work, 14,* 245–252.

Felsenfeld, S., Kirk, K. M., Zhu, G., Statham, D. J., Neale, M. C., & Martin, N. G. (2000). A study of the genetic and environmental etiology of stuttering in a selected twin sample. *Behavior Genetics, 30,* 359–366.

Felten, D. L., Cohen, N., Ader, R., Felten, S. Y, Carlson, S. L., & Roszman, T. L. (1991). Central neural circuits involved in neural-immune interactions. In R. Ader, D. L. Felten, & N. Cohen (Eds.), *Psychoneuroimmunology* (2nd ed., pp. 3–25). San Diego: Academic Press.

Fenichel, O. (1945). *The psychoanalytic theory of neuroses.* New York: Norton.

Fenton, T. S., & McGlashan, T. H. (1989). Risk of schizophrenia in character disordered patients. *American Journal of Psychiatry, 146,* 1280–1284.

Fenton, W. S., & McGlashan, T. H. (2000). Schizophrenia: Individual Psychotherapy. In B. I. Sadock & V. A. Sadock (Eds.), *Kaplan and Sadock's comprehensive textbook of psychiatry* (7th ed., pp. 1217–1231). Baltimore: Lippincott Williams & Wilkins.

Ferguson, C. P., & Pigott, T. A. (2000). Anorexia and bulimia nervosa: Neurobiology and pharmacotherapy. *Behavior Therapy, 31,* 237–263.

Fernandez, Y. M., Marshall, W. L., Lightbody, S., & O'Sullivan, C. (1999). The Child Molester Empathy measure: Description and examination of its reliability and validity. *Sexual Abuse: Journal of Research and Treatment, 11,* 17–32.

Ferrari, M. D., & Haan, J. (2001). Genetics of headaches. In S. D. Silberstein, R. B. Lipton, & D. J. Dalessio (Eds.), *Wolff's headache and other head pain* (7th ed., pp. 73–84). New York: Oxford University Press.

Fetkewicz, J., Sharma, V., & Merskey, H. (2000). A note on suicidal deterioration with recovered memory treatment. *Journal of Affective Disorders, 58,* 155–159.

Fichten, C. S., Libman, E., Bailes, S., & Alapin, I. (2000). Characteristics of older adults with insomnia. In K. L. Lichstein & C. M. Morin (Eds.), *Treatment of late-life insomnia* (pp. 37–79). Thousand Oaks, CA: Sage.

Fine, C. G. (1993). A tactical integrationist perspective on the treatment of multiple personality disorder. In R. P. Kluft & C. G. Fine (Eds.), *Clinical perspectives on multiple personality disorder* (pp. 135–153). Washington, DC: American Psychiatric Press.

Fink, M. (2001). Convulsive therapy: A review of the first 55 years. *Journal of Affective Disorders, 63,* 1–15.

Finkelhor, D. (1979). *Sexually victimized children.* New York: Free Press.

Finkelhor, D. (1984). *Child sexual abuse: New theory and research.* New York: Free Press.

Finkelhor, D. (1986). *Sourcebook on Child Sexual Abuse.* Beverly Hills, CA: Sage.

Finlay, J. M. (2001). Mesoprefrontal dopamine neurons and schizophrenia: Role of developmental abnormalities. *Schizophrenia Bulletin, 27,* 431–442.

Finn, P. R., Earleywine, M., & Pihl, R. O. (1992). Sensation seeking, stress reactivity, and alcohol dampening discriminate the density of a family history of alcoholism. *Alcoholism: Clinical and Experimental Research, 16*, 585–590.

Firenze, R. (1997). Have the creationists already won? Or the teaching of faux-biology. *Reports of the National Center for Science Education, 17*(2), 10–15.

First, M. B., Spitzer, R. L., & Williams, J. B. W. (1990). Exclusionary principles and the comorbidity of psychiatric diagnoses: A historical review and implications for the future. In J. D. Maser & C. R. Cloninger (Eds.), *Comorbidity of mood and anxiety disorders* (pp. 83–109). Washington, DC: American Psychiatric Press.

First, M. B., Spitzer, R. L., Gibbon, M., & Williams, J. B. W. (1995). *Structured clinical interview for DSM-IV Axis I disorders: Patient edition.* New York: New York State Psychiatric Institute, Biometric Research Department.

Fischer, J., & Corcoran, K. (1994a). *Measures for clinical practice: A sourcebook,* Vol. 1: *Couples, families, and children.* New York: Free Press.

Fischer, J., & Corcoran, K. (1994b). *Measures for clinical practice: A sourcebook,* Vol. 2: *Adults.* New York: Free Press.

Fischer, M. (1971). Psychosis in the offspring of schizophrenic monozygotic twins and their normal co-twins. *British Journal of Psychiatry, 118*, 43–52.

Fischman, J. (2000, March 27). Some kids' bizarre compulsions may get their start from a common germ. *U S. News and World Report, 128*(12), 61.

Fisher, S., & Goldberg, R. P. (1996). *Freud scientifically reappraised: Testing the theories and therapy.* New York: Wiley.

Fishman, B. (1992). The cognitive behavioral perspective on pain management in terminal illness. *Hospice Journal, 8*, 73–88.

Fivush, R., & Hudson, J. A. (Eds.). (1990). *Knowing and remembering in young children.* New York: Cambridge University Press.

Fletcher, A. M. (2001). *Sober for good: New solutions for drinking problems: Advice from those who have succeeded.* Boston: Houghton Mifflin.

Flor-Henry, P. (1987). Cerebral aspects of sexual deviation. In G. D. Wilson (Ed.), *Variant sexuality: Research and theory* (pp. 49–83). Baltimore: Johns Hopkins University Press.

Foa, E. B., & Franklin, M. E. (2001). Obsessive-compulsive disorder. In D. H. Barlow (Ed.), *Clinical handbook of psychological disorders: A step-by-step treatment manual* (3rd ed., pp. 209–263). New York: Guilford.

Foa, E. B., & Goldstein, A. (1978). Continuous exposure and complete response prevention of obsessive-compulsive disorder. *Behavior Therapy, 9*, 821–829.

Foa, E. B., & Meadows, E. A. (1997). Psychosocial treatments for post-traumatic stress disorder: A critical review. *Annual Review of Psychology, 48*, 449–480.

Foa, E. B., & Rothbaum, B. O. (1998). *Treating the trauma of rape: Cognitive-behavioral therapy for PTSD.* New York: Guilford.

Foa, E. B., Franklin, M. E., Perry, K. J., Herbert, J. D. (1996). Cognitive biases in generalized social phobia. *Journal of Abnormal Psychology, 105*, 433–439.

Foa, E. B., Hearst-Ikeda, D. E., & Perry, K. (1995). Evaluation of a brief cognitive-behavioral program for the prevention of chronic PTSD in recent assault victims. *Journal of Consulting and Clinical Psychology, 63*, 948–955.

Folkman, S., & Chesney, M. (1995). Coping with HIV infection. In M. Stein & A. Baum (Eds.), *Chronic diseases* (pp. 115–134). Mahwah, NJ: Erlbaum.

Ford, M., & Widiger, T. (1989). Sex bias in the diagnosis of histrionic and antisocial personality disorders. *Journal of Consulting and Clinical Psychology, 57*, 301–305.

Fornari, V. M., & Pelcovitz, D. (2000). Identity problem and borderline disorders. In B. I. Sadock & V. A. Sadock (Eds.), *Kaplan & Sadock's comprehensive textbook of psychiatry* (7th ed., pp. 2922–2932). Philadelphia: Lippincott Williams & Wilkins.

Forrest, G. G. (1994). *Chemical dependency and antisocial personality disorder.* New York: Haworth.

Fowles, D. C. (1980). The three arousal model: Implication of Gray's two-factor learning theory for heart rate, electrodermal activity, and psychopathy. *Psychophysiology, 17*, 87–104.

Fowles, D. C. (1993). Electrodermal activity and antisocial behavior: Empirical findings and theoretical issues. In J. C. Roy, W. Boucsein, D. C. Fowles, & J. H. Gruzelier (Eds.), *Progress in electrodermal research* (pp. 223–237). New York: Plenum Press.

Fowles, D. C. (2000). Electrodermal hyporeactivity and antisocial behavior: Does anxiety mediate the relationship? *Journal of Affective Disorders, 61*, 177–189.

Fowles, D. C., & Missel, K. A. (1994). Electrodermal hyporeactivity, motivation, and psychopathy: Theoretical issues. In D. C. Fowles, P. Sutker, & S. H. Goodman (Eds.), *Progress in experimental personality and psychopathology research* (pp. 263–284). New York: Springer.

Foy, D. W. (1992). *Treating PTSD: Cognitive-behavioral strategies.* New York: Guilford.

Foy, D. W., Carroll, E. M., & Donahoe, C. P. (1987). Etiological factors in the development of PTSD in clinical samples of Vietnam combat veterans. *Journal of Clinical Psychology, 43*, 17–27.

Foy, D. W., Siprelle, R. C., Rueger, D. B., & Carroll, E. M. (1984). Etiology of posttraumatic stress disorder in Vietnam veterans: Analysis of premilitary, military, and combat exposure influences. *Journal of Consulting and Clinical Psychology, 52*, 79–87.

Frances, A., Clarken, J., Gilmore, M., Hurt, S., & Brown, R. (1984). Reliability of criteria for borderline personality disorder: A comparison of DSM-III and the diagnostic interview for borderline personality disorder. *American Journal of Psychiatry, 141*, 1080–1084.

Francis, P. T., Palmer, A. M., Snape, M., & Wilcock, G. K. (1999). The cholinergic hypothesis of Alzheimer's disease: A review of progress. *Journal of Neurology, Neurosurgery and Psychiatry, 66*, 137–147.

Frank, E., Kupfer, D. J., Perel, J. M., Cornes, C., Jarrett, D. B., Mallinger, A. G., Thase, M. E., McEachran, A. B., & Grochocinski, V. J. (1990). Three-year outcomes for maintenance therapies in recurrent depression. *Archives of General Psychiatry, 47*, 1100–1105.

Frank, J. W., Moore, R. S., & Ames, G. M. (2000). Historical and cultural roots of drinking problems among American Indians. *American Journal of Public Health, 90*, 344–351.

Fray, J. C. S., & Douglas, J. G. (Eds.). (1993). *Pathophysiology of hypertension in blacks.* New York: Oxford University Press.

Freedman, B. J. (1974). The subjective experience of perceptual and cognitive disturbances in schizophrenia: A review of autobiographical accounts. *Archives of General Psychiatry, 30*, 333–340.

Freedman, B. J., & Chapman, L. J. (1973). Early subjective experiences in schizophrenic episodes. *Journal of Abnormal Psychology, 82*, 46–54.

Freedman, R., Hall, M., Adler, L. E., & Leonard, S. (1995). Evidence in postmortem brain tissue for decreased numbers of hippocampal niotinic receptors in schizophrenia. *Biological Psychiatry, 38*, 22–33.

Freestone, J., Linzer, J., McKetney, C., Basnett, D., & Prendergast, E. (2001). An innovative strategy for institutionalizing a community-based tobacco program. *American Journal of Health Promotion, 15*, 225–227.

French, C. C. (2001). Alien abductions. In R. Roberts & D. Groome (Eds.), *Parapsychology: The science of unusual experience* (pp. 102–116). London: Arnold.

Freud, S. (1892–1899). Extracts from the Fleiss papers (letter 79, dated Vienna, December 22, 1897) *Standard Edition, 1* (pp. 173–280). London: Hogarth Press.

Freud, S. (1896a/1962). The etiology of hysteria. Reprinted in *Standard edition of the complete works of Sigmund Freud,* Vol. 2 (pp. 1–31). London: Hogarth. (Trans. and ed. by J. Strachey.)

Freud, S. (1896b/1955). Further remarks on the neuro-psychosis of defense. Reprinted in the *Standard Edition of the Complete Works of Sigmund Freud,* Volume 2 (pp. 157–185). London: Hogarth Press. (Translated and edited by J. Strachey.)

Freud, S. (1900). *The interpretation of dreams,* ed. and trans. J. Strachey. New York: Wiley.

Freud, S. (1909). Analysis of a phobia of a five-year-old boy. In *Standard Edition,* Vol. 10. London: Hogarth Press (1955).

Freud, S. (1933). *New introductory lectures on psychoanalysis.* New York: Norton.

Freud, S. (1950). Mourning and melancholia. In *Collected Papers* (Vol. 4). London: Hogarth and the Institute of Psychoanalysis. (Originally published in 1917.)

Freud, S. (1957). On narcissism: An introduction. In J. Strachey (Ed. and Trans.), *The standard edition of the complete psychological works of Sigmund Freud* (Vol. 14, pp. 73–104). London: Hogarth Press. (Originally published in 1914.)

Freud, S. (1963). *A general introduction to psychoanalysis* (trans. J. Riviere). New York: Liveright. (Original work published 1917.)

Freud, S. (1963). *Sexuality and the psychology of love.* New York: Collier Books.

Freund, K. (1990). Courtship disorders. In W. L. Marshall, D. R. Laws, & H. E. Barbaree (Eds.), *Handbook of sexual assault: Issues, theories, and treatment of the offender* (pp. 195–207). New York: Plenum Press.

Freund, K., Heasman, G. A., & Roper, V. (1982). Results of the main studies on sexual offenses against children and pubescents: A review. *Canadian Journal of Criminology, 24,* 387–397.

Freund, K., Scher, H., & Hucker, S. (1983). The courtship disorders. *Archives of Sexual Behavior, 12,* 369–379.

Freund, K., Scher, H., & Hucker, S. (1984). The courtship disorders: A further investigation. *Archives of Sexual Behavior, 13,* 133–139.

Freund, K., Seto, M. C., & Kuban, M. (1997). Frotteurism: Frotteurism and the theory of courtship disorders. In D. R. Laws & W. O'Donohue (Eds.), *Sexual deviance: Theory, assessment, and treatment* (pp. 111–130). New York: Guilford.

Freyd, J. J., DePrince, A. P., & Zurbriggen, E. L. (2001). Self-reported memory for abuse depends upon victim-perpetrator relationship. *Journal of Trauma and Dissociation, 2,* 5–16.

Frick, P. J., Christian, R. E., & Wooton, J. M. (1999). Age trends in association between parenting practices and conduct problems. *Behavior Modification, 23,* 106–128.

Fried, P. A., & Smith, A. M. (2001). A literature review of the consequences of prenatal marihuana exposure: An emerging theme of a deficiency in aspects of executive function. *Neurotoxicology and Teratology, 23,* 1–11.

Friedman, A. S., & Ali, A. (1998). The interaction of SES, race/ethnicity and family organization (living arrangements) of adolescents, in relation to severity of use of drugs and alcohol. *Journal of Child and Adolescent Substance Abuse, 7,* 65–74.

Friedman, J., & Alicea, M. (1995). Women and heroin: The path of resistance and its consequences. *Gender and Society, 9,* 432–449.

Friedman, L., Benson, K., Noda, A., Zarcone, V., Wicks, D. A., O'Connell, K., Brooks, J. O., III, Bliwise, D. L., & Yesavage, J. A. (2000). An actigraphic comparison of sleep restriction and sleep hygiene treatments for insomnia in older adults. *Journal of Geriatric Psychiatry and Neurology, 13,* 17–27.

Friedman, L., Bliwise, D. L., Yesavage, J. A., & Salom, S. R. (1991). A preliminary study comparing sleep restriction and relaxation treatments for insomnia in older adults. *Journals of Gerontology, 46,* P1–P8.

Friedman, M., & Rosenman, R. H. (1959). Association of specific overt behavior pattern with blood and cardiovascular findings. *Journal of the American Medical Association, 169,* 1286.

Friedman, M., & Rosenman, R. H. (1974). *Type A behavior and your heart.* New York: Knopf.

Friedman, M., & Ulmer, D. (1984). *Treating Type A behavior and your heart.* New York: Fawcett Crest.

Friedman, M., Thoresen, C. E., Gill, J. J., Powell, L. H., Ulmer, D., Thompson, L., Price, V. A., Rabin, D. D., Breall, W. S., Dixon, T., Levy, R., & Bourg, E. (1984). Alteration of Type A behavior and reduction in cardiac recurrences in postmyocardial infarction patients. *American Heart Journal, 108,* 237–248.

Friedman, M., Thoresen, C. E., Gill, J. J., Ulmer, D., Thompson, L., Powell, L., Price, V. A., Elek, S. R., Rabin, D. D., Breall, W. S., Piaget, G., Dixon, T., Bourg, E., Levy, R., & Tasto, D. I. (1982). Feasibility of altering Type A behavior pattern after myocardial infarction. *Circulation, 66,* 83–92.

Friedman, O., & Brown, I. (2001). Assessing dementia of the Alzheimer type in people with Down syndrome. *Journal on Developmental Disabilities, 8,* 75–92.

Friedman, S., Jones, J. C., Chernen, L., & Barlow, D. H. (1992). Suicidal ideation and suicide attempts among patients with panic disorder: A survey of two outpatient clinics. *American Journal of Psychiatry, 149,* 680–685.

Fritze, J., & Moeller, H. (2001). Design of clinical trials of antidepressants: Should a placebo control arm be included? *CNS Drugs, 15,* 755–764.

Froehlich, T. E., Bofardus, S. T., Jr., & Inouye, S. K. (2001). Dementia and race: Are there differences between African Americans and Caucasians? *Journal of the American Geriatrics Society, 49,* 477–484.

Fromm-Reichmann, F. (1948). Notes on the development of treatment of schizophrenics by psychoanalytic psychotherapy, *Psychiatry, 11,* 263–273.

Frosch, J. (1983). *The psychotic process.* New York: International Universities Press.

Fukudo, S., Lane, J. D., Anderson, N. B., Kuhn, C. M., Schanberg, S. M., McCown, N., Muranaka, M., Suzuki, J., & Williams, R. B. Jr. (1992). Accentuated vagal antagonism of beta-adrenergic effects on ventricular repolarization: Evidence of weaker antagonism in hostile men. *Circulation, 85,* 2045–2053.

Fuller, R. K., Branchey, L., Brightwell, D. R., Derman, R. M., Emrick, C. D., Iber, F. L., James, K. E., & Lacoursiere, R. B. (1986). Disulfiram treatment of alcoholism: A Veterans Administration cooperative study. *Journal of the American Medical Association, 256,* 1449–1455.

Fyer, A. J., Liebowitz, M. R., Gorman, J. M., Campeas, R., Levin, A., Davies, S. O., Goetz, D., & Klein, D. F. (1987). Discontinuation of Alprazolam treatment in panic patients. *American Journal of Psychiatry, 144,* 303–308.

Gaarder, E. (2000). Gender politics: The focus on women in the memory debates. *Journal of Child Sexual Abuse, 9,* 91–106.

Gabbard, G. O. (2000). Psychoanalysis and psychoanalytic psychotherapy. In B. I. Sadock & V. A. Sadock (Eds.), *Kaplan & Sadock's comprehensive textbook of psychiatry* (7th ed., pp. 2056–2080). Philadelphia: Lippincott Williams & Wilkins.

Gabbard, G. O. (2000). Psychoanalysis. In B. I. Sadock & V. A. Sadock (Eds.), *Kaplan & Sadock's comprehensive textbook of psychiatry* (7th ed., pp. 563–607). Philadelphia: Lippincott Williams & Wilkins.

Gaily, E., & Granstrom, M. L. (1988). Minor anomalies in offspring of epileptic mothers. *Journal of Pediatrics, 112,* 520–529.

Galin, D., Diamond, R., & Braff, D. (1977). Lateralization of conversion symptoms: More frequent on the left. *American Journal of Psychiatry, 134,* 578–580.

Gallagher, A. G., Dinan, T. G., & Baker, L. J. V. (1994). The effects of varying auditory input on schizophrenic hallucinations: A replication. *British Journal of Medical Psychology, 67,* 67–76.

Ganzini, L., Nelson, H. D., Lee, M. A., Kraemer, D. F., Schmidt, T. A., & Delorit, M. A. (2001). Oregon physicians' attitudes about and experiences with end-of-life care since passage of the Oregon Death with Dignity Act. *Journal of the American Medical Association, 285,* 2363–2369.

Garcia-Toro, M., Mayol, A., Arnillas, H., Capllonch, I., Ibarra, O., Crespi, M., Mico, J., Lafau, O., & Lafuente, L. (2001). Modest adjunctive benefit with transcranial magnetic stimulation in medication-resistant depression. *Journal of Affective Disorders, 64,* 271–275.

Gardner, H., Csikszentmihalyi, M., & Damon, W. (2001). *Good work: When excellence and ethics meet.* New York: Basic Books.

Garfinkel, P. E., Lin, E., Goering, P., Spegg, C., Goldbloom, D. S., Kennedy, S., Caplan, A. S., & Woodside, D. B. (1995). Bulimia nervosa in a Canadian community sample: Prevalence in comparison of subgroups. *American Journal of Psychiatry, 152,* 1052–1058.

Garmezy, N. (1974). Children at risk: The search for the antecedents of schizophrenia: II. Ongoing research programs, issues, and interventions. *Schizophrenia Bulletin, 9,* 55–125.

Garner, D. M., Garfinkel, P. E., Schartz, D., & Thompson, M. (1980). Cultural expectation of thinness in women. *Psychological Reports, 47*, 483–491.

Garrow, B., Bartheleng, C., Savage, D., Leddert, I., & Lelord, A. (1984). Comparison of autistic syndromes with and without associated neurological problems. *Journal of Autism and Developmental Disorders, 14*, 105–111.

Garver, D. L. (1987). Methodological issues facing the interpretation of high-risk studies: Biological heterogeneity. *Schizophrenia Bulletin, 13*, 525–529.

Gay, P. (1988). *Freud: A life for our time.* New York: Norton.

Gazzaniga, M. S., Ivry, R. B., & Mangun, G. R. (1998). *Cognitive neuroscience: The biology of the mind.* New York: Norton.

Gearing M., Mirra, S. S., Hedreen, J. C., Sumi, S. M., Hansen, L. A., & Heyman, A. (1995). The Consortium to Establish a Registry for Alzheimer's Disease (CERAD). Part X. Neuropathology confirmation of the clinical diagnosis of Alzheimer's disease. *Neurology, 45*, 461–466.

Gebhard, P. H., Gagnon, J. H., Pomeroy, W. B., & Christenson, C. V. (1965). *Sex offenders: An analysis of types.* New York: Harper & Row.

Geen, R. G. (1990). *Human aggression.* Pacific Grove, CA: Brooks/Cole.

George, E. L., Friedman, J. C., & Miklowitz, D. J. (2000). Integrated family and individual therapy for bipolar disorder. In S. L. Johnson, A. M. Hayes, T. M. Field, N. Schneiderman, & P. M. McCabe (Eds.), *Stress, coping, and depression* (pp. 307–324). Mahwah, NJ: Erlbaum.

George, W. H., Stoner, S. A., Norris, J., Lopez, P. A., & Lehman, G. L. (2000). Alcohol expectancies and sexuality: A self-fulfilling prophecy analysis of dyadic perceptions and behavior. *Journal of Studies on Alcohol, 61*, 168–176.

Gerlach, A. L., Wilhelm, F. H., Gruber, K., & Roth, W. T. (2001). Blushing and physiological arousability in social phobia. *Journal of Abnormal Psychology, 110*, 247–258.

Gershon, E. S., Schreiber, J. L., Hamovit, J. R., Dibble, E. D., Kaye, W., Nurnberger, J. I., Jr., Andersen, A. E., & Ebert, M. (1984). Clinical findings in patients with anorexia nervosa and affective illness in their relatives. *American Journal of Psychiatry, 141*, 1419–1422.

Ghaziuddin, M., Butler, E., Tsai, L., & Ghaziuddin, N. (1994). Is clumsiness a marker for Asperger syndrome? *Journal of Intellectual Disability Research, 38*, 519–527.

Giacobini, E. (2000). Cholinesterase inhibitors stabilize Alzheimer's disease. *Annals of the New York Academy of Sciences, 920*, 321–327.

Gidycz, C. A., & Layman, M. J. (1996). The crime of acquaintance rape. In T. L. Jackson (Ed.), *Acquaintance rape: Assessment, treatment, and prevention* (pp. 17–54). Sarasota, FL: Professional Resource Press.

Giedd, J. N., Blumenthal, J., Molloy, E., & Castellanos, F. X. (2001). Brain imaging of attention deficit/hyperactivity disorder. In J. Wasserstein & L. E. Wolf (Eds.), *Adult attention deficit disorder: Brain mechanisms and life outcomes* (pp. 33–49). New York: New York Academy of Sciences.

Gill, M. J., & Harris, S. L. (1991). Hardiness and social support as predictors of psychological discomfort in mothers of children with autism. *Journal of Autism and Developmental Disorders, 21*, 407–416.

Gillberg, C., & Gillberg, I. C. (1983). Infantile autism: A total population study of reduced optimality in the pre-, peri-, and neonatal periods. *Journal of Autism Developmental Disorders, 13*, 153–166.

Gillberg, C., Svennerholm, L., & Hamilton-Hellberg, C. (1983). Childhood psychosis and monoamine metabolites in spinal fluid. *Journal of Autism and Developmental Disorders, 13*, 383–396.

Gillham, J. E., Reivich, K. J., Jaycox, L. H., & Seligman, M. E. P. (1995). Prevention of depressive symptoms in schoolchildren: Two-year follow-up. *Psychological Science, 6*, 343–351.

Gitlin, M. J. (1999). A psychiatrist's reaction to a patient's suicide. *American Journal of Psychiatry, 156*, 1630–1634.

Gittleson, N. L., Eacott, S. E., & Mehta, B. M. (1978). Victims of indecent exposure. *British Journal of Psychiatry, 132*, 61–66.

Givens, B. S., & Olton, D. S. (1990). Cholinergic and GABAergic modulation of medial septal area: Effect on working memory. *Behavioral Neuroscience, 104*, 849–855.

Glasgow, R. E., Strycker, L. A., Toobert, D. J., & Eakin, E. (2000). A social-ecologic approach to assessing support for disease self-management: The chronic illness resources survey. *Journal of Behavioral Medicine, 23*, 559–583.

Gleaves, D. H. (1996). The sociocognitive model of dissociative identity disorder: A reexamination of the evidence. *Psychological Bulletin, 120*, 42–59.

Gleaves, D. H., Hernandez, E., & Warner, M. S. (1999). Corroborating premorbid dissociative symptomatology in dissociative identity disorder. *Professional Psychology—Research and Practice, 30*, 341–345.

Glisky, E., Schacter, D., & Tulving, E. (1986). Computer learning by memory impaired patients: Acquisition and retention of complex knowledge. *Neuropsychologia, 24*, 313–328.

Goddard, E., Plant, M., Davidson, I., & Garretsen, H. (2000). Drinking patterns. In M. Plant & D. Cameron (Eds.), *The alcohol report* (pp. 56–78). New York: Free Association Books.

Gold, M. S. (1995). *Drugs of abuse: A comprehensive series for clinicians,* Vol. 4: *Tobacco.* New York: Plenum Medical Book Company.

Goldberg, E. M., & Morrison, S. L. (1963). Schizophrenia and social class. *British Journal of Psychiatry, 109*, 785–802.

Goldberg, L. R. (1990). An alternative "description of personality": The Big-Five factor structure. *Journal of Personality and Social Psychology, 59*, 1216–1229.

Golden, C. J. (1978). *Diagnosis and rehabilitation in clinical neuropsychology.* Springfield, IL: Charles C Thomas.

Golden, C. J. (1990). *Clinical interpretation of objective psychological tests* (2nd ed.). Boston: Allyn & Bacon.

Golden, C. J., Espe-Pfeifer, P., & Wachsler-Felder, J. (2000). *Neuropsychological interpretations of objective psychological tests.* New York: Kluwer Academic/Plenum.

Golding, J. M., Siegal, J. M., Sorenson, S. B., Burnam, M. A., & Stein, J. A. (1989). Social support sources following sexual assault. *Journal of Community Psychology, 17*, 92–107.

Goldsmith, J. B., & McFall, R. M. (1975). Development and evaluation of an interpersonal skill-training program for psychiatric inpatients. *Journal of Abnormal Psychology, 84*, 51–58.

Goldsmith, T., Shapira, N. A., Phillips, K. A., & McElroy, S. L. (1998). Conceptual foundations of obsessive-compulsive spectrum disorders. In R. P. Swinson, M. M Antony, S. Rachman, & M. A. Richter (Eds.), *Obsessive-compulsive disorder: Theory, research, and treatment* (pp. 397–425). New York: Guilford.

Goldstein, A. J., & Chambless, D. L. (1978). A reanalysis of agoraphobia. *Behavior Therapy, 9*, 47–59.

Goldstein, B. H., & Obrzut, J. E. (2001). Neuropsychological treatment of dyslexia in the classroom setting. *Journal of Learning Disabilities, 34*, 276–285.

Goldstein, D. J., Wilson, M. C., Ascroft, R. C., & Al-Banna, M. (1999). Effectiveness of fluoxetine therapy in bulimia nervosa regardless of comorbid depression. *International Journal of Eating Disorders, 25*, 19–27.

Goldstein, M. (1992). Intrafamilial communication patterns observed during adolescence and the subsequent development of schizophrenia in early adulthood. In A. Z. Schwarzberg & A. H. Esman (Eds.), *International annals of adolescent psychiatry* (Vol. 2, pp. 47–54). Chicago: University of Chicago Press.

Goldstein, M. B., Brown, C. H., & Goodrich, E. J. (1989). Public preferences and site location of residential treatment facilities. *Journal of Community Psychology, 17*, 186–193.

Goldstein, M. J. (1999). New directions in family intervention programs for psychotic patients: Implications from expressed emotion research. In D. S. Janowsky (Ed.), *Psychotherapy indications and outcomes* (pp. 323–339). Washington, DC: American Psychiatric Press.

Goldstein, M. J., & Rodnick, E. H. (1975). The family's contribution to the etiology of schizophrenia: Current status. *Schizophrenia Bulletin, 14*, 48–63.

Goldstein, M. J., Talovic, S. A., Nuechterlein, K. H., Fogelson, D. L., Subotnik, K. L., & Asarnow, R. F. (1992). Family interaction vs.

individual psychopathology: Do they indicate the same processes in the families of schizophrenics? *British Journal of Psychiatry, 161,* 97–102.

Goldstein, R. B., Prescott, C. A., & Kendler, K. S. (2001). Genetic and environmental factors in conduct problems and adult antisocial behavior among adult female twins. *Journal of Nervous and Mental Disease, 189,* 201–209.

Goode, E. (1999). *Drugs in American society* (5th ed.). New York: McGraw-Hill.

Goodman, A. (1998). *Sexual addiction: An integrated approach.* Madison, CT: International Universities Press.

Goodnick P. J., & Sandoval, R. (1993). Psychotropic treatment of chronic fatigue syndrome and related disorders. *Journal of Clinical Psychiatry, 54,* 13–20.

Goodwin, D. W. (1976). *Is alcoholism hereditary?* New York: Oxford University Press.

Goodwin, D. W., Schulsinger, F., Hermansen, L., Guze, S., & Winokur, G. (1973). Alcohol problems in adoptees raised apart from alcoholic biological parents. *Archives of General Psychiatry, 28,* 238–243.

Goodwin, D. W., Schulsinger, F., Knop, J., Mednick, S., & Guze, S. (1977). Alcoholism and depression in adopted-out daughters of alcoholics. *Archives of General Psychiatry, 34,* 751–755.

Goodwin, F., & Jamison, K. (1990). *Manic-depressive illness.* New York: Oxford University Press.

Goplerud, E., & Depue, R. A. (1985). Behavioral response to naturally occurring stress in cyclothymia and dythymia. *Journal of Abnormal Psychology, 94,* 128–139.

Gordon, J. D. (1998). Admissibility of repressed memory evidence by therapists in sexual abuse cases. *Psychology, Public Policy, and Law, 4,* 1198–1225.

Gordon, R. A. (2000). *Eating disorders: Anatomy of a social epidemic* (2nd ed.). Malden, MA: Blackwell Publishers.

Gorman, J. M., Liebowitz, M. R., Fyer, A. J., & Stein, J. A. (1989). Neuroanatomical hypothesis for panic disorder. *American Journal of Psychiatry, 146,* 148–161.

Gosselin, C., & Wilson, G. (1980). *Sexual variations.* London: Faber & Faber.

Gotlib, I. H., & Cane, D. B. (1987). Construct accessibility and clinical depression: A longitudinal investigation. *Journal of Abnormal Psychology, 96,* 199–204.

Gotlib, I. H., & Hammen, C. (1992). *Psychological aspects of depression: Toward a cognitive-interpersonal integration.* New York: Wiley.

Gotlib, I. H., & Neubauer, D. L. (2000). Information-processing approaches to the study of cognitive biases in depression. In S. L. Johnson, A. M. Hayes, T. M. Field, N. Schneiderman, & P. M. McCabe (Eds.), *Stress, coping, and depression* (pp. 117–144). Mahwah, NJ: Erlbaum.

Gottesman, I. I. (1991). *Schizophrenia genesis: The origins of madness.* New York: W. H. Freeman.

Gottesman, I. I., & Bertelsen, A. (1989). Confirming unexpressed genotypes for schizophrenia: Risk in the offspring of Fischer's Danish identical and fraternal twins. *Archives of General Psychiatry, 46,* 867–872.

Gottesman, I. I., McGuffin, P., & Farmer, A. E. (1987). Clinical genetics as a clue to the "real" genetics of schizophrenia (a decade of modest gains while playing for time). *Schizophrenia Bulletin, 13,* 23–47.

Gottlieb, A. M., Killen, J. D., Marlatt, G. A., & Taylor, C. B. (1987). Psychological and pharmacological influences in cigarette smoking withdrawal: Effects of nicotine gum and expectancy on smoking withdrawal symptoms and relapse. *Journal of Consulting and Clinical Psychology, 55,* 606–608.

Gould, M. S. (1990). Suicide clusters and media exposure. In S. J. Blumenthal & D. J. Kupfer (Eds.), *Suicide over the life cycle: Risk factors, assessment, and treatment of suicidal patients* (pp. 517–532). Washington, DC: American Psychiatric Press.

Gould, S. J. (1995). *Dinosaur in a haystack: Reflections in natural history.* New York: Harmony Books.

Gould, S. J., & Eldredge, N. (1993). Punctuated equilibrium comes of age. *Nature, 366,* 223–227.

Goyer, P., Andreason, P. J., Semle, W. E., Clayton, A. H., et al. (1994). Positron-emission tomography and personality disorders. *Neuropsychopharmacology, 10,* 21–28.

Grabowski, T. J., & Damasio, A. R. (2000). Investigating language with functional neuroimaging. In A. W. Toga & J. C Mazziotta (Eds.), *Brain mapping: The systems* (pp. 425–461). San Diego: Academic Press.

Grace, J., Bellus, S. B., Raulin, M. L., Herz, M. I., Priest, B. L., Brenner, V., Donnelly, K., Smith, P., & Gunn, S. (1996). The long-term impact of Clozapine on symptomatology and cognitive functioning in treatment-refractory schizophrenic patients. *Psychiatric Services, 47,* 41–45.

Graham, J. R. (1990). *MMPI-2: Assessing personality and psychopathology.* New York: Oxford University Press.

Graham, Jr., J. M. (1992). Congenital anomalies. In M. D. Levine, W. B. Carey, A. C. Crocker, and R. T. Gross (Eds.), *Developmental-behavioral pediatrics* (pp. 229–243). Philadephia: Saunders.

Grant, I., & Atkinson, J. H., Jr. (2000). Neuropsychiatric aspects of HIV infection and AIDS. In B. I. Sadock & V. A. Sadock (Eds.), *Kaplan & Sadock's comprehensive textbook of psychiatry* (7th ed., pp. 308–336). Philadelphia: Lippincott Williams & Wilkins.

Gray, J. A. (1982). *The neuropsychology of anxiety.* New York: Oxford University Press.

Gray, J. A., & Buffery, A. W. H. (1971). Sex differences in emotional and cognitive behavior in mammals including man: Adaptive and neural bases. *Acta Psychologica, 35,* 89–111.

Gray, J. A., & McNaughton, N. (1996). The neuropsychology of anxiety: Reprise. In D. A. Hope (Ed.), *Perspectives on anxiety, panic, and fear* (Vol. 43 of the Nebraska Symposium on Motivation, pp. 61–134). Lincoln: University of Nebraska Press.

Graziano, A. M., & Raulin, M. L. (2000). *Research Methods: A Process of Inquiry* (4th ed.). Boston: Allyn & Bacon.

Graziottin, A. (2001). Clinical approach to dyspareunia. *Journal of Sex and Marital Therapy, 27,* 489–501.

Green, L., Fein, D., Joy, S., & Waterhouse, L. (1995). Cognitive functioning in autism: An overview. In E. Schopler & G. B. Mesibov (Eds.), *Learning and cognition in autism* (pp. 13–31). New York: Plenum.

Green, M. F. (1998). *Schizophrenia from a neurocognitive perspective: Probing the impenetrable darkness.* Boston: Allyn & Bacon.

Green, M. F., & Kinsbourne, M. (1990). Subvocal activity and auditory halluncinations: Clues for behavioral treatments? *Schizophrenia Bulletin, 16,* 617–625.

Green, M. F., Nuechterlein, K. H., & Breitmeyer, B. (1997). Backward masking performance in unaffected siblings of schizophrenia patients: Evidence for a vulnerability indicator. *Archives of General Psychiatry, 54,* 465–472.

Green, R., & Fleming, D. (1990). Transsexual surgery follow-up: Status in the 1990s. In J. Bancroft, C. Davis, & R. Ruppel (Eds.), *Annual review of sex research.* Mt. Vernon, IA: Society for the Scientific Study of Sex.

Greenacre, P. (1996). Fetishism. In I. Rosen (Ed.), *Sexual deviation* (3rd ed., pp. 88–110). Oxford, England: Oxford University Press.

Greenberg, A. S., & Bailey, J. M. (1994). The irrelevance of the medical model of mental illness to law and ethics. *International Journal of Law and Psychiatry, 17,* 153–173.

Greene, R. L. (1991). *The MMPI-2/MMPI: An interpretive manual.* Boston: Allyn & Bacon.

Greene, R. W., & Ablon, J. S. (2001). What does the MTA study tell us about effective psychosocial treatment for ADHD? *Journal of Clinical Child Psychology, 30,* 114–121.

Greenhill, L. L. (2001). Clinical effects of stimulant medications in ADHD. In M. V. Solanto, A. F. T. Arnsten, & F. X. Castellanos (Eds.), *Stimulant drugs and ADHD: Basic and clinical neuroscience* (pp. 31–71). New York: Oxford University Press.

Greening, T. (1997). Posttraumatic stress disorder: An existential-humanistic perspective. In S. Krippner & S. M. Powers (Eds.), *Broken images, broken selves: Dissociative narratives in clinical practice* (pp. 125–135). Philadelphia: Brunner/Mazel.

Gregory, R. J. (1992). *Psychological testing: History, principles, and applications.* Boston: Allyn & Bacon.

Greist, J. H. (1992). An integrative approach to treatment of obsessive-compulsive disorder. *Journal of Clinical Psychiatry, 53* (Supplement), 38–41.

Griffiths, P., & Livingstone, H. (1998). Treatment of encopresis by parent-mediated biofeedback in a child with corrected imperforate anus. *Behavioural and Cognitive Psychotherapy, 26,* 143–152.

Griffiths, P., & Watson, L. (1999). Pelvic floor exercise: A novel treatment for childhood encopresis. *Behavioural and Cognitive Psychotherapy, 27,* 279–283.

Grigorenko, E. L. (2001). Developmental dyslexia: An update on genes, brains, and environments. *Journal of Child Psychology and Psychiatry and Allied Disciplines, 42,* 91–125.

Grings, W. W. (1973). Cognitive factors in electrodermal conditioning. *Psychological Bulletin, 79,* 200–210.

Grob, C. S. (1985). Single case study: Female exhibitionism. *Journal of Nervous and Mental Disease, 173,* 253–256.

Grodin, M. A., & Laurie, G. T. (2000). Susceptibility genes and neurological disorders: Learning the right lessons from the Human Genome Project. *Archives of Neurology, 57,* 1569–1574.

Grove, W. M., & Tellegen, A. (1991). Problems in the classification of personality disorders. *Journal of Personality Disorders, 5,* 31–41.

Grove, W. M., Lebow, B. S., Clementz, B. A., Cerri, A., Medus, C., & Iacono, W. G. (1991). Familial prevalence and coaggregation of schizotypy indicators: A multitrait family study. *Journal of Abnormal Psychology, 100,* 115–121.

Grunstein, R. R., Stenloef, K., Hedner, J. A., & Sjoestroem, L. (1995). Impact of self-reported sleep-breathing disturbances on psychosocial performance in the Swedish Obese Subjects (SOS) study. *Sleep, 18,* 635–643.

Gruzelier, J. H. (1999). Functional neurophysiological asymmetry in schizophrenia: A review and reorientation. *Schizophrenia Bulletin, 25,* 91–120.

Guggenheim, F. G. (2000). Somatoform disorders. In B. I. Sadock & V. A. Sadock (Eds.), *Kaplan & Sadock's comprehensive textbook of psychiatry* (7th ed., pp. 1504–1532). Philadelphia: Lippincott Williams & Wilkins.

Gunderson, J. G., & Sabo, A. N. (1993). The phenomenological and conceptual interface between borderline personality disorder and PTSD. *American Journal of Psychiatry, 150,* 19–27.

Gunderson, J. G., & Singer, M. T. (1975). Defining borderline patients: An overview. *American Journal of Psychiatry, 132,* 1–10.

Gunderson, J. G., Ronningstam, E., & Smith, L. E. (1995). Narcissistic personality disorder. In W. J. Livesley (Ed.), *The DSM-IV personality disorders* (pp. 201–212). New York: Guilford.

Gur, R. C., Skolnick, B. E., & Gur, R. E. (1994). Effects of emotional discrimination tasks on cerebral blood flow: Regional activation and its relation to performance. *Brain & Cognition, 25,* 271–286.

Gur, R. E., & Pearlson, G. D. (1993). Neuroimaging in schizophrenia research. *Schizophrenia Bulletin, 19,* 337–353.

Gurnack, A. M., Atkinson, R., & Osgood, N. J. (Eds.) (2002). *Treating alcohol and drug abuse in the elderly.* New York: Springer.

Guze, S. B. (1993). Genetics of Briquet's syndrome and somatization disorder: A review of family, adoption, and twin studies. *Annals of Clinical Psychiatry, 5,* 225–230.

Haarasilta, L., Marttunen, M., Kaprio, J., & Aro, H. (2001). The 12-month prevalence and characteristics of major depressive episodes in a representative sample of adolescents and young adults. *Psychological Medicine, 31,* 1169–1179.

Haas, H. L., & Clopton, J. R. (2001). Psychology of an eating disorder. In J. J. Robert-McComb (Ed.), *Eating disorders in women and children: Prevention, stress management, and treatment* (pp. 39–48). Boca Raton, FL: CRC Press.

Haberman, M. C., Chapman, L. J., Numbers, J. S., & McFall, R. M. (1979). Relation of social competence to scores on two scales of psychosis proneness. *Journal of Abnormal Psychology, 88,* 675–677.

Habib, M. (2000). The neurological basis of developmental dyslexia: An overview and working hypothesis. *Brain, 123,* 2373–2399.

Hafeiz, H. B. (1980). Hysterical conversion: A prognostic study. *British Journal of Psychiatry, 136,* 548–551.

Häfner, H., an der Heiden, W., Behrens, S., Gattaz, W. F., Hambrecht, M., Löffler, W., Maurer, K., Munk-Jørgensen, P., Nowotny, B., Riecher-Rössler, A., & Stein, A. (1998). Causes and consequences of the gender differences in age at onset of schizophrenia. *Schizophrenia Bulletin, 24,* 99–113.

Hagen, E. H. (1999). The functions of postpartum depression. *Evolution and Human Behavior, 20,* 325–359.

Haggarty, J. M., Cernovsky, Z., & Husni, M. (2001). The limited influence of latitude on rates of seasonal affective disorder. *Journal of Nervous and Mental Disease, 189,* 482–484.

Hall, J. G., Pauli, I., & Wilson, K. M. (1980). Maternal and fetal sequalae of anticoagulation during pregnancy. *American Journal of Medicine, 68,* 122–140.

Halmi, K. A. (2000). Eating disorders. In B. I. Sadock & V. A. Sadock (Eds.), *Kaplan and Sadock's comprehensive textbook of psychiatry* (7th ed., pp. 1663–1677). Baltimore: Lippincott Williams & Wilkins.

Hambrecht, M., Maurer, K., & Haefner, H. (1992). Gender differences in schizophrenia in three cultures: Results of the WHO Collaborative Study on psychiatric disability. *Social Psychiatry and Psychiatric Epidemiology, 27,* 117–121.

Hammen, C. (1991). The generation of stress in the course of unipolar depression. *Journal of Abnormal Psychology, 100,* 555–561.

Hammen, C., & Rudolph, K. D. (1996). Childhood depression. In E. J. Mash & R. A. Barkley (Eds.), *Child psychopathology* (pp. 153–195). New York: Guilford.

Hammen, C., Ellicott, A., & Gitlin, M. (1992). Stressors and sociotropy/autonomy: A longitudinal study of their relationship to the course of bipolar disorder. *Cognitive Therapy and Research, 16,* 409–418.

Han, L., Wang, K., Zhaoyun, D., Cheng, Y., Simons, J. S., & Rosenthal, N. E. (2000). Seasonal variations in mood and behavior among Chinese medical students. *American Journal of Psychiatry, 157,* 133–135.

Haney, C., Banks, C., & Zimbardo, P. (1973). Interpersonal dynamics in a simulated prison. *International Journal of Criminology and Penology, 1,* 69–97.

Hansen, V., Jacobsen, B. K., & Arnesen, E. (2001). Cause-specific mortality in psychiatric patients after deinstitutionalisation. *British Journal of Psychiatry, 179,* 438–443.

Hanson, D. R., & Gottesman, I. I. (1976). The genetics, if any, of infantile autism and childhood schizophrenia. *Journal of Autism and Childhood Schizophrenia, 6,* 209–234.

Hanson, J. W., Myriathopoulos, N. C., Harvey, M. A., & Smith, D. W. (1976). Risks to the offspring of women treated with hydantoin anticonvulsants, with emphasis on the fetal hydantoin syndrome. *Journal of Pediatrics, 89,* 662–668.

Hanson, R. K., & Bussiere, M. T. (1998). Predicting relapse: A meta-analysis of sexual offender recidivism studies. *Journal of Consulting and Clinical Psychology, 66,* 348–362.

Hanson, R. K., Gizzarelli, R., & Scott, H. (1994). The attitudes of incest offenders: Sexual entitlement and acceptance of sex with children. *Criminal Justice and Behavior, 21,* 187–202.

Hare, R. D. (1980). A research scale for the assessment of psychopathy in criminal populations. *Personality and Individual Differences, 1,* 111–117.

Hare, R. D. (1983). Diagnosis of antisocial personality disorder in two prison populations. *American Journal of Psychiatry, 140,* 887–890.

Hare, R. D. (1991*). Manual for the Hare Psychopathy Checklist—Revised.* Toronto, Canada: Multihealth Systems.

Hare, R. D., & Hart, S. D. (1995). Commentary on antisocial personality disorder: The DSM-IV field trial. In W. J. Livesley (Ed.), *The DSM-IV personality disorders* (pp. 127–134). New York: Guilford.

Hare, R. D., Hart, S. D., & Harpur, T. J. (1991). Psychopathy and the proposed DSM-IV criteria for antisocial personality disorder. *Journal of Abnormal Psychology, 100,* 391–398.

Harper, J. M., Schaalje, B. G., & Sandberg, J. G. (2000). Daily hassles, intimacy, and marital quality in later-life marriages. *American Journal of Family Therapy, 28,* 1–18.

Harris, G. T., Rice, M. E., & Quinsey, V. L. (1994). Psychopathy as a taxon: Evidence that psychopaths are a discrete class. *Journal of Consulting and Clinical Psychology, 62,* 387–397.

Harris, S. L. (1975). Teaching language to nonverbal children: With emphasis on problems of generalization. *Psychological Bulletin, 82,* 564–580.

Harris, S. L. (1989). Training parents of children with autism: An update on models. *Behavior Therapist, 12,* 219–221.

Harris, S. L. (1998). Behavioural and educational approaches to the pervasive developmental disorders. In F. R. Volkmar (Ed.), *Autism and pervasive developmental disorders* (pp. 195–208). Cambridge, England: Cambridge University Press.

Harris, S. L., & Handleman, J. S. (2000). Age and IQ at intake as predictors of placement for young children with autism: A four- to six-year follow-up. *Journal of Autism and Developmental Disorders, 30,* 137–142.

Harris, S. L., Handleman, J. S., Gill, M. J., & Fong, P. L. (1991). Does punishment hurt? The impact of aversives on the clinician. *Research in Developmental Disabilities, 12,* 17–24.

Hart, A. B., Craighead, W. E., & Craighead, L. W. (2001). Predicting recurrence of major depressive disorder in young adults: A prospective study. *Journal of Abnormal Psychology, 110,* 633–643.

Hart, G. (1996). Preventing HIV infection in gay men: Help and hindrance. *Sexual and Marital Therapy, 11,* 309–319.

Harter, S. L., & Taylor, T. L. (2000). Parental alcoholism, child abuse, and adult adjustment. *Journal of Substance Abuse, 11,* 31–44.

Hartman, E. (1984). *The nightmare.* New York: Basic Books.

Hartman, W. T. (1992). State funding models for special education. *RASE: Remedial and Special Education, 13*(6), 47–58.

Hartmann, D. P., & Atkinson, C. (1973). Having your cake and eating it too: A note on some apparent contradictions between therapeutic achievements and design requirements in *N*=1 studies. *Behavior Therapy, 4,* 589–591.

Harvey, B. H., & Bouwer, C. D. (2000). Neuropharmacology of paradoxic weight gain with selective serotonin reuptake inhibitors. *Clinical Neuropharmacology, 23,* 90–97.

Harvey, P. D., Weintraub, S., & Neale, J. M. (1985). Span of apprehension deficits in children vulnerable to psychopathology: A failure to replicate. *Journal of Abnormal Psychology, 94,* 410–413.

Harwood, T. M., & Beutler, L. E. (2001). Commentary on Greene and Ablon: What does the MTA study tell us about effective psychosocial treatment for ADHD? *Journal of Clinical Child Psychology, 30,* 141–143.

Hashimoto, T., Tayama, M., Murakawa, K., Yoshimoto, T., Miyazaki, M., Harada, M., & Kuroda, Y. (1995). Development of the brainstem and cerebellum in autistic patients. *Journal of Autism and Developmental Disorders, 25,* 1–18.

Haslam, N., & Beck, A. T. (1994). Subtyping major depression: A taxometric analysis. *Journal of Abnormal Psychology, 103,* 686–692.

Haverkamp, F., Propping, P., & Hilger, T. (1982). Is there an increase of reproductive rates in schizophrenics? I. Critical review of the literature. *Archiv Fuer Psychiatrie und Nervenkrankheiten, 232,* 439–450.

Hawk, B. A., Schroeder, S. R., Robinson, G., Otto, D., Mushak, P., Kleinbaum, D., & Dawson, G. (1986). Relation of lead and social factors to IQ of low-SES children: A partial replication. *Journal of Mental Deficiency, 91,* 178–183.

Head, D., Bolton, D., & Hymas, N. (1989). Deficits in cognitive shifting in obsessive-compulsive disorder. *Biological Psychiatry, 25,* 929–937.

Health Management Technology. (2000, November). The long and winding road. In the Defined Contributions section, p. 39.

Hechtman, L., Weiss, G., & Perlman, T. (1980). Hyperactives as young adults: Self-esteem and social skills. *Canadian Journal of Psychiatry, 25,* 478–483.

Henderson, V. W. (1999). The epidemiology of Alzheimer's disease: The role of estrogen in reducing risk. In R. Mayeux and Y. Christen (Eds.), *Epidemiology of Alzheimer's disease: From gene to prevention* (pp. 49–63). New York: Springer.

Henderson, V. W., Watt, L., & Buckwalter, J. G. (1996). Cognitive skills associated with estrogen replacement in women with Alzheimer's disease. *Psychoneuroendocrinology, 21,* 421–430.

Henriques, J. B., & Davidson, R. J. (1990). Regional brain electrical asymmetries discriminate between previously depressed and healthy control subjects. *Journal of Abnormal Psychology, 99,* 22–31.

Henriques, J. B., & Davidson, R. J. (1991). Left frontal hypoactivation in depression. *Journal of Abnormal Psychology, 100,* 535–545..

Herbert, M. (1998). Adolescent conduct disorders. In P. J. Graham (Ed.), *Cognitive-behaviour therapy for children and families* (pp. 194–216). New York: Cambridge University Press.

Herbert, M. E., & Jacobson, S. (1967). Late paraphrenia. *British Journal of Psychiatry, 113,* 461–469.

Herek, G. M. (2000). The psychology of sexual prejudice. *Current Directions in Psychological Science, 9,* 19–22.

Herman, C. P., & Polivy, J. (1975). Anxiety, restraint, and eating behavior. *Journal of Abnormal Psychology, 84,* 666–672.

Herman, D. (1997). *The antigay agenda: Orthodox vision and the Christian right.* Chicago: University of Chicago Press.

Hermelin, B., & Frith, U. (1971). Psychological studies of childhood autism: Can autistic children make sense of what they see and hear? *Journal of Special Education, 5,* 107–117.

Hernandez, D. E., & Glavin, G. B. (1990). *Neurobiology of stress ulcers.* New York: New York Academy of Sciences.

Hersen, M., & Turner, S. M. (Eds.). (1985). *Diagnostic interviewing.* New York: Plenum.

Hesselbrock, V. M. (1995). The genetic epidemiology of alcoholism. In H. Begleiter & B. Kissin (Eds.), *The genetics of alcoholism* (pp. 17–39). New York: Oxford University Press.

Hesselbrock, V. M., Meyer, R., & Hesselbrock, M. (1992). Psychopathology and addictive disorders: A specific case of antisocial personality disorder. In C. P. O'Brien & J. H. Jaffe (Eds.), *Addictive states* (pp. 179–191). New York: Raven.

Hettema, J. M., Neale, M. C., & Kendler, K. S. (2001a). A review and meta-analysis of the genetic epidemiology of anxiety disorders. *American Journal of Psychiatry, 158,* 1568–1578.

Hettema, J. M., Prescott, C. A., & Kendler, K. S. (2001b). A population-based twin study of generalized anxiety disorder in men and women. *Journal of Nervous and Mental Disease, 189,* 413–420.

Hewitt, P. L., Coren, S., & Steel, G. D. (2001). Death from anorexia nervosa: Age span and sex differences. *Aging and Mental Health, 5,* 41–46.

Hill, A. B., & Knowles, T. H. (1991). Depression and the emotional Stroop effect. *Personality & Individual Differences, 12,* 481–485.

Hillbrand, M., Foster, H., & Hirt, M. (1990). Rapists and child molesters: Psychometric comparisons. *Archives of Sexual Behavior, 19,* 65–71.

Hinshaw, S. P. (1994). Conduct disorder in childhood: Conceptualization, diagnosis, comorbidity, and risk status for antisocial functioning in adulthood. In D. C. Fowles, P. Sutker, & S. H. Goodman (Eds.), *Progress in experimental personality and psychopathology research* (pp. 3–44). New York: Springer.

Hirschfeld, R. M. A., Shea, M. T., & Weise, R. (1995). Dependent personality disorder. In W. J. Livesley (Ed.), *The DSM-IV personality disorders* (pp. 239–256). New York: Guilford.

Hirshkowitz, M., Moore, C. A., & Minhoto, G. (1997). The basics of sleep. In M. R. Pressman & W. C. Orr (Eds.), *Understanding sleep: The evaluation and treatment of sleep disorders* (pp. 11–34). Washington, DC: American Psychological Association.

Hitchcock, P. B., & Mathews, A. (1992). Interpretation of bodily symptoms in hypochondriasis. *Behaviour Research and Therapy, 30,* 223–234.

Hlastala, S. A., Frank, E., Kowalski, J., Sherrill, J. T., Tu, X. M., Anderson, B., & Kupfer, D. J. (2000). Stressful life events, bipolar disorder, and the "kindling model." *Journal of Abnormal Psychology, 109,* 777–786.

Ho, B., & Andreasen, N. C. (2001). Positive symptoms, negative symptoms, and beyond. In A. Breier & P. V. Tran (Eds.), *Current issues in the psychopharmacology of schizophrenia* (pp. 407–416). Philadelphia: Lippincott Williams & Wilkins.

Hobson, R. P. (1989). Beyond cognition: A theory of autism. In G. Dawson (Ed.), *Autism: Nature, diagnosis, and treatment* (pp. 22–48). New York: Guilford.

Hoch, P., & Polatin, P. (1949). Pseudoneurotic forms of schizophrenia. *Psychiatric Quarterly, 23,* 248–276.

Hodapp, R. M., & Zigler, E. (1999). Intellectual development and mental retardation: Some continuing controversies. In M. Anderson (Ed.), *The development of intelligence: Studies in developmental psychology* (pp. 295–308). Hove, England: Psychology Press/Taylor & Francis.

Hoddes, E., Zarcone, V. P., Smythe, H., Phillips, R., & Dement, W. C. (1973). Quantification of sleepiness: A new approach. *Psychophysiology, 10,* 431–436.

Hodgins, G. A., Creamer, M., & Bell, R. (2001). Risk factors for post-trauma reactions in police officers: A longitudinal study. *Journal of Nervous and Mental Disease, 189,* 541–547.

Hoehn-Saric, R., McLeod, D. R., & Zimmerli, W. D. (1989). Somatic manifestations in women with generalized anxiety disorder: Psychophysiological responses to physiological stress. *Archives of General Psychiatry, 46,* 1113–1119.

Hoehn-Saric, R., Pearson, G. D., Harris, G. J., Machlin, S. R., & Camargo, E. E. (1991). Effects of fluoxetine on regional cerebral blood flow in obsessive-compulsive patients. *American Journal of Psychiatry, 148,* 1243–1245.

Hoekstra-Weebers, J. E. H. M., Jaspers, J. P. C., Kamps, W. A., & Klip, E. C. (2001). Psychological adaptation and social support of parents of pediatric cancer patients: A prospective longitudinal study. *Journal of Pediatric Psychology, 26,* 225–235.

Hoffer, A., & Foster, H. D. (2000). Why schizophrenics smoke but have a lower incidence of lung cancer: Implications for the treatment of both disorders. *Journal of Orthomolecular Medicine, 15,* 141–144.

Hoffman, M. L. (1970). Moral development. In P. H. Mussen (Ed.), *Carmichael's manual of child psychology,* Vol. II (pp. 261–359). London: Wiley.

Hoffman, R. E., Rapaport, J., Mazure, C. M., & Quinlan, D. M. (1999). Selective speech perception alterations in schizophrenia patients reporting hallucinated "voices." *American Journal of Psychiatry, 156,* 393–399.

Hofmann, S. G., & Barlow, D. H. (2002). Social phobias (social anxiety disorder). In D. H. Barlow (Ed.), *Anxiety and its disorders: The nature and treatment of anxiety and panic* (2nd ed., pp. 454–476). New York: Guilford.

Hofstede, G. (1998). Comparative studies of sexual behavior: Sex as achievement or as relationship? In G. Hofstede (Ed.), *Masculinity and femininity: The taboo dimension of national cultures* (pp. 153–178). Thousand Oaks, CA: Sage.

Hogan, C. M. (1993). *Substance abuse: The nation's number one health problem. Key indicators for policy.* Princeton, NJ: Robert Wood Johnson Foundation.

Holinger, P. C., & Offer, D. (1991). Sociodemographic, epidemiologic, and individual attributes. In L. Davidson & M. Linnoila (Eds.), *Risk factors for youth suicide* (pp. 3–17). New York: Hemisphere.

Holinger, P. C., Offer, D., Barter, J. T., & Bell, C. C. (1994). *Suicide and homicide among adolescents.* New York: Guilford.

Hollander, E. (1991). Serotonergic drugs and the treatment of disorders related to obsessive-compulsive disorder. In M. T. Pato, & J. Zohar (Eds.), *Current treatments of obsessive-compulsive disorder* (pp. 173–191). Washington, DC: American Psychiatric Press.

Hollander, E. (1993). Introduction. In E. Hollander (Ed.), *Obsessive-compulsive related disorders* (pp. 1–16). Washington, DC: American Psychiatric Association.

Hollander, E., & Rosen, J. (2000). Impulsivity. *Journal of Psychopharmacology, 14,* S39–S44.

Hollander, E., Stein, D. J., DeCaria, C. M., Cohen, L., Saoud, J. B., Skodol, A. E., Kellman, D., Rosnick, L., & Oldham, J. M. (1994). Serotonergic sensitivity in borderline personality disorder: Preliminary findings. *American Journal of Psychiatry, 151,* 277–280.

Hollifield, M., Katon, W., Spain, D., & Pule, L. (1990). Anxiety and depression in a village in Lesotho, Africa: A comparison with the United States. *British Journal of Psychiatry, 156,* 343–350.

Hollinghead, A. B. (1957). Two-factor index of social position. Unpublished manuscript.

Hollingshead, A. B., & Redlich, F. C. (1958). *Social class and mental illness: A community study.* New York: Wiley.

Hollon, S. D. (1996). The efficacy and effectiveness of psychotherapy relative to medications. *American Psychologist, 51,* 1025–1030.

Hollon, S. D., & Beck, A. T. (1994). Cognitive and cognitive behavioral therapies. In S. L. Garfield & A. E. Bergin (Eds.), *Handbook of psychotherapy and behavioral change* (4th ed., pp. 428–466). New York: Wiley.

Hollon, S. D., DeRubeis, R. J., & Seligman, M. E. P. (1992). Cognitive therapy and the prevention of depression. *Applied and Preventive Psychology, 1,* 89–95.

Holm, A., Dodd, B., Stow, C., & Pert, S. (1999). Identification and differential diagnosis of phonological disorder in bilingual children. *Language Testing, 16,* 271–292.

Holmes, D. S. (1974). Investigations of repression: Differential recall of material experimentally or naturally associated with ego threat. *Psychological Bulletin, 81,* 632–653.

Holmes, D. S. (1978). Projection as a defense mechanism. *Psychological Bulletin, 85,* 677–688.

Holmes, T. H., & Rahe, R. H. (1967). The social readjustment rating scale. *Journal of Psychosomatic Research, 11,* 213–218. Reprinted in 1989 in T. H. Holmes & E. M. David (Eds.), *Life change, life events, and illness: Selected papers.* New York: Praeger.

Holmes, V. F., & Rich, C. L. (1990). Suicide among physicians. In S. J. Blumenthal & D. J. Kupfer (Eds.), *Suicide over the life cycle: Risk factors, assessment, and treatment of suicidal patients* (pp. 599–618). Washington, DC: American Psychiatric Press.

Holzman, P. S. (1975). Smooth pursuit eye movements in schizophrenia: Recent findings. In D. X. Freedman (Ed.), *Biology of major psychosis* (pp. 217–228). New York: Raven Press.

Holzman, P. S. (2000). Eye movements and the search for the essence of schizophrenia. *Brain Research Reviews, 31,* 350–356.

Honkonen, T., Saarinen, S., & Salokangas, R. K. R. (1999). Deinstitutionalization and schizophrenia in Finland: II. Discharged patients and their psychosocial functioning. *Schizophrenia Bulletin, 25,* 543–551.

Hope, D. A., & Heimberg, R. G. (1993). Social phobia and social anxiety. In D. H. Barlow (Ed.), *Clinical handbook of psychological disorders* (2nd ed., pp. 99–136). New York: Guilford.

Horne, A. D. (Ed.). (1981). *The wounded generation: America after Vietnam.* Englewood Cliffs, NJ: Prentice-Hall.

Horney, K. (1937). *The neurotic personality of our time.* New York: Norton.

Horowitz, M. J. (1986). Stress-response syndromes: A review of posttraumatic and adjustment disorders. *Hospital and Community Psychiatry, 28,* 354–363.

Horwath, E., & Weissman, M. M. (2000). Anxiety disorders: Epidemiology. In B. I. Sadock & V. A. Sadock (Eds.), *Kaplan & Sadock's comprehensive textbook of psychiatry* (7th ed., pp. 1444–1450). Philadelphia: Lippincott Williams & Wilkins.

Howard, J. H., Rechnitzer, P. A., Cunningham, D. A., & Donner, A. P. (1986). Change in Type A behavior a year after retirement. *Gerontologist, 26,* 643–649.

Howell, J., Hill, A., Dean, E., & Waters, D. (1993). Increasing metalinguistic awareness to assist phonological change. In D. J. Messer & G. J. Turner (Eds.), *Critical influences on child language acquisition and development* (pp. 209–228). New York: St Martin's.

Howlin, P. (1997). *Autism: Preparing for adulthood.* London: Routledge.

Howlin, P., & Goode, S. (1998). Outcome in adult life for people with autism and Asperger's syndrome. In F. R. Volkmar (Ed.), *Autism and pervasive developmental disorders* (pp. 209–241). Cambridge, England: Cambridge University Press.

Hsu, L. K. (1988). The outcome of anorexia nervosa: A reappraisal. *Psychological Medicine, 18,* 807–812.

Hsu, L. K. G. (1990). *Eating disorders.* New York: Guilford.

Hublin, C., Kaprio, J., Partinen, M., & Koskenvuo, M. (1999). Limits of self-report in assessing sleep terrors in a population survey. *Sleep, 22,* 89–93.

Hudson, C. G., Salloway, J. C., & Vissing, Y. M. (1992). The impact of state administrative practices on community mental health. *Administration and Policy in Mental Health, 19,* 417–436.

Hudson, J. I., Pope, H. G., Jonas, J. M., & Yurgelun-Todd, D. (1983). Family history study of anorexia nervosa and bulimia. *British Journal of Psychiatry, 142,* 133–138.

Hudson, S. M., & Ward, T. (1997). Rape: Psychopathology and theory. In D. R. Laws & W. O'Donohue (Eds.), *Sexual deviance* (pp. 332–355). New York: Guilford.

Hudziak, J. J. (2000). Genetics of attention-deficit/hyperactivity disorder. In T. E. Brown (Ed.), *Attention deficit disorders and comorbidities in children, adolescents, and adults* (pp. 57–78). Washington, DC: American Psychiatric Press.

Hudziak, J. J., Heath, A. C., Madden, P. F., Reich, W., Bucholz, K. K., Slutske, W., Bierut, L. J., Neuman, R. J., & Todd, R. D. (1998). Latent class and factor analysis of DSM-IV ADHD: A twin study of female adolescents. *Journal of the American Academy of Child and Adolescent Psychiatry, 37,* 848–857.

Huesmann, L. R. (1997). Observational learning of violent behavior: Social and biosocial processes. In A. Raine, P. A. Brennan, & D. P. Farrington (Eds.), *Biosocial bases of violence* (pp. 69–88). New York: Plenum.

Hugdahl, K., Frederickson, M., & Ohman, A. (1977). Preparedness and arousability determinants of electrodermal conditioning. *Behavior Research and Therapy, 15,* 345–353.

Hugdahl, K., Iversen, P. M., & Johnsen, B. H. (1993). Laterality for facial expressions: Does the sex of the subject interact with the sex of the stimulus faces? *Cortex, 29,* 325–331.

Hughes, J. R. (2000). Nicotine-related disorders. In B. I. Sadock & V. A. Sadock (Eds.), *Kaplan & Sadock's comprehensive textbook of psychiatry* (7th ed., pp. 1033–1038). Philadelphia: Lippincott Williams & Wilkins.

Hull, J. G., & Bond, C. F. (1986). Social and behavioral consequences of alcohol consumption and expectancy: A meta-analysis. *Psychological Bulletin, 99,* 347–360.

Hulter, B., Berne, C., & Lundberg, P. O. (1998). Sexual function in women with insulin dependent diabetes mellitus. *Scandinavian Journal of Sexology, 1,* 43–50.

Humphreys, K., & Kaskutas, L. A. (1995). World views of Alcoholics Anonymous, Women for Sobriety, and Adult Children of Alcoholics/Al-Anon mutual help groups. *Addiction Research, 3,* 231–243.

Hunt, M. (1993). *The story of psychology.* New York: Doubleday.

Hunter, J. A., & Mathews, R. (1997). Sexual deviance in females. In D. R. Laws & W. O'Donohue (Eds.), *Sexual deviance: Theory, assessment, and treatment* (pp. 465–480). New York: Guilford.

Hunter, R. A., & Macalpine, I. (1963). *Three hundred years of psychiatry: 1535–1860.* London: Oxford University Press.

Hurford, D. M. (1998). *To read or not to read: Answers to all your questions about dyslexia.* New York: Scribner/Simon & Schuster.

Hutchinson, M. K., & Sandall, S. R. (1995). Congenital TORCH infections in infants and young children: Neurodevelopmental sequelae and implications for intervention. *Topics in Early Childhood Special Education, 15,* 65–82.

Hyman, D. J., Ogbonnaya, K., Taylor, A. A., Ho, K., & Pavlik, V. N. (2000). Ethnic differences in nocturnal blood pressure decline in treated hypertensives. *American Journal of Hypertension, 13,* 884–891.

Idzikowski, C. (1984). Sleep and memory. *British Journal of Psychology, 75,* 439–449.

Ikonomov, O. C., & Manji, H. K. (1999). Molecular mechanisms underlying mood stabilization in manic-depressive illness: The phenotype challenge. *American Journal of Psychiatry, 156,* 1506–1514.

Ilgen, D. R., & Bell, B. S. (2001). Informed consent and dual purpose research. *American Psychologist, 56,* 1177.

Inouye, S. K., Bogardus, S. T., Jr., Charpentier, P. A., Leo-Summers, L., Acampora, D., Holford, T. R., & Cooney, L. M., Jr. (1999). A multi-component intervention to prevent delirium in hospitalized older patients. *New England Journal of Medicine, 340,* 669–676.

Insel, T. R. (1992). Toward a neuroanatomy of obsessive-compulsive disorder. *Archives of General Psychiatry, 49,* 739–744.

Insel, T. R., Donnelly, E. G., Lalakea, M. L., Alterman, I. S., & Murphy, D. L. (1983). Neurological and neuropsychological studies of patients with obsessive-compulsive disorder. *Biological Psychiatry, 18,* 741–751.

Insel, T. R., et al. (1981). Obsessive-compulsive disorder: A double-blind trial of clomipramine and clorgyline. *Archives of General Psychiatry, 40,* 605–612.

Irle, E., Exher, C., Thieleu, K., Weniger, G., & Rúther, E. (1998). Obsessive-compulsive disorder and ventromedial frontal lesions: Clinical and neuropsychological findings. *American Journal of Psychiatry, 155,* 255–263.

Irving, L. M., Seidner, A. L., Burling, T. A., Pagliarini, R., & Robbins-Sisco, D. (1998). Hope and recovery from substance dependence in homeless veterans. *Journal of Social and Clinical Psychology, 17,* 389–406.

Irwin, C., Falsetti, S. A., Lydiard, R. B., & Ballenger, J. C. (1996). Comorbidity of posttraumatic stress disorder and irritable bowel syndrome. *Journal of Clinical Psychiatry, 57,* 576–578.

Isay, R. A. (1998). Heterosexually married homosexual men: Clinical and developmental issues. *American Journal of Orthopsychiatry, 68,* 424–432.

Isometsä, E. T., & Löennqvist, J. K. (1998). Suicide attempts preceding completed suicides. *British Journal of Psychiatry, 173,* 531–538.

Ivancevich, J. M. (1986). Life events and hassles as predictors of health symptoms, job performance, and absenteeism. *Journal of Occupational Behaviour, 7,* 39–51.

Ivis, F. J., & Adlaf, E. M. (1999). A comparison of trends in drug use among students in the USA and Ontario, Canada: 1975–1997. *Drugs—Education, Prevention, and Policy, 6,* 17–27.

Ivonov, L. L., & Flynn, B. C. (1999). Utilization and satisfaction with prenatal care services. *Western Journal of Nursing Research, 21,* 372–386.

Jackson v. Indiana. (1972). 406 U.S. 715.

Jackson, T. L., & Petretic-Jackson, P. A. (1996). Introduction: The definition, incidence, and scope of acquaintance rape and sexual assault. In T. L. Jackson (Ed.), *Acquaintance rape: Assessment, treatment, and prevention* (pp. 1–15). Sarasota, FL: Professional Resource Press.

Jacob, T., & Johnson, S. L. (1999). Family influences on alcohol and substance abuse. In P. J. Ott & R. E. Tarter (Eds.), *Sourcebook on substance abuse: Etiology, epidemiology, assessment, and treatment* (pp. 166–174). Boston: Allyn & Bacon.

Jacobsen, L. K., Southwick, S. M., & Kosten, T. R. (2001). Substance use disorders in patients with posttraumatic stress disorder: A review of the literature. *American Journal of Psychiatry, 158,* 1184–1190.

Jacobson, E. (1939). *Progressive relaxation.* Chicago: University of Chicago Press.

Jacobson, N. S., Fruzzetti, A. E., Dobson, K., Whisman, M., & Hobs, H. (1993). Couple therapy as a treatment for depression. 2.: The effects of relationship quality and therapy on depressive relapse. *Journal of Consulting and Clinical Psychology, 61,* 516–519.

Jacobson, N. S., Holzworth-Monroe, A., & Schmaling, K. B. (1989). Marital therapy and spouse involvement in the treatment of depression, agoraphobia, and alcoholism. *Journal of Consulting and Clinical Psychology, 57,* 5–10.

Jacoby, L. L. (1983). Remembering the data: Analyzing interactive processes in reading. *Journal of Verbal Learning and Verbal Behavior, 17,* 649–667.

Jacoby, L. L., Lindsay, D. S., & Toth, J. P. (1992). Unconscious influences revealed: Attention, awareness, and control. *American Psychologist, 47,* 802–809.

Jacques, A., & Jackson, G. A. (2000). *Understanding dementia.* Edinberg, England: Churchill Livingstone.

Jaeger, E., Hahn, N. B., & Weinraub, M. (2000). Attachment in adult daughters of alcoholic fathers. *Addiction, 95,* 267–276.

Jaffe, J. H. (2000a). Cocaine-related disorders. In B. I. Sadock & V. A. Sadock (Eds.), *Kaplan & Sadock's comprehensive textbook of psychiatry* (7th ed., pp. 999–1015). Philadelphia: Lippincott Williams & Wilkins.

Jaffe, J. H. (2000b). Amphetamine (or amphetamine-like)-related disorders. In B. I. Sadock & V. A. Sadock (Eds.), *Kaplan & Sadock's comprehensive textbook of psychiatry* (7th ed., pp. 971–982). Philadelphia: Lippincott Williams & Wilkins.

Jaffe, J. H., & Jaffe, A. B. (2000). Opioid-related disorders. In B. I. Sadock & V. A. Sadock (Eds.), *Kaplan & Sadock's comprehensive textbook of psychiatry* (7th ed., pp. 1038–1063). Philadelphia: Lippincott Williams & Wilkins.

Jamison, K. R. (1992). *Touched with fire: Manic depressive illness and the artistic temperament.* New York: Free Press.

Jamison, K. R. (1996). Mood disorders, creativity and the artistic temperament. In J. J. Schildkraut & A. Otero (Eds.), *Depression and the spiritual in modern art: Homage to Miro* (pp. 15–32). Oxford, England: Wiley.

Janoff-Bulman, R. (1995). Victims of violence. In G. S. Everly, Jr. & J. M. Lating (Eds.), *Psychotraumatology: Key papers and core concepts in post-traumatic stress* (pp. 73–86). New York: Plenum Press.

Janowsky, D. S., Addario, D., & Risch, S. C. (1987). *Psychopharmacology case studies* (2nd ed.). New York: Guilford.

Jansson, L. M., Svikis, D., Lee, J., Paluzzi, P., Rutigliano, P., & Hackerman, F. (1996). Pregnancy and addiction: A comprehensive care model. *Journal of Substance Abuse Treatment, 13,* 321–329.

Janus, E. S. (2000). Sex predator commitment laws: Constitutional but unwise. *Psychiatric Annals, 30,* 411–420.

Janus, S. S., & Janus, C. L. (1993). *The Janus report on sexual behavior.* New York: Wiley.

Jaselskis, C. A., Cook, E. H., Jr., Fletcher, K. E., & Leventhal, B. L. (1992). Clonidine treatment of hyperactive and impulsive children with autistic disorder. *Journal of Clinical Psychopharmacology, 12,* 322–327.

Jason, L. A., McMahon, S. D., Salina, D., Hedeker, D., Stockton, M., Dunson, K., & Kimball, P. (1995). Assessing a smoking cessation intervention involving groups, incentives, and self-help manuals. *Behavior Therapy, 26,* 393–408.

Jasper, H. H. (1995). A historical perspective: The rise and fall of prefrontal lobotomy. In H. H. Jasper & S. Riggio (Eds.), *Epilepsy and the functional anatomy of the frontal lobe* (pp. 97–114). *Advances in neurology* (Vol. 66). New York: Raven Press.

Jefferson, J. W., & Greist, J. H. (1989). Lithium therapy. In H. I. Kaplan & B. J. Sadock (Eds.), *Comprehensive textbook of psychiatry* (5th ed., pp. 1655–1662). Baltimore: Williams & Wilkins.

Jellinek, E. M. (1952). Phases of alcohol addiction. *Quarterly Journal of Studies on Alcohol, 13,* 673–684.

Jellinek, E. M. (1960). *The disease concept of alcohol.* New Brunswick, NJ: Hillhouse Press.

Jenike, M. A., Baer, L., & Minichiello, W. E. (1986). *Obsessive-compulsive disorders: Theory and management.* Littleton, MA: PSG Publishing.

Jenike, M. A., Baer, L., Summergrad, P., Weilburg, J. B., Holland, A., & Seymour, R. (1989). Obsessive-compulsive disorder: A double-blind, placebo controlled trial of clomipramine in 27 patients. *American Journal of Psychiatry, 146,* 1328–1330.

Jenkins, J. H., Kleinman, A., & Good, B. J. (1991). Cross-cultural studies of depression. In J. Becker & A. Kleinman (Eds.), *Psychosocial aspects of depression* (pp. 67–99). Hillsdale, NJ: Erlbaum.

Jensen, P. S., Hinshaw, S. P., Swanson, J. M., Greenhill, L. L., Conners, C. K., Arnold, L. E., Abikoff, H. B., Elliott, G., Hechtman, L., Hoza, B., March, J. S., Newcorn, J. H., Severe, J. B., Vitiello, B., Wells, K., & Wigal, T. (2001). Findings from the NIMH Multimodal Treatment Study of ADHD (MTA): Implications and applications for primary care providers. *Journal of Developmental and Behavioral Pediatrics, 22,* 60–73.

Jeong, J., Kim, D., Kim, S. Y., Chae, J., Go, H. J., & Kim, K. (2001). Effect of total sleep deprivation on the dimensional complexity of the waking EEG. *Sleep, 24,* 197–202.

Jessor, R., & Jessor, S. L. (1977). *Problem behavior and psychosocial development: A longitudinal study of youth.* New York: Academic Press.

Jockers-Scheruebl, M. C., Godemann, F., & Pietzcker, A. (2001). Negative symptoms of schizophrenia are improved by paroxetine added to neuroleptics: A pilot study. *Journal of Clinical Psychiatry, 62,* 573.

Johnson, B. (2000). Using video vignettes to evaluate children's personal safety knowledge: Methodological and ethical issues. *Child Abuse and Neglect, 24,* 811–827.

Johnson, J., Weissman, M. M., & Klerman, G. I. (1990). Panic disorder, comorbidity and suicide attempts. *Archives of General Psychiatry, 47,* 805–808.

Johnson, R. E., Jaffe, J. H., & Fudala, P. G. (1992). A controlled trial of buprenorphine treatment for opioid dependence. *Journal of the American Medical Association, 267,* 2750–2755.

Johnson, S. L., & Roberts, J. R. (1995). Life events and bipolar disorder: Implications from biological theories. *Psychological Bulletin, 117,* 434–449.

Johnson, S. L., Winett, C. A., Meyer, B., & Miller, I. (1999). Social support and the course of bipolar disorder. *Journal of Abnormal Psychology, 108,* 558–566.

Johnston, D. W. (1997). Cardiovascular disease. In D. M. Clark & C. G. Fairburn (Eds.), *Science and practice of cognitive behaviour therapy* (pp. 341–358). New York: Oxford University Press.

Johnston, L. D., O'Malley, P. M., & Bachman, J. G. (1992). *Smoking, drinking, and illicit drug use among American secondary school students, college students, and young adults, 1975–1991: Vol. 2. College students and young adults.* Rockville, MD: U.S. Department of Health and Human Services, National Institute on Drug Abuse.

Johnston, L. D., O'Malley, P. M., & Bachman, J. G. (2001). *Monitoring the future: National survey results on drug use, 1975–2000.* Vol. I: *Secondary school students* (NIH Publication No. 01-4924). Bethesda, MD: National Institute on Drug Abuse.

Jonas, S. J. (2000). *Talking about health and wellness with patients: Integrating health promotion and disease prevention into your practice.* New York: Springer.

Jones, M. E., Russell, R. L., & Bryant, F. B. (1998). The structure of rape attitudes for men and woman: A three-factor model. *Journal of Research in Personality, 32,* 331–350.

Jones, R. (1980). Human effects: An overview. In R. Peterson (Ed.), *Marijuana Research Findings* (pp. 54–80). (NIDA Research Monograph No. 31). Washington, DC: U.S. Government Printing Office.

Jones, S. E., Oeltmann, J., Wilson, T. W., Brener, N. D., & Hill, C. V. (2001). Binge drinking among undergraduate college students in the United States: Implications for other substance use. *Journal of American College Health, 50,* 33–38.

Joormann, J., & Stoeber, J. (1999). Somatic symptoms of generalized anxiety disorder for the DSM-IV: Associations with pathological worry and depression symptoms in a nonclinical sample. *Journal of Anxiety Disorders, 13,* 491–503.

Jorm, A. F. (1991). Cross-national comparisons of the occurrence of Alzheimer's and vascular dementias. *European Archives of Psychiatry and Clinical Neuroscience, 240,* 218–222.

Jorm, A. F., Henderson, A. S., Jacomb, P. A., Christensen, H., Korten, A. E., Rodgers, B., Tan, X., & Easteal, S. (2000). Association of a functional polymorphism of the monoamine oxidase A gene promoter with personality and psychiatric symptoms. *Psychiatric Genetics, 10,* 87–90.

Jouriles, E. N., Pfiffner, L. J., & O'Leary, S. G. (1988). Marital conflict, parenting, and toddler conduct problems. *Journal of Abnormal Child Psychology, 16,* 197–206.

Junginger, J. (1997). Fetishism: Assessment and treatment. In D. R. Laws & W. O'Donohue (Eds.), *Sexual deviance: Theory, assessment, and treatment* (pp. 92–110). New York: Guilford.

Junginger, J., & Rauscher, F. P. (1987). Vocal activity in verbal hallucinations. *Journal of Psychiatric Research, 21,* 101–109.

Kaemingk, K., & Paquette, A. (1999). Effects of prenatal alcohol exposure on neuropsychological functioning. *Developmental Neuropsychology, 15,* 111–140.

Kafka, M. P. (1991). Successful antidepressant treatment of nonparaphilic sexual addictions and paraphilias in men. *Journal of Clinical Psychiatry, 52,* 60–65.

Kafka, M. P., & Prentky, R. (1992). Fluoxetine treatment of nonparaphilic sexual addictions and paraphilias in men. *Journal of Clinical Psychiatry, 53,* 351–358.

Kafka, M. P., & Prentky, R. (1994). Preliminary observations of DSM-III-R axis I comorbidity in men with paraphilias and paraphilia-related disorders. *Journal of Clinical Psychiatry, 55,* 481–487.

Kaji, L. (1960). *Alcoholism in twins.* Stockholm: Almquist and Wiksell.

Kalat, J. W. (2001). *Biological psychology* (7th ed.). Belmont, CA: Wadsworth/Thomson Learning

Kalichman, S. C. (1999). *Mandated reporting of suspected child abuse: Ethics, law, and policy* (2nd ed.). Washington, DC: American Psychological Association.

Kalinowski, L. B. (1982). The history of electroconvulsive therapy. In R. Abrams & W. B. Essman (Eds.), *Electroconvulsive therapy: Biological foundations and clinical applications* (pp. 1–5). New York: SP Medical & Scientific Books.

Kallman, F. J. (1938). *The genetics of schizophrenia.* New York: Augustin.

Kalman, D., Longabaugh, R., Clifford, P. R., Beattie, M., & Maisto, S. A. (2000). Matching alcoholics to treatment: Failure to replicate findings of an earlier study. *Journal of Substance Abuse Treatment, 19,* 183–187.

Kalus, O., Bernstein, D. P., & Siever, L. J. (1995). Schizoid personality disorder. In W. J. Livesley (Ed.), *The DSM-IV personality disorders* (pp. 58–70). New York: Guilford.

Kanarek, R. B., Mandillo, S., & Wiatr, C. (2001). Chronic sucrose intake augments antinociception induced by injections of mu but not kappa opioid receptor agonists into the periaqueductal gray matter in male and female rats. *Brain Research, 920,* 97–105.

Kandel, D. B. (2000). Gender differences in the epidemiology of substance dependence in the United States. In E. Frank (Ed.), *Gender and its effects on psychopathology* (pp. 231–252). Washington, DC: American Psychiatric Press.

Kandel, D. B., & Andrews, K. (1987). Processes of adolescent socialization by parents and peers. *International Journal of the Addictions, 22,* 319–342.

Kandel, D. B., Davies, M., Karus, D., & Yamaguchi, K. (1986). The consequences in young adulthood of adolescent drug involvement. *Archives of General Psychiatry, 43,* 746–754.

Kane, J. M., Gunduz, H., & Malhotra, A. K. (2001). Clozapine. In A. Breier & P. V. Tran (Eds.), *Current issues in the psychopharmacology of schizophrenia* (pp. 209–223). Philadelphia: Lippincott Williams & Wilkins.

Kane, J. M., Honigfeld, G., Singer, J., & Meltzer, H. (1988). Clozapine for the treatment-resistant schizophrenic: A double-blind comparison with chlorpromazine. *Archives of General Psychiatry, 45,* 789–796.

Kane, J. M., Marder, S. R., Schooler, N. R., Wirshing, W. C., Umbricht, D., Baker, R. W., Wirshing, D. A., Safferman, A., Ganguli, R., McMeniman, M., & Borenstein, M. (2001). Clozapine and haloperidol in moderately refractory schizophrenia: A 6-month randomized double-blind comparison. *Archives of General Psychiatry, 58,* 965–972.

Kanner, A. D., Coyne, J. C., Schaefer, C., & Lazarus, R. S. (1981). Comparison of two modes of stress measurement: Daily hassles and uplifts versus major life events. *Journal of Behavioral Medicine, 4,* 1–39.

Kanner, L. (1943). Autistic disturbances of affective contact. *Nervous Child, 2,* 217–250.

Kansas v. Hendricks. 117 S. Ct. 2072 (1997).

Kantor, G. K. (1993). Refining the brushstrokes in portraits of alcohol and wife assaults. In S. E. Martin (Ed.), *Alcohol and interpersonal violence: Fostering multidisciplinary perspectives* (NIAAA Research Monograph #24, pp. 280–290). Rockville, MD: U.S. Department of Health and Human Services.

Kaplan, D. S., Masand, P. S., & Gupta, S. (1996). The relationship of irritable bowel syndrome (IBS) and panic disorder. *Annals of Clinical Psychiatry, 8,* 81–88.

Kaplan, H. S. (1974). *The new sex therapy.* New York: Brunner/Mazel.

Kaplan, H. S. (1977). Hypoactive sexual desire. *Journal of Sex and Marital Therapy, 3,* 3–10.

Kaplan, H. S. (1979). *Disorders of sexual desire.* New York: Brunner/Mazel.

Kaplan, H. S. (1987a). *The illustrated manual of sex therapy* (2nd ed.). New York: Brunner/Mazel.

Kaplan, H. S. (1987b). *Sexual aversion, sexual phobias and panic disorder.* New York: Brunner/Mazel.

Kaplan, H. S. (1997). Sexual desire disorders (hypoactive sexual desire and sexual aversion). In G. O. Gabbard & S. D. Atkinson (Eds.), *Synopsis of treatments of psychiatric disorders* (2nd ed., pp. 771–780). Washington, DC: American Psychiatric Press.

Kaplan, M. S., & Krueger, R. B. (1997). Voyeurism: Psychopathology and theory. In D. R. Laws & W. O'Donohue (Eds.), *Sexual deviance: Theory, assessment, and treatment* (pp. 297–310). New York: Guilford.

Kapur, N. (1997). How can we best explain retrograde amnesia in human memory disorder? In A. R. Mayes and J. J. Downes (Eds.), *Theories of organic amnesia* (pp. 115–129). Hove, England: Psychology Press/Erlbaum.

Karlawish, J. H. T., & Casarett, D. (2001). Addressing the ethical challenges of clinical trials that involve patients with dementia. *Journal of Geriatric Psychiatry and Neurology, 14,* 222–228.

Karwautz, A., Rabe-Hesketh, S., Hu, X., Zhao, J., Sham, P., Collier, D. A., & Treasure, J. L. (2001). Individual-specific risk factors for anorexia nervosa: A pilot study using a discordant sister-pair design. *Psychological Medicine, 31,* 317–329.

Kashima, H., Kato, M., Yoshimasu, H., & Muramatsu, T. (1999). Current trends in cognitive rehabilitation for memory disorders. *Keio Journal of Medicine, 48,* 79–86.

Kass, F., Spitzer, R. L., & Williams, J. B. W. (1983). An empirical study of the issue of sex bias in the diagnostic criteria of DSM-III Axis II personality disorders. *American Psychologist, 38,* 799–801.

Katel, P., & Beck, M. (1996). Sick kid or sick mom? *Newsweek,* March 29, 73.

Katerndahl, D. A., & Realini, J. P. (1993). Lifetime prevalence of panic states. *American Journal of Psychiatry, 150,* 246–249.

Katz, M. M., Marsella, A., Dube, K. C., Olatawura, M. et al. (1988). On the expression of psychosis in different cultures: Schizophrenia in an Indian and in a Nigerian community: A report from the World Health Organization project on the determinants of outcome of severe mental disorders. *Culture, Medicine, and Psychiatry, 12,* 331–355.

Katz, R., & McGuffin, P. (1993). The genetics of affective disorders. In L. J. Chapman, J. P. Chapman, & D. C. Fowles (Eds.), *Progress in experimental personality and psychopathology research* (Vol. 16, pp. 200–221). New York: Springer.

Katzman, M. A., & Lee, S. (1997). Beyond body image: The integration of feminist and transcultural theories in the understanding of self starvation. *International Journal of Eating Disorders, 22*, 385–394.

Katzman, R., & Fox, P. J. (1999). The world-wide impact of dementia: Projections of prevalence and costs. In R. Mayeux and Y. Christen (Eds.), *Epidemiology of Alzheimer's disease: From gene to prevention* (pp. 1–17). New York: Springer.

Kawas, C. H. (1999). Inflammation, anti-inflammatory drugs, and Alzheimer's disease. In R. Mayeux and Y. Christen (Eds.), *Epidemiology of Alzheimer's disease: From gene to prevention* (pp. 65–72). New York: Springer.

Kaye, W. H. (1992). Neuropeptide abnormalities. In K. Halmi (Ed.), *Psychobiology and treatment of anorexia and bulimia nervosa* (pp. 169–192). Washington, DC: American Psychiatric Press.

Kaye, W. H., Greenco, C. G., Moss, H., Fernstrom, J., Fernstrom, M., Lilenfeld, L. R., Weltz, T. E., & Mann, J. (1998). Alterations in serotonin activity and psychiatric symptoms after recovery from bulimia nervosa. *Archives of General Psychiatry, 55*, 927–935.

Kaye, W. H., Klump, K. L., Frank, G. K. W., & Strober, M. (2000a). Anorexia and bulimia nervosa. *Annual Review of Medicine, 51*, 299–313.

Kaye, W. H., Lilenfeld, L. R., Berrettini, W. H., Strober, M., Devlin, B., Klump, K. L., Goldman, D., Bulik, C. M., Halmi, K. A., Fichter, M. M., Kaplan, A., Woodside, D. B., Treasure, J., Plotnicov, K. H., Pollice, C., Rao, R., & McConaha, C. W. (2000b). A search for susceptibility loci for anorexia nervosa: Methods and sample description. *Biological Psychiatry, 47*, 794–803.

Kaye, W. H., Nagata, T., Weltzin, T. E., Hsu, L. K. G., Sokol, M. S., McConaha, C., Plotnicov, K. H., Weise, J., & Deep, D. (2001). Double-blind placebo-controlled administration of fluoxetine in restricting- and restricting-purging-type anorexia nervosa. *Biological Psychiatry, 49*, 644–652.

Keane, T. M., & Barlow, D. H. (2002). Posttraumatic stress disorder. In D. H. Barlow (Ed.), *Anxiety and its disorders: The nature and treatment of anxiety and panic* (2nd ed., pp. 418–453). New York: Guilford.

Keefe, R. S. E., Arnold, M. C., Bayen, U. J., & Harvey, P. D. (1999a). Source monitoring deficits in patients with schizophrenia; a multinomial modeling analysis. *Psychological Medicine, 29*, 903–914.

Keefe, R. S. E., Silva, S. G., Perkins, D. O., & Lieberman, J. A. (1999b). The effects of atypical antipsychotic drugs on neurocognitive impairment in schizophrenia: A review and meta-analysis. *Schizophrenia Bulletin, 25*, 201–222.

Keel, P. K., & Mitchell, J. E. (1997). Outcome in bulimia nervosa. *American Journal of Psychiatry, 154*, 313–321.

Keel, P. K., Mitchell, J. E., Davis, T. L., & Crow, S. J. (2001). Relationship between depression and body dissatisfaction in women diagnosed with bulimia nervosa. *International Journal of Eating Disorders, 30*, 48–56.

Keeling, C. (1997). Multidisciplinary NSF document supports evolution. *Reports of the National Center for Science Education, 17*(2), 27.

Kellner, R. (1991). *Psychosomatic syndromes and somatic symptoms.* Washington, DC: American Psychiatric Press.

Kelsey, J. E., & Nemeroff, C. B (2000). Selective serotonin reuptake inhibitors. In B. I. Sadock & V. A. Sadock (Eds.), *Kaplan & Sadock's comprehensive textbook of psychiatry* (7th ed., pp. 2432–2455). Philadelphia: Lippincott Williams & Wilkins.

Kendler, K. S. (1996). Major depression and generalised anxiety disorder: Same genes, (partly) different environments—Revisited. *British Journal of Psychiatry, 168* (Supplement 30), 68–75.

Kendler, K. S., & Diehl, S. R. (1993). The genetics of schizophrenia: A current genetic-epidemiological perspective. *Schizophrenia Bulletin, 19*, 261–285.

Kendler, K. S., & Hays, P. (1981). Paranoid psychosis (delusional disorder) and schizophrenia: A family history study. *Archives of General Psychiatry, 38*, 547–551.

Kendler, K. S., Gardner, C. O., & Prescott, C. A. (1999). Clinical characteristics of major depression that predict risk of depression in relatives. *Archives of General Psychiatry, 56*, 322–327.

Kendler, K. S., Gruenberg, A. M., Strauss, J. S. (1981). An independent analysis of the Copenhagen sample of the Danish Adoption Study of Schizophrenia: III. The relationship between paranoid psychosis (delusional disorder) and the schizophrenia spectrum disorders. *Archives of General Psychiatry, 38*, 985–987.

Kendler, K. S., MaClean, C., Neale, M., Kessler, R., Heath, A., & Eaves, L. (1991). The genetic epidemiology of bulimia nervosa. *American Journal of Psychiatry, 148*, 1627–1637.

Kendler, K. S., Masterson, C. C., & Davis, K. L. (1985). Psychiatric illness in first-degree relatives of patients with paranoid psychosis, schizophrenia, and medical illness. *British Journal of Psychiatry, 147*, 524–531.

Kendler, K. S., McGuire, M., Gruenberg, A. M., O'Hara, A., Spellman, M., & Walsh, D. (1993). The Roscommon family study: III. Schizophrenia-related personality disorders in relatives. *Archives of General Psychiatry, 50*, 781–788.

Kendler, K. S., Neale, M. C., Kessler, R. C., Heath, A. C., & Eaves, L. J. (1992a). Generalized anxiety disorder in women: A population-based twin study. *Archives of General Psychiatry, 49*, 267–272.

Kendler, K. S., Neale, M. C., Kessler, R. C., Heath, A. C., & Eaves, L. J. (1992b). The genetic epidemiology of phobias in women: The interrelationship of agoraphobia, social phobia, situational phobia, and simple phobia. *Archives of General Psychiatry, 49*, 273–281.

Kendler, K. S., Och, A. L., Gorman, J. M., Hewitt, J. K., Rose, D. E., & Mirsky, A. F. (1991). The structure of schizotypy: A pilot multitrait twin study. *Psychiatry Research, 36*, 19–36.

Kennedy, S. (2000). Psychological factors and immunity in HIV infection: Stress, coping, social support, and intervention outcomes. In D. I. Mostofsky & D. H. Barlow (Eds.), *The management of stress and anxiety in medical disorders* (pp. 194–205). Boston: Allyn & Bacon.

Kentgen, L. M., Tenke, C. E., Pine, D. S., Fong, R., Klein, R. G., & Bruder, G. E. (2000). Electroencephalographic asymmetries in adolescents with major depression: Influence of comorbidity with anxiety disorders. *Journal of Abnormal Psychology, 109*, 797–802.

Kern, R. S., Green, M. F., Marshall, B. D., Jr., Wirshing, W. C., Wirshing, D., McGurk, S. R., Marder, S. R., & Mintz, J. (1999). Risperidone versus Haloperidol on secondary memory: Newer medications aid learning? *Schizophrenia Bulletin, 25*, 223–232.

Kernberg, O. (1967). Borderline personality organization. *Journal of the American Psychoanalytic Association, 15*, 641–685.

Kernberg, O. (1976). *Borderline conditions and pathological narcissism.* New York: Jason Aronson.

Kernberg, O. (1977). The structural diagnosis of borderline personality organization. In P. Hartocollis (Ed.), *Borderline personality disorders: The concept, the syndrome, the patient* (pp. 87–121). New York: International Universities Press.

Kernberg, O. (1985). *Borderline conditions and pathological narcissism.* Northvale, NJ: Jason Aronson.

Kernberg, O. (1996). A psychoanalytic theory of personality disorders. In J. F. Clarkin & M. F. Lenzweger (Eds.), *Major theories of personality disorders* (pp. 106–140). New York: Guilford.

Kerr, R. A. (1996). A piece of the dinosaur killer found? *Science, 271*, 1806.

Kessing, L. V., Andersen, E. W., & Andersen, P. K. (2000). Predictors of recurrence in affective disorder: Analyses accounting for individual heterogeneity. *Journal of Affective Disorders, 57*, 139–145.

Kessler, R. C. (1997). The effects of stressful life events on depression. *Annual Review of Psychology, 48*, 191–214.

Kessler, R. C., Avenevoli, S., & Merikangas, K. R. (2001). Mood disorders in children and adolescents: An epidemiologic perspective. *Biological Psychiatry, 49*, 1002–1014.

Kessler, R. C., McGonagle, K. A., Zhao, S., Nelson, C. B., Hughes, M., Eshleman, S., Wittchen, H., & Kendler, K. S. (1994). Lifetime and 12-month prevalence rates of DSM-III-R psychiatric disorders in the United States: Results from the national comorbidity survey. *Archives of General Psychiatry, 51*, 8–19.

Kessler, R. C., Sonnega, A., Bromet, E., Hughes, M., & Nelson, C. B. (1995). Posttraumatic stress disorder in the national comorbidity survey. *Archives of General Psychiatry, 52*, 1048–1060.

Kety, S. S. (1990). Genetic factors in suicide: Family, twin, and adoption studies. In S. J. Blumenthal & D. J. Kupfer (Eds.), *Suicide over the life cycle: Risk factors, assessment, and treatment of suicidal patients* (pp. 127–133). Washington, DC: American Psychiatric Press.

Kety, S. S., Rosenthal, D., Wender, P. H., & Schulsinger, F. (1968). The types and prevalence of mental illness in the biological and adoptive families of adopted schizophrenics. In D. Rosenthal & S. S. Kety (Eds.), *The transmission of schizophrenia* (pp. 345–362). Elmsford, NY: Pergamon.

Kety, S. S., Rosenthal, D., Wender, P. H., & Schulsinger, F. (1971). Mental illness in the biological and adoptive families of adopted schizophrenics. *American Journal of Psychiatry, 128*, 302–306.

Keys, A., Brozek, J., Henschel, A., Michelson, O., & Taylor, H. L. (1950). *The biology of human starvation* (Vol. 1). Minneapolis: University of Minnesota Press.

Kiecolt-Glaser, J. K., McGuire, L., Robles, T. F., & Glaser, R. (2002). Emotions, morbidity, and mortality. New perspectives from psychoneuroimmunology. *Annual Review of Psychology, 53*, 83–107.

Kihlstrom, J. F. (1999). The psychological unconscious. In L. A. Pervin & O. P. John (Eds.), *Handbook of personality: Theory and research* (2nd ed., pp. 424–442). New York: Guilford.

Kilgore, K., Snyder, J., & Lentz, C. (2000). The contribution of parental discipline, parental monitoring, and school risk to early-onset conduct problems in African American boys and girls. *Developmental Psychology, 36*, 835–845.

Killen, J. D. (1996). Development and evaluation of a school-based eating disorder symptoms prevention program. In L. Smolak, M. P. Levine, & R. Striegel-Moore (Eds.), *The developmental psychopathology of eating disorders: Implications for research, prevention, and treatment* (pp. 313–339). Hillsdale, NJ: Erlbaum.

Killen, J. D., Robinson, T. N., Haydel, K. F., Hayward, C., Wilson, D. M., Hammer, L. D., Litt, I. F., & Taylor, C. B. (1997). Prospective study of risk factors for the initiation of cigarette smoking. *Journal of Consulting and Clinical Psychology, 65*, 1011–1016.

Killen, J. D., Taylor, C. B., Hayward, C., Wilson, D. M., Hammer, L. D., Robinson, T. N., Litt, I., Simmonds, B. A., Varady, A., & Kraemer, H. (1994). Pursuit of thinness and onset of eating disorder symptoms in a community sample of adolescent girls: A three-year prospective analysis. *International Journal of Eating Disorders, 16*, 227–238.

Kiloh, L. G. (1982). Electroconvulsive therapy. In E. S. Paykel (Ed.), *Handbook of affective disorders* (pp. 262–275). New York: Guilford.

Kilpatrick, D. G., Edmunds, C. N., & Seymour, A. K. (1992). *Rape in America: A report to the nation.* Arlington, VA: National Victim Center.

King, A. C., Baumann, K., O'Sullivan, P., Wilcox, S., & Castro, C. (2002). Effects of moderate-intensity exercise on physiological, behavioral, and emotional responses to family caregiving: A randomized controlled trial. *Journals of Gerontology.* Series A: *Biological Sciences and Medical Sciences, 57A*, M26–M36.

King, B. H., Hodapp, R. M., & Dykens, E. M. (2000). Mental retardation. In B. I. Sadock & V. A. Sadock (Eds.), *Kaplan & Sadock's comprehensive textbook of psychiatry* (7th ed., pp. 2587–2613). Philadelphia: Lippincott Williams & Wilkins.

King, D. W., King, L. A., Gudanowski, D. M., & Vreven, D. L. (1995). Alternative representations of war-zone stressors: Relationships to posttraumatic stress disorder in male and female Vietnam veterans. *Journal of Abnormal Psychology, 104*, 184–196.

King, M. C. (1999). Realpolitik and the empirically validated treatment debate. *Canadian Psychology, 40*, 306–308.

King, N. M. P., & Churchill, L. R. (2000). Ethical principles guiding research on child and adolescent subjects. *Journal of Interpersonal Violence, 15*, 710–724.

King, S., & Dixon, M. J. (1999). Expressed emotion and relapse in young schizophrenic outpatients. *Schizophrenia Bulletin, 25*, 377–386.

King, V. L., Kidorf, M. S., Stoller, K. B., Carter, J. A., & Brooner, R. K. (2001). Influence of antisocial personality subtypes on drug abuse treatment response. *Journal of Nervous and Mental Disease, 189*, 593–601.

Kinney, D. K., Yurgelun-Todd, D. A., Toehn, M., & Tramer, S. (1998). Pre- and perinatal complications and risk for bipolar disorder: A retrospective study. *Journal of Affective Disorders, 50*, 117–124.

Kinsey, A. C., Pomeroy, W. B., & Martin, C. E. (1948). *Sexual behavior in the human male.* Philadelphia: W. B. Saunders.

Kinsey, A. C., Pomeroy, W. B., Martin, C. E., & Gebhard, P. H. (1953). *Sexual behavior in the human female.* New York: Simon & Schuster.

Kipman, A., Gorwood, P., Mouren-Simeoni, M. C., & Ades, J. (1999). Genetic factors in anorexia nervosa. *European Psychiatry, 14*, 189–198.

Kippen, H. M., Hallman, W., Kang, H., Fiedler, N., & Natelson, B. H. (1999). Prevalence of chronic fatigue and chemical sensitivities in Gulf Registry veterans. *Archives of Environmental Health, 54*, 313–318.

Kirk, S. A., & Kutchins, H. (1994). The myth of the reliability of DSM. *Journal of Mind & Behavior, 15*(1–2), 71–86.

Kirsch, I., & Lynn, S. J. (1995). Altered states of hypnosis: Changes in the theoretical landscape. *American Psychologist, 50*, 846–858.

Kleber, H. D. (1981). Detoxification from narcotics. In J. H. Lowinson & P. Ruiz (Eds.), *Substance abuse: Clinical problems and perspectives* (pp. 317–338). Baltimore: Williams & Wilkins.

Klein, D. F. (1964). Delineation of two drug responsive anxiety syndromes. *Psychopharmacologia, 5*, 397–408.

Klein, D. F., & Fink, M. (1962). Psychiatric reaction patterns to imipramine. *American Journal of Psychiatry, 119*, 432–438.

Klein, D. F., & Wender, P. H. (1993). *Understanding depression: A complete guide to its diagnosis and treatment.* New York: Oxford University Press.

Klein, D. F., Rabkin, J. G., & Gorman, J. M. (1985). Etiological and pathophysiological inferences from the pharmacological treatment of anxiety. In A. H. Tuma & J. D. Maser (Eds.), *Anxiety and the anxiety disorders* (pp. 501–532). Hillsdale, NJ: Erlbaum.

Klein, D. N., Depue, R. A., & Slater, J. F. (1985). Cyclothymia in the adolescent offspring of parents with bipolar affective disorder. *Journal of Abnormal Psychology, 94*, 115–127.

Klein, D. N., Taylor, E. B., Harding, K., Dickstein, S. (1988). Double depression and episodic major depression: Demographic, clinical, familial, personality, and socioenvironmental characteristics and short-term outcome. *American Journal of Psychiatry, 145*, 1226–1231.

Klein, M. (1934). A contribution to the psychogenesis of manic-depressive states. In *Contributions to psychoanalysis 1921–1945* (pp. 282–310). London: Hogarth Press.

Kleinman, A., & Good B. (Eds.). (1985). *Culture and depression: Studies in the anthropology and cross-cultural psychiatry of affect and disorder.* Berkeley: University of California Press.

Kleinman, P. H. (1979). Onset of addiction: A first attempt at prediction. *International Journal of the Addictions, 13*, 1217–1235.

Klerman, G. L. (1990). Treatment of recurrent unipolar major depressive disorder: Commentary on the Pittsburgh study. *Archives of General Psychiatry, 47*, 1158–1162.

Klerman, G. L., Weismann, M. M., Rounsaville, B. J., & Chevron, E. S. (1984). *Interpersonal psychotherapy of depression.* New York: Basic Books.

Klingberg, S., Buchkremer, G., Holle, R., Moenking, H. S., & Hornung, W. P. (1999). Differential therapy effects of psychoeducational psychotherapy for schizophrenia: Results of a 2-year follow-up. *European Archives of Psychiatry and Clinical Neuroscience, 249*, 66–72.

Klonoff, E. A., & Landrine, H. (2000). Is skin color a marker for racial discrimination? Explaining the skin color–hypertension relationship. *Journal of Behavioral Medicine, 23*, 329–338.

Kluft, R. P. (1984). Treatment of multiple personality disorder. *Psychiatric Clinics of North America, 7*, 9–29.

Kluft, R. P. (1988). The phenomenology of extremely complex multiple personality disorder. *Dissociation, 1*, 47–58.

Kluft, R. P. (1993). Clinical approaches to the integration of personality. In R. P. Kluft & C. G. Fine (Eds.), *Clinical perspectives on multiple personality disorder* (pp. 101–133). Washington, DC: American Psychiatric Press.

Kluft, R. P., & Fine, C. G. (Eds.). (1993). *Clinical perspectives on multiple personality disorder.* Washington, DC: American Psychiatric Press.

Klump, K. L., Kaye, W. H., & Strober, M. (2001a). The evolving genetic foundations of eating disorders. *Psychiatric Clinics of North America, 24,* 215–225.

Klump, K. L., Miller, K. B., Keel, P. K., McGue, M., & Iacono, W. G. (2001b). Genetic and environmental influences on anorexia nervosa syndromes in a population-based twin sample. *Psychological Medicine, 31,* 737–740.

Knight, R. A. (1988). A taxonomic analysis of child molesters. *Annals of the New York Academy of Science, 528,* 2–20.

Knight, R. A. (1989). An assessment of the concurrent validity of a child molester typology. *Journal of Interpersonal Violence, 4,* 131–150.

Knight, R. A. (1992). Specifying cognitive deficiencies in premorbid schizophrenics. *Progress in Experimental Personality and Psychopathology Research, 15,* 252–289.

Knight, R. A. (1999). Validation of a typology for rapists. *Journal of Interpersonal Violence, 14,* 303–330.

Knight, R. A., & Silverstein, S. M. (2001). A process-oriented approach for averting confounds resulting from general performance deficiencies in schizophrenia. *Journal of Abnormal Psychology, 110,* 15–30.

Knight, R. P. (1954). Management and psychotherapy of the borderline schizophrenic patient. In R. P. Knight & C. R. Friedman (Eds.), *Psychoanalytic psychiatry and psychology* (pp. 110–122). New York: International Universities Press.

Knopman, D. S., Berg, J. D., Thomas, R., Grundman, M., Thal, L. J., & Sano, M. (1999). Nursing home placement is related to dementia progression: Experience from a clinical trial. *Neurology, 52,* 714–718.

Koegel, R. L., O'Dell, M., & Dunlap, G. (1988). Producing speech use in nonverbal autistic children by reinforcing attempts. *Journal of Autism and Developmental Disorders, 18,* 525–538.

Kohut, H. (1971). *The analysis of the self.* New York: International Universities Press.

Kohut, H. (1977). *The restoration of the self.* New York: International Universities Press.

Konsman, J. P., Luheshi, G. N., Bluthe, R., & Dantzer, R. (2000). The vagus nerve mediates behavioural depression, but not fever, in response to peripheral immune signals: A functional anatomical analysis. *European Journal of Neuroscience, 12,* 4434–4446.

Koocher, G. P., & Pollin, I. S. (2001). Preventive psychosocial intervention in cancer treatment: Implications for managed care. In A. Baum & B. L. Andersen (Eds.), *Psychosocial interventions for cancer* (pp. 363–374). Washington, DC: American Psychological Association.

Kornetsky, C. (1976). Hyporesponsivity of chronic schizophrenic patients to dextroamphetamine. *Archives of General Psychiatry, 33,* 1425–1428.

Koss, M. P., & Cleveland, H. H. (1997). Stepping on toes: Social roots of date rape lead to intractability and politicization. In M. D. Schwartz (Ed.), *Researching sexual violence against women: Methodological and personal perspectives* (pp. 4–21). Thousand Oaks, CA: Sage.

Kottler, J. A. (1999). *Exploring and treating acquisitive desire: Living in the material world.* Thousand Oaks, CA: Sage.

Kovacs, M., Iyengar, S., Goldston, D., Stewart, J., et al. (1990). Psychological functioning of children with insulin-dependent diabetes mellitus: A longitudinal study. *Journal of Pediatric Psychology, 15,* 619–632.

Kownacki, R. J., & Shadish, W. R. (1999). Does Alcoholics Anonymous work? The results from a meta-analysis of controlled experiments. *Substance Use and Misuse, 34,* 1897–1916.

Kozak, M. J., & Foa, E. B. (1994). Obsessions, overvalued ideas, and delusions in obsessive-compulsive disorder. *Behaviour Research and Therapy, 32,* 343–353.

Kraepelin, E. (1904). *Lectures on clinical psychiatry.* (Ed. and Trans. T. Johnstone). London: Balliere, Tindall, & Cox.

Kraepelin, E. (1921). *Manic-depressive insanity and paranoia.* Edinburgh, Scotland: Livingstone.

Kramer, P. D. (1993). *Listening to Prozac.* New York: Penguin.

Kreeger, J. L., Raulin, M. L., Grace, J., & Priest, B. (1995). The effects of hearing enhancement on the mental status ratings in a geriatric psychiatric population. *American Journal of Psychiatry, 152,* 629–631.

Kreek, M. J., & Koob, G. F. (1998). Drug dependence: Stress and dysregulation of brain reward pathways. *Drug and Alcohol Dependence, 51,* 23–47.

Kribbs, N. B. (1997). Methods and problems of treatment compliance in obstructive sleep apnea. In M. R. Pressman & W. C. Orr (Eds.), *Understanding sleep: The evaluation and treatment of sleep disorders* (pp. 299–313). Washington, DC: American Psychological Association.

Krieger, N., Sidney, S., & Coakley, E. (1998). Racial discrimination and skin color in the CARDIA study: Implications for public health research. *American Journal of Public Health, 88,* 1308–1313.

Krueger, R. B., & Kaplan, M. S. (1997). Frotteurism: Assessment and treatment. In D. R. Laws & W. O'Donohue (Eds.), *Sexual deviance: Theory, assessment, and treatment* (pp. 131–151). New York: Guilford.

Kruesi, M. J. P., & Lelio, D. F. (1996). Disorders of conduct and behavior. In J. M. Wiener (Ed.), *Diagnosis and psychopharmacology of childhood and adolescent disorders* (2nd ed., pp. 401–447). Oxford, England: Wiley.

Kruesi, M. J., Fine, S., Valladares, L., Phillips, R. A. J., & Rapoport, J. L. (1992). Paraphilias: A double-blind crossover comparison of clomipramine versus desipramine. *Archives of Sexual Behavior, 21,* 587–593.

Krystal, J. H., Cramer, J. A., Krol, W. F., Kirk, G. F., & Rosenheck, R. A. (2001). Naltrexone in the treatment of alcohol dependence. *New England Journal of Medicine, 345,* 1734–1739.

Kuehnle, J., Mendelson, J. H., Davis, K. R., & New, P. F. J. (1977). Computed tomographic examinations of heavy marijuana smokers. *Journal of the American Medical Association, 237,* 1231–1232.

Kuehnle, K., Coulter, M., & Gamache, M. (2000). Incest. In V. B. Van Hasselt & M. Hersen (Eds), *Aggression and violence: An introductory text* (pp. 92–115). Boston: Allyn & Bacon.

Kuhn, T. S. (1962). *The structure of scientific revolutions.* Chicago: University of Chicago Press.

Kupfer, D. J. (1995). Sleep research in depressive illness: Clinical implicatons—A tasting menu. *Biological Psychiatry, 36,* 931–403.

Kushner, M. G., & Sher, K. J. (1993). Comorbidity of alcohol and anxiety disorders among college students: Effects of gender and family history of alcoholism. *Addictive Behaviors, 18,* 543–552.

Kwapil, T. R. (1998). Social anhedonia as a predictor of schizophrenia-spectrum disorders. *Journal of Abnormal Psychology, 107,* 558–565.

Kwapil, T. R., Mann, M. C., & Raulin, M. L. (2002). Psychometric properties and concurrent validity of the Schizotypal Ambivalence Scale. *Journal of Nervous and Mental Disease, 190,* 290–295.

La Fond, J. Q. (2000). The future of involuntary civil commitment in the U.S.A. after *Kansas v. Hendricks. Behavioral Sciences and the Law, 18,* 153–167.

La Vaque, T. J., & Rossiter, T. R. (2001). "The ethical use of placebo controls in clinical research: The Declaration of Helsinki": Reply. *Applied Psychophysiology and Biofeedback, 26,* 67–71.

Laberg, J. C., & Loeberg, T. (1989). Expectancy and tolerance: A study of acute alcohol intoxication using the balanced placebo design. *Journal of Studies on Alcohol, 50,* 448–455.

LaBuda, M. C., & Grigorenko, E. L. (Eds.). (1999). *On the way to individuality: Current methodological issues in behavioral genetics.* Huntington, NY: Nova.

Lake, C. R., Ziegler, M. G., & Murphy, D. L. (1977). Increased norepinephrine levels and decreased dopamine-β-hydroxylase activity in primary autism. *Archives of General Psychiatry, 34,* 553–556.

Lalumiere, M. L., & Quinsey, V. L. (1994). The discriminability of rapists from nonrapists using phallometric measures: A meta-analysis. *Criminal Justice and Behavior, 21,* 150–175.

Lamb, H. R., & Weinberger, L. E. (Eds.). (2001). *Deinstitutionalization: Promise and problems.* San Francisco: Jossey-Bass.

Lamb, S., Greenlick, M. R., & McCarty, D. (1998). *Bridging the gap between practice and research: Forging partnerships with community-based drug and alcohol treatment.* Washington, DC: National Academy Press.

Lancaster, M. M. (1998). Caregiver education and support. In R. C. Hamdy, J. M. Turnbull, J. Edwards, & M. M. Lancaster (Eds.), *Alzheimer's disease: A handbook for caregivers* (3rd ed., pp. 341–353). St. Louis, MO: Mosby.

Lancaster, M. M., Abusamra, L. C., & Clark, W. G. (1998). Management of difficult behaviors. In R. C. Hamdy, J. M. Turnbull, J. Edwards, & M. M. Lancaster (Eds.), *Alzheimer's disease: A handbook for caregivers* (3rd ed., pp. 150–170). St. Louis, MO: Mosby.

Landau, J., Garrett, J., Shea, R. R., Stanton, M. D., Brinkman-Sull, D., & Baciewicz, G. (2000). Strength in numbers: The ARISE method for mobilizing family and network to engage substance abusers in treatment. *American Journal of Drug and Alcohol Abuse, 26,* 379–398.

Landis, B. J. (1996). Uncertainty, spiritual well-being, and psychosocial adjustment to chronic illness. *Issues in Mental Health Nursing, 17,* 217–231.

Landry, M. J. (1994). *Understanding drugs of abuse: The process of addiction, treatment, and recovery.* Washington, DC: American Psychiatric Press.

Lane, J. (1997). Vest outlines MIT's strategies on alcohol, housing problems. *The Vest, 117*(47), 1. **www-tech.mit.edu/V117/N47/vest.47n.html.**

Lane, W. G., & Kemper, A. R. (2001). American College of Preventive Medicine Practice Policy Statement: Screening for elevated blood lead levels in children. *American Journal of Preventive Medicine, 20,* 78–82.

Lang, A. R., & Sibrel, P. A. (1989). Psychological perspectives on alcohol consumption and interpersonal aggression: The potential role of individual differences in alcohol-related criminal violence. *Criminal Justice and Behavior, 16,* 299–324.

Lang, P. J. (1985). The cognitive psychophysiology of emotion: Fear and anxiety. In A. H. Tuma and D. Maser (Eds.), *Anxiety and the anxiety disorders.* Hillsdale, NJ: Erlbaum.

Lang, P. J., & Twentyman, C. T. (1974). Learning to control heart rate: Binary vs. analogue feedback. *Psychophysiology, 11,* 616–629.

Lang, P. J., Levin, D. N., Miller, G. A., & Kozak, M. J. (1983). Fear behavior, fear imagery, and the psychophysiology of emotion: The problem of affective response integration. *Journal of Abnormal Psychology, 92,* 276–306.

Langbehn, D. R., & Cadoret, R. J. (2001). The adult antisocial syndrome with and without antecedent conduct disorder: Comparisons from an adoption study. *Comprehensive Psychiatry, 42,* 272–282.

Lapp, W. M., Collins, R. L., & Izzo, C. V. (1994). On the enhancement of creativity by alcohol: Pharmacology or expectation? *American Journal of Psychology, 107,* 173–206.

Larimer, M. E., Lydum, A. R., Anderson, B. K., & Turner, A. P. (1999). Male and female recipients of unwanted sexual contact in a college student sample: Prevalence rates, alcohol use, and depression symptoms. *Sex Roles, 40,* 295–308.

Larimer, M. E., Marlatt, G. A., Baer, J. S., Quigley, L. A., Blume, A. W., & Hawkins, E. H. (1998). Harm reduction for alcohol problems: Expanding access to and acceptability of prevention and treatment services. In G. A. Marlatt (Ed.), *Harm reduction: Pragmatic strategies for managing high-risk behaviors* (pp. 69–121). New York: Guilford.

Larose, S., & Bernier, A. (2001). Social support processes: Mediators of attachment, state of mind, and adjustment in late adolescence. *Attachment and Human Development, 3,* 96–120.

Laumann, E. O., Gagnon, J. H., Michael, R. T., & Michaels, S. (1994). *The social organization of sexuality.* Chicago: University of Chicago Press.

Laumann, E. O., Paik, A., & Rosen, R. C. (1999). Sexual dysfunction in the United States: Prevalence and predictors. *JAMA: Journal of the American Medical Association, 281,* 537–544.

Lauriello, J., Erickson, B. R., & Keith, S. J. (2000). Schizoaffective disorder, schizophreniform disorder, and brief psychotic disorder. In B. I. Sadock & V. A. Sadock (Eds.), *Kaplan and Sadock's comprehensive textbook of psychiatry* (7th ed., pp. 1232–1243). Baltimore: Lippincott Williams & Wilkins.

Lavie, P. (2001). Current concepts: Sleep disturbances in the wake of traumatic events. *New England Journal of Medicine, 345,* 1825–1832.

Lavretsky, E. P., Leiter, F. L., & Jarvik, L. F. (1998). Etiology and pathogenesis: Current concepts. In R. C. Hamdy, J. M. Turnbull, J. Edwards, & M. M. Lancaster (Eds.), *Alzheimer's disease: A handbook for caregivers* (3rd ed., pp. 60–73). St. Louis, MO: Mosby.

Lawlor, B. A. (1995). Experimental therapeutics of Alzheimer's disease. In M. Stein & A. Baum (Eds.), *Chronic diseases* (pp. 45–56). Mahwah, NJ: Erlbaum.

Laws, D. R., & O'Donohue, W. (Eds.). (1997). *Sexual deviance: Theory, assessment, and treatment.* New York: Guilford.

Layne, C., White, D., & Han, M. (1999). Do "hypochondriacal" litigants have disordered personalities? *American Journal of Forensic Psychology, 17,* 49–66.

Lazarus, R. S., & Monat, A. (1979). *Personality.* Englewood Cliffs, NJ: Prentice-Hall.

Leahey, T. H. (1980). *A history of psychology: Main currents in psychological thought.* Englewood Cliffs, NJ: Prentice-Hall.

Leckman, J. F. (1999). Incremental progress in developmental psychopathology: Simply complex. *American Journal of Psychiatry, 156,* 1495–1498.

Lecompte, D. (1987). Organic disease and associated psychopathology in a patient group with conversion symptoms. *Acta Psychiatrica Belgica, 87,* 662–669.

Lee, J. A. (1983). The social organization of sexual risk. In T. Weinberg & B. Kamel (Eds.), *S and M: Studies in sadomasochism* (pp. 175–193). Buffalo, NY: Prometheus.

Lee, K., Williams, L. M., Loughland, C. M., Davidson, D. J., & Gordon, E. (2001). Syndromes of schizophrenia and smooth-pursuit eye movement dysfunction. *Psychiatry Research, 101,* 11–21.

Lee, T., & Seeman, P. (1980). Elevation of brain neuroleptic/dopamine receptors in schizophrenia. *American Journal of Psychiatry, 137,* 191–197.

Leeper, P. (1988). Having a place to live is vital to good health. *NewsReport, 38,* 5–8.

Leff, J. (2001). Why is care in the community perceived as failure? *British Journal of Psychiatry, 179,* 381–383.

Leff, J., & Vaughn, C. (1976). Schizophrenia and family life. *Psychology Today,* November, 13–18.

Leiblum, S. R. (1997). Sex and the Net: Clinical implications. *Journal of Sex Education and Therapy, 22,* 21–27.

Leiblum, S. R. (2000). Vaginismus: A most perplexing problem. In S. R. Leiblum & R. C. Rosen (Eds.), *Principles and practice of sex therapy* (3rd ed., pp. 181–202). New York: Guilford Press.

Leiblum, S. R., & Rosen, R. C. (Eds.). (2000). *Principles and Practice of Sex Therapy* (3rd ed.). New York: Guilford.

Leiblum, S. R., Pervin, L. A., & Campbell, E. H. (1989). The treatment of vaginismus: Success and failure. In S. R. Leiblum, & R. C. Rosen (Eds.), *Principles and practice of sex therapy: Update for the 1990s* (pp. 113–140). New York: Guilford.

Leighton, A. H. (1998). A perspective on adversity, stress, and psychopathology. In B. P. Dohrenwend (Ed.), *Adversity, stress, and psychopathology* (pp. 506–520). New York: Oxford University Press.

Lennkh, C., & Simhandl, C. (2000). Current aspects of valproate in bipolar disorder. *International Clinical Psychopharmacology, 15,* 1–11.

Lenzenweger, M. F. (1999). Deeper into the schizotypy taxon: On the robust nature of maximum covariance analysis. *Journal of Abnormal Psychology, 108,* 182–187.

Lenzenweger, M. F., Cornblatt, B. A., & Putnick, M. (1991). Schizotypy and sustained attention. *Journal of Abnormal Psychology, 100,* 84–89.

Leon, A. C., Keller, M. B., Warshaw, M. G., Mueller, T. I., Soloman, D. A., Coryell, W., & Endicott, J. (1999). A prospective study of fluoxetine treatment and suicidal behavior in affectively ill subjects. *American Journal of Psychiatry, 156,* 195–201.

Leonard, B. E. (2001a). Changes in the immune system in depression and dementia: Causal or co-incidental effects? *International Journal of Developmental Neuroscience, 19,* 305–312.

Leonard, B. E. (2001b). The immune system, depression and the action of antidepressants. *Progress in Neuro-Psychopharmacology and Biological Psychiatry, 25,* 767–780.

Lepore, S. J. (2001). A social-cognitive processing model of emotional adjustment to cancer. In A. Baum & B. L. Andersen (Eds.), *Psychosocial interventions for cancer* (pp. 99–116). Washington, DC: American Psychological Association.

Lesar, M. D., Arnow, B., Stice, E., & Agras, W. S. (2001). Private high school students are at risk for bulimic pathology. *Eating Disorders: The Journal of Treatment and Prevention, 9,* 125–139.

Lester, D. (1996). *Patterns of suicide and homicide in the world.* New York: Nova Science Publishers.

Levenkron, J. C., & Moore, L. G. (1988). The Type A behavior pattern: Issues for intervention research. *Annals of Behavioral Medicine, 10,* 78–83.

Levin, R. (1998). Nightmares and schizotypy. *Psychiatry: Interpersonal and Biological Processes, 61,* 206–216.

Levin, R., & Raulin, M. L. (1991). Preliminary evidence for the proposed relationship between frequent nightmares and schizotypal symptomatology. *Journal of Personality Disorders, 5,* 8–14.

Levine, M., & Perkins, D. V. (1997). *Principles of community psychology: Perspectives and applications* (2nd ed.). New York: Oxford University Press.

Levitt, E. E., & Waldo, T. G. (1991). Hypnotically induced auditory hallucinations and the mouth-opening maneuver: A failure to duplicate findings. *American Journal of Psychiatry, 148,* 658–660.

Levy, D. L., Lajonchere, C. M., Dorogusker, B., Min, D., Lee, S., Tartaglini, A., Lieberman, J. A., & Mendell, N. R. (2000). Quantitative characterization of eye tracking dysfunction in schizophrenia. *Schizophrenia Research, 42,* 171–185.

Lewinsohn, P. M., Mischef, W., Chapion, W., & Barton, R. (1980). Social competence and depression: The role of illusory self-perceptions. *Journal of Abnormal Psychology, 89,* 203–212.

Lewinsohn, P. M., Weinstein, M., & Alper, T. (1970). A behavioral approach to the group treatment of depressed persons: A methodological contribution. *Journal of Clinical Psychology, 26,* 525–532.

Lewis, D. A., Lurigio, A. J., Riger, S., Pavkov, T. W., Reed, S. C., & Rosenberg, H. (1994). *The state mental patient and urban life: Moving in and out of the institution.* Springfield, IL: Charles C Thomas.

Lewis, N. D. (1941). *A short history of psychiatric achievement.* New York: Norton.

Lezak, M. D. (1995). *Neuropsychological assessment* (3rd ed.). New York: Oxford University Press.

Liakopoulou, M., Alifieraki, T., Katideniou, A., Peppa, M., Maniati, M., Tzikas, D., Hibbs, E. D., & Dacou-Voutetakis, C. (2001). Maternal expressed emotion and metabolic control of children and adolescents with diabetes mellitus. *Psychotherapy and Psychosomatics, 70,* 78–85.

Liberman, R. P., DeRisi, W. D., & Mueser, K. T. (1989). Social skills training for psychiatric patients. Boston: Allyn & Bacon.

Lichstein, K. L., Durrence, H. H., Riedel, B. W., & Bayen, U. J. (2001). Primary versus secondary insomnia in older adults: Subjective sleep and daytime functioning. *Psychology and Aging, 16,* 264–271.

Lichstein, K. L., Riedel, B. W., Lester, K. W., & Aguillard, R. N. (1999). Occult sleep apnea in a recruited sample of older adults with insomnia. *Journal of Consulting and Clinical Psychology, 67,* 405–410.

Lichtermann, D., Ekelund, J., Pukkala, E., Tanskanen, A., & Loennqvist, J. (2001). Incidence of cancer among persons with schizophrenia and their relatives. *Archives of General Psychiatry, 58,* 573–578.

Liddell, H. S. (1950). The role of vigilance in the development of animal neurosis. In P. Hoch & J. Zubin (Eds.), *Anxiety* (pp. 183–196). New York: Grune & Stratton.

Liddle, H. A., Dakof, G. A., Parker, K., Diamond, G. S., Barrett, K., & Tejeda, M. (2001). Multidimensional family therapy for adolescent drug abuse: Results of a randomized clinical trial. *American Journal of Drug and Alcohol Abuse, 27,* 651–688.

Lieberman, M. A., & Fisher, L. (2001). The effects of nursing home placement on family caregivers of patients with Alzheimer's disease. *Gerontologist, 41,* 819–826.

Lieberman, M., Doyle, A., & Markiewicz, D. (1999). Developmental patterns in security of attachment to mother and father in late childhood and early adolescence: Associations with peer relations. *Child Development, 70,* 202–213.

Lilienfeld, S. O. (1992). The association between antisocial personality and somatization disorders: A review and integration of theoretical models. *Clinical Psychology Review, 12,* 641–662.

Lilienfeld, S. O. (1995). *Seeing both sides: Classic controversies in abnormal psychology.* Pacific Grove, CA: Brooks/Cole.

Lilienfeld, S. O. (1996). Anxiety sensitivity is not distinct from trait anxiety. In R. M. Rapee (Ed.), *Current controversies in the anxiety disorders* (pp. 228–244). New York: Guilford.

Lilienfeld, S. O. (1997). The relationship of anxiety sensitivity to higher- and lower-order personality dimensions: Implications for etiology of panic disorder. *Journal of Abnormal Psychology, 106,* 539–544.

Lilienfeld, S. O. (2002). When worlds collide: Social science, politics, and the child sexual abuse meta-analysis. *American Psychologist, 57,* 176–188.

Lilienfeld, S. O., & Hess, T. H. (2001). Psychopathic personality traits and somatization: Sex differences and the mediating role of negative emotionality. *Journal of Psychopathology and Behavioral Assessment, 23,* 11–24.

Lilienfeld, S. O., & Marino, L. (1995). Mental disorder as a Roschian concept: A critique of Wakefield's "harmful dysfunction" analysis. *Journal of Abnormal Psychology, 104,* 411–420.

Lilienfeld, S. O., & Waldman, I. D. (1990). The relationship between childhood attention-deficit hyperactivity disorder and adult antisocial behavior reexamined: The problem of heterogeneity. *Clinical Psychology Review, 10,* 699–725.

Lilienfeld, S. O., Lynn, S. J., Kirsch, I., Chaves, J. F., Sarbin, T. R., Ganaway, G. K., & Powell, R. A. (1999). Dissociative identity disorder and the sociocognitive model: Recalling the lessons of the past. *Psychological Bulletin, 125,* 507–523.

Lilienfeld, S. O., Waldman, I. D., & Israel, A. C. (1994). A critical examination of the use of the term and concept of comorbidity in psychopathology research. *Clinical Psychology: Science and Practice, 1,* 71–83.

Lincoln, A. J., Allen, M. H., & Kilman, A. (1995). The assessment and interpretation of intellectual abilities in people with autism. In E. Schopler & G. B. Mesibov (Eds.), *Learning and cognition in autism* (pp. 89–117). New York: Plenum.

Linehan, M. M. (1993). *Cognitive-behavioral treatment of borderline personality disorder: The dialectics of effective treatment.* New York: Guilford.

Linehan, M. M. (1987). Dialectical behavior therapy for borderline personality disorder: Theory and method. *Bulletin of the Menninger Clinic, 51,* 261–276.

Linehan, M. M., & Shearin, E. N. (1988). Lethal stress: A social-behavioral model of suicide behavior. In S. Fisher & J. Reason (Eds.), *Handbook of life stress, cognition, and health* (pp. 265–285). New York: Wiley.

Linehan, M. M., Cochran, B. N., & Kehrer, C. A. (2001). Dialectical behavior therapy for borderline personality disorder. In D. H. Barlow (Ed.), *Clinical handbook of psychological disorders: A step-by-step treatment manual* (3rd ed., pp. 470–522). New York: Guilford.

Linehan, M. M., Tutek, D. A., Heard, H. L., & Armstrong, H. E. (1994). Interpersonal outcome of cognitive behavioral treatment for chronically suicidal borderline patients. *American Journal of Psychiatry, 151,* 1771–1776.

Linz, D., & Malamuth, N. (1993). *Pornography.* Newbury Park, CA: Sage.

Lipkin, M., Jr. (2000). Primary care and psychiatry. In B. I. Sadock & V. A. Sadock (Eds.), *Kaplan & Sadock's comprehensive textbook of psychiatry* (7th ed., pp. 1923–1935). Philadelphia: Lippincott Williams & Wilkins.

Lipper, S. E., Edinger, J. D., & Stein, R. M. (1989). Sleep disturbance in PTSD. *American Journal of Psychiatry, 146,* 1644–1645.

Litz, B. T., Orsillo, S. M., Friedman, M., Ehlich, P., & Batres, A. (1997). Posttraumatic stress disorder associated with peacekeeping duty in Somalia for U.S. military personnel. *American Journal of Psychiatry, 154,* 178–184.

Livesley, W. J. (1995). *The DSM-IV personality disorders.* New York: Guilford.

Lobasher, M. E., Kingerlee, P. E., & Gubbay, S. S. (1970). Childhood Autism: An investigation of aetiological factors in twenty-five cases. *British Journal of Psychiatry, 117,* 525–529.

Loeb, F. F., Jr. (1997). Conversion hysteria stemming from child abuse. *Journal of Clinical Psychoanalysis, 6,* 79–93.

Loeber, R., Burke, J. D., Lahey, B. B., Winters, A., & Zera, M. (2000). Oppositional defiant and conduct disorder: A review of the past 10 years, Part I. *Journal of the American Academy of Child and Adolescent Psychiatry, 39,* 1468–1484.

Loftus, E. F. (2001). Imagining the past. *Psychologist, 14,* 584–587.

Loftus, E. F., & Ketcham, K. (1991). *Witness for the defense: The accused, the eye witness, and the expert who puts memory on trial.* New York: St. Martin's Press.

Loftus, E. F., & Ketcham, K. (1994). *The myth of repressed memory: False memories and allegations of sexual abuse.* New York: St. Martin's Press.

Loftus, E. F., & Loftus, G. R. (1980). On the permanence of stored information in the human brain. *American Psychologist, 35,* 409–420.

Loftus, E. F., & Polage, D. C. (1999). Repressed memories: When are they real? How are they false? *Psychiatric Clinics of North America, 22,* 61–70.

Lohr, B. A., Adams, H. E., & Davis, J. M. (1997). Sexual arousal to erotic and aggressive stimuli in sexually coercive and noncoercive men. *Journal of Abnormal Psychology, 106,* 230–242.

Lohr, J. M., Tolin, D. F., & Lilienfeld, S. O. (1998). Efficacy of eye movement desensitization and reprocessing: Implications for behavior therapy. *Behavior Therapy, 29,* 123–156.

Longo, R. E., & Groth, A. N. (1983). Juvenile sexual offenses in the histories of adult rapists and child molesters. *International Journal of Offender Therapy and Comparative Criminology, 27,* 150–155.

Lonsway, K. A., & Kothari, C. (2000). First-year campus acquaintance rape education: Evaluating the impact of a mandatory intervention. *Psychology of Women Quarterly, 24,* 220–232.

LoPiccolo, J., & Freidman, J. (1988). Broad-spectrum treatment of low sexual desire: Integration of cognitive, behavioral, and systemic therapy. In S. R. Leiblum & R. C. Rosen (Eds.), *Sexual desire disorders* (pp. 107–144). New York: Guilford.

Loranger, A. W., Susman, V. L., Oldham, J. M., & Russakoff, L. M. (1987). The personality disorder examination: A preliminary report. *Journal of Personality Disorders, 1,* 1–13.

Losche, G. (1990). Sensorimotor and action development in autistic children from infancy to early adulthood. *Journal of Child Psychology and Psychiatry, 31,* 749–761.

Lovaas, O. I. (1989). Concerns about misinterpretation and placement of blame. *American Psychologist, 44,* 1243–1244.

Lovaas, O. I., Berberich, J. P., Perloff, B. F., & Schaeffer, B. (1966). Acquisition of imitative speech by schizophrenic children. *Science, 151,* 705–707.

Lovaas, O. I., Koegel, R. L., & Schreibman, L. (1979). Stimulus over-selectivity in autism: A review of research. *Psychological Bulletin, 86,* 1236–1254.

Lovaas, O. I., Koegel, R., Simmons, J. Q., & Long, J. S. (1973). Some generalization and follow-up measures on autistic children in behavior therapy. *Journal of Applied Behavior Analysis, 6,* 131–166.

Lovejoy, M. C., & Steuerwald, B. L. (1997). Subsyndromal unipolar and bipolar disorders II: Comparison of daily stress levels. *Cognitive Therapy and Research, 21,* 607–618.

Luborsky, L., Diguer, L., Cacciiola, J., Barber, J. P., Moras, K., Schmidt, K., & DeRubeis, R. J. (1996). Factors in outcome of short-term dynamic psychotherapy for chronic vs. nonchronic major depression. *Journal of Psychotherapy Practice and Research, 5,* 152–159.

Luk, E. S. L., Staiger, P. K., Mathai, J., Wong, L., Birleson, P., & Adler, R. (2001). Children with persistent conduct problems who drop out of treatment. *European Child and Adolescent Psychiatry, 10,* 28–36.

Lumsden, C. J., & Wilson, E. O. (1985). The relation between biological and cultural evolution. *Journal of Social and Biological Structures, 8,* 343–359.

Lutgendorf, S. K., Antonie, M. H., Ironson, G., Klimas, N., Kumar, M., Starr, K., McCabe, P., Cleven, K., Fletcher, M. A., & Schneiderman, N. (1997). Cognitive-behavioral stress management decreases dysphoric mood and herpes simplex virus-type 2 antibody titers in symptomatic HIV-seropositive gay men. *Journal of Consulting and Clinical Psychology, 65,* 31–43.

Luthar, S. S. (1999). *Poverty and children's adjustment.* Thousand Oaks, CA: Sage.

Lykken, D. T. (1957). A study of anxiety in the sociopathic personality. *Journal of Abnormal and Social Psychology, 55,* 6–10.

Lykken, D. T. (1982). Psychophysiology. In R. J. Corsini (Ed.), *Encyclopedia of psychology* (pp. 175–179). New York: Wiley.

Lykken, D. T. (1995). *The antisocial personalities.* Hillsdale, NJ: Erlbaum.

Lykken, D. T., McGue, M., Tellegen, A., & Bouchard, T. J. (1992). Emergenesis: Genetic traits that may not run in families. *American Psychologist, 47,* 1565–1577.

Lynam, D. R., Milich, R., Zimmerman, R., Novak, S. P., Logan, T. K., Martin, C., Leukefeld, C., & Clayton, R. (1999). Project DARE: No effects at 10-year follow-up. *Journal of Consulting and Clinical Psychology, 67,* 590–593.

Lyons, M. J., True, W. S., Eisen, A., Goldberg, J., Meyer, J. M., Faraone, S. V., Eaves, L. J., & Tsuang, M. T. (1995). Differential heritability of adults and juvenile antisocial traits. *Archives of General Psychiatry, 52,* 906–913.

Lystad, M. M. (1957). Social mobility among selected groups of schizophrenics. *American Sociological Review, 22,* 288–292.

Maas, J. B. (2002). What we should all know about sleep but are too tired to ask. Presentation at the 24th Annual National Institute on the Teaching of Psychology, January 3, St. Petersburg Beach, Florida.

Maccoby, E. E., & Jacklin, C. N. (1974). *The psychology of sex differences.* Stanford, CA: Stanford University Press.

MacCoun, R. J. (1998). Toward a psychology of harm reduction. *American Psychologist, 53,* 1199–1208.

MacDonald, J. M. (1973). *Indecent exposure.* Springfield, IL: Charles C Thomas.

MacFadden, W., & Woody, G. E. (2000). Cannabis-related disorders. In B. I. Sadock & V. A. Sadock (Eds.), *Kaplan & Sadock's comprehensive textbook of psychiatry* (7th ed., pp. 990–999). Philadelphia: Lippincott Williams & Wilkins.

Machin, G. A., Ackerman, J., & Gilbert-Barness, E. (2000). Abnormal umbilical cord coiling is associated with adverse perinatal outcomes. *Pediatric and Developmental Pathology, 3,* 462–471.

Mackintosh, N. J. (1998). *IQ and human intelligence.* New York: Oxford University Press.

Macleod, A. D. (1999). Posttraumatic stress disorder, dissociative fugue, and a locator beacon. *Australian and New Zealand Journal of Psychiatry, 33,* 102–104.

MacLeod, C., & Cohen, I. L. (1993). Anxiety and the interpretation of ambiguity: A text comprehension study. *Journal of Abnormal Psychology, 102,* 238–247.

MacLeod, C., & Mathews, A. (1991). Biased cognitive operations in anxiety: Accessibility of information or assignment of processing priorities. *Behaviour Research and Therapy, 29,* 599–610.

MacQuarrie, B. (2001). March trial date set in Wakefield killings. *Boston Globe,* December 24, B4.

Macrodimitris, S. D., & Endler, N. S. (2001). Coping, control, and adjustment in type 2 diabetes. *Health Psychology, 20,* 208–216.

Maddock, R. J. (2001). The lactic acid response to alkalosis in panic disorder: An integrative review. *Journal of Neuropsychiatry and Clinical Neurosciences, 13,* 22–34.

Magnusson, A., & Axelsson, J. (1993). The prevalence of seasonal affective disorder is low among decendants of Icelandic emigrants in Canada. *Archives of General Psychiatry, 50,* 947–951.

Magnusson, A., & Stefansson, J. G. (1993). Prevalence of seasonal affective disorder in Iceland. *Archives of General Psychiatry, 50,* 941–946.

Magnusson, A., Axelsson, J., Karlsson, M. M., & Oskarsson, J. H. (2000). Lack of seasonal mood changes in the Icelandic population: Results of a cross-sectional study. *American Journal of Psychiatry, 157,* 234–238.

Maher, J. J. (1997). Exploring effects on liver function. *Alcohol Health and Research, 2,* 5–12.

Maher, K. (2000). The new 24/7 work cycle. *Wall Street Journal,* September 20, Section B, p. 1.

Mahler, C. R., Raulin, M. L., O'Gorman, J. C., Furash, L. D., & Lowrie, G. S. (1989). Stability of schizotypic signs in a chronic schizophrenic population. Paper presented at the Eastern Psychological Association Convention, March, Boston.

Mahurin, R. K. (1998). Neural network modeling of basal ganglia function in Parkinson's disease and related disorders. In R. W. Parks, D. S. Levine, & D. L. Long (1998), *Fundamentals of neural network modeling: Neuropsychology and cognitive neuroscience* (pp. 331–355). Cambridge, MA: M.I.T. Press.

Malcom, R., Brady, K. T., Johnston, A. L., & Cunningham, M. (1993). Types of benzodiazepines abused by chemically dependent inpatients. *Journal of Psychoactive Drugs, 25,* 315–319.

Maldonado, J. R., & Spiegal, D. (1998). Trauma, dissociation, and hypnotizability. In J. D. Bremmer & C. R. Marmar (Eds.), *Trauma, memory, and dissociation* (pp. 57–106). Washington, DC: American Psychiatric Press.

Males, M. A. (1999). *Smoked: Why Joe Camel is still smiling.* Monroe, ME: Common Courage Press.

Maletsky, B. M. (1998). The paraphilias: Research and treatment. In P. E. Nathan & J. M. Gorman (Eds.), *A guide to treatments that work* (pp. 472–500). New York: Oxford University Press.

Malinowski, B. (1954). *Magic, science, and religion.* Garden City, NY: Doubleday.

Malkoff-Schwartz, S., Frank, E., Anderson, B. P., Hlastala, S. A., Luther, J. F., Sherrill, J. T., Houck, P. R., & Kupfer, D. J. (2000). Social rhythm disruption and stressful life events in the onset of bipolar and unipolar episodes. *Psychological Medicine, 30,* 1005–1016.

Malkoff-Schwartz, S., Frank, E., Anderson, B., Sherrill, J. T., Siegel, L., Patterson, D., & Kupfer, D. J. (1998). Stressful life events and social rhythm disruption in the onset of manic and depressive bipolar episodes. *Archives of General Psychiatry, 55,* 702–707.

Malkus, B. M. (1994). Family dynamic and structural correlates of adolescent substance abuse: A comparison of families of non-substance abusers and substance abusers. *Journal of Child and Adolescent Substance Abuse, 3,* 39–52.

Malone, R. P. (2000). Assessment and treatment of abnormal aggression in children and adolescents. In M. L. Crowner (Ed.), *Understanding and treating violent psychiatric patients* (pp. 21–47). Washington, DC: American Psychiatric Press.

Mander, A. (1998). Hypnosis in the treatment of dysphonia. *Australian Journal of Clinical and Experimental Hypnosis, 26,* 43–48.

Manes, F., Jorge, R., Morcuende, M., Yamada, T., Paradiso, S., & Robinson, R. G. (2001). A controlled study of repetitive transcranial magnetic stimulation as a treatment of depression in the elderly. *International Psychogeriatrics, 13,* 225–231.

Manjiviona, J., & Prior, M. (1995). Comparison of Asperger syndrome and high-functioning artistic children on a test of motor impairment. *Journal of Autism and Developmental Disorders, 25,* 23–39.

Mann, D. M. A., & Esiri, M. M. (1989). The pattern of acquisition of plaques and tangles in the brains of patients under 50 with Down's syndrome. *Journal of Neurological Science, 89,* 169–179.

Mann, L. M., Chassin, L., & Sher, K. J. (1987). Alcohol expectancies and the risk for alcoholism. *Journal of Consulting and Clinical Psychology, 55,* 411–417.

Mannuzza, S., Klein, R. G., Bessler, A., Malloy, P., & Hynes, M. E. (1997). Educational and occupational outcomes of hyperactive boys grown up. *Journal of American Academy of Child and Adolescent Psychiatry, 36,* 1222–1227.

Mannuzza, S., Klein, R. G., Bessler, A., Malloy, P., & LaPadula, M. (1993). Adult outcome of hyperactive boys. *Archives of General Psychiatry, 50,* 565–576.

Mannuzza, S., Klein, R. G., Bessler, A., Malloy, P., & LaPadula, M. (1998). Adult psychiatric status of hyperactive boys grown up. *American Journal of Psychiatry, 155,* 493–498.

Manschreck, T. C. (2000). Delusional and shared psychotic disorders. In B. I. Sadock & V. A. Sadock (Eds.), *Kaplan and Sadock's comprehensive textbook of psychiatry* (7th ed., pp. 1243–1263). Baltimore: Lippincott Williams & Wilkins.

Marazziti, D., Dell'Osso, L., Presta, S., Pfanner, C., Rossi, A., Masala, I., Baroni, S., Giannaccini, G., Lucacchini, A., & Cassano, G. B. (1999). Platelet [^{3H}]paroxetine binding in patients with OCD-related disorders. *Psychiatry Research, 89,* 223–228.

March, J. S. (1990). Sleep disturbance in PTSD. *American Journal of Psychiatry, 147,* 1697.

March, J. S. (1993). What constitutes a stressor? The criterion A issue. In J. R. T. Davidson & E. B. Foa (Eds.), *Posttraumatic stress disorder: DSM-IV and beyond* (pp. 37–54). Washington, DC: American Psychiatric Press.

Marder, S. R. (2000). Schizophrenia: Somatic treatments. In B. I. Sadock & V. A. Sadock (Eds.), *Kaplan and Sadock's comprehensive textbook of psychiatry* (7th ed., pp. 1199–1210). Baltimore: Lippincott Williams & Wilkins.

Margolis, R. D., & Zweben, J. E. (1998). *Treating patients with alcohol and other drug problems: An integrated approach.* Washington, DC: American Psychological Association.

Marini, M. M. (1988). Sociology of gender. In E. F. Borgatta & K. S. Cook (Eds.), *The future of sociology* (pp. 374–393). Newbury Park, CA: Sage.

Maris, R. W. (1981). *Pathways to suicide.* Baltimore: Johns Hopkins University Press.

Maris, R. W. (1997). Social forces in suicide: A life review, 1965–1995. In R. W. Maris, M. M. Silverman, & S. S. Canetto (Eds.), *Review of suicidology, 1997* (pp. 42–60). New York: Guilford.

Marlatt, G. A. (1983). The controlled-drinking controversy: A commentary. *American Psychologist, 38,* 1097–1110.

Marlatt, G. A., Baer, J. S., Kivlahan, D. R., Dimeff, L. A., Larimer, M. E., Quigley, L. A., Somers, J. M., & Williams, E. (1998). Screening and brief intervention for high-risk college student drinkers: Results from a 2-year follow-up assessment. *Journal of Consulting and Clinical Psychology, 66,* 604–615.

Marlatt, G. A., & Gordon, J. R. (Eds.). (1985). *Relapse prevention: Maintenance strategies in the treatment of addictive behaviors.* New York: Guilford.

Marlatt, G. A., Demming, B., & Reid, J. B. (1973). Loss of control drinking in alcoholics: An experimental analogue. *Journal of Abnormal Psychology, 81,* 233–241.

Marley, J. A., & Buila, S. (2001). Crimes against people with mental illness: Types, perpetrators, and influencing factors. *Social Work, 46,* 115–124.

Marmar, C. R., Foy, D., Kagan, B., & Pynoos, R. S. (1994). An integrated approach for treating posttraumatic stress. In R. S. Pynoos (Ed.), *Posttraumatic stress disorder: A clinical review* (pp. 99–132). Lutherville, MD: Sidran Press.

Marsella, A. J. (1987). The measurement of depressive experience and disorder across cultures. In A. J. Marsella, R. M. A. Hirschfeld, & M. M. Katz (Eds.), *The measurement of depression* (pp. 376–397). New York: Guilford.

Marshall, L. H., & Magoun, H. W. (1998). *Discoveries in the human brain: Neuroscience prehistory, brain structure, and function.* Totowa, NJ: Humana Press.

Marshall, P. J., & Fox, N. A. (2000). Emotion regulation, depression, and hemispheric asymmetry. In S. L. Johnson, A. M. Hayes, T. M. Field, N. Schneiderman, & P. M. McCabe (Eds.), *Stress, coping, and depression* (pp. 35–50). Mahwah, NJ: Erlbaum.

Marshall, W. L. (1997). Pedophilia: Psychopathology and theory. In D. R. Laws & W. O'Donohue (Eds.), *Sexual deviance: Theory, assessment, and treatment* (pp. 152–174). New York: Guilford.

Marshall, W. L., Barbaree, H. E., & Christophe, D. (1986). Early onset and deviant sexuality in child molesters. *Journal of Interpersonal Violence, 6,* 323–336.

Marshall, W. L., Barbaree, H. E., & Eccles, A. (1991). Early onset and deviant sexuality in child molesters. *Journal of Interpersonal Violence, 6,* 323–335.

Marten, P. A., Brown, T. A., Barlow, D. H., Borkovec, T. D., Shear, M. K., & Lydiard, R. B. (1993). Evaluation of the ratings comprising the associated symptom criterion of DSM-III-R generalized anxiety disorder. *Journal of Nervous and Mental Disease, 181,* 676–682.

Martens, W. H. J. (2000). Antisocial and psychopathic personality disorders: Causes, course, and remission. *International Journal of Offender Therapy and Comparative Criminology, 44,* 406–430.

Martin, R. L., & Yutzy, S. H. (1996). Somatoform disorders. In R. E. Hales & S. C. Yudofsky (Eds.), *The American Psychiatric Press synopsis of psychiatry* (pp. 547–572). Washington, DC: American Psychiatric Press.

Martin, S. E., Bryant, K., & Fitzgerald, N. (2001). Self-reported alcohol use and abuse by arrestees in the 1998 Arrestee Drug Abuse Monitoring program. *Alcohol Health and Research World, 25,* 72–79.

Marty, D. A., & Chapin, R. (2000). The legislative tenets of clients' right to treatment in the least restrictive environment and freedom from harm: Implications for community providers. *Community Mental Health Journal, 36,* 545–556.

Masand, P. S., Sousou, A. J., Gupta, S., & Kaplan, D. S. (1998). Irritable bowel syndrome (IBS) and alcohol abuse or dependence. *American Journal of Drug and Alcohol Abuse, 24,* 513–521.

Masand, P., Kaplan, D. S., Gupta, S., & Bhandary, A. N. (1997). Irritable bowel syndrome and dysthymia: Is there a relationship? *Psychosomatics, 38,* 63–69.

Masi, G., Favilla, L., & Millepiedi, S. (2000). The Kleine-Levin syndrome as a neuropsychiatric disorder: A case report. *Psychiatry: Interpersonal and Biological Processes, 63,* 93–100.

Masling, J. M., & Bornstein, R. F. (1993). *Psychoanalytic perspectives on psychopathology.* Washington, DC: American Psychological Association.

Masling, J. M., Bornstein, R. F., Poynton, F. G., Reed, S., & Katkin, E. S. (1991). Perception without awareness and electrodermal responding: A strong test of subliminal psychodynamic activation. *Journal of Mind and Behavior, 12,* 33–47.

Maslow, A. H. (1968). *Toward a psychology of being* (2nd ed.). Princeton, NJ: Van Nostrand.

Maslowski, J. (1988). Cross-cultural study of productive phenomenology of schizophrenia. *Psychiatria Polska, 22,* 193–197.

Mason, F. L. (1997). Fetishism: Psychopathology and theory. In D. R. Laws & W. O'Donohue (Eds.), *Sexual deviance: Theory, assessment, and treatment* (pp. 75–91). New York: Guilford.

Massing, W., & Angermeyer, M. C. (1985). Myocardial infarction on various days of the week. *Psychological Medicine, 15,* 851–857.

Masters, W. H., & Johnson, V. E. (1965). *Sex and Behavior.* New York: Wiley.

Masters, W. H., & Johnson, V. E. (1966). *Human sexual response.* Boston: Little, Brown.

Masters, W. H., & Johnson, V. E. (1970). *Human sexual inadequacy.* Boston: Little, Brown.

Matarazzo, J. D. (1972). *Wechsler's measurement and appraisal of adult intelligence.* Baltimore: Williams & Wilkins.

Mathews, A. M. (1993). Anxiety and the processing of emotional information. In L. J. Chapman, J. P. Chapman, & D. Fowles (Eds.), *Models and methods of psychopathology: Progress in experimental personality and psychopathology research* (pp. 254–280). New York: Springer.

Mathews, C. A., & Freimer, N. B. (2000). Genetic linkage analysis of the psychiatric disorders. In B. I. Sadock & V. A. Sadock (Eds.), *Kaplan & Sadock's comprehensive textbook of psychiatry* (7th ed., pp. 184–198). Philadelphia: Lippincott Williams & Wilkins.

Matlin, M. W. (1998). *Cognition* (4th ed.). Fort Worth, TX: Harcourt Brace.

Matson, J. L., & Hammer, D. (1996). Assessment of social functioning. In J. W. Jacobson and J. A. Mulick (Eds.), *Manual of diagnosis and professional practice in mental retardation* (pp. 157–163). Washington, DC: American Psychological Association.

Matteson, D. R. (1999). Intimate bisexual couples. In J. Carlson & L. Sperry (Eds.), *The intimate couple* (pp. 439–459). Philadelphia: Brunner/Mazel.

Maunsell, E., Brisson, J., Mondor, M., Verreault, R., & Deschenes, L. (2001). Stressful life events and survival after breast cancer. *Psychosomatic Medicine, 63,* 306–315.

May, P. A., Hymbaugh, K. J., Aase, J. M., & Samet, J. M. (1989). Epidemiology of fetal alcohol syndrome among American Indians of the Southwest. *Journal of Studies on Alcohol, 50,* 508–518.

May, P. R. A. (1968). *Treatment of schizophrenia: A comparative study of five treatment methods.* New York: Science House.

Maybery, D. J., & Graham, D. (2001). Hassles and uplifts: Including interpersonal events. *Stress and Health, 17,* 91–104.

Mayeux, R. (1999). Predicting who will develop Alzheimer's disease. In R. Mayeux and Y. Christen (Eds.), *Epidemiology of Alzheimer's disease: From gene to prevention* (pp. 21–31). New York: Springer.

McAdoo, W. G., Weinberger, M. H., Miller, J. Z., Fineberg, N. S., & Grim, C. E. (1990). Race and gender influence hemodynamic responses to psychological and physical stimuli. *Journal of Hypertension, 8,* 961–967.

McCahill, T. L., Meyer, L. C., & Fischman, A. M. (1979). *The aftermath of rape.* Lexington, MA: Heath.

McCann, S. J. H., & Stewin, L. L. (1984). Environmental threat and parapsychological contributions to the psychological literature. *Journal of Social Psychology, 122,* 227–235.

McClelland, D. C. (1985). *Human motivation.* Glenview, IL: Scott, Foresman.

McDaniel, S. H., & Speice, J. (2001). What family psychology has to offer women's health: The examples of conversion, somatization, infertility treatment, and genetic testing. *Professional Psychology—Research and Practice, 32,* 44–51.

McDermott, M. R., Ramsay, J. M. C., & Bray, C. (2001). Components of the anger-hostility complex as risk factors for coronary artery disease severity: A multi-measure study. *Journal of Health Psychology, 6,* 309–319.

McDougle, C. J. (1998). Psychopharmacology. In F. R. Volkmar (Ed.), *Autism and pervasive developmental disorders* (pp. 169–194). Cambridge, England: Cambridge University Press.

McDougle, C. J., Brodkin, E. S., Yeung, P. P., Naylor, S. T., Cohen, D. J., & Price, L. H. (1995). Risperidone in adults with autism or pervasive developmental disorder. *Journal of Child and Adolescent Psychopharmacology, 5,* 273–282.

McDowell, D. M., Levin, F. R., & Nunes, E. V. (1999). Dissociative identity disorder and substance abuse: The forgotten relationship. *Journal of Psychoactive Drugs, 31,* 71–83.

McElroy, S. L., Hudson, J. I., Pope, H. G., Keck, P. E., & Aizley, H. G. (1992). The DSM-III-R impulse control disorders not elsewhere classified: Clinical characteristics and relationship to other psychiatric disorders. *American Journal of Psychiatry, 149,* 318–327.

McFall, R. M. (1990). The enhancement of social skills: An information-processing analysis. In W. L. Marshall, D. R. Laws, & H. E. Barbaree (Eds.), *Handbook of sexual assault: Issues, theories and treatment of the offender* (pp. 311–330). New York: Plenum.

McFall, R. M. (2000). Elaborate reflections on a simple manifesto. *Applied and Preventive Psychology, 9,* 5–21.

McFarlane, A. C. (1988). The etiology of post-traumatic stress disorder following a natural disaster. *British Journal of Psychiatry, 152,* 116–121.

McFarlane, T., McCabe, R. E. A., Jarry, J., Olmsted, M. P., & Polivy, J. (2001). Weight-related and shape-related self-evaluation in eating-disordered and non-eating-disordered women. *International Journal of Eating Disorders, 29*, 328–335.

McFarlin, S. K., & Fals-Stewart, W. (2002). Workplace absenteeism and alcohol use: A sequential analysis. *Psychology of Addictive Behaviors, 16*, 17–21.

McGee, G. G., Krantz, P. J., Mason, D., & McClannahan, L. E. (1983). A modified incidental-teaching procedure for autistic youth: Acquisition and generalization of receptive object labels. *Journal of Applied Behavior Analysis, 16*, 329–338.

McGhie, A., & Chapman, J. S. (1961). Disorders of attention and perception in early schizophrenia. *British Journal of Medical Psychology, 34*, 103–116.

McGlashan, T. H. (1983). The borderline syndrome: II. Is it a variant of schizophrenia or affective disorder? *Archives of General Psychiatry, 40*, 1319–1323.

McGlashan, T. H., & Hoffman, R. E.. (2000). Schizophrenia: Psychodynamic and neurodynamic theories. In B. I. Sadock & V. A. Sadock (Eds.), *Kaplan and Sadock's comprehensive textbook of psychiatry* (7th ed., pp. 1159–1169). Baltimore: Lippincott Williams & Wilkins.

McGue, M. (1999). The behavioral genetics of alcoholism. *Current Directions in Psychological Science, 8*, 109–115.

McGuffin, P., Reveley, A., & Holland, A. (1982). Identical triplets: Nonidentical psychoses? *British Journal of Psychiatry, 140*, 1–6.

McGuire, P. K., Shaah, G. M. S., & Murray, R. M. (1993). Increased blood flow in Broca's area during auditory hallucinations in schizophrenia. *Lancet, 342*, 703–706.

McGuire, P. K., Silberswieg, D. A., Wright, I., Murray, R. M., Frackowiak, R. S. J., & Frith, C. D. (1996). The neural correlates of inner speech and auditory verbal imagery in schizophrenia: Relationships to auditory verbal hallucinations. *British Journal of Psychiatry, 169*, 148–159.

McInnis, M. G. (1997). Recent advances in the genetics of bipolar disorder. *Psychiatric Annals, 27*, 482–488.

McIntosh, J. L. (1991). Epidemiology of suicide in the U.S. In A. A. Leenaars (Ed.), *Life span perspectives of suicide.* New York: Plenum.

McIntosh, J. L. (1992). Epidemiology of suicide in the elderly. *Suicide and Life-Threatening Behavior, 22*, 15–35.

McKay, A. (2000). Prevention of sexually transmitted infections in different populations: A review of behaviourally effective and cost-effective interventions. *The Canadian Journal of Human Sexuality, 9*, 95–120.

McKay, D., Neziroglu, F., Yaryura-Tobias, J. A. (1997). Comparison of clinical characteristics in obsessive-compulsive disorder and body dysmorphic disorder. *Journal of Anxiety Disorders, 11*, 447–454.

McLean, P. D., & Woody, S. R. (2001). *Anxiety disorders in adults: An evidence-based approach to psychological treatment.* New York: Oxford University Press.

McLeer, S. V., Deblinger, E., Atkins, M. S., Foa, E. B., & Ralphe, D. L. (1988). Posttraumatic stress disorder in sexually abused children. *Journal of the American Academy of Child and Adolescent Psychiatry, 27*, 650–665.

McNally, R. J. (1992). Anxiety sensitivity distinguishes panic disorder from generalized anxiety disorder. *Journal of Nervous and Mental Disease, 180*, 737–738.

McNally, R. J. (1994). *Panic disorder: A critical analysis.* New York: Guilford.

McNally, R. J. (1996). Anxiety sensitivity is distinguishable from trait anxiety. In R. M. Rapee (Ed.), *Current controversies in the anxiety disorders* (pp. 214–227). New York: Guilford.

McNally, R. J. (1999). Posttraumatic stress disorder. In T. E. Millon, P. H. Blaney, & R. D. Davis (Eds.), *Oxford textbook of psychopathology* (pp. 144–165). New York: Oxford University Press.

McNally, R. J., & Louro, C. E. (1992). Fear of flying in agoraphobia and simple phobia: Distinguishing features. *Journal of Anxiety Disorders, 6*, 319–324.

McNamara, B., Ray, J. L., Arthurs, O. J., & Boniface, S. (2001). Transcranial magnetic stimulation for depression and other psychiatric disorders. *Psychological Medicine, 31*, 1141–1146.

McNeal, E. T., & Cimbolic, P. (1986). Antidepressants and biochemical theories of depression. *Psychological Bulletin, 99*, 361–374.

McNeil, T. F. (1987). Perinatal influences in the development of schizophrenia. In H. Helmchen & F. A. Henn (Eds.), *Biological perspectives on schizophrenia* (pp. 125–138). New York: Wiley.

McNeil, T. F., Cantor-Graae, E., & Weinberger, D. R. (2000). Relationship of obstetric complications and differences in size of brain structures in monozygotic twin pairs discordant for schizophrenia. *American Journal of Psychiatry, 157*, 203–212.

McNeilly, M., & Zeichner, A. (1989). Neuropeptide and cardiovascular responses to intravenous catheterization in normotensive and hypertensive Blacks and Whites. *Health Psychology, 8*, 487–501.

McQuaid, J. R., Monroe, S. M., Roberts, J. E., Kupfer, D. J., & Frank, E. (2000). A comparison of two life stress assessment approaches: Prospective prediction of treatment outcome in recurrent depression. *Journal of Abnormal Psychology, 109*, 787–791.

Meador-Woodruff, J. H., Hogg, A. J., Jr., & Smith, R. E. (2001). Striatal ionotropic glutamate receptor expression in schizophrenia, bipolar disorder, and major depressive disorder. *Brain Research Bulletin, 55*, 631–640.

Mealey, L. (1995) The sociobiology of sociopathy: An integrated evolutionary model. *Behavior and Brain Sciences, 18*, 523–599.

Mednick, S. A., & McNeil, T. (1968). Current methodology in research on the etiology of schizophrenia: Serious difficulties which suggest the use of the high risk group method. *Psychological Bulletin, 70*, 681–693.

Mednick, S. A., & Schulsinger, F. (1968). Some premorbid characteristics related to breakdown in children with schizophrenic mothers. In D. Rosenthal & S. S. Kety (Eds.), *The transmission of schizophrenia.* Elmsford, NY: Pergamon.

Mednick, S. A., Machon, R. A., Huttunen, M. O., & Bonett, D. (1988). Adult schizophrenia following prenatal exposure to an influenza epidemic. *Archives of General Psychiatry, 45*, 189–192.

Mednick, S. A., Watson, J. B., Huttunen, M., Cannon, T. D., Katila, H., Machon, R., Mednick, B., Hollister, M., Parnas, J., Schulsinger, F., Sajaniemi, N., Voldgaard, P., Pyhala, R., Gutkind, D., & Wang, X. (1998). A two-hit working model of the etiology of schizophrenia. In M. Lenzenweger & R. H. Dworkin (Eds.), *Origins and development of schizophrenia: Advances in experimental psychopathology* (pp. 27–66). Washington, DC: American Psychological Association.

Meehl, P. E. (1962). Schizotaxia, schizotypy, schizophrenia. *American Psychologist, 17*, 827–838.

Meehl, P. E. (1964). *Manual for use with checklist of schizotypic signs.* Minneapolis: Psychiatric Research Unit, University of Minnesota Medical School.

Meehl, P. E. (1971). High school yearbooks: A reply to Schwarz. *Journal of Abnormal Psychology, 77*, 143–148.

Meehl, P. E. (1990). Toward an integrated theory of schizotaxia, schizotypy, and schizophrenia. *Journal of Personality Disorders, 4*, 1–99.

Meehl, P. E., & Rosen, A. (1955). Antecedent probability and the efficiency of psychometric signs, patterns, or cutting scores. *Psychological Bulletin, 52*, 194–216.

Meesters, Y., & Letsch, M. C. (1998). The dark side of light treatment for seasonal affective disorder. *International Journal of Risk and Safety in Medicine, 11*, 115–120.

Mehta, M. A., Sahakian, B. J., & Robbins, T. W. (2001). Comparative psychopharmacology of methylphenidate and related drugs in human volunteers, patients with ADHD, and experimental animals. In M. V. Solanto, A. F. T. Arnsten, & F. X. Castellanos (Eds.), *Stimulant drugs and ADHD: Basic and clinical neuroscience* (pp. 303–331). New York: Oxford University Press.

Meichenbaum, D., & Turk, D. C. (1987). *Facilitating treatment adherence: A practitioner's guidebook.* New York: Plenum.

Meisler, A. W. (1999). Group treatment of PTSD and comorbid alcohol abuse. In B. H. Young & D. D. Blake (Eds.), *Group treatments for posttraumatic stress disorder* (pp. 117–136). Philadelphia: Brunner/Mazel.

Mellman, T. A. (2000). Sleep and the pathogenesis of PTSD. In A. Y. Shalev, R. Yehuda, & A. C. McFarlane (Eds.), *International handbook of human response to trauma* (pp. 299–306). New York: Kluwer Academic/Plenum Publishers.

Melman, A., Tiefer, L., & Pedersen, R. (1988). Evaluation of the first 406 patients in a urology-department-based center for male sexual dysfunction. *Urology, 32,* 6–10.

Meltzer, H. Y. (1999). Treatment of schizophrenia and spectrum disorders: Pharmacotherapy, psychosocial treatments, and neurotransmitter interactions. *Biological Psychiatry, 46,* 1321–1327.

Meltzer, H. Y., & McGurk, S. R. (1999). The effects of clozapine, risperidone, and olanzapine on cognitive function in schizophrenia. *Schizophrenia Bulletin, 25,* 233–255.

Mendels, J., Stinnett, J. L., Burns, D., & Frazer, A. (1975). Amine precursors and depression. *Archives of General Psychiatry, 32,* 22–30.

Mendes de Leon, C. F., Powell, L. H., & Kaplan, B. H. (1991). Change in coronary-prone behaviors in the Recurrent Coronary Prevention Project. *Psychosomatic Medicine, 53,* 407–419.

Mendlewicz, J. (1985). Genetic research in depressive disorders. In E. E. Beckham & W. R. Leber (Eds.), *Handbook of depression: Treatment, assessment, and research* (pp. 795–815). Homewood, IL: Dorsey Press.

Mendlewicz, J., & Rainer, J. D. (1977). Adoption study supporting genetic transmission in the manic depressive illness. *Nature, 268*(5618), 327–329.

Menkes, J. H. (1995). *Textbook of child neurology.* Baltimore: Williams & Wilkins.

Merrill, J., Milner, G., Owens, J., & Vale, A. (1992). Alcohol and attempted suicide. *British Journal of Addiction, 87,* 83–89.

Mersch, P. P. A., Middendorp, H. M., Bouhuys, A. L., Beersma, D. G. M., & van den Hoofdakker, R. H. (1999). The prevalence of seasonal affective disorder in the Netherlands: A prospective and retrospective study of seasonal mood variation in the general population. *Biological Psychiatry, 45,* 1013–1022.

Merskey, H. (1995). *The analysis of hysteria: Understanding conversion and dissocation* (2nd ed.). London: Gaskell/Royal College of Psychiatrists.

Meston, C. M., & Gorzalka, B. B. (1996). Differential effects of sympathetic activation on sexual arousal in sexually dysfunctional and functional women. *Journal of Abnormal Psychology, 105,* 582–591.

Meston, C. M., Gorzalka, B. B., & Wright, J. M. (1997). Inhibition of subjective and physiological sexual arousal in women by clonidine. *Psychosomatic Medicine, 59,* 399–407.

Metalsky, G. I., Haberstadt, L. J., & Abramson, L. Y. (1987). Vulnerability and invulnerability to depressive mood reactions: Toward a more powerful test of the diathesis-stress and causal medication components of the reformulated theory of depression. *Journal of Personality and Social Psychology, 52,* 386–393.

Metz, M. E., & Prior, J. L. (2000). Premature ejaculation: A psychophysiological approach for assessment and management. *Journal of Sex and Marital Therapy, 26,* 293–320.

Mezzich, A. C., Moss, H., Tarter, R. E., Wolfenstein, M., et al. (1994). Gender differences in the pattern and progression of substance use in conduct-disordered adolescents. *American Journal on Addictions, 3,* 289–295.

Michael, R. P., & Zumpe, D. (1998). Developmental changes in behavior and in steroid uptake by the male and female macaque brain. *Developmental Neuropsychology, 14,* 233–260.

Miech, R. A., Breitner, J. C. S., Zandi, P. P., Khachaturian, A. S., Anthony, J. C., & Mayer, L. (2002). Incidence of AD may decline in the early 90s for men, later for women: The Cache County study. *Neurology, 58,* 209–218.

Miers, T. C., & Raulin, M. L. (1985). The development of a scale to measure cognitive slippage. Paper presented in March at the Eastern Psychological Association Convention, Boston.

Miesen, B. M. L. (1999). *Dementia in close-up.* London: Routledge.

Mignot, E. (1998). Genetic and familial aspects of narcolepsy. *Neurology, 50,* S16–S22.

Miklowitz, D. J. (1994). Family risk indicators in schizophrenia. *Schizophrenia Bulletin, 20,* 137-149.

Miklowitz, D. J. (1996). Psychotherapy in combination with drug treatment for bipolar disorder. *Journal of Clinical Psychopharmacology, 16* (Supplement 1), 56s–66s.

Milam, J. R., & Ketcham, K. (1983). *Under the influence.* New York: Bantam.

Milich, R., Balentine, A. C., & Lynam, D. R. (2001). ADHD combined type and ADHD predominantly inattentive type are distinct and unrelated disorders. *Clinical Psychology: Science and Practice, 8,* 463–488.

Miller, F., Barasch, A., Sacks, M., Levitan, J., & Ashcroft, L. (1986). Serum prolactin correlates with depressed mood during alcohol withdrawal. *Drug and Alcohol Dependence, 17,* 331–338.

Miller, N. E. (1985). The value of behavioral research with animals. *American Psychologist, 40,* 423–440.

Miller, N. S. (1995). *Addiction psychiatry: Current diagnosis and treatment.* New York: Wiley-Liss.

Miller, W. M., & Seligman, M. E. P. (1975). Depression and learned helplessness in man. *Journal of Abnormal Psychology, 84,* 228–238.

Miller, W. R. (2000). Rediscovering fire: Small interventions, large effects. *Psychology of Addictive Behaviors, 14,* 6–18.

Miller, W. R., & Heather, N. (1998). *Treating addictive behaviors* (2nd ed.). New York: Plenum.

Miller, W. R., Leckman, A. L., Delaney, H. D., & Tinkcom, M. (1992). Long-term follow-up of behavioral self-control training. *Journal of Studies on Alcohol, 53,* 249–261.

Millon, T. (1969). *Modern psychopathology.* Philadelphia: Saunders.

Millon, T. (1990). *Toward a new personology: An evolutionary model.* New York: Wiley-Interscience.

Millon, T. (1996). *Disorders of personality: DSM-IV and beyond* (2nd ed.). New York: Wiley.

Millon, T., & Davis, R. (1995). Conceptions of personality disorders: Historical perspectives, the DSMs, and future directions. In W. J. Livesley (Ed.), *The DSM-IV personality disorders* (pp. 3–28). New York: Guilford.

Millon, T., & Davis, R. (1999). Developmental pathogenesis. In T. Millon, P. H. Blaney, & R. D. Davis (Eds.), *Oxford textbook of psychopathology* (pp. 29–48). New York: Oxford University Press.

Millon, T., & Martinez, A. (1995). Avoidant personality disorder. In W. J. Livesley (Ed.), *The DSM-IV personality disorders* (pp. 218–233). New York: Guilford.

Millon, T., Blaney, P. H., & Davis, R. D. (Eds.). (1999). *Oxford textbook of psychopathology.* New York: Oxford University Press.

Millsaps, C. L., Azrin, R. L., & Mittenberg, W. (1994). Neuropsychological effects of chronic cannabis use on the memory and intelligence of adolescents. *Journal of Child and Adolescent Substance Abuse, 3,* 47–55.

Mindell, J. A. (1993). Sleep disorders in children. *Health Psychology, 12,* 151–162.

Mineka, S., & Cook, M. (1993). Mechanisms underlying observational conditioning of fear in monkeys. *Journal of Experimental Psychology: General, 122,* 23–38.

Mineka, S., & Henderson, R. (1985). Controllability and predictability in acquired motivation. *Annual Review of Psychology, 36,* 495–529.

Mineka, S., Davidson, M., Cook, M., & Keir, R. (1984). Observational conditioning of snake fears in rhesus monkeys. *Journal of Abnormal Psychology, 93,* 355–372.

Minshew, N. J. (1991). Indices of neural function in autism: Clinical and biological implications. *Pediatrics, 31,* 774–780.

Minshew, N. J., Goldstein, G., Taylor, H. G., & Siegel, D. J. (1994). Academic achievement in high-functioning autistic individuals. *Journal of Clinical and Experimental Neuropsychology, 16,* 261–270.

Minuchin, S., Lee, W. Y., & Simon, G. M. (1996). *Mastering family therapy: Journeys of growth and transformation.* New York: Wiley.

Minuchin, S., Rosman, B. L., & Baker, L. (1978). *Psychosomatic families.* Cambridge, MA: Harvard University Press.

Mischel, W. (1968). *Personality and assessment.* New York: Wiley.

Mishler, E. G., & Waxler, N. E. (1968). *Family processes and schizophrenia: Theory and selected experimental studies.* New York: Science House.

Mitchell, J. E. (1986). Bulimia: Medical and physiological aspects. In K. D. Brownell & J. P. Foreyt (Eds.), *Handbook of eating disorders: Physiology, psychology, and treatment of obesity, anorexia, and bulimia* (pp. 379–388). New York: Basic Books.

Mitchell, J. E., Fletcher, L., Hanson, K., Mussell, M. P., Seim, H., Crosby, R., & Al-Banna, M. (2001). The relative efficacy of fluoxetine and manual-based self-help in the treatment of outpatients with bulimia nervosa. *Journal of Clinical Psychopharmacology, 21,* 298–304.

Mitchell, P. B. (1999a). On the 50th anniversary of John Cade's discovery of the anti-manic effect of lithium. *Australian and New Zealand Journal of Psychiatry, 33,* 623–628.

Mitchell, P. B. (1999b). The place of anticonvulsants and other putative mood stabilizers in the treatment of bipolar disorder. *Australian and New Zealand Journal of Psychiatry, 33,* S99–S107.

Mitchell, P. B., Mackinnon, A. J., & Waters, B. (1993). The genetics of bipolar disorder. *Australian and New Zealand Journal of Psychiatry, 27,* 560–580.

Mitler, M. M., Van den Hoed, J., Carskadon, M. A., Richardson, G. S., Park, R., Guilleminault, C., & Dement, W. C. (1979). REM sleep episodes during the Multiple Sleep Latency Test in narcoleptic patients. *Electroencephalography and Clinical Neurophysiology, 46,* 479–481.

Mitton, J. B. (1997). *Selection in natural populations.* New York: Oxford University Press.

Moeller, H. J. (1995). The psychopathology of schizophrenia: An integrated view on positive symptoms and negative symptoms. *International Clinical Psychopharmacology, 10,* 57–64.

Moffitt, T. E. (1990). Juvenile delinquency and attention-deficit disorder: Developmental trajectories from age 3 to 15. *Child Development, 61,* 893–910.

Moffitt, T. E. (1993). Adolescence-limited and life-course-persistent antisocial behavior: A developmental taxonomy. *Psychological Review, 100,* 674–701.

Moffitt, T. E., Mednick, S. A., & Gabrielli, W. F. (1989). Predicting criminal violence: Descriptive data and predispositional factors. In D. Brizer & M. Crowner (Eds.), *Current approaches to the prediction of violence* (pp. 13–34). Washington, DC: American Psychiatric Association.

Moller-Madsen, S., Nystrup, J., & Nielsen, S. (1996). Mortality in anorexia nervosa in Denmark during the period 1970–1987. *Acta Psychiatrica Scandinavica, 94,* 454–459.

Monahan, J. (1992). Mental disorder and violent behavior: Perceptions and evidence. *American Psychologist, 47,* 511–521.

Monahan, J. (1993). Mental disorder and violence: Another look. In S. Hodgins (Ed.), *Mental disorder and crime* (pp. 287–302). Thousand Oaks, CA: Sage.

Monahan, J., & Steadman, H. J. (2001). Violence risk assessment: A quarter century of research. In L. E. Frost & R. J. Bonnie (Eds.), *The evolution of mental health law* (pp. 195–211). Washington, DC: American Psychological Association.

Moniz, E. (1994). Prefrontal leucotomy in the treatment of mental disorders. *American Journal of Psychiatry, 151*(6, supplement), 237–239. Originally published in 1937.

Monroe, S. A., & Johnson, S. L. (1992). Social support, depression, and other mental disorders: In retrospect and toward future prospects. In H. O. F. Veiel & U. Baumann (Eds.), *The meaning and measurement of social support.* New York: Hemisphere.

Monroe, S. A., Thase, M. E., & Simons, A. D. (1992). Social factors and the psychobiology of depression: Relationships between life stress and rapid eye movement sleep latency. *Journal of Abnormal Psychology, 101,* 528–537.

Moore, J. (1994). The chola life course: Chicana heroin users and the barrio gang. *International Journal of the Addictions, 29,* 1115–1126.

Moore, S. W. (1998). Specific drug therapy. In R. C. Hamdy, J. M. Turnbull, J. Edwards, & M. M. Lancaster (Eds.), *Alzheimer's disease: A handbook for caregivers* (3rd ed., pp. 183–198). St. Louis, MO: Mosby.

Moore, S., Grunberg, L., & Greenberg, E. (2000). The relationships between alcohol problems and well-being, work attitudes, and performance: Are they monotonic? *Journal of Substance Abuse, 11,* 183–204.

Moore-Ede, M. C., Sulzman, F. M., & Fuller, C. F. (1982). *The clocks that time us.* Cambridge, MA: Harvard University Press.

Moran, P. W. (2000). The adaptive practice of psychotherapy in the managed care era. *Psychiatric Clinics of North America, 23,* 383–402.

Moretti, M. M., Charlton, S., & Taylor, S. (1996). The effects of hemispheric asymmetries and depression on the perception of emotion. *Brain & Cognition, 32,* 67–82.

Morganstern, J., Langenbucher, J., Lavouvie, E., & Miller, K. J. (1997). The comorbidity of alcoholism and personality disorders in a clinical population: Prevalence rates and relationship to alcohol typology variables. *Journal of Abnormal Psychology, 106,* 74–84.

Morin, C. M. (1993). *Insomnia: Psychological assessment and management.* New York: Guilford.

Morokoff, P. J., & Gillilland, R. (1993). Stress, sexual functioning, and marital satisfaction. *Journal of Sex Research, 30,* 43–53.

Morokoff, P. J., & LoPiccolo, J. L. (1986). A comparative evaluation of minimal therapist contact and 15-session treatment for female orgasmic dysfunction. *Journal of Consulting and Clinical Psychology, 54,* 294–300.

Morrison, J. (1997). *When psychological problems mask medical disorders: A guide for psychotherapists.* New York: Guilford.

Morse, J. (2002). Women on a binge. *Time, 159*(13), 56–61.

Mortimer, A. M. (2001). First-line atypical antipsychotics for schizophrenia are appropriate—with psychosocial interventions. *Psychiatric Bulletin, 25,* 287–288.

Moser, C., & Levitt, E. E. (1987). An exploratory-descriptive study of a sadomasochistically oriented sample. *Journal of Sex Research, 23,* 322–337.

Moser, R. P., & Jacob, T. (1997). Parent-child interactions and child outcomes as related to gender of alcoholic parent. *Journal of Substance Abuse, 9,* 189–208.

Mottaghipour, Y., Pourmand, D., Maleki, H., & Davidian, L. (2001). Expressed emotion and the course of schizophrenia in Iran. *Social Psychiatry and Psychiatric Epidemiology, 36,* 195–199.

Mowrer, O. H. (1947). On the dual nature of learning: A reinterpretation of "conditioning" and "problem solving." *Harvard Educational Review, 17,* 102–148.

Mpofu, E., & Crystal, R. (2001). Conduct disorder in children: Challenges, and prospective cognitive behavioural treatments. *Counseling Psychology Quarterly, 14,* 21–32.

Muehlberger, A., Herrmann, M. J., Wiedemann, G., Ellgring, H., & Pauli, P. (2001). Repeated exposure of flight phobics to flights in virtual reality. *Behaviour Research and Therapy, 39,* 1033–1050.

Muehlenhard, C. L., & Kimes, L. A. (1999). The social construction of violence: The case of sexual and domestic violence. *Personality and Social Psychology Review, 3,* 234–245.

Muir, J. L. (1997). Acetylcholine, aging, and Alzheimer's disease. *Pharmacological Biochemical Behavior, 56,* 687–696.

Mulhall, J. P. (2000). Current concepts in erectile dysfunction. *American Journal of Managed Care, 6,* S625–S631.

Mulhern, S. (1991). Satanism and psychotherapy: A rumor in search of an inquisition. In J. T. Richardson, J. Best, & D. H. Bromley (Eds.), *The Satanism scare* (pp. 145–172). New York: Aldine.

Multimodal Treatment Study of Children with ADHD Cooperative Group. (1999). Moderators and mediators of treatment response for children with attention-deficit/hyperactivity disorder: The multimodal treatment study of children with attention-deficit/hyperactivity disorder. *Archives of General Psychiatry, 56,* 1088–1096.

Mumenthaler, M. S., Taylor, J. L., O'Hara, R., & Yesavage, J. A. (1999). Gender differences in moderate drinking effects. *Alcohol Health and Research World, 23,* 55–61.

Mundy, P., & Sigman, M. (1989). The theoretical implications of joint-attention deficits in autism. *Development and Psychopathology, 1,* 173–184.

Munoz, R. F., Le, H., & Ghosh Ippen, C. (2000). We should screen for major depression. *Applied and Preventive Psychology, 9,* 123–133.

Murialdo, G., Nobili, F., Rollero, A., Gianelli, M. V., Copello, F., Rodriguez, G., & Polleri, A. (2000). Hippocampal perfusion and pituitary-adrenal axis in Alzheimer's disease. *Neuropsychobiology, 42,* 51–57.

Muris, P., Schmidt, H., & Merckelbach, H. (1999). The structure of specific phobia symptoms among children and adolescents. *Behaviour Research and Therapy, 37,* 863–868.

Murphy, D. L., Brodie, H. K. H., Goodwin, F. K., & Bunney, W. E. (1971). Regular induction of hypomania by L-dopa in "bipolar" manic-depressive patients. *Nature, 229,* 135–136.

Murphy, E., & Carr, A. (2000). Enuresis and encopresis. In A. Carr (Ed.), *What works with children and adolescents: A critical review of psychological interventions with children, adolescents and their families* (pp. 49–64). Florence, KY: Taylor & Francis/Routledge.

Murphy, F., Troop, N. A., & Treasure, J. L. (2000). Differential environmental factors in anorexia nervosa: A sibling pair study. *British Journal of Clinical Psychology, 39,* 193–203.

Murphy, W. D. (1997). Exhibitionism: Psychopathology and theory. In D. R. Laws & W. O'Donohue (Eds.), *Sexual deviance: Theory, assessment, and treatment* (pp. 22–39). New York: Guilford.

Murphy, W. D., Krisak, J., Stalgaitis, S., & Anderson, K. (1984). The use of penile tumescence measures with incarcerated rapists: Further validity issues. *Archives of Sexual Behavior, 13,* 545–554.

Muscettola, G., Potter, W. Z., Pickar, D., & Goodwin, F. K. (1984). Urinary 3-methoxy-4-hydroxyphenyl glycol and major affective disorders. *Archives of General Psychiatry, 41,* 337–342.

Myers, D. G. (1999). Social psychology (6th ed.). New York: McGraw-Hill.

Myers, G. J., & Davidson, P. W. (1998). Prenatal methylmercury exposure and children: neurologic, developmental, and behavioral research. *Environmental Health Perspectives, 106* (Supplement 3), 841–847.

Nader, K. (1996). Children's traumatic dreams. In D. Barrett (Ed.), *Trauma and dreams* (pp. 9–24). Cambridge, MA: Harvard University Press.

Naegele, T., & Clark, A. (2001). Forensic Munchausen syndrome by proxy: An emerging subspecies of child sexual abuse. *Forensic Examiner, 10,* 21–23.

Nagel, K. L., & Jones, K. H. (1992). Predisposition factors in anorexia nervosa. *Adolescence, 27,* 381–386.

Nakatani, H., Munesue, T., Kaneda, M., Yagishita, K., & Koshino, Y. (2000). The estimated prevalence of delayed sleep phase syndrome in high school students. *Seishin Igaku, 42,* 1095–1099.

Naliboff, B. D., Heitkemper, M. M., Chang, L., & Mayer, E. A. (2000). Sex and gender in irritable bowel syndrome. In R. B. Fillingim (Ed.), *Sex, gender, and pain,* Vol. 17: *Progress in pain research and management* (pp. 327–353). Seattle, WA: IASP Press.

Narrow, W. E., Rae, D. S., Robins, L. N., & Regier, D. A. (2002). Revised prevalence estimates of mental disorders in the United States: Using a clinical significance criterion to reconcile two surveys' estimates. *Archives of General Psychiatry, 59,* 115–123.

Natelson, B. H. (2001). Chronic fatigue syndrome. *JAMA, The Journal of the American Medical Association, 285,* 2557–2559.

National Academies of Sciences and Engineering and Institute of Medicine. (1995). *On being a scientist: Responsible conduct in research* (2nd ed.). Washington, DC: National Academy Press.

Ndetei, D. M., & Singh, A. (1983). Hallucinations in Kenyan schizophrenic patients. *Acta Psychiatrica Scandinavica, 67,* 144–147.

Neal, A. M., & Turner, S. M. (1991). Anxiety disorders research with African Americans: Current status. *Psychological Bulletin, 109,* 400–410.

Neale, M. C., Walters, E. E., Eaves, L. J., Kessler, R. C., Heath, A. C., & Kendler, K. S. (1994). Genetics of blood-injury fears and phobias: A population-based twin study. *American Journal of Medical Genetics, 54,* 326–334.

Needle, R., McCubbin, H., Wilson, M., Reineck, R., Lazar, A., & Mederer, H. (1986). Interpersonal influences in adolescent drug use: The role of older siblings, parents, and peers. *International Journal of the Addictions, 21,* 739–766.

Needleman, H. L. (1992). Childhood exposure to lead: A common cause of school failure. *Phi Delta Kappan, 74,* 35–37.

Neisser, U., & Harsch, N. (1992). Phantom flashbulbs: False recollection of hearing the news about Challenger. In E. Winograd & U. Neisser (Eds.), *Affect and accuracy in recall: Studies of "flashbulb" memories* (pp. 9–31). New York: Cambridge University Press.

Nelson, J. C., & Davis, J. M. (1997). DST studies in psychotic depression: A meta-analysis. *American Journal of Psychiatry, 154,* 1497–1503.

Nemeroff, C. B., & Schatzberg, A. F. (1998). Pharmacological treatment of unipolar depression. In P. E. Nathan & J. M. Gorman (Eds.), *A guide to treatments that work* (pp. 212–225). New York: Oxford University Press.

Nemiah, J. C. (1998). Early concepts of trauma, dissociation, and the unconscious: Their history and current implications. In J. D. Bremmer & C. R. Marmar (Eds.), *Trauma, memory, and dissociation* (pp. 1–26). Washington, DC: American Psychiatric Press.

Nemiah, J. C., & Uhde, T. W. (1989). Obsessive-compulsive disorder. In H. I. Kaplan & B. J. Sadock (Eds.), *Comprehensive textbook of psychiatry* (5th ed., pp. 984–1000). Baltimore, MD: Williams & Wilkins.

Nesse, R. M. (1988). Panic disorder: An evolutionary view. *Psychiatric Annals, 18,* 478–483.

Nesse, R. M. (1999). Proximate and evolutionary studies of anxiety, stress and depression: Synergy at the interface. *Neuroscience and Biobehavioral Reviews, 23,* 895–903.

Nesse, R. M., & Williams, G. (1994). *Why we get sick: The new science of Darwinian medicine.* New York: New York Times Books.

Neuger, J., El Khoury, A., Kjellman, B. F., Wahlund, B., Aberg-Wistedt, A, & Stain-Malmgren, R. (1999). Platelet serotonin functions in untreated major depression. *Psychiatry Research, 85,* 189–198.

Neumaerker, K., Bettle, N., Neumaerker, U., & Bettle, O. (2000). Age- and gender-related psychological characteristics of adolescent ballet dancers. *Psychopathology, 33,* 137–142.

Newton, J. D. (1987). *Uncommon friends : Life with Thomas Edison, Henry Ford, Harvey Firestone, Alexis Carrel, and Charles Lindbergh.* San Diego: Harcourt.

Newton, L., Rosen, A., Tennant, C., & Hobbs, C. (2001). Moving out and moving on: Some ethnographic observations of deinstitutionalization in an Australian community. *Psychiatric Rehabilitation Journal, 25,* 152–162.

NHSDA. (1997). *Preliminary results of the 1997 national household survey on drug abuse* (H6, DDHS Publication # SMA 98–3251). Rockville, MD: Substance Abuse and Mental Health Services Administration.

NHTSA (National Highway Traffic Safety Association). (1994). *FEARS.* Washington, DC: U.S. Department of Transportation.

NHTSA (National Highway Traffic Safety Association). (2001). *The visual detection of DWI motorists.* Washington, DC: U.S. Department of Transportation.

NIAAA (National Institute on Alcohol Abuse and Alcoholism). (1990). *Seventh special report to the U.S. Congress on alcohol and health:* DHHS Publication ADM 90-1656. Washington, DC: U.S. Government Printing Office.

NIAAA (National Institute on Alcohol Abuse and Alcoholism). (1991). Fetal alcohol syndrome. *Alcohol Alert, no. 13,* 297.

NIAAA (National Institute on Alcohol Abuse and Alcoholism). (1997). *Alcohol and Health: Ninth special report to the U.S. Congress* (NIH Publication Number 97–4017). Bethesda, MD: National Institute of Health.

Nichols, M. P., & Minuchin, S. (1999). Short-term structural family therapy with couples. In J. M. Donovan (Ed.), *Short-term couple therapy. The Guilford family therapy series* (pp. 124–143). New York: Guilford.

NIDA (National Institute on Drug Abuse). (1982). *National survey on drug abuse.* Washington, DC: Department of Health and Human Services.

NIDA (National Institute on Drug Abuse). (1996). *National household survey on drug abuse: Population estimates 1995.* Washington, DC: Department of Health and Human Services.

NIDA (National Institute on Drug Abuse). (1999). *Cocaine abuse and addiction.* Washington, DC: National Institutes of Health (Publication Number 99-4342).

NIDA (National Institute on Drug Abuse). (2001). *Nicotine addiction.* Washington, DC: National Institutes of Health (Publication Number 01-4342).

Nigg, J. T. (2001). Is ADHD a disinhibitory disorder? *Psychological Bulletin, 127,* 571–598.

Nihira, K., Foster, R., Shenhaas, M., & Leland, H. (1975). *AAMD-Adaptive Behavior Scale.* Washington, DC: American Association on Mental Deficiency.

Nijenhuis, E. R. S., Spinhoven, P., Vanderlinden, J., van Dyck, R., & van der Hart, O. (1998a). Somatoform dissociative symptoms as related to animal defensive reactions to predatory imminence and injury. *Journal of Abnormal Psychology, 107,* 63–73.

Nijenhuis, E. R. S., Vanderlinden, J., & Spinhoven, P. (1998b). Animal defensive reactions as a model for trauma-induced dissociative reactions. *Journal of Traumatic Stress, 11,* 243–260.

Nishith, P., Resick, P. A., & Mueser, K. T. (2001). Sleep difficulties and alcohol use motives in female rape victims with posttraumatic stress disorder. *Journal of Traumatic Stress, 14,* 469–479.

Noback, C. R., Strominger, N. L., & Demarest, R. J. (1991). *The human nervous system: Introduction and review* (4th ed.). Philadelphia: Lea & Febiger.

Nolen-Hoeksema, S. (1987). Sex differences in unipolar depression: Evidence and theory. *Psychological Bulletin, 101,* 259–282.

Nolen-Hoeksema, S. (1990). Sex differences in depression. Stanford, CA: Stanford University Press.

Nolen-Hoeksema, S., & Girgus, J. S. (1994). The emergence of gender differences in depression during adolescence. *Psychological Bulletin, 115,* 424–443.

Nolen-Hoeksema, S., Girgus, J. S., & Seligman, M. E. (1992). Predictors and consequences of childhood depressive symptoms: A 5-year longitudinal study. *Journal of Abnormal Psychology, 101,* 405–422.

Novak, V. (2001). New Ritalin ad blitz makes parents jumpy. *Time, 158*(10), 62–63.

Noyes, R., Clarkson, C., Crowe, R. R., Yates, W. R., & McChesney, C. M. (1987). A family study of generalized anxiety disorder. *American Journal of Psychiatry, 144,* 1019–1024.

Noyes, R., Garvey, M. J., Cook, B., & Suelzer, M. (1991). Controlled discontinuation of benzodiazepine treatment for patients with panic disorder. *American Journal of Psychiatry, 148,* 517–523.

Nuechterlein, K. H. (1991). Vigilance in schizophrenia and related disorders. In S. R. Steinhauer, J. H. Gruzelier, & J. Zubin (Eds.), *Handbook of schizophrenia* (Vol. 5, pp. 397–433). Amsterdam: Elsevier.

Nugter, A., Dingemans, P., Van der Does, J. W., Linszen, D., & Gersons, B. (1997). Family treatment, expressed emotion, and relapse in recent-onset schizophrenia. *Psychiatry Research, 72,* 23–31.

Nutter, D., & Condron, M. (1983). Sexual fantasy and activity pattern of females with inhibited sexual desire versus normal controls. *Journal of Sex and Marital Therapy, 9,* 276–282.

Nutter, D., & Condron, M. (1985). Sexual fantasy and activity pattern of males with inhibited sexual desire and males with erectile dysfunction versus normal controls. *Journal of Sex and Marital Therapy, 11,* 91–98.

Nye, C. L., Zucker, R. A., & Fitzgerald, H. E. (1999). Early family-based intervention in the path to alcohol problems: Rationale and relationship between treatment process characteristics and child and parenting outcomes. *Journal of Studies on Alcohol.* Vol. Supp. 13, 10–21.

Nykamp, K., Rosenthal, L., Folkerts, M., Roehrs, T., Guido, P., & Roth, T. (1998). The effects of REM sleep deprivation on the level of sleepiness/alertness. *Sleep, 21,* 609–613.

Oakes, K. E., Allen, J. P., & Ciarrocchi, J. W. (2000). Spirituality, religious problem-solving, and sobriety in Alcoholics Anonymous. *Alcoholism Treatment Quarterly, 18,* 37–50.

Oates, R. K. (1996). *The spectrum of child abuse: Assessment, treatment, and prevention.* Philadelphia: Brunner/Mazel.

O'Connor, M. K. (1993). Hypotheses regarding the mechanism of action of electroconvulsive therapy, past and present. *Psychiatric Annals, 23,* 15–18.

Ødegaard, Ø. (1972). Epidemiology of the psychosis. In K. P. Kisker, J. E. Meyer, C. Müller, & E. Strömgren (Eds.), *Psychiatrie der gegenwart* (Vol. 2, pp. 213–258). Berlin: Springer-Verlag.

Odom, S. L., & Strain, P. S. (1986). A comparison of peer-initiation and teacher-antecedent intervention for promoting reciprocal social interaction of autistic preschoolers. *Journal of Applied Behavior Analysis, 19,* 59–71.

O'Farrell, T. J., Hooley, J., Fals-Stewart, W., & Henry, S. G. (1998). Expressed emotion and relapse in alcoholic patients. *Journal of Consulting and Clinical Psychology, 66,* 744–752.

O'Halloran, R. L., & Deitz, P. E. (1993). Autoerotic fatalities with power hydraulics. *Journal of Forensic Sciences, 38,* 359–364.

O'Hara, M. W., Rehm, L. P., & Campbell, S. B. (1982). Predicting depressive symptomatology: Cognitive-behavioral models and postpartum depression. *Journal of Abnormal Psychology, 91,* 457–461.

O'Hara, M. W., Zekoski, E. M., Philipps, L. H., & Wright, E. J. (1990). Controlled prospective study of postpartum mood disorders: Comparison of childbearing and nonchildbearing women. *Journal of Abnormal Psychology, 99,* 3–15.

O'Hare, A. E., Brown, J. K., & Aitken, K. (1991). Dyscalculia in children. *Developmental Medicine and Child Neurology, 33,* 356–361.

O'Hare, T. (2001). Substance abuse and risky sex in young people: The development and validation of the Risky Sex Scale. *Journal of Primary Prevention, 22,* 89–101.

Ohayon, M. M., Guilleminault, C., & Priest, R. G. (1999). Night terrors, sleepwalking, and confusional arousals in the general population: Their frequency and relationship to other sleep and mental disorders. *Journal of Clinical Psychiatry, 60,* 268–276.

Ohayon, M. M., Morselli, P. L., & Guilleminault, C. (1997). Prevalence of nightmares and their relationship to psychopathology and daytime functioning in insomnia subjects. *Sleep, 20,* 340–348.

O'Leary, A. (2000). Women at risk for HIV from a primary partner: Balancing risk and intimacy. *Annual Review of Sex Research, 11,* 191–234.

Olincy, A., Ross, R. G., Young, D. A., Roath, M., & Freedman, R. (1996). Smooth pursuit eye movements after smoking in schizophrenia patients. *Biological Psychiatry, 39,* 574.

Olivardia, R. (2001). Mirror, mirror on the wall, who's the largest of them all? The features and phenomenology of muscle dysmorphia. *Harvard Review of Psychiatry, 9,* 254–259.

Ollendick, T. H., & King, N. J. (1991). Origins of childhood fears: An evaluation of Rachman's theory of fear acquisition. *Behavior Research and Therapy, 29,* 117–123.

Ormond, K. E. (1997). Update and review: Maternal serum screening. *Journal of Genetic Counseling, 6,* 395–417.

Orne, M. T., Dinges, D. F., & Orne, E. C. (1984). On the differential diagnosis of multiple personality in the forensic context. *International Journal of Clinical and Experimental Hypnosis, 32,* 118–169.

Orr, S. P., Lasko, N. B., Shalev, A. Y., & Pitman, R. K. (1995). Physiological responses to loud tones in Vietnam veterans with posttraumatic stress disorder. *Journal of Abnormal Psychology, 104,* 75–82.

Orr, W. C. (1997). Obstructive sleep apnea: Natural history and varieties of the clinical presentation. In M. R. Pressman & W. C. Orr

(Eds.), *Understanding sleep: The evaluation and treatment of sleep disorders* (pp. 267–281). Washington, DC: American Psychological Association.

Orvaschel, H., & Puig-Antich, J. (1986). *Schedule for affective disorders and schizophrenia for school-age children, epidemiologic version.* Philadelphia: Medical College of Pennsylvania.

Osborn, M., Hawton, K., & Gath, D. (1988). Sexual dysfunction among middle aged women in the community. *British Medical Journal, 296,* 959–962.

O'Shanick, G. J., & O'Shanick, A. M. (1994). Personality and intellectual changes. In J. M. Silver & S. C. Yudofsky (Eds.), *Neuropsychiatry of traumatic brain injury* (pp. 163–188). Washington, DC: American Psychiatric Press.

Öst, L. G. (1992). Blood and injection phobia: Background and cognitive, physiological, and behavioral variables. *Journal of Abnormal Psychology, 101,* 68–74.

O'Sullivan, E., & Carlton, A. (2001). Victim services, community outreach, and contemporary rape crisis centers. *Journal of Interpersonal Violence, 16,* 343–360.

Osvold, L. L., & Sodowsky, G. R. (1993). Eating disorders of white American, racial and ethnic minority American, and international women. *Journal of Multicultural Counseling and Development, 21,* 143–154.

Ott, J. (1991). *Analysis of human genetic linkage,* revised edition. Baltimore: Johns Hopkins University Press.

Otto, M. W., Tuby, K. S., Gould, R. A., McLean, R. Y. S., & Pollack, M. H. (2001). An effect-size analysis of the relative efficacy and tolerability of serotonin selective reuptake inhibitors for panic disorder. *American Journal of Psychiatry, 158,* 1989–1992.

Ouimette, P. C., Finney, J. W., & Moos, R. H. (1997). Twelve-step and cognitive-behavioral treatment for substance abuse: A comparison of treatment effectiveness. *Journal of Consulting and Clinical Psychology, 65,* 230–240.

Oyewumi, L. K., & Al-Semaan, Y. (2000). Olanzapine: Safe during clozapine-induced agranulocytosis. *Journal of Clinical Psychopharmacology, 20,* 279–281.

Ozaki, N., Ono, Y., Ito, A., & Rosenthal, N. E. (1995). Prevalence of seasonal difficulties in mood and behavior among Japanese civil servants. *American Journal of Psychiatry, 152,* 1225–1227.

Padgett, V. R., & Jorgenson, D. O. (1982). Superstition and economic threat: Germany, 1918–1940. *Personality and Social Psychology Bulletin, 8,* 736–741.

Panksepp, J. (1998). Attention deficit hyperactivity disorders, psychostimulants, and intolerance of childhood playfulness: A tragedy in the making? *Current Directions in Psychological Science, 7,* 91–98.

Panksepp, J., Siviy, S., & Normansell, L. A. (1984). The psychobiology of play: Theoretical and methodological problems. *Neuroscience and Biobehavioral Reviews, 8,* 465–492.

Papp, L. A. (2000). Anxiety disorders: Somatic treatments. In B. I. Sadock & V. A. Sadock (Eds.), *Kaplan & Sadock's comprehensive textbook of psychiatry* (7th ed., pp. 1490–1498). Philadelphia: Lippincott Williams & Wilkins.

Paris, J. (1991). Personality disorders, parasuicide, and culture. *Transcultural Psychiatric Research Review, 28,* 25–39.

Paris, J., Zweig, F. M., & Guzder, J. (1994). Psychological risk factors for borderline personality disorder in female patients. *Comprehensive Psychiatry, 35,* 301–305.

Parker, G., & Hadzi-Pavlovic, D. (1990). Expressed emotion as a predictor of schizophrenic relapse: An analysis of aggregated data. *Psychological Medicine, 20,* 961–965.

Parkes, J. D., & Lock, C. B. (1989). Genetic factors in sleep disorders. *Journal of Neurology, Neurosurgery and Psychiatry* (Special Supplement), 101–108.

Parks, G. A., Anderson, B. K., & Marlatt, G. A. (2001). Relapse prevention therapy. In N. Heather & T. J. Peters (Eds.), *International handbook of alcohol dependence and problems* (pp. 575–592). New York: Wiley.

Parmeggiani, P. L. (1994). The autonomic nervous system in sleep. In M. H. Kryger, T. Roth, & W. C. Dement (Eds.), *Principles and practice of sleep medicine* (2nd ed., pp. 194–203). Philadelphia: Saunders.

Parry, B. L., & Newton, R. P. (2001). Chronobiological basis of female-specific mood disorders. *Neuropsychopharmacology, 25* (Supplement 5), S102–S108.

Parsons, O. A. (1998). Neurocognitive deficits in alcoholics and social drinkers: A continuum? *Alcoholism: Clinical and Experimental Research, 22,* 954–961.

Partinen, M., & Telakivi, T. (1992). Epidemiology of obstructive sleep apnea syndrome. *Sleep, 15*(6, Supplement), S1–S4.

Partlett, D. F., & Nurcombe, B. (1998). Recovered memories of child sexual abuse and liability: Society, science, and the law in a comparative setting. *Psychology, Public Policy, and Law, 4,* 1253–1306.

Paschall, M. J., & Hubbard, M. L. (1998). Effects of neighborhood and family stressors on African American adolescents' self-worth and propensity for violent behavior. *Journal of Consulting and Clinical Psychology, 66,* 825–831.

Pasewark, R. A., & Pantle, M. L. (1979). Insanity plea: Legislators' view. *American Journal of Psychiatry, 136,* 222–223.

Pasewark, R. A., & Seidenzahl, D. (1979). Opinions concerning the insanity plea and criminality among mental patients. *Bulletin of the American Academy of Psychiatry and Law, 7,* 199–202.

Patrick, M., Hobson, R. P., Castle, D., Howard, R., & Maughan, B. (1994). Personality disorder and the mental representation of early social experience. *Development and Psychopathology, 6,* 375–388.

Patton, C. J. (1992). Fear of abandonment and binge eating: A subliminal psychodynamic activation investigation. *Journal of Nervous and Mental Disease, 180,* 484–490.

Paul, G. L., & Lentz, R. (1977). Psychosocial treatment of the chronic mental patient. Cambridge, MA: Harvard University Press.

Pauls, D. L., Alsobrook, J. P., II., Goodman, W., Rasmussen, S., & Leckman, J. F. (1995). A family study of obsessive-compulsive disorder. *American Journal of Psychiatry, 152,* 76–84.

Paulson, R. I. (1988). People and garbage are not the same: Issues in contracting for public mental health services. *Community Mental Health Journal, 24,* 91–102.

Payami, H., Zaareparsi, S., Montee, K. R., Sexton, G. J., Kaye, J. A., Bird, T. D., Yu, C. E., Wijsman, E. M., Heston, L. L., Litrt, M., & Schellenberg, G. D. (1996). Gender differences in apolipoprotein E–associated risk for familial Alzheimer disease: A possible clue to the higher incidence of Alzheimer's in women. *American Journal of Human Genetics, 58,* 803–811.

Paykel, E. S., Emms, E. M., Fletcher, J., & Rassaby, E. S. (1980). Life events and social support in puerperal depression. *British Journal of Psychiatry, 136,* 339–346.

Payte, T. J. (1989). Combined treatment modalities: The need for innovative approaches. Third national forum on AIDS and chemical dependency of the American Society of Addiction Medicine. *Journal of Psychoactive Drugs, 21,* 431–434.

Pelham, W. E., Jr., & Gnagy, E. M. (1999). Psychosocial and combined treatments for ADHD. *Mental Retardation and Developmental Disabilities Research Reviews, 5,* 225–236.

Pelham, W. E., Jr., & Waschbusch, D. A. (1999). Behavioral intervention in attention-deficit/hyperactivity disorder. In H. C. Quay & A. E. Hogan (Eds.), *Handbook of disruptive behavior disorders* (pp. 255–278). New York: Plenum.

Pelham, W. E., Jr., Gnagy, E. M., Greiner, A. R., Hoza, B., Hinshaw, S. P., Swanson, J. M., Simpson, S., Shapiro, C., Bukstein, O., Baron-Myak, C., & McBurnett, K. (2000). Behavioral versus behavioral and pharmacological treatment in ADHD children attending a summer treatment program. *Journal of Abnormal Child Psychology, 28,* 507–525.

Pelissier, B. M. M., & O'Neil, J. A. (2000). Antisocial personality and depression among incarcerated drug treatment participants. *Journal of Substance Abuse, 11,* 379–393.

Peltzer, K., & Machleidt, W. (1992). A traditional (African) approach towards the therapy of schizophrenia and its comparison with Western models. *Therapeutic Communities: The International Journal of Therapeutic and Supportive Organizations, 13*, 229–242.

Pendery, M. L., Maltzman, I. M., & West, L. J. (1982). Controlled drinking by alcoholics? New findings and a reevaluation of a major affirmative study. *Science, 217*, 169–174.

Penn, D. L., Kommana, S., Mansfield, M., & Link, B. G. (1999). Dispelling the stigma of schizophrenia: II. The impact of information on dangerousness. *Schizophrenia Bulletin, 25*, 437–446.

Pepper, B., Ryglewicz, H., & Kirshner, M. C. (2001). The uninstitutionalization generation: A new breed of psychiatric patient. In H. R. Lamb (Ed.), *Best of new directions for mental health services, 1979–2001. New directions for mental health services* (pp. 5–15). San Francisco: Jossey-Bass.

Perelman, M. A. (1994). Sex and fatigue. *Contemporary Urology, 6*, 10–12.

Perlis, M. L., Giles, D. E., Buysse, D. J., Tu, X., & Kupfer, D. J. (1997). Self-reported sleep disturbance as a prodromal symptom in recurrent depression. *Journal of Affective Disorders, 42*, 209–212.

Perls, F. (1969). *Gestalt therapy verbatim.* Lafayette, CA: Real People Press.

Perse, T. L., Greist, J. H., Jefferson, J. W., Rosenfeld, R., & Dar, R. (1987). Fluvoxamine treatment of obsessive-compulsive disorder. *American Journal of Psychiatry, 144*, 1543–1548.

Person, E., & Ovesey, L. (1978). Transvestism: New perspectives. *Journal of the American Academy of Psychoanalysis, 6*, 301–323.

Petersen, R. C., Stevens , J. C., Ganguli, M., Tangalos, E. G., Cummings, J. L., & DeKosky, S. T. (2001). Practice parameter: Early detection of dementia: Mild cognitive impairment (an evidence-based review). *Neurology, 56*, 1133–1142.

Peterson, C., Maier, S. F., & Seligman, M. E. P. (1993). *Learned helplessness: A theory for the age of personal control.* New York: Oxford University Press.

Peterson, C., Semmel, A., von Baeyer, C. Abramson, L. Y., Metalsky, G. I., & Seligman, M. E. P. (1982). The attributional style questionnaire. *Cognitive Therapy and Research, 6*, 287–299.

Peterson, R. (Ed.) (1980). *Marijuana research findings.* (NIDA Research Monograph No. 31). Washington, DC: U.S. Government Printing Office.

Petty, R. G. (1999). Structural asymmetries of the human brain and their disturbance in schizophrenia. *Schizophrenia Bulletin, 25*, 121–139.

Pfohl, B. (1995). Histrionic personality disorder. In W. J. Livesley (Ed.), *The DSM-IV personality disorders* (pp. 173–192). New York: Guilford.

Pfohl, B., & Blum, N. (1995). Obsessive-compulsive personality disorder. In W. J. Livesley (Ed.), *The DSM-IV personality disorders* (pp. 261–276). New York: Guilford.

Pfohl, B., Blum, N., Zimmerman, M., & Stranl, D. (1997). *The structured interview for DSM-IV personality disorders.* Iowa City: University of Iowa.

Phelps, L. (1999). Low-level lead exposure: Implications for research and practice. *School Psychology Review, 28*, 477–492.

Phillip, M., & Fickinger, M. (1993). Psychotropic drugs in the management of chronic pain syndromes. *Pharmacopsychiatry, 26*, 221–234.

Phillips, K. A. (1996). *The broken mirror: Understanding and treating body dysmorphic disorder.* New York: Oxford University Press.

Phillips, K. A., Dwight, M. M., & McElroy, S. L. (1998). Efficacy and safety of fluvoxamine in body dysmorphic disorder. *Journal of Clinical Psychiatry, 59*, 165–171.

Physician's Desk Reference (PDR). (2002). 56th edition. Montvale, NJ: Medical Economics Data Production Company.

Piacentini, J., & Bergman, R. L. (2000). Obsessive-compulsive disorder in children. In B. I. Sadock & V. A. Sadock (Eds.), *Kaplan & Sadock's comprehensive textbook of psychiatry* (7th ed., pp. 2758–2763). Philadelphia: Lippincott Williams & Wilkins.

Piasecki, J., & Hollon, S. D. (1987). Cognitive therapy for depression: Unexplicated schemata and scripts. In N. S. Jacobson (Ed.),

Psychotherapists in clinical practice: Cognitive and behavioral perspectives (pp. 121–152). New York: Guilford.

Pickens, R. W., Svikis, D. S., McGue, M., Lykken, D. T., Heston, L. L., & Clayton, P. J. (1991). Heterogeneity in the inheritance of alcoholism: A study of male and female twins. *Archives of General Psychiatry, 48*, 19–28.

Pickworth, W. B., Rohrer, M. S., & Fant, R. V. (1997). Effects of abused drugs on psychomotor performance. *Experimental and Clinical Psychopharmacology, 5*, 235–241.

Piercy, F. P., Volk, R. J., Trepper, T., & Sprenkle, D. H. (1991). The relationship of family factors to patterns of adolescent substance abuse. *Family Dynamics of Addiction Quarterly, 1*, 41–54.

Pinel, P. (1962). *A treatise on insanity.* New York: Hafner. (Originally published in 1801.)

Piper, A., Jr. (1993). "Truth serum" and "recovered memories" of sexual abuse: A review of the evidence. *Journal of Psychiatry and Law, 21*, 447–471.

Piper, A., Jr., Pope, H. G., Jr., & Borowiecki, J. J., III. (2000). Custer's last stand: Brown, Scheflin, and Whitfield's latest attempt to salvage "dissociative amnesia." *Journal of Psychiatry and Law, 28*, 149–213.

Pirke, K. M. (1996). Central and peripheral noradrenalin regulation in eating disorders. *Psychiatry Research, 62*, 43–49.

Pitts, F. N., & McClure, J. N. (1967). Lactate metabolism in anxiety neurosis. *New England Journal of Medicine, 277*, 1329–1336.

Piven, J. (2002). Genetics of personality: The example of the broad autism phenotype. In J. Benjamin & R. P. Ebstein (Eds.), *Molecular genetics and the human personality* (pp. 43–62). Washington, DC: American Psychiatric Publishing.

Piven, J., Arndt, S., Bailey, J., Havercamp, S., Andreasen, N. C., & Palmer, P. (1995). An MRI study of brain size in autism. *American Journal of Psychiatry, 152*, 1145–1149.

Place, E. J. S., & Gilmore, G. C. (1980). Perceptual organization in schizophrenia. *Journal of Abnormal Psychology, 89*, 409–418.

Plassman, B.L., Havlik, R. J., Steffens, D. C., Helms, M. J., Newman, T. N., Drosdick, D., Phillips, C., Gau, B. A., Welsh-Bohmer, K. A., Burke, J. R., Guralnik, J. M., & Breitner, J. C. S. (2000). Documented head injury in early adulthood and risk of Alzheimer's disease and other dementias. *Neurology, 55*, 1158–1166.

Pliszka, S. R., Sherman, J. O., Barrow, M. V., & Irick, S. (2000). Affective disorder in juvenile offenders: A preliminary study. *American Journal of Psychiatry, 157*, 130–132.

Plomin, R. (2001). Genetic factors contributing to learning and language delays and disabilities. *Child and Adolescent Psychiatric Clinics of North America, 10*, 259–277.

Plomin, R., DeFries, J. C., & McClearn, G. E. (1990). *Behavioral genetics: A primer* (2nd ed.). New York: Freeman.

Poirier, J. (1994). Apolipoprotein E in animal models of CNS injury and in Alzheimer's disease. *Trends in Neuroscience, 17*, 525–530.

Polivy, J., & Herman, C. P. (2002). Causes of eating disorders. *Annual Review of Psychology, 53*, 187–213.

Pollack, J. M. (1979). Obsessive-compulsive personality: A review. *Psychological Bulletin, 86*, 225–241.

Pollack, J. M. (1987). Relationship of obsessive-compulsive personality to obsessive-compulsive disorder: A review of the literature. *Journal of Psychology, 121*, 137–148.

Pollack, V. E., Gabrielli, W. F., Mednick, S. A., & Goodwin, D. W. (1988). EEG identification of subgroups of men at risk for alcoholism? *Psychiatry Research, 26*, 101–114.

Polvan, N. (1969). Historical aspects of mental ills in Middle East discussed. *Roche Reports, 6*, 3.

Pomerleau, O. V. (1992). Nicotine and the central nervous system: Biobehavioral effects of cigarette smoking. *American Journal of Medicine, 93* (Supplement 1A), 2–7.

Pope, H. G., Jr., Olivardia, R., Borowiecki, J. J., III., & Cohane, G. H. (2001). The growing commercial value of the male body: A longitudinal survey of advertising in women's magazines. *Psychotherapy and Psychosomatics, 70*, 189–192.

Porter, S., Birt, A., & Boer, D. P. (2001). Investigation of the criminal and conditional release profiles of Canadian federal offenders as a function of psychopathy and age. *Law and Human Behavior, 25,* 647–661.

Porzelius, L. K., Berel, S., & Howard, C. (1999). Cognitive behavior therapy. In M. Hersen & A. S. Bellack (Eds.), *Handbook of comparative interventions for adult disorders* (2nd ed., pp. 491–512). New York: Wiley.

Post, R. M. (2000). Mood disorders: Treatment of bipolar disorder. In B. I. Sadock & V. A. Sadock (Eds.), *Kaplan & Sadock's comprehensive textbook of psychiatry* (7th ed., pp. 1385–1430). Philadelphia: Lippincott Williams & Wilkins.

Post, R. M., et al. (1978). Cerebrospinal fluid norepinephrine in affective illness. *American Journal of Psychiatry, 135,* 907–912.

Poustka, F. (1998). Neurobiology of autism. In F. R. Volkmar (Ed.), *Autism and pervasive developmental disorders* (pp. 130–168). Cambridge, England: Cambridge University Press.

Powell, A. L. (1994). Senile dementia of extreme aging: A common disorder of centenarians. *Dementia, 5,* 106–109.

Powell, J. E., Edwards, A., Edwards, M., Pandit, B. S., Sungum-Paliwal, S. R., & Whitehouse, W. (2000). Changes in the incidence of childhood autism and other autistic spectrum disorders in preschool children from two areas of the West Midlands, UK. *Developmental Medicine and Child Neurology, 42,* 624–628.

Pratap, S., Chaudhary, G., Kavathekar, S. A., & Saxena, S. (1996). Preliminary report of psychiatric disorders in survivors of a severe earthquake. *American Journal of Psychiatry, 1996, 153,* 556–558.

Prentky, R. A., & Knight, R. A. (1991). Identifying critical dimensions for discriminating among rapists. *Journal of Consulting and Clinical Psychology, 59,* 643–661.

Price, L. H. (1990). Serotonin reuptake inhibitors in depression and anxiety: An overview. *Annals of Clinical Psychiatry, 2,* 165–172.

Prigatano, G. P. (1999). *Principles of neuropsychological rehabilitation.* New York: Oxford University Press.

Pring, L., Hermelin, B., & Heavey, L. (1995). Savants, segments, art and autism. *Journal of Child Psychology and Psychiatry and Allied Disciplines, 36,* 1065–1076.

Prior, M., & Ozonoff, S. (1998). Psychological factors in autism. In F. R. Volkmar (Ed.), *Autism and pervasive developmental disorders* (pp. 64–108). New York: Cambridge University Press.

Prior, M., Perry, D., & Gajzago, C. (1975). Kanner's syndrome or early-onset psychosis: A taxometric analysis of 142 cases. *Journal of Autism and Childhood Schizophrenia, 5,* 71–80.

Procci, W. R. (1989). Schizoaffective disorder, schizophreniform disorder, and brief reactive psychosis. In H. I. Kaplan & B. J. Sadock (Eds.), *Comprehensive textbook of psychiatry* (5th ed., Vol. II, pp. 830–842). Baltimore: Williams & Wilkins.

Prudic, J., & Sackeim, H. A. (1999). Electroconvulsive therapy and suicide risk. *Journal of Clinical Psychiatry, 60* (Supplement 2), 104–110.

Prudic, J., Olfson, M., & Sackeim, H. A. (2001). Electro-convulsive therapy practices in the community. *Psychological Medicine, 31,* 929–934.

Purves, D., Augustine, G. J., Fitzpatrick, D., Katz, L. C., LaMantia, A., McNamara, J. O., & Williams, S. M. (Eds.). (2001). *Neuroscience* (2nd ed.). Sunderland, MA: Sinauer Associates.

Putnam, F. W. (1986). The scientific investigation of multiple personality disorder. In J. Quen (Ed.), *Split minds, split brains: Historical and current perspectives* (pp. 109–125). New York: New York University Press.

Putnam, F. W. (1989). *Diagnosis and treatment of multiple personality disorder.* New York: Guilford.

Putnam, F. W. (1997). *Dissociation in children and adolescents: A developmental perspective.* New York: Guilford.

Putnam, F. W. (1999). Pierre Janet and modern views of dissociation. In M. J. Horowitz (Ed.), *Essential papers on posttraumatic stress disorder* (pp. 116–135). New York: New York University Press.

Putnam, F. W., & Carlson, E. B. (1998). Hypnosis, dissociation, and trauma: Myths, metaphors, and mechanisms. In J. D. Bremmer & C.

R. Marmar (Eds.), *Trauma, memory, and dissociation* (pp. 27–55). Washington, DC: American Psychiatric Press.

Putnam, F. W., Carlson, E. B., Ross, C. A., Anderson, G., Clark, P., Torem, M., Bowman, E. S., Coons, P., Chu, J. A., Dill, D. L., Loewenstein, R. J., & Braun, B. G. (1996). Patterns of dissociation in clinical and nonclinical samples. *Journal of Nervous and Mental Disease, 184,* 673–679.

Putnam, F. W., Guroff, J. J., Silberman, E. K., Barban, L., & Post, R. M. (1986). The clinical phenomenology of multiple personality disorder: Review of 100 recent cases. *Journal of Clinical Psychiatry, 47,* 285–293.

Putnam, F. W., Zahn, T. P., & Post, R. M. (1990). Differential autonomic nervous system activity in multiple personality disorder. *Psychiatry Research, 31,* 251–260.

Quinlan, D. M. (2000). Assessment of attention-deficit/hyperactivity disorder and comorbidities. In T. E. Brown (Ed.), *Attention deficit disorders and comorbidities in children, adolescents, and adults* (pp. 455–508). Washington, DC: American Psychiatric Press.

Quinsey, V. L., Chaplin, T. C., & Carrigan, W. F. (1979). Sexual preferences among incestuous and nonincestuous child molesters. *Behavior Therapy, 10,* 562–565.

Quinsey, V. L., Chaplin, T. C., & Upfold, D. (1984). Sexual arousal to nonsexual violence and sadomasochistic themes among rapists and non-sex-offenders. *Journal of Consulting and Clinical Psychology, 52,* 651–657.

Rabavilas, A. D., Boulougouris, J. C., & Stefanis, C. (1976). Duration of flooding sessions in the treatment of obsessive-compulsive patients. *Behaviour Research and Therapy, 14,* 349–355.

Rachman, S. (1977). The conditioning theory of fear-acquisition: A critical examination. *Behaviour Research and Therapy, 15,* 373–387.

Rachman, S., & Hodgson, R. (1968). Experimentally induced "sexual fetishism": Replication and development. *Psychological Record, 18,* 25–27.

Rachman, S., & Hodgson, R. (1980). *Obsessions and compulsions.* Englewood Cliffs, NJ: Prentice-Hall.

Rachman, S., Hodgson, R., & Marks, I. M. (1971). Treatment of a chronic obsessive-compulsive neurosis. *Behavior Research and Therapy, 9,* 237–247.

Rado, S. (1959). Obsessive behavior: So-called obsessive-compulsive neuroses. In S. Arieti (Ed.), *American handbook of psychiatry* (Vol. 1, pp. 324–344). New York: Basic Books.

Raine, A. (1989). Evoked potentials and psychopathy. *International Journal of Psychophysiology, 8,* 1–16.

Ramana, R., & Bebbington, P. (1995). Social influences on bipolar affective disorders. *Social Psychiatry and Psychiatric Epidemiology, 30,* 152–160.

Ramey, C. T., & Ramey, S. L. (1998). Early intervention and early experience. *American Psychologist, 53,* 109–120.

Ramey, C. T., Mulvihill, B. A., & Ramey, S. L. (1996). Prevention: Social and educational factors and early intervention. In J. W. Jacobson, & J. A. Mulick (Eds.), *Manual of diagnosis and professional practice in mental retardation* (pp. 215–227). Washington, DC: American Psychological Association.

Rapaport, D., Gill, M., & Schafer, R. (1946). *Diagnostic psychological testing:* Vol. II. Chicago: Year Book Publishers.

Rapaport, S. I. (1988). Brain evolution and Alzheimer's disease. *Revue Neurologique, 144,* 79–90.

Rapaport, S. I. (1990). Integrated phylogeny of the primate brain, with special reference to humans and their diseases. *Brain Research: Brain Research Reviews, 15,* 267–294.

Raphael, M. J. (2000). *Bill W. and Mr. Wilson: The legend and life of A.A.'s cofounder.* Amherst: University of Massachusetts Press.

Rapoport, J. L., & Castellanos, F. X. (1996). Attention-deficit/hyperactivity disorder. In J. M. Wiener (Ed.), *Diagnosis and psychopharmacology of childhood and adolescent disorders* (2nd ed., pp. 265–292). Oxford, England: Wiley.

Rapoport, J. L., & Wise, S. P. (1988). Obsessive-compulsive disorder: Evidence for basal ganglia dysfunction. *Psychopharmacology Bulletin, 24,* 380–384.

Rapoport, J. L., Castellanos, F. X., Gogate, N., Janson, K., Kohler, S., & Nelson, P. (2001). Imaging normal and abnormal brain development: New perspectives for child psychiatry. *Australian and New Zealand Journal of Psychiatry, 35,* 272–281.

Raskin, V. D. (1993). Psychiatric aspects of substance use disorders in child bearing populations. *Psychiatric Clinics of North America, 16,* 157–165.

Raskind, W. H., Hsu, L., Berninger, V. W., Thomson, J. B., & Wijsman, E. M. (2000). Familial aggregation of dyslexia phenotypes. *Behavior Genetics, 30,* 385–396.

Rasmussen, S. A., & Tsuang, M. T. (1986). Clinical characteristics and family history in DSM-III obsessive-compulsive disorder. *American Journal of Psychiatry, 143,* 317–322.

Ratey, J. J., Bemporad, J., Sorgi, P., Bick, P., Polakoff, S., O'Driscoll, G., & Mikkelsen, E. (1987). Brief report: Open trial effects of beta-blockers on speech and social behaviors in 8 autistic adults. *Journal of Autism and Developmental Disorders, 17,* 439–446.

Rattenborg, N. C., Amlaner, C. J., & Lima, S. L. (2000). Behavioral, neurophysiological and evolutionary perspectives on unihemispheric sleep. *Neuroscience and Biobehavioral Reviews, 24,* 817–842.

Rauch, S. A. M., Hembree, E. A., & Foa, E. B. (2001). Acute psychosocial preventive interventions for posttraumatic stress disorder. *Advances in Mind-Body Medicine, 17,* 187–190.

Rauch, S. L., Dougherty, D. D., Cosgrove, G. R., Cassem, E. H., Alpert, N. M., Price, B. H., Nierenberg, A. A., Mayberg, H. S., Baer, L., Jenike, M. A., & Fischman, A. J. (2001). Cerebral metabolic correlates as potential predictors of response to anterior cingulotomy for obsessive compulsive disorder, *Biological Psychiatry, 50,* 659–667.

Rauch, S. L., Jenike, M. A., Alpert, N. M., Baer, L, Breiter, H. C. R., Savage, C. R., & Fischman, A. J. (1994). Regional cerebral blood flow measured during symptom provocation in obsessive-compulsive disorder using oxygen 15–labeled carbon dioxide and positron emission tomography. *Archives of General Psychiatry, 51,* 62–70.

Raulin, M. L. (1984). Development of a scale to measure intense ambivalence. *Journal of Consulting and Clinical Psychology, 52,* 63–72.

Raulin, M. L., & Brenner, V. (1993). Ambivalence. In C. G. Costello (Ed.), *Symptoms of schizophrenia* (pp. 201–226). New York: Wiley.

Raulin, M. L., & Lilienfeld, S. O. (1999). Research strategies for studying psychopathology. In T. Millon, P. H. Blaney, & R. D. Davis (Eds.), *Oxford textbook of psychopathology* (pp. 49–78). New York: Oxford University Press.

Raulin, M. L., & Wee, J. L. (1984). The development and initial validation of a scale to measure social fear. *Journal of Clinical Psychology, 40,* 780–784.

Ravidran, A. V., Anisman, H., Merali, Z., Charbonneau, Y., Telner, J., Bialik, R. J., Wiens, A., Ellis, J., & Griffiths, J. (1999). Treatment of primary dysthymia with group cognitive therapy and pharmacotherapy: Clinical symptoms and functional impairments. *American Journal of Psychiatry, 156,* 1608–1617.

Read, J. D. (1997). Memory issues in the diagnosis of unreported trauma. In J. D. Read & D. S. Lindsay (Eds.), *Recollections of trauma: Scientific evidence and clinical practice* (pp. 79–108). New York: Plenum.

Rechtschaffen, A., Bergmann, B. M., Everson, C. A., Kushida, C. A., & Gilliland, M. A. (1989). Sleep deprivation in the rat: X. Integration and discussion of the findings. *Sleep, 12,* 68–87.

Redmond, D. E. (1977). Alterations in the function of the nucleus locus coeruleus: A possible model for studies of anxiety. In I. Hanan & E. Usdin (Eds.), *Animal models in psychiatry and neurology.* New York: Pergamon.

Reed, D. B. (2001). Outpatient civil commitment: A growing trend in state law. In G. Landsberg & A. Smiley (Eds.), *Forensic mental health: Working with offenders with mental illness* (pp. 31.1–31.8). Kingston, NJ: Civic Research Institute.

Reeves, S. B., & Nagoshi, C. T. (1993). Effects of alcohol administration on the disinhibition of racial prejudice. *Alcoholism: Clinical and Experimental Research, 17,* 1066–1071.

Regenbrecht, H. T., Schubert, T. W., & Friedmann, F. (1998). Measuring the sense of presence and its relations to fear of heights in virtual environments. *International Journal of Human–Computer Interaction, 10,* 233–249.

Regier, D. A., & Burke, J. D. (1985). Epidemiology. In H. I. Kaplan & B. J. Sadock (Eds.), *Comprehensive textbook of psychiatry* (4th ed., pp. 295–312). Baltimore: Williams & Wilkins.

Reich, J. (1987). Sex distribution of DSM-III personality disorders in psychiatric outpatients. *American Journal of Psychiatry, 144,* 485–488.

Reich, W. (1972). *Character analysis.* New York: Farrar, Straus & Giroux. (Originally published in 1933.)

Reid, S. A., Duke, L. M., & Allen, J. J. B. (1998). Resting frontal electroencephalographic asymmetry in depression: Inconsistencies suggest the need to identify mediating factors. *Psychophysiology, 35,* 389–404.

Reilly, J. L., Murphy, P. T., Byrne, M., Larkin, C., Gill, M., O'Callaghan, E., & Lane, A. (2001). Dermatoglyphic fluctuating asymmetry and atypical handedness in schizophrenia. *Schizophrenia Research, 50,* 159–168.

Reilly-Harrington, N. A., Alloy, L. B., Fresco, D. M., & Whitehouse, W. G. (1999). Cognitive styles and life events interact to predict bipolar and unipolar symptomatology. *Journal of Abnormal Psychology, 108,* 567–578.

Reinvang, I. (1998). Amnestic disorders and their role in cognitive theory. *Scandinavian Journal of Psychology, 39,* 141–143.

Reisberg, D. (1997). *Cognition: Exploring the science of the mind.* New York: Norton.

Reiss, S., & McNally, R. J. (1985). Expectancy model of fear. In S. Reiss & R. R. Bootzin (Eds.), *Theoretical issues in behavior therapy* (pp. 107–121). San Diego, CA: Academic Press.

Reneman, L., Booij, J., Schmand, B., van den Brink, W., & Gunning, B. (2000). Memory disturbances in "Ecstasy" users are correlated with an altered brain serotonin neurotransmission. *Outcomes Management, 148,* 322–324.

Rescorla, R. A. (1988). Pavlovian conditioning: It's not what you think. *American Psychologist, 43,* 151–160.

Reuter, P., & MacCoun, R. (1995). Drawing lessons from the absence of harm reduction in American drug policy. *Tobacco Control, 4,* S28–S32.

Reuter-Lorenz, P., & Davidson, R. J. (1981). Differential contribution of the two cerebral hemispheres to the perception of happy and sad faces. *Neuropsychologia, 19,* 609–614.

Revonsuo, A. (2000). Did ancestral humans dream for their lives? *Behavioral and Brain Sciences, 23,* 1063–1121.

Reynolds, C. F., III, Frank, E., Perel, J. M., Imber, S. D., Cornes, C., Morycz, R. K., Mazumdar, S., Miller, M. D., Pollock, B. G., Rifai, A. H., Stack, J. A., George, C. J., Houck, P. R., & Kupfer, D. J. (1992). Combined pharmacotherapy and psychotherapy in the acute and continuation treatment of elderly patients with recurrent major depression: A preliminary report. *American Journal of Psychiatry, 149,* 1687–1692.

Reynolds, C. F., III, Frank, E., Perel, J. M., Mazumdar, S., Dew, M. A., Begley, A., Houck, P. R., Hall, M., Mulsant, B., Shear, M. K., Miller, M D., Cornes, C., & Kupfer, D. J. (1996). High relapse rate after discontinuation of adjunctive medication for elderly patients with recurrent major depression. *American Journal of Psychiatry, 153,* 1418–1422.

Rice, M. E., Chaplin, T. E., Harris, G. E., & Coutts, J. (1994). Empathy for the victim and sexual arousal among rapists and nonrapists. *Journal of Interpersonal Violence, 9,* 435–449.

Richter, J. S. (2001). Eating disorders and sexuality. In J. J. Robert-McComb (Ed.), *Eating disorders in women and children: Prevention, stress management, and treatment* (pp. 201–208). Boca Raton, FL: CRC Press.

Rickels, K., Schweizer, E., Case, W. G., & Greenblatt, D. J. (1990). Long-term therapeutic use of benzodiazepines. I. Effects of abrupt discontinuation. *Archives of General Psychiatry, 47*, 899–907.

Ridley, M. (1996). *Evolution* (2nd ed.). Cambridge, MA: Blackwell Science.

Rief, W., Hessel, A., & Braehler, E. (2001). Somatization symptoms and hypochondriacal features in the general population. *Psychosomatic Medicine, 63*, 595–602.

Rieger, E., Touyz, S. W., Swain, T., & Beumont, P. J. V. (2001). Cross-cultural research on anorexia nervosa: Assumptions regarding the role of body weight. *International Journal of Eating Disorders, 29*, 205–215.

Rifkin, A., Ghisalbert, D., Dimatou, S., Jin, C., & Sethi, M. (1998). Dissociative identity disorder in psychiatric inpatients. *American Journal of Psychiatry, 155*, 844–845.

Riggs, D. S., & Foa, E. B. (1993). Obsessive compulsive disorder. In D. H. Barlow (Ed.), *Clinical handbook of psychological disorders* (2nd ed., pp. 189–239). New York: Guilford.

Rimland, B. (1978). Inside the mind of the autistic savant. *Psychology Today*, August, 69–80.

Rimm, D. C., & Litvak, S. B. (1969). Self verbalization and emotional arousal. *Journal of Abnormal Psychology, 74*, 181–187.

Rind, B., Tromovitch, P., & Bauserman, R. (1998). A meta-analytic examination of assumed properties of child sexual abuse using college samples. *Psychological Bulletin, 124*, 22–53.

Rinehart, N. J., & McCabe, M. P. (1998). An empirical investigation of hypersexuality. *Sexual and Marital Therapy, 13*, 369–384.

Risch, N., Baron, M., & Mendlewicz, J. (1986). Assessing the role of X-linked inheritance in bipolar-related major affective disorder. *Journal of Psychiatric Research, 20*, 275–288.

Ritvo, E. R., Freeman, B. J., Scheibel, A. B., Duong, T., Robinson, H., Guthrie, D., & Ritvo, A. (1986). Lower Purkinje cell counts in the cerebella of four autistic subjects: Initial findings of the UCLA-NSAC autopsy research report. *American Journal of Psychiatry, 143*, 862–866.

Ritzler, B. A. (1981). Paranoia—Prognosis and treatment: A review. *Schizophrenia Bulletin, 7*, 710–728.

Rivers, P. C., & Shore, E. R. (Eds.). (1997). *Substance abuse on campus: A handbook for college and university personnel*. Westport, CT: Greenwood Press.

Robert-McComb, J. J. (Ed.). (2001). *Eating disorders in women and children: Prevention, stress management, and treatment*. Boca Raton, FL: CRC Press.

Roberts, R. E., Shema, S. J., & Kaplan, G. A. (1999). Prospective data on sleep complaints and associated risk factors in an older cohort. *Psychosomatic Medicine, 61*, 188–196.

Robins, E., & Guze, S. B. (1970). Establishment of diagnostic validity in psychiatric illness: Its application to schizophrenia. *American Journal of Psychiatry, 126*, 983–987.

Robinson, D., Wu, H., Munne, R. A., Ashtari, M., Alvir, J. M. J., Lerner, G., Koreen, A., Cole, K., & Bogerts, B. (1995). Reduced caudate nucleus volume in obsessive-compulsive disorder. *Archives of General Psychiatry, 52*, 393–398.

Robinson, G. C., Conry, J. L., & Conry, R. F. (1987). Clinical profile and prevalence of fetal alcohol syndrome in an isolated community in British Columbia. *Canadian Medical Association Journal, 137*, 203–207.

Robison, W. L. (2002). The changing form of psychiatric care. In J. M. Humber & R. F. Almeder (Eds.), *Mental illness and public health care: Biomedical ethics reviews. Contemporary issues in biomedicine, ethics, and society* (pp. 105–126). Totowa, NJ: Humana.

Robitschek, C., & Kashubeck, S. (1999). A structural model of parental alcoholism, family functioning, and psychological health: The mediating effects of hardiness and personal growth orientation. *Journal of Counseling Psychology, 46*, 159–172.

Rochefort, D. A. (1997). *From poorhouses to homelessness: Policy analysis and mental health care* (2nd ed.). Westport, CT: Auburn House/Greenwood.

Roehrs, T., & Roth, T. (1997). Hypnotics, alcohol, and caffeine: Relation to insomnia. In M. R. Pressman & W. C. Orr (Eds.), *Understanding sleep: The evaluation and treatment of sleep disorders* (pp. 339–355). Washington, DC: American Psychological Association.

Rogers, C. R. (1951). *Client-Centered therapy*. Boston: Houghton Mifflin.

Rogers, C. R. (1961). *On becoming a person*. Boston: Houghton Mifflin.

Rogers, C. R. (1967). *The therapeutic relationship and its impact: A study of psychotherapy with schizophrenics*. Madison: University of Wisconsin Press.

Rogers, C. R., & Sandford, R. C. (1989). Client-centered psychotherapy. In H. I. Kaplan & B. J. Sadock (Eds.), *Comprehensive textbook of psychiatry* (5th ed., pp. 1482–1501). Baltimore: Williams & Wilkins.

Rogers, J. R. (1992). Suicide and alcohol: Conceptualizing the relationship from a cognitive-social paradigm. *Journal of Counseling and Development, 70*, 540–543.

Rokach, A. (2000). Terminal illness and coping with loneliness. *Journal of Psychology, 134*, 283–296.

Rolland, J. P. (1993). Validité de construct de "marqueurs´des dimensions de personnalité du module en cinq facteurs. *Revue Européenne de Psychologie Appliquée, 44*, 17–24.

Romano, S., Goodman, W., Tamura, R., Gonzales, G., and the Collaborative Research Group. (2001). Long-term treatment of obsessive-compulsive disorder after an acute response: A comparison of fluoxetine versus placebo. *Journal of Clinical Psychopharmacology, 21*, 46–52.

Rona, R. J., Li, L., & Chinn, S. (1997). Determinants of nocturnal enuresis in England and Scotland in the '90s. *Developmental Medicine and Child Neurology, 39*, 677–681.

Root, M. (1991). Persistent disordered eating as a gender-specific post-traumatic stress response to sexual assault. *Psychotherapy, 28*, 96–102.

Rorschach, H. (1942). *Psychodiagnostics*. Bern, Switzerland: Hans Huber.

Rorty, M., Yager, J., Buckwalter, J. G., & Rossotto, E. (1999). Social support, social adjustment, and recovery status in bulimia nervosa. *International Journal of Eating Disorders, 26*, 1–12.

Roscoe, J. A., Hickok, J. T., & Morrow, G. R. (2000). Patient expectations as predictor of chemotherapy-induced nausea. *Annals of Behavioral Medicine, 22*, 121–126.

Rose, L. (1991). Swaziland: Witchcraft and deviance. In M. Freilich, D. Raybeck, & J. Savishinsky (Eds.), *Deviance: Anthropological perspectives* (pp. 93–113). New York: Bergin & Garvey.

Rosecrans, J. A., & Karan, L. D. (1993). Neurobehavioral mechanisms of nicotine action: Role in the initiation and maintenance of tobacco dependence. *Journal of Substance Abuse Treatment, 10*, 161–170.

Rosen, G. M., Ferber, R., & Mahowald, M. W. (1996). Evaluation of parasomnias in children. *Child and Adolescent Psychiatric Clinics of North America, 5*, 601–616.

Rosen, M. D. (1997, April). My husband is a control freak: Can this marriage be saved? *Ladies' Home Journal, 114*(4), 14.

Rosen, R. C. (1991). Alcohol and drug effects on sexual response: Human experimental and clinical studies. *Annual Review of Sex Research, 2*, 119–180.

Rosen, R. C., & Leiblum, S. R. (1995). Treatment of sexual disorders in the 1990s: An integrated approach. *Journal of Consulting and Clinical Psychology, 63*, 877–890.

Rosen, R. C., Taylor, J. F., Leiblum, S. R., & Bachmann, G. A. (1993). Prevalence of sexual dysfunction in women: Results of a survey study of 329 women in an outpatient gynecological clinic. *Journal of Sex and Marital Therapy, 19*, 171–188.

Rosenfield, S. (1999). Gender and mental health: Do women have more psychopathology, men more, or both the same (and why)? In A. V. Horwitz & T. L. Scheid (Eds.), *A handbook for the study of mental health: Social contexts, theories, and systems* (pp. 348–360). New York: Cambridge University Press.

Rosenman, R. H., Brand, R. J., Jenkins, C. D., Friedman, M., Straus, R., & Wurm, M. (1975). Coronary heart disease in the Western Collaborative Group Study: Final follow-up experience of 8 years. *Journal of the American Medical Association, 233*, 872–877.

Rosenthal, D. (1970). *Genetic theory and abnormal behavior*. New York: McGraw-Hill.

Rosenthal, D., Wender, P. H., Kety, S. S., Schulsinger, F., Welner, J., & Østergard, L. (1968). Schizophrenics' offspring reared in adoptive homes. In D. Rosenthal & S. S. Kety (Eds.), *The transmission of schizophrenia* (pp. 377–391). Elmsford, NY: Pergamon.

Rosenthal, N. E. (1998). *Winter blues: Seasonal affective disorder: What it is and how to overcome it* (rev. and updated). New York: Guilford.

Rosenthal, N. E., & Blehar, M. C. (Eds.). (1989). *Seasonal affective disorders and phototherapy*. New York: Guilford.

Ross, C. A. (1990). Twelve cognitive errors about multiple personality disorder. *American Journal of Psychotherapy, 44*, 348–356.

Ross, C. A. (1997). *Dissociative identity disorder: Diagnosis, clinical features, and treatment of multiple personality* (2nd ed.). New York: Wiley.

Ross, C. A. (1999). Dissociative disorders. In T. Millon, P. H. Blaney, & R. D. Davis (Eds.), *Oxford textbook of psychopathology* (pp. 466–481). New York: Oxford University Press.

Ross, C. A., Anderson, G., Fleisher, W. P., & Norton, G. R. (1991). The frequency of multiple personality disorder among psychiatric inpatients. *American Journal of Psychiatry, 148*, 1717–1720.

Ross, C. A., Heber, S., Norton, G. R., & Anderson, G. (1989). Somatic symptoms in multiple personality disorder. *Psychosomatics, 30*, 154–160.

Ross, C. A., Heber, S., Norton, G.R., Anderson, D., Anderson, G., & Burchet. P. (1989). The Dissociative Disorders Interview Schedule: A structured interview. *Dissociation, 2*, 169–189.

Rothbaum, B. O., Foa, E. B., Riggs, D., Murdock, T., & Walsh, W. (1992). A prospective examination of posttraumatic stress disorder in rape victims. *Journal of Traumatic Stress, 5*, 455–475.

Rothholz, D. A., & Massey, P. S. (1996). Comparison of states' utilization of large residential settings for persons with mental retardation. *Mental Retardation, 34*, 303–311.

Rothschild, A. J. (2000). Sexual side effects of antidepressants. *Journal of Clinical Psychiatry, 61*(Supplement 11), 28–36.

Rourke, B. P. (Ed.). (1991). *Neuropsychological validation of learning disability subtypes*. New York: Guilford.

Rowland, D. L., Cooper, S. E., & Slob, A. K. (1996). Genital and psycho-affective response to erotic stimulation in sexually functional and dysfunctional men. *Journal of Abnormal Psychology, 105*, 194–203.

Rowland, D. L., Haensel, S. M., Blom, J. H. M., & Slob, A. K. (1993). Penile sensitivity in men with premature ejaculation and erectile dysfunction. *Journal of Sex and Marital Therapy, 19*, 189–197.

Roy, A. (1982). Suicide in chronic schizophrenia. *British Journal of Psychiatry, 141*, 171–180.

Roy, A. (1992). Genetics, biology, and suicide in the family. In R. W. Maris, A. L. Berman, J. T. Maltsberger, & R. I. Yufit (Eds.), *Assessment and prediction of suicide* (pp. 574–588). New York: Guilford.

Roy, A. (2000). Suicide. In B. I. Sadock & V. A. Sadock (Eds.), *Kaplan & Sadock's comprehensive textbook of psychiatry* (7th ed., pp. 2031–2040). Philadelphia: Lippincott Williams & Wilkins.

Roy, A., Nielsen, D., Rylander, G., Sarchiapone, M., & Segal, N. L. (1999). Genetics of suicide in depression. *Journal of Clinical Psychiatry, 60* (Supplement 2), 12–17.

Roy, A., Segal, N., Centerwall, B. S., & Robinette, C. D. (1991). Suicide in twins. *Archives of General Psychiatry, 48*, 29–32.

Rubens, R. D., & Coleman R. E. (1999). Twenty-five years of reviewing cancer treatment. *Cancer Treatment Reviews, 25*, 1–2.

Ruggiero, G. M., Laini, V., Mauri, M. C., Ferrari, V. M. S., Clemente, A., Lugo, F., Mantero, M., Redaelli, G., Zappulli, D., & Cavagnini, F. (2001). A single-blind comparison of amisulpride, fluoxetine, and clomipramine in the treatment of restricting anorectics. *Progress in Neuro-Psychopharmacology and Biological Psychiatry, 25*, 1049–1059.

Rugh, R. (1958). X-irradiation effects on the human fetus. *Journal of Pediatrics, 52*, 531–538.

Rumelhart, D. E. (1997). The architecture of mind: A connectionist approach. In J. Haugeland (Ed.), *Mind design 2: Philosophy, psychology, artificial intelligence* (2nd ed., pp. 205–232). Cambridge, MA: M.I.T. Press.

Rumelhart, D. E., McClelland, J. L., & the PDP Research Group. (1986). *Parallel distributed processing: Explorations in the microstructure of cognition*, Vol. 1: *Foundations*. Cambridge, MA: M.I.T. Press.

Rush, A. J. (2000). Mood disorders: Treatment of depression. In B. I. Sadock & V. A. Sadock (Eds.), *Kaplan & Sadock's comprehensive textbook of psychiatry* (7th ed., pp. 1377–1385). Philadelphia: Lippincott Williams & Wilkins.

Rush, A. J., Beck, A. T., Kovacs, M., & Hollon, S. D. (1977). Comparative efficacy of cognitive therapy and pharmacotherapy in the treatment of depressed outpatients. *Cognitive Therapy and Research, 1*, 17–39.

Rush, B. (1812). *Medical inquires and observations on the diseases of the mind*. Philadelphia: Kimber & Richardson.

Ryder, A. G., & Bagby, R. M. (1999). Diagnostic viability of depressive personality disorder: Theoretical and conceptual issues. *Journal of Personality Disorders, 13*, 99–117.

Sackeim, H. A. (1989). The efficacy of electroconvulsive therapy in the treatment of major depression disorder. In S. Fisher & R. P. Greenberg (Eds.), *The limits of biological treatments for psychological distress: Comparisons with therapy and placebo* (pp. 275–307). Hillsdale, NY: Erlbaum.

Sackeim, H. A., & Lisanby, S. H. (2001). Physical treatments in psychiatry: Advances in electroconvulsive therapy, transcranial magnetic stimulation, and vagus nerve stimulation. In M. M. Weissman (Ed.), *Treatment of depression: Bridging the 21st century* (pp. 151–174). Washington, DC: American Psychiatric Press.

Safer, D. L., Telch, C. F., & Agras, W. S. (2001). Dialectical behavior therapy for bulimia nervosa. *American Journal of Psychiatry, 158*, 632–634.

Safferman, A., Lieberman, J. A., Kane, J. M., Szymanski, S., & Kinon, B. (1991). Update on the clinical efficacy and side effects of clozapine. *Schizophrenia Bulletin, 17*, 247–261.

Safyer, A. W., Hauser, S. T., Jacobson, A. M., Bliss, R., et al. (1993). The impact of the family on diabetes adjustment: A developmental perspective. *Child and Adolescent Social Work Journal, 10*, 123–140.

Saigh, P. A. (1998). Effects of flooding on memories of patients with posttraumatic stress disorder. In J. D. Bremner & C. R. Marmar (Eds.), *Trauma, memory, and dissociation* (pp. 285–320). Washington, DC: American Psychiatric Press.

Salkovskis, P. M., & Warwick, H. M. C. (2001). Meaning, misinterpretations, and medicine: A cognitive-behavioral approach to understanding health anxiety and hypochondriasis. In V. Starcevic & D. R. Lipsitt (Eds.), *Hypochondriasis: Modern perspectives on an ancient malady* (pp. 202–222). New York: Oxford University Press.

Sallee, F. R., Sethuraman, G., Sine, L., & Liu, H. (2000). Yohimbine challenge in children with anxiety disorders. *American Journal of Psychiatry, 157*, 1236–1242.

Salzman, L. (1968). *The obsessive personality*. New York: Science House.

SAMHSA (Substance Abuse and Mental Health Services Administration). (1996). *National household survey on drug abuse: 1994 and 1995*. Washington, DC: U.S. Department of Health and Human Services, Office of Applied Studies.

Sanchez-Carbonell, X., & Seus, L. (2000). Ten-year survival analysis of a cohort of heroin addicts in Catalonia: The EMETYST project. *Addiction, 95*, 941–948.

Sanders, M. R. (1996). New directions in behavioral family intervention with children. In T. H. Ollendick & R. J. Prinz (Eds.), *Advances in clinical child psychology*, Vol. 18 (pp. 283–330). New York: Plenum.

Sanders, M. R., Markie-Dadds, C., & Nicholson, J. M. (1997). Concurrent interventions for marital and children's problems. In W. K. Halford & H. J. Markman (Eds.), *Clinical handbook of marriage and couples interventions* (pp. 509–535). Chichester, England: Wiley.

Sanderson, W. C., Beck, A. T., & McGinn, L. K. (1994). Cognitive therapy for generalized anxiety disorder: Significance of comorbid personality disorders. *Journal of Cognitive Psychotherapy, 8*, 13–18.

Sanderson, W. C., Rapee, R., & Barlow, D. H. (1989). The influence of an illusion of control on panic attacks induced via inhalation of

5.5% carbon dioxide–enriched air. *Archives of General Psychiatry, 46,* 157–162.

Sanderson, W. C., Wetzler, S., & Asnis, G. M. (1994). Alprazolam blockade of CO_2-provoked panic in patients with panic disorder. *American Journal of Psychiatry, 151,* 1220–1222.

Saskin, P. (1997). Obstructive sleep apneas. In M. R. Pressman & W. C. Orr (Eds.), *Understanding sleep: The evaluation and treatment of sleep disorders* (pp. 283–297). Washington, DC: American Psychological Association.

Sattin, A. (1999). The role of TRH and related peptides in the mechanism of action of ECT. *Journal of ECT, 15,* 76–92.

Satz, P., & Green, M. F. (1999). Atypical handedness in schizophrenia: Some methodological and theoretical issues. *Schizophrenia Bulletin, 25,* 63–78.

Saugstad, L. F. (1989). Social class, marriage, and fertility in schizophrenia. *Schizophrenia Bulletin, 15,* 9–43.

Saunders, B. E., Kilpatrick, D. G., Resnick, H. S., & Tidwell, R. P. (1989). Brief screening for lifetime history of criminal victimization at mental health intake: A preliminary study. *Journal of Interpersonal Violence, 4,* 267–277.

Savela, T., Robinson, G., & Crow, S. (2000). *Contracting for public mental health services: Opinions of managed behavioral health care organizations.* (DHHS Publication No. SMA 00-3438)

Schachter, J., & Luborsky, L. (1998). Who's afraid of psychoanalytic research? Analysts' attitudes towards reading clinical versus empirical research papers. *International Journal of Psychoanalysis, 79,* 965–969.

Schacter, D. (1992). Understanding implicit memory: A cognitive neuroscience approach. *American Psychologist, 47,* 559–569.

Schacter, D., & Tulving, E. (1982). Amnesia and memory research. In L. S. Cermak (Ed.), *Human memory and amnesia.* Hillsdale, NJ: Erlbaum.

Schacter, D. L., Verfaellie, M., Anes, M. D., & Racine, C. (1998). When true recognition suppresses false recognition: Evidence from amnesic patients. *Journal of Cognitive Neuroscience, 10,* 668–679.

Scharf, M. B., & Jennings, S. W. (1990). Sleep disorders. In D. Bienenfeld (Ed.), *Verwoerdt's clinical geropsychiatry* (3rd ed., pp. 178–194). Baltimore: Williams & Wilkins.

Scheier, M. F., & Carver, C. S. (2001). Adapting to cancer: The importance of hope and purpose. In A. Baum & B. L. Andersen (Eds.), *Psychosocial interventions for cancer* (pp. 15–36). Washington, DC: American Psychological Association.

Scherrer, J. F., True, W. R., Xian, H., Lyons, M. J., Eisen, S. A., Goldberg, J., Lin, N., & Tsuang, M. T. (2000). Evidence for genetic influences common and specific to symptoms of generalized anxiety and panic. *Journal of Affective Disorders, 57,* 25–35.

Scheuner, D., Eckman, C., Jensen, M., Song, X., Citron, M., Suzuki, N., Bird, T. D., Hardy, J., Hutton, M., Kukull, W., Larson, E., Levy-Lahad, E., Viitanen, M., Peskind, E., Poorkaj, P., Schellenberg, G., Tanzi, R., Wasco, W., Lannfelt, I., Selkoe, D., & Younkin, S. (1996). Secreted amyloid β-protein similar to that in senile plaques in Alzheimer's disease is increased in vivo in the presenile 1 and 2 and APP mutations linked to familial Alzheimer's disease. *Nature and Medicine, 2,* 864–870.

Schilder, P. (1938). The organic background of obsessions and compulsions. *American Journal of Psychiatry, 94,* 1397.

Schlank, A., & Bidelman, P. (2001). Transition: Challenges for the offender and the community. In A. Schlank (Ed.), *The sexual predator,* Vol. 2, *Legal issues, clinical issues, and special populations* (pp. 10.1–10.13). Kingston, NJ: Civic Research Institute.

Schlank, A., & Cohen, F. (Eds.). (1999). *The sexual predator: Law, policy, evaluation and treatment.* Kingston, NJ: Civic Research Institute.

Schlessinger, L. (1999). Article on pedophilia is just "junk science." Universal Press Syndicate, April 18, 1999. (Available through the Internet).

Schlundt, O. G., & Johnson, W. G. (1990). *Eating disorders: Assessment and treatment.* Boston: Allyn & Bacon.

Schmidt, C. W., Jr. (1995). Sexual psychopathology and DSM-IV. *American Psychiatric Press Review of Psychiatry, 14,* 719–733.

Schmidt, N. B., Lerew, D. R., & Jackson, R. J. (1997). The role of anxiety sensitivity in the pathogenesis of panic: Prospective evaluation of spontaneous panic attacks during acute stress. *Journal of Abnormal Psychology, 106,* 355–364.

Schmidt-Nowara, W. W., Meade, T. E., & Hays, M. B. (1991). Treatment for snoring and obstructive sleep apnea with a dental orthosis. *Chest, 99,* 1378–1385.

Schneider, K. (1923). *Die psychopathischen personlichkeiten.* Berlin: Springer.

Schneider, L. S. (2000). Psychopharmacology: Antidementia drugs. In B. I. Sadock & V. A. Sadock (Eds.), *Kaplan & Sadock's comprehensive textbook of psychiatry* (7th ed., pp. 3101–3107). Philadelphia: Lippincott Williams & Wilkins.

Schneiderman, N., Antoni, M. H., Ironson, G., LaPerriere, A., et al. (1992). Applied psychological science and HIV-1 spectrum disease. *Applied and Preventive Psychology, 1,* 67–82.

Schneier, F. R., Johnson, J., Hornig, C. D., Liebowitz, M. R., & Weisman, M. M. (1992). Social phobia: Comorbidity and morbidity in an epidemiologic sample. *Archives of General Psychiatry, 49,* 282–288.

Schoeneman, T. J. (1984). The mentally ill witch in textbooks of abnormal psychology: Current status and implications of a fallacy. *Professional psychology, 15,* 299–314.

Schopp, R. F. (2001). *Competence, condemnation, and commitment: An integrated theory of mental health law.* Washington, DC: American Psychological Association.

Schramke, C. J., Stowe, R. M., Ratcliff, G., Goldstein, G., & Condray, R. (1998). Poststroke depression and anxiety: Different assessment methods result in variations in incidence and severity estimates. *Journal of Clinical and Experimental Neuropsychology, 20,* 723–737.

Schreiber, F. R. (1973). *Sybil.* Chicago: Regnery.

Schuckit, M. A. (2000). Alcohol-related disorders. In B. I. Sadock & V. A. Sadock (Eds.), *Kaplan & Sadock's comprehensive textbook of psychiatry* (7th ed., pp. 953–971). Philadelphia: Lippincott Williams & Wilkins.

Schuckit, M. A., & Smith, T. L. (1996). An 8-year follow-up of 450 sons of alcoholic and control subjects. *Archives of General Psychiatry, 53,* 202–210.

Schultz, S. K., Scherman, A., & Marshall, L. J. (2000). Evaluation of a university-based date rape prevention program: Effect on attitudes and behavior related to rape. *Journal of College Student Development, 41,* 193–201.

Schwartz, J. M., Stoessel, P. W., Baxter, L. R., Jr., Martin, K. M., & Phelps, M. E. (1996). Systematic changes in cerebral glucose metabolic rate after successful behavior modification treatment of obsessive-compulsive disorder. *Archives of General Psychiatry, 53,* 109–113.

Schwartz, M. S., & Olson, R. P. (1995). A historical perspective on the field of biofeedback and applied psychophysiology. In M. S. Schwartz (Ed.), *Biofeedback: A practitioner's guide* (2nd ed., pp. 3–18). New York: Guilford.

Scott, G. G. (1983). *Erotic power: An exploration of dominance and submission.* Secaucus, NJ: Citadel Press.

Scott, J. E., & Hochberg, M. C. (1998). Arthritis and other musculoskeletal diseases. In R. C. Brownson, P. L. Remington, & J. R. Davis (Eds.), *Chronic disease: Epidemiology and control* (2nd ed., pp. 465–489). Washington, DC: American Public Health Association.

Scott, M. J., & Stradling, S. G. (1994). Post-traumatic stress disorder without the trauma. *British Journal of Clinical Psychology, 33,* 71–74.

Scully, J. A., Tosi, H., & Banning, K. (2000). Life event checklists: Revisiting the Social Readjustment Rating Scale after 30 years. *Educational and Psychological Measurement, 60,* 864–876.

Segal, N. L. (1999). *Entwined lives: Twins and what they tell us about human behavior.* New York: Dutton.

Segall, M. H., Dasen, P. R., Berry, J. W., & Poortinga, Y. H. (1990). *Human behavior in global perspective: An introduction to cross-cultural psychology.* New York: Pergamon.

Segraves, K., & Segraves, R. T. (1991). Hypoactive sexual desire disorder: Prevalence and comorbidity in 906 subjects. *Journal of Sex and Marital Therapy, 17*, 55–58.

Seidman, L. J., Biederman, J., Monuteaux, M. C., Doyle, A. E., & Faraone, S. V. (2001). Learning disabilities and executive dysfunction in boys with attention-deficit/hyperactivity disorder. *Neuropsychology, 15*, 544–556.

Seligman, M. E. P. (1971). Phobias and preparedness. *Behavior Therapy, 2*, 307–320.

Seligman, M. E. P. (1975). *Helplessness: On depression, development, and death.* San Francisco: Freeman.

Seligman, M. E. P. (1990). Why is there so much depression today? The wasting of the individual and the waning of the commons. In R. E. Ingram (Ed.), *Contemporary psychological approaches to depression: Theory, research, and treatment* (pp. 1–9). New York: Plenum Press.

Seligman, M. E. P. (1992). *Learned optimism.* New York: Pocket Books.

Selling, L. S. (1943). *Men against madness.* New York: Garden City Books.

Selye, H. (1936). A syndrome produced by diverse noxious agents. *Nature, 138*, 32.

Selye, H. (1950). *The physiology and pathology of exposure to stress.* Montreal: Acta.

Serban, G., Conte, H. R., & Plutchik, R. (1987). Borderline and schizotypal personality disorders: Mutually exclusive or overlapping? *Journal of Personality Assessment, 5*, 15–22.

Serra, M., Minderaa, R. B., van Geert, P. L. C., Jackson, A. E., Althaus, M., & Til, R. (1995). Emotional role-taking abilities of children with a pervasive developmental disorder not otherwise specified. *Journal of Child Psychology and Psychiatry, 36*, 475–490.

Servan-Schreiber, D., & Cohen, J. D. (1998). Stroop task, language, and neuromodulation: Models of cognitive deficits in schizophrenia. In R. W. Parks, D. S. Levine, & D. L. Long (Eds.), *Fundamentals of neural network modeling: Neuropsychology and cognitive neuroscience* (pp. 192–208). Cambridge, MA: M.I.T. Press.

Seto, M. C., & Barbaree, H. E. (1995). The role of alcohol in sexual aggression. *Clinical Psychology Review, 15*, 545–566.

Seymour, P. H. K., & Evans, H. M. (1999). Foundation-level dyslexia: Assessment and treatment. *Journal of Learning Disabilities, 32*, 394–405.

Shaffer, I. A. (2001). Managed care: Cost and effectiveness. In N. A. Cummings & W. O'Donohue (Eds.), *Integrated behavioral healthcare: Positioning mental health practice with medical/surgical practice* (pp. 187–206). San Diego, CA: Academic.

Shapiro, F. (1989). Efficacy of the eye movement desensitization procedure in the treatment of traumatic memories. *Journal of Traumatic Stress, 2*, 199–223.

Shapiro, F. (1995). *Eye movement desensitization and reprocessing: Basic principles, protocols, and procedures.* New York: Guilford.

Shapiro, F. (1997). Eye movement desensitization and reprocessing (EMDR): Research and clinical significance. In P. Gosselin and W. Matthews (Eds.), *Current thinking and research in brief therapy: Solutions, strategies, and narratives* (pp. 239–260). Philadelphia: Brunner Mazel.

Shaw, D. S., Owens, E. B., Giovannelli, J., & Winslow, E. B. (2001). Infant and toddler pathways leading to early externalizing disorders. *Journal of the American Academy of Child and Adolescent Psychiatry, 40*, 36–43.

Shea, M. T., Elkin, I., Imber, S. D., Sotsky, S. M., Watkins, J. T., Collins, J. F., Pilkonis, P. A., Beckham, E., Glass, D. R., Dolan, R. T., & Parloff, M. B. (1992). Course of depressive symptoms over follow-up: Findings from the National Institute of Mental Health treatment of depression collaborative research program. *Archives of General Psychiatry, 49*, 782–787.

Sher, K. J., Frost, R. O., & Otto, R. (1983). Cognitive deficits in compulsive checkers: An exploratory study. *Behaviour Research and Therapy, 21*, 357–363.

Sher, K. J., Frost, R. O., Kushner, M., Crews, T. M., & Alexander, J. E. (1989). Memory deficits in compulsive checkers: Replication and extension in a clinical sample. *Behaviour Research and Therapy, 27*, 65–69.

Sher, K. J., Mann, B., & Frost, R. O. (1984). Cognitive dysfunction in compulsive checkers: Further exploration. *Behaviour Research and Therapy, 22*, 493–502.

Sher, L., Matthews, J. R., Turner, E. H., Postolache, T. T., Katz, K. S., & Rosenthal, N. E. (2001). Early response to light therapy partially predicts long-term antidepressant effects in patients with seasonal affective disorder. *Journal of Psychiatry and Neuroscience, 26*, 336–338.

Shergill, S. S., Murray, R. M., & McGuire, P. K. (1998). Auditory hallucinations: A review of psychological treatments. *Schizophrenia Research, 32*, 137–150.

Sherlock, R. (1983). Suicide and public policy: A critique of the "new consensus." *Journal of Bioethics, 4*, 58–70.

Sherwin, B. (1988). A comparative analysis of the role of androgen in human male and female sexual behavior: Behavioral specificity, critical thresholds, and sensitivity. *Psychobiology, 16*, 416–425.

Sheth, N., & Imbroglia, G. (1999). Images in psychiatry: Trenton Psychiatric Hospital. *American Journal of Psychiatry, 156*, 1982.

Shisslak, C. M., Perse, T., & Crago, Marjorie. (1991). Coexistence of bulimia nervosa and mania: A literature review and case report. *Comprehensive Psychiatry, 32*, 181–184.

Shisslak, C. M., Renger, R., Sharpe, T., Crago, M., McKnight, K. M., Gray, N., Bryson, S., Estes, L. S., Parnby, O. G., Killen, J., & Taylor, C. B. (1999). Development and evaluation of the McKnight Risk Factor Survey for assessing potential risk and protective factors for disordered eating in preadolescent and adolescent girls. *International Journal of Eating Disorders, 25*, 195–214.

Shneidman, E. S. (1973). Suicide notes reconsidered. *Psychiatry, 36*, 379–394.

Shneidman, E. S. (1979). A bibliography of suicide notes: 1856–1979. *Suicide and Life-Threatening Behavior, 9*, 57–59.

Shneidman, E. S. (1985). *Definition of suicide.* New York: Wiley.

Shneidman, E. S. (1987). A psychological approach to suicide. In G. R. VandenBos & B. K. Bryant (Eds.), *Cataclysms, crisis, and catastrophes: Psychology in action.* Washington, DC: American Psychological Association.

Shneidman, E. S. (1993). *Suicide as psyche: A clinical approach to self-destructive behavior.* Northvale, NJ: Jason Aronson.

Shneidman, E. S., Farberow, N. L., & Litman, R. E. (Eds.) (1994). *The psychology of suicide: A clinician's guide to evaluation and treatment* (rev. ed.). Northvale, NJ: Jason Aronson.

Sholevar, G. P. (2001). Family therapy for conduct disorders. *Child and Adolescent Psychiatric Clinics of North America, 10*, 501–517.

Shopsin, B., Friedman, E., & Gershon, S. (1976). Parachlorophenylalanine reversal of tranylcypromine effects in depressed patients. *Archives of General Psychiatry, 33*, 811–819.

Shore, R. (1997). *Rethinking the brain: New insights into early development.* New York: Families and Work Institute.

Shrout, P. E., Canino, G. J., Bird, H. R., Rubio-Stipec, M., et al. (1992). Mental health status among Puerto Ricans, Mexican Americans, and non-Hispanic Whites. *American Journal of Community Psychology, 20*, 729–752.

Siegfried, B., Frischknecht, H. R., & Nunez de Souza, R. (1990). An ethological model for the study of activation and interaction of pain, memory, and defensive systems in the attacked mouse: Role of endogenous opioids. *Neuroscience and Biobehavioral Reviews, 14*, 481–490.

Siegler, I. C., Peterson, B. L., Barefoot, J. C., & Williams, R. B. (1992). Hostility in late adolescence predicts coronary risk factors at mid-life. *American Journal of Epidemiology, 136*, 146–156.

Siever, L. J., & Davis, K. (1991). A psychobiologic perspective on the personality disorders. *American Journal of Psychiatry, 148*, 1647–1658.

Siever, L. J., Bernstein, D. P., & Silverman, J. M. (1995). Schizotypal personality disorder. In W. J. Livesley (Ed.), *The DSM-IV personality disorders* (pp. 71–90). New York: Guilford.

Siever, L. J., Keefe, R., Bernstein, D. P., Coccaro, E. F., Klar, H. M., Zemishlany, Z., Peterson, A. E., Davidson, M., Mahon, T., Horvath, T., & Mohs, R. (1990). Eye tracking impairment in clinically identified patients with schizotypal personality disorder. *American Journal of Psychiatry, 147*, 740–745.

Sigman, M. D., Kasari, C., Kwon, J., & Yirmiya, N. (1992). Responses to the negative emotions of others by autistic, mentally retarded, and normal children. *Child Development, 63*, 796–807.

Sihver, W., Langstroem, B., & Nordberg, A. (2000). Ligands for in vivo imaging of nicotinic receptor subtypes in Alzheimer brain. *Acta Neurologica Scandinavica, 102* (Supplement 176), 27–33.

Silberman, E. K. (1999). Pharmacotherapy. In M. Hersen & A. S. Bellack (Eds.), *Handbook of comparative interventions for adult disorders* (2nd ed., pp. 256–283). New York: Wiley.

Silberstein, S. D. (2001). Hormone-related headache. *Medical Clinics of North America, 85*, 1017–1035.

Silberstein, S. D., Lipton, R. B., & Dalessio, D. J. (2001a). Overview, diagnosis, and classification of headache. In S. D. Silberstein, R. B. Lipton, & D. J. Dalessio (Eds.), *Wolff's headache and other head pain* (7th ed., pp. 6–26). New York: Oxford University Press.

Silberstein, S. D., Saper, J. R., & Freitag, F. G. (2001b). Migraine: Diagnosis and treatment. In S. D. Silberstein, R. B. Lipton, & D. J. Dalessio (Eds.), *Wolff's headache and other head pain* (7th ed., pp. 121–237). New York: Oxford University Press.

Silver, E., Cirincione, C., & Steadman, H. J. (1994). Demythologizing inaccurate perceptions of the insanity defense. *Law and Human Behavior, 18*, 63–70.

Silverman, F. H. (1996). *Stuttering and other fluency disorders* (2nd ed.). Boston: Allyn & Bacon.

Silverman, L. H. (1983). The subliminal psychodynamic activation method. In J. M. Masling (Ed.), *Empirical studies of psychoanalytic theories*, Vol. 1 (pp. 69–100). Hillsdale, NJ: Erlbaum.

Silverman, L. H., Bronstein, A., & Mendelsohn, E. (1976). The further use of the subliminal psychodynamic activation method for the experimental study of the clinical theory of psychoanalysis: On the specificity of the relationship between symptoms and unconscious conflicts. *Psychotherapy: Theory, Research, & Practice, 13*, 2–16.

Silverstein, B., & Perlick, D. (1995). *The cost of competence: Why inequality causes depression, eating disorders, and illness in women*. New York: Oxford University Press.

Silvia, P. J., & Duval, T. S. (2001). Predicting the interpersonal targets of self-serving attributions. *Journal of Experimental Social Psychology, 37*, 333–340.

Simeon, D., Hollander, E., Stein, D. J., Cohen, L., & Aronowitz, B. (1995). Body dysmorphic disorder in the DSM-IV field trial for obsessive-compulsive disorder. *American Journal of Psychiatry, 152*, 1207–1209.

Simon, R. I. (2001). *Concise guide to psychiatry and law for clinicians* (3rd ed.). Washington, DC: American Psychiatric Association.

Simon, R. J. (1999). *The jury and the defense of insanity*. New Brunswick, NJ: Transaction Publishers.

Simoneau, T. L., Miklowitz, D. J., & Saleem, R. (1998). Expressed emotion and interactional patterns in the families of bipolar patients. *Journal of Abnormal Psychology, 107*, 497–507.

Simonoff, E. (2001). Gene-environment interplay in oppositional defiant and conduct disorder. *Child and Adolescent Psychiatric Clinics of North America, 10*, 351–374.

Simons, R. F. (1981). Electrodermal and cardiac orienting in psychometrically defined high-risk subjects. *Psychiatric Research, 4*, 347–356.

Simons, R. F., & Katkin, W. (1985). Smooth pursuit eye movement in subjects reporting physical anhedonia and perceptual aberration. *Psychiatry Research, 14*, 275–289.

Simpson, J. M. (2001). Infant stress and sleep deprivation as an aetiological basis for the sudden infant death syndrome. *Early Human Development, 61*, 1–43.

Singer, M., & Wynne, L. C. (1963). Differentiating characteristics of the parents of childhood schizophrenics. *American Journal of Psychiatry, 120*, 234–243.

Singer, M., & Wynne, L. C. (1965). Thought disorder and family relations of schizophrenia. III. Methodology using projective techniques. *Archives of General Psychiatry, 12*, 187–200.

Singh, A., Herrmann, N., & Black, S. E. (1998). The importance of lesion location in poststroke depression: A critical review. *Canadian Journal of Psychiatry, 43*, 921–927.

Sipprelle, R. C. (1992). A vet center experience: Multievent trauma, delayed treatment type. In D. W. Foy (Ed.), *Treating PTSD: Cognitive-behavioral strategies* (pp. 13–38). New York: Guilford.

Skinner, B. F. (1956). A case history in scientific method. *American Psychologist, 11*, 221–233.

Skinner, B. F. (1972). *Cumulative record: A selection of papers* (3rd ed.). New York: Appleton-Century-Crofts.

Skwerer, R. G., Jacobsen, F. M., Duncan, C. C., Kelley, K. A., Sack, D. A., Tamarkin, L., Gaist, P. A., Kasper, S., & Rosenthal, N. E. (1989). Neurobiology of seasonal affective disorder and phototherapy. In N. E. Rosenthal & M. C. Blehar (Eds.), *Seasonal affective disorders and phototherapy* (pp. 311–332). New York: Guilford.

Sleep Research Society (1993). *Basics of sleep behavior*. Los Angeles: UCLA and the Sleep Research Society.

Sloan, E. P., & Shapiro, C. M. (1995). Obstructive sleep apnea in a consecutive series of obese women. *International Journal of Eating Disorders, 17*, 167–173.

Slutske, W. S., Heath, A. C., Dinwiddie, S. H., Madden, P. A. F., Bucholz, K. K., Dunne, M. P., Statham, D. J., & Martin, N. G. (1998). Common genetic risk factors for conduct disorder and alcohol dependence. *Journal of Abnormal Psychology, 107*, 363–374.

Smalley, S. L., Asarnow, R. F., & Spence, A. (1988). Autism and genetics: A decade of research. *Archives of General Psychiatry, 45*, 953–961.

Smith, B. K., Kelly, L. A., Pina, R., York, D. A., & Bray, G. A. (1998). Preferential fat intake increases adiposity but not body weight in Sprague-Dawley rats. *Appetite, 31*, 127–139.

Smith, D. W., Bierman, E. L., & Robinson, N. M. (1978). *The biological ages of man: From conception through old age*. Philadelphia: Saunders.

Smith, G. S., Reynolds, C. F., III, Pollock, B., Derbyshire, S., Nofzinger, E., Dew, M. A., Houck, P. R., Milko, D., Meltzer, C. C., & Kupfer, D. J. (1999). Cerebral glucose metabolic response to combined total sleep deprivation and antidepressant treatment in geriatric depression. *American Journal of Psychiatry, 156*, 683–689.

Smith, H., & Cox, C. (1983). Dialogue with a dominatrix. In T. Weinberg & G. Kamel (Eds.), *S and M: Studies in sadomasochism* (pp. 80–86). Buffalo, NY: Prometheus.

Smolak, L., Murnen, S. K., & Ruble, A. E. (2000). Female athletes and eating problems: A meta-analysis. *International Journal of Eating Disorders, 27*, 371–380.

Smoller, J. W., Finn, C., & White, C. (2000). The genetics of anxiety disorders: An overview. *Psychiatric Annals, 30*, 745–753.

Smukler, A. J., & Schiebel, D. (1975). Personality characteristics of exhibitionists. *Diseases of the Nervous System, 36*, 600–603.

Snowden, D. A., Kemper, S. J., Mortimer, J. A., Greiner, L. H., Wekstein, D. R., & Markesbery, W. R. (1996). Linguistic ability in early life and cognitive function and Alzheimer's disease in late life: Findings from the nun study. *Journal of the American Medical Association, 275*, 528–534.

Sobell, M. B., & Sobell, L. C. (1973). Individualized behavior therapy for alcoholics. *Behavior Therapy, 4*, 49–72.

Sobell, M. B., & Sobell, L. C. (1976). Second-year treatment outcome of alcoholics treated by individualized behavior therapy: Results. *Behaviour Research and Therapy, 14*, 195–215.

Sobell, M. B., & Sobell, L. C. (1978). *Behavioral treatment of alcohol problems*. New York: Plenum.

Sobell, M. B., & Sobell, L. C. (1993). *Problem drinkers: Guided self-change treatment.* New York: Guilford.

Sokol, R. J., Ager, J., Martier, S., Debanne, S., Ernhart, C., Kuzma, J., & Miller, S. I. (1986). Significant determinants of susceptibility to alcohol teratogenicity. *Annals of the New York Academy of Sciences, 477,* 87–102.

Soloff, P. H., Lynch, K. G., & Moss, H. B. (2000). Serotonin, impulsivity, and alcohol use disorders in the older adolescent: A psychobiological study. *Alcoholism: Clinical and Experimental Research, 24,* 1609–1619.

Soloff, P. H., Lynch, K. G., Kelley, T. M., Malone, K. M., & Mann, J. J. (2000). Characteristics of suicide attempts of patients with major depressive episode and borderline personality disorder: A comparative study. *American Journal of Psychiatry, 157,* 601–608.

Solomon, D. A., Keller, M. B., Leon, A. C., Mueller, T. I., Lavori, P. W., Shea, M. T., Coryell, W., Warshaw, M., Turvey, C., Maser, J. D., & Endicott, J. (2000). Multiple recurrences of major depression. *American Journal of Psychiatry, 157,* 229–233.

Solomon, K., & Hart, R. (1978). Pitfalls and prospects in clinical research on antianxiety drugs: Benzodiazepines and placebos. *Journal of Clinical Psychiatry, 39,* 238–246.

Solomon, S., & Newman, L. C. (2001). Episodic tension-type headaches. In S. D. Silberstein, R. B. Lipton, & D. J. Dalessio (Eds.), *Wolff's headache and other head pain* (7th ed., pp. 238–248). New York: Oxford University Press.

Sommer, I., Aleman, A., Ramsey, N., Bouma, A., & Kahn, R. (2001). Handedness, language lateralisation and anatomical asymmetry in schizophrenia. *British Journal of Psychiatry, 178,* 344–351.

Songer, D. A., & Roman, B. (1996). Treatment of somatic delusional disorder with atypical antipsychotic agents. *American Journal of Psychiatry, 153,* 578–579.

Sonuga-Barke, E. J. S., Daley, D., Thompson, M., Laver-Bradbury, C., & Weeks, A. (2001). Parent-based therapies for preschool attention-deficit/hyperactivity disorder: A randomized, controlled trial with a community sample. *Journal of the American Academy of Child and Adolescent Psychiatry, 40,* 402–408.

Southwick, S. M., Bremner, D., Krystal, J. H., & Charney, D. S. (1994). Psychobiologic research in post-traumatic stress disorder. *Psychiatric Clinics of North America, 17,* 251–264.

Spangler, W. J., Cosgrove, G. R., Ballantine, H. T., Jr., Cassem, E. H., Rauch, S. L., Nierenberg, A., & Price, B. H. (1996). Magnetic resonance image–guided stereotactic cingulotomy for intractable psychiatric disease. *Neurosurgery, 38,* 1071–1076.

Spanos, N. P. (1994). Multiple identity enactments and multiple personality disorder: A sociocognitive perspective. *Psychological Bulletin, 116,* 143–165.

Sparrow, S. S., Ballo, D. A., & Cicchetti, D. V. (1984). *Vineland Adaptive Behavior Scales.* Circle Pines, MI: American Guidance Services.

Spector, I. P., & Carey, M. P. (1990). Incidence and prevalence of the sexual dysfunctions: A critical review of the empirical literature. *Archives of Sexual Behavior, 19,* 389–408.

Speed, N., Engdahl, B., Schwartz, J., & Eberly, R. (1989). Posttraumatic stress disorder as a consequence of the POW experience. *Journal of Nervous and Mental Disease, 177,* 147–153.

Spencer, T., Wilens, T., Biederman, J., Wozniak, J., & Harding-Crawford, M. (2000). Attention-deficit/hyperactivity disorder with mood disorder. In T. E. Brown (Ed.), *Attention deficit disorders and comorbidities in children, adolescents, and adults* (pp. 79–124). Washington, DC: American Psychiatric Press.

Spiegel, D. (1996). Dissociative disorders. In R. E. Hales & S. C. Yudofsky (Eds.), *The American Psychiatric Press textbook of psychiatry* (pp. 583–604). Washington, DC: American Psychiatric Press.

Spiegel, H., & Spiegel, D. (1987). *Trance and treatment: Clinical uses of hypnosis.* New York: Basic Books.

Spielman, A. J., & Glovinsky, P. B. (1997). The diagnostic interview and differential diagnosis for complaints of insomnia. In M. R. Pressman & W. C. Orr (Eds.), *Understanding sleep: The evaluation and treat-

ment of sleep disorders* (pp. 125–160). Washington, DC: American Psychological Association.

Spielman, A. J., Caruso, L. S., & Glovinsky, P. B. (1987). A behavioral perspective on insomnia treatment. *Psychiatric Clinics of North America, 10,* 541–553.

Spitzer, R. L., & Endicott, J. (1977). *Schedule for affective disorders and schizophrenia—lifetime version (SADS-L).* New York: New York State Psychiatric Institute.

Spitzer, R. L., & Fleiss, J. L. (1974). A re-analysis of the reliability of psychiatric diagnosis. *British Journal of Psychiatry, 125,* 341–347.

Spitzer, R. L., & Wakefield, J. C. (1999). DSM-IV diagnostic criterion for clinical significance: Does it help solve the false-positives problem? *American Journal of Psychiatry, 156,* 1856–1864.

Spitzer, R. L., & Williams, J. B. W. (1988). Basic principles in the development of DSM-III. In J. E. Mezzich & M. von Cranach (Eds.), *International classification in psychiatry: Unity and diversity* (pp. 81–86). New York: Cambridge University Press.

Spitzer, R. L., Endicott, J., & Robins, E. (1975). Clinical criteria for psychiatric diagnosis and DSM-III. *American Journal of Psychiatry, 132,* 1187–1192.

Spitzer, R. L., Williams, J. B. W., Kroenke, K., Linzer, M., deGruy, F. I., Hahan, S., Brody, D., & Johnson, J. (1994). Utility of a new procedure for diagnosing mental disorders in primary care: The PRIME-MD 1000 study. *Journal of the American Medical Association, 272,* 1749–1756.

Spoont, M. R. (1996). Emotional instability. In C. G. Costello (Ed.), *Personality characteristics of the personality disordered* (pp. 48–90). New York: Wiley.

St. Lawrence, J. S., & Madakasira, S. (1992). Evaluation and treatment of premature ejaculation: A critical review. *International Journal of Psychiatry in Medicine, 22,* 77–97.

Staal, W. G., Hulshoff Pol, H. E., & Kahn, R. S. (1999). Outcome of schizophrenia in relationship to brain abnormalities. *Schizophrenia Bulletin, 25,* 337–348.

Stahl, S. M. (2000). The new cholinesterase inhibitors for Alzheimer's disease. Part 1: Their similarities are different. *Journal of Clinical Psychiatry, 61,* 710–711.

Stampfl, T. G., & Levis, D. J. (1967). Essentials of implosive therapy: A learning theory–based psychodynamic behavioral therapy. *Journal of Abnormal Psychology, 72,* 496–503.

Stanley, M. A., & Turner, S. M. (1995). Current status of pharmacological and behavioral treatment of obsessive-compulsive disorder. *Behavior Therapy, 26,* 163–186.

Staples, R. (1990). Substance abuse and the black family crisis: An overview. *Western Journal of Black Studies, 14,* 196–204.

Starkstein, S. E., Mayberg, H. S., Berthier, M. L., Fedoroff, P., Price, T. R., Dannals, R. F., Wagner, H. N., Leiguiarda, R., & Robinson, R. G. (1990). Mania after brain injury: Neuroradiologic and metabolic findings. *Annals of Neurology, 27,* 652–659.

Staudacher, C. (1991). *Men and grief.* Oakland, CA: New Harbinger.

Steadman, H. J. (1979). *Beating a rap: Defendants found incompetent to stand trial.* Chicago: University of Chicago Press.

Steege, J. F. (1984). Dyspareunia and vaginismus. *Clinics in Obstetrics and Gynecology, 27,* 750–759.

Steege, J. F., & Ling, F. W. (1993). Dyspareunia: A special type of chronic pelvic pain. *Obstetrics and Gynecology Clinics of North America, 20,* 779–793.

Stege, P., Visco-Dangler, L., & Rye, L. (1982). Anorexia nervosa: Review including oral and dental manifestations. *Journal of the American Dental Association, 104,* 548–552.

Stein, D. J., & Niehaus, D. J. H. (2001). Stereotypic self-injurious behaviors: Neurobiology and psychopharmacology. In D. Simeon & E. Hollander (Eds.), *Self-injurious behaviors: Assessment and treatment* (pp. 29–48). Washington, DC: American Psychiatric Association.

Stein, D. J., Hollander, E., Anthony, D. T., Schneier, F. R., Fallon, B. A., Liebowitz, M. R., & Klein, D. F. (1992). Serotonergic medications for sexual obsessions, sexual addictions, and paraphilias. *Journal of Clinical Psychiatry, 53,* 267–271.

Stein, L., & Wise, C. D. (1971). Possible etiology of schizophrenia: Progressive damage to the noradrenergic reward system by 6-hydroxydopamine. *Science, 171,* 1032–1036.

Stein, M. B., Forde, D. R., Anderson, G., & Walker, J. R. (1997b). Obsessive-compulsive disorder in the community: An epidemiologic survey with clinical reappraisal. *American Journal of Psychiatry, 154,* 1120–1126.

Stein, M. B., Walker, J. R., Hazen, A. L., & Forde, D. R. (1997a). Full and partial posttraumatic stress disorder: Findings from a community survey. *American Journal of Psychiatry, 154,* 1114–1119.

Steinberg, M. (2000). Depersonalization disorder. In B. I. Sadock & V. A. Sadock (Eds.), *Kaplan & Sadock's comprehensive textbook of psychiatry* (7th ed., pp. 1564–1570). Philadelphia: Lippincott Williams & Wilkins.

Steketee, G. (1999). *Overcoming obsessive-compulsive disorder: Therapist protocol.* Oakland, CA: New Harbinger Publications.

Steketee, G. S. (1993). *Treatment of obsessive compulsive disorder.* New York: Guilford.

Steketee, G., & White, K. (1990). *When once is not enough.* Oakland, CA: New Harbinger Publications.

Steptoe, A., & Wardle, J. (Eds.). (1994). *Psychosocial processes and health: A reader.* Cambridge, England: Cambridge University Press.

Sterk-Elifson, C. (1996). Just for fun?: Cocaine use among middle-class women. *Journal of Drug Issues, 26,* 63–76.

Stermac, L. E., & Quinsey, V. L. (1986). Social competence among rapists. *Behavioral Assessment, 8,* 171–185.

Stern, S. L., Dixon, K. N., Nemzer, E., Lake, M. D., Sansone, R. A., Smeltzer, D. J., Lantz, S., & Schrier, S. S. (1984). Affective disorder in the families of women with normal weight bulimia. *American Journal of Psychiatry, 141,* 1224–1227.

Stern, Y., Gurland, B., Tatemichi, T., Tang, M. X., Wilder, D., & Mayeux, R. (1994). Influence of education and occupation on the incidence of Alzheimer disease. *Journal of the American Medical Association, 271,* 1004–1010.

Sternbach, H. (1998). Age-associated testosterone decline in men: Clinical issues for psychiatry. *American Journal of Psychiatry, 155,* 1310–1318.

Sternberg, R. J. (1994). Thinking styles: Theory and assessment of the interface between intelligence and personality. In R. J. Sternberg & P. Ruzgis (Eds.), *Personality and intelligence* (pp. 169–187). New York: Cambridge University Press.

Sternberg, R. J. (2001). Successful intelligence: Understanding what Spearman had rather than what he studied. In J. M. Collis & S. Messick (Eds.), *Intelligence and personality: Bridging the gap in theory and measurement* (pp. 347–373). Mahwah, NJ: Erlbaum.

Sternberg, R. J., & Wagner, R. K. (Eds.). (1994). *Minds in context: Interactionist perspectives on human intelligence.* New York: Cambridge University Press.

Stevens, L. J., & Price, M. (1992). Meeting the challenge of educating children at risk. *Phi Delta Kappan, 74,* 18–23.

Stevenson, J. (2001). Comorbidity of reading/spelling disability and ADHD. In F. Levy & D. A. Hay (Eds.), *Attention, genes, and ADHD* (pp. 99–114). Philadelphia: Brunner-Routledge.

Stewart, J. W., Quitkin, F. M., McGrath, P. J., & Bruder, G. E. (1999). Do tricyclic responders have different brain laterality? *Journal of Abnormal Psychology, 108,* 707–710.

Stice, E. (2001). A prospective test of the dual-pathway model of bulimic pathology: Mediating effects of dieting and negative affect. *Journal of Abnormal Psychology, 110,* 124–135.

Stillion, J. M. (1985). *Death and the sexes: An examination of the differential longevity, attitudes, behaviors, and coping skills.* Washington, DC: Hemisphere.

Stinson, S. (Ed.). (2000). *Human biology: An evolutionary and biocultural perspective.* New York: Wiley.

Stoll, A. L. (2001). *The omega-3 connection: The groundbreaking omega-3 antidepression diet and brain program.* New York: Simon & Schuster.

Stone, A. A., Bovbjerg, D. H., Neale, J. M., Napoli, A., et al. (1992). Development of common cold symptoms following experimental rhinovirus infection is related to prior stressful life events. *Behavioral Medicine, 18,* 115–120.

Stone, B., & Archer, J. (1990). College and university counseling centers in the 1990s: Challenges and limits. *Counseling Psychologist, 18,* 539–607.

Stone, M. (1985). Schizotypal personality: Psychotherapeutic aspects. *Schizophrenia Bulletin, 11,* 554–563.

Stoney, C. M., & Engebretson, T. O. (1994). Anger and hostility: Potential mediators of the gender difference in coronary heart disease. In A. W. Siegman & T. W. Smith (Eds.), *Anger, hostility, and the heart* (pp. 215–237). Hillsdale, NJ: Erlbaum.

Stoohs, R. A., Guilleminault, C., & Dement, W. C. (1993). Sleep apnea and hypertension in commercial truck drivers. *Sleep, 16*(8, Supplement), S11–S14.

Stover, E., & Nightingale, E. O. (1985). Introduction. In E. Stover & E. O. Nightingale (Eds.), *The breaking of minds and bodies* (pp. 1–26). New York: Freeman.

Strain, E. C., Bigelow, G. E., Liebson, I. A., & Stitzer, M. L. (1999). Moderate- vs low-dose methadone in the treatment of opioid dependence. *Journal of the American Medical Association, 281,* 1000–1005.

Strand, V. C. (2000). *Treating secondary victims: Intervention with the nonoffending mother in the incest family.* Thousand Oaks, CA: Sage.

Strang, S., & Strang, P. (2001). Spiritual thoughts, coping and "sense of coherence" in brain tumour patients and their spouses. *Palliative Medicine, 15,* 127–134.

Straus, S. E., Tosata, G., Armstrong, G., Lawley, T., Preble, O. T., Henle, W., Davey, R., Pearson, G., Epstein, J., Brus, I., & Blaese, R. M. (1985). Persisting illness and fatigue in adults with evidence of Epstein-Barr virus infection. *Annals of Internal Medicine, 102,* 7–16.

Strauss, M. E. (2001). Demonstrating specific cognitive deficits: A psychometric perspective. *Journal of Abnormal Psychology, 110,* 6–14.

Street, L., Craske, M. G., & Barlow, D. H. (1989). Sensations, cognitions, and the perception of cues associated with expected and unexpected panic attacks. *Behaviour Research and Therapy, 27,* 189–198.

Strittmatter, W. J., Saunders, A. M., Schmechel, D., Pericak-Vance, M., Enghild, J., Salvesen, G. S., & Roses, A. D. (1993). Apolipoprotein E: High-avidity binding to β-amyloid and increased frequency of type 4 allele in late-onset familial Alzheimer disease. *Proceedings of the National Academy of Science, 90,* 1977–1981.

Strober, M., Pataki, C., Freeman, R., & DeAntonio, M. (1999). No effect of adjunctive fluoxetine on eating behavior or weight phobia during the inpatient treatment of anorexia nervosa: An historical case-control study. *Journal of Child and Adolescent Psychopharmacology, 9,* 195–201.

Strunin, L., & Hingson, R. W. (1993). Alcohol use and risk for HIV infection. *Alcohol Health and Research World, 17,* 35–38.

Stunkard, A., Sorensen, T., & Schulsinger, F. (1980). Use of the Danish Adoption Register for the study of obesity and thinness. In S. Kety (Ed.), *The genetics of neurological and psychiatric disorders* (pp. 115–120). New York: Raven Press.

Suarez, E. C., Kuhn, C. M., Schanberg, S. M., Williams, R. B., Jr., & Zimmermann, E. A. (1998). Neuroendocrine, cardiovascular, and emotional responses of hostile men: The role of interpersonal challenge. *Psychosomatic Medicine, 60,* 78–88.

Suarez, T., & Reese, F. L. (2000). Coping, psychological adjustment, and complementary and alternative medicine use in persons living with HIV and AIDS. *Psychology and Health, 15,* 635–649.

Suddath, R. L., Christison, G. W., Torrey, E. F., Cassonova, M. F., Weinberger, D. R., et al. (1990). Anatomical abnormalities in the brains of monozygotic twins discordant for schizophrenia. *New England Journal of Medicine, 322,* 789–793.

Sullivan, C. E., Berthon-Jones, M., Issa, F. G., & Eves, L. (1981). Reversal of obstructive sleep apnoea by continuous positive airway pressure applied through the nares. *Lancet, 1,* 862–865.

Surgeon General. (1999). Mental health: A report of the surgeon general. (**www.surgeongeneral.gov/Library/MentalHealth/home.html**)

Sussman, S., Dent, C. W., Stacy, A. W., Burciaga, C., Raynor, A., Turner, G. E., Charlin, V., Craig, S., Hansen, W. B., Burton, D., & Flay, B. R. (1990). Peer-group association and adolescent tobacco use. *Journal of Abnormal Psychology, 99,* 349–352.

Sutker, P. B., & Allain, A. N. (1983). Behavior and personality assessment in men labeled adaptive sociopaths. *Journal of Behavioral Assessment, 5,* 65–79.

Sutker, P. B., Allain, A. N., & Winstead, D. K. (1993). Psychopathology and psychiatric diagnoses of World War II Pacific theater prisoner-of-war survivors and combat veterans. *American Journal of Psychiatry, 150,* 240–245.

Swadi, H. (1996). Nocturnal enuresis and psychopathology: Associations in a community sample. *Arab Journal of Psychiatry, 7,* 111–118.

Swan, N. (1995). Marijuana, other drug use among teens continue to rise. *National Institute on Drug Abuse Notes, 10*(2), 8–9.

Swanson, H. L., Hoskyn, M., & Lee, C. (1999). *Interventions for students with learning disabilities: A meta-analysis of treatment outcomes.* New York: Guilford.

Swayze, V. W. (1995). Frontal leukotomy and related psychosurgical procedures in the era before antipsychotics (1935–1954): A historical overview. *American Journal of Psychiatry, 152,* 505–515.

Swedo, S. E., Pietrini, P., Leonard, H. L., Schapiro, M. B., Rettew, D. C., Goldberger, E. L., Rapoport, S. I., Rapoport, J. L., & Grady, C. L. (1992). Cerebral glucose metabolism in childhood-onset obsessive-compulsive disorder: Revisualization during pharmacotherapy. *Archives of General Psychiatry, 49,* 690–694.

Swedo, S. E., Rapoport, J. L., Cheslow, D. L., Leonard, H. L., Ayoub, E. M., Hosier, D. M., & Wald, E. R. (1989). High prevalence of obsessive-compulsive symptoms in patients with Sydenham's chorea. *American Journal of Psychiatry, 146,* 246–249.

Swerdlow, N. R., & Koob, G. F. (1987). Dopamine, schizophrenia, mania, and depression: Toward a unified hypothesis of cortico-striato-pallido-thalamic function. *Behavior and Brain Science, 10,* 197–245.

Swift, R., & Davidson, D. (1998). Alcohol hangover: Mechanisms and mediators. *Alcohol Health and Research World, 22,* 54–60.

Szasz, T. S. (1961). *The myth of mental illness.* New York: Harper & Row.

Szasz, T. S. (1963). *Law, liberty, and psychiatry.* New York: Macmillan.

Szatmari, P., & Jones, M. B. (1998). Genetic epidemiology of autism and other pervasive developmental disorders. In F. R. Volkmar (Ed.), *Autism and pervasive developmental disorders* (pp. 109–129). New York: Cambridge University Press.

Szczepanski, R., Napolitano, M., Feaganes, J. R., Barefoot, J. C., Luecken, L., Swoap, R., Kuhn, C., Suarez, E., Siegler, I. C., Williams, R. B., & Blumenthal, J. A. (1997). Relation of mood ratings and neuro-hormonal responses during daily life in employed women. *International Journal of Behavioral Medicine, 4,* 1–16.

Szmukler, G. I., & Patton, G. (1995). Sociocultural models of eating disorders. In G. I. Szmukler & C. Dare (Eds.), *Handbook of eating disorders: Theory, treatment and research* (pp. 177–192). Chichester, England: Wiley.

Taleb, M., Rouillon, F., Petitjean, F., & Gorwood, P. (1996). Cross-cultural study of schizophrenia. *Psychopathology, 29,* 85–94.

Tannock, R. (2000). Attention-deficit/hyperactivity disorder with anxiety disorders. In T. E. Brown (Ed.), *Attention deficit disorders and comorbidities in children, adolescents, and adults* (pp. 125–170). Washington, DC: American Psychiatric Press.

Tannock, R., & Brown, T. E. (2000). Attention deficit disorders with learning disorders in children and adolescents. In T. E. Brown (Ed.), *Attention deficit disorders and comorbidities in children, adolescents, and adults* (pp. 231–296). Washington, DC: American Psychiatric Press.

Tarosoff v. Regents of University of California. (1974). 529 P.2d 553 (Cal. Sup. Ct.).

Tauscher, J., & Kapur, S. (2001). Choosing the right dose of antipsychotics in schizophrenia: Lessons from neuroimaging studies. *CNS Drugs, 15,* 671–678.

Tavris, C. (1992). The mismeasure of woman. New York: Simon & Schuster.

Taylor, C. B., & Arnow, B. (1988). *The nature and treatment of anxiety disorders.* New York: Free Press.

Taylor, C. B., Sharpe, T., Shisslak, C., Bryson, S., Estes, L. S., Gray, N., McKnight, K. M., Crago, M., Kraemer, H. C., & Killen, J. D. (1998). Factors associated with weight concerns in adolescent girls. *International Journal of Eating Disorders, 24,* 31–42.

Taylor, D. M., & Duncan-McConnell, D. (2000). Refractory schizophrenia and atypical antipsychotics. *Journal of Psychopharmacology, 14,* 409–418.

Taylor, G. R. (2001). Direct intervention techniques for teaching social skills to individuals with exceptionalities. In G. R. Taylor (Ed.), *Educational interventions and services for children with exceptionalities: Strategies and perspectives* (2nd ed., pp. 125–140). Springfield, IL: Charles C Thomas.

Taylor, R. R., Friedberg, F., & Jason, L. A. (2001). *A clinician's guide to controversial illnesses: Chronic fatigue syndrome, fibromyalgia, multiple chemical sensitivities.* Sarasota, FL: Professional Resource Press/Professional Resource Exchange.

Taylor, S. (2000). *Understanding and treating panic disorder: Cognitive-behavioural approaches.* New York: Wiley.

Taylor, S. E., & Aspinwall, L. G. (1996). Mediating and moderating processes in psychosocial stress: Appraisal, coping, resistance, and vulnerability. In H. Kaplan (Ed.), *Psychosocial stress: Perspective on structure, theory, life-course, and methods* (pp. 71–110). San Diego: Academic.

Taylor, T. K., Eddy, J. M., & Biglan, A. (1999). Interpersonal skills training to reduce aggressive and delinquent behavior: Limited evidence and the need for an evidence-based system of care. *Clinical Child and Family Psychology Review, 2,* 169–182.

Teichner, G., & Golden, C. J. (2000). The relationship of neuropsychological impairment to conduct disorder in adolescence: A conceptual review. *Aggression and Violent Behavior, 5,* 509–528.

Teigen, K. H. (1994). Yerkes-Dodson: A law for all seasons. *Theory and Psychology, 4,* 525–547.

Teitelbaum, P. (1961). Disturbance in feeding and drinking behavior after hypothalamic lesions. In M. R. Jones (Ed.), *Nebraska symposium on motivation* (pp. 39–65). Lincoln: University of Nebraska Press.

Teplin, L. A. (1985). The criminality of the mentally ill: A dangerous misconception. *American Journal of Psychiatry, 142,* 593–599.

Terenius, L. T., & O'Brien, C. P. (1992). Receptors and endogenous ligands: Implications for addiction. In C. P. O'Brien & J. H. Jaffe (Eds.), *Addictive states. Research publications: Association for Research in Nervous and Mental Disease,* Vol. 70 (pp. 123–130). New York: Raven.

Teri, L., & Lewinsohn, P. M. (1986). Individual and group treatment of unipolar depression: Comparison of treatment outcome and identification of predictors of successful treatment outcome. *Behavior Therapy, 17,* 215–228.

Terman, L. M. (1919). *Intelligence of school children.* Boston: Houghton Mifflin.

Terman, M., & Schlager, D. S. (1990). Twilight therapeutics, winter depression, melatonin, and sleep. In J. Montplaisir & R. Godbout (Eds.), *Sleep and biological rhythms: Basic mechanisms and applications to psychiatry* (pp. 113–128). New York: Oxford University Press.

Terry, G. C., & Rennie, T. (1938). Analysis of paraergesia. *American Journal of Orthopsychiatry, 9*, 817–918.

Tescavage, K. (1999). Teaching women a lesson: Sexually aggressive and sexually nonaggressive men's perceptions of acquaintance and date rape. *Violence Against Women, 5*, 796–812.

Testa, M., & Leonard, K. E. (2001). The impact of husband physical aggression and alcohol use on marital functioning: Does alcohol "excuse" the violence? *Violence and Victims, 16*, 507–516.

Tew, J. D., Jr., Mulsant, B. H., Haskett, R. F., Prudic, J., Thase, M. E., Crowe, R. R., Dolata, D., Begley, A. E., Reynolds., C. F., III, & Sackeim, H. A. (1999). Acute efficacy of ECT in the treatment of major depression in the old. *American Journal of Psychiatry, 156*, 1865–1870.

Thagard, P. (1999). *How scientists explain disease.* Princeton, NJ: Princeton University Press.

Thase, M. E. (2000). Mood disorders: Neurobiology. In B. I. Sadock & V. A. Sadock (Eds.), *Kaplan & Sadock's comprehensive textbook of psychiatry* (7th ed., pp. 1318–1328). Philadelphia: Lippincott Williams & Wilkins.

Thase, M. E., Dubé, S., Bowler, K., Howland, R. H., Myers, J. E., Friedman, E., & Jarrett, D. B. (1996). Hypothalamic-pituitary-adrenocortical activity and response to cognitive behavioral therapy in unmedicated, hospitalized depressed patients. *American Journal of Psychiatry, 153*, 886–891.

Thayer, J. F., Friedman, B. H., Borkovec, T. D., Johnsen, B. H., & Molina, S. (2000). Phasic heart period reactions to cued threat and nonthreat stimuli in generalized anxiety disorder. *Psychophysiology, 37*, 361–368.

The Economist. (2002). Treatment of choice. January 19, Business section.

Thigpen, C. H., & Cleckley, H. M. (1957). *The three faces of Eve.* New York: McGraw-Hill.

Thom, A., Sartory, G., & Joehren, P. (2000). Comparison between one-session psychological treatment and benzodiazepine in dental phobia. *Journal of Consulting and Clinical Psychology, 68*, 378–387.

Thombs, D. L. (1999). *Introduction to addictive behaviors* (2nd ed.). New York: Guilford.

Thompson v. County of Alameda. (1980). 614 P.2d 728 (Cal. Sup. Ct.)

Thornhill, N., & Thornhill, R. (1990a). Evolutionary analysis of psychological pain of rape victims. I: The effects of victim's age and marital status. *Ethology and Sociobiology, 11*, 155–176.

Thornhill, N., & Thornhill, R. (1990b). Evolutionary analysis of psychological pain following rape. II: The effects of stranger, friend and family member offenders. *Ethology and Sociobiology, 11*, 177–193.

Thornhill, N., & Thornhill, R. (1990c). Evolutionary analysis of psychological pain following rape. III: The effects of force and violence. *Aggressive Behavior, 16*, 297–320.

Thornhill, R., & Palmer, C. T. (2000). *A natural history of rape: Biological bases of sexual coercion.* Cambridge, MA: M.I.T. Press.

Thorpy, M. J. (1992). Report from the American Sleep Disorders Association. The clinical use of Multiple Sleep Latency Test. *Sleep, 15*, 268–276.

Thyer, B. A., Himle, J., & Curtis, G. C. (1985). Blood-injury-illness phobia: A review. *Journal of Clinical Psychology, 41*, 451–459.

Tierney, A. J. (2000). Egas Moniz and the origins of psychosurgery: A review commemorating the 50th anniversary of Moniz's Nobel Prize. *Journal of the History of the Neurosciences, 9*, 22–36.

Tiet, Q. Q., Bird, H. R., Hoven, C. W., Moore, R., Wu, P., Wicks, J., Jensen, P. S., Goodman, S., & Cohen, P. (2001). Relationship between specific adverse life events and psychiatric disorders. *Journal of Abnormal Child Psychology, 29*, 153–164.

Timmerman, I. G. H., & Emmelkamp, P. M. G. (2001). The prevalence and comobidity of Axis I and Axis II pathology in a group of forensic patients. *International Journal of Offender Therapy and Comparative Criminology, 45*, 198–213.

Tolat, R. D., O'Dell, M. W., Golamco-Estrella, S. P., & Avella, H. (2000). Cocaine-associated stroke: Three cases and rehabilitation considerations. *Brain Injury, 14*, 383–391.

Tollefson, G. D., Rampey, A. H., Potvin, J. H., Jenike, M. A., Rush, A. J., Dominquez, R. A., Koran, L. M., Shear, K., Goodman, M. D., & Gendusa, L. A. (1994). A multicenter investigation of fixed-dose fluoxetine in the treatment of obsessive-compulsive disorder. *Archives of General Psychiatry, 51*, 559–567.

Tollefson, G. D., Tollefson, S. L., Pederson, M., Luxenberg, M., et al. (1991). Comorbid irritable bowel syndrome in patients with generalized anxiety and major depression. *Annals of Clinical Psychiatry, 3*, 215–222.

Tomblin, J. B., & Buckwalter, P. R. (1998). Heritability of poor language achievement among twins. *Journal of Speech Language and Hearing Research, 41*, 188–199.

Tompson, M. C., Asarnow, J. R., Goldstein, M. J., & Miklowitz, D. J. (1990). Thought disorder and communication problems in children with schizophrenia spectrum and depressive disorders and their parents. *Journal of Clinical Child Psychology, 19*, 159–168.

Torgersen, S. (1994). Personality deviations within the schizophrenia spectrum. *Acta Psychiatrica Scandinavica, 90*, 40–44.

Torrey, E. F. (1988). Stalking the schizovirus. *Schizophrenia Bulletin, 14*, 223–229.

Torrey, E. F., Miller, J., Rawlings, R., & Yolken, R. H. (1997). Seasonality of births in schizophrenia and bipolar disorder: A review of the literature. *Schizophrenia Research, 28*, 1–38.

Toth, J. P., Reingold, E. M., & Jacoby, L. L. (1994). Toward a redefinition of implicit memory: Process dissociations following elaborative processing and self-generation. *Journal of Experimental Psychology: Learning, Memory, and Cognition, 20*, 290–303.

Toufexis, A. (1994). Are smokers junkies? *Time*, March 21, 1994, 62.

Towbin, A. (1978). Cerebral dysfunctions related to perinatal organic damage: Clinical neuropathologic correlations. *Journal of Abnormal Psychology, 87*, 617–635.

Treuting, J. J., & Hinshaw, S. P. (2001). Depression and self-esteem in boys with attention-deficit/hyperactivity disorder: Associations with comorbid aggression and explanatory attributional mechanisms. *Journal of Abnormal Child Psychology, 29*, 23–39.

Trimble, M. R. (1996). *Biological Psychiatry* (2nd ed.). New York: Wiley.

True, W. R., Rice, J., Eisen, S. A., Heath, A. C., Goldberg, J., Lyons, M. J., & Nowak, J. (1993). A twin study of genetic and environmental contributions to liability for posttraumatic stress symptoms. *Archives of General Psychiatry, 50*, 257–264.

Trull, T. J., Widiger, T. A., & Guthrie, P. (1990). Categorical versus dimensional status of borderline personality disorder. *Journal of Abnormal Psychology, 99*, 40–48.

Trull, T. J., Widiger, T. A., Useda, J. D., Holcomb, J., Doan, B, Axelrod, S. R., Stern, B. L., & Gershuny, B. S. (1998). A structured interview for the assessment of the five-factor model of personality. *Psychological Assessment, 10*, 229–240.

Tsai, G. E., Condie, D., Wu, M., & Chang, I. (1999). Functional magnetic resonance imaging of personality switches in a woman with dissociative identity disorder. *Harvard Review of Psychiatry, 7*, 119–122.

Tsai, G., Gastfriend, D. R., & Coyle, J. T. (1995). The glutamatergic basis of human alcoholism. *American Journal of Psychiatry, 152*, 332–340.

Tsai, L. Y., Tsai, M. C., & August, G. J. (1985). Brief report: Implication of EEG diagnoses in the subclassification of infantile autism. *Journal of Autism and Developmental Disorders, 15*, 339–344.

Tsuang, M. T., Perkins, K., & Simpson, J. C. (1983). Physical diseases in schizophrenia and affective disorder. *Journal of Clinical Psychiatry, 44*, 42–46.

Tsuang, M., Simpson, J., & Fleming, J. (1992). Epidemiology of suicide. *International Review of Psychiatry, 92*, 117.

Tuchman, R. F., Rapin, I., & Shinnar, S. (1991). Autistic and dysphasic children. II. Epilepsy. *Pediatrics, 88*, 1219–1225.

Tuck, I., & Wallace, D. (2000). Chronic fatigue syndrome: A woman's dilemma. *Health Care for Women International, 21,* 457–466.

Tucker, P., Pfefferbaum, B., Nixon, S. J., & Dickson, W. (2000). Predictors of post-traumatic stress symptoms in Oklahoma City: Exposure, social support, peri-traumatic responses. *Journal of Behavioral Health Services and Research, 27,* 406–416.

Turchiano, T. P. (2000). A meta-analysis of behavioral and cognitive therapies for children and adolescents with attention deficit hyperactivity and/or impulsivity disorders. *Dissertation Abstracts International: Section B: The Sciences and Engineering, 60* (June), 5760.

Turk, C. L., Heimberg, R. G., & Hope, D. A. (2001). Social anxiety disorder. In D. H. Barlow (Ed.), *Clinical handbook of psychological disorders* (3rd ed., pp. 114–153). New York: Guilford.

Turkat, I. D. (1990). *The personality disorders: A psychological approach to clinical management.* New York: Pergamon.

Turnbull, J. M. (1998). Psychopharmacology in dementia. In R. C. Hamdy, J. M. Turnbull, J. Edwards, & M. M. Lancaster (Eds.), *Alzheimer's disease: A handbook for caregivers* (3rd ed., pp. 171–182). St. Louis, MO: Mosby.

Turner, R. J., & Wagonfeld, M. O. (1967). Occupational mobility and schizophrenia. *American Sociological Review, 32,* 104–113.

Turner, S. M., Beidel, D. C., & Cooley, M. R. (1994). *Social effectiveness therapy: A program for overcoming social anxiety and social phobia. A therapist's guide.* Charleston, SC: Turndel Publishing.

Tursz, A. (1997). Problems in conceptualizing adolescent risk behaviors: International comparisons. *Journal of Adolescent Health, 21,* 116–127.

Twombly, R. (1994). The trouble with me. *New Scientist, 142*(1925), 23–25.

Tyler, D. B. (1955). Psychological changes during experimental sleep deprivation. *Diseases of the Nervous System, 16,* 293–299.

Tyrer, P. (1995). Are personality disorders well classified in DSM-IV? In W. J. Livesley (Ed.), *The DSM-IV personality disorders* (pp. 29–42). New York: Guilford.

Tyrer, P., Seivewright, N., & Seivewright, H. (1999). Long-term outcome of hypochondriacal personality disorder. *Journal of Psychosomatic Research, 46,* 177–185.

Uhde, T. W., Roy-Byrne, P. P., Vittone, B. J., Boulenger, J. P., & Post, R. M. (1985). Phenomenology and neurobiology of panic disorder. In A. H. Tuma & J. D. Maser (Eds.), *Anxiety and the anxiety disorders* (pp. 557–576). Hillsdale, NJ: Erlbaum.

Ullman, S. E., & Seigel, J. M. (1993). Victim-offender relationship and sexual assault. *Violence and Victims, 8,* 121–134.

Ullmann, L. P., & Krasner, L. (1975). *A psychological approach to abnormal behavior* (2nd ed.). Englewood Cliffs, NJ: Prentice-Hall.

Ulrich, R. E. (1991). Animal rights, animal wrongs and the question of balance. *Psychological Science, 2,* 197–201.

Unis, A. S., Cook, E. H., Vincent, J. G., Gjerde, D. K., Perry, B. D., Mason, C., & Mitchell, J. (1997). Platelet serotonin measures in adolescents with conduct disorder. *Biological Psychiatry, 42,* 553–559.

United States v. DeBellis. (1981). 649 f.2d 1 (1st Cir.).

Vaillant, G. E. (1995). *The natural history of alcoholism revisited.* Cambridge, MA: Harvard University Press.

Valentiner, D. P., Foa, E. B., Riggs, D. S., & Gershuny, B. S. (1996). Coping strategies and posttraumatic stress disorder in female victims of sexual and nonsexual assault. *Journal of Abnormal Psychology, 105,* 455–458.

van Berlo, W., & Ensink, B. (2000). Problems with sexuality after sexual assault. *Annual Review of Sex Research, 11,* 235–257.

van Dam-Baggen, R., & Kraaimaat, F. (2000). Group social skills training or cognitive group therapy as the clinical treatment of choice for generalized social phobia? *Journal of Anxiety Disorders, 14,* 437–451.

van der Hart, O., van der Kolb, B. A., & Boon, S. (1998). Treatment of dissociative disorders. In J. D. Bremmer & C. R. Marmar (Eds.), *Trauma, memory, and dissociation* (pp. 253–283). Washington, DC: American Psychiatric Press.

van der Kolk, B. A., Greenberg, M. S., Boyd, H., & Krystal, J. (1985). Inescapable shock, neurotransmitters, and addiction to trauma: Toward a psychobiology of posttraumatic stress. *Biological Psychiatry, 20,* 314–325.

van der Kolk, B. A., Greenberg, M. S., Orr, S. P., & Pitman, R. K. (1989). Endogenous opioids, stress induced analgesia, and posttraumatic stress disorder. *Psychopharmacology Bulletin, 25,* 417–422.

van der Kolk, B. A., Herron, N., & Hostetler, A. (1994). The history of trauma in psychiatry. *Psychiatric Clinics of North America, 17,* 583–600.

Van Praag, H. M., & Korf, J. (1975). Neuroleptics, catecholamines, and psychoses: A study of their interrelations. *American Journal of Psychiatry, 132,* 593–597.

van Reekum, R., Conway, C. A., Gansler, D., & White, R. (1993). Neurobehavioral study of borderline personality disorder. *Journal of Psychiatry and Neuroscience, 18,* 121–129.

van Weel-Baumgarten, E. M., van den Bosch, W. J., van den Hoogen, H. J., & Zitman, F. G. (2000). The long-term perspective: A study of psychopathology and health status of patients with a history of depression more than 15 years after the first episode. *General Hospital Psychiatry, 22,* 399–404.

van Zijderveld, G. A., Veltman, D. J., van Dyck, R., & van Doornen, L. J. P. (1999). Epinephrine-induced panic attacks and hyperventilation. *Journal of Psychiatric Research, 33,* 73–78.

Vaughn, C. E., & Leff, J. P. (1976a). The influence of family and social factors on the course of psychiatric illness: A comparison of schizophrenic and depressed neurotic patients. *British Journal of Psychiatry, 129,* 125–137.

Vaughn, C., & Leff, J. (1976b). The measurement of expressed emotion in the families of psychiatric patients. *British Journal of Social and Clinical Psychology, 15,* 157–165.

Veale, D. (2000). Outcome of cosmetic surgery and "DIY" surgery in patients with body dysmorphic disorder. *Psychiatric Bulletin, 24,* 218–221.

Veiel, H. O. F., & Baumann, U. (Eds.) (1992). *The meaning and measurement of social support.* New York: Hemisphere.

Velakoulis, D., Stuart, G. W., Wood, S. J., Smith, D. J., Brewer, W. J., Desmond, P., Singh, B., Copolov, D., & Pantelis, C. (2001). Selective bilateral hippocampal volume loss in chronic schizophrenia. *Biological Psychiatry, 50,* 531–539.

Vermetten, E., Bremner, J. D., & Spiegel, D. (1998). Dissociation and hypnotizability: A conceptual and methodological perspective on two distinct concepts. In J. D. Bremmer & C. R. Marmar (Eds.), *Trauma, memory, and dissociation* (pp. 107–159). Washington, DC: American Psychiatric Press.

Viguera, A. C., Nonacs, R., Cohen, L. S., Tondo, L., Murray, A., & Baldessarini, R. J. (2000). Risk of recurrence of bipolar disorder in pregnant and nonpregnant women after discontinuing lithium maintenance. *American Journal of Psychiatry, 157,* 179–184.

Virag, R., Frydman, D., Legman, M., & Virag, H. (1984). Intracavernous injection of papaverine as a diagnostic and therapeutic method in erectile failure. *Angiology, 35,* 79–87.

Virgin, C. E., Jr., Ha, T. P., Packan, D. R., Tombaugh, G. C., Yang, S. H., Horner, H. C., & Sapolsky R. M. (1991). Glucocorticoids inhibit glucose transport and glutamate uptake in hippocampal astrocytes: Implications for glucocorticoid neurotoxicity. *Journal of Neurochemistry, 57,* 1422–1428.

Visser, J. T., De Kloet, E. R., & Nagelkerken, L. (2000). Altered glucocorticoid regulation of the immune response in the chronic fatigue syndrome. *Annals of the New York Academy of Sciences, 917,* 868–875.

Volkmar, F. R., & Lord, C. (1998). Diagnosis and definition of autism and other pervasive developmental disorders. In F. R. Volkmar (Ed.), *Autism and pervasive developmental disorders* (pp. 1–31). Cambridge, England: Cambridge University Press.

Volkmar, F. R., & Nelson, D. S. (1990). Seizure disorders in autism. *Journal of the American Academy of Child and Adolescent Psychiatry, 29,* 127–129.

Volkow, N. D., Wang, G. J., Fischman, M. W., & Foltin, R. W. (1997). Relationship between subjective effects of cocaine and dopamine transporter occupancy. *Nature, 386,* 827–830.

Volpicelli, J. R., Rhines, K. D., Rhines, J. S., Volpicelli, L. A., Alterman, A. I., & O'Brien, C. P. (1997). Naltrexone and alcohol dependence: Role of subject compliance. *Archives of General Psychiatry, 54,* 737–743.

Volpicelli, J. R., Watson, N. T., King, A. C., Sherman, C. E., & O'Brien, C. P. (1995). Effects of naltrexone on alcohol "high" in alcoholics. *American Journal of Psychiatry, 152,* 613–617.

Von Burg, M., & Hibbard, R. (1995). Munchausen syndrome by proxy: A different kind of child abuse. *Indiana Medicine, 88,* 378–382.

von Gontard, A. (1998). Annotation: Day and night wetting in children—A paediatric and child psychiatric perspective. *Journal of Child Psychology and Psychiatry and Allied Disciplines, 39,* 439–451.

Von Knorring, A. L., Cloninger, C. R., Bohman, M., & Sigvardsson, S. (1983). An adoption study of depressive disorders and substance abuse. *Archives of General Psychiatry, 40,* 943–950.

Wachtel, P. L. (1977). *Psychoanalysis and behavior therapy: Toward an integration.* New York: Basic Books.

Wade, T. D., Bulik, C. M., & Kendler, K. S. (2001). Investigation of quality of the parental relationship as a risk factor for subclinical bulimia nervosa. *International Journal of Eating Disorders, 30,* 389–400.

Wade, T. D., Bulik, C. M., Neale, M., & Kendler, K. S. (2000). Anorexia nervosa and major depression: Shared genetic and environmental risk factors. *American Journal of Psychiatry, 157,* 469–471.

Wadsworth, S. J., Knopik, V. S., & DeFries, J. C. (2000). Reading disability in boys and girls: No evidence for a differential genetic etiology. *Reading and Writing, 13,* 133–145.

Wagner, A. W., & Linehan, M. M. (1997). The relationship between childhood sexual abuse and suicidal behaviors in borderline patients. In M. Zanarini (Ed.), *The role of sexual abuse in the etiology of borderline personality disorder* (pp. 203–223). Washington, DC: American Psychiatric Association.

Wakefield, J. C. (1992). Disorder as harmful dysfunction: A conceptual critique of DSM-III-R's definition of mental disorder. *Psychological Review, 99,* 232–247.

Waldman, I. D., Lilienfeld, S. O., & Lahey, B. B. (1995). Toward construct validity in the childhood disruptive behavior disorders: Classification and diagnosis in DSM-IV and beyond. In T. H. Ollendick & R. J. Prinz (Eds.), *Advances in Clinical Child Psychology* (Vol. 17, pp. 323–363). New York: Plenum Press.

Walker, E. A., Katon, W. J., Roy-Byrne, P. P., Jemelka, R. P., & Russo, J. (1993). Histories of sexual victimization in patients with irritable bowel syndrome or inflammatory bowel disease. *American Journal of Psychiatry, 150,* 1502–1506.

Walker, E. F. (2002). Adolescent neurodevelopment and psychopathology. *Current Directions in Psychological Science, 11,* 24–28.

Walker, E. F., Davis, D. M., & Savoie, T. D. (1994). Neuromotor precursors of schizophrenia. *Schizophrenia Bulletin, 20,* 441–451.

Walker, E. F., Grimes, K. E., Davis, D. M., & Adina, J. (1993). Childhood precursors of schizophrenia: Facial expressions of emotion. *American Journal of Psychiatry, 150,* 1654–1660.

Walker, J. G., Johnson, S., Manion, I., & Cloutier, P. (1996). Emotionally focused marital intervention for couples with chronically ill children. *Journal of Consulting and Clinical Psychology, 64,* 1029–1036.

Waller, N. G., & Meehl, P. E. (1998). *Multivariate taxometric procedures: Distinguishing types from continua.* Thousand Oaks, CA: Sage.

Walsh, B. T., Agras, W. S., Devlin, M. J., Fairburn, C. G., Wilson, G. T., Kahn, C., & Chally, M. K. (2000). Fluoxetine for bulimia nervosa following poor response to psychotherapy. *American Journal of Psychiatry, 157,* 1332–1334.

Walsh, J. K., & Lindblom, S. S. (1997). Psychophysiology of sleep deprivation and disruption. In M. R. Pressman & W. C. Orr (Eds.), *Understanding sleep: The evaluation and treatment of sleep disorders* (pp. 73–110). Washington, DC: American Psychological Association.

Walters, E. E., Neale, M. C., Eaves, L. J., Heath, A. C., Kessler, R. C., & Kendler, K. S. (1992). Bulimia nervosa and major depression: A study of common genetic and environmental factors. *Psychological Medicine, 22,* 617–622.

Walters, G. D. (2000). Behavioral self-control training for problem drinkers: A meta-analysis of randomized control studies. *Behavior Therapy, 31,* 135–149.

Ward, T., McCormack, J., Hudson, S. M., & Polaschek, D. (1997). Rape: Assessment and treatment. In D. R. Laws & W. O'Donohue (Eds.), *Sexual deviance: Theory, assessment, and treatment* (pp. 356–393). New York: Guilford.

Wardle, J., Rapoport, L., Miles, A., Afuape, T., & Duman, M. (2001). Mass education for obesity prevention: The penetration of the BBC's "Fighting Fat, Fighting Fit" campaign. *Health Education Research, 16,* 343–355.

Ware, J. C., & Morin, C. M. (1997). Sleep in depression and anxiety. In M. R. Pressman & W. C. Orr (Eds.), *Understanding sleep: The evaluation and treatment of sleep disorders* (pp. 483–503). Washington, DC: American Psychological Association.

Ware, J. C., & Orr, W. C. (1992). Evaluation and treatment of sleep disorders in children. In C. E. Walker & M. C. Roberts (Eds.), *Handbook of clinical child psychology* (2nd ed., pp. 261–282). New York: Wiley.

Warwick, H. M. C., & Salkovskis, P. M. (2001). Cognitive-behavioral treatment of hypochondriasis. In V. Starcevic & D. R. Lipsitt (Eds.), *Hypochondriasis: Modern perspectives on an ancient malady* (pp. 314–328). New York: Oxford University Press.

Warwick, H. M. C., Clark, D. M., Cobb, A. M., & Salkovskis, P. M. (1996). A controlled trial of cognitive-behavioural treatment of hypochondriasis. *British Journal of Psychiatry, 169,* 189–195.

Wassermann, E. M., & Lisanby, S. H. (2001). Therapeutic application of repetitive transcranial magnetic stimulation: A review. *Clinical Neurophysiology, 112,* 1367–1377.

Watkins, J. O., & Stauffacher, J. C. (1952). An index of pathological thinking in the Rorschach. *Journal of Projective Techniques, 16,* 276–286.

Watson, D., & Pennebaker, J. W. (1989). Health complaints, stress, and distress: Exploring the central role of negative affectivity. *Psychological Review, 96,* 234–254.

Watson, D., Clark, L. A., & Carey, G. (1988). Positive and negative affectivity and their relation to anxiety and depressive disorders. *Journal of Abnormal Psychology, 97,* 346–353.

Watson, J. B. (1913). Psychology as the behaviorist views it. *Psychological Review, 20,* 158–177.

Watson, J., & Hewlett, N. (1998). Perceptual strategies in phonological disorder: Assessment, remediation and evaluation. *International Journal of Language and Communication Disorders, 33* (Supplement), 475–480.

Watson, J., & Raynor, R. (1920). Conditioned emotional reactions. *Journal of Genetic Psychology, 37,* 394–419.

Watson, T. L., Bowers, W. A., & Andersen, A. E. (2000). Involuntary treatment of eating disorders. *American Journal of Psychiatry, 157,* 1806–1810.

Weaver, M. F., & Schnoll, S. H. (1999). Stimulants: Amphetamines and cocaine. In B. S. McCrady & E. E. Epstein (Eds.), *Addictions: A comprehensive guidebook* (pp. 105–120). New York: Oxford University Press.

Webster-Stratton, C. H. (1996). Early intervention with videotape modeling: Programs for families of children with oppositional defiant disorder or conduct disorder. In E. D. Hibbs & P. S. Jensen (Eds.), *Psychosocial treatments for child and adolescent disorders: Empirically based strategies for clinical practice* (pp. 435–474). Washington, DC: American Psychological Association.

Wechsler, H., & Isaac, N. E. (1992). Binge drinkers at Massachusetts colleges: Prevalence, drinking styles, time trends and associated problems. *Journal of the American Medical Association, 267,* 2929–2931.

Wechsler, H., Davenport, A., Dowdall, G., Moeykens, B., & Castillo, S. (1994). Health and behavioral consequences of binge drinking in college: A national survey of students at 140 campuses. *Journal of the American Medical Association, 272,* 1672–1677.

Wechsler, H., Dowdall, G. W., Maenner, G., Gledhill-Hoyt, J., & Lee, H. (1998). Changes in binge drinking and related problems among American college students between 1993 and 1997: Results of the Harvard School of Public Health college alcohol survey. *Journal of American College Health, 47,* 57–68.

Weeks, S. J., & Hobson, R. P. (1987). The salience of facial expression for autistic children. *Journal of Child Psychology and Psychiatry, 28,* 137–152.

Wehmeyer, M. L., & Bolding, N. (1999). Self-determination across living and working environments: A matched-samples study of adults with mental retardation. *Mental Retardation, 37,* 353–363.

Weinberger, D. R., & Gallhofer, B. (1997). Cognitive function in schizophrenia. *International Clinical Psychopharmacology, 12,* S29–S36.

Weinberger, D. R., Berman, K. F., Suddath, R., & Torrey, E. F. (1992). Evidence of dysfunction of the prefrontal-limbic network in schizophrenia: A magnetic resonance imaging and regional cerebral blood flow study of discordant monozygotic twins. *American Journal of Psychiatry, 149,* 890–897.

Weiner, R. D. (1989). Electroconvulsive therapy. In H. I. Kaplan & B. J. Sadock (Eds.), *Comprehensive textbook of psychiatry* (5th ed., pp. 1670–1678). Baltimore: Williams & Wilkins.

Weisberg, R. B., Brown, T. A., Wincze, J. P., & Barlow, D. H. (2001). Causal attributions and male sexual arousal: The impact of attributions for a bogus erectile difficulty on sexual arousal, cognitions, and affect. *Journal of Abnormal Psychology, 110,* 324–334.

Weiss, C. J., & Millman, R. B. (1998). Hallucinogens, phencyclidine, marijuana, inhalants. In R. J. Frances & S. I. Miller (Ed.), *Clinical textbook of addictive disorders* (2nd ed., pp. 202–232). New York: Guilford.

Weiss, G., & Hechtman, L. T. (1993). *Hyperactive children grown up: ADHD in children, adolescents, and adulthood* (2nd ed.). New York: Guilford.

Weiss, G., Hechtman, L. T., Milroy, T., & Perlman, T. (1985). Psychiatric status of hyperactives as adults: A controlled 15-year follow-up of 63 hyperactive children. *Journal of American Academy of Child Psychiatry, 23,* 211–220.

Weiss, G., Minde, K., Werry, J. S., Douglas, V., & Nemeth E. (1971). Studies of the hyperactive child, VIII: Five-year follow-up. *Archives of General Psychiatry, 24,* 409–414.

Weiss, M., Hechtman, L. T., & Weiss, G. (1999). *ADHD in adulthood: A guide to current theory, diagnosis, and treatment.* Baltimore: Johns Hopkins University Press.

Weissman, M. M. (1995). *Mastery of your depression through interpersonal psychotherapy.* Albany, NY: Graywind Publications.

Weissman, M. M., Klerman, G. L., Markowitz, J. S., & Ouellette, R. (1989). Suicidal ideation and suicide attempts in panic disorder and attacks. *New England Journal of Medicine, 321,* 1209–1214.

Wekstein, L. (1979). *Handbook of suicidology: Principles, problems, and practice.* New York: Brunner/Mazel.

Welkowitz, L. A. (2000). Anxiety disorders: Psychological treatments. In B. I. Sadock & V. A. Sadock (Eds.), *Kaplan & Sadock's comprehensive textbook of psychiatry* (7th ed., pp. 1498–1503). Philadelphia: Lippincott Williams & Wilkins.

Wells, K. C., Epstein, J. N., Hinshaw, S. P., Conners, C. K., Klaric, J., Abikoff, H. B., Abramowitz, A., Arnold, L. E., Elliott, G., Greenhill, L. L., Hechtman, L., Hoza, B., Jensen, P. S., March, J. S., Pelham, W., Jr., Pfiffner, L., Severe, J., Swanson, J. M., Vitiello, B., & Wigal, T. (2000). Parenting and family stress treatment outcomes in attention deficit hyperactivity disorder (ADHD): An empirical analysis in the MTA study. *Journal of Abnormal Child Psychology, 28,* 543–553.

Wender, P. H., Kety, S. S., Rosenthal, D., Schulsinger, F., Ortmann, J., & Lunde, I. (1986). Psychiatric disorders in the biological and adoptive families of adopted individuals with affective disorders. *Archives of General Psychiatry, 43,* 923–929.

Wender, P. H., Rosenthal, D., Rainer, J. D., Greenhill, L., & Sarlin, M. B. (1977). Schizophrenics' adopting parents: Psychiatric status. *Archives of General Psychiatry, 34,* 777–784.

Wert, R. C., & Raulin, M. L. (1986a). The chronic cerebral effects of cannabis use: I. Methodological issues and neurological findings. *International Journal of the Addictions, 21,* 605–628.

Wert, R. C., & Raulin, M. L. (1986b). The chronic cerebral effects of cannabis use: II. Psychological findings and conclusions. *International Journal of the Addictions, 21,* 629–642.

Werth, J. L., Jr. (2001). U.S. involuntary mental health commitment statutes: Requirements for persons perceived to be a potential harm to self. *Suicide and Life-Threatening Behavior, 31,* 348–357.

Wessely, S. (2001). Chronic fatigue: Symptom and syndrome. *Annals of Internal Medicine, 134,* 838–843.

Westermeyer, J. (1987). Public health and chronic mental illness. *American Journal of Public Health, 77,* 667–668.

Westphal, V. K., & Smith, J. E. (1996). Overeaters anonymous: Who goes and who succeeds? *Eating Disorders: The Journal of Treatment and Prevention, 4,* 160–170.

Whalen, C. K. (2001). ADHD treatment in the 21st century: Pushing the envelope. *Journal of Clinical Child Psychology, 30,* 136–40.

Whiffen, V. E. (1992). Is postpartum depression a distinct diagnosis? *Clinical Psychology Review, 12,* 485–508.

Whiffen, V. E., & Gotlib, I. H. (1993). Comparison of postpartum and non-postpartum depression: Clinical presentation, psychiatric history, and psychosocial functioning. *Journal of Consulting and Clinical Psychology, 61,* 485–494.

White, H. K., & Levin, E. D. (1999). Four-week nicotine skin patch treatment effects on cognitive performance in Alzheimer's disease. *Outcomes Management, 143,* 158–165.

White, J. L., & Mitler, M. M. (1997). The diagnostic interview and differential diagnosis for complaints of excessive daytime sleepiness. In M. R. Pressman & W. C. Orr (Eds.), *Understanding sleep: The evaluation and treatment of sleep disorders* (pp. 161–175). Washington, DC: American Psychological Association.

White, W. L. (2000a). The history of recovered people as wounded healers: I. From Native America to the rise of the modern alcoholism movement. *Alcoholism Treatment Quarterly, 18*(1), 1–23.

White, W. L. (2000b). The history of recovered people as wounded healers: II. The era of professionalization and specialization. *Alcoholism Treatment Quarterly, 18*(2), 1–25.

Whittal, M. L., & Zaretsky, A. (1996). Cognitive-behavioral strategies for the treatment of eating disorders. In M. H. Pollack & M. W. Otto (Eds.), *Challenges in clinical practice: Pharmacologic and psychosocial strategies* (pp. 276–307). New York,: Guilford Press.

Whittal, M. L., Suchday, S., & Goetsch, V. L. (1994). The panic attack questionnaire: Factor analysis of symptom profiles and characteristics of undergraduates who panic. *Journal of Anxiety Disorders, 8,* 237–245.

Whybrow, P. C. (1997). *A mood apart.* New York: Basic Books.

Widiger, T. A., & Corbitt, E. M. (1995). Antisocial personality disorder. In W. J. Livesley (Ed.), *The DSM-IV personality disorders* (pp. 103–126). New York: Guilford.

Widiger, T., & Spitzer, R. L. (1991). Sex bias in the diagnosis of personality disorders: Conceptual and methodological issues. *Clinical Psychology Review, 11,* 1–22.

Widiger, T., Frances, A., Warner, L., & Bluhm, C. (1986). Diagnostic criteria for the borderline and schizotypal personality disorders. *Journal of Abnormal Psychology, 95,* 43–51.

Widiger, T., Trull, T., Hurt, S., Clarkin, J., & Frances, A. (1987). A multi-dimensional scaling of the DSM-III personality disorders. *Archives of General Psychiatry, 44,* 557–563.

Widom, C. P., & Morris, S. (1997). Accuracy of adult recollections of childhood victimization, Part 2: Childhood sexual abuse. *Psychological Assessment, 9,* 34–46.

Widom, C. S. (1977). A methodology for studying noninstitutionalized psychopaths. *Journal of Consulting and Clinical Psychology, 45,* 674–683.

Wiederman, M. W. (1996). Women, sex, and food: A review of research on eating disorders and sexuality. *Journal of Sex Research, 33,* 301–311.

Wierzbicka, A. (1998). Russian emotional expression. *Ethos, 26,* 456–483.

Wiese, J. G., Shlipak, M. G., & Browner, W. S. (2000). The alcohol hangover. *Annals of Internal Medicine, 132,* 897–902.

Wiggins, J. S. (1973). *Personality and prediction: Principles of personality assessment.* Reading, MA: Addison-Wesley.

Wilens, T. E., Spencer, T. J., & Biederman, J. (2000). Attention-deficit/hyperactivity disorder with substance use disorders. In T. E. Brown (Ed.), *Attention deficit disorders and comorbidities in children, adolescents, and adults* (pp. 319–340). Washington, DC: American Psychiatric Press.

Wilensky, M., & Myers, M. F. (1987). Retarded ejaculation in homosexual patients: A report of nine cases. *Journal of Sex Research, 23,* 85–91.

Wiliszowski, C. H., Lacey, J. H., Jones, R. K., Marchetti, L. M., & Smith, E. J. (1998). *Develop and test messages to deter drinking and driving.* Washington, DC: U.S. Department of Transportation, National Highway Traffic Safety Administration (Publication number DOT HS 808 726).

Williams, J. M. G., Mathews, A., & MacLeod, C. (1996). The Emotional Stroop Task and psychopathology. *Psychological Bulletin, 120,* 3–24.

Williams, R. B. (1996). Coronary-prone behaviors, hostility, and cardiovascular health: Implications for behavioral and pharmacological interventions. In K. Orth-Gomér & N. Schneiderman (Eds.), *Behavioral medicine approaches to cardiovascular disease prevention* (pp. 161–168). Mahwah, NJ: Erlbaum.

Williams, S. L., Kinney, P. J., Harap, S. T., & Liebmann, M. (1997). Thoughts of agoraphobic people during scary tasks. *Journal of Abnormal Psychology, 106,* 511–520.

Wills, C. (1993). *The runaway brain: The evolution of human uniqueness.* New York: Basic Books.

Wills, T. A., Sandy, J. M., & Shinar, O. (1999). Cloninger's constructs related to substance use level and problems in late adolescence: A mediational model based on self-control and coping motives. *Experimental and Clinical Psychopharmacology, 7,* 122–134.

Wilmoth, G. H., Silver, S., & Severy, L. J. (1987). Receptivity and planned change: Community attitudes and deinstitutionalization. *Journal of Applied Psychology, 72,* 138–145.

Wilson, E. O. (1975). *Sociobiology: The new synthesis.* Cambridge, MA: The Belknap Press of Harvard University Press.

Wilson, E. O. (1978). *On human nature.* Cambridge, MA: Harvard University Press.

Wilson, J. R., McClearn, G. E., & Johnson, R. C. (1978). Ethnic variation in the use and effect of alcohol. *Drug and Alcohol Dependence, 3,* 147–151.

Wilson, M. A., & Leith, S. (2001). Acquaintances, lovers, and friends: Rape within relationships. *Journal of Applied Social Psychology, 31,* 1709–1726.

Wilson, S. A., Becker, L. A., & Tinker, R. H. (1995). Eye movement desensitization and reprocessing (EMDR) treatment for psychologically traumatized individuals. *Journal of Consulting and Clinical Psychology, 63,* 928–937.

Wilson, S. A., Becker, L. A., & Tinker, R. H. (1997). Fifteen-month follow-up of eye movement desensitization and reprocessing (EMDR) treatment for PTSD and psychological trauma. *Journal of Consulting and Clinical Psychology, 65,* 1047–1056.

Wilson, S. A., Tinker, R. H., Becker, L. A., & Logan, C. R. (2001). Stress management with law enforcement personnel: A controlled outcome study of EMDR versus a traditional stress management program. *International Journal of Stress Management, 8,* 179–200.

Wincze, J. P., & Carey, M. P. (1991). *Sexual dysfunction: A guide for assessment and treatment.* New York: Guilford.

Wingard, D. L., & Berkman, L. F. (1983). Mortality risk associated with sleeping patterns among adults. *Sleep, 6,* 102–107.

Winick, B. J. (2001). The civil commitment hearing: Applying the law therapeutically. In L. E. Frost & R. J. Bonnie (Eds.), *The evolution of mental health law* (pp. 291–308). Washington, DC: American Psychological Association.

Winkelman, J. W. (2001). Schizophrenia, obesity, and obstructive sleep apnea. *Journal of Clinical Psychiatry, 62,* 8–11.

Winokur, G. (1985). Familial psychopathology in delusional disorder. *Comprehensive Psychiatry, 26,* 241–248.

Winokur, G., Turvey, C., Akiskal, H., Coyell, W., Solomon, D., Leon, A., Mueller, T., Endicott, J., Maser, J., & Keller, M. (1998). Alcoholism and drug abuse in three groups—Bipolar I, unipolars, and their acquaintances. *Journal of Affective Disorders, 50,* 81–89.

Winstock, A. R., Griffiths, P., & Stewart, D. (2001). Drugs and the dance music scene: A survey of current drug use patterns among a sample of dance music enthusiasts in the UK. *Drug and Alcohol Dependence, 64,* 9–17.

Winters, K. C., Stinchfield, R., & Fulkerson, J. (1993). Patterns and characteristics of adolescent gambling. *Journal of Gambling Studies, 9,* 415–418.

Wirshing, D. A., Marshall, B. D., Jr., Green, M. F., Mintz, J., Marder, S. R., & Wirshing, W. C. (1999). Risperidone in treatment-refractory schizophrenia. *American Journal of Psychiatry, 156,* 1374–1379.

Wirtz, P. W., & Harrell, A. V. (1987). Effects of postassault exposure to attack-similar stimuli on long-term recovery victims. *Journal of Consulting and Clinical Psychology, 55,* 10–16.

Wise, C. D., & Stein, L. (1973). Dopamine-β-hydroxylase deficits in the brains of schizophrenic patients. *Science, 181,* 344–347.

Wiseman, C. V., Gray, J. J., Mosimann, J. E., & Ahrens, A. H. (1992). Cultural expectations of thinness in women: An update. *International Journal of Eating Disorders, 11,* 85–89.

Wiseman, C. V., Sunday, S. R., Klapper, F., Harris, W. A., & Halmi, K. A. (2001). Changing patterns of hospitalization in eating disorder patients. *International Journal of Eating Disorders, 30,* 69–74.

Wittchen, H. U., Zhao, S., Kessler, R. C., & Eaton, W. W. (1994). DSM-III-R generalized anxiety disorder in the National Comorbidity Survey. *Archives of General Psychiatry, 51,* 355–364.

Wixted, J. T., Morrison, R. L., & Bellack, A. S. (1988). Social skills training in the treatment of negative symptoms. *International Journal of Mental Health, 17,* 3–21.

Wohlgemuth, W. K., & Edinger, J. D. (2000). Sleep restriction therapy. In K. L. Lichstein & C. M. Morin (Eds.), *Treatment of late-life insomnia* (pp. 147–166). Thousand Oaks, CA: Sage.

Wolf, M. E., Mosnaim, A. D., Puente, J., & Ignacio, R. (1991). Plasma methionine-enkephalin in PTSD. *Biological Psychiatry, 29,* 305–307.

Wolf, P. H. (1972). Ethnic differences in alcohol sensitivity. *Science, 175,* 449–450.

Wolf, P. H. (1973). Vasomotor sensitivity to alcohol in diverse mongoloid populations. *American Journal of Human Genetics, 25,* 193–199.

Wolff, S., & Chick, J. (1980). Schizoid personality disorder in childhood. *Psychological Medicine, 10,* 85–101.

Wolpe, J. (1958). *Psychotherapy by reciprocal inhibition.* Stanford, CA: Stanford University Press.

Wong, D. F., Wagner, H. N., Jr., Tune, L. E., Dannals, R. F., Perlson, G. D., Links, J. M., Tamminga, C. A., Broussoule, E. P., Ravert, H. T., Wilson, A. A., Toung, J. K. T., Malat, J., Williams, J. A., O'Tuama, L. A., Snyder, S. H., Kuhar, M. J., & Gjedde, A. (1986). Positron emission tomography reveals elevated D_2 dopamine receptors in drug-naïve schizophrenics. *Science, 234,* 1558.

Wong, M. R., & Cook, D. (1992). Shame and its contribution to PTSD. *Journal of Traumatic Stress, 5,* 557–562.

Wood, J. M., Lilienfeld, S. O., Nezworski, M. T., & Garb, H. N. (2001). Coming to grips with negative evidence for the comprehensive system for the Rorschach: A comment on Gacono, Loving, and Bodholdt; Ganellen; and Bornstein. *Journal of Personality Assessment, 77,* 48–70.

Woods, P. J. (1961). A test of Mednick's analysis of the thinking disorder in schizophrenia. *Psychological Reports, 9,* 441–446.

Woodside, D. B., & Kennedy, S. H. (1995). Gender differences in eating disorders. In M. V. Seeman (Ed.), *Gender and psychopathology* (pp. 253–268). Washington, DC: American Psychiatric Press.

Woodward, S. H., Arsenault, N. J., Murray, C., & Bliwise, D. L. (2000). Laboratory sleep correlates of nightmare complaint in PTSD inpatients. *Biological Psychiatry, 48,* 1081–1087.

Woody, S. R. (1996). Effect of focus of attention on anxiety levels and social performance of indviduals with social phobia. *Journal of Abnormal Psychology, 105,* 61–69.

Wooley, S. C., & Kearney-Cooke, A. (1986). Intensive treatment of bulimia and body-image disturbance. In K. D. Brownell & J. P. Foreyt (Eds.), *Handbook of eating disorders: Physiology, psychology, and treatment of obesity, anorexia, and bulimia* (pp. 476–502). New York: Basic Books.

World Health Organization (WHO) (1988). *Correlates of youth suicide.* Geneva: World Health Organization, Division of Mental Health.

Wray, H. (1997). The hysteria over "Hystories." *U.S. News & World Report, 122*(19), 14.

Wu, J. C., & Bunney, W. E., Jr. (1990). The biological basis of an antidepressant response to sleep deprivation and relapse: Review and hypothesis. *American Journal of Psychiatry, 147,* 14–21.

Wu, J. C., Amen, D. G., & Bracha, H. S. (2000). Neuroimaging in clinical practice. In B. I. Sadock & V. A. Sadock (Eds.), *Kaplan & Sadock's comprehensive textbook of psychiatry* (7th ed., pp. 373–385). Philadelphia: Lippincott Williams & Wilkins.

Wurmser, L. (1974). Psychoanalytic considerations of the etiology of compulsive drug use. *Journal of the American Psychoanalytic Association, 22,* 820–843.

Wurmser, L. (1978). *The hidden dimension: Psychodynamics in compulsive drug use.* New York: Aronson.

Wyatt v. Stickney. (1972). 325 F.Supp 781 (M.D.Ala. 1971), enforced in 334 F.Supp. 1341 (M.D.Ala. 1971),344 F.Supp. 373, 379 (M.D.Ala. 1972), aff'd sub nom *Wyatt v. Anderholt,* 503 F.2d 1305 (5th Cir. 1974).

Wyatt, S. A., & Ziedonis, D. (1998). Psychological and psychiatric consequences of amphetamines. In R. E. Tarter & R. T. Ammerman (Eds.), *Handbook of substance abuse: Neurobehavioral pharmacology* (pp. 529–544). New York: Plenum.

Wykes, T., Parr, A. M., & Landau, S. (1999). Group treatment of auditory hallucinations: Exploratory study of effectiveness. *British Journal of Psychiatry, 175,* 180–185.

Wynne, L. C., & Singer, M. T. (1963). Thought disorder and family relations of schizophrenics: I. A research strategy. *Archives of General Psychiatry, 9,* 191–198.

Wynne, L. C., Singer, M. T., & Toohey, M. (1976). Communication of the adoptive parents of schizophrenics. In J. Jorstad and E. Ugelstad (Eds.), *Schizophrenia 75: Psychotherapy, family studies, research* (pp. 413–452). Olso, Norway: Universitetsforlaget.

Wynne, L. C., Singer, M. T., Bartko, J., & Toohey, M. (1977). Schizophrenics and their families: Recent research on parental communication. In J. M. Tanner (Ed.), *Developments in psychiatric research* (pp. 254–286). London: Hodder & Stoughton.

Wynne, L. C., Tookey, M. L., & Doane, J. (1979). Family studies. In L. Bellak (Ed.), *Disorders of the schizophrenic syndrome.* New York: Basic Books.

Wysocki, T., Greco, P., Harris, M. A., & White, N. H. (2000). Behavioral family systems therapy for adolescents with diabetes. In D. Drotar (Ed.), *Promoting adherence to medical treatment in chronic childhood illness: Concepts, methods, and interventions* (pp. 367–381). Mahwah, NJ: Erlbaum.

Xian, H., Chantarujikapong, S. I., Scherrer, J. F., Eisen, S. A., Lyons, M. J., Goldberg, J., Tsuang, M., & True, W. R. (2000). Genetic and environmental influences on posttraumatic stress disorder, alcohol and drug dependence in twin pairs. *Drug and Alcohol Dependence, 61,* 95–102.

Xiao, X. Q., Wang, R., & Tang, X. C. (2000). Huperzine A and tacrine attenuate beta-amyloid peptide-induced oxidative injury. *Journal of Neuroscience Research, 61,* 564–569.

Yairi, E. (1999). Epidemiologic factors and stuttering research. In N. B. Ratner & E. C. Healey (Eds.), *Stuttering research and practice: Bridging the gap* (pp. 45–53). Mahwah, NJ: Erlbaum.

Yalom, I. D. (1980). *Existential psychotherapy.* New York: Basic Books.

Yamashita, I., Koyaman, T., & Ohmori, T. (1995). Ethnic differences in alcohol metabolism and physiological responses to alcohol: Implications in alcohol abuse. In B. Tabakoff & P. L., Hoffman (Eds.), *Biological aspects of alcoholism* (pp. 49–61). Seattle: Hogrefe & Huber.

Yates, W. R. (1999). Medical problems of the athlete with an eating disorder. In P. S. Mehler & A. E. Andersen (Eds.), *Eating disorders: A guide to medical care and complications* (pp. 153–166). Baltimore: Johns Hopkins University Press.

Yegorov, V. F. (1992). And how is it over there, across the ocean? *Schizophrenia Bulletin, 18,* 7–14.

Yehuda, R., Giller, E. L., Jr., Levengood, R. A., Southwick, S. M., & Siever, L. J. (1995). Hypothalamic-pituitary-adrenal functioning in post-traumatic stress disorder: Expanding the concept of the stress response spectrum. In M. J. Friedman, D. S. Charney, & A. Y. Deutch (Eds.), *Neurobiological and clinical consequences of stress: From normal adaptation to post-traumatic stress disorder* (pp. 351–365). Philadelphia: Lippincott-Raven.

Yehuda, R., Giller, E. L., Southwick, S. M., Lowy, M. T., & Mason, J. W. (1991). Hypothalamic-pituitary-adrenal dysfunction in posttraumatic stress disorder. *Biological Psychiatry, 30,* 1031–1048.

Yerkes, R. M., & Dodson, J. D. (1908). The relation of strength of stimulus to rapidity of habit-formation. *Journal of Comparative Neurology and Psychology, 18,* 459–482.

Yoast, R., Williams, M. A., Deitchman, S. D., & Champion, H. C. (2001). Report of the Council on Scientific Affairs: Methadone maintenance and needle-exchange programs to reduce the medical and public health consequences of drug abuse. *Journal of Addictive Diseases, 20,* 15–40.

Yoder, J. D. (1999). *Women and gender: Transforming psychology.* Upper Saddle River, NJ: Prentice-Hall.

Young, J. E., Beck, A. T., & Weinberger, A. (1993). Depression. In D. H. Barlow (Ed.), *Clinical handbook of psychological disorders* (2nd ed., pp. 240–277). New York: Guilford.

Young, L. T., Joffe, R. T., Robb, J. C., MacQueen, G. M., Marriott, M., & Patelis-Siotis, I. (2000). Double-blind comparison of addition of a second mood stabilizer versus an antidepressant to an initial mood stabilizer for treatment of patients with bipolar depression. *American Journal of Psychiatry, 157,* 124–126.

Young, M. A., Fogg, L. F., Scheftner, W. A., & Fawcett, J. A. (1994). Interactions of risk factors in predicting suicide. *American Journal of Psychiatry, 151,* 434–435.

Young, M. A., Meaden, P. M., Fogg, L. F., Cherin, E. A., & Eastman, C. I. (1997). Which environmental variables are related to the onset of seasonal affective disorders? *Journal of Abnormal Psychology, 106,* 554–562.

Young, M. A., Watel, L. G., Lahmeyer, H. W., & Eastman, C. I. (1991). The temporal onset of individual symptoms in winter depression.

Differentiating underlying mechanisms. *Journal of Affective Disorders, 22,* 191–197.

Yovel, G., Sirota, P., Mazeh, D., Shakhar, G., Rosenne, E., & Ben-Eliyahu, S. (2000). Higher natural killer cell activity in schizophrenic patients: The impact of serum factors, medication, and smoking. *Brain, Behavior, and Immunity, 14,* 153–169.

Zadra, A., & Donderi, D. C. (2000). Nightmares and bad dreams: Their prevalence and relationship to well-being. *Journal of Abnormal Psychology, 109,* 273–281.

Zanarini, M., Jermaineenburg, F., Chauncey, D., & Gunderson, J. G. (1987). The diagnostic interview for personality disorders: Interrater and test-retest reliability. *Comprehensive Psychiatry, 28,* 467–480.

Zarit, S. H., Orr, N., & Zarit, J. M. (1985). *The hidden victims of Alzheimer's disease: Families under stress.* New York: New York University Press.

Zgourides, G. D., & Warren, R. (1989). Retarded ejaculation: Overview and treatment implications. *Journal of Psychology and Human Sexuality, 2,* 139–150.

Zigler (1967). Familial mental retardation: A continuing dilemma. *Science, 155,* 292–298.

Zilboorg, G., & Henry, G. W. (1941). *A history of medical psychology.* New York: Norton.

Zimmer, C. (2001). *Evolution: The triumph of an idea.* New York: HarperCollins.

Zimmer, L., & Morgan, J. P. (1995). *Exposing marijuana myths: A review of the scientific evidence.* New York: The Lindemith Center.

Zimmerman, M., & Coryell, W. (1989). DSM-III personality disorder diagnoses in a nonpatient sample. *Archives of General Psychiatry, 46,* 682–689.

Zimmerman, M., & Coryell, W. (1990). Diagnosing personality disorders in the community: A comparison of self-report and interview measures. *Archives of General Psychiatry, 47,* 527–531.

Zinbarg, R. E., & Mineka, S. (2001). Understanding, treating, and preventing anxiety, phobias, and anxiety disorders. In M. E. Carroll & J. B. Overmier (Eds.), *Animal research and human health: Advancing human welfare through behavioral science* (pp. 19–28). Washington, DC: American Psychological Association.

Zisapel, N. (2001). Circadian rhythm sleep disorders: Pathophysiology and potential approaches to management. *CNS Drugs, 15,* 311–328.

Zohar, J., Mueller, E. A., Insel, T. R., Zohar-Kadouch, R. C., & Murphy, D. L. (1987). Serotonergic responsivity in obsessive-compulsive disorder. *Archives of General Psychiatry, 44,* 946–951.

Zoratti, R. (1998). A review on ethnic differences in plasma triglycerides and high-density-lipoprotein cholesterol: Is the lipid pattern the key factor for the low coronary heart disease rate in people of African origin? *European Journal of Epidemiology, 14,* 9–21.

Zucker, K. J., & Blanchard, R. (1997). Transvestic fetishism: Psychopathology and theory. In D. R. Laws & W. O'Donohue (Eds.), *Sexual deviance: Theory, assessment, and treatment* (pp. 253–279). New York: Guilford.

Zuroff, D. C., & Mongrain, M. (1987). Dependency and self-criticism: Vulnerability factors for depressive affective states. *Journal of Abnormal Psychology, 96,* 14–22.

Zusne, L., & Jones, W. H. (1989). *Anomalistic psychology: A study of magical thinking.* Hillsdale, NJ: Erlbaum.

Name Index

Subject Index